KU-680-861

University of Liverpool

Withdrawn from stock

# Introduction
# to Econometrics

# MyEconLab® Provides the Power of Practice

Optimize your study time with **MyEconLab**, the online assessment and tutorial system. When you take a sample test online, **MyEconLab** gives you targeted feedback and a personalized Study Plan to identify the topics you need to review.

## Study Plan

The Study Plan shows you the sections you should study next, gives easy access to practice problems, and provides you with an automatically generated quiz to prove mastery of the course material.

## Unlimited Practice

As you work each exercise, instant feedback helps you understand and apply the concepts. Many Study Plan exercises contain algorithmically generated values to ensure that you get as much practice as you need.

## Learning Resources

Study Plan problems link to learning resources that further reinforce concepts you need to master.

- **Help Me Solve This** learning aids help you break down a problem much the same way as an instructor would do during office hours. Help Me Solve This is available for select problems.

- **eText links** are specific to the problem at hand so that related concepts are easy to review just when they are needed.

- A **graphing tool** enables you to build and manipulate graphs to better understand how concepts, numbers, and graphs connect.

Find out more at www.myeconlab.com

## Current News Exercises

Posted weekly, we find the latest microeconomic and macroeconomic news stories, post them, and write auto-graded multi-part exercises that illustrate the economic way of thinking about the news.

## Interactive Homework Exercises

Participate in a fun and engaging activity that helps promote active learning and mastery of important economic concepts.

Pearson's experiments program is flexible and easy for instructors and students to use. For a complete list of available experiments, visit *www.myeconlab.com*.

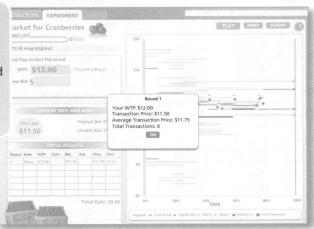

# The Pearson Series in Economics

**Abel/Bernanke/Croushore**
*Macroeconomics\**

**Bade/Parkin**
*Foundations of Economics\**

**Berck/Helfand**
*The Economics of the Environment*

**Bierman/Fernandez**
*Game Theory with Economic Applications*

**Blanchard**
*Macroeconomics\**

**Blau/Ferber/Winkler**
*The Economics of Women, Men, and Work*

**Boardman/Greenberg/Vining/Weimer**
*Cost-Benefit Analysis*

**Boyer**
*Principles of Transportation Economics*

**Branson**
*Macroeconomic Theory and Policy*

**Bruce**
*Public Finance and the American Economy*

**Carlton/Perloff**
*Modern Industrial Organization*

**Case/Fair/Oster**
*Principles of Economics\**

**Chapman**
*Environmental Economics: Theory, Application, and Policy*

**Cooter/Ulen**
*Law & Economics*

**Daniels/VanHoose**
*International Monetary & Financial Economics*

**Downs**
*An Economic Theory of Democracy*

**Ehrenberg/Smith**
*Modern Labor Economics*

**Farnham**
*Economics for Managers*

**Folland/Goodman/Stano**
*The Economics of Health and Health Care*

**Fort**
*Sports Economics*

**Froyen**
*Macroeconomics*

**Fusfeld**
*The Age of the Economist*

**Gerber**
*International Economics\**

**González-Rivera**
*Forecasting for Economics and Business*

**Gordon**
*Macroeconomics\**

**Greene**
*Econometric Analysis*

**Gregory**
*Essentials of Economics*

**Gregory/Stuart**
*Russian and Soviet Economic Performance and Structure*

**Hartwick/Olewiler**
*The Economics of Natural Resource Use*

**Heilbroner/Milberg**
*The Making of the Economic Society*

**Heyne/Boettke/Prychitko**
*The Economic Way of Thinking*

**Holt**
*Markets, Games, and Strategic Behavior*

**Hubbard/O'Brien**
*Economics\**
*Money, Banking, and the Financial System\**

**Hubbard/O'Brien/Rafferty**
*Macroeconomics\**

**Hughes/Cain**
*American Economic History*

**Husted/Melvin**
*International Economics*

**Jehle/Reny**
*Advanced Microeconomic Theory*

**Johnson-Lans**
*A Health Economics Primer*

**Keat/Young/Erfle**
*Managerial Economics*

**Klein**
*Mathematical Methods for Economics*

**Krugman/Obstfeld/Melitz**
*International Economics: Theory & Policy\**

**Laidler**
*The Demand for Money*

**Leeds/von Allmen**
*The Economics of Sports*

**Leeds/von Allmen/Schiming**
*Economics\**

**Lynn**
*Economic Development: Theory and Practice for a Divided World*

**Miller**
*Economics Today\**
*Understanding Modern Economics*

**Miller/Benjamin**
*The Economics of Macro Issues*

**Miller/Benjamin/North**
*The Economics of Public Issues*

**Mills/Hamilton**
*Urban Economics*

**Mishkin**
*The Economics of Money, Banking, and Financial Markets\**

*The Economics of Money, Banking, and Financial Markets, Business School Edition\**

*Macroeconomics: Policy and Practice\**

**Murray**
*Econometrics: A Modern Introduction*

**O'Sullivan/Sheffrin/Perez**
*Economics: Principles, Applications, and Tools\**

**Parkin**
*Economics\**

**Perloff**
*Microeconomics\**
*Microeconomics: Theory and Applications with Calculus\**

**Perloff/Brander**
*Managerial Economics and Strategy\**

**Phelps**
*Health Economics*

**Pindyck/Rubinfeld**
*Microeconomics\**

**Riddell/Shackelford/ Stamos/Schneider**
*Economics: A Tool for Critically Understanding Society*

**Roberts**
*The Choice: A Fable of Free Trade and Protection*

**Rohlf**
*Introduction to Economic Reasoning*

**Roland**
*Development Economics*

**Scherer**
*Industry Structure, Strategy, and Public Policy*

**Schiller**
*The Economics of Poverty and Discrimination*

**Sherman**
*Market Regulation*

**Stock/Watson**
*Introduction to Econometrics*

**Studenmund**
*Using Econometrics: A Practical Guide*

**Tietenberg/Lewis**
*Environmental and Natural Resource Economics*
*Environmental Economics and Policy*

**Todaro/Smith**
*Economic Development*

**Waldman/Jensen**
*Industrial Organization: Theory and Practice*

**Walters/Walters/Appel/ Callahan/Centanni/ Maex/O'Neill**
*Econversations: Today's Students Discuss Today's Issues*

**Weil**
*Economic Growth*

**Williamson**
*Macroeconomics*

*denotes MyEconLab titles. Visit www.myeconlab.com to learn more.

# Introduction to Econometrics

## UPDATED THIRD EDITION
## GLOBAL EDITION

**James H. Stock**
Harvard University

**Mark W. Watson**
Princeton University

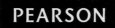

Boston  Columbus  Indianapolis  New York  San Francisco  Hoboken
Amsterdam  Cape Town  Dubai  London  Madrid  Milan  Munich  Paris  Montréal  Toronto
Delhi  Mexico City  São Paulo  Sydney  Hong Kong  Seoul  Singapore  Taipei  Tokyo

Vice President, Product Management: Donna Battista
Acquisitions Editor: Christina Masturzo
Editorial Assistant: Christine Mallon
Head of Learning Asset Acquisition, Global Editions:
Laura Dent
Senior Acquisitions Editor, Global Editions: Sandhya Ghoshal
Assistant Project Editor, Global Editions: Paromita Banerjee
Vice President, Marketing: Maggie Moylan
Director, Strategy and Marketing: Scott Dustan
Manager, Field Marketing: Leigh Ann Sims
Product Marketing Manager: Alison Haskins
Executive Field Marketing Manager: Lori DeShazo
Senior Strategic Marketing Manager: Erin Gardner

Senior Production Manufacturing Controller, Global
Editions: Trudy Kimber
Team Lead, Program Management: Ashley Santora
Program Manager: Carolyn Philips
Team Lead, Project Management: Jeff Holcomb
Project Manager: Liz Napolitano
Media Producer, Global Editions: Pallavi Pandit
Operations Specialist: Carol Melville
Cover Designer: Jon Boylan
Cover Art: © URRRA/Shutterstock
Full-Service Project Management, Design, and Electronic
Composition: Cenveo® Publisher Services

Credits and acknowledgments borrowed from other sources and reproduced, with permission, in this textbook appear on appropriate page within text.

Photo Credits: page 410 left: Henrik Montgomery/Pressens Bild/AP Photo; page 410 right: Paul Sakuma/AP Photo; page 428 left: Courtesy of Allison Harris; page 428 right: Courtesy of Allison Harris; page 669 top left: John McCombe/AP Photo; bottom left: New York University/AFP/Newscom; top right: Denise Applewhite/Princeton University/AP Photo; bottom right: Courtesy of the University of Chicago/AP Photo.

Pearson Education Limited
Edinburgh Gate
Harlow
Essex CM20 2JE
England

and Associated Companies throughout the world

Visit us on the World Wide Web at:
www.pearsonglobaleditions.com

© Pearson Education Limited 2015

The rights of James H. Stock and Mark W. Watson to be identified as the author of this work have been asserted by him in accordance with the Copyright, Designs and Patents Act 1988.

Authorized adaptation from the United States edition, entitled Introduction to Econometrics, Update, 3rd Edition, ISBN 978-0-13-348687-2 by James H. Stock and Mark W. Watson, published by Pearson Education © 2015.

All rights reserved. No part of this publication may be reproduced, stored in a retrieval system, or transmitted in any form or by any means, electronic, mechanical, photocopying, recording or otherwise, without either the prior written permission of the publisher or a license permitting restricted copying in the United Kingdom issued by the Copyright Licensing Agency Ltd, Saffron House, 6–10 Kirby Street, London EC1N 8TS.

All trademarks used herein are the property of their respective owners. The use of any trademark in this text does not vest in the author or publisher any trademark ownership rights in such trademarks, nor does the use of such trademarks imply any affiliation with or endorsement of this book by such owners.

ISBN 10: 1-292-07131-1
ISBN 13: 978-1-292-07131-2

**British Library Cataloguing-in-Publication Data**
A catalogue record for this book is available from the British Library

10 9 8 7 6

Typeset in Minion Pro by Cenveo Publishing Services/Nesbitt
Printed and bound by Malaysia, CTP-PJB

# Brief Contents

# Contents

# Key Concepts

## PART THREE     Further Topics in Regression Analysis

## PART FOUR     Regression Analysis of Economic Time Series Data

## PART FIVE    Regression Analysis of Economic Time Series Data

# General Interest Boxes

# Preface

Econometrics can be a fun course for both teacher and student. The real world of economics, business, and government is a complicated and messy place, full of competing ideas and questions that demand answers. Is it more effective to tackle drunk driving by passing tough laws or by increasing the tax on alcohol? Can you make money in the stock market by buying when prices are historically low, relative to earnings, or should you just sit tight, as the random walk theory of stock prices suggests? Can we improve elementary education by reducing class sizes, or should we simply have our children listen to Mozart for 10 minutes a day? Econometrics helps us sort out sound ideas from crazy ones and find quantitative answers to important quantitative questions. Econometrics opens a window on our complicated world that lets us see the relationships on which people, businesses, and governments base their decisions.

*Introduction to Econometrics* is designed for a first course in undergraduate econometrics. It is our experience that to make econometrics relevant in an introductory course, interesting applications must motivate the theory and the theory must match the applications. This simple principle represents a significant departure from the older generation of econometrics books, in which theoretical models and assumptions do not match the applications. It is no wonder that some students question the relevance of econometrics after they spend much of their time learning assumptions that they subsequently realize are unrealistic so that they must then learn "solutions" to "problems" that arise when the applications do not match the assumptions. We believe that it is far better to motivate the need for tools with a concrete application and then to provide a few simple assumptions that match the application. Because the theory is immediately relevant to the applications, this approach can make econometrics come alive.

## New to the Third Edition

- Updated treatment of standard errors for panel data regression

- Discussion of when and why missing data can present a problem for regression analysis

- The use of regression discontinuity design as a method for analyzing quasi-experiments

- Updated discussion of weak instruments

- Discussion of the use and interpretation of control variables integrated into the core development of regression analysis

- Introduction of the "potential outcomes" framework for experimental data

- Additional general interest boxes

- Additional exercises, both pencil-and-paper and empirical

This third edition builds on the philosophy of the first and second editions that applications should drive the theory, not the other way around.

One substantial change in this edition concerns inference in regression with panel data (Chapter 10). In panel data, the data within an entity typically are correlated over time. For inference to be valid, standard errors must be computed using a method that is robust to this correlation. The chapter on panel data now uses one such method, clustered standard errors, from the outset. Clustered standard errors are the natural extension to panel data of the heteroskedasticity-robust standard errors introduced in the initial treatment of regression analysis in Part II. Recent research has shown that clustered standard errors have a number of desirable properties, which are now discussed in Chapter 10 and in a revised appendix to Chapter 10.

Another substantial set of changes concerns the treatment of experiments and quasi-experiments in Chapter 13. The discussion of differences-in-differences regression has been streamlined and draws directly on the multiple regression principles introduced in Part II. Chapter 13 now discusses regression discontinuity design, which is an intuitive and important framework for the analysis of quasi-experimental data. In addition, Chapter 13 now introduces the potential outcomes framework and relates this increasingly commonplace terminology to concepts that were introduced in Parts I and II.

This edition has a number of other significant changes. One is that it incorporates a precise but accessible treatment of control variables into the initial discussion of multiple regression. Chapter 7 now discusses conditions for control variables being successful in the sense that the coefficient on the variable of interest is unbiased even though the coefficients on the control variables generally are not. Other changes include a new discussion of missing data in Chapter 9, a new optional calculus-based appendix to Chapter 8 on slopes and elasticities of nonlinear regression functions, and an updated discussion in Chapter 12 of what to do if you have weak instruments. This edition also includes new general interest boxes, updated empirical examples, and additional exercises.

# The Updated Third Edition

- The time series data used in Chapters 14–16 have been extended through the beginning of 2013 and now include the Great Recession.

- The empirical analysis in Chapter 14 now focuses on forecasting the growth rate of real GDP using the term spread, replacing the Phillips curve forecasts from earlier editions.

- Several new empirical exercises have been added to each chapter. Rather than include all of the empirical exercises in the text, we have moved many of them to the Companion Website, **www.pearsonglobaleditions.com/Stock_Watson**. This has two main advantages: first, we can offer more and more in-depth exercises, and second, we can add and update exercises between editions. We encourage you to browse the empirical exercises available on the Companion Website.

# Features of This Book

*Introduction to Econometrics* differs from other textbooks in three main ways. First, we integrate real-world questions and data into the development of the theory, and we take seriously the substantive findings of the resulting empirical analysis. Second, our choice of topics reflects modern theory and practice. Third, we provide theory and assumptions that match the applications. Our aim is to teach students to become sophisticated consumers of econometrics and to do so at a level of mathematics appropriate for an introductory course.

## Real-World Questions and Data

We organize each methodological topic around an important real-world question that demands a specific numerical answer. For example, we teach single-variable regression, multiple regression, and functional form analysis in the context of estimating the effect of school inputs on school outputs. (Do smaller elementary school class sizes produce higher test scores?) We teach panel data methods in the context of analyzing the effect of drunk driving laws on traffic fatalities. We use possible racial discrimination in the market for home loans as the empirical application for teaching regression with a binary dependent variable (logit and probit). We teach instrumental variable estimation in the context of estimating the demand elasticity for cigarettes. Although these examples involve economic reasoning, all can be understood with only a single introductory course in economics, and many can be understood without any previous economics coursework. Thus the instructor can focus on teaching econometrics, not microeconomics or macroeconomics.

We treat all our empirical applications seriously and in a way that shows students how they can learn from data but at the same time be self-critical and aware of the limitations of empirical analyses. Through each application, we teach students to explore alternative specifications and thereby to assess whether their substantive findings are robust. The questions asked in the empirical applications are important, and we provide serious and, we think, credible answers. We encourage students and instructors to disagree, however, and invite them to reanalyze the data, which are provided on the textbook's Companion Website (**www .pearsonglobaleditions.com/Stock_Watson**).

## Contemporary Choice of Topics

Econometrics has come a long way since the 1980s. The topics we cover reflect the best of contemporary applied econometrics. One can only do so much in an introductory course, so we focus on procedures and tests that are commonly used in practice. For example:

- *Instrumental variables regression.* We present instrumental variables regression as a general method for handling correlation between the error term and a regressor, which can arise for many reasons, including omitted variables and simultaneous causality. The two assumptions for a valid instrument—exogeneity and relevance—are given equal billing. We follow that presentation with an extended discussion of where instruments come from and with tests of overidentifying restrictions and diagnostics for weak instruments, and we explain what to do if these diagnostics suggest problems.

- *Program evaluation.* An increasing number of econometric studies analyze either randomized controlled experiments or quasi-experiments, also known as natural experiments. We address these topics, often collectively referred to as program evaluation, in Chapter 13. We present this research strategy as an alternative approach to the problems of omitted variables, simultaneous causality, and selection, and we assess both the strengths and the weaknesses of studies using experimental or quasi-experimental data.

- *Forecasting.* The chapter on forecasting (Chapter 14) considers univariate (autoregressive) and multivariate forecasts using time series regression, not large simultaneous equation structural models. We focus on simple and reliable tools, such as autoregressions and model selection via an information criterion, that work well in practice. This chapter also features a practically oriented treatment of stochastic trends (unit roots), unit root tests, tests for structural breaks (at known and unknown dates), and pseudo out-of-sample forecasting, all in the context of developing stable and reliable time series forecasting models.

- *Time series regression.* We make a clear distinction between two very different applications of time series regression: forecasting and estimation of dynamic causal effects. The chapter on causal inference using time series data (Chapter 15) pays careful attention to when different estimation methods, including generalized least squares, will or will not lead to valid causal inferences and when it is advisable to estimate dynamic regressions using OLS with heteroskedasticity- and autocorrelation-consistent standard errors.

## Theory That Matches Applications

Although econometric tools are best motivated by empirical applications, students need to learn enough econometric theory to understand the strengths and limitations of those tools. We provide a modern treatment in which the fit between theory and applications is as tight as possible, while keeping the mathematics at a level that requires only algebra.

Modern empirical applications share some common characteristics: The data sets typically are large (hundreds of observations, often more); regressors are not fixed over repeated samples but rather are collected by random sampling (or some other mechanism that makes them random); the data are not normally distributed; and there is no *a priori* reason to think that the errors are homoskedastic (although often there are reasons to think that they are heteroskedastic).

These observations lead to important differences between the theoretical development in this textbook and other textbooks:

- *Large-sample approach.* Because data sets are large, from the outset we use large-sample normal approximations to sampling distributions for hypothesis testing and confidence intervals. In our experience, it takes less time to teach the rudiments of large-sample approximations than to teach the Student $t$ and exact $F$ distributions, degrees-of-freedom corrections, and so forth. This large-sample approach also saves students the frustration of discovering that, because of nonnormal errors, the exact distribution theory they just mastered is irrelevant. Once taught in the context of the sample mean, the large-sample approach to hypothesis testing and confidence intervals carries directly through multiple regression analysis, logit and probit, instrumental variables estimation, and time series methods.

- ***Random sampling.*** Because regressors are rarely fixed in econometric applications, from the outset we treat data on all variables (dependent and independent) as the result of random sampling. This assumption matches our initial applications to cross-sectional data, it extends readily to panel and time series data, and because of our large-sample approach, it poses no additional conceptual or mathematical difficulties.

- ***Heteroskedasticity.*** Applied econometricians routinely use heteroskedasticity-robust standard errors to eliminate worries about whether heteroskedasticity is present or not. In this book, we move beyond treating heteroskedasticity as an exception or a "problem" to be "solved"; instead, we allow for heteroskedasticity from the outset and simply use heteroskedasticity-robust standard errors. We present homoskedasticity as a special case that provides a theoretical motivation for OLS.

## Skilled Producers, Sophisticated Consumers

We hope that students using this book will become sophisticated consumers of empirical analysis. To do so, they must learn not only how to use the tools of regression analysis but also how to assess the validity of empirical analyses presented to them.

Our approach to teaching how to assess an empirical study is threefold. First, immediately after introducing the main tools of regression analysis, we devote Chapter 9 to the threats to internal and external validity of an empirical study. This chapter discusses data problems and issues of generalizing findings to other settings. It also examines the main threats to regression analysis, including omitted variables, functional form misspecification, errors-in-variables, selection, and simultaneity—and ways to recognize these threats in practice.

Second, we apply these methods for assessing empirical studies to the empirical analysis of the ongoing examples in the book. We do so by considering alternative specifications and by systematically addressing the various threats to validity of the analyses presented in the book.

Third, to become sophisticated consumers, students need firsthand experience as producers. Active learning beats passive learning, and econometrics is an ideal course for active learning. For this reason, the textbook website features data sets, software, and suggestions for empirical exercises of different scopes.

## Approach to Mathematics and Level of Rigor

Our aim is for students to develop a sophisticated understanding of the tools of modern regression analysis, whether the course is taught at a "high" or a "low" level of mathematics. Parts I through IV of the text (which cover the substantive material) are accessible to students with only precalculus mathematics. Parts I through IV have fewer equations and more applications than many introductory econometrics books and far fewer equations than books aimed at mathematical sections of undergraduate courses. But more equations do not imply a more sophisticated treatment. In our experience, a more mathematical treatment does not lead to a deeper understanding for most students.

That said, different students learn differently, and for mathematically well-prepared students, learning can be enhanced by a more explicitly mathematical treatment. Part V therefore contains an introduction to econometric theory that is appropriate for students with a stronger mathematical background. When the mathematical chapters in Part V are used in conjunction with the material in Parts I through IV, this book is suitable for advanced undergraduate or master's level econometrics courses.

## Contents and Organization

There are five parts to *Introduction to Econometrics*. This textbook assumes that the student has had a course in probability and statistics, although we review that material in Part I. We cover the core material of regression analysis in Part II. Parts III, IV, and V present additional topics that build on the core treatment in Part II.

### Part I

Chapter 1 introduces econometrics and stresses the importance of providing quantitative answers to quantitative questions. It discusses the concept of causality in statistical studies and surveys the different types of data encountered in econometrics. Material from probability and statistics is reviewed in Chapters 2 and 3, respectively; whether these chapters are taught in a given course or are simply provided as a reference depends on the background of the students.

### Part II

Chapter 4 introduces regression with a single regressor and ordinary least squares (OLS) estimation, and Chapter 5 discusses hypothesis tests and confidence intervals in the regression model with a single regressor. In Chapter 6, students learn how they can address omitted variable bias using multiple regression, thereby estimating the effect of one independent variable while holding other independent variables constant. Chapter 7 covers hypothesis tests, including $F$-tests, and confidence intervals in multiple regression. In Chapter 8, the linear regression model is extended to models with nonlinear population regression functions, with a focus on regression functions that are linear in the parameters (so that the parameters can be estimated by OLS). In Chapter 9, students step back and learn how to identify the strengths and limitations of regression studies, seeing in the process how to apply the concepts of internal and external validity.

## Part III

Part III presents extensions of regression methods. In Chapter 10, students learn how to use panel data to control for unobserved variables that are constant over time. Chapter 11 covers regression with a binary dependent variable. Chapter 12 shows how instrumental variables regression can be used to address a variety of problems that produce correlation between the error term and the regressor, and examines how one might find and evaluate valid instruments. Chapter 13 introduces students to the analysis of data from experiments and quasi-, or natural, experiments, topics often referred to as "program evaluation."

## Part IV

Part IV takes up regression with time series data. Chapter 14 focuses on forecasting and introduces various modern tools for analyzing time series regressions, such as unit root tests and tests for stability. Chapter 15 discusses the use of time series data to estimate causal relations. Chapter 16 presents some more advanced tools for time series analysis, including models of conditional heteroskedasticity.

## Part V

Part V is an introduction to econometric theory. This part is more than an appendix that fills in mathematical details omitted from the text. Rather, it is a self-contained treatment of the econometric theory of estimation and inference in the linear regression model. Chapter 17 develops the theory of regression analysis for a single regressor; the exposition does not use matrix algebra, although it does demand a higher level of mathematical sophistication than the rest of the text. Chapter 18 presents and studies the multiple regression model, instrumental variables regression, and generalized method of moments estimation of the linear model, all in matrix form.

## Prerequisites Within the Book

Because different instructors like to emphasize different material, we wrote this book with diverse teaching preferences in mind. To the maximum extent possible, the chapters in Parts III, IV, and V are "stand-alone" in the sense that they do not require first teaching all the preceding chapters. The specific prerequisites for each chapter are described in Table I. Although we have found that the sequence of topics adopted in the textbook works well in our own courses, the chapters are written in a way that allows instructors to present topics in a different order if they so desire.

## Sample Courses

This book accommodates several different course structures.

| TABLE I | Guide to Prerequisites for Special-Topic Chapters in Parts III, IV, and V | | | | | | | | | |
|---|---|---|---|---|---|---|---|---|---|---|
| | **Prerequisite parts or chapters** | | | | | | | | | |
| | Part I | Part II | | Part III | | Part IV | | | Part V |
| Chapter | 1–3 | 4–7, 9 | 8 | 10.1, 10.2 | 12.1, 12.2 | 14.1–14.4 | 14.5–14.8 | 15 | 17 |
| 10 | X[a] | X[a] | X | | | | | | |
| 11 | X[a] | X[a] | X | | | | | | |
| 12.1, 12.2 | X[a] | X[a] | X | | | | | | |
| 12.3–12.6 | X[a] | X[a] | X | X | X | | | | |
| 13 | X[a] | X[a] | X | X | X | | | | |
| 14 | X[a] | X[a] | b | | | | | | |
| 15 | X[a] | X[a] | b | | | X | | | |
| 16 | X[a] | X[a] | b | | | X | X | X | |
| 17 | X | X | X | | | | | | |
| 18 | X | X | X | | X | | | | X |

This table shows the minimum prerequisites needed to cover the material in a given chapter. For example, estimation of dynamic causal effects with time series data (Chapter 15) first requires Part I (as needed, depending on student preparation, and except as noted in footnote a), Part II (except for Chapter 8; see footnote b), and Sections 14.1 through 14.4.

[a]Chapters 10 through 16 use exclusively large-sample approximations to sampling distributions, so the optional Sections 3.6 (the Student $t$ distribution for testing means) and 5.6 (the Student $t$ distribution for testing regression coefficients) can be skipped.
[b]Chapters 14 through 16 (the time series chapters) can be taught without first teaching Chapter 8 (nonlinear regression functions) if the instructor pauses to explain the use of logarithmic transformations to approximate percentage changes.

## Standard Introductory Econometrics

This course introduces econometrics (Chapter 1) and reviews probability and statistics as needed (Chapters 2 and 3). It then moves on to regression with a single regressor, multiple regression, the basics of functional form analysis, and the evaluation of regression studies (all Part II). The course proceeds to cover regression with panel data (Chapter 10), regression with a limited dependent variable (Chapter 11), and instrumental variables regression (Chapter 12), as time permits. The course concludes with experiments and quasi-experiments in Chapter 13, topics that provide an opportunity to return to the questions of estimating causal effects raised at the beginning of the semester and to recapitulate core regression methods. *Prerequisites: Algebra II and introductory statistics.*

## Introductory Econometrics with Time Series and Forecasting Applications

Like a standard introductory course, this course covers all of Part I (as needed) and Part II. Optionally, the course next provides a brief introduction to panel data (Sections 10.1 and 10.2) and takes up instrumental variables regression (Chapter 12, or just Sections 12.1 and 12.2). The course then proceeds to Part IV, covering forecasting (Chapter 14) and estimation of dynamic causal effects (Chapter 15). If time permits, the course can include some advanced topics in time series analysis such as volatility clustering and conditional heteroskedasticity (Section 16.5). *Prerequisites: Algebra II and introductory statistics.*

## Applied Time Series Analysis and Forecasting

This book also can be used for a short course on applied time series and forecasting, for which a course on regression analysis is a prerequisite. Some time is spent reviewing the tools of basic regression analysis in Part II, depending on student preparation. The course then moves directly to Part IV and works through forecasting (Chapter 14), estimation of dynamic causal effects (Chapter 15), and advanced topics in time series analysis (Chapter 16), including vector autoregressions and conditional heteroskedasticity. An important component of this course is hands-on forecasting exercises, available to instructors on the book's accompanying website. *Prerequisites: Algebra II and basic introductory econometrics or the equivalent.*

## Introduction to Econometric Theory

This book is also suitable for an advanced undergraduate course in which the students have a strong mathematical preparation or for a master's level course in econometrics. The course briefly reviews the theory of statistics and probability as necessary (Part I). The course introduces regression analysis using the nonmathematical, applications-based treatment of Part II. This introduction is followed by the theoretical development in Chapters 17 and 18 (through Section 18.5). The course then takes up regression with a limited dependent variable (Chapter 11) and maximum likelihood estimation (Appendix 11.2). Next, the course optionally turns to instrumental variables regression and generalized method of moments (Chapter 12 and Section 18.7), time series methods (Chapter 14), and the estimation of causal effects using time series data and generalized least squares (Chapter 15 and Section 18.6). *Prerequisites: Calculus and introductory statistics. Chapter 18 assumes previous exposure to matrix algebra.*

## Pedagogical Features

This textbook has a variety of pedagogical features aimed at helping students understand, retain, and apply the essential ideas. *Chapter introductions* provide real-world grounding and motivation, as well as brief road maps highlighting the sequence of the discussion. *Key terms* are boldfaced and defined in context throughout each chapter, and *Key Concept boxes* at regular intervals recap the central ideas. *General interest boxes* provide interesting excursions into related topics and highlight real-world studies that use the methods or concepts being discussed in the text. A *Summary* concluding each chapter serves as a helpful framework for reviewing the main points of coverage. The questions in the *Review the Concepts* section check students' understanding of the core content, *Exercises* give more intensive practice working with the concepts and techniques introduced in the chapter, and *Empirical Exercises* allow students to apply what they have learned to answer real-world empirical questions. At the end of the textbook, the *Appendix* provides statistical tables, the *References* section lists sources for further reading, and a *Glossary* conveniently defines many key terms in the book.

## Supplements to Accompany the Textbook

The online supplements accompanying the third edition update of *Introduction to Econometrics* include the Instructor's Resource Manual, Test Bank, and PowerPoint® slides with text figures, tables, and Key Concepts. The Instructor's Resource Manual includes solutions to all the end-of-chapter exercises, while the Test Bank, offered in Testgen, provides a rich supply of easily edited test problems and questions of various types to meet specific course needs. These resources are available for download from the Instructor's Resource Center at **www.pearsonglobaleditions .com/Stock_Watson**.

## Companion Website

The Companion Website, found at **www.pearsonglobaleditions.com/Stock_ Watson**, provides a wide range of additional resources for students and faculty. These resources include more and more in depth empirical exercises, data sets for the empirical exercises, replication files for empirical results reported in the text, practice quizzes, answers to end-of-chapter Review the Concepts questions and Exercises, and EViews tutorials.

## MyEconLab

The third edition update is accompanied by a robust MyEconLab course. The MyEconLab course includes all the Review the Concepts questions as well as some Exercises and Empirical Exercises. In addition, the enhanced eText available in MyEconLab for the third edition update includes URL links from the Exercises and Empirical Exercises to questions in the MyEconLab course and to the data that accompanies them. To register for MyEconLab and to learn more, log on to **www.myeconlab.com**.

## Acknowledgments

A great many people contributed to the first edition of this book. Our biggest debts of gratitude are to our colleagues at Harvard and Princeton who used early drafts of this book in their classrooms. At Harvard's Kennedy School of Government, Suzanne Cooper provided invaluable suggestions and detailed comments on multiple drafts. As a coteacher with one of the authors (Stock), she also helped vet much of the material in this book while it was being developed for a required course for master's students at the Kennedy School. We are also indebted to two other Kennedy School colleagues, Alberto Abadie and Sue Dynarski, for their patient explanations of quasi-experiments and the field of program evaluation and for their detailed comments on early drafts of the text. At Princeton, Eli Tamer taught from an early draft and also provided helpful comments on the penultimate draft of the book.

We also owe much to many of our friends and colleagues in econometrics who spent time talking with us about the substance of this book and who collectively made so many helpful suggestions. Bruce Hansen (University of Wisconsin–Madison) and Bo Honore (Princeton) provided helpful feedback on very early outlines and preliminary versions of the core material in Part II. Joshua Angrist (MIT) and Guido Imbens (University of California, Berkeley) provided thoughtful suggestions about our treatment of materials on program evaluation. Our presentation of the material on time series has benefited from discussions with Yacine Ait-Sahalia (Princeton), Graham Elliott (University of California, San Diego), Andrew Harvey (Cambridge University), and Christopher Sims (Princeton). Finally, many people made helpful suggestions on parts of the manuscript close to their area of expertise: Don Andrews (Yale), John Bound (University of Michigan), Gregory Chow (Princeton), Thomas Downes (Tufts), David Drukker (StataCorp.), Jean Baldwin Grossman (Princeton), Eric Hanushek (Hoover Institution), James Heckman (University of Chicago), Han Hong (Princeton), Caroline Hoxby (Harvard), Alan Krueger (Princeton), Steven Levitt (University of Chicago), Richard Light (Harvard), David Neumark (Michigan State University), Joseph Newhouse (Harvard), Pierre Perron (Boston University), Kenneth Warner (University of Michigan), and Richard Zeckhauser (Harvard).

Many people were very generous in providing us with data. The California test score data were constructed with the assistance of Les Axelrod of the Standards and Assessments Division, California Department of Education. We are grateful to Charlie DePascale, Student Assessment Services, Massachusetts Department of Education, for his help with aspects of the Massachusetts test score data set. Christopher Ruhm (University of North Carolina, Greensboro) graciously provided us with his data set on drunk driving laws and traffic fatalities. The research department at the Federal Reserve Bank of Boston deserves thanks for putting together its data on racial discrimination in mortgage lending; we particularly thank Geoffrey Tootell for providing us with the updated version of the data set we use in Chapter 9 and Lynn Browne for explaining its policy context. We thank Jonathan Gruber (MIT) for sharing his data on cigarette sales, which we analyze in Chapter 12, and Alan Krueger (Princeton) for his help with the Tennessee STAR data that we analyze in Chapter 13.

We thank several people for carefully checking the page proof for errors. Kerry Griffin and Yair Listokin read the entire manuscript, and Andrew Fraker, Ori Heffetz, Amber Henry, Hong Li, Alessandro Tarozzi, and Matt Watson worked through several chapters.

In the first edition, we benefited from the help of an exceptional development editor, Jane Tufts, whose creativity, hard work, and attention to detail improved the book in many ways, large and small. Pearson provided us with first-rate support, starting with our excellent editor, Sylvia Mallory, and extending through the entire publishing team. Jane and Sylvia patiently taught us a lot about writing, organization, and presentation, and their efforts are evident on every page of this book. We extend our thanks to the superb Pearson team, who worked with us on the second edition: Adrienne D'Ambrosio (senior acquisitions editor), Bridget Page (associate media producer), Charles Spaulding (senior designer), Nancy Fenton (managing editor) and her selection of Nancy Freihofer and Thompson Steele Inc. who handled the entire production process, Heather McNally (supplements coordinator), and Denise Clinton (editor-in-chief). Finally, we had the benefit of Kay Ueno's skilled editing in the second edition. We are also grateful to the excellent third edition Pearson team of Adrienne D'Ambrosio, Nancy Fenton, and Jill Kolongowski, as well as Mary Sanger, the project manager with Nesbitt Graphics. We also wish to thank the Pearson team who worked on the third edition update: Christina Masturzo, Carolyn Philips, Liz Napolitano, and Heidi Allgair, project manager with Cenveo® Publisher Services.

We also received a great deal of help and suggestions from faculty, students, and researchers as we prepared the third edition and its update. The changes made in the third edition incorporate or reflect suggestions, corrections, comments, data, and help provided by a number of researchers and instructors: Donald Andrews (Yale University), Jushan Bai (Columbia), James Cobbe (Florida State University), Susan Dynarski (University of Michigan), Nicole Eichelberger (Texas Tech University), Boyd Fjeldsted (University of Utah), Martina Grunow, Daniel Hamermesh (University of Texas–Austin), Keisuke Hirano (University of Arizona), Bo Honore (Princeton University), Guido Imbens (Harvard University), Manfred Keil (Claremont McKenna College), David Laibson (Harvard University), David Lee (Princeton University), Brigitte Madrian (Harvard University), Jorge Marquez (University of Maryland), Karen Bennett Mathis (Florida Department of Citrus), Alan Mehlenbacher (University of Victoria), Ulrich Müller (Princeton University), Serena Ng (Columbia University), Harry Patrinos (World Bank), Zhuan Pei (Brandeis University), Peter Summers (Texas Tech University), Andrey Vasnov (University of Sydney), and Douglas Young (Montana State University). We also benefited from student input from F. Hoces dela Guardia and Carrie Wilson.

Thoughtful reviews for the third edition were prepared for Addison-Wesley by Steve DeLoach (Elon University), Jeffrey DeSimone (University of Texas at Arlington), Gary V. Engelhardt (Syracuse University), Luca Flabbi (Georgetown University), Steffen Habermalz (Northwestern University), Carolyn J. Heinrich (University of Wisconsin–Madison), Emma M. Iglesias-Vazquez (Michigan State

University), Carlos Lamarche (University of Oklahoma), Vicki A. McCracken (Washington State University), Claudiney M. Pereira (Tulane University), and John T. Warner (Clemson University). We also received very helpful input on draft revisions of Chapters 7 and 10 from John Berdell (DePaul University), Janet Kohlhase (University of Houston), Aprajit Mahajan (Stanford University), Xia Meng (Brandeis University), and Chan Shen (Georgetown University).

Above all, we are indebted to our families for their endurance throughout this project. Writing this book took a long time, and for them, the project must have seemed endless. They, more than anyone else, bore the burden of this commitment, and for their help and support we are deeply grateful.

Pearson would also like to thank and acknowledge Anisha Sharma (University of Oxford) and Samprit Chakrabarti (International School of Business and Media) for their contributions and reviews for the Global Edition, and Indrani Chkarborty (Institute of Development Studies), Gagari Chakrabarti ( Presidency University), Sukanya Das (Madras School of Economics), and Abhik Kumar Mukherjee (St. Xavier's College) for their guidance and recommendations to improve the global content.

# Introduction
# to Econometrics

# 1 Economic Questions and Data

Ask a half dozen econometricians what econometrics is, and you could get a half dozen different answers. One might tell you that econometrics is the science of testing economic theories. A second might tell you that econometrics is the set of tools used for forecasting future values of economic variables, such as a firm's sales, the overall growth of the economy, or stock prices. Another might say that econometrics is the process of fitting mathematical economic models to real-world data. A fourth might tell you that it is the science and art of using historical data to make numerical, or quantitative, policy recommendations in government and business.

In fact, all these answers are right. At a broad level, econometrics is the science and art of using economic theory and statistical techniques to analyze economic data. Econometric methods are used in many branches of economics, including finance, labor economics, macroeconomics, microeconomics, marketing, and economic policy. Econometric methods are also commonly used in other social sciences, including political science and sociology.

This book introduces you to the core set of methods used by econometricians. We will use these methods to answer a variety of specific, quantitative questions from the worlds of business and government policy. This chapter poses four of those questions and discusses, in general terms, the econometric approach to answering them. The chapter concludes with a survey of the main types of data available to econometricians for answering these and other quantitative economic questions.

## 1.1 Economic Questions We Examine

Many decisions in economics, business, and government hinge on understanding relationships among variables in the world around us. These decisions require quantitative answers to quantitative questions.

This book examines several quantitative questions taken from current issues in economics. Four of these questions concern education policy, racial bias in mortgage lending, cigarette consumption, and macroeconomic forecasting.

## Question #1: Does Reducing Class Size Improve Elementary School Education?

Proposals for reform of the U.S. public education system generate heated debate. Many of the proposals concern the youngest students, those in elementary schools. Elementary school education has various objectives, such as developing social skills, but for many parents and educators, the most important objective is basic academic learning: reading, writing, and basic mathematics. One prominent proposal for improving basic learning is to reduce class sizes at elementary schools. With fewer students in the classroom, the argument goes, each student gets more of the teacher's attention, there are fewer class disruptions, learning is enhanced, and grades improve.

But what, precisely, is the effect on elementary school education of reducing class size? Reducing class size costs money: It requires hiring more teachers and, if the school is already at capacity, building more classrooms. A decision maker contemplating hiring more teachers must weigh these costs against the benefits. To weigh costs and benefits, however, the decision maker must have a precise quantitative understanding of the likely benefits. Is the beneficial effect on basic learning of smaller classes large or small? Is it possible that smaller class size actually has no effect on basic learning?

Although common sense and everyday experience may suggest that more learning occurs when there are fewer students, common sense cannot provide a quantitative answer to the question of what exactly is the effect on basic learning of reducing class size. To provide such an answer, we must examine empirical evidence—that is, evidence based on data—relating class size to basic learning in elementary schools.

In this book, we examine the relationship between class size and basic learning, using data gathered from 420 California school districts in 1999. In the California data, students in districts with small class sizes tend to perform better on standardized tests than students in districts with larger classes. While this fact is consistent with the idea that smaller classes produce better test scores, it might simply reflect many other advantages that students in districts with small classes have over their counterparts in districts with large classes. For example, districts with small class sizes tend to have wealthier residents than districts with large classes, so students in small-class districts could have more opportunities for learning outside the classroom. It could be these extra learning opportunities that lead to higher test scores, not smaller class sizes. In Part II, we use multiple regression analysis to isolate the effect of changes in class size from changes in other factors, such as the economic background of the students.

## Question #2: Is There Racial Discrimination in the Market for Home Loans?

Most people buy their homes with the help of a mortgage, a large loan secured by the value of the home. By law, U.S. lending institutions cannot take race into account when deciding to grant or deny a request for a mortgage: Applicants who are identical in all ways except their race should be equally likely to have their mortgage applications approved. In theory, then, there should be no racial bias in mortgage lending.

In contrast to this theoretical conclusion, researchers at the Federal Reserve Bank of Boston found (using data from the early 1990s) that 28% of black applicants are denied mortgages, while only 9% of white applicants are denied. Do these data indicate that, in practice, there is racial bias in mortgage lending? If so, how large is it?

The fact that more black than white applicants are denied in the Boston Fed data does not by itself provide evidence of discrimination by mortgage lenders because the black and white applicants differ in many ways other than their race. Before concluding that there is bias in the mortgage market, these data must be examined more closely to see if there is a difference in the probability of being denied for *otherwise identical* applicants and, if so, whether this difference is large or small. To do so, in Chapter 11 we introduce econometric methods that make it possible to quantify the effect of race on the chance of obtaining a mortgage, *holding constant* other applicant characteristics, notably their ability to repay the loan.

## Question #3: How Much Do Cigarette Taxes Reduce Smoking?

Cigarette smoking is a major public health concern worldwide. Many of the costs of smoking, such as the medical expenses of caring for those made sick by smoking and the less quantifiable costs to nonsmokers who prefer not to breathe secondhand cigarette smoke, are borne by other members of society. Because these costs are borne by people other than the smoker, there is a role for government intervention in reducing cigarette consumption. One of the most flexible tools for cutting consumption is to increase taxes on cigarettes.

Basic economics says that if cigarette prices go up, consumption will go down. But by how much? If the sales price goes up by 1%, by what percentage will the quantity of cigarettes sold decrease? The percentage change in the quantity demanded resulting from a 1% increase in price is the *price elasticity of demand*.

If we want to reduce smoking by a certain amount, say 20%, by raising taxes, then we need to know the price elasticity of demand to calculate the price increase necessary to achieve this reduction in consumption. But what is the price elasticity of demand for cigarettes?

Although economic theory provides us with the concepts that help us answer this question, it does not tell us the numerical value of the price elasticity of demand. To learn the elasticity, we must examine empirical evidence about the behavior of smokers and potential smokers; in other words, we need to analyze data on cigarette consumption and prices.

The data we examine are cigarette sales, prices, taxes, and personal income for U.S. states in the 1980s and 1990s. In these data, states with low taxes, and thus low cigarette prices, have high smoking rates, and states with high prices have low smoking rates. However, the analysis of these data is complicated because causality runs both ways: Low taxes lead to high demand, but if there are many smokers in the state, then local politicians might try to keep cigarette taxes low to satisfy their smoking constituents. In Chapter 12, we study methods for handling this "simultaneous causality" and use those methods to estimate the price elasticity of cigarette demand.

## Question #4: By How Much Will U.S. GDP Grow Next Year?

It seems that people always want a sneak preview of the future. What will sales be next year at a firm that is considering investing in new equipment? Will the stock market go up next month, and, if it does, by how much? Will city tax receipts next year cover planned expenditures on city services? Will your microeconomics exam next week focus on externalities or monopolies? Will Saturday be a nice day to go to the beach?

One aspect of the future in which macroeconomists are particularly interested is the growth of real economic activity, as measured by real gross domestic product (GDP), during the next year. A management consulting firm might advise a manufacturing client to expand its capacity based on an upbeat forecast of economic growth. Economists at the Federal Reserve Board in Washington, D.C., are mandated to set policy to keep real GDP near its potential in order to maximize employment. If they forecast anemic GDP growth over the next year, they might expand liquidity in the economy by reducing interest rates or other measures, in an attempt to boost economic activity.

Professional economists who rely on precise numerical forecasts use econometric models to make those forecasts. A forecaster's job is to predict the future by using the past, and econometricians do this by using economic theory and statistical techniques to quantify relationships in historical data.

The data we use to forecast the growth rate of GDP are past values of GDP and the "term spread" in the United States. The *term spread* is the difference between long-term and short-term interest rates. It measures, among other things, whether investors expect short-term interest rates to rise or fall in the future. The term spread is usually positive, but it tends to fall sharply before the onset of a recession. One of the GDP growth rate forecasts we develop and evaluate in Chapter 14 is based on the term spread.

### Quantitative Questions, Quantitative Answers

Each of these four questions requires a numerical answer. Economic theory provides clues about that answer—for example, cigarette consumption ought to go down when the price goes up—but the actual value of the number must be learned empirically, that is, by analyzing data. Because we use data to answer quantitative questions, our answers always have some uncertainty: A different set of data would produce a different numerical answer. Therefore, the conceptual framework for the analysis needs to provide both a numerical answer to the question and a measure of how precise the answer is.

The conceptual framework used in this book is the multiple regression model, the mainstay of econometrics. This model, introduced in Part II, provides a mathematical way to quantify how a change in one variable affects another variable, holding other things constant. For example, what effect does a change in class size have on test scores, *holding constant* or *controlling for* student characteristics (such as family income) that a school district administrator cannot control? What effect does your race have on your chances of having a mortgage application granted, *holding constant* other factors such as your ability to repay the loan? What effect does a 1% increase in the price of cigarettes have on cigarette consumption, *holding constant* the income of smokers and potential smokers? The multiple regression model and its extensions provide a framework for answering these questions using data and for quantifying the uncertainty associated with those answers.

## 1.2   Causal Effects and Idealized Experiments

Like many other questions encountered in econometrics, the first three questions in Section 1.1 concern causal relationships among variables. In common usage, an action is said to cause an outcome if the outcome is the direct result, or consequence, of that action. Touching a hot stove causes you to get burned; drinking water causes you to be less thirsty; putting air in your tires causes them to inflate; putting fertilizer on your tomato plants causes them to produce more tomatoes. Causality means that a specific action (applying fertilizer) leads to a specific, measurable consequence (more tomatoes).

## Estimation of Causal Effects

How best might we measure the causal effect on tomato yield (measured in kilograms) of applying a certain amount of fertilizer, say 100 grams of fertilizer per square meter?

One way to measure this causal effect is to conduct an experiment. In that experiment, a horticultural researcher plants many plots of tomatoes. Each plot is tended identically, with one exception: Some plots get 100 grams of fertilizer per square meter, while the rest get none. Moreover, whether a plot is fertilized or not is determined randomly by a computer, ensuring that any other differences between the plots are unrelated to whether they receive fertilizer. At the end of the growing season, the horticulturalist weighs the harvest from each plot. The difference between the average yield per square meter of the treated and untreated plots is the effect on tomato production of the fertilizer treatment.

This is an example of a **randomized controlled experiment**. It is controlled in the sense that there are both a **control group** that receives no treatment (no fertilizer) and a **treatment group** that receives the treatment (100 g/m$^2$ of fertilizer). It is randomized in the sense that the treatment is assigned randomly. This random assignment eliminates the possibility of a systematic relationship between, for example, how sunny the plot is and whether it receives fertilizer so that the only systematic difference between the treatment and control groups is the treatment. If this experiment is properly implemented on a large enough scale, then it will yield an estimate of the causal effect on the outcome of interest (tomato production) of the treatment (applying 100 g/m$^2$ of fertilizer).

In this book, the **causal effect** is defined to be the effect on an outcome of a given action or treatment, as measured in an ideal randomized controlled experiment. In such an experiment, the only systematic reason for differences in outcomes between the treatment and control groups is the treatment itself.

It is possible to imagine an ideal randomized controlled experiment to answer each of the first three questions in Section 1.1. For example, to study class size, one can imagine randomly assigning "treatments" of different class sizes to different groups of students. If the experiment is designed and executed so that the only systematic difference between the groups of students is their class size, then in theory this experiment would estimate the effect on test scores of reducing class size, holding all else constant.

The concept of an ideal randomized controlled experiment is useful because it gives a definition of a causal effect. In practice, however, it is not possible to perform ideal experiments. In fact, experiments are relatively rare in econometrics because often they are unethical, impossible to execute satisfactorily, or prohibitively expensive. The concept of the ideal randomized controlled experiment does, however, provide a theoretical benchmark for an econometric analysis of causal effects using actual data.

### Forecasting and Causality

Although the first three questions in Section 1.1 concern causal effects, the fourth—forecasting the growth rate of GDP—does not. You do not need to know a causal relationship to make a good forecast. A good way to "forecast" whether it is raining is to observe whether pedestrians are using umbrellas, but the act of using an umbrella does not cause it to rain.

Even though forecasting need not involve causal relationships, economic theory suggests patterns and relationships that might be useful for forecasting. As we see in Chapter 14, multiple regression analysis allows us to quantify historical relationships suggested by economic theory, to check whether those relationships have been stable over time, to make quantitative forecasts about the future, and to assess the accuracy of those forecasts.

## 1.3   Data: Sources and Types

In econometrics, data come from one of two sources: experiments or nonexperimental observations of the world. This book examines both experimental and nonexperimental data sets.

### Experimental Versus Observational Data

**Experimental data** come from experiments designed to evaluate a treatment or policy or to investigate a causal effect. For example, the state of Tennessee financed a large randomized controlled experiment examining class size in the 1980s. In that experiment, which we examine in Chapter 13, thousands of students were randomly assigned to classes of different sizes for several years and were given standardized tests annually.

The Tennessee class size experiment cost millions of dollars and required the ongoing cooperation of many administrators, parents, and teachers over several years. Because real-world experiments with human subjects are difficult to administer and to control, they have flaws relative to ideal randomized controlled experiments. Moreover, in some circumstances, experiments are not only expensive and difficult to administer but also unethical. (Would it be ethical to offer randomly selected teenagers inexpensive cigarettes to see how many they buy?) Because of these financial, practical, and ethical problems, experiments in economics are relatively rare. Instead, most economic data are obtained by observing real-world behavior.

Data obtained by observing actual behavior outside an experimental setting are called **observational data**. Observational data are collected using surveys, such as telephone surveys of consumers, and administrative records, such as historical records on mortgage applications maintained by lending institutions.

Observational data pose major challenges to econometric attempts to estimate causal effects, and the tools of econometrics are designed to tackle these challenges. In the real world, levels of "treatment" (the amount of fertilizer in the tomato example, the student–teacher ratio in the class size example) are not assigned at random, so it is difficult to sort out the effect of the "treatment" from other relevant factors. Much of econometrics, and much of this book, is devoted to methods for meeting the challenges encountered when real-world data are used to estimate causal effects.

Whether the data are experimental or observational, data sets come in three main types: cross-sectional data, time series data, and panel data. In this book, you will encounter all three types.

## Cross-Sectional Data

Data on different entities—workers, consumers, firms, governmental units, and so forth—for a single time period are called **cross-sectional data**. For example, the data on test scores in California school districts are cross sectional. Those data are for 420 entities (school districts) for a single time period (1999). In general, the number of entities on which we have observations is denoted $n$; so, for example, in the California data set, $n = 420$.

The California test score data set contains measurements of several different variables for each district. Some of these data are tabulated in Table 1.1. Each row lists data for a different district. For example, the average test score for the first district ("district #1") is 690.8; this is the average of the math and science test scores for all fifth graders in that district in 1999 on a standardized test (the Stanford

| TABLE 1.1 | Selected Observations on Test Scores and Other Variables for California School Districts in 1999 | | | |
|---|---|---|---|---|
| Observation (District) Number | District Average Test Score (fifth grade) | Student–Teacher Ratio | Expenditure per Pupil ($) | Percentage of Students Learning English |
| 1 | 690.8 | 17.89 | $6385 | 0.0% |
| 2 | 661.2 | 21.52 | 5099 | 4.6 |
| 3 | 643.6 | 18.70 | 5502 | 30.0 |
| 4 | 647.7 | 17.36 | 7102 | 0.0 |
| 5 | 640.8 | 18.67 | 5236 | 13.9 |
| ⋮ | ⋮ | ⋮ | ⋮ | ⋮ |
| 418 | 645.0 | 21.89 | 4403 | 24.3 |
| 419 | 672.2 | 20.20 | 4776 | 3.0 |
| 420 | 655.8 | 19.04 | 5993 | 5.0 |

*Note:* The California test score data set is described in Appendix 4.1.

Achievement Test). The average student–teacher ratio in that district is 17.89; that is, the number of students in district #1 divided by the number of classroom teachers in district #1 is 17.89. Average expenditure per pupil in district #1 is $6385. The percentage of students in that district still learning English—that is, the percentage of students for whom English is a second language and who are not yet proficient in English—is 0%.

The remaining rows present data for other districts. The order of the rows is arbitrary, and the number of the district, which is called the **observation number**, is an arbitrarily assigned number that organizes the data. As you can see in the table, all the variables listed vary considerably.

With cross-sectional data, we can learn about relationships among variables by studying differences across people, firms, or other economic entities during a single time period.

## Time Series Data

**Time series data** are data for a single entity (person, firm, country) collected at multiple time periods. Our data set on the growth rate of GDP and the term spread in the United States is an example of a time series data set. The data set

| TABLE 1.2 | Selected Observations on the Growth Rate of GDP and the Term Spread in the United States: Quarterly Data, 1960:Q1–2013:Q1 | | |
|---|---|---|---|
| Observation Number | Date (year:quarter) | GDP Growth Rate (% at an annual rate) | Term Spread (% per year) |
| 1 | 1960:Q1 | 8.8% | 0.6% |
| 2 | 1960:Q2 | −1.5 | 1.3 |
| 3 | 1960:Q3 | 1.0 | 1.5 |
| 4 | 1960:Q4 | −4.9 | 1.6 |
| 5 | 1961:Q1 | 2.7 | 1.4 |
| ⋮ | ⋮ | ⋮ | ⋮ |
| 211 | 2012:Q3 | 2.7 | 1.5 |
| 212 | 2012:Q4 | 0.1 | 1.6 |
| 213 | 2013:Q1 | 1.1 | 1.9 |

*Note:* The United States GDP and term spread data set is described in Appendix 14.1.

contains observations on two variables (the growth rate of GDP and the term spread) for a single entity (the United States) for 213 time periods. Each time period in this data set is a quarter of a year (the first quarter is January, February, and March; the second quarter is April, May, and June; and so forth). The observations in this data set begin in the first quarter of 1960, which is denoted 1960:Q1, and end in the first quarter of 2013 (2013:Q1). The number of observations (that is, time periods) in a time series data set is denoted $T$. Because there are 213 quarters from 1960:Q1 to 2013:Q1, this data set contains $T = 213$ observations.

Some observations in this data set are listed in Table 1.2. The data in each row correspond to a different time period (year and quarter). In the first quarter of 1960, for example, GDP grew 8.8% at an annual rate. In other words, if GDP had continued growing for four quarters at its rate during the first quarter of 1960, the level of GDP would have increased by 8.8%. In the first quarter of 1960, the long-term interest rate was 4.5%, the short-term interest rate was 3.9%, so their difference, the term spread, was 0.6%.

By tracking a single entity over time, time series data can be used to study the evolution of variables over time and to forecast future values of those variables.

| TABLE 1.3 | Selected Observations on Cigarette Sales, Prices, and Taxes, by State and Year for U.S. States, 1985–1995 | | | | |
|---|---|---|---|---|---|
| Observation Number | State | Year | Cigarette Sales (packs per capita) | Average Price per Pack (including taxes) | Total Taxes (cigarette excise tax + sales tax) |
| 1 | Alabama | 1985 | 116.5 | $1.022 | $0.333 |
| 2 | Arkansas | 1985 | 128.5 | 1.015 | 0.370 |
| 3 | Arizona | 1985 | 104.5 | 1.086 | 0.362 |
| . | . | . | . | . | . |
| . | . | . | . | . | . |
| . | . | . | . | . | . |
| 47 | West Virginia | 1985 | 112.8 | 1.089 | 0.382 |
| 48 | Wyoming | 1985 | 129.4 | 0.935 | 0.240 |
| 49 | Alabama | 1986 | 117.2 | 1.080 | 0.334 |
| . | . | . | . | . | . |
| . | . | . | . | . | . |
| . | . | . | . | . | . |
| 96 | Wyoming | 1986 | 127.8 | 1.007 | 0.240 |
| 97 | Alabama | 1987 | 115.8 | 1.135 | 0.335 |
| . | . | . | . | . | . |
| . | . | . | . | . | . |
| . | . | . | . | . | . |
| 528 | Wyoming | 1995 | 112.2 | 1.585 | 0.360 |

*Note:* The cigarette consumption data set is described in Appendix 12.1.

## Panel Data

**Panel data**, also called **longitudinal data**, are data for multiple entities in which each entity is observed at two or more time periods. Our data on cigarette consumption and prices are an example of a panel data set, and selected variables and observations in that data set are listed in Table 1.3. The number of entities in a panel data set is denoted $n$, and the number of time periods is denoted $T$. In the cigarette data set, we have observations on $n = 48$ continental U.S. states (entities) for $T = 11$ years (time periods) from 1985 to 1995. Thus there is a total of $n \times T = 48 \times 11 = 528$ observations.

**KEY CONCEPT**

**1.1**

## Cross-Sectional, Time Series, and Panel Data

- Cross-sectional data consist of multiple entities observed at a single time period.
- Time series data consist of a single entity observed at multiple time periods.
- Panel data (also known as longitudinal data) consist of multiple entities, where each entity is observed at two or more time periods.

Some data from the cigarette consumption data set are listed in Table 1.3. The first block of 48 observations lists the data for each state in 1985, organized alphabetically from Alabama to Wyoming. The next block of 48 observations lists the data for 1986, and so forth, through 1995. For example, in 1985, cigarette sales in Arkansas were 128.5 packs per capita (the total number of packs of cigarettes sold in Arkansas in 1985 divided by the total population of Arkansas in 1985 equals 128.5). The average price of a pack of cigarettes in Arkansas in 1985, including tax, was $1.015, of which 37¢ went to federal, state, and local taxes.

Panel data can be used to learn about economic relationships from the experiences of the many different entities in the data set and from the evolution over time of the variables for each entity.

The definitions of cross-sectional data, time series data, and panel data are summarized in Key Concept 1.1.

## Summary

1. Many decisions in business and economics require quantitative estimates of how a change in one variable affects another variable.
2. Conceptually, the way to estimate a causal effect is in an ideal randomized controlled experiment, but performing such experiments in economic applications is usually unethical, impractical, or too expensive.
3. Econometrics provides tools for estimating causal effects using either observational (nonexperimental) data or data from real-world, imperfect experiments.
4. Cross-sectional data are gathered by observing multiple entities at a single point in time; time series data are gathered by observing a single entity at multiple points in time; and panel data are gathered by observing multiple entities, each of which is observed at multiple points in time.

## Key Terms

randomized controlled experiment
(52)
control group (52)
treatment group (52)
causal effect (52)
experimental data (53)

observational data (54)
cross-sectional data (54)
observation number (55)
time series data (55)
panel data (57)
longitudinal data (57)

---

**MyEconLab Can Help You Get a Better Grade**

MyEconLab    If your exam were tomorrow, would you be ready? For each chapter, **MyEconLab** Practice Tests and Study Plan help you prepare for your exams. You can also find similar Exercises and Review the Concepts Questions now in **MyEconLab**. To see how it works, turn to the **MyEconLab** spread on pages 2 and 3 of this book and then go to **www.myeconlab.com**.

For additional Empirical Exercises and Data Sets, log on to the Companion Website at **www.pearsonglobaleditions.com/Stock_Watson**.

---

## Review the Concepts

**1.1** Design a hypothetical ideal randomized controlled experiment to study the effect of reading on the improvement of a person's vocabulary. Suggest some impediments to implementing this experiment in practice.

**1.2** Design a hypothetical ideal randomized controlled experiment to study the effect of the consumption of alcohol on long-term memory loss. Suggest some impediments to implementing this experiment in practice.

**1.3** You are asked to study the causal effect of hours spent in remedial classes at schools by students who are struggling in mathematics on their final test scores and performance in the subject. Describe:

   **a.** an ideal randomized controlled experiment to measure this causal effect;

   **b.** an observational cross-sectional data set with which you could study this effect;

   **c.** an observational time series data set for studying this effect; and

   **d.** an observational panel data set for studying this effect.

2

# Review of Probability

This chapter reviews the core ideas of the theory of probability that are needed to understand regression analysis and econometrics. We assume that you have taken an introductory course in probability and statistics. If your knowledge of probability is stale, you should refresh it by reading this chapter. If you feel confident with the material, you still should skim the chapter and the terms and concepts at the end to make sure you are familiar with the ideas and notation.

Most aspects of the world around us have an element of randomness. The theory of probability provides mathematical tools for quantifying and describing this randomness. Section 2.1 reviews probability distributions for a single random variable, and Section 2.2 covers the mathematical expectation, mean, and variance of a single random variable. Most of the interesting problems in economics involve more than one variable, and Section 2.3 introduces the basic elements of probability theory for two random variables. Section 2.4 discusses three special probability distributions that play a central role in statistics and econometrics: the normal, chi-squared, and *F* distributions.

The final two sections of this chapter focus on a specific source of randomness of central importance in econometrics: the randomness that arises by randomly drawing a sample of data from a larger population. For example, suppose you survey ten recent college graduates selected at random, record (or "observe") their earnings, and compute the average earnings using these ten data points (or "observations"). Because you chose the sample at random, you could have chosen ten different graduates by pure random chance; had you done so, you would have observed ten different earnings and you would have computed a different sample average. Because the average earnings vary from one randomly chosen sample to the next, the sample average is itself a random variable. Therefore, the sample average has a probability distribution, which is referred to as its sampling distribution because this distribution describes the different possible values of the sample average that might have occurred had a different sample been drawn.

Section 2.5 discusses random sampling and the sampling distribution of the sample average. This sampling distribution is, in general, complicated. When the sample size is sufficiently large, however, the sampling distribution of the sample average is approximately normal, a result known as the central limit theorem, which is discussed in Section 2.6.

## 2.1   Random Variables and Probability Distributions

### Probabilities, the Sample Space, and Random Variables

*Probabilities and outcomes.*   The gender of the next new person you meet, your grade on an exam, and the number of times your computer will crash while you are writing a term paper all have an element of chance or randomness. In each of these examples, there is something not yet known that is eventually revealed.

The mutually exclusive potential results of a random process are called the **outcomes**. For example, your computer might never crash, it might crash once, it might crash twice, and so on. Only one of these outcomes will actually occur (the outcomes are mutually exclusive), and the outcomes need not be equally likely.

The **probability** of an outcome is the proportion of the time that the outcome occurs in the long run. If the probability of your computer not crashing while you are writing a term paper is 80%, then over the course of writing many term papers you will complete 80% without a crash.

*The sample space and events.*   The set of all possible outcomes is called the **sample space**. An **event** is a subset of the sample space, that is, an event is a set of one or more outcomes. The event "my computer will crash no more than once" is the set consisting of two outcomes: "no crashes" and "one crash."

*Random variables.*   A random variable is a numerical summary of a random outcome. The number of times your computer crashes while you are writing a term paper is random and takes on a numerical value, so it is a random variable.

Some random variables are discrete and some are continuous. As their names suggest, a **discrete random variable** takes on only a discrete set of values, like 0, 1, 2, . . . , whereas a **continuous random variable** takes on a continuum of possible values.

## Probability Distribution of a Discrete Random Variable

*Probability distribution.* The **probability distribution** of a discrete random variable is the list of all possible values of the variable and the probability that each value will occur. These probabilities sum to 1.

For example, let $M$ be the number of times your computer crashes while you are writing a term paper. The probability distribution of the random variable $M$ is the list of probabilities of each possible outcome: The probability that $M = 0$, denoted $\Pr(M = 0)$, is the probability of no computer crashes; $\Pr(M = 1)$ is the probability of a single computer crash; and so forth. An example of a probability distribution for $M$ is given in the second row of Table 2.1; in this distribution, if your computer crashes four times, you will quit and write the paper by hand. According to this distribution, the probability of no crashes is 80%; the probability of one crash is 10%; and the probability of two, three, or four crashes is, respectively, 6%, 3%, and 1%. These probabilities sum to 100%. This probability distribution is plotted in Figure 2.1.

*Probabilities of events.* The probability of an event can be computed from the probability distribution. For example, the probability of the event of one or two crashes is the sum of the probabilities of the constituent outcomes. That is, $\Pr(M = 1 \text{ or } M = 2) = \Pr(M = 1) + \Pr(M = 2) = 0.10 + 0.06 = 0.16$, or 16%.

*Cumulative probability distribution.* The **cumulative probability distribution** is the probability that the random variable is less than or equal to a particular value. The last row of Table 2.1 gives the cumulative probability distribution of the random variable $M$. For example, the probability of at most one crash, $\Pr(M \leq 1)$, is 90%, which is the sum of the probabilities of no crashes (80%) and of one crash (10%).

| TABLE 2.1 | Probability of Your Computer Crashing $M$ Times | | | | |
|---|---|---|---|---|---|
| | Outcome (number of crashes) | | | | |
| | 0 | 1 | 2 | 3 | 4 |
| Probability distribution | 0.80 | 0.10 | 0.06 | 0.03 | 0.01 |
| Cumulative probability distribution | 0.80 | 0.90 | 0.96 | 0.99 | 1.00 |

**FIGURE 2.1**    **Probability Distribution of the Number of Computer Crashes**

The height of each bar is the probability that the computer crashes the indicated number of times. The height of the first bar is 0.8, so the probability of 0 computer crashes is 80%. The height of the second bar is 0.1, so the probability of 1 computer crash is 10%, and so forth for the other bars.

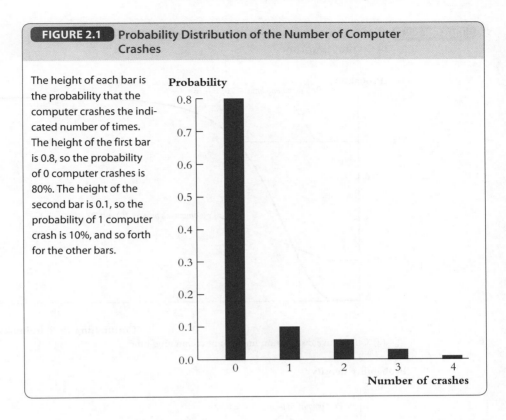

A cumulative probability distribution is also referred to as a **cumulative distribution function**, a **c.d.f.**, or a **cumulative distribution**.

*The Bernoulli distribution.* An important special case of a discrete random variable is when the random variable is binary, that is, the outcomes are 0 or 1. A binary random variable is called a **Bernoulli random variable** (in honor of the seventeenth-century Swiss mathematician and scientist Jacob Bernoulli), and its probability distribution is called the **Bernoulli distribution**.

For example, let $G$ be the gender of the next new person you meet, where $G = 0$ indicates that the person is male and $G = 1$ indicates that she is female. The outcomes of $G$ and their probabilities thus are

$$G = \begin{cases} 1 \text{ with probability } p \\ 0 \text{ with probability } 1 - p, \end{cases} \tag{2.1}$$

where $p$ is the probability of the next new person you meet being a woman. The probability distribution in Equation (2.1) is the Bernoulli distribution.

**FIGURE 2.2** Cumulative Distribution and Probability Density Functions of Commuting Time

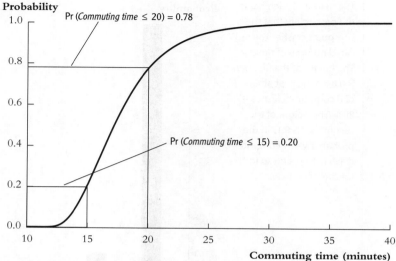

**(a)** Cumulative distribution function of commuting time

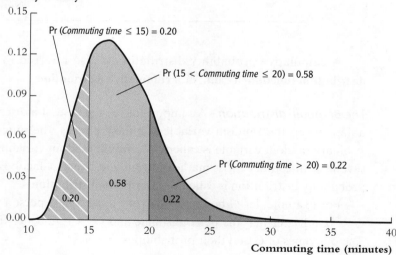

**(b)** Probability density function of commuting time

Figure 2.2a shows the cumulative probability distribution (or c.d.f.) of commuting times. The probability that a commuting time is less than 15 minutes is 0.20 (or 20%), and the probability that it is less than 20 minutes is 0.78 (78%). Figure 2.2b shows the probability density function (or p.d.f.) of commuting times. Probabilities are given by areas under the p.d.f. The probability that a commuting time is between 15 and 20 minutes is 0.58 (58%) and is given by the area under the curve between 15 and 20 minutes.

## Probability Distribution of a Continuous Random Variable

*Cumulative probability distribution.*  The cumulative probability distribution for a continuous variable is defined just as it is for a discrete random variable. That is, the cumulative probability distribution of a continuous random variable is the probability that the random variable is less than or equal to a particular value.

For example, consider a student who drives from home to school. This student's commuting time can take on a continuum of values and, because it depends on random factors such as the weather and traffic conditions, it is natural to treat it as a continuous random variable. Figure 2.2a plots a hypothetical cumulative distribution of commuting times. For example, the probability that the commute takes less than 15 minutes is 20% and the probability that it takes less than 20 minutes is 78%.

*Probability density function.*  Because a continuous random variable can take on a continuum of possible values, the probability distribution used for discrete variables, which lists the probability of each possible value of the random variable, is not suitable for continuous variables. Instead, the probability is summarized by the **probability density function**. The area under the probability density function between any two points is the probability that the random variable falls between those two points. A probability density function is also called a **p.d.f.**, a **density function**, or simply a **density**.

Figure 2.2b plots the probability density function of commuting times corresponding to the cumulative distribution in Figure 2.2a. The probability that the commute takes between 15 and 20 minutes is given by the area under the p.d.f. between 15 minutes and 20 minutes, which is 0.58, or 58%. Equivalently, this probability can be seen on the cumulative distribution in Figure 2.2a as the difference between the probability that the commute is less than 20 minutes (78%) and the probability that it is less than 15 minutes (20%). Thus the probability density function and the cumulative probability distribution show the same information in different formats.

## 2.2  Expected Values, Mean, and Variance

### The Expected Value of a Random Variable

*Expected value.*  The **expected value** of a random variable $Y$, denoted $E(Y)$, is the long-run average value of the random variable over many repeated trials or occurrences. The expected value of a discrete random variable is computed as a weighted average of the possible outcomes of that random variable, where the weights are the probabilities of that outcome. The expected value of $Y$ is also called the **expectation** of $Y$ or the **mean** of $Y$ and is denoted $\mu_Y$.

For example, suppose you loan a friend $100 at 10% interest. If the loan is repaid, you get $110 (the principal of $100 plus interest of $10), but there is a risk of 1% that your friend will default and you will get nothing at all. Thus the amount you are repaid is a random variable that equals $110 with probability 0.99 and equals $0 with probability 0.01. Over many such loans, 99% of the time you would be paid back $110, but 1% of the time you would get nothing, so on average you would be repaid $110 × 0.99 + $0 × 0.01 = $108.90. Thus the expected value of your repayment (or the "mean repayment") is $108.90.

As a second example, consider the number of computer crashes $M$ with the probability distribution given in Table 2.1. The expected value of $M$ is the average number of crashes over many term papers, weighted by the frequency with which a crash of a given size occurs. Accordingly,

$$E(M) = 0 \times 0.80 + 1 \times 0.10 + 2 \times 0.06 + 3 \times 0.03 + 4 \times 0.01 = 0.35. \quad (2.2)$$

That is, the expected number of computer crashes while writing a term paper is 0.35. Of course, the actual number of crashes must always be an integer; it makes no sense to say that the computer crashed 0.35 times while writing a particular term paper! Rather, the calculation in Equation (2.2) means that the average number of crashes over many such term papers is 0.35.

The formula for the expected value of a discrete random variable $Y$ that can take on $k$ different values is given as Key Concept 2.1. (Key Concept 2.1 uses "summation notation," which is reviewed in Exercise 2.25.)

**KEY CONCEPT 2.1**

## Expected Value and the Mean

Suppose the random variable $Y$ takes on $k$ possible values, $y_1, \ldots, y_k$, where $y_1$ denotes the first value, $y_2$ denotes the second value, and so forth, and that the probability that $Y$ takes on $y_1$ is $p_1$, the probability that $Y$ takes on $y_2$ is $p_2$, and so forth. The expected value of $Y$, denoted $E(Y)$, is

$$E(Y) = y_1 p_1 + y_2 p_2 + \cdots + y_k p_k = \sum_{i=1}^{k} y_i p_i, \quad (2.3)$$

where the notation $\sum_{i=1}^{k} y_i p_i$ means "the sum of $y_i p_i$ for $i$ running from 1 to $k$." The expected value of $Y$ is also called the mean of $Y$ or the expectation of $Y$ and is denoted $\mu_Y$.

*Expected value of a Bernoulli random variable.*   An important special case of the general formula in Key Concept 2.1 is the mean of a Bernoulli random variable. Let $G$ be the Bernoulli random variable with the probability distribution in Equation (2.1). The expected value of $G$ is

$$E(G) = 1 \times p + 0 \times (1 - p) = p. \tag{2.4}$$

Thus the expected value of a Bernoulli random variable is $p$, the probability that it takes on the value "1."

*Expected value of a continuous random variable.*   The expected value of a continuous random variable is also the probability-weighted average of the possible outcomes of the random variable. Because a continuous random variable can take on a continuum of possible values, the formal mathematical definition of its expectation involves calculus and its definition is given in Appendix 17.1.

## The Standard Deviation and Variance

The variance and standard deviation measure the dispersion or the "spread" of a probability distribution. The **variance** of a random variable $Y$, denoted var($Y$), is the expected value of the square of the deviation of $Y$ from its mean: var($Y$) $= E[(Y - \mu_Y)^2]$.

Because the variance involves the square of $Y$, the units of the variance are the units of the square of $Y$, which makes the variance awkward to interpret. It is therefore common to measure the spread by the **standard deviation**, which is the square root of the variance and is denoted $\sigma_Y$. The standard deviation has the same units as $Y$. These definitions are summarized in Key Concept 2.2.

## Variance and Standard Deviation

**KEY CONCEPT**

**2.2**

The variance of the discrete random variable $Y$, denoted $\sigma_Y^2$, is

$$\sigma_Y^2 = \text{var}(Y) = E[(Y - \mu_Y)^2] = \sum_{i=1}^{k} (y_i - \mu_Y)^2 p_i. \tag{2.5}$$

The standard deviation of $Y$ is $\sigma_Y$, the square root of the variance. The units of the standard deviation are the same as the units of $Y$.

For example, the variance of the number of computer crashes $M$ is the probability-weighted average of the squared difference between $M$ and its mean, 0.35:

$$\text{var}(M) = (0 - 0.35)^2 \times 0.80 + (1 - 0.35)^2 \times 0.10 + (2 - 0.35)^2 \times 0.06$$
$$+ (3 - 0.35)^2 \times 0.03 + (4 - 0.35)^2 \times 0.01 = 0.6475. \qquad (2.6)$$

The standard deviation of $M$ is the square root of the variance, so $\sigma_M = \sqrt{0.64750} \cong 0.80$.

*Variance of a Bernoulli random variable.* The mean of the Bernoulli random variable $G$ with probability distribution in Equation (2.1) is $\mu_G = p$ [Equation (2.4)], so its variance is

$$\text{var}(G) = \sigma_G^2 = (0 - p)^2 \times (1 - p) + (1 - p)^2 \times p = p(1 - p). \quad (2.7)$$

Thus the standard deviation of a Bernoulli random variable is $\sigma_G = \sqrt{p(1 - p)}$.

## Mean and Variance of a Linear Function of a Random Variable

This section discusses random variables (say, $X$ and $Y$) that are related by a linear function. For example, consider an income tax scheme under which a worker is taxed at a rate of 20% on his or her earnings and then given a (tax-free) grant of $2000. Under this tax scheme, after-tax earnings $Y$ are related to pre-tax earnings $X$ by the equation

$$Y = 2000 + 0.8X. \qquad (2.8)$$

That is, after-tax earnings $Y$ is 80% of pre-tax earnings $X$, plus $2000.

Suppose an individual's pre-tax earnings next year are a random variable with mean $\mu_X$ and variance $\sigma_X^2$. Because pre-tax earnings are random, so are after-tax earnings. What are the mean and standard deviations of her after-tax earnings under this tax? After taxes, her earnings are 80% of the original pre-tax earnings, plus $2000. Thus the expected value of her after-tax earnings is

$$E(Y) = \mu_Y = 2000 + 0.8\mu_X. \qquad (2.9)$$

The variance of after-tax earnings is the expected value of $(Y - \mu_Y)^2$. Because $Y = 2000 + 0.8X$, $Y - \mu_Y = 2000 + 0.8X - (2000 + 0.8\mu_X) = 0.8(X - \mu_X)$.

Thus $E[(Y - \mu_Y)^2] = E\{[0.8(X - \mu_X)]^2\} = 0.64E[(X - \mu_X)^2]$. It follows that $var(Y) = 0.64var(X)$, so, taking the square root of the variance, the standard deviation of $Y$ is

$$\sigma_Y = 0.8\sigma_X. \tag{2.10}$$

That is, the standard deviation of the distribution of her after-tax earnings is 80% of the standard deviation of the distribution of pre-tax earnings.

This analysis can be generalized so that $Y$ depends on $X$ with an intercept $a$ (instead of $2000) and a slope $b$ (instead of 0.8) so that

$$Y = a + bX. \tag{2.11}$$

Then the mean and variance of $Y$ are

$$\mu_Y = a + b\mu_X \quad \text{and} \tag{2.12}$$

$$\sigma_Y^2 = b^2\sigma_X^2, \tag{2.13}$$

and the standard deviation of $Y$ is $\sigma_Y = b\sigma_X$. The expressions in Equations (2.9) and (2.10) are applications of the more general formulas in Equations (2.12) and (2.13) with $a = 2000$ and $b = 0.8$.

## Other Measures of the Shape of a Distribution

The mean and standard deviation measure two important features of a distribution: its center (the mean) and its spread (the standard deviation). This section discusses measures of two other features of a distribution: the skewness, which measures the lack of symmetry of a distribution, and the kurtosis, which measures how thick, or "heavy," are its tails. The mean, variance, skewness, and kurtosis are all based on what are called the **moments of a distribution**.

*Skewness.* Figure 2.3 plots four distributions, two which are symmetric (Figures 2.3a and 2.3b) and two which are not (Figures 2.3c and 2.3d). Visually, the distribution in Figure 2.3d appears to deviate more from symmetry than does the distribution in Figure 2.3c. The skewness of a distribution provides a mathematical way to describe how much a distribution deviates from symmetry.

The **skewness** of the distribution of a random variable $Y$ is

$$\text{Skewness} = \frac{E[(Y - \mu_Y)^3]}{\sigma_Y^3}, \tag{2.14}$$

**FIGURE 2.3**   Four Distributions with Different Skewness and Kurtosis

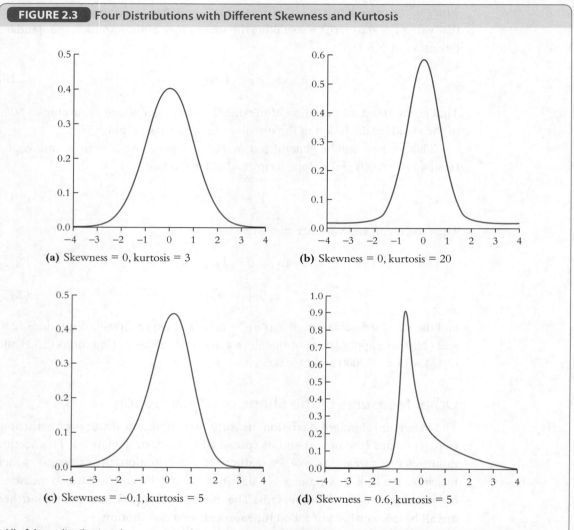

**(a)** Skewness = 0, kurtosis = 3

**(b)** Skewness = 0, kurtosis = 20

**(c)** Skewness = −0.1, kurtosis = 5

**(d)** Skewness = 0.6, kurtosis = 5

All of these distributions have a mean of 0 and a variance of 1. The distributions with skewness of 0 (a and b) are symmetric; the distributions with nonzero skewness (c and d) are not symmetric. The distributions with kurtosis exceeding 3 (b–d) have heavy tails.

where $\sigma_Y$ is the standard deviation of $Y$. For a symmetric distribution, a value of $Y$ a given amount above its mean is just as likely as a value of $Y$ the same amount below its mean. If so, then positive values of $(Y - \mu_Y)^3$ will be offset on average (in expectation) by equally likely negative values. Thus, for a symmetric distribution, $E[(Y - \mu_Y)^3] = 0$; the skewness of a symmetric distribution is zero. If a distribution is not symmetric, then a positive value of $(Y - \mu_Y)^3$ generally is not offset on average by an equally likely negative value, so the skewness is nonzero for a distribution that is not symmetric. Dividing by $\sigma_Y^3$ in the denominator of Equation (2.14) cancels the units of $Y^3$ in the numerator, so the skewness is unit free; in other words, changing the units of $Y$ does not change its skewness.

Below each of the four distributions in Figure 2.3 is its skewness. If a distribution has a long right tail, positive values of $(Y - \mu_Y)^3$ are not fully offset by negative values, and the skewness is positive. If a distribution has a long left tail, its skewness is negative.

*Kurtosis.* The **kurtosis** of a distribution is a measure of how much mass is in its tails and, therefore, is a measure of how much of the variance of $Y$ arises from extreme values. An extreme value of $Y$ is called an **outlier**. The greater the kurtosis of a distribution, the more likely are outliers.

The kurtosis of the distribution of $Y$ is

$$\text{Kurtosis} = \frac{E[(Y - \mu_Y)^4]}{\sigma_Y^4}. \tag{2.15}$$

If a distribution has a large amount of mass in its tails, then some extreme departures of $Y$ from its mean are likely, and these departures will lead to large values, on average (in expectation), of $(Y - \mu_Y)^4$. Thus, for a distribution with a large amount of mass in its tails, the kurtosis will be large. Because $(Y - \mu_Y)^4$ cannot be negative, the kurtosis cannot be negative.

The kurtosis of a normally distributed random variable is 3, so a random variable with kurtosis exceeding 3 has more mass in its tails than a normal random variable. A distribution with kurtosis exceeding 3 is called **leptokurtic** or, more simply, heavy-tailed. Like skewness, the kurtosis is unit free, so changing the units of $Y$ does not change its kurtosis.

Below each of the four distributions in Figure 2.3 is its kurtosis. The distributions in Figures 2.3b–d are heavy-tailed.

*Moments.* The mean of $Y$, $E(Y)$, is also called the first moment of $Y$, and the expected value of the square of $Y$, $E(Y^2)$, is called the second moment of $Y$. In general, the expected value of $Y^r$ is called the $r^{\text{th}}$ **moment** of the random variable $Y$. That is, the $r^{\text{th}}$ moment of $Y$ is $E(Y^r)$. The skewness is a function of the first, second, and third moments of $Y$, and the kurtosis is a function of the first through fourth moments of $Y$.

# 2.3 Two Random Variables

Most of the interesting questions in economics involve two or more variables. Are college graduates more likely to have a job than nongraduates? How does the distribution of income for women compare to that for men? These questions concern the distribution of two random variables, considered together (education and employment status in the first example, income and gender in the second). Answering such questions requires an understanding of the concepts of joint, marginal, and conditional probability distributions.

## Joint and Marginal Distributions

*Joint distribution.* The **joint probability distribution** of two discrete random variables, say $X$ and $Y$, is the probability that the random variables simultaneously take on certain values, say $x$ and $y$. The probabilities of all possible $(x, y)$ combinations sum to 1. The joint probability distribution can be written as the function $\Pr(X = x, Y = y)$.

For example, weather conditions—whether or not it is raining—affect the commuting time of the student commuter in Section 2.1. Let $Y$ be a binary random variable that equals 1 if the commute is short (less than 20 minutes) and equals 0 otherwise and let $X$ be a binary random variable that equals 0 if it is raining and 1 if not. Between these two random variables, there are four possible outcomes: it rains and the commute is long ($X = 0, Y = 0$); rain and short commute ($X = 0, Y = 1$); no rain and long commute ($X = 1, Y = 0$); and no rain and short commute ($X = 1, Y = 1$). The joint probability distribution is the frequency with which each of these four outcomes occurs over many repeated commutes.

An example of a joint distribution of these two variables is given in Table 2.2. According to this distribution, over many commutes, 15% of the days have rain and a long commute ($X = 0, Y = 0$); that is, the probability of a long, rainy commute is 15%, or $\Pr(X = 0, Y = 0) = 0.15$. Also, $\Pr(X = 0, Y = 1) = 0.15$,

| TABLE 2.2 | Joint Distribution of Weather Conditions and Commuting Times | | |
|---|---|---|---|
| | Rain ($X = 0$) | No Rain ($X = 1$) | Total |
| Long commute ($Y = 0$) | 0.15 | 0.07 | 0.22 |
| Short commute ($Y = 1$) | 0.15 | 0.63 | 0.78 |
| **Total** | 0.30 | 0.70 | 1.00 |

$\Pr(X = 1, Y = 0) = 0.07$, and $\Pr(X = 1, Y = 1) = 0.63$. These four possible outcomes are mutually exclusive and constitute the sample space so the four probabilities sum to 1.

*Marginal probability distribution.* The **marginal probability distribution** of a random variable $Y$ is just another name for its probability distribution. This term is used to distinguish the distribution of $Y$ alone (the marginal distribution) from the joint distribution of $Y$ and another random variable.

The marginal distribution of $Y$ can be computed from the joint distribution of $X$ and $Y$ by adding up the probabilities of all possible outcomes for which $Y$ takes on a specified value. If $X$ can take on $l$ different values $x_1, \ldots, x_l$, then the marginal probability that $Y$ takes on the value $y$ is

$$\Pr(Y = y) = \sum_{i=1}^{l} \Pr(X = x_i, Y = y). \tag{2.16}$$

For example, in Table 2.2, the probability of a long rainy commute is 15% and the probability of a long commute with no rain is 7%, so the probability of a long commute (rainy or not) is 22%. The marginal distribution of commuting times is given in the final column of Table 2.2. Similarly, the marginal probability that it will rain is 30%, as shown in the final row of Table 2.2.

## Conditional Distributions

*Conditional distribution.* The distribution of a random variable $Y$ conditional on another random variable $X$ taking on a specific value is called the **conditional distribution** of $Y$ given $X$. The conditional probability that $Y$ takes on the value $y$ when $X$ takes on the value $x$ is written $\Pr(Y = y \mid X = x)$.

For example, what is the probability of a long commute ($Y = 0$) if you know it is raining ($X = 0$)? From Table 2.2, the joint probability of a rainy short commute is 15% and the joint probability of a rainy long commute is 15%, so if it is raining a long commute and a short commute are equally likely. Thus the probability of a long commute ($Y = 0$), conditional on it being rainy ($X = 0$), is 50%, or $\Pr(Y = 0 \mid X = 0) = 0.50$. Equivalently, the marginal probability of rain is 30%; that is, over many commutes it rains 30% of the time. Of this 30% of commutes, 50% of the time the commute is long ($0.15/0.30$).

In general, the conditional distribution of $Y$ given $X = x$ is

$$\Pr(Y = y \mid X = x) = \frac{\Pr(X = x, Y = y)}{\Pr(X = x)}. \tag{2.17}$$

**TABLE 2.3**  Joint and Conditional Distributions of Computer Crashes (*M*) and Computer Age (*A*)

**A. Joint Distribution**

|  | M = 0 | M = 1 | M = 2 | M = 3 | M = 4 | Total |
|---|---|---|---|---|---|---|
| Old computer ($A = 0$) | 0.35 | 0.065 | 0.05 | 0.025 | 0.01 | 0.50 |
| New computer ($A = 1$) | 0.45 | 0.035 | 0.01 | 0.005 | 0.00 | 0.50 |
| **Total** | 0.80 | 0.10 | 0.06 | 0.03 | 0.01 | 1.00 |

**B. Conditional Distributions of *M* given *A***

|  | M = 0 | M = 1 | M = 2 | M = 3 | M = 2 | Total |
|---|---|---|---|---|---|---|
| $\Pr(M \mid A = 0)$ | 0.70 | 0.13 | 0.10 | 0.05 | 0.02 | 1.00 |
| $\Pr(M \mid A = 1)$ | 0.90 | 0.07 | 0.02 | 0.01 | 0.00 | 1.00 |

For example, the conditional probability of a long commute given that it is rainy is $\Pr(Y = 0 \mid X = 0) = \Pr(X = 0, Y = 0)/\Pr(X = 0) = 0.15/0.30 = 0.50$.

As a second example, consider a modification of the crashing computer example. Suppose you use a computer in the library to type your term paper and the librarian randomly assigns you a computer from those available, half of which are new and half of which are old. Because you are randomly assigned to a computer, the age of the computer you use, $A$ ($= 1$ if the computer is new, $= 0$ if it is old), is a random variable. Suppose the joint distribution of the random variables $M$ and $A$ is given in Part A of Table 2.3. Then the conditional distribution of computer crashes, given the age of the computer, is given in Part B of the table. For example, the joint probability $M = 0$ and $A = 0$ is 0.35; because half the computers are old, the conditional probability of no crashes, given that you are using an old computer, is $\Pr(M = 0 \mid A = 0) = \Pr(M = 0, A = 0)/\Pr(A = 0) = 0.35/0.50 = 0.70$, or 70%. In contrast, the conditional probability of no crashes given that you are assigned a new computer is 90%. According to the conditional distributions in Part B of Table 2.3, the newer computers are less likely to crash than the old ones; for example, the probability of three crashes is 5% with an old computer but 1% with a new computer.

*Conditional expectation.* The **conditional expectation** of $Y$ given $X$, also called the **conditional mean** of $Y$ given $X$, is the mean of the conditional distribution of $Y$ given $X$. That is, the conditional expectation is the expected value of $Y$, computed using the conditional distribution of $Y$ given $X$. If $Y$ takes on $k$ values $y_1, \ldots, y_k$, then the conditional mean of $Y$ given $X = x$ is

$$E(Y \mid X = x) = \sum_{i=1}^{k} y_i \Pr(Y = y_i \mid X = x). \tag{2.18}$$

For example, based on the conditional distributions in Table 2.3, the expected number of computer crashes, given that the computer is old, is $E(M \mid A = 0) = 0 \times 0.70 + 1 \times 0.13 + 2 \times 0.10 + 3 \times 0.05 + 4 \times 0.02 = 0.56$. The expected number of computer crashes, given that the computer is new, is $E(M \mid A = 1) = 0.14$, less than for the old computers.

The conditional expectation of $Y$ given $X = x$ is just the mean value of $Y$ when $X = x$. In the example of Table 2.3, the mean number of crashes is 0.56 for old computers, so the conditional expectation of $Y$ given that the computer is old is 0.56. Similarly, among new computers, the mean number of crashes is 0.14, that is, the conditional expectation of $Y$ given that the computer is new is 0.14.

*The law of iterated expectations.* The mean of $Y$ is the weighted average of the conditional expectation of $Y$ given $X$, weighted by the probability distribution of $X$. For example, the mean height of adults is the weighted average of the mean height of men and the mean height of women, weighted by the proportions of men and women. Stated mathematically, if $X$ takes on the $l$ values $x_1, \ldots, x_l$, then

$$E(Y) = \sum_{i=1}^{l} E(Y \mid X = x_i)\Pr(X = x_i). \tag{2.19}$$

Equation (2.19) follows from Equations (2.18) and (2.17) (see Exercise 2.19).

Stated differently, the expectation of $Y$ is the expectation of the conditional expectation of $Y$ given $X$,

$$E(Y) = E[E(Y \mid X)], \tag{2.20}$$

where the inner expectation on the right-hand side of Equation (2.20) is computed using the conditional distribution of $Y$ given $X$ and the outer expectation is computed using the marginal distribution of $X$. Equation (2.20) is known as the **law of iterated expectations**.

For example, the mean number of crashes $M$ is the weighted average of the conditional expectation of $M$ given that it is old and the conditional expectation of

$M$ given that it is new, so $E(M) = E(M \mid A = 0) \times \Pr(A = 0) + E(M \mid A = 1) \times \Pr(A = 1) = 0.56 \times 0.50 + 0.14 \times 0.50 = 0.35$. This is the mean of the marginal distribution of $M$, as calculated in Equation (2.2).

The law of iterated expectations implies that if the conditional mean of $Y$ given $X$ is zero, then the mean of $Y$ is zero. This is an immediate consequence of Equation (2.20): if $E(Y \mid X) = 0$, then $E(Y) = E[E(Y \mid X)] = E[0] = 0$. Said differently, if the mean of $Y$ given $X$ is zero, then it must be that the probability-weighted average of these conditional means is zero, that is, the mean of $Y$ must be zero.

The law of iterated expectations also applies to expectations that are conditional on multiple random variables. For example, let $X$, $Y$, and $Z$ be random variables that are jointly distributed. Then the law of iterated expectations says that $E(Y) = E[E(Y \mid X, Z)]$, where $E(Y \mid X, Z)$ is the conditional expectation of $Y$ given both $X$ and $Z$. For example, in the computer crash illustration of Table 2.3, let $P$ denote the number of programs installed on the computer; then $E(M \mid A, P)$ is the expected number of crashes for a computer with age $A$ that has $P$ programs installed. The expected number of crashes overall, $E(M)$, is the weighted average of the expected number of crashes for a computer with age $A$ and number of programs $P$, weighted by the proportion of computers with that value of both $A$ and $P$.

Exercise 2.20 provides some additional properties of conditional expectations with multiple variables.

*Conditional variance.* The variance of $Y$ conditional on $X$ is the variance of the conditional distribution of $Y$ given $X$. Stated mathematically, the **conditional variance** of $Y$ given $X$ is

$$\text{var}(Y \mid X = x) = \sum_{i=1}^{k} [y_i - E(Y \mid X = x)]^2 \Pr(Y = y_i \mid X = x). \quad (2.21)$$

For example, the conditional variance of the number of crashes given that the computer is old is $\text{var}(M \mid A = 0) = (0 - 0.56)^2 \times 0.70 + (1 - 0.56)^2 \times 0.13 + (2 - 0.56)^2 \times 0.10 + (3 - 0.56)^2 \times 0.05 + (4 - 0.56)^2 \times 0.02 \cong 0.99$. The standard deviation of the conditional distribution of $M$ given that $A = 0$ is thus $\sqrt{0.99} = 0.99$. The conditional variance of $M$ given that $A = 1$ is the variance of the distribution in the second row of Panel B of Table 2.3, which is 0.22, so the standard deviation of $M$ for new computers is $\sqrt{0.22} = 0.47$. For the conditional distributions in Table 2.3, the expected number of crashes for new computers (0.14) is less than that for old computers (0.56), and the spread of the distribution of the number of crashes, as measured by the conditional standard deviation, is smaller for new computers (0.47) than for old (0.99).

## Independence

Two random variables $X$ and $Y$ are **independently distributed**, or **independent**, if knowing the value of one of the variables provides no information about the other. Specifically, $X$ and $Y$ are independent if the conditional distribution of $Y$ given $X$ equals the marginal distribution of $Y$. That is, $X$ and $Y$ are independently distributed if, for all values of $x$ and $y$,

$$\Pr(Y = y \mid X = x) = \Pr(Y = y) \quad \text{(independence of } X \text{ and } Y\text{).} \quad (2.22)$$

Substituting Equation (2.22) into Equation (2.17) gives an alternative expression for independent random variables in terms of their joint distribution. If $X$ and $Y$ are independent, then

$$\Pr(X = x, Y = y) = \Pr(X = x)\Pr(Y = y). \quad (2.23)$$

That is, the joint distribution of two independent random variables is the product of their marginal distributions.

## Covariance and Correlation

*Covariance.* One measure of the extent to which two random variables move together is their covariance. The **covariance** between $X$ and $Y$ is the expected value $E[(X - \mu_X)(Y - \mu_Y)]$, where $\mu_X$, where $\mu_X$ is the mean of $X$ and $\mu_Y$ is the mean of $Y$. The covariance is denoted $\text{cov}(X, Y)$ or $\sigma_{XY}$. If $X$ can take on $l$ values and $Y$ can take on $k$ values, then the covariance is given by the formula

$$\begin{aligned}
\text{cov}(X, Y) = \sigma_{XY} &= E[(X - \mu_X)(Y - \mu_Y)] \\
&= \sum_{i=1}^{k}\sum_{j=1}^{l}(x_j - \mu_X)(y_i - \mu_Y)\Pr(X = x_j, Y = y_i).
\end{aligned} \quad (2.24)$$

To interpret this formula, suppose that when $X$ is greater than its mean (so that $X - \mu_X$ is positive), then $Y$ tends be greater than its mean (so that $Y - \mu_Y$ is positive), and when $X$ is less than its mean (so that $X - \mu_X < 0$), then $Y$ tends to be less than its mean (so that $Y - \mu_Y < 0$). In both cases, the product $(X - \mu_X) \times (Y - \mu_Y)$ tends to be positive, so the covariance is positive. In contrast, if $X$ and $Y$ tend to move in opposite directions (so that $X$ is large when $Y$ is small, and vice versa), then the covariance is negative. Finally, if $X$ and $Y$ are independent, then the covariance is zero (see Exercise 2.19).

*Correlation.* Because the covariance is the product of $X$ and $Y$, deviated from their means, its units are, awkwardly, the units of $X$ multiplied by the units of $Y$. This "units" problem can make numerical values of the covariance difficult to interpret.

The correlation is an alternative measure of dependence between $X$ and $Y$ that solves the "units" problem of the covariance. Specifically, the **correlation** between $X$ and $Y$ is the covariance between $X$ and $Y$ divided by their standard deviations:

$$\text{corr}(X, Y) = \frac{\text{cov}(X, Y)}{\sqrt{\text{var}(X)\,\text{var}(Y)}} = \frac{\sigma_{XY}}{\sigma_X \sigma_Y}. \qquad (2.25)$$

Because the units of the numerator in Equation (2.25) are the same as those of the denominator, the units cancel and the correlation is unitless. The random variables $X$ and $Y$ are said to be **uncorrelated** if $\text{corr}(X, Y) = 0$.

The correlation always is between –1 and 1; that is, as proven in Appendix 2.1,

$$-1 \leq \text{corr}(X, Y) \leq 1 \quad \text{(correlation inequality)}. \qquad (2.26)$$

*Correlation and conditional mean.* If the conditional mean of $Y$ does not depend on $X$, then $Y$ and $X$ are uncorrelated. That is,

$$\text{if } E(Y \mid X) = \mu_Y, \text{ then cov}(Y, X) = 0 \text{ and corr}(Y, X) = 0. \qquad (2.27)$$

We now show this result. First suppose that $Y$ and $X$ have mean zero so that $\text{cov}(Y, X) = E[(Y - \mu_Y)(X - \mu_X)] = E(YX)$. By the law of iterated expectations [Equation (2.20)], $E(YX) = E[E(YX \mid X)] = E[E(Y \mid X)X] = 0$ because $E(Y \mid X) = 0$, so $\text{cov}(Y, X) = 0$. Equation (2.27) follows by substituting $\text{cov}(Y, X) = 0$ into the definition of correlation in Equation (2.25). If $Y$ and $X$ do not have mean zero, first subtract off their means, then the preceding proof applies.

It is *not* necessarily true, however, that if $X$ and $Y$ are uncorrelated, then the conditional mean of $Y$ given $X$ does not depend on $X$. Said differently, it is possible for the conditional mean of $Y$ to be a function of $X$ but for $Y$ and $X$ nonetheless to be uncorrelated. An example is given in Exercise 2.23.

## The Mean and Variance of Sums of Random Variables

The mean of the sum of two random variables, $X$ and $Y$, is the sum of their means:

$$E(X + Y) = E(X) + E(Y) = \mu_X + \mu_Y. \qquad (2.28)$$

## The Distribution of Earnings in the United States in 2012

Some parents tell their children that they will be able to get a better, higher-paying job if they get a college degree than if they skip higher education. Are these parents right? Does the distribution of earnings differ between workers who are college graduates and workers who have only a high school diploma, and, if so, how? Among workers with a similar education, does the distribution of earnings for men and women differ?

For example, do the best-paid college-educated women earn as much as the best-paid college-educated men?

One way to answer these questions is to examine the distribution of earnings of full-time workers, conditional on the highest educational degree achieved (high school diploma or bachelor's degree) and on gender. These four conditional distributions are shown in Figure 2.4, and the mean, standard deviation, and

**FIGURE 2.4** Conditional Distribution of Average Hourly Earnings of U.S. Full-Time Workers in 2012, Given Education Level and Gender

The four distributions of earnings are for women and men, for those with only a high school diploma (a and c) and those whose highest degree is from a four-year college (b and d).

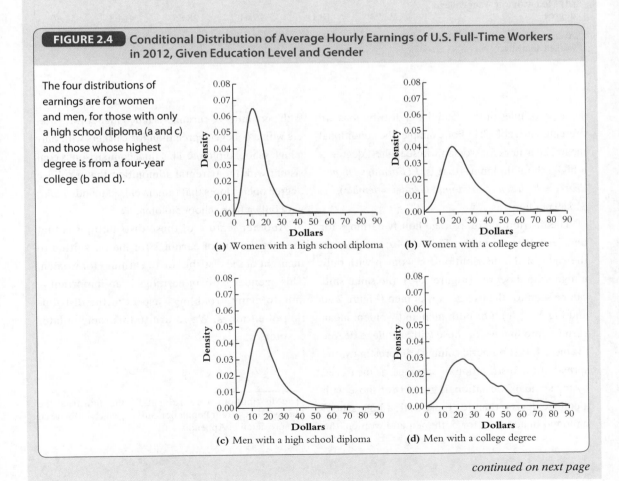

(a) Women with a high school diploma
(b) Women with a college degree
(c) Men with a high school diploma
(d) Men with a college degree

*continued on next page*

| TABLE 2.4 | Summaries of the Conditional Distribution of Average Hourly Earnings of U.S. Full-Time Workers in 2012 Given Education Level and Gender | | | | | | |
|---|---|---|---|---|---|---|---|
| | | | | **Percentile** | | | |
| | **Mean** | **Standard Deviation** | **25%** | **50% (median)** | **75%** | **90%** | |
| (a) Women with high school diploma | $15.49 | $8.42 | $10.10 | $14.03 | $18.75 | $24.52 | |
| (b) Women with four-year college degree | 25.42 | 13.81 | 16.15 | 22.44 | 31.34 | 43.27 | |
| (c) Men with high school diploma | 20.25 | 11.00 | 12.92 | 17.86 | 24.83 | 33.78 | |
| (d) Men with four-year college degree | 32.73 | 18.11 | 19.61 | 28.85 | 41.68 | 57.30 | |

Average hourly earnings are the sum of annual pretax wages, salaries, tips, and bonuses divided by the number of hours worked annually.

some percentiles of the conditional distributions are presented in Table 2.4.[1] For example, the conditional mean of earnings for women whose highest degree is a high school diploma—that is, $E(Earnings|Highest\ degree = high\ school\ diploma,\ Gender = female)$—is $15.49 per hour.

The distribution of average hourly earnings for female college graduates (Figure 2.4b) is shifted to the right of the distribution for women with only a high school degree (Figure 2.4a); the same shift can be seen for the two groups of men (Figure 2.4d and Figure 2.4c). For both men and women, mean earnings are higher for those with a college degree (Table 2.4, first numeric column). Interestingly, the spread of the distribution of earnings, as measured by the standard deviation, is greater for those with a college degree than for those with a high school diploma. In addition, for both men and women, the 90th percentile of earnings is much higher for workers with a college degree than for workers with only a high school diploma. This final comparison is consistent with the parental admonition that a college degree opens doors that remain closed to individuals with only a high school diploma.

Another feature of these distributions is that the distribution of earnings for men is shifted to the right of the distribution of earnings for women. This "gender gap" in earnings is an important—and, to many, troubling—aspect of the distribution of earnings. We return to this topic in later chapters.

---

[1]The distributions were estimated using data from the March 2013 Current Population Survey, which is discussed in more detail in Appendix 3.1.

## Means, Variances, and Covariances of Sums of Random Variables

Let $X$, $Y$, and $V$ be random variables, let $\mu_X$ and $\sigma_X^2$ be the mean and variance of $X$, let $\sigma_{XY}$ be the covariance between $X$ and $Y$ (and so forth for the other variables), and let $a$, $b$, and $c$ be constants. Equations (2.29) through (2.35) follow from the definitions of the mean, variance, and covariance:

$$E(a + bX + cY) = a + b\mu_X + c\mu_Y, \qquad (2.29)$$

$$\text{var}(a + bY) = b^2\sigma_Y^2, \qquad (2.30)$$

$$\text{var}(aX + bY) = a^2\sigma_X^2 + 2ab\sigma_{XY} + b^2\sigma_Y^2, \qquad (2.31)$$

$$E(Y^2) = \sigma_Y^2 + \mu_Y^2, \qquad (2.32)$$

$$\text{cov}(a + bX + cV, Y) = b\sigma_{XY} + c\sigma_{VY}, \qquad (2.33)$$

$$E(XY) = \sigma_{XY} + \mu_X\mu_Y, \qquad (2.34)$$

$$|\text{corr}(X, Y)| \le 1 \text{ and } |\sigma_{XY}| \le \sqrt{\sigma_X^2\sigma_Y^2} \text{ (correlation inequality).} \qquad (2.35)$$

The variance of the sum of $X$ and $Y$ is the sum of their variances plus two times their covariance:

$$\text{var}(X + Y) = \text{var}(X) + \text{var}(Y) + 2\,\text{cov}(X, Y) = \sigma_X^2 + \sigma_Y^2 + 2\sigma_{XY}. \quad (2.36)$$

If $X$ and $Y$ are independent, then the covariance is zero and the variance of their sum is the sum of their variances:

$$\text{var}(X + Y) = \text{var}(X) + \text{var}(Y) = \sigma_X^2 + \sigma_Y^2$$

$$\text{(if } X \text{ and } Y \text{ are independent).} \qquad (2.37)$$

Useful expressions for means, variances, and covariances involving weighted sums of random variables are collected in Key Concept 2.3. The results in Key Concept 2.3 are derived in Appendix 2.1.

## 2.4 The Normal, Chi-Squared, Student $t$, and $F$ Distributions

The probability distributions most often encountered in econometrics are the normal, chi-squared, Student $t$, and $F$ distributions.

### The Normal Distribution

A continuous random variable with a **normal distribution** has the familiar bell-shaped probability density shown in Figure 2.5. The function defining the normal probability density is given in Appendix 17.1. As Figure 2.5 shows, the normal density with mean $\mu$ and variance $\sigma^2$ is symmetric around its mean and has 95% of its probability between $\mu - 1.96\sigma$ and $\mu + 1.96\sigma$.

Some special notation and terminology have been developed for the normal distribution. The normal distribution with mean $\mu$ and variance $\sigma^2$ is expressed concisely as "$N(\mu, \sigma^2)$." The **standard normal distribution** is the normal distribution with mean $\mu = 0$ and variance $\sigma^2 = 1$ and is denoted $N(0, 1)$. Random variables that have a $N(0, 1)$ distribution are often denoted $Z$, and the standard normal cumulative distribution function is denoted by the Greek letter $\Phi$; accordingly, $\Pr(Z \leq c) = \Phi(c)$, where $c$ is a constant. Values of the standard normal cumulative distribution function are tabulated in Appendix Table 1.

To look up probabilities for a normal variable with a general mean and variance, we must **standardize the variable** by first subtracting the mean, then by dividing

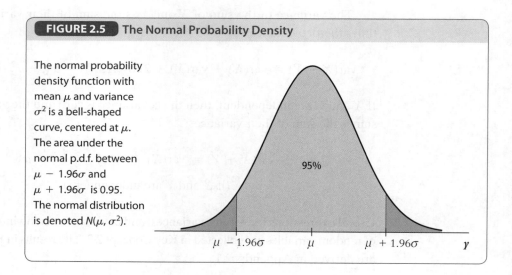

**FIGURE 2.5    The Normal Probability Density**

The normal probability density function with mean $\mu$ and variance $\sigma^2$ is a bell-shaped curve, centered at $\mu$. The area under the normal p.d.f. between $\mu - 1.96\sigma$ and $\mu + 1.96\sigma$ is 0.95. The normal distribution is denoted $N(\mu, \sigma^2)$.

95%

$\mu - 1.96\sigma$      $\mu$      $\mu + 1.96\sigma$      $y$

## Computing Probabilities Involving Normal Random Variables

Suppose $Y$ is normally distributed with mean $\mu$ and variance $\sigma^2$; in other words, $Y$ is distributed $N(\mu, \sigma^2)$. Then $Y$ is standardized by subtracting its mean and dividing by its standard deviation, that is, by computing $Z = (Y - \mu)/\sigma$.

Let $c_1$ and $c_2$ denote two numbers with $c_1 < c_2$ and let $d_1 = (c_1 - \mu)/\sigma$ and $d_2 = (c_2 - \mu)/\sigma$. Then

$$\Pr(Y \le c_2) = \Pr(Z \le d_2) = \Phi(d_2), \qquad (2.38)$$

$$\Pr(Y \ge c_1) = \Pr(Z \ge d_1) = 1 - \Phi(d_1), \qquad (2.39)$$

$$\Pr(c_1 \le Y \le c_2) = \Pr(d_1 \le Z \le d_2) = \Phi(d_2) - \Phi(d_1). \qquad (2.40)$$

The normal cumulative distribution function $\Phi$ is tabulated in Appendix Table 1.

the result by the standard deviation. For example, suppose $Y$ is distributed $N(1, 4)$—that is, $Y$ is normally distributed with a mean of 1 and a variance of 4. What is the probability that $Y \le 2$—that is, what is the shaded area in Figure 2.6a? The standardized version of $Y$ is $Y$ minus its mean, divided by its standard deviation, that is, $(Y - 1)/\sqrt{4} = \frac{1}{2}(Y - 1)$. Accordingly, the random variable $\frac{1}{2}(Y - 1)$ is normally distributed with mean zero and variance one (see Exercise 2.8); it has the standard normal distribution shown in Figure 2.6b. Now $Y \le 2$ is equivalent to $\frac{1}{2}(Y - 1) \le \frac{1}{2}(2 - 1)$—that is, $\frac{1}{2}(Y - 1) \le \frac{1}{2}$. Thus,

$$\Pr(Y \le 2) = \Pr[\tfrac{1}{2}(Y - 1) \le \tfrac{1}{2}] = \Pr(Z \le \tfrac{1}{2}) = \Phi(0.5) = 0.691, \quad (2.41)$$

where the value 0.691 is taken from Appendix Table 1.

The same approach can be applied to compute the probability that a normally distributed random variable exceeds some value or that it falls in a certain range. These steps are summarized in Key Concept 2.4. The box "A Bad Day on Wall Street" presents an unusual application of the cumulative normal distribution.

The normal distribution is symmetric, so its skewness is zero. The kurtosis of the normal distribution is 3.

**FIGURE 2.6** Calculating the Probability That $Y \leq 2$ When $Y$ Is Distributed $N(1, 4)$

To calculate $\Pr(Y \leq 2)$, standardize $Y$, then use the standard normal distribution table. $Y$ is standardized by subtracting its mean ($\mu = 1$) and dividing by its standard deviation ($\sigma = 2$). The probability that $Y \leq 2$ is shown in Figure 2.6a, and the corresponding probability after standardizing $Y$ is shown in Figure 2.6b. Because the standardized random variable, $(Y - 1)/2$, is a standard normal ($Z$) random variable, $\Pr(Y \leq 2) = \Pr\left(\frac{Y-1}{2} \leq \frac{2-1}{2}\right) = \Pr(Z \leq 0.5)$. From Appendix Table 1, $\Pr(Z \leq 0.5) = \Phi(0.5) = 0.691$.

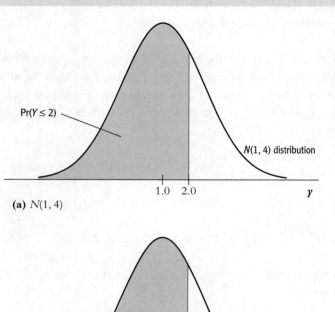

**(a)** $N(1, 4)$

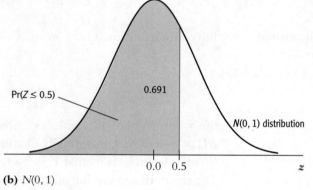

**(b)** $N(0, 1)$

*The multivariate normal distribution.* The normal distribution can be generalized to describe the joint distribution of a set of random variables. In this case, the distribution is called the **multivariate normal distribution**, or, if only two variables are being considered, the **bivariate normal distribution**. The formula for the bivariate normal p.d.f. is given in Appendix 17.1, and the formula for the general multivariate normal p.d.f. is given in Appendix 18.1.

The multivariate normal distribution has four important properties. If $X$ and $Y$ have a bivariate normal distribution with covariance $\sigma_{XY}$ and if $a$ and $b$ are two constants, then $aX + bY$ has the normal distribution:

$$aX + bY \text{ is distributed } N(a\mu_X + b\mu_Y, a^2\sigma_X^2 + b^2\sigma_Y^2 + 2ab\sigma_{XY})$$
$$(X, Y \text{ bivariate normal}). \tag{2.42}$$

## A Bad Day on Wall Street

On a typical day the overall value of stocks traded on the U.S. stock market can rise or fall by 1% or even more. This is a lot—but nothing compared to what happened on Monday, October 19, 1987. On "Black Monday," the Dow Jones Industrial Average (an average of 30 large industrial stocks) fell by 22.6%! From January 1, 1980, to December 31, 2012, the standard deviation of daily percentage price changes on the Dow was 1.12%, so the drop of 22.6% was a negative return of 20(= 22.6/1.12)

standard deviations. The enormity of this drop can be seen in Figure 2.7, a plot of the daily returns on the Dow during the 1980s.

If daily percentage price changes are normally distributed, then the probability of a change of at least 20 standard deviations is $\Pr(|Z| \geq 20) = 2 \times \Phi(-20)$. You will not find this value in Appendix Table 1, but you can calculate it using a computer (try it!). This probability is $5.5 \times 10^{-89}$, that is, 0.000 . . . 00055, where there are a total of 88 zeros!

---

**FIGURE 2.7** Daily Percentage Changes in the Dow Jones Industrial Average in the 1980s

From 1980 through 2012, the average percentage daily change of "the Dow" index was 0.04% and its standard deviation was 1.12%. On October 19, 1987— "Black Monday" — the Dow fell 22.6%, or more than 20 standard deviations.

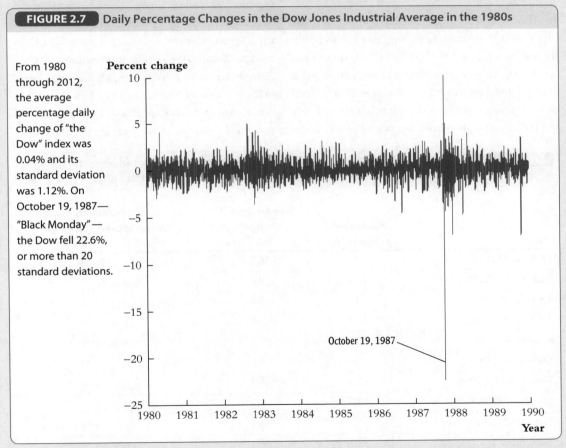

*continued on next page*

How small is $5.5 \times 10^{-89}$? Consider the following:

- The world population is about 7 billion, so the probability of winning a random lottery among all living people is about one in 7 billion, or $1.4 \times 10^{-10}$.
- The universe is believed to have existed for 14 billion years, or about $5 \times 10^{17}$ seconds, so the probability of choosing a particular second at random from all the seconds since the beginning of time is $2 \times 10^{-18}$.
- There are approximately $10^{43}$ molecules of gas in the first kilometer above the earth's surface. The probability of choosing one at random is $10^{-43}$.

Although Wall Street *did* have a bad day, the fact that it happened at all suggests its probability was more than $5.5 \times 10^{-89}$. In fact, there have been many days—good and bad—with stock price changes too large to be consistent with a normal distribution with a constant variance. Table 2.5 lists the ten largest daily percentage price changes in the

Dow Jones Industrial Average in the 8325 trading days between January 1, 1980, and December 31, 2012, along with the standardized change using the mean and variance over this period. All ten changes exceed 6.4 standard deviations, an extremely rare event if stock prices are normally distributed.

Clearly, stock price percentage changes have a distribution with heavier tails than the normal distribution. For this reason, finance professionals use other models of stock price changes. One such model treats stock price changes as normally distributed with a variance that evolves over time, so periods like October 1987 and the financial crisis in the fall of 2008 have higher volatility than others (models with time-varying variances are discussed in Chapter 16). Other models abandon the normal distribution in favor of distributions with heavier tails, an idea popularized in Nassim Taleb's 2007 book, *The Black Swan*. These models are more consistent with the very bad—and very good—days we actually see on Wall Street.

**TABLE 2.5** The Ten Largest Daily Percentage Changes in the Dow Jones Industrial Index, 1980–2012, and the Normal Probability of a Change at Least as Large

| Date | Percentage Change (x) | Standardized Change $Z = (x - \mu)/\sigma$ | Normal Probability of a Change at Least This Large $\Pr(|Z| \geq z) = 2\Phi(-z)$ |
|---|---|---|---|
| October 19, 1987 | −22.6 | −20.2 | $5.5 \times 10^{-89}$ |
| October 13, 2008 | 11.1 | 9.9 | $6.4 \times 10^{-23}$ |
| October 28, 2008 | 10.9 | 9.7 | $3.8 \times 10^{-22}$ |
| October 21, 1987 | 10.1 | 9.0 | $1.8 \times 10^{-19}$ |
| October 26, 1987 | −8.0 | −7.2 | $5.6 \times 10^{-13}$ |
| October 15, 2008 | −7.9 | −7.1 | $1.6 \times 10^{-12}$ |
| December 01, 2008 | −7.7 | −6.9 | $4.9 \times 10^{-12}$ |
| October 09, 2008 | −7.3 | −6.6 | $4.7 \times 10^{-11}$ |
| October 27, 1997 | −7.2 | −6.4 | $1.2 \times 10^{-10}$ |
| September 17, 2001 | −7.1 | −6.4 | $1.6 \times 10^{-10}$ |

More generally, if $n$ random variables have a multivariate normal distribution, then any linear combination of these variables (such as their sum) is normally distributed.

Second, if a set of variables has a multivariate normal distribution, then the marginal distribution of each of the variables is normal [this follows from Equation (2.42) by setting $a = 1$ and $b = 0$].

Third, if variables with a multivariate normal distribution have covariances that equal zero, then the variables are independent. Thus, if $X$ and $Y$ have a bivariate normal distribution and $\sigma_{XY} = 0$, then $X$ and $Y$ are independent. In Section 2.3 it was shown that if $X$ and $Y$ are independent, then, regardless of their joint distribution, $\sigma_{XY} = 0$. If $X$ and $Y$ are jointly normally distributed, then the converse is also true. This result—that zero covariance implies independence—is a special property of the multivariate normal distribution that is not true in general.

Fourth, if $X$ and $Y$ have a bivariate normal distribution, then the conditional expectation of $Y$ given $X$ is linear in $X$; that is, $E(Y \mid X = x) = a + bx$, where $a$ and $b$ are constants (Exercise 17.11). Joint normality implies linearity of conditional expectations, but linearity of conditional expectations does not imply joint normality.

## The Chi-Squared Distribution

The chi-squared distribution is used when testing certain types of hypotheses in statistics and econometrics.

The **chi-squared distribution** is the distribution of the sum of $m$ squared independent standard normal random variables. This distribution depends on $m$, which is called the degrees of freedom of the chi-squared distribution. For example, let $Z_1, Z_2$, and $Z_3$ be independent standard normal random variables. Then $Z_1^2 + Z_2^2 + Z_3^2$ has a chi-squared distribution with 3 degrees of freedom. The name for this distribution derives from the Greek letter used to denote it: A chi-squared distribution with $m$ degrees of freedom is denoted $\chi_m^2$.

Selected percentiles of the $\chi_m^2$ distribution are given in Appendix Table 3. For example, Appendix Table 3 shows that the 95th percentile of the $\chi_m^2$ distribution is 7.81, so $\Pr(Z_1^2 + Z_2^2 + Z_3^3 \le 7.81) = 0.95$.

## The Student *t* Distribution

The **Student *t* distribution** with $m$ degrees of freedom is defined to be the distribution of the ratio of a standard normal random variable, divided by the square root of an independently distributed chi-squared random variable with $m$ degrees of freedom divided by $m$. That is, let $Z$ be a standard normal random variable, let $W$ be a random variable with a chi-squared distribution with $m$ degrees of freedom, and let $Z$ and $W$ be independently distributed. Then the random variable $Z/\sqrt{W/m}$ has a Student $t$ distribution (also called the *t* **distribution**) with $m$ degrees of freedom. This distribution is denoted $t_m$. Selected percentiles of the Student $t$ distribution are given in Appendix Table 2.

The Student $t$ distribution depends on the degrees of freedom $m$. Thus the 95th percentile of the $t_m$ distribution depends on the degrees of freedom $m$. The Student $t$ distribution has a bell shape similar to that of the normal distribution, but when $m$ is small (20 or less), it has more mass in the tails—that is, it is a "fatter" bell shape than the normal. When $m$ is 30 or more, the Student $t$ distribution is well approximated by the standard normal distribution and the $t_\infty$ distribution equals the standard normal distribution.

## The *F* Distribution

The **F distribution** with $m$ and $n$ degrees of freedom, denoted $F_{m,n}$, is defined to be the distribution of the ratio of a chi-squared random variable with degrees of freedom $m$, divided by $m$, to an independently distributed chi-squared random variable with degrees of freedom $n$, divided by $n$. To state this mathematically, let $W$ be a chi-squared random variable with $m$ degrees of freedom and let $V$ be a chi-squared random variable with $n$ degrees of freedom, where $W$ and $V$ are independently distributed. Then $\frac{W/m}{V/n}$ has an $F_{m,n}$ distribution—that is, an $F$ distribution with numerator degrees of freedom $m$ and denominator degrees of freedom $n$.

In statistics and econometrics, an important special case of the $F$ distribution arises when the denominator degrees of freedom is large enough that the $F_{m,n}$ distribution can be approximated by the $F_{m,\infty}$ distribution. In this limiting case, the denominator random variable $V/n$ is the mean of infinitely many squared standard normal random variables, and that mean is 1 because the mean of a squared standard normal random variable is 1 (see Exercise 2.24). Thus the $F_{m,\infty}$ distribution is the distribution of a chi-squared random variable with $m$ degrees of freedom, divided by $m$: $W/m$ is distributed $F_{m,\infty}$. For example, from Appendix Table 4, the 95th percentile of the $F_{3,\infty}$ distribution is 2.60, which is the same as the 95th percentile of the $\chi^2_3$ distribution, 7.81 (from Appendix Table 2), divided by the degrees of freedom, which is 3 ($7.81/3 = 2.60$).

The 90th, 95th, and 99th percentiles of the $F_{m,n}$ distribution are given in Appendix Table 5 for selected values of $m$ and $n$. For example, the 95th percentile of the $F_{3,30}$ distribution is 2.92, and the 95th percentile of the $F_{3,90}$ distribution is 2.71. As the denominator degrees of freedom $n$ increases, the 95th percentile of the $F_{3,n}$ distribution tends to the $F_{3,\infty}$ limit of 2.60.

# 2.5  Random Sampling and the Distribution of the Sample Average

Almost all the statistical and econometric procedures used in this book involve averages or weighted averages of a sample of data. Characterizing the distributions of sample averages therefore is an essential step toward understanding the performance of econometric procedures.

This section introduces some basic concepts about random sampling and the distributions of averages that are used throughout the book. We begin by discussing random sampling. The act of random sampling—that is, randomly drawing a sample from a larger population—has the effect of making the sample average itself a random variable. Because the sample average is a random variable, it has a probability distribution, which is called its sampling distribution. This section concludes with some properties of the sampling distribution of the sample average.

## Random Sampling

*Simple random sampling.*  Suppose our commuting student from Section 2.1 aspires to be a statistician and decides to record her commuting times on various days. She selects these days at random from the school year, and her daily commuting time has the cumulative distribution function in Figure 2.2a. Because these days were selected at random, knowing the value of the commuting time on one of these randomly selected days provides no information about the commuting time on another of the days; that is, because the days were selected at random, the values of the commuting time on each of the different days are independently distributed random variables.

The situation described in the previous paragraph is an example of the simplest sampling scheme used in statistics, called **simple random sampling**, in which $n$ objects are selected at random from a **population** (the population of commuting days) and each member of the population (each day) is equally likely to be included in the sample.

The $n$ observations in the sample are denoted $Y_1, \ldots, Y_n$, where $Y_1$ is the first observation, $Y_2$ is the second observation, and so forth. In the commuting example, $Y_1$ is the commuting time on the first of her $n$ randomly selected days and $Y_i$ is the commuting time on the $i^{\text{th}}$ of her randomly selected days.

Because the members of the population included in the sample are selected at random, the values of the observations $Y_1, \ldots, Y_n$ are themselves random. If

**KEY CONCEPT**

**2.5**

## Simple Random Sampling and i.i.d. Random Variables

In a simple random sample, $n$ objects are drawn at random from a population and each object is equally likely to be drawn. The value of the random variable $Y$ for the $i^{\text{th}}$ randomly drawn object is denoted $Y_i$. Because each object is equally likely to be drawn and the distribution of $Y_i$ is the same for all $i$, the random variables $Y_1, \ldots, Y_n$ are independently and identically distributed (i.i.d.); that is, the distribution of $Y_i$ is the same for all $i = 1, \ldots, n$ and $Y_1$ is distributed independently of $Y_2, \ldots, Y_n$ and so forth.

different members of the population are chosen, their values of $Y$ will differ. Thus the act of random sampling means that $Y_1, \ldots, Y_n$ can be treated as random variables. Before they are sampled, $Y_1, \ldots, Y_n$ can take on many possible values; after they are sampled, a specific value is recorded for each observation.

*i.i.d. draws.*  Because $Y_1, \ldots, Y_n$ are randomly drawn from the same population, the marginal distribution of $Y_i$ is the same for each $i = 1, \ldots, n$; this marginal distribution is the distribution of $Y$ in the population being sampled. When $Y_i$ has the same marginal distribution for $i = 1, \ldots, n$, then $Y_1, \ldots, Y_n$ are said to be **identically distributed**.

Under simple random sampling, knowing the value of $Y_1$ provides no information about $Y_2$, so the conditional distribution of $Y_2$ given $Y_1$ is the same as the marginal distribution of $Y_2$. In other words, under simple random sampling, $Y_1$ is distributed independently of $Y_2, \ldots, Y_n$.

When $Y_1, \ldots, Y_n$ are drawn from the same distribution and are independently distributed, they are said to be **independently and identically distributed** (or **i.i.d.**).

Simple random sampling and i.i.d. draws are summarized in Key Concept 2.5.

## The Sampling Distribution of the Sample Average

The **sample average** or **sample mean**, $\overline{Y}$, of the $n$ observations $Y_1, \ldots, Y_n$ is

$$\overline{Y} = \frac{1}{n}(Y_1 + Y_2 + \cdots + Y_n) = \frac{1}{n}\sum_{i=1}^{n} Y_i. \tag{2.43}$$

An essential concept is that the act of drawing a random sample has the effect of making the sample average $\overline{Y}$ a random variable. Because the sample was drawn at random, the value of each $Y_i$ is random. Because $Y_1, \ldots, Y_n$ are random, their average is random. Had a different sample been drawn, then the observations and their sample average would have been different: The value of $\overline{Y}$ differs from one randomly drawn sample to the next.

For example, suppose our student commuter selected five days at random to record her commute times, then computed the average of those five times. Had she chosen five different days, she would have recorded five different times—and thus would have computed a different value of the sample average.

Because $\overline{Y}$ is random, it has a probability distribution. The distribution of $\overline{Y}$ is called the **sampling distribution** of $\overline{Y}$ because it is the probability distribution associated with possible values of $\overline{Y}$ that could be computed for different possible samples $Y_1, \ldots, Y_n$.

The sampling distribution of averages and weighted averages plays a central role in statistics and econometrics. We start our discussion of the sampling distribution of $\overline{Y}$ by computing its mean and variance under general conditions on the population distribution of $Y$.

*Mean and variance of* $\overline{Y}$. Suppose that the observations $Y_1, \ldots, Y_n$ are i.i.d., and let $\mu_Y$ and $\sigma_Y^2$ denote the mean and variance of $Y_i$ (because the observations are i.i.d. the mean and variance is the same for all $i = 1, \ldots, n$). When $n = 2$, the mean of the sum $Y_1 + Y_2$ is given by applying Equation (2.28): $E(Y_1 + Y_2) = \mu_Y + \mu_Y = 2\mu_Y$. Thus the mean of the sample average is $E[\frac{1}{2}(Y_1 + Y_2)] = \frac{1}{2} \times 2\mu_Y = \mu_Y$. In general,

$$E(\overline{Y}) = \frac{1}{n}\sum_{i=1}^{n} E(Y_i) = \mu_Y. \tag{2.44}$$

The variance of $\overline{Y}$ is found by applying Equation (2.37). For example, for $n = 2$, $\text{var}(Y_1 + Y_2) = 2\sigma_Y^2$, so [by applying Equation (2.31) with $a = b = \frac{1}{2}$ and $\text{cov}(Y_1, Y_2) = 0$], $\text{var}(\overline{Y}) = \frac{1}{2}\sigma_Y^2$. For general $n$, because $Y_1, \ldots, Y_n$ are i.i.d., $Y_i$ and $Y_j$ are independently distributed for $i \neq j$, so $\text{cov}(Y_i, Y_j) = 0$. Thus,

$$\text{var}(\overline{Y}) = \text{var}\left(\frac{1}{n}\sum_{i=1}^{n} Y_i\right)$$

$$= \frac{1}{n^2}\sum_{i=1}^{n} \text{var}(Y_i) + \frac{1}{n^2}\sum_{i=1}^{n}\sum_{j=1, j \neq i}^{n} \text{cov}(Y_i, Y_j)$$

$$= \frac{\sigma_Y^2}{n}. \tag{2.45}$$

The standard deviation of $\overline{Y}$ is the square root of the variance, $\sigma_Y \sqrt{n}$.

## Financial Diversification and Portfolios

The principle of diversification says that you can reduce your risk by holding small investments in multiple assets, compared to putting all your money into one asset. That is, you shouldn't put all your eggs in one basket.

The math of diversification follows from Equation (2.45). Suppose you divide $1 equally among $n$ assets. Let $Y_i$ represent the payout in 1 year of $1 invested in the $i^{\text{th}}$ asset. Because you invested $1/n$ dollars in each asset, the actual payoff of your portfolio after 1 year is $(Y_1 + Y_2 + \cdots + Y_n)/n = \overline{Y}$. To keep things simple, suppose that each asset has the same expected payout, $\mu_Y$, the same variance, $\sigma^2$, and the same positive correlation $\rho$ across assets [so that $\text{cov}(Y_i, Y_j) = \rho\sigma^2$]. Then the expected payout is

$E(\overline{Y}) = \mu_Y$, and, for large $n$, the variance of the portfolio payout is $\text{var}(\overline{Y}) = \rho\sigma^2$ (Exercise 2.26). Putting all your money into one asset or spreading it equally across all $n$ assets has the same expected payout, but diversifying reduces the variance from $\sigma^2$ to $\rho\sigma^2$.

The math of diversification has led to financial products such as stock mutual funds, in which the fund holds many stocks and an individual owns a share of the fund, thereby owning a small amount of many stocks. But diversification has its limits: For many assets, payouts are positively correlated, so $\text{var}(\overline{Y})$ remains positive even if $n$ is large. In the case of stocks, risk is reduced by holding a portfolio, but that portfolio remains subject to the unpredictable fluctuations of the overall stock market.

In summary, the mean, the variance, and the standard deviation of $\overline{Y}$ are

$$E(\overline{Y}) = \mu_Y. \tag{2.46}$$

$$\text{var}(\overline{Y}) = \sigma_{\overline{Y}}^2 = \frac{\sigma_Y^2}{n}, \text{ and} \tag{2.47}$$

$$\text{std.dev}(\overline{Y}) = \sigma_{\overline{Y}} = \frac{\sigma_Y}{\sqrt{n}}. \tag{2.48}$$

These results hold whatever the distribution of $Y_i$ is; that is, the distribution of $Y_i$ does not need to take on a specific form, such as the normal distribution, for Equations (2.46) through (2.48) to hold.

The notation $\sigma_{\overline{Y}}^2$ denotes the variance of the sampling distribution of the sample average $\overline{Y}$. In contrast, $\sigma_Y^2$ is the variance of each individual $Y_i$, that is, the variance of the population distribution from which the observation is drawn. Similarly, $\sigma_{\overline{Y}}$ denotes the standard deviation of the sampling distribution of $\overline{Y}$.

*Sampling distribution of $\overline{Y}$ when Y is normally distributed.* Suppose that $Y_1, \ldots, Y_n$ are i.i.d. draws from the $N(\mu_Y, \sigma_Y^2)$ distribution. As stated following Equation (2.42), the sum of $n$ normally distributed random variables is itself normally distributed. Because the mean of $\overline{Y}$ is $\mu_Y$ and the variance of $\overline{Y}$ is $\sigma_Y^2/n$, this means that, if $Y_1, \ldots, Y_n$ are i.i.d. draws from the $N(\mu_Y, \sigma_Y^2)$, then $\overline{Y}$ is distributed $N(\mu_Y, \sigma_Y^2/n)$.

## 2.6 Large-Sample Approximations to Sampling Distributions

Sampling distributions play a central role in the development of statistical and econometric procedures, so it is important to know, in a mathematical sense, what the sampling distribution of $\overline{Y}$ is. There are two approaches to characterizing sampling distributions: an "exact" approach and an "approximate" approach.

The "exact" approach entails deriving a formula for the sampling distribution that holds exactly for any value of $n$. The sampling distribution that exactly describes the distribution of $\overline{Y}$ for any $n$ is called the **exact distribution** or **finite-sample distribution** of $\overline{Y}$. For example, if $Y$ is normally distributed and $Y_1, \ldots, Y_n$ are i.i.d., then (as discussed in Section 2.5) the exact distribution of $\overline{Y}$ is normal with mean $\mu_Y$ and variance $\sigma_Y^2/n$. Unfortunately, if the distribution of $Y$ is not normal, then in general the exact sampling distribution of $\overline{Y}$ is very complicated and depends on the distribution of $Y$.

The "approximate" approach uses approximations to the sampling distribution that rely on the sample size being large. The large-sample approximation to the sampling distribution is often called the **asymptotic distribution**—"asymptotic" because the approximations become exact in the limit that $n \rightarrow \infty$. As we see in this section, these approximations can be very accurate even if the sample size is only $n = 30$ observations. Because sample sizes used in practice in econometrics typically number in the hundreds or thousands, these asymptotic distributions can be counted on to provide very good approximations to the exact sampling distribution.

This section presents the two key tools used to approximate sampling distributions when the sample size is large: the law of large numbers and the central limit theorem. The law of large numbers says that, when the sample size is large, $\overline{Y}$ will be close to $\mu_Y$ with very high probability. The central limit theorem says that, when the sample size is large, the sampling distribution of the standardized sample average, $(\overline{Y} - \mu_Y)/\sigma_{\overline{Y}}$, is approximately normal.

Although exact sampling distributions are complicated and depend on the distribution of $Y$, the asymptotic distributions are simple. Moreover—remarkably—the asymptotic normal distribution of $(\overline{Y} - \mu_Y)/\sigma_{\overline{Y}}$ does *not* depend on the distribution of $Y$. This normal approximate distribution provides enormous simplifications and underlies the theory of regression used throughout this book.

## Convergence in Probability, Consistency, and the Law of Large Numbers

The sample average $\overline{Y}$ converges in probability to $\mu_Y$ (or, equivalently, $\overline{Y}$ is consistent for $\mu_Y$) if the probability that $\overline{Y}$ is in the range $(\mu_Y - c)$ to $(\mu_Y + c)$ becomes arbitrarily close to 1 as $n$ increases for any constant $c > 0$. The convergence of $\overline{Y}$ to $\mu_Y$ in probability is written, $\overline{Y} \xrightarrow{p} \mu_Y$.

The law of large numbers says that if $Y_i, i = 1, \ldots, n$ are independently and identically distributed with $E(Y_i) = \mu_Y$ and if large outliers are unlikely (technically if $\mathrm{var}(Y_i) = \sigma_Y^2 < \infty$), then $\overline{Y} \xrightarrow{p} \mu_Y$.

### The Law of Large Numbers and Consistency

The **law of large numbers** states that, under general conditions, $\overline{Y}$ will be near $\mu_Y$ with very high probability when $n$ is large. This is sometimes called the "law of averages." When a large number of random variables with the same mean are averaged together, the large values balance the small values and their sample average is close to their common mean.

For example, consider a simplified version of our student commuter's experiment in which she simply records whether her commute was short (less than 20 minutes) or long. Let $Y_i = 1$ if her commute was short on the $i^{\text{th}}$ randomly selected day and $Y_i = 0$ if it was long. Because she used simple random sampling, $Y_1, \ldots, Y_n$ are i.i.d. Thus $Y_i, i = 1, \ldots, n$ are i.i.d. draws of a Bernoulli random variable, where (from Table 2.2) the probability that $Y_i = 1$ is 0.78. Because the expectation of a Bernoulli random variable is its success probability, $E(Y_i) = \mu_Y = 0.78$. The sample average $\overline{Y}$ is the fraction of days in her sample in which her commute was short.

Figure 2.8 shows the sampling distribution of $\overline{Y}$ for various sample sizes $n$. When $n = 2$ (Figure 2.8a), $\overline{Y}$ can take on only three values: $0, \frac{1}{2}$, and 1 (neither commute was short, one was short, and both were short), none of which is particularly close to the true proportion in the population, 0.78. As $n$ increases, however (Figures 2.8b–d), $\overline{Y}$ takes on more values and the sampling distribution becomes tightly centered on $\mu_Y$.

The property that $\overline{Y}$ is near $\mu_Y$ with increasing probability as $n$ increases is called **convergence in probability** or, more concisely, **consistency** (see Key Concept 2.6). The law of large numbers states that, under certain conditions, $\overline{Y}$ converges in probability to $\mu_Y$ or, equivalently, that $\overline{Y}$ is consistent for $\mu_Y$.

---

**FIGURE 2.8** Sampling Distribution of the Sample Average of $n$ Bernoulli Random Variables

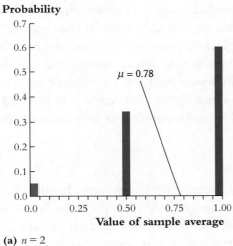

**(a)** $n = 2$

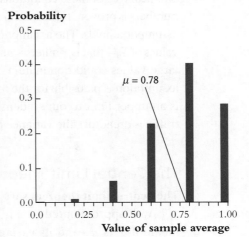

**(b)** $n = 5$

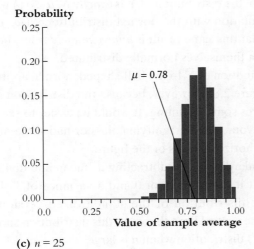

**(c)** $n = 25$

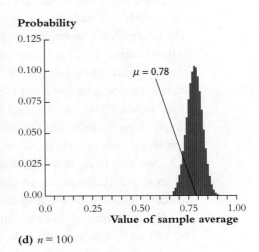

**(d)** $n = 100$

The distributions are the sampling distributions of $\overline{Y}$, the sample average of $n$ independent Bernoulli random variables with $p = \Pr(Y_i = 1) = 0.78$ (the probability of a short commute is 78%). The variance of the sampling distribution of $\overline{Y}$ decreases as $n$ gets larger, so the sampling distribution becomes more tightly concentrated around its mean $\mu = 0.78$ as the sample size $n$ increases.

The conditions for the law of large numbers that we will use in this book are that $Y_i, i = 1, \ldots, n$ are i.i.d. and that the variance of $Y_i$, $\sigma_Y^2$, is finite. The mathematical role of these conditions is made clear in Section 17.2, where the law of large numbers is proven. If the data are collected by simple random sampling, then the i.i.d. assumption holds. The assumption that the variance is finite says that extremely large values of $Y_i$—that is, outliers—are unlikely and observed infrequently; otherwise, these large values could dominate $\overline{Y}$ and the sample average would be unreliable. This assumption is plausible for the applications in this book. For example, because there is an upper limit to our student's commuting time (she could park and walk if the traffic is dreadful), the variance of the distribution of commuting times is finite.

## The Central Limit Theorem

The **central limit theorem** says that, under general conditions, the distribution of $\overline{Y}$ is well approximated by a normal distribution when $n$ is large. Recall that the mean of $\overline{Y}$ is $\mu_Y$ and its variance is $\sigma_{\overline{Y}}^2 = \sigma_Y^2/n$. According to the central limit theorem, when $n$ is large, the distribution of $\overline{Y}$ is approximately $N(\mu_Y, \sigma_{\overline{Y}}^2)$. As discussed at the end of Section 2.5, the distribution of $\overline{Y}$ is *exactly* $N(\mu_Y, \sigma_{\overline{Y}}^2)$ when the sample is drawn from a population with the normal distribution $N(\mu_Y, \sigma_Y^2)$. The central limit theorem says that this same result is *approximately* true when $n$ is large even if $Y_1, \ldots, Y_n$ are not themselves normally distributed.

The convergence of the distribution of $\overline{Y}$ to the bell-shaped, normal approximation can be seen (a bit) in Figure 2.8. However, because the distribution gets quite tight for large $n$, this requires some squinting. It would be easier to see the shape of the distribution of $\overline{Y}$ if you used a magnifying glass or had some other way to zoom in or to expand the horizontal axis of the figure.

One way to do this is to standardize $\overline{Y}$ by subtracting its mean and dividing by its standard deviation so that it has a mean of 0 and a variance of 1. This process leads to examining the distribution of the standardized version of $\overline{Y}$, $(\overline{Y} - \mu_Y)/\sigma_{\overline{Y}}$. According to the central limit theorem, this distribution should be well approximated by a $N(0, 1)$ distribution when $n$ is large.

The distribution of the standardized average $(\overline{Y} - \mu_Y)/\sigma_{\overline{Y}}$ is plotted in Figure 2.9 for the distributions in Figure 2.8; the distributions in Figure 2.9 are exactly the same as in Figure 2.8, except that the scale of the horizontal axis is changed so that the standardized variable has a mean of 0 and a variance of 1. After this change of scale, it is easy to see that, if $n$ is large enough, the distribution of $\overline{Y}$ is well approximated by a normal distribution.

One might ask, how large is "large enough"? That is, how large must $n$ be for the distribution of $\overline{Y}$ to be approximately normal? The answer is, "It depends." The

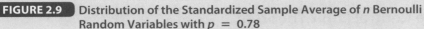

**FIGURE 2.9**  Distribution of the Standardized Sample Average of *n* Bernoulli
Random Variables with $p = 0.78$

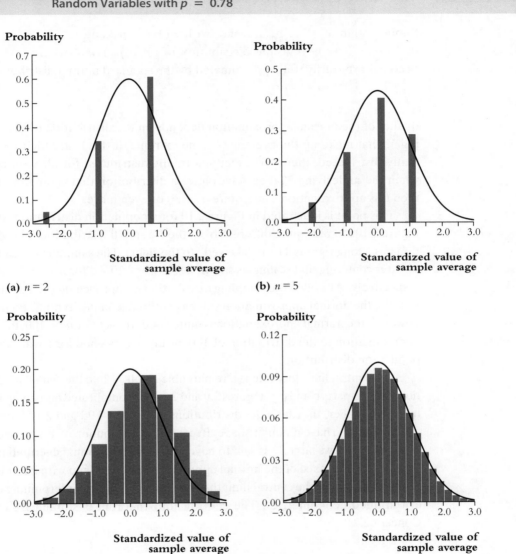

The sampling distribution of $\overline{Y}$ in Figure 2.8 is plotted here after standardizing $\overline{Y}$. This plot centers the distributions in Figure 2.8 and magnifies the scale on the horizontal axis by a factor of $\sqrt{n}$. When the sample size is large, the sampling distributions are increasingly well approximated by the normal distribution (the solid line), as predicted by the central limit theorem. The normal distribution is scaled so that the height of the distributions is approximately the same in all figures.

**KEY CONCEPT**

**2.7**

## The Central Limit Theorem

Suppose that $Y_1, \ldots, Y_n$ are i.i.d. with $E(Y_i) = \mu_Y$ and $\text{var}(Y_i) = \sigma_Y^2$, where $0 < \sigma_Y^2 < \infty$. As $n \to \infty$, the distribution of $(\overline{Y} - \mu_Y)/\sigma_{\overline{Y}}$ (where $\sigma_{\overline{Y}}^2 = \sigma_Y^2/n$) becomes arbitrarily well approximated by the standard normal distribution.

quality of the normal approximation depends on the distribution of the underlying $Y_i$ that make up the average. At one extreme, if the $Y_i$ are themselves normally distributed, then $\overline{Y}$ is exactly normally distributed for all $n$. In contrast, when the underlying $Y_i$ themselves have a distribution that is far from normal, then this approximation can require $n = 30$ or even more.

This point is illustrated in Figure 2.10 for a population distribution, shown in Figure 2.10a, that is quite different from the Bernoulli distribution. This distribution has a long right tail (it is "skewed" to the right). The sampling distribution of $\overline{Y}$, after centering and scaling, is shown in Figures 2.10b–d for $n = 5, 25$, and $100$, respectively. Although the sampling distribution is approaching the bell shape for $n = 25$, the normal approximation still has noticeable imperfections. By $n = 100$, however, the normal approximation is quite good. In fact, for $n \geq 100$, the normal approximation to the distribution of $\overline{Y}$ typically is very good for a wide variety of population distributions.

The central limit theorem is a remarkable result. While the "small $n$" distributions of $\overline{Y}$ in parts b and c of Figures 2.9 and 2.10 are complicated and quite different from each other, the "large $n$" distributions in Figures 2.9d and 2.10d are simple and, amazingly, have a similar shape. Because the distribution of $\overline{Y}$ approaches the normal as $n$ grows large, $\overline{Y}$ is said to have an **asymptotic normal distribution**.

The convenience of the normal approximation, combined with its wide applicability because of the central limit theorem, makes it a key underpinning of modern applied econometrics. The central limit theorem is summarized in Key Concept 2.7.

## Summary

1.  The probabilities with which a random variable takes on different values are summarized by the cumulative distribution function, the probability distribution function (for discrete random variables), and the probability density function (for continuous random variables).

**FIGURE 2.10**  Distribution of the Standardized Sample Average of *n* Draws from a Skewed Distribution

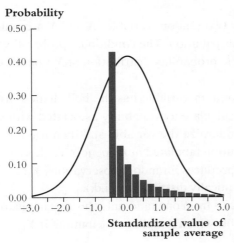

**(a)** *n* = 1

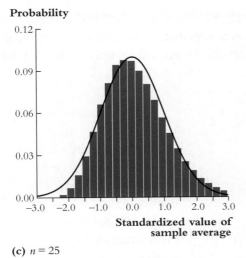

**(c)** *n* = 25

**(b)** *n* = 5

**(d)** *n* = 100

The figures show the sampling distribution of the standardized sample average of *n* draws from the skewed (asymmetric) population distribution shown in Figure 2.10a. When *n* is small (*n* = 5), the sampling distribution, like the population distribution, is skewed. But when *n* is large (*n* = 100), the sampling distribution is well approximated by a standard normal distribution (solid line), as predicted by the central limit theorem. The normal distribution is scaled so that the height of the distributions is approximately the same in all figures.

2. The expected value of a random variable $Y$ (also called its mean, $\mu_Y$), denoted $E(Y)$, is its probability-weighted average value. The variance of $Y$ is $\sigma_Y^2 = E[(Y - \mu_Y)^2]$, and the standard deviation of $Y$ is the square root of its variance.

3. The joint probabilities for two random variables $X$ and $Y$ are summarized by their joint probability distribution. The conditional probability distribution of $Y$ given $X = x$ is the probability distribution of $Y$, conditional on $X$ taking on the value $x$.

4. A normally distributed random variable has the bell-shaped probability density in Figure 2.5. To calculate a probability associated with a normal random variable, first standardize the variable and then use the standard normal cumulative distribution tabulated in Appendix Table 1.

5. Simple random sampling produces $n$ random observations $Y_1, \ldots, Y_n$ that are independently and identically distributed (i.i.d.).

6. The sample average, $\overline{Y}$, varies from one randomly chosen sample to the next and thus is a random variable with a sampling distribution. If $Y_1, \ldots, Y_n$ are i.i.d., then:

   a. the sampling distribution of $\overline{Y}$ has mean $\mu_Y$ and variance $\sigma_{\overline{Y}}^2 = \sigma_Y^2/n$;

   b. the law of large numbers says that $\overline{Y}$ converges in probability to $\mu_Y$; and

   c. the central limit theorem says that the standardized version of $\overline{Y}$, $(\overline{Y} - \mu_Y)/\sigma_{\overline{Y}}$, has a standard normal distribution [$N(0, 1)$ distribution] when $n$ is large.

## Key Terms

outcomes (61)
probability (61)
sample space (61)
event (61)
discrete random variable (61)
continuous random variable (61)
probability distribution (62)
cumulative probability
   distribution (62)
cumulative distribution function
   (c.d.f.) (63)
Bernoulli random variable (63)
Bernoulli distribution (63)

probability density
   function (p.d.f.) (65)
density function (65)
density (65)
expected value (65)
expectation (65)
mean (65)
variance (67)
standard deviation (67)
moments of a distribution (69)
skewness (69)
kurtosis (71)
outlier (71)

leptokurtic (71)

$r^{th}$ moment (71)

joint probability distribution (72)

marginal probability distribution (73)

conditional distribution (73)

conditional expectation (74)

conditional mean (74)

law of iterated expectations (75)

conditional variance (76)

independently distributed (77)

independent (77)

covariance (77)

correlation (78)

uncorrelated (78)

normal distribution (82)

standard normal distribution (82)

standardize a variable (82)

multivariate normal distribution (84)

bivariate normal distribution (84)

chi-squared distribution (87)

Student $t$ distribution (87)

$t$ distribution (88)

$F$ distribution (88)

simple random sampling (89)

population (89)

identically distributed (90)

independently and identically
distributed (i.i.d.) (90)

sample average (90)

sample mean (90)

sampling distribution (91)

exact (finite-sample) distribution (93)

asymptotic distribution (93)

law of large numbers (94)

convergence in probability (94)

consistency (94)

central limit theorem (96)

asymptotic normal distribution (98)

---

**MyEconLab Can Help You Get a Better Grade**

MyEconLab    If your exam were tomorrow, would you be ready? For each chapter,
**MyEconLab** Practice Tests and Study Plan help you prepare for your exams.
You can also find similar Exercises and Review the Concepts Questions now in **MyEconLab**.
To see how it works, turn to the **MyEconLab** spread on pages 2 and 3 of this book and then go to
**www.myeconlab.com**.

For additional Empirical Exercises and Data Sets, log on to the Companion Website at
**www.pearsonglobaleditions.com/Stock_Watson**.

---

## Review the Concepts

**2.1.** Examples of random variables used in this chapter included (a) the gender of the next person you meet, (b) the number of times a computer crashes, (c) the time it takes to commute to school, (d) whether the computer you are assigned in the library is new or old, and (e) whether it is raining or not. Explain why each can be thought of as random.

**2.2.** Suppose that the random variables $X$ and $Y$ are independent and you know their distributions. Explain why knowing the value of $X$ tells you nothing about the value of $Y$.

**2.3.** Suppose that $X$ denotes the amount of rainfall in your hometown during a randomly selected month and $Y$ denotes the number of children born in Los Angeles during the same month. Are $X$ and $Y$ independent? Explain.

**2.4.** An econometrics class has 80 students, and the mean student weight is 145 lb. A random sample of 4 students is selected from the class, and their average weight is calculated. Will the average weight of the students in the sample equal 145 lb? Why or why not? Use this example to explain why the sample average, $\overline{Y}$, is a random variable.

**2.5.** Suppose that $Y_1, \ldots, Y_n$ are i.i.d. random variables with a $N(1, 4)$ distribution. Sketch the probability density of $\overline{Y}$ when $n = 2$. Repeat this for $n = 10$ and $n = 100$. In words, describe how the densities differ. What is the relationship between your answer and the law of large numbers?

**2.6.** Suppose that $Y_1, \ldots, Y_n$ are i.i.d. random variables with the probability distribution given in Figure 2.10a. You want to calculate $\Pr(\overline{Y} \leq 0.1)$. Would it be reasonable to use the normal approximation if $n = 5$? What about $n = 25$ or $n = 100$? Explain.

**2.7.** $Y$ is a random variable with $\mu_Y = 0, \sigma_Y = 1$, skewness $= 0$, and kurtosis $= 100$. Sketch a hypothetical probability distribution of $Y$. Explain why $n$ random variables drawn from this distribution might have some large outliers.

## Exercises

**2.1** Let $Y$ denote the number of "heads" that occur when two loaded coins are tossed. Assume the probability of getting "heads" is 0.4 on either coin.

   **a.** Derive the probability distribution of $Y$.

   **b.** Derive the mean and variance of $Y$.

**2.2** Use the probability distribution given in Table 2.2 to compute (a) $E(Y)$ and $E(X)$; (b) $\sigma_X^2$ and $\sigma_Y^2$; and (c) $\sigma_{XY}$ and corr$(X, Y)$.

**2.3** Using the random variables $X$ and $Y$ from Table 2.2, consider two new random variables $W = 4 + 8X$ and $V = 11 - 2Y$. Compute (a) $E(W)$ and $E(V)$; (b) $\sigma_W^2$ and $\sigma_V^2$; and (c) $\sigma_{WV}$ and corr$(W, V)$.

**2.4** Suppose $X$ is a Bernoulli random variable with $P(X = 1) = p$.

   **a.** Show $E(X^3) = p$.

   **b.** Show $E(X^k) = p$ for $k > 0$.

**c.** Suppose that $p = 0.3$. Compute the mean, variance, skewness, and kurtosis of $X$. (*Hint:* You might find it helpful to use the formulas given in Exercise 2.21.)

**2.5** In July, Fairtown's daily maximum temperature has a mean of 65°F and a standard deviation of 5°F. What are the mean, standard deviation, and variance in °C?

**2.6** The following table gives the joint probability distribution between employment status and college graduation among those either employed or looking for work (unemployed) in the working-age population of country A.

|  | Unemployed ($Y = 0$) | Employed ($Y = 1$) | Total |
|---|---|---|---|
| Non–college grads ($X = 0$) | 0.078 | 0.673 | 0.751 |
| College grads ($X = 1$) | 0.042 | 0.207 | 0.249 |
| **Total** | 0.12 | 0.88 | 1.000 |

**a.** Compute $E(Y)$.

**b.** The unemployment rate is a fraction of the labor force that is unemployed. Show that the unemployment rate is given by $1 - E(Y)$.

**c.** Calculate $E(Y|X = 1)$ and $E(Y|X = 0)$.

**d.** Calculate the unemployment rate for (i) college graduates and (ii) non–graduates.

**e.** A randomly selected member of this population reports being unemployed. What is the probability that this worker is a (i) college graduate, (ii) non–graduate?

**f.** Are educational achievement and employment status independent? Explain.

**2.7** In a given population of two-earning male-female couples, male earnings have a mean of $50,000 per year and a standard deviation of $15,000. Female earnings have a mean of $48,000 per year and a standard deviation of $13,000. The correlation between male and female earnings for a couple is 0.90. Let $C$ denote the combined earnings for a randomly selected couple.

**a.** What is the mean of $C$?

**b.** What is the covariance between male and female earnings?

**c.** What is the standard deviation of $C$?

**d.** Convert the answers to (a) through (c) from U.S. dollars (\$) to euros (€).

**2.8** The random variable $Y$ has a mean of 4 and a variance of 1/9. Let $Z = 3(Y - 4)$. Find the mean and the variance of Z.

**2.9** $X$ and $Y$ are discrete random variables with the following joint distribution:

|  |  | Value of Y | | | | |
|---|---|---|---|---|---|---|
|  |  | 2 | 4 | 6 | 8 | 10 |
|  | 3 | 0.04 | 0.09 | 0.03 | 0.12 | 0.01 |
| Value of X | 6 | 0.10 | 0.06 | 0.15 | 0.03 | 0.02 |
|  | 9 | 0.13 | 0.11 | 0.04 | 0.06 | 0.01 |

That is, $\Pr(X = 3, Y = 2) = 0.04$, and so forth.

**a.** Calculate the probability distribution, mean, and variance of $Y$.

**b.** Calculate the probability distribution, mean, and variance of $Y$ given $X = 6$.

**c.** Calculate the covariance and correlation between $X$ and $Y$.

**2.10** Compute the following probabilities:

**a.** If $Y$ is distributed $N(4, 9)$, find $\Pr(Y \leq 5)$.

**b.** If $Y$ is distributed $N(5, 16)$, find $\Pr(Y > 2)$.

**c.** If $Y$ is distributed $N(1, 4)$, find $\Pr(2 \leq Y \leq 5)$.

**d.** If $Y$ is distributed $N(2, 1)$, find $\Pr(1 \leq Y \leq 4)$.

**2.11** Compute the following probabilities:

**a.** If $Y$ is distributed $\chi^2_3$, find $\Pr(Y \leq 6.25)$.

**b.** If $Y$ is distributed $\chi^2_8$, find $\Pr(Y \leq 15.51)$.

**c.** If $Y$ is distributed $F_{8,\infty}$, find $\Pr(Y \leq 1.94)$.

**d.** Why are the answers to (b) and (c) the same?

**e.** If $Y$ is distributed $\chi^2_1$, find $\Pr(Y \leq 0.5)$. (*Hint:* Use the definition of the $\chi^2_1$ distribution.)

**2.12** Compute the following probabilities:

**a.** If $Y$ is distributed $t_{12}$, find $\Pr(Y \leq 1.36)$.

**b.** If $Y$ is distributed $t_{30}$, find $\Pr(-1.70 \leq Y \leq 1.70)$.

**c.** If $Y$ is distributed $N(0, 1)$, find $\Pr(-1.70 \leq Y \leq 1.70)$.

**d.** When do the critical values of the normal and the $t$ distribution coincide?

**e.** If $Y$ is distributed $F_{4,11}$, find $\Pr(Y > 3.36)$.

**f.** If $Y$ is distributed $F_{3,21}$, find $\Pr(Y > 4.87)$.

**2.13** $X$ is a Bernoulli random variable with $\Pr(X = 1) = 0.90$, $Y$ is distributed $N(0, 4)$, $W$ is distributed $N(0, 16)$, and $X$, $Y$, and $W$ are independent. Let $S = XY + (1 - X)W$. (That is, $S = Y$ when $X = 1$, and $S = W$ when $X = 0$.)

**a.** Show that $E(Y^2) = 4$ and $E(W^2) = 16$.

**b.** Show that $E(Y^3) = 0$ and $E(W^3) = 0$. (*Hint:* What is the skewness for a symmetric distribution?)

**c.** Show that $E(Y^4) = 3 \times 4^2$ and $E(W^4) = 3 \times 16^2$. (*Hint:* Use the fact that the kurtosis is 3 for a normal distribution.)

**d.** Derive $E(S)$, $E(S^2)$, $E(S^3)$ and $E(S^4)$. (*Hint:* Use the law of iterated expectations conditioning on $X = 0$ and $X = 1$.)

**e.** Derive the skewness and kurtosis for $S$.

**2.14** In a population $\mu_Y = 50$ and $J_Y^2 = 21$. Use the central limit theorem to answer the following questions:

**a.** In a random sample of size $n = 50$, find $\Pr(\overline{Y} \leq 51)$.

**b.** In a random sample of size $n = 150$, find $\Pr(\overline{Y} > 49)$.

**c.** In a random sample of size $n = 45$, find $\Pr(50.5 \leq \overline{Y} \leq 51)$.

**2.15** Suppose $Y_i, i = 1, 2, \ldots, n$, are i.i.d. random variables, each distributed $N(10, 4)$.

**a.** Compute $\Pr(9.6 \leq \overline{Y} \leq 10.4)$ when (i) $n = 20$, (ii) $n = 100$, and (iii) $n = 1000$.

**b.** Suppose $c$ is a positive number. Show that $\Pr(10 - c \leq \overline{Y} \leq 10 + c)$ becomes close to 1.0 as $n$ grows large.

**c.** Use your answer in (b) to argue that $\overline{Y}$ converges in probability to 10.

**2.16** $Y$ is distributed $N(5, 100)$ and you want to calculate $\Pr(Y < 3.6)$. Unfortunately, you do not have your textbook, and do not have access to a normal probability table like Appendix Table 1. However, you do have your computer and a computer program that can generate i.i.d. draws from the $N(5, 100)$ distribution. Explain how you can use your computer to compute an accurate approximation for $\Pr(Y < 3.6)$.

**2.17** $Y_i, i = 1, c, n$, are i.i.d. Bernoulli random variables with $p = 0.6$. Let $\overline{Y}$ denote the sample mean.

    **a.** Use the central limit to compute approximations for

        i. $\Pr(\overline{Y} > 0.64)$ when $n = 50$.

        ii. $\Pr(\overline{Y} < 0.56)$ when $n = 200$.

    **b.** How large would $n$ need to be to ensure that $\Pr(0.65 > \overline{Y} > 0.55) = 0.95$? (*Hint:* Use the central limit theorem to compute an approximate answer.)

**2.18** In any year, the weather may cause damages to a home. On a year-to-year basis, the damage is random. Let $Y$ denote the dollar value of damages in any given year. Suppose that during 95% of the year $Y = \$0$, but during the other 5% $Y = \$30,000$.

    **a.** What are the mean and standard deviation of damages caused in a year?

    **b.** Consider an "insurance pool" of 120 people whose homes are sufficiently dispersed so that, in any year, the damage to different homes can be viewed as independently distributed random variables. Let $\overline{Y}$ denote the average damage caused to these 120 homes in one year. (i) What is the expected value of the average damage $\overline{Y}$? (ii) What is the probability that $\overline{Y}$ exceeds $\$3,000$?

**2.19** Consider two random variables $X$ and $Y$. Suppose that $Y$ takes on $k$ values $y_1, \ldots, y_k$ and that $X$ takes on $l$ values $x_1, \ldots, x_l$.

    **a.** Show that $\Pr(Y = y_j) = \sum_{i=1}^{l} \Pr(Y = y_j \mid X = x_i) \Pr(X = x_i)$. [*Hint:* Use the definition of $\Pr(Y = y_j \mid X = x_i)$.]

    **b.** Use your answer to (a) to verify Equation (2.19).

    **c.** Suppose that $X$ and $Y$ are independent. Show that $\sigma_{XY} = 0$ and $\text{corr}(X, Y) = 0$.

**2.20** Consider three random variables $X$, $Y$, and $Z$. Suppose that $Y$ takes on $k$ values $y_1, \ldots, y_k$, that $X$ takes on $l$ values $x_1, \ldots, x_l$, and that $Z$ takes on $m$ values $z_1, \ldots, z_m$. The joint probability distribution of $X, Y, Z$ is $\Pr(X = x, Y = y, Z = z)$, and the conditional probability distribution of $Y$ given $X$ and $Z$ is $\Pr(Y = y \mid X = x, Z = z) = \frac{\Pr(Y = y, X = x, Z = z)}{\Pr(X = x, Z = z)}$.

**a.** Explain how the marginal probability that $Y = y$ can be calculated from the joint probability distribution. [*Hint:* This is a generalization of Equation (2.16).]

**b.** Show that $E(Y) = E[E(Y|X, Z)]$. [*Hint:* This is a generalization of Equations (2.19) and (2.20).]

**2.21** $X$ is a random variable with moments $E(X)$, $E(X^2)$, $E(X^3)$, and so forth.

**a.** Show $E(X - \mu)^3 = E(X^3) - 3[E(X^2)][E(X)] + 2[E(X)]^3$.

**b.** Show $E(X - \mu)^4 = E(X^4) - 4[E(X)][E(X^3)] + 6[E(X)]^2[E(X^2)] - 3[E(X)]^4$.

**2.22** Suppose you have some money to invest—for simplicity, $1—and you are planning to put a fraction $w$ into a stock market mutual fund and the rest, $1 - w$, into a bond mutual fund. Suppose that $1 invested in a stock fund yields $R_s$ after 1 year and that $1 invested in a bond fund yields $R_b$, suppose that $R_s$ is random with mean 0.08 (8%) and standard deviation 0.07, and suppose that $R_b$ is random with mean 0.05 (5%) and standard deviation 0.04. The correlation between $R_s$ and $R_b$ is 0.25. If you place a fraction $w$ of your money in the stock fund and the rest, $1 - w$, in the bond fund, then the return on your investment is $R = wR_s + (1 - w)R_b$.

**a.** Suppose that $w = 0.5$. Compute the mean and standard deviation of $R$.

**b.** Suppose that $w = 0.75$. Compute the mean and standard deviation of $R$.

**c.** What value of $w$ makes the mean of $R$ as large as possible? What is the standard deviation of $R$ for this value of $w$?

**d.** (Harder) What is the value of $w$ that minimizes the standard deviation of $R$? (Show using a graph, algebra, or calculus.)

**2.23** This exercise provides an example of a pair of random variables $X$ and $Y$ for which the conditional mean of $Y$ given $X$ depends on $X$ but $\text{corr}(X, Y) = 0$. Let $X$ and $Z$ be two independently distributed standard normal random variables, and let $Y = X^2 + Z$.

**a.** Show that $E(Y|X) = X^2$.

**b.** Show that $\mu_Y = 1$.

**c.** Show that $E(XY) = 0$. (*Hint:* Use the fact that the odd moments of a standard normal random variable are all zero.)

**d.** Show that $\text{cov}(X, Y) = 0$ and thus $\text{corr}(X, Y) = 0$.

**2.24** Suppose $Y_i$ is distributed i.i.d. $N(0, \sigma^2)$ for $i = 1, 2, \ldots, n$.

    **a.** Show that $E(Y_i^2/\sigma^2) = 1$.

    **b.** Show that $W = (1/\sigma^2)\sum_{i=1}^{n} Y_i^2$ is distributed $\chi_n^2$.

    **c.** Show that $E(W) = n$. [*Hint:* Use your answer to (a).]

    **d.** Show that $V = Y_1 \Big/ \sqrt{\dfrac{\sum_{i=2}^{n} Y_i^2}{n-1}}$ is distributed $t_{n-1}$.

**2.25** (Review of summation notation) Let $x_1, \ldots, x_n$ denote a sequence of numbers, $y_1, \ldots, y_n$ denote another sequence of numbers, and $a$, $b$, and $c$ denote three constants. Show that

    **a.** $\displaystyle\sum_{i=1}^{n} ax_i = a\sum_{i=1}^{n} x_i$

    **b.** $\displaystyle\sum_{i=1}^{n} (x_i + y_i) = \sum_{i=1}^{n} x_i + \sum_{i=1}^{n} y_i$

    **c.** $\displaystyle\sum_{i=1}^{n} a = na$

    **d.** $\displaystyle\sum_{i=1}^{n} (a + bx_i + cy_i)^2 = na^2 + b^2\sum_{i=1}^{n} x_i^2 + c^2\sum_{i=1}^{n} y_i^2 + 2ab\sum_{i=1}^{n} x_i +$
    $2ac\displaystyle\sum_{i=1}^{n} y_i + 2bc\sum_{i=1}^{n} x_i y_i$

**2.26** Suppose that $Y_1, Y_2, \ldots, Y_n$ are random variables with a common mean $\mu_Y$, a common variance $\sigma_Y^2$, and the same correlation $\rho$ (so that the correlation between $Y_i$ and $Y_j$ is equal to $\rho$ for all pairs $i$ and $j$, where $i \neq j$).

    **a.** Show that $\text{cov}(Y_i, Y_j) = \rho\sigma_Y^2$ for $i \neq j$.

    **b.** Suppose that $n = 2$. Show that $E(\overline{Y}) = \mu_Y$ and $\text{var}(\overline{Y}) = \frac{1}{2}\sigma_Y^2 + \frac{1}{2}\rho\sigma_Y^2$.

    **c.** For $n \geq 2$, show that $E(\overline{Y}) = \mu_Y$ and $\text{var}(\overline{Y}) = \sigma_Y^2/n + [(n-1)/n]\rho\sigma_Y^2$.

    **d.** When $n$ is very large, show that $\text{var}(\overline{Y}) \approx \rho\sigma_Y^2$.

**2.27** $X$ and $Z$ are two jointly distributed random variables. Suppose you know the value of $Z$, but not the value of $X$. Let $\tilde{X} = E(X \mid Z)$ denote a guess of the value of $X$ using the information on $Z$, and let $W = X - \tilde{X}$ denote the error associated with this guess.

    **a.** Show that $E(W) = 0$. (*Hint:* Use the law of iterated expectations.)

    **b.** Show that $E(WZ) = 0$.

**c.** Let $\hat{X} = g(Z)$ denote another guess of $X$ using $Z$, and $V = X - \hat{X}$ denote its error. Show that $E(V^2) \geq E(W^2)$. [*Hint:* Let $h(Z) = g(Z) - E(X \mid Z)$, so that $V = [X - E(X \mid Z)] - h(Z)$. Derive $E(V^2)$.]

## Empirical Exercise

**E2.1**   On the text website, **http://www.pearsonglobaleditions.com/Stock_Watson**, you will find the spreadsheet **Age_HourlyEarnings**, which contains the joint distribution of age (*Age*) and average hourly earnings (*AHE*) for 25- to 34-year-old full-time workers in 2012 with an education level that exceeds a high school diploma. Use this joint distribution to carry out the following exercises. (*Note:* For these exercises, you need to be able to carry out calculations and construct charts using a spreadsheet.)

   **a.** Compute the marginal distribution of *Age*.

   **b.** Compute the mean of *AHE* for each value of *Age*; that is, compute, $E(AHE|Age = 25)$, and so forth.

   **c.** Compute and plot the mean of *AHE* versus *Age*. Are average hourly earnings and age related? Explain.

   **d.** Use the law of iterated expectations to compute the mean of *AHE*; that is, compute $E(AHE)$.

   **e.** Compute the variance of *AHE*.

   **f.** Compute the covariance between *AHE* and *Age*.

   **g.** Compute the correlation between *AHE* and *Age*.

   **h.** Relate your answers in parts (f) and (g) to the plot you constructed in (c).

**APPENDIX**

## 2.1   Derivation of Results in Key Concept 2.3

This appendix derives the equations in Key Concept 2.3.

Equation (2.29) follows from the definition of the expectation.

To derive Equation (2.30), use the definition of the variance to write $\text{var}(a + bY) = E\{[a + bY - E(a + bY)]^2\} = E\{[b(Y - \mu_Y)]^2\} = b^2 E[(Y - \mu_Y)^2] = b^2 \sigma_Y^2$.

To derive Equation (2.31), use the definition of the variance to write

$$
\begin{aligned}
\text{var}(aX + bY) &= E\big\{[(aX + bY) - (a\mu_X + b\mu_Y)]^2\big\} \\
&= E\big\{[a(X - \mu_X) + b(Y - \mu_Y)]^2\big\} \\
&= E[a^2(X - \mu_X)^2] + 2E[ab(X - \mu_X)(Y - \mu_Y)] \\
&\quad + E[b^2(Y - \mu_Y)^2] \\
&= a^2\,\text{var}(X) + 2ab\,\text{cov}(X, Y) + b^2\,\text{var}(Y) \\
&= a^2\sigma_X^2 + 2ab\sigma_{XY} + b^2\sigma_Y^2,
\end{aligned}
\tag{2.49}
$$

where the second equality follows by collecting terms, the third equality follows by expanding the quadratic, and the fourth equality follows by the definition of the variance and covariance.

To derive Equation (2.32), write $E(Y^2) = E\big\{[(Y - \mu_Y) + \mu_Y]^2\big\} = E[(Y - \mu_Y)^2] + 2\mu_Y E(Y - \mu_Y) + \mu_Y^2 = \sigma_Y^2 + \mu_Y^2$ because $E(Y - \mu_Y) = 0$.

To derive Equation (2.33), use the definition of the covariance to write

$$
\begin{aligned}
\text{cov}(a + bX + cV, Y) &= E\big\{[a + bX + cV - E(a + bX + cV)][Y - \mu_Y]\big\} \\
&= E\big\{[b(X - \mu_X) + c(V - \mu_V)][Y - \mu_Y]\big\} \\
&= E\big\{[b(X - \mu_X)][Y - \mu_Y]\big\} + E\big\{[c(V - \mu_V)][Y - \mu_Y]\big\} \\
&= b\sigma_{XY} + c\sigma_{VY},
\end{aligned}
\tag{2.50}
$$

which is Equation (2.33).

To derive Equation (2.34), write $E(XY) = E\big\{[(X - \mu_X) + \mu_X][(Y - \mu_Y) + \mu_Y]\big\} = E[(X - \mu_X)(Y - \mu_Y)] + \mu_X E(Y - \mu_Y) + \mu_Y E(X - \mu_X) + \mu_X \mu_Y = \sigma_{XY} + \mu_X \mu_Y$.

We now prove the correlation inequality in Equation (2.35); that is, $|\text{corr}\,(X, Y)| \leq 1$. Let $a = -\sigma_{XY}/\sigma_X^2$ and $b = 1$. Applying Equation (2.31), we have that

$$
\begin{aligned}
\text{var}(aX + Y) &= a^2\sigma_X^2 + \sigma_Y^2 + 2a\sigma_{XY} \\
&= (-\sigma_{XY}/\sigma_X^2)^2\,\sigma_X^2 + \sigma_Y^2 + 2(-\sigma_{XY}/\sigma_X^2)\sigma_{XY} \\
&= \sigma_Y^2 - \sigma_{XY}^2/\sigma_X^2.
\end{aligned}
\tag{2.51}
$$

Because $\text{var}(aX + Y)$ is a variance, it cannot be negative, so from the final line of Equation (2.51), it must be that $\sigma_Y^2 - \sigma_{XY}^2/\sigma_X^2 \geq 0$. Rearranging this inequality yields

$$
\sigma_{XY}^2 \leq \sigma_X^2\sigma_Y^2 \quad \text{(covariance inequality).}
\tag{2.52}
$$

The covariance inequality implies that $\sigma_{XY}^2/(\sigma_X^2\sigma_Y^2) \leq 1$ or, equivalently, $|\sigma_{XY}/(\sigma_X\sigma_Y)| \leq 1$, which (using the definition of the correlation) proves the correlation inequality, $|\text{corr}\,(X\,Y)| \leq 1$.

# 3 Review of Statistics

Statistics is the science of using data to learn about the world around us. Statistical tools help us answer questions about unknown characteristics of distributions in populations of interest. For example, what is the mean of the distribution of earnings of recent college graduates? Do mean earnings differ for men and women, and, if so, by how much?

These questions relate to the distribution of earnings in the population of workers. One way to answer these questions would be to perform an exhaustive survey of the population of workers, measuring the earnings of each worker and thus finding the population distribution of earnings. In practice, however, such a comprehensive survey would be extremely expensive. The only comprehensive survey of the U.S. population is the decennial census, which cost $13 billion to carry out in 2010. The process of designing the census forms, managing and conducting the surveys, and compiling and analyzing the data takes ten years. Despite this extraordinary commitment, many members of the population slip through the cracks and are not surveyed. Thus a different, more practical approach is needed.

The key insight of statistics is that one can learn about a population distribution by selecting a random sample from that population. Rather than survey the entire U.S. population, we might survey, say, 1000 members of the population, selected at random by simple random sampling. Using statistical methods, we can use this sample to reach tentative conclusions—to draw statistical inferences—about characteristics of the full population.

Three types of statistical methods are used throughout econometrics: estimation, hypothesis testing, and confidence intervals. Estimation entails computing a "best guess" numerical value for an unknown characteristic of a population distribution, such as its mean, from a sample of data. Hypothesis testing entails formulating a specific hypothesis about the population, then using sample evidence to decide whether it is true. Confidence intervals use a set of data to estimate an interval or range for an unknown population characteristic. Sections 3.1, 3.2, and 3.3 review estimation, hypothesis testing, and confidence intervals in the context of statistical inference about an unknown population mean.

Most of the interesting questions in economics involve relationships between two or more variables or comparisons between different populations. For example, is there a gap between the mean earnings for male and female recent college graduates? In Section 3.4, the methods for learning about the mean of a single population in Sections 3.1 through 3.3 are extended to compare means in two different populations. Section 3.5 discusses how the methods for comparing the means of two populations can be used to estimate causal effects in experiments. Sections 3.2 through 3.5 focus on the use of the normal distribution for performing hypothesis tests and for constructing confidence intervals when the sample size is large. In some special circumstances, hypothesis tests and confidence intervals can be based on the Student $t$ distribution instead of the normal distribution; these special circumstances are discussed in Section 3.6. The chapter concludes with a discussion of the sample correlation and scatterplots in Section 3.7.

# 3.1    Estimation of the Population Mean

Suppose you want to know the mean value of $Y$ (that is, $\mu_Y$) in a population, such as the mean earnings of women recently graduated from college. A natural way to estimate this mean is to compute the sample average $\overline{Y}$ from a sample of $n$ independently and identically distributed (i.i.d.) observations, $Y_1, \ldots, Y_n$ (recall that $Y_1, \ldots, Y_n$ are i.i.d. if they are collected by simple random sampling). This section discusses estimation of $\mu_Y$ and the properties of $\overline{Y}$ as an estimator of $\mu_Y$.

## Estimators and Their Properties

*Estimators.* The sample average $\overline{Y}$ is a natural way to estimate $\mu_Y$, but it is not the only way. For example, another way to estimate $\mu_Y$ is simply to use the first observation, $Y_1$. Both $\overline{Y}$ and $Y_1$ are functions of the data that are designed to estimate $\mu_Y$; using the terminology in Key Concept 3.1, both are estimators of $\mu_Y$. When evaluated in repeated samples, $\overline{Y}$ and $Y_1$ take on different values (they produce different estimates) from one sample to the next. Thus the estimators $\overline{Y}$ and $Y_1$ both have sampling distributions. There are, in fact, many estimators of $\mu_Y$, of which $\overline{Y}$ and $Y_1$ are two examples.

There are many possible estimators, so what makes one estimator "better" than another? Because estimators are random variables, this question can be phrased more precisely: What are desirable characteristics of the sampling distribution of an estimator? In general, we would like an estimator that gets as close as possible to the unknown true value, at least in some average sense; in other words, we would like the sampling distribution of an estimator to be as tightly

## Estimators and Estimates

An **estimator** is a function of a sample of data to be drawn randomly from a population. An **estimate** is the numerical value of the estimator when it is actually computed using data from a specific sample. An estimator is a random variable because of randomness in selecting the sample, while an estimate is a nonrandom number.

centered on the unknown value as possible. This observation leads to three specific desirable characteristics of an estimator: unbiasedness (a lack of bias), consistency, and efficiency.

*Unbiasedness.* Suppose you evaluate an estimator many times over repeated randomly drawn samples. It is reasonable to hope that, on average, you would get the right answer. Thus a desirable property of an estimator is that the mean of its sampling distribution equals $\mu_Y$; if so, the estimator is said to be unbiased.

To state this concept mathematically, let $\hat{\mu}_Y$ denote some estimator of $\mu_Y$, such as $\overline{Y}$ or $Y_1$. The estimator $\hat{\mu}_Y$ is unbiased if $E(\hat{\mu}_Y) = \mu_Y$, where $E(\hat{\mu}_Y)$ is the mean of the sampling distribution of $\hat{\mu}_Y$; otherwise, $\hat{\mu}_Y$ is biased.

*Consistency.* Another desirable property of an estimator $\mu_Y$ is that, when the sample size is large, the uncertainty about the value of $\mu_Y$ arising from random variations in the sample is very small. Stated more precisely, a desirable property of $\hat{\mu}_Y$ is that the probability that it is within a small interval of the true value $\mu_Y$ approaches 1 as the sample size increases, that is, $\hat{\mu}_Y$ is consistent for $\mu_Y$ (Key Concept 2.6).

*Variance and efficiency.* Suppose you have two candidate estimators, $\hat{\mu}_Y$ and $\tilde{\mu}_Y$, both of which are unbiased. How might you choose between them? One way to do so is to choose the estimator with the tightest sampling distribution. This suggests choosing between $\hat{\mu}_Y$ and $\tilde{\mu}_Y$ by picking the estimator with the smallest variance. If $\hat{\mu}_Y$ has a smaller variance than $\tilde{\mu}_Y$, then $\hat{\mu}_Y$ is said to be more efficient than $\tilde{\mu}_Y$. The terminology "efficiency" stems from the notion that if $\hat{\mu}_Y$ has a smaller variance than $\tilde{\mu}_Y$, then it uses the information in the data more efficiently than does $\tilde{\mu}_Y$.

## Bias, Consistency, and Efficiency

Let $\hat{\mu}_Y$ be an estimator of $\mu_Y$. Then:

- The *bias* of $\hat{\mu}_Y$ is $E(\hat{\mu}_Y) - \mu_Y$.
- $\hat{\mu}_Y$ is an *unbiased estimator* of $\mu_Y$ if $E(\hat{\mu}_Y) = \mu_Y$.
- $\hat{\mu}_Y$ is a *consistent estimator* of $\mu_Y$ if $\hat{\mu}_Y \xrightarrow{p} \mu_Y$.
- Let $\tilde{\mu}_Y$ be another estimator of $\mu_Y$ and suppose that both $\hat{\mu}_Y$ and $\tilde{\mu}_Y$ are unbiased. Then $\hat{\mu}_Y$ is said to be more *efficient* than $\hat{\mu}_Y$ if $\text{var}(\hat{\mu}_Y) < \text{var}(\tilde{\mu}_Y)$.

**Bias**, **consistency**, and **efficiency** are summarized in Key Concept 3.2.

### Properties of $\overline{Y}$

How does $\overline{Y}$ fare as an estimator of $\mu_Y$ when judged by the three criteria of bias, consistency, and efficiency?

*Bias and consistency.* The sampling distribution of $\overline{Y}$ has already been examined in Sections 2.5 and 2.6. As shown in Section 2.5, $E(\overline{Y}) = \mu_Y$, so $\overline{Y}$ is an unbiased estimator of $\mu_Y$. Similarly, the law of large numbers (Key Concept 2.6) states that $\overline{Y} \xrightarrow{p} \mu_Y$; that is, $\overline{Y}$ is consistent.

*Efficiency.* What can be said about the efficiency of $\overline{Y}$? Because efficiency entails a comparison of estimators, we need to specify the estimator or estimators to which $\overline{Y}$ is to be compared.

We start by comparing the efficiency of $\overline{Y}$ to the estimator $Y_1$. Because $Y_1, \ldots, Y_n$ are i.i.d., the mean of the sampling distribution of $Y_1$ is $E(Y_1) = \mu_Y$; thus $Y_1$ is an unbiased estimator of $\mu_Y$. Its variance is $\text{var}(Y_1) = \sigma_Y^2$. From Section 2.5, the variance of $\overline{Y}$ is $\sigma_Y^2/n$. Thus, for $n \geq 2$, the variance of $\overline{Y}$ is less than the variance of $Y_1$; that is, $\overline{Y}$ is a more efficient estimator than $Y_1$, so, according to the criterion of efficiency, $\overline{Y}$ should be used instead of $Y_1$. The estimator $Y_1$ might strike you as an obviously poor estimator—why would you go to the trouble of collecting a sample of $n$ observations only to throw away all but the first?—and the concept of efficiency provides a formal way to show that $\overline{Y}$ is a more desirable estimator than $Y_1$.

## Efficiency of $\overline{Y}$: $\overline{Y}$ Is BLUE

KEY CONCEPT

3.3

Let $\hat{\mu}_Y$ be an estimator of $\mu_Y$ that is a weighted average of $Y_1, \ldots, Y_n$, that is, $\hat{\mu}_Y = (1/n)\sum_{i=1}^{n} a_i Y_i$, where $a_1, \ldots, a_n$ are nonrandom constants. If $\hat{\mu}_Y$ is unbiased, then $\text{var}(\overline{Y}) < \text{var}(\hat{\mu}_Y)$ unless $\hat{\mu}_Y = \overline{Y}$. Thus $\overline{Y}$ is the Best Linear Unbiased Estimator (BLUE); that is, $\overline{Y}$ is the most efficient estimator of $\mu_Y$ among all unbiased estimators that are weighted averages of $Y_1, \ldots, Y_n$.

What about a less obviously poor estimator? Consider the weighted average in which the observations are alternately weighted by $\frac{1}{2}$ and $\frac{3}{2}$:

$$\widetilde{Y} = \frac{1}{n}\left(\frac{1}{2}Y_1 + \frac{3}{2}Y_2 + \frac{1}{2}Y_3 + \frac{3}{2}Y_4 + \cdots + \frac{1}{2}Y_{n-1} + \frac{3}{2}Y_n\right), \quad (3.1)$$

where the number of observations $n$ is assumed to be even for convenience. The mean of $\widetilde{Y}$ is $\mu_Y$ and its variance is $\text{var}(\widetilde{Y}) = 1.25\sigma_Y^2/n$ (Exercise 3.11). Thus $\widetilde{Y}$ is unbiased and, because $\text{var}(\widetilde{Y}) \to 0$ as $n \to \infty$, $\widetilde{Y}$ is consistent. However, $\widetilde{Y}$ has a larger variance than $\overline{Y}$. Thus $\overline{Y}$ is more efficient than $\widetilde{Y}$.

The estimators $\overline{Y}$, $Y_1$, and $\widetilde{Y}$ have a common mathematical structure: They are weighted averages of $Y_1, \ldots, Y_n$. The comparisons in the previous two paragraphs show that the weighted averages $Y_1$ and $\widetilde{Y}$ have larger variances than $\overline{Y}$. In fact, these conclusions reflect a more general result: $\overline{Y}$ is the most efficient estimator of *all* unbiased estimators that are weighted averages of $Y_1, \ldots, Y_n$. Said differently, $\overline{Y}$ is the **B**est **L**inear **U**nbiased **E**stimator (**BLUE**); that is, it is the most efficient (best) estimator among all estimators that are unbiased and are linear functions of $Y_1, \ldots, Y_n$. This result is stated in Key Concept 3.3 and is proved in Chapter 5.

$\overline{Y}$ *is the least squares estimator of* $\mu_Y$. The sample average $\overline{Y}$ provides the best fit to the data in the sense that the average squared differences between the observations and $\overline{Y}$ are the smallest of all possible estimators.

Consider the problem of finding the estimator $m$ that minimizes

$$\sum_{i=1}^{n}(Y_i - m)^2, \quad (3.2)$$

which is a measure of the total squared gap or distance between the estimator $m$ and the sample points. Because $m$ is an estimator of $E(Y)$, you can think of it as a

## Off the Mark!

In 2009, just before India's National Elections, pollsters predicted a close fight between the coalition parties, UPA and NDA. Psephologists envisaged that while UPA might have had the upper hand, NDA could not be written off. They predicted UPA would get between 201 and 235 seats, and NDA between 165 and 186. The actual results were surprising: UPA got 262 seats, while NDA could only manage to get 157 seats.

What could be the possible reasons for opinion polls being wide off the mark?

In countries that do not have a homogenous population, such as India, caste, religion, and region influence electoral outcomes greatly. Vulnerable sections of the population may be afraid to disclose their actual preference. If opinion polls do not randomly select samples across various locations and sections of people they may not hit the mark.

*Source: http://timesofindia.indiatimes.com/news/Why-opinion-polls-are-often-wide-of-the-mark/articleshow/33678070.cms?*

prediction of the value of $Y_i$, so the gap $Y_i - m$ can be thought of as a prediction mistake. The sum of squared gaps in Expression (3.2) can be thought of as the sum of squared prediction mistakes.

The estimator $m$ that minimizes the sum of squared gaps $Y_i - m$ in Expression (3.2) is called the **least squares estimator**. One can imagine using trial and error to solve the least squares problem: Try many values of $m$ until you are satisfied that you have the value that makes Expression (3.2) as small as possible. Alternatively, as is done in Appendix 3.2, you can use algebra or calculus to show that choosing $m = \overline{Y}$ minimizes the sum of squared gaps in Expression (3.2) so that $\overline{Y}$ is the least squares estimator of $\mu_Y$.

## The Importance of Random Sampling

We have assumed that $Y_1, \ldots, Y_n$ are i.i.d. draws, such as those that would be obtained from simple random sampling. This assumption is important because nonrandom sampling can result in $\overline{Y}$ being biased. Suppose that, to estimate the monthly national unemployment rate, a statistical agency adopts a sampling scheme in which interviewers survey working-age adults sitting in city parks at 10 A.M. on the second Wednesday of the month. Because most employed people are at work at that hour (not sitting in the park!), the unemployed are overly represented in the sample, and an estimate of the unemployment rate based on this sampling plan would be biased. This bias arises because this sampling scheme overrepresents, or oversamples, the unemployed members of the population. This example is fictitious, but the "Off the Mark!" box gives a real-world example of biases introduced by sampling that is not entirely random.

It is important to design sample selection schemes in a way that minimizes bias. Appendix 3.1 includes a discussion of what the Bureau of Labor Statistics actually does when it conducts the U.S. Current Population Survey (CPS), the survey it uses to estimate the monthly U.S. unemployment rate.

## 3.2 Hypothesis Tests Concerning the Population Mean

Many hypotheses about the world around us can be phrased as yes/no questions. Do the mean hourly earnings of recent U.S. college graduates equal $20 per hour? Are mean earnings the same for male and female college graduates? Both these questions embody specific hypotheses about the population distribution of earnings. The statistical challenge is to answer these questions based on a sample of evidence. This section describes **hypothesis tests** concerning the population mean (Does the population mean of hourly earnings equal $20?). Hypothesis tests involving two populations (Are mean earnings the same for men and women?) are taken up in Section 3.4.

### Null and Alternative Hypotheses

The starting point of statistical hypotheses testing is specifying the hypothesis to be tested, called the **null hypothesis**. Hypothesis testing entails using data to compare the null hypothesis to a second hypothesis, called the **alternative hypothesis**, that holds if the null does not.

The null hypothesis is that the population mean, $E(Y)$, takes on a specific value, denoted $\mu_{Y,0}$. The null hypothesis is denoted $H_0$ and thus is

$$H_0: E(Y) = \mu_{Y,0}. \tag{3.3}$$

For example, the conjecture that, on average in the population, college graduates earn $20 per hour constitutes a null hypothesis about the population distribution of hourly earnings. Stated mathematically, if $Y$ is the hourly earning of a randomly selected recent college graduate, then the null hypothesis is that $E(Y) = 20$; that is, $\mu_{Y,0} = 20$ in Equation (3.3).

The alternative hypothesis specifies what is true if the null hypothesis is not. The most general alternative hypothesis is that $E(Y) \neq \mu_{Y,0}$, which is called a **two-sided alternative hypothesis** because it allows $E(Y)$ to be either less than or greater than $\mu_{Y,0}$. The two-sided alternative is written as

$$H_1: E(Y) \neq \mu_{Y,0} \quad \text{(two-sided alternative)}. \tag{3.4}$$

One-sided alternatives are also possible, and these are discussed later in this section.

The problem facing the statistician is to use the evidence in a randomly selected sample of data to decide whether to accept the null hypothesis $H_0$ or to reject it in favor of the alternative hypothesis $H_1$. If the null hypothesis is "accepted," this does not mean that the statistician declares it to be true; rather, it is accepted tentatively with the recognition that it might be rejected later based on additional evidence. For this reason, statistical hypothesis testing can be posed as either rejecting the null hypothesis or failing to do so.

## The p-Value

In any given sample, the sample average $\overline{Y}$ will rarely be exactly equal to the hypothesized value $\mu_{Y,0}$. Differences between $\overline{Y}$ and $\mu_{Y,0}$ can arise because the true mean in fact does not equal $\mu_{Y,0}$ (the null hypothesis is false) or because the true mean equals $\mu_{Y,0}$ (the null hypothesis is true) but $\overline{Y}$ differs from $\mu_{Y,0}$ because of random sampling. It is impossible to distinguish between these two possibilities with certainty. Although a sample of data cannot provide conclusive evidence about the null hypothesis, it is possible to do a probabilistic calculation that permits testing the null hypothesis in a way that accounts for sampling uncertainty. This calculation involves using the data to compute the p-value of the null hypothesis.

The **p-value**, also called the **significance probability**, is the probability of drawing a statistic at least as adverse to the null hypothesis as the one you actually computed in your sample, assuming the null hypothesis is correct. In the case at hand, the p-value is the probability of drawing $\overline{Y}$ at least as far in the tails of its distribution under the null hypothesis as the sample average you actually computed.

For example, suppose that, in your sample of recent college graduates, the average wage is $22.64. The p-value is the probability of observing a value of $\overline{Y}$ at least as different from $20 (the population mean under the null) as the observed value of $22.64 by pure random sampling variation, assuming that the null hypothesis is true. If this p-value is small, say 0.5%, then it is very unlikely that this sample would have been drawn if the null hypothesis is true; thus it is reasonable to conclude that the null hypothesis is not true. By contrast, if this p-value is large, say 40%, then it is quite likely that the observed sample average of $22.64 could have arisen just by random sampling variation if the null hypothesis is true; accordingly, the evidence against the null hypothesis is weak in this probabilistic sense, and it is reasonable not to reject the null hypothesis.

To state the definition of the p-value mathematically, let $\overline{Y}^{act}$ denote the value of the sample average actually computed in the data set at hand and let $\text{Pr}_{H_0}$

denote the probability computed under the null hypothesis (that is, computed assuming that $E(Y_i) = \mu_{Y,0}$). The $p$-value is

$$p\text{-value} = \Pr_{H_0}\big[|\overline{Y} - \mu_{Y,0}| > |\overline{Y}^{act} - \mu_{Y,0}|\big]. \qquad (3.5)$$

That is, the $p$-value is the area in the tails of the distribution of $\overline{Y}$ under the null hypothesis beyond $\mu_{Y,0} \pm |\overline{Y}^{act} - \mu_{Y,0}|$. If the $p$-value is large, then the observed value $\overline{Y}^{act}$ is consistent with the null hypothesis, but if the $p$-value is small, it is not.

To compute the $p$-value, it is necessary to know the sampling distribution of $\overline{Y}$ under the null hypothesis. As discussed in Section 2.6, when the sample size is small this distribution is complicated. However, according to the central limit theorem, when the sample size is large, the sampling distribution of $\overline{Y}$ is well approximated by a normal distribution. Under the null hypothesis the mean of this normal distribution is $\mu_{Y,0}$, so under the null hypothesis $\overline{Y}$ is distributed $N(\mu_{Y,0}, \sigma_{\overline{Y}}^2)$, where $\sigma_{\overline{Y}}^2 = \sigma_Y^2/n$. This large-sample normal approximation makes it possible to compute the $p$-value without needing to know the population distribution of $Y$, as long as the sample size is large. The details of the calculation, however, depend on whether $\sigma_Y^2$ is known.

## Calculating the $p$-Value When $\sigma_Y$ Is Known

The calculation of the $p$-value when $\sigma_Y$ is known is summarized in Figure 3.1. If the sample size is large, then under the null hypothesis the sampling distribution of $\overline{Y}$ is $N(\mu_{Y,0}, \sigma_{\overline{Y}}^2)$, where $\sigma_{\overline{Y}}^2 = \sigma_Y^2/n$. Thus, under the null hypothesis, the standardized version of $\overline{Y}$, $(\overline{Y} - \mu_{Y,0})/\sigma_{\overline{Y}}$, has a standard normal distribution. The $p$-value is the probability of obtaining a value of $\overline{Y}$ farther from $\mu_{Y,0}$ than $\overline{Y}^{act}$ under the null hypothesis or, equivalently, is the probability of obtaining $(\overline{Y} - \mu_{Y,0})/\sigma_{\overline{Y}}$ greater than $(\overline{Y}^{act} - \mu_{Y,0})/\sigma_{\overline{Y}}$ in absolute value. This probability is the shaded area shown in Figure 3.1. Written mathematically, the shaded tail probability in Figure 3.1 (that is, the $p$-value) is

$$p\text{-value} = \Pr_{H_0}\left(\left|\frac{\overline{Y} - \mu_{Y,0}}{\sigma_{\overline{Y}}}\right| > \left|\frac{\overline{Y}^{act} - \mu_{Y,0}}{\sigma_{\overline{Y}}}\right|\right) = 2\Phi\left(-\left|\frac{\overline{Y}^{act} - \mu_{Y,0}}{\sigma_{\overline{Y}}}\right|\right), \quad (3.6)$$

where $\Phi$ is the standard normal cumulative distribution function. That is, the $p$-value is the area in the tails of a standard normal distribution outside $\pm|\overline{Y}^{act} - \mu_{Y,0}|/\sigma_{\overline{Y}}$.

The formula for the $p$-value in Equation (3.6) depends on the variance of the population distribution, $\sigma_Y^2$. In practice, this variance is typically unknown. [An exception is when $Y_i$ is binary so that its distribution is Bernoulli, in which case

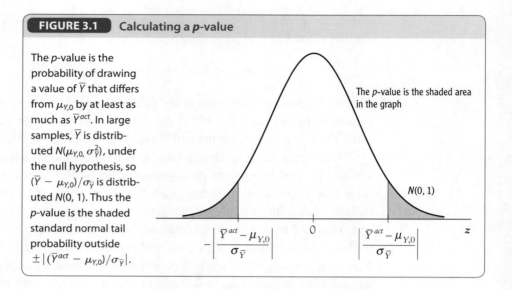

**FIGURE 3.1** Calculating a *p*-value

The *p*-value is the probability of drawing a value of $\overline{Y}$ that differs from $\mu_{Y,0}$ by at least as much as $\overline{Y}^{act}$. In large samples, $\overline{Y}$ is distributed $N(\mu_{Y,0}, \sigma_{\overline{Y}}^2)$, under the null hypothesis, so $(\overline{Y} - \mu_{Y,0})/\sigma_{\overline{Y}}$ is distributed $N(0, 1)$. Thus the *p*-value is the shaded standard normal tail probability outside $\pm|(\overline{Y}^{act} - \mu_{Y,0})/\sigma_{\overline{Y}}|$.

The *p*-value is the shaded area in the graph

the variance is determined by the null hypothesis; see Equation (2.7) and Exercise 3.2.] Because in general $\sigma_{\overline{Y}}^2$ must be estimated before the *p*-value can be computed, we now turn to the problem of estimating $\sigma_{\overline{Y}}^2$.

## The Sample Variance, Sample Standard Deviation, and Standard Error

The sample variance $s_Y^2$ is an estimator of the population variance $\sigma_Y^2$, the sample standard deviation $s_Y$ is an estimator of the population standard deviation $\sigma_Y$, and the standard error of the sample average $\overline{Y}$ is an estimator of the standard deviation of the sampling distribution of $\overline{Y}$.

***The sample variance and standard deviation.*** The **sample variance**, $s_Y^2$, is

$$s_Y^2 = \frac{1}{n-1} \sum_{i=1}^{n} (Y_i - \overline{Y})^2. \tag{3.7}$$

The **sample standard deviation**, $s_Y$, is the square root of the sample variance.

The formula for the sample variance is much like the formula for the population variance. The population variance, $E(Y - \mu_Y)^2$, is the average value of $(Y - \mu_Y)^2$ in the population distribution. Similarly, the sample variance is the sample average of $(Y_i - \mu_Y)^2, i = 1, \ldots, n$, with two modifications: First, $\mu_Y$ is replaced by $\overline{Y}$, and second, the average uses the divisor $n - 1$ instead of $n$.

## The Standard Error of $\overline{Y}$

The standard error of $\overline{Y}$ is an estimator of the standard deviation of $\overline{Y}$. The standard error of $\overline{Y}$ is denoted $SE(\overline{Y})$ or $\hat{\sigma}_{\overline{Y}}$. When $Y_1, \ldots, Y_n$ are i.i.d.,

$$SE(\overline{Y}) = \hat{\sigma}_{\overline{Y}} = s_Y / \sqrt{n}. \tag{3.8}$$

The reason for the first modification—replacing $\mu_Y$ by $\overline{Y}$—is that $\mu_Y$ is unknown and thus must be estimated; the natural estimator of $\mu_Y$ is $\overline{Y}$. The reason for the second modification—dividing by $n - 1$ instead of by $n$—is that estimating $\mu_Y$ by $\overline{Y}$ introduces a small downward bias in $(Y_i - \overline{Y})^2$. Specifically, as is shown in Exercise 3.18, $E[(Y_i - \overline{Y})^2] = [(n - 1)/n]\sigma_Y^2$. Thus $E\sum_{i=1}^{n}(Y_i - \overline{Y})^2 = nE[(Y_i - \overline{Y})^2] = (n - 1)\sigma_Y^2$. Dividing by $n - 1$ in Equation (3.7) instead of $n$ corrects for this small downward bias, and as a result $s_Y^2$ is unbiased.

Dividing by $n - 1$ in Equation (3.7) instead of $n$ is called a **degrees of freedom** correction: Estimating the mean uses up some of the information—that is, uses up 1 "degree of freedom"—in the data, so that only $n - 1$ degrees of freedom remain.

*Consistency of the sample variance.* The sample variance is a consistent estimator of the population variance:

$$s_Y^2 \longrightarrow \sigma_Y^2. \tag{3.9}$$

In other words, the sample variance is close to the population variance with high probability when $n$ is large.

The result in Equation (3.9) is proven in Appendix 3.3 under the assumptions that $Y_1, \ldots, Y_n$ are i.i.d. and $Y_i$ has a finite fourth moment; that is, $E(Y_i^4) < \infty$. Intuitively, the reason that $s_Y^2$ is consistent is that it is a sample average, so $s_Y^2$ obeys the law of large numbers. But for $s_Y^2$ to obey the law of large numbers in Key Concept 2.6, $(Y_i - \mu_Y)^2$ must have finite variance, which in turn means that $E(Y_i^4)$ must be finite; in other words, $Y_i$ must have a finite fourth moment.

*The standard error of $\overline{Y}$.* Because the standard deviation of the sampling distribution of $\overline{Y}$ is $\sigma_{\overline{Y}} = \sigma_Y / \sqrt{n}$, Equation (3.9) justifies using $s_Y / \sqrt{n}$ as an estimator of $\sigma_{\overline{Y}}$. The estimator of $\sigma_{\overline{Y}}$, $s_Y / \sqrt{n}$, is called the **standard error of $\overline{Y}$** and is denoted $SE(\overline{Y})$ or $\hat{\sigma}_{\overline{Y}}$ (the caret "^" over the symbol means that it is an estimator of $\sigma_{\overline{Y}}$). The standard error of $\overline{Y}$ is summarized as in Key Concept 3.4.

When $Y_1, \ldots, Y_n$ are i.i.d. draws from a Bernoulli distribution with success probability $p$, the formula for the variance of $\overline{Y}$ simplifies to $p(1-p)/n$ (see Exercise 3.2). The formula for the standard error also takes on a simple form that depends only on $\overline{Y}$ and $n$: $SE(\overline{Y}) = \sqrt{\overline{Y}(1-\overline{Y})/n}$.

## Calculating the p-Value When $\sigma_Y$ Is Unknown

Because $s_Y^2$ is a consistent estimator of $\sigma_Y^2$, the $p$-value can be computed by replacing $\sigma_{\overline{Y}}$ in Equation (3.6) by the standard error, $SE(\overline{Y}) = \hat{\sigma}_{\overline{Y}}$. That is, when $\sigma_Y$ is unknown and $Y_1, \ldots, Y_n$ are i.i.d., the $p$-value is calculated using the formula

$$p\text{-value} = 2\Phi\left(-\left|\frac{\overline{Y}^{act} - \mu_{Y,0}}{SE(\overline{Y})}\right|\right). \tag{3.10}$$

## The t-Statistic

The standardized sample average $(\overline{Y} - \mu_{Y,0})/SE(\overline{Y})$ plays a central role in testing statistical hypotheses and has a special name, the **t-statistic** or **t-ratio**:

$$t = \frac{\overline{Y} - \mu_{Y,0}}{SE(\overline{Y})}. \tag{3.11}$$

In general, a **test statistic** is a statistic used to perform a hypothesis test. The $t$-statistic is an important example of a test statistic.

*Large-sample distribution of the t-statistic.* When $n$ is large, $s_Y^2$ is close to $\sigma_Y^2$ with high probability. Thus the distribution of the $t$-statistic is approximately the same as the distribution of $(\overline{Y} - \mu_{Y,0})/\sigma_{\overline{Y}}$, which in turn is well approximated by the standard normal distribution when $n$ is large because of the central limit theorem (Key Concept 2.7). Accordingly, under the null hypothesis,

$$t \text{ is approximately distributed } N(0,1) \text{ for large } n. \tag{3.12}$$

The formula for the $p$-value in Equation (3.10) can be rewritten in terms of the $t$-statistic. Let $t^{act}$ denote the value of the $t$-statistic actually computed:

$$t^{act} = \frac{\overline{Y}^{act} - \mu_{Y,0}}{SE(\overline{Y})}. \tag{3.13}$$

Accordingly, when $n$ is large, the $p$-value can be calculated using

$$p\text{-value} = 2\Phi(-|t^{act}|). \tag{3.14}$$

As a hypothetical example, suppose that a sample of $n = 200$ recent college graduates is used to test the null hypothesis that the mean wage, $E(Y)$, is $20 per hour. The sample average wage is $\overline{Y}^{act} = \$22.64$, and the sample standard deviation is $s_Y = \$18.14$. Then the standard error of $\overline{Y}$ is $s_Y/\sqrt{n} = 18.14/\sqrt{200} = 1.28$. The value of the $t$-statistic is $t^{act} = (22.64 - 20)/1.28 = 2.06$. From Appendix Table 1, the $p$-value is $2\Phi(-2.06) = 0.039$, or 3.9%. That is, assuming the null hypothesis to be true, the probability of obtaining a sample average at least as different from the null as the one actually computed is 3.9%.

## Hypothesis Testing with a Prespecified Significance Level

When you undertake a statistical hypothesis test, you can make two types of mistakes: You can incorrectly reject the null hypothesis when it is true, or you can fail to reject the null hypothesis when it is false. Hypothesis tests can be performed without computing the $p$-value if you are willing to specify in advance the probability you are willing to tolerate of making the first kind of mistake—that is, of incorrectly rejecting the null hypothesis when it is true. If you choose a prespecified probability of rejecting the null hypothesis when it is true (for example, 5%), then you will reject the null hypothesis if and only if the $p$-value is less than 0.05. This approach gives preferential treatment to the null hypothesis, but in many practical situations this preferential treatment is appropriate.

*Hypothesis tests using a fixed significance level.* Suppose it has been decided that the hypothesis will be rejected if the $p$-value is less than 5%. Because the area under the tails of the standard normal distribution outside $\pm 1.96$ is 5%, this gives a simple rule:

$$\text{Reject } H_0 \text{ if } |t^{act}| > 1.96. \tag{3.15}$$

That is, reject if the absolute value of the $t$-statistic computed from the sample is greater than 1.96. If $n$ is large enough, then under the null hypothesis the $t$-statistic has a $N(0, 1)$ distribution. Thus the probability of erroneously rejecting the null hypothesis (rejecting the null hypothesis when it is in fact true) is 5%.

**KEY CONCEPT**

**3.5**

## The Terminology of Hypothesis Testing

A statistical hypothesis test can make two types of mistakes: a **type I error**, in which the null hypothesis is rejected when in fact it is true, and a **type II error**, in which the null hypothesis is not rejected when in fact it is false. The prespecified rejection probability of a statistical hypothesis test when the null hypothesis is true—that is, the prespecified probability of a type I error—is the **significance level** of the test. The **critical value** of the test statistic is the value of the statistic for which the test just rejects the null hypothesis at the given significance level. The set of values of the test statistic for which the test rejects the null hypothesis is the **rejection region**, and the values of the test statistic for which it does not reject the null hypothesis is the **acceptance region**. The probability that the test actually incorrectly rejects the null hypothesis when it is true is the **size of the test**, and the probability that the test correctly rejects the null hypothesis when the alternative is true is the **power of the test**.

The $p$-value is the probability of obtaining a test statistic, by random sampling variation, at least as adverse to the null hypothesis value as is the statistic actually observed, assuming that the null hypothesis is correct. Equivalently, the $p$-value is the smallest significance level at which you can reject the null hypothesis.

This framework for testing statistical hypotheses has some specialized terminology, summarized in Key Concept 3.5. The significance level of the test in Equation (3.15) is 5%, the critical value of this two-sided test is 1.96, and the rejection region is the values of the $t$-statistic outside ±1.96. If the test rejects at the 5% significance level, the population mean $\mu_Y$ is said to be statistically significantly different from $\mu_{Y,0}$ at the 5% significance level.

Testing hypotheses using a prespecified significance level does not require computing $p$-values. In the previous example of testing the hypothesis that the mean earnings of recent college graduates is $20 per hour, the $t$-statistic was 2.06. This value exceeds 1.96, so the hypothesis is rejected at the 5% level. Although performing the test with a 5% significance level is easy, reporting only whether the null hypothesis is rejected at a prespecified significance level conveys less information than reporting the $p$-value.

*What significance level should you use in practice?*   In many cases, statisticians and econometricians use a 5% significance level. If you were to test many statistical

**Testing the Hypothesis $E(Y) = \mu_{Y,0}$**
**Against the Alternative $E(Y) \neq \mu_{Y,0}$**

KEY CONCEPT

## 3.6

1. Compute the standard error of $\overline{Y}$, $SE(\overline{Y})$ [Equation (3.8)].
2. Compute the $t$-statistic [Equation (3.13)].
3. Compute the $p$-value [Equation (3.14)]. Reject the hypothesis at the 5% significance level if the $p$-value is less than 0.05 (equivalently, if $|t^{act}| > 1.96$).

hypotheses at the 5% level, you would incorrectly reject the null on average once in 20 cases. Sometimes a more conservative significance level might be in order. For example, legal cases sometimes involve statistical evidence, and the null hypothesis could be that the defendant is not guilty; then one would want to be quite sure that a rejection of the null (conclusion of guilt) is not just a result of random sample variation. In some legal settings, the significance level used is 1%, or even 0.1%, to avoid this sort of mistake. Similarly, if a government agency is considering permitting the sale of a new drug, a very conservative standard might be in order so that consumers can be sure that the drugs available in the market actually work.

Being conservative, in the sense of using a very low significance level, has a cost: The smaller the significance level, the larger the critical value and the more difficult it becomes to reject the null when the null is false. In fact, the most conservative thing to do is never to reject the null hypothesis—but if that is your view, then you never need to look at any statistical evidence for you will never change your mind! The lower the significance level, the lower the power of the test. Many economic and policy applications can call for less conservatism than a legal case, so a 5% significance level is often considered to be a reasonable compromise.

Key Concept 3.6 summarizes hypothesis tests for the population mean against the two-sided alternative.

## One-Sided Alternatives

In some circumstances, the alternative hypothesis might be that the mean exceeds $\mu_{Y,0}$. For example, one hopes that education helps in the labor market, so the relevant alternative to the null hypothesis that earnings are the same for college graduates and non–college graduates is not just that their earnings differ, but rather that graduates earn more than nongraduates. This is called a **one-sided alternative hypothesis** and can be written

$$H_1: E(Y) > \mu_{Y,0} \quad \text{(one-sided alternative)}. \tag{3.16}$$

The general approach to computing $p$-values and to hypothesis testing is the same for one-sided alternatives as it is for two-sided alternatives, with the modification that only large positive values of the $t$-statistic reject the null hypothesis rather than values that are large in absolute value. Specifically, to test the one-sided hypothesis in Equation (3.16), construct the $t$-statistic in Equation (3.13). The $p$-value is the area under the standard normal distribution to the right of the calculated $t$-statistic. That is, the $p$-value, based on the $N(0, 1)$ approximation to the distribution of the $t$-statistic, is

$$p\text{-value} = \text{Pr}_{H_0}(Z > t^{act}) = 1 - \Phi(t^{act}). \tag{3.17}$$

The $N(0, 1)$ critical value for a one-sided test with a 5% significance level is 1.64. The rejection region for this test is all values of the $t$-statistic exceeding 1.64.

The one-sided hypothesis in Equation (3.16) concerns values of $\mu_Y$ exceeding $\mu_{Y,0}$. If instead the alternative hypothesis is that $E(Y) < \mu_{Y,0}$, then the discussion of the previous paragraph applies except that the signs are switched; for example, the 5% rejection region consists of values of the $t$-statistic less than $-1.64$.

# 3.3 Confidence Intervals for the Population Mean

Because of random sampling error, it is impossible to learn the exact value of the population mean of $Y$ using only the information in a sample. However, it is possible to use data from a random sample to construct a set of values that contains the true population mean $\mu_Y$ with a certain prespecified probability. Such a set is called a **confidence set**, and the prespecified probability that $\mu_Y$ is contained in this set is called the **confidence level**. The confidence set for $\mu_Y$ turns out to be all the possible values of the mean between a lower and an upper limit, so that the confidence set is an interval, called a **confidence interval**.

Here is one way to construct a 95% confidence set for the population mean. Begin by picking some arbitrary value for the mean; call it $\mu_{Y,0}$. Test the null hypothesis that $\mu_Y = \mu_{Y,0}$ against the alternative that $\mu_Y \neq \mu_{Y,0}$ by computing the $t$-statistic; if its absolute value is less than 1.96, this hypothesized value $\mu_{Y,0}$ is not rejected at the 5% level, and write down this nonrejected value $\mu_{Y,0}$. Now pick another arbitrary value of $\mu_{Y,0}$ and test it; if you cannot reject it, write this value on your list.

## Confidence Intervals for the Population Mean

**KEY CONCEPT**

**3.7**

A 95% two-sided confidence interval for $\mu_Y$ is an interval constructed so that it contains the true value of $\mu_Y$ in 95% of all possible random samples. When the sample size $n$ is large, 95%, 90%, and 99% confidence intervals for $\mu_Y$ are

95% confidence interval for $\mu_Y = \{\overline{Y} \pm 1.96SE(\overline{Y})\}$.

90% confidence interval for $\mu_Y = \{\overline{Y} \pm 1.64SE(\overline{Y})\}$.

99% confidence interval for $\mu_Y = \{\overline{Y} \pm 2.58SE(\overline{Y})\}$.

Do this again and again; indeed, do so for all possible values of the population mean. Continuing this process yields the set of all values of the population mean that cannot be rejected at the 5% level by a two-sided hypothesis test.

This list is useful because it summarizes the set of hypotheses you can and cannot reject (at the 5% level) based on your data: If someone walks up to you with a specific number in mind, you can tell him whether his hypothesis is rejected or not simply by looking up his number on your handy list. A bit of clever reasoning shows that this set of values has a remarkable property: The probability that it contains the true value of the population mean is 95%.

The clever reasoning goes like this: Suppose the true value of $\mu_Y$ is 21.5 (although we do not know this). Then $\overline{Y}$ has a normal distribution centered on 21.5, and the $t$-statistic testing the null hypothesis $\mu_Y = 21.5$ has a $N(0, 1)$ distribution. Thus, if $n$ is large, the probability of rejecting the null hypothesis $\mu_Y = 21.5$ at the 5% level is 5%. But because you tested all possible values of the population mean in constructing your set, in particular you tested the true value, $\mu_Y = 21.5$. In 95% of all samples, you will correctly accept 21.5; this means that in 95% of all samples, your list will contain the true value of $\mu_Y$. Thus the values on your list constitute a 95% confidence set for $\mu_Y$.

This method of constructing a confidence set is impractical, for it requires you to test all possible values of $\mu_Y$ as null hypotheses. Fortunately, there is a much easier approach. According to the formula for the $t$-statistic in Equation (3.13), a trial value of $\mu_{Y,0}$ is rejected at the 5% level if it is more than 1.96 standard errors away from $\overline{Y}$. Thus the set of values of $\mu_Y$ that are not rejected at the 5% level consists of those values within $\pm 1.96SE(\overline{Y})$ of $\overline{Y}$; that is, a 95% confidence interval for $\mu_Y$ is $\overline{Y} - 1.96SE(\overline{Y}) \leq \mu_Y \leq \overline{Y} + 1.96SE(\overline{Y})$. Key Concept 3.7 summarizes this approach.

As an example, consider the problem of constructing a 95% confidence interval for the mean hourly earnings of recent college graduates using a hypothetical random sample of 200 recent college graduates where $\overline{Y}$ = \$22.64 and $SE(\overline{Y})$ = 1.28. The 95% confidence interval for mean hourly earnings is $22.64 \pm 1.96 \times 1.28 = 22.64 \pm 2.51 = [\$20.13, \$25.15]$.

This discussion so far has focused on two-sided confidence intervals. One could instead construct a one-sided confidence interval as the set of values of $\mu_Y$ that cannot be rejected by a one-sided hypothesis test. Although one-sided confidence intervals have applications in some branches of statistics, they are uncommon in applied econometric analysis.

*Coverage probabilities.* The **coverage probability** of a confidence interval for the population mean is the probability, computed over all possible random samples, that it contains the true population mean.

## 3.4 Comparing Means from Different Populations

Do recent male and female college graduates earn the same amount on average? This question involves comparing the means of two different population distributions. This section summarizes how to test hypotheses and how to construct confidence intervals for the difference in the means from two different populations.

### Hypothesis Tests for the Difference Between Two Means

To illustrate a **test for the difference between two means**, let $\mu_w$ be the mean hourly earning in the population of women recently graduated from college and let $\mu_m$ be the population mean for recently graduated men. Consider the null hypothesis that mean earnings for these two populations differ by a certain amount, say $d_0$. Then the null hypothesis and the two-sided alternative hypothesis are

$$H_0\text{: } \mu_m - \mu_w = d_0 \text{ vs. } H_1\text{: } \mu_m - \mu_w \neq d_0. \tag{3.18}$$

The null hypothesis that men and women in these populations have the same mean earnings corresponds to $H_0$ in Equation (3.18) with $d_0 = 0$.

Because these population means are unknown, they must be estimated from samples of men and women. Suppose we have samples of $n_m$ men and $n_w$ women drawn at random from their populations. Let the sample average annual earnings be $\overline{Y}_m$ for men and $\overline{Y}_w$ for women. Then an estimator of $\mu_m - \mu_w$ is $\overline{Y}_m - \overline{Y}_w$.

To test the null hypothesis that $\mu_m - \mu_w = d_0$ using $\overline{Y}_m - \overline{Y}_w$, we need to know the distribution of $\overline{Y}_m - \overline{Y}_w$. Recall that $\overline{Y}_m$ is, according to the central limit theorem, approximately distributed $N(\mu_m, \sigma_m^2/n_m)$, where $\sigma_m^2$ is the population variance of earnings for men. Similarly, $\overline{Y}_w$ is approximately distributed $N(\mu_w, \sigma_w^2/n_w)$ where $\sigma_w^2$ is the population variance of earnings for women. Also, recall from Section 2.4 that a weighted average of two normal random variables is itself normally distributed. Because $\overline{Y}_m$ and $\overline{Y}_w$ are constructed from different randomly selected samples, they are independent random variables. Thus $\overline{Y}_m - \overline{Y}_w$ is distributed $N[\mu_m - \mu_w, (\sigma_m^2/n_m) + (\sigma_w^2/n_w)]$.

If $\sigma_m^2$ and $\sigma_w^2$ are known, then this approximate normal distribution can be used to compute $p$-values for the test of the null hypothesis that $\mu_m - \mu_w = d_0$. In practice, however, these population variances are typically unknown so they must be estimated. As before, they can be estimated using the sample variances, $s_m^2$ and $s_w^2$ where $s_m^2$ is defined as in Equation (3.7), except that the statistic is computed only for the men in the sample, and $s_w^2$ is defined similarly for the women. Thus the standard error of $\overline{Y}_m - \overline{Y}_w$ is

$$SE(\overline{Y}_m - \overline{Y}_w) = \sqrt{\frac{s_m^2}{n_m} + \frac{s_w^2}{n_w}}. \qquad (3.19)$$

For a simplified version of Equation (3.19) when $Y$ is a Bernoulli random variable, see Exercise 3.15.

The $t$-statistic for testing the null hypothesis is constructed analogously to the $t$-statistic for testing a hypothesis about a single population mean, by subtracting the null hypothesized value of $\mu_m - \mu_w$ from the estimator $\overline{Y}_m - \overline{Y}_w$ and dividing the result by the standard error of $\overline{Y}_m - \overline{Y}_w$:

$$t = \frac{(\overline{Y}_m - \overline{Y}_w) - d_0}{SE(\overline{Y}_m - \overline{Y}_w)} \qquad (\textit{t-statistic for comparing two means}). \qquad (3.20)$$

If both $n_m$ and $n_w$ are large, then this $t$-statistic has a standard normal distribution when the null hypothesis is true.

Because the $t$-statistic in Equation (3.20) has a standard normal distribution under the null hypothesis when $n_m$ and $n_w$ are large, the $p$-value of the two-sided test is computed exactly as it was in the case of a single population. That is, the *p*-value is computed using Equation (3.14).

To conduct a test with a prespecified significance level, simply calculate the *t*-statistic in Equation (3.20) and compare it to the appropriate critical value. For example, the null hypothesis is rejected at the 5% significance level if the absolute value of the *t*-statistic exceeds 1.96.

If the alternative is one-sided rather than two-sided (that is, if the alternative is that $\mu_m - \mu_w > d_0$), then the test is modified as outlined in Section 3.2. The *p*-value is computed using Equation (3.17), and a test with a 5% significance level rejects when $t > 1.64$.

## Confidence Intervals for the Difference Between Two Population Means

The method for constructing confidence intervals summarized in Section 3.3 extends to constructing a confidence interval for the difference between the means, $d = \mu_m - \mu_w$. Because the hypothesized value $d_0$ is rejected at the 5% level if $|t| > 1.96$, $d_0$ will be in the confidence set if $|t| \leq 1.96$. But $|t| \leq 1.96$ means that the estimated difference, $\overline{Y}_m - \overline{Y}_w$, is less than 1.96 standard errors away from $d_0$. Thus the 95% two-sided confidence interval for $d$ consists of those values of $d$ within $\pm$ 1.96 standard errors of $\overline{Y}_m - \overline{Y}_w$:

95% confidence interval for $d = \mu_m - \mu_w$ is

$$(\overline{Y}_m - \overline{Y}_w) \pm 1.96SE(\overline{Y}_m - \overline{Y}_w). \quad (3.21)$$

With these formulas in hand, the box "The Gender Gap of Earnings of College Graduates in the United States" contains an empirical investigation of gender differences in earnings of U.S. college graduates.

## 3.5 Differences-of-Means Estimation of Causal Effects Using Experimental Data

Recall from Section 1.2 that a randomized controlled experiment randomly selects subjects (individuals or, more generally, entities) from a population of interest, then randomly assigns them either to a treatment group, which receives the experimental treatment, or to a control group, which does not receive the treatment. The difference between the sample means of the treatment and control groups is an estimator of the causal effect of the treatment.

## The Causal Effect as a Difference of Conditional Expectations

The causal effect of a treatment is the expected effect on the outcome of interest of the treatment as measured in an ideal randomized controlled experiment. This effect can be expressed as the difference of two conditional expectations. Specifically, the **causal effect** on $Y$ of treatment level $x$ is the difference in the conditional expectations, $E(Y|X = x) - E(Y|X = 0)$, where $E(Y|X = x)$ is the expected value of $Y$ for the treatment group (which receives treatment level $X = x$) in an ideal randomized controlled experiment and $E(Y|X = 0)$ is the expected value of $Y$ for the control group (which receives treatment level $X = 0$). In the context of experiments, the causal effect is also called the **treatment effect**. If there are only two treatment levels (that is, if the treatment is binary), then we can let $X = 0$ denote the control group and $X = 1$ denote the treatment group. If the treatment is binary treatment, then the causal effect (that is, the treatment effect) is $E(Y|X = 1) - E(Y|X = 0)$ in an ideal randomized controlled experiment.

## Estimation of the Causal Effect Using Differences of Means

If the treatment in a randomized controlled experiment is binary, then the causal effect can be estimated by the difference in the sample average outcomes between the treatment and control groups. The hypothesis that the treatment is ineffective is equivalent to the hypothesis that the two means are the same, which can be tested using the $t$-statistic for comparing two means, given in Equation (3.20). A 95% confidence interval for the difference in the means of the two groups is a 95% confidence interval for the causal effect, so a 95% confidence interval for the causal effect can be constructed using Equation (3.21).

A well-designed, well-run experiment can provide a compelling estimate of a causal effect. For this reason, randomized controlled experiments are commonly conducted in some fields, such as medicine. The box "A Way to Increase Voter Turnout" provides an example of such a randomized experiment that yielded such casual effects. In economics, however, experiments tend to be expensive, difficult to administer, and, in some cases, ethically questionable, so they are used less often. For this reason, econometricians sometimes study "natural experiments," also called quasi-experiments, in which some event unrelated to the treatment or subject characteristics has the effect of assigning different treatments to different subjects *as if* they had been part of a randomized controlled experiment.

## The Gender Gap of Earnings of College Graduates in the United States

The box in Chapter 2 "The Distribution of Earnings in the United States in 2012" shows that, on average, male college graduates earn more than female college graduates. What are the recent trends in this "gender gap" in earnings? Social norms and laws governing gender discrimination in the workplace have changed substantially in the United States. Is the gender gap in earnings of college graduates stable, or has it diminished over time?

Table 3.1 gives estimates of hourly earnings for college-educated full-time workers ages 25–34 in the United States in 1992, 1996, 2000, 2004, 2008, and 2012, using data collected by the Current Population Survey. Earnings for 1992, 1996, 2000, 2004, and 2008 were adjusted for inflation by putting them in 2012 dollars using the Consumer Price Index (CPI).[1] In 2012, the average hourly earnings of the 2004 men surveyed was $25.30, and the standard deviation of earnings for men was $12.09. The average hourly earnings in 2012 of the 1951 women surveyed was $21.50, and the standard deviation of earnings was $9.99. Thus the estimate of the gender gap in earnings for 2012 is $3.80 (= $25.30 − $21.50), with a standard error of $0.35 (= $\sqrt{12.09^2/2004 + 9.99^2/1951}$). The 95% confidence interval for the gender gap in earnings in 2012 is $3.80 \pm 1.96 \times 0.35 = (\$3.11, \$4.49)$.

The results in Table 3.1 suggest four conclusions. First, the gender gap is large. An hourly gap of $3.80 might not sound like much, but over a year it adds up to $7600, assuming a 40-hour workweek and 50 paid weeks per year. Second, from 1992 to 2012, the estimated gender gap increased by $0.36 per hour in real terms, from $3.44 per hour to $3.80 per hour;

| | **Men** | | | **Women** | | | **Difference, Men vs. Women** | | |
|---|---|---|---|---|---|---|---|---|---|
| Year | $\bar{Y}_m$ | $s_m$ | $n_m$ | $\bar{Y}_w$ | $s_w$ | $n_w$ | $\bar{Y}_m - \bar{Y}_w$ | $SE(\bar{Y}_m - \bar{Y}_w)$ | 95% Confidence Interval for $d$ |
| 1992 | 24.83 | 10.85 | 1594 | 21.39 | 8.39 | 1368 | 3.44** | 0.35 | 2.75–4.14 |
| 1996 | 23.97 | 10.79 | 1380 | 20.26 | 8.48 | 1230 | 3.71** | 0.38 | 2.97–4.46 |
| 2000 | 26.55 | 12.38 | 1303 | 22.13 | 9.98 | 1181 | 4.42** | 0.45 | 3.54–5.30 |
| 2004 | 26.80 | 12.81 | 1894 | 22.43 | 9.99 | 1735 | 4.37** | 0.38 | 3.63–5.12 |
| 2008 | 26.63 | 12.57 | 1839 | 22.26 | 10.30 | 1871 | 4.36** | 0.38 | 3.62–5.10 |
| 2012 | 25.30 | 12.09 | 2004 | 21.50 | 9.99 | 1951 | 3.80** | 0.35 | 3.11–4.49 |

**TABLE 3.1** Trends in Hourly Earnings in the United States of Working College Graduates, Ages 25–34, 1992 to 2012, in 2012 Dollars

These estimates are computed using data on all full-time workers ages 25–34 surveyed in the Current Population Survey conducted in March of the next year (for example, the data for 2012 were collected in March 2013). The difference is significantly different from zero at the **1% significance level.

*(continued)*

however, this increase is not statistically significant at the 5% significance level (Exercise 3.17). Third, the gap is large if it is measured instead in percentage terms: According to the estimates in Table 3.1, in 2012 women earned 15% less per hour than men did ($3.80/$25.30), slightly more than the gap of 14% seen in 1992 ($3.44/$24.83). Fourth, the gender gap is smaller for young college graduates (the group analyzed in Table 3.1) than it is for all college graduates (analyzed in Table 2.4): As reported in Table 2.4, the mean earnings for all college-educated women working full-time in 2012 was $25.42, while for men this mean was $32.73, which corresponds to a gender gap of 22% $[ = (32.73 - 25.42)/32.73]$ among all full-time college-educated workers.

This empirical analysis documents that the "gender gap" in hourly earnings is large and has been fairly stable (or perhaps increased slightly) over the recent past. The analysis does not, however, tell us *why* this gap exists. Does it arise from gender discrimination in the labor market? Does it reflect differences in skills, experience, or education between men and women? Does it reflect differences in choice of jobs? Or is there some other cause? We return to these questions once we have in hand the tools of multiple regression analysis, the topic of Part II.

_____

[1]Because of inflation, a dollar in 1992 was worth more than a dollar in 2012, in the sense that a dollar in 1992 could buy more goods and services than a dollar in 2012 could. Thus earnings in 1992 cannot be directly compared to earnings in 2012 without adjusting for inflation. One way to make this adjustment is to use the CPI, a measure of the price of a "market basket" of consumer goods and services constructed by the Bureau of Labor Statistics. Over the 20 years from 1992 to 2012, the price of the CPI market basket rose by 63.6%; in other words, the CPI basket of goods and services that cost $100 in 1992 cost $163.64 in 2012. To make earnings in 1992 and 2012 comparable in Table 3.1, 1992 earnings are inflated by the amount of overall CPI price inflation, that is, by multiplying 1992 earnings by 1.636 to put them into "2012 dollars."

## 3.6    Using the *t*-Statistic When the Sample Size Is Small

In Sections 3.2 through 3.5, the *t*-statistic is used in conjunction with critical values from the standard normal distribution for hypothesis testing and for the construction of confidence intervals. The use of the standard normal distribution is justified by the central limit theorem, which applies when the sample size is large. When the sample size is small, the standard normal distribution can provide a poor approximation to the distribution of the *t*-statistic. If, however, the population distribution is itself normally distributed, then the exact distribution (that is, the finite-sample distribution; see Section 2.6) of the *t*-statistic testing the mean of a single population is the Student *t* distribution with $n - 1$ degrees of freedom, and critical values can be taken from the Student *t* distribution.

### The *t*-Statistic and the Student *t* Distribution

**The t-*statistic testing the mean.***   Consider the *t*-statistic used to test the hypothesis that the mean of $Y$ is $\mu_{Y,0}$, using data $Y_1, \ldots, Y_n$. The formula for this statistic is given by Equation (3.10), where the standard error of $\overline{Y}$ is given by Equation (3.8). Substitution of the latter expression into the former yields the formula for the $t$-statistic:

$$t = \frac{\overline{Y} - \mu_{Y,0}}{\sqrt{s_Y^2/n}}, \tag{3.22}$$

where $s_Y^2$ is given in Equation (3.7).

As discussed in Section 3.2, under general conditions the $t$-statistic has a standard normal distribution if the sample size is large and the null hypothesis is true [see Equation (3.12)]. Although the standard normal approximation to the $t$-statistic is reliable for a wide range of distributions of $Y$ if $n$ is large, it can be unreliable if $n$ is small. The exact distribution of the $t$-statistic depends on the distribution of $Y$, and it can be very complicated. There is, however, one special case in which the exact distribution of the $t$-statistic is relatively simple: If $Y$ is normally distributed, then the $t$-statistic in Equation (3.22) has a Student $t$ distribution with $n - 1$ degrees of freedom. (The mathematics behind this result is provided in Sections 17.4 and 18.4.)

If the population distribution is normally distributed, then critical values from the Student $t$ distribution can be used to perform hypothesis tests and to construct confidence intervals. As an example, consider a hypothetical problem in which $t^{act} = 2.15$ and $n = 20$ so that the degrees of freedom is $n - 1 = 19$. From Appendix Table 2, the 5% two-sided critical value for the $t_{19}$ distribution is 2.09. Because the $t$-statistic is larger in absolute value than the critical value $(2.15 > 2.09)$, the null hypothesis would be rejected at the 5% significance level against the two-sided alternative. The 95% confidence interval for $\mu_Y$, constructed using the $t_{19}$ distribution, would be $\overline{Y} \pm 2.09\,SE(\overline{Y})$. This confidence interval is somewhat wider than the confidence interval constructed using the standard normal critical value of 1.96.

*The t-statistic testing differences of means.*  The $t$-statistic testing the difference of two means, given in Equation (3.20), does not have a Student $t$ distribution, even if the population distribution of $Y$ is normal. (The Student $t$ distribution does not apply here because the variance estimator used to compute the standard error in Equation (3.19) does not produce a denominator in the $t$-statistic with a chi-squared distribution.)

A modified version of the differences-of-means $t$-statistic, based on a different standard error formula—the "pooled" standard error formula—has an exact Student $t$ distribution when $Y$ is normally distributed; however, the pooled standard error formula applies only in the special case that the two groups have the same variance or that each group has the same number of observations (Exercise 3.21). Adopt the notation of Equation (3.19) so that the two groups are denoted as $m$ and $w$. The pooled variance estimator is

$$s^2_{pooled} = \frac{1}{n_m + n_w - 2}\left[\underbrace{\sum_{i=1}^{n_m} (Y_i - \overline{Y}_m)^2}_{\text{group }m} + \underbrace{\sum_{i=1}^{n_w} (Y_i - \overline{Y}_m)^2}_{\text{group }w}\right], \quad (3.23)$$

where the first summation is for the observations in group $m$ and the second summation is for the observations in group $w$. The pooled standard error of the difference in means is $SE_{pooled}(\overline{Y}_m - \overline{Y}_w) = s_{pooled} \times \sqrt{1/n_m + 1/n_w}$, and the pooled $t$-statistic is computed using Equation (3.20), where the standard error is the pooled standard error, $SE_{pooled}(\overline{Y}_m - \overline{Y}_w)$.

If the population distribution of $Y$ in group $m$ is $N(\mu_m, \sigma^2_m)$, if the population distribution of $Y$ in group $w$ is $N(\mu_w, \sigma^2_w)$, *and* if the two group variances are the same (that is, $\sigma^2_m = \sigma^2_w$), then under the null hypothesis the $t$-statistic computed using the pooled standard error has a Student $t$ distribution with $n_m + n_w - 2$ degrees of freedom.

The drawback of using the pooled variance estimator $s^2_{pooled}$ is that it applies only if the two population variances are the same (assuming $n_m \neq n_w$). If the population variances are different, the pooled variance estimator is biased and inconsistent. If the population variances are different but the pooled variance formula is used, the null distribution of the pooled $t$-statistic is not a Student $t$ distribution, even if the data are normally distributed; in fact, it does not even have a standard normal distribution in large samples. Therefore, the pooled standard error and the pooled $t$-statistic should not be used unless you have a good reason to believe that the population variances are the same.

## Use of the Student *t* Distribution in Practice

For the problem of testing the mean of $Y$, the Student $t$ distribution is applicable if the underlying population distribution of $Y$ is normal. For economic variables, however, normal distributions are the exception (for example, see the boxes in Chapter 2 "The Distribution of Earnings in the United States in 2012" and "A Bad Day on Wall Street"). Even if the underlying data are not normally distributed, the normal approximation to the distribution of the $t$-statistic is valid if the sample size is large. Therefore, inferences—hypothesis tests and confidence intervals—about the mean of a distribution should be based on the large-sample normal approximation.

## A Way to Increase Voter Turnout

Apathy among citizens toward political participation, especially in voting, has been noted in the United Kingdom and other democratic countries. This kind of behavior is generally seen in economies where people have greater mobility, maintain an intensive work culture, and work for private corporate entities. Apart from these there could be other dominant factors like politicians failing to keep their promises, inappropriately using public funds that have had a negative impact on the citizens' willingness to participate in elections.

A study was conducted in a Manchester constituency in the United Kingdom, in 2005, during the campaign period before the general election. The constituency's voter turnout rate in the 2001 general election had been 48.6%, while the national average had been 59.4%. Thus, voter participation in this constituency was far below the national average. For the experiment, three groups (two treatment groups and one control group) were randomly selected out of the registered voters from whom landline numbers could be obtained. One of the treatment groups was exposed to strong canvassing in the form of telephone calls, and the other treatment group was exposed to strong canvassing in the form of door-to-door visits. No contacts were made with the control group. The callers and the door-to-door canvassers were given instructions to ask respondents three questions, namely, whether the respondents thought voting is important, whether the respondents intended to vote, and whether they would vote by post. The conversations were informal and the main objective of this exercise was to persuade citizens to vote, by focusing on the importance of voting. The callers and canvassers were also advised to respond to any concerns of the voters regarding the voting process.

The researchers got interesting results from the elections. The participation rate was 55.1% in the group which was exposed to canvassing. The participation rate for the treatment group which was treated with telephone calls was 55%. Both these rates had a difference with the control group, which was not exposed to any experiment. Further calculations using suitable methodologies gave estimates of the effects of canvassing and telephone calls. 6.7% and 7.3% were the estimates of the two. The overall experiment was a success as the two interventions done on the two treatments groups by a non-partisan source had impacts that were statistically significant.

This exercise showed that citizens can be nudged to participate in elections by creating awareness through personal contacts. In yet another democracy, India, the 2014 general election saw a record voter turnout. A top Election Commission official has said that the Election Commission's efforts to increase voters' awareness and their registration has helped the process.

*Sources: 1. http://www.bloomsburycollections.com/book/nudge
-nudge-think-think-experimenting-with-ways-to-change-civic-
behaviour/*
*2. Lok Sabha polls 2014: Country records highest voter turnout since
independence, The Economic Times*

When comparing two means, any economic reason for two groups having different means typically implies that the two groups also could have different variances. Accordingly, the pooled standard error formula is inappropriate, and the correct standard error formula, which allows for different group variances, is as given in Equation (3.19). Even if the population distributions are normal, the $t$-statistic computed using the standard error formula in Equation (3.19) does not have a Student $t$ distribution. In practice, therefore, inferences about differences in means should be based on Equation (3.19), used in conjunction with the large-sample standard normal approximation.

Even though the Student $t$ distribution is rarely applicable in economics, some software uses the Student $t$ distribution to compute $p$-values and confidence intervals. In practice, this does not pose a problem because the difference between the Student $t$ distribution and the standard normal distribution is negligible if the sample size is large. For $n > 15$, the difference in the $p$-values computed using the Student $t$ and standard normal distributions never exceeds 0.01; for $n > 80$, the difference never exceeds 0.002. In most modern applications, and in all applications in this textbook, the sample sizes are in the hundreds or thousands, large enough for the difference between the Student $t$ distribution and the standard normal distribution to be negligible.

# 3.7 Scatterplots, the Sample Covariance, and the Sample Correlation

What is the relationship between age and earnings? This question, like many others, relates one variable, $X$ (age), to another, $Y$ (earnings). This section reviews three ways to summarize the relationship between variables: the scatterplot, the sample covariance, and the sample correlation coefficient.

## Scatterplots

A **scatterplot** is a plot of $n$ observations on $X_i$ and $Y_i$, in which each observation is represented by the point $(X_i, Y_i)$. For example, Figure 3.2 is a scatterplot of age ($X$) and hourly earnings ($Y$) for a sample of 200 managers in the information industry from the March 2009 CPS. Each dot in Figure 3.2 corresponds to an $(X, Y)$ pair for one of the observations. For example, one of the workers in this sample is 40 years old and earns $35.78 per hour; this worker's age and earnings are indicated by the highlighted dot in Figure 3.2. The scatterplot shows a positive

---

**FIGURE 3.2**    **Scatterplot of Average Hourly Earnings vs. Age**

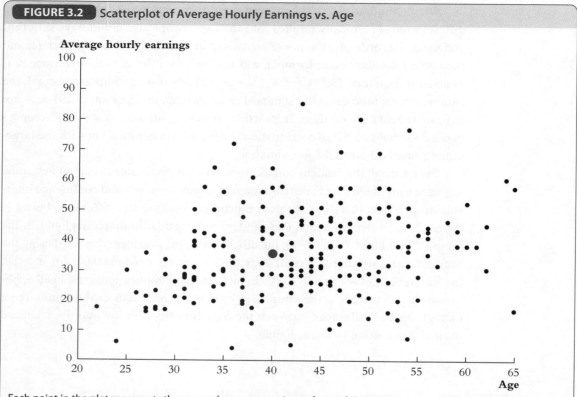

Each point in the plot represents the age and average earnings of one of the 200 workers in the sample. The high-lighted dot corresponds to a 40-year-old worker who earns $35.78 per hour. The data are for computer and information systems managers from the March 2009 CPS.

---

relationship between age and earnings in this sample: Older workers tend to earn more than younger workers. This relationship is not exact, however, and earnings could not be predicted perfectly using only a person's age.

## Sample Covariance and Correlation

The covariance and correlation were introduced in Section 2.3 as two properties of the joint probability distribution of the random variables $X$ and $Y$. Because the population distribution is unknown, in practice we do not know the population covariance or correlation. The population covariance and correlation can, however, be estimated by taking a random sample of $n$ members of the population and collecting the data $(X_i, Y_i), i = 1, \ldots, n$.

The sample covariance and correlation are estimators of the population covariance and correlation. Like the estimators discussed previously in this chapter, they are computed by replacing a population mean (the expectation) with a sample mean. The **sample covariance**, denoted $s_{XY}$, is

$$s_{XY} = \frac{1}{n-1} \sum_{i=1}^{n} (X_i - \overline{X})(Y_i - \overline{Y}). \tag{3.24}$$

Like the sample variance, the average in Equation (3.24) is computed by dividing by $n-1$ instead of $n$; here, too, this difference stems from using $\overline{X}$ and $\overline{Y}$ to estimate the respective population means. When $n$ is large, it makes little difference whether division is by $n$ or $n-1$.

The **sample correlation coefficient**, or **sample correlation**, is denoted $r_{XY}$ and is the ratio of the sample covariance to the sample standard deviations:

$$r_{XY} = \frac{s_{XY}}{s_X s_Y}. \tag{3.25}$$

The sample correlation measures the strength of the linear association between $X$ and $Y$ in a sample of $n$ observations. Like the population correlation, the sample correlation is unitless and lies between –1 and 1: $|r_{XY}| \leq 1$.

The sample correlation equals 1 if $X_i = Y_i$ for all $i$ and equals –1 if $X_i = -Y_i$ for all $i$. More generally, the correlation is ±1 if the scatterplot is a straight line. If the line slopes upward, then there is a positive relationship between $X$ and $Y$ and the correlation is 1. If the line slopes down, then there is a negative relationship and the correlation is –1. The closer the scatterplot is to a straight line, the closer is the correlation to ±1. A high correlation coefficient does not necessarily mean that the line has a steep slope; rather, it means that the points in the scatterplot fall very close to a straight line.

*Consistency of the sample covariance and correlation.*  Like the sample variance, the sample covariance is consistent. That is,

$$s_{XY} \xrightarrow{p} \sigma_{XY}. \tag{3.26}$$

In other words, in large samples the sample covariance is close to the population covariance with high probability.

The proof of the result in Equation (3.26) under the assumption that $(X_i, Y_i)$ are i.i.d. and that $X_i$ and $Y_i$ have finite fourth moments is similar to the proof in Appendix 3.3 that the sample covariance is consistent and is left as an exercise (Exercise 3.20).

---

**FIGURE 3.3** Scatterplots for Four Hypothetical Data Sets

The scatterplots in Figures 3.3a and 3.3b show strong linear relationships between X and Y. In Figure 3.3c, X is independent of Y and the two variables are uncorrelated. In Figure 3.3d, the two variables also are uncorrelated even though they are related nonlinearly.

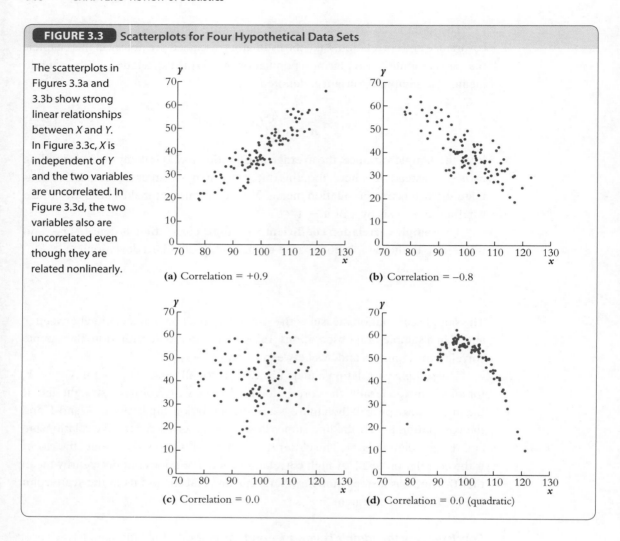

**(a)** Correlation = +0.9

**(b)** Correlation = −0.8

**(c)** Correlation = 0.0

**(d)** Correlation = 0.0 (quadratic)

---

Because the sample variance and sample covariance are consistent, the sample correlation coefficient is consistent, that is, $r_{XY} \xrightarrow{p} \text{corr}(X_i, Y_i)$.

*Example.* As an example, consider the data on age and earnings in Figure 3.2. For these 200 workers, the sample standard deviation of age is $s_A = 9.07$ years and the sample standard deviation of earnings is $s_E = \$14.37$ per hour. The sample covariance between age and earnings is $s_{AE} = 33.16$ (the units are years × dollars per hour, not readily interpretable). Thus the sample correlation coefficient is $r_{AE} = 33.16/(9.07 \times 14.37) = 0.25$ or 25%. The correlation of 0.25 means that there is a positive relationship between age and earnings, but as is evident in the scatterplot, this relationship is far from perfect.

To verify that the correlation does not depend on the units of measurement, suppose that earnings had been reported in cents, in which case the sample standard deviations of earnings is 1437¢ per hour and the covariance between age and earnings is 3316 (units are years × cents per hour); then the correlation is $3316/(9.07 \times 1437) = 0.25$ or 25%.

Figure 3.3 gives additional examples of scatterplots and correlation. Figure 3.3a shows a strong positive linear relationship between these variables, and the sample correlation is 0.9.

Figure 3.3b shows a strong negative relationship with a sample correlation of −0.8. Figure 3.3c shows a scatterplot with no evident relationship, and the sample correlation is zero. Figure 3.3d shows a clear relationship: As $X$ increases, $Y$ initially increases, but then decreases. Despite this discernable relationship between $X$ and $Y$, the sample correlation is zero; the reason is that, for these data, small values of $Y$ are associated with *both* large and small values of $X$.

This final example emphasizes an important point: The correlation coefficient is a measure of *linear* association. There is a relationship in Figure 3.3d, but it is not linear.

## Summary

1. The sample average, $\overline{Y}$, is an estimator of the population mean, $\mu_Y$. When $Y_1, \ldots, Y_n$ are i.i.d.,
   a. the sampling distribution of $\overline{Y}$ has mean $\mu_Y$ and variance $\sigma_{\overline{Y}}^2 = \sigma_Y^2/n$;
   b. $\overline{Y}$ is unbiased;
   c. by the law of large numbers, $\overline{Y}$ is consistent; and
   d. by the central limit theorem, $\overline{Y}$ has an approximately normal sampling distribution when the sample size is large.
2. The $t$-statistic is used to test the null hypothesis that the population mean takes on a particular value. If $n$ is large, the $t$-statistic has a standard normal sampling distribution when the null hypothesis is true.
3. The $t$-statistic can be used to calculate the $p$-value associated with the null hypothesis. A small $p$-value is evidence that the null hypothesis is false.
4. A 95% confidence interval for $\mu_Y$ is an interval constructed so that it contains the true value of $\mu_Y$ in 95% of all possible samples.
5. Hypothesis tests and confidence intervals for the difference in the means of two populations are conceptually similar to tests and intervals for the mean of a single population.

6.  The sample correlation coefficient is an estimator of the population correlation coefficient and measures the linear relationship between two variables—that is, how well their scatterplot is approximated by a straight line.

## Key Terms

estimator (113)

estimate (113)

bias, consistency, and
    efficiency (114)

BLUE (Best Linear Unbiased
    Estimator) (115)

least squares estimator (116)

hypothesis tests (117)

null hypothesis (117)

alternative hypothesis (117)

two-sided alternative
    hypothesis (117)

*p*-value (significance
    probability) (118)

sample variance (120)

sample standard deviation (120)

degrees of freedom (121)

standard error of $\overline{Y}$ (121)

*t*-statistic (*t*-ratio) (122)

test statistic (122)

type I error (124)

type II error (124)

significance level (124)

critical value (124)

rejection region (124)

acceptance region (124)

size of a test (124)

power of a test (124)

one-sided alternative
    hypothesis (126)

confidence set (126)

confidence level (126)

confidence interval (126)

coverage probability (128)

test for the difference between two
    means (128)

causal effect (131)

treatment effect (131)

scatterplot (137)

sample covariance (139)

sample correlation coefficient
    (sample correlation) (139)

---

**MyEconLab Can Help You Get a Better Grade**

MyEconLab    If your exam were tomorrow, would you be ready? For each chapter, **MyEconLab** Practice Tests and Study Plan help you prepare for your exams. You can also find similar Exercises and Review the Concepts Questions now in **MyEconLab**. To see how it works, turn to the **MyEconLab** spread on pages 2 and 3 of this book and then go to **www.myeconlab.com**.

For additional Empirical Exercises and Data Sets, log on to the Companion Website at **www.pearsonglobaleditions.com/Stock_Watson**.

## Review the Concepts

**3.1**  What is the difference between an unbiased estimator and a consistent estimator?

**3.2**  What is meant by the efficiency of an estimator? Which estimator is known as BLUE?

**3.3**  A population distribution has a mean of 15 and a variance of 10. Determine the mean and variance of $\overline{Y}$ from an i.i.d. sample from this population for (a) $n = 50$; (b) $n = 500$; and (c) $n = 5000$. Relate your answers to the law of large numbers.

**3.4**  Differentiate between standard error and standard deviation. How is the standard error of a sample mean calculated?

**3.5**  What is the difference between a null hypothesis and an alternative hypothesis? Among size, significance level, and power? Between a one-sided alternative hypothesis and a two-sided alternative hypothesis?

**3.6**  Why does a confidence interval contain more information than the result of a single hypothesis test?

**3.7**  What is a scatterplot? What statistical features of a dataset can be represented using a scatterplot diagram?

**3.8**  Sketch a hypothetical scatterplot for a sample of size 10 for two random variables with a population correlation of (a) 1.0; (b) –1.0; (c) 0.9; (d) –0.5; (e) 0.0.

## Exercises

**3.1**  In a population, $\mu_Y = 75$ and $\sigma_Y^2 = 45$. Use the central limit theorem to answer the following questions:

**a.**  In a random sample of size $n = 50$, find $\Pr(\overline{Y} < 73)$.

**b.**  In a random sample of size $n = 90$, find $\Pr(76 < \overline{Y} < 78)$.

**c.**  In a random sample of size $n = 120$, find $\Pr(\overline{Y} > 68)$.

**3.2**  Let $Y$ be a Bernoulli random variable with success probability $\Pr(Y = 1) = p$, and let $Y_1, \ldots, Y_n$ be i.i.d. draws from this distribution. Let $\hat{p}$ be the fraction of successes (1s) in this sample.

  **a.** Show that $\hat{p} = \overline{Y}$.

  **b.** Show that $\hat{p}$ is an unbiased estimator of $p$.

  **c.** Show that $\text{var}(\hat{p}) = p(1 - p)/n$.

**3.3**  In a survey of 400 likely voters, 215 responded that they would vote for the incumbent, and 185 responded that they would vote for the challenger. Let $p$ denote the fraction of all likely voters who preferred the incumbent at the time of the survey, and let $\hat{p}$ be the fraction of survey respondents who preferred the incumbent.

  **a.** Use the survey results to estimate $p$.

  **b.** Use the estimator of the variance of $\hat{p}$, $\hat{p}(1 - \hat{p})/n$, to calculate the standard error of your estimator.

  **c.** What is the $p$-value for the test $H_0: p = 0.5$ vs. $H_1: p \neq 0.5$?

  **d.** What is the $p$-value for the test $H_0: p = 0.5$ vs. $H_1: p > 0.5$?

  **e.** Why do the results from (c) and (d) differ?

  **f.** Did the survey contain statistically significant evidence that the incumbent was ahead of the challenger at the time of the survey? Explain.

**3.4**  Using the data in Exercise 3.3:

  **a.** Construct a 95% confidence interval for $p$.

  **b.** Construct a 99% confidence interval for $p$.

  **c.** Why is the interval in (b) wider than the interval in (a)?

  **a.** Without doing any additional calculations, test the hypothesis $H_0: p = 0.50$ vs. $H_1: p \neq 0.50$ at the 5% significance level.

**3.5**  A survey is conducted using 1000 registered voters, who are asked to choose between candidate A and candidate B. Let $p$ denote the fraction of voters in the population who prefer candidate A, and let $\hat{p}$ denote the fraction of voters who prefer Candidate B.

  **a.** You are interested in the competing hypotheses $H_0: p = 0.4$ vs. $H_1: p \neq 0.4$. Suppose that you decide to reject $H_0$ if $|\hat{p} - 0.4| > 0.01$. Then

  i. What is the size of this test?

  ii. Compute the power of this test if $p = 0.45$.

**b.** In the survey, $\hat{p} = 0.44$.

    i. Test $H_0: p = 0.4$ vs. $H_1: p \neq 0.4$ using a 10% significance level.

    ii. Test $H_0: p = 0.4$ vs. $H_1: p < 0.4$ using a 10% significance level.

    iii. Construct a 90% confidence interval for $p$.

    iv. Construct a 99% confidence interval for $p$.

    v. Construct a 60% confidence interval for $p$.

**c.** Suppose the survey is carried out 30 times, using independently selected voters in each survey. For each of these 30 surveys, a 90% confidence interval for $p$ is constructed.

    i. What is the probability that the true value of $p$ is contained in all 30 of these confidence intervals?

    ii. How many of these confidence intervals do you expect to contain the true value of $p$?

**d.** In survey jargon, the "margin of error" is $1.96 \times SE(\hat{p})$; that means it is half the length of 95% confidence interval. Suppose you want to design a survey that has a margin of error of at most 0.5%, i.e., $Pr(|\hat{p} - p| > 0.005) \leq 0.05$. How large should $n$ be if the survey uses simple random sampling?

**3.6** Let $Y_1, \ldots, Y_n$ be i.i.d. draws from a distribution with mean $\mu$. A test of $H_0: \mu = 10$ vs. $H_1: \mu \neq 10$ using the usual $t$-statistic yields a $p$-value of 0.07.

**a.** Does the 90% confidence interval contain $\mu = 10$? Explain.

**b.** Can you determine if $\mu = 8$ is contained in the 95% confidence interval? Briefly explain your answers.

**3.7** In a given population, 50% of the likely voters are women. A survey using a simple random sample of 1000 landline telephone numbers finds the percentage of female voters to be 55%. Is there evidence that this survey is biased? Explain.

**3.8** A new version of the SAT is given to 1500 randomly selected high school seniors. The sample mean test score is 1230, and the sample standard deviation is 145. Construct a 95% confidence interval for the population mean test score for high school seniors.

**3.9** Suppose a light bulb manufacturing plant produces bulbs with a mean life of 1000 hours, and a standard deviation of 100 hours. An inventor claims to have developed an improved process that produces bulbs with a longer mean life and the same standard deviation. The plant manager randomly selects 50 bulbs produced by the process. She says that she will believe the inventor's claim if the sample mean life of the bulbs is greater than 1100 hours; otherwise, she will conclude that the new process is no better than the old one. Let $\mu$ denote the mean of the new process. Consider the null and alternative hypotheses $H_0: \mu = 1000$ vs. $H_1: \mu > 1000$.

a. What is the size of the plant manager's testing procedure?

b. Suppose the new process is, in fact, better and has a mean bulb life of 1150 hours. What is the power of the plant manager's testing procedure?

c. What testing procedure should the plant manager use if she wants the size of her test to be 1%?

**3.10** Suppose a new standardized test is given to 150 randomly selected third-grade students in New Jersey. The sample average score $Y$ on the test is 42 points, and the sample standard deviation, $s_Y$, is 6 points.

a. The authors plan to administer the test to all third-grade students in New Jersey. Construct a 99% confidence interval for the mean score of all New Jersey third graders.

b. Suppose the same test is given to 300 randomly selected third graders from Iowa, producing a sample average of 48 points and sample standard deviation of 10 points. Construct a 95% confidence interval for the difference in mean scores between Iowa and New Jersey.

c. Can you conclude with a high degree of confidence that the population means for Iowa and New Jersey students are different? (What is the standard error of the difference in the two sample means? What is the $p$-value of the test of no difference in means versus some difference?)

**3.11** Consider the estimator $\tilde{Y}$, defined in Equation (3.1). Show that (a) $E(\tilde{Y}) = \mu_Y$ and (b) $\text{var}(\tilde{Y}) = 1.25\sigma_Y^2/n$.

**3.12** To investigate possible gender discrimination in a firm, a sample of 120 men and 150 women with similar job descriptions are selected at random. A summary of the resulting monthly salaries follows:

|  | **Average Salary** | **Standard Deviation** | **$n$** |
|---|---|---|---|
| Men | $8,200 | $450 | 120 |
| Women | $7,900 | $520 | 150 |

a. What do the data suggest about wage differences in the firm? Do they represent statistically significant evidence that average wages of men and women are different? (To answer this question, first state the null and alternative hypotheses; second, compute the relevant $t$-statistic; third, compute the $p$-value associated with the $t$-statistic; and finally, use the $p$-value to answer the question.)

b. Does the data suggest that the firm is guilty of gender discrimination in its compensation policies? Explain.

**3.13** Data on fifth-grade test scores (reading and mathematics) for 400 school districts in California yield $\overline{Y} = 712.1$ and standard deviation $s_Y = 23.2$.

a. Construct a 90% confidence interval for the mean test score in the population.

b. When the districts were divided into districts with small classes ($< 20$ students per teacher) and large classes ($\geq 20$ students per teacher), the following results were found:

| Class Size | Average Score | Standard Deviation | n |
|---|---|---|---|
| Small | 721.8 | 24.4 | 150 |
| Large | 710.9 | 20.6 | 250 |

Is there statistically significant evidence that the districts with smaller classes have higher average test scores? Explain.

**3.14** Values of height in inches ($X$) and weight in pounds ($Y$) are recorded from a sample of 200 male college students. The resulting summary statistics are $\overline{X} = 71.2$ in, $\overline{Y} = 164$ lb., $s_X = 1.9$ in, $s_Y = 16.4$ lb., $s_{XY} = 22.54$ in. $\times$ lb., and $r_{XY} = 0.8$. Convert these statistics to the metric system (meters and kilograms).

**3.15** Let $Y_a$ and $Y_b$ denote Bernoulli random variables from two different populations, denoted $a$ and $b$. Suppose that $E(Y_a) = p_a$ and $E(Y_b) = p_b$. A random sample of size $n_a$ is chosen from population $a$, with sample average denoted $\hat{p}_a$, and a random sample of size $n_b$ is chosen from population $b$, with sample average denoted $\hat{p}_b$. Suppose the sample from population $a$ is independent of the sample from population $b$.

a. Show that $E(\hat{p}_a) = p_a$ and var$(\hat{p}_a) = p_a(1 - p_a)/n_a$. Show that $E(\hat{p}_b) = p_b$ and var$(\hat{p}_b) = p_b(1 - p_b)/n_b$.

**b.** Show that $\text{var}(\hat{p}_a - \hat{p}_b) = \frac{p_a(1 - p_a)}{n_a} + \frac{p_b(1 - p_b)}{n_b}$. (*Hint:* Remember that the samples are independent.)

**c.** Suppose that $n_a$ and $n_b$ are large. Show that a 95% confidence interval for $p_a - p_b$ is given by $(\hat{p}_a - \hat{p}_b) \pm 1.96 \sqrt{\frac{\hat{p}_a(1 - \hat{p}_a)}{n_a} + \frac{\hat{p}_b(1 - \hat{p}_b)}{n_b}}$. How would you construct a 90% confidence interval for $p_a - p_b$?

**3.16** Grades on a standardized test are known to have a mean of 500 for students in the United States. The test is administered to 600 randomly selected students in Florida; in this sample, the mean is 508, and the standard deviation ($s$) is 75.

**a.** Construct a 95% confidence interval for the average test score for students in Florida.

**b.** Is there statistically significant evidence that students in Florida perform differently from other students in the United States?

**c.** Another 500 students are selected at random from Florida. They are given a 3-hour preparation course before the test is administered. Their average test score is 514, with a standard deviation of 65.

   i.  Construct a 95% confidence interval for the change in average test score associated with the prep course.

   ii. Is there statistically significant evidence that the prep course helped?

**d.** The original 600 students are given the prep course and are then asked to take the test a second time. The average change in their test scores is 7 points, and the standard deviation of the change is 40 points.

   i.  Construct a 95% confidence interval for the change in average test scores.

   ii. Is there statistically significant evidence that students will perform better on their second attempt, after taking the prep course?

   iii. Students may have performed better in their second attempt because of the prep course or because they gained test-taking experience in their first attempt. Describe an experiment that would quantify these two effects.

**3.17** Read the box "The Gender Gap of Earnings of College Graduates in the United States" in Section 3.5.

    **a.** Construct a 95% confidence interval for the change in men's average hourly earnings between 1992 and 2012.

    **b.** Construct a 95% confidence interval for the change in women's average hourly earnings between 1992 and 2012.

    **c.** Construct a 95% confidence interval for the change in the gender gap in average hourly earnings between 1992 and 2012. (*Hint:* $\overline{Y}_{m,1992} - \overline{Y}_{w,1992}$ is independent of $\overline{Y}_{m,2012} - \overline{Y}_{w,2012}$.)

**3.18** This exercise shows that the sample variance is an unbiased estimator of the population variance when $Y_1, \ldots, Y_n$ are i.i.d. with mean $\mu_Y$ and variance $\sigma_Y^2$.

    **a.** Use Equation (2.31) to show that
$$E[(Y_i - \overline{Y})^2] = \mathrm{var}(Y_i) - 2\mathrm{cov}(Y_i, \overline{Y}) + \mathrm{var}(\overline{Y}).$$

    **b.** Use Equation (2.33) to show that $\mathrm{cov}(\overline{Y}, Y_i) = \sigma_Y^2/n$.

    **c.** Use the results in (a) and (b) to show that $E(s_Y^2) = \sigma_Y^2$.

**3.19** **a.** $\overline{Y}$ is an unbiased estimator of $\mu_Y$. Is $\overline{Y}^2$ an unbiased estimator of $\mu_Y^2$?

    **b.** $\overline{Y}$ is a consistent estimator of $\mu_Y$. Is $\overline{Y}^2$ a consistent estimator of $\mu_Y^2$?

**3.20** Suppose that $(X_i, Y_i)$ are i.i.d. with finite fourth moments. Prove that the sample covariance is a consistent estimator of the population covariance, that is, $s_{XY} \xrightarrow{p} \sigma_{XY}$, where $s_{XY}$ is defined in Equation (3.24). (*Hint:* Use the strategy of Appendix 3.3.)

**3.21** Show that the pooled standard error $[SE_{pooled}(\overline{Y}_m - \overline{Y}_w)]$ given following Equation (3.23) equals the usual standard error for the difference in means in Equation (3.19) when the two group sizes are the same $(n_m = n_w)$.

## Empirical Exercises

**E3.1** On the text website, **www.pearsonglobaleditions.com/Stock_Watson**, you will find the data file **CPS92_12**, which contains an extended version of the data set used in Table 3.1 of the text for the years 1992 and 2012. It contains data on full-time workers, ages 25–34, with a high school diploma or B.A./B.S. as their highest degree. A detailed description is given in

**CPS92_12_Description**, available on the website. Use these data to answer the following questions.

**a.**  i.  Compute the sample mean for average hourly earnings (*AHE*) in 1992 and 2012.

    ii.  Compute the sample standard deviation for *AHE* in 1992 and 2012.

    iii.  Construct a 95% confidence interval for the population means of *AHE* in 1992 and 2012.

    iv.  Construct a 95% confidence interval for the change in the population mean of *AHE* between 1992 and 2012.

**b.**  In 2012, the value of the Consumer Price Index (CPI) was 229.6. In 1992, the value of the CPI was 140.3. Repeat (a) but use *AHE* measured in real 2012 dollars ($2012); that is, adjust the 1992 data for the price inflation that occurred between 1992 and 2012.

**c.**  If you were interested in the change in workers' purchasing power from 1992 to 2012, would you use the results from (a) or (b)? Explain.

**d.**  Using the data for 2012:

    i.  Construct a 95% confidence interval for the mean of *AHE* for high school graduates.

    ii.  Construct a 95% confidence interval for the mean of *AHE* for workers with a college degree.

    iii.  Construct a 95% confidence interval for the difference between the two means.

**e.**  Repeat (d) using the 1992 data expressed in $2012.

**f.**  Using appropriate estimates, confidence intervals, and test statistics, answer the following questions:

    i.  Did real (inflation-adjusted) wages of high school graduates increase from 1992 to 2012?

    ii.  Did real wages of college graduates increase?

    iii.  Did the gap between earnings of college and high school graduates increase? Explain.

**g.**  Table 3.1 presents information on the gender gap for college graduates. Prepare a similar table for high school graduates, using the 1992 and 2012 data. Are there any notable differences between the results for high school and college graduates?

**E3.2**    A consumer is given the chance to buy a baseball card for $1, but he declines the trade. If the consumer is now given the baseball card, will he be willing to sell it for $1? Standard consumer theory suggests yes, but behavioral economists have found that "ownership" tends to increase the value of goods to consumers. That is, the consumer may hold out for some amount more than $1 (for example, $1.20) when selling the card, even though he was willing to pay only some amount less than $1 (for example, $0.88) when buying it. Behavioral economists call this phenomenon the "endowment effect." John List investigated the endowment effect in a randomized experiment involving sports memorabilia traders at a sports-card show. Traders were randomly given one of two sports collectibles, say good A or good B, that had approximately equal market value.[1] Those receiving good A were then given the option of trading good A for good B with the experimenter; those receiving good B were given the option of trading good B for good A with the experimenter. Data from the experiment and a detailed description can be found on the textbook website, **www .pearsonglobaleditions.com/Stock_Watson**, in the files **Sportscards** and **Sportscards_Description**.[2]

**a.**  i. Suppose that, absent any endowment effect, all the subjects prefer good A to good B. What fraction of the experiment's subjects would you expect to trade the good that they were given for the other good? (*Hint:* Because of random assignment of the two treatments, approximately 50% of the subjects received good A and 50% received good B.)

   ii. Suppose that, absent any endowment effect, 50% of the subjects prefer good A to good B, and the other 50% prefer good B to good A. What fraction of the subjects would you expect to trade the good that they were given for the other good?

   iii. Suppose that, absent any endowment effect, $X$% of the subjects prefer good A to good B, and the other $(100 - X)$% prefer good B to good A. Show that you would expect 50% of the subjects to trade the good that they were given for the other good.

---

[1]Good A was a ticket stub from the game in which Cal Ripken, Jr., set the record for consecutive games played, and good B was a souvenir from the game in which Nolan Ryan won his 300th game.

[2]These data were provided by Professor John List of the University of Chicago and were used in his paper "Does Market Experience Eliminate Market Anomalies," *Quarterly Journal of Economics*, 2003, 118(1): 41–71.

**b.** Using the sports-card data, what fraction of the subjects traded the good they were given? Is the fraction significantly different from 50%? Is there evidence of an endowment effect? (*Hint:* Review Exercises 3.2 and 3.3)

**c.** Some have argued that the endowment effect may be present, but that it is likely to disappear as traders gain more trading experience. Half of the experimental subjects were dealers, and the other half were nondealers. Dealers have more experience than nondealers. Repeat (b) for dealers and nondealers. Is there a significant difference in their behavior? Is the evidence consistent with the hypothesis that the endowment effect disappears as traders gain more experience? (*Hint:* Review Exercise 3.15).

**APPENDIX**

# 3.1 The U.S. Current Population Survey

Each month, the U.S. Census Bureau and the U.S. Bureau of Labor Statistics conduct the Current Population Survey (CPS), which provides data on labor force characteristics of the population, including the levels of employment, unemployment, and earnings. Approximately 60,000 U.S. households are surveyed each month. The sample is chosen by randomly selecting addresses from a database of addresses from the most recent decennial census augmented with data on new housing units constructed after the last census. The exact random sampling scheme is rather complicated (first, small geographical areas are randomly selected, then housing units within these areas are randomly selected); details can be found in the *Handbook of Labor Statistics* and on the Bureau of Labor Statistics website (www.bls.gov).

The survey conducted each March is more detailed than in other months and asks questions about earnings during the previous year. The statistics in Tables 2.4 and 3.1 were computed using the March surveys. The CPS earnings data are for full-time workers, defined to be somebody employed more than 35 hours per week for at least 48 weeks in the previous year.

APPENDIX

## 3.2 Two Proofs That $\overline{Y}$ Is the Least Squares Estimator of $\mu_Y$

This appendix provides two proofs, one using calculus and one not, that $\overline{Y}$ minimizes the sum of squared prediction mistakes in Equation (3.2)—that is, that $\overline{Y}$ is the least squares estimator of $E(Y)$.

### Calculus Proof

To minimize the sum of squared prediction mistakes, take its derivative and set it to zero:

$$\frac{d}{dm}\sum_{i=1}^{n}(Y_i - m)^2 = -2\sum_{i=1}^{n}(Y_i - m) = -2\sum_{i=1}^{n}Y_i + 2nm = 0. \quad (3.27)$$

Solving for the final equation for $m$ shows that $\sum_{i=1}^{n}(Y_i - m)^2$ is minimized when $m = \overline{Y}$.

### Noncalculus Proof

The strategy is to show that the difference between the least squares estimator and $\overline{Y}$ must be zero, from which it follows that $\overline{Y}$ is the least squares estimator. Let $d = \overline{Y} - m$, so that $m = \overline{Y} - d$. Then $(Y_i - m)^2 = (Y_i - [\overline{Y} - d])^2 = ([Y_i - \overline{Y}] + d)^2 = (Y_i - \overline{Y})^2 + 2d(Y_i - \overline{Y}) + d^2$. Thus the sum of squared prediction mistakes [Equation (3.2)] is

$$\sum_{i=1}^{n}(Y_i - m)^2 = \sum_{i=1}^{n}(Y_i - \overline{Y})^2 + 2d\sum_{i=1}^{n}(Y_i - \overline{Y}) + nd^2 = \sum_{i=1}^{n}(Y_i - \overline{Y})^2 + nd^2,$$

$$(3.28)$$

where the second equality uses the fact that $\sum_{i=1}^{n}(Y_i - \overline{Y}) = 0$. Because both terms in the final line of Equation (3.28) are nonnegative and because the first term does not depend on $d$, $\sum_{i=1}^{n}(Y_i - m)^2$ is minimized by choosing $d$ to make the second term, $nd^2$, as small as possible. This is done by setting $d = 0$—that is, by setting $m = \overline{Y}$—so that $\overline{Y}$ is the least squares estimator of $E(Y)$.

## 3.3 A Proof That the Sample Variance Is Consistent

This appendix uses the law of large numbers to prove that the sample variance $s_Y^2$ is a consistent estimator of the population variance $\sigma_Y^2$, as stated in Equation (3.9), when $Y_1, \ldots, Y_n$ are i.i.d. and $E(Y_i^4) < \infty$.

First, consider a version of the sample variance that uses $n$ instead of $n-1$ as a divisor:

$$
\begin{aligned}
\frac{1}{n}\sum_{i=1}^{n}(Y_i - \overline{Y})^2 &= \frac{1}{n}\sum_{i=1}^{n}Y_i^2 - 2\overline{Y}\frac{1}{n}\sum_{i=1}^{n}Y_i + \overline{Y}^2 \\
&= \frac{1}{n}\sum_{i=1}^{n}Y_i^2 - \overline{Y}^2 \\
&\xrightarrow{p} (\sigma_Y^2 + \mu_Y^2) - \mu_Y^2 \\
&= \sigma_Y^2, \quad\quad\quad\quad\quad\quad\quad\quad (3.29)
\end{aligned}
$$

where the first equality uses $(Y_i - \overline{Y})^2 = Y_i^2 - 2\overline{Y}Y_i + \overline{Y}^2$, and the second uses $\frac{1}{n}\sum_{i=1}^{n}Y_i := \overline{Y}$. The convergence in the third line follows from (i) applying the law of large numbers to $\frac{1}{n}\sum_{i=1}^{n}Y_i^2 \xrightarrow{p} E(Y^2)$ (which follows because $Y_i^2$ are i.i.d. and have finite variance because $E(Y_i^4)$ is finite), (ii) recognizing that $E(Y_i^2) = \sigma_Y^2 + \mu_Y^2$ (Key Concept 2.3), and (iii) noting that $\overline{Y} \xrightarrow{p} \mu_Y$ so that $\overline{Y}^2 \xrightarrow{p} \mu_Y^2$. Finally, $s_Y^2 = \left(\frac{n}{n-1}\right)\left(\frac{1}{n}\sum_{i=1}^{n}(Y_i - \overline{Y})^2\right) \xrightarrow{p} \sigma_Y^2$ follows from Equation (3.29) and $\left(\frac{n}{n-1}\right) \to 1$.

# CHAPTER 4

# Linear Regression with One Regressor

A state implements tough new penalties on drunk drivers: What is the effect on highway fatalities? A school district cuts the size of its elementary school classes: What is the effect on its students' standardized test scores? You successfully complete one more year of college classes: What is the effect on your future earnings?

All three of these questions are about the unknown effect of changing one variable, $X$ ($X$ being penalties for drunk driving, class size, or years of schooling), on another variable, $Y$ ($Y$ being highway deaths, student test scores, or earnings).

This chapter introduces the linear regression model relating one variable, $X$, to another, $Y$. This model postulates a linear relationship between $X$ and $Y$; the slope of the line relating $X$ and $Y$ is the effect of a one-unit change in $X$ on $Y$. Just as the mean of $Y$ is an unknown characteristic of the population distribution of $Y$, the slope of the line relating $X$ and $Y$ is unknown characteristic of the population joint distribution of $X$ and $Y$. The econometric problem is to estimate this slope—that is, to estimate the effect on $Y$ of a unit change in $X$—using a sample of data on these two variables.

This chapter describes methods for estimating this slope using a random sample of data on $X$ and $Y$. For instance, using data on class sizes and test scores from different school districts, we show how to estimate the expected effect on test scores of reducing class sizes by, say, one student per class. The slope and the intercept of the line relating $X$ and $Y$ can be estimated by a method called ordinary least squares (OLS).

## 4.1 The Linear Regression Model

The superintendent of an elementary school district must decide whether to hire additional teachers and she wants your advice. If she hires the teachers, she will reduce the number of students per teacher (the student–teacher ratio) by two. She faces a trade-off. Parents want smaller classes so that their children can receive more individualized attention. But hiring more teachers means spending more money, which is not to the liking of those paying the bill! So she asks you: If she cuts class sizes, what will the effect be on student performance?

In many school districts, student performance is measured by standardized tests, and the job status or pay of some administrators can depend in part on how well their students do on these tests. We therefore sharpen the superintendent's question: If she reduces the average class size by two students, what will the effect be on standardized test scores in her district?

A precise answer to this question requires a quantitative statement about changes. If the superintendent *changes* the class size by a certain amount, what would she expect the *change* in standardized test scores to be? We can write this as a mathematical relationship using the Greek letter beta, $\beta_{ClassSize}$, where the subscript *ClassSize* distinguishes the effect of changing the class size from other effects. Thus,

$$\beta_{ClassSize} = \frac{change\ in\ TestScore}{change\ in\ ClassSize} = \frac{\Delta TestScore}{\Delta ClassSize}, \tag{4.1}$$

where the Greek letter $\Delta$ (delta) stands for "change in." That is, $\beta_{ClassSize}$ is the change in the test score that results from changing the class size divided by the change in the class size.

If you were lucky enough to know $\beta_{ClassSize}$, you would be able to tell the superintendent that decreasing class size by one student would change district-wide test scores by $\beta_{ClassSize}$. You could also answer the superintendent's actual question, which concerned changing class size by two students per class. To do so, rearrange Equation (4.1) so that

$$\Delta TestScore = \beta_{ClassSize} \times \Delta ClassSize. \tag{4.2}$$

Suppose that $\beta_{ClassSize} = -0.6$. Then a reduction in class size of two students per class would yield a predicted change in test scores of $(-0.6) \times (-2) = 1.2$; that is, you would predict that test scores would *rise* by 1.2 points as a result of the *reduction* in class sizes by two students per class.

Equation (4.1) is the definition of the slope of a straight line relating test scores and class size. This straight line can be written

$$TestScore = \beta_0 + \beta_{ClassSize} \times ClassSize, \tag{4.3}$$

where $\beta_0$ is the intercept of this straight line and, as before, $\beta_{ClassSize}$ is the slope. According to Equation (4.3), if you knew $\beta_0$ and $\beta_{ClassSize}$, not only would you be able to determine the *change* in test scores at a district associated with a *change* in class size, but you also would be able to predict the average test score itself for a given class size.

When you propose Equation (4.3) to the superintendent, she tells you that something is wrong with this formulation. She points out that class size is just one of many facets of elementary education and that two districts with the same class sizes will have different test scores for many reasons. One district might have better teachers or it might use better textbooks. Two districts with comparable class sizes, teachers, and textbooks still might have very different student populations; perhaps one district has more immigrants (and thus fewer native English speakers) or wealthier families. Finally, she points out that even if two districts are the same in all these ways they might have different test scores for essentially random reasons having to do with the performance of the individual students on the day of the test. She is right, of course; for all these reasons, Equation (4.3) will not hold exactly for all districts. Instead, it should be viewed as a statement about a relationship that holds *on average* across the population of districts.

A version of this linear relationship that holds for *each* district must incorporate these other factors influencing test scores, including each district's unique characteristics (for example, quality of their teachers, background of their students, how lucky the students were on test day). One approach would be to list the most important factors and to introduce them explicitly into Equation (4.3) (an idea we return to in Chapter 6). For now, however, we simply lump all these "other factors" together and write the relationship for a given district as

$$TestScore = \beta_0 + \beta_{ClassSize} \times ClassSize + \text{other factors}. \qquad (4.4)$$

Thus the test score for the district is written in terms of one component, $\beta_0 + \beta_{ClassSize} \times ClassSize$, that represents the average effect of class size on scores in the population of school districts and a second component that represents all other factors.

Although this discussion has focused on test scores and class size, the idea expressed in Equation (4.4) is much more general, so it is useful to introduce more general notation. Suppose you have a sample of $n$ districts. Let $Y_i$ be the average test score in the $i^{th}$ district, let $X_i$ be the average class size in the $i^{th}$ district, and let $u_i$ denote the other factors influencing the test score in the $i^{th}$ district. Then Equation (4.4) can be written more generally as

$$Y_i = \beta_0 + \beta_1 X_i + u_i, \qquad (4.5)$$

for each district (that is, $i = 1, \ldots, n$), where $\beta_0$ is the intercept of this line and $\beta_1$ is the slope. [The general notation $\beta_1$ is used for the slope in Equation (4.5) instead of $\beta_{ClassSize}$ because this equation is written in terms of a general variable $X_i$.]

Equation (4.5) is the **linear regression model with a single regressor**, in which $Y$ is the **dependent variable** and $X$ is the **independent variable** or the **regressor**.

The first part of Equation (4.5), $\beta_0 + \beta_1 X_i$, is the **population regression line** or the **population regression function**. This is the relationship that holds between $Y$ and $X$ on average over the population. Thus, if you knew the value of $X$, according to this population regression line you would predict that the value of the dependent variable, $Y$, is $\beta_0 + \beta_1 X$.

The **intercept** $\beta_0$ and the **slope** $\beta_1$ are the **coefficients** of the population regression line, also known as the **parameters** of the population regression line. The slope $\beta_1$ is the change in $Y$ associated with a unit change in $X$. The intercept is the value of the population regression line when $X = 0$; it is the point at which the population regression line intersects the $Y$ axis. In some econometric applications, the intercept has a meaningful economic interpretation. In other applications, the intercept has no real-world meaning; for example, when $X$ is the class size, strictly speaking the intercept is the predicted value of test scores when there are no students in the class! When the real-world meaning of the intercept is nonsensical, it is best to think of it mathematically as the coefficient that determines the level of the regression line.

The term $u_i$ in Equation (4.5) is the **error term**. The error term incorporates all of the factors responsible for the difference between the $i^{th}$ district's average test score and the value predicted by the population regression line. This error term contains all the other factors besides $X$ that determine the value of the dependent variable, $Y$, for a specific observation, $i$. In the class size example, these other factors include all the unique features of the $i^{th}$ district that affect the performance of its students on the test, including teacher quality, student economic background, luck, and even any mistakes in grading the test.

The linear regression model and its terminology are summarized in Key Concept 4.1.

Figure 4.1 summarizes the linear regression model with a single regressor for seven hypothetical observations on test scores ($Y$) and class size ($X$). The population regression line is the straight line $\beta_0 + \beta_1 X$. The population regression line slopes down ($\beta_1 < 0$), which means that districts with lower student–teacher ratios (smaller classes) tend to have higher test scores. The intercept $\beta_0$ has a mathematical meaning as the value of the $Y$ axis intersected by the population regression line, but, as mentioned earlier, it has no real-world meaning in this example.

Because of the other factors that determine test performance, the hypothetical observations in Figure 4.1 do not fall exactly on the population regression line. For example, the value of $Y$ for district #1, $Y_1$, is above the population regression line. This means that test scores in district #1 were better than predicted by the

## Terminology for the Linear Regression Model with a Single Regressor

**KEY CONCEPT**

**4.1**

The linear regression model is

$$Y_i = \beta_0 + \beta_1 X_i + u_i,$$

where

the subscript $i$ runs over observations, $i = 1, \ldots, n$;

$Y_i$ is the *dependent variable*, the *regressand*, or simply the *left-hand variable*;

$X_i$ is the *independent variable*, the *regressor*, or simply the *right-hand variable*;

$\beta_0 + \beta_1 X$ is the *population regression line* or the *population regression function*;

$\beta_0$ is the *intercept* of the population regression line;

$\beta_1$ is the *slope* of the population regression line; and

$u_i$ is the *error term*.

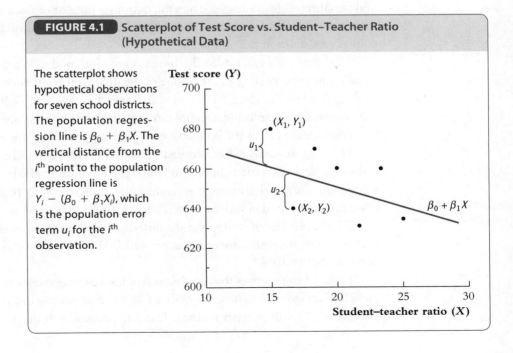

**FIGURE 4.1**  Scatterplot of Test Score vs. Student–Teacher Ratio (Hypothetical Data)

The scatterplot shows hypothetical observations for seven school districts. The population regression line is $\beta_0 + \beta_1 X$. The vertical distance from the $i^{th}$ point to the population regression line is $Y_i - (\beta_0 + \beta_1 X_i)$, which is the population error term $u_i$ for the $i^{th}$ observation.

population regression line, so the error term for that district, $u_1$, is positive. In contrast, $Y_2$ is below the population regression line, so test scores for that district were worse than predicted, and $u_2 < 0$.

Now return to your problem as advisor to the superintendent: What is the expected effect on test scores of reducing the student–teacher ratio by two students per teacher? The answer is easy: The expected change is $(-2) \times \beta_{ClassSize}$. But what is the value of $\beta_{ClassSize}$?

# 4.2 Estimating the Coefficients of the Linear Regression Model

In a practical situation such as the application to class size and test scores, the intercept $\beta_0$ and slope $\beta_1$ of the population regression line are unknown. Therefore, we must use data to estimate the unknown slope and intercept of the population regression line.

This estimation problem is similar to others you have faced in statistics. For example, suppose you want to compare the mean earnings of men and women who recently graduated from college. Although the population mean earnings are unknown, we can estimate the population means using a random sample of male and female college graduates. Then the natural estimator of the unknown population mean earnings for women, for example, is the average earnings of the female college graduates in the sample.

The same idea extends to the linear regression model. We do not know the population value of $\beta_{ClassSize}$, the slope of the unknown population regression line relating $X$ (class size) and $Y$ (test scores). But just as it was possible to learn about the population mean using a sample of data drawn from that population, so is it possible to learn about the population slope $\beta_{ClassSize}$ using a sample of data.

The data we analyze here consist of test scores and class sizes in 1999 in 420 California school districts that serve kindergarten through eighth grade. The test score is the districtwide average of reading and math scores for fifth graders. Class size can be measured in various ways. The measure used here is one of the broadest, which is the number of students in the district divided by the number of teachers— that is, the districtwide student–teacher ratio. These data are described in more detail in Appendix 4.1.

Table 4.1 summarizes the distributions of test scores and class sizes for this sample. The average student–teacher ratio is 19.6 students per teacher, and the standard deviation is 1.9 students per teacher. The 10th percentile of the distribution of the

| TABLE 4.1 | Summary of the Distribution of Student–Teacher Ratios and Fifth-Grade Test Scores for 420 K–8 Districts in California in 1999 | | | | | | | | |
|---|---|---|---|---|---|---|---|---|---|

| | | | Percentile | | | | | | |
|---|---|---|---|---|---|---|---|---|---|
| | Average | Standard Deviation | 10% | 25% | 40% | 50% (median) | 60% | 75% | 90% |
| Student–teacher ratio | 19.6 | 1.9 | 17.3 | 18.6 | 19.3 | 19.7 | 20.1 | 20.9 | 21.9 |
| Test score | 654.2 | 19.1 | 630.4 | 640.0 | 649.1 | 654.5 | 659.4 | 666.7 | 679.1 |

student–teacher ratio is 17.3 (that is, only 10% of districts have student–teacher ratios below 17.3), while the district at the 90th percentile has a student–teacher ratio of 21.9.

A scatterplot of these 420 observations on test scores and the student–teacher ratio is shown in Figure 4.2. The sample correlation is −0.23, indicating a weak negative relationship between the two variables. Although larger classes in this sample tend to have lower test scores, there are other determinants of test scores that keep the observations from falling perfectly along a straight line.

Despite this low correlation, if one could somehow draw a straight line through these data, then the slope of this line would be an estimate of $\beta_{ClassSize}$

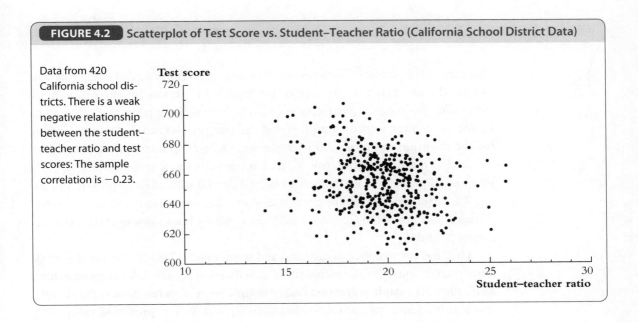

**FIGURE 4.2** Scatterplot of Test Score vs. Student–Teacher Ratio (California School District Data)

Data from 420 California school districts. There is a weak negative relationship between the student–teacher ratio and test scores: The sample correlation is −0.23.

based on these data. One way to draw the line would be to take out a pencil and a ruler and to "eyeball" the best line you could. While this method is easy, it is very unscientific, and different people will create different estimated lines.

How, then, should you choose among the many possible lines? By far the most common way is to choose the line that produces the "least squares" fit to these data—that is, to use the ordinary least squares (OLS) estimator.

## The Ordinary Least Squares Estimator

The OLS estimator chooses the regression coefficients so that the estimated regression line is as close as possible to the observed data, where closeness is measured by the sum of the squared mistakes made in predicting $Y$ given $X$.

As discussed in Section 3.1, the sample average, $\overline{Y}$, is the least squares estimator of the population mean, $E(Y)$; that is, $\overline{Y}$ minimizes the total squared estimation mistakes $\sum_{i=1}^{n}(Y_i - m)^2$ among all possible estimators $m$ [see Expression (3.2)].

The OLS estimator extends this idea to the linear regression model. Let $b_0$ and $b_1$ be some estimators of $\beta_0$ and $\beta_1$. The regression line based on these estimators is $b_0 + b_1 X$, so the value of $Y_i$ predicted using this line is $b_0 + b_1 X_i$. Thus the mistake made in predicting the $i^{\text{th}}$ observation is $Y_i - (b_0 + b_1 X_i) = Y_i - b_0 - b_1 X_i$. The sum of these squared prediction mistakes over all $n$ observations is

$$\sum_{i=1}^{n}(Y_i - b_0 - b_1 X_i)^2. \tag{4.6}$$

The sum of the squared mistakes for the linear regression model in Expression (4.6) is the extension of the sum of the squared mistakes for the problem of estimating the mean in Expression (3.2). In fact, if there is no regressor, then $b_1$ does not enter Expression (4.6) and the two problems are identical except for the different notation [$m$ in Expression (3.2), $b_0$ in Expression (4.6)]. Just as there is a unique estimator, $\overline{Y}$, that minimizes the Expression (3.2), so is there a unique pair of estimators of $\beta_0$ and $\beta_1$ that minimize Expression (4.6).

The estimators of the intercept and slope that minimize the sum of squared mistakes in Expression (4.6) are called the **ordinary least squares (OLS) estimators** of $\beta_0$ and $\beta_1$.

OLS has its own special notation and terminology. The OLS estimator of $\beta_0$ is denoted $\hat{\beta}_0$, and the OLS estimator of $\beta_1$ is denoted $\hat{\beta}_1$. The **OLS regression line**, also called the **sample regression line** or **sample regression function**, is the straight line constructed using the OLS estimators: $\hat{\beta}_0 + \hat{\beta}_1 X$. The **predicted value** of $Y_i$

## The OLS Estimator, Predicted Values, and Residuals

The OLS estimators of the slope $\beta_1$ and the intercept $\beta_0$ are

$$\hat{\beta}_1 = \frac{\sum_{i=1}^{n}(X_i - \overline{X})(Y_i - \overline{Y})}{\sum_{i=1}^{n}(X_i - \overline{X})^2} = \frac{s_{XY}}{s_X^2} \tag{4.7}$$

$$\hat{\beta}_0 = \overline{Y} - \hat{\beta}_1\overline{X}. \tag{4.8}$$

The OLS predicted values $\hat{Y}_i$ and residuals $\hat{u}_i$ are

$$\hat{Y}_i = \hat{\beta}_0 + \hat{\beta}_1 X_i, \quad i = 1, \ldots, n \tag{4.9}$$

$$\hat{u}_i = Y_i - \hat{Y}_i, \quad i = 1, \ldots, n. \tag{4.10}$$

The estimated intercept ($\hat{\beta}_0$), slope ($\hat{\beta}_1$), and residual ($\hat{u}_i$) are computed from a sample of $n$ observations of $X_i$ and $Y_i$, $i = 1, \ldots, n$. These are estimates of the unknown true population intercept ($\beta_0$), slope ($\beta_1$), and error term ($u_i$).

given $X_i$, based on the OLS regression line, is $\hat{Y}_i = \hat{\beta}_0 + \hat{\beta}_1 X_i$. The **residual** for the $i^{\text{th}}$ observation is the difference between $Y_i$ and its predicted value: $\hat{u}_i = Y_i - \hat{Y}_i$.

The OLS estimators, $\hat{\beta}_0$ and $\hat{\beta}_1$, are sample counterparts of the population coefficients, $\beta_0$ and $\beta_1$. Similarly, the OLS regression line $\hat{\beta}_0 + \hat{\beta}_1 X$ is the sample counterpart of the population regression line $\beta_0 + \beta_1 X$, and the OLS residuals $\hat{u}_i$ are sample counterparts of the population errors $u_i$.

You could compute the OLS estimators $\hat{\beta}_0$ and $\hat{\beta}_1$ by trying different values of $b_0$ and $b_1$ repeatedly until you find those that minimize the total squared mistakes in Expression (4.6); they are the least squares estimates. This method would be quite tedious, however. Fortunately, there are formulas, derived by minimizing Expression (4.6) using calculus, that streamline the calculation of the OLS estimators.

The OLS formulas and terminology are collected in Key Concept 4.2. These formulas are implemented in virtually all statistical and spreadsheet programs. These formulas are derived in Appendix 4.2.

## OLS Estimates of the Relationship Between Test Scores and the Student–Teacher Ratio

When OLS is used to estimate a line relating the student–teacher ratio to test scores using the 420 observations in Figure 4.2, the estimated slope is −2.28 and the estimated intercept is 698.9. Accordingly, the OLS regression line for these 420 observations is

$$\widehat{TestScore} = 698.9 - 2.28 \times STR, \tag{4.11}$$

where *TestScore* is the average test score in the district and *STR* is the student–teacher ratio. The "^" over *TestScore* in Equation (4.11) indicates that it is the predicted value based on the OLS regression line. Figure 4.3 plots this OLS regression line superimposed over the scatterplot of the data previously shown in Figure 4.2.

The slope of −2.28 means that an increase in the student–teacher ratio by one student per class is, on average, associated with a decline in districtwide test scores by 2.28 points on the test. A decrease in the student–teacher ratio by two students per class is, on average, associated with an increase in test scores of 4.56 points [$= -2 \times (-2.28)$]. The negative slope indicates that more students per teacher (larger classes) is associated with poorer performance on the test.

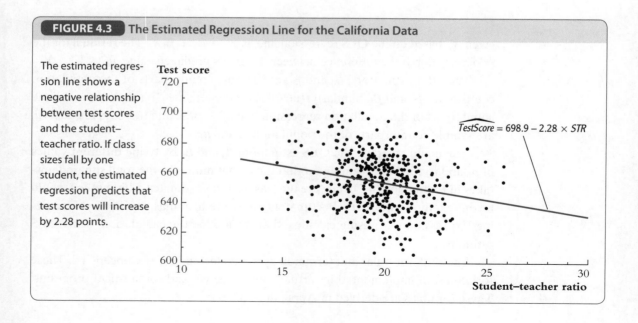

**FIGURE 4.3** The Estimated Regression Line for the California Data

The estimated regression line shows a negative relationship between test scores and the student–teacher ratio. If class sizes fall by one student, the estimated regression predicts that test scores will increase by 2.28 points.

It is now possible to predict the districtwide test score given a value of the student–teacher ratio. For example, for a district with 20 students per teacher, the predicted test score is $698.9 - 2.28 \times 20 = 653.3$. Of course, this prediction will not be exactly right because of the other factors that determine a district's performance. But the regression line does give a prediction (the OLS prediction) of what test scores would be for that district, based on their student–teacher ratio, absent those other factors.

Is this estimate of the slope large or small? To answer this, we return to the superintendent's problem. Recall that she is contemplating hiring enough teachers to reduce the student–teacher ratio by 2. Suppose her district is at the median of the California districts. From Table 4.1, the median student–teacher ratio is 19.7 and the median test score is 654.5. A reduction of two students per class, from 19.7 to 17.7, would move her student–teacher ratio from the 50th percentile to very near the 10th percentile. This is a big change, and she would need to hire many new teachers. How would it affect test scores?

According to Equation (4.11), cutting the student–teacher ratio by 2 is predicted to increase test scores by approximately 4.6 points; if her district's test scores are at the median, 654.5, they are predicted to increase to 659.1. Is this improvement large or small? According to Table 4.1, this improvement would move her district from the median to just short of the 60th percentile. Thus a decrease in class size that would place her district close to the 10% with the smallest classes would move her test scores from the 50th to the 60th percentile. According to these estimates, at least, cutting the student–teacher ratio by a large amount (two students per teacher) would help and might be worth doing depending on her budgetary situation, but it would not be a panacea.

What if the superintendent were contemplating a far more radical change, such as reducing the student–teacher ratio from 20 students per teacher to 5? Unfortunately, the estimates in Equation (4.11) would not be very useful to her. This regression was estimated using the data in Figure 4.2, and, as the figure shows, the smallest student–teacher ratio in these data is 14. These data contain no information on how districts with extremely small classes perform, so these data alone are not a reliable basis for predicting the effect of a radical move to such an extremely low student–teacher ratio.

## Why Use the OLS Estimator?

There are both practical and theoretical reasons to use the OLS estimators $\hat{\beta}_0$ and $\hat{\beta}_1$. Because OLS is the dominant method used in practice, it has become the common language for regression analysis throughout economics, finance (see "The 'Beta' of a Stock" box), and the social sciences more generally. Presenting results

## The "Beta" of a Stock

A fundamental idea of modern finance is that an investor needs a financial incentive to take a risk. Said differently, the expected return[1] on a risky investment, $R$, must exceed the return on a safe, or risk-free, investment, $R_f$. Thus the expected excess return, $R - R_f$, on a risky investment, like owning stock in a company, should be positive.

At first it might seem like the risk of a stock should be measured by its variance. Much of that risk, however, can be reduced by holding other stocks in a "portfolio"—in other words, by diversifying your financial holdings. This means that the right way to measure the risk of a stock is not by its *variance* but rather by its *covariance* with the market.

The capital asset pricing model (CAPM) formalizes this idea. According to the CAPM, the expected excess return on an asset is proportional to the expected excess return on a portfolio of all available assets (the "market portfolio"). That is, the CAPM says that

$$R - R_f = \beta(R_m - R_f), \qquad (4.12)$$

where $R_m$ is the expected return on the market portfolio and $\beta$ is the coefficient in the population regression of $R - R_f$ on $R_m - R_f$. In practice, the risk-free return is often taken to be the rate of interest on short-term U.S. government debt. According to the CAPM, a stock with a $\beta < 1$ has less risk than the market portfolio and therefore has a lower expected excess return than the market portfolio. In contrast, a stock with a $\beta > 1$ is riskier than the market portfolio and thus commands a higher expected excess return.

The "beta" of a stock has become a workhorse of the investment industry, and you can obtain estimated betas for hundreds of stocks on investment firm websites. Those betas typically are estimated by OLS regression of the actual excess return on the stock against the actual excess return on a broad market index.

The table below gives estimated betas for seven U.S. stocks. Low-risk producers of consumer staples like Kellogg have stocks with low betas; riskier stocks have high betas.

| Company | Estimated $\beta$ |
|---|---|
| Verizon (telecommunications) | 0.0 |
| Wal-Mart (discount retailer) | 0.3 |
| Kellogg (breakfast cereal) | 0.5 |
| Waste Management (waste disposal) | 0.6 |
| Google (information technology) | 1.0 |
| Ford Motor Company (auto producer) | 1.3 |
| Bank of America (bank) | 2.2 |

*Source:* finance.yahoo.com.

---

[1]The return on an investment is the change in its price plus any payout (dividend) from the investment as a percentage of its initial price. For example, a stock bought on January 1 for \$100, which then paid a \$2.50 dividend during the year and sold on December 31 for \$105, would have a return of $R = [(\$105 - \$100) + \$2.50]/\$100 = 7.5\%$.

using OLS (or its variants discussed later in this book) means that you are "speaking the same language" as other economists and statisticians. The OLS formulas are built into virtually all spreadsheet and statistical software packages, making OLS easy to use.

The OLS estimators also have desirable theoretical properties. They are analogous to the desirable properties, studied in Section 3.1, of $\overline{Y}$ as an estimator of the population mean. Under the assumptions introduced in Section 4.4, the OLS estimator is unbiased and consistent. The OLS estimator is also efficient among a certain class of unbiased estimators; however, this efficiency result holds under some additional special conditions, and further discussion of this result is deferred until Section 5.5.

# 4.3  Measures of Fit

Having estimated a linear regression, you might wonder how well that regression line describes the data. Does the regressor account for much or for little of the variation in the dependent variable? Are the observations tightly clustered around the regression line, or are they spread out?

The $R^2$ and the standard error of the regression measure how well the OLS regression line fits the data. The $R^2$ ranges between 0 and 1 and measures the fraction of the variance of $Y_i$ that is explained by $X_i$. The standard error of the regression measures how far $Y_i$ typically is from its predicted value.

## The $R^2$

The **regression $R^2$** is the fraction of the sample variance of $Y_i$ explained by (or predicted by) $X_i$. The definitions of the predicted value and the residual (see Key Concept 4.2) allow us to write the dependent variable $Y_i$ as the sum of the predicted value, $\hat{Y}_i$, plus the residual $\hat{u}_i$:

$$Y_i = \hat{Y}_i + \hat{u}_i. \tag{4.13}$$

In this notation, the $R^2$ is the ratio of the sample variance of $\hat{Y}_i$ to the sample variance of $Y_i$.

Mathematically, the $R^2$ can be written as the ratio of the explained sum of squares to the total sum of squares. The **explained sum of squares (ESS)** is the sum of squared deviations of the predicted value, $\hat{Y}_i$, from its average, and the **total sum of squares (TSS)** is the sum of squared deviations of $Y_i$ from its average:

$$ESS = \sum_{i=1}^{n}(\hat{Y}_i - \overline{Y})^2 \tag{4.14}$$

$$TSS = \sum_{i=1}^{n}(Y_i - \overline{Y})^2. \tag{4.15}$$

Equation (4.14) uses the fact that the sample average OLS predicted value equals $\overline{Y}$ (proven in Appendix 4.3).

The $R^2$ is the ratio of the explained sum of squares to the total sum of squares:

$$R^2 = \frac{ESS}{TSS}. \tag{4.16}$$

Alternatively, the $R^2$ can be written in terms of the fraction of the variance of $Y_i$ *not* explained by $X_i$. The **sum of squared residuals**, or **SSR**, is the sum of the squared OLS residuals:

$$SSR = \sum_{i=1}^{n} \hat{u}_i^2. \tag{4.17}$$

It is shown in Appendix 4.3 that $TSS = ESS + SSR$. Thus the $R^2$ also can be expressed as 1 minus the ratio of the sum of squared residuals to the total sum of squares:

$$R^2 = 1 - \frac{SSR}{TSS}. \tag{4.18}$$

Finally, the $R^2$ of the regression of $Y$ on the single regressor $X$ is the square of the correlation coefficient between $Y$ and $X$ (Exercise 4.12).

The $R^2$ ranges between 0 and 1. If $\hat{\beta}_1 = 0$, then $X_i$ explains none of the variation of $Y_i$ and the predicted value of $Y_i$ is $\hat{Y}_i = \hat{\beta}_0 = \overline{Y}$ [from Equation (4.8)]. In this case, the explained sum of squares is zero and the sum of squared residuals equals the total sum of squares; thus the $R^2$ is zero. In contrast, if $X_i$ explains all of the variation of $Y_i$, then $Y_i = \hat{Y}_i$ for all $i$ and every residual is zero (that is, $\hat{u}_i = 0$), so that $ESS = TSS$ and $R^2 = 1$. In general, the $R^2$ does not take on the extreme values of 0 or 1 but falls somewhere in between. An $R^2$ near 1 indicates that the regressor is good at predicting $Y_i$, while an $R^2$ near 0 indicates that the regressor is not very good at predicting $Y_i$.

## The Standard Error of the Regression

The **standard error of the regression (SER)** is an estimator of the standard deviation of the regression error $u_i$. The units of $u_i$ and $Y_i$ are the same, so the SER is a measure of the spread of the observations around the regression line, measured in the units of the dependent variable. For example, if the units of the dependent variable are dollars, then the SER measures the magnitude of a typical deviation from the regression line—that is, the magnitude of a typical regression error—in dollars.

Because the regression errors $u_1, \ldots, u_n$ are unobserved, the *SER* is computed using their sample counterparts, the OLS residuals $\hat{u}_1, \ldots, \hat{u}_n$. The formula for the *SER* is

$$SER = s_{\hat{u}} = \sqrt{s_{\hat{u}}^2}, \text{ where } s_{\hat{u}}^2 = \frac{1}{n-2}\sum_{i=1}^{n}\hat{u}_i^2 = \frac{SSR}{n-2}, \tag{4.19}$$

where the formula for $s_{\hat{u}}^2$ uses the fact (proven in Appendix 4.3) that the sample average of the OLS residuals is zero.

The formula for the *SER* in Equation (4.19) is similar to the formula for the sample standard deviation of $Y$ given in Equation (3.7) in Section 3.2, except that $Y_i - \overline{Y}$ in Equation (3.7) is replaced by $\hat{u}_i$ and the divisor in Equation (3.7) is $n-1$, whereas here it is $n-2$. The reason for using the divisor $n-2$ here (instead of $n$) is the same as the reason for using the divisor $n-1$ in Equation (3.7): It corrects for a slight downward bias introduced because two regression coefficients were estimated. This is called a "degrees of freedom" correction because two coefficients were estimated ($\beta_0$ and $\beta_1$), two "degrees of freedom" of the data were lost, so the divisor in this factor is $n-2$. (The mathematics behind this is discussed in Section 5.6.) When $n$ is large, the difference between dividing by $n$, by $n-1$, or by $n-2$ is negligible.

## Application to the Test Score Data

Equation (4.11) reports the regression line, estimated using the California test score data, relating the standardized test score (*TestScore*) to the student–teacher ratio (*STR*). The $R^2$ of this regression is 0.051, or 5.1%, and the *SER* is 18.6.

The $R^2$ of 0.051 means that the regressor *STR* explains 5.1% of the variance of the dependent variable *TestScore*. Figure 4.3 superimposes this regression line on the scatterplot of the *TestScore* and *STR* data. As the scatterplot shows, the student–teacher ratio explains some of the variation in test scores, but much variation remains unaccounted for.

The *SER* of 18.6 means that standard deviation of the regression residuals is 18.6, where the units are points on the standardized test. Because the standard deviation is a measure of spread, the *SER* of 18.6 means that there is a large spread of the scatterplot in Figure 4.3 around the regression line as measured in points on the test. This large spread means that predictions of test scores made using only the student–teacher ratio for that district will often be wrong by a large amount.

What should we make of this low $R^2$ and large $SER$? The fact that the $R^2$ of this regression is low (and the $SER$ is large) does not, by itself, imply that this regression is either "good" or "bad." What the low $R^2$ *does* tell us is that other important factors influence test scores. These factors could include differences in the student body across districts, differences in school quality unrelated to the student–teacher ratio, or luck on the test. The low $R^2$ and high $SER$ do not tell us what these factors are, but they do indicate that the student–teacher ratio alone explains only a small part of the variation in test scores in these data.

# 4.4   The Least Squares Assumptions

This section presents a set of three assumptions on the linear regression model and the sampling scheme under which OLS provides an appropriate estimator of the unknown regression coefficients, $\beta_0$ and $\beta_1$. Initially, these assumptions might appear abstract. They do, however, have natural interpretations, and understanding these assumptions is essential for understanding when OLS will—and will not—give useful estimates of the regression coefficients.

## Assumption #1: The Conditional Distribution of $u_i$ Given $X_i$ Has a Mean of Zero

The first of the three **least squares assumptions** is that the conditional distribution of $u_i$ given $X_i$ has a mean of zero. This assumption is a formal mathematical statement about the "other factors" contained in $u_i$ and asserts that these other factors are unrelated to $X_i$ in the sense that, given a value of $X_i$, the mean of the distribution of these other factors is zero.

This assumption is illustrated in Figure 4.4. The population regression is the relationship that holds on average between class size and test scores in the population, and the error term $u_i$ represents the other factors that lead test scores at a given district to differ from the prediction based on the population regression line. As shown in Figure 4.4, at a given value of class size, say 20 students per class, sometimes these other factors lead to better performance than predicted ($u_i > 0$) and sometimes to worse performance ($u_i < 0$), but on average over the population the prediction is right. In other words, given $X_i = 20$, the mean of the distribution of $u_i$ is zero. In Figure 4.4, this is shown as the distribution of $u_i$ being centered on the population regression line at $X_i = 20$ and, more generally, at other values $x$ of $X_i$ as well. Said differently, the distribution of $u_i$, conditional on $X_i = x$, has a mean of zero; stated mathematically, $E(u_i | X_i = x) = 0$, or, in somewhat simpler notation, $E(u_i | X_i) = 0$.

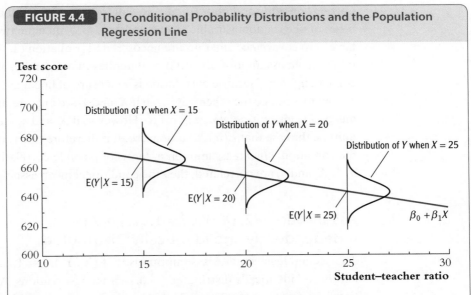

**FIGURE 4.4** The Conditional Probability Distributions and the Population Regression Line

The figure shows the conditional probability of test scores for districts with class sizes of 15, 20, and 25 students. The mean of the conditional distribution of test scores, given the student–teacher ratio, $E(Y|X)$, is the population regression line. At a given value of $X$, $Y$ is distributed around the regression line and the error, $u = Y - (\beta_0 + \beta_1 X)$, has a conditional mean of zero for all values of $X$.

As shown in Figure 4.4, the assumption that $E(u_i|X_i) = 0$ is equivalent to assuming that the population regression line is the conditional mean of $Y_i$ given $X_i$ (a mathematical proof of this is left as Exercise 4.6).

***The conditional mean of u in a randomized controlled experiment.*** In a randomized controlled experiment, subjects are randomly assigned to the treatment group ($X = 1$) or to the control group ($X = 0$). The random assignment typically is done using a computer program that uses no information about the subject, ensuring that $X$ is distributed independently of all personal characteristics of the subject. Random assignment makes $X$ and $u$ independent, which in turn implies that the conditional mean of $u$ given $X$ is zero.

In observational data, $X$ is not randomly assigned in an experiment. Instead, the best that can be hoped for is that $X$ is *as if* randomly assigned, in the precise sense that $E(u_i|X_i) = 0$. Whether this assumption holds in a given empirical application with observational data requires careful thought and judgment, and we return to this issue repeatedly.

*Correlation and conditional mean.* Recall from Section 2.3 that if the conditional mean of one random variable given another is zero, then the two random variables have zero covariance and thus are uncorrelated [Equation (2.27)]. Thus the conditional mean assumption $E(u_i | X_i) = 0$ implies that $X_i$ and $u_i$ are uncorrelated, or $corr(X_i, u_i) = 0$. Because correlation is a measure of linear association, this implication does not go the other way; even if $X_i$ and $u_i$ are uncorrelated, the conditional mean of $u_i$ given $X_i$ might be nonzero. However, if $X_i$ and $u_i$ are correlated, then it must be the case that $E(u_i | X_i)$ is nonzero. It is therefore often convenient to discuss the conditional mean assumption in terms of possible correlation between $X_i$ and $u_i$. If $X_i$ and $u_i$ are correlated, then the conditional mean assumption is violated.

## Assumption #2: $(X_i, Y_i)$, $i = 1, \ldots, n$, Are Independently and Identically Distributed

The second least squares assumption is that $(X_i, Y_i)$, $i = 1, \ldots, n$, are independently and identically distributed (i.i.d.) across observations. As discussed in Section 2.5 (Key Concept 2.5), this assumption is a statement about how the sample is drawn. If the observations are drawn by simple random sampling from a single large population, then $(X_i, Y_i)$, $i = 1, \ldots, n$, are i.i.d. For example, let $X$ be the age of a worker and $Y$ be his or her earnings, and imagine drawing a person at random from the population of workers. That randomly drawn person will have a certain age and earnings (that is, $X$ and $Y$ will take on some values). If a sample of $n$ workers is drawn from this population, then $(X_i, Y_i)$, $i = 1, \ldots, n$, necessarily have the same distribution. If they are drawn at random they are also distributed independently from one observation to the next; that is, they are i.i.d.

The i.i.d. assumption is a reasonable one for many data collection schemes. For example, survey data from a randomly chosen subset of the population typically can be treated as i.i.d.

Not all sampling schemes produce i.i.d. observations on $(X_i, Y_i)$, however. One example is when the values of $X$ are not drawn from a random sample of the population but rather are set by a researcher as part of an experiment. For example, suppose a horticulturalist wants to study the effects of different organic weeding methods $(X)$ on tomato production $(Y)$ and accordingly grows different plots of tomatoes using different organic weeding techniques. If she picks the techniques (the level of $X$) to be used on the $i^{th}$ plot and applies the same technique to the $i^{th}$ plot in all repetitions of the experiment, then the value of $X_i$ does not change from one sample to the next. Thus $X_i$ is nonrandom (although the outcome $Y_i$ is random), so the sampling scheme is not i.i.d. The results presented in this chapter developed for i.i.d. regressors are also true if the regressors are nonrandom. The case of a nonrandom regressor is, however, quite special. For example, modern experimental protocols would have the horticulturalist assign the level of $X$ to the different plots using a computerized random number generator, thereby circumventing any possible bias by the horticulturalist (she might use her favorite weeding method for the tomatoes in the sunniest plot). When this modern experimental protocol is used, the level of $X$ is random and $(X_i, Y_i)$ are i.i.d.

Another example of non-i.i.d. sampling is when observations refer to the same unit of observation over time. For example, we might have data on inventory levels $(Y)$ at a firm and the interest rate at which the firm can borrow $(X)$, where these data are collected over time from a specific firm; for example, they might be recorded four times a year (quarterly) for 30 years. This is an example of time series data, and a key feature of time series data is that observations falling close to each other in time are not independent but rather tend to be correlated with each other; if interest rates are low now, they are likely to be low next quarter. This pattern of correlation violates the "independence" part of the i.i.d. assumption. Time series data introduce a set of complications that are best handled after developing the basic tools of regression analysis, so we postpone discussion of time series data until Chapter 14.

## Assumption #3: Large Outliers Are Unlikely

The third least squares assumption is that large outliers—that is, observations with values of $X_i$, $Y_i$, or both that are far outside the usual range of the data—are unlikely. Large outliers can make OLS regression results misleading. This potential sensitivity of OLS to extreme outliers is illustrated in Figure 4.5 using hypothetical data.

In this book, the assumption that large outliers are unlikely is made mathematically precise by assuming that $X$ and $Y$ have nonzero finite fourth moments: $0 < E(X_i^4) < \infty$ and $0 < E(Y_i^4) < \infty$. Another way to state this assumption is that $X$ and $Y$ have finite kurtosis.

The assumption of finite kurtosis is used in the mathematics that justify the large-sample approximations to the distributions of the OLS test statistics. For example, we encountered this assumption in Chapter 3 when discussing the consistency of the sample variance. Specifically, Equation (3.9) states that the sample variance is a consistent estimator of the population variance $\sigma_Y^2$ ($s_Y^2 \xrightarrow{p} \sigma_Y^2$). If $Y_1, \ldots, Y_n$ are i.i.d. and the fourth moment of $Y_i$ is finite, then the law of large numbers in Key Concept 2.6 applies to the average, $\frac{1}{n}\sum_{i=1}^{n}Y_i^2$, a key step in the proof in Appendix 3.3 showing that $s_Y^2$ is consistent.

One source of large outliers is data entry errors, such as a typographical error or incorrectly using different units for different observations. Imagine collecting data on the height of students in meters, but inadvertently recording one student's

**FIGURE 4.5**    The Sensitivity of OLS to Large Outliers

This hypothetical data set has one outlier. The OLS regression line estimated with the outlier shows a strong positive relationship between *X* and *Y*, but the OLS regression line estimated without the outlier shows no relationship.

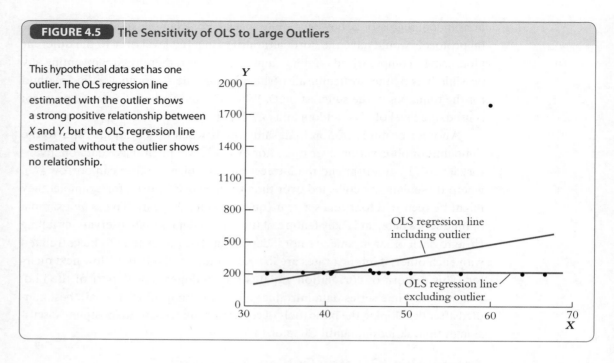

height in centimeters instead. This would create a large outlier in the sample. One way to find outliers is to plot your data. If you decide that an outlier is due to a data entry error, then you can either correct the error or, if that is impossible, drop the observation from your data set.

Data entry errors aside, the assumption of finite kurtosis is a plausible one in many applications with economic data. Class size is capped by the physical capacity of a classroom; the best you can do on a standardized test is to get all the questions right and the worst you can do is to get all the questions wrong. Because class size and test scores have a finite range, they necessarily have finite kurtosis. More generally, commonly used distributions such as the normal distribution have four moments. Still, as a mathematical matter, some distributions have infinite fourth moments, and this assumption rules out those distributions. If the assumption of finite fourth moments holds, then it is unlikely that statistical inferences using OLS will be dominated by a few observations.

## Use of the Least Squares Assumptions

The three least squares assumptions for the linear regression model are summarized in Key Concept 4.3. The least squares assumptions play twin roles, and we return to them repeatedly throughout this textbook.

## The Least Squares Assumptions

KEY CONCEPT

4.3

$$Y_i = \beta_0 + \beta_1 X_i + u_i, i = 1, \ldots, n, \text{ where}$$

1. The error term $u_i$ has conditional mean zero given $X_i$: $E(u_i | X_i) = 0$;
2. $(X_i, Y_i), i = 1, \ldots, n$, are independent and identically distributed (i.i.d.) draws from their joint distribution; and
3. Large outliers are unlikely: $X_i$ and $Y_i$ have nonzero finite fourth moments.

Their first role is mathematical: If these assumptions hold, then, as is shown in the next section, in large samples the OLS estimators have sampling distributions that are normal. In turn, this large-sample normal distribution lets us develop methods for hypothesis testing and constructing confidence intervals using the OLS estimators.

Their second role is to organize the circumstances that pose difficulties for OLS regression. As we will see, the first least squares assumption is the most important to consider in practice. One reason why the first least squares assumption might not hold in practice is discussed in Chapter 6, and additional reasons are discussed in Section 9.2.

It is also important to consider whether the second assumption holds in an application. Although it plausibly holds in many cross-sectional data sets, the independence assumption is inappropriate for panel and time series data. Therefore, the regression methods developed under assumption 2 require modification for some applications with time series data. These modifications are developed in Chapters 10 and 14–16.

The third assumption serves as a reminder that OLS, just like the sample mean, can be sensitive to large outliers. If your data set contains large outliers, you should examine those outliers carefully to make sure those observations are correctly recorded and belong in the data set.

## 4.5 Sampling Distribution of the OLS Estimators

Because the OLS estimators $\hat{\beta}_0$ and $\hat{\beta}_1$ are computed from a randomly drawn sample, the estimators themselves are random variables with a probability distribution—the sampling distribution—that describes the values they could take over different possible random samples. This section presents these sampling distributions.

In small samples, these distributions are complicated, but in large samples, they are approximately normal because of the central limit theorem.

## The Sampling Distribution of the OLS Estimators

***Review of the sampling distribution of $\overline{Y}$.*** Recall the discussion in Sections 2.5 and 2.6 about the sampling distribution of the sample average, $\overline{Y}$, an estimator of the unknown population mean of $Y$, $\mu_Y$. Because $\overline{Y}$ is calculated using a randomly drawn sample, $\overline{Y}$ is a random variable that takes on different values from one sample to the next; the probability of these different values is summarized in its sampling distribution. Although the sampling distribution of $\overline{Y}$ can be complicated when the sample size is small, it is possible to make certain statements about it that hold for all $n$. In particular, the mean of the sampling distribution is $\mu_Y$, that is, $E(\overline{Y}) = \mu_Y$, so $\overline{Y}$ is an unbiased estimator of $\mu_Y$. If $n$ is large, then more can be said about the sampling distribution. In particular, the central limit theorem (Section 2.6) states that this distribution is approximately normal.

***The sampling distribution of $\hat{\beta}_0$ and $\hat{\beta}_1$.*** These ideas carry over to the OLS estimators $\hat{\beta}_0$ and $\hat{\beta}_1$ of the unknown intercept $\beta_0$ and slope $\beta_1$ of the population regression line. Because the OLS estimators are calculated using a random sample, $\hat{\beta}_0$ and $\hat{\beta}_1$ are random variables that take on different values from one sample to the next; the probability of these different values is summarized in their sampling distributions.

Although the sampling distribution of $\hat{\beta}_0$ and $\hat{\beta}_1$ can be complicated when the sample size is small, it is possible to make certain statements about it that hold for all $n$. In particular, the mean of the sampling distributions of $\hat{\beta}_0$ and $\hat{\beta}_1$ are $\beta_0$ and $\beta_1$. In other words, under the least squares assumptions in Key Concept 4.3,

$$E(\hat{\beta}_0) = \beta_0 \text{ and } E(\hat{\beta}_1) = \beta_1; \tag{4.20}$$

that is, $\hat{\beta}_0$ and $\hat{\beta}_1$ are unbiased estimators of $\beta_0$ and $\beta_1$. The proof that $\hat{\beta}_1$ is unbiased is given in Appendix 4.3, and the proof that $\hat{\beta}_0$ is unbiased is left as Exercise 4.7.

If the sample is sufficiently large, by the central limit theorem the sampling distribution of $\hat{\beta}_0$ and $\hat{\beta}_1$ is well approximated by the bivariate normal distribution (Section 2.4). This implies that the marginal distributions of $\hat{\beta}_0$ and $\hat{\beta}_1$ are normal in large samples.

This argument invokes the central limit theorem. Technically, the central limit theorem concerns the distribution of averages (like $\overline{Y}$). If you examine the numerator in Equation (4.7) for $\hat{\beta}_1$, you will see that it, too, is a type of average—not a simple average, like $\overline{Y}$, but an average of the product, $(Y_i - \overline{Y})(X_i - \overline{X})$. As discussed

## Large-Sample Distributions of $\hat{\beta}_0$ and $\hat{\beta}_1$

**KEY CONCEPT**

4.4

If the least squares assumptions in Key Concept 4.3 hold, then in large samples $\hat{\beta}_0$ and $\hat{\beta}_1$ have a jointly normal sampling distribution. The large-sample normal distribution of $\hat{\beta}_1$ is $N(\beta_1, \sigma_{\hat{\beta}_1}^2)$, where the variance of this distribution, $\sigma_{\hat{\beta}_1}^2$, is

$$\sigma_{\hat{\beta}_1}^2 = \frac{1}{n} \frac{\text{var}[(X_i - \mu_X)u_i]}{[\text{var}(X_i)]^2}. \tag{4.21}$$

The large-sample normal distribution of $\hat{\beta}_0$ is $N(\beta_0, \sigma_{\hat{\beta}_0}^2)$, where

$$\sigma_{\hat{\beta}_0}^2 = \frac{1}{n} \frac{\text{var}(H_i u_i)}{[E(H_i^2)]^2}, \text{ where } H_i = 1 - \left[\frac{\mu_X}{E(X_i^2)}\right]X_i. \tag{4.22}$$

further in Appendix 4.3, the central limit theorem applies to this average so that, like the simpler average $\overline{Y}$, it is normally distributed in large samples.

The normal approximation to the distribution of the OLS estimators in large samples is summarized in Key Concept 4.4. (Appendix 4.3 summarizes the derivation of these formulas.) A relevant question in practice is how large $n$ must be for these approximations to be reliable. In Section 2.6, we suggested that $n = 100$ is sufficiently large for the sampling distribution of $\overline{Y}$ to be well approximated by a normal distribution, and sometimes smaller $n$ suffices. This criterion carries over to the more complicated averages appearing in regression analysis. In virtually all modern econometric applications, $n > 100$, so we will treat the normal approximations to the distributions of the OLS estimators as reliable unless there are good reasons to think otherwise.

The results in Key Concept 4.4 imply that the OLS estimators are consistent — that is, when the sample size is large, $\hat{\beta}_0$ and $\hat{\beta}_1$ will be close to the true population coefficients $\beta_0$ and $\beta_1$ with high probability. This is because the variances $\sigma_{\hat{\beta}_0}^2$ and $\sigma_{\hat{\beta}_1}^2$ of the estimators decrease to zero as $n$ increases ($n$ appears in the denominator of the formulas for the variances), so the distribution of the OLS estimators will be tightly concentrated around their means, $\beta_0$ and $\beta_1$, when $n$ is large.

Another implication of the distributions in Key Concept 4.4 is that, in general, the larger is the variance of $X_i$, the smaller is the variance $\sigma_{\hat{\beta}_1}^2$ of $\hat{\beta}_1$. Mathematically, this implication arises because the variance of $\hat{\beta}_1$ in Equation (4.21) is inversely proportional to the square of the variance of $X_i$: the larger is $\text{var}(X_i)$, the larger is the denominator in Equation (4.21) so the smaller is $\sigma_{\hat{\beta}_1}^2$. To get a better sense

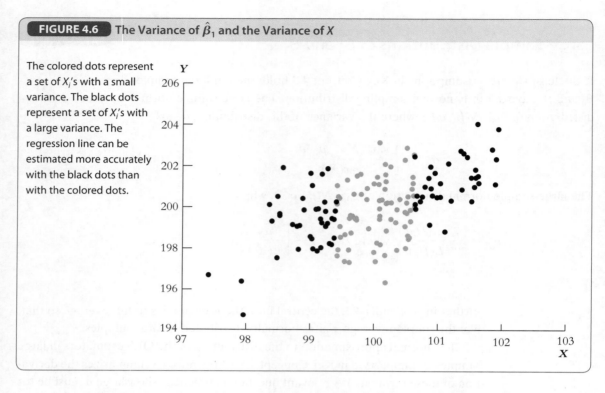

**FIGURE 4.6** The Variance of $\hat{\beta}_1$ and the Variance of $X$

The colored dots represent a set of $X_i$'s with a small variance. The black dots represent a set of $X_i$'s with a large variance. The regression line can be estimated more accurately with the black dots than with the colored dots.

of why this is so, look at Figure 4.6, which presents a scatterplot of 150 artificial data points on $X$ and $Y$. The data points indicated by the colored dots are the 75 observations closest to $\overline{X}$. Suppose you were asked to draw a line as accurately as possible through *either* the colored or the black dots—which would you choose? It would be easier to draw a precise line through the black dots, which have a larger variance than the colored dots. Similarly, the larger the variance of $X$, the more precise is $\hat{\beta}_1$.

The distributions in Key Concept 4.4 also imply that the smaller is the variance of the error $u_i$, the smaller is the variance of $\hat{\beta}_1$. This can be seen mathematically in Equation (4.21) because $u_i$ enters the numerator, but not denominator, of $\sigma^2_{\hat{\beta}_1}$: If all $u_i$ were smaller by a factor of one-half but the $X$'s did not change, then $\sigma_{\hat{\beta}_1}$ would be smaller by a factor of one-half and $\sigma^2_{\hat{\beta}_1}$ would be smaller by a factor of one-fourth (Exercise 4.13). Stated less mathematically, if the errors are smaller (holding the $X$'s fixed), then the data will have a tighter scatter around the population regression line so its slope will be estimated more precisely.

The normal approximation to the sampling distribution of $\hat{\beta}_0$ and $\hat{\beta}_1$ is a powerful tool. With this approximation in hand, we are able to develop methods for making inferences about the true population values of the regression coefficients using only a sample of data.

# 4.6   Conclusion

This chapter has focused on the use of ordinary least squares to estimate the intercept and slope of a population regression line using a sample of $n$ observations on a dependent variable, $Y$, and a single regressor, $X$. There are many ways to draw a straight line through a scatterplot, but doing so using OLS has several virtues. If the least squares assumptions hold, then the OLS estimators of the slope and intercept are unbiased, are consistent, and have a sampling distribution with a variance that is inversely proportional to the sample size $n$. Moreover, if $n$ is large, then the sampling distribution of the OLS estimator is normal.

These important properties of the sampling distribution of the OLS estimator hold under the three least squares assumptions.

The first assumption is that the error term in the linear regression model has a conditional mean of zero, given the regressor $X$. This assumption implies that the OLS estimator is unbiased.

The second assumption is that $(X_i, Y_i)$ are i.i.d., as is the case if the data are collected by simple random sampling. This assumption yields the formula, presented in Key Concept 4.4, for the variance of the sampling distribution of the OLS estimator.

The third assumption is that large outliers are unlikely. Stated more formally, $X$ and $Y$ have finite fourth moments (finite kurtosis). The reason for this assumption is that OLS can be unreliable if there are large outliers. Taken together, the three least squares assumptions imply that the OLS estimator is normally distributed in large samples as described in Key Concept 4.4.

The results in this chapter describe the sampling distribution of the OLS estimator. By themselves, however, these results are not sufficient to test a hypothesis about the value of $\beta_1$ or to construct a confidence interval for $\beta_1$. Doing so requires an estimator of the standard deviation of the sampling distribution—that is, the standard error of the OLS estimator. This step—moving from the sampling distribution of $\hat{\beta}_1$ to its standard error, hypothesis tests, and confidence intervals—is taken in the next chapter.

## Summary

1. The population regression line, $\beta_0 + \beta_1 X$, is the mean of $Y$ as a function of the value of $X$. The slope, $\beta_1$, is the expected change in $Y$ associated with a one-unit change in $X$. The intercept, $\beta_0$, determines the level (or height) of the regression line. Key Concept 4.1 summarizes the terminology of the population linear regression model.

2. The population regression line can be estimated using sample observations $(Y_i, X_i)$, $i = 1, \ldots, n$ by ordinary least squares (OLS). The OLS estimators of the regression intercept and slope are denoted $\hat{\beta}_0$ and $\hat{\beta}_1$.

3. The $R^2$ and standard error of the regression ($SER$) are measures of how close the values of $Y_i$ are to the estimated regression line. The $R^2$ is between 0 and 1, with a larger value indicating that the $Y_i$'s are closer to the line. The standard error of the regression is an estimator of the standard deviation of the regression error.

4. There are three key assumptions for the linear regression model: (1) The regression errors, $u_i$, have a mean of zero, conditional on the regressors $X_i$; (2) the sample observations are i.i.d. random draws from the population; and (3) large outliers are unlikely. If these assumptions hold, the OLS estimators $\hat{\beta}_0$ and $\hat{\beta}_1$ are (1) unbiased, (2) consistent, and (3) normally distributed when the sample is large.

## Key Terms

linear regression model with a single regressor (158)
dependent variable (158)
independent variable (158)
regressor (158)
population regression line (158)
population regression function (158)
population intercept (158)
population slope (158)
population coefficients (158)
parameters (158)
error term (158)
ordinary least squares (OLS) estimators (162)

OLS regression line (162)
sample regression line (162)
sample regression function (162)
predicted value (162)
residual (163)
regression $R^2$ (167)
explained sum of squares ($ESS$) (167)
total sum of squares ($TSS$) (167)
sum of squared residuals ($SSR$) (168)
standard error of the regression ($SER$) (168)
least squares assumptions (170)

---

**MyEconLab Can Help You Get a Better Grade**

MyEconLab     If your exam were tomorrow, would you be ready? For each chapter, **MyEconLab** Practice Tests and Study Plan help you prepare for your exams. You can also find similar Exercises and Review the Concepts Questions now in **MyEconLab**.

To see how it works, turn to the **MyEconLab** spread on pages 2 and 3 of this book and then go to **www.myeconlab.com**.

For additional Empirical Exercises and Data Sets, log on to the Companion Website at **www.pearsonglobaleditions.com/Stock_Watson**.

## Review the Concepts

**4.1**  What is a linear regression model? What is measured by the coefficients of a linear regression model? What is the ordinary least squares estimator?

**4.2**  Explain what is meant by an error term. What assumptions do we make about an error term when estimating an ordinary least squares regression?

**4.3**  What is meant by the assumption that the paired sample observations of $Y_i$ and $X_i$ are independently and identically distributed? Why is this an important assumption for ordinary least-squares estimation? When is this assumption likely to be violated?

**4.4**  Distinguish between the $R^2$ and the standard error of a regression. How do each of these measures describe the fit of a regression?

## Exercises

**4.1**  Suppose that a researcher, using data on class size ($CS$) and average test scores from 50 third-grade classes, estimates the OLS regression:

$$\widehat{TestScore} = 640.3 - 4.93 \times CS, R^2 = 0.11, SER = 8.7.$$

**a.**  A classroom has 25 students. What is the regression's prediction for that classroom's average test score?

**b.**  Last year a classroom had 21 students, and this year it has 24 students. What is the regression's prediction for the change in the classroom average test score?

**c.**  The sample average class size across the 50 classrooms is 22.8. What is the sample average of the test scores across the 50 classrooms? (*Hint:* Review the formulas for the OLS estimators.)

**d.**  What is the sample standard deviation of test scores across the 50 classrooms? (*Hint:* Review the formulas for the $R^2$ and $SER$.)

**4.2**  Suppose a random sample of 100 20-year-old men is selected from a population and that these men's height and weight are recorded. A regression of weight on height yields

$$\widehat{Weight} = -79.24 + 4.16 \times Height, R^2 = 0.72, SER = 12.6,$$

where *Weight* is measured in pounds and *Height* is measured in inches.

a. What is the regression's weight prediction for someone who is (i) 64 in. tall, (ii) 68 in. tall, (iii) 72 in. tall?

b. A man has a late growth spurt and grows 2 in. over the course of a year. What is the regression's prediction for the increase in this man's weight?

c. Suppose, that instead of measuring *Weight* and *Height* in pounds and inches, these variables are measured in centimeters and kilograms. What are the regression estimates from this new centimeter-kilogram regression? (Give all results, estimated coefficients, $R^2$, and *SER*.)

4.3  A regression of average weekly earnings (*AWE*, measured in dollars) on age (measured in years) using a random sample of college-educated full-time workers aged 25–65 yields the following:

$$\widehat{AWE} = 696.7 + 9.6 \times Age, R^2 = 0.023, SER = 624.1.$$

a. Explain what the coefficient values 696.7 and 9.6 mean.

b. The standard error of the regression (*SER*) is 624.1. What are the units of measurement for the *SER*? (Dollars? Years? Or is *SER* unit-free?)

c. The regression $R^2$ is 0.023. What are the units of measurement for the $R^2$? (Dollars? Years? Or is $R^2$ unit-free?)

d. What does the regression predict will be the earnings for a 25-year-old worker? For a 45-year-old worker?

e. Will the regression give reliable predictions for a 99-year-old worker? Why or why not?

f. Given what you know about the distribution of earnings, do you think it is plausible that the distribution of errors in the regression is normal? (*Hint:* Do you think that the distribution is symmetric or skewed? What is the smallest value of earnings, and is it consistent with a normal distribution?)

g. The average age in this sample is 41.6 years. What is the average value of *AWE* in the sample? (*Hint:* Review Key Concept 4.2.)

4.4  Read the box "The 'Beta' of a Stock" in Section 4.2.

a. Suppose that the value of $\beta$ is greater than 1 for a particular stock. Show that the variance of $(R - R_f)$ for this stock is greater than the variance of $(R_m - R_t)$.

b. Suppose that the value of $\beta$ is less than 1 for a particular stock. Is it possible that variance of $(R - R_f)$ for this stock is greater than the variance of $(R_m - R_t)$? (*Hint:* Don't forget the regression error.)

    **c.** In a given year, the rate of return on 3-month Treasury bills is 2.0% and the rate of return on a large diversified portfolio of stocks (the S&P 500) is 5.3%. For each company listed in the table in the box, use the estimated value of $\beta$ to estimate the stock's expected rate of return.

**4.5** A researcher runs an experiment to measure the impact a short nap has on memory. 200 participants in the sample are allowed to take a short nap of either 60 minutes or 75 minutes. After waking up, each of the participants takes a short test on short-term recall. Each participant is randomly assigned one of the examination times, based on the flip of a coin. Let $Y_i$ denote the number of points scored on the test by the $i^{th}$ participant $(0 \ldots Y_i \ldots 100)$, let $X_i$ denote the amount of time for which the participant slept prior to taking the test ($X_i = 60$ or $75$), and consider the regression model $Y_i = b_0 + b_1 X_i + u_i$.

    **a.** Explain what the term $u_i$ represents. Why will different students have different values of $u_i$?

    **b.** What is $E(u_i|X_i)$? Are the estimated coefficients unbiased?

    **c.** What concerns might you have about ensuring compliance among participants?

    **d.** The estimated regression is $Y_i = 55 + 0.17 X_i$.

       i. Compute the estimated regression's prediction for the average score of participants who slept for 60 minutes before taking the test. Repeat for 75 minutes and 90 minutes.

       ii. Compute the estimated gain in score for a participant who is given an additional 5 minutes on the exam.

**4.6** Show that the first least squares assumption, $E(u_i|X_i) = 0$, implies that $E(Y_i|X_i) = \beta_0 + \beta_1 X_i$.

**4.7** Show that $\hat{\beta}_0$ is an unbiased estimator of $\beta_0$. (*Hint:* Use the fact that $\hat{\beta}_1$ is unbiased, which is shown in Appendix 4.3.)

**4.8** Suppose that all of the regression assumptions in Key Concept 4.3 are satisfied except that the first assumption is replaced with $E(u_i|X_i) = 2$. Which parts of Key Concept 4.4 continue to hold? Which change? Why? (Is $\hat{\beta}_1$ normally distributed in large samples with mean and variance given in Key Concept 4.4? What about $\hat{\beta}_0$?)

**4.9**   **a.** A linear regression yields $\hat{\beta}_1 = 0$. Show that $R^2 = 0$.

    **b.** A linear regression yields $R^2 = 0$. Does this imply that $\hat{\beta}_1 = 0$?

**4.10** Suppose that $Y_i = \beta_0 + \beta_1 X_i + u_i$, where $(X_i, u_i)$ are i.i.d., and $X_i$ is a Bernoulli random variable with $\Pr(X = 1) = 0.20$. When $X = 1, u_i$ is $N(0, 4)$; when $X = 0, u_i$ is $N(0, 1)$.

   **a.** Show that the regression assumptions in Key Concept 4.3 are satisfied.

   **b.** Derive an expression for the large-sample variance of $\hat{\beta}_1$. [*Hint:* Evaluate the terms in Equation (4.21).]

**4.11** Consider the regression model $Y_i = \beta_0 + \beta_1 X_i + u_i$.

   **a.** Suppose you know that $\beta_0 = 0$. Derive a formula for the least squares estimator of $\beta_1$.

   **b.** Suppose you know that $\beta_0 = 4$. Derive a formula for the least squares estimator of $\beta_1$.

**4.12** **a.** Show that the regression $R^2$ in the regression of $Y$ on $X$ is the squared value of the sample correlation between $X$ and $Y$. That is, show that $R^2 = r_{XY}^2$.

   **b.** Show that the $R^2$ from the regression of $Y$ on $X$ is the same as the $R^2$ from the regression of $X$ on $Y$.

   **c.** Show that $\hat{\beta}_1 = r_{XY}(s_Y/s_X)$, where $r_{XY}$ is the sample correlation between $X$ and $Y$, and $s_X$ and $s_Y$ are the sample standard deviations of $X$ and $Y$.

**4.13** Suppose that $Y_i = \beta_0 + \beta_1 X_i + \kappa u_i$, where $\kappa$ is a nonzero constant and $(Y_i, X_i)$ satisfy the three least squares assumptions. Show that the large sample variance of $\hat{\beta}_1$ is given by $\sigma_{\hat{\beta}_1}^2 = \kappa^2 \frac{1}{n} \frac{\operatorname{var}[(X_i - \mu_X)u_i]}{[\operatorname{var}(X_i)^2]}$. [*Hint:* This equation is the variance given in Equation (4.21) multiplied by $\kappa^2$.]

**4.14** Show that the sample regression line passes through the point $(\overline{X}, \overline{Y})$.

## Empirical Exercises

(Only two empirical exercises for this chapter are given in the text, but you can find more on the text website, **www.pearsonglobaleditions.com/Stock_Watson**.)

**E4.1** On the text website, **www.pearsonglobaleditions.com/Stock_Watson**, you will find the data file **Growth**, which contains data on average growth rates from 1960 through 1995 for 65 countries, along with variables that are potentially related to growth. A detailed description is given in

**Growth_Description**, also available on the website. In this exercise, you will investigate the relationship between growth and trade.[1]

**a.** Construct a scatterplot of average annual growth rate (*Growth*) on the average trade share (*TradeShare*). Does there appear to be a relationship between the variables?

**b.** One country, Malta, has a trade share much larger than the other countries. Find Malta on the scatterplot. Does Malta look like an outlier?

**c.** Using all observations, run a regression of *Growth* on *TradeShare*. What is the estimated slope? What is the estimated intercept? Use the regression to predict the growth rate for a country with a trade share of 0.5 and with a trade share equal to 1.0.

**d.** Estimate the same regression, excluding the data from Malta. Answer the same questions in (c).

**e.** Plot the estimated regression functions from (c) and (d). Using the scatterplot in (a), explain why the regression function that includes Malta is steeper than the regression function that excludes Malta.

**f.** Where is Malta? Why is the Malta trade share so large? Should Malta be included or excluded from the analysis?

**E4.2** On the text website, **www.pearsonglobaleditions.com/Stock_Watson**, you will find the data file **Earnings_and_Height**, which contains data on earnings, height, and other characteristics of a random sample of U.S. workers.[2] A detailed description is given in **Earnings_and_Height_Description**, also available on the website. In this exercise, you will investigate the relationship between earnings and height.

**a.** What is the median value of height in the sample?

**b.** i. Estimate average earnings for workers whose height is at most 67 inches.

   ii. Estimate average earnings for workers whose height is greater than 67 inches.

---

[1]These data were provided by Professor Ross Levine of the University of California at Berkeley and were used in his paper with Thorsten Beck and Norman Loayza, "Finance and the Sources of Growth," *Journal of Financial Economics*, 2000, 58: 261–300.

[2]These data were provided by Professors Anne Case (Princeton University) and Christina Paxson (Brown University) and were used in their paper "Stature and Status: Height, Ability, and Labor Market Outcomes," *Journal of Political Economy*, 2008, 116(3): 499–532.

      iii. On average, do taller workers earn more than shorter workers? How much more? What is a 95% confidence interval for the difference in average earnings?

  **c.** Construct a scatterplot of annual earnings (*Earnings*) on height (*Height*). Notice that the points on the plot fall along horizontal lines. (There are only 23 distinct values of *Earnings*). Why? (*Hint:* Carefully read the detailed data description.)

  **d.** Run a regression of *Earnings* on *Height*.

      i. What is the estimated slope?

      ii. Use the estimated regression to predict earnings for a worker who is 67 inches tall, for a worker who is 70 inches tall, and for a worker who is 65 inches tall.

  **e.** Suppose height were measured in centimeters instead of inches. Answer the following questions about the *Earnings* on *Height* (in cm) regression.

      i. What is the estimated slope of the regression?

      ii. What is the estimated intercept?

      iii. What is the $R^2$?

      iv. What is the standard error of the regression?

  **f.** Run a regression of *Earnings* on *Height*, using data for female workers only.

      i. What is the estimated slope?

      ii. A randomly selected woman is 1 inch taller than the average woman in the sample. Would you predict her earnings to be higher or lower than the average earnings for women in the sample? By how much?

  **g.** Repeat (f) for male workers.

  **h.** Do you think that height is uncorrelated with other factors that cause earning? That is, do you think that the regression error term, say $u_i$, has a conditional mean of zero, given *Height* $(X_i)$? (You will investigate this more in the *Earnings* and *Height* exercises in later chapters.)

**APPENDIX**

## 4.1  The California Test Score Data Set

The California Standardized Testing and Reporting data set contains data on test performance, school characteristics, and student demographic backgrounds. The data used here are from all 420 K–6 and K–8 districts in California with data available for 1999. Test scores are the average of the reading and math scores on the Stanford 9 Achievement Test, a standardized test administered to fifth-grade students. School characteristics (averaged across the district) include enrollment, number of teachers (measured as "full-time equivalents"), number of computers per classroom, and expenditures per student. The student–teacher ratio used here is the number of students in the district divided by the number of full-time equivalent teachers. Demographic variables for the students also are averaged across the district. The demographic variables include the percentage of students who are in the public assistance program CalWorks (formerly AFDC), the percentage of students who qualify for a reduced-price lunch, and the percentage of students who are English learners (that is, students for whom English is a second language). All of these data were obtained from the California Department of Education (www.cde.ca.gov).

**APPENDIX**

## 4.2  Derivation of the OLS Estimators

This appendix uses calculus to derive the formulas for the OLS estimators given in Key Concept 4.2. To minimize the sum of squared prediction mistakes $\sum_{i=1}^{n}(Y_i - b_0 - b_1 X_i)^2$ [Equation (4.6)], first take the partial derivatives with respect to $b_0$ and $b_1$:

$$\frac{\partial}{\partial b_0}\sum_{i=1}^{n}(Y_i - b_0 - b_1 X_i)^2 = -2\sum_{i=1}^{n}(Y_i - b_0 - b_1 X_i) \text{ and} \tag{4.23}$$

$$\frac{\partial}{\partial b_1}\sum_{i=1}^{n}(Y_i - b_0 - b_1 X_i)^2 = -2\sum_{i=1}^{n}(Y_i - b_0 - b_1 X_i)X_i. \tag{4.24}$$

The OLS estimators, $\hat{\beta}_0$ and $\hat{\beta}_1$, are the values of $b_0$ and $b_1$ that minimize $\sum_{i=1}^{n}(Y_i - b_0 - b_1 X_i)^2$, or, equivalently, the values of $b_0$ and $b_1$ for which the derivatives in Equations (4.23) and (4.24) equal zero. Accordingly, setting these derivatives equal to zero, collecting terms, and dividing by $n$ shows that the OLS estimators, $\hat{\beta}_0$ and $\hat{\beta}_1$, must satisfy the two equations

$$\overline{Y} - \hat{\beta}_0 - \hat{\beta}_1\overline{X} = 0 \text{ and} \tag{4.25}$$

$$\frac{1}{n}\sum_{i=1}^{n}X_iY_i - \hat{\beta}_0\overline{X} - \hat{\beta}_1\frac{1}{n}\sum_{i=1}^{n}X_i^2 = 0. \tag{4.26}$$

Solving this pair of equations for $\hat{\beta}_0$ and $\hat{\beta}_1$ yields

$$\hat{\beta}_1 = \frac{\frac{1}{n}\sum_{i=1}^{n}X_iY_i - \overline{X}\,\overline{Y}}{\frac{1}{n}\sum_{i=1}^{n}X_i^2 - (\overline{X})^2} = \frac{\sum_{i=1}^{n}(X_i - \overline{X})(Y_i - \overline{Y})}{\sum_{i=1}^{n}(X_i - \overline{X})^2} \text{ and} \tag{4.27}$$

$$\hat{\beta}_0 = \overline{Y} - \hat{\beta}_1\overline{X}. \tag{4.28}$$

Equations (4.27) and (4.28) are the formulas for $\hat{\beta}_0$ and $\hat{\beta}_1$ given in Key Concept 4.2; the formula $\hat{\beta}_1 = s_{XY}/s_X^2$ is obtained by dividing the numerator and denominator in Equation (4.27) by $n - 1$.

## 4.3 Sampling Distribution of the OLS Estimator

In this appendix, we show that the OLS estimator $\hat{\beta}_1$ is unbiased and, in large samples, has the normal sampling distribution given in Key Concept 4.4.

### Representation of $\hat{\beta}_1$ in Terms of the Regressors and Errors

We start by providing an expression for $\hat{\beta}_1$ in terms of the regressors and errors. Because $Y_i = \beta_0 + \beta_1X_i + u_i$, $Y_i - \overline{Y} = \beta_1(X_i - \overline{X}) + u_i - \overline{u}$, so the numerator of the formula for $\hat{\beta}_1$ in Equation (4.27) is

$$\sum_{i=1}^{n}(X_i - \overline{X})(Y_i - \overline{Y}) = \sum_{i=1}^{n}(X_i - \overline{X})[\beta_1(X_i - \overline{X}) + (u_i - \overline{u})]$$

$$= \beta_1\sum_{i=1}^{n}(X_i - \overline{X})^2 + \sum_{i=1}^{n}(X_i - \overline{X})(u_i - \overline{u}). \tag{4.29}$$

Now $\sum_{i=1}^{n}(X_i - \overline{X})(u_i - \overline{u}) = \sum_{i=1}^{n}(X_i - \overline{X})u_i - \sum_{i=1}^{n}(X_i - \overline{X})\overline{u} = \sum_{i=1}^{n}(X_i - \overline{X})u_i$, where the final equality follows from the definition of $\overline{X}$, which implies that $\sum_{i=1}^{n}(X_i - \overline{X})\overline{u} = [\sum_{i=1}^{n}X_i - n\overline{X}]\overline{u} = 0$. Substituting $\sum_{i=1}^{n}(X_i - \overline{X})(u_i - \overline{u}) = \sum_{i=1}^{n}(X_i - \overline{X})u_i$ into the final expression in Equation (4.29) yields $\sum_{i=1}^{n}(X_i - \overline{X})(Y_i - \overline{Y}) = \beta_1\sum_{i=1}^{n}(X_i - \overline{X})^2 + \sum_{i=1}^{n}(X_i - \overline{X})u_i$. Substituting this expression in turn into the formula for $\hat{\beta}_1$ in Equation (4.27) yields

$$\hat{\beta}_1 = \beta_1 + \frac{\frac{1}{n}\sum_{i=1}^{n}(X_i - \overline{X})u_i}{\frac{1}{n}\sum_{i=1}^{n}(X_i - \overline{X})^2}. \tag{4.30}$$

## Proof That $\hat{\beta}_1$ Is Unbiased

The expectation of $\hat{\beta}_1$ is obtained by taking the expectation of both sides of Equation (4.30). Thus,

$$E(\hat{\beta}_1) = \beta_1 + E\left[\frac{\frac{1}{n}\sum_{i=1}^{n}(X_i - \overline{X})u_i}{\frac{1}{n}\sum_{i=1}^{n}(X_i - \overline{X})^2}\right]$$

$$= \beta_1 + E\left[\frac{\frac{1}{n}\sum_{i=1}^{n}(X_i - \overline{X})E(u_i|X_i, \ldots, X_n)}{\frac{1}{n}\sum_{i=1}^{n}(X_i - \overline{X})^2}\right] = \beta_1, \tag{4.31}$$

where the second equality in Equation (4.31) follows by using the law of iterated expectations (Section 2.3). By the second least squares assumption, $u_i$ is distributed independently of $X$ for all observations other than $i$, so $E(u_i|X_1, \ldots, X_n) = E(u_i|X_i)$. By the first least squares assumption, however, $E(u_i|X_i) = 0$. It follows that the conditional expectation in large brackets in the second line of Equation (4.31) is zero, so that $E(\hat{\beta}_1 - \beta_1|X_1, \ldots X_n) = 0$. Equivalently, $E(\hat{\beta}_1|X_1, \ldots, X_n) = \beta_1$; that is, $\hat{\beta}_1$ is conditionally unbiased, given $X_1, \ldots, X_n$. By the law of iterated expectations, $E(\hat{\beta}_1 - \beta_1) = E[E(\hat{\beta}_1 - \beta_1|X_1, \ldots, X_n)] = 0$, so that $E(\hat{\beta}_1) = \beta_1$; that is, $\hat{\beta}_1$ is unbiased.

## Large-Sample Normal Distribution of the OLS Estimator

The large-sample normal approximation to the limiting distribution of $\hat{\beta}_1$ (Key Concept 4.4) is obtained by considering the behavior of the final term in Equation (4.30).

First consider the numerator of this term. Because $\overline{X}$ is consistent, if the sample size is large, $\overline{X}$ is nearly equal to $\mu_X$. Thus, to a close approximation, the term in the numerator of Equation (4.30) is the sample average $\overline{v}$, where $v_i = (X_i - \mu_X)u_i$. By the first least squares assumption, $v_i$ has a mean of zero. By the second least squares assumption, $v_i$ is i.i.d. The variance of $v_i$ is $\sigma_v^2 = [\text{var}(X_i - \mu_X)u_i]$, which, by the third least squares assumption, is nonzero and finite. Therefore, $\overline{v}$ satisfies all the requirements of the central limit theorem (Key Concept 2.7). Thus $\overline{v}/\sigma_{\overline{v}}$ is, in large samples, distributed $N(0, 1)$, where $\sigma_{\overline{v}}^2 = \sigma_v^2/n$. Thus the distribution of $\overline{v}$ is well approximated by the $N(0, \sigma_v^2/n)$ distribution.

Next consider the expression in the denominator in Equation (4.30); this is the sample variance of $X$ (except dividing by $n$ rather than $n - 1$, which is inconsequential if $n$ is large). As discussed in Section 3.2 [Equation (3.8)], the sample variance is a consistent estimator of the population variance, so in large samples it is arbitrarily close to the population variance of $X$.

Combining these two results, we have that, in large samples, $\hat{\beta}_1 - \beta_1 \cong \overline{v}/\text{var}(X_i)$, so that the sampling distribution of $\hat{\beta}_1$ is, in large samples, $N(\beta_1, \sigma_{\hat{\beta}_1}^2)$, where $\sigma_{\hat{\beta}_1}^2 = \text{var}(\overline{v})/[\text{var}(X_i)]^2 = \text{var}[(X_i - \mu_X)u_i]/\{n[\text{var}(X_i)]^2\}$, which is the expression in Equation (4.21).

## Some Additional Algebraic Facts About OLS

The OLS residuals and predicted values satisfy

$$\frac{1}{n}\sum_{i=1}^{n}\hat{u}_i = 0, \tag{4.32}$$

$$\frac{1}{n}\sum_{i=1}^{n}\hat{Y}_i = \overline{Y}, \tag{4.33}$$

$$\sum_{i=1}^{n}\hat{u}_i X_i = 0 \text{ and } s_{\hat{u}X} = 0, \text{ and} \tag{4.34}$$

$$TSS = SSR + ESS. \tag{4.35}$$

Equations (4.32) through (4.35) say that the sample average of the OLS residuals is zero; the sample average of the OLS predicted values equals $\overline{Y}$; the sample covariance $s_{\hat{u}X}$ between the OLS residuals and the regressors is zero; and the total sum of squares is the sum of squared residuals and the explained sum of squares. [The $ESS$, $TSS$, and $SSR$ are defined in Equations (4.14), (4.15), and (4.17).]

To verify Equation (4.32), note that the definition of $\hat{\beta}_0$ lets us write the OLS residuals as $\hat{u}_i = Y_i - \hat{\beta}_0 - \hat{\beta}_1 X_i = (Y_i - \overline{Y}) - \hat{\beta}_1(X_i - \overline{X})$; thus

$$\sum_{i=1}^{n}\hat{u}_i = \sum_{i=1}^{n}(Y_i - \overline{Y}) - \hat{\beta}_1\sum_{i=1}^{n}(X_i - \overline{X}).$$

But the definitions of $\overline{Y}$ and $\overline{X}$ imply that $\sum_{i=1}^{n}(Y_i - \overline{Y}) = 0$ and $\sum_{i=1}^{n}(X_i - \overline{X}) = 0$, so $\sum_{i=1}^{n}\hat{u}_i = 0$.

To verify Equation (4.33), note that $Y_i = \hat{Y}_i + \hat{u}_i$, so $\sum_{i=1}^{n} Y_i = \sum_{i=1}^{n} \hat{Y}_i + \sum_{i=1}^{n} \hat{u}_1 = \sum_{i=1}^{n} \hat{Y}_i$, where the second equality is a consequence of Equation (4.32).

To verify Equation (4.34), note that $\sum_{i=1}^{n} \hat{u}_i = 0$ implies $\sum_{i=1}^{n} \hat{u}_i X_i = \sum_{i=1}^{n} \hat{u}_i (X_i - \overline{X})$, so

$$\sum_{i=1}^{n} \hat{u}_i X_i = \sum_{i=1}^{n} [(Y_i - \overline{Y}) - \hat{\beta}_1 (X_i - \overline{X})](X_i - \overline{X})$$
$$= \sum_{i=1}^{n} (Y_i - \overline{Y})(X_i - \overline{X}) - \hat{\beta}_1 \sum_{i=1}^{n} (X_i - \overline{X})^2 = 0, \qquad (4.36)$$

where the final equality in Equation (4.36) is obtained using the formula for $\hat{\beta}_1$ in Equation (4.27). This result, combined with the preceding results, implies that $s_{\hat{u}X} = 0$.

Equation (4.35) follows from the previous results and some algebra:

$$TSS = \sum_{i=1}^{n} (Y_i - \overline{Y})^2 = \sum_{i=1}^{n} (Y_i - \hat{Y}_i + \hat{Y}_i - \overline{Y})^2$$
$$= \sum_{i=1}^{n} (Y_i - \hat{Y}_i)^2 + \sum_{i=1}^{n} (\hat{Y}_i - \overline{Y})^2 + 2 \sum_{i=1}^{n} (Y_i - \hat{Y}_i)(\hat{Y}_i - \overline{Y})$$
$$= SSR + ESS + 2 \sum_{i=1}^{n} \hat{u}_i \hat{Y}_i = SSR + ESS, \qquad (4.37)$$

where the final equality follows from $\sum_{i=1}^{n} \hat{u}_i \hat{Y}_i = \sum_{i=1}^{n} \hat{u}_i (\hat{\beta}_0 + \hat{\beta}_1 X_i) = \hat{\beta}_0 \sum_{i=1}^{n} \hat{u}_i + \hat{\beta}_1 \sum_{i=1}^{n} \hat{u}_i X_i = 0$ by the previous results.

# 5 Regression with a Single Regressor: Hypothesis Tests and Confidence Intervals

This chapter continues the treatment of linear regression with a single regressor. Chapter 4 explained how the OLS estimator $\hat{\beta}_1$ of the slope coefficient $\beta_1$ differs from one sample to the next—that is, how $\hat{\beta}_1$ has a sampling distribution. In this chapter, we show how knowledge of this sampling distribution can be used to make statements about $\beta_1$ that accurately summarize the sampling uncertainty. The starting point is the standard error of the OLS estimator, which measures the spread of the sampling distribution of $\hat{\beta}_1$. Section 5.1 provides an expression for this standard error (and for the standard error of the OLS estimator of the intercept), then shows how to use $\hat{\beta}_1$ and its standard error to test hypotheses. Section 5.2 explains how to construct confidence intervals for $\beta_1$. Section 5.3 takes up the special case of a binary regressor.

Sections 5.1 through 5.3 assume that the three least squares assumptions of Chapter 4 hold. If, in addition, some stronger conditions hold, then some stronger results can be derived regarding the distribution of the OLS estimator. One of these stronger conditions is that the errors are homoskedastic, a concept introduced in Section 5.4. Section 5.5 presents the Gauss–Markov theorem, which states that, under certain conditions, OLS is efficient (has the smallest variance) among a certain class of estimators. Section 5.6 discusses the distribution of the OLS estimator when the population distribution of the regression errors is normal.

## 5.1 Testing Hypotheses About One of the Regression Coefficients

Your client, the superintendent, calls you with a problem. She has an angry taxpayer in her office who asserts that cutting class size will not help boost test scores, so reducing them is a waste of money. Class size, the taxpayer claims, has no effect on test scores.

The taxpayer's claim can be rephrased in the language of regression analysis. Because the effect on test scores of a unit change in class size is $\beta_{ClassSize}$, the taxpayer is asserting that the population regression line is flat—that is, the slope $\beta_{ClassSize}$ of the population regression line is zero. Is there, the superintendent asks,

## General Form of the *t*-Statistic

In general, the *t*-statistic has the form

$$t = \frac{\text{estimator} - \text{hypothesized value}}{\text{standard error of the estimator}}. \qquad (5.1)$$

evidence in your sample of 420 observations on California school districts that this slope is nonzero? Can you reject the taxpayer's hypothesis that $\beta_{ClassSize} = 0$, or should you accept it, at least tentatively pending further new evidence?

This section discusses tests of hypotheses about the slope $\beta_1$ or intercept $\beta_0$ of the population regression line. We start by discussing two-sided tests of the slope $\beta_1$ in detail, then turn to one-sided tests and to tests of hypotheses regarding the intercept $\beta_0$.

### Two-Sided Hypotheses Concerning $\beta_1$

The general approach to testing hypotheses about the coefficient $\beta_1$ is the same as to testing hypotheses about the population mean, so we begin with a brief review.

*Testing hypotheses about the population mean.* Recall from Section 3.2 that the null hypothesis that the mean of $Y$ is a specific value $\mu_{Y,0}$ can be written as $H_0$: $E(Y) = \mu_{Y,0}$, and the two-sided alternative is $H_1$: $E(Y) \neq \mu_{Y,0}$.

The test of the null hypothesis $H_0$ against the two-sided alternative proceeds as in the three steps summarized in Key Concept 3.6. The first is to compute the standard error of $\overline{Y}$, $SE(\overline{Y})$, which is an estimator of the standard deviation of the sampling distribution of $\overline{Y}$. The second step is to compute the *t*-statistic, which has the general form given in Key Concept 5.1; applied here, the *t*-statistic is $t = (\overline{Y} - \mu_{Y,0})/SE(\overline{Y})$.

The third step is to compute the *p*-value, which is the smallest significance level at which the null hypothesis could be rejected, based on the test statistic actually observed; equivalently, the *p*-value is the probability of obtaining a statistic, by random sampling variation, at least as different from the null hypothesis value as is the statistic actually observed, assuming that the null hypothesis is correct (Key Concept 3.5). Because the *t*-statistic has a standard normal distribution in large samples under the null hypothesis, the *p*-value for a two-sided hypothesis test is $2\Phi(-|t^{act}|)$, where $t^{act}$ is the value of the *t*-statistic actually computed and $\Phi$ is the cumulative standard normal distribution tabulated in Appendix Table 1. Alternatively, the third step can be replaced by simply comparing the $t$-statistic to the critical value appropriate for the test with the desired significance level. For example, a two-sided test with a 5% significance level would reject the null hypothesis if $|t^{act}| > 1.96$. In this case, the population mean is said to be statistically significantly different from the hypothesized value at the 5% significance level.

*Testing hypotheses about the slope $\beta_1$.* At a theoretical level, the critical feature justifying the foregoing testing procedure for the population mean is that, in large samples, the sampling distribution of $\overline{Y}$ is approximately normal. Because $\hat{\beta}_1$ also has a normal sampling distribution in large samples, hypotheses about the true value of the slope $\beta_1$ can be tested using the same general approach.

The null and alternative hypotheses need to be stated precisely before they can be tested. The angry taxpayer's hypothesis is that $\beta_{ClassSize} = 0$. More generally, under the null hypothesis the true population slope $\beta_1$ takes on some specific value, $\beta_{1,0}$. Under the two-sided alternative, $\beta_1$ does not equal $\beta_{1,0}$. That is, the **null hypothesis** and the **two-sided alternative hypothesis** are

$$H_0: \beta_1 = \beta_{1,0} \text{ vs. } H_1: \beta_1 \neq \beta_{1,0} \quad \text{(two-sided alternative).} \quad (5.2)$$

To test the null hypothesis $H_0$, we follow the same three steps as for the population mean.

The first step is to compute the **standard error of $\hat{\beta}_1$, $SE(\hat{\beta}_1)$**. The standard error of $\hat{\beta}_1$ is an estimator of $\sigma_{\hat{\beta}_1}$ the standard deviation of the sampling distribution of $\hat{\beta}_1$. Specifically,

$$SE(\hat{\beta}_1) = \sqrt{\hat{\sigma}^2_{\hat{\beta}_1}}, \quad (5.3)$$

where

$$\hat{\sigma}^2_{\hat{\beta}_1} = \frac{1}{n} \times \frac{\dfrac{1}{n-2}\sum_{i=1}^{n}(X_i - \overline{X})^2 \hat{u}_i^2}{\left[\dfrac{1}{n}\sum_{i=1}^{n}(X_i - \overline{X})^2\right]^2}. \quad (5.4)$$

The estimator of the variance in Equation (5.4) is discussed in Appendix (5.1). Although the formula for $\hat{\sigma}^2_{\hat{\beta}_1}$ is complicated, in applications the standard error is computed by regression software so that it is easy to use in practice.

The second step is to compute the *t*-**statistic**,

$$t = \frac{\hat{\beta}_1 - \beta_{1,0}}{SE(\hat{\beta}_1)}. \quad (5.5)$$

## Testing the Hypothesis $\beta_1 = \beta_{1,0}$ Against the Alternative $\beta_1 \neq \beta_{1,0}$

**KEY CONCEPT**

**5.2**

1. Compute the standard error of $\hat{\beta}_1$, $SE(\hat{\beta}_1)$ [Equation (5.3)].
2. Compute the $t$-statistic [Equation (5.5)].
3. Compute the $p$-value [Equation (5.7)]. Reject the hypothesis at the 5% significance level if the $p$-value is less than 0.05 or, equivalently, if $|t^{act}| > 1.96$.

The standard error and (typically) the $t$-statistic and $p$-value testing $\beta_1 = 0$ are computed automatically by regression software.

The third step is to compute the **$p$-value**, the probability of observing a value of $\hat{\beta}_1$ at least as different from $\beta_{1,0}$ as the estimate actually computed ($\hat{\beta}_1^{act}$), assuming that the null hypothesis is correct. Stated mathematically,

$$p\text{-value} = \Pr_{H_0}\left[|\hat{\beta}_1 - \beta_{1,0}| > |\hat{\beta}_1^{act} - \beta_{1,0}|\right]$$

$$= \Pr_{H_0}\left[\left|\frac{\hat{\beta}_1 - \beta_{1,0}}{SE(\hat{\beta}_1)}\right| > \left|\frac{\hat{\beta}_1^{act} - \beta_{1,0}}{SE(\hat{\beta}_1)}\right|\right] = \Pr_{H_0}(|t| > |t^{act}|), \quad (5.6)$$

where $\Pr_{H_0}$ denotes the probability computed under the null hypothesis, the second equality follows by dividing by $SE(\hat{\beta}_1)$, and $t^{act}$ is the value of the $t$-statistic actually computed. Because $\hat{\beta}_1$ is approximately normally distributed in large samples, under the null hypothesis the $t$-statistic is approximately distributed as a standard normal random variable, so in large samples,

$$p\text{-value} = \Pr(|Z| > |t^{act}|) = 2\Phi(-|t^{act}|). \quad (5.7)$$

A $p$-value of less than 5% provides evidence against the null hypothesis in the sense that, under the null hypothesis, the probability of obtaining a value of $\hat{\beta}_1$ at least as far from the null as that actually observed is less than 5%. If so, the null hypothesis is rejected at the 5% significance level.

Alternatively, the hypothesis can be tested at the 5% significance level simply by comparing the absolute value of the $t$-statistic to 1.96, the critical value for a two-sided test, and rejecting the null hypothesis at the 5% level if $|t^{act}| > 1.96$.

These steps are summarized in Key Concept 5.2.

*Reporting regression equations and application to test scores.* The OLS regression of the test score against the student–teacher ratio, reported in Equation (4.11), yielded $\hat{\beta}_0 = 698.9$ and $\hat{\beta}_1 = -2.28$. The standard errors of these estimates are $SE(\hat{\beta}_0) = 10.4$ and $SE(\hat{\beta}_1) = 0.52$.

Because of the importance of the standard errors, by convention they are included when reporting the estimated OLS coefficients. One compact way to report the standard errors is to place them in parentheses below the respective coefficients of the OLS regression line:

$$\widehat{TestScore} = 698.9 - 2.28 \times STR, R^2 = 0.051, SER = 18.6. \qquad (5.8)$$
$$\quad\quad\quad (10.4) \quad (0.52)$$

Equation (5.8) also reports the regression $R^2$ and the standard error of the regression ($SER$) following the estimated regression line. Thus Equation (5.8) provides the estimated regression line, estimates of the sampling uncertainty of the slope and the intercept (the standard errors), and two measures of the fit of this regression line (the $R^2$ and the $SER$). This is a common format for reporting a single regression equation, and it will be used throughout the rest of this book.

Suppose you wish to test the null hypothesis that the slope $\beta_1$ is zero in the population counterpart of Equation (5.8) at the 5% significance level. To do so, construct the $t$-statistic and compare its absolute value to 1.96, the 5% (two-sided) critical value taken from the standard normal distribution. The $t$-statistic is constructed by substituting the hypothesized value of $\beta_1$ under the null hypothesis (zero), the estimated slope, and its standard error from Equation (5.8) into the general formula in Equation (5.5); the result is $t^{act} = (-2.28 - 0)/0.52 = -4.38$. The absolute value of this $t$-statistic exceeds the 5% two-sided critical value of 1.96, so the null hypothesis is rejected in favor of the two-sided alternative at the 5% significance level.

Alternatively, we can compute the $p$-value associated with $t^{act} = -4.38$. This probability is the area in the tails of standard normal distribution, as shown in Figure 5.1. This probability is extremely small, approximately 0.00001, or 0.001%. That is, if the null hypothesis $\beta_{ClassSize} = 0$ is true, the probability of obtaining a value of $\hat{\beta}_1$ as far from the null as the value we actually obtained is extremely small, less than 0.001%. Because this event is so unlikely, it is reasonable to conclude that the null hypothesis is false.

## One-Sided Hypotheses Concerning $\beta_1$

The discussion so far has focused on testing the hypothesis that $\beta_1 = \beta_{1,0}$ against the hypothesis that $\beta_1 \neq \beta_{1,0}$. This is a two-sided hypothesis test, because under the alternative $\beta_1$ could be either larger or smaller than $\beta_{1,0}$. Sometimes, however, it

---

**FIGURE 5.1** Calculating the *p*-Value of a Two-Sided Test When $t^{act} = -4.38$

The *p*-value of a two-sided test is the probability that $|Z| > |t^{act}|$ where $Z$ is a standard normal random variable and $t^{act}$ is the value of the *t*-statistic calculated from the sample. When $t^{act} = -4.38$, the *p*-value is only 0.00001.

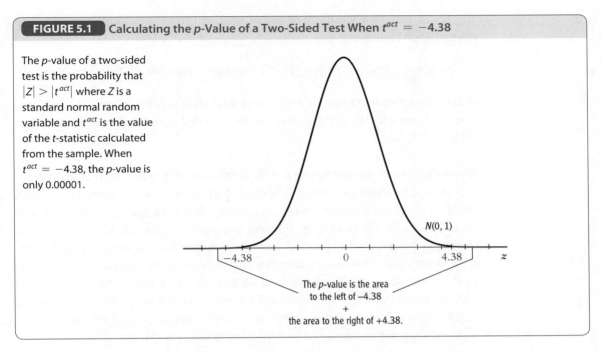

$N(0, 1)$

−4.38    0    4.38    $z$

The *p*-value is the area
to the left of –4.38
+
the area to the right of +4.38.

---

is appropriate to use a one-sided hypothesis test. For example, in the student–teacher ratio/test score problem, many people think that smaller classes provide a better learning environment. Under that hypothesis, $\beta_1$ is negative: Smaller classes lead to higher scores. It might make sense, therefore, to test the null hypothesis that $\beta_1 = 0$ (no effect) against the one-sided alternative that $\beta_1 < 0$.

For a one-sided test, the null hypothesis and the one-sided alternative hypothesis are

$$H_0: \beta_1 = \beta_{1,0} \text{ vs. } H_1: \beta_1 < \beta_{1,0} \quad \text{(one-sided alternative).} \tag{5.9}$$

where $\beta_{1,0}$ is the value of $\beta_1$ under the null (0 in the student–teacher ratio example) and the alternative is that $\beta_1$ is less than $\beta_{1,0}$. If the alternative is that $\beta_1$ is greater than $\beta_{1,0}$, the inequality in Equation (5.9) is reversed.

Because the null hypothesis is the same for a one- and a two-sided hypothesis test, the construction of the *t*-statistic is the same. The only difference between a one- and two-sided hypothesis test is how you interpret the *t*-statistic. For the one-sided alternative in Equation (5.9), the null hypothesis is rejected against the one-sided alternative for large negative, but not large positive, values of the *t*-statistic: Instead of rejecting if $|t^{act}| > 1.96$, the hypothesis is rejected at the 5% significance level if $t^{act} < -1.64$.

The $p$-value for a one-sided test is obtained from the cumulative standard normal distribution as

$$p\text{-value} = \Pr(Z < t^{act}) = \Phi(t^{act}) \quad (p\text{-value, one-sided left-tail test}). \quad (5.10)$$

If the alternative hypothesis is that $\beta_1$ is greater than $\beta_{1,0}$, the inequalities in Equations (5.9) and (5.10) are reversed, so the $p$-value is the right-tail probability, $\Pr(Z > t^{act})$.

*When should a one-sided test be used?* In practice, one-sided alternative hypotheses should be used only when there is a clear reason for doing so. This reason could come from economic theory, prior empirical evidence, or both. However, even if it initially seems that the relevant alternative is one-sided, upon reflection this might not necessarily be so. A newly formulated drug undergoing clinical trials actually could prove harmful because of previously unrecognized side effects. In the class size example, we are reminded of the graduation joke that a university's secret of success is to admit talented students and then make sure that the faculty stays out of their way and does as little damage as possible. In practice, such ambiguity often leads econometricians to use two-sided tests.

*Application to test scores.* The $t$-statistic testing the hypothesis that there is no effect of class size on test scores [so $\beta_{1,0} = 0$ in Equation (5.9)] is $t^{act} = -4.38$. This value is less than $-2.33$ (the critical value for a one-sided test with a 1% significance level), so the null hypothesis is rejected against the one-sided alternative at the 1% level. In fact, the $p$-value is less than 0.0006%. Based on these data, you can reject the angry taxpayer's assertion that the negative estimate of the slope arose purely because of random sampling variation at the 1% significance level.

## Testing Hypotheses About the Intercept $\beta_0$

This discussion has focused on testing hypotheses about the slope, $\beta_1$. Occasionally, however, the hypothesis concerns the intercept $\beta_0$. The null hypothesis concerning the intercept and the two-sided alternative are

$$H_0: \beta_0 = \beta_{0,0} \text{ vs. } H_1: \beta_0 \neq \beta_{0,0} \quad (\text{two-sided alternative}). \quad (5.11)$$

The general approach to testing this null hypothesis consists of the three steps in Key Concept 5.2 applied to $\beta_0$ (the formula for the standard error of $\hat{\beta}_0$ is given in Appendix 5.1). If the alternative is one-sided, this approach is modified as was discussed in the previous subsection for hypotheses about the slope.

Hypothesis tests are useful if you have a specific null hypothesis in mind (as did our angry taxpayer). Being able to accept or reject this null hypothesis based on the statistical evidence provides a powerful tool for coping with the uncertainty inherent in using a sample to learn about the population. Yet, there are many times that no single hypothesis about a regression coefficient is dominant, and instead one would like to know a range of values of the coefficient that are consistent with the data. This calls for constructing a confidence interval.

# 5.2 Confidence Intervals for a Regression Coefficient

Because any statistical estimate of the slope $\beta_1$ necessarily has sampling uncertainty, we cannot determine the true value of $\beta_1$ exactly from a sample of data. It is possible, however, to use the OLS estimator and its standard error to construct a confidence interval for the slope $\beta_1$ or for the intercept $\beta_0$.

*Confidence interval for $\beta_1$.* Recall from the discussion of confidence intervals in Section 3.3 that a 95% **confidence interval for $\beta_1$** has two equivalent definitions. First, it is the set of values that cannot be rejected using a two-sided hypothesis test with a 5% significance level. Second, it is an interval that has a 95% probability of containing the true value of $\beta_1$; that is, in 95% of possible samples that might be drawn, the confidence interval will contain the true value of $\beta_1$. Because this interval contains the true value in 95% of all samples, it is said to have a **confidence level** of 95%.

The reason these two definitions are equivalent is as follows. A hypothesis test with a 5% significance level will, by definition, reject the true value of $\beta_1$ in only 5% of all possible samples; that is, in 95% of all possible samples, the true value of $\beta_1$ will *not* be rejected. Because the 95% confidence interval (as defined in the first definition) is the set of all values of $\beta_1$ that are *not* rejected at the 5% significance level, it follows that the true value of $\beta_1$ will be contained in the confidence interval in 95% of all possible samples.

As in the case of a confidence interval for the population mean (Section 3.3), in principle a 95% confidence interval can be computed by testing all possible values of $\beta_1$ (that is, testing the null hypothesis $\beta_1 = \beta_{1,0}$ for all values of $\beta_{1,0}$) at the 5% significance level using the $t$-statistic. The 95% confidence interval is then the collection of all the values of $\beta_1$ that are not rejected. But constructing the $t$-statistic for all values of $\beta_1$ would take forever.

An easier way to construct the confidence interval is to note that the $t$-statistic will reject the hypothesized value $\beta_{1,0}$ whenever $\beta_{1,0}$ is outside the range

**KEY CONCEPT**

**5.3**

## Confidence Interval for $\beta_1$

A 95% two-sided confidence interval for $\beta_1$ is an interval that contains the true value of $\beta_1$ with a 95% probability; that is, it contains the true value of $\beta_1$ in 95% of all possible randomly drawn samples. Equivalently, it is the set of values of $\beta_1$ that cannot be rejected by a 5% two-sided hypothesis test. When the sample size is large, it is constructed as

$$95\% \text{ confidence interval for } \beta_1 = [\hat{\beta}_1 - 1.96SE(\hat{\beta}_1), \hat{\beta}_1 + 1.96SE(\hat{\beta}_1)]. \quad (5.12)$$

$\hat{\beta}_1 \pm 1.96SE(\hat{\beta}_1)$. This implies that the 95% confidence interval for $\beta_1$ is the interval $[\hat{\beta}_1 - 1.96SE(\hat{\beta}_1), \hat{\beta}_1 + 1.96SE(\hat{\beta}_1)]$. This argument parallels the argument used to develop a confidence interval for the population mean.

The construction of a confidence interval for $\beta_1$ is summarized as Key Concept 5.3.

*Confidence interval for $\beta_0$.* A 95% confidence interval for $\beta_0$ is constructed as in Key Concept 5.3, with $\hat{\beta}_0$ and $SE(\hat{\beta}_0)$ replacing $\hat{\beta}_1$ and $SE(\hat{\beta}_1)$.

*Application to test scores.* The OLS regression of the test score against the student–teacher ratio, reported in Equation (5.8), yielded $\hat{\beta}_1 = -2.28$ and $SE(\hat{\beta}_1) = 0.52$. The 95% two-sided confidence interval for $\beta_1$ is $\{-2.28 \pm 1.96 \times 0.52\}$, or $-3.30 \le \beta_1 \le -1.26$. The value $\beta_1 = 0$ is not contained in this confidence interval, so (as we knew already from Section 5.1) the hypothesis $\beta_1 = 0$ can be rejected at the 5% significance level.

*Confidence intervals for predicted effects of changing X.* The 95% confidence interval for $\beta_1$ can be used to construct a 95% confidence interval for the predicted effect of a general change in $X$.

Consider changing $X$ by a given amount, $\Delta x$. The predicted change in $Y$ associated with this change in $X$ is $\beta_1 \Delta x$. The population slope $\beta_1$ is unknown, but because we can construct a confidence interval for $\beta_1$, we can construct a confidence interval for the predicted effect $\beta_1 \Delta x$. Because one end of a 95% confidence interval for $\beta_1$ is $\hat{\beta}_1 - 1.96SE(\hat{\beta}_1)$, the predicted effect of the change $\Delta x$ using this estimate of $\beta_1$ is $[\hat{\beta}_1 - 1.96SE(\hat{\beta}_1)] \times \Delta x$. The other end of the confidence interval is $\hat{\beta}_1 + 1.96SE(\hat{\beta}_1)$, and the predicted effect of the change using that estimate is $[\hat{\beta}_1 + 1.96SE(\hat{\beta}_1)] \times \Delta x$. Thus a 95% confidence interval for the effect of changing $x$ by the amount $\Delta x$ can be expressed as

95% confidence interval for $\beta_1 \Delta x$

$$= [(\hat{\beta}_1 - 1.96SE(\hat{\beta}_1))\Delta x, (\hat{\beta}_1 + 1.96SE(\hat{\beta}_1))\Delta x]. \tag{5.13}$$

For example, our hypothetical superintendent is contemplating reducing the student–teacher ratio by 2. Because the 95% confidence interval for $\beta_1$ is $[-3.30, -1.26]$, the effect of reducing the student–teacher ratio by 2 could be as great as $-3.30 \times (-2) = 6.60$ or as little as $-1.26 \times (-2) = 2.52$. Thus decreasing the student–teacher ratio by 2 is predicted to increase test scores by between 2.52 and 6.60 points, with a 95% confidence level.

## 5.3  Regression When *X* Is a Binary Variable

The discussion so far has focused on the case that the regressor is a continuous variable. Regression analysis can also be used when the regressor is binary—that is, when it takes on only two values, 0 or 1. For example, $X$ might be a worker's gender ($=1$ if female, $= 0$ if male), whether a school district is urban or rural ($=1$ if urban, $= 0$ if rural), or whether the district's class size is small or large ($= 1$ if small, $= 0$ if large). A binary variable is also called an **indicator variable** or sometimes a **dummy variable**.

### Interpretation of the Regression Coefficients

The mechanics of regression with a binary regressor are the same as if it is continuous. The interpretation of $\beta_1$, however, is different, and it turns out that regression with a binary variable is equivalent to performing a difference of means analysis, as described in Section 3.4.

To see this, suppose you have a variable $D_i$ that equals either 0 or 1, depending on whether the student–teacher ratio is less than 20:

$$D_i = \begin{cases} 1 \text{ if the student–teacher ratio in } i^{\text{th}} \text{ district} < 20 \\ 0 \text{ if the student–teacher ratio in } i^{\text{th}} \text{ district} \geq 20 \end{cases} \tag{5.14}$$

The population regression model with $D_i$ as the regressor is

$$Y_i = \beta_0 + \beta_1 D_i + u_i, i = 1, \ldots, n. \tag{5.15}$$

This is the same as the regression model with the continuous regressor $X_i$ except that now the regressor is the binary variable $D_i$. Because $D_i$ is not continuous, it is not useful to think of $\beta_1$ as a slope; indeed, because $D_i$ can take on only two values, there is no "line," so it makes no sense to talk about a slope. Thus we will not refer to $\beta_1$ as the slope in Equation (5.15); instead we will simply refer to $\beta_1$ as the **coefficient multiplying $D_i$** in this regression or, more compactly, the **coefficient on $D_i$**.

If $\beta_1$ in Equation (5.15) is not a slope, what is it? The best way to interpret $\beta_0$ and $\beta_1$ in a regression with a binary regressor is to consider, one at a time, the two possible cases, $D_i = 0$ and $D_i = 1$. If the student–teacher ratio is high, then $D_i = 0$ and Equation (5.15) becomes

$$Y_i = \beta_0 + u_i \quad (D_i = 0). \tag{5.16}$$

Because $E(u_i \mid D_i) = 0$, the conditional expectation of $Y_i$ when $D_i = 0$ is $E(Y_i \mid D_i = 0) = \beta_0$; that is, $\beta_0$ is the population mean value of test scores when the student–teacher ratio is high. Similarly, when $D_i = 1$,

$$Y_i = \beta_0 + \beta_1 + u_i \quad (D_i = 1). \tag{5.17}$$

Thus, when $D_i = 1$, $E(Y_i \mid D_i = 1) = \beta_0 + \beta_1$; that is, $\beta_0 + \beta_1$ is the population mean value of test scores when the student–teacher ratio is low.

Because $\beta_0 + \beta_1$ is the population mean of $Y_i$ when $D_i = 1$ and $\beta_0$ is the population mean of $Y_i$ when $D_i = 0$, the difference $(\beta_0 + \beta_1) - \beta_0 = \beta_1$ is the difference between these two means. In other words, $\beta_1$ is the difference between the conditional expectation of $Y_i$ when $D_i = 1$ and when $D_i = 0$, or $\beta_1 = E(Y_i \mid D_i = 1) - E(Y_i \mid D_i = 0)$. In the test score example, $\beta_1$ is the difference between mean test score in districts with low student–teacher ratios and the mean test score in districts with high student–teacher ratios.

Because $\beta_1$ is the difference in the population means, it makes sense that the OLS estimator $\beta_1$ is the difference between the sample averages of $Y_i$ in the two groups, and, in fact, this is the case.

*Hypothesis tests and confidence intervals.* If the two population means are the same, then $\beta_1$ in Equation (5.15) is zero. Thus the null hypothesis that the two population means are the same can be tested against the alternative hypothesis that they differ by testing the null hypothesis $\beta_1 = 0$ against the alternative $\beta_1 \neq 0$. This hypothesis can be tested using the procedure outlined in Section 5.1. Specifically, the null hypothesis can be rejected at the 5% level against the two-sided alternative when the OLS $t$-statistic $t = \hat{\beta}_1 / SE(\hat{\beta}_1)$ exceeds 1.96 in absolute value. Similarly, a 95% confidence interval for $\beta_1$, constructed as $\hat{\beta}_1 \pm 1.96SE(\hat{\beta}_1)$. as described in Section 5.2, provides a 95% confidence interval for the difference between the two population means.

*Application to test scores.* As an example, a regression of the test score against the student–teacher ratio binary variable $D$ defined in Equation (5.14) estimated by OLS using the 420 observations in Figure 4.2 yields

$$\widehat{TestScore} = 650.0 + 7.4D, R^2 = 0.037, SER = 18.7,$$
$$\phantom{\widehat{TestScore} = 650.0 + }(1.3) \quad (1.8) \tag{5.18}$$

where the standard errors of the OLS estimates of the coefficients $\beta_0$ and $\beta_1$ are given in parentheses below the OLS estimates. Thus the average test score for the subsample with student–teacher ratios greater than or equal to 20 (that is, for which $D = 0$) is 650.0, and the average test score for the subsample with student–teacher ratios less than 20 (so $D = 1$) is $650.0 + 7.4 = 657.4$. The difference between the sample average test scores for the two groups is 7.4. This is the OLS estimate of $\beta_1$, the coefficient on the student–teacher ratio binary variable $D$.

Is the difference in the population mean test scores in the two groups statistically significantly different from zero at the 5% level? To find out, construct the $t$-statistic on $\beta_1$: $t = 7.4 / 1.8 = 4.04$. This value exceeds 1.96 in absolute value, so the hypothesis that the population mean test scores in districts with high and low student–teacher ratios is the same can be rejected at the 5% significance level.

The OLS estimator and its standard error can be used to construct a 95% confidence interval for the true difference in means. This is $7.4 \pm 1.96 \times 1.8 = (3.9, 10.9)$. This confidence interval excludes $\beta_1 = 0$, so that (as we know from the previous paragraph) the hypothesis $\beta_1 = 0$ can be rejected at the 5% significance level.

## 5.4 Heteroskedasticity and Homoskedasticity

Our only assumption about the distribution of $u_i$ conditional on $X_i$ is that it has a mean of zero (the first least squares assumption). If, furthermore, the *variance* of this conditional distribution does not depend on $X_i$, then the errors are said to be homoskedastic. This section discusses homoskedasticity, its theoretical implications, the simplified formulas for the standard errors of the OLS estimators that arise if the errors are homoskedastic, and the risks you run if you use these simplified formulas in practice.

## What Are Heteroskedasticity and Homoskedasticity?

***Definitions of heteroskedasticity and homoskedasticity.***  The error term $u_i$ is **homoskedastic** if the variance of the conditional distribution of $u_i$ given $X_i$ is constant for $i = 1, \ldots, n$ and in particular does not depend on $X_i$. Otherwise, the error term is **heteroskedastic**.

As an illustration, return to Figure 4.4. The distribution of the errors $u_i$ is shown for various values of $x$. Because this distribution applies specifically for the indicated value of $x$, this is the conditional distribution of $u_i$ given $X_i = x$. As drawn in that figure, all these conditional distributions have the same spread; more precisely, the variance of these distributions is the same for the various values of $x$. That is, in Figure 4.4, the conditional variance of $u_i$ given $X_i = x$ does not depend on $x$, so the errors illustrated in Figure 4.4 are homoskedastic.

In contrast, Figure 5.2 illustrates a case in which the conditional distribution of $u_i$ spreads out as $x$ increases. For small values of $x$, this distribution is tight, but for larger values of $x$, it has a greater spread. Thus in Figure 5.2 the variance of $u_i$ given $X_i = x$ increases with $x$, so that the errors in Figure 5.2 are heteroskedastic.

The definitions of heteroskedasticity and homoskedasticity are summarized in Key Concept 5.4.

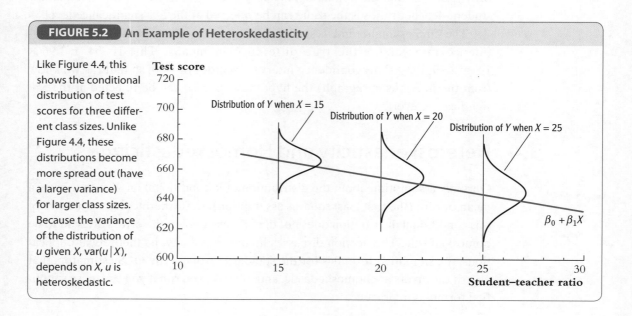

**FIGURE 5.2**    **An Example of Heteroskedasticity**

Like Figure 4.4, this shows the conditional distribution of test scores for three different class sizes. Unlike Figure 4.4, these distributions become more spread out (have a larger variance) for larger class sizes. Because the variance of the distribution of $u$ given $X$, $\text{var}(u \mid X)$, depends on $X$, $u$ is heteroskedastic.

## Heteroskedasticity and Homoskedasticity

The error term $u_i$ is homoskedastic if the variance of the conditional distribution of $u_i$ given $X_i$, $var(u_i|X_i = x)$, is constant for $i = 1, \ldots, n$ and in particular does not depend on $x$. Otherwise, the error term is heteroskedastic.

*Example.* These terms are a mouthful, and the definitions might seem abstract. To help clarify them with an example, we digress from the student–teacher ratio/test score problem and instead return to the example of earnings of male versus female college graduates considered in the box in Chapter 3 "The Gender Gap in Earnings of College Graduates in the United States." Let $MALE_i$ be a binary variable that equals 1 for male college graduates and equals 0 for female graduates. The binary variable regression model relating a college graduate's earnings to his or her gender is

$$Earnings_i = \beta_0 + \beta_1 MALE_i + u_i \qquad (5.19)$$

for $i = 1, \ldots, n$. Because the regressor is binary, $\beta_1$ is the difference in the population means of the two groups—in this case, the difference in mean earnings between men and women who graduated from college.

The definition of homoskedasticity states that the variance of $u_i$ does not depend on the regressor. Here the regressor is $MALE_i$, so at issue is whether the variance of the error term depends on $MALE_i$. In other words, is the variance of the error term the same for men and for women? If so, the error is homoskedastic; if not, it is heteroskedastic.

Deciding whether the variance of $u_i$ depends on $MALE_i$ requires thinking hard about what the error term actually is. In this regard, it is useful to write Equation (5.19) as two separate equations, one for men and one for women:

$$Earnings_i = \beta_0 + u_i \quad \text{(women) and} \qquad (5.20)$$

$$Earnings_i = \beta_0 + \beta_1 + u_i \quad \text{(men)}. \qquad (5.21)$$

Thus, for women, $u_i$ is the deviation of the $i^{th}$ woman's earnings from the population mean earnings for women ($\beta_0$), and for men, $u_i$ is the deviation of the $i^{th}$ man's earnings from the population mean earnings for men ($\beta_0 + \beta_1$). It follows that the statement "the variance of $u_i$ does not depend on $MALE$" is equivalent to the statement "the variance of earnings is the same for men as it is for women." In other words, in this example, the error term is homoskedastic if the variance of the population distribution of earnings is the same for men and women; if these variances differ, the error term is heteroskedastic.

## Mathematical Implications of Homoskedasticity

*The OLS estimators remain unbiased and asymptotically normal.*  Because the least squares assumptions in Key Concept 4.3 place no restrictions on the conditional variance, they apply to both the general case of heteroskedasticity and the special case of homoskedasticity. Therefore, the OLS estimators remain unbiased and consistent even if the errors are homoskedastic. In addition, the OLS estimators have sampling distributions that are normal in large samples even if the errors are homoskedastic. Whether the errors are homoskedastic or heteroskedastic, the OLS estimator is unbiased, consistent, and asymptotically normal.

*Efficiency of the OLS estimator when the errors are homoskedastic.*  If the least squares assumptions in Key Concept 4.3 hold and the errors are homoskedastic, then the OLS estimators $\hat{\beta}_0$ and $\hat{\beta}_1$ are efficient among all estimators that are linear in $Y_1, \ldots, Y_n$ and are unbiased, conditional on $X_1, \ldots, X_n$. This result, which is called the Gauss–Markov theorem, is discussed in Section 5.5.

*Homoskedasticity-only variance formula.*  If the error term is homoskedastic, then the formulas for the variances of $\hat{\beta}_0$ and $\hat{\beta}_1$ in Key Concept 4.4 simplify. Consequently, if the errors are homoskedastic, then there is a specialized formula that can be used for the standard errors of $\hat{\beta}_0$ and $\hat{\beta}_1$. The **homoskedasticity-only standard error** of $\hat{\beta}_1$, derived in Appendix (5.1), is $SE(\hat{\beta}_1) = \sqrt{\tilde{\sigma}^2_{\hat{\beta}_1}}$ where $\tilde{\sigma}^2_{\hat{\beta}_1}$ is the homoskedasticity-only estimator of the variance of $\hat{\beta}_1$:

$$\tilde{\sigma}^2_{\hat{\beta}_1} = \frac{s^2_{\hat{u}}}{\sum_{i=1}^{n}(X_i - \overline{X})^2} \quad \text{(homoskedasticity-only),} \qquad (5.22)$$

where $s^2_{\hat{u}}$ is given in Equation (4.19). The homoskedasticity-only formula for the standard error of $\hat{\beta}_0$ is given in Appendix (5.1). In the special case that $X$ is a binary variable, the estimator of the variance of $\hat{\beta}_1$ under homoskedasticity (that is, the square of the standard error of $\hat{\beta}_1$ under homoskedasticity) is the so-called pooled variance formula for the difference in means, given in Equation (3.23).

Because these alternative formulas are derived for the special case that the errors are homoskedastic and do not apply if the errors are heteroskedastic, they will be referred to as the "homoskedasticity-only" formulas for the variance and standard error of the OLS estimators. As the name suggests, if the errors are heteroskedastic, then the homoskedasticity-only standard errors are inappropriate. Specifically, if the errors are heteroskedastic, then the $t$-statistic computed using the homoskedasticity-only standard error does not have a standard normal distribution, even in large samples. In fact, the correct critical values to use for this homoskedasticity-only $t$-statistic depend on the precise nature of the heteroskedasticity, so those critical values cannot be tabulated. Similarly, if the errors are heteroskedastic but a confidence interval is constructed as $\pm 1.96$ homoskedasticity-only standard errors, in general the probability that this interval contains the true value of the coefficient is not 95%, even in large samples.

In contrast, because homoskedasticity is a special case of heteroskedasticity, the estimators $\hat{\sigma}^2_{\hat{\beta}_1}$ and $\hat{\sigma}^2_{\hat{\beta}_0}$ of the variances of $\hat{\beta}_1$ and $\hat{\beta}_0$ given in Equations (5.4) and (5.26) produce valid statistical inferences whether the errors are heteroskedastic or homoskedastic. Thus hypothesis tests and confidence intervals based on those standard errors are valid whether or not the errors are heteroskedastic. Because the standard errors we have used so far [that is, those based on Equations (5.4) and (5.26)] lead to statistical inferences that are valid whether or not the errors are heteroskedastic, they are called **heteroskedasticity-robust standard errors**. Because such formulas were proposed by Eicker (1967), Huber (1967), and White (1980), they are also referred to as Eicker–Huber–White standard errors.

## What Does This Mean in Practice?

*Which is more realistic, heteroskedasticity or homoskedasticity?* The answer to this question depends on the application. However, the issues can be clarified by returning to the example of the gender gap in earnings among college graduates. Familiarity with how people are paid in the world around us gives some clues as to which assumption is more sensible. For many years—and, to a lesser extent, today—women were not found in the top-paying jobs: There have always been poorly paid men, but there have rarely been highly paid women. This suggests that the distribution of earnings among women is tighter than among men (see the box in Chapter 3 "The Gender Gap in Earnings of College Graduates in the United States"). In other words, the variance of the error term in Equation (5.20) for women is plausibly less than the variance of the error term in Equation (5.21) for men. Thus the presence of a "glass ceiling" for women's jobs and pay suggests that the error term in the binary variable regression model in Equation (5.19) is heteroskedastic. Unless there are compelling reasons to the contrary—and we can think of none—it makes sense to treat the error term in this example as heteroskedastic.

## The Economic Value of a Year of Education: Homoskedasticity or Heteroskedasticity?

On average, workers with more education have higher earnings than workers with less education. But if the best-paying jobs mainly go to the college educated, it might also be that the *spread* of the distribution of earnings is greater for workers with more education. Does the distribution of earnings spread out as education increases?

This is an empirical question, so answering it requires analyzing data. Figure 5.3 is a scatterplot of the hourly earnings and the number of years of education for a sample of 2829 full-time workers in the United States in 2012, ages 29 and 30, with between 6 and 18 years of education. The data come from the March 2013 Current Population Survey, which is described in Appendix 3.1.

Figure 5.3 has two striking features. The first is that the mean of the distribution of earnings increases with the number of years of education. This increase is summarized by the OLS regression line,

$$\widehat{Earnings} = -7.29 + 1.93\,Years\,Education,$$
$$(1.10) \quad (0.08)$$
$$R^2 = 0.162, SER = 10.29. \qquad (5.23)$$

This line is plotted in Figure 5.3. The coefficient of 1.93 in the OLS regression line means that, on average, hourly earnings increase by $1.93 for each additional year of education. The 95% confidence interval for this coefficient is $1.93 \pm 1.96 \times 0.08$, or 1.77 to 2.09.

The second striking feature of Figure 5.3 is that the spread of the distribution of earnings increases with the years of education. While some workers with many years of education have low-paying jobs, very few workers with low levels of education have high-paying jobs. This can be quantified by looking at the spread of the residuals around the OLS regression line. For workers with ten years of education, the standard deviation of the residuals is $4.32; for workers with a high school diploma, this standard deviation is $7.80; and for workers with a college degree, this standard deviation increases to $12.46. Because these standard deviations differ for different levels of education, the variance of the residuals in the regression of Equation (5.23) depends on the value of the regressor (the years of education); in other words, the regression errors are heteroskedastic. In real-world terms, not all college graduates will be earning $50 per hour by the time they are 29, but some will, and workers with only ten years of education have no shot at those jobs.

---

**FIGURE 5.3** Scatterplot of Hourly Earnings and Years of Education for 29- to 30-Year-Olds in the United States in 2012

Hourly earnings are plotted against years of education for 2,829 full-time 29- to 30-year-old workers. The spread around the regression line increases with the years of education, indicating that the regression errors are heteroskedastic.

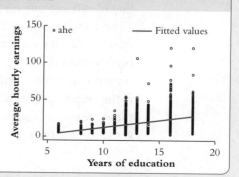

As this example of modeling earnings illustrates, heteroskedasticity arises in many econometric applications. At a general level, economic theory rarely gives any reason to believe that the errors are homoskedastic. It therefore is prudent to assume that the errors might be heteroskedastic unless you have compelling reasons to believe otherwise.

*Practical implications.*   The main issue of practical relevance in this discussion is whether one should use heteroskedasticity-robust or homoskedasticity-only standard errors. In this regard, it is useful to imagine computing both, then choosing between them. If the homoskedasticity-only and heteroskedasticity-robust standard errors are the same, nothing is lost by using the heteroskedasticity-robust standard errors; if they differ, however, then you should use the more reliable ones that allow for heteroskedasticity. The simplest thing, then, is always to use the heteroskedasticity-robust standard errors.

For historical reasons, many software programs report homoskedasticity-only standard errors as their default setting, so it is up to the user to specify the option of heteroskedasticity-robust standard errors. The details of how to implement heteroskedasticity-robust standard errors depend on the software package you use.

All of the empirical examples in this book employ heteroskedasticity-robust standard errors unless explicitly stated otherwise.[1]

## *5.5  The Theoretical Foundations of Ordinary Least Squares

As discussed in Section 4.5, the OLS estimator is unbiased, is consistent, has a variance that is inversely proportional to $n$, and has a normal sampling distribution when the sample size is large. In addition, under certain conditions the OLS estimator is more efficient than some other candidate estimators. Specifically, if the least squares assumptions hold and if the errors are homoskedastic, then the OLS estimator has the smallest variance of all conditionally unbiased estimators that are linear functions of $Y_1, \ldots, Y_n$. This section explains and discusses this result, which is a consequence of the Gauss–Markov theorem. The section concludes

[1]In case this book is used in conjunction with other texts, it might be helpful to note that some textbooks add homoskedasticity to the list of least squares assumptions. As just discussed, however, this additional assumption is not needed for the validity of OLS regression analysis as long as heteroskedasticity-robust standard errors are used.

*This section is optional and is not used in later chapters.

with a discussion of alternative estimators that are more efficient than OLS when the conditions of the Gauss–Markov theorem do not hold.

## Linear Conditionally Unbiased Estimators and the Gauss–Markov Theorem

If the three least squares assumptions (Key Concept 4.3) hold and if the error is homoskedastic, then the OLS estimator has the smallest variance, conditional on $X_1, \ldots, X_n$, among all estimators in the class of linear conditionally unbiased estimators. In other words, the OLS estimator is the **B**est **L**inear conditionally **U**nbiased **E**stimator—that is, it is BLUE. This result is an extension of the result, summarized in Key Concept 3.3, that the sample average $\overline{Y}$ is the most efficient estimator of the population mean among the class of all estimators that are unbiased and are linear functions (weighted averages) of $Y_1, \ldots, Y_n$.

*Linear conditionally unbiased estimators.*  The class of linear conditionally unbiased estimators consists of all estimators of $\beta_1$ that are linear functions of $Y_1, \ldots, Y_n$ and that are unbiased, conditional on $X_1, \ldots, X_n$. That is, if $\widetilde{\beta}_1$ is a linear estimator, then it can be written as

$$\widetilde{\beta}_1 = \sum_{i=1}^{n} a_i Y_i \quad (\widetilde{\beta}_1 \text{ is linear}), \tag{5.24}$$

where the weights $a_1, \ldots, a_n$ can depend on $X_1, \ldots, X_n$ but *not* on $Y_1, \ldots, Y_n$. The estimator $\widetilde{\beta}_1$ is conditionally unbiased if the mean of its conditional sampling distribution, given $X_1, \ldots, X_n$, is $\beta_1$. That is, the estimator $\widetilde{\beta}_1$ is conditionally unbiased if

$$E(\widetilde{\beta}_1 \mid X_1, \ldots, X_n) = \beta_1 \quad (\widetilde{\beta}_1 \text{ is conditionally unbiased}). \tag{5.25}$$

The estimator $\widetilde{\beta}_1$ is a linear conditionally unbiased estimator if it can be written in the form of Equation (5.24) (it is linear) and if Equation (5.25) holds (it is conditionally unbiased). It is shown in Appendix 5.2 that the OLS estimator is linear and conditionally unbiased.

*The Gauss–Markov theorem.*  The **Gauss–Markov theorem** states that, under a set of conditions known as the Gauss–Markov conditions, the OLS estimator $\hat{\beta}_1$ has the smallest conditional variance, given $X_1, \ldots, X_n$, of all linear conditionally unbiased estimators of $\beta_1$; that is, the OLS estimator is BLUE. The Gauss–Markov conditions, which are stated in Appendix 5.2, are implied by the three least

**KEY CONCEPT**

**5.5**

## The Gauss–Markov Theorem for $\hat{\beta}_1$

If the three least squares assumptions in Key Concept 4.3 hold *and* if errors are homoskedastic, then the OLS estimator $\hat{\beta}_1$ is the **B**est (most efficient) **L**inear conditionally **U**nbiased **E**stimator (**BLUE**).

squares assumptions plus the assumption that the errors are homoskedastic. Consequently, if the three least squares assumptions hold and the errors are homoskedastic, then OLS is BLUE. The Gauss–Markov theorem is stated in Key Concept 5.5 and proven in Appendix 5.2.

*Limitations of the Gauss–Markov theorem.* The Gauss–Markov theorem provides a theoretical justification for using OLS. However, the theorem has two important limitations. First, its conditions might not hold in practice. In particular, if the error term is heteroskedastic—as it often is in economic applications—then the OLS estimator is no longer BLUE. As discussed in Section 5.4, the presence of heteroskedasticity does not pose a threat to inference based on heteroskedasticity-robust standard errors, but it does mean that OLS is no longer the efficient linear conditionally unbiased estimator. An alternative to OLS when there is heteroskedasticity of a known form, called the weighted least squares estimator, is discussed below.

The second limitation of the Gauss–Markov theorem is that even if the conditions of the theorem hold, there are other candidate estimators that are not linear and conditionally unbiased; under some conditions, these other estimators are more efficient than OLS.

## Regression Estimators Other Than OLS

Under certain conditions, some regression estimators are more efficient than OLS.

*The weighted least squares estimator.* If the errors are heteroskedastic, then OLS is no longer BLUE. If the nature of the heteroskedasticity is known—specifically, if the conditional variance of $u_i$ given $X_i$ is known up to a constant factor of proportionality—then it is possible to construct an estimator that has a smaller variance than the OLS estimator. This method, called **weighted least squares (WLS)**, weights the $i^{\text{th}}$ observation by the inverse of the square root of the conditional variance of $u_i$ given $X_i$. Because of this weighting, the errors in this weighted regression are homoskedastic, so OLS, when applied to the weighted data, is BLUE.

Although theoretically elegant, the practical problem with weighted least squares is that you must know how the conditional variance of $u_i$ depends on $X_i$, something that is rarely known in econometric applications. Weighted least squares is therefore used far less frequently than OLS, and further discussion of WLS is deferred to Chapter 17.

*The least absolute deviations estimator.* As discussed in Section 4.3, the OLS estimator can be sensitive to outliers. If extreme outliers are not rare, then other estimators can be more efficient than OLS and can produce inferences that are more reliable. One such estimator is the least absolute deviations (LAD) estimator, in which the regression coefficients $\beta_0$ and $\beta_1$ are obtained by solving a minimization problem like that in Equation (4.6) except that the absolute value of the prediction "mistake" is used instead of its square. That is, the LAD estimators of $\beta_0$ and $\beta_1$ are the values of $b_0$ and $b_1$ that minimize $\sum_{i=1}^{n} |Y_i - b_0 - b_1 X_i|$. The LAD estimator is less sensitive to large outliers in $u$ than is OLS.

In many economic data sets, severe outliers in $u$ are rare, so use of the LAD estimator, or other estimators with reduced sensitivity to outliers, is uncommon in applications. Thus the treatment of linear regression throughout the remainder of this text focuses exclusively on least squares methods.

## *5.6 Using the *t*-Statistic in Regression When the Sample Size Is Small

When the sample size is small, the exact distribution of the *t*-statistic is complicated and depends on the unknown population distribution of the data. If, however, the three least squares assumptions hold, the regression errors are homoskedastic, *and* the regression errors are normally distributed, then the OLS estimator is normally distributed and the homoskedasticity-only *t*-statistic has a Student *t* distribution. These five assumptions—the three least squares assumptions, that the errors are homoskedastic, and that the errors are normally distributed—are collectively called the **homoskedastic normal regression assumptions**.

### The *t*-Statistic and the Student *t* Distribution

Recall from Section 2.4 that the Student *t* distribution with $m$ degrees of freedom is defined to be the distribution of $Z/\sqrt{W/m}$, where $Z$ is a random variable with a standard normal distribution, $W$ is a random variable with a chi-squared distribution

---

*This section is optional and is not used in later chapters.

with $m$ degrees of freedom, and $Z$ and $W$ are independent. Under the null hypothesis, the *t*-statistic computed using the homoskedasticity-only standard error can be written in this form.

The details of the calculation is presented in Sections 17.4 and 18.4, but the main ideas are as follows. The homoskedasticity-only *t*-statistic testing $\beta_1 = \beta_{1,0}$ is $\tilde{t} = (\hat{\beta}_1 - \beta_{1,0})/\tilde{\sigma}_{\hat{\beta}_1}$, where $\tilde{\sigma}^2_{\hat{\beta}_1}$ is defined in Equation (5.22). Under the homoskedastic normal regression assumptions, $Y$ has a normal distribution, conditional on $X_1, \ldots, X_n$. As discussed in Section 5.5, the OLS estimator is a weighted average of $Y_1, \ldots, Y_n$, where the weights depend on $X_1, \ldots, X_n$ [see Equation (5.32) in Appendix 5.2]. Because a weighted average of independent normal random variables is normally distributed, $\hat{\beta}_1$ has a normal distribution, conditional on $X_1, \ldots, X_n$. Thus $(\hat{\beta}_1 - \beta_{1,0})$ has a normal distribution under the null hypothesis, conditional on $X_1, \ldots, X_n$. In addition, sections 17.4 and 18.4 show that the (normalized) homoskedasticity-only variance estimator has a chi-squared distribution with $n - 2$ degrees of freedom, divided by $n - 2$, and $\tilde{\sigma}^2_{\hat{\beta}_1}$ and $\hat{\beta}_1$ are independently distributed. Consequently, the homoskedasticity-only *t*-statistic has a Student *t* distribution with $n - 2$ degrees of freedom.

This result is closely related to a result discussed in Section 3.5 in the context of testing for the equality of the means in two samples. In that problem, if the two population distributions are normal with the same variance and if the *t*-statistic is constructed using the pooled standard error formula [Equation (3.23)], then the (pooled) *t*-statistic has a Student *t* distribution. When $X$ is binary, the homoskedasticity-only standard error for $\hat{\beta}_1$ simplifies to the pooled standard error formula for the difference of means. It follows that the result of Section 3.5 is a special case of the result that if the homoskedastic normal regression assumptions hold, then the homoskedasticity-only regression *t*-statistic has a Student *t* distribution (see Exercise 5.10).

## Use of the Student *t* Distribution in Practice

If the regression errors are homoskedastic and normally distributed and if the homoskedasticity-only *t*-statistic is used, then critical values should be taken from the Student *t* distribution (Appendix Table 2) instead of the standard normal distribution. Because the difference between the Student *t* distribution and the normal distribution is negligible if $n$ is moderate or large, this distinction is relevant only if the sample size is small.

In econometric applications, there is rarely a reason to believe that the errors are homoskedastic and normally distributed. Because sample sizes typically are large, however, inference can proceed as described in Section 5.1 and 5.2—that is, by first computing heteroskedasticity-robust standard errors and then by using the standard normal distribution to compute *p*-values, hypothesis tests, and confidence intervals.

## 5.7  Conclusion

Return for a moment to the problem that started Chapter 4: the superintendent who is considering hiring additional teachers to cut the student–teacher ratio. What have we learned that she might find useful?

Our regression analysis, based on the 420 observations for 1998 in the California test score data set, showed that there was a negative relationship between the student–teacher ratio and test scores: Districts with smaller classes have higher test scores. The coefficient is moderately large, in a practical sense: Districts with two fewer students per teacher have, on average, test scores that are 4.6 points higher. This corresponds to moving a district at the 50th percentile of the distribution of test scores to approximately the 60th percentile.

The coefficient on the student–teacher ratio is statistically significantly different from 0 at the 5% significance level. The population coefficient might be 0, and we might simply have estimated our negative coefficient by random sampling variation. However, the probability of doing so (and of obtaining a $t$-statistic on $\beta_1$ as large as we did) purely by random variation over potential samples is exceedingly small, approximately 0.001%. A 95% confidence interval for $\beta_1$ is $-3.30 \leq \beta_1 \leq -1.26$.

This result represents considerable progress toward answering the superintendent's question yet a nagging concern remains. There is a negative relationship between the student–teacher ratio and test scores, but is this relationship necessarily the *causal* one that the superintendent needs to make her decision? Districts with lower student–teacher ratios have, on average, higher test scores. But does this mean that reducing the student–teacher ratio will, in fact, increase scores?

There is, in fact, reason to worry that it might not. Hiring more teachers, after all, costs money, so wealthier school districts can better afford smaller classes. But students at wealthier schools also have other advantages over their poorer neighbors, including better facilities, newer books, and better-paid teachers. Moreover, students at wealthier schools tend themselves to come from more affluent families and thus have other advantages not directly associated with their school. For example, California has a large immigrant community; these immigrants tend to be poorer than the overall population, and in many cases, their children are not native English speakers. It thus might be that our negative estimated relationship between test scores and the student–teacher ratio is a consequence of large classes being found in conjunction with many other factors that are, in fact, the real cause of the lower test scores.

These other factors, or "omitted variables," could mean that the OLS analysis done so far has little value to the superintendent. Indeed, it could be misleading:

Changing the student–teacher ratio alone would not change these other factors that determine a child's performance at school. To address this problem, we need a method that will allow us to isolate the effect on test scores of changing the student–teacher ratio, *holding these other factors constant*. That method is multiple regression analysis, the topic of Chapters 6 and 7.

## Summary

1. Hypothesis testing for regression coefficients is analogous to hypothesis testing for the population mean: Use the $t$-statistic to calculate the $p$-values and either accept or reject the null hypothesis. Like a confidence interval for the population mean, a 95% confidence interval for a regression coefficient is computed as the estimator $\pm 1.96$ standard errors.

2. When $X$ is binary, the regression model can be used to estimate and test hypotheses about the difference between the population means of the "$X = 0$" group and the "$X = 1$" group.

3. In general, the error $u_i$ is heteroskedastic—that is, the variance of $u_i$ at a given value of $X_i$, $\text{var}(u_i \mid X_i = x)$, depends on $x$. A special case is when the error is homoskedastic—that is, $\text{var}(u_i \mid X_i = x)$ is constant. Homoskedasticity-only standard errors do not produce valid statistical inferences when the errors are heteroskedastic, but heteroskedasticity-robust standard errors do.

4. If the three least squares assumption hold *and* if the regression errors are homoskedastic, then, as a result of the Gauss–Markov theorem, the OLS estimator is BLUE.

5. If the three least squares assumptions hold, if the regression errors are homoskedastic, *and* if the regression errors are normally distributed, then the OLS $t$-statistic computed using homoskedasticity-only standard errors has a Student $t$ distribution when the null hypothesis is true. The difference between the Student $t$ distribution and the normal distribution is negligible if the sample size is moderate or large.

## Key Terms

null hypothesis (194)
two-sided alternative hypothesis (194)
standard error of $\hat{\beta}_1$ (194)

$t$-statistic (194)
$p$-value (195)
confidence interval for $\beta_1$ (199)
confidence level (199)

---

**MyEconLab Can Help You Get a Better Grade**

MyEconLab   If your exam were tomorrow, would you be ready? For each chapter,
**MyEconLab** Practice Tests and Study Plan help you prepare for your exams.
You can also find similar Exercises and Review the Concepts Questions now in **MyEconLab**.
To see how it works, turn to the **MyEconLab** spread on pages 2 and 3 of this book and then go to
**www.myeconlab.com**.

For additional Empirical Exercises and Data Sets, log on to the Companion Website at
**www.pearsonglobaleditions.com/Stock_Watson**.

---

## Review the Concepts

**5.1** Outline the procedures for computing the $p$-value of a two-sided test of $H_0: \mu_Y = 0$ using an i.i.d. set of observations $Y_i, i = 1, \ldots, n$. Outline the procedures for computing the $p$-value of a two-sided test of $H_0: \beta_1 = 0$ in a regression model using an i.i.d. set of observations $(Y_i, X_i), i = 1, \ldots, n$.

**5.2** When are one-sided hypothesis tests constructed for estimated regression coefficients as opposed to two-sided hypothesis tests? When are confidence intervals constructed instead of hypothesis tests?

**5.3** Describe the important characteristics of the variance of a conditional distribution of an error term in a linear regression. What are the implications for OLS estimation?

**5.4** What is a dummy variable or an indicator variable? Describe the differences in interpretation of the coefficients of a linear regression when the independent variable is continuous and when it is binary. Give an example of each case. How are the construction of confidence intervals and hypothesis tests different when the independent variable is binary compared to when it is continuous?

## Exercises

**5.1** Suppose that a researcher, using data on class size ($CS$) and average test scores from 50 third-grade classes, estimates the OLS regression

$$\widehat{TestScore} = 640.3 - 4.93 \times CS, R^2 = 0.11, SER = 8.7.$$
$$(23.5) \quad (2.02)$$

**a.** Construct a 95% confidence interval for $\beta_1$, the regression slope coefficient.

**b.** Calculate the $p$-value for the two-sided test of the null hypothesis $H_0: \beta_1 = 0$. Do you reject the null hypothesis (i) at the 5% level (ii) at the 1% level?

**c.** Calculate the $p$-value for the two-sided test of the null hypothesis $H_0: b_1 = -5.0$. Without doing any additional calculations, determine whether $-5.0$ is contained in the 95% confidence interval for $\beta_1$.

**d.** Construct a 90% confidence interval for $\beta_0$.

**5.2** Suppose a researcher, using wage data on 200 randomly selected male workers and 240 female workers, estimates the OLS regression

$$\widehat{Wage} = 10.73 + 1.78 \times Male, R^2 = 0.09, SER = 3.8,$$
$$(0.16) \quad (0.29)$$

where *Wage* is measured in dollars per hour and *Male* is a binary variable that is equal to 1 if the person is a male and 0 if the person is a female. Define the wage-gender gap as the difference in mean earnings between men and women.

**a.** What is the estimated gender gap?

**b.** Is the estimated gender gap significantly different from 0? (Compute the $p$-value for testing the null hypothesis that there is no gender gap.)

**c.** Construct a 95% confidence interval for the gender gap.

**d.** In the sample, what is the mean wage of women? What is the mean wage of men?

**e.** Another researcher uses these same data but regresses *Wages* on *Female*, a variable that is equal to 1 if the person is female and 0 if the person is male. What are the regression estimates calculated from this regression?

$$\widehat{Wage} = \underline{\quad} + \underline{\quad} \times Female, R^2 = \underline{\quad}, SER = \underline{\quad}.$$

**5.3** Suppose a random sample of 100 20-year-old men is selected from a population, and that these men's height and weight are recorded. A regression of weight on height yields

$$\widehat{Weight} = -79.24 + 4.16 \times Height, R^2 = 0.72, SER = 12.6,$$
$$\phantom{xxxxxxxxxxx}(3.42)\phantom{xx}(.42)$$

where weight is measured in pounds and height is measured in inches. A man has a late growth spurt and grows 2 inches over the course of a year. Construct a 95% confidence interval for the person's weight gain.

**5.4** Read the box "The Economic Value of a Year of Education: Homoskedasticity or Heteroskedasticity?" in Section 5.4. Use the regression reported in Equation (5.23) to answer the following.

**a.** A randomly selected 30-year-old worker reports an education level of 16 years. What is the worker's expected average hourly earnings?

**b.** A high school graduate (12 years of education) is contemplating going to a community college for a 2-year degree. How much is this worker's average hourly earnings expected to increase?

**c.** A high school counselor tells a student that, on average, college graduates earn $10 per hour more than high school graduates. Is this statement consistent with the regression evidence? What range of values is consistent with the regression evidence?

**5.5** In the 1980s, Tennessee conducted an experiment in which kindergarten students were randomly assigned to "regular" and "small" classes and given standardized tests at the end of the year. (Regular classes contained approximately 24 students, and small classes contained approximately 15 students.) Suppose that, in the population, the standardized tests have a mean score of 925 points and a standard deviation of 75 points. Let *SmallClass* denote a binary variable equal to 1 if the student is assigned to a small class and equal to 0 otherwise. A regression of *TestScore* on *SmallClass* yields

$$\widehat{TestScore} = 918.0 + 13.9 \times SmallClass, R^2 = 0.01, SER = 74.6.$$
$$\phantom{xxxxxxxxx}(1.6)\phantom{xxx}(2.5)$$

**a.** Do small classes improve test scores? By how much? Is the effect large? Explain.

**b.** Is the estimated effect of class size on test scores statistically significant? Carry out a test at the 5% level.

    **c.** Construct a 99% confidence interval for the effect of *SmallClass* on *Test Score*.

**5.6**   Refer to the regression described in Exercise 5.5.

    **a.** Do you think that the regression errors are plausibly homoskedastic? Explain.

    **b.** $SE(\hat{\beta}_1)$ was computed using Equation (5.3). Suppose that the regression errors were homoskedastic: Would this affect the validity of the confidence interval constructed in Exercise 5.5(c)? Explain.

**5.7**   Suppose that $(Y_i, X_i)$ satisfy the least squares assumptions in Key Concept 4.3. A random sample of size $n = 250$ is drawn and yields

$$\hat{Y} = 5.4 + 3.2X, R^2 = 0.26, SER = 6.2.$$
$$(3.1) \quad (1.5)$$

    **a.** Test $H_0: \beta_1 = 0$ vs. $H_1: \beta_1 \neq 0$ at the 5% level.

    **b.** Construct a 95% confidence interval for $\beta_1$.

    **c.** Suppose you learned that $Y_i$ and $X_i$ were independent. Would you be surprised? Explain.

    **d.** Suppose that $Y_i$ and $X_i$ are independent and many samples of size $n = 250$ are drawn, regressions estimated, and (a) and (b) answered. In what fraction of the samples would $H_0$ from (a) be rejected? In what fraction of samples would the value $\beta_1 = 0$ be included in the confidence interval from (b)?

**5.8**   Suppose that $(Y_i, X_i)$ satisfy the least squares assumptions in Key Concept 4.3 and, in addition, $u_i$ is $N(0, \sigma_u^2)$ and is independent of $X_i$. A sample of size $n = 30$ yields

$$\hat{Y} = 43.2 + 61.5X, R^2 = 0.54, SER = 1.52,$$
$$(10.2) \quad (7.4)$$

where the numbers in parentheses are the homoskedastic-only standard errors for the regression coefficients.

    **a.** Construct a 95% confidence interval for $\beta_0$.

    **b.** Test $H_0: \beta_1 = 55$ vs. $H_1: \beta_1 \neq 55$ at the 5% level.

    **c.** Test $H_0: \beta_1 = 55$ vs. $H_1: \beta_1 > 55$ at the 5% level.

**5.9** Consider the regression model

$$Y_i = \beta X_i + u_i,$$

where $u_i$ and $X_i$ satisfy the least squares assumptions in Key Concept 4.3. Let $\bar{\beta}$ denote an estimator of $\beta$ that is constructed as $\bar{\beta} = \bar{Y}/\bar{X}$, where $\bar{Y}$ and $\bar{X}$ are the sample means of $Y_i$ and $X_i$, respectively.

   **a.** Show that $\bar{\beta}$ is a linear function of $Y_1, Y_2, \ldots, Y_n$.

   **b.** Show that $\bar{\beta}$ is conditionally unbiased.

**5.10** Let $X_i$ denote a binary variable and consider the regression $Y_i = \beta_0 + \beta_1 X_i + u_i$. Let $\bar{Y}_0$ denote the sample mean for observations with $X = 0$ and let $\bar{Y}_1$ denote the sample mean for observations with $X = 1$. Show that $\hat{\beta}_0 = \bar{Y}_0$, $\hat{\beta}_0 + \hat{\beta}_1 = \bar{Y}_1$, and $\hat{\beta}_1 = \bar{Y}_1 - \bar{Y}_0$.

**5.11** A random sample of workers contains $n_m = 100$ men and $n_w = 150$ women. The sample average of men's weekly earnings $\bar{Y}_m = \$565.89$, and the sample standard deviation is $s_m = \$75.62$. The corresponding values for women are $\bar{Y}_w = \$502.37$ and $s_w = \$53.40$. Let *Women* denote an indicator variable that is equal to 1 for women and 0 for men and suppose that all 250 observations are used in the regression $Y_i = \beta_0 + \beta_1 Women_i + u_i$. Find the OLS estimates of $\beta_0$ and $\beta_1$ and their corresponding standard errors.

**5.12** Starting from Equation (4.22), derive the variance of $\hat{\beta}_0$ under homoskedasticity given in Equation (5.28) in Appendix 5.1.

**5.13** Suppose that $(Y_i, X_i)$ satisfy the least squares assumptions in Key Concept 4.3 and, in addition, $u_i$ is $N(0, \sigma_u^2)$ and is independent of $X_i$.

   **a.** Is $\hat{\beta}_1$ conditionally unbiased?

   **b.** Is $\hat{\beta}_1$ the best linear conditionally unbiased estimator of $\beta_1$?

   **c.** How would your answers to (a) and (b) change if you assumed only that $(Y_i, X_i)$ satisfied the least squares assumptions in Key Concept 4.3 and var$(u_i \mid X_i = x)$ is constant?

   **d.** How would your answers to (a) and (b) change if you assumed only that $(Y_i, X_i)$ satisfied the least squares assumptions in Key Concept 4.3?

**5.14** Suppose that $Y_i = \beta X_i + u_i$, where $(u_i, X_i)$ satisfy the Gauss–Markov conditions given in Equation (5.31).

   **a.** Derive the least squares estimator of $\beta$ and show that it is a linear function of $Y_1, \ldots, Y_n$.

    **b.** Show that the estimator is conditionally unbiased.

    **c.** Derive the conditional variance of the estimator.

    **d.** Prove that the estimator is BLUE.

**5.15** A researcher has two independent samples of observations on $(Y_i, X_i)$. To be specific, suppose that $Y_i$ denotes earnings, $X_i$ denotes years of schooling, and the independent samples are for men and women. Write the regression for men as $Y_{m,i} = \beta_{m,0} + \beta_{m,1} X_{m,i} + u_{m,i}$ and the regression for women as $Y_{w,i} = \beta_{w,0} + \beta_{w,1} X_{w,i} + u_{w,i}$. Let $\hat{\beta}_{m,1}$ denote the OLS estimator constructed using the sample of men, $\hat{\beta}_{w,1}$ denote the OLS estimator constructed from the sample of women, and $SE(\hat{\beta}_{m,1})$ and $SE(\hat{\beta}_{w,1})$ denote the corresponding standard errors. Show that the standard error of $\hat{\beta}_{m,1} - \hat{\beta}_{w,1}$ is given by $SE(\hat{\beta}_{m,1} - \hat{\beta}_{w,1}) = \sqrt{[SE(\hat{\beta}_{m,1})]^2 + [SE(\hat{\beta}_{w,1})]^2}$.

## Empirical Exercises

(Only three empirical exercises for this chapter are given in the text, but you can find more on the text website, **www.pearsonglobaleditions.com/Stock_Watson**.)

**E5.1** Use the data set **Earnings_and_Height** described in Empirical Exercise 4.2 to carry out the following exercises.

    **a.** Run a regression of *Earnings* on *Height*.

        i. Is the estimated slope statistically significant?

        ii. Construct a 95% confidence interval for the slope coefficient.

    **b.** Repeat (a) for women.

    **c.** Repeat (a) for men.

    **d.** Test the null hypothesis that the effect of height on earnings is the same for men and women. (*Hint:* See Exercise 5.15.)

    **e.** One explanation for the effect on height on earnings is that some professions require strength, which is correlated with height. Does the effect of height on earnings disappear when the sample is restricted to occupations in which strength is unlikely to be important?

**E5.2** Using the data set **Growth** described in Empirical Exercise 4.1, but excluding the data for Malta, run a regression of *Growth* on *TradeShare*.

    **a.** Is the estimated regression slope statistically significant? This is, can you reject the null hypothesis $H_0: \beta_1 = 0$ vs. a two-sided alternative hypothesis at the 10%, 5%, or 1% significance level?

**b.** What is the *p*-value associated with the coefficient's *t*-statistic?

**c.** Construct a 90% confidence interval for $\beta_1$.

**E5.3** On the text website, **www.pearsonglobaleditions.com/Stock_Watson**, you will find the data file **Birthweight_Smoking**, which contains data for a random sample of babies born in Pennsylvania in 1989. The data include the baby's birth weight together with various characteristics of the mother, including whether she smoked during the pregnancy.[2] A detailed description is given in **Birthweight_Smoking_Description**, also available on the website. In this exercise you will investigate the relationship between birth weight and smoking during pregnancy.

**a.** In the sample:

   i. What is the average value of *Birthweight* for all mothers?

   ii. For mothers who smoke?

   iii. For mothers who do not smoke?

**b.** i. Use the data in the sample to estimate the difference in average birth weight for smoking and nonsmoking mothers.

   ii. What is the standard error for the estimated difference in (i)?

   iii. Construct a 95% confidence interval for the difference in the average birth weight for smoking and nonsmoking mothers.

**c.** Run a regression of *Birthweight* on the binary variable *Smoker*.

   i. Explain how the estimated slope and intercept are related to your answers in parts (a) and (b).

   ii. Explain how the $SE(\hat{\beta}_1)$ is related to your answer in b(ii).

   iii. Construct a 95% confidence interval for the effect of smoking on birth weight.

**d.** Do you think smoking is uncorrelated with other factors that cause low birth weight? That is, do you think that the regression error term, say $u_i$, has a conditional mean of zero, given *Smoking* $(X_i)$? (You will investigate this further in *Birthweight* and *Smoking* exercises in later chapters.)

---

[2]These data were provided by Professors Douglas Almond (Columbia University), Ken Chay (Brown University), and David Lee (Princeton University) and were used in their paper "The Costs of Low Birth Weight," *Quarterly Journal of Economics*, August 2005, 120(3): 1031–1083.

# 5.1   Formulas for OLS Standard Errors

This appendix discusses the formulas for OLS standard errors. These are first presented under the least squares assumptions in Key Concept 4.3, which allow for heteroskedasticity; these are the "heteroskedasticity-robust" standard errors. Formulas for the variance of the OLS estimators and the associated standard errors are then given for the special case of homoskedasticity.

## Heteroskedasticity-Robust Standard Errors

The estimator $\hat{\sigma}^2_{\hat{\beta}_1}$ defined in Equation (5.4) is obtained by replacing the population variances in Equation (4.21) by the corresponding sample variances, with a modification. The variance in the numerator of Equation (4.21) is estimated by $\frac{1}{n-2}\Sigma_{i=1}^n (X_i - \overline{X})^2 \hat{u}_i^2$, where the divisor $n - 2$ (instead of $n$) incorporates a degrees-of-freedom adjustment to correct for downward bias, analogously to the degrees-of-freedom adjustment used in the definition of the *SER* in Section 4.3. The variance in the denominator is estimated by $(1/n)\Sigma_{i=1}^n (X_i - \overline{X})^2$. Replacing $\text{var}[(X_i - \mu_X)u_i]$ and $\text{var}(X_i)$ in Equation (4.21) by these two estimators yields $\hat{\sigma}^2_{\hat{\beta}_1}$ in Equation (5.4). The consistency of heteroskedasticity-robust standard errors is discussed in Section 17.3.

The estimator of the variance of $\hat{\beta}_0$ is

$$\hat{\sigma}^2_{\hat{\beta}_0} = \frac{1}{n} \times \frac{\dfrac{1}{n-2}\sum_{i=1}^n \hat{H}_i^2 \hat{u}_i^2}{\left(\dfrac{1}{n}\sum_{i=1}^n \hat{H}_i^2\right)^2}, \tag{5.26}$$

where $\hat{H}_i = 1 - (\overline{X}/\frac{1}{n}\Sigma_{i=1}^n X_i^2)X_i$. The standard error of $\hat{\beta}_0$ is $SE(\hat{\beta}_0) = \sqrt{\hat{\sigma}^2_{\hat{\beta}_0}}$. The reasoning behind the estimator $\hat{\sigma}^2_{\hat{\beta}_0}$ is the same as behind $\hat{\sigma}^2_{\hat{\beta}_1}$ and stems from replacing population expectations with sample averages.

## Homoskedasticity-Only Variances

Under homoskedasticity, the conditional variance of $u_i$ given $X_i$ is a constant: $\text{var}(u_i \mid X_i) = \sigma_u^2$. If the errors are homoskedastic, the formulas in Key Concept 4.4 simplify to

$$\sigma^2_{\hat{\beta}_1} = \frac{\sigma_u^2}{n\sigma_X^2} \text{ and} \tag{5.27}$$

$$\sigma^2_{\hat{\beta}_0} = \frac{E(X_i^2)}{n\sigma_X^2}\sigma_u^2. \tag{5.28}$$

To derive Equation (5.27), write the numerator in Equation (4.21) as $\text{var}[(X_i - \mu_X)u_i]$ $= E(\{(X_i - \mu_X)u_i - E[(X_i - \mu_X)u_i]\}^2) = E\{[(X_i - \mu_X)u_i]^2\} = E[(X_i - \mu_X)^2 u_i^2] = E[(X_i - \mu_X)^2 \text{var}(u_i \mid X_i)]$, where the second equality follows because $E[(X_i - \mu_X)u_i] = 0$ (by the first least squares assumption) and where the final equality follows from the law of iterated expectations (Section 2.3). If $u_i$ is homoskedastic, then $\text{var}(u_i \mid X_i) = \sigma_u^2$, so $E[(X_i - \mu_X)^2 \text{var}(u_i \mid X_i)] = \sigma_u^2 E[(X_i - \mu_X)^2] = \sigma_u^2 \sigma_X^2$. The result in Equation (5.27) follows by substituting this expression into the numerator of Equation (4.21) and simplifying. A similar calculation yields Equation (5.28).

## Homoskedasticity-Only Standard Errors

The homoskedasticity-only standard errors are obtained by substituting sample means and variances for the population means and variances in Equations (5.27) and (5.28) and by estimating the variance of $u_i$ by the square of the *SER*. The homoskedasticity-only estimators of these variances are

$$\tilde{\sigma}_{\hat{\beta}_1}^2 = \frac{s_{\hat{u}}^2}{\sum_{i=1}^{n}(X_i - \overline{X})^2} \quad \text{(homoskedasticity-only) and} \tag{5.29}$$

$$\tilde{\sigma}_{\hat{\beta}_0}^2 = \frac{\left(\frac{1}{n}\sum_{i=1}^{n}X_i^2\right)s_{\hat{u}}^2}{\sum_{i=1}^{n}(X_i - \overline{X})^2} \quad \text{(homoskedasticity-only),} \tag{5.30}$$

where $s_{\hat{u}}^2$ is given in Equation (4.19). The homoskedasticity-only standard errors are the square roots of $\tilde{\sigma}_{\hat{\beta}_0}^2$ and $\tilde{\sigma}_{\hat{\beta}_1}^2$.

**APPENDIX**

## 5.2 The Gauss–Markov Conditions and a Proof of the Gauss–Markov Theorem

As discussed in Section 5.5, the Gauss–Markov theorem states that if the Gauss–Markov conditions hold, then the OLS estimator is the best (most efficient) conditionally linear unbiased estimator (is BLUE). This appendix begins by stating the Gauss–Markov conditions and showing that they are implied by the three least squares condition plus homoskedasticity.

We next show that the OLS estimator is a linear conditionally unbiased estimator. Finally, we turn to the proof of the theorem.

## The Gauss–Markov Conditions

The three Gauss–Markov conditions are

(i) $E(u_i|X_1, \ldots, X_n) = 0$

(ii) $\operatorname{var}(u_i|X_1, \ldots, X_n) = \sigma_u^2, \quad 0 < \sigma_u^2 < \infty$

(iii) $E(u_iu_j|X_1, \ldots, X_n) = 0, i \neq j,$ (5.31)

where the conditions hold for $i, j = 1, \ldots, n$. The three conditions, respectively, state that $u_i$ has mean zero, that $u_i$ has a constant variance, and that the errors are uncorrelated for different observations, where all these statements hold conditionally on all observed $X$'s $(X_1, \ldots, X_n)$.

The **Gauss–Markov conditions** are implied by the three least squares assumptions (Key Concept 4.3), plus the additional assumptions that the errors are homoskedastic. Because the observations are i.i.d. (Assumption 2), $E(u_i|X_1, \ldots, X_n) = E(u_i|X_i)$, and by Assumption 1, $E(u_i|X_i) = 0$; thus condition (i) holds. Similarly, by Assumption 2, $\operatorname{var}(u_i|X_1, \ldots, X_n) = \operatorname{var}(u_i|X_i)$, and because the errors are assumed to be homoskedastic, $\operatorname{var}(u_i|X_i) = \sigma_u^2$, which is constant. Assumption 3 (nonzero finite fourth moments) ensures that $0 < \sigma_u^2 < \infty$, so condition (ii) holds. To show that condition (iii) is implied by the least squares assumptions, note that $E(u_iu_j|X_1, \ldots, X_n) = E(u_iu_j|X_i, X_j)$ because $(X_i, Y_i)$ are i.i.d. by Assumption 2. Assumption 2 also implies that $E(u_iu_j|X_i, X_j) = E(u_i|X_i)\,E(u_j|X_j)$ for $i \neq j$; because $E(u_i|X_i) = 0$ for all $i$, it follows that $E(u_iu_j|X_1, \ldots, X_n) = 0$ for all $i \neq j$, so condition (iii) holds. Thus the least squares assumptions in Key Concept 4.3, plus homoskedasticity of the errors, imply the Gauss–Markov conditions in Equation (5.31).

## The OLS Estimator $\hat{\beta}_1$ Is a Linear Conditionally Unbiased Estimator

To show that $\hat{\beta}_1$ is linear, first note that, because $\sum_{i=1}^{n}(X_i - \overline{X}) = 0$ (by the definition of $\overline{X}$), $\sum_{i=1}^{n}(X_i - \overline{X})(Y_i - \overline{Y}) = \sum_{i=1}^{n}(X_i - \overline{X})Y_i - \overline{Y}\sum_{i=1}^{n}(X_i - \overline{X}) = \sum_{i=1}^{n}(X_i - \overline{X})Y_i$. Substituting this result into the formula for $\hat{\beta}_1$ in Equation (4.7) yields

$$\hat{\beta}_1 = \frac{\sum_{i=1}^{n}(X_i - \overline{X})Y_i}{\sum_{j=1}^{n}(X_j - \overline{X})^2} = \sum_{i=1}^{n}\hat{a}_iY_i, \text{ where } \hat{a}_i = \frac{(X_i - \overline{X})}{\sum_{j=1}^{n}(X_j - \overline{X})^2} \tag{5.32}$$

Because the weights $\hat{a}_i, i = 1, \ldots, n$, in Equation (5.32) depend on $X_1, \ldots, X_n$ but not on $Y_1, \ldots, Y_n$, the OLS estimator $\hat{\beta}_1$ is a linear estimator.

Under the Gauss–Markov conditions, $\hat{\beta}_1$ is conditionally unbiased, and the variance of the conditional distribution of $\hat{\beta}_1$, given $X_1, \ldots, X_n$, is

$$\text{var}(\hat{\beta}_1 \mid X_1, \ldots, X_n) = \frac{\sigma_u^2}{\sum_{i=1}^{n}(X_i - \overline{X})^2}. \tag{5.33}$$

The result that $\hat{\beta}_1$ is conditionally unbiased was previously shown in Appendix 4.3.

## Proof of the Gauss–Markov Theorem

We start by deriving some facts that hold for all linear conditionally unbiased estimators— that is, for all estimators $\widetilde{\beta}_1$ satisfying Equations (5.24) and (5.25). Substituting $Y_i = \beta_0 + \beta_1 X_i + u_i$ into $\widetilde{\beta}_1 = \sum_{i=1}^{n} a_i Y_i$ and collecting terms, we have that

$$\widetilde{\beta}_1 = \beta_0 \left( \sum_{i=1}^{n} a_i \right) + \beta_1 \left( \sum_{i=1}^{n} a_i X_i \right) + \sum_{i=1}^{n} a_i u_i. \tag{5.34}$$

By the first Gauss–Markov condition, $E(\sum_{i=1}^{n} a_i u_i \mid X_1, \ldots, X_n) = \sum_{i=1}^{n} a_i E(u_i \mid X_1, \ldots, X_n) = 0$; thus taking conditional expectations of both sides of Equation (5.34) yields $E(\widetilde{\beta}_1 \mid X_1, \ldots, X_n) = \beta_0(\sum_{i=1}^{n} a_i) + \beta_1(\sum_{i=1}^{n} a_i X_i)$. Because $\widetilde{\beta}_1$ is conditionally unbiased by assumption, it must be that $\beta_0(\sum_{i=1}^{n} a_i) + \beta_1(\sum_{i=1}^{n} a_i X_i) = \beta_1$, but for this equality to hold for all values of $\beta_0$ and $\beta_1$, it must be the case that, for $\widetilde{\beta}_1$ to be conditionally unbiased,

$$\sum_{i=1}^{n} a_i = 0 \text{ and } \sum_{i=1}^{n} a_i X_i = 1. \tag{5.35}$$

Under the Gauss–Markov conditions, the variance of $\widetilde{\beta}_1$, conditional on $X_1, \ldots, X_n$, has a simple form. Substituting Equation (5.35) into Equation (5.34) yields $\widetilde{\beta}_1 - \beta_1 = \sum_{i=1}^{n} a_i u_i$. Thus $\text{var}(\widetilde{\beta}_1 \mid X_1, \ldots, X_n) = \text{var}(\sum_{i=1}^{n} a_i u_i \mid X_1, \ldots, X_n) = \sum_{i=1}^{n} \sum_{j=1}^{n} a_i a_j \text{cov}(u_i, u_j \mid X_1, \ldots, X_n)$; applying the second and third Gauss–Markov conditions, the cross terms in the double summation vanish, and the expression for the conditional variance simplifies to

$$\text{var}(\widetilde{\beta}_1 \mid X_1, \ldots, X_n) = \sigma_u^2 \sum_{i=1}^{n} a_i^2. \tag{5.36}$$

Note that Equations (5.35) and (5.36) apply to $\hat{\beta}_1$ with weights $a_i = \hat{a}_i$, given in Equation (5.32).

We now show that the two restrictions in Equation (5.35) and the expression for the conditional variance in Equation (5.36) imply that the conditional variance of $\widetilde{\beta}_1$ exceeds the conditional variance of $\hat{\beta}_1$ unless $\widetilde{\beta}_1 = \hat{\beta}_1$. Let $a_i = \hat{a}_i + d_i$, so $\sum_{i=1}^{n} a_i^2 = \sum_{i=1}^{n} (\hat{a}_i + d_i)^2 = \sum_{i=1}^{n} \hat{a}_i^2 + 2\sum_{i=1}^{n} \hat{a}_i d_i + \sum_{i=1}^{n} d_i^2$.

Using the definition of $\hat{a}_i$ in Equation (5.32), we have that

$$
\sum_{i=1}^{n} \hat{a}_i d_i = \frac{\sum_{i=1}^{n} (X_i - \overline{X}) d_i}{\sum_{j=1}^{n} (X_j - \overline{X})^2} = \frac{\sum_{i=1}^{n} d_i X_i - \overline{X} \sum_{i=1}^{n} d_i}{\sum_{j=1}^{n} (X_j - \overline{X})^2}
$$

$$
= \frac{\left( \sum_{i=1}^{n} a_i X_i - \sum_{i=1}^{n} \hat{a}_i X_i \right) - \overline{X} \left( \sum_{i=1}^{n} a_i - \sum_{i=1}^{n} \hat{a}_i \right)}{\sum_{j=1}^{n} (X_j - \overline{X})^2} = 0,
$$

where the penultimate equality follows from $d_i = a_i - \hat{a}_i$ and the final equality follows from Equation (5.35) (which holds for both $a_i$ and $\hat{a}_i$). Thus $\sigma_u^2 \sum_{i=1}^{n} a_i^2 = \sigma_u^2 \sum_{i=1}^{n} \hat{a}_i^2 + \sigma_u^2 \sum_{i=1}^{n} d_i^2 = \mathrm{var}(\hat{\beta}_1 \mid X_1, \ldots, X_n) + \sigma_u^2 \sum_{i=1}^{n} d_i^2$; substituting this result into Equation (5.36) yields

$$
\mathrm{var}(\widetilde{\beta}_1 \mid X_1, \ldots, X_n) - \mathrm{var}(\hat{\beta}_1 \mid X_1, \ldots, X_n) = \sigma_u^2 \sum_{i=1}^{n} d_i^2. \tag{5.37}
$$

Thus $\widetilde{\beta}_1$ has a greater conditional variance than $\hat{\beta}_1$ if $d_i$ is nonzero for any $i = 1, \ldots, n$. But if $d_i = 0$ for all $i$, then $a_i = \hat{a}_i$ and $\widetilde{\beta}_1 = \hat{\beta}_1$, which proves that OLS is BLUE.

## The Gauss–Markov Theorem When *X* Is Nonrandom

With a minor change in interpretation, the Gauss–Markov theorem also applies to nonrandom regressors; that is, it applies to regressors that do not change their values over repeated samples. Specifically, if the second least squares assumption is replaced by the assumption that $X_1, \ldots, X_n$ are nonrandom (fixed over repeated samples) and $u_1, \ldots, u_n$ are i.i.d., then the foregoing statement and proof of the Gauss–Markov theorem apply directly, except that all of the "conditional on $X_1, \ldots, X_n$" statements are unnecessary because $X_1, \ldots, X_n$ take on the same values from one sample to the next.

## The Sample Average Is the Efficient Linear Estimator of *E*(*Y*)

An implication of the Gauss–Markov theorem is that the sample average, $\overline{Y}$, is the most efficient linear estimator of $E(Y_i)$ when $Y_i, \ldots, Y_n$ are i.i.d. To see this, consider the case of regression without an "$X$" so that the only regressor is the constant regressor $X_{0i} = 1$. Then the OLS estimator $\hat{\beta}_0 = \overline{Y}$. It follows that, under the Gauss–Markov assumptions, $\overline{Y}$ is BLUE. Note that the Gauss–Markov requirement that the error be homoskedastic is automatically satisfied in this case because there is no regressor, so it follows that $\overline{Y}$ is BLUE if $Y_1, \ldots, Y_n$ are i.i.d. This result was stated previously in Key Concept 3.3.

# Linear Regression with Multiple Regressors

C hapter 5 ended on a worried note. Although school districts with lower student–teacher ratios tend to have higher test scores in the California data set, perhaps students from districts with small classes have other advantages that help them perform well on standardized tests. Could this have produced misleading results, and, if so, what can be done?

Omitted factors, such as student characteristics, can, in fact, make the ordinary least squares (OLS) estimator of the effect of class size on test scores misleading or, more precisely, biased. This chapter explains this "omitted variable bias" and introduces multiple regression, a method that can eliminate omitted variable bias. The key idea of multiple regression is that if we have data on these omitted variables, then we can include them as additional regressors and thereby estimate the effect of one regressor (the student–teacher ratio) while holding constant the other variables (such as student characteristics).

This chapter explains how to estimate the coefficients of the multiple linear regression model. Many aspects of multiple regression parallel those of regression with a single regressor, studied in Chapters 4 and 5. The coefficients of the multiple regression model can be estimated from data using OLS; the OLS estimators in multiple regression are random variables because they depend on data from a random sample; and in large samples the sampling distributions of the OLS estimators are approximately normal.

## 6.1 Omitted Variable Bias

By focusing only on the student–teacher ratio, the empirical analysis in Chapters 4 and 5 ignored some potentially important determinants of test scores by collecting their influences in the regression error term. These omitted factors include school characteristics, such as teacher quality and computer usage, and student characteristics, such as family background. We begin by considering an omitted student characteristic that is particularly relevant in California because of its large immigrant population: the prevalence in the school district of students who are still learning English.

By ignoring the percentage of English learners in the district, the OLS estimator of the slope in the regression of test scores on the student–teacher ratio could be biased; that is, the mean of the sampling distribution of the OLS estimator might not equal the true effect on test scores of a unit change in the student–teacher ratio. Here is the reasoning. Students who are still learning English might perform worse on standardized tests than native English speakers. If districts with large classes also have many students still learning English, then the OLS regression of test scores on the student–teacher ratio could erroneously find a correlation and produce a large estimated coefficient, when in fact the true causal effect of cutting class sizes on test scores is small, even zero. Accordingly, based on the analysis of Chapters 4 and 5, the superintendent might hire enough new teachers to reduce the student–teacher ratio by 2, but her hoped-for improvement in test scores will fail to materialize if the true coefficient is small or zero.

A look at the California data lends credence to this concern. The correlation between the student–teacher ratio and the percentage of English learners (students who are not native English speakers and who have not yet mastered English) in the district is 0.19. This small but positive correlation suggests that districts with more English learners tend to have a higher student–teacher ratio (larger classes). If the student–teacher ratio were unrelated to the percentage of English learners, then it would be safe to ignore English proficiency in the regression of test scores against the student–teacher ratio. But because the student–teacher ratio and the percentage of English learners are correlated, it is possible that the OLS coefficient in the regression of test scores on the student–teacher ratio reflects that influence.

## Definition of Omitted Variable Bias

If the regressor (the student–teacher ratio) is correlated with a variable that has been omitted from the analysis (the percentage of English learners) and that determines, in part, the dependent variable (test scores), then the OLS estimator will have **omitted variable bias**.

Omitted variable bias occurs when two conditions are true: (1) when the omitted variable is correlated with the included regressor and (2) when the omitted variable is a determinant of the dependent variable. To illustrate these conditions, consider three examples of variables that are omitted from the regression of test scores on the student–teacher ratio.

*Example #1: Percentage of English learners.* Because the percentage of English learners is correlated with the student–teacher ratio, the first condition for omitted variable bias holds. It is plausible that students who are still learning English will do worse on standardized tests than native English speakers, in which case the percentage of English learners is a determinant of test scores and the second condition for omitted variable bias holds. Thus the OLS estimator in the regression of test scores on the student–teacher ratio could incorrectly reflect the influence of the omitted variable, the percentage of English learners. That is, omitting the percentage of English learners may introduce omitted variable bias.

*Example #2: Time of day of the test.*  Another variable omitted from the analysis is the time of day that the test was administered. For this omitted variable, it is plausible that the first condition for omitted variable bias does not hold but that the second condition does. For example, if the time of day of the test varies from one district to the next in a way that is unrelated to class size, then the time of day and class size would be uncorrelated so the first condition does not hold. Conversely, the time of day of the test could affect scores (alertness varies through the school day), so the second condition holds. However, because in this example the time of day the test is administered is uncorrelated with the student–teacher ratio, the student–teacher ratio could not be incorrectly picking up the "time of day" effect. Thus omitting the time of day of the test does not result in omitted variable bias.

*Example #3: Parking lot space per pupil.*  Another omitted variable is parking lot space per pupil (the area of the teacher parking lot divided by the number of students). This variable satisfies the first but not the second condition for omitted variable bias. Specifically, schools with more teachers per pupil probably have more teacher parking space, so the first condition would be satisfied. However, under the assumption that learning takes place in the classroom, not the parking lot, parking lot space has no direct effect on learning; thus the second condition does not hold. Because parking lot space per pupil is not a determinant of test scores, omitting it from the analysis does not lead to omitted variable bias.

Omitted variable bias is summarized in Key Concept 6.1.

*Omitted variable bias and the first least squares assumption.*  Omitted variable bias means that the first least squares assumption—that $E(u_i | X_i) = 0$, as listed in Key Concept 4.3—is incorrect. To see why, recall that the error term $u_i$ in the linear regression model with a single regressor represents all factors, other than $X_i$, that are determinants of $Y_i$. If one of these other factors is correlated with $X_i$, this means that the error term (which contains this factor) is correlated with $X_i$. In other words, if an omitted variable is a determinant of $Y_i$, then it is in the error term, and if it is correlated with $X_i$, then the error term is correlated with $X_i$.

**KEY CONCEPT**

**6.1**

## Omitted Variable Bias in Regression with a Single Regressor

Omitted variable bias is the bias in the OLS estimator that arises when the regressor, $X$, is correlated with an omitted variable. For omitted variable bias to occur, two conditions must be true:

1. $X$ is correlated with the omitted variable.

2. The omitted variable is a determinant of the dependent variable, $Y$.

Because $u_i$ and $X_i$ are correlated, the conditional mean of $u_i$ given $X_i$ is nonzero. This correlation therefore violates the first least squares assumption, and the consequence is serious: The OLS estimator is biased. This bias does not vanish even in very large samples, and the OLS estimator is inconsistent.

### A Formula for Omitted Variable Bias

The discussion of the previous section about omitted variable bias can be summarized mathematically by a formula for this bias. Let the correlation between $X_i$ and $u_i$ be $\text{corr}(X_i, u_i) = \rho_{Xu}$. Suppose that the second and third least squares assumptions hold, but the first does not because $\rho_{Xu}$ is nonzero. Then the OLS estimator has the limit (derived in Appendix 6.1)

$$\hat{\beta}_1 \xrightarrow{p} \beta_1 + \rho_{Xu}\frac{\sigma_u}{\sigma_X}. \tag{6.1}$$

That is, as the sample size increases, $\hat{\beta}_1$ is close to $\beta_1 + \rho_{Xu}(\sigma_u/\sigma_X)$ with increasingly high probability.

The formula in Equation (6.1) summarizes several of the ideas discussed above about omitted variable bias:

1. Omitted variable bias is a problem whether the sample size is large or small. Because $\hat{\beta}_1$ does not converge in probability to the true value $\beta_1$, $\hat{\beta}_1$ is biased and inconsistent; that is, $\hat{\beta}_1$ is not a consistent estimator of $\beta_1$ when there is omitted variable bias. The term $\rho_{Xu}(\sigma_u/\sigma_X)$ in Equation (6.1) is the bias in $\hat{\beta}_1$ that persists even in large samples.

## The Mozart Effect: Omitted Variable Bias?

A study published in *Nature* in 1993 (Rauscher, Shaw, and Ky, 1993) suggested that listening to Mozart for 10 to 15 minutes could temporarily raise your IQ by 8 or 9 points. That study made big news—and politicians and parents saw an easy way to make their children smarter. For a while, the state of Georgia even distributed classical music CDs to all infants in the state.

What is the evidence for the "Mozart effect"? A review of dozens of studies found that students who take optional music or arts courses in high school do, in fact, have higher English and math test scores than those who don't.[1] A closer look at these studies, however, suggests that the real reason for the better test performance has little to do with those courses. Instead, the authors of the review suggested that the correlation between testing well and taking art or music could arise from any number of things. For example, the academically better students might have more time to take optional music courses or more interest in doing so, or those schools with a deeper music curriculum might just be better schools across the board.

In the terminology of regression, the estimated relationship between test scores and taking optional music courses appears to have omitted variable bias. By omitting factors such as the student's innate ability or the overall quality of the school, studying music appears to have an effect on test scores when in fact it has none.

So is there a Mozart effect? One way to find out is to do a randomized controlled experiment. (As discussed in Chapter 4, randomized controlled experiments eliminate omitted variable bias by randomly assigning participants to "treatment" and "control" groups.) Taken together, the many controlled experiments on the Mozart effect fail to show that listening to Mozart improves IQ or general test performance. For reasons not fully understood, however, it seems that listening to classical music *does* help temporarily in one narrow area: folding paper and visualizing shapes. So the next time you cram for an origami exam, try to fit in a little Mozart, too.

---

[1]See the fall/winter 2000 issue of *Journal of Aesthetic Education* 34, especially the article by Ellen Winner and Monica Cooper (pp. 11–76) and the one by Lois Hetland (pp. 105–148).

2. Whether this bias is large or small in practice depends on the correlation $\rho_{Xu}$ between the regressor and the error term. The larger $|\rho_{Xu}|$ is, the larger the bias.

3. The direction of the bias in $\hat{\beta}_1$ depends on whether $X$ and $u$ are positively or negatively correlated. For example, we speculated that the percentage of students learning English has a *negative* effect on district test scores (students still learning English have lower scores), so that the percentage of English learners enters the error term with a negative sign. In our data, the fraction of English learners is *positively* correlated with the student–teacher

ratio (districts with more English learners have larger classes). Thus the student–teacher ratio ($X$) would be *negatively* correlated with the error term ($u$), so $\rho_{Xu} < 0$ and the coefficient on the student–teacher ratio $\hat{\beta}_1$ would be biased toward a negative number. In other words, having a small percentage of English learners is associated both with *high* test scores and *low* student–teacher ratios, so one reason that the OLS estimator suggests that small classes improve test scores may be that the districts with small classes have fewer English learners.

## Addressing Omitted Variable Bias by Dividing the Data into Groups

What can you do about omitted variable bias? Our superintendent is considering increasing the number of teachers in her district, but she has no control over the fraction of immigrants in her community. As a result, she is interested in the effect of the student–teacher ratio on test scores, *holding constant* other factors, including the percentage of English learners. This new way of posing her question suggests that, instead of using data for all districts, perhaps we should focus on districts with percentages of English learners comparable to hers. Among this subset of districts, do those with smaller classes do better on standardized tests?

Table 6.1 reports evidence on the relationship between class size and test scores within districts with comparable percentages of English learners. Districts are divided into eight groups. First, the districts are broken into four categories

| TABLE 6.1 | Differences in Test Scores for California School Districts with Low and High Student–Teacher Ratios, by the Percentage of English Learners in the District | | | | | |
|---|---|---|---|---|---|---|
| | Student–Teacher Ratio < 20 | | Student–Teacher Ratio ≥ 20 | | Difference in Test Scores, Low vs. High STR | |
| | Average Test Score | n | Average Test Score | n | Difference | t-statistic |
| All districts | 657.4 | 238 | 650.0 | 182 | 7.4 | 4.04 |
| Percentage of English learners | | | | | | |
| < 1.9% | 664.5 | 76 | 665.4 | 27 | −0.9 | −0.30 |
| 1.9–8.8% | 665.2 | 64 | 661.8 | 44 | 3.3 | 1.13 |
| 8.8–23.0% | 654.9 | 54 | 649.7 | 50 | 5.2 | 1.72 |
| > 23.0% | 636.7 | 44 | 634.8 | 61 | 1.9 | 0.68 |

that correspond to the quartiles of the distribution of the percentage of English learners across districts. Second, within each of these four categories, districts are further broken down into two groups, depending on whether the student–teacher ratio is small ($STR < 20$) or large ($STR \geq 20$).

The first row in Table 6.1 reports the overall difference in average test scores between districts with low and high student–teacher ratios, that is, the difference in test scores between these two groups without breaking them down further into the quartiles of English learners. (Recall that this difference was previously reported in regression form in Equation (5.18) as the OLS estimate of the coefficient on $D_i$ in the regression of *TestScore* on $D_i$, where $D_i$ is a binary regressor that equals 1 if $STR_i < 20$ and equals 0 otherwise.) Over the full sample of 420 districts, the average test score is 7.4 points higher in districts with a low student–teacher ratio than a high one; the *t*-statistic is 4.04, so the null hypothesis that the mean test score is the same in the two groups is rejected at the 1% significance level.

The final four rows in Table 6.1 report the difference in test scores between districts with low and high student–teacher ratios, broken down by the quartile of the percentage of English learners. This evidence presents a different picture. Of the districts with the fewest English learners ($< 1.9\%$), the average test score for those 76 with low student–teacher ratios is 664.5 and the average for the 27 with high student–teacher ratios is 665.4. Thus, for the districts with the fewest English learners, test scores were on average 0.9 points *lower* in the districts with low student–teacher ratios! In the second quartile, districts with low student–teacher ratios had test scores that averaged 3.3 points higher than those with high student–teacher ratios; this gap was 5.2 points for the third quartile and only 1.9 points for the quartile of districts with the most English learners. Once we hold the percentage of English learners constant, the difference in performance between districts with high and low student–teacher ratios is perhaps half (or less) of the overall estimate of 7.4 points.

At first this finding might seem puzzling. How can the overall effect of test scores be twice the effect of test scores within any quartile? The answer is that the districts with the most English learners tend to have *both* the highest student–teacher ratios *and* the lowest test scores. The difference in the average test score between districts in the lowest and highest quartile of the percentage of English learners is large, approximately 30 points. The districts with few English learners tend to have lower student–teacher ratios: 74% (76 of 103) of the districts in the first quartile of English learners have small classes ($STR < 20$), while only 42% (44 of 105) of the districts in the quartile with the most English learners have small classes. So, the districts with the most English learners have both lower test scores and higher student–teacher ratios than the other districts.

This analysis reinforces the superintendent's worry that omitted variable bias is present in the regression of test scores against the student–teacher ratio. By looking within quartiles of the percentage of English learners, the test score differences in the second part of Table 6.1 improve on the simple difference-of-means analysis in the first line of Table 6.1. Still, this analysis does not yet provide the superintendent with a useful estimate of the effect on test scores of changing class size, holding constant the fraction of English learners. Such an estimate can be provided, however, using the method of multiple regression.

# 6.2 The Multiple Regression Model

The **multiple regression model** extends the single variable regression model of Chapters 4 and 5 to include additional variables as regressors. This model permits estimating the effect on $Y_i$ of changing one variable ($X_{1i}$) while holding the other regressors ($X_{2i}$, $X_{3i}$, and so forth) constant. In the class size problem, the multiple regression model provides a way to isolate the effect on test scores ($Y_i$) of the student–teacher ratio ($X_{1i}$) while holding constant the percentage of students in the district who are English learners ($X_{2i}$).

## The Population Regression Line

Suppose for the moment that there are only two independent variables, $X_{1i}$ and $X_{2i}$. In the linear multiple regression model, the average relationship between these two independent variables and the dependent variable, $Y$, is given by the linear function

$$E(Y_i | X_{1i} = x_1, X_{2i} = x_2) = \beta_0 + \beta_1 x_1 + \beta_2 x_2, \tag{6.2}$$

where $E(Y_i | X_{1i} = x_1, X_{2i} = x_2)$ is the conditional expectation of $Y_i$ given that $X_{1i} = x_1$ and $X_{2i} = x_2$. That is, if the student–teacher ratio in the $i^{\text{th}}$ district ($X_{1i}$) equals some value $x_1$ and the percentage of English learners in the $i^{\text{th}}$ district ($X_{2i}$) equals $x_2$, then the expected value of $Y_i$ given the student–teacher ratio and the percentage of English learners is given by Equation (6.2).

Equation (6.2) is the **population regression line** or **population regression function** in the multiple regression model. The coefficient $\beta_0$ is the **intercept**; the coefficient $\beta_1$ is the **slope coefficient of $X_{1i}$** or, more simply, the **coefficient on $X_{1i}$**; and the coefficient $\beta_2$ is the **slope coefficient of $X_{2i}$** or, more simply, the **coefficient on $X_{2i}$**. One or more of the independent variables in the multiple regression model are sometimes referred to as control variables.

The interpretation of the coefficient $\beta_1$ in Equation (6.2) is different than it was when $X_{1i}$ was the only regressor: In Equation (6.2), $\beta_1$ is the effect on $Y$ of a unit change in $X_1$, **holding $X_2$ constant** or **controlling for $X_2$**.

This interpretation of $\beta_1$ follows from the definition that the expected effect on $Y$ of a change in $X_1$, $\Delta X_1$, holding $X_2$ constant, is the difference between the expected value of $Y$ when the independent variables take on the values $X_1 + \Delta X_1$ and $X_2$ and the expected value of $Y$ when the independent variables take on the values $X_1$ and $X_2$. Accordingly, write the population regression function in Equation (6.2) as $Y = \beta_0 + \beta_1 X_1 + \beta_2 X_2$ and imagine changing $X_1$ by the amount $\Delta X_1$ while not changing $X_2$, that is, while holding $X_2$ constant. Because $X_1$ has changed, $Y$ will change by some amount, say $\Delta Y$. After this change, the new value of $Y$, $Y + \Delta Y$, is

$$Y + \Delta Y = \beta_0 + \beta_1(X_1 + \Delta X_1) + \beta_2 X_2. \tag{6.3}$$

An equation for $\Delta Y$ in terms of $\Delta X_1$ is obtained by subtracting the equation $Y = \beta_0 + \beta_1 X_1 + \beta_2 X_2$ from Equation (6.3), yielding $\Delta Y = \beta_1 \Delta X_1$. Rearranging this equation shows that

$$\beta_1 = \frac{\Delta Y}{\Delta X_1} \text{ holding } X_2 \text{ constant.} \tag{6.4}$$

The coefficient $\beta_1$ is the effect on $Y$ (the expected change in $Y$) of a unit change in $X_1$, holding $X_2$ fixed. Another phrase used to describe $\beta_1$ is the **partial effect** on $Y$ of $X_1$, holding $X_2$ fixed.

The interpretation of the intercept in the multiple regression model, $\beta_0$, is similar to the interpretation of the intercept in the single-regressor model: It is the expected value of $Y_i$ when $X_{1i}$ and $X_{2i}$ are zero. Simply put, the intercept $\beta_0$ determines how far up the $Y$ axis the population regression line starts.

## The Population Multiple Regression Model

The population regression line in Equation (6.2) is the relationship between $Y$ and $X_1$ and $X_2$ that holds on average in the population. Just as in the case of regression with a single regressor, however, this relationship does not hold exactly because many other factors influence the dependent variable. In addition to the student–teacher ratio and the fraction of students still learning English, for example, test scores are influenced by school characteristics, other student characteristics, and luck. Thus the population regression function in Equation (6.2) needs to be augmented to incorporate these additional factors.

Just as in the case of regression with a single regressor, the factors that determine $Y_i$ in addition to $X_{1i}$ and $X_{2i}$ are incorporated into Equation (6.2) as an "error" term $u_i$. This error term is the deviation of a particular observation (test scores in the $i^{\text{th}}$ district in our example) from the average population relationship. Accordingly, we have

$$Y_i = \beta_0 + \beta_1 X_{1i} + \beta_2 X_{2i} + u_i, i = 1, \ldots, n, \tag{6.5}$$

where the subscript $i$ indicates the $i^{\text{th}}$ of the $n$ observations (districts) in the sample.

Equation (6.5) is the **population multiple regression model** when there are two regressors, $X_{1i}$ and $X_{2i}$.

In regression with binary regressors, it can be useful to treat $\beta_0$ as the coefficient on a regressor that always equals 1; think of $\beta_0$ as the coefficient on $X_{0i}$, where $X_{0i} = 1$ for $i = 1, \ldots, n$. Accordingly, the population multiple regression model in Equation (6.5) can alternatively be written as

$$Y_i = \beta_0 X_{0i} + \beta_1 X_{1i} + \beta_2 X_{2i} + u_i, \text{ where } X_{0i} = 1, i = 1, \ldots, n. \tag{6.6}$$

The variable $X_{0i}$ is sometimes called the **constant regressor** because it takes on the same value—the value 1—for all observations. Similarly, the intercept, $\beta_0$, is sometimes called the **constant term** in the regression.

The two ways of writing the population regression model, Equations (6.5) and (6.6), are equivalent.

The discussion so far has focused on the case of a single additional variable, $X_2$. In practice, however, there might be multiple factors omitted from the single-regressor model. For example, ignoring the students' economic background might result in omitted variable bias, just as ignoring the fraction of English learners did. This reasoning leads us to consider a model with three regressors or, more generally, a model that includes $k$ regressors. The multiple regression model with $k$ regressors, $X_{1i}, X_{2i}, \ldots, X_{ki}$, is summarized as Key Concept 6.2.

The definitions of homoskedasticity and heteroskedasticity in the multiple regression model are extensions of their definitions in the single-regressor model. The error term $u_i$ in the multiple regression model is **homoskedastic** if the variance of the conditional distribution of $u_i$ given $X_{1i}, \ldots, X_{ki}$, $\text{var}(u_i | X_{1i}, \ldots, X_{ki})$, is constant for $i = 1, \ldots, n$ and thus does not depend on the values of $X_{1i}, \ldots, X_{ki}$. Otherwise, the error term is **heteroskedastic**.

The multiple regression model holds out the promise of providing just what the superintendent wants to know: the effect of changing the student–teacher ratio, holding constant other factors that are beyond her control.

KEY CONCEPT

6.2

## The Multiple Regression Model

The multiple regression model is

$$Y_i = \beta_0 + \beta_1 X_{1i} + \beta_2 X_{2i} + \cdots + \beta_k X_{ki} + u_i, i = 1, \ldots, n, \qquad (6.7)$$

where

- $Y_i$ is $i^{th}$ observation on the dependent variable; $X_{1i}, X_{2i}, \ldots, X_{ki}$ are the $i^{th}$ observations on each of the $k$ regressors; and $u_i$ is the error term.

- The population regression line is the relationship that holds between $Y$ and the $X$'s on average in the population:

$$E(Y|X_{1i} = x_1, X_{2i} = x_2, \ldots, X_{ki} = x_k) = \beta_0 + \beta_1 x_1 + \beta_2 x_2 + \cdots + \beta_k x_k.$$

- $\beta_1$ is the slope coefficient on $X_1$, $\beta_2$ is the coefficient on $X_2$, and so on. The coefficient $\beta_1$ is the expected change in $Y_i$ resulting from changing $X_{1i}$ by one unit, holding constant $X_{2i}, \ldots, X_{ki}$. The coefficients on the other $X$'s are interpreted similarly.

- The intercept $\beta_0$ is the expected value of $Y$ when all the $X$'s equal 0. The intercept can be thought of as the coefficient on a regressor, $X_{0i}$, that equals 1 for all $i$.

These factors include not just the percentage of English learners, but other measurable factors that might affect test performance, including the economic background of the students. To be of practical help to the superintendent, however, we need to provide her with estimates of the unknown population coefficients $\beta_0, \ldots, \beta_k$ of the population regression model calculated using a sample of data. Fortunately, these coefficients can be estimated using ordinary least squares.

## 6.3 The OLS Estimator in Multiple Regression

This section describes how the coefficients of the multiple regression model can be estimated using OLS.

## The OLS Estimator

Section 4.2 shows how to estimate the intercept and slope coefficients in the single-regressor model by applying OLS to a sample of observations of $Y$ and $X$. The key idea is that these coefficients can be estimated by minimizing the sum of squared prediction mistakes, that is, by choosing the estimators $b_0$ and $b_1$ so as to minimize $\sum_{i=1}^{n}(Y_i - b_0 - b_1 X_i)^2$. The estimators that do so are the OLS estimators, $\hat{\beta}_0$ and $\hat{\beta}_1$.

The method of OLS also can be used to estimate the coefficients $\beta_0, \beta_1, \ldots, \beta_k$ in the multiple regression model. Let $b_0, b_1, \ldots, b_k$ be estimates of $\beta_0, \beta_1, \ldots, \beta_k$. The predicted value of $Y_i$, calculated using these estimates, is $b_0 + b_1 X_{1i} + \cdots + b_k X_{ki}$, and the mistake in predicting $Y_i$ is $Y_i - (b_0 + b_1 X_{1i} + \cdots + b_k X_{ki}) = Y_i - b_0 - b_1 X_{1i} - \cdots - b_k X_{ki}$. The sum of these squared prediction mistakes over all $n$ observations is thus

$$\sum_{i=1}^{n}(Y_i - b_0 - b_1 X_{1i} - \cdots - b_k X_{ki})^2. \tag{6.8}$$

The sum of the squared mistakes for the linear regression model in Expression (6.8) is the extension of the sum of the squared mistakes given in Equation (4.6) for the linear regression model with a single regressor.

The estimators of the coefficients $\beta_0, \beta_1, \ldots, \beta_k$ that minimize the sum of squared mistakes in Expression (6.8) are called the **ordinary least squares (OLS) estimators of $\beta_0, \beta_1, \ldots, \beta_k$**. The OLS estimators are denoted $\hat{\beta}_0, \hat{\beta}_1, \ldots, \hat{\beta}_k$.

The terminology of OLS in the linear multiple regression model is the same as in the linear regression model with a single regressor. The **OLS regression line** is the straight line constructed using the OLS estimators: $\hat{\beta}_0 + \hat{\beta}_1 X_1 + \cdots + \hat{\beta}_k X_k$. The **predicted value** of $Y_i$ given $X_{1i}, \ldots, X_{ki}$, based on the OLS regression line, is $\hat{Y}_i = \hat{\beta}_0 + \hat{\beta}_1 X_{1i} + \cdots + \hat{\beta}_k X_{ki}$. The **OLS residual** for the $i^{th}$ observation is the difference between $Y_i$ and its OLS predicted value; that is, the OLS residual is $\hat{u}_i = Y_i - \hat{Y}_i$.

The OLS estimators could be computed by trial and error, repeatedly trying different values of $b_0, \ldots, b_k$ until you are satisfied that you have minimized the total sum of squares in Expression (6.8). It is far easier, however, to use explicit formulas for the OLS estimators that are derived using calculus. The formulas for the OLS estimators in the multiple regression model are similar to those in Key Concept 4.2 for the single-regressor model. These formulas are incorporated into modern statistical software. In the multiple regression model, the formulas are best expressed and discussed using matrix notation, so their presentation is deferred to Section 18.1.

**KEY CONCEPT**

**6.3**

## The OLS Estimators, Predicted Values, and Residuals in the Multiple Regression Model

The OLS estimators $\hat{\beta}_0, \hat{\beta}_1, \ldots, \hat{\beta}_k$ are the values of $b_0, b_1, \ldots, b_k$ that minimize the sum of squared prediction mistakes $\sum_{i=1}^{n}(Y_i - b_0 - b_1 X_{1i} - \cdots - b_k X_{ki})^2$. The OLS predicted values $\hat{Y}_i$ and residuals $\hat{u}_i$ are

$$\hat{Y}_i = \hat{\beta}_0 + \hat{\beta}_1 X_{1i} + \cdots + \hat{\beta}_k X_{ki}, i = 1, \ldots, n, \text{ and} \tag{6.9}$$

$$\hat{u}_i = Y_i - \hat{Y}_i, i = 1, \ldots, n. \tag{6.10}$$

The OLS estimators $\hat{\beta}_0, \hat{\beta}_1, \ldots, \hat{\beta}_k$ and residual $\hat{u}_i$ are computed from a sample of $n$ observations of $(X_{1i}, \ldots, X_{ki}, Y_i), i = 1, \ldots, n$. These are estimators of the unknown true population coefficients $\beta_0, \beta_1, \ldots, \beta_k$ and error term, $u_i$.

The definitions and terminology of OLS in multiple regression are summarized in Key Concept 6.3.

## Application to Test Scores and the Student–Teacher Ratio

In Section 4.2, we used OLS to estimate the intercept and slope coefficient of the regression relating test scores (*TestScore*) to the student–teacher ratio (*STR*), using our 420 observations for California school districts; the estimated OLS regression line, reported in Equation (4.11), is

$$\widehat{TestScore} = 698.9 - 2.28 \times STR. \tag{6.11}$$

Our concern has been that this relationship is misleading because the student–teacher ratio might be picking up the effect of having many English learners in districts with large classes. That is, it is possible that the OLS estimator is subject to omitted variable bias.

We are now in a position to address this concern by using OLS to estimate a multiple regression in which the dependent variable is the test score ($Y_i$) and there are two regressors: the student–teacher ratio ($X_{1i}$) and the percentage of

English learners in the school district ($X_{2i}$) for our 420 districts ($i = 1, \ldots, 420$). The estimated OLS regression line for this multiple regression is

$$\widehat{TestScore} = 686.0 - 1.10 \times STR - 0.65 \times PctEL, \tag{6.12}$$

where *PctEL* is the percentage of students in the district who are English learners. The OLS estimate of the intercept ($\hat{\beta}_0$) is 686.0, the OLS estimate of the coefficient on the student–teacher ratio ($\hat{\beta}_1$) is −1.10, and the OLS estimate of the coefficient on the percentage English learners ($\hat{\beta}_2$) is −0.65.

The estimated effect on test scores of a change in the student–teacher ratio in the multiple regression is approximately half as large as when the student–teacher ratio is the only regressor: In the single-regressor equation [Equation (6.11)], a unit decrease in the *STR* is estimated to increase test scores by 2.28 points, but in the multiple regression equation [Equation (6.12)], it is estimated to increase test scores by only 1.10 points. This difference occurs because the coefficient on *STR* in the multiple regression is the effect of a change in *STR*, holding constant (or controlling for) *PctEL*, whereas in the single-regressor regression, *PctEL* is not held constant.

These two estimates can be reconciled by concluding that there is omitted variable bias in the estimate in the single-regressor model in Equation (6.11). In Section 6.1, we saw that districts with a high percentage of English learners tend to have not only low test scores but also a high student–teacher ratio. If the fraction of English learners is omitted from the regression, reducing the student–teacher ratio is estimated to have a larger effect on test scores, but this estimate reflects *both* the effect of a change in the student–teacher ratio *and* the omitted effect of having fewer English learners in the district.

We have reached the same conclusion that there is omitted variable bias in the relationship between test scores and the student–teacher ratio by two different paths: the tabular approach of dividing the data into groups (Section 6.1) and the multiple regression approach [Equation (6.12)]. Of these two methods, multiple regression has two important advantages. First, it provides a quantitative estimate of the effect of a unit decrease in the student–teacher ratio, which is what the superintendent needs to make her decision. Second, it readily extends to more than two regressors so that multiple regression can be used to control for measurable factors other than just the percentage of English learners.

The rest of this chapter is devoted to understanding and using OLS in the multiple regression model. Much of what you learned about the OLS estimator with a single regressor carries over to multiple regression with few or no modifications, so we will focus on that which is new with multiple regression. We begin by discussing measures of fit for the multiple regression model.

## 6.4  Measures of Fit in Multiple Regression

Three commonly used summary statistics in multiple regression are the standard error of the regression, the regression $R^2$, and the adjusted $R^2$ (also known as $\overline{R}^2$). All three statistics measure how well the OLS estimate of the multiple regression line describes, or "fits," the data.

### The Standard Error of the Regression (SER)

The standard error of the regression ($SER$) estimates the standard deviation of the error term $u_i$. Thus the $SER$ is a measure of the spread of the distribution of $Y$ around the regression line. In multiple regression, the $SER$ is

$$SER = s_{\hat{u}} = \sqrt{s_{\hat{u}}^2} \quad \text{where } s_{\hat{u}}^2 = \frac{1}{n-k-1} \sum_{i=1}^{n} \hat{u}_i^2 = \frac{SSR}{n-k-1} \quad (6.13)$$

and where $SSR$ is the sum of squared residuals, $SSR = \sum_{i=1}^{n} \hat{u}_i^2$.

The only difference between the definition in Equation (6.13) and the definition of the $SER$ in Section 4.3 for the single-regressor model is that here the divisor is $n - k - 1$ rather than $n - 2$. In Section 4.3, the divisor $n - 2$ (rather than $n$) adjusts for the downward bias introduced by estimating two coefficients (the slope and intercept of the regression line). Here, the divisor $n - k - 1$ adjusts for the downward bias introduced by estimating $k + 1$ coefficients (the $k$ slope coefficients plus the intercept). As in Section 4.3, using $n - k - 1$ rather than $n$ is called a degrees-of-freedom adjustment. If there is a single regressor, then $k = 1$, so the formula in Section 4.3 is the same as in Equation (6.13). When $n$ is large, the effect of the degrees-of-freedom adjustment is negligible.

### The $R^2$

The regression $\boldsymbol{R^2}$ is the fraction of the sample variance of $Y_i$ explained by (or predicted by) the regressors. Equivalently, the $R^2$ is 1 minus the fraction of the variance of $Y_i$ *not* explained by the regressors.

The mathematical definition of the $R^2$ is the same as for regression with a single regressor:

$$R^2 = \frac{ESS}{TSS} = 1 - \frac{SSR}{TSS}, \quad (6.14)$$

where the explained sum of squares is $ESS = \sum_{i=1}^{n}(\hat{Y}_i - \overline{Y})^2$ and the total sum of squares is $TSS = \sum_{i=1}^{n}(Y_i - \overline{Y})^2$.

In multiple regression, the $R^2$ increases whenever a regressor is added, unless the estimated coefficient on the added regressor is exactly zero. To see this, think about starting with one regressor and then adding a second. When you use OLS to estimate the model with both regressors, OLS finds the values of the coefficients that minimize the sum of squared residuals. If OLS happens to choose the coefficient on the new regressor to be exactly zero, then the $SSR$ will be the same whether or not the second variable is included in the regression. But if OLS chooses any value other than zero, then it must be that this value reduced the $SSR$ relative to the regression that excludes this regressor. In practice, it is extremely unusual for an estimated coefficient to be exactly zero, so in general the $SSR$ will decrease when a new regressor is added. But this means that the $R^2$ generally increases (and never decreases) when a new regressor is added.

## The "Adjusted $R^2$"

Because the $R^2$ increases when a new variable is added, an increase in the $R^2$ does not mean that adding a variable actually improves the fit of the model. In this sense, the $R^2$ gives an inflated estimate of how well the regression fits the data. One way to correct for this is to deflate or reduce the $R^2$ by some factor, and this is what the adjusted $R^2$, or $\overline{R}^2$, does.

The **adjusted $R^2$**, or $\overline{R}^2$, is a modified version of the $R^2$ that does not necessarily increase when a new regressor is added. The $\overline{R}^2$ is

$$\overline{R}^2 = 1 - \frac{n-1}{n-k-1} \frac{SSR}{TSS} = 1 - \frac{s_{\hat{u}}^2}{s_Y^2}. \tag{6.15}$$

The difference between this formula and the second definition of the $R^2$ in Equation (6.14) is that the ratio of the sum of squared residuals to the total sum of squares is multiplied by the factor $(n-1)/(n-k-1)$. As the second expression in Equation (6.15) shows, this means that the adjusted $R^2$ is 1 minus the ratio of the sample variance of the OLS residuals [with the degrees-of-freedom correction in Equation (6.13)] to the sample variance of $Y$.

There are three useful things to know about the $\overline{R}^2$. First, $(n-1)/(n-k-1)$ is always greater than 1, so $\overline{R}^2$ is always less than $R^2$.

Second, adding a regressor has two opposite effects on the $\overline{R}^2$. On the one hand, the $SSR$ falls, which increases the $\overline{R}^2$. On the other hand, the factor $(n-1)/(n-k-1)$ increases. Whether the $\overline{R}^2$ increases or decreases depends on which of these two effects is stronger.

Third, the $\overline{R}^2$ can be negative. This happens when the regressors, taken together, reduce the sum of squared residuals by such a small amount that this reduction fails to offset the factor $(n-1)/(n-k-1)$.

## Application to Test Scores

Equation (6.12) reports the estimated regression line for the multiple regression relating test scores (*TestScore*) to the student–teacher ratio (*STR*) and the percentage of English learners (*PctEL*). The $R^2$ for this regression line is $R^2 = 0.426$, the adjusted $R^2$ is $\overline{R}^2 = 0.424$, and the standard error of the regression is $SER = 14.5$.

Comparing these measures of fit with those for the regression in which *PctEL* is excluded [Equation (5.8)] shows that including *PctEL* in the regression increased the $R^2$ from 0.051 to 0.426. When the only regressor is *STR*, only a small fraction of the variation in *TestScore* is explained; however, when *PctEL* is added to the regression, more than two-fifths (42.6%) of the variation in test scores is explained. In this sense, including the percentage of English learners substantially improves the fit of the regression. Because $n$ is large and only two regressors appear in Equation (6.12), the difference between $R^2$ and adjusted $R^2$ is very small ($R^2 = 0.426$ versus $\overline{R}^2 = 0.424$).

The *SER* for the regression excluding *PctEL* is 18.6; this value falls to 14.5 when *PctEL* is included as a second regressor. The units of the *SER* are points on the standardized test. The reduction in the *SER* tells us that predictions about standardized test scores are substantially more precise if they are made using the regression with both *STR* and *PctEL* than if they are made using the regression with only *STR* as a regressor.

*Using the* $R^2$ *and adjusted* $R^2$. The $\overline{R}^2$ is useful because it quantifies the extent to which the regressors account for, or explain, the variation in the dependent variable. Nevertheless, heavy reliance on the $\overline{R}^2$ (or $R^2$) can be a trap. In applications, "maximize the $\overline{R}^2$" is rarely the answer to any economically or statistically meaningful question. Instead, the decision about whether to include a variable in a multiple regression should be based on whether including that variable allows you better to estimate the causal effect of interest. We return to the issue of how to decide which variables to include—and which to exclude—in Chapter 7. First, however, we need to develop methods for quantifying the sampling uncertainty of the OLS estimator. The starting point for doing so is extending the least squares assumptions of Chapter 4 to the case of multiple regressors.

# 6.5 The Least Squares Assumptions in Multiple Regression

There are four least squares assumptions in the multiple regression model. The first three are those of Section 4.3 for the single regressor model (Key Concept 4.3), extended to allow for multiple regressors, and these are discussed only briefly. The fourth assumption is new and is discussed in more detail.

## Assumption #1: The Conditional Distribution of $u_i$ Given $X_{1i}, X_{2i}, \ldots, X_{ki}$ Has a Mean of Zero

The first assumption is that the conditional distribution of $u_i$ given $X_{1i}, \ldots, X_{ki}$ has a mean of zero. This assumption extends the first least squares assumption with a single regressor to multiple regressors. This assumption means that sometimes $Y_i$ is above the population regression line and sometimes $Y_i$ is below the population regression line, but on average over the population $Y_i$ falls on the population regression line. Therefore, for any value of the regressors, the expected value of $u_i$ is zero. As is the case for regression with a single regressor, this is the key assumption that makes the OLS estimators unbiased. We return to omitted variable bias in multiple regression in Section 7.5.

## Assumption #2: $(X_{1i}, X_{2i}, \ldots, X_{ki}, Y_i), i = 1, \ldots, n,$ Are i.i.d.

The second assumption is that $(X_{1i}, \ldots, X_{ki}, Y_i), i = 1, \ldots, n$, are independently and identically distributed (i.i.d.) random variables. This assumption holds automatically if the data are collected by simple random sampling. The comments on this assumption appearing in Section 4.3 for a single regressor also apply to multiple regressors.

## Assumption #3: Large Outliers Are Unlikely

The third least squares assumption is that large outliers—that is, observations with values far outside the usual range of the data—are unlikely. This assumption serves as a reminder that, as in single-regressor case, the OLS estimator of the coefficients in the multiple regression model can be sensitive to large outliers.

The assumption that large outliers are unlikely is made mathematically precise by assuming that $X_{1i}, \ldots, X_{ki}$, and $Y_i$ have nonzero finite fourth moments: $0 < E(X_{1i}^4) < \infty, \ldots, 0 < E(X_{ki}^4) < \infty$ and $0 < E(Y_i^4) < \infty$. Another way to state this assumption is that the dependent variable and regressors have finite kurtosis. This assumption is used to derive the properties of OLS regression statistics in large samples.

## Assumption #4: No Perfect Multicollinearity

The fourth assumption is new to the multiple regression model. It rules out an inconvenient situation, called perfect multicollinearity, in which it is impossible to compute the OLS estimator. The regressors are said to exhibit **perfect multicollinearity**, (or to be perfectly multicollinear) if one of the regressors is a perfect linear function of the other regressors. The fourth least squares assumption is that the regressors are not perfectly multicollinear.

Why does perfect multicollinearity make it impossible to compute the OLS estimator? Suppose you want to estimate the coefficient on $STR$ in a regression of $TestScore_i$ on $STR_i$ and $PctEL_i$, except that you make a typographical error and accidentally type in $STR_i$ a second time instead of $PctEL_i$; that is, you regress $TestScore_i$ on $STR_i$ and $STR_i$. This is a case of perfect multicollinearity because one of the regressors (the first occurrence of $STR$) is a perfect linear function of another regressor (the second occurrence of $STR$). Depending on how your software package handles perfect multicollinearity, if you try to estimate this regression the software will do one of two things: Either it will drop one of the occurrences of $STR$ or it will refuse to calculate the OLS estimates and give an error message. The mathematical reason for this failure is that perfect multicollinearity produces division by zero in the OLS formulas.

At an intuitive level, perfect multicollinearity is a problem because you are asking the regression to answer an illogical question. In multiple regression, the coefficient on one of the regressors is the effect of a change in that regressor, holding the other regressors constant. In the hypothetical regression of $TestScore$ on $STR$ and $STR$, the coefficient on the first occurrence of $STR$ is the effect on test scores of a change in $STR$, holding constant $STR$. This makes no sense, and OLS cannot estimate this nonsensical partial effect.

The solution to perfect multicollinearity in this hypothetical regression is simply to correct the typo and to replace one of the occurrences of $STR$ with the variable you originally wanted to include. This example is typical: When perfect multicollinearity occurs, it often reflects a logical mistake in choosing the regressors or some previously unrecognized feature of the data set. In general, the solution to perfect multicollinearity is to modify the regressors to eliminate the problem.

Additional examples of perfect multicollinearity are given in Section 6.7, which also defines and discusses imperfect multicollinearity.

## The Least Squares Assumptions in the Multiple Regression Model

$$Y_i = \beta_0 + \beta_1 X_{1i} + \beta_2 X_{2i} + \cdots + \beta_k X_{ki} + u_i, i = 1, \ldots, n,$$

where

1. $u_i$ has conditional mean zero given $X_{1i}, X_{2i}, \ldots, X_{ki}$; that is,

$$E(u_i \mid X_{1i}, X_{2i}, \ldots, X_{ki}) = 0$$

2. $(X_{1i}, X_{2i}, \ldots, X_{ki}, Y_i), i = 1, \ldots, n$, are independently and identically distributed (i.i.d.) draws from their joint distribution.

3. Large outliers are unlikely: $X_{1i}, \ldots, X_{ki}$ and $Y_i$ have nonzero finite fourth moments.

4. There is no perfect multicollinearity.

The least squares assumptions for the multiple regression model are summarized in Key Concept 6.4.

## 6.6 The Distribution of the OLS Estimators in Multiple Regression

Because the data differ from one sample to the next, different samples produce different values of the OLS estimators. This variation across possible samples gives rise to the uncertainty associated with the OLS estimators of the population regression coefficients, $\beta_0, \beta_1, \ldots, \beta_k$. Just as in the case of regression with a single regressor, this variation is summarized in the sampling distribution of the OLS estimators.

Recall from Section 4.4 that, under the least squares assumptions, the OLS estimators ($\hat{\beta}_0$ and $\hat{\beta}_1$) are unbiased and consistent estimators of the unknown coefficients ($\beta_0$ and $\beta_1$) in the linear regression model with a single regressor. In addition, in large samples, the sampling distribution of $\hat{\beta}_0$ and $\hat{\beta}_1$ is well approximated by a bivariate normal distribution.

These results carry over to multiple regression analysis. That is, under the least squares assumptions of Key Concept 6.4, the OLS estimators $\hat{\beta}_0, \hat{\beta}_1, \ldots, \hat{\beta}_k$ are unbiased and consistent estimators of $\beta_0, \beta_1, \ldots, \beta_k$ in the linear multiple

**KEY CONCEPT**

**6.5**

## Large-Sample Distribution of $\hat{\beta}_0, \hat{\beta}_1, \ldots, \hat{\beta}_k$

If the least squares assumptions (Key Concept 6.4) hold, then in large samples the OLS estimators $\hat{\beta}_0, \hat{\beta}_1, \ldots, \hat{\beta}_k$ are jointly normally distributed and each $\hat{\beta}_j$ is distributed $N(\beta_j, \sigma^2_{\hat{\beta}_j})$, $j = 0, \ldots, k$.

regression model. In large samples, the joint sampling distribution of $\hat{\beta}_0, \hat{\beta}_1, \ldots, \hat{\beta}_k$ is well approximated by a multivariate normal distribution, which is the extension of the bivariate normal distribution to the general case of two or more jointly normal random variables (Section 2.4).

Although the algebra is more complicated when there are multiple regressors, the central limit theorem applies to the OLS estimators in the multiple regression model for the same reason that it applies to $\overline{Y}$ and to the OLS estimators when there is a single regressor: The OLS estimators $\hat{\beta}_0, \hat{\beta}_1, \ldots, \hat{\beta}_k$ are averages of the randomly sampled data, and if the sample size is sufficiently large, the sampling distribution of those averages becomes normal. Because the multivariate normal distribution is best handled mathematically using matrix algebra, the expressions for the joint distribution of the OLS estimators are deferred to Chapter 18.

Key Concept 6.5 summarizes the result that, in large samples, the distribution of the OLS estimators in multiple regression is approximately jointly normal. In general, the OLS estimators are correlated; this correlation arises from the correlation between the regressors. The joint sampling distribution of the OLS estimators is discussed in more detail for the case that there are two regressors and homoskedastic errors in Appendix (6.2), and the general case is discussed in Section 18.2.

## 6.7  Multicollinearity

As discussed in Section 6.5, perfect multicollinearity arises when one of the regressors is a perfect linear combination of the other regressors. This section provides some examples of perfect multicollinearity and discusses how perfect multicollinearity can arise, and can be avoided, in regressions with multiple binary regressors. Imperfect multicollinearity arises when one of the regressors is very highly correlated—but not perfectly correlated—with the other regressors. Unlike perfect multicollinearity, imperfect multicollinearity does not prevent estimation of the regression, nor does it imply a logical problem with the choice of regressors. However, it does mean that one or more regression coefficients could be estimated imprecisely.

## Examples of Perfect Multicollinearity

We continue the discussion of perfect multicollinearity from Section 6.5 by examining three additional hypothetical regressions. In each, a third regressor is added to the regression of $TestScore_i$ on $STR_i$ and $PctEL_i$ in Equation (6.12).

*Example #1: Fraction of English learners.* Let $FracEL_i$ be the fraction of English learners in the $i^{th}$ district, which varies between 0 and 1. If the variable $FracEL_i$ were included as a third regressor in addition to $STR_i$ and $PctEL_i$, the regressors would be perfectly multicollinear. The reason is that $PctEL$ is the *percentage* of English learners, so that $PctEL_i = 100 \times FracEL_i$ for every district. Thus one of the regressors ($PctEL_i$) can be written as a perfect linear function of another regressor ($FracEL_i$).

Because of this perfect multicollinearity, it is impossible to compute the OLS estimates of the regression of $TestScore_i$ on $STR_i$, $PctEL_i$, and $FracEL_i$. At an intuitive level, OLS fails because you are asking, What is the effect of a unit change in the *percentage* of English learners, holding constant the *fraction* of English learners? Because the percentage of English learners and the fraction of English learners move together in a perfect linear relationship, this question makes no sense and OLS cannot answer it.

*Example #2: "Not very small" classes.* Let $NVS_i$ be a binary variable that equals 1 if the student–teacher ratio in the $i^{th}$ district is "not very small," specifically, $NVS_i$ equals 1 if $STR_i \geq 12$ and equals 0 otherwise. This regression also exhibits perfect multicollinearity, but for a more subtle reason than the regression in the previous example. There are in fact no districts in our data set with $STR_i < 12$; as you can see in the scatterplot in Figure 4.2, the smallest value of $STR$ is 14. Thus $NVS_i = 1$ for all observations. Now recall that the linear regression model with an intercept can equivalently be thought of as including a regressor, $X_{0i}$, that equals 1 for all $i$, as shown in Equation (6.6). Thus we can write $NVS_i = 1 \times X_{0i}$ for all the observations in our data set; that is, $NVS_i$ can be written as a perfect linear combination of the regressors; specifically, it equals $X_{0i}$.

This illustrates two important points about perfect multicollinearity. First, when the regression includes an intercept, then one of the regressors that can be implicated in perfect multicollinearity is the constant regressor $X_{0i}$. Second, perfect multicollinearity is a statement about the data set you have on hand. While it is possible to imagine a school district with fewer than 12 students per teacher, there are no such districts in our data set so we cannot analyze them in our regression.

*Example #3: Percentage of English speakers.* Let $PctES_i$ be the percentage of "English speakers" in the $i^{th}$ district, defined to be the percentage of students who are not English learners. Again the regressors will be perfectly multicollinear.

Like the previous example, the perfect linear relationship among the regressors involves the constant regressor $X_{0i}$: For every district, $PctES_i = 100 - PctEL_i = 100 \times X_{0i} - PctEL_i$, because $X_{0i} = 1$ for all $i$.

This example illustrates another point: Perfect multicollinearity is a feature of the entire set of regressors. If either the intercept (that is, the regressor $X_{0i}$) or $PctEL_i$ were excluded from this regression, the regressors would not be perfectly multicollinear.

*The dummy variable trap.*   Another possible source of perfect multicollinearity arises when multiple binary, or dummy, variables are used as regressors. For example, suppose you have partitioned the school districts into three categories: rural, suburban, and urban. Each district falls into one (and only one) category. Let these binary variables be $Rural_i$, which equals 1 for a rural district and equals 0 otherwise; $Suburban_i$; and $Urban_i$. If you include all three binary variables in the regression along with a constant, the regressors will be perfect multicollinearity: Because each district belongs to one and only one category, $Rural_i + Suburban_i + Urban_i = 1 = X_{0i}$, where $X_{0i}$ denotes the constant regressor introduced in Equation (6.6). Thus, to estimate the regression, you must exclude one of these four variables, either one of the binary indicators or the constant term. By convention, the constant term is retained, in which case one of the binary indicators is excluded. For example, if $Rural_i$ were excluded, then the coefficient on $Suburban_i$ would be the average difference between test scores in suburban and rural districts, holding constant the other variables in the regression.

In general, if there are $G$ binary variables, if each observation falls into one and only one category, if there is an intercept in the regression, and if all $G$ binary variables are included as regressors, then the regression will fail because of perfect multicollinearity. This situation is called the **dummy variable trap**. The usual way to avoid the dummy variable trap is to exclude one of the binary variables from the multiple regression, so only $G - 1$ of the $G$ binary variables are included as regressors. In this case, the coefficients on the included binary variables represent the incremental effect of being in that category, relative to the base case of the omitted category, holding constant the other regressors. Alternatively, all $G$ binary regressors can be included if the intercept is omitted from the regression.

*Solutions to perfect multicollinearity.*   Perfect multicollinearity typically arises when a mistake has been made in specifying the regression. Sometimes the mistake is easy to spot (as in the first example) but sometimes it is not (as in the second example). In one way or another, your software will let you know if you make such a mistake because it cannot compute the OLS estimator if you have.

When your software lets you know that you have perfect multicollinearity, it is important that you modify your regression to eliminate it. Some software is unreliable when there is perfect multicollinearity, and at a minimum you will be ceding control over your choice of regressors to your computer if your regressors are perfectly multicollinear.

## Imperfect Multicollinearity

Despite its similar name, imperfect multicollinearity is conceptually quite different from perfect multicollinearity. **Imperfect multicollinearity** means that two or more of the regressors are highly correlated in the sense that there is a linear function of the regressors that is highly correlated with another regressor. Imperfect multicollinearity does not pose any problems for the theory of the OLS estimators; indeed, a purpose of OLS is to sort out the independent influences of the various regressors when these regressors are potentially correlated.

If the regressors are imperfectly multicollinear, then the coefficients on at least one individual regressor will be imprecisely estimated. For example, consider the regression of *TestScore* on *STR* and *PctEL*. Suppose we were to add a third regressor, the percentage of the district's residents who are first-generation immigrants. First-generation immigrants often speak English as a second language, so the variables *PctEL* and percentage immigrants will be highly correlated: Districts with many recent immigrants will tend to have many students who are still learning English. Because these two variables are highly correlated, it would be difficult to use these data to estimate the partial effect on test scores of an increase in *PctEL*, holding constant the percentage immigrants. In other words, the data set provides little information about what happens to test scores when the percentage of English learners is low but the fraction of immigrants is high, or vice versa. If the least squares assumptions hold, then the OLS estimator of the coefficient on *PctEL* in this regression will be unbiased; however, it will have a larger variance than if the regressors *PctEL* and percentage immigrants were uncorrelated.

The effect of imperfect multicollinearity on the variance of the OLS estimators can be seen mathematically by inspecting Equation (6.17) in Appendix (6.2), which is the variance of $\hat{\beta}_1$ in a multiple regression with two regressors ($X_1$ and $X_2$) for the special case of a homoskedastic error. In this case, the variance of $\hat{\beta}_1$ is inversely proportional to $1 - \rho_{X_1,X_2}^2$, where $\rho_{X_1,X_2}$ is the correlation between $X_1$ and $X_2$. The larger the correlation between the two regressors, the closer this term is to zero and the larger is the variance of $\hat{\beta}_1$. More generally, when multiple regressors are imperfectly multicollinear, the coefficients on one or more of these regressors will be imprecisely estimated—that is, they will have a large sampling variance.

Perfect multicollinearity is a problem that often signals the presence of a logical error. In contrast, imperfect multicollinearity is not necessarily an error, but rather just a feature of OLS, your data, and the question you are trying to answer. If the variables in your regression are the ones you meant to include—the ones you chose to address the potential for omitted variable bias—then imperfect multicollinearity implies that it will be difficult to estimate precisely one or more of the partial effects using the data at hand.

## 6.8  Conclusion

Regression with a single regressor is vulnerable to omitted variable bias: If an omitted variable is a determinant of the dependent variable and is correlated with the regressor, then the OLS estimator of the slope coefficient will be biased and will reflect both the effect of the regressor and the effect of the omitted variable. Multiple regression makes it possible to mitigate omitted variable bias by including the omitted variable in the regression. The coefficient on a regressor, $X_1$, in multiple regression is the partial effect of a change in $X_1$, holding constant the other included regressors. In the test score example, including the percentage of English learners as a regressor made it possible to estimate the effect on test scores of a change in the student–teacher ratio, holding constant the percentage of English learners. Doing so reduced by half the estimated effect on test scores of a change in the student–teacher ratio.

The statistical theory of multiple regression builds on the statistical theory of regression with a single regressor. The least squares assumptions for multiple regression are extensions of the three least squares assumptions for regression with a single regressor, plus a fourth assumption ruling out perfect multicollinearity. Because the regression coefficients are estimated using a single sample, the OLS estimators have a joint sampling distribution and therefore have sampling uncertainty. This sampling uncertainty must be quantified as part of an empirical study, and the ways to do so in the multiple regression model are the topic of the next chapter.

## Summary

1. Omitted variable bias occurs when an omitted variable (1) is correlated with an included regressor and (2) is a determinant of $Y$.
2. The multiple regression model is a linear regression model that includes multiple regressors, $X_1, X_2, \ldots, X_k$. Associated with each regressor is a regression coefficient, $\beta_1, \beta_2, \ldots, \beta_k$. The coefficient $\beta_1$ is the expected change in $Y$ associated with a one-unit change in $X_1$, holding the other regressors constant. The other regression coefficients have an analogous interpretation.

3.  The coefficients in multiple regression can be estimated by OLS. When the four least squares assumptions in Key Concept 6.4 are satisfied, the OLS estimators are unbiased, consistent, and normally distributed in large samples.

4.  Perfect multicollinearity, which occurs when one regressor is an exact linear function of the other regressors, usually arises from a mistake in choosing which regressors to include in a multiple regression. Solving perfect multicollinearity requires changing the set of regressors.

5.  The standard error of the regression, the $R^2$, and the $\overline{R}^2$ are measures of fit for the multiple regression model.

## Key Terms

omitted variable bias (229)

multiple regression model (235)

population regression line (235)

population regression function (235)

intercept (235)

slope coefficient of $X_{1i}$ (235)

coefficient on $X_{1i}$ (235)

slope coefficient of $X_{2i}$ (235)

coefficient on $X_{2i}$ (235)

holding $X_2$ constant (236)

controlling for $X_2$ (236)

partial effect (236)

population multiple regression model (237)

constant regressor (237)

constant term (237)

homoskedastic (237)

heteroskedastic (237)

ordinary least squares (OLS) estimators of $\beta_0, \beta_1, \ldots, \beta_k$ (239)

OLS regression line (239)

predicted value (239)

OLS residual (239)

$R^2$ (242)

adjusted $R^2 (\overline{R}^2)$ (243)

perfect multicollinearity (246)

dummy variable trap (250)

imperfect multicollinearity (251)

---

**MyEconLab Can Help You Get a Better Grade**

**MyEconLab**  If your exam were tomorrow, would you be ready? For each chapter, **MyEconLab** Practice Tests and Study Plan help you prepare for your exams. You can also find similar Exercises and Review the Concepts Questions now in **MyEconLab**. To see how it works, turn to the **MyEconLab** spread on pages 2 and 3 of this book and then go to **www.myeconlab.com**.

For additional Empirical Exercises and Data Sets, log on to the Companion Website at **www.pearsonglobaleditions.com/Stock_Watson**.

---

## Review the Concepts

**6.1**  A researcher is estimating the effect of studying on the test scores of student's from a private school. She is concerned, however, that she does not have information on the class size to include in the regression. What effect would the omission of the class size variable have on her estimated coefficient on the private school indicator variable? Will the effect of this omission disappear if she uses a larger sample of students?

**6.2** A multiple regression includes two regressors: $Y_i = b_0 + b_1 X_{1i} + b_2 X_{2i} + u_i$. What is the expected change in $Y$ if $X_1$ increases by 8 units and $X_2$ is unchanged? What is the expected change in $Y$ if $X_2$ decreases by 3 units and $X_1$ is unchanged? What is the expected change in $Y$ if $X_1$ increases by 4 units and $X_2$ decreases by 7 units?

**6.3** What are the measures of fit that are commonly used for multiple regressions? How can an adjusted $R^2$ take on negative values?

**6.4** What is a dummy variable trap and how is it related to multicollinearity of regressors? What is the solution for this form of multicollinearity?

**6.5** How is imperfect collinearity of regressors different from perfect collinearity? Compare the solutions for these two concerns with multiple regression estimation.

## Exercises

The first four exercises refer to the table of estimated regressions on page 255, computed using data for 2012 from the CPS. The data set consists of information on 7440 full-time, full-year workers. The highest educational achievement for each worker was either a high school diploma or a bachelor's degree. The workers' ages ranged from 25 to 34 years. The data set also contains information on the region of the country where the person lived, marital status, and number of children. For the purposes of these exercises, let

$AHE$ = average hourly earnings (in 2012 dollars)
*College* = binary variable (1 if college, 0 if high school)
*Female* = binary variable (1 if female, 0 if male)
*Age* = age (in years)
*Ntheast* = binary variable (1 if Region = Northeast, 0 otherwise)
*Midwest* = binary variable (1 if Region = Midwest, 0 otherwise)
*South* = binary variable (1 if Region = South, 0 otherwise)
*West* = binary variable (1 if Region = West, 0 otherwise)

**6.1** Compute $\overline{R}^2$ for each of the regressions.

**6.2**  Using the regression results in column (1):

  **a.** Do workers with college degrees earn more, on average, than workers with only high school degrees? How much more?

  **b.** Do men earn more than women, on average? How much more?

**6.3**  Using the regression results in column (2):

  **a.** Is age an important determinant of earnings? Explain.

  **b.** Sally is a 29-year-old female college graduate. Betsy is a 34-year-old female college graduate. Predict Sally's and Betsy's earnings.

**6.4**  Using the regression results in column (3):

  **a.** Do there appear to be important regional differences?

  **b.** Why is the regressor *West* omitted from the regression? What would happen if it were included?

| Results of Regressions of Average Hourly Earnings on Gender and Education Binary Variables and Other Characteristics, Using 2012 Data from the Current Population Survey | | | |
|---|---|---|---|
| **Dependent variable: average hourly earnings (AHE).** | | | |
| **Regressor** | **(1)** | **(2)** | **(3)** |
| College ($X_1$) | 8.31 | 8.32 | 8.34 |
| Female ($X_2$) | −3.85 | −3.81 | −3.80 |
| Age ($X_3$) | | 0.51 | 0.52 |
| Northeast ($X_4$) | | | 0.18 |
| Midwest ($X_5$) | | | −1.23 |
| South ($X_6$) | | | −0.43 |
| Intercept | 17.02 | 1.87 | 2.05 |
| **Summary Statistics** | | | |
| SER | 9.79 | 9.68 | 9.67 |
| $R^2$ | 0.162 | 0.180 | 0.182 |
| $\bar{R}^2$ | | | |
| $n$ | 7440 | 7440 | 7440 |

    **c.** Juanita is a 28-year-old female college graduate from the South. Jennifer is a 28-year-old female college graduate from the Midwest. Calculate the expected difference in earnings between Juanita and Jennifer.

**6.5** Data were collected from a random sample of 200 home sales from a community in 2013. Let *Price* denote the selling price (in $1000), *BDR* denote the number of bedrooms, *Bath* denote the number of bathrooms, *Hsize* denote the size of the house (in square feet), *Lsize* denote the lot size (in square feet), *Age* denote the age of the house (in years), and *Poor* denote a binary variable that is equal to 1 if the condition of the house is reported as "poor." An estimated regression yields

$$\widehat{Price} = 109.7 + 0.567BDR + 26.9Bath + 0.239Hsize + 0.005Lsize$$
$$+ 0.1Age - 56.9Poor, R^2 = 0.85, SER = 45.8.$$

    **a.** Suppose a homeowner converts part of an existing family room in their house into a new bathroom. What is the expected increase in the value of the house?

    **b.** Suppose that a homeowner adds a new bathroom to their house, which increases the size of the house by 80 square feet. What is the expected increase in the value of the house?

    **c.** What is the loss in value if a homeowner lets their house run down, such that its condition becomes "poor?"

    **d.** Compute the $R^2$ for the regression.

**6.6** A researcher plans to study the causal effect of a strong legal system on the economy, using data from a sample of countries. The researcher plans to regress national income per capita on whether the country has a strong legal system or not (an indicator variable taking the value 1 or 0, based on expert opinion).

    **a.** Do you think this regression suffers from omitted variable bias? Which variables would you add to the regression?

    **b.** Assess whether the regression will likely over- or underestimate the effect of police on the crime rate, based on the variables you think are omitted. (That is, do you think that $\hat{\beta} > \beta$ or $\hat{\beta} < \beta$?)

**6.7** Critique each of the following proposed research plans. Your critique should explain any problems with the proposed research and describe how the research plan might be improved. Include a discussion of any additional data that need to be collected and the appropriate statistical techniques for analyzing those data.

**a.** A researcher wants to determine whether a leading global university is biased against Black students in admissions. To determine potential bias, the researcher collects race information on all applicants to the university for a given year. The researcher plans to conduct a difference in means test to determine whether the proportion of acceptances among Black candidates is systematically different from the proportion of acceptances among other candidates.

**b.** A researcher is interested in identifying the impact of a mother's education on the educational attainment of her children. The researcher collects data on a random sample of individuals aged between 25 and 40 who have exited the schooling system. The data set contains information on each person's level of schooling, type of school, gender, and ethnicity, as well as information on the schooling of their parents and the demographic characteristics of the household in which they grew up. The researcher plans to regress years of schooling achieved by an individual on the years of schooling of their mother, including as controls in the regression the other potential determinants of schooling (gender, ethnicity, number of siblings, whether parents lived together or were separated).

**6.8** A government study found that people who eat chocolate frequently weigh less than people who don't. Researchers questioned 1000 individuals from California between the ages of 20 and 85 about their eating habits, and measured their weight and height. On average, participants ate chocolate twice a week and had a body mass index (BMI) of 28. There was an observed difference of five to seven pounds in weight between those who ate chocolate five times a week and those who did not eat any chocolate at all, with the chocolate eaters weighing less on average. Frequent chocolate eaters also consumed more calories, on average, than people who consumed less chocolate. Based on this summary, would you recommend that American's who do not presently eat chocolate, consider eating chocolate up to five times a week if they want to lose weight? Why or why not? Explain.

**6.9** $(Y_i, X_{1i}, X_{2i})$ satisfy the assumptions in Key Concept 6.4. You are interested in $\beta_1$, the causal effect of $X_1$ on $Y$. Suppose that $X_1$ and $X_2$ are uncorrelated. You estimate $\beta_1$ by regressing $Y$ onto $X_1$ (so that $X_2$ is not included in the regression). Does this estimator suffer from omitted variable bias? Explain.

**6.10** $(Y_i, X_{1i}, X_{2i})$ satisfy the assumptions in Key Concept 6.4; in addition, $\text{var}(u_i | X_{1i}, X_{2i}) = 4$ and $\text{var}(X_{1i}) = 6$. A random sample of size $n = 400$ is drawn from the population.

   **a.** Assume that $X_1$ and $X_2$ are uncorrelated. Compute the variance of $\hat{\beta}_1$. [*Hint:* Look at Equation (6.17) in Appendix 6.2.]

   **b.** Assume that $\text{corr}(X_1, X_2) = 0.5$. Compute the variance of $\hat{\beta}_1$.

   **c.** Comment on the following statements: "When $X_1$ and $X_2$ are correlated, the variance of $\hat{\beta}_1$ is larger than it would be if $X_1$ and $X_2$ were uncorrelated. Thus, if you are interested in $\beta_1$, it is best to leave $X_2$ out of the regression if it is correlated with $X_1$."

**6.11** (Requires calculus) Consider the regression model

$$Y_i = \beta_1 X_{1i} + \beta_2 X_{2i} + u_i$$

for $i = 1, \ldots, n$. (Notice that there is no constant term in the regression.) Following analysis like that used in Appendix (4.2):

   **a.** Specify the least squares function that is minimized by OLS.

   **b.** Compute the partial derivatives of the objective function with respect to $b_1$ and $b_2$.

   **c.** Suppose that $\sum_{i=1}^{n} X_{1i} X_{2i} = 0$. Show that $\hat{\beta}_1 = \sum_{i=1}^{n} X_{1i} Y_i / \sum_{i=1}^{n} X_{1i}^2$.

   **d.** Suppose that $\sum_{i=1}^{n} X_{1i} X_{2i} \neq 0$. Derive an expression for $\hat{\beta}_1$ as a function of the data $(Y_i, X_{1i}, X_{2i})$, $i = 1, \ldots, n$.

   **e.** Suppose that the model includes an intercept: $Y_i = \beta_0 + \beta_1 X_{1i} + \beta_2 X_{2i} + u_i$. Show that the least squares estimators satisfy $\hat{\beta}_0 = \overline{Y} - \hat{\beta}_1 \overline{X}_1 - \hat{\beta}_2 \overline{X}_2$.

   **f.** As in (e), suppose that the model contains an intercept. Also suppose that $\sum_{i=1}^{n} (X_{1i} - \overline{X}_1)(X_{2i} - \overline{X}_2) = 0$. Show that $\hat{\beta}_1 = \sum_{i=1}^{n} (X_{1i} - \overline{X}_1)(Y_i - \overline{Y}) / \sum_{i=1}^{n} (X_{1i} - \overline{X}_1)^2$. How does this compare to the OLS estimator of $\beta_1$ from the regression that omits $X_2$?

## Empirical Exercises

(Only two empirical exercises for this chapter are given in the text, but you can find more on the text website, **www.pearsonglobaleditions.com/Stock_Watson**.)

**E6.1** Use the **Birthweight_Smoking** data set introduced in Empirical Exercise E5.3 to answer the following questions.

**a.** Regress *Birthweight* on *Smoker*. What is the estimated effect of smoking on birth weight?

**b.** Regress *Birthweight* on *Smoker*, *Alcohol*, and *Nprevist*.

   i. Using the two conditions in Key Concept 6.1, explain why the exclusion of *Alcohol* and *Nprevist* could lead to omitted variable bias in the regression estimated in (a).

   ii. Is the estimated effect of smoking on birth weight substantially different from the regression that excludes *Alcohol* and *Nprevist*? Does the regression in (a) seem to suffer from omitted variable bias?

   iii. Jane smoked during her pregnancy, did not drink alcohol, and had 8 prenatal care visits. Use the regression to predict the birth weight of Jane's child.

   iv. Compute $R^2$ and $\overline{R}^2$. Why are they so similar?

**c.** Estimate the coefficient on *Smoking* for the multiple regression model in (b), using the three-step process in Appendix (6.3) (the Frisch-Waugh theorem). Verify that the three-step process yields the same estimated coefficient for *Smoking* as that obtained in (b).

**d.** An alternative way to control for prenatal visits is to use the binary variables *Tripre0* through *Tripre3*. Regress *Birthweight* on *Smoker*, *Alcohol*, *Tripre0*, *Tripre2*, and *Tripre3*.

   i. Why is *Tripre1* excluded from the regression? What would happen if you included it in the regression?

   ii. The estimated coefficient on *Tripre0* is large and negative. What does this coefficient measure? Interpret its value.

   iii. Interpret the value of the estimated coefficients on *Tripre2* and *Tripre3*.

   iv. Does the regression in (d) explain a larger fraction of the variance in birth weight than the regression in (b)?

**E6.2** Using the data set **Growth** described in Empirical Exercise E4.1, but excluding the data for Malta, carry out the following exercises.

**a.** Construct a table that shows the sample mean, standard deviation, and minimum and maximum values for the series *Growth*, *TradeShare*, *YearsSchool*, *Oil*, *Rev_Coups*, *Assassinations*, and *RGDP60*. Include the appropriate units for all entries.

**b.** Run a regression of *Growth* on *TradeShare*, *YearsSchool*, *Rev_Coups*, *Assassinations*, and *RGDP60*. What is the value of the coefficient on *Rev_Coups*? Interpret the value of this coefficient. Is it large or small in a real-world sense?

**c.** Use the regression to predict the average annual growth rate for a country that has average values for all regressors.

**d.** Repeat (c) but now assume that the country's value for *TradeShare* is one standard deviation above the mean.

**e.** Why is *Oil* omitted from the regression? What would happen if it were included?

APPENDIX

## 6.1  Derivation of Equation (6.1)

This appendix presents a derivation of the formula for omitted variable bias in Equation (6.1). Equation (4.30) in Appendix (4.3) states

$$\hat{\beta}_1 = \beta_1 + \frac{\frac{1}{n}\sum_{i=1}^{n}(X_i - \overline{X})u_i}{\frac{1}{n}\sum_{i=1}^{n}(X_i - \overline{X})^2}. \tag{6.16}$$

Under the last two assumptions in Key Concept 4.3, $(1/n)\sum_{i=1}^{n}(X_i - \overline{X})^2 \xrightarrow{p} \sigma_X^2$ and $(1/n)\sum_{i=1}^{n}(X_i - \overline{X})u_i \xrightarrow{p} \text{cov}(u_i, X_i) = \rho_{Xu}\sigma_u\sigma_X$. Substitution of these limits into Equation (6.16) yields Equation (6.1).

APPENDIX

## 6.2  Distribution of the OLS Estimators When There Are Two Regressors and Homoskedastic Errors

Although the general formula for the variance of the OLS estimators in multiple regression is complicated, if there are two regressors ($k = 2$) and the errors are homoskedastic, then the formula simplifies enough to provide some insights into the distribution of the OLS estimators.

Because the errors are homoskedastic, the conditional variance of $u_i$ can be written as $\text{var}(u_i | X_{1i}, X_{2i}) = \sigma_u^2$. When there are two regressors, $X_{1i}$ and $X_{2i}$, and the error term is homoskedastic, in large samples the sampling distribution of $\hat{\beta}_1$ is $N(\beta_1, \sigma_{\hat{\beta}_1}^2)$ where the variance of this distribution, $\sigma_{\hat{\beta}_1}^2$, is

$$\sigma_{\hat{\beta}_1}^2 = \frac{1}{n}\left(\frac{1}{1 - \rho_{X_1, X_2}^2}\right)\frac{\sigma_u^2}{\sigma_{X_1}^2}, \tag{6.17}$$

where $\rho_{X_1, X_2}$ is the population correlation between the two regressors $X_1$ and $X_2$ and $\sigma_{X_1}^2$ is the population variance of $X_1$.

The variance $\sigma_{\hat{\beta}_1}^2$ of the sampling distribution of $\hat{\beta}_1$ depends on the squared correlation between the regressors. If $X_1$ and $X_2$ are highly correlated, either positively or negatively, then $\rho_{X_1, X_2}^2$ is close to 1, and thus the term $1 - \rho_{X_1, X_2}^2$ in the denominator of Equation (6.17) is small and the variance of $\hat{\beta}_1$ is larger than it would be if $\rho_{X_1, X_2}$ were close to 0.

Another feature of the joint normal large-sample distribution of the OLS estimators is that $\hat{\beta}_1$ and $\hat{\beta}_2$ are in general correlated. When the errors are homoskedastic, the correlation between the OLS estimators $\hat{\beta}_1$ and $\hat{\beta}_2$ is the negative of the correlation between the two regressors:

$$\text{corr}(\hat{\beta}_1, \hat{\beta}_2) = -\rho_{X_1, X_2}. \tag{6.18}$$

APPENDIX

## 6.3  The Frisch–Waugh Theorem

The OLS estimator in multiple regression can be computed by a sequence of shorter regressions. Consider the multiple regression model in Equation (6.7). The OLS estimator of $\beta_1$ can be computed in three steps:

1. Regress $X_1$ on $X_2, X_3, \ldots, X_k$, and let $\widetilde{X}_1$ denote the residuals from this regression;
2. Regress $Y$ on $X_2, X_3, \ldots, X_k$, and let $\widetilde{Y}$ denote the residuals from this regression; and
3. Regress $\widetilde{Y}$ on $\widetilde{X}_1$,

where the regressions include a constant term (intercept). The Frisch-Waugh theorem states that the OLS coefficient in step 3 equals the OLS coefficient on $X_1$ in the multiple regression model [Equation (6.7)].

This result provides a mathematical statement of how the multiple regression coefficient $\hat{\beta}_1$ estimates the effect on $Y$ of $X_1$, controlling for the other $X$'s: Because the first two regressions (steps 1 and 2) remove from $Y$ and $X_1$ their variation associated with the other $X$'s, the third regression estimates the effect on $Y$ of $X_1$ using what is left over after removing (controlling for) the effect of the other $X$'s. The Frisch-Waugh theorem is proven in Exercise 18.17.

This theorem suggests how Equation (6.17) can be derived from Equation (5.27). Because $\hat{\beta}_1$ is the OLS regression coefficient from the regression of $\widetilde{Y}$ onto $\widetilde{X}_1$, Equation (5.27) suggests that the homoskedasticity-only variance of $\hat{\beta}_1$ is $\sigma^2_{\hat{\beta}_1} = \frac{\sigma^2_{\tilde{u}}}{n\sigma^2_{\tilde{X}_1}}$, where $\sigma^2_{\tilde{X}_1}$ is the variance of $\widetilde{X}_1$. Because $\widetilde{X}_1$ is the residual from the regression of $X_1$ onto $X_2$ (recall that Equation (6.17) pertains to the model with $k = 2$ regressors), Equation (6.15) implies that $s^2_{\tilde{X}_1} = (1 - \overline{R}^2_{X_1, X_2})s^2_{X_1}$, where $\overline{R}^2_{X_1, X_2}$ is the adjusted $R^2$ from the regression of $X_1$ onto $X_2$. Equation (6.17) follows from $s^2_{\tilde{X}_1} \xrightarrow{p} \sigma^2_{\tilde{X}_1}$, $\overline{R}^2_{X_1, X_2} \xrightarrow{p} \rho^2_{X_1, X_2}$ and $s^2_{X_1} \xrightarrow{p} \sigma^2_{X_1}$.

# 7 Hypothesis Tests and Confidence Intervals in Multiple Regression

As discussed in Chapter 6, multiple regression analysis provides a way to mitigate the problem of omitted variable bias by including additional regressors, thereby controlling for the effects of those additional regressors. The coefficients of the multiple regression model can be estimated by OLS. Like all estimators, the OLS estimator has sampling uncertainty because its value differs from one sample to the next.

This chapter presents methods for quantifying the sampling uncertainty of the OLS estimator through the use of standard errors, statistical hypothesis tests, and confidence intervals. One new possibility that arises in multiple regression is a hypothesis that simultaneously involves two or more regression coefficients. The general approach to testing such "joint" hypotheses involves a new test statistic, the *F*-statistic.

Section 7.1 extends the methods for statistical inference in regression with a single regressor to multiple regression. Sections 7.2 and 7.3 show how to test hypotheses that involve two or more regression coefficients. Section 7.4 extends the notion of confidence intervals for a single coefficient to confidence sets for multiple coefficients. Deciding which variables to include in a regression is an important practical issue, so Section 7.5 discusses ways to approach this problem. In Section 7.6, we apply multiple regression analysis to obtain improved estimates of the effect on test scores of a reduction in the student–teacher ratio using the California test score data set.

## 7.1 Hypothesis Tests and Confidence Intervals for a Single Coefficient

This section describes how to compute the standard error, how to test hypotheses, and how to construct confidence intervals for a single coefficient in a multiple regression equation.

### Standard Errors for the OLS Estimators

Recall that, in the case of a single regressor, it was possible to estimate the variance of the OLS estimator by substituting sample averages for expectations, which led to the estimator $\hat{\sigma}_{\hat{\beta}_1}^2$ given in Equation (5.4). Under the least squares assumptions, the law of large numbers implies that these sample averages converge to their population counterparts, so, for example, $\hat{\sigma}_{\hat{\beta}_1}^2 / \sigma_{\hat{\beta}_1}^2 \xrightarrow{p} 1$. The square root of $\hat{\sigma}_{\hat{\beta}_1}^2$ is the standard error of $\hat{\beta}_1$, $SE(\hat{\beta}_1)$, an estimator of the standard deviation of the sampling distribution of $\hat{\beta}_1$.

All this extends directly to multiple regression. The OLS estimator $\hat{\beta}_j$ of the $j^{\text{th}}$ regression coefficient has a standard deviation, and this standard deviation is estimated by its standard error, $SE(\hat{\beta}_j)$. The formula for the standard error is most easily stated using matrices (see Section 18.2). The important point is that, as far as standard errors are concerned, there is nothing conceptually different between the single- or multiple-regressor cases. The key ideas—the large-sample normality of the estimators and the ability to estimate consistently the standard deviation of their sampling distribution—are the same whether one has one, two, or 12 regressors.

## Hypothesis Tests for a Single Coefficient

Suppose that you want to test the hypothesis that a change in the student–teacher ratio has no effect on test scores, holding constant the percentage of English learners in the district. This corresponds to hypothesizing that the true coefficient $\beta_1$ on the student–teacher ratio is zero in the population regression of test scores on $STR$ and $PctEL$. More generally, we might want to test the hypothesis that the true coefficient $\beta_j$ on the $j^{\text{th}}$ regressor takes on some specific value, $\beta_{j,0}$. The null value $\beta_{j,0}$ comes either from economic theory or, as in the student–teacher ratio example, from the decision-making context of the application. If the alternative hypothesis is two-sided, then the two hypotheses can be written mathematically as

$$H_0: \beta_j = \beta_{j,0} \text{ vs. } H_1: \beta_j \neq \beta_{j,0} \quad \text{(two-sided alternative).} \tag{7.1}$$

For example, if the first regressor is $STR$, then the null hypothesis that changing the student–teacher ratio has no effect on class size corresponds to the null hypothesis that $\beta_1 = 0$ (so $\beta_{1,0} = 0$). Our task is to test the null hypothesis $H_0$ against the alternative $H_1$ using a sample of data.

Key Concept 5.2 gives a procedure for testing this null hypothesis when there is a single regressor. The first step in this procedure is to calculate the standard error of the coefficient. The second step is to calculate the $t$-statistic using the general formula in Key Concept 5.1. The third step is to compute the $p$-value of the test using the cumulative normal distribution in Appendix Table 1 or, alternatively, to compare the $t$-statistic to the critical value corresponding to the

**KEY CONCEPT**

**7.1**

**Testing the Hypothesis $\beta_j = \beta_{j,0}$**
**Against the Alternative $\beta_j \neq \beta_{j,0}$**

1. Compute the standard error of $\hat{\beta}_j$, $SE(\hat{\beta}_j)$.
2. Compute the $t$-statistic,

$$t = \frac{\hat{\beta}_j - \beta_{j,0}}{SE(\hat{\beta}_j)}. \tag{7.2}$$

3. Compute the $p$-value,

$$p\text{-value} = 2\Phi(-|t^{act}|), \tag{7.3}$$

where $t^{act}$ is the value of the $t$-statistic actually computed. Reject the hypothesis at the 5% significance level if the $p$-value is less than 0.05 or, equivalently, if $|t^{act}| > 1.96$.

The standard error and (typically) the $t$-statistic and $p$-value testing $\beta_j = 0$ are computed automatically by regression software.

desired significance level of the test. The theoretical underpinnings of this procedure are that the OLS estimator has a large-sample normal distribution that, under the null hypothesis, has as its mean the hypothesized true value and that the variance of this distribution can be estimated consistently.

This underpinning is present in multiple regression as well. As stated in Key Concept 6.5, the sampling distribution of $\hat{\beta}_j$ is approximately normal. Under the null hypothesis the mean of this distribution is $\beta_{j,0}$. The variance of this distribution can be estimated consistently. Therefore we can simply follow the same procedure as in the single-regressor case to test the null hypothesis in Equation (7.1).

The procedure for testing a hypothesis on a single coefficient in multiple regression is summarized as Key Concept 7.1. The $t$-statistic actually computed is denoted $t^{act}$ in this box. However, it is customary to denote this simply as $t$, and we adopt this simplified notation for the rest of the book.

## Confidence Intervals for a Single Coefficient

The method for constructing a confidence interval in the multiple regression model is also the same as in the single-regressor model. This method is summarized as Key Concept 7.2.

**KEY CONCEPT**

**7.2**

## Confidence Intervals for a Single Coefficient in Multiple Regression

A 95% two-sided confidence interval for the coefficient $\beta_j$ is an interval that contains the true value of $\beta_j$ with a 95% probability; that is, it contains the true value of $\beta_j$ in 95% of all possible randomly drawn samples. Equivalently, it is the set of values of $\beta_j$ that cannot be rejected by a 5% two-sided hypothesis test. When the sample size is large, the 95% confidence interval is

$$95\% \text{ confidence interval for } \beta_j = [\hat{\beta}_j - 1.96\,SE(\hat{\beta}_j), \hat{\beta}_j + 1.96\,SE(\hat{\beta}_j)]. \quad (7.4)$$

A 90% confidence interval is obtained by replacing 1.96 in Equation (7.4) with 1.64.

The method for conducting a hypothesis test in Key Concept 7.1 and the method for constructing a confidence interval in Key Concept 7.2 rely on the large-sample normal approximation to the distribution of the OLS estimator $\hat{\beta}_j$. Accordingly, it should be kept in mind that these methods for quantifying the sampling uncertainty are only guaranteed to work in large samples.

## Application to Test Scores and the Student–Teacher Ratio

Can we reject the null hypothesis that a change in the student–teacher ratio has no effect on test scores, once we control for the percentage of English learners in the district? What is a 95% confidence interval for the effect on test scores of a change in the student–teacher ratio, controlling for the percentage of English learners? We are now able to find out. The regression of test scores against $STR$ and $PctEL$, estimated by OLS, was given in Equation (6.12) and is restated here with standard errors in parentheses below the coefficients:

$$\widehat{TestScore} = 686.0 - 1.10 \times STR - 0.650 \times PctEL. \quad (7.5)$$
$$\phantom{\widehat{TestScore} = } (8.7) \quad (0.43) \qquad\quad (0.031)$$

To test the hypothesis that the true coefficient on $STR$ is 0, we first need to compute the $t$-statistic in Equation (7.2). Because the null hypothesis says that the true value of this coefficient is zero, the $t$-statistic is $t = (-1.10 - 0)/0.43 = -2.54$.

The associated $p$-value is $2\Phi(-2.54) = 1.1\%$; that is, the smallest significance level at which we can reject the null hypothesis is 1.1%. Because the $p$-value is less than 5%, the null hypothesis can be rejected at the 5% significance level (but not quite at the 1% significance level).

A 95% confidence interval for the population coefficient on $STR$ is $-1.10 \pm 1.96 \times 0.43 = (-1.95, -0.26)$; that is, we can be 95% confident that the true value of the coefficient is between $-1.95$ and $-0.26$. Interpreted in the context of the superintendent's interest in decreasing the student–teacher ratio by 2, the 95% confidence interval for the effect on test scores of this reduction is $(-1.95 \times 2, -0.26 \times 2) = (-3.90, -0.52)$.

***Adding expenditures per pupil to the equation.*** Your analysis of the multiple regression in Equation (7.5) has persuaded the superintendent that, based on the evidence so far, reducing class size will improve test scores in her district. Now, however, she moves on to a more nuanced question. If she is to hire more teachers, she can pay for those teachers either through cuts elsewhere in the budget (no new computers, reduced maintenance, and so on) or by asking for an increase in her budget, which taxpayers do not favor. What, she asks, is the effect on test scores of reducing the student–teacher ratio, holding expenditures per pupil (and the percentage of English learners) constant?

This question can be addressed by estimating a regression of test scores on the student–teacher ratio, total spending per pupil, and the percentage of English learners. The OLS regression line is

$$\widehat{TestScore} = 649.6 - 0.29 \times STR + 3.87 \times Expn - 0.656 \times PctEL, \quad (7.6)$$
$$\phantom{xxx}(15.5)\ \ (0.48)\phantom{xxxxx}(1.59)\phantom{xxxxxx}(0.032)$$

where $Expn$ is total annual expenditures per pupil in the district in thousands of dollars.

The result is striking. Holding expenditures per pupil and the percentage of English learners constant, changing the student–teacher ratio is estimated to have a very small effect on test scores: The estimated coefficient on $STR$ is $-1.10$ in Equation (7.5) but, after adding $Expn$ as a regressor in Equation (7.6), it is only $-0.29$. Moreover, the $t$-statistic for testing that the true value of the coefficient is zero is now $t = (-0.29 - 0)/0.48 = -0.60$, so the hypothesis that the population value of this coefficient is indeed zero cannot be rejected even at the 10% significance level ($|-0.60| < 1.64$). Thus Equation (7.6) provides no evidence that hiring more teachers improves test scores if overall expenditures per pupil are held constant.

One interpretation of the regression in Equation (7.6) is that, in these California data, school administrators allocate their budgets efficiently. Suppose, counterfactually, that the coefficient on *STR* in Equation (7.6) were negative and large. If so, school districts could raise their test scores simply by decreasing funding for other purposes (textbooks, technology, sports, and so on) and transferring those funds to hire more teachers, thereby reducing class sizes while holding expenditures constant. However, the small and statistically insignificant coefficient on *STR* in Equation (7.6) indicates that this transfer would have little effect on test scores. Put differently, districts are already allocating their funds efficiently.

Note that the standard error on *STR* increased when *Expn* was added, from 0.43 in Equation (7.5) to 0.48 in Equation (7.6). This illustrates the general point, introduced in Section 6.7 in the context of imperfect multicollinearity, that correlation between regressors (the correlation between *STR* and *Expn* is −0.62) can make the OLS estimators less precise.

What about our angry taxpayer? He asserts that the population values of *both* the coefficient on the student–teacher ratio ($\beta_1$) *and* the coefficient on spending per pupil ($\beta_2$) are zero; that is, he hypothesizes that both $\beta_1 = 0$ and $\beta_2 = 0$. Although it might seem that we can reject this hypothesis because the $t$-statistic testing $\beta_2 = 0$ in Equation (7.6) is $t = 3.87/1.59 = 2.43$, this reasoning is flawed. The taxpayer's hypothesis is a joint hypothesis, and to test it we need a new tool, the $F$-statistic.

## 7.2 Tests of Joint Hypotheses

This section describes how to formulate joint hypotheses on multiple regression coefficients and how to test them using an $F$-statistic.

### Testing Hypotheses on Two or More Coefficients

*Joint null hypotheses.*  Consider the regression in Equation (7.6) of the test score against the student–teacher ratio, expenditures per pupil, and the percentage of English learners. Our angry taxpayer hypothesizes that neither the student–teacher ratio nor expenditures per pupil have an effect on test scores, once we control for the percentage of English learners. Because *STR* is the first regressor in Equation (7.6) and *Expn* is the second, we can write this hypothesis mathematically as

$$H_0: \beta_1 = 0 \text{ and } \beta_2 = 0 \text{ vs. } H_1: \beta_1 \neq 0 \text{ and/or } \beta_2 \neq 0. \qquad (7.7)$$

The hypothesis that *both* the coefficient on the student–teacher ratio ($\beta_1$) *and* the coefficient on expenditures per pupil ($\beta_2$) are zero is an example of a joint hypothesis on the coefficients in the multiple regression model. In this case, the null hypothesis restricts the value of two of the coefficients, so as a matter of terminology we can say that the null hypothesis in Equation (7.7) imposes two **restrictions** on the multiple regression model: $\beta_1 = 0$ *and* $\beta_2 = 0$.

In general, a **joint hypothesis** is a hypothesis that imposes two or more restrictions on the regression coefficients. We consider joint null and alternative hypotheses of the form

$$H_0: \beta_j = \beta_{j,0}, \beta_m = \beta_{m,0}, \ldots, \text{ for a total of } q \text{ restrictions, vs.}$$
$$H_1: \text{one or more of the } q \text{ restrictions under } H_0 \text{ does not hold,} \qquad (7.8)$$

where $\beta_j, \beta_m, \ldots$, refer to different regression coefficients and $\beta_{j,0}, \beta_{m,0}, \ldots$, refer to the values of these coefficients under the null hypothesis. The null hypothesis in Equation (7.7) is an example of Equation (7.8). Another example is that, in a regression with $k = 6$ regressors, the null hypothesis is that the coefficients on the $2^{nd}$, $4^{th}$, and $5^{th}$ regressors are zero; that is, $\beta_2 = 0, \beta_4 = 0$, and $\beta_5 = 0$ so that there are $q = 3$ restrictions. In general, under the null hypothesis $H_0$ there are $q$ such restrictions.

If any one (or more than one) of the equalities under the null hypothesis $H_0$ in Equation (7.8) is false, then the joint null hypothesis itself is false. Thus the alternative hypothesis is that at least one of the equalities in the null hypothesis $H_0$ does not hold.

*Why can't I just test the individual coefficients one at a time?* Although it seems it should be possible to test a joint hypothesis by using the usual $t$-statistics to test the restrictions one at a time, the following calculation shows that this approach is unreliable. Specifically, suppose that you are interested in testing the joint null hypothesis in Equation (7.6) that $\beta_1 = 0$ and $\beta_2 = 0$. Let $t_1$ be the $t$-statistic for testing the null hypothesis that $\beta_1 = 0$ and let $t_2$ be the $t$-statistic for testing the null hypothesis that $\beta_2 = 0$. What happens when you use the "one-at-a-time" testing procedure: Reject the joint null hypothesis if either $t_1$ or $t_2$ exceeds 1.96 in absolute value?

Because this question involves the two random variables $t_1$ and $t_2$, answering it requires characterizing the joint sampling distribution of $t_1$ and $t_2$. As mentioned in Section 6.6, in large samples $\hat{\beta}_1$ and $\hat{\beta}_2$ have a joint normal distribution, so under the joint null hypothesis the $t$-statistics $t_1$ and $t_2$ have a bivariate normal distribution, where each $t$-statistic has mean equal to 0 and variance equal to 1.

First consider the special case in which the $t$-statistics are uncorrelated and thus are independent. What is the size of the one-at-a-time testing procedure; that is, what is the probability that you will reject the null hypothesis when it is true? More than 5%! In this special case we can calculate the rejection probability of this method exactly. The null is *not* rejected only if both $|t_1| \leq 1.96$ and $|t_2| \leq 1.96$. Because the $t$-statistics are independent, $Pr(|t_1| \leq 1.96$ and $|t_2| \leq 1.96) = Pr(|t_1| \leq 1.96) \times Pr(|t_2| \leq 1.96) = 0.95^2 = 0.9025 = 90.25\%$. So the probability of rejecting the null hypothesis when it is true is $1 - 0.95^2 = 9.75\%$. This "one at a time" method rejects the null too often because it gives you too many chances: If you fail to reject using the first $t$-statistic, you get to try again using the second.

If the regressors are correlated, the situation is even more complicated. The size of the "one at a time" procedure depends on the value of the correlation between the regressors. Because the "one at a time" testing approach has the wrong size—that is, its rejection rate under the null hypothesis does not equal the desired significance level—a new approach is needed.

One approach is to modify the "one at a time" method so that it uses different critical values that ensure that its size equals its significance level. This method, called the Bonferroni method, is described in Appendix (7.1). The advantage of the Bonferroni method is that it applies very generally. Its disadvantage is that it can have low power: It frequently fails to reject the null hypothesis when in fact the alternative hypothesis is true.

Fortunately, there is another approach to testing joint hypotheses that is more powerful, especially when the regressors are highly correlated. That approach is based on the $F$-statistic.

## The F-Statistic

The **F-statistic** is used to test joint hypothesis about regression coefficients. The formulas for the $F$-statistic are integrated into modern regression software. We first discuss the case of two restrictions, then turn to the general case of $q$ restrictions.

*The F-statistic with q = 2 restrictions.* When the joint null hypothesis has the two restrictions that $\beta_1 = 0$ and $\beta_2 = 0$, the $F$-statistic combines the two $t$-statistics $t_1$ and $t_2$ using the formula

$$F = \frac{1}{2}\left(\frac{t_1^2 + t_2^2 - 2\hat{\rho}_{t_1,t_2}t_1t_2}{1 - \hat{\rho}_{t_1,t_2}^2}\right), \tag{7.9}$$

where $\hat{\rho}_{t_1,t_2}$ is an estimator of the correlation between the two $t$-statistics.

To understand the $F$-statistic in Equation (7.9), first suppose that we know that the $t$-statistics are uncorrelated so we can drop the terms involving $\hat{\rho}_{t_1, t_2}$. If so, Equation (7.9) simplifies and $F = \frac{1}{2}(t_1^2 + t_2^2)$; that is, the $F$-statistic is the average of the squared $t$-statistics. Under the null hypothesis, $t_1$ and $t_2$ are independent standard normal random variables (because the $t$-statistics are uncorrelated by assumption), so under the null hypothesis $F$ has an $F_{2,\infty}$ distribution (Section 2.4). Under the alternative hypothesis that either $\beta_1$ is nonzero or $\beta_2$ is nonzero (or both), then either $t_1^2$ or $t_2^2$ (or both) will be large, leading the test to reject the null hypothesis.

In general the $t$-statistics are correlated, and the formula for the $F$-statistic in Equation (7.9) adjusts for this correlation. This adjustment is made so that, under the null hypothesis, the $F$-statistic has an $F_{2,\infty}$ distribution in large samples whether or not the $t$-statistics are correlated.

**The F-statistic with q restrictions.**  The formula for the heteroskedasticity-robust $F$-statistic testing the $q$ restrictions of the joint null hypothesis in Equation (7.8) is given in Section 18.3. This formula is incorporated into regression software, making the $F$-statistic easy to compute in practice.

Under the null hypothesis, the $F$-statistic has a sampling distribution that, in large samples, is given by the $F_{q,\infty}$ distribution. That is, in large samples, under the null hypothesis

$$\text{the } F\text{-statistic is distributed } F_{q,\infty}. \tag{7.10}$$

Thus the critical values for the $F$-statistic can be obtained from the tables of the $F_{q,\infty}$ distribution in Appendix Table 4 for the appropriate value of $q$ and the desired significance level.

**Computing the heteroskedasticity-robust F-statistic in statistical software.**  If the $F$-statistic is computed using the general heteroskedasticity-robust formula, its large-$n$ distribution under the null hypothesis is $F_{q,\infty}$ regardless of whether the errors are homoskedastic or heteroskedastic. As discussed in Section 5.4, for historical reasons most statistical software computes homoskedasticity-only standard errors by default. Consequently, in some software packages you must select a "robust" option so that the $F$-statistic is computed using heteroskedasticity-robust standard errors (and, more generally, a heteroskedasticity-robust estimate of the "covariance matrix"). The homoskedasticity-only version of the $F$-statistic is discussed at the end of this section.

**Computing the p-value using the F-statistic.**  The $p$-value of the $F$-statistic can be computed using the large-sample $F_{q,\infty}$ approximation to its distribution. Let

$F^{act}$ denote the value of the $F$-statistic actually computed. Because the $F$-statistic has a large-sample $F_{q,\infty}$ distribution under the null hypothesis, the $p$-value is

$$p\text{-value} = \Pr\left[F_{q,\infty} > F^{act}\right]. \tag{7.11}$$

The $p$-value in Equation (7.11) can be evaluated using a table of the $F_{q,\infty}$ distribution (or, alternatively, a table of the $\chi_q^2$ distribution, because a $\chi_q^2$-distributed random variable is $q$ times an $F_{q,\infty}$-distributed random variable). Alternatively, the $p$-value can be evaluated using a computer, because formulas for the cumulative chi-squared and $F$ distributions have been incorporated into most modern statistical software.

***The "overall" regression F-statistic.*** The "overall" regression $F$-statistic tests the joint hypothesis that *all* the slope coefficients are zero. That is, the null and alternative hypotheses are

$$H_0: \beta_1 = 0, \beta_2 = 0, \ldots, \beta_k = 0 \text{ vs. } H_1: \beta_j \neq 0, \text{ at least one } j, j = 1, \ldots, k. \tag{7.12}$$

Under this null hypothesis, none of the regressors explains any of the variation in $Y_i$, although the intercept (which under the null hypothesis is the mean of $Y_i$) can be nonzero. The null hypothesis in Equation (7.12) is a special case of the general null hypothesis in Equation (7.8), and the overall regression $F$-statistic is the $F$-statistic computed for the null hypothesis in Equation (7.12). In large samples, the overall regression $F$-statistic has an $F_{k,\infty}$ distribution when the null hypothesis is true.

***The F-statistic when q = 1.*** When $q = 1$, the $F$-statistic tests a single restriction. Then the joint null hypothesis reduces to the null hypothesis on a single regression coefficient, and the $F$-statistic is the square of the $t$-statistic.

## Application to Test Scores and the Student–Teacher Ratio

We are now able to test the null hypothesis that the coefficients on *both* the student–teacher ratio *and* expenditures per pupil are zero, against the alternative that at least one coefficient is nonzero, controlling for the percentage of English learners in the district.

To test this hypothesis, we need to compute the heteroskedasticity-robust $F$-statistic of the test that $\beta_1 = 0$ and $\beta_2 = 0$ using the regression of *TestScore* on *STR*, *Expn*, and *PctEL* reported in Equation (7.6). This $F$-statistic is 5.43. Under the null hypothesis, in large samples this statistic has an $F_{2,\infty}$ distribution. The 5% critical value of the $F_{2,\infty}$ distribution is 3.00 (Appendix Table 4), and the 1% critical value is 4.61. The value of the $F$-statistic computed from the data, 5.43, exceeds 4.61, so the null hypothesis is rejected at the 1% level. It is very unlikely that we would have drawn a sample that produced an $F$-statistic as large as 5.43 if the null hypothesis really were true (the $p$-value is 0.005). Based on the evidence in Equation (7.6) as summarized in this $F$-statistic, we can reject the taxpayer's hypothesis that *neither* the student–teacher ratio *nor* expenditures per pupil have an effect on test scores (holding constant the percentage of English learners).

## The Homoskedasticity-Only $F$-Statistic

One way to restate the question addressed by the $F$-statistic is to ask whether relaxing the $q$ restrictions that constitute the null hypothesis improves the fit of the regression by enough that this improvement is unlikely to be the result merely of random sampling variation if the null hypothesis is true. This restatement suggests that there is a link between the $F$-statistic and the regression $R^2$: A large $F$-statistic should, it seems, be associated with a substantial increase in the $R^2$. In fact, if the error $u_i$ is homoskedastic, this intuition has an exact mathematical expression. Specifically, if the error term is homoskedastic, the $F$-statistic can be written in terms of the improvement in the fit of the regression as measured either by the decrease in the sum of squared residuals or by the increase in the regression $R^2$. The resulting $F$-statistic is referred to as the homoskedasticity-only $F$-statistic, because it is valid only if the error term is homoskedastic. In contrast, the heteroskedasticity-robust $F$-statistic computed using the formula in Section 18.3 is valid whether the error term is homoskedastic or heteroskedastic. Despite this significant limitation of the homoskedasticity-only $F$-statistic, its simple formula sheds light on what the $F$-statistic is doing. In addition, the simple formula can be computed using standard regression output, such as might be reported in a table that includes regression $R^2$'s but not $F$-statistics.

The homoskedasticity-only $F$-statistic is computed using a simple formula based on the sum of squared residuals from two regressions. In the first regression, called the **restricted regression**, the null hypothesis is forced to be true. When the null hypothesis is of the type in Equation (7.8), where all the hypothesized values are zero, the restricted regression is the regression in which those coefficients are set to zero; that is, the relevant regressors are excluded from the regression. In the second regression, called the **unrestricted regression**, the alternative hypothesis is allowed to be true. If the sum of squared residuals is sufficiently smaller in the unrestricted than the restricted regression, then the test rejects the null hypothesis.

The **homoskedasticity-only F-statistic** is given by the formula

$$F = \frac{(SSR_{restricted} - SSR_{unrestricted})/q}{SSR_{unrestricted}/(n - k_{unrestricted} - 1)}, \tag{7.13}$$

where $SSR_{restricted}$ is the sum of squared residuals from the restricted regression, $SSR_{unrestricted}$ is the sum of squared residuals from the unrestricted regression, $q$ is the number of restrictions under the null hypothesis, and $k_{unrestricted}$ is the number of regressors in the unrestricted regression. An alternative equivalent formula for the homoskedasticity-only F-statistic is based on the $R^2$ of the two regressions:

$$F = \frac{(R^2_{unrestricted} - R^2_{restricted})/q}{(1 - R^2_{unrestricted})(n - k_{unrestricted} - 1)}. \tag{7.14}$$

If the errors are homoskedastic, then the difference between the homoskedasticity-only F-statistic computed using Equation (7.13) or (7.14) and the heteroskedasticity-robust F-statistic vanishes as the sample size $n$ increases. Thus, if the errors are homoskedastic, the sampling distribution of the homoskedasticity-only F-statistic under the null hypothesis is, in large samples, $F_{q,\infty}$.

These formulas are easy to compute and have an intuitive interpretation in terms of how well the unrestricted and restricted regressions fit the data. Unfortunately, the formulas apply only if the errors are homoskedastic. Because homoskedasticity is a special case that cannot be counted on in applications with economic data, or more generally with data sets typically found in the social sciences, in practice the homoskedasticity-only F-statistic is not a satisfactory substitute for the heteroskedasticity-robust F-statistic.

*Using the homoskedasticity-only F-statistic when n is small.* If the errors are homoskedastic and are i.i.d. normally distributed, then the homoskedasticity-only F-statistic defined in Equations (7.13) and (7.14) has an $F_{q,n-k_{unrestricted}-1}$ distribution under the null hypothesis. Critical values for this distribution, which depend on both $q$ and $n - k_{unrestricted} - 1$, are given in Appendix Table 5. As discussed in Section 2.4, the $F_{q,n-k_{unrestricted}-1}$ distribution converges to the $F_{q,\infty}$ distribution as $n$ increases; for large sample sizes, the differences between the two distributions are negligible. For small samples, however, the two sets of critical values differ.

*Application to test scores and the student–teacher ratio.* To test the null hypothesis that the population coefficients on *STR* and *Expn* are 0, controlling for *PctEL*, we need to compute the $R^2$ (or *SSR*) for the restricted and unrestricted regression. The unrestricted regression has the regressors *STR*, *Expn*, and *PctEL*, and is given in Equation (7.6); its $R^2$ is 0.4366; that is, $R^2_{unrestricted} = 0.4366$. The restricted regression imposes the joint null hypothesis that the true coefficients on *STR* and *Expn* are zero; that is, under the null hypothesis *STR* and *Expn* do not enter the population regression, although *PctEL* does (the null hypothesis does not restrict the coefficient on *PctEL*). The restricted regression, estimated by OLS, is

$$\widehat{TestScore} = 664.7 - 0.671 \times PctEL, R^2 = 0.4149, \qquad (7.15)$$
$$\phantom{\widehat{TestScore} = 664.7}(1.0) \quad (0.032)$$

so $R^2_{restricted} = 0.4149$. The number of restrictions is $q = 2$, the number of observations is $n = 420$, and the number of regressors in the unrestricted regression is $k = 3$. The homoskedasticity-only $F$-statistic, computed using Equation (7.14), is

$$F = \frac{(0.4366 - 0.4149)/2}{(1 - 0.4366)(420 - 3 - 1)} = 8.01.$$

Because 8.01 exceeds the 1% critical value of 4.61, the hypothesis is rejected at the 1% level using the homoskedasticity-only test.

This example illustrates the advantages and disadvantages of the homoskedasticity-only $F$-statistic. Its advantage is that it can be computed using a calculator. Its disadvantage is that the values of the homoskedasticity-only and heteroskedasticity-robust $F$-statistics can be very different: The heteroskedasticity-robust $F$-statistic testing this joint hypothesis is 5.43, quite different from the less reliable homoskedasticity-only value of 8.01.

## 7.3 Testing Single Restrictions Involving Multiple Coefficients

Sometimes economic theory suggests a single restriction that involves two or more regression coefficients. For example, theory might suggest a null hypothesis of the form $\beta_1 = \beta_2$; that is, the effects of the first and second regressor are the same. In this case, the task is to test this null hypothesis against the alternative that the two coefficients differ:

$$H_0: \beta_1 = \beta_2 \text{ vs. } H_1: \beta_1 \neq \beta_2. \qquad (7.16)$$

This null hypothesis has a single restriction, so $q = 1$, but that restriction involves multiple coefficients ($\beta_1$ and $\beta_2$). We need to modify the methods presented so far to test this hypothesis. There are two approaches; which is easier depends on your software.

***Approach #1: Test the restriction directly.*** Some statistical packages have a specialized command designed to test restrictions like Equation (7.16) and the result is an $F$-statistic that, because $q = 1$, has an $F_{1,\infty}$ distribution under the null hypothesis. (Recall from Section 2.4 that the square of a standard normal random variable has an $F_{1,\infty}$ distribution, so the 95% percentile of the $F_{1,\infty}$ distribution is $1.96^2 = 3.84$.)

***Approach #2: Transform the regression.*** If your statistical package cannot test the restriction directly, the hypothesis in Equation (7.16) can be tested using a trick in which the original regression equation is rewritten to turn the restriction in Equation (7.16) into a restriction on a single regression coefficient. To be concrete, suppose there are only two regressors, $X_{1i}$ and $X_{2i}$, in the regression, so the population regression has the form

$$Y_i = \beta_0 + \beta_1 X_{1i} + \beta_2 X_{2i} + u_i. \tag{7.17}$$

Here is the trick: By subtracting and adding $\beta_2 X_{1i}$, we have that $\beta_1 X_{1i} + \beta_2 X_{2i} = \beta_1 X_{1i} - \beta_2 X_{1i} + \beta_2 X_{1i} + \beta_2 X_{2i} = (\beta_1 - \beta_2)X_{1i} + \beta_2(X_{1i} + X_{2i}) = \gamma_1 X_{1i} + \beta_2 W_i$, where $\gamma_1 = \beta_1 - \beta_2$ and $W_i = X_{1i} + X_{2i}$. Thus the population regression in Equation (7.17) can be rewritten as

$$Y_i = \beta_0 + \gamma_1 X_{1i} + \beta_2 W_i + u_i. \tag{7.18}$$

Because the coefficient $\gamma_1$ in this equation is $\gamma_1 = \beta_1 - \beta_2$, under the null hypothesis in Equation (7.16), $\gamma_1 = 0$, while under the alternative, $\gamma_1 \neq 0$. Thus, by turning Equation (7.17) into Equation (7.18), we have turned a restriction on two regression coefficients into a restriction on a single regression coefficient.

Because the restriction now involves the single coefficient $\gamma_1$, the null hypothesis in Equation (7.16) can be tested using the $t$-statistic method of Section 7.1. In practice, this is done by first constructing the new regressor $W_i$ as the sum of the two original regressors, then estimating the regression of $Y_i$ on $X_{1i}$ and $W_i$. A 95% confidence interval for the difference in the coefficients $\beta_1 - \beta_2$ can be calculated as $\hat{\gamma}_1 \pm 1.96\, SE(\hat{\gamma}_1)$.

This method can be extended to other restrictions on regression equations using the same trick (see Exercise 7.9).

The two methods (Approaches #1 and #2) are equivalent, in the sense that the $F$-statistic from the first method equals the square of the $t$-statistic from the second method.

*Extension to q > 1.* In general, it is possible to have $q$ restrictions under the null hypothesis in which some or all of these restrictions involve multiple coefficients. The $F$-statistic of Section 7.2 extends to this type of joint hypothesis. The $F$-statistic can be computed by either of the two methods just discussed for $q = 1$. Precisely how best to do this in practice depends on the specific regression software being used.

## 7.4 Confidence Sets for Multiple Coefficients

This section explains how to construct a confidence set for two or more regression coefficients. The method is conceptually similar to the method in Section 7.1 for constructing a confidence set for a single coefficient using the $t$-statistic, except that the confidence set for multiple coefficients is based on the $F$-statistic.

A **95% confidence set** for two or more coefficients is a set that contains the true population values of these coefficients in 95% of randomly drawn samples. Thus a confidence set is the generalization to two or more coefficients of a confidence interval for a single coefficient.

Recall that a 95% confidence interval is computed by finding the set of values of the coefficients that are not rejected using a $t$-statistic at the 5% significance level. This approach can be extended to the case of multiple coefficients. To make this concrete, suppose you are interested in constructing a confidence set for two coefficients, $\beta_1$ and $\beta_2$. Section 7.2 showed how to use the $F$-statistic to test a joint null hypothesis that $\beta_1 = \beta_{1,0}$ and $\beta_2 = \beta_{2,0}$. Suppose you were to test every possible value of $\beta_{1,0}$ and $\beta_{2,0}$ at the 5% level. For each pair of candidates $(\beta_{1,0}, \beta_{2,0})$, you compute the $F$-statistic and reject it if it exceeds the 5% critical value of 3.00. Because the test has a 5% significance level, the true population values of $\beta_1$ and $\beta_2$ will not be rejected in 95% of all samples. Thus the set of values not rejected at the 5% level by this $F$-statistic constitutes a 95% confidence set for $\beta_1$ and $\beta_2$.

Although this method of trying all possible values of $\beta_{1,0}$ and $\beta_{2,0}$ works in theory, in practice it is much simpler to use an explicit formula for the confidence set. This formula for the confidence set for an arbitrary number of coefficients is based on the formula for the $F$-statistic. When there are two coefficients, the resulting confidence sets are ellipses.

As an illustration, Figure 7.1 shows a 95% confidence set (confidence ellipse) for the coefficients on the student–teacher ratio and expenditure per pupil, holding constant the percentage of English learners, based on the estimated regression in Equation (7.6). This ellipse does not include the point (0,0). This means that the

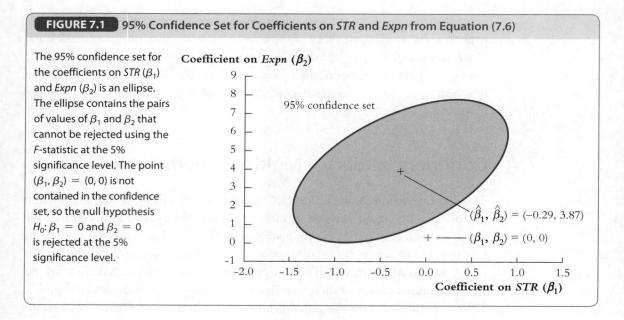

**FIGURE 7.1** 95% Confidence Set for Coefficients on *STR* and *Expn* from Equation (7.6)

The 95% confidence set for the coefficients on *STR* ($\beta_1$) and *Expn* ($\beta_2$) is an ellipse. The ellipse contains the pairs of values of $\beta_1$ and $\beta_2$ that cannot be rejected using the *F*-statistic at the 5% significance level. The point $(\beta_1, \beta_2) = (0, 0)$ is not contained in the confidence set, so the null hypothesis $H_0: \beta_1 = 0$ and $\beta_2 = 0$ is rejected at the 5% significance level.

null hypothesis that these two coefficients are both zero is rejected using the *F*-statistic at the 5% significance level, which we already knew from Section 7.2. The confidence ellipse is a fat sausage with the long part of the sausage oriented in the lower-left/upper-right direction. The reason for this orientation is that the estimated correlation between $\hat{\beta}_1$ and $\hat{\beta}_2$ is positive, which in turn arises because the correlation between the regressors *STR* and *Expn* is negative (schools that spend more per pupil tend to have fewer students per teacher).

## 7.5 Model Specification for Multiple Regression

The job of determining which variables to include in multiple regression—that is, the problem of choosing a regression specification—can be quite challenging, and no single rule applies in all situations. But do not despair, because some useful guidelines are available. The starting point for choosing a regression specification is thinking through the possible sources of omitted variable bias. It is important to rely on your expert knowledge of the empirical problem and to focus on obtaining an unbiased estimate of the causal effect of interest; do not rely solely on purely statistical measures of fit such as the $R^2$ or $\overline{R}^2$.

## Omitted Variable Bias in Multiple Regression

Omitted variable bias is the bias in the OLS estimator that arises when one or more included regressors are correlated with an omitted variable. For omitted variable bias to arise, two things must be true:

1. At least one of the included regressors must be correlated with the omitted variable.
2. The omitted variable must be a determinant of the dependent variable, $Y$.

## Omitted Variable Bias in Multiple Regression

The OLS estimators of the coefficients in multiple regression will have omitted variable bias if an omitted determinant of $Y_i$ is correlated with at least one of the regressors. For example, students from affluent families often have more learning opportunities outside the classroom (reading material at home, travel, museum visits, etc.) than do their less affluent peers, which could lead to better test scores. Moreover, if the district is a wealthy one, then the schools will tend to have larger budgets and lower student–teacher ratios. If so, the availability of outside learning opportunities and the student–teacher ratio would be negatively correlated, and the OLS estimate of the coefficient on the student–teacher ratio would pick up the effect of outside learning opportunities, even after controlling for the percentage of English learners. In short, omitting outside learning opportunities (and other variables related to the students' economic background) could lead to omitted variable bias in the regression of test scores on the student–teacher ratio and the percentage of English learners.

The general conditions for omitted variable bias in multiple regression are similar to those for a single regressor: If an omitted variable is a determinant of $Y_i$ and if it is correlated with at least one of the regressors, then the OLS estimator of at least one of the coefficients will have omitted variable bias. The two conditions for omitted variable bias in multiple regression are summarized in Key Concept 7.3.

At a mathematical level, if the two conditions for omitted variable bias are satisfied, then at least one of the regressors is correlated with the error term. This means that the conditional expectation of $u_i$ given $X_{1i}, \ldots, X_{ki}$ is nonzero, so the first least squares assumption is violated. As a result, the omitted variable bias persists even if the sample size is large; that is, omitted variable bias implies that the OLS estimators are inconsistent.

## The Role of Control Variables in Multiple Regression

So far, we have implicitly distinguished between a regressor for which we wish to estimate a causal effect—that is, a variable of interest—and control variables. We now discuss this distinction in more detail.

A **control variable** is not the object of interest in the study; rather it is a regressor included to hold constant factors that, if neglected, could lead the estimated causal effect of interest to suffer from omitted variable bias. The least squares assumptions for multiple regression (Section 6.5) treat the regressors symmetrically. In this subsection, we introduce an alternative to the first least squares assumption in which the distinction between a variable of interest and a control variable is explicit. If this alternative assumption holds, the OLS estimator of the effect of interest is unbiased, but the OLS coefficients on control variables are in general biased and do not have a causal interpretation.

For example, consider the potential omitted variable bias arising from omitting outside learning opportunities from a test score regression. Although "outside learning opportunities" is a broad concept that is difficult to measure, those opportunities are correlated with the students' economic background, which can be measured. Thus a measure of economic background can be included in a test score regression to control for omitted income-related determinants of test scores, like outside learning opportunities. To this end, we augment the regression of test scores on $STR$ and $PctEL$ with the percentage of students receiving a free or subsidized school lunch ($LchPct$). Because students are eligible for this program if their family income is less than a certain threshold (approximately 150% of the poverty line), $LchPct$ measures the fraction of economically disadvantaged children in the district. The estimated regression is

$$\widehat{TestScore} = 700.2 - 1.00 \times STR - 0.122 \times PctEL - 0.547 \times LchPct. \quad (7.19)$$
$$\phantom{\widehat{TestScore} = }(5.6) \quad (0.27) \quad\quad\quad (0.033) \quad\quad\quad\quad (0.024)$$

Including the control variable $LchPct$ does not substantially change any conclusions about the class size effect: The coefficient on $STR$ changes only slightly from its value of −1.10 in Equation (7.5) to −1.00 in Equation (7.19), and it remains statistically significant at the 1% level.

What does one make of the coefficient on $LchPct$ in Equation (7.19)? That coefficient is very large: The difference in test scores between a district with $LchPct = 0\%$

and one with $LchPct = 50\%$ is estimated to be 27.4 points $[= 0.547 \times (50 - 0)]$, approximately the difference between the 75th and 25th percentiles of test scores in Table 4.1. Does this coefficient have a causal interpretation? Suppose that upon seeing Equation (7.19) the superintendent proposed eliminating the reduced-price lunch program so that, for her district, $LchPct$ would immediately drop to zero. Would eliminating the lunch program boost her district's test scores? Common sense suggests that the answer is no; in fact, by leaving some students hungry, eliminating the reduced-price lunch program could have the opposite effect. But does it make sense to treat the coefficient on the variable of interest $STR$ as causal, but not the coefficient on the control variable $LchPct$?

The distinction between variables of interest and control variables can be made mathematically precise by replacing the first least squares assumption of Key Concept 6.4—that is, the conditional mean-zero assumption—with an assumption called conditional mean independence. Consider a regression with two variables, in which $X_{1i}$ is the variable of interest and $X_{2i}$ is the control variable. **Conditional mean independence** requires that the conditional expectation of $u_i$ given $X_{1i}$ and $X_{2i}$ does not depend on (is independent of) $X_{1i}$, although it can depend on $X_{2i}$. That is

$$E(u_i | X_{1i}, X_{2i}) = E(u_i | X_{2i}) \quad \text{(conditional mean independence).} \quad (7.20)$$

As is shown in Appendix (7.2), under the conditional mean independence assumption in Equation (7.20), the coefficient on $X_{1i}$ has a causal interpretation but the coefficient on $X_{2i}$ does not.

The idea of conditional mean independence is that once you control for $X_{2i}$, $X_{1i}$ can be treated as if it were randomly assigned, in the sense that the conditional mean of the error term no longer depends on $X_{1i}$. Including $X_{2i}$ as a control variable makes $X_{1i}$ uncorrelated with the error term so that OLS can estimate the causal effect on $Y_{1i}$ of a change in $X_{1i}$. The control variable, however, remains correlated with the error term, so the coefficient on the control variable is subject to omitted variable bias and does not have a causal interpretation.

The terminology of control variables can be confusing. The control variable $X_{2i}$ is included because it controls for omitted factors that affect $Y_i$ and are correlated with $X_{1i}$ and because it might (but need not) have a causal effect itself. Thus the coefficient on $X_{1i}$ is the effect on $Y_i$ of $X_{1i}$, using the control variable $X_{2i}$ both to hold constant the direct effect of $X_{2i}$ and to control for factors correlated with $X_{2i}$. Because this terminology is awkward, it is conventional simply to say that the coefficient on $X_{1i}$ is the effect on $Y_i$, controlling for $X_{2i}$. When a control variable is used, it is controlling both for its own direct causal effect (if any) and for the effect of correlated omitted factors, with the aim of ensuring that conditional mean independence holds.

In the class size example, *LchPct* can be correlated with factors, such as learning opportunities outside school, that enter the error term; indeed, it is *because* of this correlation that *LchPct* is a useful control variable. This correlation between *LchPct* and the error term means that the estimated coefficient on *LchPct* does not have a causal interpretation. What the conditional mean independence assumption requires is that, given the control variables in the regression (*PctEL* and *LchPct*), the mean of the error term does not depend on the student–teacher ratio. Said differently, conditional mean independence says that among schools with the same values of *PctEL* and *LchPct*, class size is "as if" randomly assigned: including *PctEL* and *LchPct* in the regression controls for omitted factors so that *STR* is uncorrelated with the error term. If so, the coefficient on the student–teacher ratio has a causal interpretation even though the coefficient on *LchPct* does not: For the superintendent struggling to increase test scores, there is no free lunch.

## Model Specification in Theory and in Practice

In theory, when data are available on the omitted variable, the solution to omitted variable bias is to include the omitted variable in the regression. In practice, however, deciding whether to include a particular variable can be difficult and requires judgment.

Our approach to the challenge of potential omitted variable bias is twofold. First, a core or base set of regressors should be chosen using a combination of expert judgment, economic theory, and knowledge of how the data were collected; the regression using this base set of regressors is sometimes referred to as a **base specification**. This base specification should contain the variables of primary interest and the control variables suggested by expert judgment and economic theory. Expert judgment and economic theory are rarely decisive, however, and often the variables suggested by economic theory are not the ones on which you have data. Therefore the next step is to develop a list of candidate **alternative specifications**, that is, alternative sets of regressors. If the estimates of the coefficients of interest are numerically similar across the alternative specifications, then this provides evidence that the estimates from your base specification are reliable. If, on the other hand, the estimates of the coefficients of interest change substantially across specifications, this often provides evidence that the original specification had omitted variable bias. We elaborate on this approach to model specification in Section 9.2 after studying some tools for specifying regressions.

## Interpreting the $R^2$ and the Adjusted $R^2$ in Practice

An $R^2$ or an $\overline{R}^2$ near 1 means that the regressors are good at predicting the values of the dependent variable in the sample, and an $R^2$ or an $\overline{R}^2$ near 0 means that they are not. This makes these statistics useful summaries of the predictive ability of the regression. However, it is easy to read more into them than they deserve.

There are four potential pitfalls to guard against when using the $R^2$ or $\overline{R}^2$:

1. ***An increase in the $R^2$ or $\overline{R}^2$ does not necessarily mean that an added variable is statistically significant.*** The $R^2$ increases whenever you add a regressor, whether or not it is statistically significant. The $\overline{R}^2$ does not always increase, but if it does, this does not necessarily mean that the coefficient on that added regressor is statistically significant. To ascertain whether an added variable is statistically significant, you need to perform a hypothesis test using the $t$-statistic.

2. ***A high $R^2$ or $\overline{R}^2$ does not mean that the regressors are a true cause of the dependent variable.*** Imagine regressing test scores against parking lot area per pupil. Parking lot area is correlated with the student–teacher ratio, with whether the school is in a suburb or a city, and possibly with district income—all things that are correlated with test scores. Thus the regression of test scores on parking lot area per pupil could have a high $R^2$ and $\overline{R}^2$, but the relationship is not causal (try telling the superintendent that the way to increase test scores is to increase parking space!).

3. ***A high $R^2$ or $\overline{R}^2$ does not mean that there is no omitted variable bias.*** Recall the discussion of Section 6.1, which concerned omitted variable bias in the regression of test scores on the student–teacher ratio. The $R^2$ of the regression never came up because it played no logical role in this discussion. Omitted variable bias can occur in regressions with a low $R^2$, a moderate $R^2$, or a high $R^2$. Conversely, a low $R^2$ does not imply that there necessarily is omitted variable bias.

4. ***A high $R^2$ or $\overline{R}^2$ does not necessarily mean that you have the most appropriate set of regressors, nor does a low $R^2$ or $\overline{R}^2$ necessarily mean that you have an inappropriate set of regressors.*** The question of what constitutes the right set of regressors in multiple regression is difficult, and we return to it throughout this textbook. Decisions about the regressors must weigh issues of omitted variable bias, data availability, data quality, and, most importantly, economic theory and the nature of the substantive questions being addressed. None of these questions can be answered simply by having a high (or low) regression $R^2$ or $\overline{R}^2$.

These points are summarized in Key Concept 7.4.

KEY CONCEPT

**7.4**

## $R^2$ and $\bar{R}^2$: What They Tell You—and What They Don't

*The $R^2$ and $\bar{R}^2$ tell you* whether the regressors are good at predicting, or "explaining," the values of the dependent variable in the sample of data on hand. If the $R^2$ (or $\bar{R}^2$) is nearly 1, then the regressors produce good predictions of the dependent variable in that sample, in the sense that the variance of the OLS residual is small compared to the variance of the dependent variable. If the $R^2$ (or $\bar{R}^2$) is nearly 0, the opposite is true.

*The $R^2$ and $\bar{R}^2$ do NOT tell you* whether:

1. An included variable is statistically significant,

2. The regressors are a true cause of the movements in the dependent variable,

3. There is omitted variable bias, or

4. You have chosen the most appropriate set of regressors.

## 7.6 Analysis of the Test Score Data Set

This section presents an analysis of the effect on test scores of the student–teacher ratio using the California data set. Our primary purpose is to provide an example in which multiple regression analysis is used to mitigate omitted variable bias. Our secondary purpose is to demonstrate how to use a table to summarize regression results.

*Discussion of the base and alternative specifications.* This analysis focuses on estimating the effect on test scores of a change in the student–teacher ratio, holding constant student characteristics that the superintendent cannot control. Many factors potentially affect the average test score in a district. Some of these factors are correlated with the student–teacher ratio, so omitting them from the regression results in omitted variable bias. Because these factors, such as outside learning opportunities, are not directly measured, we include control variables that are correlated with these omitted factors. If the control variables are adequate in the sense that the conditional mean independence assumption holds, then the coefficient on the student–teacher ratio is the effect of a change in the student–teacher ratio, holding constant these other factors.

Here we consider three variables that control for background characteristics of the students that could affect test scores: the fraction of students who are still learning English, the percentage of students who are eligible for receiving a subsidized or free lunch at school, and a new variable, the percentage of students in the district whose families qualify for a California income assistance program. Eligibility for this income assistance program depends in part on family income, with a lower (stricter) threshold than the subsidized lunch program. The final two variables thus are different measures of the fraction of economically disadvantaged children in the district (their correlation coefficient is 0.74). Theory and expert judgment do not tell us which of these two variables to use to control for determinants of test scores related to economic background. For our base specification, we use the percentage eligible for a subsidized lunch, but we also consider an alternative specification that uses the fraction eligible for the income assistance program.

Scatterplots of tests scores and these variables are presented in Figure 7.2. Each of these variables exhibits a negative correlation with test scores. The correlation between test scores and the percentage of English learners is $-0.64$; between test scores and the percentage eligible for a subsidized lunch is $-0.87$; and between test scores and the percentage qualifying for income assistance is $-0.63$.

*What scale should we use for the regressors?*   A practical question that arises in regression analysis is what scale you should use for the regressors. In Figure 7.2, the units of the variables are percent, so the maximum possible range of the data is 0 to 100. Alternatively, we could have defined these variables to be a *decimal fraction* rather than a percent; for example, $PctEL$ could be replaced by the *fraction* of English learners, $FracEL (= PctEL / 100)$, which would range between 0 and 1 instead of between 0 and 100. More generally, in regression analysis some decision usually needs to be made about the scale of both the dependent and independent variables. How, then, should you choose the scale, or units, of the variables?

The general answer to the question of choosing the scale of the variables is to make the regression results easy to read and to interpret. In the test score application, the natural unit for the dependent variable is the score of the test itself. In the regression of *TestScore* on *STR* and *PctEL* reported in Equation (7.5), the coefficient on *PctEL* is $-0.650$. If instead the regressor had been *FracEL*, the regression would have had an identical $R^2$ and *SER*; however, the coefficient on *FracEL* would have been $-65.0$. In the specification with *PctEL*, the coefficient is the predicted change in test scores for a 1-percentage-point increase in English learners, holding *STR* constant; in the specification with *FracEL*, the coefficient is the predicted change in test scores for an increase by 1 in the fraction of English learners—that is, for a 100-percentage-point-increase—holding *STR* constant. Although these two specifications are mathematically equivalent, for the purposes of interpretation the one with *PctEL* seems, to us, more natural.

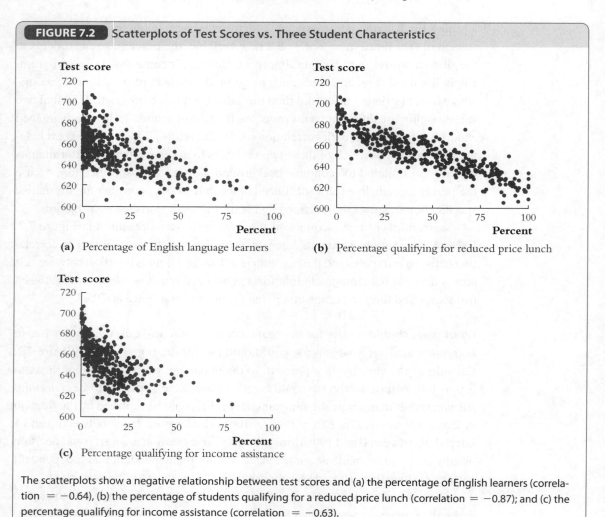

**FIGURE 7.2**    Scatterplots of Test Scores vs. Three Student Characteristics

(a)  Percentage of English language learners

(b)  Percentage qualifying for reduced price lunch

(c)  Percentage qualifying for income assistance

The scatterplots show a negative relationship between test scores and (a) the percentage of English learners (correlation = −0.64), (b) the percentage of students qualifying for a reduced price lunch (correlation = −0.87); and (c) the percentage qualifying for income assistance (correlation = −0.63).

Another consideration when deciding on a scale is to choose the units of the regressors so that the resulting regression coefficients are easy to read. For example, if a regressor is measured in dollars and has a coefficient of 0.00000356, it is easier to read if the regressor is converted to millions of dollars and the coefficient 3.56 is reported.

*Tabular presentation of result.*  We are now faced with a communication problem. What is the best way to show the results from several multiple regressions that contain different subsets of the possible regressors? So far, we have presented

**TABLE 7.1** Results of Regressions of Test Scores on the Student–Teacher Ratio and Student Characteristic Control Variables Using California Elementary School Districts

**Dependent variable: average test score in the district.**

| Regressor | (1) | (2) | (3) | (4) | (5) |
|---|---|---|---|---|---|
| Student–teacher ratio ($X_1$) | −2.28** | −1.10* | −1.00** | −1.31* | −1.01* |
| | (0.52) | (0.43) | (0.27) | (0.34) | (0.27) |
| Percent English learners ($X_2$) | | −0.650** | −0.122** | −0.488** | −0.130** |
| | | (0.031) | (0.033) | (0.030) | (0.036) |
| Percent eligible for subsidized lunch ($X_3$) | | | −0.547* | | −0.529* |
| | | | (0.024) | | (0.038) |
| Percent on public income assistance ($X_4$) | | | | −0.790** | 0.048 |
| | | | | (0.068) | (0.059) |
| Intercept | 698.9** | 686.0** | 700.2** | 698.0** | 700.4** |
| | (10.4) | (8.7) | (5.6) | (6.9) | (5.5) |
| **Summary Statistics** | | | | | |
| $SER$ | 18.58 | 14.46 | 9.08 | 11.65 | 9.08 |
| $\overline{R}^2$ | 0.049 | 0.424 | 0.773 | 0.626 | 0.773 |
| $n$ | 420 | 420 | 420 | 420 | 420 |

These regressions were estimated using the data on K–8 school districts in California, described in Appendix (4.1). Heteroskedasticity-robust standard errors are given in parentheses under coefficients. The individual coefficient is statistically significant at the *5% level or **1% significance level using a two-sided test.

regression results by writing out the estimated regression equations, as in Equations (7.6) and (7.19). This works well when there are only a few regressors and only a few equations, but with more regressors and equations this method of presentation can be confusing. A better way to communicate the results of several regressions is in a table.

Table 7.1 summarizes the results of regressions of the test score on various sets of regressors. Each column summarizes a separate regression. Each regression has the same dependent variable, test score. The entries in the first five rows are the estimated regression coefficients, with their standard errors below them in parentheses. The asterisks indicate whether the $t$-statistics, testing the hypothesis that the relevant coefficient is zero, is significant at the 5% level (one asterisk) or the 1% level (two asterisks). The final three rows contain summary statistics for the regression (the standard error of the regression, $SER$, and the adjusted $R^2$, $\overline{R}^2$) and the sample size (which is the same for all of the regressions, 420 observations).

All the information that we have presented so far in equation format appears as a column of this table. For example, consider the regression of the test score against the student–teacher ratio, with no control variables. In equation form, this regression is

$$\widehat{TestScore} = 698.9 - 2.28 \times STR, \overline{R}^2 = 0.049, SER = 18.58, n = 420. \quad (7.21)$$
$$\phantom{\widehat{TestScore} = }(10.4) \ (0.52)$$

All this information appears in column (1) of Table 7.1. The estimated coefficient on the student–teacher ratio ($-2.28$) appears in the first row of numerical entries, and its standard error (0.52) appears in parentheses just below the estimated coefficient. The intercept (698.9) and its standard error (10.4) are given in the row labeled "Intercept." (Sometimes you will see this row labeled "constant" because, as discussed in Section 6.2, the intercept can be viewed as the coefficient on a regressor that is always equal to 1.) Similarly, the $\overline{R}^2$ (0.049), the SER (18.58), and the sample size $n$ (420) appear in the final rows. The blank entries in the rows of the other regressors indicate that those regressors are not included in this regression.

Although the table does not report $t$-statistics, they can be computed from the information provided; for example, the $t$-statistic testing the hypothesis that the coefficient on the student–teacher ratio in column (1) is zero is $-2.28/0.52 = -4.38$. This hypothesis is rejected at the 1% level, which is indicated by the double asterisk next to the estimated coefficient in the table.

Regressions that include the control variables measuring student characteristics are reported in columns (2) through (5). Column (2), which reports the regression of test scores on the student–teacher ratio and on the percentage of English learners, was previously stated as Equation (7.5).

Column (3) presents the base specification, in which the regressors are the student–teacher ratio and two control variables, the percentage of English learners and the percentage of students eligible for a free lunch.

Columns (4) and (5) present alternative specifications that examine the effect of changes in the way the economic background of the students is measured. In column (4) the percentage of students on income assistance is included as a regressor, and in column (5) both of the economic background variables are included.

*Discussion of empirical results.* These results suggest three conclusions:

1. Controlling for these student characteristics cuts the effect of the student–teacher ratio on test scores approximately in half. This estimated effect is not very sensitive to which specific control variables are included in the regression. In all cases the coefficient on the student–teacher ratio remains statistically significant at the 5% level. In the four specifications with control variables, regressions (2) through (5), reducing the student–teacher ratio

by one student per teacher is estimated to increase average test scores by approximately 1 point, holding constant student characteristics.

2. The student characteristic variables are potent predictors of test scores. The student–teacher ratio alone explains only a small fraction of the variation in test scores: The $\overline{R}^2$ in column (1) is 0.049. The $\overline{R}^2$ jumps, however, when the student characteristic variables are added. For example, the $\overline{R}^2$ in the base specification, regression (3), is 0.773. The signs of the coefficients on the student demographic variables are consistent with the patterns seen in Figure 7.2: Districts with many English learners and districts with many poor children have lower test scores.

3. The control variables are not always individually statistically significant: In specification (5), the hypothesis that the coefficient on the percentage qualifying for income assistance is zero is not rejected at the 5% level (the $t$-statistic is $-0.82$). Because adding this control variable to the base specification (3) has a negligible effect on the estimated coefficient for the student–teacher ratio and its standard error, and because the coefficient on this control variable is not significant in specification (5), this additional control variable is redundant, at least for the purposes of this analysis.

## 7.7 Conclusion

Chapter 6 began with a concern: In the regression of test scores against the student–teacher ratio, omitted student characteristics that influence test scores might be correlated with the student–teacher ratio in the district, and, if so, the student–teacher ratio in the district would pick up the effect on test scores of these omitted student characteristics. Thus the OLS estimator would have omitted variable bias. To mitigate this potential omitted variable bias, we augmented the regression by including variables that control for various student characteristics (the percentage of English learners and two measures of student economic background). Doing so cuts the estimated effect of a unit change in the student–teacher ratio in half, although it remains possible to reject the null hypothesis that the population effect on test scores, holding these control variables constant, is zero at the 5% significance level. Because they eliminate omitted variable bias arising from these student characteristics, these multiple regression estimates, hypothesis tests, and confidence intervals are much more useful for advising the superintendent than the single-regressor estimates of Chapters 4 and 5.

The analysis in this and the preceding chapter has presumed that the population regression function is linear in the regressors—that is, that the conditional expectation of $Y_i$ given the regressors is a straight line. There is, however, no particular reason to think this is so. In fact, the effect of reducing the student–teacher ratio might be quite different in districts with large classes than in districts that already have small classes. If so, the population regression line is not linear in the $X$'s but rather is a nonlinear function of the $X$'s. To extend our analysis to regression functions that are nonlinear in the $X$'s, however, we need the tools developed in the next chapter.

## Summary

1.  Hypothesis tests and confidence intervals for a single regression coefficient are carried out using essentially the same procedures used in the one-variable linear regression model of Chapter 5. For example, a 95% confidence interval for $\beta_1$ is given by $\hat{\beta}_1 \pm 1.96 \, SE(\hat{\beta}_1)$.
2.  Hypotheses involving more than one restriction on the coefficients are called joint hypotheses. Joint hypotheses can be tested using an $F$-statistic.
3.  Regression specification proceeds by first determining a base specification chosen to address concern about omitted variable bias. The base specification can be modified by including additional regressors that address other potential sources of omitted variable bias. Simply choosing the specification with the highest $R^2$ can lead to regression models that do not estimate the causal effect of interest.

## Key Terms

restrictions (269)                         95% confidence set (277)
joint hypothesis (269)                     control variable (280)
$F$-statistic (270)                        conditional mean independence (281)
restricted regression (273)                base specification (282)
unrestricted regression (273)              alternative specifications (282)
homoskedasticity-only $F$-statistic (274)  Bonferroni test (297)

---

**MyEconLab Can Help You Get a Better Grade**

**MyEconLab**  If your exam were tomorrow, would you be ready? For each chapter, **MyEconLab** Practice Tests and Study Plan help you prepare for your exams. You can also find similar Exercises and Review the Concepts Questions now in **MyEconLab**. To see how it works, turn to the **MyEconLab** spread on pages 2 and 3 of this book and then go to **www.myeconlab.com**.

For additional Empirical Exercises and Data Sets, log on to the Companion Website at **www.pearsonglobaleditions.com/Stock_Watson**.

## Review the Concepts

**7.1**  What is a joint hypothesis? Explain how an F-statistic is constructed to test a joint hypothesis. What is the hypothesis that is tested by constructing the overall regression F-statistic in the multiple regression model $Y_i = \beta_0 + \beta_1 X_{1i} + \beta_2 X_{2i} + u_i$? Explain, using the concepts of restricted and unrestricted regressions. Why is it important for a researcher to have information on the distribution of the error terms when implementing these tests?

**7.2**  Describe the recommended approach towards determining model specification. How does the $R^2$ help in determining an appropriate model? Is the ideal model the one with the highest $R^2$? Should a regressor be included in the model if it increases the model $R^2$?

**7.3**  What is a control variable, and how does it differ from a variable of interest? Looking at Table 7.1, which variables are control variables? What is the variable of interest? Do coefficients on control variables measure causal effects? Explain.

## Exercises

The first six exercises refer to the table of estimated regressions on page 292, computed using data on employees. The data set consists of information on over 10000 full-time, full-year workers. The highest educational achievement for each worker was either a high school diploma or a bachelor's degree. The workers' ages ranged from 25 to 40 years. The data set also contains information on the region of the country where the person lived, and the individual's gender and age. For the purposes of these exercises, let

$AWE$ = logarithm of average weekly earnings (in 2007 units)

*High school* = binary variable (1 if High school, 0 if less)

*Male* = binary variable (1 if male, 0 if female)

*Age* = age (in years)

*North* = binary variable (1 if Region = North, 0 otherwise)

*East* = binary variable (1 if Region = East, 0 otherwise)

*South* = binary variable (1 if Region = South, 0 otherwise)

*West* = binary variable (1 if Region = West, 0 otherwise)

**Results of Regressions of Average Hourly Earnings on Gender and Education Binary Variables and Other Characteristics Using 2007 Data from the Current Population Survey**

**Dependent variable: average hourly earnings (AHE).**

| Regressor | 1 | 2 | 3 |
|---|---|---|---|
| Graduated high school $(X_1)$ | 0.352 (0.021) | 0.373 (0.021) | 0.371 (0.021) |
| Male $(X_2)$ | 0.458 (0.021) | 0.457 (0.020) | 0.451 (0.020) |
| Age $(X_3)$ | | 0.011 (0.001) | 0.011 (0.001) |
| North $(X_4)$ | | | 0.175 (0.37) |
| South $(X_5)$ | | | 0.103 (0.033) |
| East $(X_6)$ | | | −0.102 (0.043) |
| Intercept | 12.84 (0.018) | 12.471 (0.049) | 12.390 (0.057) |
| $F$-statistic for regional effects = 0 | | | 21.87 |
| SER | 1.026 | 1.023 | 1.020 |
| $R^2$ | 0.0710 | 0.0761 | 0.0814 |
| $n$ | 10973 | 10973 | 10973 |

**7.1** Add * (5%) and ** (1%) to the table to indicate the statistical significance of the coefficients.

**7.2** Using the regression results in column (1):
   **a.** Is the college–high school earnings difference, estimated from this regression, statistically significant at the 5% level? Construct a 95% confidence interval of the difference.

   **b.** Is the male–female earnings difference, estimated from this regression, statistically significant at the 5% level? Construct a 95% confidence interval for the difference.

**7.3** Using the regression results in column (2):
   **a.** Is age an important determinant of earnings? Use an appropriate statistical test and/or confidence interval to explain your answer.

   **b.** Alvo is a 30-year-old male college graduate. Kal is a 40-year-old male college graduate. Construct a 95% confidence interval for the expected difference between their earnings.

**7.4** Using the regression results in column (3):

    **a.** Are there important regional differences? Use an appropriate hypothesis test to explain your answer.

    **b.** Juan is a 32-year-old male high school graduate from the North. Ali is a 32-year-old male college graduate from the West. Mayank is a 32-year-old male college graduate from the East.

        i. Construct a 95% confidence interval for the difference in expected earnings between Juan and Ali.

        ii. Explain how you would construct a 95% confidence interval for the difference in expected earnings between Juan and Mayank. (*Hint:* What would happen if you included *West* and excluded *East* from the regression?)

**7.5** The regression shown in column (2) was estimated again, this time using data from 1993 (5000 observations selected at random and converted into 2007 units using the consumer price index). The results are

$$\widehat{logAWE} = 9.32 + 0.301 High\ school + 0.562 Male + 0.011 Age;\ SER = 1.25,\ \overline{R}^2 = 0.08.$$
$$\phantom{\widehat{logAWE} = }(0.20)\ \ (0.019)\phantom{xxxxxx}(0.047)\phantom{xxxx}(0.002)$$

Comparing this regression to the regression for 2012 shown in column (2), was there a statistically significant change in the coefficient on *High school*?

**7.6** In all the regressions, the coefficient of *High school* is positive, large, and statistically significant. Do you believe this provides strong statistical evidence of the high returns to schooling in the labor market?

**7.7** Question 6.5 reported the following regression (where standard errors have been added):

$$\widehat{Price} = 109.7 + 0.567 BDR + 26.9 Bath + 0.239 Hsize + 0.005 Lsize$$
$$\phantom{\widehat{Price} = }(22.1)\ \ \ (1.23)\phantom{xxx}(9.76)\phantom{xxx}(0.021)\phantom{xxx}(0.00072)$$

$$\phantom{\widehat{Price} = }+ 0.1 Age - 56.9 Poor,\ R^2 = 0.85,\ SER = 45.8$$
$$\phantom{\widehat{Price} = }(0.23)\phantom{xxx}(12.23)$$

    **a.** Is the coefficient on *BDR* statistically significantly different from zero?

    **b.** Typically four-bedroom houses sell for more than three-bedroom houses. Is this consistent with your answer to (a), and with the regression in general?

    **c.** A homeowner purchases 2500 square feet from an adjacent lot. Construct a 95% confident interval for the change in the value of their house.

    **d.** Lot size is measured in square feet. Do you think that another scale might be more appropriate? Why or why not?

    **e.** The $F$-statistic for omitting $BDR$ and $Age$ from the regression is $F = 2.38$. Are the coefficients on $BDR$ and $Age$ statistically different from zero at the 10% level?

**7.8** Referring to the table on page 292 used for exercises 7.1–7.6:

    **a.** Construct the $R^2$ for each of the regressions.

    **b.** Show how to construct the homoskedasticity-only $F$-statistic for testing $\beta_4 = \beta_5 = \beta_6 = 0$ in the regression shown in column (3).

    **c.** Test $\beta_4 = \beta_5 = \beta_6 = 0$ in the regression shown in column (3) using the Bonferroni test discussed in Appendix 7.1.

    **d.** Construct a 99% confidence interval for $\beta_1$ for the regression in column (3).

**7.9** Consider the regression model $Y_i = \beta_0 + \beta_1 X_{1i} + \beta_2 X_{2i} + u_i$. Use Approach #2 from Section 7.3 to transform the regression so that you can use a $t$-statistic to test

    **a.** $\beta_1 = \beta_2$.

    **b.** $\beta_1 + 2\beta_2 = 0$.

    **c.** $\beta_1 + \beta_2 = 1$. (*Hint:* You must redefine the dependent variable in the regression.)

**7.10** Equations (7.13) and (7.14) show two formulas for the homoskedasticity-only $F$-statistic. Show that the two formulas are equivalent.

**7.11** A school district undertakes an experiment to estimate the effect of class size on test scores in second-grade classes. The district assigns 50% of its previous year's first graders to small second-grade classes (18 students per classroom) and 50% to regular-size classes (21 students per classroom). Students new to the district are handled differently: 20% are randomly assigned to small classes and 80% to regular-size classes. At the end of the second-grade school year, each student is given a standardized exam. Let $Y_i$ denote the exam score for the $i^{\text{th}}$ student, $X_{1i}$ denote a binary variable that equals 1 if the student is assigned to a small class, and $X_{2i}$ denote a binary variable that equals 1 if the student is newly enrolled. Let $\beta_1$ denote the causal effect on test scores of reducing class size from regular to small.

**a.** Consider the regression $Y_i = \beta_0 + \beta_1 X_{1i} + u_i$. Do you think that $E(u_i|X_{1i}) = 0$? Is the OLS estimator of $\beta_1$ unbiased and consistent? Explain.

**b.** Consider the regression $Y_i = \beta_0 + \beta_1 X_{1i} + \beta_2 X_{2i} + u_i$. Do you think that $E(u_i|X_{1i}, X_{2i})$ depends on $X_1$? Is the OLS estimator of $\beta_1$ unbiased and consistent? Explain. Do you think that $E(u_i|X_{1i}, X_{2i})$ depends on $X_2$? Will the OLS estimator of $\beta_2$ provide an unbiased and consistent estimate of the causal effect of transferring to a new school (that is, being a newly enrolled student)? Explain.

## Empirical Exercises

(Only two empirical exercises for this chapter are given in the text, but you can find more on the text website, **www.pearsonglobaleditions.com/Stock_Watson**.)

**E7.1** Use the **Birthweight_Smoking** data set introduced in Empirical Exercise E5.3 to answer the following questions. To begin, run three regressions:

(1) *Birthweight* on *Smoker*

(2) *Birthweight* on *Smoker*, *Alcohol*, and *Nprevist*

(3) *Birthweight* on *Smoker*, *Alcohol*, *Nprevist*, and *Unmarried*

**a.** What is the value of the estimated effect of smoking on birth weight in each of the regressions?

**b.** Construct a 95% confidence interval for the effect of smoking on birth weight, using each of the regressions.

**c.** Does the coefficient on *Smoker* in regression (1) suffer from omitted variable bias? Explain.

**d.** Does the coefficient on *Smoker* in regression (2) suffer from omitted variable bias? Explain.

**e.** Consider the coefficient on *Unmarried* in regression (3).

  i. Construct a 95% confidence interval for the coefficient.

  ii. Is the coefficient statistically significant? Explain.

  iii. Is the magnitude of the coefficient large? Explain.

  iv. A family advocacy group notes that the large coefficient suggests that public policies that encourage marriage will lead, on average, to healthier babies. Do you agree? (*Hint:* Review the discussion of control variables in Section 7.5. Discuss some of the various factors that *Unmarried* may be controlling for and how this affects the interpretation of its coefficient.)

**f.** Consider the various other control variables in the data set. Which do you think should be included in the regression? Using a table like Table 7.1, examine the robustness of the confidence interval you constructed in (b). What is a reasonable 95% confidence interval for the effect of smoking on birth weight?

**E7.2** In the empirical exercises on earning and height in Chapters 4 and 5, you estimated a relatively large and statistically significant effect of a worker's height on his or her earnings. One explanation for this result is omitted variable bias: Height is correlated with an omitted factor that affects earnings. For example, Case and Paxson (2008) suggest that cognitive ability (or intelligence) is the omitted factor. The mechanism they describe is straightforward: Poor nutrition and other harmful environmental factors in utero and in early childhood have, on average, deleterious effects on both cognitive and physical development. Cognitive ability affects earnings later in life and thus is an omitted variable in the regression.

**a.** Suppose that the mechanism described above is correct. Explain how this leads to omitted variable bias in the OLS regression of *Earnings* on *Height*. Does the bias lead the estimated slope to be too large or too small? [*Hint:* Review Equation (6.1).]

If the mechanism described above is correct, the estimated effect of height on earnings should disappear if a variable measuring cognitive ability is included in the regression. Unfortunately, there isn't a direct measure of cognitive ability in the data set, but the data set does include "years of education" for each individual. Because students with higher cognitive ability are more likely to attend school longer, years of education might serve as a control variable for cognitive ability; in this case, including education in the regression will eliminate, or at least attenuate, the omitted variable bias problem.

Use the years of education variable (*educ*) to construct four indicator variables for whether a worker has less than a high school diploma ($LT\_HS = 1$ if $educ < 12$, 0 otherwise), a high school diploma ($HS = 1$ if $educ = 12$, 0 otherwise), some college ($Some\_Col = 1$ if $12 < educ < 16$, 0 otherwise), or a bachelor's degree or higher ($College = 1$ if $educ \geq 16$, 0 otherwise).

**b.** Focusing first on women only, run a regression of (1) *Earnings* on *Height* and (2) *Earnings* on *Height*, including $LT\_HS$, $HS$, and *Some_Col* as control variables.

i. Compare the estimated coefficient on *Height* in regressions (1) and (2). Is there a large change in the coefficient? Has it changed in a way consistent with the cognitive ability explanation? Explain.

ii. The regression omits the control variable *College*. Why?

iii. Test the joint null hypothesis that the coefficients on the education variables are equal to zero.

iv. Discuss the values of the estimated coefficients on *LT_HS*, *HS*, and *Some_Col*. (Each of the estimated coefficients is negative, and the coefficient on *LT_HS* is more negative than the coefficient on *HS*, which in turn is more negative than the coefficient on *Some_Col*. Why? What do the coefficients measure?)

c. Repeat (b), using data for men.

---

**APPENDIX**

## 7.1 The Bonferroni Test of a Joint Hypothesis

The method of Section 7.2 is the preferred way to test joint hypotheses in multiple regression. However, if the author of a study presents regression results but did not test a joint restriction in which you are interested and if you do not have the original data, then you will not be able to compute the $F$-statistic as in Section 7.2. This appendix describes a way to test joint hypotheses that can be used when you only have a table of regression results. This method is an application of a very general testing approach based on Bonferroni's inequality.

The Bonferroni test is a test of a joint hypothesis based on the $t$-statistics for the individual hypotheses; that is, the Bonferroni test is the one-at-a-time $t$-statistic test of Section 7.2 done properly. The **Bonferroni test** of the joint null hypothesis $\beta_1 = \beta_{1,0}$ and $\beta_2 = \beta_{2,0}$ based on the critical value $c > 0$, uses the following rule:

$$\text{Accept if } |t_1| \leq c \text{ and if } |t_2| \leq c; \text{ otherwise, reject} \qquad (7.22)$$
$$\text{(Bonferroni one-at-a-time } t\text{-statistic test)}$$

where $t_1$ and $t_2$ are the $t$-statistics that test the restrictions on $\beta_1$ and $\beta_2$, respectfully.

The trick is to choose the critical value $c$ in such a way that the probability that the one-at-a-time test rejects when the null hypothesis is true is no more than the desired significance level, say 5%. This is done by using Bonferroni's inequality to choose the critical value $c$ to allow both for the fact that two restrictions are being tested and for any possible correlation between $t_1$ and $t_2$.

## Bonferroni's Inequality

Bonferroni's inequality is a basic result of probability theory. Let $A$ and $B$ be events. Let $A \cap B$ be the event "both $A$ and $B$" (the intersection of $A$ and $B$), and let $A \cup B$ be the event "$A$ or $B$ or both" (the union of $A$ and $B$). Then $\Pr(A \cup B) = \Pr(A) + \Pr(B) - \Pr(A \cap B)$. Because $\Pr(A \cap B) \geq 0$, it follows that $\Pr(A \cup B) \leq \Pr(A) + \Pr(B)$.[1] Now let $A$ be the event that $|t_1| > c$ and $B$ be the event that $|t_2| > c$. Then the inequality $\Pr(A \cup B) \leq \Pr(A) + \Pr(B)$ yields

$$\Pr(|t_1| > c \text{ or } |t_2| > c \text{ or both}) \leq \Pr(|t_1| > c) + \Pr(|t_2| > c). \qquad (7.23)$$

## Bonferroni Tests

Because the event "$|t_1| > c$ or $|t_2| > c$ or both" is the rejection region of the one-at-a-time test, Equation (7.23) leads to a valid critical value for the one-at-a-time test. Under the null hypothesis in large samples, $\Pr(|t_1| > c) = \Pr(|t_2| > c) = \Pr(|Z| > c)$. Thus Equation (7.23) implies that, in large samples, the probability that the one-at-a-time test rejects under the null is

$$\Pr_{H_0}(\text{one-at-a-time test rejects}) \leq 2\Pr(|Z| > c). \qquad (7.24)$$

The inequality in Equation (7.24) provides a way to choose a critical value $c$ so that the probability of the rejection under the null hypothesis equals the desired significance level. The Bonferroni approach can be extended to more than two coefficients; if there are $q$ restrictions under the null, the factor of 2 on the right-hand side in Equation (7.24) is replaced by $q$.

Table 7.2 presents critical values $c$ for the one-at-a-time Bonferroni test for various significance levels and $q = 2, 3$, and 4. For example, suppose the desired significance level is 5% and $q = 2$. According to Table 7.2, the critical value $c$ is 2.241. This critical value is

**TABLE 7.2** Bonferroni Critical Values $c$ for the One-at-a-Time $t$-Statistic Test of a Joint Hypothesis

| Number of Restrictions ($q$) | Significance Level | | |
| --- | --- | --- | --- |
| | 10% | 5% | 1% |
| 2 | 1.960 | 2.241 | 2.807 |
| 3 | 2.128 | 2.394 | 2.935 |
| 4 | 2.241 | 2.498 | 3.023 |

---

[1]This inequality can be used to derive other interesting inequalities. For example, it implies that $1 - \Pr(A \cup B) \geq 1 - [\Pr(A) + \Pr(B)]$. Let $A^c$ and $B^c$ be the complements of $A$ and $B$—that is, the events "not $A$" and "not $B$." Because the complement of $A \cup B$ is $A^c \cap B^c$, $1 - \Pr(A \cup B) = \Pr(A^c \cap B^c)$, which yields Bonferroni's inequality, $\Pr(A^c \cap B^c) \geq 1 - [\Pr(A) + \Pr(B)]$.

the 1.25% percentile of the standard normal distribution, so $\Pr(|Z| > 2.241) = 2.5\%$. Thus Equation (7.24) tells us that, in large samples, the one-at-a-time test in Equation (7.22) will reject at most 5% of the time under the null hypothesis.

The critical values in Table 7.2 are larger than the critical values for testing a single restriction. For example, with $q = 2$, the one-at-a-time test rejects if at least one $t$-statistic exceeds 2.241 in absolute value. This critical value is greater than 1.96 because it properly corrects for the fact that, by looking at two $t$-statistics, you get a second chance to reject the joint null hypothesis, as discussed in Section 7.2.

If the individual $t$-statistics are based on heteroskedasticity-robust standard errors, then the Bonferroni test is valid whether or not there is heteroskedasticity, but if the $t$-statistics are based on homoskedasticity-only standard errors, the Bonferroni test is valid only under homoskedasticity.

### Application to Test Scores

The $t$-statistics testing the joint null hypothesis that the true coefficients on test scores and expenditures per pupil in Equation (7.6) are, respectively, $t_1 = -0.60$ and $t_2 = 2.43$. Although $|t_1| < 2.241$, because $|t_2| > 2.241$, we can reject the joint null hypothesis at the 5% significance level using the Bonferroni test. However, both $t_1$ and $t_2$ are less than 2.807 in absolute value, so we cannot reject the joint null hypothesis at the 1% significance level using the Bonferroni test. In contrast, using the $F$-statistic in Section 7.2, we were able to reject this hypothesis at the 1% significance level.

---

APPENDIX

## 7.2   Conditional Mean Independence

This appendix shows that, under the assumption of conditional mean independence introduced in Section 7.5 [Equation (7.20)], the OLS coefficient estimator is unbiased for the variable of interest but not for the control variable.

Consider a regression with two regressors, $Y_i = \beta_0 + \beta_1 X_{1i} + \beta_2 X_{2i} + u_i$. If $E(u_i | X_{1i}, X_{2i}) = 0$, as would be true if $X_{1i}$ and $X_{2i}$ are randomly assigned in an experiment, then the OLS estimators $\hat{\beta}_1$ and $\hat{\beta}_2$ are unbiased estimators of the causal effects $\beta_1$ and $\beta_2$.

Now suppose that $X_{1i}$ is the variable of interest and $X_{2i}$ is a control variable that is correlated with omitted factors in the error term. Although the conditional mean zero assumption does not hold, suppose that conditional mean independence does so that $E(u_i | X_{1i}, X_{2i}) = E(u_i | X_{2i})$. For convenience, further suppose that $E(u_i | X_{2i})$ is linear in $X_{2i}$ so that $E(u_i | X_{2i}) = \gamma_0 + \gamma_2 X_{2i}$, where $\gamma_0$ and $\gamma_1$ are constants. (This linearity assumption is discussed below.) Define $v_i$ to be the difference between $u_i$ and the conditional expectation of

$u_i$ given $X_{1i}$ and $X_{2i}$—that is, $v_i = u_i - E(u_i | X_{1i}, X_{2i})$—so that $v_i$ has conditional mean zero:
$E(v_i | X_{1i}, X_{2i}) = E[u_i - E(u_i | X_{1i}, X_{2i}) | X_{1i}, X_{2i}] = E(u_i | X_{1i}, X_{2i}) - E(u_i | X_{1i}, X_{2i}) = 0$.
Thus,

$$
\begin{aligned}
Y_i &= \beta_0 + \beta_1 X_{1i} + \beta_2 X_{2i} + u_i \\
&= \beta_0 + \beta_1 X_{1i} + \beta_2 X_{2i} + E(u_i | X_{1i}, X_{2i}) + v_i \quad \text{(using the definition of } v_i\text{)} \\
&= \beta_0 + \beta_1 X_{1i} + \beta_2 X_{2i} + E(u_i | X_{2i}) + v_i \quad \text{(using conditional mean independence)} \\
&= \beta_0 + \beta_1 X_{1i} + \beta_2 X_{2i} + (\gamma_0 + \gamma_2 X_{2i}) + v_i \quad [\text{using linearity of } E(u_i | X_{2i})] \\
&= (\beta_0 + \gamma_0) + \beta_1 X_{1i} + (\beta_2 + \gamma_2) X_{2i} + v_i \quad \text{(collecting terms)} \\
&= \delta_0 + \beta_1 X_{1i} + \delta_2 X_{2i} + v_i,
\end{aligned}
\tag{7.25}
$$

where $\delta_0 = \beta_0 + \gamma_0$ and $\delta_2 = \beta_2 + \gamma_2$.

The error $v_i$ in Equation (7.25) has conditional mean zero; that is, $E(v_i | X_{1i}, X_{2i}) = 0$. Therefore, the first least squares assumption for multiple regression applies to the final line of Equation (7.25), and if the other three least squares assumptions for multiple regression also hold, then the OLS regression of $Y_i$ on a constant, $X_{1i}$, and $X_{2i}$ will yield unbiased and consistent estimators of $\delta_0, \beta_1$, and $\delta_2$. Thus the OLS estimator of the coefficient on $X_{1i}$ is unbiased for the causal effect $\beta_1$. However, the OLS estimator of the coefficient on $X_{2i}$ is *not* unbiased for $\beta_2$ and instead estimates the sum of the causal effect $\beta_2$ and the coefficient $\gamma_2$ arising from the correlation of the control variable $X_{2i}$ with the original error term $u_i$.

The derivation in Equation (7.25) works for any value of $\beta_2$, including zero. A variable $X_{2i}$ is a useful control variable if conditional mean independence holds; it need not have a direct causal effect on $Y_i$.

The fourth line in Equation (7.25) uses the assumption that $E(u_i | X_{2i})$ is linear in $X_{2i}$. As discussed in Section 2.4, this will be true if $u_i$ and $X_{2i}$ are jointly normally distributed. The assumption of linearity can be relaxed using methods discussed in Chapter 8. Exercise 18.9 works through the steps in Equation (7.25) for multiple variables of interest and multiple control variables.

In terms of the example in Section 7.5 [the regression in Equation (7.19)], if $X_{2i}$ is *LchPct*, then $\beta_2$ is the causal effect of the subsidized lunch program ($\beta_2$ is positive if the program's nutritional benefits improve test scores), $\gamma_2$ is negative because *LchPct* is negatively correlated with (controls for) omitted learning advantages that improve test scores, and $\delta_2 = \beta_2 + \gamma_2$ would be negative if the omitted variable bias contribution through $\gamma_2$ outweighs the positive causal effect $\beta_2$.

To better understand the conditional mean independence assumption, return to the concept of an ideal randomized controlled experiment. As discussed in Section 4.4, if $X_{1i}$ is randomly assigned, then in a regression of $Y_i$ on $X_{1i}$, the conditional mean zero assumption holds. If, however, $X_{1i}$ is randomly assigned, conditional on another variable $X_{2i}$, then the conditional mean independence assumption holds, but if $X_{2i}$ is correlated with $u_i$, the conditional mean zero assumption does not. For example, consider an experiment to study the effect on grades in econometrics of mandatory versus optional homework. Among economics majors ($X_{2i} = 1$), 75% are assigned to the treatment group (mandatory homework: $X_{1i} = 1$), while among non-economics majors ($X_{2i} = 0$), only 25% are assigned to the treatment group. Because treatment is randomly assigned within majors and within nonmajors, $u_i$ is independent of $X_{1i}$, given $X_{2i}$, so in particular, $E(u_i | X_{1i}, X_{2i}) = E(u_i | X_{2i})$. If choice of major is correlated with other characteristics (like prior math) that determine performance in an econometrics course, then $E(u_i | X_{2i}) \neq 0$, and the regression of the final exam grade ($Y_i$) on $X_{1i}$ alone will be subject to omitted variable bias ($X_{1i}$ is correlated with major and thus with other omitted determinants of grade). Including major ($X_{2i}$) in the regression eliminates this omitted variable bias (treatment is randomly assigned, given major), making the OLS estimator of the coefficient on $X_{1i}$ an unbiased estimator of the causal effect on econometrics grades of requiring homework. However, the OLS estimator of the coefficient on major is not unbiased for the causal effect of switching into economics because major is not randomly assigned and is correlated with other omitted factors that would not change (like prior math) were a student to switch majors.

# 8  Nonlinear Regression Functions

In Chapters 4 through 7, the population regression function was assumed to be linear. In other words, the slope of the population regression function was constant, so the effect on $Y$ of a unit change in $X$ does not itself depend on the value of $X$. But what if the effect on $Y$ of a change in $X$ does depend on the value of one or more of the independent variables? If so, the population regression function is nonlinear.

This chapter develops two groups of methods for detecting and modeling nonlinear population regression functions. The methods in the first group are useful when the effect on $Y$ of a change in one independent variable, $X_1$, depends on the value of $X_1$ itself. For example, reducing class sizes by one student per teacher might have a greater effect if class sizes are already manageably small than if they are so large that the teacher can do little more than keep the class under control. If so, the test score ($Y$) is a nonlinear function of the student–teacher ratio ($X_1$), where this function is steeper when $X_1$ is small. An example of a nonlinear regression function with this feature is shown in Figure 8.1. Whereas the linear population regression function in Figure 8.1a has a constant slope, the nonlinear population regression function in Figure 8.1b has a steeper slope when $X_1$ is small than when it is large. This first group of methods is presented in Section 8.2.

The methods in the second group are useful when the effect on $Y$ of a change in $X_1$ depends on the value of another independent variable, say $X_2$. For example, students still learning English might especially benefit from having more one-on-one attention; if so, the effect on test scores of reducing the student–teacher ratio will be greater in districts with many students still learning English than in districts with few English learners. In this example, the effect on test scores ($Y$) of a reduction in the student–teacher ratio ($X_1$) depends on the percentage of English learners in the district ($X_2$). As shown in Figure 8.1c, the slope of this type of population regression function depends on the value of $X_2$. This second group of methods is presented in Section 8.3.

In the models of Sections 8.2 and 8.3, the population regression function is a nonlinear function of the independent variables; that is, the conditional expectation $E(Y_i | X_{1i}, \ldots, X_{ki})$ is a nonlinear function of one or more of the $X$'s. Although they are nonlinear in the $X$'s, these models are linear functions of the unknown coefficients

**FIGURE 8.1**    Population Regression Functions with Different Slopes

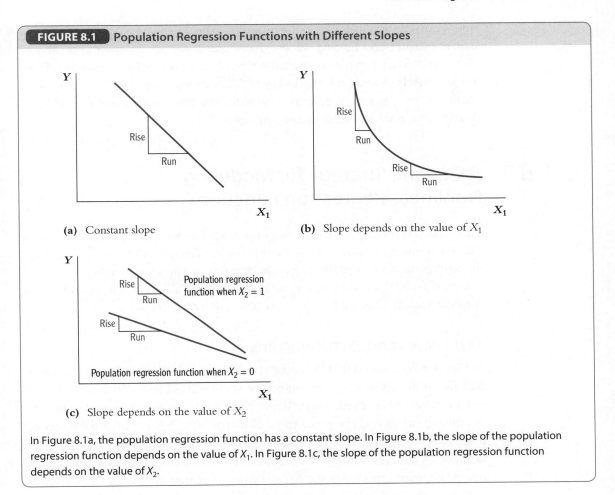

**(a)** Constant slope

**(b)** Slope depends on the value of $X_1$

**(c)** Slope depends on the value of $X_2$

In Figure 8.1a, the population regression function has a constant slope. In Figure 8.1b, the slope of the population regression function depends on the value of $X_1$. In Figure 8.1c, the slope of the population regression function depends on the value of $X_2$.

(or parameters) of the population regression model and thus are versions of the multiple regression model of Chapters 6 and 7. Therefore, the unknown parameters of these nonlinear regression functions can be estimated and tested using OLS and the methods of Chapters 6 and 7.

Sections 8.1 and 8.2 introduce nonlinear regression functions in the context of regression with a single independent variable, and Section 8.3 extends this to two independent variables. To keep things simple, additional control variables are omitted in the empirical examples of Sections 8.1 through 8.3. In practice, however, it is important to analyze nonlinear regression functions in models that control for omitted factors by including control variables as well. In Section 8.5, we combine nonlinear regression functions and additional control variables when we take a close look at possible nonlinearities in the relationship between test scores and the student–teacher ratio, holding student characteristics constant. In some applications, the regression function is a nonlinear function of the X's *and* of the parameters. If so, the parameters cannot be estimated by OLS, but they can be estimated using nonlinear least squares. Appendix 8.1 provides examples of such functions and describes the nonlinear least squares estimator.

## 8.1  A General Strategy for Modeling Nonlinear Regression Functions

This section lays out a general strategy for modeling nonlinear population regression functions. In this strategy, the nonlinear models are extensions of the multiple regression model and therefore can be estimated and tested using the tools of Chapters 6 and 7. First, however, we return to the California test score data and consider the relationship between test scores and district income.

### Test Scores and District Income

In Chapter 7, we found that the economic background of the students is an important factor in explaining performance on standardized tests. That analysis used two economic background variables (the percentage of students qualifying for a subsidized lunch and the percentage of district families qualifying for income assistance) to measure the fraction of students in the district coming from poor families. A different, broader measure of economic background is the average annual per capita income in the school district ("district income"). The California data set includes district income measured in thousands of 1998 dollars. The sample contains a wide range of income levels: For the 420 districts in our sample, the median district income is 13.7 (that is, $13,700 per person), and it ranges from 5.3 ($5300 per person) to 55.3 ($55,300 per person).

Figure 8.2 shows a scatterplot of fifth-grade test scores against district income for the California data set, along with the OLS regression line relating these two variables. Test scores and average income are strongly positively correlated, with a correlation coefficient of 0.71; students from affluent districts do better on the tests than students from poor districts. But this scatterplot has a peculiarity: Most of the points are below the OLS line when income is very low (under $10,000) or very high (over $40,000), but are above the line when income is between $15,000 and $30,000. There seems to be some curvature in the relationship between test scores and income that is not captured by the linear regression.

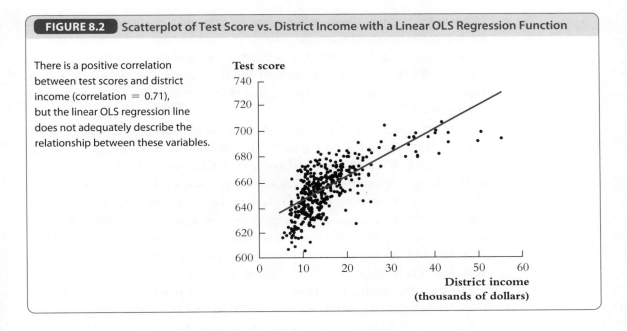

**FIGURE 8.2**    Scatterplot of Test Score vs. District Income with a Linear OLS Regression Function

There is a positive correlation between test scores and district income (correlation = 0.71), but the linear OLS regression line does not adequately describe the relationship between these variables.

In short, it seems that the relationship between district income and test scores is not a straight line. Rather, it is nonlinear. A nonlinear function is a function with a slope that is not constant: The function $f(X)$ is linear if the slope of $f(X)$ is the same for all values of $X$, but if the slope depends on the value of $X$, then $f(X)$ is nonlinear.

If a straight line is not an adequate description of the relationship between district income and test scores, what is? Imagine drawing a curve that fits the points in Figure 8.2. This curve would be steep for low values of district income and then would flatten out as district income gets higher. One way to approximate such a curve mathematically is to model the relationship as a quadratic function. That is, we could model test scores as a function of income *and* the square of income.

A quadratic population regression model relating test scores and income is written mathematically as

$$TestScore_i = \beta_0 + \beta_1 Income_i + \beta_2 Income_i^2 + u_i, \tag{8.1}$$

where $\beta_0, \beta_1$, and $\beta_2$ are coefficients, $Income_i$ is the income in the $i^{th}$ district, $Income_i^2$ is the square of income in the $i^{th}$ district, and $u_i$ is an error term that, as usual, represents all the other factors that determine test scores. Equation (8.1) is called the **quadratic regression model** because the population regression function,

$E(TestScore_i | Income_i) = \beta_0 + \beta_1 Income_i + \beta_2 Income_i^2$, is a quadratic function of the independent variable, *Income*.

If you knew the population coefficients $\beta_0, \beta_1$, and $\beta_2$ in Equation (8.1), you could predict the test score of a district based on its average income. But these population coefficients are unknown and therefore must be estimated using a sample of data.

At first, it might seem difficult to find the coefficients of the quadratic function that best fits the data in Figure 8.2. If you compare Equation (8.1) with the multiple regression model in Key Concept 6.2, however, you will see that Equation (8.1) is in fact a version of the multiple regression model with two regressors: The first regressor is *Income*, and the second regressor is *Income²*. Mechanically, you can create this second regressor by generating a new variable that equals the square of *Income*, for example as an additional column in a spreadsheet. Thus, after defining the regressors as *Income* and *Income²*, the nonlinear model in Equation (8.1) is simply a multiple regression model with two regressors!

Because the quadratic regression model is a variant of multiple regression, its unknown population coefficients can be estimated and tested using the OLS methods described in Chapters 6 and 7. Estimating the coefficients of Equation (8.1) using OLS for the 420 observations in Figure 8.2 yields

$$\widehat{TestScore} = 607.3 + 3.85\,Income - 0.0423\,Income^2, \overline{R}^2 = 0.554, \quad (8.2)$$
$$\phantom{\widehat{TestScore} = }(2.9) \quad (0.27) \qquad\quad (0.0048)$$

where (as usual) standard errors of the estimated coefficients are given in parentheses. The estimated regression function of Equation (8.2) is plotted in Figure 8.3, superimposed over the scatterplot of the data. The quadratic function captures the curvature in the scatterplot: It is steep for low values of district income but flattens out when district income is high. In short, the quadratic regression function seems to fit the data better than the linear one.

We can go one step beyond this visual comparison and formally test the hypothesis that the relationship between income and test scores is linear against the alternative that it is nonlinear. If the relationship is linear, then the regression function is correctly specified as Equation (8.1), except that the regressor *Income²* is absent; that is, if the relationship is linear, then Equation (8.1) holds with $\beta_2 = 0$. Thus we can test the null hypothesis that the population regression function is linear against the alternative that it is quadratic by testing the null hypothesis that $\beta_2 = 0$ against the alternative that $\beta_2 \neq 0$.

Because Equation (8.1) is just a variant of the multiple regression model, the null hypothesis that $\beta_2 = 0$ can be tested by constructing the *t*-statistic for this

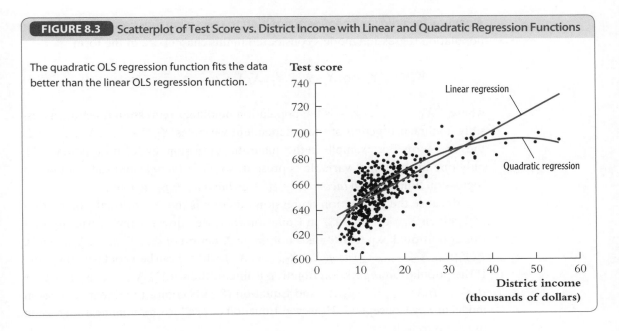

**FIGURE 8.3**   Scatterplot of Test Score vs. District Income with Linear and Quadratic Regression Functions

The quadratic OLS regression function fits the data better than the linear OLS regression function.

hypothesis. This $t$-statistic is $t = (\hat{\beta}_2 - 0)/SE(\hat{\beta}_2)$, which from Equation (8.2) is $t = -0.0423/0.0048 = -8.81$. In absolute value, this exceeds the 5% critical value of this test (which is 1.96). Indeed the $p$-value for the $t$-statistic is less than 0.01%, so we can reject the hypothesis that $\beta_2 = 0$ at all conventional significance levels. Thus this formal hypothesis test supports our informal inspection of Figures 8.2 and 8.3: The quadratic model fits the data better than the linear model.

## The Effect on $Y$ of a Change in $X$ in Nonlinear Specifications

Put aside the test score example for a moment and consider a general problem. You want to know how the dependent variable $Y$ is expected to change when the independent variable $X_1$ changes by the amount $\Delta X_1$, holding constant other independent variables $X_2, \ldots, X_k$. When the population regression function is linear, this effect is easy to calculate: As shown in Equation (6.4), the expected change in $Y$ is $\Delta Y = \beta_1 \Delta X_1$, where $\beta_1$ is the population regression coefficient multiplying $X_1$. When the regression function is nonlinear, however, the expected change in $Y$ is more complicated to calculate because it can depend on the values of the independent variables.

*A general formula for a nonlinear population regression function.*[1] The nonlinear population regression models considered in this chapter are of the form

$$Y_i = f(X_{1i}, X_{2i}, \ldots, X_{ki}) + u_i, i = 1, \ldots, n, \tag{8.3}$$

where $f(X_{1i}, X_{2i}, \ldots, X_{ki})$ is the population **nonlinear regression function**, a possibly nonlinear function of the independent variables $X_{1i}, X_{2i}, \ldots, X_{ki}$, and $u_i$ is the error term. For example, in the quadratic regression model in Equation (8.1), only one independent variable is present, so $X_1$ is *Income* and the population regression function is $f(Income_i) = \beta_0 + \beta_1 Income_i + \beta_2 Income_i^2$.

Because the population regression function is the conditional expectation of $Y_i$ given $X_{1i}, X_{2i}, \ldots, X_{ki}$, in Equation (8.3) we allow for the possibility that this conditional expectation is a nonlinear function of $X_{1i}, X_{2i}, \ldots, X_{ki}$; that is, $E(Y_i | X_{1i}, X_{2i}, \ldots, X_{ki}) = f(X_{1i}, X_{2i}, \ldots, X_{ki})$, where $f$ can be a nonlinear function. If the population regression function is linear, then $f(X_{1i}, X_{2i}, \ldots, X_{ki}) = \beta_0 + \beta_1 X_{1i} + \beta_2 X_{2i} + \cdots + \beta_k X_{ki}$, and Equation (8.3) becomes the linear regression model in Key Concept 6.2. However, Equation (8.3) allows for nonlinear regression functions as well.

*The effect on Y of a change in $X_1$.* As discussed in Section 6.2, the effect on $Y$ of a change in $X_1$, $\Delta X_1$, holding $X_2, \ldots, X_k$ constant, is the difference in the expected value of $Y$ when the independent variables take on the values $X_1 + \Delta X_1, X_2, \ldots, X_k$ and the expected value of $Y$ when the independent variables take on the values $X_1, X_2, \ldots, X_k$. The difference between these two expected values, say $\Delta Y$, is what happens to $Y$ on average in the population when $X_1$ changes by an amount $\Delta X_1$, holding constant the other variables $X_2, \ldots, X_k$. In the nonlinear regression model of Equation (8.3), this effect on $Y$ is $\Delta Y = f(X_1 + \Delta X_1, X_2, \ldots, X_k) - f(X_1, X_2, \ldots, X_k)$.

Because the regression function $f$ is unknown, the population effect on $Y$ of a change in $X_1$ is also unknown. To estimate the population effect, first estimate the population regression function. At a general level, denote this estimated function

---

[1] The term *nonlinear regression* applies to two conceptually different families of models. In the first family, the population regression function is a nonlinear function of the $X$'s but is a linear function of the unknown parameters (the $\beta$'s). In the second family, the population regression function is a nonlinear function of the unknown parameters and may or may not be a nonlinear function of the $X$'s. The models in the body of this chapter are all in the first family. Appendix 8.1 takes up models from the second family.

## The Expected Change on $Y$ of a Change in $X_1$ in the Nonlinear Regression Model (8.3)

The expected change in $Y$, $\Delta Y$, associated with the change in $X_1$, $\Delta X_1$, holding $X_2, \ldots, X_k$ constant, is the difference between the value of the population regression function before and after changing $X_1$, holding $X_2, \ldots, X_k$ constant. That is, the expected change in $Y$ is the difference:

$$\Delta Y = f(X_1 + \Delta X_1, X_2, \ldots, X_k) - f(X_1, X_2, \ldots, X_k). \tag{8.4}$$

The estimator of this unknown population difference is the difference between the predicted values for these two cases. Let $\hat{f}(X_1, X_2, \ldots, X_k)$ be the predicted value of $Y$ based on the estimator $\hat{f}$ of the population regression function. Then the predicted change in $Y$ is

$$\Delta \hat{Y} = \hat{f}(X_1 + \Delta X_1, X_2, \ldots, X_k) - \hat{f}(X_1, X_2, \ldots, X_k). \tag{8.5}$$

by $\hat{f}$; an example of such an estimated function is the estimated quadratic regression function in Equation (8.2). The estimated effect on $Y$ (denoted $\Delta \hat{Y}$) of the change in $X_1$ is the difference between the predicted value of $Y$ when the independent variables take on the values $X_1 + \Delta X_1, X_2, \ldots, X_k$ and the predicted value of $Y$ when they take on the values $X_1, X_2, \ldots, X_k$.

The method for calculating the expected effect on $Y$ of a change in $X_1$ is summarized in Key Concept 8.1. The method in Key Concept 8.1 always works, whether $\Delta X_1$ is large or small and whether the regressors are continuous or discrete. Appendix 8.2 shows how to evaluate the slope using calculus for the special case of a single continuous regressor when $\Delta X_1$ small.

*Application to test scores and income.* What is the predicted change in test scores associated with a change in district income of $1000, based on the estimated quadratic regression function in Equation (8.2)? Because that regression function is quadratic, this effect depends on the initial district income. We therefore consider two cases: an increase in district income from 10 to 11 (i.e., from $10,000 per capita to $11,000) and an increase in district income from 40 to 41.

To compute $\Delta \hat{Y}$ associated with the change in income from 10 to 11, we can apply the general formula in Equation (8.5) to the quadratic regression model. Doing so yields

$$\Delta \hat{Y} = (\hat{\beta}_0 + \hat{\beta}_1 \times 11 + \hat{\beta}_2 \times 11^2) - (\hat{\beta}_0 + \hat{\beta}_1 \times 10 + \hat{\beta}_2 \times 10^2), \quad (8.6)$$

where $\hat{\beta}_0$, $\hat{\beta}_1$, and $\hat{\beta}_2$ are the OLS estimators.

The term in the first set of parentheses in Equation (8.6) is the predicted value of $Y$ when $Income = 11$, and the term in the second set of parentheses is the predicted value of $Y$ when $Income = 10$. These predicted values are calculated using the OLS estimates of the coefficients in Equation (8.2). Accordingly, when $Income = 10$, the predicted value of test scores is $607.3 + 3.85 \times 10 - 0.0423 \times 10^2 = 641.57$. When $Income = 11$, the predicted value is $607.3 + 3.85 \times 11 - 0.0423 \times 11^2 = 644.53$. The difference in these two predicted values is $\Delta \hat{Y} = 644.53 - 641.57 = 2.96$ points; that is, the predicted difference in test scores between a district with average income of \$11,000 and one with average income of \$10,000 is 2.96 points.

In the second case, when income changes from \$40,000 to \$41,000, the difference in the predicted values in Equation (8.6) is $\Delta \hat{Y} = (607.3 + 3.85 \times 41 - 0.0423 \times 41^2) - (607.3 + 3.85 \times 40 - 0.0423 \times 40^2) = 694.04 - 693.62 = 0.42$ points. Thus a change of income of \$1000 is associated with a larger change in predicted test scores if the initial income is \$10,000 than if it is \$40,000 (the predicted changes are 2.96 points versus 0.42 point). Said differently, the slope of the estimated quadratic regression function in Figure 8.3 is steeper at low values of income (like \$10,000) than at the higher values of income (like \$40,000).

*Standard errors of estimated effects.* The estimator of the effect on $Y$ of changing $X_1$ depends on the estimator of the population regression function, $\hat{f}$, which varies from one sample to the next. Therefore, the estimated effect contains a sampling error. One way to quantify the sampling uncertainty associated with the estimated effect is to compute a confidence interval for the true population effect. To do so, we need to compute the standard error of $\Delta \hat{Y}$ in Equation (8.5).

It is easy to compute a standard error for $\Delta \hat{Y}$ when the regression function is linear. The estimated effect of a change in $X_1$ is $\hat{\beta}_1 \Delta X_1$, so the standard error of $\Delta \hat{Y}$ is $SE(\Delta \hat{Y}) = SE(\hat{\beta}_1) \Delta X_1$ and a 95% confidence interval for the estimated change is $\hat{\beta}_1 \Delta X_1 \pm 1.96 \, SE(\hat{\beta}_1) \Delta X_1$.

In the nonlinear regression models of this chapter, the standard error of $\Delta \hat{Y}$ can be computed using the tools introduced in Section 7.3 for testing a single restriction involving multiple coefficients. To illustrate this method, consider the estimated change in test scores associated with a change in income from 10 to 11 in

Equation (8.6), which is $\Delta \hat{Y} = \hat{\beta}_1 \times (11 - 10) + \hat{\beta}_2 \times (11^2 - 10^2) = \hat{\beta}_1 + 21\hat{\beta}_2$. The standard error of the predicted change therefore is

$$SE(\Delta \hat{Y}) = SE(\hat{\beta}_1 + 21\hat{\beta}_2). \tag{8.7}$$

Thus, if we can compute the standard error of $\hat{\beta}_1 + 21\hat{\beta}_2$, then we have computed the standard error of $\Delta \hat{Y}$. There are two methods for doing this using standard regression software, which correspond to the two approaches in Section 7.3 for testing a single restriction on multiple coefficients.

The first method is to use Approach #1 of Section 7.3, which is to compute the $F$-statistic testing the hypothesis that $\beta_1 + 21\beta_2 = 0$. The standard error of $\Delta \hat{Y}$ is then given by[2]

$$SE(\Delta \hat{Y}) = \frac{|\Delta \hat{Y}|}{\sqrt{F}}. \tag{8.8}$$

When applied to the quadratic regression in Equation (8.2), the $F$-statistic testing the hypothesis that $\beta_1 + 21\beta_2 = 0$ is $F = 299.94$. Because $\Delta \hat{Y} = 2.96$, applying Equation (8.8) gives $SE(\Delta \hat{Y}) = 2.96 / \sqrt{299.94} = 0.17$. Thus a 95% confidence interval for the change in the expected value of $Y$ is $2.96 \pm 1.96 \times 0.17$ or (2.63, 3.29).

The second method is to use Approach #2 of Section 7.3, which entails transforming the regressors so that, in the transformed regression, one of the coefficients is $\beta_1 + 21\beta_2$. Doing this transformation is left as an exercise (Exercise 8.9).

*A comment on interpreting coefficients in nonlinear specifications.* In the multiple regression model of Chapters 6 and 7, the regression coefficients had a natural interpretation. For example, $\beta_1$ is the expected change in $Y$ associated with a change in $X_1$, holding the other regressors constant. But, as we have seen, this is not generally the case in a nonlinear model. That is, it is not very helpful to think of $\beta_1$ in Equation (8.1) as being the effect of changing the district's income, holding the square of the district's income constant. In nonlinear models the regression function is best interpreted by graphing it and by calculating the predicted effect on $Y$ of changing one or more of the independent variables.

---

[2]Equation (8.8) is derived by noting that the $F$-statistic is the square of the $t$-statistic testing this hypothesis—that is, $F = t^2 = [(\hat{\beta}_1 + 21\hat{\beta}_2)/SE(\hat{\beta}_1 + 21\hat{\beta}_1)]^2 = [\Delta \hat{Y}/SE(\Delta \hat{Y})]^2$—and solving for $SE(\Delta \hat{Y})$.

## A General Approach to Modeling Nonlinearities Using Multiple Regression

The general approach to modeling nonlinear regression functions taken in this chapter has five elements:

1. ***Identify a possible nonlinear relationship.*** The best thing to do is to use economic theory and what you know about the application to suggest a possible nonlinear relationship. Before you even look at the data, ask yourself whether the slope of the regression function relating $Y$ and $X$ might reasonably depend on the value of $X$ or on another independent variable. Why might such nonlinear dependence exist? What nonlinear shapes does this suggest? For example, thinking about classroom dynamics with 11-year-olds suggests that cutting class size from 18 students to 17 could have a greater effect than cutting it from 30 to 29.

2. ***Specify a nonlinear function and estimate its parameters by OLS.*** Sections 8.2 and 8.3 contain various nonlinear regression functions that can be estimated by OLS. After working through these sections you will understand the characteristics of each of these functions.

3. ***Determine whether the nonlinear model improves upon a linear model.*** Just because you think a regression function is nonlinear does not mean it really is! You must determine empirically whether your nonlinear model is appropriate. Most of the time you can use $t$-statistics and $F$-statistics to test the null hypothesis that the population regression function is linear against the alternative that it is nonlinear.

4. ***Plot the estimated nonlinear regression function.*** Does the estimated regression function describe the data well? Looking at Figures 8.2 and 8.3 suggested that the quadratic model fit the data better than the linear model.

5. ***Estimate the effect on Y of a change in X.*** The final step is to use the estimated regression to calculate the effect on $Y$ of a change in one or more regressors $X$ using the method in Key Concept 8.1.

# 8.2 Nonlinear Functions of a Single Independent Variable

This section provides two methods for modeling a nonlinear regression function. To keep things simple, we develop these methods for a nonlinear regression function that involves only one independent variable, $X$. As we see in Section 8.5, however, these models can be modified to include multiple independent variables.

The first method discussed in this section is polynomial regression, an extension of the quadratic regression used in the last section to model the relationship between test scores and income. The second method uses logarithms of $X$, of $Y$, or of both $X$ and $Y$. Although these methods are presented separately, they can be used in combination.

Appendix 8.2 provides a calculus-based treatment of the models in this section.

## Polynomials

One way to specify a nonlinear regression function is to use a polynomial in $X$. In general, let $r$ denote the highest power of $X$ that is included in the regression. The **polynomial regression model** of degree $r$ is

$$Y_i = \beta_0 + \beta_1 X_i + \beta_2 X_i^2 + \cdots + \beta_r X_i^r + u_i. \tag{8.9}$$

When $r = 2$, Equation (8.9) is the quadratic regression model discussed in Section 8.1. When $r = 3$ so that the highest power of $X$ included is $X^3$, Equation (8.9) is called the **cubic regression model**.

The polynomial regression model is similar to the multiple regression model of Chapter 6 except that in Chapter 6 the regressors were distinct independent variables whereas here the regressors are powers of the same dependent variable, $X$; that is, the regressors are $X, X^2, X^3$, and so on. Thus the techniques for estimation and inference developed for multiple regression can be applied here. In particular, the unknown coefficients $\beta_0, \beta_1, \ldots, \beta_r$ in Equation (8.9) can be estimated by OLS regression of $Y_i$ against $X_i, X_i^2, \ldots, X_i^r$.

*Testing the null hypothesis that the population regression function is linear.* If the population regression function is linear, then the quadratic and higher-degree terms do not enter the population regression function. Accordingly, the null hypothesis $(H_0)$ that the regression is linear and the alternative $(H_1)$ that it is a polynomial of degree $r$ correspond to

$$H_0: \beta_2 = 0, \beta_3 = 0, \ldots, \beta_r = 0 \text{ vs. } H_1: \text{at least one } \beta_j \neq 0, j = 2, \ldots, r. \tag{8.10}$$

The null hypothesis that the population regression function is linear can be tested against the alternative that it is a polynomial of degree $r$ by testing $H_0$ against $H_1$ in Equation (8.10). Because $H_0$ is a joint null hypothesis with $q = r - 1$ restrictions on the coefficients of the population polynomial regression model, it can be tested using the $F$-statistic as described in Section 7.2.

*Which degree polynomial should I use?* That is, how many powers of $X$ should be included in a polynomial regression? The answer balances a trade-off between flexibility and statistical precision. Increasing the degree $r$ introduces more flexibility into the regression function and allows it to match more shapes; a polynomial of degree $r$ can have up to $r - 1$ bends (that is, inflection points) in its graph. But increasing $r$ means adding more regressors, which can reduce the precision of the estimated coefficients.

Thus the answer to the question of how many terms to include is that you should include enough to model the nonlinear regression function adequately, but no more. Unfortunately, this answer is not very useful in practice!

A practical way to determine the degree of the polynomial is to ask whether the coefficients in Equation (8.9) associated with largest values of $r$ are zero. If so, then these terms can be dropped from the regression. This procedure, which is called sequential hypothesis testing because individual hypotheses are tested sequentially, is summarized in the following steps:

1. Pick a maximum value of $r$ and estimate the polynomial regression for that $r$.

2. Use the $t$-statistic to test the hypothesis that the coefficient on $X^r$ [$\beta_r$ in Equation (8.9)] is zero. If you reject this hypothesis, then $X^r$ belongs in the regression, so use the polynomial of degree $r$.

3. If you do not reject $\beta_r = 0$ in step 2, eliminate $X^r$ from the regression and estimate a polynomial regression of degree $r - 1$. Test whether the coefficient on $X^{r-1}$ is zero. If you reject, use the polynomial of degree $r - 1$.

4. If you do not reject $\beta_{r-1} = 0$ in step 3, continue this procedure until the coefficient on the highest power in your polynomial is statistically significant.

This recipe has one missing ingredient: the initial degree $r$ of the polynomial. In many applications involving economic data, the nonlinear functions are smooth, that is, they do not have sharp jumps, or "spikes." If so, then it is appropriate to choose a small maximum degree for the polynomial, such as 2, 3, or 4—that is, begin with $r = 2$ or 3 or 4 in step 1.

*Application to district income and test scores.* The estimated cubic regression function relating district income to test scores is

$$\widehat{TestScore} = 600.1 + 5.02\,Income - 0.096\,Income^2 + 0.00069\,Income^3,$$
$$\phantom{\widehat{TestScore} = }(5.1) \quad (0.71) \qquad\quad (0.029) \qquad\qquad (0.00035)$$
$$\overline{R}^2 = 0.555. \tag{8.11}$$

The $t$-statistic on $Income^3$ is 1.97, so the null hypothesis that the regression function is a quadratic is rejected against the alternative that it is a cubic at the 5%

level. Moreover, the *F*-statistic testing the joint null hypothesis that the coefficients on *Income*$^2$ and *Income*$^3$ are both zero is 37.7, with a *p*-value less than 0.01%, so the null hypothesis that the regression function is linear is rejected against the alternative that it is either a quadratic or a cubic.

***Interpretation of coefficients in polynomial regression models.*** The coefficients in polynomial regressions do not have a simple interpretation. The best way to interpret polynomial regressions is to plot the estimated regression function and calculate the estimated effect on *Y* associated with a change in *X* for one or more values of *X*.

## Logarithms

Another way to specify a nonlinear regression function is to use the natural logarithm of *Y* and/or *X*. Logarithms convert changes in variables into percentage changes, and many relationships are naturally expressed in terms of percentages. Here are some examples:

- A box in Chapter 3, "The Gender Gap of Earnings of College Graduates in the United States," examined the wage gap between male and female college graduates. In that discussion, the wage gap was measured in terms of dollars. However, it is easier to compare wage gaps across professions and over time when they are expressed in percentage terms.

- In Section 8.1, we found that district income and test scores were nonlinearly related. Would this relationship be linear using percentage changes? That is, might it be that a change in district income of 1%—rather than $1000—is associated with a change in test scores that is approximately constant for different values of income?

- In the economic analysis of consumer demand, it is often assumed that a 1% increase in price leads to a certain *percentage* decrease in the quantity demanded. The percentage decrease in demand resulting from a 1% increase in price is called the price **elasticity**.

Regression specifications that use natural logarithms allow regression models to estimate percentage relationships such as these. Before introducing those specifications, we review the exponential and natural logarithm functions.

***The exponential function and the natural logarithm.*** The exponential function and its inverse, the natural logarithm, play an important role in modeling nonlinear regression functions. The **exponential function** of *x* is $e^x$ (that is, *e* raised

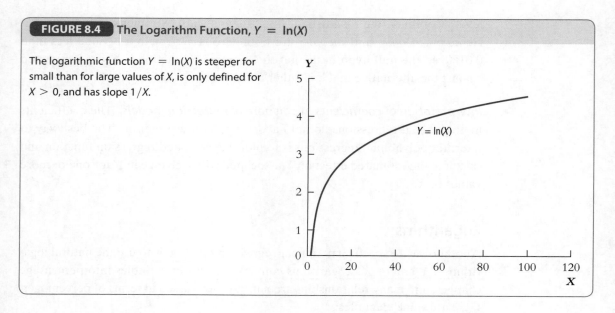

**FIGURE 8.4**    The Logarithm Function, $Y = \ln(X)$

The logarithmic function $Y = \ln(X)$ is steeper for small than for large values of $X$, is only defined for $X > 0$, and has slope $1/X$.

to the power $x$), where $e$ is the constant 2.71828 . . . ; the exponential function is also written as $\exp(x)$. The **natural logarithm** is the inverse of the exponential function; that is, the natural logarithm is the function for which $x = \ln(e^x)$ or, equivalently, $x = \ln[\exp(x)]$. The base of the natural logarithm is $e$. Although there are logarithms in other bases, such as base 10, in this book we consider only logarithms in base $e$—that is, the natural logarithm—so when we use the term *logarithm* we always mean "natural logarithm."

The logarithm function, $y = \ln(x)$, is graphed in Figure 8.4. Note that the logarithm function is defined only for positive values of $x$. The logarithm function has a slope that is steep at first and then flattens out (although the function continues to increase). The slope of the logarithm function $\ln(x)$ is $1/x$.

The logarithm function has the following useful properties:

$$\ln(1/x) = -\ln(x); \tag{8.12}$$

$$\ln(ax) = \ln(a) + \ln(x); \tag{8.13}$$

$$\ln(x/a) = \ln(x) - \ln(a); \text{ and} \tag{8.14}$$

$$\ln(x^a) = a \ln(x). \tag{8.15}$$

*Logarithms and percentages.* The link between the logarithm and percentages relies on a key fact: When $\Delta x$ is small, the difference between the logarithm of

$x + \Delta x$ and the logarithm of $x$ is approximately $\Delta x / x$, the percentage change in $x$ divided by 100. That is,

$$\ln(x + \Delta x) - \ln(x) \cong \frac{\Delta x}{x} \quad \left( \text{when } \frac{\Delta x}{x} \text{ is small} \right), \tag{8.16}$$

where "$\cong$" means "approximately equal to." The derivation of this approximation relies on calculus, but it is readily demonstrated by trying out some values of $x$ and $\Delta x$. For example, when $x = 100$ and $\Delta x = 1$, then $\Delta x / x = 1/100 = 0.01$ (or 1%), while $\ln(x + \Delta x) - \ln(x) = \ln(101) - \ln(100) = 0.00995$ (or 0.995%). Thus $\Delta x / x$ (which is 0.01) is very close to $\ln(x + \Delta x) - \ln(x)$ (which is 0.00995). When $\Delta x = 5$, $\Delta x / x = 5/100 = 0.05$, while $\ln(x + \Delta x) - \ln(x) = \ln(105) - \ln(100) = 0.04879$.

*The three logarithmic regression models.* There are three different cases in which logarithms might be used: when $X$ is transformed by taking its logarithm but $Y$ is not; when $Y$ is transformed to its logarithm but $X$ is not; and when both $Y$ and $X$ are transformed to their logarithms. The interpretation of the regression coefficients is different in each case. We discuss these three cases in turn.

*Case I: X is in logarithms, Y is not.* In this case, the regression model is

$$Y_i = \beta_0 + \beta_1 \ln(X_i) + u_i, i = 1, \dots, n. \tag{8.17}$$

Because $Y$ is not in logarithms but $X$ is, this is sometimes referred to as a **linear-log model**.

In the linear-log model, a 1% change in $X$ is associated with a change in $Y$ of $0.01\beta_1$. To see this, consider the difference between the population regression function at values of $X$ that differ by $\Delta X$: This is $[\beta_0 + \beta_1 \ln(X + \Delta X)] - [\beta_0 + \beta_1 \ln(X)] = \beta_1[\ln(X + \Delta X) - \ln(X)] \cong \beta_1(\Delta X / X)$, where the final step uses the approximation in Equation (8.16). If $X$ changes by 1%, then $\Delta X / X = 0.01$; thus in this model a 1% change in $X$ is associated with a change of $Y$ of $0.01\beta_1$.

The only difference between the regression model in Equation (8.17) and the regression model of Chapter 4 with a single regressor is that the right-hand variable is now the logarithm of $X$ rather than $X$ itself. To estimate the coefficients $\beta_0$ and $\beta_1$ in Equation (8.17), first compute a new variable, $\ln(X)$, which is readily done using a spreadsheet or statistical software. Then $\beta_0$ and $\beta_1$ can be estimated by the OLS regression of $Y_i$ on $\ln(X_i)$, hypotheses about $\beta_1$ can be tested using the $t$-statistic, and a 95% confidence interval for $\beta_1$ can be constructed as $\hat{\beta}_1 \pm 1.96\, SE(\hat{\beta}_1)$.

As an example, return to the relationship between district income and test scores. Instead of the quadratic specification, we could use the linear-log specification in Equation (8.17). Estimating this regression by OLS yields

$$\widehat{TestScore} = 557.8 + 36.42\ln(Income), \overline{R}^2 = 0.561.$$
$$\quad\quad\quad\quad (3.8) \quad\quad (1.40)$$
(8.18)

According to Equation (8.18), a 1% increase in income is associated with an increase in test scores of $0.01 \times 36.42 = 0.36$ point.

To estimate the effect on $Y$ of a change in $X$ in its original units of thousands of dollars (not in logarithms), we can use the method in Key Concept 8.1. For example, what is the predicted difference in test scores for districts with average incomes of $10,000 versus $11,000? The estimated value of $\Delta Y$ is the difference between the predicted values: $\Delta\hat{Y} = [557.8 + 36.42\ln(11)] - [557.8 + 36.42\ln(10)] = 36.42 \times [\ln(11) - \ln(10)] = 3.47$. Similarly, the predicted difference between a district with average income of $40,000 and a district with average income of $41,000 is $36.42 \times [\ln(41) - \ln(40)] = 0.90$. Thus, like the quadratic specification, this regression predicts that a $1000 increase in income has a larger effect on test scores in poor districts than it does in affluent districts.

The estimated linear-log regression function in Equation (8.18) is plotted in Figure 8.5. Because the regressor in Equation (8.18) is the natural logarithm of income rather than income, the estimated regression function is not a straight line. Like the quadratic regression function in Figure 8.3, it is initially steep but then flattens out for higher levels of income.

*Case II: Y is in logarithms, X is not.* In this case, the regression model is

$$\ln(Y_i) = \beta_0 + \beta_1 X_i + u_i.$$
(8.19)

Because $Y$ is in logarithms but $X$ is not, this is referred to as a **log-linear model**.

In the log-linear model, a one-unit change in $X$ ($\Delta X = 1$) is associated with a $(100 \times \beta_1)\%$ change in $Y$. To see this, compare the expected values of $\ln(Y)$ for values of $X$ that differ by $\Delta X$. The expected value of $\ln(Y)$ given $X$ is $\ln(Y) = \beta_0 + \beta_1 X$. When $X$ is $X + \Delta X$, the expected value is given by $\ln(Y + \Delta Y) = \beta_0 + \beta_1(X + \Delta X)$. Thus the difference between these expected values is $\ln(Y + \Delta Y) - \ln(Y) = [\beta_0 + \beta_1(X + \Delta X)] - [\beta_0 + \beta_1 X] = \beta_1\Delta X$. From the approximation in Equation (8.16), however, if $\beta_1\Delta X$ is small, then $\ln(Y + \Delta Y) - \ln(Y) \cong \Delta Y/Y$. Thus $\Delta Y/Y \cong \beta_1\Delta X$. If $\Delta X = 1$ so that $X$ changes by one unit, then $\Delta Y/Y$ changes

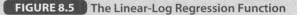

**FIGURE 8.5**   The Linear-Log Regression Function

The estimated linear-log regression function $\hat{Y} = \hat{\beta}_0 + \hat{\beta}_1 \ln(X)$ captures much of the nonlinear relation between test scores and district income.

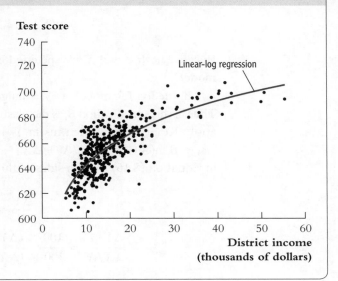

by $\beta_1$. Translated into percentages, a one-unit change in $X$ is associated with a $(100 \times \beta_1)\%$ change in $Y$.

As an illustration, we return to the empirical example of Section 3.7, the relationship between age and earnings of college graduates. Many employment contracts specify that, for each additional year of service, a worker gets a certain percentage increase in his or her wage. This percentage relationship suggests estimating the log-linear specification in Equation (8.19) so that each additional year of age ($X$) is, on average in the population, associated with some constant percentage increase in earnings ($Y$). By first computing the new dependent variable, $\ln(Earnings_i)$, the unknown coefficients $\beta_0$ and $\beta_1$ can be estimated by the OLS regression of $\ln(Earnings_i)$ against $Age_i$. When estimated using the 14,752 observations on college graduates in the March 2013 Current Population Survey (the data are described in Appendix 3.1), this relationship is

$$\widehat{\ln(Earnings)} = 2.811 + 0.0096\,Age, \overline{R}^2 = 0.034. \qquad (8.20)$$
$$\qquad\qquad (0.018) \quad (0.0004)$$

According to this regression, earnings are predicted to increase by 0.96% $[(100 \times 0.0096)\%]$ for each additional year of age.

*Case III: Both X and Y are in logarithms.* In this case, the regression model is

$$\ln(Y_i) = \beta_0 + \beta_1 \ln(X_i) + u_i. \tag{8.21}$$

Because both $Y$ and $X$ are specified in logarithms, this is referred to as a **log-log model**.

In the log-log model, a 1% change in $X$ is associated with a $\beta_1$% change in $Y$. Thus in this specification $\beta_1$ is the elasticity of $Y$ with respect to $X$. To see this, again apply Key Concept 8.1; thus $\ln(Y + \Delta Y) - \ln(Y) = [\beta_0 + \beta_1 \ln(X + \Delta X)] - [\beta_0 + \beta_1 \ln(X)] = \beta_1 [\ln(X + \Delta X) - \ln(X)]$. Application of the approximation in Equation (8.16) to both sides of this equation yields

$$\frac{\Delta Y}{Y} \cong \beta_1 \frac{\Delta X}{X} \text{ or}$$

$$\beta_1 = \frac{\Delta Y/Y}{\Delta X/X} = \frac{100 \times (\Delta Y/Y)}{100 \times (\Delta X/X)} = \frac{\text{percentage change in } Y}{\text{percentage change in } X}. \tag{8.22}$$

Thus in the log-log specification $\beta_1$ is the ratio of the percentage change in $Y$ associated with the percentage change in $X$. If the percentage change in $X$ is 1% (that is, if $\Delta X = 0.01X$), then $\beta_1$ is the percentage change in $Y$ associated with a 1% change in $X$. That is, $\beta_1$ is the elasticity of $Y$ with respect to $X$.

As an illustration, return to the relationship between income and test scores. When this relationship is specified in this form, the unknown coefficients are estimated by a regression of the logarithm of test scores against the logarithm of income. The resulting estimated equation is

$$\widehat{\ln(TestScore)} = 6.336 + 0.0554 \ln(Income), \overline{R}^2 = 0.557. \tag{8.23}$$
$$(0.006) \quad (0.0021)$$

According to this estimated regression function, a 1% increase in income is estimated to correspond to a 0.0554% increase in test scores.

The estimated log-log regression function in Equation (8.23) is plotted in Figure 8.6. Because $Y$ is in logarithms, the vertical axis in Figure 8.6 is the logarithm of the test score and the scatterplot is the logarithm of test scores versus district income. For comparison purposes, Figure 8.6 also shows the estimated regression function for a log-linear specification, which is

$$\widehat{\ln(TestScore)} = 6.439 + 0.00284 \, Income, \overline{R}^2 = 0.497. \tag{8.24}$$
$$(0.003) \quad (0.00018)$$

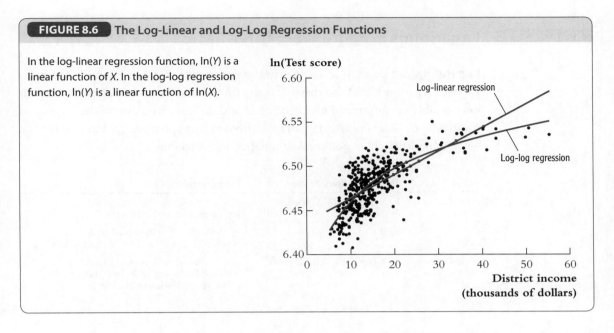

**FIGURE 8.6**    The Log-Linear and Log-Log Regression Functions

In the log-linear regression function, $\ln(Y)$ is a linear function of $X$. In the log-log regression function, $\ln(Y)$ is a linear function of $\ln(X)$.

Because the vertical axis is in logarithms, the regression function in Equation (8.24) is the straight line in Figure 8.6.

As you can see in Figure 8.6, the log-log specification fits better than the log-linear specification. This is consistent with the higher $\overline{R}^2$ for the log-log regression (0.557) than for the log-linear regression (0.497). Even so, the log-log specification does not fit the data especially well: At the lower values of income most of the observations fall below the log-log curve, while in the middle income range most of the observations fall above the estimated regression function.

The three logarithmic regression models are summarized in Key Concept 8.2.

*A difficulty with comparing logarithmic specifications.* Which of the log regression models best fits the data? As we saw in the discussion of Equations (8.23) and (8.24), the $\overline{R}^2$ can be used to compare the log-linear and log-log models; as it happened, the log-log model had the higher $\overline{R}^2$. Similarly, the $\overline{R}^2$ can be used to compare the linear-log regression in Equation (8.18) and the linear regression of $Y$ against $X$. In the test score and income regression, the linear-log regression has an $\overline{R}^2$ of 0.561 while the linear regression has an $\overline{R}^2$ of 0.508, so the linear-log model fits the data better.

How can we compare the linear-log model and the log-log model? Unfortunately, the $\overline{R}^2$ *cannot* be used to compare these two regressions because their dependent variables are different [one is $Y$, the other is $\ln(Y)$]. Recall that the $\overline{R}^2$

| KEY CONCEPT | **Logarithms in Regression: Three Cases** |

**8.2**

Logarithms can be used to transform the dependent variable $Y$, an independent variable $X$, or both (but the variable being transformed must be positive). The following table summarizes these three cases and the interpretation of the regression coefficient $\beta_1$. In each case, $\beta_1$ can be estimated by applying OLS after taking the logarithm of the dependent and/or independent variable.

| Case | Regression Specification | Interpretation of $\beta_1$ |
|------|--------------------------|------------------------------|
| I | $Y_i = \beta_0 + \beta_1 \ln(X_i) + u_i$ | A 1% change in $X$ is associated with a change in $Y$ of $0.01\beta_1$. |
| II | $\ln(Y_i) = \beta_0 + \beta_1 X_i + u_i$ | A change in $X$ by one unit ($\Delta X = 1$) is associated with a $100\beta_1\%$ change in $Y$. |
| III | $\ln(Y_i) = \beta_0 + \beta_1 \ln(X_i) + u_i$ | A 1% change in $X$ is associated with a $\beta_1\%$ change in $Y$, so $\beta_1$ is the elasticity of $Y$ with respect to $X$. |

measures the fraction of the variance of the dependent variable explained by the regressors. Because the dependent variables in the log-log and linear-log models are different, it does not make sense to compare their $\overline{R}^2$'s.

Because of this problem, the best thing to do in a particular application is to decide, using economic theory and either your or other experts' knowledge of the problem, whether it makes sense to specify $Y$ in logarithms. For example, labor economists typically model earnings using logarithms because wage comparisons, contract wage increases, and so forth are often most naturally discussed in percentage terms. In modeling test scores, it seems (to us, anyway) natural to discuss test results in terms of points on the test rather than percentage increases in the test scores, so we focus on models in which the dependent variable is the test score rather than its logarithm.

*Computing predicted values of Y when Y is in logarithms.*[3] If the dependent variable $Y$ has been transformed by taking logarithms, the estimated regression can be used to compute directly the predicted value of $\ln(Y)$. However, it is a bit trickier to compute the predicted value of $Y$ itself.

---

[3] This material is more advanced and can be skipped without loss of continuity.

To see this, consider the log-linear regression model in Equation (8.19) and rewrite it so that it is specified in terms of $Y$ rather than $\ln(Y)$. To do so, take the exponential function of both sides of the Equation (8.19); the result is

$$Y_i = \exp(\beta_0 + \beta_1 X_i + u_i) = e^{\beta_0 + \beta_1 X_i} e^{u_i}. \tag{8.25}$$

The expected value of $Y_i$ given $X_i$ is $E(Y_i | X_i) = E(e^{\beta_0 + \beta_1 X_i} e^{u_i} | X_i) = e^{\beta_0 + \beta_1 X_i}$ $E(e^{u_i} | X_i)$. The problem is that even if $E(u_i | X_i) = 0$, $E(e^{u_i} | X_i) \neq 1$. Thus the appropriate predicted value of $Y_i$ is not simply obtained by taking the exponential function of $\hat{\beta}_0 + \hat{\beta}_1 X_i$, that is, by setting $\hat{Y}_i = e^{\hat{\beta}_0 + \hat{\beta}_1 X_i}$: This predicted value is biased because of the missing factor $E(e^{u_i} | X_i)$.

One solution to this problem is to estimate the factor $E(e^{u_i} | X_i)$ and use this estimate when computing the predicted value of $Y$. Exercise 17.12 works through several ways to estimate $E(e^{u_i} | X_i)$, but this gets complicated, particularly if $u_i$ is heteroskedastic, and we do not pursue it further.

Another solution, which is the approach used in this book, is to compute predicted values of the logarithm of $Y$ but not transform them to their original units. In practice, this is often acceptable because when the dependent variable is specified as a logarithm, it is often most natural just to use the logarithmic specification (and the associated percentage interpretations) throughout the analysis.

## Polynomial and Logarithmic Models of Test Scores and District Income

In practice, economic theory or expert judgment might suggest a functional form to use, but in the end the true form of the population regression function is unknown. In practice, fitting a nonlinear function therefore entails deciding which method or combination of methods works best. As an illustration, we compare logarithmic and polynomial models of the relationship between district income and test scores.

*Polynomial specifications.* We considered two polynomial specifications specified using powers of *Income*, quadratic [Equation (8.2)] and cubic [Equation (8.11)]. Because the coefficient on *Income*$^3$ in Equation (8.11) was significant at the 5% level, the cubic specification provided an improvement over the quadratic, so we select the cubic model as the preferred polynomial specification.

*Logarithmic specifications.* The logarithmic specification in Equation (8.18) seemed to provide a good fit to these data, but we did not test this formally. One way to do so is to augment it with higher powers of the logarithm of income. If these additional terms are not statistically different from zero, then we can conclude that the specification in Equation (8.18) is adequate in the sense that it cannot be rejected against a polynomial function of the logarithm. Accordingly, the estimated cubic regression (specified in powers of the logarithm of income) is

$$\widehat{TestScore} = 486.1 + 113.4\ln(Income) - 26.9[\ln(Income)^2]$$
$$\phantom{xx}(79.4) \phantom{xx} (87.9) \phantom{xxxxxxxxxx} (31.7)$$
$$+ \phantom{x} 3.06[\ln(Income)]^3, \overline{R}^2 = 0.560. \tag{8.26}$$
$$(3.74)$$

The $t$-statistic on the coefficient on the cubic term is 0.818, so the null hypothesis that the true coefficient is zero is not rejected at the 10% level. The $F$-statistic testing the joint hypothesis that the true coefficients on the quadratic and cubic term are both zero is 0.44, with a $p$-value of 0.64, so this joint null hypothesis is not rejected at the 10% level. Thus the cubic logarithmic model in Equation (8.26) does not provide a statistically significant improvement over the model in Equation (8.18), which is linear in the logarithm of income.

*Comparing the cubic and linear-log specifications.*  Figure 8.7 plots the estimated regression functions from the cubic specification in Equation (8.11) and the linear-log specification in Equation (8.18). The two estimated regression functions are quite similar. One statistical tool for comparing these specifications is the $\overline{R}^2$. The $\overline{R}^2$ of the logarithmic regression is 0.561, and for the cubic regression it is 0.555. Because the logarithmic specification has a slight edge in terms of the $\overline{R}^2$ and because this specification does not need higher-degree polynomials in the logarithm of income to fit these data, we adopt the logarithmic specification in Equation (8.18).

## 8.3 Interactions Between Independent Variables

In the introduction to this chapter we wondered whether reducing the student–teacher ratio might have a bigger effect on test scores in districts where many students are still learning English than in those with few still learning English. This could arise, for example, if students who are still learning English benefit differentially from one-on-one or small-group instruction. If so, the presence of many English learners in a district would interact with the student–teacher ratio in such a way that the effect on test scores of a change in the student–teacher ratio would depend on the fraction of English learners.

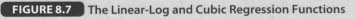

**FIGURE 8.7** The Linear-Log and Cubic Regression Functions

The estimated cubic regression function [Equation (8.11)] and the estimated linear-log regression function [Equation (8.18)] are nearly identical in this sample.

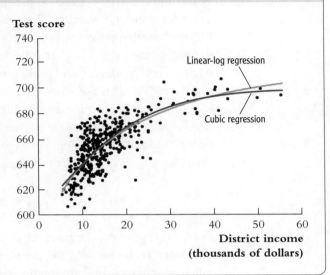

This section explains how to incorporate such interactions between two independent variables into the multiple regression model. The possible interaction between the student–teacher ratio and the fraction of English learners is an example of the more general situation in which the effect on $Y$ of a change in one independent variable depends on the value of another independent variable. We consider three cases: when both independent variables are binary, when one is binary and the other is continuous, and when both are continuous.

## Interactions Between Two Binary Variables

Consider the population regression of log earnings [$Y_i$, where $Y_i = \ln(Earnings_i)$] against two binary variables: whether a worker has a college degree ($D_{1i}$, where $D_{1i} = 1$ if the $i^{\text{th}}$ person graduated from college) and the worker's gender ($D_{2i}$, where $D_{2i} = 1$ if the $i^{\text{th}}$ person is female). The population linear regression of $Y_i$ on these two binary variables is

$$Y_i = \beta_0 + \beta_1 D_{1i} + \beta_2 D_{2i} + u_i. \tag{8.27}$$

In this regression model, $\beta_1$ is the effect on log earnings of having a college degree, holding gender constant, and $\beta_2$ is the effect of being female, holding schooling constant.

The specification in Equation (8.27) has an important limitation: The effect of having a college degree in this specification, holding constant gender, is the same for men and women. There is, however, no reason that this must be so. Phrased mathematically, the effect on $Y_i$ of $D_{1i}$, holding $D_{2i}$ constant, could depend on the value of $D_{2i}$. In other words, there could be an interaction between having a college degree and gender so that the value in the job market of a degree is different for men and women.

Although the specification in Equation (8.27) does not allow for this interaction between having a college degree and gender, it is easy to modify the specification so that it does by introducing another regressor, the product of the two binary variables, $D_{1i} \times D_{2i}$. The resulting regression is

$$Y_i = \beta_0 + \beta_1 D_{1i} + \beta_2 D_{2i} + \beta_3(D_{1i} \times D_{2i}) + u_i. \qquad (8.28)$$

The new regressor, the product $D_{1i} \times D_{2i}$, is called an **interaction term** or an **interacted regressor**, and the population regression model in Equation (8.28) is called a binary variable **interaction regression model**.

The interaction term in Equation (8.28) allows the population effect on log earnings ($Y_i$) of having a college degree (changing $D_{1i}$ from $D_{1i} = 0$ to $D_{1i} = 1$) to depend on gender ($D_{2i}$). To show this mathematically, calculate the population effect of a change in $D_{1i}$ using the general method laid out in Key Concept 8.1. The first step is to compute the conditional expectation of $Y_i$ for $D_{1i} = 0$, given a value of $D_{2i}$; this is $E(Y_i | D_{1i} = 0, D_{2i} = d_2) = \beta_0 + \beta_1 \times 0 + \beta_2 \times d_2 + \beta_3 \times (0 \times d_2) = \beta_0 + \beta_2 d_2$, where we use the conditional mean zero assumption, $E(u_i | D_{1i}, D_{2i}) = 0$. The next step is to compute the conditional expectation of $Y_i$ after the change—that is, for $D_{1i} = 1$—given the same value of $D_{2i}$; this is $E(Y_i | D_{1i} = 1, D_{2i} = d_2) = \beta_0 + \beta_1 \times 1 + \beta_2 \times d_2 + \beta_3 \times (1 \times d_2) = \beta_0 + \beta_1 + \beta_2 d_2 + \beta_3 d_2$. The effect of this change is the difference of expected values [that is, the difference in Equation (8.4)], which is

$$E(Y_i | D_{1i} = 1, D_{2i} = d_2) - E(Y_i | D_{1i} = 0, D_{2i} = d_2) = \beta_1 + \beta_3 d_2. \quad (8.29)$$

Thus, in the binary variable interaction specification in Equation (8.28), the effect of acquiring a college degree (a unit change in $D_{1i}$) depends on the person's gender [the value of $D_{2i}$, which is $d_2$ in Equation (8.29)]. If the person is male ($d_2 = 0$), the effect of acquiring a college degree is $\beta_1$, but if the person is female ($d_2 = 1$), the effect is $\beta_1 + \beta_3$. The coefficient $\beta_3$ on the interaction term is the difference in the effect of acquiring a college degree for women versus men.

# A Method for Interpreting Coefficients in Regressions with Binary Variables

**KEY CONCEPT**

**8.3**

First compute the expected values of $Y$ for each possible case described by the set of binary variables. Next compare these expected values. Each coefficient can then be expressed either as an expected value or as the difference between two or more expected values.

Although this example was phrased using log earnings, having a college degree, and gender, the point is a general one. The binary variable interaction regression allows the effect of changing one of the binary independent variables to depend on the value of the other binary variable.

The method we used here to interpret the coefficients was, in effect, to work through each possible combination of the binary variables. This method, which applies to all regressions with binary variables, is summarized in Key Concept 8.3.

*Application to the student–teacher ratio and the percentage of English learners.* Let $HiSTR_i$ be a binary variable that equals 1 if the student–teacher ratio is 20 or more and equals 0 otherwise, and let $HiEL_i$ be a binary variable that equals 1 if the percentage of English learners is 10% or more and equals 0 otherwise. The interacted regression of test scores against $HiSTR_i$ and $HiEL_i$ is

$$\widehat{TestScore} = 664.1 - 1.9\,HiSTR - 18.2\,HiEL - 3.5(HiSTR \times HiEL),$$
$$(1.4)\quad(1.9)\qquad(2.3)\qquad(3.1)$$

$$\overline{R}^2 = 0.290. \tag{8.30}$$

The predicted effect of moving from a district with a low student–teacher ratio to one with a high student–teacher ratio, holding constant whether the percentage of English learners is high or low, is given by Equation (8.29), with estimated coefficients replacing the population coefficients. According to the estimates in Equation (8.30), this effect thus is $-1.9 - 3.5HiEL$. That is, if the fraction of English learners is low ($HiEL = 0$), then the effect on test scores of moving from $HiSTR = 0$ to $HiSTR = 1$ is for test scores to decline by 1.9 points. If the fraction of English learners is high, then test scores are estimated to decline by $1.9 + 3.5 = 5.4$ points.

The estimated regression in Equation (8.30) also can be used to estimate the mean test scores for each of the four possible combinations of the binary variables.

This is done using the procedure in Key Concept 8.3. Accordingly, the sample average test score for districts with low student–teacher ratios ($HiSTR_i = 0$) and low fractions of English learners ($HiEL_i = 0$) is 664.1. For districts with $HiSTR_i = 1$ (high student–teacher ratios) and $HiEL_i = 0$ (low fractions of English learners), the sample average is 662.2 ($= 664.1 - 1.9$). When $HiSTR_i = 0$ and $HiEL_i = 1$, the sample average is 645.9 ($= 664.1 - 18.2$), and when $HiSTR_i = 1$ and $HiEL_i = 1$, the sample average is 640.5 ($= 664.1 - 1.9 - 18.2 - 3.5$).

## Interactions Between a Continuous and a Binary Variable

Next consider the population regression of log earnings [$Y_i = \ln(Earnings_i)$] against one continuous variable, the individual's years of work experience ($X_i$), and one binary variable, whether the worker has a college degree ($D_i$, where $D_i = 1$ if the $i^{\text{th}}$ person is a college graduate). As shown in Figure 8.8, the population regression line relating $Y$ and the continuous variable $X$ can depend on the binary variable $D$ in three different ways.

In Figure 8.8a, the two regression lines differ only in their intercept. The corresponding population regression model is

$$Y_i = \beta_0 + \beta_1 X_i + \beta_2 D_i + u_i. \tag{8.31}$$

This is the familiar multiple regression model with a population regression function that is linear in $X_i$ and $D_i$. When $D_i = 0$, the population regression function is $\beta_0 + \beta_1 X_i$, so the intercept is $\beta_0$ and the slope is $\beta_1$. When $D_i = 1$, the population regression function is $\beta_0 + \beta_1 X_i + \beta_2$, so the slope remains $\beta_1$ but the intercept is $\beta_0 + \beta_2$. Thus $\beta_2$ is the difference between the intercepts of the two regression lines, as shown in Figure 8.8a. Stated in terms of the earnings example, $\beta_1$ is the effect on log earnings of an additional year of work experience, holding college degree status constant, and $\beta_2$ is the effect of a college degree on log earnings, holding years of experience constant. In this specification, the effect of an additional year of work experience is the same for college graduates and nongraduates; that is, the two lines in Figure 8.8a have the same slope.

In Figure 8.8b, the two lines have different slopes and intercepts. The different slopes permit the effect of an additional year of work to differ for college graduates and nongraduates. To allow for different slopes, add an interaction term to Equation (8.31):

$$Y_i = \beta_0 + \beta_1 X_i + \beta_2 D_i + \beta_3 (X_i \times D_i) + u_i, \tag{8.32}$$

**FIGURE 8.8**   Regression Functions Using Binary and Continuous Variables

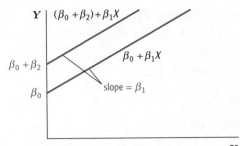

**(a)** Different intercepts, same slope

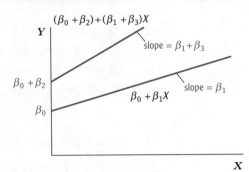

**(b)** Different intercepts, different slopes

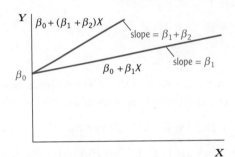

**(c)** Same intercept, different slopes

Interactions of binary variables and continuous variables can produce three different population regression functions: (a) $\beta_0 + \beta_1 X + \beta_2 D$ allows for different intercepts but has the same slope, (b) $\beta_0 + \beta_1 X + \beta_2 D + \beta_3 (X \times D)$ allows for different intercepts and different slopes, and (c) $\beta_0 + \beta_1 X + \beta_2 (X \times D)$ has the same intercept but allows for different slopes.

where $X_i \times D_i$ is a new variable, the product of $X_i$ and $D_i$. To interpret the coefficients of this regression, apply the procedure in Key Concept 8.3. Doing so shows that, if $D_i = 0$, the population regression function is $\beta_0 + \beta_1 X_i$, whereas if $D_i = 1$, the population regression function is $(\beta_0 + \beta_2) + (\beta_1 + \beta_3)X_i$. Thus this specification allows for two different population regression functions relating $Y_i$ and $X_i$, depending on the value of $D_i$, as is shown in Figure 8.8b. The difference between the two intercepts is $\beta_2$, and the difference between the two slopes is $\beta_3$. In the earnings example, $\beta_1$ is the effect of an additional year of work experience for nongraduates ($D_i = 0$) and $\beta_1 + \beta_3$ is this effect for graduates, so $\beta_3$ is the *difference* in the effect of an additional year of work experience for college graduates versus nongraduates.

**KEY CONCEPT**

**8.4**

## Interactions Between Binary and Continuous Variables

Through the use of the interaction term $X_i \times D_i$, the population regression line relating $Y_i$ and the continuous variable $X_i$ can have a slope that depends on the binary variable $D_i$. There are three possibilities:

1. Different intercept, same slope (Figure 8.8a):

$$Y_i = \beta_0 + \beta_1 X_i + \beta_2 D_i + u_i;$$

2. Different intercept and slope (Figure 8.8b):

$$Y_i = \beta_0 + \beta_1 X_i + \beta_2 D_i + \beta_3 (X_i \times D_i) + u_i;$$

3. Same intercept, different slope (Figure 8.8c):

$$Y_i = \beta_0 + \beta_1 X_i + \beta_2 (X_i \times D_i) + u_i.$$

A third possibility, shown in Figure 8.8c, is that the two lines have different slopes but the same intercept. The interacted regression model for this case is

$$Y_i = \beta_0 + \beta_1 X_i + \beta_2 (X_i \times D_i) + u_i. \qquad (8.33)$$

The coefficients of this specification also can be interpreted using Key Concept 8.3. In terms of the earnings example, this specification allows for different effects of experience on log earnings between college graduates and nongraduates, but requires that expected log earnings be the same for both groups when they have no prior experience. Said differently, this specification corresponds to the population mean entry-level wage being the same for college graduates and nongraduates. This does not make much sense in this application, and in practice this specification is used less frequently than Equation (8.32), which allows for different intercepts and slopes.

All three specifications—Equations (8.31), (8.32), and (8.33)—are versions of the multiple regression model of Chapter 6, and once the new variable $X_i \times D_i$ is created, the coefficients of all three can be estimated by OLS.

The three regression models with a binary and a continuous independent variable are summarized in Key Concept 8.4.

*Application to the student–teacher ratio and the percentage of English learners.* Does the effect on test scores of cutting the student–teacher ratio depend on whether the percentage of students still learning English is high or low? One way to answer this question is to use a specification that allows for two different regression lines, depending on whether there is a high or a low percentage of English learners. This is achieved using the different intercept/different slope specification:

$$\widehat{TestScore} = 682.2 - 0.97\,STR + 5.6\,HiEL - 1.28(STR \times HiEL),$$
$$\qquad\qquad (11.9) \quad (0.59) \qquad (19.5) \qquad\quad (0.97)$$
$$\overline{R}^2 = 0.305, \tag{8.34}$$

where the binary variable $HiEL_i$ equals 1 if the percentage of students still learning English in the district is greater than 10% and equals 0 otherwise.

For districts with a low fraction of English learners ($HiEL_i = 0$), the estimated regression line is $682.2 - 0.97STR_i$. For districts with a high fraction of English learners ($HiEL_i = 1$), the estimated regression line is $682.2 + 5.6 - 0.97STR_i - 1.28STR_i = 687.8 - 2.25STR_i$. According to these estimates, reducing the student–teacher ratio by 1 is predicted to increase test scores by 0.97 point in districts with low fractions of English learners but by 2.25 points in districts with high fractions of English learners. The difference between these two effects, 1.28 points, is the coefficient on the interaction term in Equation (8.34).

The interaction regression model in Equation (8.34) allows us to estimate the effect of more nuanced policy interventions than the across-the-board class size reduction considered so far. For example, suppose that the state considered a policy to reduce the student–teacher ratio by 2 in districts with a high fraction of English learners ($HiEL_i = 1$) but to leave class size unchanged in other districts. Applying the method of Key Concept 8.1 to Equations (8.32) and (8.34) shows that the estimated effect of this reduction for the districts for which $HiEL = 1$ is $-2(\hat{\beta}_1 + \hat{\beta}_3) = 4.50$. The standard error of this estimated effect is $SE(-2\hat{\beta}_1 - 2\hat{\beta}_3) = 1.53$, which can be computed using Equation (8.8) and the methods of Section 7.3.

The OLS regression in Equation (8.34) can be used to test several hypotheses about the population regression line. First, the hypothesis that the two lines are in fact the same can be tested by computing the $F$-statistic testing the joint hypothesis that the coefficient on $HiEL_i$ and the coefficient on the interaction term $STR_i \times HiEL_i$ are both zero. This $F$-statistic is 89.9, which is significant at the 1% level.

Second, the hypothesis that two lines have the same slope can be tested by testing whether the coefficient on the interaction term is zero. The $t$-statistic, $-1.28/0.97 = -1.32$, is less than 1.64 in absolute value, so the null hypothesis that the two lines have the same slope cannot be rejected using a two-sided test at the 10% significance level.

Third, the hypothesis that the lines have the same intercept corresponds to the restriction that the population coefficient on $HiEL$ is zero. The $t$-statistic testing this restriction is $t = 5.6/19.5 = 0.29$, so the hypothesis that the lines have the same intercept cannot be rejected at the 5% level.

These three tests produce seemingly contradictory results: The joint test using the $F$-statistic rejects the joint hypothesis that the slope and the intercept are the same, but the tests of the individual hypotheses using the $t$-statistic fail to reject. The reason is that the regressors, $HiEL$ and $STR \times HiEL$, are highly correlated. This results in large standard errors on the individual coefficients. Even though it is impossible to tell which of the coefficients is nonzero, there is strong evidence against the hypothesis that *both* are zero.

Finally, the hypothesis that the student–teacher ratio does not enter this specification can be tested by computing the $F$-statistic for the joint hypothesis that the coefficients on $STR$ and on the interaction term are both zero. This $F$-statistic is 5.64, which has a $p$-value of 0.004. Thus the coefficients on the student–teacher ratio are statistically significant at the 1% significance level.

## Interactions Between Two Continuous Variables

Now suppose that both independent variables ($X_{1i}$ and $X_{2i}$) are continuous. An example is when $Y_i$ is log earnings of the $i^{\text{th}}$ worker, $X_{1i}$ is his or her years of work experience, and $X_{2i}$ is the number of years he or she went to school. If the population regression function is linear, the effect on wages of an additional year of experience does not depend on the number of years of education, or, equivalently, the effect of an additional year of education does not depend on the number of years of work experience. In reality, however, there might be an interaction between these two variables so that the effect on wages of an additional year of experience depends on the number of years of education. This interaction can be modeled by augmenting the linear regression model with an interaction term that is the product of $X_{1i}$ and $X_{2i}$:

$$Y_i = \beta_0 + \beta_1 X_{1i} + \beta_2 X_{2i} + \beta_3 (X_{1i} \times X_{2i}) + u_i. \tag{8.35}$$

The interaction term allows the effect of a unit change in $X_1$ to depend on $X_2$. To see this, apply the general method for computing effects in nonlinear regression models in Key Concept 8.1. The difference in Equation (8.4), computed for the interacted regression function in Equation (8.35), is $\Delta Y = (\beta_1 + \beta_3 X_2)\Delta X_1$ [Exercise 8.10(a)]. Thus the effect on $Y$ of a change in $X_1$, holding $X_2$ constant, is

$$\frac{\Delta Y}{\Delta X_1} = \beta_1 + \beta_3 X_2, \tag{8.36}$$

which depends on $X_2$. For example, in the earnings example, if $\beta_3$ is positive, then the effect on log earnings of an additional year of experience is greater, by the amount $\beta_3$, for each additional year of education the worker has.

## The Return to Education and the Gender Gap

In addition to its intellectual pleasures, education has economic rewards. As the boxes in Chapters 3 and 5 show, workers with more education tend to earn more than their counterparts with less education. The analysis in those boxes was incomplete, however, for at least three reasons. First, it failed to control for other determinants of earnings that might be correlated with educational achievement, so the OLS estimator of the coefficient on education could have omitted variable bias. Second, the functional form used in Chapter 5—a simple linear relation—implies that earnings change by a constant dollar amount for each additional year of education, whereas one might suspect that the dollar change in earnings is actually larger at higher levels of education. Third, the box in Chapter 5 ignores the gender differences in earnings highlighted in the box in Chapter 3.

All these limitations can be addressed by a multiple regression analysis that controls for determinants of earnings that, if omitted, could cause omitted variable bias and that uses a nonlinear functional form relating education and earnings. Table 8.1 summarizes regressions estimated using data on full-time workers, ages 30 through 64, from the Current Population Survey (the CPS data are described in Appendix 3.1). The dependent variable is the logarithm of hourly earnings, so another year of education is associated with a constant percentage increase (not dollar increase) in earnings.

Table 8.1 has four salient results. First, the omission of gender in regression (1) does not result in substantial omitted variable bias: Even though gender enters regression (2) significantly and with a large coefficient, gender and years of education are uncorrelated; that is, on average men and women have nearly the same levels of education. Second, the returns to education are economically and statistically significantly different for men and women: In regression (3), the $t$-statistic testing the hypothesis that they are the same is 4.55 ($= 0.008/0.0018$). Third, regression (4) controls for the region of the country in which the individual lives, thereby addressing potential omitted variable bias that might arise if years of education differ systematically by region. Controlling for region makes a small difference to the estimated coefficients on the education terms, relative to those reported in regression (3). Fourth, regression (4) controls for the potential experience of the worker, as measured by years since completion of schooling. The estimated coefficients imply a declining marginal value for each year of potential experience.

The estimated economic return to education in regression (4) is 11.26% for each year of education for men and 12.25% ($= 0.1126 + 0.0099$, in percent) for women. Because the regression functions for men and women have different slopes, the gender gap depends on the years of education. For 12 years of education, the gender gap is estimated to be 27.3% ($= 0.0099 \times 12 - 0.392$, in percent); for 16 years of education, the gender gap is less in percentage terms, 23.4%.

These estimates of the return to education and the gender gap still have limitations, including the possibility of other omitted variables, notably the native ability of the worker, and potential problems associated with the way variables are measured in the CPS. Nevertheless, the estimates in Table 8.1

*continued on next page*

**TABLE 8.1** The Return to Education and the Gender Gap: Regression Results for the United States in 2012

Dependent variable: logarithm of *Hourly Earnings*.

| Regressor | (1) | (2) | (3) | (4) |
|---|---|---|---|---|
| *Years of education* | 0.1082** (0.0009) | 0.1111** (0.0009) | 0.1078** (0.0012) | 0.1126** (0.0012) |
| *Female* | | −0.251** (0.005) | −0.367** (0.026) | −0.392** (0.025) |
| *Female × Years of education* | | | 0.0081** (0.0018) | 0.0099** (0.0018) |
| *Potential experience* | | | | 0.0186** (0.0012) |
| *Potential experience$^2$* | | | | −0.000263** (0.000024) |
| *Midwest* | | | | −0.080** (0.007) |
| *South* | | | | −0.083** (0.007) |
| *West* | | | | −0.018** (0.007) |
| *Intercept* | 1.515** (0.013) | 1.585** (0.013) | 1.632** (0.016) | 1.335** (0.024) |
| $\bar{R}^2$ | 0.221 | 0.263 | 0.264 | 0.276 |

The data are from the March 2013 Current Population Survey (see Appendix 3.1). The sample size is $n$ = 50,174 observations for each regression. *Female* is an indicator variable that equals 1 for women and 0 for men. *Midwest*, *South*, and *West* are indicator variables denoting the region of the United States in which the worker lives: For example, *Midwest* equals 1 if the worker lives in the Midwest and equals 0 otherwise (the omitted region is *Northeast*). Standard errors are reported in parentheses below the estimated coefficients. Individual coefficients are statistically significant at the *5% or **1% significance level.

are consistent with those obtained by economists who carefully address these limitations. A survey by the econometrician David Card (1999) of dozens of empirical studies concludes that labor economists' best estimates of the return to education generally fall between 8% and 11%, and that the return depends on the quality of the education. If you are interested in learning more about the economic return to education, see Card (1999).

## Interactions in Multiple Regression

The interaction term between the two independent variables $X_1$ and $X_2$ is their product $X_1 \times X_2$. Including this interaction term allows the effect on $Y$ of a change in $X_1$ to depend on the value of $X_2$ and, conversely, allows the effect of a change in $X_2$ to depend on the value of $X_1$.

The coefficient on $X_1 \times X_2$ is the effect of a one-unit increase in $X_1$ *and* $X_2$, above and beyond the sum of the individual effects of a unit increase in $X_1$ alone and a unit increase in $X_2$ alone. This is true whether $X_1$ and/or $X_2$ are continuous or binary.

A similar calculation shows that the effect on $Y$ of a change $\Delta X_2$ in $X_2$, holding $X_1$ constant, is $\Delta Y / \Delta X_2 = (\beta_2 + \beta_3 X_1)$.

Putting these two effects together shows that the coefficient $\beta_3$ on the interaction term is the effect of a unit increase in $X_1$ and $X_2$, above and beyond the sum of the effects of a unit increase in $X_1$ alone and a unit increase in $X_2$ alone. That is, if $X_1$ changes by $\Delta X_1$ and $X_2$ changes by $\Delta X_2$, then the expected change in $Y$ is $\Delta Y = (\beta_1 + \beta_3 X_2)\Delta X_1 + (\beta_2 + \beta_3 X_1)\Delta X_2 + \beta_3 \Delta X_1 \Delta X_2$ [Exercise 8.10(c)]. The first term is the effect from changing $X_1$ holding $X_2$ constant; the second term is the effect from changing $X_2$ holding $X_1$ constant; and the final term, $\beta_3 \Delta X_1 \Delta X_2$, is the extra effect from changing both $X_1$ and $X_2$.

Interactions between two variables are summarized as Key Concept 8.5.

When interactions are combined with logarithmic transformations, they can be used to estimate price elasticities when the price elasticity depends on the characteristics of the good (see the box "The Demand for Economics Journals" on page 336 for an example).

*Application to the student–teacher ratio and the percentage of English learners.* The previous examples considered interactions between the student–teacher ratio and a binary variable indicating whether the percentage of English learners is large or small. A different way to study this interaction is to examine the interaction between the student–teacher ratio and the continuous variable,

## The Demand for Economics Journals

Professional economists follow the most recent research in their areas of specialization. Most research in economics first appears in economics journals, so economists—or their libraries—subscribe to economics journals.

How elastic is the demand by libraries for economics journals? To find out, we analyzed the relationship between the number of subscriptions to a journal at U.S. libraries ($Y_i$) and the journal's library subscription price using data for the year 2000 for 180 economics journals. Because the product of a journal is not the paper on which it is printed but rather the ideas it contains, its price is logically measured not in dollars per year or dollars per page but instead in dollars per idea. Although we cannot measure "ideas" directly, a good indirect measure is the number of times that articles in a journal are subsequently cited by other researchers. Accordingly, we measure price

---

**FIGURE 8.9** Library Subscriptions and Prices of Economics Journals

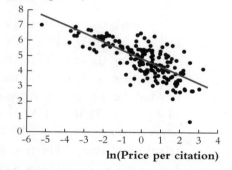

**(a)** Subscriptions and Price per citation

**(b)** ln(Subscriptions) and ln(Price per citation)

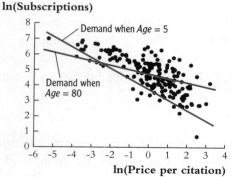

**(c)** ln(Subscriptions) and ln(Price per citation)

There is a nonlinear inverse relation between the number of U.S. library subscriptions (quantity) and the library price per citation (price), as shown in Figure 8.9a for 180 economics journals in 2000. But as seen in Figure 8.9b, the relation between log quantity and log price appears to be approximately linear. Figure 8.9c shows that demand is more elastic for young journals (Age = 5) than for old journals (Age = 80).

*continued on next page*

as the "price per citation" in the journal. The price range is enormous, from $\frac{1}{2}$¢ per citation (the *American Economic Review*) to 20¢ per citation or more. Some journals are expensive per citation because they have few citations, others because their library subscription price per year is very high. In 2014, a library print subscription to the *Journal of Econometrics* cost $4089, compared to only $455 for a bundled subscription to all seven journals published by the American

Economics Association, including the *American Economic Review*!

Because we are interested in estimating elasticities, we use a log-log specification (Key Concept 8.2). The scatterplots in Figures 8.9a and 8.9b provide empirical support for this transformation. Because some of the oldest and most prestigious journals are the cheapest per citation, a regression of log quantity against log price could have omitted variable bias.

| TABLE 8.2 | Estimates of the Demand for Economics Journals | | | |
| --- | --- | --- | --- | --- |
| **Dependent variable: logarithm of subscriptions at U.S. libraries in the Year 2000; 180 observations.** | | | | |
| Regressor | (1) | (2) | (3) | (4) |
| ln(*Price per citation*) | −0.533** (0.034) | −0.408** (0.044) | −0.961** (0.160) | −0.899** (0.145) |
| [ln(*Price per citation*)]$^2$ | | | 0.017 (0.025) | |
| [ln(*Price per citation*)]$^3$ | | | 0.0037 (0.0055) | |
| ln(*Age*) | | 0.424** (0.119) | 0.373** (0.118) | 0.374** (0.118) |
| ln(*Age*) × ln(*Price per citation*) | | | 0.156** (0.052) | 0.141** (0.040) |
| ln(*Characters* ÷ 1,000,000) | | 0.206* (0.098) | 0.235* (0.098) | 0.229* (0.096) |
| Intercept | 4.77** (0.055) | 3.21** (0.38) | 3.41** (0.38) | 3.43** (0.38) |
| **F Statistics and Summary Statistics** | | | | |
| *F*-statistic testing coefficients on quadratic and cubic terms (*p*-value) | | | 0.25 (0.779) | |
| *SER* | 0.750 | 0.705 | 0.691 | 0.688 |
| $\overline{R}^2$ | 0.555 | 0.607 | 0.622 | 0.626 |

The *F*-statistic tests the hypothesis that the coefficients on [ln(*Price per citation*)]$^2$ and [ln(*Price per citation*)]$^3$ are both zero. Standard errors are given in parentheses under coefficients, and *p*-values are given in parentheses under *F*-statistics. Individual coefficients are statistically significant at the *5% level or **1% level.

*continued on next page*

Our regressions therefore include two control variables: the logarithm of age and the logarithm of the number of characters per year in the journal.

The regression results are summarized in Table 8.2. Those results yield the following conclusions (see if you can find the basis for these conclusions in the table!):

1. Demand is less elastic for older than for newer journals.

2. The evidence supports a linear, rather than a cubic, function of log price.

3. Demand is greater for journals with more characters, holding price and age constant.

So what is the elasticity of demand for economics journals? It depends on the age of the journal. Demand curves for an 80-year-old journal and a 5-year-old upstart are superimposed on the scatterplot in Figure 8.9c; the older journal's demand elasticity is $-0.28$ ($SE = 0.06$), while the younger journal's is $-0.67$($SE = 0.08$).

This demand is very inelastic: Demand is very insensitive to price, especially for older journals. For libraries, having the most recent research on hand is a necessity, not a luxury. By way of comparison, experts estimate the demand elasticity for cigarettes to be in the range of $-0.3$ to $-0.5$. Economics journals are, it seems, as addictive as cigarettes, but a lot better for your health![1]

---

[1]These data were graciously provided by Professor Theodore Bergstrom of the Department of Economics at the University of California, Santa Barbara. If you are interested in learning more about the economics of economics journals, see Bergstrom (2001).

the percentage of English learners (*PctEL*). The estimated interaction regression is

$$\widehat{TestScore} = 686.3 - 1.12\,STR - 0.67\,PctEL + 0.0012(STR \times PctEL),$$
$$\quad\quad\quad (11.8) \quad (0.59) \quad\quad (0.37) \quad\quad\quad (0.019)$$
$$\overline{R}^2 = 0.422. \tag{8.37}$$

When the percentage of English learners is at the median (*PctEL* = 8.85), the slope of the line relating test scores and the student–teacher ratio is estimated to be $-1.11$ ($= -1.12 + 0.0012 \times 8.85$). When the percentage of English learners is at the 75th percentile (*PctEL* = 23.0), this line is estimated to be flatter, with a slope of $-1.09$ ($= -1.12 + 0.0012 \times 23.0$). That is, for a district with 8.85% English learners, the estimated effect of a one-unit reduction in the student–teacher ratio is to increase test scores by 1.11 points, but for a district with 23.0% English learners, reducing the student–teacher ratio by one unit is predicted to increase test scores by only 1.09 points. The difference between these estimated effects is not statistically significant, however: The *t*-statistic testing whether the coefficient on the interaction term is zero is $t = 0.0012/0.019 = 0.06$, which is not significant at the 10% level.

To keep the discussion focused on nonlinear models, the specifications in Sections 8.1 through 8.3 exclude additional control variables such as the students' economic background. Consequently, these results arguably are subject to omitted variable bias. To draw substantive conclusions about the effect on test scores of reducing the student–teacher ratio, these nonlinear specifications must be augmented with control variables, and it is to such an exercise that we now turn.

## 8.4 Nonlinear Effects on Test Scores of the Student–Teacher Ratio

This section addresses three specific questions about test scores and the student–teacher ratio. First, after controlling for differences in economic characteristics of different districts, does the effect on test scores of reducing the student–teacher ratio depend on the fraction of English learners? Second, does this effect depend on the value of the student–teacher ratio? Third, and most important, after taking economic factors and nonlinearities into account, what is the estimated effect on test scores of reducing the student–teacher ratio by two students per teacher, as our superintendent from Chapter 4 proposes to do?

We answer these questions by considering nonlinear regression specifications of the type discussed in Sections 8.2 and 8.3, extended to include two measures of the economic background of the students: the percentage of students eligible for a subsidized lunch and the logarithm of average district income. The logarithm of income is used because the empirical analysis of Section 8.2 suggests that this specification captures the nonlinear relationship between test scores and income. As in Section 7.6, we do not include expenditures per pupil as a regressor and in so doing we are considering the effect of decreasing the student–teacher ratio, allowing expenditures per pupil to increase (that is, we are not holding expenditures per pupil constant).

### Discussion of Regression Results

The OLS regression results are summarized in Table 8.3. The columns labeled (1) through (7) each report separate regressions. The entries in the table are the coefficients, standard errors, certain $F$-statistics and their $p$-values, and summary statistics, as indicated by the description in each row.

The first column of regression results, labeled regression (1) in the table, is regression (3) in Table 7.1 repeated here for convenience. This regression does not

### TABLE 8.3    Nonlinear Regression Models of Test Scores

**Dependent variable: average test score in district; 420 observations.**

| Regressor | (1) | (2) | (3) | (4) | (5) | (6) | (7) |
|---|---|---|---|---|---|---|---|
| Student–teacher ratio ($STR$) | −1.00** (0.27) | −0.73** (0.26) | −0.97 (0.59) | −0.53 (0.34) | 64.33** (24.86) | 83.70** (28.50) | 65.29** (25.26) |
| $STR^2$ | | | | | −3.42** (1.25) | −4.38** (1.44) | −3.47** (1.27) |
| $STR^3$ | | | | | 0.059** (0.021) | 0.075** (0.024) | 0.060** (0.021) |
| % English learners | −0.122** (0.033) | −0.176** (0.034) | | | | | −0.166** (0.034) |
| % English learners $\geq$ 10%? (Binary, $HiEL$) | | | 5.64 (19.51) | 5.50 (9.80) | −5.47** (1.03) | 816.1* (327.7) | |
| $HiEL \times STR$ | | | −1.28 (0.97) | −0.58 (0.50) | | −123.3* (50.2) | |
| $HiEL \times STR^2$ | | | | | | 6.12* (2.54) | |
| $HiEL \times STR^3$ | | | | | | −0.101* (0.043) | |
| % Eligible for subsidized lunch | −0.547** (0.024) | −0.398** (0.033) | | −0.411** (0.029) | −0.420** (0.029) | −0.418** (0.029) | −0.402** (0.033) |
| Average district income (logarithm) | | 11.57** (1.81) | | 12.12** (1.80) | 11.75** (1.78) | 11.80** (1.78) | 11.51** (1.81) |
| Intercept | 700.2** (5.6) | 658.6** (8.6) | 682.2** (11.9) | 653.6** (9.9) | 252.0 (163.6) | 122.3 (185.5) | 244.8 (165.7) |

**F-Statistics and p-Values on Joint Hypotheses**

| | | | | | | | |
|---|---|---|---|---|---|---|---|
| (a) All $STR$ variables and interactions = 0 | | | 5.64 (0.004) | 5.92 (0.003) | 6.31 (< 0.001) | 4.96 (< 0.001) | 5.91 (0.001) |
| (b) $STR^2$, $STR^3$ = 0 | | | | | 6.17 (< 0.001) | 5.81 (0.003) | 5.96 (0.003) |
| (c) $HiEL \times STR$, $HiEL \times STR^2$, $HiEL \times STR^3$ = 0 | | | | | | 2.69 (0.046) | |
| $SER$ | 9.08 | 8.64 | 15.88 | 8.63 | 8.56 | 8.55 | 8.57 |
| $\overline{R}^2$ | 0.773 | 0.794 | 0.305 | 0.795 | 0.798 | 0.799 | 0.798 |

These regressions were estimated using the data on K–8 school districts in California, described in Appendix 4.1. Standard errors are given in parentheses under coefficients, and p-values are given in parentheses under F-statistics. Individual coefficients are statistically significant at the *5% or **1% significance level.

control for income, so the first thing we do is check whether the results change substantially when log income is included as an additional economic control variable. The results are given in regression (2) in Table 8.3. The log of income is statistically significant at the 1% level and the coefficient on the student–teacher ratio becomes somewhat closer to zero, falling from $-1.00$ to $-0.73$, although it remains statistically significant at the 1% level. The change in the coefficient on $STR$ is large enough between regressions (1) and (2) to warrant including the logarithm of income in the remaining regressions as a deterrent to omitted variable bias.

Regression (3) in Table 8.3 is the interacted regression in Equation (8.34) with the binary variable for a high or low percentage of English learners, but with no economic control variables. When the economic control variables (percentage eligible for subsidized lunch and log income) are added [regression (4) in the table], the coefficients change, but in neither case is the coefficient on the interaction term significant at the 5% level. Based on the evidence in regression (4), the hypothesis that the effect of $STR$ is the same for districts with low and high percentages of English learners cannot be rejected at the 5% level (the $t$-statistic is $t = -0.58/0.50 = -1.16$).

Regression (5) examines whether the effect of changing the student–teacher ratio depends on the value of the student–teacher ratio by including a cubic specification in $STR$ in addition to the other control variables in regression (4) [the interaction term, $HiEL \times STR$, was dropped because it was not significant in regression (4) at the 10% level]. The estimates in regression (5) are consistent with the student–teacher ratio having a nonlinear effect. The null hypothesis that the relationship is linear is rejected at the 1% significance level against the alternative that it is cubic (the $F$-statistic testing the hypothesis that the true coefficients on $STR^2$ and $STR^3$ are zero is 6.17, with a $p$-value of $< 0.001$).

Regression (6) further examines whether the effect of the student–teacher ratio depends not just on the value of the student–teacher ratio but also on the fraction of English learners. By including interactions between $HiEL$ and $STR$, $STR^2$, and $STR^3$, we can check whether the (possibly cubic) population regressions functions relating test scores and $STR$ are different for low and high percentages of English learners. To do so, we test the restriction that the coefficients on the three interaction terms are zero. The resulting $F$-statistic is 2.69, which has a $p$-value of 0.046 and thus is significant at the 5% but not the 1% significance level. This provides some evidence that the regression functions are different for districts with high and low percentages of English learners; however, comparing regressions (6) and (4) makes it clear that these differences are associated with the quadratic and cubic terms.

Regression (7) is a modification of regression (5), in which the continuous variable $PctEL$ is used instead of the binary variable $HiEL$ to control for the percentage of English learners in the district. The coefficients on the other regressors

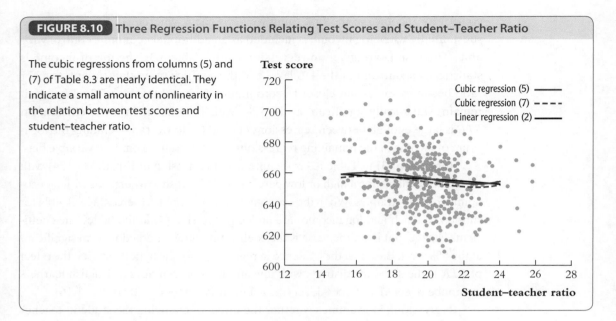

**FIGURE 8.10** Three Regression Functions Relating Test Scores and Student–Teacher Ratio

The cubic regressions from columns (5) and (7) of Table 8.3 are nearly identical. They indicate a small amount of nonlinearity in the relation between test scores and student–teacher ratio.

do not change substantially when this modification is made, indicating that the results in regression (5) are not sensitive to what measure of the percentage of English learners is actually used in the regression.

In all the specifications, the hypothesis that the student–teacher ratio does not enter the regressions is rejected at the 1% level.

The nonlinear specifications in Table 8.3 are most easily interpreted graphically. Figure 8.10 graphs the estimated regression functions relating test scores and the student–teacher ratio for the linear specification (2) and the cubic specifications (5) and (7), along with a scatterplot of the data.[4] These estimated regression functions show the predicted value of test scores as a function of the student–teacher ratio, holding fixed other values of the independent variables in the regression. The estimated regression functions are all close to one another, although the cubic regressions flatten out for large values of the student–teacher ratio.

Regression (6) indicates a statistically significant difference in the cubic regression functions relating test scores and $STR$, depending on whether the percentage of English learners in the district is large or small. Figure 8.11 graphs these two estimated regression functions so that we can see whether this difference, in addition

---

[4]For each curve, the predicted value was computed by setting each independent variable, other than $STR$, to its sample average value and computing the predicted value by multiplying these fixed values of the independent variables by the respective estimated coefficients from Table 8.3. This was done for various values of $STR$, and the graph of the resulting adjusted predicted values is the estimated regression function relating test scores and the $STR$, holding the other variables constant at their sample averages.

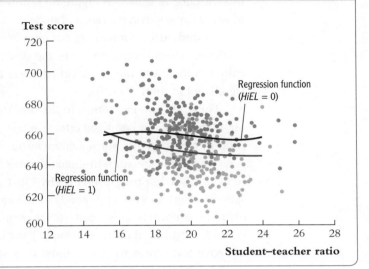

**FIGURE 8.11**   Regression Functions for Districts with High and Low Percentages of English Learners

Districts with low percentages of English learners ($HiEL = 0$) are shown by gray dots, and districts with $HiEL = 1$ are shown by colored dots. The cubic regression function for $HiEL = 1$ from regression (6) in Table 8.3 is approximately 10 points below the cubic regression function for $HiEL = 0$ for $17 \leq STR \leq 23$, but otherwise the two functions have similar shapes and slopes in this range. The slopes of the regression functions differ most for very large and small values of $STR$, for which there are few observations.

to being statistically significant, is of practical importance. As Figure 8.11 shows, for student–teacher ratios between 17 and 23—a range that includes 88% of the observations—the two functions are separated by approximately 10 points but otherwise are very similar; that is, for $STR$ between 17 and 23, districts with a lower percentage of English learners do better, holding constant the student–teacher ratio, but the effect of a change in the student–teacher ratio is essentially the same for the two groups. The two regression functions are different for student–teacher ratios below 16.5, but we must be careful not to read more into this than is justified. The districts with $STR < 16.5$ constitute only 6% of the observations, so the differences between the nonlinear regression functions are reflecting differences in these very few districts with very low student–teacher ratios. Thus, based on Figure 8.11, we conclude that the effect on test scores of a change in the student–teacher ratio does not depend on the percentage of English learners for the range of student–teacher ratios for which we have the most data.

## Summary of Findings

These results let us answer the three questions raised at the start of this section.

First, after controlling for economic background, whether there are many or few English learners in the district does not have a substantial influence on the effect on test scores of a change in the student–teacher ratio. In the linear specifications, there is no statistically significant evidence of such a difference. The cubic specification in regression (6) provides statistically significant evidence (at the 5% level) that the regression functions are different for districts with high and low percentages of English learners; as shown in Figure 8.11, however, the estimated regression functions have similar slopes in the range of student–teacher ratios containing most of our data.

Second, after controlling for economic background, there is evidence of a nonlinear effect on test scores of the student–teacher ratio. This effect is statistically significant at the 1% level (the coefficients on $STR^2$ and $STR^3$ are always significant at the 1% level).

Third, we now can return to the superintendent's problem that opened Chapter 4. She wants to know the effect on test scores of reducing the student–teacher ratio by two students per teacher. In the linear specification (2), this effect does not depend on the student–teacher ratio itself, and the estimated effect of this reduction is to improve test scores by 1.46 ($= -0.73 \times -2$) points. In the nonlinear specifications, this effect depends on the value of the student–teacher ratio. If her district currently has a student–teacher ratio of 20 and she is considering cutting it to 18, then based on regression (5) the estimated effect of this reduction is to improve test scores by 3.00 points, while based on regression (7) this estimate is 2.93. If her district currently has a student–teacher ratio of 22 and she is considering cutting it to 20, then based on regression (5) the estimated effect of this reduction is to improve test scores by 1.93 points, while based on regression (7) this estimate is 1.90. The estimates from the nonlinear specifications suggest that cutting the student–teacher ratio has a greater effect if this ratio is already small.

## 8.5 Conclusion

This chapter presented several ways to model nonlinear regression functions. Because these models are variants of the multiple regression model, the unknown coefficients can be estimated by OLS, and hypotheses about their values can be tested using $t$- and $F$-statistics as described in Chapter 7. In these models, the expected effect on $Y$ of a change in one of the independent variables, $X_1$, holding the other independent variables $X_2, \ldots, X_k$ constant in general depends on the values of $X_1, X_2, \ldots, X_k$.

There are many different models in this chapter, and you could not be blamed for being a bit bewildered about which to use in a given application. How should you analyze possible nonlinearities in practice? Section 8.1 laid out a general approach for such an analysis, but this approach requires you to make decisions and exercise judgment along the way. It would be convenient if there were a single recipe you could follow that would always work in every application, but in practice data analysis is rarely that simple.

The single most important step in specifying nonlinear regression functions is to "use your head." Before you look at the data, can you think of a reason, based on economic theory or expert judgment, why the slope of the population regression function might depend on the value of that, or another, independent variable? If so, what sort of dependence might you expect? And, most important, which nonlinearities (if any) could have major implications for the substantive issues addressed by your study? Answering these questions carefully will focus your analysis. In the test score application, for example, such reasoning led us to investigate whether hiring more teachers might have a greater effect in districts with a large percentage of students still learning English, perhaps because those students would differentially benefit from more personal attention. By making the question precise, we were able to find a precise answer: After controlling for the economic background of the students, we found no statistically significant evidence of such an interaction.

## Summary

1. In a nonlinear regression, the slope of the population regression function depends on the value of one or more of the independent variables.
2. The effect on $Y$ of a change in the independent variable(s) can be computed by evaluating the regression function at two values of the independent variable(s). The procedure is summarized in Key Concept 8.1.
3. A polynomial regression includes powers of $X$ as regressors. A quadratic regression includes $X$ and $X^2$, and a cubic regression includes $X$, $X^2$, and $X^3$.
4. Small changes in logarithms can be interpreted as proportional or percentage changes in a variable. Regressions involving logarithms are used to estimate proportional changes and elasticities.
5. The product of two variables is called an interaction term. When interaction terms are included as regressors, they allow the regression slope of one variable to depend on the value of another variable.

## Key Terms

quadratic regression model (305)
nonlinear regression function (308)
polynomial regression model (313)
cubic regression model (313)
elasticity (315)
exponential function (315)
natural logarithm (316)
linear-log model (317)

log-linear model (320)
log-log model (320)
interaction term (326)
interacted regressor (326)
interaction regression model (326)
nonlinear least squares (357)
nonlinear least squares
     estimators (357)

**MyEconLab Can Help You Get a Better Grade**

MyEconLab  If your exam were tomorrow, would you be ready? For each chapter, **MyEconLab** Practice Tests and Study Plan help you prepare for your exams. You can also find similar Exercises and Review the Concepts Questions now in **MyEconLab**.
To see how it works, turn to the **MyEconLab** spread on pages 2 and 3 of this book and then go to **www.myeconlab.com**.

For additional Empirical Exercises and Data Sets, log on to the Companion Website at **www.pearsonglobaleditions.com/Stock_Watson**.

## Review the Concepts

**8.1** A researcher tells you that there are non-linearities in the relationship between wages and years of schooling. What does this mean? How would you test for non-linearities in the relationship between wages and schooling? How would you estimate the rate of change in wages with respect to years of schooling?

**8.2** A "Cobb–Douglas" production function relates production ($Q$) to factors of production, capital ($K$), labor ($L$), and raw materials ($M$), and an error term $u$ using the equation $Q = \lambda K^{\beta_1} L^{\beta_2} M^{\beta_3} e^u$, where $\lambda$, $\beta_1$, $\beta_2$, and $\beta_3$ are production parameters. Suppose that you have data on production and the factors of production from a random sample of firms with the same Cobb–Douglas production function. How would you use regression analysis to estimate the production parameters?

**8.3** How is the slope coefficient interpreted in a log-linear model, where the dependent variable is (i) in logarithms but the independent variable is not, (ii) in a linear-log model, (iii) in a log-log model?

**8.4** Suppose the regression in Equation (8.30) is estimated using $LoSTR$ and $LoEL$ in place of $HiSTR$ and $HiEL$, where $LoSTR = 1 - HiSTR$ is an indicator for a low-class-size district and $LoEL = 1 - HiEL$ is an indicator for a district with a low percentage of English learners. What are the values of the estimated regression coefficients?

**8.5** Suppose that in Exercise 8.2 you thought that the value of $\beta_2$ was not constant but rather increased when $K$ increased. How could you use an interaction term to capture this effect?

**8.6** What types of independent variables—binary or continuous—may interact with one another in a regression? How do you interpret the coefficient on the interaction between two continuous regressors and two binary regressors?

## Exercises

**8.1**  Sales of a company is \$243 million in 2013, and it increases to \$250 million in 2014.

    **a.**  Compute the percentage increase in sales, using the usual formula $100 \times \frac{(\text{Sales}_{2014} - \text{Sales}_{2013})}{\text{Sales}_{2013}}$. Compare this value to the approximation. $100 \times [\ln(\text{Sales}_{2014}) - \ln(\text{Sales}_{2013})]$.

    **b.**  Repeat (a), assuming that $\text{Sales}_{2014} = 255$, $\text{Sales}_{2014} = 260$, and $\text{Sales}_{2014} = 265$.

    **c.**  How good is the approximation when the change is small? Does the quality of the approximation deteriorate as the percentage change increases?

**8.2**  Suppose a researcher collects data on houses that have been sold in a particular neighborhood over the past year, and obtains the regression results in the table shown below.

    **a.**  Using the results in column (1), what is the expected change in price of building a 1500-square-foot addition to a house? Construct a 99% confidence interval for the percentage change in price.

    **b.**  How is the coefficient on size interpreted in column (2)? What is the effect of a doubling of the size of a house on its price?

    **c.**  Using column (2), what is the estimated effect of view on price? Construct a 99% confidence interval for this effect. Is the effect statistically different from 0?

    **d.**  Use the results from the regression in column (3) to calculate the effect of adding 2 bedrooms to a house. Is the effect statistically significant? Which of the two variables—size or number of bedrooms—do you think is relatively more important in determining the price of a house?

    **e.**  Is the coefficient on condition significant in column (4)?

    **f.**  Is the interaction term between pool and view statistically significant in column (5)? Find the effect of adding a view on the price of a house with a pool, as well as a house without a pool.

**8.3**  After reading this chapter's analysis of test scores and class size, an educator comments, "In my experience, student performance depends on class

**Regression Results for Exercise 8.2**

**Dependent variable: ln(*Price*)**

| Regressor | (1) | (2) | (3) | (4) | (5) |
|---|---|---|---|---|---|
| *Size* | 0.00042 (0.000038) | | | | |
| ln(*Size*) | | 0.69 (0.054) | 0.68 (0.087) | 0.57 (2.03) | 0.69 (0.055) |
| ln(*Size*)$^2$ | | | | 0.0078 (0.14) | |
| *Bedrooms* | | | 0.0036 (0.037) | | |
| *Pool* | 0.082 (0.032) | 0.071 (0.034) | 0.071 (0.034) | 0.071 (0.036) | 0.071 (0.035) |
| *View* | 0.037 (0.029) | 0.027 (0.028) | 0.026 (0.026) | 0.027 (0.029) | 0.027 (0.030) |
| *Pool* × *View* | | | | | 0.0022 (0.10) |
| *Condition* | 0.13 (0.045) | 0.12 (0.035) | 0.12 (0.035) | 0.12 (0.036) | 0.12 (0.035) |
| Intercept | 10.97 (0.069) | 6.60 (0.39) | 6.63 (0.53) | 7.02 (7.50) | 6.60 (0.40) |
| **Summary Statistics** | | | | | |
| *SER* | 0.102 | 0.098 | 0.099 | 0.099 | 0.099 |
| $\overline{R}^2$ | 0.72 | 0.74 | 0.73 | 0.73 | 0.73 |

Variable definitions: *Price* = sale price ($); *Size* = house size (in square feet); *Bedrooms* = number of bedrooms; *Pool* = binary variable (1 if house has a swimming pool, 0 otherwise); *View* = binary variable (1 if house has a nice view, 0 otherwise); *Condition* = binary variable (1 if real estate agent reports house is in excellent condition, 0 otherwise).

size, but not in the way your regressions say. Rather, students do well when class size is less than 20 students and do very poorly when class size is greater than 25. There are no gains from reducing class size below 20 students, the relationship is constant in the intermediate region between 20 and 25 students, and there is no loss to increasing class size when it is already greater than 25." The educator is describing a "threshold effect" in which performance is constant for class sizes less than 20, then jumps and is constant for class sizes between 20 and 25, and then jumps again for class sizes greater than 25. To model these threshold effects, define the binary variables

$$STRsmall = 1 \text{ if } STR < 20, \text{ and } STRsmall = 0 \text{ otherwise};$$

$$STRmoderate = 1 \text{ if } 20 \le STR \le 25, \text{ and } STRmoderate = 0 \text{ otherwise; and}$$

$$STRlarge = 1 \text{ if } STR > 25, \text{ and } STRlarge = 0 \text{ otherwise.}$$

**a.** Consider the regression $TestScore_i = \beta_0 + \beta_1 STRsmall_i + \beta_2 STRlarge_i + u_i$. Sketch the regression function relating $TestScore$ to $STR$ for hypothetical values of the regression coefficients that are consistent with the educator's statement.

**b.** A researcher tries to estimate the regression $TestScore_i = \beta_0 + \beta_1 STRsmall_i + \beta_2 STRmoderate_i + \beta_3 STRlarge_i + u_i$ and finds that the software gives an error message. Why?

**8.4** Read the box "The Return to Education and the Gender Gap" in Section 8.3.

**a.** Consider a man with 16 years of education and 2 years of experience who is from a western state. Use the results from column (4) of Table 8.1 and the method in Key Concept 8.1 to estimate the expected change in the logarithm of average hourly earnings ($AHE$) associated with an additional year of experience.

**b.** Repeat (a), assuming 10 years of experience.

**c.** Explain why the answers to (a) and (b) are different.

**d.** Is the difference in the answers to (a) and (b) statistically significant at the 5% level? Explain.

**e.** Would your answers to (a) through (d) change if the person were a woman? If the person were from the South? Explain.

**f.** How would you change the regression if you suspected that the effect of experience on earnings was different for men than for women?

**8.5** Read the box "The Demand for Economics Journals" in Section 8.3.

**a.** The box reaches three conclusions. Looking at the results in the table, what is the basis for each of these conclusions?

**b.** Using the results in regression (4), the box reports that the elasticity of demand for an 80-year-old journal is $-0.28$.

  i. How was this value determined from the estimated regression?

  ii. The box reports that the standard error for the estimated elasticity is 0.06. How would you calculate this standard error?

(*Hint:* See the discussion "Standard errors of estimated effects" on page 310.)

   **c.** Suppose that the variable *Characters* had been divided by 1000 instead of 1,000,000. How would the results in column (4) change?

**8.6** Refer to Table 8.3.

   **a.** A researcher suspects that the effect of *%Eligible for subsidized lunch* has a nonlinear effect on test scores. In particular, he conjectures that increases in this variable from 10% to 20% have little effect on test scores but that changes from 50% to 60% have a much larger effect.

   i. Describe a nonlinear specification that can be used to model this form of nonlinearity.

   ii. How would you test whether the researcher's conjecture was better than the linear specification in column (7) of Table 8.3?

   **b.** A researcher suspects that the effect of income on test scores is different in districts with small classes than in districts with large classes.

   i. Describe a nonlinear specification that can be used to model this form of nonlinearity.

   ii. How would you test whether the researcher's conjecture was better than the linear specification in column (7) of Table 8.3?

**8.7** This problem is inspired by a study of the "gender gap" in earnings in top corporate jobs [Bertrand and Hallock (2001)]. The study compares total compensation among top executives in a large set of U.S. public corporations in the 1990s. (Each year these publicly traded corporations must report total compensation levels for their top five executives.)

   **a.** Let *Female* be an indicator variable that is equal to 1 for females and 0 for males. A regression of the logarithm of earnings onto *Female* yields

$$\widehat{\ln(Earnings)} = 6.48 - 0.44\,Female,\; SER = 2.65.$$
$$\quad\quad\quad (0.01)\;\; (0.05)$$

   i. The estimated coefficient on *Female* is $-0.44$. Explain what this value means.

   ii. The *SER* is 2.65. Explain what this value means.

   iii. Does this regression suggest that female top executives earn less than top male executives? Explain.

   iv. Does this regression suggest that there is gender discrimination? Explain.

**b.** Two new variables, the market value of the firm (a measure of firm size, in millions of dollars) and stock return (a measure of firm performance, in percentage points), are added to the regression:

$$\widehat{\ln(Earnings)} = 3.86 - 0.28\,Female + 0.37\ln(MarketValue) + 0.004\,Return,$$
$$\qquad\quad (0.03)\quad (0.04)\qquad\qquad (0.004)\qquad\qquad\qquad (0.003)$$
$$n = 46{,}670, \overline{R}^2 = 0.345.$$

    i. The coefficient on $\ln(MarketValue)$ is 0.37. Explain what this value means.

    ii. The coefficient on *Female* is now $-0.28$. Explain why it has changed from the regression in (a).

**c.** Are large firms more likely than small firms to have female top executives? Explain.

**8.8** $X$ is a continuous variable that takes on values between 5 and 100. $Z$ is a binary variable. Sketch the following regression functions (with values of $X$ between 5 and 100 on the horizontal axis and values of $\hat{Y}$ on the vertical axis):

    **a.** $\hat{Y} = 2.0 + 3.0 \times \ln(X)$.

    **b.** $\hat{Y} = 2.0 - 3.0 \times \ln(X)$.

    **c.** i. $\hat{Y} = 2.0 + 3.0 \times \ln(X) + 4.0Z$, with $Z = 1$.

       ii. Same as (i), but with $Z = 0$.

    **d.** i. $\hat{Y} = 2.0 + 3.0 \times \ln(X) + 4.0Z - 1.0 \times Z \times \ln(X)$, with $Z = 1$.

       ii. Same as (i), but with $Z = 0$.

    **e.** $\hat{Y} = 1.0 + 125.0X - 0.01X^2$.

**8.9** Explain how you would use Approach #2 from Section 7.3 to calculate the confidence interval discussed below Equation (8.8). [*Hint:* This requires estimating a new regression using a different definition of the regressors and the dependent variable. See Exercise (7.9).]

**8.10** Consider the regression model $Y_i = \beta_0 + \beta_1 X_{1i} + \beta_2 X_{2i} + \beta_3(X_{1i} \times X_{2i}) + u_i$. Use Key Concept 8.1 to show:

    **a.** $\Delta Y/\Delta X_1 = \beta_1 + \beta_3 X_2$ (effect of change in $X_1$, holding $X_2$ constant).

    **b.** $\Delta Y/\Delta X_2 = \beta_2 + \beta_3 X_1$ (effect of change in $X_2$, holding $X_1$ constant).

    **c.** If $X_1$ changes by $\Delta X_1$ and $X_2$ changes by $\Delta X_2$, then $\Delta Y = (\beta_1 + \beta_3 X_2)\Delta X_1 + (\beta_2 + \beta_3 X_1)\Delta X_2 + \beta_3 \Delta X_1 \Delta X_2$.

**8.11** Derive the expressions for the elasticities given in Appendix 8.2 for the linear and log-log models. (*Hint:* For the log-log model, assume that $u$

and $X$ are independent, as is done in Appendix 8.2 for the log-linear model.)

**8.12** The discussion following Equation (8.28) interprets the coefficient on interacted binary variables using the conditional mean zero assumption. This exercise shows that interpretation also applies under conditional mean independence. Consider the hypothetical experiment in Exercise 7.11.

   **a.** Suppose that you estimate the regression $Y_i = \gamma_0 + \gamma_1 X_{1i} + u_i$ using only the data on returning students. Show that $\gamma_1$ is the class size effect for returning students—that is, that $\gamma_1 = E(Y_i | X_{1i} = 1, X_{2i} = 0) - E(Y_i | X_{1i} = 0, X_{2i} = 0)$. Explain why $\hat{\gamma}_1$ is an unbiased estimator of $\gamma_1$.

   **b.** Suppose that you estimate the regression $Y_i = \delta_0 + \delta_1 X_{1i} + u_i$ using only the data on new students. Show that $\delta_1$ is the class size effect for new students—that is, that $\delta_1 = E(Y_i | X_{1i} = 1, X_{2i} = 1) - E(Y_i | X_{1i} = 0, X_{2i} = 1)$. Explain why $\hat{\delta}_1$ is an unbiased estimator of $\delta_1$.

   **c.** Consider the regression for both returning and new students, $Y_i = \beta_0 + \beta_1 X_{1i} + \beta_2 X_{2i} + \beta_3(X_{1i} \times X_{2i}) + u_i$. Use the conditional mean independence assumption $E(u_i | X_{1i}, X_{2i}) = E(u_i | X_{2i})$ to show that $\beta_1 = \gamma_1$, $\beta_1 + \beta_3 = \delta_1$, and $\beta_3 = \delta_1 - \gamma_1$ (the difference in the class size effects).

   **d.** Suppose that you estimate the interaction regression in (c) using the combined data and that $E(u_i | X_{1i}, X_{2i}) = E(u_i | X_{2i})$. Show that $\hat{\beta}_1$ and $\hat{\beta}_3$ are unbiased but that $\hat{\beta}_2$ is in general biased.

## Empirical Exercises

(Only two empirical exercises for this chapter are given in the text, but you can find more on the text website **www.pearsonglobaleditions.com/Stock_Watson**.)

**E8.1** Lead is toxic, particularly for young children, and for this reason government regulations severely restrict the amount of lead in our environment. But this was not always the case. In the early part of the 20th century, the underground water pipes in many U.S. cities contained lead, and lead from these pipes leached into drinking water. In this exercise you will investigate the effect of these lead water pipes on infant mortality. On the text website **www.pearsonglobaleditions.com/Stock_Watson**, you will find the data file **Lead_Mortality**, which contains data on infant mortality, type of water pipes (lead or non-lead), water acidity (pH), and several demographic variables for 172 U.S. cities in 1900.[5] A detailed description is given in **Lead_Mortality_ Description**, also available on the website.

**a.** Compute the average infant mortality rate (*Inf*) for cities with lead pipes and for cities with non-lead pipes. Is there a statistically significant difference in the averages?

**b.** The amount of lead leached from lead pipes depends on the chemistry of the water running through the pipes. The more acidic the water (that is, the lower its pH), the more lead is leached. Run a regression of *Inf* on *Lead*, *pH*, and the interaction term *Lead* $\times$ *pH*.

   i. The regression includes four coefficients (the intercept and the three coefficients multiplying the regressors). Explain what each coefficient measures.

   ii. Plot the estimated regression function relating *Inf* to *pH* for *Lead* = 0 and for *Lead* = 1. Describe the differences in the regression functions and relate these differences to the coefficients you discussed in (i).

   iii. Does *Lead* have a statistically significant effect on infant mortality? Explain.

   iv. Does the effect of *Lead* on infant mortality depend on *pH*? Is this dependence statistically significant?

   v. What is the average value of *pH* in the sample? At this *pH* level, what is the estimated effect of *Lead* on infant mortality? What is the standard deviation of *pH*? Suppose that the *pH* level is one standard deviation lower than the average level of *pH* in the sample; what is the estimated effect of *Lead* on infant mortality? What if *pH* is one standard deviation higher than the average value?

   vi. Construct a 95% confidence interval for the effect of *Lead* on infant mortality when *pH* = 6.5.

**c.** The analysis in (b) may suffer from omitted variable bias because it neglects factors that affect infant mortality and that might potentially be correlated with *Lead* and *pH*. Investigate this concern, using the other variables in the data set.

---

[5]These data were provided by Professor Karen Clay of Carnegie Mellon University and were used in her paper with Werner Troesken and Michael Haines, "Lead and Mortality," *The Review of Economics and Statistics,* 2014, 96(3).

**E8.2**    On the text website **www.pearsonglobaleditions.com/Stock_Watson** you will find a data file **CPS12**, which contains data for full-time, full-year workers, ages 25–34, with a high school diploma or B.A./B.S. as their highest degree. A detailed description is given in **CPS12_Description**, also available on the website. (These are the same data as in **CPS92_12**, used in Empirical Exercise 3.1, but are limited to the year 2012.) In this exercise, you will investigate the relationship between a worker's age and earnings. (Generally, older workers have more job experience, leading to higher productivity and higher earnings.)

**a.** Run a regression of average hourly earnings (*AHE*) on age (*Age*), gender (*Female*), and education (*Bachelor*). If *Age* increases from 25 to 26, how are earnings expected to change? If *Age* increases from 33 to 34, how are earnings expected to change?

**b.** Run a regression of the logarithm of average hourly earnings, ln(*AHE*), on *Age*, *Female*, and *Bachelor*. If *Age* increases from 25 to 26, how are earnings expected to change? If *Age* increases from 33 to 34, how are earnings expected to change?

**c.** Run a regression of the logarithm of average hourly earnings, ln(*AHE*), on ln(*Age*), *Female*, and *Bachelor*. If *Age* increases from 25 to 26, how are earnings expected to change? If *Age* increases from 33 to 34, how are earnings expected to change?

**d.** Run a regression of the logarithm of average hourly earnings, ln(*AHE*), on *Age*, $Age^2$, *Female*, and *Bachelor*. If *Age* increases from 25 to 26, how are earnings expected to change? If *Age* increases from 33 to 34, how are earnings expected to change?

**e.** Do you prefer the regression in (c) to the regression in (b)? Explain.

**f.** Do you prefer the regression in (d) to the regression in (b)? Explain.

**g.** Do you prefer the regression in (d) to the regression in (c)? Explain.

**h.** Plot the regression relation between *Age* and ln(*AHE*) from (b), (c), and (d) for males with a high school diploma. Describe the similarities and differences between the estimated regression functions. Would your answer change if you plotted the regression function for females with college degrees?

   i. Run a regression of ln(*AHE*) on *Age*, $Age^2$, *Female*, *Bachelor*, and the interaction term *Female* × *Bachelor*. What does the coefficient on the interaction term measure? Alexis is a 30-year-old female with a bachelor's degree. What does the regression predict for her value of ln(*AHE*)? Jane is a 30-year-old female with a high school degree. What does the regression predict for her value of ln(*AHE*)? What is the predicted difference between Alexis's and Jane's earnings? Bob is a 30-year-old male with a bachelor's degree. What does the regression predict for his value of ln(*AHE*)? Jim is a 30-year-old male with a high school degree. What does the regression predict for his value of ln(*AHE*)? What is the predicted difference between Bob's and Jim's earnings?

**j.** Is the effect of *Age* on earnings different for men than for women? Specify and estimate a regression that you can use to answer this question.

**k.** Is the effect of *Age* on earnings different for high school graduates than for college graduates? Specify and estimate a regression that you can use to answer this question.

**l.** After running all these regressions (and any others that you want to run), summarize the effect of age on earnings for young workers.

APPENDIX

# 8.1  Regression Functions That Are Nonlinear in the Parameters

The nonlinear regression functions considered in Sections 8.2 and 8.3 are nonlinear functions of the *X*'s but are linear functions of the unknown parameters. Because they are linear in the unknown parameters, those parameters can be estimated by OLS after defining new regressors that are nonlinear transformations of the original *X*'s. This family of nonlinear regression functions is both rich and convenient to use. In some applications, however, economic reasoning leads to regression functions that are not linear in the parameters. Although such regression functions cannot be estimated by OLS, they can be estimated using an extension of OLS called nonlinear least squares.

## Functions That Are Nonlinear in the Parameters

We begin with two examples of functions that are nonlinear in the parameters. We then provide a general formulation.

*Logistic curve.* Suppose that you are studying the market penetration of a technology, such as the adoption of database management software in different industries. The dependent variable is the fraction of firms in the industry that have adopted the software, a single

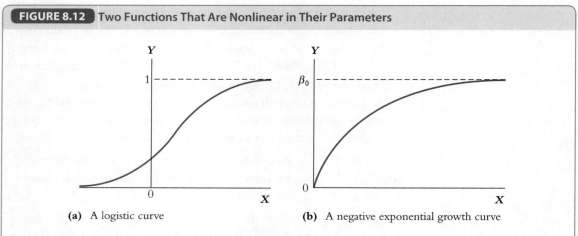

**FIGURE 8.12** Two Functions That Are Nonlinear in Their Parameters

(a) A logistic curve

(b) A negative exponential growth curve

Part (a) plots the logistic function of Equation (8.38), which has predicted values that lie between 0 and 1. Part (b) plots the negative exponential growth function of Equation (8.39), which has a slope that is always positive and decreases as $X$ increases, and an asymptote at $\beta_0$ as $X$ tends to infinity.

independent variable $X$ describes an industry characteristic, and you have data on $n$ industries. The dependent variable is between 0 (no adopters) and 1 (100% adoption). Because a linear regression model could produce predicted values less than 0 or greater than 1, it makes sense to use instead a function that produces predicted values between 0 and 1.

The logistic function smoothly increases from a minimum of 0 to a maximum of 1. The logistic regression model with a single $X$ is

$$Y_i = \frac{1}{1 + e^{-(\beta_0 + \beta_1 X_i)}} + u_i. \tag{8.38}$$

The logistic function with a single $X$ is graphed in Figure 8.12a. As can be seen in the graph, the logistic function has an elongated "S" shape. For small values of $X$, the value of the function is nearly 0 and the slope is flat; the curve is steeper for moderate values of $X$; and for large values of $X$, the function approaches 1 and the slope is flat again.

*Negative exponential growth.* The functions used in Section 8.2 to model the relation between test scores and income have some deficiencies. For example, the polynomial models can produce a negative slope for some values of income, which is implausible. The logarithmic specification has a positive slope for all values of income; however, as income gets very large, the predicted values increase without bound, so for some incomes the predicted value for a district will exceed the maximum possible score on the test.

The negative exponential growth model provides a nonlinear specification that has a positive slope for all values of income, has a slope that is greatest at low values of income and decreases as income rises, and has an upper bound (that is, an asymptote as income increases to infinity). The negative exponential growth regression model is

$$Y_i = \beta_0[1 - e^{-\beta_1(X_i - \beta_2)}] + u_i. \tag{8.39}$$

The negative exponential growth function is graphed in Figure 8.12b. The slope is steep for low values of $X$, but as $X$ increases, it reaches an asymptote of $\beta_0$.

*General functions that are nonlinear in the parameters.* The logistic and negative exponential growth regression models are special cases of the general nonlinear regression model

$$Y_i = f(X_{1i}, \ldots, X_{ki}; \beta_0, \ldots, \beta_m) + u_i, \tag{8.40}$$

in which there are $k$ independent variables and $m + 1$ parameters, $\beta_0, \ldots, \beta_m$. In the models of Sections 8.2 and 8.3, the $X$'s entered this function nonlinearly, but the parameters entered linearly. In the examples of this appendix, the parameters enter nonlinearly as well. If the parameters are known, then predicted effects can be computed using the method described in Section 8.1. In applications, however, the parameters are unknown and must be estimated from the data. Parameters that enter nonlinearly cannot be estimated by OLS, but they can be estimated by nonlinear least squares.

## Nonlinear Least Squares Estimation

Nonlinear least squares is a general method for estimating the unknown parameters of a regression function when those parameters enter the population regression function nonlinearly.

Recall the discussion in Section 5.3 of the OLS estimator of the coefficients of the linear multiple regression model. The OLS estimator minimizes the sum of squared prediction mistakes in Equation (5.8), $\sum_{i=1}^{n}[Y_i - (b_0 + b_1X_{1i} + \cdots + b_kX_{ki})]^2$. In principle, the OLS estimator can be computed by checking many trial values of $b_0, \ldots, b_k$ and settling on the values that minimize the sum of squared mistakes.

This same approach can be used to estimate the parameters of the general nonlinear regression model in Equation (8.40). Because the regression function is nonlinear in the coefficients, this method is called **nonlinear least squares**. For a set of trial parameter values $b_0, b_1, \ldots, b_m$ construct the sum of squared prediction mistakes:

$$\sum_{i=1}^{n}[Y_i - f(X_{1i}, \ldots, X_{ki}; b_1, \ldots, b_m)]^2. \tag{8.41}$$

The **nonlinear least squares estimators** of $\beta_0, \beta_1, \ldots, \beta_m$ are the values of $b_0, b_1, \ldots, b_m$ that minimize the sum of squared prediction mistakes in Equation (8.41).

---

**FIGURE 8.13** The Negative Exponential Growth and Linear-Log Regression Functions

The negative exponential growth regression function [Equation (8.42)] and the linear-log regression function [Equation (8.18)] both capture the nonlinear relation between test scores and district income. One difference between the two functions is that the negative exponential growth model has an asymptote as *Income* increases to infinity, but the linear-log regression function does not.

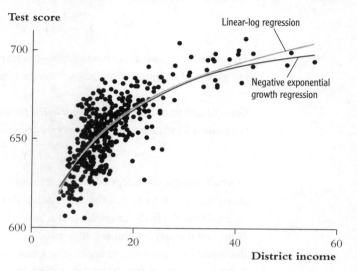

---

In linear regression, a relatively simple formula expresses the OLS estimator as a function of the data. Unfortunately, no such general formula exists for nonlinear least squares, so the nonlinear least squares estimator must be found numerically using a computer. Regression software incorporates algorithms for solving the nonlinear least squares minimization problem, which simplifies the task of computing the nonlinear least squares estimator in practice.

Under general conditions on the function $f$ and the $X$'s, the nonlinear least squares estimator shares two key properties with the OLS estimator in the linear regression model: It is consistent, and it is normally distributed in large samples. In regression software that supports nonlinear least squares estimation, the output typically reports standard errors for the estimated parameters. As a consequence, inference concerning the parameters can proceed as usual; in particular, $t$-statistics can be constructed using the general approach in Key Concept 5.1, and a 95% confidence interval can be constructed as the estimated coefficient, plus or minus 1.96 standard errors. Just as in linear regression, the error term in the nonlinear regression model can be heteroskedastic, so heteroskedasticity-robust standard errors should be used.

## Application to the Test Score–Income Relation

A negative exponential growth model, fit to district income ($X$) and test scores ($Y$), has the desirable features of a slope that is always positive [if $\beta_1$ in Equation (8.39) is positive] and an asymptote of $\beta_0$ as income increases to infinity. The result of estimating $\beta_0$, $\beta_1$, and $\beta_2$ in

Equation (8.39) using the California test score data yields $\hat{\beta}_0 = 703.2$ (heteroskedasticity-robust standard error $= 4.44$), $\hat{\beta}_1 = 0.0552$ ($SE = 0.0068$), and $\hat{\beta}_2 = -34.0$ ($SE = 4.48$). Thus the estimated nonlinear regression function (with standard errors reported below the parameter estimates) is

$$\widehat{TestScore} = 703.2[1 - e^{-0.0552(Income + 34.0)}].$$
$$\quad\quad\quad\quad\quad (4.44) \quad\quad\quad (0.0068) \quad (4.48) \tag{8.42}$$

This estimated regression function is plotted in Figure 8.13, along with the logarithmic regression function and a scatterplot of the data. The two specifications are, in this case, quite similar. One difference is that the negative exponential growth curve flattens out at the highest levels of income, consistent with having an asymptote.

---

**APPENDIX**

# 8.2 Slopes and Elasticities for Nonlinear Regression Functions

This appendix uses calculus to evaluate slopes and elasticities of nonlinear regression functions with continuous regressors. We focus on the case of Section 8.2, in which there is a single $X$. This approach extends to multiple $X$'s, using partial derivatives.

Consider the nonlinear regression model, $Y_i = f(X_i) + u_i$, with $E(u_i|X_i) = 0$. The slope of the population regression function, $f(X)$, evaluated at the point $X = x$, is the derivative of $f$, that is, $df(X)/dX|_{X=x}$. For the polynomial regression function in Equation (8.9), $f(X) = \beta_0 + \beta_1 X + \beta_2 X^2 + \cdots + \beta_r X^r$ and $dX^a/dX = aX^{a-1}$ for any constant $a$, so $df(X)/dX|_{X=x} = \beta_1 + 2\beta_2 x + \cdots + r\beta_r x^{r-1}$. The estimated slope at $x$ is $d\hat{f}(X)/dX|_{X=x} = \hat{\beta}_1 + 2\hat{\beta}_2 x + \cdots + r\hat{\beta}_r x^{r-1}$. The standard error of the estimated slope is $SE(\hat{\beta}_1 + 2\hat{\beta}_2 x + \cdots + r\hat{\beta}_r x^{r-1})$; for a given value of $x$, this is the standard error of a weighted sum of regression coefficients, which can be computed using the methods of Section 7.3 and Equation (8.8).

The elasticity of $Y$ with respect to $X$ is the percentage change in $Y$ for a given percentage change in $X$. Formally, this definition applies in the limit that the percentage change in $X$ goes to zero, so the slope appearing in the definition in Equation (8.22) is replaced by the derivative and the elasticity is

$$\text{elasticity of } Y \text{ with respect to } X = \frac{dY}{dX} \times \frac{X}{Y} = \frac{d \ln Y}{d \ln X}.$$

In a regression model, $Y$ depends both on $X$ and on the error term $u$. Because $u$ is random, it is conventional to evaluate the elasticity as the percentage change not of $Y$ but of the predicted component of $Y$—that is, the percentage change in $E(Y|X)$. Accordingly, the elasticity of $E(Y|X)$ with respect to $X$ is

$$\frac{dE(Y|X)}{dX} \times \frac{X}{E(Y|X)} = \frac{d \ln E(Y|X)}{d \ln X}.$$

The elasticities for the linear model and for the three logarithmic models summarized in Key Concept 8.2 are given in the table below.

| Case | Population Regression Model | Elasticity of $E(Y\|X)$ with Respect to $X$ |
|---|---|---|
| linear | $Y = \beta_0 + \beta_1 X + u$ | $\dfrac{\beta_1 X}{\beta_0 + \beta_1 X}$ |
| linear-log | $Y = \beta_0 + \beta_1 \ln(X) + u$ | $\dfrac{\beta_1}{\beta_0 + \beta_1 \ln(X)}$ |
| log-linear | $\ln(Y) = \beta_0 + \beta_1 X + u$ | $\beta_1 X$ |
| log-log | $\ln(Y) = \beta_0 + \beta_1 \ln(X) + u$ | $\beta_1$ |

The log-log specification has a constant elasticity, but in the other three specifications, the elasticity depends on $X$.

We now derive the expressions for the linear-log and log-linear models. For the linear-log model, $E(Y|X) = \beta_0 + \beta_1 \ln(X)$. Because $d\ln(X)/dX = 1/X$, applying the chain rule yields $dE(Y|X)/dX = \beta_1/X$. Thus the elasticity is $dE(Y|X)/dX \times X/E(Y|X) = (\beta_1/X) \times X/[\beta_0 + \beta_1\ln(X)] = \beta_1/[\beta_0 + \beta_1\ln(X)]$, as is given in the table. For the log-linear model, it is conventional to make the additional assumption that $u$ and $X$ are independently distributed, so the expression for $E(Y|X)$ given following Equation (8.25) becomes $E(Y|X) = ce^{\beta_0 + \beta_1 X}$, where $c = E(e^u)$ is a constant that does not depend on $X$ because of the additional assumption that $u$ and $X$ are independent. Thus $dE(Y|X)/dX = ce^{\beta_0+\beta_1 X}\beta_1$ and the elasticity is $dE(Y|X)/dX \times X/E(Y|X) = ce^{\beta_0+\beta_1 X}\beta_1 \times X/(ce^{\beta_0+\beta_1 X}) = \beta_1 X$. The derivations for the linear and log-log models are left as Exercise 8.11.

# Assessing Studies Based on Multiple Regression

The preceding five chapters explain how to use multiple regression to analyze the relationship among variables in a data set. In this chapter, we step back and ask, What makes a study that uses multiple regression reliable or unreliable? We focus on statistical studies that have the objective of estimating the causal effect of a change in some independent variable, such as class size, on a dependent variable, such as test scores. For such studies, when will multiple regression provide a useful estimate of the causal effect, and, just as importantly, when will it fail to do so?

To answer these questions, this chapter presents a framework for assessing statistical studies in general, whether or not they use regression analysis. This framework relies on the concepts of internal and external validity. A study is internally valid if its statistical inferences about causal effects are valid for the population and setting studied; it is externally valid if its inferences can be generalized to other populations and settings. In Sections 9.1 and 9.2, we discuss internal and external validity, list a variety of possible threats to internal and external validity, and discuss how to identify those threats in practice. The discussion in Sections 9.1 and 9.2 focuses on the estimation of causal effects from observational data. Section 9.3 discusses a different use of regression models—forecasting—and provides an introduction to the threats to the validity of forecasts made using regression models.

As an illustration of the framework of internal and external validity, in Section 9.4 we assess the internal and external validity of the study of the effect on test scores of cutting the student–teacher ratio presented in Chapters 4 through 8.

## 9.1 Internal and External Validity

The concepts of internal and external validity, defined in Key Concept 9.1, provide a framework for evaluating whether a statistical or econometric study is useful for answering a specific question of interest.

Internal and external validity distinguish between the population and setting studied and the population and setting to which the results are generalized. The **population studied** is the population of entities—people, companies, school districts, and so forth—from which the sample was drawn. The population to which

**KEY CONCEPT**

**9.1**

## Internal and External Validity

A statistical analysis is said to have **internal validity** if the statistical inferences about causal effects are valid for the population being studied. The analysis is said to have **external validity** if its inferences and conclusions can be generalized from the population and setting studied to other populations and settings.

the results are generalized, or the **population of interest**, is the population of entities to which the causal inferences from the study are to be applied. For example, a high school (grades 9 through 12) principal might want to generalize our findings on class sizes and test scores in California elementary school districts (the population studied) to the population of high schools (the population of interest).

By "setting," we mean the institutional, legal, social, and economic environment. For example, it would be important to know whether the findings of a laboratory experiment assessing methods for growing organic tomatoes could be generalized to the field, that is, whether the organic methods that work in the setting of a laboratory also work in the setting of the real world. We provide other examples of differences in populations and settings later in this section.

## Threats to Internal Validity

Internal validity has two components. First, the estimator of the causal effect should be unbiased and consistent. For example, if $\hat{\beta}_{STR}$ is the OLS estimator of the effect on test scores of a unit change in the student–teacher ratio in a certain regression, then $\hat{\beta}_{STR}$ should be an unbiased and consistent estimator of the true population causal effect of a change in the student–teacher ratio, $\beta_{STR}$.

Second, hypothesis tests should have the desired significance level (the actual rejection rate of the test under the null hypothesis should equal its desired significance level), and confidence intervals should have the desired confidence level. For example, if a confidence interval is constructed as $\hat{\beta}_{STR} \pm 1.96\,SE(\hat{\beta}_{STR})$, this confidence interval should contain the true population causal effect, $\beta_{STR}$, with probability 95% over repeated samples.

In regression analysis, causal effects are estimated using the estimated regression function, and hypothesis tests are performed using the estimated regression coefficients and their standard errors. Accordingly, in a study based on OLS regression, the requirements for internal validity are that the OLS estimator is unbiased and consistent, and that standard errors are computed in a way that makes confidence intervals have the desired confidence level. For various reasons these requirements might not be met, and these reasons constitute threats to internal validity. These threats lead to failures of one or more of the least squares assumptions in Key Concept 6.4. For example, one threat that we have discussed at length is omitted variable bias; it leads to correlation between one or more regressors and the error term, which violates the first least squares assumption. If data are available on the omitted variable or on an adequate control variable, then this threat can be avoided by including that variable as an additional regressor.

Section 9.2 provides a detailed discussion of the various threats to internal validity in multiple regression analysis and suggests how to mitigate them.

## Threats to External Validity

Potential threats to external validity arise from differences between the population and setting studied and the population and setting of interest.

*Differences in populations.*  Differences between the population studied and the population of interest can pose a threat to external validity. For example, laboratory studies of the toxic effects of chemicals typically use animal populations like mice (the population studied), but the results are used to write health and safety regulations for human populations (the population of interest). Whether mice and men differ sufficiently to threaten the external validity of such studies is a matter of debate.

More generally, the true causal effect might not be the same in the population studied and the population of interest. This could be because the population was chosen in a way that makes it different from the population of interest, because of differences in characteristics of the populations, because of geographical differences, or because the study is out of date.

*Differences in settings.*  Even if the population being studied and the population of interest are identical, it might not be possible to generalize the study results if the settings differ. For example, a study of the effect on college binge drinking of an antidrinking advertising campaign might not generalize to another identical group of college students if the legal penalties for drinking at the two colleges differ. In this case, the legal setting in which the study was conducted differs from the legal setting to which its results are applied.

More generally, examples of differences in settings include differences in the institutional environment (public universities versus religious universities), differences in laws (differences in legal penalties), or differences in the physical environment (tailgate-party binge drinking in southern California versus Fairbanks, Alaska).

*Application to test scores and the student–teacher ratio.* Chapters 7 and 8 reported statistically significant, but substantively small, estimated improvements in test scores resulting from reducing the student–teacher ratio. This analysis was based on test results for California school districts. Suppose for the moment that these results are internally valid. To what other populations and settings of interest could this finding be generalized?

The closer the population and setting of the study are to those of interest, the stronger the case for external validity. For example, college students and college instruction are very different from elementary school students and instruction, so it is implausible that the effect of reducing class sizes estimated using the California elementary school district data would generalize to colleges. On the other hand, elementary school students, curriculum, and organization are broadly similar throughout the United States, so it is plausible that the California results might generalize to performance on standardized tests in other U.S. elementary school districts.

*How to assess the external validity of a study.* External validity must be judged using specific knowledge of the populations and settings studied and those of interest. Important differences between the two will cast doubt on the external validity of the study.

Sometimes there are two or more studies on different but related populations. If so, the external validity of both studies can be checked by comparing their results. For example, in Section 9.4 we analyze test score and class size data for elementary school districts in Massachusetts and compare the Massachusetts and California results. In general, similar findings in two or more studies bolster claims to external validity, while differences in their findings that are not readily explained cast doubt on their external validity.[1]

*How to design an externally valid study.* Because threats to external validity stem from a lack of comparability of populations and settings, these threats are best minimized at the early stages of a study, before the data are collected. Study design is beyond the scope of this textbook, and the interested reader is referred to Shadish, Cook, and Campbell (2002).

---

[1]A comparison of many related studies on the same topic is called a meta-analysis. The discussion in the box "The Mozart Effect: Omitted Variable Bias?" in Chapter 6 is based on a meta-analysis, for example. Performing a meta-analysis of many studies has its own challenges. How do you sort the good studies from the bad? How do you compare studies when the dependent variables differ? Should you put more weight on studies with larger samples? A discussion of meta-analysis and its challenges goes beyond the scope of this textbook. The interested reader is referred to Hedges and Olkin (1985) and Cooper and Hedges (1994).

# 9.2   Threats to Internal Validity of Multiple Regression Analysis

Studies based on regression analysis are internally valid if the estimated regression coefficients are unbiased and consistent, and if their standard errors yield confidence intervals with the desired confidence level. This section surveys five reasons why the OLS estimator of the multiple regression coefficients might be biased, even in large samples: omitted variables, misspecification of the functional form of the regression function, imprecise measurement of the independent variables ("errors in variables"), sample selection, and simultaneous causality. All five sources of bias arise because the regressor is correlated with the error term in the population regression, violating the first least squares assumption in Key Concept 6.4. For each, we discuss what can be done to reduce this bias. The section concludes with a discussion of circumstances that lead to inconsistent standard errors and what can be done about it.

## Omitted Variable Bias

Recall that omitted variable bias arises when a variable that both determines $Y$ and is correlated with one or more of the included regressors is omitted from the regression. This bias persists even in large samples, so the OLS estimator is inconsistent. How best to minimize omitted variable bias depends on whether or not variables that adequately control for the potential omitted variable are available.

*Solutions to omitted variable bias when the variable is observed or there are adequate control variables.* If you have data on the omitted variable, then you can include that variable in a multiple regression, thereby addressing the problem. Alternatively, if you have data on one or more control variables and if these control variables are adequate in the sense that they lead to conditional mean independence [Equation (7.20)], then including those control variables eliminates the potential bias in the coefficient on the variable of interest.

Adding a variable to a regression has both costs and benefits. On the one hand, omitting the variable could result in omitted variable bias. On the other hand, including the variable when it does not belong (that is, when its population regression coefficient is zero) reduces the precision of the estimators of the other regression coefficients. In other words, the decision whether to include a variable involves a trade-off between bias and variance of the coefficient of interest. In practice, there are four steps that can help you decide whether to include a variable or set of variables in a regression.

The first step is to identify the key coefficient or coefficients of interest in your regression. In the test score regressions, this is the coefficient on the student–teacher ratio, because the question originally posed concerns the effect on test scores of reducing the student–teacher ratio.

The second step is to ask yourself: What are the most likely sources of important omitted variable bias in this regression? Answering this question requires applying economic theory and expert knowledge, and should occur before you actually run any regressions; because this step is done before analyzing the data, it is referred to as *a priori* ("before the fact") reasoning. In the test score example, this step entails identifying those determinants of test scores that, if ignored, could bias our estimator of the class size effect. The results of this step are a base regression specification, the starting point for your empirical regression analysis, and a list of additional "questionable" variables that might help to mitigate possible omitted variable bias.

The third step is to augment your base specification with the additional questionable control variables identified in the second step. If the coefficients on the additional control variables are statistically significant or if the estimated coefficients of interest change appreciably when the additional variables are included, then they should remain in the specification and you should modify your base specification. If not, then these variables can be excluded from the regression.

The fourth step is to present an accurate summary of your results in tabular form. This provides "full disclosure" to a potential skeptic, who can then draw his or her own conclusions. Table 7.1 and 8.3 are examples of this strategy. For example, in Table 8.3, we could have presented only the regression in column (7), because that regression summarizes the relevant effects and nonlinearities in the other regressions in that table. Presenting the other regressions, however, permits the skeptical reader to draw his or her own conclusions.

These steps are summarized in Key Concept 9.2.

*Solutions to omitted variable bias when adequate control variables are not available.* Adding an omitted variable to a regression is not an option if you do not have data on that variable and if there are no adequate control variables. Still, there are three other ways to solve omitted variable bias. Each of these three solutions circumvents omitted variable bias through the use of different types of data.

The first solution is to use data in which the same observational unit is observed at different points in time. For example, test score and related data might be collected for the same districts in 1995 and again in 2000. Data in this form are called panel data. As explained in Chapter 10, panel data make it possible to control for unobserved omitted variables as long as those omitted variables do not change over time.

## Omitted Variable Bias: Should I Include More Variables in My Regression?

If you include another variable in your multiple regression, you will eliminate the possibility of omitted variable bias from excluding that variable, but the variance of the estimator of the coefficients of interest can increase. Here are some guidelines to help you decide whether to include an additional variable:

1. Be specific about the coefficient or coefficients of interest.

2. Use *a priori* reasoning to identify the most important potential sources of omitted variable bias, leading to a base specification and some "questionable" variables.

3. Test whether additional "questionable" control variables have nonzero coefficients.

4. Provide "full disclosure" representative tabulations of your results so that others can see the effect of including the questionable variables on the coefficient(s) of interest. Do your results change if you include a questionable control variable?

The second solution is to use instrumental variables regression. This method relies on a new variable, called an instrumental variable. Instrumental variables regression is discussed in Chapter 12.

The third solution is to use a study design in which the effect of interest (for example, the effect of reducing class size on student achievement) is studied using a randomized controlled experiment. Randomized controlled experiments are discussed in Chapter 13.

### Misspecification of the Functional Form of the Regression Function

If the true population regression function is nonlinear but the estimated regression is linear, then this **functional form misspecification** makes the OLS estimator biased. This bias is a type of omitted variable bias, in which the omitted variables are the terms that reflect the missing nonlinear aspects of the regression function. For example, if the population regression function is a quadratic polynomial, then a regression that omits the square of the independent variable would suffer from omitted variable bias. Bias arising from functional form misspecification is summarized in Key Concept 9.3.

KEY CONCEPT

9.3

## Functional Form Misspecification

Functional form misspecification arises when the functional form of the estimated regression function differs from the functional form of the population regression function. If the functional form is misspecified, then the estimator of the partial effect of a change in one of the variables will, in general, be biased. Functional form misspecification often can be detected by plotting the data and the estimated regression function, and it can be corrected by using a different functional form.

*Solutions to functional form misspecification.* When the dependent variable is continuous (like test scores), this problem of potential nonlinearity can be solved using the methods of Chapter 8. If, however, the dependent variable is discrete or binary (for example, $Y_i$ equals 1 if the $i^{th}$ person attended college and equals 0 otherwise), things are more complicated. Regression with a discrete dependent variable is discussed in Chapter 11.

## Measurement Error and Errors-in-Variables Bias

Suppose that in our regression of test scores against the student–teacher ratio we had inadvertently mixed up our data so that we ended up regressing test scores for fifth graders on the student–teacher ratio for tenth graders in that district. Although the student–teacher ratio for elementary school students and tenth graders might be correlated, they are not the same, so this mix-up would lead to bias in the estimated coefficient. This is an example of **errors-in-variables bias** because its source is an error in the measurement of the independent variable. This bias persists even in very large samples, so the OLS estimator is inconsistent if there is measurement error.

There are many possible sources of measurement error. If the data are collected through a survey, a respondent might give the wrong answer. For example, one question in the Current Population Survey involves last year's earnings. A respondent might not know his or her exact earnings or might misstate the amount for some other reason. If instead the data are obtained from computerized administrative records, there might have been typographical errors when the data were first entered.

To see that errors in variables can result in correlation between the regressor and the error term, suppose that there is a single regressor $X_i$ (say, actual earnings) but that $X_i$ is measured imprecisely by $\widetilde{X}_i$ (the respondent's stated earnings). Because $\widetilde{X}_i$, not $X_i$, is observed, the regression equation actually estimated is the one based on $\widetilde{X}_i$. Written in terms of the imprecisely measured variable $\widetilde{X}_i$, the population regression equation $Y_i = \beta_0 + \beta_1 X_i + u_i$ is

$$Y_i = \beta_0 + \beta_1 \widetilde{X}_i + [\beta_1(X_i - \widetilde{X}_i) + u_i]$$
$$= \beta_0 + \beta_1 \widetilde{X}_i + v_i, \tag{9.1}$$

where $v_i = \beta_1(X_i - \widetilde{X}_i) + u_i$. Thus the population regression equation written in terms of $\widetilde{X}_i$ has an error term that contains the measurement error, the difference between $\widetilde{X}_i$ and $X_i$. If this difference is correlated with the measured value $\widetilde{X}_i$, then the regressor $\widetilde{X}_i$ will be correlated with the error term and $\hat{\beta}_1$ will be biased and inconsistent.

The precise size and direction of the bias in $\hat{\beta}_1$ depend on the correlation between $\widetilde{X}_i$ and the measurement error, $\widetilde{X}_i - X_i$. This correlation depends, in turn, on the specific nature of the measurement error.

For example, suppose that the measured value, $\widetilde{X}_i$, equals the actual, unmeasured value, $X_i$, plus a purely random component, $w_i$, which has mean zero and variance $\sigma_w^2$. Because the error is purely random, we might suppose that $w_i$ is uncorrelated with $X_i$ and with the regression error $u_i$. This assumption constitutes the **classical measurement error model** in which $\widetilde{X}_i = X_i + w_i$, where $\text{corr}(w_i, X_i) = 0$ and $\text{corr}(w_i, u_i) = 0$. Under the classical measurement error model, a bit of algebra[2] shows that $\hat{\beta}_1$ has the probability limit

$$\hat{\beta}_1 \xrightarrow{p} \frac{\sigma_X^2}{\sigma_X^2 + \sigma_w^2}\beta_1. \tag{9.2}$$

That is, if the measurement error has the effect of simply adding a random element to the actual value of the independent variable, then $\hat{\beta}_1$ is inconsistent. Because the ratio $\frac{\sigma_X^2}{\sigma_X^2 + \sigma_w^2}$ is less than 1, $\hat{\beta}_1$ will be biased toward 0, even in large samples. In the extreme case that the measurement error is so large that essentially no information about $X_i$ remains, the ratio of the variances in the final expression in Equation (9.2) is 0 and $\hat{\beta}_1$ converges in probability to 0. In the other extreme, when there is no measurement error, $\sigma_w^2 = 0$, so $\hat{\beta}_1 \xrightarrow{p} \beta_1$.

A different model of measurement error supposes that the respondent makes his or her best estimate of the true value. In this "best guess" model the response

---

[2]Under this measurement error assumption, $v_i = \beta_1(X_i - \widetilde{X}_i) + u_i = -\beta_1 w_i + u_i$, $\text{cov}(X_i, u_i) = 0$, and $\text{cov}(\widetilde{X}_1, w_i) = \text{cov}(X_i + w_i, w_i) = \sigma_w^2$, so $\text{cov}(\widetilde{X}_i, v_i) = -\beta_1\text{cov}(\widetilde{X}_1, w_i) + \text{cov}(\widetilde{X}_i, u_i) = -\beta_1\sigma_w^2$. Thus, from Equation (6.1), $\hat{\beta}_1 \xrightarrow{p} \beta_1 - \beta_1\sigma_w^2/\sigma_{\widetilde{X}}^2$. Now $\sigma_{\widetilde{X}}^2 = \sigma_X^2 + \sigma_w^2$, so $\hat{\beta}_1 \xrightarrow{p} \beta_1 - \beta_1\sigma_w^2/(\sigma_X^2 + \sigma_w^2) = [\sigma_X^2/(\sigma_X^2 + \sigma_w^2)]\beta_1$.

**KEY CONCEPT**

**9.4**

## Errors-in-Variables Bias

Errors-in-variables bias in the OLS estimator arises when an independent variable is measured imprecisely. This bias depends on the nature of the measurement error and persists even if the sample size is large. If the measured variable equals the actual value plus a mean-zero, independently distributed measurement error, then the OLS estimator in a regression with a single right-hand variable is biased toward zero, and its probability limit is given in Equation (9.2).

$\widetilde{X}_i$ is modeled as the conditional mean of $X_i$, given the information available to the respondent. Because $\widetilde{X}_i$ is the best guess, the measurement error $\widetilde{X}_i - X_i$ is uncorrelated with the response $\widetilde{X}_i$ (if the measurement error were correlated with $\widetilde{X}_i$, then that would be useful information for predicting $X_i$, in which case $\widetilde{X}_i$ would not have been the best guess of $X_i$). That is, $E[(\widetilde{X}_i - X_i)\widetilde{X}_i] = 0$, and if the respondent's information is uncorrelated with $u_i$, then $\widetilde{X}_i$ is uncorrelated with the error term $v_i$. Thus, in this "best guess" measurement error model, $\hat{\beta}_1$ is consistent, but because $\text{var}(v_i) > \text{var}(u_i)$, the variance of $\hat{\beta}_1$ is larger than it would be absent measurement error. The "best guess" measurement error model is examined further in Exercise 9.12.

Problems created by measurement error can be even more complicated if there is intentional misreporting. For example, suppose that survey respondents provide the income reported on their income taxes but intentionally underreport their true taxable income by not including cash payments. If, for example, all respondents report only 90% of income, then $\widetilde{X}_i = 0.90X_i$ and $\hat{\beta}_1$ will be biased *up* by 10%.

Although the result in Equation (9.2) is specific to classical measurement error, it illustrates the more general proposition that if the independent variable is measured imprecisely, then the OLS estimator is biased, even in large samples. Errors-in-variables bias is summarized in Key Concept 9.4.

*Measurement error in Y.* The effect of measurement error in $Y$ is different from measurement error in $X$. If $Y$ has classical measurement error, then this measurement error increases the variance of the regression and of $\hat{\beta}_1$ but does not induce bias in $\hat{\beta}_1$. To see this, suppose that measured $Y_i$ is $\widetilde{Y}_i$, which equals true $Y_i$ plus random measurement error $w_i$. Then the regression model estimated is $\widetilde{Y}_i = \beta_0 + \beta_1 X_i + v_i$, where $v_i = w_i + u_i$. If $w_i$ is truly random, then $w_i$ and $X_i$ are independently distributed so that $E(w_i|X_i) = 0$, in which case $E(v_i|X_i) = 0$, so $\hat{\beta}_1$ is unbiased. However, because $\text{var}(v_i) > \text{var}(u_i)$, the variance of $\hat{\beta}_1$ is larger than it would be without measurement error. In the test score/class size example, suppose that test scores have purely random grading errors that are independent of the regressors; then the classical measurement error model of this paragraph applies to $\widetilde{Y}_i$, and $\hat{\beta}_1$ is unbiased. More generally, measurement error in $Y$ that has conditional mean zero given the regressors will not induce bias in the OLS coefficients.

*Solutions to errors-in-variables bias.*  The best way to solve the errors-in-variables problem is to get an accurate measure of $X$. If this is impossible, however, econometric methods can be used to mitigate errors-in-variables bias.

One such method is instrumental variables regression. It relies on having another variable (the "instrumental" variable) that is correlated with the actual value $X_i$ but is uncorrelated with the measurement error. This method is studied in Chapter 12.

A second method is to develop a mathematical model of the measurement error and, if possible, to use the resulting formulas to adjust the estimates. For example, if a researcher believes that the classical measurement error model applies and if she knows or can estimate the ratio $\sigma_w^2/\sigma_X^2$, then she can use Equation (9.2) to compute an estimator of $\beta_1$ that corrects for the downward bias. Because this approach requires specialized knowledge about the nature of the measurement error, the details typically are specific to a given data set and its measurement problems and we shall not pursue this approach further in this textbook.

## Missing Data and Sample Selection

Missing data are a common feature of economic data sets. Whether missing data pose a threat to internal validity depends on why the data are missing. We consider three cases: when the data are missing completely at random, when the data are missing based on $X$, and when the data are missing because of a selection process that is related to $Y$ beyond depending on $X$.

When the data are missing completely at random—that is, for random reasons unrelated to the values of $X$ or $Y$—the effect is to reduce the sample size but not introduce bias. For example, suppose that you conduct a simple random sample of 100 classmates, then randomly lose half the records. It would be as if you had never surveyed those individuals. You would be left with a simple random sample of 50 classmates, so randomly losing the records does not introduce bias.

When the data are missing based on the value of a regressor, the effect also is to reduce the sample size but not introduce bias. For example, in the class size/student–teacher ratio example, suppose that we used only the districts in which the student–teacher ratio exceeds 20. Although we would not be able to draw conclusions about what happens when $STR \leq 20$, this would not introduce bias into our analysis of the class size effect for districts with $STR > 20$.

KEY CONCEPT

9.5

## Sample Selection Bias

Sample selection bias arises when a selection process influences the availability of data and that process is related to the dependent variable, beyond depending on the regressors. Sample selection induces correlation between one or more regressors and the error term, leading to bias and inconsistency of the OLS estimator.

In contrast to the first two cases, if the data are missing because of a selection process that is related to the value of the dependent variable ($Y$), beyond depending on the regressors ($X$), then this selection process can introduce correlation between the error term and the regressors. The resulting bias in the OLS estimator is called **sample selection bias**. An example of sample selection bias in polling was given in the box "Landon Wins!" in Section 3.1. In that example, the sample selection method (randomly selecting phone numbers of automobile owners) was related to the dependent variable (who the individual supported for president in 1936), because in 1936 car owners with phones were more likely to be Republicans. The sample selection problem can be cast either as a consequence of nonrandom sampling or as a missing data problem. In the 1936 polling example, the sample was a random sample of car owners with phones, not a random sample of voters. Alternatively, this example can be cast as a missing data problem by imagining a random sample of voters, but with missing data for those without cars and phones. The mechanism by which the data are missing is related to the dependent variable, leading to sample selection bias.

The box "Do Stock Mutual Funds Outperform the Market?" provides an example of sample selection bias in financial economics. Sample selection bias is summarized in Key Concept 9.5.[3]

*Solutions to selection bias.* The methods we have discussed so far cannot eliminate sample selection bias. The methods for estimating models with sample selection are beyond the scope of this book. Those methods build on the techniques introduced in Chapter 11, where further references are provided.

## Simultaneous Causality

So far, we have assumed that causality runs from the regressors to the dependent variable ($X$ causes $Y$). But what if causality also runs from the dependent variable to

---

[3]Exercise 18.16 provides a mathematical treatment of the three missing data cases discussed here.

## Do Stock Mutual Funds Outperform the Market?

Stock mutual funds are investment vehicles that hold a portfolio of stocks. By purchasing shares in a mutual fund, a small investor can hold a broadly diversified portfolio without the hassle and expense (transaction cost) of buying and selling shares in individual companies. Some mutual funds simply track the market (for example, by holding the stocks in the S&P 500), whereas others are actively managed by full-time professionals whose job is to make the fund earn a better return than the overall market—and competitors' funds. But do these actively managed funds achieve this goal? Do some mutual funds consistently beat other funds and the market?

One way to answer these questions is to compare future returns on mutual funds that had high returns over the past year to future returns on other funds and on the market as a whole. In making such comparisons, financial economists know that it is important to select the sample of mutual funds carefully. This task is not as straightforward as it seems, however. Some databases include historical data on funds currently available for purchase, but this approach means that the dogs—the most poorly performing funds—are omitted from the data set because they went out of business or were merged into other funds. For this

reason, a study using data on historical performance of currently available funds is subject to sample selection bias: The sample is selected based on the value of the dependent variable, returns, because funds with the lowest returns are eliminated. The mean return of all funds (including the defunct) over a ten-year period will be less than the mean return of those funds still in existence at the end of those ten years, so a study of only the latter funds will overstate performance. Financial economists refer to this selection bias as "survivorship bias" because only the better funds survive to be in the data set.

When financial econometricians correct for survivorship bias by incorporating data on defunct funds, the results do not paint a flattering portrait of mutual fund managers. Corrected for survivorship bias, the econometric evidence indicates that actively managed stock mutual funds do not outperform the market on average and that past good performance does not predict future good performance. For further reading on mutual funds and survivorship bias, see Malkiel (2012), Chapter 11 and Carhart (1997). The problem of survivorship bias also arises in evaluating hedge fund performance; for further reading, see Aggarwal and Jorion (2010).

one or more regressors ($Y$ causes $X$)? If so, causality runs "backward" as well as forward; that is, there is **simultaneous causality**. If there is simultaneous causality, an OLS regression picks up both effects, so the OLS estimator is biased and inconsistent.

For example, our study of test scores focused on the effect on test scores of reducing the student–teacher ratio, so causality is presumed to run from the student–teacher ratio to test scores. Suppose, however, that a government initiative subsidized hiring teachers in school districts with poor test scores. If so, causality would run in both directions: For the usual educational reasons low student–teacher ratios would arguably lead to high test scores, but because of the government program low test scores would lead to low student–teacher ratios.

Simultaneous causality leads to correlation between the regressor and the error term. In the test score example, suppose that there is an omitted factor that leads to poor test scores; because of the government program, this factor that produces low scores in turn results in a low student–teacher ratio. Thus a negative error term in the population regression of test scores on the student–teacher ratio reduces test scores, but because of the government program it also leads to a decrease in the student–teacher ratio. In other words, the student–teacher ratio is positively correlated with the error term in the population regression. This in turn leads to simultaneous causality bias and inconsistency of the OLS estimator.

This correlation between the error term and the regressor can be made mathematically precise by introducing an additional equation that describes the reverse causal link. For convenience, consider just the two variables $X$ and $Y$ and ignore other possible regressors. Accordingly, there are two equations, one in which $X$ causes $Y$ and one in which $Y$ causes $X$:

$$Y_i = \beta_0 + \beta_1 X_i + u_i \quad \text{and} \tag{9.3}$$

$$X_i = \gamma_0 + \gamma_1 Y_i + v_i. \tag{9.4}$$

Equation (9.3) is the familiar one in which $\beta_1$ is the effect on $Y$ of a change in $X$, where $u$ represents other factors. Equation (9.4) represents the reverse causal effect of $Y$ on $X$. In the test score problem, Equation (9.3) represents the educational effect of class size on test scores, while Equation (9.4) represents the reverse causal effect of test scores on class size induced by the government program.

Simultaneous causality leads to correlation between $X_i$ and the error term $u_i$ in Equation (9.3). To see this, imagine that $u_i$ is positive, which increases $Y_i$. However, this higher value of $Y_i$ affects the value of $X_i$ through the second of these equations, and if $\gamma_1$ is positive, a high value of $Y_i$ will lead to a high value of $X_i$. Thus, if $\gamma_1$ is positive, $X_i$ and $u_i$ will be positively correlated.[4]

Because this can be expressed mathematically using two simultaneous equations, the simultaneous causality bias is sometimes called **simultaneous equations bias**. Simultaneous causality bias is summarized in Key Concept 9.6.

*Solutions to simultaneous causality bias.* There are two ways to mitigate simultaneous causality bias. One is to use instrumental variables regression, the topic

[4]To show this mathematically, note that Equation (9.4) implies that $\text{cov}(X_i, u_i) = \text{cov}(\gamma_0 + \gamma_1 Y_i + v_i, u_i) = \gamma_1 \text{cov}(Y_i, u_i) + \text{cov}(v_i, u_i)$. Assuming that $\text{cov}(v_i, u_i) = 0$ by Equation (9.3) this in turn implies that $\text{cov}(X_i, u_i) = \gamma_1 \text{cov}(Y_i, u_i) = \gamma_1 \text{cov}(\beta_0 + \beta_1 X_i + u_i, u_i) = \gamma_1 \beta_1 \text{cov}(X_i, u_i) + \gamma_1 \sigma_u^2$. Solving for $\text{cov}(X_i, u_i)$ then yields the result $\text{cov}(X_i, u_i) = \gamma_1 \sigma_u^2 / (1 - \gamma_1 \beta_1)$.

## Simultaneous Causality Bias

**KEY CONCEPT**

9.6

Simultaneous causality bias, also called simultaneous equations bias, arises in a regression of $Y$ on $X$ when, in addition to the causal link of interest from $X$ to $Y$, there is a causal link from $Y$ to $X$. This reverse causality makes $X$ correlated with the error term in the population regression of interest.

of Chapter 12. The second is to design and implement a randomized controlled experiment in which the reverse causality channel is nullified, and such experiments are discussed in Chapter 13.

### Sources of Inconsistency of OLS Standard Errors

Inconsistent standard errors pose a different threat to internal validity. Even if the OLS estimator is consistent and the sample is large, inconsistent standard errors will produce hypothesis tests with size that differs from the desired significance level and "95%" confidence intervals that fail to include the true value in 95% of repeated samples.

There are two main reasons for inconsistent standard errors: improperly handled heteroskedasticity and correlation of the error term across observations.

*Heteroskedasticity.*  As discussed in Section 5.4, for historical reasons some regression software report homoskedasticity-only standard errors. If, however, the regression error is heteroskedastic, those standard errors are not a reliable basis for hypothesis tests and confidence intervals. The solution to this problem is to use heteroskedasticity-robust standard errors and to construct $F$-statistics using a heteroskedasticity-robust variance estimator. Heteroskedasticity-robust standard errors are provided as an option in modern software packages.

*Correlation of the error term across observations.*  In some settings, the population regression error can be correlated across observations. This will not happen if the data are obtained by sampling at random from the population because the randomness of the sampling process ensures that the errors are independently distributed from one observation to the next. Sometimes, however, sampling is only partially random. The most common circumstance is when the data are repeated observations on the same entity over time, such as the same school district for different years. If the omitted variables that constitute the regression error are persistent (like district demographics), "serial" correlation is induced in the regression error over time.

| KEY CONCEPT | **Threats to the Internal Validity of a Multiple Regression Study** |
|---|---|

9.7

There are five primary threats to the internal validity of a multiple regression study:

1. Omitted variables
2. Functional form misspecification
3. Errors in variables (measurement error in the regressors)
4. Sample selection
5. Simultaneous causality

Each of these, if present, results in failure of the first least squares assumption, $E(u_i | X_{1i}, \ldots, X_{ki}) \neq 0$, which in turn means that the OLS estimator is biased and inconsistent.

Incorrect calculation of the standard errors also poses a threat to internal validity. Homoskedasticity-only standard errors are invalid if heteroskedasticity is present. If the variables are not independent across observations, as can arise in panel and time series data, then a further adjustment to the standard error formula is needed to obtain valid standard errors.

Applying this list of threats to a multiple regression study provides a systematic way to assess the internal validity of that study.

Serial correlation in the error term can arise in panel data (data on multiple districts for multiple years) and in time series data (data on a single district for multiple years).

Another situation in which the error term can be correlated across observations is when sampling is based on a geographical unit. If there are omitted variables that reflect geographic influences, these omitted variables could result in correlation of the regression errors for adjacent observations.

Correlation of the regression error across observations does not make the OLS estimator biased or inconsistent, but it does violate the second least squares assumption in Key Concept 6.4. The consequence is that the OLS standard errors—both homoskedasticity-only *and* heteroskedasticity-robust—are incorrect in the sense that they do not produce confidence intervals with the desired confidence level.

In many cases, this problem can be fixed by using an alternative formula for standard errors. We provide formulas for computing standard errors that are robust to both heteroskedasticity and serial correlation in Chapter 10 (regression with panel data) and in Chapter 15 (regression with time series data).

Key Concept 9.7 summarizes the threats to internal validity of a multiple regression study.

# 9.3   Internal and External Validity When the Regression Is Used for Forecasting

Up to now, the discussion of multiple regression analysis has focused on the estimation of causal effects. Regression models can be used for other purposes, however, including forecasting. When regression models are used for forecasting, concerns about external validity are very important, but concerns about unbiased estimation of causal effects are not.

## Using Regression Models for Forecasting

Chapter 4 began by considering the problem of a school superintendent who wants to know how much test scores would increase if she reduced class sizes in her school district; that is, the superintendent wants to know the causal effect on test scores of a change in class size. Accordingly, Chapters 4 through 8 focused on using regression analysis to estimate causal effects using observational data.

Now consider a different problem. A parent moving to a metropolitan area plans to choose where to live based in part on the quality of the local schools. The parent would like to know how different school districts perform on standardized tests. Suppose, however, that test score data are not available (perhaps they are confidential) but data on class sizes are. In this situation, the parent must guess at how well the different districts perform on standardized tests based on a limited amount of information. That is, the parent's problem is to forecast average test scores in a given district based on information related to test scores—in particular, class size.

How can the parent make this forecast? Recall the regression of test scores on the student–teacher ratio ($STR$) from Chapter 4:

$$\widehat{TestScore} = 698.9 - 2.28 \times STR. \tag{9.5}$$

We concluded that this regression is not useful for the superintendent: The OLS estimator of the slope is biased because of omitted variables such as the composition of the student body and students' other learning opportunities outside school.

Nevertheless, Equation (9.5) could be useful to the parent trying to choose a home. To be sure, class size is not the only determinant of test performance, but from the parent's perspective what matters is whether it is a reliable predictor of test performance. The parent interested in forecasting test scores does not care whether the coefficient in Equation (9.5) estimates the causal effect on test scores of class size. Rather, the parent simply wants the regression to explain much of the variation in test scores across districts and to be stable—that is, to apply to the districts to which the parent is considering moving. Although omitted variable bias renders Equation (9.5) useless for answering the causal question, it still can be useful for forecasting purposes.

More generally, regression models can produce reliable forecasts, even if their coefficients have no causal interpretation. This recognition underlies much of the use of regression models for forecasting.

### Assessing the Validity of Regression Models for Forecasting

Because the superintendent's problem and the parent's problem are conceptually very different, the requirements for the validity of the regression are different for their respective problems. To obtain credible estimates of causal effects, we must address the threats to internal validity summarized in Key Concept 9.7.

In contrast, if we are to obtain reliable forecasts, the estimated regression must have good explanatory power, its coefficients must be estimated precisely, and it must be stable in the sense that the regression estimated on one set of data can be reliably used to make forecasts using other data. When a regression model is used for forecasting, a paramount concern is that the model is externally valid in the sense that it is stable and quantitatively applicable to the circumstance in which the forecast is made. In Part IV, we return to the problem of assessing the validity of a regression model for forecasting future values of time series data.

## 9.4 Example: Test Scores and Class Size

The framework of internal and external validity helps us to take a critical look at what we have learned—and what we have not—from our analysis of the California test score data.

### External Validity

Whether the California analysis can be generalized—that is, whether it is externally valid—depends on the population and setting to which the generalization is made. Here, we consider whether the results can be generalized to performance on other standardized tests in other elementary public school districts in the United States.

Section 9.1 noted that having more than one study on the same topic provides an opportunity to assess the external validity of both studies by comparing their results. In the case of test scores and class size, other comparable data sets are, in fact, available. In this section, we examine a different data set, based on standardized test results for fourth graders in 220 public school districts in Massachusetts in 1998. Both the Massachusetts and California tests are broad measures of student knowledge and academic skills, although the details differ. Similarly, the organization of classroom instruction is broadly similar at the elementary school level in the two states (as it is in most U.S. elementary school districts), although aspects of elementary school funding and curriculum differ. Thus finding similar results about the effect of the student–teacher ratio on test performance in the California and Massachusetts data would be evidence of external validity of the findings in California. Conversely, finding different results in the two states would raise questions about the internal or external validity of at least one of the studies.

***Comparison of the California and Massachusetts data.***   Like the California data, the Massachusetts data are at the school district level. The definitions of the variables in the Massachusetts data set are the same as those in the California data set, or nearly so. More information on the Massachusetts data set, including definitions of the variables, is given in Appendix 9.1.

Table 9.1 presents summary statistics for the California and Massachusetts samples. The average test score is higher in Massachusetts, but the test is different, so a direct comparison of scores is not appropriate. The average student–teacher ratio is higher in California (19.6 versus 17.3). Average district income is 20% higher in Massachusetts, but the standard deviation of income is greater in

| **TABLE 9.1** | Summary Statistics for California and Massachusetts Test Score Data Sets | | | |
|---|---|---|---|---|
| | **California** | | **Massachusetts** | |
| | **Average** | **Standard Deviation** | **Average** | **Standard Deviation** |
| Test scores | 654.1 | 19.1 | 709.8 | 15.1 |
| Student–teacher ratio | 19.6 | 1.9 | 17.3 | 2.3 |
| % English learners | 15.8% | 18.3% | 1.1% | 2.9% |
| % Receiving lunch subsidy | 44.7% | 27.1% | 15.3% | 15.1% |
| Average district income ($) | $15,317 | $7226 | $18,747 | $5808 |
| Number of observations | 420 | | 220 | |
| Year | 1999 | | 1998 | |

California; that is, there is a greater spread in average district incomes in California than in Massachusetts. The average percentage of students still learning English and the average percentage of students receiving subsidized lunches are both much higher in the California than in the Massachusetts districts.

*Test scores and average district income.* To save space, we do not present scatterplots of all the Massachusetts data. Because it was a focus in Chapter 8, however, it is interesting to examine the relationship between test scores and average district income in Massachusetts. This scatterplot is presented in Figure 9.1. The general pattern of this scatterplot is similar to that in Figure 8.2 for the California data: The relationship between income and test scores appears to be steep for low values of income and flatter for high values. Evidently, the linear regression plotted in the figure misses this apparent nonlinearity. Cubic and logarithmic regression functions are also plotted in Figure 9.1. The cubic regression function has a slightly higher $\overline{R}^2$ than the logarithmic specification (0.486 versus 0.455). Comparing Figures 8.7 and 9.1 shows that the general pattern of nonlinearity found in the California income and test score data is also present in the Massachusetts data.

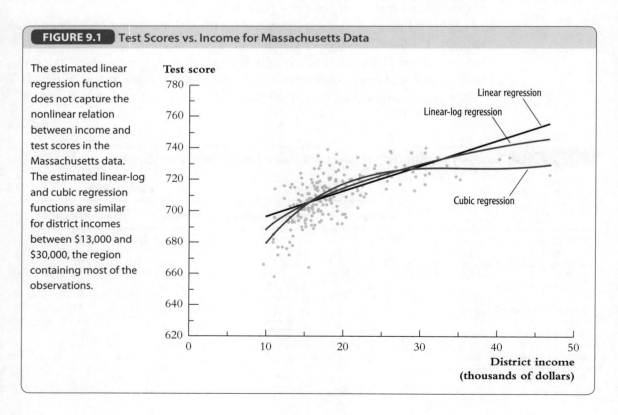

**FIGURE 9.1** Test Scores vs. Income for Massachusetts Data

The estimated linear regression function does not capture the nonlinear relation between income and test scores in the Massachusetts data. The estimated linear-log and cubic regression functions are similar for district incomes between $13,000 and $30,000, the region containing most of the observations.

The precise functional forms that best describe this nonlinearity differ, however, with the cubic specification fitting best in Massachusetts but the linear-log specification fitting best in California.

*Multiple regression results.* Regression results for the Massachusetts data are presented in Table 9.2. The first regression, reported in column (1) in the table, has only the student–teacher ratio as a regressor. The slope is negative ($-1.72$),

| TABLE 9.2 | Multiple Regression Estimates of the Student–Teacher Ratio and Test Scores: Data from Massachusetts |
|---|---|

Dependent variable: average combined English, math, and science test score in the school district, fourth grade; 220 observations.

| Regressor | (1) | (2) | (3) | (4) | (5) | (6) |
|---|---|---|---|---|---|---|
| Student–teacher ratio ($STR$) | $-1.72$** | $-0.69$* | $-0.64$* | 12.4 | $-1.02$** | $-0.67$* |
| | (0.50) | (0.27) | (0.27) | (14.0) | (0.37) | (0.27) |
| $STR^2$ | | | | $-0.680$ | | |
| | | | | (0.737) | | |
| $STR^3$ | | | | 0.011 | | |
| | | | | (0.013) | | |
| % English learners | | $-0.411$ | $-0.437$ | $-0.434$ | | |
| | | (0.306) | (0.303) | (0.300) | | |
| % English learners > median? (Binary, $HiEL$) | | | | | $-12.6$ | |
| | | | | | (9.8) | |
| $HiEL \times STR$ | | | | | 0.80 | |
| | | | | | (0.56) | |
| % Eligible for free lunch | | $-0.521$** | $-0.582$** | $-0.587$** | $-0.709$** | $-0.653$** |
| | | (0.077) | (0.097) | (0.104) | (0.091) | (0.72) |
| District income (logarithm) | | 16.53** | | | | |
| | | (3.15) | | | | |
| District income | | | $-3.07$ | $-3.38$ | $-3.87$* | $-3.22$ |
| | | | (2.35) | (2.49) | (2.49) | (2.31) |
| District income$^2$ | | | 0.164 | 0.174 | 0.184* | 0.165 |
| | | | (0.085) | (0.089) | (0.090) | (0.085) |
| District income$^3$ | | | $-0.0022$* | $-0.0023$* | $-0.0023$* | $-0.0022$* |
| | | | (0.0010) | (0.0010) | (0.0010) | (0.0010) |
| Intercept | 739.6** | 682.4** | 744.0** | 665.5** | 759.9** | 747.4** |
| | (8.6) | (11.5) | (21.3) | (81.3) | (23.2) | (20.3) |

*(Table 9.2 continued)*

*(Table 9.2 continued)*

| **F-Statistics and p-Values Testing Exclusion of Groups of Variables** | | | | | | |
|---|---|---|---|---|---|---|
| | (1) | (2) | (3) | (4) | (5) | (6) |
| All *STR* variables and interactions = 0 | | | | 2.86 (0.038) | 4.01 (0.020) | |
| $STR^2$, $STR^3 = 0$ | | | | 0.45 (0.641) | | |
| $Income^2$, $Income^3$ | | | 7.74 (< 0.001) | 7.75 (< 0.001) | 5.85 (0.003) | 6.55 (0.002) |
| $HiEL$, $HiEL \times STR$ | | | | | 1.58 (0.208) | |
| *SER* | 14.64 | 8.69 | 8.61 | 8.63 | 8.62 | 8.64 |
| $\overline{R}^2$ | 0.063 | 0.670 | 0.676 | 0.675 | 0.675 | 0.674 |

These regressions were estimated using the data on Massachusetts elementary school districts described in Appendix 9.1. Standard errors are given in parentheses under the coefficients, and *p*-values are given in parentheses under the *F*-statistics. Individual coefficients are statistically significant at the *5% level or **1% level.

and the hypothesis that the coefficient is zero can be rejected at the 1% significance level ($t = -1.72/0.50 = -3.44$).

The remaining columns report the results of including additional variables that control for student characteristics and of introducing nonlinearities into the estimated regression function. Controlling for the percentage of English learners, the percentage of students eligible for a free lunch, and the average district income reduces the estimated coefficient on the student–teacher ratio by 60%, from −1.72 in regression (1) to −0.69 in regression (2) and −0.64 in regression (3).

Comparing the $\overline{R}^2$'s of regressions (2) and (3) indicates that the cubic specification (3) provides a better model of the relationship between test scores and income than does the logarithmic specification (2), even holding constant the student–teacher ratio. There is no statistically significant evidence of a nonlinear relationship between test scores and the student–teacher ratio: The *F*-statistic in regression (4) testing whether the population coefficients on $STR^2$ and $STR^3$ are zero has a *p*-value of 0.641. Similarly, there is no evidence that a reduction in the student–teacher ratio has a different effect in districts with many English learners than with few [the *t*-statistic on $HiEL \times STR$ in regression (5) is $0.80/0.56 = 1.43$]. Finally, regression (6) shows that the estimated coefficient on the student–teacher ratio does not change substantially when the percentage of English learners [which is insignificant in regression (3)] is excluded. In short, the results in regression (3) are not sensitive to the changes in functional form and specification considered in regressions (4) through (6) in Table 9.2. Therefore, we adopt regression (3) as our base estimate of the effect in test scores of a change in the student–teacher ratio based on the Massachusetts data.

***Comparison of Massachusetts and California results.*** For the California data, we found the following:

1.  Adding variables that control for student background characteristics reduced the coefficient on the student–teacher ratio from −2.28 [Table 7.1, regression (1)] to −0.73 [Table 8.3, regression (2)], a reduction of 68%.
2.  The hypothesis that the true coefficient on the student–teacher ratio is zero was rejected at the 1% significance level, even after adding variables that control for student background and district economic characteristics.
3.  The effect of cutting the student–teacher ratio did not depend in an important way on the percentage of English learners in the district.
4.  There is some evidence that the relationship between test scores and the student–teacher ratio is nonlinear.

Do we find the same things in Massachusetts? For findings (1), (2), and (3), the answer is yes. Including the additional control variables reduces the coefficient on the student–teacher ratio from −1.72 [Table 9.2, regression (1)] to −0.69 [Table 9.2, regression (2)], a reduction of 60%. The coefficients on the student–teacher ratio remain significant after adding the control variables. Those coefficients are only significant at the 5% level in the Massachusetts data, whereas they are significant at the 1% level in the California data. However, there are nearly twice as many observations in the California data, so it is not surprising that the California estimates are more precise. As in the California data, there is no statistically significant evidence in the Massachusetts data of an interaction between the student–teacher ratio and the binary variable indicating a large percentage of English learners in the district.

Finding (4), however, does not hold up in the Massachusetts data: The hypothesis that the relationship between the student–teacher ratio and test scores is linear cannot be rejected at the 5% significance level when tested against a cubic specification.

Because the two standardized tests are different, the coefficients themselves cannot be compared directly: One point on the Massachusetts test is not the same as one point on the California test. If, however, the test scores are put into the

| TABLE 9.3 | Student–Teacher Ratios and Test Scores: Comparing the Estimates from California and Massachusetts | | | |
|---|---|---|---|---|

| | | | Estimated Effect of Two Fewer Students per Teacher, In Units of: | |
|---|---|---|---|---|
| | OLS Estimate $\hat{\beta}_{STR}$ | Standard Deviation of Test Scores Across Districts | Points on the Test | Standard Deviations |
| **California** | | | | |
| Linear: Table 9.3(2) | −0.73 (0.26) | 19.1 | 1.46 (0.52) | 0.076 (0.027) |
| Cubic: Table 9.3(7) *Reduce STR from 20 to 18* | — | 19.1 | 2.93 (0.70) | 0.153 (0.037) |
| Cubic: Table 9.3(7) *Reduce STR from 22 to 20* | — | 19.1 | 1.90 (0.69) | 0.099 (0.036) |
| **Massachusetts** | | | | |
| Linear: Table 9.2(3) | −0.64 (0.27) | 15.1 | 1.28 (0.54) | 0.085 (0.036) |

Standard errors are given in parentheses.

same units, then the estimated class size effects can be compared. One way to do this is to transform the test scores by standardizing them: Subtract the sample average and divide by the standard deviation so that they have a mean of 0 and a variance of 1. The slope coefficients in the regression with the standardized test score equal the slope coefficients in the original regression divided by the standard deviation of the test. Thus the coefficient on the student–teacher ratio divided by the standard deviation of test scores can be compared across the two data sets.

This comparison is undertaken in Table 9.3. The first column reports the OLS estimates of the coefficient on the student–teacher ratio in a regression with the percentage of English learners, the percentage of students eligible for a free lunch, and the average district income included as control variables. The second column reports the standard deviation of the test scores across districts. The final two columns report the estimated effect on test scores of reducing the student–teacher ratio by two students per teacher (our superintendent's proposal), first in the units of the test and second in standard deviation units. For the linear specification, the OLS coefficient estimate using California data is −0.73, so cutting the student–teacher ratio by two is estimated to increase district test scores by −0.73 × (−2) = 1.46

points. Because the standard deviation of test scores is 19.1 points, this corresponds to $1.46/19.1 = 0.076$ standard deviation of the distribution of test scores across districts. The standard error of this estimate is $0.26 \times 2/19.1 = 0.027$. The estimated effects for the nonlinear models and their standard errors were computed using the method described in Section 8.1.

Based on the linear model using California data, a reduction of two students per teacher is estimated to increase test scores by 0.076 standard deviation unit, with a standard error of 0.027. The nonlinear models for California data suggest a somewhat larger effect, with the specific effect depending on the initial student–teacher ratio. Based on the Massachusetts data, this estimated effect is 0.085 standard deviation unit, with a standard error of 0.036.

These estimates are essentially the same. Cutting the student–teacher ratio is predicted to raise test scores, but the predicted improvement is small. In the California data, for example, the difference in test scores between the median district and a district at the 75th percentile is 12.2 test score points (Table 4.1), or $0.64 (= 12.2/19.1)$ standard deviations. The estimated effect from the linear model is just over one-tenth this size; in other words, according to this estimate, cutting the student teacher–ratio by two would move a district only one-tenth of the way from the median to the 75th percentile of the distribution of test scores across districts. Reducing the student–teacher ratio by two is a large change for a district, but the estimated benefits shown in Table 9.3, while nonzero, are small.

This analysis of Massachusetts data suggests that the California results are externally valid, at least when generalized to elementary school districts elsewhere in the United States.

## Internal Validity

The similarity of the results for California and Massachusetts does not ensure their *internal* validity. Section 9.2 listed five possible threats to internal validity that could induce bias in the estimated effect on test scores on class size. We consider these threats in turn.

*Omitted variables.* The multiple regressions reported in this and previous chapters control for a student characteristic (the percentage of English learners), a family economic characteristic (the percentage of students receiving a subsidized lunch), and a broader measure of the affluence of the district (average district income).

If these control variables are adequate, then for the purpose of regression analysis it is as if the student–teacher ratio is randomly assigned among districts with the same values of these control variables, in which case the conditional mean independence assumption holds. There still could be, however, some omitted factors for which these three variables might not be adequate controls. For example, if the student–teacher ratio is correlated with teacher quality even among districts with the same fraction of immigrants and the same socioeconomic characteristics (perhaps because better teachers are attracted to schools with smaller student–teacher ratios) and if teacher quality affects test scores, then omission of teacher quality could bias the coefficient on the student–teacher ratio. Similarly, among districts with the same socioeconomic characteristics, districts with a low student–teacher ratio might have families that are more committed to enhancing their children's learning at home. Such omitted factors could lead to omitted variable bias.

One way to eliminate omitted variable bias, at least in theory, is to conduct an experiment. For example, students could be randomly assigned to different size classes, and their subsequent performance on standardized tests could be compared. Such a study was in fact conducted in Tennessee, and we examine it in Chapter 13.

*Functional form.* The analysis here and in Chapter 8 explored a variety of functional forms. We found that some of the possible nonlinearities investigated were not statistically significant, while those that were did not substantially alter the estimated effect of reducing the student–teacher ratio. Although further functional form analysis could be carried out, this suggests that the main findings of these studies are unlikely to be sensitive to using different nonlinear regression specifications.

*Errors in variables.* The average student–teacher ratio in the district is a broad and potentially inaccurate measure of class size. For example, because students move in and out of districts, the student–teacher ratio might not accurately represent the actual class sizes experienced by the students taking the test, which in turn could lead to the estimated class size effect being biased toward zero. Another variable with potential measurement error is average district income. Those data were taken from the 1990 census, while the other data pertain to 1998 (Massachusetts) or 1999 (California). If the economic composition of the district changed substantially over the 1990s, this would be an imprecise measure of the actual average district income.

*Selection.* The California and the Massachusetts data cover all the public elementary school districts in the state that satisfy minimum size restrictions, so there is no reason to believe that sample selection is a problem here.

*Simultaneous causality.* Simultaneous causality would arise if the performance on standardized tests affected the student–teacher ratio. This could happen, for example, if there is a bureaucratic or political mechanism for increasing the funding of poorly performing schools or districts that in turn resulted in hiring more teachers. In Massachusetts, no such mechanism for equalization of school financing was in place during the time of these tests. In California, a series of court cases led to some equalization of funding, but this redistribution of funds was not based on student achievement. Thus in neither Massachusetts nor California does simultaneous causality appear to be a problem.

***Heteroskedasticity and correlation of the error term across observations.*** All the results reported here and in earlier chapters use heteroskedastic-robust standard errors, so heteroskedasticity does not threaten internal validity. Correlation of the error term across observations, however, could threaten the consistency of the standard errors because simple random sampling was not used (the sample consists of all elementary school districts in the state). Although there are alternative standard error formulas that could be applied to this situation, the details are complicated and specialized and we leave them to more advanced texts.

## Discussion and Implications

The similarity between the Massachusetts and California results suggest that these studies are externally valid, in the sense that the main findings can be generalized to performance on standardized tests at other elementary school districts in the United States.

Some of the most important potential threats to internal validity have been addressed by controlling for student background, family economic background, and district affluence, and by checking for nonlinearities in the regression function. Still, some potential threats to internal validity remain. A leading candidate is omitted variable bias, perhaps arising because the control variables do not capture other characteristics of the school districts or extracurricular learning opportunities.

Based on both the California and the Massachusetts data, we are able to answer the superintendent's question from Section 4.1: After controlling for family economic background, student characteristics, and district affluence, and after modeling nonlinearities in the regression function, cutting the student–teacher ratio by two students per teacher is predicted to increase test scores by approximately 0.08 standard deviation of the distribution of test scores across districts. This effect is statistically significant, but it is quite small. This small estimated effect is in line with the results of the many studies that have investigated the effects on test scores of class size reductions.[5]

---

[5]If you are interested in learning more about the relationship between class size and test scores, see the reviews by Ehrenberg et al. (2001a, 2001b).

The superintendent can now use this estimate to help her decide whether to reduce class sizes. In making this decision, she will need to weigh the costs of the proposed reduction against the benefits. The costs include teacher salaries and expenses for additional classrooms. The benefits include improved academic performance, which we have measured by performance on standardized tests, but there are other potential benefits that we have not studied, including lower drop-out rates and enhanced future earnings. The estimated effect of the proposal on standardized test performance is one important input into her calculation of costs and benefits.

## 9.5 Conclusion

The concepts of internal and external validity provide a framework for assessing what has been learned from an econometric study.

A study based on multiple regression is internally valid if the estimated coefficients are unbiased and consistent, and if standard errors are consistent. Threats to the internal validity of such a study include omitted variables, misspecification of functional form (nonlinearities), imprecise measurement of the independent variables (errors in variables), sample selection, and simultaneous causality. Each of these introduces correlation between the regressor and the error term, which in turn makes OLS estimators biased and inconsistent. If the errors are correlated across observations, as they can be with time series data, or if they are heteroskedastic but the standard errors are computed using the homoskedasticity-only formula, then internal validity is compromised because the standard errors will be inconsistent. These latter problems can be addressed by computing the standard errors properly.

A study using regression analysis, like any statistical study, is externally valid if its findings can be generalized beyond the population and setting studied. Sometimes it can help to compare two or more studies on the same topic. Whether or not there are two or more such studies, however, assessing external validity requires making judgments about the similarities of the population and setting studied and the population and setting to which the results are being generalized.

The next two parts of this textbook develop ways to address threats to internal validity that cannot be mitigated by multiple regression analysis alone. Part III extends the multiple regression model in ways designed to mitigate all five sources of potential bias in the OLS estimator; Part III also discusses a different approach to obtaining internal validity, randomized controlled experiments. Part IV develops methods for analyzing time series data and for using time series data to estimate so-called dynamic causal effects, which are causal effects that vary over time.

## Summary

1. Statistical studies are evaluated by asking whether the analysis is internally and externally valid. A study is internally valid if the statistical inferences about causal effects are valid for the population being studied. A study is externally valid if its inferences and conclusions can be generalized from the population and setting studied to other populations and settings.

2. In regression estimation of causal effects, there are two types of threats to internal validity. First, OLS estimators are biased and inconsistent if the regressors and error terms are correlated. Second, confidence intervals and hypothesis tests are not valid when the standard errors are incorrect.

3. Regressors and error terms may be correlated when there are omitted variables, an incorrect functional form is used, one or more of the regressors are measured with error, the sample is chosen nonrandomly from the population, or there is simultaneous causality between the regressors and dependent variables.

4. Standard errors are incorrect when the errors are heteroskedastic and the computer software uses the homoskedasticity-only standard errors, or when the error term is correlated across different observations.

5. When regression models are used solely for forecasting, it is not necessary for the regression coefficients to be unbiased estimates of causal effects. It is critical, however, that the regression model be externally valid for the forecasting application at hand.

## Key Terms

population studied (361)
internal validity (362)
external validity (362)
population of interest (362)
functional form misspecification (367)

errors-in-variables bias (368)
classical measurement error model (369)
sample selection bias (372)
simultaneous causality (373)
simultaneous equations bias (374)

---

**MyEconLab Can Help You Get a Better Grade**

MyEconLab   If your exam were tomorrow, would you be ready? For each chapter, MyEconLab Practice Tests and Study Plan help you prepare for your exams. You can also find similar Exercises and Review the Concepts Questions now in **MyEconLab**.
To see how it works, turn to the **MyEconLab** spread on pages 2 and 3 of this book and then go to **www.myeconlab.com**.

For additional Empirical Exercises and Data Sets, log on to the Companion Website at **www.pearsonglobaleditions.com/Stock_Watson**.

## Review the Concepts

**9.1**   Is it possible for an econometric study to have internal validity but not external validity?

**9.2**   Key Concept 9.2 describes the problem of variable selection in terms of a trade-off between bias and variance. What is this trade-off? Why could including an additional regressor decrease bias? Increase variance?

**9.3**   What is the effect of measurement error in $Y$? How is this different from the effect of measurement error in $X$?

**9.4**   What is sample selection bias? Suppose you read a study using data on college graduates of the effects of an additional year of schooling on earnings. What is the potential sample selection bias?

**9.5**   Define simultaneous causality bias. Explain the potential for simultaneous causality in a study of the effects of high levels of bureaucratic corruption on national income.

**9.6**   A researcher estimates a regression using two different software packages. The first uses the homoskedasticity-only formula for standard errors. The second uses the heteroskedasticity-robust formula. The standard errors are very different. Which should the researcher use? Why?

## Exercises

**9.1**   Suppose you just read a careful statistical study of the effect of improved health of children on their test scores at school. Using data from a project in a West African district, in 2000, the study concluded that students who received multivitamin supplements performed substantially better at school. Use the concept of external validity to determine if these results are likely to apply to India in 2000, the United Kingdom in 2000, and West Africa in 2015.

**9.2**   Consider the one-variable regression model $Y_i = \beta_0 + \beta_1 X_i + u_i$ and suppose that it satisfies the least squares assumptions in Key Concept 4.3. Suppose that $Y_i$ is measured with error, so the data are $\tilde{Y}_i = Y_i + w_i$, where $w_i$ is the measurement error, which is i.i.d. and independent of $Y_i$ and $X_i$. Consider the population regression $\tilde{Y}_i = \beta_0 + \beta_1 X_i + v_i$, where $v_i$ is the regression error, using the mismeasured dependent variable, $\tilde{Y}_i$.

   **a.**  Show that $v_i = u_i + w_i$.

**b.** Show that the regression $\widetilde{Y}_i = \beta_0 + \beta_1 X_i + v_i$ satisfies the least squares assumptions in Key Concept 4.3. (Assume that $w_i$ is independent of $Y_j$ and $X_j$ for all values of $i$ and $j$ and has a finite fourth moment.)

**c.** Are the OLS estimators consistent?

**d.** Can confidence intervals be constructed in the usual way?

**e.** Evaluate these statements: "Measurement error in the $X$'s is a serious problem. Measurement error in $Y$ is not."

**9.3** Labor economists studying the determinants of women's earnings discovered a puzzling empirical result. Using randomly selected employed women, they regressed earnings on the women's number of children and a set of control variables (age, education, occupation, and so forth). They found that women with more children had higher wages, controlling for these other factors. Explain how sample selection might be the cause of this result. (*Hint:* Notice that women who do not work outside the home are missing from the sample.) [This empirical puzzle motivated James Heckman's research on sample selection that led to his 2000 Nobel Prize in Economics. See Heckman (1974).]

**9.4** Using the regressions shown in columns (2) of Table 8.3 and 9.3, and column (2) of Table 9.2, construct a table like Table 9.3 to compare the estimated effects of a 10 percentage point increase in the students eligible for free lunch on test scores in California and Massachusetts.

**9.5** The demand for a commodity is given by $Q = \beta_0 + \beta_1 P + u$, where $Q$ denotes quantity, $P$ denotes price, and $u$ denotes factors other than price that determine demand. Supply for the commodity is given by $Q = \gamma_0 + \gamma_1 P + v$, where $v$ denotes factors other than price that determine supply. Suppose that $u$ and $v$ both have a mean of zero, have variances $\sigma_u^2$ and $\sigma_v^2$, and are mutually uncorrelated.

**a.** Solve the two simultaneous equations to show how $Q$ and $P$ depend on $u$ and $v$.

**b.** Derive the means of $P$ and $Q$.

**c.** Derive the variance of $P$, the variance of $Q$, and the covariance between $Q$ and $P$.

**d.** A random sample of observations of $(Q_i, P_i)$ is collected, and $Q_i$ is regressed on $P_i$. (That is, $Q_i$ is the regressand, and $P_i$ is the regressor.) Suppose that the sample is very large.

    i. Use your answers to (b) and (c) to derive values of the regression coefficients. [*Hint:* Use Equations (4.7) and (4.8).]

    ii. A researcher uses the slope of this regression as an estimate of the slope of the demand function ($\beta_1$). Is the estimated slope too large or too small? (*Hint:* Remember that demand curves slope down and supply curves slope up.)

**9.6** Suppose that $n = 50$, i.i.d. observations for $(Y_i, X_i)$ yield the following regression results:

$$\hat{Y} = 49.2 + 73.9X, SER = 13.4, R^2 = 0.78.$$
$$\quad\quad (23.5)\quad (16.4)$$

Another researcher is interested in the same regression, but makes an error when entering the data into a regression program: The researcher enters each observation twice, ending up with 100 observations (with observation 1 entered twice, observation 2 entered twice and so forth).

**a.** Using these 100 observations, what results will be produced by the regression program? (*Hint:* Write the "incorrect" values of the sample means, variances, and covariances of $Y$ and $X$ as functions of the "correct" values. Use these to determine the regression statistics.)

$$\hat{Y} = \underline{\quad} + \underline{\quad}X, SER = \underline{\quad}, R^2 = \underline{\quad}.$$
$$\quad (\underline{\quad})\ (\underline{\quad})$$

**b.** Which (if any) of the internal validity conditions are violated?

**9.7** Are the following statements true or false? Explain your answer.

**a.** "An ordinary least squares regression of $Y$ onto $X$ will not be internally valid if $Y$ is correlated with the error term."

**b.** "If the error term exhibits heteroskedasticity, then the estimates of $X$ will always be biased."

**9.8** Would the regression in Equation (9.5) be useful for predicting test scores in a school district in Massachusetts? Why or why not?

**9.9** Consider the linear regression of *TestScore* on *Income* shown in Figure 8.2 and the nonlinear regression in Equation (8.18). Would either of these regressions provide a reliable estimate of the effect of income on test scores? Would either of these regressions provide a reliable method for forecasting test scores? Explain.

**9.10** Read the box "The Return to Education and the Gender Gap" in Section 8.3. Discuss the internal and external validity of the estimated effect of education on earnings.

**9.11** Read the box "The Demand for Economics Journals" in Section 8.3. Discuss the internal and external validity of the estimated effect of price per citation on subscriptions.

**9.12** Consider the one-variable regression model $Y_i = \beta_0 + \beta_1 X_i + u_i$ and suppose that it satisfies the least squares assumptions in Key Concept 4.3. The regressor $X_i$ is missing, but data on a related variable, $Z_i$, are available, and the value of $X_i$ is estimated using $\widetilde{X}_i = E(X_i|Z_i)$. Let $w_i = \widetilde{X}_i - X_i$.

   **a.** Show that $\widetilde{X}_i$ is the minimum mean square error estimator of $X_i$ using $Z_i$. That is, let $\hat{X}_i = g(Z_i)$ be some other guess of $X_i$ based on $Z_i$, and show that $E[(\hat{X}_i - X_i)^2] \geq E[(\widetilde{X}_i - X_i)^2]$. (*Hint:* Review Exercise 2.27.)

   **b.** Show that $E(w_i|\widetilde{X}_i) = 0$.

   **c.** Suppose that $E(u_i|Z_i) = 0$ and that $\widetilde{X}_i$ is used as the regressor in place of $X_i$. Show that $\hat{\beta}_1$ is consistent. Is $\hat{\beta}_0$ consistent?

**9.13** Assume that the regression model $Y_i = \beta_0 + \beta_1 X_i + u_i$ satisfies the least squares assumptions in Key Concept 4.3 in Section 4.4. You and a friend collect a random sample of 300 observations on $Y$ and $X$.

   **a.** Your friend reports the he inadvertently scrambled the $X$ observations for 20% of the sample. For these scrambled observations, the value of $X$ does not correspond to $X_i$ for the $i^{\text{th}}$ observation; rather, it corresponds to the value of $X$ for some other observation. In the notation of Section 9.2, the measured value of the regressor, $\widetilde{X}_i$, is equal to $X_i$ for 80% of the observations, but it is equal to a randomly selected $X_j$ for the remaining 20% of the observations. You regress $Y_i$ on $\widetilde{X}_i$. Show that $E(\hat{\beta}_1) = 0.8\beta_1$.

   **b.** Explain how you could construct an unbiased estimate of $\beta_1$ using the OLS estimator in (a).

   **c.** Suppose now that your friend tells you that the $X$'s were scrambled for the first 60 observations but that the remaining 240 observations are correct. You estimate $\beta_1$ by regressing $Y$ on $X$, using only the correctly measured 240 observations. Is this estimator of $\beta_1$ better than the estimator you proposed in (b)? Explain.

## Empirical Exercises

(Only two empirical exercises for this chapter are given in the text, but you can find more on the text website, **www.pearsonglobaleditions.com/Stock_Watson**.)

**E9.1** Use the data set **CPS12**, described in Empirical Exercise 8.2, to answer the following questions.

    **a.** Discuss the internal validity of the regressions that you used to answer Empirical Exercise 8.2(l). Include a discussion of possible omitted variable bias, misspecification of the functional form of the regression, errors in variables, sample selection, simultaneous causality, and inconsistency of the OLS standard errors.

    **b.** The data set **CPS92_12** described in Empirical Exercise 3.1 includes data from 2012 and 1992. Use these data to investigate the (temporal) external validity of the conclusions that you reached in Empirical Exercise 8.2(l). [*Note:* Remember to adjust for inflation, as explained in Empirical Exercise 3.1(b).]

**E9.2** Use the data set **Birthweight_Smoking** introduced in Empirical Exercise 5.1 to answer the following questions.

    **a.** In Empirical Exercise 7.1(f), you estimated several regressions and were asked: "What is a reasonable 95% confidence interval for the effect of smoking on birth weight?"

      i. In Chapter 8 you learned about nonlinear regressions. Can you think of any nonlinear regressions that can potentially improve your answer to Empirical Exercise E7.1(f)? After estimating these additional regressions, what is a reasonable 95% confidence interval for the effect of smoking on birth weight?

      ii. Discuss the internal validity of the regressions you used to construct the confidence interval. Include a discussion of possible omitted variable bias, misspecification of the functional form of the regression, errors in variables, sample selection, simultaneous causality, and inconsistency of the OLS standard errors.

    **b.** The data set **Birthweight_Smoking** includes babies born in Pennsylvania in 1989. Discuss the external validity of your analysis for (i) California in 1989, (ii) Illinois in 2015, and (iii) South Korea in 2014.

APPENDIX

# 9.1 The Massachusetts Elementary School Testing Data

The Massachusetts data are districtwide averages for public elementary school districts in 1998. The test score is taken from the Massachusetts Comprehensive Assessment System (MCAS) test administered to all fourth graders in Massachusetts public schools in the spring of 1998. The test is sponsored by the Massachusetts Department of Education and is mandatory for all public schools. The data analyzed here are the overall total score, which is the sum of the scores on the English, math, and science portions of the test.

Data on the student–teacher ratio, the percentage of students receiving a subsidized lunch, and the percentage of students still learning English are averages for each elementary school district for the 1997–1998 school year and were obtained from the Massachusetts Department of Education. Data on average district income were obtained from the 1990 U.S. Census.

# 10 Regression with Panel Data

M ultiple regression is a powerful tool for controlling for the effect of variables on which we have data. If data are not available for some of the variables, however, they cannot be included in the regression and the OLS estimators of the regression coefficients could have omitted variable bias.

This chapter describes a method for controlling for some types of omitted variables without actually observing them. This method requires a specific type of data, called panel data, in which each observational unit, or entity, is observed at two or more time periods. By studying *changes* in the dependent variable over time, it is possible to eliminate the effect of omitted variables that differ across entities but are constant over time.

The empirical application in this chapter concerns drunk driving: What are the effects of alcohol taxes and drunk driving laws on traffic fatalities? We address this question using data on traffic fatalities, alcohol taxes, drunk driving laws, and related variables for the 48 contiguous U.S. states for each of the seven years from 1982 to 1988. This panel data set lets us control for unobserved variables that differ from one state to the next, such as prevailing cultural attitudes toward drinking and driving, but do not change over time. It also allows us to control for variables that vary through time, like improvements in the safety of new cars, but do not vary across states.

Section 10.1 describes the structure of panel data and introduces the drunk driving data set. Fixed effects regression, the main tool for regression analysis of panel data, is an extension of multiple regression that exploits panel data to control for variables that differ across entities but are constant over time. Fixed effects regression is introduced in Sections 10.2 and 10.3, first for the case of only two time periods and then for multiple time periods. In Section 10.4, these methods are extended to incorporate so-called time fixed effects, which control for unobserved variables that are constant across entities but change over time. Section 10.5 discusses the panel data regression assumptions and standard errors for panel data regression. In Section 10.6, we use these methods to study the effect of alcohol taxes and drunk driving laws on traffic deaths.

## Notation for Panel Data

Panel data consist of observations on the same $n$ entities at two or more time periods $T$, as is illustrated in Table 1.3. If the data set contains observations on the variables $X$ and $Y$, then the data are denoted

$$(X_{it}, Y_{it}), i = 1, \ldots, n \text{ and } t = 1, \ldots, T, \tag{10.1}$$

where the first subscript, $i$, refers to the entity being observed and the second subscript, $t$, refers to the date at which it is observed.

## 10.1   Panel Data

Recall from Section 1.3 that **panel data** (also called longitudinal data) refers to data for $n$ different entities observed at $T$ different time periods. The state traffic fatality data studied in this chapter are panel data. Those data are for $n = 48$ entities (states), where each entity is observed in $T = 7$ time periods (each of the years 1982, . . . , 1988), for a total of $7 \times 48 = 336$ observations.

When describing cross-sectional data it was useful to use a subscript to denote the entity; for example, $Y_i$ referred to the variable $Y$ for the $i^{th}$ entity. When describing panel data, we need some additional notation to keep track of both the entity and the time period. We do so by using two subscripts rather than one: The first, $i$, refers to the entity, and the second, $t$, refers to the time period of the observation. Thus $Y_{it}$ denotes the variable $Y$ observed for the $i^{th}$ of $n$ entities in the $t^{th}$ of $T$ periods. This notation is summarized in Key Concept 10.1.

Some additional terminology associated with panel data describes whether some observations are missing. A **balanced panel** has all its observations; that is, the variables are observed for each entity and each time period. A panel that has some missing data for at least one time period for at least one entity is called an **unbalanced panel**. The traffic fatality data set has data for all 48 contiguous U.S. states for all seven years, so it is balanced. If, however, some data were missing (for example, if we did not have data on fatalities for some states in 1983), then the data set would be unbalanced. The methods presented in this chapter are described for a balanced panel; however, all these methods can be used with an unbalanced panel, although precisely how to do so in practice depends on the regression software being used.

## Example: Traffic Deaths and Alcohol Taxes

There are approximately 40,000 highway traffic fatalities each year in the United States. Approximately one-fourth of fatal crashes involve a driver who was drinking, and this fraction rises during peak drinking periods. One study (Levitt and Porter, 2001) estimates that as many as 25% of drivers on the road between 1 A.M. and 3 A.M. have been drinking and that a driver who is legally drunk is at least 13 times as likely to cause a fatal crash as a driver who has not been drinking.

In this chapter, we study how effective various government policies designed to discourage drunk driving actually are in reducing traffic deaths. The panel data set contains variables related to traffic fatalities and alcohol, including the number of traffic fatalities in each state in each year, the type of drunk driving laws in each state in each year, and the tax on beer in each state. The measure of traffic deaths we use is the fatality rate, which is the number of annual traffic deaths per 10,000 people in the population in the state. The measure of alcohol taxes we use is the "real" tax on a case of beer, which is the beer tax, put into 1988 dollars by adjusting for inflation.[1] The data are described in more detail in Appendix 10.1.

Figure 10.1a is a scatterplot of the data for 1982 on two of these variables, the fatality rate and the real tax on a case of beer. A point in this scatterplot represents the fatality rate in 1982 and the real beer tax in 1982 for a given state. The OLS regression line obtained by regressing the fatality rate on the real beer tax is also plotted in the figure; the estimated regression line is

$$\widehat{FatalityRate} = 2.01 + 0.15\,BeerTax \quad \text{(1982 data)}. \qquad (10.2)$$
$$\phantom{\widehat{FatalityRate} = } (0.15) \quad (0.13)$$

The coefficient on the real beer tax is positive, but not statistically significant at the 10% level.

Because we have data for more than one year, we can reexamine this relationship for another year. This is done in Figure 10.1b, which is the same scatterplot as before except that it uses the data for 1988. The OLS regression line through these data is

$$\widehat{FatalityRate} = 1.86 + 0.44\,BeerTax \quad \text{(1988 data)}. \qquad (10.3)$$
$$\phantom{\widehat{FatalityRate} = } (0.11) \quad (0.13)$$

---

[1]To make the taxes comparable over time, they are put into "1988 dollars" using the Consumer Price Index (CPI). For example, because of inflation a tax of $1 in 1982 corresponds to a tax of $1.23 in 1988 dollars.

**FIGURE 10.1**    The Traffic Fatality Rate and the Tax on Beer

Panel (a) is a scatterplot of traffic fatality rates and the real tax on a case of beer (in 1988 dollars) for 48 states in 1982. Panel (b) shows the data for 1988. Both plots show a positive relationship between the fatality rate and the real beer tax.

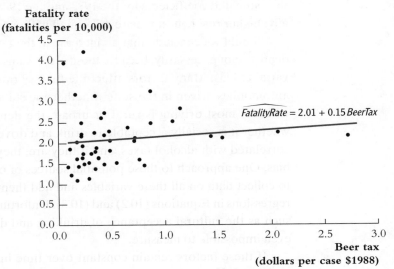

$\widehat{FatalityRate} = 2.01 + 0.15\,BeerTax$

(a) 1982 data

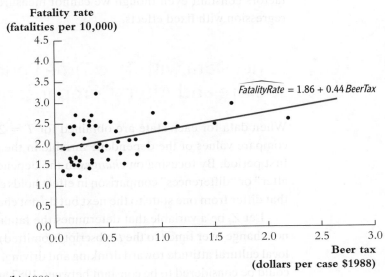

$\widehat{FatalityRate} = 1.86 + 0.44\,BeerTax$

(b) 1988 data

In contrast to the regression using the 1982 data, the coefficient on the real beer tax is statistically significant at the 1% level (the $t$-statistic is 3.43). Curiously, the estimated coefficients for the 1982 and the 1988 data are *positive*: Taken literally, higher real beer taxes are associated with *more*, not fewer, traffic fatalities.

Should we conclude that an increase in the tax on beer leads to more traffic deaths? Not necessarily, because these regressions could have substantial omitted variable bias. Many factors affect the fatality rate, including the quality of the automobiles driven in the state, whether the state highways are in good repair, whether most driving is rural or urban, the density of cars on the road, and whether it is socially acceptable to drink and drive. Any of these factors may be correlated with alcohol taxes, and if they are, they will lead to omitted variable bias. One approach to these potential sources of omitted variable bias would be to collect data on all these variables and add them to the annual cross-sectional regressions in Equations (10.2) and (10.3). Unfortunately, some of these variables, such as the cultural acceptance of drinking and driving, might be very hard or even impossible to measure.

If these factors remain constant over time in a given state, however, then another route is available. Because we have panel data, we can in effect hold these factors constant even though we cannot measure them. To do so, we use OLS regression with fixed effects.

## 10.2 Panel Data with Two Time Periods: "Before and After" Comparisons

When data for each state are obtained for $T = 2$ time periods, it is possible to compare values of the dependent variable in the second period to values in the first period. By focusing on *changes* in the dependent variable, this "before and after" or "differences" comparison in effect holds constant the unobserved factors that differ from one state to the next but do not change over time within the state.

Let $Z_i$ be a variable that determines the fatality rate in the $i^{\text{th}}$ state but does not change over time (so the $t$ subscript is omitted). For example, $Z_i$ might be the local cultural attitude toward drinking and driving, which changes slowly and thus could be considered to be constant between 1982 and 1988. Accordingly, the population linear regression relating $Z_i$ and the real beer tax to the fatality rate is

$$FatalityRate_{it} = \beta_0 + \beta_1 BeerTax_{it} + \beta_2 Z_i + u_{it}, \tag{10.4}$$

where $u_{it}$ is the error term and $i = 1, \ldots, n$ *and* $t = 1, \ldots, T$.

Because $Z_i$ does not change over time, in the regression model in Equation (10.4) it will not produce any *change* in the fatality rate between 1982 and 1988. Thus, in this regression model, the influence of $Z_i$ can be eliminated by analyzing the change in the fatality rate between the two periods. To see this mathematically, consider Equation (10.4) for each of the two years 1982 and 1988:

$$FatalityRate_{i1982} = \beta_0 + \beta_1 BeerTax_{i1982} + \beta_2 Z_i + u_{i1982}, \qquad (10.5)$$

$$FatalityRate_{i1988} = \beta_0 + \beta_1 BeerTax_{i1988} + \beta_2 Z_i + u_{i1988}. \qquad (10.6)$$

Subtracting Equation (10.5) from Equation (10.6) eliminates the effect of $Z_i$:

$$FatalityRate_{i1988} - FatalityRate_{i1982}$$
$$= \beta_1 (BeerTax_{i1988} - BeerTax_{i1982}) + u_{i1988} - u_{i1982}. \qquad (10.7)$$

This specification has an intuitive interpretation. Cultural attitudes toward drinking and driving affect the level of drunk driving and thus the traffic fatality rate in a state. If, however, they did not change between 1982 and 1988, then they did not produce any *change* in fatalities in the state. Rather, any changes in traffic fatalities over time must have arisen from other sources. In Equation (10.7), these other sources are changes in the tax on beer and changes in the error term (which captures changes in other factors that determine traffic deaths).

Specifying the regression in changes in Equation (10.7) eliminates the effect of the unobserved variables $Z_i$ that are constant over time. In other words, analyzing changes in $Y$ and $X$ has the effect of controlling for variables that are constant over time, thereby eliminating this source of omitted variable bias.

Figure 10.2 presents a scatterplot of the *change* in the fatality rate between 1982 and 1988 against the *change* in the real beer tax between 1982 and 1988 for the 48 states in our data set. A point in Figure 10.2 represents the change in the fatality rate and the change in the real beer tax between 1982 and 1988 for a given state. The OLS regression line, estimated using these data and plotted in the figure, is

$$\widehat{FatalityRate_{1988} - FatalityRate_{1982}} = -0.072 - 1.04(BeerTax_{1988} - BeerTax_{1982}).$$
$$\quad (0.065) \quad (0.36) \qquad\qquad (10.8)$$

Including an intercept in Equation (10.8) allows for the possibility that the mean change in the fatality rate, in the absence of a change in the real beer tax, is non-zero. For example, the negative intercept ($-0.072$) could reflect improvements in auto safety from 1982 to 1988 that reduced the average fatality rate.

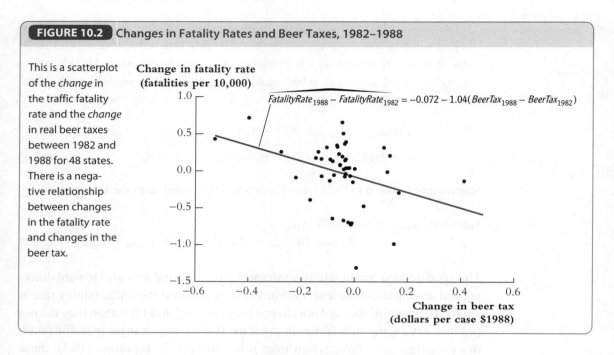

**FIGURE 10.2**    Changes in Fatality Rates and Beer Taxes, 1982–1988

This is a scatterplot of the *change* in the traffic fatality rate and the *change* in real beer taxes between 1982 and 1988 for 48 states. There is a negative relationship between changes in the fatality rate and changes in the beer tax.

Change in fatality rate (fatalities per 10,000)

$$FatalityRate_{1988} - FatalityRate_{1982} = -0.072 - 1.04(BeerTax_{1988} - BeerTax_{1982})$$

Change in beer tax (dollars per case $1988)

In contrast to the cross-sectional regression results, the estimated effect of a change in the real beer tax is negative, as predicted by economic theory. The hypothesis that the population slope coefficient is zero is rejected at the 5% significance level. According to this estimated coefficient, an increase in the real beer tax by $1 per case reduces the traffic fatality rate by 1.04 deaths per 10,000 people. This estimated effect is very large: The average fatality rate is approximately 2 in these data (that is, 2 fatalities per year per 10,000 members of the population), so the estimate suggests that traffic fatalities can be cut in half merely by increasing the real tax on beer by $1 per case.

By examining changes in the fatality rate over time, the regression in Equation (10.8) controls for fixed factors such as cultural attitudes toward drinking and driving. But there are many factors that influence traffic safety, and if they change over time and are correlated with the real beer tax, then their omission will produce omitted variable bias. In Section 10.5, we undertake a more careful analysis that controls for several such factors, so for now it is best to refrain from drawing any substantive conclusions about the effect of real beer taxes on traffic fatalities.

This "before and after" analysis works when the data are observed in two different years. Our data set, however, contains observations for seven different years, and it seems foolish to discard those potentially useful additional data. But the "before and after" method does not apply directly when $T > 2$. To analyze all the observations in our panel data set, we use the method of fixed effects regression.

# 10.3   Fixed Effects Regression

Fixed effects regression is a method for controlling for omitted variables in panel data when the omitted variables vary across entities (states) but do not change over time. Unlike the "before and after" comparisons of Section 10.2, fixed effects regression can be used when there are two or more time observations for each entity.

The fixed effects regression model has $n$ different intercepts, one for each entity. These intercepts can be represented by a set of binary (or indicator) variables. These binary variables absorb the influences of all omitted variables that differ from one entity to the next but are constant over time.

## The Fixed Effects Regression Model

Consider the regression model in Equation (10.4) with the dependent variable (*FatalityRate*) and observed regressor (*BeerTax*) denoted as $Y_{it}$ and $X_{it}$, respectively:

$$Y_{it} = \beta_0 + \beta_1 X_{it} + \beta_2 Z_i + u_{it}, \tag{10.9}$$

where $Z_i$ is an unobserved variable that varies from one state to the next but does not change over time (for example, $Z_i$ represents cultural attitudes toward drinking and driving). We want to estimate $\beta_1$, the effect on $Y$ of $X$ holding constant the unobserved state characteristics $Z$.

Because $Z_i$ varies from one state to the next but is constant over time, the population regression model in Equation (10.9) can be interpreted as having $n$ intercepts, one for each state. Specifically, let $\alpha_i = \beta_0 + \beta_2 Z_i$. Then Equation (10.9) becomes

$$Y_{it} = \beta_1 X_{it} + \alpha_i + u_{it}. \tag{10.10}$$

Equation (10.10) is the **fixed effects regression model**, in which $\alpha_1, \ldots, \alpha_n$ are treated as unknown intercepts to be estimated, one for each state. The interpretation of $\alpha_i$ as a state-specific intercept in Equation (10.10) comes from considering the population regression line for the $i^{\text{th}}$ state; this population regression line is $\alpha_i + \beta_1 X_{it}$. The slope coefficient of the population regression line, $\beta_1$, is the same for all states, but the intercept of the population regression line varies from one state to the next.

Because the intercept $\alpha_i$ in Equation (10.10) can be thought of as the "effect" of being in entity $i$ (in the current application, entities are states), the terms $\alpha_1, \ldots, \alpha_n$ are known as **entity fixed effects**. The variation in the entity fixed effects comes from omitted variables that, like $Z_i$ in Equation (10.9), vary across entities but not over time.

The state-specific intercepts in the fixed effects regression model also can be expressed using binary variables to denote the individual states. Section 8.3 considered the case in which the observations belong to one of two groups and the population regression line has the same slope for both groups but different intercepts (see Figure 8.8a). That population regression line was expressed mathematically using a single binary variable indicating one of the groups (case #1 in Key Concept 8.4). If we had only two states in our data set, that binary variable regression model would apply here. Because we have more than two states, however, we need additional binary variables to capture all the state-specific intercepts in Equation (10.10).

To develop the fixed effects regression model using binary variables, let $D1_i$ be a binary variable that equals 1 when $i = 1$ and equals 0 otherwise, let $D2_i$ equal 1 when $i = 2$ and equal 0 otherwise, and so on. We cannot include all $n$ binary variables plus a common intercept, for if we do the regressors will be perfectly multicollinear (this is the "dummy variable trap" of Section 6.7), so we arbitrarily omit the binary variable $D1_i$ for the first group. Accordingly, the fixed effects regression model in Equation (10.10) can be written equivalently as

$$Y_{it} = \beta_0 + \beta_1 X_{it} + \gamma_2 D2_i + \gamma_3 D3_i + \cdots + \gamma_n Dn_i + u_{it}, \qquad (10.11)$$

where $\beta_0, \beta_1, \gamma_2, \ldots, \gamma_n$ are unknown coefficients to be estimated. To derive the relationship between the coefficients in Equation (10.11) and the intercepts in Equation (10.10), compare the population regression lines for each state in the two equations. In Equation (10.11), the population regression equation for the first state is $\beta_0 + \beta_1 X_{it}$, so $\alpha_1 = \beta_0$. For the second and remaining states, it is $\beta_0 + \beta_1 X_{it} + \gamma_i$, so $\alpha_i = \beta_0 + \gamma_i$ for $i \geq 2$.

Thus there are two equivalent ways to write the fixed effects regression model, Equations (10.10) and (10.11). In Equation (10.10), it is written in terms of $n$ state-specific intercepts. In Equation (10.11), the fixed effects regression model has a common intercept and $n - 1$ binary regressors. In both formulations, the slope coefficient on $X$ is the same from one state to the next. The state-specific intercepts in Equation (10.10) and the binary regressors in Equation (10.11) have the same source: the unobserved variable $Z_i$ that varies across states but not over time.

*Extension to multiple X's.* If there are other observed determinants of $Y$ that are correlated with $X$ and that change over time, then these should also be included in the regression to avoid omitted variable bias. Doing so results in the fixed effects regression model with multiple regressors, summarized in Key Concept 10.2.

## The Fixed Effects Regression Model

KEY CONCEPT

**10.2**

The fixed effects regression model is

$$Y_{it} = \beta_1 X_{1,it} + \cdots + \beta_k X_{k,it} + \alpha_i + u_{it}, \tag{10.12}$$

where $i = 1, \ldots, n$; $t = 1, \ldots, T$; $X_{1,it}$ is the value of the first regressor for entity $i$ in time period $t$, $X_{2,it}$ is the value of the second regressor, and so forth; and $\alpha_1, \ldots, \alpha_n$ are entity-specific intercepts.

Equivalently, the fixed effects regression model can be written in terms of a common intercept, the $X$'s, and $n - 1$ binary variables representing all but one entity:

$$\begin{aligned} Y_{it} = \beta_0 &+ \beta_1 X_{1,it} + \cdots + \beta_k X_{k,it} + \gamma_2 D2_i \\ &+ \gamma_3 D3_i + \cdots + \gamma_n Dn_i + u_{it}, \end{aligned} \tag{10.13}$$

where $D2_i = 1$ if $i = 2$ and $D2_i = 0$ otherwise, and so forth.

### Estimation and Inference

In principle the binary variable specification of the fixed effects regression model [Equation (10.13)] can be estimated by OLS. This regression, however, has $k + n$ regressors (the $k$ $X$'s, the $n - 1$ binary variables, and the intercept), so in practice this OLS regression is tedious or, in some software packages, impossible to implement if the number of entities is large. Econometric software therefore has special routines for OLS estimation of fixed effects regression models. These special routines are equivalent to using OLS on the full binary variable regression, but are faster because they employ some mathematical simplifications that arise in the algebra of fixed effects regression.

*The "entity-demeaned" OLS algorithm.* Regression software typically computes the OLS fixed effects estimator in two steps. In the first step, the entity-specific average is subtracted from each variable. In the second step, the regression is estimated using "entity-demeaned" variables. Specifically, consider the case of a single regressor in the version of the fixed effects model in Equation (10.10) and take the average of both sides of Equation (10.10); then $\overline{Y}_i = \beta_1 \overline{X}_i + \alpha_i + \overline{u}_i$, where $\overline{Y}_i = (1/T)\sum_{t=1}^{T} Y_{it}$, and $\overline{X}_i$ and $\overline{u}_i$ are defined similarly. Thus Equation (10.10) implies that $Y_{it} - \overline{Y}_i = \beta_1(X_{it} - \overline{X}_i) + (u_{it} - \overline{u}_i)$. Let $\widetilde{Y}_{it} = Y_{it} - \overline{Y}_i, \widetilde{X}_{it} = X_{it} - \overline{X}_i$ and $\widetilde{u}_{it} = u_{it} - \overline{u}_i$; accordingly,

$$\widetilde{Y}_{it} = \beta_1 \widetilde{X}_{it} + \widetilde{u}_{it}. \tag{10.14}$$

Thus $\beta_1$ can be estimated by the OLS regression of the "entity-demeaned" variables $\widetilde{Y}_{it}$ on $\widetilde{X}_{it}$. In fact, this estimator is identical to the OLS estimator of $\beta_1$ obtained by estimation of the fixed effects model in Equation (10.11) using $n - 1$ binary variables (Exercise 18.6).

***The "before and after" (differences) regression versus the binary variables specification.*** Although Equation (10.11) with its binary variables looks quite different from the "before and after" regression model in Equation (10.7), in the special case that $T = 2$ the OLS estimator of $\beta_1$ from the binary variable specification and that from the "before and after" specification are identical if the intercept is excluded from the "before and after" specifications. Thus, when $T = 2$, there are three ways to estimate $\beta_1$ by OLS: the "before and after" specification in Equation (10.7) (without an intercept), the binary variable specification in Equation (10.11), and the "entity-demeaned" specification in Equation (10.14). These three methods are equivalent; that is, they produce identical OLS estimates of $\beta_1$ (Exercise 10.11).

***The sampling distribution, standard errors, and statistical inference.*** In multiple regression with cross-sectional data, if the four least squares assumptions in Key Concept 6.4 hold, then the sampling distribution of the OLS estimator is normal in large samples. The variance of this sampling distribution can be estimated from the data, and the square root of this estimator of the variance—that is, the standard error—can be used to test hypotheses using a $t$-statistic and to construct confidence intervals.

Similarly, in multiple regression with panel data, if a set of assumptions—called the fixed effects regression assumptions—hold, then the sampling distribution of the fixed effects OLS estimator is normal in large samples, the variance of that distribution can be estimated from the data, the square root of that estimator is the standard error, and the standard error can be used to construct $t$-statistics and confidence intervals. Given the standard error, statistical inference—testing hypotheses (including joint hypotheses using $F$-statistics) and constructing confidence intervals—proceeds in exactly the same way as in multiple regression with cross-sectional data.

The fixed effects regression assumptions and standard errors for fixed effects regression are discussed further in Section 10.5.

## Application to Traffic Deaths

The OLS estimate of the fixed effects regression line relating the real beer tax to the fatality rate, based on all 7 years of data (336 observations), is

$$\widehat{FatalityRate} = -0.66\,BeerTax + StateFixedEffects, \qquad (10.15)$$
$$(0.29)$$

where, as is conventional, the estimated state fixed intercepts are not listed to save space and because they are not of primary interest in this application.

Like the "differences" specification in Equation (10.8), the estimated coefficient in the fixed effects regression in Equation (10.15) is negative, so, as predicted by economic theory, higher real beer taxes are associated with fewer traffic deaths, which is the opposite of what we found in the initial cross-sectional regressions of Equations (10.2) and (10.3). The two regressions are not identical because the "differences" regression in Equation (10.8) uses only the data for 1982 and 1988 (specifically, the difference between those two years), whereas the fixed effects regression in Equation (10.15) uses the data for all 7 years. Because of the additional observations, the standard error is smaller in Equation (10.15) than in Equation (10.8).

Including state fixed effects in the fatality rate regression lets us avoid omitted variables bias arising from omitted factors, such as cultural attitudes toward drinking and driving, that vary across states but are constant over time within a state. Still, a skeptic might suspect that other factors could lead to omitted variables bias. For example, over this period cars were getting safer and occupants were increasingly wearing seat belts; if the real tax on beer rose on average during the mid-1980s, then *BeerTax* could be picking up the effect of overall automobile safety improvements. If, however, safety improvements evolved over time but were the same for all states, then we can eliminate their influence by including time fixed effects.

## 10.4   Regression with Time Fixed Effects

Just as fixed effects for each entity can control for variables that are constant over time but differ across entities, so can time fixed effects control for variables that are constant across entities but evolve over time.

Because safety improvements in new cars are introduced nationally, they serve to reduce traffic fatalities in all states. So, it is plausible to think of automobile safety as an omitted variable that changes over time but has the same value for all states. The population regression in Equation (10.9) can be modified to make explicit the effect of automobile safety, which we will denote $S_t$:

$$Y_{it} = \beta_0 + \beta_1 X_{it} + \beta_2 Z_i + \beta_3 S_t + u_{it}, \qquad (10.16)$$

where $S_t$ is unobserved and where the single $t$ subscript emphasizes that safety changes over time but is constant across states. Because $\beta_3 S_t$ represents variables that determine $Y_{it}$, if $S_t$ is correlated with $X_{it}$, then omitting $S_t$ from the regression leads to omitted variable bias.

## Time Effects Only

For the moment, suppose that the variables $Z_i$ are not present so that the term $\beta_2 Z_i$ can be dropped from Equation (10.16), although the term $\beta_3 S_t$ remains. Our objective is to estimate $\beta_1$, controlling for $S_t$.

Although $S_t$ is unobserved, its influence can be eliminated because it varies over time but not across states, just as it is possible to eliminate the effect of $Z_i$, which varies across states but not over time. In the entity fixed effects model, the presence of $Z_i$ leads to the fixed effects regression model in Equation (10.10), in which each state has its own intercept (or fixed effect). Similarly, because $S_t$ varies over time but not over states, the presence of $S_t$ leads to a regression model in which each time period has its own intercept.

The **time fixed effects regression model** with a single $X$ regressor is

$$Y_{it} = \beta_1 X_{it} + \lambda_t + u_{it}. \qquad (10.17)$$

This model has a different intercept, $\lambda_t$, for each time period. The intercept $\lambda_t$ in Equation (10.17) can be thought of as the "effect" on $Y$ of year $t$ (or, more generally, time period $t$), so the terms $\lambda_1, \ldots, \lambda_T$ are known as **time fixed effects**. The variation in the time fixed effects comes from omitted variables that, like $S_t$ in Equation (10.16), vary over time but not across entities.

Just as the entity fixed effects regression model can be represented using $n - 1$ binary indicators, so, too, can the time fixed effects regression model be represented using $T - 1$ binary indicators:

$$Y_{it} = \beta_0 + \beta_1 X_{it} + \delta_2 B2_t + \cdots + \delta_T BT_t + u_{it}, \qquad (10.18)$$

where $\delta_2, \ldots, \delta_T$ are unknown coefficients and where $B2_t = 1$ if $t = 2$ and $B2_t = 0$ otherwise, and so forth. As in the fixed effects regression model in Equation (10.11), in this version of the time effects model the intercept is included, and the first binary variable ($B1_t$) is omitted to prevent perfect multicollinearity.

When there are additional observed "$X$" regressors, then these regressors appear in Equations (10.17) and (10.18) as well.

In the traffic fatalities regression, the time fixed effects specification allows us to eliminate bias arising from omitted variables like nationally introduced safety standards that change over time but are the same across states in a given year.

## Both Entity and Time Fixed Effects

If some omitted variables are constant over time but vary across states (such as cultural norms) while others are constant across states but vary over time (such as national safety standards), then it is appropriate to include *both* entity (state) *and* time effects.

The combined **entity and time fixed effects regression model** is

$$Y_{it} = \beta_1 X_{it} + \alpha_i + \lambda_t + u_{it}, \tag{10.19}$$

where $\alpha_i$ is the entity fixed effect and $\lambda_t$ is the time fixed effect. This model can equivalently be represented using $n - 1$ entity binary indicators and $T - 1$ time binary indicators, along with an intercept:

$$\begin{aligned} Y_{it} = \beta_0 + \beta_1 X_{it} + \gamma_2 D2_i + \cdots + \gamma_n Dn_i \\ + \delta_2 B2_t + \cdots + \delta_T BT_t + u_{it}, \end{aligned} \tag{10.20}$$

where $\beta_0, \beta_1, \gamma_2, \ldots, \gamma_n$, and $\delta_2, \ldots, \delta_T$ are unknown coefficients.

When there are additional observed "$X$" regressors, then these appear in Equations (10.19) and (10.20) as well.

The combined state and time fixed effects regression model eliminates omitted variables bias arising both from unobserved variables that are constant over time and from unobserved variables that are constant across states.

*Estimation.* The time fixed effects model and the entity and time fixed effects model are both variants of the multiple regression model. Thus their coefficients can be estimated by OLS by including the additional time binary variables. Alternatively, in a balanced panel the coefficients on the $X$'s can be computed by first deviating $Y$ and the $X$'s from their entity *and* time-period means and then by estimating the multiple regression equation of deviated $Y$ on the deviated $X$'s. This algorithm, which is commonly implemented in regression software, eliminates the need to construct the full set of binary indicators that appear in Equation (10.20). An equivalent approach is to deviate $Y$, the $X$'s, and the time indicators from their entity (but not time) means and to estimate $k + T$ coefficients by multiple regression of the deviated $Y$ on the deviated $X$'s and the deviated time indicators. Finally, if $T = 2$, the entity and time fixed effects regression can be estimated using the "before and after" approach of Section 10.2, including the intercept in the regression. Thus the "before and after" regression reported in Equation (10.8), in which the change in *FatalityRate* from 1982 to 1988 is regressed on the change in *BeerTax* from 1982 to 1988 including an intercept, provides the same estimate of the slope coefficient as the OLS regression of *FatalityRate* on *BeerTax*, including entity and time fixed effects, estimated using data for the two years 1982 and 1988.

*Application to traffic deaths.*  Adding time effects to the state fixed effects regression results in the OLS estimate of the regression line:

$$\widehat{FatalityRate} = -0.64\,BeerTax + StateFixedEffects + TimeFixedEffects. \quad (10.21)$$
$$(0.36)$$

This specification includes the beer tax, 47 state binary variables (state fixed effects), 6 single-year binary variables (time fixed effects), and an intercept, so this regression actually has $1 + 47 + 6 + 1 = 55$ right-hand variables! The coefficients on the time and state binary variables and the intercept are not reported because they are not of primary interest.

Including time effects has little impact on the coefficient on the real beer tax [compare Equations (10.15) and (10.21)]. Although this coefficient is less precisely estimated when time effects are included, it is still significant at the 10%, but not 5%, significance level ($t = -0.64/0.36 = -1.78$).

This estimated relationship between the real beer tax and traffic fatalities is immune to omitted variable bias from variables that are constant either over time or across states. However, many important determinants of traffic deaths do not fall into this category, so this specification could still be subject to omitted variable bias. Section 10.6 therefore undertakes a more complete empirical examination of the effect of the beer tax and of laws aimed directly at eliminating drunk driving, controlling for a variety of factors. Before turning to that study, we first discuss the assumptions underlying panel data regression and the construction of standard errors for fixed effects estimators.

## 10.5 The Fixed Effects Regression Assumptions and Standard Errors for Fixed Effects Regression

In panel data, the regression error can be correlated over time within an entity. Like heteroskedasticity, this correlation does not introduce bias into the fixed effects estimator, but it affects the variance of the fixed effects estimator and therefore it affects how one computes standard errors. The standard errors for fixed effects regressions reported in this chapter are so-called clustered standard errors, which are robust both to heteroskedasticity and to correlation over time within an entity. When there are many entities (when $n$ is large), hypothesis tests and confidence intervals can be computed using the usual large-sample normal and $F$ critical values.

This section describes clustered standard errors. We begin with the fixed effects regression assumptions, which extend the least squares regression assumptions to panel data; under these assumptions, the fixed effects estimator is asymptotically normally distributed when $n$ is large. To keep the notation as simple as possible, this section focuses on the entity fixed effects regression model of Section 10.3, in which there are no time effects.

### The Fixed Effects Regression Assumptions

The four fixed effects regression assumptions are summarized in Key Concept 10.3. These assumptions extend the four least squares assumptions, stated for cross-sectional data in Key Concept 6.4, to panel data.

The first assumption is that the error term has conditional mean zero, given all $T$ values of $X$ for that entity. This assumption plays the same role as the first least squares assumption for cross-sectional data in Key Concept 6.4 and implies that there is no omitted variable bias. The requirement that the conditional mean of $u_{it}$ not depend on *any* of the values of $X$ for that entity—past, present, or future—adds an important subtlety beyond the first least squares assumption for cross-sectional data. This assumption is violated if current $u_{it}$ is correlated with past, present, or future values of $X$.

The second assumption is that the variables for one entity are distributed identically to, but independently of, the variables for another entity; that is, the variables are i.i.d. across entities for $i = 1, \ldots, n$. Like the second least squares assumption in Key Concept 6.4, the second assumption for fixed effects regression holds if entities are selected by simple random sampling from the population.

## The Fixed Effects Regression Assumptions

$$Y_{it} = \beta_1 X_{it} + \alpha_i + u_{it}, i = 1, \ldots, n, t = 1, \ldots, T,$$

where

1. $u_{it}$ has conditional mean zero: $E(u_{it} \mid X_{i1}, X_{i2}, \ldots, X_{iT}, \alpha_i) = 0$.
2. $(X_{i1}, X_{i2}, \ldots, X_{iT}, u_{i1}, u_{i2}, \ldots, u_{iT}), i = 1, \ldots, n$ are i.i.d. draws from their joint distribution.
3. Large outliers are unlikely: $(X_{it}, u_{it})$ have nonzero finite fourth moments.
4. There is no perfect multicollinearity.

For multiple regressors, $X_{it}$ should be replaced by the full list $X_{1,it}, X_{2,it}, \ldots, X_{k,it}$.

The third and fourth assumptions for fixed effects regression are analogous to the third and fourth least squares assumptions for cross-sectional data in Key Concept 6.4.

Under the least squares assumptions for panel data in Key Concept 10.3, the fixed effects estimator is consistent and is normally distributed when $n$ is large. The details are discussed in Appendix 10.2.

An important difference between the panel data assumptions in Key Concept 10.3 and the assumptions for cross-sectional data in Key Concept 6.4 is Assumption 2. The cross-sectional counterpart of Assumption 2 holds that each observation is independent, which arises under simple random sampling. In contrast, Assumption 2 for panel data holds that the variables are independent across entities but makes no such restriction within an entity. For example, Assumption 2 allows $X_{it}$ to be correlated over time within an entity.

If $X_{it}$ is correlated with $X_{is}$ for different values of $s$ and $t$—that is, if $X_{it}$ is correlated over time for a given entity—then $X_{it}$ is said to be **autocorrelated** (correlated with itself, at different dates) or **serially correlated**. Autocorrelation is a pervasive feature of time series data: What happens one year tends to be correlated with what happens the next year. In the traffic fatality example, $X_{it}$, the beer tax in state $i$ in year $t$, is autocorrelated: Most of the time, the legislature does not change the beer tax, so if it is high one year relative to its mean value for state $i$, it will tend to be high the next year, too. Similarly, it is possible to think of reasons why $u_{it}$ would be autocorrelated. Recall that $u_{it}$ consists of time-varying factors that are determinants of $Y_{it}$ but are not included as regressors, and some of these omitted factors might be autocorrelated. For example, a downturn in the local economy might produce layoffs and diminish commuting traffic, thus reducing traffic fatalities for 2 or more years. Similarly, a major road improvement project might reduce traffic accidents not only in the year of completion but also in future years. Such omitted factors, which persist over multiple years, produce autocorrelated regression errors. Not all omitted factors will produce autocorrelation in $u_{it}$; for example, severe winter driving conditions plausibly affect fatalities, but if winter weather conditions for a given state are independently distributed from one year to the next, then this component of the error term would be serially uncorrelated. In general, though, as long as some omitted factors are autocorrelated, then $u_{it}$ will be autocorrelated.

## Standard Errors for Fixed Effects Regression

If the regression errors are autocorrelated, then the usual heteroskedasticity-robust standard error formula for cross-section regression [Equations (5.3) and (5.4)] is not valid. One way to see this is to draw an analogy to heteroskedasticity. In a regression with cross-sectional data, if the errors are heteroskedastic, then (as discussed in Section 5.4) the homoskedasticity-only standard errors are not valid because they were derived under the false assumption of homoskedasticity. Similarly, if the errors are autocorrelated, then the usual standard errors will not be valid because they were derived under the false assumption of no serial correlation.

Standard errors that are valid if $u_{it}$ is potentially heteroskedastic and potentially correlated over time within an entity are referred to as **heteroskedasticity- and autocorrelation-consistent (HAC) standard errors**. The standard errors used in this chapter are one type of HAC standard errors, **clustered standard errors**. The term *clustered* arises because these standard errors allow the regression errors to have an arbitrary correlation within a cluster, or grouping, but assume that the regression errors are uncorrelated across clusters. In the context of panel data, each cluster consists of an entity. Thus clustered standard errors allow for heteroskedasticity and for arbitrary autocorrelation within an entity, but treat the errors as uncorrelated across entities. That is, clustered standard errors allow for heteroskedasticity and autocorrelation in a way that is consistent with the second fixed effects regression assumption in Key Concept 10.3.

Like heteroskedasticity-robust standard errors in regression with cross-sectional data, clustered standard errors are valid whether or not there is heteroskedasticity, autocorrelation, or both. If the number of entities $n$ is large, inference using clustered standard errors can proceed using the usual large-sample normal critical values for $t$-statistics and $F_{q,\infty}$ critical values for $F$-statistics testing $q$ restrictions.

In practice, there can be a large difference between clustered standard errors and standard errors that do not allow for autocorrelation of $u_{it}$. For example, the usual (cross-sectional data) heteroskedasticity-robust standard error for the *BeerTax* coefficient in Equation (10.21) is 0.25, substantially smaller than the clustered standard error, 0.36, and the respective $t$-statistics testing $\beta_1 = 0$ are $-2.51$ and $-1.78$. The reason we report the clustered standard error is that it allows for serial correlation of $u_{it}$ within an entity, whereas the usual heteroskedasticity-robust standard error does not. The formula for clustered standard errors is given in Appendix 10.2.

## 10.6  Drunk Driving Laws and Traffic Deaths

Alcohol taxes are only one way to discourage drinking and driving. States differ in their punishments for drunk driving, and a state that cracks down on drunk driving could do so by toughening driving laws as well as raising taxes. If so, omitting these laws could produce omitted variable bias in the OLS estimator of the effect of real beer taxes on traffic fatalities, even in regressions with state and time fixed effects. In addition, because vehicle use depends in part on whether drivers have jobs and because tax changes can reflect economic conditions (a state budget deficit can lead to tax hikes), omitting state economic conditions also could result in omitted variable bias. In this section, we therefore extend the preceding analysis of traffic fatalities to include other driving laws and economic conditions.

The results are summarized in Table 10.1. The format of the table is the same as that of the tables of regression results in Chapters 7 through 9: Each column reports a different regression, and each row reports a coefficient estimate and standard error, $F$-statistic and $p$-value, or other information about the regression.

Column (1) in Table 10.1 presents results for the OLS regression of the fatality rate on the real beer tax without state and time fixed effects. As in the cross-sectional regressions for 1982 and 1988 [Equations (10.2) and (10.3)], the coefficient on the real beer tax is *positive* (0.36): According to this estimate, increasing beer taxes *increases* traffic fatalities! However, the regression in column (2) [reported previously as Equation (10.15)], which includes state fixed effects, suggests that the positive coefficient in regression (1) is the result of omitted variable bias (the coefficient on the real beer tax is $-0.66$). The regression $\overline{R}^2$ jumps from 0.091 to 0.889 when fixed effects are included; evidently, the state fixed effects account for a large amount of the variation in the data.

Little changes when time effects are added, as reported in column (3) [reported previously as Equation (10.21)], except that the beer tax coefficient is now estimated less precisely. The results in columns (1) through (3) are consistent with the omitted fixed factors—historical and cultural factors, general road conditions, population density, attitudes toward drinking and driving, and so forth—being important determinants of the variation in traffic fatalities across states.

| TABLE 10.1 | Regression Analysis of the Effect of Drunk Driving Laws on Traffic Deaths |
|---|---|

**Dependent variable: Traffic fatality rate (deaths per 10,000).**

| Regressor | (1) | (2) | (3) | (4) | (5) | (6) | (7) |
|---|---|---|---|---|---|---|---|
| Beer tax | 0.36** (0.05) | −0.66* (0.29) | −0.64+ (0.36) | −0.45 (0.30) | −0.69* (0.35) | −0.46 (0.31) | −0.93** (0.34) |
| Drinking age 18 | | | | 0.028 (0.070) | −0.010 (0.083) | | 0.037 (0.102) |
| Drinking age 19 | | | | −0.018 (0.050) | −0.076 (0.068) | | −0.065 (0.099) |
| Drinking age 20 | | | | 0.032 (0.051) | −0.100+ (0.056) | | −0.113 (0.125) |
| Drinking age | | | | | | −0.002 (0.021) | |
| Mandatory jail or community service? | | | | 0.038 (0.103) | 0.085 (0.112) | 0.039 (0.103) | 0.089 (0.164) |
| Average vehicle miles per driver | | | | 0.008 (0.007) | 0.017 (0.011) | 0.009 (0.007) | 0.124 (0.049) |
| Unemployment rate | | | | −0.063** (0.013) | | −0.063** (0.013) | −0.091** (0.021) |
| Real income per capita (logarithm) | | | | 1.82** (0.64) | | 1.79** (0.64) | 1.00 (0.68) |
| Years | 1982–88 | 1982–88 | 1982–88 | 1982–88 | 1982–88 | 1982–88 | 1982 & 1988 only |
| State effects? | no | yes | yes | yes | yes | yes | yes |
| Time effects? | no | no | yes | yes | yes | yes | yes |
| Clustered standard errors? | no | yes | yes | yes | yes | yes | yes |

**F-Statistics and p-Values Testing Exclusion of Groups of Variables**

| | | | | | | | |
|---|---|---|---|---|---|---|---|
| Time effects = 0 | | | 4.22 (0.002) | 10.12 (< 0.001) | 3.48 (0.006) | 10.28 (< 0.001) | 37.49 (< 0.001) |
| Drinking age coefficients = 0 | | | | 0.35 (0.786) | 1.41 (0.253) | | 0.42 (0.738) |
| Unemployment rate, income per capita = 0 | | | | 29.62 (< 0.001) | | 31.96 (< 0.001) | 25.20 (< 0.001) |
| $\overline{R}^2$ | 0.091 | 0.889 | 0.891 | 0.926 | 0.893 | 0.926 | 0.899 |

These regressions were estimated using panel data for 48 U.S. states. Regressions (1) through (6) use data for all years 1982 to 1988, and regression (7) uses data from 1982 and 1988 only. The data set is described in Appendix 10.1. Standard errors are given in parentheses under the coefficients, and p-values are given in parentheses under the F-statistics. The individual coefficient is statistically significant at the +10%, *5%, or **1% significance level.

The next four regressions in Table 10.1 include additional potential determinants of fatality rates along with state and time effects. The base specification, reported in column (4), includes variables related to drunk driving laws plus variables that control for the amount of driving and overall state economic conditions. The first legal variables are the minimum legal drinking age, represented by three binary variables for a minimum legal drinking age of 18, 19, and 20 (so the omitted group is a minimum legal drinking age of 21 or older). The other legal variable is the punishment associated with the first conviction for driving under the influence of alcohol, either mandatory jail time or mandatory community service (the omitted group is less severe punishment). The three measures of driving and economic conditions are average vehicle miles per driver, the unemployment rate, and the logarithm of real (1988 dollars) personal income per capita (using the logarithm of income permits the coefficient to be interpreted in terms of percentage changes of income; see Section 8.2). The final regression in Table 10.1 follows the "before and after" approach of Section 10.2 and uses only data from 1982 and 1988; thus regression (7) extends the regression in Equation (10.8) to include the additional regressors.

The regression in column (4) has four interesting results.

1. Including the additional variables reduces the estimated effect of the beer tax from $-0.64$ in column (3) to $-0.45$ in column (4). One way to evaluate the magnitude of this coefficient is to imagine a state with an average real beer tax doubling its tax; because the average real beer tax in these data is approximately \$0.50 per case (in 1988 dollars), this entails increasing the tax by \$0.50 per case. The estimated effect of a \$0.50 increase in the beer tax is to decrease the expected fatality rate by $0.45 \times 0.50 = 0.23$ death per 10,000. This estimated effect is large: Because the average fatality rate is 2 per 10,000, a reduction of 0.23 corresponds to reducing traffic deaths by nearly one-eighth. This said, the estimate is quite imprecise: Because the standard error on this coefficient is 0.30, the 95% confidence interval for this effect is $-0.45 \times 0.50 \pm 1.96 \times 0.30 \times 0.50 = (-0.52, 0.07)$. This wide 95% confidence interval includes zero, so the hypothesis that the beer tax has no effect cannot be rejected at the 5% significance level.

2. The minimum legal drinking age is precisely estimated to have a small effect on traffic fatalities. According to the regression in column (4), the 95% confidence interval for the increase in the fatality rate in a state with a minimum legal drinking age of 18, relative to age 21, is $(-0.11, 0.17)$. The joint hypothesis that the coefficients on the minimum legal drinking age variables are zero cannot be rejected at the 10% significance level: The $F$-statistic testing the joint hypothesis that the three coefficients are zero is 0.35, with a $p$-value of 0.786.

3. The coefficient on the first offense punishment variable is also estimated to be small and is not significantly different from zero at the 10% significance level.

4. The economic variables have considerable explanatory power for traffic fatalities. High unemployment rates are associated with fewer fatalities: An increase in the unemployment rate by one percentage point is estimated to reduce traffic fatalities by 0.063 death per 10,000. Similarly, high values of real per capita income are associated with high fatalities: The coefficient is 1.82, so a 1% increase in real per capita income is associated with an increase in traffic fatalities of 0.0182 death per 10,000 (see Case I in Key Concept 8.2 for interpretation of this coefficient). According to these estimates, good economic conditions are associated with higher fatalities, perhaps because of increased traffic density when the unemployment rate is low or greater alcohol consumption when income is high. The two economic variables are jointly significant at the 0.1% significance level (the $F$-statistic is 29.62).

Columns (5) through (7) of Table 10.1 report regressions that check the sensitivity of these conclusions to changes in the base specification. The regression in column (5) drops the variables that control for economic conditions. The result is an increase in the estimated effect of the real beer tax, which becomes significant at the 5% level, but no appreciable change in the other coefficients. The sensitivity of the estimated beer tax coefficient to including the economic variables, combined with the statistical significance of the coefficients on those variables in column (4), indicates that the economic variables should remain in the base specification. The regression in column (6) shows that the results in column (4) are not sensitive to changing the functional form when the three drinking age indicator variables are replaced by the drinking age itself. When the coefficients are estimated using the changes of the variables from 1982 to 1988 [column (7)], as in Section 10.2, the findings from column (4) are largely unchanged except that the coefficient on the beer tax is larger and is significant at the 1% level.

The strength of this analysis is that including state and time fixed effects mitigates the threat of omitted variable bias arising from unobserved variables that either do not change over time (like cultural attitudes toward drinking and driving) or do not vary across states (like safety innovations). As always, however, it is important to think about possible threats to validity. One potential source of omitted variable bias is that the measure of alcohol taxes used here, the real tax on beer, could move with other alcohol taxes, which suggests interpreting the results as pertaining more broadly than just to beer. A subtler possibility is that hikes in the real beer tax could be associated with public education campaigns. If so, changes in the real beer tax could pick up the effect of a broader campaign to reduce drunk driving.

Taken together, these results present a provocative picture of measures to control drunk driving and traffic fatalities. According to these estimates, neither stiff punishments nor increases in the minimum legal drinking age have important effects on fatalities. In contrast, there is some evidence that increasing alcohol taxes, as measured by the real tax on beer, does reduce traffic deaths, presumably through reduced alcohol consumption. The imprecision of the estimated beer tax coefficient means, however, that we should be cautious about drawing policy conclusions from this analysis and that additional research is warranted.[2]

## 10.7  Conclusion

This chapter showed how multiple observations over time on the same entity can be used to control for unobserved omitted variables that differ across entities but are constant over time. The key insight is that if the unobserved variable does not change over time, then any changes in the dependent variable must be due to influences other than these fixed characteristics. If cultural attitudes toward drinking and driving do not change appreciably over 7 years within a state, then explanations for changes in the traffic fatality rate over those 7 years must lie elsewhere.

To exploit this insight, you need data in which the same entity is observed at two or more time periods; that is, you need panel data. With panel data, the multiple regression model of Part II can be extended to include a full set of entity binary variables; this is the fixed effects regression model, which can be estimated by OLS. A twist on the fixed effects regression model is to include time fixed effects, which control for unobserved variables that change over time but are constant across entities. Both entity and time fixed effects can be included in the regression to control for variables that vary across entities but are constant over time and for variables that vary over time but are constant across entities.

Despite these virtues, entity and time fixed effects regression cannot control for omitted variables that vary *both* across entities *and* over time. And, obviously, panel data methods require panel data, which often are not available. Thus there

---

[2]For further analysis of these data, see Ruhm (1996). A recent meta-analysis of 112 studies of the effect of alcohol prices and taxes on consumption found elasticities of −0.46 for beer, −0.69 for wine, and −0.80 for spirits, and concluded that alcohol taxes have large effects on reducing consumption, relative to other programs [Wagenaar, Salois, and Komro (2009)]. To learn more about drunk driving and alcohol, and about the economics of alcohol more generally, also see Cook and Moore (2000), Chaloupka, Grossman, and Saffer (2002), Young and Bielinska-Kwapisz (2006), and Dang (2008).

remains a need for a method that can eliminate the influence of unobserved omitted variables when panel data methods cannot do the job. A powerful and general method for doing so is instrumental variables regression, the topic of Chapter 12.

## Summary

1. Panel data consist of observations on multiple ($n$) entities—states, firms, people, and so forth—where each entity is observed at two or more time periods ($T$).
2. Regression with entity fixed effects controls for unobserved variables that differ from one entity to the next but remain constant over time.
3. When there are two time periods, fixed effects regression can be estimated by a "before and after" regression of the change in $Y$ from the first period to the second on the corresponding change in $X$.
4. Entity fixed effects regression can be estimated by including binary variables for $n - 1$ entities plus the observable independent variables (the $X$'s) and an intercept.
5. Time fixed effects control for unobserved variables that are the same across entities but vary over time.
6. A regression with time and entity fixed effects can be estimated by including binary variables for $n - 1$ entities and binary variables for $T - 1$ time periods plus the $X$'s and an intercept.
7. In panel data, variables are typically autocorrelated—that is, correlated over time within an entity. Standard errors need to allow both for this autocorrelation and for potential heteroskedasticity, and one way to do so is to use clustered standard errors.

## Key Terms

panel data (397)
balanced panel (397)
unbalanced panel (397)
fixed effects regression model (403)
entity fixed effects (403)
time fixed effects regression model (408)
time fixed effects (408)

entity and time fixed effects regression model (409)
autocorrelated (412)
serially correlated (412)
heteroskedasticity- and autocorrelation-consistent (HAC) standard errors (413)
clustered standard errors (413)

**MyEconLab Can Help You Get a Better Grade**

MyEconLab   If your exam were tomorrow, would you be ready? For each chapter, **MyEconLab** Practice Tests and Study Plan help you prepare for your exams. You can also find similar Exercises and Review the Concepts Questions now in **MyEconLab**. To see how it works, turn to the **MyEconLab** spread on pages 2 and 3 of this book and then go to **www.myeconlab.com**.

For additional Empirical Exercises and Data Sets, log on to the Companion Website at **www.pearsonglobaleditions.com/Stock_Watson**.

## Review the Concepts

**10.1**   Define panel data. What is the advantage of using such data to make statistical and economic inferences? Why is it necessary to use two subscripts, $i$ and $t$, to describe panel data? What does $i$ refer to? What does $t$ refer to?

**10.2**   A researcher is using a panel data set on $n = 1000$ workers over $T = 10$ years (from 2001 through 2010) that contains the workers' earnings, gender, education, and age. The researcher is interested in the effect of education on earnings. Give some examples of unobserved person-specific variables that are correlated with both education and earnings. Can you think of examples of time-specific variables that might be correlated with education and earnings? How would you control for these person-specific and time-specific effects in a panel data regression?

**10.3**   Can the regression that you suggested in response to Question 10.2 be used to estimate the effect of gender on an individual's earnings? Can that regression be used to estimate the effect of the national unemployment rate on an individual's earnings? Explain.

**10.4**   In the context of the regression you suggested for Question 10.2, explain why the regression error for a given individual might be serially correlated.

## Exercises

**10.1**   This exercise refers to the drunk driving panel data regression, summarized in Table 10.1.

     **a.**   New Jersey has a population of 8.85 million people. Suppose that New Jersey increased the tax on a case of beer by $2 (in 1988 dollars). Use the results in column (5) to predict the number of lives that would be saved over the next year. Construct a 99% confidence interval for your answer.

**b.** The drinking age in New Jersey is 21. Suppose that New Jersey lowered its drinking age to 19. Use the results in column (5) to predict the change in the number of traffic fatalities in the next year. Construct a 95% confidence interval for your answer.

**c.** Suppose that real income per capita in New Jersey increases by 3% in the next year. Use the results in column (6) to predict the change in the number of traffic fatalities in the next year. Construct a 95% confidence interval for your answer.

**d.** How should standard errors be clustered in the regressions in columns (2) through (7)?

**e.** How should minimum drinking age be included in the regressions? Should it enter as a continuous variable or as a series of indicator variables? Be specific about the information you use to assess this question.

**10.2**  Consider the binary variable version of the fixed effects model in Equation (10.11), except with an additional regressor, $D1_i$; that is, let

$$Y_{it} = \beta_0 + \beta_1 X_{it} + \gamma_1 D1_i + \gamma_2 D2_i + \cdots + \gamma_n Dn_i + u_{it}.$$

**a.** Suppose that $n = 3$. Show that the binary regressors and the "constant" regressor are perfectly multicollinear; that is, express one of the variables $D1_i$, $D2_i$, $D3_i$, and $X_{0,it}$ as a perfect linear function of the others, where $X_{0,it} = 1$ for all $i, t$.

**b.** Show the result in (a) for general $n$.

**c.** What will happen if you try to estimate the coefficients of the regression by OLS?

**10.3**  Section 9.2 gave a list of five potential threats to the internal validity of a regression study. Apply that list to the empirical analysis in Section 10.6 and thereby draw conclusions about its internal validity.

**10.4**  Using the regression in Equation (10.11), what is the slope and intercept for

**a.** Entity 1 in time period 1?

**b.** Entity 1 in time period 3?

**c.** Entity 3 in time period 1?

**d.** Entity 3 in time period 3?

**10.5**   Consider the model with a single regressor $Y_{it} = \beta_1 X_{1,it} + \alpha_i + \lambda_t + u_{it}$. This model also can be written as

$$Y_{it} = \beta_0 + \beta_1 X_{1,it} + \delta_2 B2_t + \cdots + \delta_T BT_t + \gamma_2 D2_i + \cdots + \gamma_n Dn_i + u_{it},$$

where $B2_t = 1$ if $t = 2$ and 0 otherwise, $D2_i = 1$ if $i = 2$ and 0 otherwise, and so forth. How are the coefficients $(\beta_0, \delta_2, \ldots, \delta_T, \gamma_2, \ldots, \gamma_n)$ related to the coefficients $(\alpha_1, \ldots, \alpha_n, \lambda_1, \ldots, \lambda_T)$?

**10.6**   Do the fixed effects regression assumptions in Key Concept 10.3 imply that $\text{cov}(\tilde{v}_{it}, \tilde{v}_{is}) = 0$ for $t \neq s$ in Equation (10.28)? Explain.

**10.7**   Suppose a researcher believes that the occurrence of natural disasters, such as earthquakes, leads to increased activity in the construction industry. The researcher decides to collect province-level data on employment in the construction industry of an earthquake-prone country, and regress this variable on an indicator variable that equals 1 if an earthquake took place in that province in the last five years.

   **a.** Should the researcher include province fixed effects in order to control for location-specific characteristics of the labor market?

   **b.** What can the researcher do to control for location effects?

**10.8**   Consider observations $(Y_{it}, X_{it})$ from the linear panel data model

$$Y_{it} = X_{it}\beta_1 + \alpha_i + \lambda_i t + u_{it},$$

where $t = 1, \ldots, T; i = 1, \ldots, n$; and $\alpha_i + \lambda_i t$ is an unobserved entity-specific time trend. How would you estimate $\beta_1$?

**10.9**   **a.** In the fixed effects regression model, are the fixed entity effects, $\alpha_i$, consistently estimated as $n \longrightarrow \infty$ with $T$ fixed? (*Hint:* Analyze the model with no $X$'s: $Y_{it} = \alpha_i + u_{it}$.)

   **b.** If $n$ is large (say, $n = 2000$) but $T$ is small (say, $T = 4$), do you think that the estimated values of $\alpha_i$ are approximately normally distributed? Why or why not? (*Hint:* Analyze the model $Y_{it} = \alpha_i + u_{it}$.)

**10.10**   A researcher wants to estimate the determinants of annual earnings: age, gender, schooling, union status, occupation, and sector of employment. The researcher has been told that if they collect panel data on a large number of randomly chosen individuals over time, they will be able to regress annual earnings on these determinant variables while using fixed effects to control for individual-specific time-invariant characteristics. What estimation problems is the researcher likely to run into if they use this strategy?

**10.11** Let $\hat{\beta}_1^{DM}$ denote the entity-demeaned estimator given in Equation (10.22), and let $\hat{\beta}_1^{BA}$ denote the "before and after" estimator without an intercept, so that $\hat{\beta}_1^{BA} = [\Sigma_{i=1}^n (X_{i2} - X_{i1})(Y_{i2} - Y_{i1})]/[\Sigma_{i=1}^n (X_{i2} - X_{i1})^2]$. Show that, if $T = 2$, $\hat{\beta}_1^{DM} = \hat{\beta}_1^{BA}$. [*Hint:* Use the definition of $\widetilde{X}_{it}$ before Equation (10.22) to show that $\widetilde{X}_{i1} = -\frac{1}{2}(X_{i2} - X_{i1})$ and $\widetilde{X}_{i2} = \frac{1}{2}(X_{i2} - X_{i1})$.]

## Empirical Exercises

(Only two empirical exercises for this chapter are given in the text, but you can find more on the text website, **www.pearsonglobaleditions.com/Stock_Watson**.)

**E10.1** Some U.S. states have enacted laws that allow citizens to carry concealed weapons. These laws are known as "shall-issue" laws because they instruct local authorities to issue a concealed weapons permit to all applicants who are citizens, are mentally competent, and have not been convicted of a felony. (Some states have some additional restrictions.) Proponents argue that if more people carry concealed weapons, crime will decline because criminals will be deterred from attacking other people. Opponents argue that crime will increase because of accidental or spontaneous use of the weapons. In this exercise, you will analyze the effect of concealed weapons laws on violent crimes. On the textbook website, **www.pearsonglobaleditions .com/Stock_Watson**, you will find the data file **Guns**, which contains a balanced panel of data from the 50 U.S. states plus the District of Columbia for the years 1977 through 1999.[3] A detailed description is given in **Guns_ Description**, available on the website.

   **a.** Estimate (1) a regression of ln(*vio*) against *shall* and (2) a regression of ln(*vio*) against *shall, incarc_rate, density, avginc, pop, pb1064, pw1064*, and *pm1029*.

      **i.** Interpret the coefficient on *shall* in regression (2). Is this estimate large or small in a "real-world" sense?

---

[3]These data were provided by Professor John Donohue of Stanford University and were used in his paper with Ian Ayres, "Shooting Down the 'More Guns Less Crime' Hypothesis," *Stanford Law Review*, 2003, 55: 1193–1312.

    ii. Does adding the control variables in regression (2) change the estimated effect of a shall-carry law in regression (1) as measured by statistical significance? As measured by the "real-world" significance of the estimated coefficient?

    iii. Suggest a variable that varies across states but plausibly varies little—or not at all—over time and that could cause omitted variable bias in regression (2).

**b.** Do the results change when you add fixed state effects? If so, which set of regression results is more credible, and why?

**c.** Do the results change when you add fixed time effects? If so, which set of regression results is more credible, and why?

**d.** Repeat the analysis using ln(*rob*) and ln(*mur*) in place of ln(*vio*).

**e.** In your view, what are the most important remaining threats to the internal validity of this regression analysis?

**f.** Based on your analysis, what conclusions would you draw about the effects of concealed weapons laws on these crime rates?

**E10.2** Do citizens demand more democracy and political freedom as their incomes grow? That is, is democracy a normal good? On the textbook website, **www.pearsonglobaleditions.com/Stock_Watson**, you will find the data file **Income_Democracy**, which contains a panel data set from 195 countries for the years 1960, 1965, ... , 2000. A detailed description is given in **Income_Democracy_Description**, available on the website.[4] The dataset contains an index of political freedom/democracy for each country in each year, together with data on the country's income and various demographic controls. (The income and demographic controls are lagged five years relative to the democracy index to allow time for democracy to adjust to changes in these variables.)

**a.** Is the data set a balanced panel? Explain.

**b.** The index of political freedom/democracy is labeled *Dem_ind*.

    i. What are the minimum and maximum values of *Dem_ind* in the data set? What are the mean and standard deviation of *Dem_ind*

---

[4]These data were provided by Daron Acemoglu of M.I.T. and were used in his paper with Simon Johnson, James Robinson, and Pierre Yared, "Income and Democracy," *American Economic Review*, 2008, 98:3, 808–842.

in the data set? What are the 10th, 25th, 50th, 75th, and 90th percentiles of its distribution?

    ii. What is the value of *Dem_ind* for the United States in 2000? Averaged over all years in the data set?

    iii. What is the value of *Dem_ind* for Libya in 2000? Averaged over all years in the data set?

    iv. List five countries with an average value of *Dem_ind* greater than 0.95; less than 0.10; and between 0.3 and 0.7.

**c.** The logarithm of per capita income is labeled *Log_GDPPC*. Regress *Dem_ind* on *Log_GDPPC*. Use standard errors that are clustered by country.

    i. How large is the estimated coefficient on *Log_GDPPC*? Is the coefficient statistically significant?

    ii. If per capita income in a country increases by 20%, by how much is *Dem_ind* predicted to increase? What is a 95% confidence interval for the prediction? Is the predicted increase in *Dem_ind* large or small? (Explain what you mean by large or small.)

    iii. Why is it important to use clustered standard errors for the regression? Do the results change if you do not use clustered standard errors?

**d.** i. Suggest a variable that varies across countries but plausibly varies little—or not at all—over time and that could cause omitted variable bias in the regression in (c).

    ii. Estimate the regression in (c), allowing for country fixed effects. How do your answers to (c)(i) and (c)(ii) change?

    iii. Exclude the data for Azerbaijan and rerun the regression. Do the results change? Why or why not?

    iv. Suggest a variable that varies over time but plausibly varies little—or not at all—across countries and that could cause omitted variable bias in the regression in (c).

    v. Estimate the regression in (c), allowing for time and country fixed effects. How do your answers to (c)(i) and (c)(ii) change?

    vi. There are addition demographic controls in the data set. Should these variables be included in the regression? If so, how do the results change when they are included?

**e.** Based on your analysis, what conclusions do you draw about the effects of income on democracy?

# 10.1 The State Traffic Fatality Data Set

The data are for the contiguous 48 U.S. states (excluding Alaska and Hawaii), annually for 1982 through 1988. The traffic fatality rate is the number of traffic deaths in a given state in a given year, per 10,000 people living in that state in that year. Traffic fatality data were obtained from the U.S. Department of Transportation Fatal Accident Reporting System. The beer tax (the tax on a case of beer) was obtained from Beer Institute's *Brewers Almanac*. The drinking age variables in Table 10.1 are binary variables indicating whether the legal drinking age is 18, 19, or 20. The binary punishment variable in Table 10.1 describes the state's minimum sentencing requirements for an initial drunk driving conviction: This variable equals 1 if the state requires jail time or community service and equals 0 otherwise (a lesser punishment). Data on the total vehicle miles traveled annually by state were obtained from the Department of Transportation. Personal income data were obtained from the U.S. Bureau of Economic Analysis, and the unemployment rate was obtained from the U.S. Bureau of Labor Statistics.

These data were graciously provided by Professor Christopher J. Ruhm of the Department of Economics at the University of North Carolina.

# 10.2 Standard Errors for Fixed Effects Regression

This appendix provides formulas for standard errors for fixed effects regression with a single regressor. These formulas are extended to multiple regressors in Exercise 18.15.

## The Asymptotic Distribution of the Fixed Effects Estimator with Large *n*

*The fixed effects estimator.* The fixed effects estimator of $\beta_1$ is the OLS estimator obtained using the entity-demeaned regression of Equation (10.14), in which $\widetilde{Y}_{it}$ is regressed on $\widetilde{X}_{it}$, where $\widetilde{Y}_{it} = Y_{it} - \overline{Y}_i$, $\widetilde{X}_{it} = X_{it} - \overline{X}_i$, $\overline{Y}_i = T^{-1}\sum_{t=1}^{T}Y_{it}$, and $\overline{X}_i = T^{-1}\sum_{t=1}^{T}X_{it}$. The formula for the OLS estimator is obtained by replacing $X_i - \overline{X}$ by $\widetilde{X}_{it}$ and $Y_i - \overline{Y}$ by $\widetilde{Y}_{it}$ in

Equation (4.7) and by replacing the single summation in Equation (4.7) by two summations, one over entities ($i = 1, \ldots, n$) and one over time periods ($t = 1, \ldots, T$),[5] so

$$\hat{\beta}_1 = \frac{\sum\limits_{i=1}^{n}\sum\limits_{t=1}^{T}\widetilde{X}_{it}\widetilde{Y}_{it}}{\sum\limits_{i=1}^{n}\sum\limits_{t=1}^{T}\widetilde{X}_{it}^2}. \tag{10.22}$$

The derivation of the sampling distribution of $\hat{\beta}_1$ parallels the derivation in Appendix 4.3 of the sampling distribution of the OLS estimator with cross-sectional data. First, substitute $\widetilde{Y}_{it} = \beta_1\widetilde{X}_{it} + \widetilde{u}_{it}$ [Equation (10.14)] into the numerator of Equation (10.22) to obtain the panel data counterpart of Equation (4.30):

$$\hat{\beta}_1 = \beta_1 + \frac{\frac{1}{nT}\sum\limits_{i=1}^{n}\sum\limits_{t=1}^{T}\widetilde{X}_{it}\widetilde{u}_{it}}{\frac{1}{nT}\sum\limits_{i=1}^{n}\sum\limits_{t=1}^{T}\widetilde{X}_{it}^2}. \tag{10.23}$$

Next, rearrange this expression and multiply both sides by $\sqrt{nT}$ to obtain

$$\sqrt{nT}(\hat{\beta}_1 - \beta_1) = \frac{\sqrt{\frac{1}{n}\sum\limits_{i=1}^{n}\eta_i}}{\hat{Q}_{\widetilde{X}}}, \text{ where } \eta_i = \sqrt{\frac{1}{T}\sum\limits_{t=1}^{T}\widetilde{X}_{it}\widetilde{u}_{it}} \text{ and } \hat{Q}_{\widetilde{X}} = \frac{1}{nT}\sum\limits_{i=1}^{n}\sum\limits_{t=1}^{T}\widetilde{X}_{it}^2. \tag{10.24}$$

The scaling factor in Equation (10.24), $nT$, is the total number of observations.

***Distribution and standard errors when*** n ***is large.*** In most panel data applications, $n$ is much larger than $T$, which motivates approximating sampling distributions by letting $n \to \infty$ while keeping $T$ fixed. Under the fixed effects regression assumptions of Key Concept 10.3, $\hat{Q}_{\widetilde{X}} \xrightarrow{p} Q_{\widetilde{X}} = ET^{-1}\sum_{t=1}^{T}\widetilde{X}_{it}^2$ as $n \to \infty$. Also, $\eta_i$ is i.i.d. over $i = 1, \ldots, n$ (by Assumption 2) with mean zero (by Assumption 1) and variance $\sigma_\eta^2$ (which is finite by Assumption 3), so by the central limit theorem, $\sqrt{1/n}\sum_{i=1}^{n}\eta_i \xrightarrow{d} N(0, \sigma_\eta^2)$. It follows from Equation (10.24) that

$$\sqrt{nT}(\hat{\beta}_1 - \beta_1) \xrightarrow{d} N\left(0, \frac{\sigma_\eta^2}{Q_{\widetilde{X}}^2}\right), \tag{10.25}$$

---

[5]The double summation is the extension to double subscripts of a single summation:

$$\sum_{i=1}^{n}\sum_{t=1}^{T}X_{it} = \sum_{i=1}^{n}\left(\sum_{t=1}^{T}X_{it}\right)$$
$$= \sum_{i=1}^{n}(X_{i1} + X_{i2} + \cdots + X_{iT})$$
$$= (X_{11} + X_{12} + \cdots + X_{1T}) + (X_{21} + X_{22} + \cdots + X_{2T}) + \cdots + (X_{n1} + X_{n2} + \cdots + X_{nT}).$$

From Equation (10.25), the variance of the large-sample distribution of $\hat{\beta}_1$ is

$$\text{var}(\hat{\beta}_1) = \frac{1}{nT}\frac{\sigma_\eta^2}{Q_{\tilde{X}}^2}. \tag{10.26}$$

The clustered standard error formula replaces the population moments in Equation (10.26) by their sample counterparts:

$$SE(\hat{\beta}_1) = \sqrt{\frac{1}{nT}\frac{s_\eta^2}{\hat{Q}_{\tilde{X}}^2}},$$

$$\text{where } s_\eta^2 = \frac{1}{n-1}\sum_{i=1}^n (\hat{\eta}_i - \overline{\hat{\eta}})^2 = \frac{1}{n-1}\sum_{i=1}^n \hat{\eta}_i^2 \tag{10.27}$$

where $\hat{\eta}_i = \sqrt{1/T}\sum_{t=1}^T \tilde{X}_{it}\hat{u}_{it}$ is the sample counterpart of $\eta_i$ [$\hat{\eta}_i$ is $\eta_i$ in Equation (10.24), with $\tilde{u}_{it}$ replaced by the fixed effects regression residual $\hat{u}_{it}$] and $\overline{\hat{\eta}} = (1/n)\sum_{i=1}^n \hat{\eta}_i$. The final equality in Equation (10.27) arises because $\overline{\hat{\eta}} = 0$, which in turn follows from the residuals and regressors being uncorrelated [Equation (4.34)]. Note that $s_\eta^2$ is just the sample variance of $\hat{\eta}_i$ [see Equation (3.7)].

The estimator $s_\eta^2$ is a consistent estimator of $\sigma_\eta^2$ as $n \to \infty$, even if there is heteroskedasticity or autocorrelation (Exercise 18.15); thus the clustered standard error in Equation (10.27) is heteroskedasticity- and autocorrelation-consistent. Because the clustered standard error is consistent, the $t$-statistic testing $\beta_1 = \beta_{1,0}$ has a standard normal distribution under the null hypothesis as $n \to \infty$.

All the foregoing results apply if there are multiple regressors. In addition, if $n$ is large, then the $F$-statistic testing $q$ restrictions (computed using the clustered variance formula) has its usual asymptotic $F_{q,\infty}$ distribution.

*Why isn't the usual heteroskedasticity-robust estimator of Chapter 5 valid for panel data?* There are two reasons. The most important reason is that the heteroskedasticity-robust estimator of Chapter 5 does not allow for serial correlation within a cluster. Recall that, for two random variables $U$ and $V$, $\text{var}(U + V) = \text{var}(U) + \text{var}(V) + 2\text{cov}(U, V)$. The variance $\eta_i$ in Equation (10.24) therefore can be written as the sum of variances plus covariances. Let $\tilde{v}_{it} = \tilde{X}_{it}\tilde{u}_{it}$; then

$$\text{var}(\eta_i) = \text{var}\left(\sqrt{\frac{1}{T}\sum_{t=1}^T \tilde{v}_{it}}\right) = \frac{1}{T}\text{var}(\tilde{v}_{i1} + \tilde{v}_{i2} + \cdots + \tilde{v}_{iT})$$

$$= \frac{1}{T}[\text{var}(\tilde{v}_{i1}) + \text{var}(\tilde{v}_{i2}) + \cdots + \text{var}(\tilde{v}_{iT})$$

$$+ 2\text{cov}(\tilde{v}_{i1}, \tilde{v}_{i2}) + \cdots + 2\text{cov}(\tilde{v}_{iT-1}, \tilde{v}_{iT})]. \tag{10.28}$$

The heteroskedasticity-robust variance formula of Chapter 5 misses all the covariances in the final part of Equation (10.28), so if there is serial correlation, the usual heteroskedasticity-robust variance estimator is inconsistent.

The second reason is that if $T$ is small, the estimation of the fixed effects introduces bias into the Chapter 5 heteroskedasticity-robust variance estimator. This problem does not arise in cross-sectional regression.

The one case in which the usual heteroskedasticity-robust standard errors can be used with panel data is with fixed effects regression with $T = 2$ observations. In this case, fixed effects regression is equivalent to the "before and after" differences regression in Section 10.2, and heteroskedasticity-robust and clustered standard errors are equivalent.

For empirical examples showing the importance of using clustered standard errors in economic panel data, see Bertrand, Duflo, and Mullainathan (2004).

*Standard Errors When $u_{it}$ Is Correlated Across Entities.*  In some cases, $u_{it}$ might be correlated across entities. For example, in a study of earnings, suppose that the sampling scheme selects families by simple random sampling, then tracks all siblings within a family. Because the omitted factors that enter the error term could have common elements for siblings, it is not reasonable to assume that the errors are independent for siblings (even though they are independent across families).

In the siblings example, families are natural clusters, or groupings, of observations, where $u_{it}$ is correlated within the cluster but not across clusters. The derivation leading to Equation (10.27) can be modified to allow for clusters across entities (for example, families) or across both entities and time, as long as there are many clusters.

## Distribution and Standard Errors When $n$ Is Small

If $n$ is small and $T$ is large, then it remains possible to use clustered standard errors; however, $t$-statistics need to be compared with critical values from the $t_{n-1}$ tables, and the $F$-statistic testing $q$ restrictions needs to be compared to the $F_{q,\,n-q}$ critical value multiplied by $(n - 1)/(n - q)$. These distributions are valid under the assumptions in Key Concept 10.3, plus some additional assumptions on the joint distribution of $X_{it}$ and $u_{it}$ over time within an entity. Although the validity of the $t$-distribution in cross-sectional regression requires normality and homoskedasticity of the regression errors (Section 5.6), neither requirement is needed to justify using the $t$-distribution with clustered standard errors in panel data when $T$ is large.

To see why the cluster $t$-statistic has a $t_{n-1}$ distribution when $n$ is small and $T$ is large, even if $u_{it}$ is neither normally distributed nor homoskedastic, first note that if $T$ is large, then under additional assumptions, $\eta_i$ in Equation (10.24) will obey a central limit theorem, so $\eta_i \overset{d}{\longrightarrow} N(0, \sigma_\eta^2)$. (The additional assumptions required for this result are substantial and technical, and we defer further discussion of them to our treatment of time series data in Chapter 14.) Thus, if $T$ is large, then $\sqrt{nT}(\hat{\beta}_1 - \beta_1)$ in Equation (10.24) is a scaled average of the $n$ normal random variables $\eta_i$. Moreover, the clustered formula $s_{\hat{\eta}}^2$ in Equation (10.27) is the usual formula for the sample variance, and if it could be computed using $\eta_i$, then $(n-1)s_{\eta}^2/\sigma_{\eta}^2$ would have a $\chi_{n-1}^2$ distribution, so the $t$-statistic would have a $t_{n-1}$ distribution [see Section 3.6]. Using the residuals to compute $\hat{\eta}_i$ and $s_{\hat{\eta}}^2$ does not change this conclusion. In the case of multiple regressors, analogous reasoning leads to the conclusion that the $F$-statistic testing $q$ restrictions, computed using the cluster variance estimator, is distributed as $(\frac{n-1}{n-q})F_{q,n-q}$. [For example, the 5% critical value for this $F$-statistic when $n = 10$ and $q = 4$ is $(\frac{10-1}{10-4}) \times 4.53 = 6.80$, where 4.53 is the 5% critical value from the $F_{4,6}$ distribution given in Appendix Table 5B.] Note that, as $n$ increases, the $t_{n-1}$ and $(\frac{n-1}{n-q})F_{q,n-q}$ distributions approach the usual standard normal and $F_{q,\infty}$ distributions.[6]

If both $n$ and $T$ are small, then in general $\hat{\beta}_1$ will not be normally distributed, and clustered standard errors will not provide reliable inference.

---

[6]Not all software implements clustered standard errors using the $t_{n-1}$ and $(\frac{n-1}{n-q})F_{q,n-q}$ distributions that apply if $n$ is small, so you should check how your software implements and treats clustered standard errors.

# Regression with a Binary Dependent Variable

Two people, identical but for their race, walk into a bank and apply for a mortgage, a large loan so that each can buy an identical house. Does the bank treat them the same way? Are they both equally likely to have their mortgage application accepted? By law they must receive identical treatment. But whether they actually do is a matter of great concern among bank regulators.

Loans are made and denied for many legitimate reasons. For example, if the proposed loan payments take up most or all of the applicant's monthly income, a loan officer might justifiably deny the loan. Also, even loan officers are human and they can make honest mistakes, so the denial of a single minority applicant does not prove anything about discrimination. Many studies of discrimination thus look for statistical evidence of discrimination, that is, evidence contained in large data sets showing that whites and minorities are treated differently.

But how, precisely, should one check for statistical evidence of discrimination in the mortgage market? A start is to compare the fraction of minority and white applicants who were denied a mortgage. In the data examined in this chapter, gathered from mortgage applications in 1990 in the Boston, Massachusetts, area, 28% of black applicants were denied mortgages but only 9% of white applicants were denied. But this comparison does not really answer the question that opened this chapter, because the black applicants and the white applicants were not necessarily "identical but for their race." Instead, we need a method for comparing rates of denial, *holding other applicant characteristics constant*.

This sounds like a job for multiple regression analysis—and it is, but with a twist. The twist is that the dependent variable—whether the applicant is denied—is binary. In Part II, we regularly used binary variables as regressors, and they caused no particular problems. But when the dependent variable is binary, things are more difficult: What does it mean to fit a line to a dependent variable that can take on only two values, 0 and 1?

The answer to this question is to interpret the regression function as a conditional probability. This interpretation is discussed in Section 11.1, and it allows us to apply the multiple regression models from Part II to binary dependent variables. Section 11.1 goes over this "linear probability model." But the predicted probability interpretation also suggests that alternative, nonlinear regression models can do a better job modeling these probabilities. These methods, called "probit" and "logit" regression, are discussed in Section 11.2. Section 11.3, which is optional, discusses the method used to estimate the coefficients of the probit and logit regressions, the method of maximum likelihood estimation. In Section 11.4, we apply these methods to the Boston mortgage application data set to see whether there is evidence of racial bias in mortgage lending.

The binary dependent variable considered in this chapter is an example of a dependent variable with a limited range; in other words, it is a **limited dependent variable**. Models for other types of limited dependent variables, for example, dependent variables that take on multiple discrete values, are surveyed in Appendix 11.3.

# 11.1  Binary Dependent Variables and the Linear Probability Model

Whether a mortgage application is accepted or denied is one example of a binary variable. Many other important questions also concern binary outcomes. What is the effect of a tuition subsidy on an individual's decision to go to college? What determines whether a teenager takes up smoking? What determines whether a country receives foreign aid? What determines whether a job applicant is successful? In all these examples, the outcome of interest is binary: The student does or does not go to college, the teenager does or does not take up smoking, a country does or does not receive foreign aid, the applicant does or does not get a job.

This section discusses what distinguishes regression with a binary dependent variable from regression with a continuous dependent variable and then turns to the simplest model to use with binary dependent variables, the linear probability model.

## Binary Dependent Variables

The application examined in this chapter is whether race is a factor in denying a mortgage application; the binary dependent variable is whether a mortgage application is denied. The data are a subset of a larger data set compiled by researchers at the Federal Reserve Bank of Boston under the Home Mortgage Disclosure Act (HMDA) and relate to mortgage applications filed in the Boston, Massachusetts, area in 1990. The Boston HMDA data are described in Appendix 11.1.

Mortgage applications are complicated and so is the process by which the bank loan officer makes a decision. The loan officer must forecast whether the applicant will make his or her loan payments. One important piece of information is the size of the required loan payments relative to the applicant's income. As anyone who has borrowed money knows, it is much easier to make payments that are 10% of your income than 50%! We therefore begin by looking at the relationship between two variables: the binary dependent variable *deny*, which equals 1 if the mortgage application was denied and equals 0 if it was accepted, and the continuous variable *P/I ratio*, which is the ratio of the applicant's anticipated total monthly loan payments to his or her monthly income.

Figure 11.1 presents a scatterplot of *deny* versus *P/I ratio* for 127 of the 2380 observations in the data set. (The scatterplot is easier to read using this subset of the data.) This scatterplot looks different from the scatterplots of Part II because the variable *deny* is binary. Still, it seems to show a relationship between *deny* and *P/I ratio*: Few applicants with a payment-to-income ratio less than 0.3 have their application denied, but most applicants with a payment-to-income ratio exceeding 0.4 are denied.

This positive relationship between *P/I ratio* and *deny* (the higher the *P/I ratio*, the greater the fraction of denials) is summarized in Figure 11.1 by the OLS regression line estimated using these 127 observations. As usual, this line plots the predicted value of *deny* as a function of the regressor, the payment-to-income ratio. For example, when *P/I ratio* = 0.3, the predicted value of deny is 0.20. But what, precisely, does it mean for the predicted value of the binary variable *deny* to be 0.20?

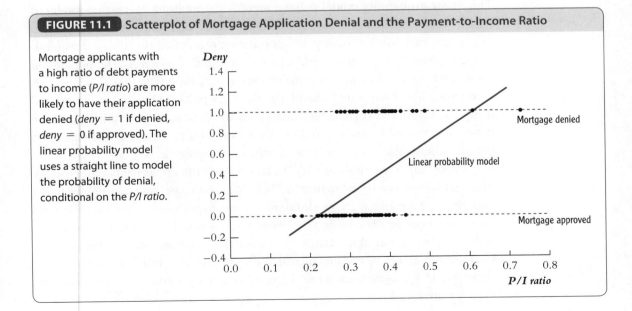

**FIGURE 11.1**  Scatterplot of Mortgage Application Denial and the Payment-to-Income Ratio

Mortgage applicants with a high ratio of debt payments to income (*P/I ratio*) are more likely to have their application denied (*deny* = 1 if denied, *deny* = 0 if approved). The linear probability model uses a straight line to model the probability of denial, conditional on the *P/I ratio*.

The key to answering this question—and more generally to understanding regression with a binary dependent variable—is to interpret the regression as modeling the *probability* that the dependent variable equals 1. Thus the predicted value of 0.20 is interpreted as meaning that, when *P/I ratio* is 0.3, the probability of denial is estimated to be 20%. Said differently, if there were many applications with *P/I ratio* = 0.3, then 20% of them would be denied.

This interpretation follows from two facts. First, from Part II, the population regression function is the expected value of $Y$ given the regressors, $E(Y|X_1, \ldots, X_k)$. Second, from Section 2.2, if $Y$ is a 0–1 binary variable, its expected value (or mean) is the probability that $Y = 1$; that is, $E(Y) = 0 \times \Pr(Y = 0) + 1 \times \Pr(Y = 1) = \Pr(Y = 1)$. In the regression context the expected value is conditional on the value of the regressors, so the probability is conditional on $X$. Thus for a binary variable, $E(Y|X_1, \ldots, X_k) = \Pr(Y = 1|X_1, \ldots, X_k)$. In short, for a binary dependent variable, the predicted value from the population regression is the probability that $Y = 1$, given $X$.

The linear multiple regression model applied to a binary dependent variable is called the linear probability model: "linear" because it is a straight line and "probability model" because it models the probability that the dependent variable equals 1 (in our example, the probability of loan denial).

## The Linear Probability Model

The **linear probability model** is the name for the multiple regression model of Part II when the dependent variable is binary rather than continuous. Because the dependent variable $Y$ is binary, the population regression function corresponds to the probability that the dependent variable equals 1, given $X$. The population coefficient $\beta_1$ on a regressor $X$ is the *change in the probability* that $Y = 1$ associated with a *unit change* in $X$. Similarly, the OLS predicted value, $\hat{Y}_i$, computed using the estimated regression function, is the predicted probability that the dependent variable equals 1, and the OLS estimator $\hat{\beta}_1$ estimates the change in the probability that $Y = 1$ associated with a unit change in $X$.

Almost all of the tools of Part II carry over to the linear probability model. The coefficients can be estimated by OLS. Ninety-five percent confidence intervals can be formed as ±1.96 standard errors, hypotheses concerning several coefficients can be tested using the $F$-statistic discussed in Chapter 7, and interactions between variables can be modeled using the methods of Section 8.3. Because the errors of the linear probability model are always heteroskedastic (Exercise 11.8), it is essential that heteroskedasticity-robust standard errors be used for inference.

One tool that does not carry over is the $R^2$. When the dependent variable is continuous, it is possible to imagine a situation in which the $R^2$ equals 1: All the data lie exactly on the regression line. This is impossible when the dependent variable is binary, unless the regressors are also binary. Accordingly, the $R^2$ is not a particularly useful statistic here. We return to measures of fit in the next section.

The linear probability model is summarized in Key Concept 11.1.

***Application to the Boston HMDA data.*** The OLS regression of the binary dependent variable, *deny*, against the payment-to-income ratio, *P/I ratio*, estimated using all 2380 observations in our data set is

$$\widehat{deny} = -0.080 + 0.604 \, P/I \, ratio. \tag{11.1}$$
$$\phantom{\widehat{deny} = } (0.032) \quad (0.098)$$

The estimated coefficient on *P/I ratio* is positive, and the population coefficient is statistically significantly different from zero at the 1% level (the *t*-statistic is 6.13). Thus applicants with higher debt payments as a fraction of income are more likely to have their application denied. This coefficient can be used to compute the predicted change in the probability of denial, given a change in the regressor.

---

## The Linear Probability Model

**KEY CONCEPT**

**11.1**

The linear probability model is the linear multiple regression model,

$$Y_i = \beta_0 + \beta_1 X_{1i} + \beta_2 X_{2i} + \cdots + \beta_k X_{ki} + u_i, \tag{11.2}$$

applied to a binary dependent variable $Y_i$. Because $Y$ is binary, $E(Y|X_1, X_2, \ldots, X_k)$ $= \Pr(Y = 1|X_1, X_2, \ldots, X_k)$, so for the linear probability model,

$$\Pr(Y = 1|X_1, X_2, \ldots, X_k) = \beta_0 + \beta_1 X_1 + \beta_2 X_2 + \cdots + \beta_k X_k.$$

The regression coefficient $\beta_1$ is the change in the probability that $Y = 1$ associated with a unit change in $X_1$, holding constant the other regressors, and so forth for $\beta_2, \ldots, \beta_k$. The regression coefficients can be estimated by OLS, and the usual (heteroskedasticity-robust) OLS standard errors can be used for confidence intervals and hypothesis tests.

For example, according to Equation (11.1), if *P/I ratio* increases by 0.1, the probability of denial increases by $0.604 \times 0.1 \cong 0.060$, that is, by 6.0 percentage points.

The estimated linear probability model in Equation (11.1) can be used to compute predicted denial probabilities as a function of *P/I ratio*. For example, if projected debt payments are 30% of an applicant's income, *P/I ratio* is 0.3 and the predicted value from Equation (11.1) is $-0.080 + 0.604 \times 0.3 = 0.101$. That is, according to this linear probability model, an applicant whose projected debt payments are 30% of income has a probability of 10.1% that his or her application will be denied. [This is different from the probability of 20% based on the regression line in Figure 11.1, because that line was estimated using only 127 of the 2380 observations used to estimate Equation (11.1).]

What is the effect of race on the probability of denial, holding constant the *P/I ratio*? To keep things simple, we focus on differences between black applicants and white applicants. To estimate the effect of race, holding constant *P/I ratio*, we augment Equation (11.1) with a binary regressor that equals 1 if the applicant is black and equals 0 if the applicant is white. The estimated linear probability model is

$$\widehat{deny} = -0.091 + 0.559\,P/I\,ratio + 0.177\,black. \tag{11.3}$$
$$\phantom{\widehat{deny} = }(0.029)\quad(0.089)\qquad\qquad(0.025)$$

The coefficient on *black*, 0.177, indicates that an African American applicant has a 17.7% higher probability of having a mortgage application denied than a white applicant, holding constant their payment-to-income ratio. This coefficient is significant at the 1% level (the *t*-statistic is 7.11).

Taken literally, this estimate suggests that there might be racial bias in mortgage decisions, but such a conclusion would be premature. Although the payment-to-income ratio plays a role in the loan officer's decision, so do many other factors, such as the applicant's earning potential and the individual's credit history. If any of these variables are correlated with the regressors *black* or *P/I ratio*, their omission from Equation (11.3) will cause omitted variable bias. Thus we must defer any conclusions about discrimination in mortgage lending until we complete the more thorough analysis in Section 11.3.

*Shortcomings of the linear probability model.* The linearity that makes the linear probability model easy to use is also its major flaw. Because probabilities cannot exceed 1, the effect on the probability that $Y = 1$ of a given change in $X$ must be nonlinear: Although a change in *P/I ratio* from 0.3 to 0.4 might have a large effect on the probability of denial, once *P/I ratio* is so large that the loan is very likely to be denied, increasing *P/I ratio* further will have little effect. In contrast, in the linear probability model, the effect of a given change in *P/I ratio* is constant, which leads to predicted probabilities in Figure 11.1 that drop below 0 for very low values of *P/I ratio* and exceeds 1 for high values! But this is non-sense: A probability cannot be less than 0 or greater than 1. This nonsensical feature is an inevitable consequence of the linear regression. To address this problem, we introduce new nonlinear models specifically designed for binary dependent variables, the probit and logit regression models.

# 11.2 Probit and Logit Regression

**Probit** and **logit**[1] regression are nonlinear regression models specifically designed for binary dependent variables. Because a regression with a binary dependent variable $Y$ models the probability that $Y = 1$, it makes sense to adopt a nonlinear formulation that forces the predicted values to be between 0 and 1. Because cumulative probability distribution functions (c.d.f.'s) produce probabilities between 0 and 1 (Section 2.1), they are used in logit and probit regressions. Probit regression uses the standard normal c.d.f. Logit regression, also called **logistic regression**, uses the "logistic" c.d.f.

## Probit Regression

*Probit regression with a single regressor.* The probit regression model with a single regressor $X$ is

$$\Pr(Y = 1 | X) = \Phi(\beta_0 + \beta_1 X), \tag{11.4}$$

where $\Phi$ is the cumulative standard normal distribution function (tabulated in Appendix Table 1).

For example, suppose that $Y$ is the binary mortgage denial variable (*deny*), $X$ is the payment-to-income ratio (*P/I ratio*), $\beta_0 = -2$, and $\beta_1 = 3$. What then is the probability of denial if *P/I ratio* $= 0.4$? According to Equation (11.4), this probability is $\Phi(\beta_0 + \beta_1 P/I \, ratio) = \Phi(-2 + 3 P/I \, ratio) = \Phi(-2 + 3 \times 0.4) = \Phi(-0.8)$. According to the cumulative normal distribution table (Appendix Table 1), $\Phi(-0.8) = \Pr(Z \leq -0.8) = 21.2\%$. That is, when *P/I ratio* is 0.4, the predicted

---

[1]Pronounced prō-bit and lō-jit.

probability that the application will be denied is 21.2%, computed using the probit model with the coefficients $\beta_0 = -2$ and $\beta_1 = 3$.

In the probit model, the term $\beta_0 + \beta_1 X$ plays the role of "$z$" in the cumulative standard normal distribution table in Appendix Table 1. Thus the calculation in the previous paragraph can, equivalently, be done by first computing the "$z$-value," $z = \beta_0 + \beta_1 X = -2 + 3 \times 0.4 = -0.8$, and then looking up the probability in the tail of the normal distribution to the left of $z = -0.8$, which is 21.2%.

The probit coefficient $\beta_1$ in Equation (11.4) is the change in the $z$-value associated with a unit change in $X$. If $\beta_1$ is positive, an increase in $X$ increases the $z$-value and thus increases the probability that $Y = 1$; if $\beta_1$ is negative, an increase in $X$ decreases the probability that $Y = 1$. Although the effect of $X$ on the $z$-value is linear, its effect on the probability is nonlinear. Thus in practice the easiest way to interpret the coefficients of a probit model is to compute the predicted probability, or the change in the predicted probability, for one or more values of the regressors. When there is just one regressor, the predicted probability can be plotted as a function of $X$.

Figure 11.2 plots the estimated regression function produced by the probit regression of *deny* on *P/I ratio* for the 127 observations in the scatterplot. The estimated probit regression function has a stretched "S" shape: It is nearly 0 and flat for small values of *P/I ratio*, it turns and increases for intermediate values, and it

---

**FIGURE 11.2**  Probit Model of the Probability of Denial, Given *P/I Ratio*

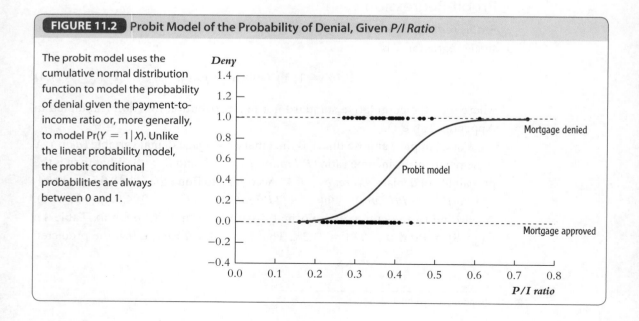

The probit model uses the cumulative normal distribution function to model the probability of denial given the payment-to-income ratio or, more generally, to model $\Pr(Y = 1 \mid X)$. Unlike the linear probability model, the probit conditional probabilities are always between 0 and 1.

flattens out again and is nearly 1 for large values. For small values of the payment-to-income ratio, the probability of denial is small. For example, for $P/I\ ratio = 0.2$, the estimated probability of denial based on the estimated probit function in Figure 11.2 is $\Pr(deny = 1 \mid P/I\ ratio = 0.2) = 2.1\%$ When $P/I\ ratio = 0.3$, the estimated probability of denial is 16.1%. When $P/I\ ratio = 0.4$, the probability of denial increases sharply to 51.9%, and when $P/I\ ratio = 0.6$, the denial probability is 98.3%. According to this estimated probit model, for applicants with high payment-to-income ratios, the probability of denial is nearly 1.

***Probit regression with multiple regressors.*** In all the regression problems we have studied so far, leaving out a determinant of $Y$ that is correlated with the included regressors results in omitted variable bias. Probit regression is no exception. In linear regression, the solution is to include the additional variable as a regressor. This is also the solution to omitted variable bias in probit regression.

The probit model with multiple regressors extends the single-regressor probit model by adding regressors to compute the $z$-value. Accordingly, the probit population regression model with two regressors, $X_1$ and $X_2$, is

$$\Pr(Y = 1 \mid X_1, X_2) = \Phi(\beta_0 + \beta_1 X_1 + \beta_2 X_2). \qquad (11.5)$$

For example, suppose that $\beta_0 = -1.6, \beta_1 = 2$, and $\beta_2 = 0.5$. If $X_1 = 0.4$ and $X_2 = 1$, the $z$-value is $z = -1.6 + 2 \times 0.4 + 0.5 \times 1 = -0.3$. So, the probability that $Y = 1$ given $X_1 = 0.4$ and $X_2 = 1$ is $\Pr(Y = 1 \mid X_1 = 0.4, X_2 = 1) = \Phi(-0.3) = 38\%$.

***Effect of a change in X.*** In general, the regression model can be used to determine the expected change in $Y$ arising from a change in $X$. When $Y$ is binary, its conditional expectation is the conditional probability that it equals 1, so the expected change in $Y$ arising from a change in $X$ is the change in the probability that $Y = 1$.

Recall from Section 8.1 that, when the population regression function is a nonlinear function of $X$, this expected change is estimated in three steps: First, compute the predicted value at the original value of $X$ using the estimated regression function; next, compute the predicted value at the changed value of $X, X + \Delta X$; finally, compute the difference between the two predicted values. This procedure is summarized in Key Concept 8.1. As emphasized in Section 8.1, this method *always* works for computing predicted effects of a change in $X$, no matter how complicated the nonlinear model. When applied to the probit model, the method of Key Concept 8.1 yields the estimated effect on the probability that $Y = 1$ of a change in $X$.

The probit regression model, predicted probabilities, and estimated effects are summarized in Key Concept 11.2.

**KEY CONCEPT**

**11.2**

## The Probit Model, Predicted Probabilities, and Estimated Effects

The population probit model with multiple regressors is

$$\Pr(Y = 1 | X_1, X_2, \ldots, X_k) = \Phi(\beta_0 + \beta_1 X_1 + \beta_2 X_2 + \cdots + \beta_k X_k) \quad (11.6)$$

where the dependent variable $Y$ is binary, $\Phi$ is the cumulative standard normal distribution function, and $X_1$, $X_2$, and so on are regressors. The model is best interpreted by computing predicted probabilities and the effect of a change in a regressor.

The predicted probability that $Y = 1$, given values of $X_1, X_2, \ldots, X_k$, is calculated by computing the $z$-value, $z = \beta_0 + \beta_1 X_1 + \beta_2 X_2 + \cdots + \beta_k X_k$, and then looking up this $z$-value in the normal distribution table (Appendix Table 1).

The coefficient $\beta_1$ is the change in the $z$-value arising from a unit change in $X_1$, holding constant $X_2, \ldots, X_k$.

The effect on the predicted probability of a change in a regressor is computed by (1) computing the predicted probability for the initial value of the regressors, (2) computing the predicted probability for the new or changed value of the regressors, and (3) taking their difference.

*Application to the mortgage data.* As an illustration, we fit a probit model to the 2380 observations in our data set on mortgage denial (*deny*) and the payment-to-income ratio (*P/I ratio*):

$$\widehat{\Pr(deny = 1 | P/I\, ratio)} = \Phi(-2.19 + 2.97\, P/I\, ratio). \quad (11.7)$$
$$\qquad\qquad\quad (0.16) \quad (0.47)$$

The estimated coefficients of $-2.19$ and $2.97$ are difficult to interpret because they affect the probability of denial via the $z$-value. Indeed, the only things that can be readily concluded from the estimated probit regression in Equation (11.7) are that the payment-to-income ratio is positively related to probability of denial (the coefficient on *P/I ratio* is positive) and that this relationship is statistically significant ($t = 2.97/0.47 = 6.32$).

What is the change in the predicted probability that an application will be denied when the payment-to-income ratio increases from 0.3 to 0.4? To answer this question, we follow the procedure in Key Concept 8.1: Compute the probability of denial for *P/I ratio* = 0.3 and then for *P/I ratio* = 0.4, and then compute the difference. The probability of denial when *P/I ratio* = 0.3 is $\Phi(-2.19 + 2.97 \times 0.3) = \Phi(-1.30) = 0.097$. The probability of denial when *P/I ratio* = 0.4 is $\Phi(-2.19 + 2.97 \times 0.4) = \Phi(-1.00) = 0.159$. The estimated change in the probability of denial is $0.159 - 0.097 = 0.062$. That is, an increase in the payment-to-income ratio from 0.3 to 0.4 is associated with an increase in the probability of denial of 6.2 percentage points, from 9.7% to 15.9%.

Because the probit regression function is nonlinear, the effect of a change in $X$ depends on the starting value of $X$. For example, if *P/I ratio* = 0.5, the estimated denial probability based on Equation (11.7) is $\Phi(-2.19 + 2.97 \times 0.5) = \Phi(-0.71) = 0.239$. Thus the change in the predicted probability when *P/I ratio* increases from 0.4 to 0.5 is $0.239 - 0.159$, or 8.0 percentage points, larger than the increase of 6.2 percentage points when *P/I ratio* increases from 0.3 to 0.4.

What is the effect of race on the probability of mortgage denial, holding constant the payment-to-income ratio? To estimate this effect, we estimate a probit regression with both *P/I ratio* and *black* as regressors:

$$\overbrace{\Pr(deny = 1 \mid P/I\,ratio, black)} = \Phi(-2.26 + 2.74\,P/I\,ratio + 0.71\,black). \quad (11.8)$$
$$\qquad\qquad\qquad\quad (0.16) \quad (0.44) \qquad\qquad (0.083)$$

Again, the values of the coefficients are difficult to interpret but the sign and statistical significance are not. The coefficient on *black* is positive, indicating that an African American applicant has a higher probability of denial than a white applicant, holding constant their payment-to-income ratio. This coefficient is statistically significant at the 1% level (the *t*-statistic on the coefficient multiplying *black* is 8.55). For a white applicant with *P/I ratio* = 0.3, the predicted denial probability is 7.5%, while for a black applicant with *P/I ratio* = 0.3, it is 23.3%; the difference in denial probabilities between these two hypothetical applicants is 15.8 percentage points.

*Estimation of the probit coefficients.* The probit coefficients reported here were estimated using the method of maximum likelihood, which produces efficient (minimum variance) estimators in a wide variety of applications, including regression with a binary dependent variable. The maximum likelihood estimator is consistent and normally distributed in large samples, so *t*-statistics and confidence intervals for the coefficients can be constructed in the usual way.

Regression software for estimating probit models typically uses maximum likelihood estimation, so this is a simple method to apply in practice. Standard errors produced by such software can be used in the same way as the standard errors of regression coefficients; for example, a 95% confidence interval for the

**KEY CONCEPT**

**11.3**

## Logit Regression

The population logit model of the binary dependent variable $Y$ with multiple regressors is

$$\Pr(Y = 1 \mid X_1, X_2, \ldots, X_k) = F(\beta_0 + \beta_1 X_1 + \beta_2 X_2 + \cdots + \beta_k X_k)$$

$$= \frac{1}{1 + e^{-(\beta_0 + \beta_1 X_1 + \beta_2 X_2 + \cdots + \beta_k X_k)}}. \tag{11.9}$$

Logit regression is similar to probit regression except that the cumulative distribution function is different.

true probit coefficient can be constructed as the estimated coefficient $\pm 1.96$ standard errors. Similarly, $F$-statistics computed using maximum likelihood estimators can be used to test joint hypotheses. Maximum likelihood estimation is discussed further in Section 11.3, with additional details given in Appendix 11.2.

## Logit Regression

*The logit regression model.* The logit regression model is similar to the probit regression model except that the cumulative standard normal distribution function $\Phi$ in Equation (11.6) is replaced by the cumulative standard logistic distribution function, which we denote by $F$. Logit regression is summarized in Key Concept 11.3. The logistic cumulative distribution function has a specific functional form, defined in terms of the exponential function, which is given as the final expression in Equation (11.9).

As with probit, the logit coefficients are best interpreted by computing predicted probabilities and differences in predicted probabilities.

The coefficients of the logit model can be estimated by maximum likelihood. The maximum likelihood estimator is consistent and normally distributed in large samples, so $t$-statistics and confidence intervals for the coefficients can be constructed in the usual way.

The logit and probit regression functions are similar. This is illustrated in Figure 11.3, which graphs the probit and logit regression functions for the dependent variable *deny* and the single regressor *P/I ratio*, estimated by maximum likelihood

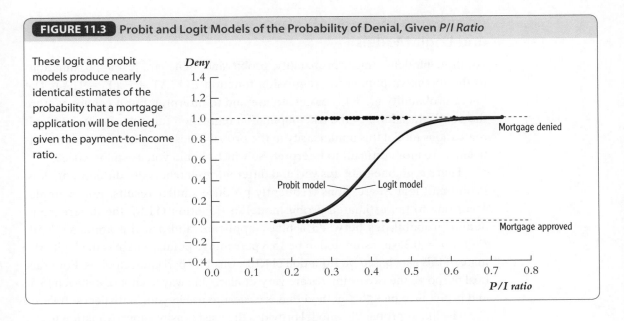

**FIGURE 11.3** Probit and Logit Models of the Probability of Denial, Given *P/I Ratio*

These logit and probit models produce nearly identical estimates of the probability that a mortgage application will be denied, given the payment-to-income ratio.

*Deny*

Mortgage denied

Probit model — Logit model

Mortgage approved

*P/I ratio*

using the same 127 observations as in Figures 11.1 and 11.2. The differences between the two functions are small.

Historically, the main motivation for logit regression was that the logistic cumulative distribution function could be computed faster than the normal cumulative distribution function. With the advent of more efficient computers, this distinction is no longer important.

***Application to the Boston HMDA data.*** A logit regression of *deny* against *P/I ratio* and *black*, using the 2380 observations in the data set, yields the estimated regression function

$$\overline{\Pr(deny = 1 | P/I\,ratio, black)} = F(-4.13 + 5.37\,P/I\,ratio + 1.27\,black). \quad (11.10)$$
$$(0.35) \quad (0.96) \qquad\qquad (0.15)$$

The coefficient on *black* is positive and statistically significant at the 1% level (the *t*-statistic is 8.47). The predicted denial probability of a white applicant with *P/I ratio* = 0.3 is $1/[1 + e^{-(-4.13+5.37\times0.3+1.27\times0)}] = 1/[1 + e^{2.52}] = 0.074$, or 7.4%. The predicted denial probability of an African American applicant with *P/I ratio* = 0.3 is $1/[1 + e^{1.25}] = 0.222$, or 22.2 %, so the difference between the two probabilities is 14.8 percentage points.

## Comparing the Linear Probability, Probit, and Logit Models

All three models—linear probability, probit, and logit—are just approximations to the unknown population regression function $E(Y|X) = \Pr(Y = 1|X)$. The linear probability model is easiest to use and to interpret, but it cannot capture the nonlinear nature of the true population regression function. Probit and logit regressions model this nonlinearity in the probabilities, but their regression coefficients are more difficult to interpret. So which should you use in practice?

There is no one right answer, and different researchers use different models. Probit and logit regressions frequently produce similar results. For example, according to the estimated probit model in Equation (11.8), the difference in denial probabilities between a black applicant and a white applicant with *P/I ratio* = 0.3 was estimated to be 15.8 percentage points, whereas the logit estimate of this gap, based on Equation (11.10), was 14.9 percentage points. For practical purposes the two estimates are very similar. One way to choose between logit and probit is to pick the method that is easiest to use in your statistical software.

The linear probability model provides the least sensible approximation to the nonlinear population regression function. Even so, in some data sets there may be few extreme values of the regressors, in which case the linear probability model still can provide an adequate approximation. In the denial probability regression in Equation (11.3), the estimated black/white gap from the linear probability model is 17.7 percentage points, larger than the probit and logit estimates but still qualitatively similar. The only way to know this, however, is to estimate both a linear and nonlinear model and to compare their predicted probabilities.

## 11.3 Estimation and Inference in the Logit and Probit Models[2]

The nonlinear models studied in Sections 8.2 and 8.3 are nonlinear functions of the independent variables but are linear functions of the unknown coefficients ("parameters"). Consequently, the unknown coefficients of those nonlinear regression functions can be estimated by OLS. In contrast, the probit and logit regression functions are a nonlinear function of the coefficients. That is, the probit coefficients $\beta_0, \beta_1, \ldots, \beta_k$, in Equation (11.6) appear *inside* the cumulative standard normal distribution function $\Phi$, and the logit coefficients in Equation (11.9)

---

[2]This section contains more advanced material that can be skipped without loss of continuity.

appear *inside* the cumulative standard logistic distribution function $F$. Because the population regression function is a nonlinear function of the coefficients $\beta_0, \beta_1, \ldots, \beta_k$, those coefficients cannot be estimated by OLS.

This section provides an introduction to the standard method for estimation of probit and logit coefficients, maximum likelihood; additional mathematical details are given in Appendix 11.2. Because it is built into modern statistical software, maximum likelihood estimation of the probit and logit coefficients is easy in practice. The theory of maximum likelihood estimation, however, is more complicated than the theory of least squares. We therefore first discuss another estimation method, nonlinear least squares, before turning to maximum likelihood.

## Nonlinear Least Squares Estimation

Nonlinear least squares is a general method for estimating the unknown parameters of a regression function when, like the probit coefficients, those parameters enter the population regression function nonlinearly. The nonlinear least squares estimator, which was introduced in Appendix 8.1, extends the OLS estimator to regression functions that are nonlinear functions of the parameters. Like OLS, nonlinear least squares finds the values of the parameters that minimize the sum of squared prediction mistakes produced by the model.

To be concrete, consider the nonlinear least squares estimator of the parameters of the probit model. The conditional expectation of $Y$ given the $X$'s is   $E(Y|X_1, \ldots, X_k) = \Pr(Y = 1|X_1, \ldots, X_k) = \Phi(\beta_0 + \beta_1 X_1 + \cdots + \beta_k X_k)$. Estimation by nonlinear least squares fits this conditional expectation function, which is a nonlinear function of the parameters, to the dependent variable. That is, the nonlinear least squares estimator of the probit coefficients are those values of $b_0, \ldots, b_k$ that minimize the sum of squared prediction mistakes:

$$\sum_{i=1}^{n} [Y_i - \Phi(b_0 + b_1 X_{1i} + \cdots + b_k X_{ki})]^2. \tag{11.11}$$

The nonlinear least squares estimator shares two key properties with the OLS estimator in linear regression: It is consistent (the probability that it is close to the true value approaches 1 as the sample size gets large), and it is normally distributed in large samples. There are, however, estimators that have a smaller variance than the nonlinear least squares estimator; that is, the nonlinear least squares estimator is inefficient. For this reason, the nonlinear least squares estimator of the probit coefficients is rarely used in practice, and instead the parameters are estimated by maximum likelihood.

## Maximum Likelihood Estimation

The **likelihood function** is the joint probability distribution of the data, treated as a function of the unknown coefficients. The **maximum likelihood estimator (MLE)** of the unknown coefficients consists of the values of the coefficients that maximize the likelihood function. Because the MLE chooses the unknown coefficients to maximize the likelihood function, which is in turn the joint probability distribution, in effect the MLE chooses the values of the parameters to maximize the probability of drawing the data that are actually observed. In this sense, the MLEs are the parameter values "most likely" to have produced the data.

To illustrate maximum likelihood estimation, consider two i.i.d. observations, $Y_1$ and $Y_2$, on a binary dependent variable with no regressors. Thus $Y$ is a Bernoulli random variable, and the only unknown parameter to estimate is the probability $p$ that $Y = 1$, which is also the mean of $Y$.

To obtain the maximum likelihood estimator, we need an expression for the likelihood function, which in turn requires an expression for the joint probability distribution of the data. The joint probability distribution of the two observations $Y_1$ and $Y_2$ is $\Pr(Y_1 = y_1, Y_2 = y_2)$. Because $Y_1$ and $Y_2$ are independently distributed, the joint distribution is the product of the individual distributions [Equation (2.23)], so $\Pr(Y_1 = y_1, Y_2 = y_2) = \Pr(Y_1 = y_1)\Pr(Y_2 = y_2)$. The Bernoulli distribution can be summarized in the formula $\Pr(Y = y) = p^y(1 - p)^{1-y}$: When $y = 1, \Pr(Y = 1) = p^1(1 - p)^0 = p$, and when $y = 0, \Pr(Y = 0) = p^0(1 - p)^1 = 1 - p$. Thus the joint probability distribution of $Y_1$ and $Y_2$ is $\Pr(Y_1 = y_1, Y_2 = y_2) = [p^{y_1}(1 - p)^{1-y_1}] \times [p^{y_2}(1 - p)^{1-y_2}] = p^{(y_1+y_2)}(1 - p)^{2-(y_1+y_2)}$.

The likelihood function is the joint probability distribution, treated as a function of the unknown coefficients. For $n = 2$ i.i.d. observations on Bernoulli random variables, the likelihood function is

$$f(p; Y_1, Y_2) = p^{(Y_1+Y_2)}(1 - p)^{2-(Y_1+Y_2)}. \tag{11.12}$$

The maximum likelihood estimator of $p$ is the value of $p$ that maximizes the likelihood function in Equation (11.12). As with all maximization or minimization problems, this can be done by trial and error; that is, you can try different values of $p$ and compute the likelihood $f(p; Y_1, Y_2)$ until you are satisfied that you have maximized this function. In this example, however, maximizing the likelihood function using calculus produces a simple formula for the MLE: The MLE is $\hat{p} = \frac{1}{2}(Y_1 + Y_2)$. In other words, the MLE of $p$ is just the sample average! In fact, for general $n$, the MLE $\hat{p}$ of the Bernoulli probability $p$ is the sample average; that is, $\hat{p} = \overline{Y}$ (this is shown in Appendix 11.2). In this example, the MLE is the usual estimator of $p$, the fraction of times $Y_i = 1$ in the sample.

This example is similar to the problem of estimating the unknown coefficients of the probit and logit regression models. In those models, the success probability $p$ is not constant, but rather depends on $X$; that is, it is the success probability conditional on $X$, which is given in Equation (11.6) for the probit model and Equation (11.9) for the logit model. Thus the probit and logit likelihood functions are similar to the likelihood function in Equation (11.12) except that the success probability varies from one observation to the next (because it depends on $X_i$). Expressions for the probit and logit likelihood functions are given in Appendix 11.2.

Like the nonlinear least squares estimator, the MLE is consistent and normally distributed in large samples. Because regression software commonly computes the MLE of the probit coefficients, this estimator is easy to use in practice. All the estimated probit and logit coefficients reported in this chapter are MLEs.

*Statistical inference based on the MLE.* Because the MLE is normally distributed in large samples, statistical inference about the probit and logit coefficients based on the MLE proceeds in the same way as inference about the linear regression function coefficients based on the OLS estimator. That is, hypothesis tests are performed using the $t$-statistic and 95% confidence intervals are formed as $\pm 1.96$ standard errors. Tests of joint hypotheses on multiple coefficients use the $F$-statistic in a way similar to that discussed in Chapter 7 for the linear regression model. All of this is completely analogous to statistical inference in the linear regression model.

An important practical point is that some statistical software reports tests of joint hypotheses using the $F$-statistic, while other software uses the chi-squared statistic. The chi-squared statistic is $q \times F$, where $q$ is the number of restrictions being tested. Because the $F$-statistic is, under the null hypothesis, distributed as $\chi_q^2 / q$ in large samples, $q \times F$ is distributed as $\chi_q^2$ in large samples. Because the two approaches differ only in whether they divide by $q$, they produce identical inferences, but you need to know which approach is implemented in your software so that you use the correct critical values.

## Measures of Fit

In Section 11.1, it was mentioned that the $R^2$ is a poor measure of fit for the linear probability model. This is also true for probit and logit regression. Two measures of fit for models with binary dependent variables are the "fraction correctly predicted" and the "pseudo-$R^2$." The **fraction correctly predicted** uses the following rule: If $Y_i = 1$ and the predicted probability exceeds 50% or if $Y_i = 0$ and the predicted probability is less than 50%, then $Y_i$ is said to be correctly predicted.

Otherwise, $Y_i$ is said to be incorrectly predicted. The "fraction correctly predicted" is the fraction of the $n$ observations $Y_1, \ldots, Y_n$ that are correctly predicted.

An advantage of this measure of fit is that it is easy to understand. A disadvantage is that it does not reflect the quality of the prediction: If $Y_i = 1$, the observation is treated as correctly predicted whether the predicted probability is 51% or 90%.

The **pseudo-$R^2$** measures the fit of the model using the likelihood function. Because the MLE maximizes the likelihood function, adding another regressor to a probit or logit model increases the value of the maximized likelihood, just like adding a regressor necessarily reduces the sum of squared residuals in linear regression by OLS. This suggests measuring the quality of fit of a probit model by comparing values of the maximized likelihood function with all the regressors to the value of the likelihood with none. This is, in fact, what the pseudo-$R^2$ does. A formula for the pseudo-$R^2$ is given in Appendix 11.2.

# 11.4  Application to the Boston HMDA Data

The regressions of the previous two sections indicated that denial rates were higher for black than white applicants, holding constant their payment-to-income ratio. Loan officers, however, legitimately weigh many factors when deciding on a mortgage application, and if any of those other factors differ systematically by race, the estimators considered so far have omitted variable bias.

In this section, we take a closer look at whether there is statistical evidence of discrimination in the Boston HMDA data. Specifically, our objective is to estimate the effect of race on the probability of denial, holding constant those applicant characteristics that a loan officer might legally consider when deciding on a mortgage application.

The most important variables available to loan officers through the mortgage applications in the Boston HMDA data set are listed in Table 11.1; these are the variables we will focus on in our empirical models of loan decisions. The first two variables are direct measures of the financial burden the proposed loan would place on the applicant, measured in terms of his or her income. The first of these is the *P/I ratio*; the second is the ratio of housing-related expenses to income. The next variable is the size of the loan, relative to the assessed value of the home; if the loan-to-value ratio is nearly 1, the bank might have trouble recouping the full amount of the loan if the applicant defaults on the loan and the bank forecloses. The final three financial variables summarize the applicant's credit history. If an applicant has been unreliable paying off debts in the past, the loan officer legitimately

| TABLE 11.1 | Variables Included in Regression Models of Mortgage Decisions | |
|---|---|---|
| **Variable** | **Definition** | **Sample Average** |
| **Financial Variables** | | |
| *P/I ratio* | Ratio of total monthly debt payments to total monthly income | 0.331 |
| *housing expense-to-income ratio* | Ratio of monthly housing expenses to total monthly income | 0.255 |
| *loan-to-value ratio* | Ratio of size of loan to assessed value of property | 0.738 |
| *consumer credit score* | 1  if no "slow" payments or delinquencies<br>2  if one or two slow payments or delinquencies<br>3  if more than two slow payments<br>4  if insufficient credit history for determination<br>5  if delinquent credit history with payments 60 days overdue<br>6  if delinquent credit history with payments 90 days overdue | 2.1 |
| *mortgage credit score* | 1  if no late mortgage payments<br>2  if no mortgage payment history<br>3  if one or two late mortgage payments<br>4  if more than two late mortgage payments | 1.7 |
| *public bad credit record* | 1  if any public record of credit problems (bankruptcy, charge-offs, collection actions)<br>0  otherwise | 0.074 |
| **Additional Applicant Characteristics** | | |
| *denied mortgage insurance* | 1  if applicant applied for mortgage insurance and was denied,<br>0  otherwise | 0.020 |
| *self-employed* | 1  if self-employed, 0 otherwise | 0.116 |
| *single* | 1  if applicant reported being single, 0 otherwise | 0.393 |
| *high school diploma* | 1  if applicant graduated from high school, 0 otherwise | 0.984 |
| *unemployment rate* | 1989 Massachusetts unemployment rate in the applicant's industry | 3.8 |
| *condominium* | 1  if unit is a condominium, 0 otherwise | 0.288 |
| *black* | 1  if applicant is black, 0 if white | 0.142 |
| *deny* | 1  if mortgage application denied, 0 otherwise | 0.120 |

might worry about the applicant's ability or desire to make mortgage payments in the future. The three variables measure different types of credit histories, which the loan officer might weigh differently. The first concerns consumer credit, such as credit card debt; the second is previous mortgage payment history; and the third measures credit problems so severe that they appeared in a public legal record, such as filing for bankruptcy.

Table 11.1 also lists some other variables relevant to the loan officer's decision. Sometimes the applicant must apply for private mortgage insurance.[3] The loan officer knows whether that application was denied, and that denial would weigh negatively with the loan officer. The next three variables, which concern the employment status, marital status, and educational attainment of the applicant, relate to the prospective ability of the applicant to repay. In the event of foreclosure, characteristics of the property are relevant as well, and the next variable indicates whether the property is a condominium. The final two variables in Table 11.1 are whether the applicant is black or white and whether the application was denied or accepted. In these data, 14.2% of applicants are black and 12.0% of applications are denied.

Table 11.2 presents regression results based on these variables. The base specifications, reported in columns (1) through (3), include the financial variables in Table 11.1 plus the variables indicating whether private mortgage insurance was denied and whether the applicant is self-employed. In the 1990s, loan officers commonly used thresholds, or cutoff values, for the loan-to-value ratio, so the base specification for that variable uses binary variables for whether the loan-to-value ratio is high ($\geq 0.95$), medium (between 0.8 and 0.95), or low ($<0.8$; this case is omitted to avoid perfect multicollinearity). The regressors in the first three columns are similar to those in the base specification considered by the Federal Reserve Bank of Boston researchers in their original analysis of these data.[4] The regressions in columns (1) through (3) differ only in how the denial probability is modeled, using a linear probability model, a logit model, and a probit model, respectively.

Because the regression in column (1) is a linear probability model, its coefficients are estimated changes in predicted probabilities arising from a unit change in the independent variable. Accordingly, an increase in *P/I ratio* of 0.1 is estimated to

---

[3]Mortgage insurance is an insurance policy under which the insurance company makes the monthly payment to the bank if the borrower defaults. During the period of this study, if the loan-to-value ratio exceeds 80%, the applicant typically was required to buy mortgage insurance.

[4]The difference between the regressors in columns (1) through (3) and those in Munnell et al. (1996), table 2(1), is that Munnell et al. include additional indicators for the location of the home and the identity of the lender, data that are not publicly available; an indicator for a multifamily home, which is irrelevant here because our subset focuses on single-family homes; and net wealth, which we omit because this variable has a few very large positive and negative values and thus risks making the results sensitive to a few specific outlier observations.

| TABLE 11.2 | Mortgage Denial Regressions Using the Boston HMDA Data |

**Dependent variable: *deny* = 1 if mortgage application is denied, = 0 if accepted; 2380 observations.**

| Regression Model<br>Regressor | LPM<br>(1) | Logit<br>(2) | Probit<br>(3) | Probit<br>(4) | Probit<br>(5) | Probit<br>(6) |
|---|---|---|---|---|---|---|
| black | 0.084**<br>(0.023) | 0.688**<br>(0.182) | 0.389**<br>(0.098) | 0.371**<br>(0.099) | 0.363**<br>(0.100) | 0.246<br>(0.448) |
| P/I ratio | 0.449**<br>(0.114) | 4.76**<br>(1.33) | 2.44**<br>(0.61) | 2.46**<br>(0.60) | 2.62**<br>(0.61) | 2.57**<br>(0.66) |
| housing expense-to-<br>income ratio | −0.048<br>(0.110) | −0.11<br>(1.29) | −0.18<br>(0.68) | −0.30<br>(0.68) | −0.50<br>(0.70) | −0.54<br>(0.74) |
| medium loan-to-value ratio<br>(0.80 ≤ loan-value ratio ≤ 0.95) | 0.031*<br>(0.013) | 0.46**<br>(0.16) | 0.21**<br>(0.08) | 0.22**<br>(0.08) | 0.22**<br>(0.08) | 0.22**<br>(0.08) |
| high loan-to-value ratio<br>(loan-value ratio > 0.95) | 0.189**<br>(0.050) | 1.49**<br>(0.32) | 0.79**<br>(0.18) | 0.79**<br>(0.18) | 0.84**<br>(0.18) | 0.79**<br>(0.18) |
| consumer credit score | 0.031**<br>(0.005) | 0.29**<br>(0.04) | 0.15**<br>(0.02) | 0.16**<br>(0.02) | 0.34**<br>(0.11) | 0.16**<br>(0.02) |
| mortgage credit score | 0.021<br>(0.011) | 0.28*<br>(0.14) | 0.15*<br>(0.07) | 0.11<br>(0.08) | 0.16<br>(0.10) | 0.11<br>(0.08) |
| public bad credit record | 0.197**<br>(0.035) | 1.23**<br>(0.20) | 0.70**<br>(0.12) | 0.70**<br>(0.12) | 0.72**<br>(0.12) | 0.70**<br>(0.12) |
| denied mortgage insurance | 0.702**<br>(0.045) | 4.55**<br>(0.57) | 2.56**<br>(0.30) | 2.59**<br>(0.29) | 2.59**<br>(0.30) | 2.59**<br>(0.29) |
| self-employed | 0.060**<br>(0.021) | 0.67**<br>(0.21) | 0.36**<br>(0.11) | 0.35**<br>(0.11) | 0.34**<br>(0.11) | 0.35**<br>(0.11) |
| single | | | | 0.23**<br>(0.08) | 0.23**<br>(0.08) | 0.23**<br>(0.08) |
| high school diploma | | | | −0.61**<br>(0.23) | −0.60*<br>(0.24) | −0.62**<br>(0.23) |
| unemployment rate | | | | 0.03<br>(0.02) | 0.03<br>(0.02) | 0.03<br>(0.02) |
| condominium | | | | | −0.05<br>(0.09) | |
| black × P/I ratio | | | | | | −0.58<br>(1.47) |
| black × housing expense-<br>to-income ratio | | | | | | 1.23<br>(1.69) |
| additional credit rating<br>indicator variables | no | no | no | no | yes | no |
| constant | −0.183**<br>(0.028) | −5.71**<br>(0.48) | −3.04**<br>(0.23) | −2.57**<br>(0.34) | −2.90**<br>(0.39) | −2.54**<br>(0.35) |

*(continued)*

*(Table 11.2 continued)*

**F-Statistics and p-Values Testing Exclusion of Groups of Variables**

| | (1) | (2) | (3) | (4) | (5) | (6) |
|---|---|---|---|---|---|---|
| *applicant single; high school diploma; industry unemployment rate* | | | | 5.85 (< 0.001) | 5.22 (0.001) | 5.79 (< 0.001) |
| *additional credit rating indicator variables* | | | | | 1.22 (0.291) | |
| *race interactions and black* | | | | | | 4.96 (0.002) |
| *race interactions only* | | | | | | 0.27 (0.766) |
| *difference in predicted probability of denial, white vs. black (percentage points)* | 8.4% | 6.0% | 7.1% | 6.6% | 6.3% | 6.5% |

These regressions were estimated using the $n = 2380$ observations in the Boston HMDA data set described in Appendix 11.1. The linear probability model was estimated by OLS, and probit and logit regressions were estimated by maximum likelihood. Standard errors are given in parentheses under the coefficients, and $p$-values are given in parentheses under the $F$-statistics. The change in predicted probability in the final row was computed for a hypothetical applicant whose values of the regressors, other than race, equal the sample mean. Individual coefficients are statistically significant at the *5% or **1% level.

increase the probability of denial by 4.5 percentage points (the coefficient on *P/I ratio* in column (1) is 0.449, and $0.449 \times 0.1 \cong 0.045$). Similarly, having a high loan-to-value ratio increases the probability of denial: A loan-to-value ratio exceeding 95% is associated with an 18.9 percentage point increase (the coefficient is 0.189) in the denial probability, relative to the omitted case of a loan-to-value ratio less than 80%, holding the other variables in column (1) constant. Applicants with a poor credit rating also have a more difficult time getting a loan, all else being constant, although interestingly the coefficient on consumer credit is statistically significant but the coefficient on mortgage credit is not. Applicants with a public record of credit problems, such as filing for bankruptcy, have much greater difficulty obtaining a loan: All else equal, a public bad credit record is estimated to increase the probability of denial by 0.197, or 19.7 percentage points. Being denied private mortgage insurance is estimated to be virtually decisive: The estimated coefficient of 0.702 means that being denied mortgage insurance increases your chance of being denied a mortgage by 70.2 percentage points, all else equal. Of the nine variables (other than race) in the regression, the coefficients on all but two are statistically significant at the 5% level, which is consistent with loan officers' considering many factors when they make their decisions.

The coefficient on *black* in regression (1) is 0.084, indicating that the difference in denial probabilities for black and white applicants is 8.4 percentage points, holding constant the other variables in the regression. This is statistically significant at the 1% significance level ($t = 3.65$).

The logit and probit estimates reported in columns (2) and (3) yield similar conclusions. In the logit and probit regressions, eight of the nine coefficients on variables other than race are individually statistically significantly different from zero at the 5% level, and the coefficient on *black* is statistically significant at the 1% level. As discussed in Section 11.2, because these models are nonlinear, specific values of all the regressors must be chosen to compute the difference in predicted probabilities for white applicants and black applicants. A conventional way to make this choice is to consider an "average" applicant who has the sample average values of all the regressors other than race. The final row in Table 11.2 reports this estimated difference in probabilities, evaluated for this average applicant. The estimated racial differentials are similar to each other: 8.4 percentage points for the linear probability model [column (1)], 6.0 percentage points for the logit model [column (2)], and 7.1 percentage points for the probit model [column (3)]. These estimated race effects and the coefficients on *black* are less than in the regressions of the previous sections, in which the only regressors were *P/I ratio* and *black*, indicating that those earlier estimates had omitted variable bias.

The regressions in columns (4) through (6) investigate the sensitivity of the results in column (3) to changes in the regression specification. Column (4) modifies column (3) by including additional applicant characteristics. These characteristics help to predict whether the loan is denied; for example, having at least a high school diploma reduces the probability of denial (the estimate is negative and the coefficient is statistically significant at the 1% level). However, controlling for these personal characteristics does not change the estimated coefficient on *black* or the estimated difference in denial probabilities (6.6%) in an important way.

Column (5) breaks out the six consumer credit categories and four mortgage credit categories to test the null hypothesis that these two variables enter linearly; this regression also adds a variable indicating whether the property is a condominium. The null hypothesis that the credit rating variables enter the expression for the $z$-value linearly is not rejected, nor is the condominium indicator significant, at the 5% level. Most importantly, the estimated racial difference in denial probabilities (6.3%) is essentially the same as in columns (3) and (4).

Column (6) examines whether there are interactions. Are different standards applied to evaluating the payment-to-income and housing expense-to-income ratios for black applicants versus white applicants? The answer appears to be no: The interaction terms are not jointly statistically significant at the 5% level. However, race continues to have a significant effect, because the race indicator and the interaction terms are jointly statistically significant at the 1% level. Again, the estimated racial difference in denial probabilities (6.5%) is essentially the same as in the other probit regressions.

In all six specifications, the effect of race on the denial probability, holding other applicant characteristics constant, is statistically significant at the 1% level. The estimated difference in denial probabilities between black applicants and white applicants ranges from 6.0 percentage points to 8.4 percentage points.

One way to assess whether this differential is large or small is to return to a variation on the question posed at the beginning of this chapter. Suppose two individuals apply for a mortgage, one white and one black, but otherwise having the same values of the other independent variables in regression (3); specifically, aside from race, the values of the other variables in regression (3) are the sample average values in the HMDA data set. The white applicant faces a 7.4% chance of denial, but the black applicant faces a 14.5% chance of denial. The estimated racial difference in denial probabilities, 7.1 percentage points, means that the black applicant is nearly twice as likely to be denied as the white applicant.

The results in Table 11.2 (and in the original Boston Fed study) provide statistical evidence of racial patterns in mortgage denial that, by law, ought not be there. This evidence played an important role in spurring policy changes by bank regulators.[5] But economists love a good argument, and not surprisingly these results have also stimulated a vigorous debate.

Because the suggestion that there is (or was) racial discrimination in lending is charged, we briefly review some points of this debate. In so doing, it is useful to adopt the framework of Chapter 9, that is, to consider the internal and external validity of the results in Table 11.2, which are representative of previous analyses of the Boston HMDA data. A number of the criticisms made of the original Federal Reserve Bank of Boston study concern internal validity: possible errors in the data, alternative nonlinear functional forms, additional interactions, and so forth. The original data were subjected to a careful audit, some errors were found, and the results reported here (and in the final published Boston Fed study) are based

---

[5]These policy shifts include changes in the way that fair lending examinations were done by federal bank regulators, changes in inquiries made by the U.S. Department of Justice, and enhanced education programs for banks and other home loan origination companies.

on the "cleaned" data set. Estimation of other specifications—different functional forms and/or additional regressors—also produces estimates of racial differentials comparable to those in Table 11.2. A potentially more difficult issue of internal validity is whether there is relevant nonracial financial information obtained during in-person loan interviews, not recorded on the loan application itself, that is correlated with race; if so, there still might be omitted variable bias in the Table 11.2 regressions. Finally, some have questioned external validity: Even if there was racial discrimination in Boston in 1990, it is wrong to implicate lenders elsewhere today. Moreover, racial discrimination might be less likely using modern online applications, because the mortgage can be approved or denied without a face-to-face meeting. The only way to resolve the question of external validity is to consider data from other locations and years.[6]

## 11.5   Conclusion

When the dependent variable $Y$ is binary, the population regression function is the probability that $Y = 1$, conditional on the regressors. Estimation of this population regression function entails finding a functional form that does justice to its probability interpretation, estimating the unknown parameters of that function, and interpreting the results. The resulting predicted values are predicted probabilities, and the estimated effect of a change in a regressor $X$ is the estimated change in the probability that $Y = 1$ arising from the change in $X$.

A natural way to model the probability that $Y = 1$ given the regressors is to use a cumulative distribution function, where the argument of the c.d.f. depends on the regressors. Probit regression uses a normal c.d.f. as the regression function, and logit regression uses a logistic c.d.f. Because these models are nonlinear functions of the unknown parameters, those parameters are more complicated to estimate than linear regression coefficients. The standard estimation method is maximum likelihood. In practice, statistical inference using the maximum likelihood estimates proceeds the same way as it does in linear multiple regression; for

---

[6]If you are interested in further reading on this topic, a good place to start is the symposium on racial discrimination and economics in the Spring 1998 issue of the *Journal of Economic Perspectives*. The article in that symposium by Helen Ladd (1998) surveys the evidence and debate on racial discrimination in mortgage lending. A more detailed treatment is given in Goering and Wienk (1996). The U.S. mortgage market has changed dramatically since the Boston Fed study, including a relaxation of lending standards, a bubble in housing prices, the financial crisis of 2008–2009, and a return to tighter lending standards. For an introduction to changes in mortgage markets, see Green and Wachter (2008).

## James Heckman and Daniel McFadden, Nobel Laureates

The 2000 Nobel Prize in economics was awarded jointly to two econometricians, James J. Heckman of the University of Chicago and Daniel L. McFadden of the University of California at Berkeley, for fundamental contributions to the analysis of data on individuals and firms. Much of their work addressed difficulties that arise with limited dependent variables.

Heckman was awarded the prize for developing tools for handling sample selection. As discussed in Section 9.2, sample selection bias occurs when the availability of data is influenced by a selection process related to the value of dependent variable. For example, suppose you want to estimate the relationship between earnings and some regressor, $X$, using a random sample from the population. If you estimate the regression using the subsample of employed workers—that is, those reporting positive earnings—the OLS estimate could be subject to selection bias. Heckman's solution was to specify a preliminary equation with a binary dependent variable indicating whether the worker is in or out of the labor force (in or out of the subsample) and to treat this equation and the earnings equation as a system of simultaneous equations. This general strategy has been extended to selection problems that arise in many fields, ranging from labor economics to industrial organization to finance.

McFadden was awarded the prize for developing models for analyzing discrete choice data (does a high school graduate join the military, go to college, or get a job?). He started by considering the problem of an individual maximizing the expected utility of each possible choice, which could depend on observable variables (such as wages, job characteristics, and family background). He then derived models for the individual choice probabilities with unknown coefficients, which in turn could be estimated by maximum likelihood. These models and their extensions have proven widely useful in analyzing discrete choice data in many fields, including labor economics, health economics, and transportation economics.

For more information on these and other Nobel laureates in economics, visit the Nobel Foundation website, http://www.nobel.se/economics.

James J. Heckman

Daniel L. McFadden

example, 95% confidence intervals for a coefficient are constructed as the estimated coefficient $\pm 1.96$ standard errors.

Despite its intrinsic nonlinearity, sometimes the population regression function can be adequately approximated by a linear probability model, that is, by the straight line produced by linear multiple regression. The linear probability model, probit regression, and logit regression all give similar "bottom line" answers when they are applied to the Boston HMDA data: All three methods estimate substantial differences in mortgage denial rates for otherwise similar black applicants and white applicants.

Binary dependent variables are the most common example of limited dependent variables, which are dependent variables with a limited range. The final quarter of the twentieth century saw important advances in econometric methods for analyzing other limited dependent variables (see the Nobel Laureates box). Some of these methods are reviewed in Appendix 11.3.

## Summary

1. When $Y$ is a binary variable, the population regression function shows the probability that $Y = 1$ given the value of the regressors, $X_1, X_2, \ldots, X_k$.

2. The linear multiple regression model is called the linear probability model when $Y$ is a binary variable because the probability that $Y = 1$ is a linear function of the regressors.

3. Probit and logit regression models are nonlinear regression models used when $Y$ is a binary variable. Unlike the linear probability model, probit and logit regressions ensure that the predicted probability that $Y = 1$ is between 0 and 1 for all values of $X$.

4. Probit regression uses the standard normal cumulative distribution function. Logit regression uses the logistic cumulative distribution function. Logit and probit coefficients are estimated by maximum likelihood.

5. The values of coefficients in probit and logit regressions are not easy to interpret. Changes in the probability that $Y = 1$ associated with changes in one or more of the $X$'s can be calculated using the general procedure for nonlinear models outlined in Key Concept 8.1.

6. Hypothesis tests on coefficients in the linear probability, logit, and probit models are performed using the usual $t$- and $F$-statistics.

## Key Terms

limited dependent variable (432)
linear probability model (434)
probit (437)
logit (437)
logistic regression (437)

likelihood function (447)
maximum likelihood estimator
  (MLE) (447)
fraction correctly predicted (447)
pseudo-$R^2$ (448)

**MyEconLab Can Help You Get a Better Grade**

**MyEconLab** If your exam were tomorrow, would you be ready? For each chapter, **MyEconLab** Practice Tests and Study Plan help you prepare for your exams. You can also find similar Exercises and Review the Concepts Questions now in **MyEconLab**. To see how it works, turn to the **MyEconLab** spread on pages 2 and 3 of this book and then go to **www.myeconlab.com**.

For additional Empirical Exercises and Data Sets, log on to the Companion Website at **www.pearsonglobaleditions.com/Stock_Watson**.

## Review the Concepts

**11.1**  Suppose that a linear probability model yields a predicted value of $Y$ that is equal to 1.3. Explain why this is nonsensical.

**11.2**  In Table 11.2 the estimated coefficient on *black* is 0.084 in column (1), 0.688 in column (2), and 0.389 in column (3). In spite of these large differences, all three models yield similar estimates of the marginal effect of race on the probability of mortgage denial. How can this be?

**11.3**  What is a maximum likelihood estimation? What are the advantages of using maximum likelihood estimators such as the probit and the logit, instead of the linear probability model? How would you choose between the probit and the logit?

**11.4**  What measures of fit are typically used to assess binary dependent variable regression models?

## Exercises

Exercises 11.1 through 11.5 are based on the following scenario: 700 income-earning individuals from a district were randomly selected and asked whether they were employed by the government ($Gov_i = 1$) or failed their entrance test ($Gov_i = 0$); data were also collected on their gender ($Male_i = 1$) if male and $= 0$ if female) and their years of schooling ($Schooling_i$, in years). The following table summarizes several estimated models.

**11.1**  Using the results in column (1):

    **a.** Does the probability of working in the government depend on *Schooling*? Explain.

**Dependent Variable:** *Gov*

| | Probit (1) | Logit (2) | Linear Probability (3) | Probit (4) | Logit (5) | Linear Probability (6) | Probit (7) |
|---|---|---|---|---|---|---|---|
| Schooling | 0.272 (0.029) | 0.551 (0.062) | 0.035 (0.003) | | | | 0.548 (0.091) |
| Male | | | | −0.242 (0.125) | −0.455 (0.234) | −0.050 (0.025) | 4.352 (1.291) |
| Male × Schooling | | | | | | | −.344 (0.096) |
| Constant | −4.107 (0.358) | −8.146 (0.800) | −0.172 (0.027) | −1.027 (0.098) | −1.717 (0.179) | 0.152 (0.021) | −7.702 (1.238) |

    **b.** Matthew has 16 years of schooling. What is the probability that he will pass the test?

    **c.** Christopher never went to college (12 years of schooling). What is the probability that he will get a job with the government?

    **d.** The sample included values of *Schooling* between 0 and 18 years, and only five people in the sample had more than 15 years of schooling. Jed has completed a PhD and has been a student for 24 years. What is the model's prediction for the probability that Jed will get a job with the government? Do you think that this prediction is reliable? Why or why not?

**11.2**  **a.** Answer (a) through (c) from Exercise 11.1 using the results in column (2).

    **b.** Sketch the predicted probabilities from the probit and logit in columns (1) and (2) for values of *Schooling* between 0 and 18. Are the probit and logit models similar?

**11.3**  **a.** Answer (a) through (c) from Exercise 11.1 using the results in column (3).

    **b.** Sketch the predicted probabilities from the probit and linear probability in columns (1) and (3) as a function of *Schooling$_i$* for values of *Schooling* between 0 and 18. Do you think that the linear probability is appropriate here? Why or why not?

**11.4**  Using the results in columns (4) through (6):

    **a.** Compute the estimated probability of passing the test for men and for women.

    **b.** Are the models in (4) through (6) different? Why or why not?

**11.5** Using the results in column (7):

    **a.** Akira is a man with 10 years of schooling. What is the probability that the government will employ him?

    **b.** Jane is a woman with 12 years of schooling. What is the probability that the government will employ her?

    **c.** Does the effect of the years of schooling on employment in the government depend on gender? Explain.

**11.6** Use the estimated probit model in Equation (11.8) to answer the following questions:

    **a.** A black mortgage applicant has a *P/I ratio* of 0.35. What is the probability that his application will be denied?

    **b.** Suppose that the applicant reduced this ratio to 0.30. What effect would this have on his probability of being denied a mortgage?

    **c.** Repeat (a) and (b) for a white applicant.

    **d.** Does the marginal effect of the *P/I ratio* on the probability of mortgage denial depend on race? Explain.

**11.7** Repeat Exercise 11.6 using the logit model in Equation (11.10). Are the logit and probit results similar? Explain.

**11.8** Consider the linear probability model $Y_i = \beta_0 + \beta_1 X_i + u_i$, where $\Pr(Y_i = 1 | X_i) = \beta_0 + \beta_1 X_i$.

    **a.** Show that $E(u_i | X_i) = 0$.

    **b.** Show that $\text{var}(u_i | X_i) = (\beta_0 + \beta_1 X_i)[1 - (\beta_0 + \beta_1 X_i)]$. [*Hint:* Review Equation (2.7).]

    **c.** Is $u_i$ heteroskedastic? Explain.

    **d.** (Requires Section 11.3) Derive the likelihood function.

**11.9** Use the estimated linear probability model shown in column (1) of Table 11.2 to answer the following:

    **a.** Two applicants—one self-employed and one salaried—apply for a mortgage. They have the same values for all the regressors other than employment status. How much more likely is it for the self-employed applicant to be denied a mortgage?

    **b.** Construct a 95% confidence interval for your answer to (a).

    **c.** Think of an important omitted variable that might create a bias in the answer to part (a). What is the variable, and how would it create a bias in the results?

**11.10** (Requires Section 11.3 and calculus) Suppose that a random variable $Y$ has the following probability distribution: $\Pr(Y = 1) = p$, $\Pr(Y = 2) = q$, and $\Pr(Y = 3) = 1 - p - q$. A random sample of size $n$ is drawn from this distribution, and the random variables are denoted $Y_1, Y_2, \ldots, Y_n$.

    **a.** Derive the likelihood function for the parameters $p$ and $q$.

    **b.** Derive formulas for the MLE of $p$ and $q$.

**11.11** (Refer to Appendix 11.3) Which model would you use for:

    **a.** A study explaining the number of hours spent by a person working for income during a week.

    **b.** A study explaining the level of satisfaction a person has with their job (on a scale of 0 to 5).

    **c.** A study of a consumer's choice of mode of transport between bus, car, and bicycle.

    **d.** A study of the number of rainy days in a week.

## Empirical Exercises

(Only two empirical exercises for this chapter are given in the text, but you can find more on the text website, **www.pearsonglobaleditions.com/Stock_Watson.**)

**E11.1** In April 2008 the unemployment rate in the United States stood at 5.0%. By April 2009 it had increased to 9.0%, and it had increased further, to 10.0%, by October 2009. Were some groups of workers more likely to lose their jobs than others during the Great Recession? For example, were young workers more likely to lose their jobs than middle-aged workers? What about workers with a college degree versus those without a degree, or women versus men? On the textbook website, **www.pearsonglobaleditions .com/Stock_Watson**, you will find the data file **Employment_08_09**, which contains a random sample of 5440 workers who were surveyed in April 2008 and reported that they were employed full time. A detailed description is given in **Employment_08_09_Description**, available on the website. These workers were surveyed one year later, in April 2009, and asked about their employment status (employed, unemployed, or out of the labor force). The data set also includes various demographic measures for each individual. Use these data to answer the following questions.

    **a.** What fraction of workers in the sample were employed in April 2009? Use your answer to compute a 95% confidence interval for the probability that a worker was employed in April 2009, conditional on being employed in April 2008.

**b.** Regress *Employed* on *Age* and *Age*$^2$, using a linear probability model.

   i.  Based on this regression, was age a statistically significant determinant of employment in April 2009?

   ii.  Is there evidence of a nonlinear effect of age on the probability of being employed?

   iii.  Compute the predicted probability of employment for a 20-year-old worker, a 40-year-old worker, and a 60-year-old worker.

**c.** Repeat (b) using a probit regression.

**d.** Repeat (b) using a logit regression.

**e.** Are there important differences in your answers to (b)–(d)? Explain.

**f.** The data set includes variables measuring the workers' educational attainment, sex, race, marital status, region of the country, and weekly earnings in April 2008.

   i.  Construct a table like Table 11.2 to investigate whether the conclusions on the effect of age on employment from (b)–(d) are affected by omitted variable bias.

   ii.  Use the regressions in your table to discuss the characteristics of workers who were hurt most by the Great Recession.

**g.** The results in (a)–(f) were based on the probability of employment. Workers who are not employed can either be (i) unemployed or (ii) out the labor force. Do the conclusions you reached in (a)–(f) also hold for workers who became unemployed? (*Hint:* Use the binary variable *Unemployed* instead of *Employed*.)

**h.** These results have covered employment transitions during the Great Recession, but what about transitions during normal times? On the textbook website, you will find the data file **Employment_06_07**, which measures the same variables but for the years 2006–2007. Analyze these data and comment on the differences in employment transitions during recessions and normal times.

**E11.2**  Believe it or not, workers used to be able to smoke inside office buildings. Smoking bans were introduced in several areas during the 1990s. In addition to eliminating the externality of secondhand smoke, supporters of these bans argued that they would encourage smokers to quit by reducing their opportunities to smoke. In this assignment you will estimate the effect of workplace smoking bans on smoking, using data on a sample of 10,000 U.S. indoor workers from 1991 to 1993, available on the textbook website, **www.pearsonglobaleditions.com/Stock_Watson**, in the file **Smoking**. The data set contains information on whether individuals were or were not subject to a workplace smoking ban, whether the individuals smoked, and other individual characteristics.[7] A detailed description is given in **Smoking_Description**, available on the website.

**a.** Estimate the probability of smoking for (i) all workers, (ii) workers affected by workplace smoking bans, and (iii) workers not affected by workplace smoking bans.

**b.** What is the difference in the probability of smoking between workers affected by a workplace smoking ban and workers not affected by a workplace smoking ban? Use a linear probability model to determine whether this difference is statistically significant.

**c.** Estimate a linear probability model with *smoker* as the dependent variable and the following regressors: *smkban*, *female*, *age*, *age*$^2$, *hsdrop*, *hsgrad*, *colsome*, *colgrad*, *black*, and *hispanic*. Compare the estimated effect of a smoking ban from this regression with your answer from (b). Suggest a reason, based on the substance of this regression, explaining the change in the estimated effect of a smoking ban between (b) and (c).

**d.** Test the hypothesis that the coefficient on *smkban* is zero in the population version of the regression in (c) against the alternative that it is nonzero, at the 5% significance level.

**e.** Test the hypothesis that the probability of smoking does not depend on the level of education in the regression in (c). Does the probability of smoking increase or decrease with the level of education?

**f.** Repeat (c)–(e) using a probit model.

**g.** Repeat (c)–(e) using a logit model.

**h.** i. Mr. A is white, non-Hispanic, 20 years old, and a high school dropout. Using the probit regression and assuming that Mr. A is not subject to a workplace smoking ban, calculate the probability that Mr. A smokes. Carry out the calculation again, assuming that

[7]These data were provided by Professor William Evans of the University of Maryland and were used in his paper with Matthew Farrelly and Edward Montgomery, "Do Workplace Smoking Bans Reduce Smoking?" *American Economic Review*, 1999, 89(4): 728–747.

he is subject to a workplace smoking ban. What is the effect of the smoking ban on the probability of smoking?

ii. Repeat (i) for Ms. B, a female, black, 40-year-old college graduate.

iii. Repeat (i)–(ii) using the linear probability model.

iv. Repeat (i)–(ii) using the logit model.

v. Based on your answers to (i)–(iv), do the logit, probit, and linear probability models differ? If they do, which results make most sense? Are the estimated effects large in a real work sense?

---

APPENDIX

## 11.1  The Boston HMDA Data Set

The Boston HMDA data set was collected by researchers at the Federal Reserve Bank of Boston. The data set combines information from mortgage applications and a follow-up survey of the banks and other lending institutions that received these mortgage applications. The data pertain to mortgage applications made in 1990 in the greater Boston metropolitan area. The full data set has 2925 observations, consisting of all mortgage applications by blacks and Hispanics plus a random sample of mortgage applications by whites.

To narrow the scope of the analysis in this chapter, we use a subset of the data for single-family residences only (thereby excluding data on multifamily homes) and for black applicants and white applicants only (thereby excluding data on applicants from other minority groups). This leaves 2380 observations. Definitions of the variables used in this chapter are given in Table 11.1.

These data were graciously provided to us by Geoffrey Tootell of the Research Department of the Federal Reserve Bank of Boston. More information about this data set, along with the conclusions reached by the Federal Reserve Bank of Boston researchers, is available in the article by Alicia H. Munnell, Geoffrey M. B. Tootell, Lynne E. Browne, and James McEneaney, "Mortgage Lending in Boston: Interpreting HMDA Data," *American Economic Review*, 1996, pp. 25–53.

---

APPENDIX

## 11.2  Maximum Likelihood Estimation

This appendix provides a brief introduction to maximum likelihood estimation in the context of the binary response models discussed in this chapter. We start by deriving the MLE of the success probability $p$ for $n$ i.i.d. observations of a Bernoulli random variable. We then turn to the probit and logit models and discuss the pseudo-$R^2$. We conclude with a discussion of standard errors for predicted probabilities. This appendix uses calculus at two points.

## MLE for $n$ i.i.d. Bernoulli Random Variables

The first step in computing the MLE is to derive the joint probability distribution. For $n$ i.i.d. observations on a Bernoulli random variable, this joint probability distribution is the extension of the $n = 2$ case in Section 11.3 to general $n$:

$$\Pr(Y_1 = y_1, Y_2 = y_2, \ldots, Y_n = y_n)$$
$$= [p^{y_1}(1-p)^{(1-y_1)}] \times [p^{y_2}(1-p)^{(1-y_2)}] \times \cdots \times [p^{y_n}(1-p)^{(1-y_n)}]$$
$$= p^{(y_1+\cdots+y_n)}(1-p)^{n-(y_1+\cdots+y_n)}. \tag{11.13}$$

The likelihood function is the joint probability distribution, treated as a function of the unknown coefficients. Let $S = \sum_{i=1}^{n} Y_i$; then the likelihood function is

$$f_{Bernoulli}(p; Y_1, \ldots, Y_n) = p^S(1-p)^{n-S}. \tag{11.14}$$

The MLE of $p$ is the value of $p$ that maximizes the likelihood in Equation (11.14). The likelihood function can be maximized using calculus. It is convenient to maximize not the likelihood but rather its logarithm (because the logarithm is a strictly increasing function, maximizing the likelihood or its logarithm gives the same estimator). The log likelihood is $S\ln(p) + (n - S)\ln(1 - p)$, and the derivative of the log likelihood with respect to $p$ is

$$\frac{d}{dp} \ln [f_{Bernoulli}(p; Y_1, \ldots, Y_n)] = \frac{S}{p} - \frac{n-S}{1-p}. \tag{11.15}$$

Setting the derivative in Equation (11.15) to zero and solving for $p$ yields the MLE $\hat{p} = S/n = \overline{Y}$.

## MLE for the Probit Model

For the probit model, the probability that $Y_i = 1$, conditional on $X_{1i}, \ldots, X_{ki}$, is $p_i = \Phi(\beta_0 + \beta_1 X_{1i} + \cdots + \beta_k X_{ki})$. The conditional probability distribution for the $i^{th}$ observation is $\Pr[Y_i = y_i | X_{1i}, \ldots, X_{ki}] = p_i^{y_i}(1 - p_i)^{1-y_i}$. Assuming that $(X_{1i}, \ldots, X_{ki}, Y_i)$ are i.i.d., $i = 1, \ldots, n$, the joint probability distribution of $Y_1, \ldots, Y_n$, conditional on the $X$'s, is

$$\Pr(Y_1 = y_1, \ldots, Y_n = y_n | X_{1i}, \ldots, X_{ki}, i = 1, \ldots, n)$$
$$= \Pr(Y_1 = y_1 | X_{11}, \ldots, X_{k1}) \times \cdots \times \Pr(Y_n = y_n | X_{1n}, \ldots, X_{kn})$$
$$= p_1^{y_1}(1 - p_1)^{1-y_1} \times \cdots \times p_n^{y_n}(1 - p_n)^{1-y_n}. \tag{11.16}$$

The likelihood function is the joint probability distribution, treated as a function of the unknown coefficients. It is conventional to consider the logarithm of the likelihood. Accordingly, the log likelihood function is

$$
\ln[f_{probit}(\beta_0, \ldots, \beta_k; Y_1, \ldots, Y_n \mid X_{1i}, \ldots, X_{ki}, i = 1, \ldots, n)]
$$

$$
= \sum_{i=1}^{n} Y_i \ln [\Phi(\beta_0 + \beta_1 X_{1i} + \cdots + \beta_k X_{ki})]
$$

$$
+ \sum_{i=1}^{n} (1 - Y_i) \ln[1 - \Phi(\beta_0 + \beta_1 X_{1i} + \cdots + \beta_k X_{ki})], \qquad (11.17)
$$

where this expression incorporates the probit formula for the conditional probability, $p_i = \Phi(\beta_0 + \beta_1 X_{1i} + \cdots + \beta_k X_{ki})$.

The MLE for the probit model maximizes the likelihood function or, equivalently, the logarithm of the likelihood function given in Equation (11.17). Because there is no simple formula for the MLE, the probit likelihood function must be maximized using a numerical algorithm on the computer.

Under general conditions, maximum likelihood estimators are consistent and have a normal sampling distribution in large samples.

## MLE for the Logit Model

The likelihood for the logit model is derived in the same way as the likelihood for the probit model. The only difference is that the conditional success probability $p_i$ for the logit model is given by Equation (11.9). Accordingly, the log likelihood of the logit model is given by Equation (11.17), with $\Phi(\beta_0 + \beta_1 X_{1i} + \cdots + \beta_k X_{ki})$ replaced by $[1 + e^{-(\beta_0 + \beta_1 X_{1i} + \beta_2 X_{2i} + \cdots + \beta_k X_{ki})}]^{-1}$. As with the probit model, there is no simple formula for the MLE of the logit coefficients, so the log likelihood must be maximized numerically.

## Pseudo-$R^2$

The pseudo-$R^2$ compares the value of the likelihood of the estimated model to the value of the likelihood when none of the $X$'s are included as regressors. Specifically, the pseudo-$R^2$ for the probit model is

$$
\text{pseudo-}R^2 = 1 - \frac{\ln(f_{probit}^{max})}{\ln(f_{Bernoulli}^{max})}, \qquad (11.18)
$$

where $f_{probit}^{max}$ is the value of the maximized probit likelihood (which includes the $X$'s) and $f_{Bernoulli}^{max}$ is the value of the maximized Bernoulli likelihood (the probit model excluding all the $X$'s).

## Standard Errors for Predicted Probabilities

For simplicity, consider the case of a single regressor in the probit model. Then the predicted probability at a fixed value of that regressor, $x$, is $\hat{p}(x) = \Phi(\hat{\beta}_0^{MLE} + \hat{\beta}_1^{MLE}x)$, where $\hat{\beta}_0^{MLE}$ and $\hat{\beta}_1^{MLE}$ are the MLEs of the two probit coefficients. Because this predicted probability depends on the estimators $\hat{\beta}_0^{MLE}$ and $\hat{\beta}_1^{MLE}$, and because those estimators have a sampling distribution, the predicted probability will also have a sampling distribution.

The variance of the sampling distribution of $\hat{p}(x)$ is calculated by approximating the function $\Phi(\hat{\beta}_0^{MLE} + \hat{\beta}_1^{MLE}x)$, a nonlinear function of $\hat{\beta}_0^{MLE}$ and $\hat{\beta}_1^{MLE}$, by a linear function of $\hat{\beta}_0^{MLE}$ and $\hat{\beta}_1^{MLE}$. Specifically, let

$$\hat{p}(x) = \Phi(\hat{\beta}_0^{MLE} + \hat{\beta}_1^{MLE}x) \cong c + a_0(\hat{\beta}_0^{MLE} - \beta_0) + a_1(\hat{\beta}_1^{MLE} - \beta_1) \qquad (11.19)$$

where the constant $c$ and factors $a_0$ and $a_1$ depend on $x$ and are obtained from calculus. [Equation (11.19) is a first-order Taylor series expansion; $c = \Phi(\beta_0 + \beta_1 x)$; and $a_0$ and $a_1$ are the partial derivatives, $a_0 = \partial\Phi(\beta_0 + \beta_1 x)/\partial\beta_0|_{\hat{\beta}_0^{MLE}, \hat{\beta}_1^{MLE}}$ and $a_1 = \partial\Phi(\beta_0 + \beta_1 x)/\partial\beta_1|_{\hat{\beta}_0^{MLE}, \hat{\beta}_1^{MLE}}$.] The variance of $\hat{p}(x)$ now can be calculated using the approximation in Equation (11.19) and the expression for the variance of the sum of two random variables in Equation (2.31):

$$\begin{aligned}
\text{var}[\hat{p}(x)] &\cong \text{var}[c + a_0(\hat{\beta}_0^{MLE} - \beta_0) + a_1(\hat{\beta}_1^{MLE} - \beta_1)] \\
&= a_0^2\text{var}(\hat{\beta}_0^{MLE}) + a_1^2\text{var}(\hat{\beta}_1^{MLE}) + 2a_0a_1\text{cov}(\hat{\beta}_0^{MLE}, \hat{\beta}_1^{MLE}).
\end{aligned} \qquad (11.20)$$

Using Equation (11.20), the standard error of $\hat{p}(x)$ can be calculated using estimates of the variances and covariance of the MLEs.

---

**APPENDIX**

# 11.3 Other Limited Dependent Variable Models

This appendix surveys some models for limited dependent variables, other than binary variables, found in econometric applications. In most cases the OLS estimators of the parameters of limited dependent variable models are inconsistent, and estimation is routinely done using maximum likelihood. There are several advanced references available to the reader interested in further details; see, for example, Ruud (2000) and Wooldridge (2010).

## Censored and Truncated Regression Models

Suppose that you have cross-sectional data on car purchases by individuals in a given year. Car buyers have positive expenditures, which can reasonably be treated as continuous random variables, but nonbuyers spent $0. Thus the distribution of car expenditures is a combination of a discrete distribution (at zero) and a continuous distribution.

Nobel laureate James Tobin developed a useful model for a dependent variable with a partly continuous and partly discrete distribution (Tobin, 1958). Tobin suggested modeling the $i^{th}$ individual in the sample as having a desired level of spending, $Y_i^*$, that is related to the regressors (for example, family size) according to a linear regression model. That is, when there is a single regressor, the desired level of spending is

$$Y_i^* = \beta_0 + \beta_1 X_i + u_i, i = 1, \ldots, n. \tag{11.21}$$

If $Y_i^*$ (what the consumer wants to spend) exceeds some cutoff, such as the minimum price of a car, the consumer buys the car and spends $Y_i = Y_i^*$, which is observed. However, if $Y_i^*$ is less than the cutoff, spending of $Y_i = 0$ is observed instead of $Y_i^*$.

When Equation (11.21) is estimated using observed expenditures $Y_i$ in place of $Y_i^*$, the OLS estimator is inconsistent. Tobin solved this problem by deriving the likelihood function using the additional assumption that $u_i$ has a normal distribution, and the resulting MLE has been used by applied econometricians to analyze many problems in economics. In Tobin's honor, Equation (11.21), combined with the assumption of normal errors, is called the *tobit* regression model. The tobit model is an example of a *censored regression model*, so called because the dependent variable has been "censored" above or below a certain cutoff.

## Sample Selection Models

In the censored regression model, there are data on buyers and nonbuyers, as there would be if the data were obtained via simple random sampling of the adult population. If, however, the data are collected from sales tax records, then the data would include only buyers: There would be no data at all for nonbuyers. Data in which observations are unavailable above or below a threshold (data for buyers only) are called truncated data. The *truncated regression model* is a regression model applied to data in which observations are simply unavailable when the dependent variable is above or below a certain cutoff.

The truncated regression model is an example of a sample selection model, in which the selection mechanism (an individual is in the sample by virtue of buying a car) is related to the value of the dependent variable (expenditure on a car). As discussed in the box in Section 11.4, one approach to estimation of sample selection models is to develop two equations, one for $Y_i^*$ and one for whether $Y_i^*$ is observed. The parameters of the model can then be estimated by maximum likelihood, or in a stepwise procedure, estimating the selection equation first and then estimating the equation for $Y_i^*$. For additional discussion, see Ruud (2000, Chapter 28), Greene (2012, Chapter 19), or Wooldridge (2010, Chapter 17).

## Count Data

*Count data* arise when the dependent variable is a counting number—for example, the number of restaurant meals eaten by a consumer in a week. When these numbers are large, the variable can be treated as approximately continuous, but when they are small, the continuous approximation is a poor one. The linear regression model, estimated by OLS, can be used for count data, even if the number of counts is small. Predicted values from the regression are interpreted as the expected value of the dependent variable, conditional on the regressors. So, when the dependent variable is the number of restaurant meals eaten, a predicted value of 1.7 means, on average, 1.7 restaurant meals per week. As in the binary regression model, however, OLS does not take advantage of the special structure of count data and can yield nonsense predictions, for example, −0.2 restaurant meal per week. Just as probit and logit eliminate nonsense predictions when the dependent variable is binary, special models do so for count data. The two most widely used models are the Poisson and negative binomial regression models.

## Ordered Responses

*Ordered response data* arise when mutually exclusive qualitative categories have a natural ordering, such as obtaining a high school degree, obtaining some college education (but not graduating), or graduating from college. Like count data, ordered response data have a natural ordering, but unlike count data, they do not have natural numerical values.

Because there are no natural numerical values for ordered response data, OLS is inappropriate. Instead, ordered data are often analyzed using a generalization of probit called the *ordered probit model*, in which the probabilities of each outcome (e.g., a college education), conditional on the independent variables (such as parents' income), are modeled using the cumulative normal distribution.

## Discrete Choice Data

A *discrete choice* or *multiple choice* variable can take on multiple unordered qualitative values. One example in economics is the mode of transport chosen by a commuter: She might take the subway, ride the bus, drive, or make her way under her own power (walk, bicycle). If we were to analyze these choices, the dependent variable would have four possible outcomes (subway, bus, car, human-powered). These outcomes are not ordered in any natural way. Instead, the outcomes are a choice among distinct qualitative alternatives.

The econometric task is to model the probability of choosing the various options, given various regressors such as individual characteristics (how far the commuter's house is from the subway station) and the characteristics of each option (the price of the subway). As discussed in the box in Section 11.3, models for analysis of discrete choice data can be developed from principles of utility maximization. Individual choice probabilities can be expressed in probit or logit form, and those models are called *multinomial probit* and *multinomial logit* regression models.

# Instrumental Variables Regression

Chapter 9 discussed several problems, including omitted variables, errors in variables, and simultaneous causality, that make the error term correlated with the regressor. Omitted variable bias can be addressed directly by including the omitted variable in a multiple regression, but this is only feasible if you have data on the omitted variable. And sometimes, such as when causality runs *both* from $X$ to $Y$ and from $Y$ to $X$ so that there is simultaneous causality bias, multiple regression simply cannot eliminate the bias. If a direct solution to these problems is either infeasible or unavailable, a new method is required.

**Instrumental variables (IV) regression** is a general way to obtain a consistent estimator of the unknown coefficients of the population regression function when the regressor, $X$, is correlated with the error term, $u$. To understand how IV regression works, think of the variation in $X$ as having two parts: one part that, for whatever reason, is correlated with $u$ (this is the part that causes the problems) and a second part that is uncorrelated with $u$. If you had information that allowed you to isolate the second part, you could focus on those variations in $X$ that are uncorrelated with $u$ and disregard the variations in $X$ that bias the OLS estimates. This is, in fact, what IV regression does. The information about the movements in $X$ that are uncorrelated with $u$ is gleaned from one or more additional variables, called **instrumental variables** or simply **instruments**. Instrumental variables regression uses these additional variables as tools or "instruments" to isolate the movements in $X$ that are uncorrelated with $u$, which in turn permit consistent estimation of the regression coefficients.

The first two sections of this chapter describe the mechanics and assumptions of IV regression: why IV regression works, what is a valid instrument, and how to implement and to interpret the most common IV regression method, two stage least squares. The key to successful empirical analysis using instrumental variables is finding valid instruments, and Section 12.3 takes up the question of how to assess whether a set of instruments is valid. As an illustration, Section 12.4 uses IV regression to estimate the elasticity of demand for cigarettes. Finally, Section 12.5 turns to the difficult question of where valid instruments come from in the first place.

# 12.1 The IV Estimator with a Single Regressor and a Single Instrument

We start with the case of a single regressor, $X$, which might be correlated with the regression error, $u$. If $X$ and $u$ are correlated, the OLS estimator is inconsistent; that is, it may not be close to the true value of the regression coefficient even when the sample is very large [see Equation (6.1)]. As discussed in Section 9.2, this correlation between $X$ and $u$ can stem from various sources, including omitted variables, errors in variables (measurement errors in the regressors), and simultaneous causality (when causality runs "backward" from $Y$ to $X$ as well as "forward" from $X$ to $Y$). Whatever the source of the correlation between $X$ and $u$, if there is a valid instrumental variable, $Z$, the effect on $Y$ of a unit change in $X$ can be estimated using the instrumental variables estimator.

## The IV Model and Assumptions

The population regression model relating the dependent variable $Y_i$ and regressor $X_i$ is

$$Y_i = \beta_0 + \beta_1 X_i + u_i, i = 1, \ldots, n, \tag{12.1}$$

where as usual $u_i$ is the error term representing omitted factors that determine $Y_i$. If $X_i$ and $u_i$ are correlated, the OLS estimator is inconsistent. Instrumental variables estimation uses an additional, "instrumental" variable $Z$ to isolate that part of $X$ that is uncorrelated with $u_i$.

*Endogeneity and exogeneity.* Instrumental variables regression has some specialized terminology to distinguish variables that are correlated with the population error term $u$ from ones that are not. Variables correlated with the error term are called **endogenous variables**, while variables uncorrelated with the error term are called **exogenous variables**. The historical source of these terms traces to models with multiple equations, in which an "endogenous" variable is determined within the model while an "exogenous" variable is determined outside the model. For example, Section 9.2 considered the possibility that if low test scores produced decreases in the student–teacher ratio because of political intervention and increased funding, causality would run *both* from the student–teacher ratio to test scores *and* from test scores to the student–teacher ratio. This was represented mathematically as a system of two simultaneous equations [Equations (9.3) and (9.4)], one for each causal connection. As discussed in Section 9.2, because both test scores and the student–teacher ratio are determined within the model, both are correlated with the population error term $u$; that is, in this example, both variables are endogenous. In contrast, an exogenous variable, which is determined outside the model, is uncorrelated with $u$.

*The two conditions for a valid instrument.*   A valid instrumental variable ("instrument") must satisfy two conditions, known as the **instrument relevance condition** and the **instrument exogeneity condition**:

1.   Instrument relevance: corr $(Z_i, X_i) \neq 0$.
2.   Instrument exogeneity: corr $(Z_i, u_i) = 0$.

If an instrument is relevant, then variation in the instrument is related to variation in $X_i$. If in addition the instrument is exogenous, then that part of the variation of $X_i$ captured by the instrumental variable is exogenous. Thus an instrument that is relevant and exogenous can capture movements in $X_i$ that are exogenous. This exogenous variation can in turn be used to estimate the population coefficient $\beta_1$.

The two conditions for a valid instrument are vital for instrumental variables regression, and we return to them (and their extension to a multiple regressors and multiple instruments) repeatedly throughout this chapter.

## The Two Stage Least Squares Estimator

If the instrument $Z$ satisfies the conditions of instrument relevance and exogeneity, the coefficient $\beta_1$ can be estimated using an IV estimator called **two stage least squares (TSLS)**. As the name suggests, the two stage least squares estimator is calculated in two stages. The first stage decomposes $X$ into two components: a problematic component that may be correlated with the regression error and another problem-free component that is uncorrelated with the error. The second stage uses the problem-free component to estimate $\beta_1$.

The first stage begins with a population regression linking $X$ and $Z$:

$$X_i = \pi_0 + \pi_1 Z_i + v_i, \tag{12.2}$$

where $\pi_0$ is the intercept, $\pi_1$ is the slope, and $v_i$ is the error term. This regression provides the needed decomposition of $X_i$. One component is $\pi_0 + \pi_1 Z_i$, the part of $X_i$ that can be predicted by $Z_i$. Because $Z_i$ is exogenous, this component of $X_i$ is uncorrelated with $u_i$, the error term in Equation (12.1). The other component of $X_i$ is $v_i$, which is the problematic component of $X_i$ that is correlated with $u_i$.

The idea behind TSLS is to use the problem-free component of $X_i$, $\pi_0 + \pi_1 Z_i$, and to disregard $v_i$. The only complication is that the values of $\pi_0$ and $\pi_1$ are unknown, so $\pi_0 + \pi_1 Z_i$ cannot be calculated. Accordingly, the first stage of TSLS applies OLS to Equation (12.2) and uses the predicted value from the OLS regression, $\hat{X}_i = \hat{\pi}_0 + \hat{\pi}_1 Z_i$, where $\hat{\pi}_0$ and $\hat{\pi}_1$ are the OLS estimates.

The second stage of TSLS is easy: Regress $Y_i$ on $\hat{X}_i$ using OLS. The resulting estimators from the second-stage regression are the TSLS estimators, $\hat{\beta}_0^{TSLS}$ and $\hat{\beta}_1^{TSLS}$.

## Why Does IV Regression Work?

Two examples provide some intuition for why IV regression solves the problem of correlation between $X_i$ and $u_i$.

*Example #1: Philip Wright's problem.* The method of instrumental variables estimation was first published in 1928 in an appendix to a book written by Philip G. Wright (Wright, 1928), although the key ideas of IV regression appear to have been developed collaboratively with his son, Sewall Wright (see the box). Philip Wright was concerned with an important economic problem of his day: how to set an import tariff (a tax on imported goods) on animal and vegetable oils and fats, such as butter and soy oil. In the 1920s, import tariffs were a major source of tax revenue for the United States. The key to understanding the economic effect of a tariff was having quantitative estimates of the demand and supply curves of the goods. Recall that the supply elasticity is the percentage change in the quantity supplied arising from a 1% increase in the price and that the demand elasticity is the percentage change in the quantity demanded arising from a 1% increase in the price. Philip Wright needed estimates of these elasticities of supply and demand.

To be concrete, consider the problem of estimating the elasticity of demand for butter. Recall from Key Concept 8.2 that the coefficient in a linear equation relating $\ln(Y_i)$ to $\ln(X_i)$ has the interpretation of the elasticity of $Y$ with respect to $X$. In Wright's problem, this suggests the demand equation

$$\ln(Q_i^{butter}) = \beta_0 + \beta_1 \ln(P_i^{butter}) + u_i, \tag{12.3}$$

where $Q_i^{butter}$ is the $i$th observation on the quantity of butter consumed, $P_i^{butter}$ is its price, and $u_i$ represents other factors that affect demand, such as income and consumer tastes. In Equation (12.3), a 1% increase in the price of butter yields a $\beta_1$ percent change in demand, so $\beta_1$ is the demand elasticity.

## Who Invented Instrumental Variables Regression?

Instrumental variables regression was first proposed as a solution to the simultaneous causation problem in econometrics in the appendix to Philip G. Wright's 1928 book, *The Tariff on Animal and Vegetable Oils*. If you want to know how animal and vegetable oils were produced, transported, and sold in the early twentieth century, the first 285 pages of the book are for you. Econometricians, however, will be more interested in Appendix B. The appendix provides two derivations of "the method of introducing external factors"—what we now call the instrumental variables estimator—and uses IV regression to estimate the supply and demand elasticities for butter and flaxseed oil. Philip was an obscure economist with a scant intellectual legacy other than this appendix, but his son Sewall went on to become a preeminent population geneticist and statistician. Because the mathematical material in the appendix is so different than the rest of the book, many econometricians assumed that Philip's son Sewall Wright wrote the appendix anonymously. So who wrote Appendix B?

In fact, either father or son could have been the author. Philip Wright (1861–1934) received a master's degree in economics from Harvard University in 1887, and he taught mathematics and economics (as well as literature and physical education) at a small college in Illinois. In a book review [Wright (1915)], he used a figure like Figures 12.1a and 12.1b to show how a regression of quantity on price will not, in general, estimate a demand curve, but instead estimates a combination of the supply and demand curves. In the early 1920s, Sewall Wright (1889–1988) was researching the statistical analysis of multiple equations with multiple causal variables in the context of genetics, research that in part led to his assuming a professorship in 1930 at the University of Chicago.

Although it is too late to ask Philip or Sewall who wrote Appendix B, it is never too late to do some statistical detective work. Stylometrics is the subfield of statistics, invented by Frederick Mosteller and David Wallace (1963), that uses subtle, subconscious differences in writing styles to identify authorship of disputed texts using statistical analysis of grammatical constructions and word choice. The field has had verified successes, such as Donald Foster's (1996) uncovering of Joseph Klein as the author of the political novel *Primary Colors*. When Appendix B is compared statistically to texts known to have been written independently by Philip and by Sewall, the results are clear: Philip was the author.

Does this mean that Philip G. Wright invented IV regression? Not quite. Recently, correspondence between Philip and Sewall in the mid-1920s has come to light, and this correspondence shows that the development of IV regression was a joint intellectual collaboration between father and son. To learn more, see Stock and Trebbi (2003).

Philip G. Wright

Sewall Wright

Philip Wright had data on total annual butter consumption and its average annual price in the United States for 1912 to 1922. It would have been easy to use these data to estimate the demand elasticity by applying OLS to Equation (12.3), but he had a key insight: Because of the interactions between supply and demand, the regressor, $\ln (P_i^{butter})$, was likely to be correlated with the error term.

To see this, look at Figure 12.1a, which shows the market demand and supply curves for butter for three different years. The demand and supply curves for the first period are denoted $D_1$ and $S_1$, and the first period's equilibrium price and quantity are determined by their intersection. In year 2, demand increases from $D_1$ to $D_2$ (say, because of an increase in income) and supply decreases from $S_1$ to $S_2$ (because of an increase in the cost of producing butter); the equilibrium price and quantity are determined by the intersection of the new supply and demand curves. In year 3, the factors affecting demand and supply change again; demand increases again to $D_3$, supply increases to $S_3$, and a new equilibrium quantity and price are determined. Figure 12.1b shows the equilibrium quantity and price pairs for these three periods and for eight subsequent years, where in each year the supply and demand curves are subject to shifts associated with factors other than price that affect market supply and demand. This scatterplot is like the one that Wright would have seen when he plotted his data. As he reasoned, fitting a line to these points by OLS will estimate neither a demand curve nor a supply curve, because the points have been determined by changes in both demand and supply.

Wright realized that a way to get around this problem was to find some third variable that shifted supply but did not shift demand. Figure 12.1c shows what happens when such a variable shifts the supply curve, but demand remains stable. Now all of the equilibrium price and quantity pairs lie on a stable demand curve, and the slope of the demand curve is easily estimated. In the instrumental variable formulation of Wright's problem, this third variable — the instrumental variable — is correlated with price (it shifts the supply curve, which leads to a change in price) but is uncorrelated with $u$ (the demand curve remains stable). Wright considered several potential instrumental variables; one was the weather. For example, below-average rainfall in a dairy region could impair grazing and thus reduce butter production at a given price (it would shift the supply curve to the left and increase the equilibrium price), so dairy-region rainfall satisfies the condition for instrument relevance. But dairy-region rainfall should not have a direct influence on the demand for butter, so the correlation between dairy-region rainfall and $u_i$ would be zero; that is, dairy-region rainfall satisfies the condition for instrument exogeneity.

*Example #2: Estimating the effect on test scores of class size.*  Despite controlling for student and district characteristics, the estimates of the effect on test scores of

## FIGURE 12.1    Equilibrium Price and Quantity Data

(a) Price and quantity are determined by the intersection of the supply and demand curves. The equilibrium in the first period is determined by the intersection of the demand curve $D_1$ and the supply curve $S_1$. Equilibrium in the second period is the intersection of $D_2$ and $S_2$, and equilibrium in the third period is the intersection of $D_3$ and $S_3$.

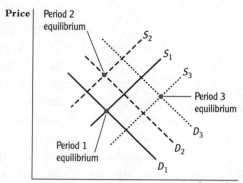

**(a)** Demand and supply in three time periods

(b) This scatterplot shows equilibrium price and quantity in 11 different time periods. The demand and supply curves are hidden. Can you determine the demand and supply curves from the points on the scatterplot?

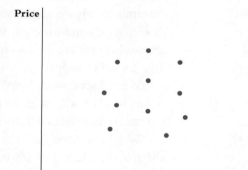

**(b)** Equilibrium price and quantity for 11 time periods

(c) When the supply curve shifts from $S_1$ to $S_2$ to $S_3$ but the demand curve remains at $D_1$, the equilibrium prices and quantities trace out the demand curve.

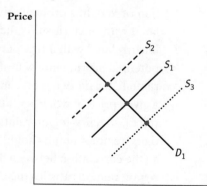

**(c)** Equilibrium price and quantity when only the supply curve shifts

class size reported in Part II still might have omitted variables bias resulting from unmeasured variables such as learning opportunities outside school or the quality of the teachers. If data on these variables are unavailable, this omitted variables bias cannot be addressed by including the variables in the multiple regressions.

Instrumental variables regression provides an alternative approach to this problem. Consider the following hypothetical example: Some California schools are forced to close for repairs because of a summer earthquake. Districts closest to the epicenter are most severely affected. A district with some closed schools needs to "double up" its students, temporarily increasing class size. This means that distance from the epicenter satisfies the condition for instrument relevance because it is correlated with class size. But if distance to the epicenter is unrelated to any of the other factors affecting student performance (such as whether the students are still learning English, or other disruptive effects of the earthquake on student performance), then it will be exogenous because it is uncorrelated with the error term. Thus the instrumental variable, distance to the epicenter, could be used to circumvent omitted variables bias and to estimate the effect of class size on test scores.

## The Sampling Distribution of the TSLS Estimator

The exact distribution of the TSLS estimator in small samples is complicated. However, like the OLS estimator, its distribution in large samples is simple: The TSLS estimator is consistent and is normally distributed.

*Formula for the TSLS estimator.* Although the two stages of TSLS make the estimator seem complicated, when there is a single $X$ and a single instrument $Z$, as we assume in this section, there is a simple formula for the TSLS estimator. Let $s_{ZY}$ be the sample covariance between $Z$ and $Y$ and let $s_{ZX}$ be the sample covariance between $Z$ and $X$. As shown in Appendix 12.2, the TSLS estimator with a single instrument is

$$\hat{\beta}_1^{TSLS} = \frac{s_{ZY}}{s_{ZX}}. \tag{12.4}$$

That is, the TSLS estimator of $\beta_1$ is the ratio of the sample covariance between $Z$ and $Y$ to the sample covariance between $Z$ and $X$.

*Sampling distribution of $\hat{\beta}_1^{TSLS}$ when the sample size is large.* The formula in Equation (12.4) can be used to show that $\hat{\beta}_1^{TSLS}$ is consistent and, in large samples, normally distributed. The argument is summarized here, with mathematical details given in Appendix 12.3.

The argument that $\hat{\beta}_1^{TSLS}$ is consistent combines the assumptions that $Z_i$ is relevant and exogenous with the consistency of sample covariances for population covariances. To begin, note that because $Y_i = \beta_0 + \beta_1 X_i + u_i$ in Equation (12.1),

$$\text{cov}(Z_i, Y_i) = \text{cov}[Z_i, (\beta_0 + \beta X_i + u_i)] = \beta_1 \text{cov}(Z_i, X_i) + \text{cov}(Z_i, u_i), \quad (12.5)$$

where the second equality follows from the properties of covariances [Equation (2.33)]. By the instrument exogeneity assumption, $\text{cov}(Z_i, u_i) = 0$, and by the instrument relevance assumption, $\text{cov}(Z_i, X_i) \neq 0$. Thus, if the instrument is valid, Equation (12.5) implies that

$$\beta_1 = \frac{\text{cov}(Z_i, Y_i)}{\text{cov}(Z_i, X_i)}. \quad (12.6)$$

That is, the population coefficient $\beta_1$ is the ratio of the population covariance between $Z$ and $Y$ to the population covariance between $Z$ and $X$.

As discussed in Section 3.7, the sample covariance is a consistent estimator of the population covariance; that is, $s_{ZY} \xrightarrow{p} \text{cov}(Z_i, Y_i)$ and $s_{ZX} \xrightarrow{p} \text{cov}(Z_i, X_i)$. It follows from Equations (12.4) and (12.6) that the TSLS estimator is consistent:

$$\hat{\beta}_1^{TSLS} = \frac{s_{ZY}}{s_{ZX}} \xrightarrow{p} \frac{\text{cov}(Z_i, Y_i)}{\text{cov}(Z_i, X_i)} = \beta_1. \quad (12.7)$$

The formula in Equation (12.4) also can be used to show that the sampling distribution of $\hat{\beta}_1^{TSLS}$ is normal in large samples. The reason is the same as for every other least squares estimator we have considered: The TSLS estimator is an average of random variables, and when the sample size is large, the central limit theorem tells us that averages of random variables are normally distributed. Specifically, the numerator of the expression for $\hat{\beta}_1^{TSLS}$ in Equation (12.4) is $s_{ZY} = \frac{1}{n-1}\sum_{i=1}^{n}(Z_i - \overline{Z})(Y_i - \overline{Y})$, an average of $(Z_i - \overline{Z})(Y_i - \overline{Y})$. A bit of algebra, sketched out in Appendix 12.3, shows that because of this averaging the central limit theorem implies that, in large samples, $\hat{\beta}_1^{TSLS}$ has a sampling distribution that is approximately $N(\beta_1, \sigma^2_{\hat{\beta}_1^{TSLS}})$, where

$$\sigma^2_{\hat{\beta}_1^{TSLS}} = \frac{1}{n}\frac{\text{var}\left[(Z_i - \mu_Z)u_i\right]}{\left[\text{cov}(Z_i, X_i)\right]^2}. \quad (12.8)$$

***Statistical inference using the large-sample distribution.*** The variance $\sigma^2_{\hat{\beta}_1^{TSLS}}$ can be estimated by estimating the variance and covariance terms appearing in

Equation (12.8), and the square root of the estimate of $\sigma^2_{\hat\beta_1^{TSLS}}$ is the standard error of the IV estimator. This is done automatically in TSLS regression commands in econometric software packages. Because $\hat\beta_1^{TSLS}$ is normally distributed in large samples, hypothesis tests about $\beta_1$ can be performed by computing the $t$-statistic, and a 95% large-sample confidence interval is given by $\hat\beta_1^{TSLS} \pm 1.96\,SE(\hat\beta_1^{TSLS})$.

## Application to the Demand for Cigarettes

Philip Wright was interested in the demand elasticity of butter, but today other commodities, such as cigarettes, figure more prominently in public policy debates. One tool in the quest for reducing illnesses and deaths from smoking—and the costs, or externalities, imposed by those illnesses on the rest of society—is to tax cigarettes so heavily that current smokers cut back and potential new smokers are discouraged from taking up the habit. But precisely how big a tax hike is needed to make a dent in cigarette consumption? For example, what would the after-tax sales price of cigarettes need to be to achieve a 20% reduction in cigarette consumption?

The answer to this question depends on the elasticity of demand for cigarettes. If the elasticity is −1, then the 20% target in consumption can be achieved by a 20% increase in price. If the elasticity is −0.5, then the price must rise 40% to decrease consumption by 20%. Of course, we do not know the demand elasticity of cigarettes: We must estimate it from data on prices and sales. But, as with butter, because of the interactions between supply and demand, the elasticity of demand for cigarettes cannot be estimated consistently by an OLS regression of log quantity on log price.

We therefore use TSLS to estimate the elasticity of demand for cigarettes using annual data for the 48 contiguous U.S. states for 1985 through 1995 (the data are described in Appendix 12.1). For now, all the results are for the cross section of states in 1995; results using data for earlier years (panel data) are presented in Section 12.4.

The instrumental variable, $SalesTax_i$, is the portion of the tax on cigarettes arising from the general sales tax, measured in dollars per pack (in real dollars, deflated by the Consumer Price Index). Cigarette consumption, $Q_i^{cigarettes}$, is the number of packs of cigarettes sold per capita in the state, and the price, $P_i^{cigarettes}$, is the average real price per pack of cigarettes including all taxes.

Before using TSLS it is essential to ask whether the two conditions for instrument validity hold. We return to this topic in detail in Section 12.3, where we provide some statistical tools that help in this assessment. Even with those statistical tools, judgment plays an important role, so it is useful to think about whether the sales tax on cigarettes plausibly satisfies the two conditions.

First consider instrument relevance. Because a high sales tax increases the after-tax sales price $P_i^{cigarettes}$, the sales tax per pack plausibly satisfies the condition for instrument relevance.

Next consider instrument exogeneity. For the sales tax to be exogenous, it must be uncorrelated with the error in the demand equation; that is, the sales tax must affect the demand for cigarettes only indirectly through the price. This seems plausible: General sales tax rates vary from state to state, but they do so mainly because different states choose different mixes of sales, income, property, and other taxes to finance public undertakings. Those choices about public finance are driven by political considerations, not by factors related to the demand for cigarettes. We discuss the credibility of this assumption more in Section 12.4, but for now we keep it as a working hypothesis.

In modern statistical software, the first stage of TSLS is estimated automatically, so you do not need to run this regression yourself to compute the TSLS estimator. Even so, it is a good idea to look at the first-stage regression. Using data for the 48 states in 1995, it is

$$\widehat{\ln(P_i^{cigarettes})} = 4.62 + 0.031 Sales\,Tax_i. \tag{12.9}$$
$$(0.03) \quad (0.005)$$

As expected, higher sales taxes mean higher after-tax prices. The $R^2$ of this regression is 47%, so the variation in sales tax on cigarettes explains 47% of the variance of cigarette prices across states.

In the second stage of TSLS, $\ln(Q_i^{cigarettes})$ is regressed on $\widehat{\ln(P_i^{cigarettes})}$ using OLS. The resulting estimated regression function is

$$\widehat{\ln(Q_i^{cigarettes})} = 9.72 - 1.08\widehat{\ln(P_i^{cigarettes})}. \tag{12.10}$$

This estimated regression function is written using the regressor in the second stage, the predicted value $\widehat{\ln(P_i^{cigarettes})}$. It is, however, conventional and less cumbersome simply to report the estimated regression function with $\ln(P_i^{cigarettes})$ rather than $\widehat{\ln(P_i^{cigarettes})}$. Reported in this notation, the TSLS estimates and heteroskedasticity-robust standard errors are

$$\widehat{\ln(Q_i^{cigarettes})} = 9.72 - 1.08\ln(P_i^{cigarettes}). \tag{12.11}$$
$$(1.53) \quad (0.32)$$

The TSLS estimate suggests that the demand for cigarettes is surprisingly elastic, in light of their addictive nature: An increase in the price of 1% reduces consumption by 1.08%. But, recalling our discussion of instrument exogeneity, perhaps this estimate should not yet be taken too seriously. Even though the elasticity was estimated using an instrumental variable, there might still be omitted variables that are correlated with the sales tax per pack. A leading candidate is income: States with higher incomes might depend relatively less on a sales tax and more on an income tax to finance state government. Moreover, the demand for cigarettes presumably depends on income. Thus we would like to reestimate our demand equation including income as an additional regressor. To do so, however, we must first extend the IV regression model to include additional regressors.

## 12.2  The General IV Regression Model

The general IV regression model has four types of variables: the dependent variable, $Y$; problematic endogenous regressors, like the price of cigarettes, which are correlated with the error term and which we will label $X$; additional regressors, called **included exogenous variables**, which we will label $W$; and instrumental variables, $Z$. In general, there can be multiple endogenous regressors ($X$'s), multiple included exogenous regressors ($W$'s), and multiple instrumental variables ($Z$'s).

For IV regression to be possible, there must be at least as many instrumental variables ($Z$'s) as endogenous regressors ($X$'s). In Section 12.1, there was a single endogenous regressor and a single instrument. Having (at least) one instrument for this single endogenous regressor was essential. Without the instrument we could not have computed the instrumental variables estimator: there would be no first-stage regression in TSLS.

The relationship between the number of instruments and the number of endogenous regressors has its own terminology. The regression coefficients are said to be **exactly identified** if the number of instruments ($m$) equals the number of endogenous regressors ($k$); that is, $m = k$. The coefficients are **overidentified** if the number of instruments exceeds the number of endogenous regressors; that is, $m > k$. They are **underidentified** if the number of instruments is less than the number of endogenous regressors; that is, $m < k$. The coefficients must be either exactly identified or overidentified if they are to be estimated by IV regression.

The general IV regression model and its terminology are summarized in Key Concept 12.1.

*Included exogenous variables and control variables in IV regression.*  The $W$ variables in Equation (12.12) can be either exogenous variables, in which case $E(u_i|W_i) = 0$, or they can be control variables that need not have a causal

KEY CONCEPT

## 12.1

## The General Instrumental Variables Regression Model and Terminology

The general IV regression model is

$$Y_i = \beta_0 + \beta_1 X_{1i} + \cdots + \beta_k X_{ki} + \beta_{k+1} W_{1i} + \cdots + \beta_{k+r} W_{ri} + u_i, \quad (12.12)$$

$i = 1, \ldots, n$, where

- $Y_i$ is the dependent variable;
- $\beta_0, \beta_1, \ldots, \beta_{k+r}$ are unknown regression coefficients;
- $X_{1i}, \ldots, X_{ki}$ are $k$ endogenous regressors, which are potentially correlated with $u_i$;
- $W_{1i}, \ldots, W_{ri}$ are $r$ included exogenous regressors, which are uncorrelated with $u_i$ or are control variables;
- $u_i$ is the error term, which represents measurement error and/or omitted factors; and
- $Z_{1i}, \ldots, Z_{mi}$ are $m$ instrumental variables.

The coefficients are overidentified if there are more instruments than endogenous regressors ($m > k$), they are underidentified if $m < k$, and they are exactly identified if $m = k$. Estimation of the IV regression model requires exact identification or overidentification.

interpretation but are included to ensure that the instrument is uncorrelated with the error term. For example, Section 12.1 raised the possibility that the sales tax might be correlated with income, which economic theory tells us is a determinant of cigarette demand. If so, the sales tax would be correlated with the error term in the cigarette demand equation, $\ln(Q_i^{cigarettes}) = \beta_0 + \beta_1 \ln(P_i^{cigarettes}) + u_i$, and thus would not be an exogenous instrument. Including income in the regression, or including variables that control for income, would remove this source of potential correlation between the instrument and the error term. In general, if $W$ is an effective control variable in IV regression, then including $W$ makes the instrument uncorrelated with $u$, so the TSLS estimator of the coefficient on $X$ is consistent; if $W$ is correlated with $u$, however, then the TSLS coefficient on $W$ is subject to omitted variable bias and does not have a causal interpretation. The logic of control variables in IV regression therefore parallels the logic of control variables in OLS, discussed in Section 7.5.

The mathematical condition for $W$ to be an effective control variable in IV regression is similar to the condition on control variables in OLS discussed in Section 7.5. Specifically, including $W$ must ensure that the conditional mean of $u$ does not depend on $Z$, so conditional mean independence holds; that is, $E(u_i|Z_i, W_i) = E(u_i|W_i)$. For clarity, in the body of this chapter we focus on the case that $W$ variables are exogenous so that $E(u_i|W_i) = 0$. Appendix 12.6 explains how the results of this chapter extend to the case that $W$ is a control variable, in which case the conditional mean zero condition, $E(u_i|W_i) = 0$, is replaced by the conditional mean independence condition, $E(u_i|Z_i, W_i) = E(u_i|W_i)$.

## TSLS in the General IV Model

*TSLS with a single endogenous regressor.* When there is a single endogenous regressor $X$ and some additional included exogenous variables, the equation of interest is

$$Y_i = \beta_0 + \beta_1 X_i + \beta_2 W_{1i} + \cdots + \beta_{1+r} W_{ri} + u_i, \tag{12.13}$$

where, as before, $X_i$ might be correlated with the error term, but $W_{1i}, \ldots, W_{ri}$ are not.

The population first-stage regression of TSLS relates $X$ to the exogenous variables, that is, the $W$'s and the instruments ($Z$'s):

$$X_i = \pi_0 + \pi_1 Z_{1i} + \cdots + \pi_m Z_{mi} + \pi_{m+1} W_{1i} + \cdots + \pi_{m+r} W_{ri} + v_i, \tag{12.14}$$

where $\pi_0, \pi_1, \ldots, \pi_{m+r}$ are unknown regression coefficients and $v_i$ is an error term.

Equation (12.14) is sometimes called the **reduced form** equation for $X$. It relates the endogenous variable $X$ to all the available exogenous variables, both those included in the regression of interest ($W$) and the instruments ($Z$).

In the first stage of TSLS, the unknown coefficients in Equation (12.14) are estimated by OLS, and the predicted values from this regression are $\hat{X}_1, \ldots, \hat{X}_n$.

In the second stage of TSLS, Equation (12.13) is estimated by OLS, except that $X_i$ is replaced by its predicted value from the first stage. That is, $Y_i$ is regressed on $\hat{X}_i, W_{1i}, \ldots, W_{ri}$ using OLS. The resulting estimator of $\beta_0, \beta_1, \ldots, \beta_{1+r}$ is the TSLS estimator.

*Extension to multiple endogenous regressors.* When there are multiple endogenous regressors $X_{1i}, \ldots, X_{ki}$, the TSLS algorithm is similar, except that each endogenous regressor requires its own first-stage regression. Each of these first-stage regressions has the same form as Equation (12.14); that is, the dependent

KEY CONCEPT
## Two Stage Least Squares

**12.2**

The TSLS estimator in the general IV regression model in Equation (12.12) with multiple instrumental variables is computed in two stages:

1. **First-stage regression(s)**: Regress $X_{1i}$ on the instrumental variables $(Z_{1i}, \ldots, Z_{mi})$ and the included exogenous variables $(W_{1i}, \ldots, W_{ri})$ using OLS, including an intercept. Compute the predicted values from this regression; call these $\hat{X}_{1i}$. Repeat this for all the endogenous regressors $X_{2i}, \ldots, X_{ki}$, thereby computing the predicted values $\hat{X}_{1i}, \ldots, \hat{X}_{ki}$.

2. **Second-stage regression**: Regress $Y_i$ on the predicted values of the endogenous variables $(\hat{X}_{1i}, \ldots, \hat{X}_{ki})$ and the included exogenous variables $(W_{1i}, \ldots, W_{ri})$ using OLS, including an intercept. The TSLS estimators $\hat{\beta}_0^{TSLS}, \ldots, \hat{\beta}_{k+r}^{TSLS}$ are the estimators from the second-stage regression.

In practice, the two stages are done automatically within TSLS estimation commands in modern econometric software.

variable is one of the $X$'s, and the regressors are all the instruments ($Z$'s) and all the included exogenous variables ($W$'s). Together, these first-stage regressions produce predicted values of each of the endogenous regressors.

In the second stage of TSLS, Equation (12.12) is estimated by OLS, except that the endogenous regressors ($X$'s) are replaced by their respective predicted values ($\hat{X}$'s). The resulting estimator of $\beta_0, \beta_1, \ldots, \beta_{k+r}$ is the TSLS estimator.

In practice, the two stages of TSLS are done automatically within TSLS estimation commands in modern econometric software. The general TSLS estimator is summarized in Key Concept 12.2.

## Instrument Relevance and Exogeneity in the General IV Model

The conditions of instrument relevance and exogeneity need to be modified for the general IV regression model.

When there is one included endogenous variable but multiple instruments, the condition for instrument relevance is that at least one $Z$ is useful for predicting $X$, given $W$. When there are multiple included endogenous variables, this condition is more complicated because we must rule out perfect multicollinearity in the

KEY CONCEPT

12.3

## The Two Conditions for Valid Instruments

A set of $m$ instruments $Z_{1i}, \ldots, Z_{mi}$ must satisfy the following two conditions to be valid:

1. **Instrument Relevance**

- *In general*, let $\hat{X}_{1i}^*$ be the predicted value of $X_{1i}$ from the population regression of $X_{1i}$ on the instruments ($Z$'s) and the included exogenous regressors ($W$'s), and let "1" denote the constant regressor that takes on the value 1 for all observations. Then $(\hat{X}_{1i}^*, \ldots, \hat{X}_{ki}^*, W_{1i}, \ldots, W_{ri}, 1)$ are not perfectly multicollinear.

- *If there is only one* $X$, then for the previous condition to hold, at least one $Z$ must have a non-zero coefficient in the population regression of $X$ on the $Z$'s and the $W$'s.

2. **Instrument Exogeneity**

   The instruments are uncorrelated with the error term; that is, $\text{corr}(Z_{1i}, u_i) = 0, \ldots,$ $\text{corr}(Z_{mi}, u_i) = 0$.

second-stage population regression. Intuitively, when there are multiple included endogenous variables, the instruments must provide enough information about the exogenous movements in these variables to sort out their separate effects on $Y$.

The general statement of the instrument exogeneity condition is that each instrument must be uncorrelated with the error term $u_i$. The general conditions for valid instruments are given in Key Concept 12.3.

## The IV Regression Assumptions and Sampling Distribution of the TSLS Estimator

Under the IV regression assumptions, the TSLS estimator is consistent and has a sampling distribution that, in large samples, is approximately normal.

*The IV regression assumptions.* The IV regression assumptions are modifications of the least squares assumptions for the multiple regression model in Key Concept 6.4.

The first IV regression assumption modifies the conditional mean assumption in Key Concept 6.4 to apply only to the included exogenous variables. Just like the second least squares assumption for the multiple regression model, the second

**KEY CONCEPT**

**12.4**

## The IV Regression Assumptions

The variables and errors in the IV regression model in Key Concept 12.1 satisfy the following:

1. $E(u_i | W_{1i}, \ldots, W_{ri}) = 0$;

2. $(X_{1i}, \ldots, X_{ki}, W_{1i}, \ldots, W_{ri}, Z_{1i}, \ldots, Z_{mi}, Y_i)$ are i.i.d. draws from their joint distribution;

3. Large outliers are unlikely: The $X$'s, $W$'s, $Z$'s, and $Y$ have nonzero finite fourth moments; and

4. The two conditions for a valid instrument in Key Concept 12.3 hold.

IV regression assumption is that the draws are i.i.d., as they are if the data are collected by simple random sampling. Similarly, the third IV assumption is that large outliers are unlikely.

The fourth IV regression assumption is that the two conditions for instrument validity in Key Concept 12.3 hold. The instrument relevance condition in Key Concept 12.3 subsumes the fourth least squares assumption in Key Concept 4.6 (no perfect multicollinearity) by assuming that the regressors in the second-stage regression are not perfectly multicollinear. The IV regression assumptions are summarized in Key Concept 12.4.

***Sampling distribution of the TSLS estimator.*** Under the IV regression assumptions, the TSLS estimator is consistent and normally distributed in large samples. This is shown in Section 12.1 (and Appendix 12.3) for the special case of a single endogenous regressor, a single instrument, and no included exogenous variables. Conceptually, the reasoning in Section 12.1 carries over to the general case of multiple instruments and multiple included endogenous variables. The expressions in the general case are complicated, however, and are deferred to Chapter 18.

## Inference Using the TSLS Estimator

Because the sampling distribution of the TSLS estimator is normal in large samples, the general procedures for statistical inference (hypothesis tests and confidence intervals) in regression models extend to TSLS regression. For example, 95% confidence intervals are constructed as the TSLS estimator $\pm 1.96$ standard errors. Similarly, joint hypotheses about the population values of the coefficients can be tested using the $F$-statistic, as described in Section 7.2.

*Calculation of TSLS standard errors.*  There are two points to bear in mind about TSLS standard errors. First, the standard errors reported by OLS estimation of the second-stage regression are incorrect because they do not recognize that it is the second stage of a two-stage process. Specifically, the second-stage OLS standard errors fail to adjust for the second-stage regression using the predicted values of the included endogenous variables. Formulas for standard errors that make the necessary adjustment are incorporated into (and automatically used by) TSLS regression commands in econometric software. Therefore, this issue is not a concern in practice if you use a specialized TSLS regression command.

Second, as always the error $u$ might be heteroskedastic. It is therefore important to use heteroskedasticity-robust versions of the standard errors for precisely the same reason as it is important to use heteroskedasticity-robust standard errors for the OLS estimators of the multiple regression model.

## Application to the Demand for Cigarettes

In Section 12.1, we estimated the elasticity of demand for cigarettes using data on annual consumption in 48 U.S. states in 1995 using TSLS with a single regressor (the logarithm of the real price per pack) and a single instrument (the real sales tax per pack). Income also affects demand, however, so it is part of the error term of the population regression. As discussed in Section 12.1, if the state sales tax is related to state income, it is correlated with a variable in the error term of the cigarette demand equation, which violates the instrument exogeneity condition. If so, the IV estimator in Section 12.1 is inconsistent. That is, the IV regression suffers from a version of omitted variable bias. To solve this problem, we need to include income in the regression.

We therefore consider an alternative specification in which the logarithm of income is included in the demand equation. In the terminology of Key Concept 12.1, the dependent variable $Y$ is the logarithm of consumption, $\ln(Q_i^{cigarettes})$; the endogenous regressor $X$ is the logarithm of the real after-tax price, $\ln(P_i^{cigarettes})$; the included exogenous variable $W$ is the logarithm of the real per capita state income, $\ln(Inc_i)$; and the instrument $Z$ is the real sales tax per pack, $SalesTax_i$. The TSLS estimates and (heteroskedasticity-robust) standard errors are

$$\widehat{\ln(Q_i^{cigarettes})} = 9.43 - 1.14\ln(P_i^{cigarettes}) + 0.21\ln(Inc_i). \qquad (12.15)$$
$$\qquad\quad (1.26) \quad (0.37) \qquad\qquad (0.31)$$

This regression uses a single instrument, $SalesTax_i$, but in fact another candidate instrument is available. In addition to general sales taxes, states levy special taxes that apply only to cigarettes and other tobacco products. These cigarette-specific taxes ($CigTax_i$) constitute a possible second instrumental variable. The cigarette-specific tax increases the price of cigarettes paid by the consumer, so it arguably meets the condition for instrument relevance. If it is uncorrelated with the error term in the state cigarette demand equation, it is an exogenous instrument.

With this additional instrument in hand, we now have two instrumental variables, the real sales tax per pack and the real state cigarette-specific tax per pack. With two instruments and a single endogenous regressor, the demand elasticity is overidentified; that is, the number of instruments ($SalesTax_i$ and $CigTax_i$, so $m = 2$) exceeds the number of included endogenous variables ($P_i^{cigarettes}$, so $k = 1$). We can estimate the demand elasticity using TSLS, where the regressors in the first-stage regression are the included exogenous variable, $\ln(Inc_i)$, and both instruments.

The resulting TSLS estimate of the regression function using the two instruments $SalesTax_i$ and $CigTax_i$ is

$$\widehat{\ln(Q_i^{cigarettes})} = 9.89 - 1.28\ln(P_i^{cigarettes}) + 0.28\ln(Inc_i). \qquad (12.16)$$
$$\phantom{\widehat{\ln(Q_i^{cigarettes})} = }(0.96) \quad (0.25) \qquad\qquad\quad (0.25)$$

Compare Equations (12.15) and (12.16): The standard error of the estimated price elasticity is smaller by one-third in Equation (12.16) [0.25 in Equation (12.16) versus 0.37 in Equation (12.15)]. The reason the standard error is smaller in Equation (12.16) is that this estimate uses more information than Equation (12.15): In Equation (12.15), only one instrument is used (the sales tax), but in Equation (12.16), two instruments are used (the sales tax and the cigarette-specific tax). Using two instruments explains more of the variation in cigarette prices than using just one, and this is reflected in smaller standard errors on the estimated demand elasticity.

Are these estimates credible? Ultimately, credibility depends on whether the set of instrumental variables—here, the two taxes—plausibly satisfies the two conditions for valid instruments. It is therefore vital that we assess whether these instruments are valid, and it is to this topic that we now turn.

## 12.3 Checking Instrument Validity

Whether instrumental variables regression is useful in a given application hinges on whether the instruments are valid: Invalid instruments produce meaningless results. It therefore is essential to assess whether a given set of instruments is valid in a particular application.

## Assumption #1: Instrument Relevance

The role of the instrument relevance condition in IV regression is subtle. One way to think of instrument relevance is that it plays a role akin to the sample size: The more relevant the instruments—that is, the more the variation in $X$ is explained by the instruments—the more information is available for use in IV regression. A more relevant instrument produces a more accurate estimator, just as a larger sample size produces a more accurate estimator. Moreover, statistical inference using TSLS is predicated on the TSLS estimator having a normal sampling distribution, but according to the central limit theorem the normal distribution is a good approximation in large—but not necessarily small—samples. If having a more relevant instrument is like having a larger sample size, this suggests, correctly, that the more relevant is the instrument, the better is the normal approximation to the sampling distribution of the TSLS estimator and its $t$-statistic.

Instruments that explain little of the variation in $X$ are called **weak instruments**. In the cigarette example, the distance of the state from cigarette manufacturing plants arguably would be a weak instrument: Although a greater distance increases shipping costs (thus shifting the supply curve in and raising the equilibrium price), cigarettes are lightweight, so shipping costs are a small component of the price of cigarettes. Thus the amount of price variation explained by shipping costs, and thus distance to manufacturing plants, probably is quite small.

This section discusses why weak instruments are a problem, how to check for weak instruments, and what to do if you have weak instruments. It is assumed throughout that the instruments are exogenous.

*Why weak instruments are a problem.*   If the instruments are weak, then the normal distribution provides a poor approximation to the sampling distribution of the TSLS estimator, even if the sample size is large. Thus there is no theoretical justification for the usual methods for performing statistical inference, even in large samples. In fact, if instruments are weak, then the TSLS estimator can be badly biased in the direction of the OLS estimator. In addition, 95% confidence intervals constructed as the TSLS estimator $\pm 1.96$ standard errors can contain the true value the coefficient far less than 95% of the time. In short, if instruments are weak, TSLS is no longer reliable.

To see that there is a problem with the large-sample normal approximation to the sampling distribution of the TSLS estimator, consider the special case, introduced in Section 12.1, of a single included endogenous variable, a single instrument, and no included exogenous regressor. If the instrument is valid, then $\hat{\beta}_1^{TSLS}$ is consistent because the sample covariances $s_{ZY}$ and $s_{ZX}$ are consistent; that

**KEY CONCEPT**

**12.5**

## A Rule of Thumb for Checking for Weak Instruments

The first-stage $F$-statistic is the $F$-statistic testing the hypothesis that the coefficients on the instruments $Z_{1i}, \ldots, Z_{mi}$ equal zero in the first stage of two stage least squares. When there is a single endogenous regressor, a first-stage $F$-statistic less than 10 indicates that the instruments are weak, in which case the TSLS estimator is biased (even in large samples) and TSLS $t$-statistics and confidence intervals are unreliable.

is, $\hat{\beta}_1^{TSLS} = s_{ZY}/s_{ZX} \xrightarrow{p} \text{cov}(Z_i, Y_i)/\text{cov}(Z_i, X_i) = \beta_1$ [Equation (12.7)]. But now suppose that the instrument is not just weak but irrelevant so that $\text{cov}(Z_i, X_i) = 0$. Then $s_{ZX} \xrightarrow{p} \text{cov}(Z_i, X_i) = 0$, so, taken literally, the denominator on the right-hand side of the limit $\text{cov}(Z_i, Y_i)/\text{cov}(Z_i, X_i)$ is zero! Clearly, the argument that $\hat{\beta}_1^{TSLS}$ is consistent breaks down when the instrument relevance condition fails. As shown in Appendix 12.4, this breakdown results in the TSLS estimator having a nonnormal sampling distribution, even if the sample size is very large. In fact, when the instrument is irrelevant, the large-sample distribution of $\hat{\beta}_1^{TSLS}$ is not that of a normal random variable, but rather the distribution of a *ratio* of two normal random variables!

While this circumstance of totally irrelevant instruments might not be encountered in practice, it raises a question: How relevant must the instruments be for the normal distribution to provide a good approximation in practice? The answer to this question in the general IV model is complicated. Fortunately, however, there is a simple rule of thumb available for the most common situation in practice, the case of a single endogenous regressor.

*Checking for weak instruments when there is a single endogenous regressor.* One way to check for weak instruments when there is a single endogenous regressor is to compute the $F$-statistic testing the hypothesis that the coefficients on the instruments are all zero in the first-stage regression of TSLS. This **first-stage $F$-statistic** provides a measure of the information content contained in the instruments: The more information content, the larger is the expected value of the $F$-statistic. One simple rule of thumb is that you do not need to worry about weak instruments if the first-stage $F$-statistic exceeds 10. (Why 10? See Appendix 12.5.) This is summarized in Key Concept 12.5.

*What do I do if I have weak instruments?* If you have many instruments, some of those instruments are probably weaker than others. If you have a small number of strong instruments and many weak ones, you will be better off discarding the weakest instruments and using the most relevant subset for your TSLS analysis. Your TSLS standard errors might increase when you drop weak instruments, but keep in mind that your original standard errors were not meaningful anyway!

If, however, the coefficients are exactly identified, you cannot discard the weak instruments. Even if the coefficients are overidentified, you might not have enough strong instruments to achieve identification, so discarding some weak instruments will not help. In this case, you have two options. The first option is to find additional, stronger instruments. This is easier said than done: It requires an intimate knowledge of the problem at hand and can entail redesigning the data set and the nature of the empirical study. The second option is to proceed with your empirical analysis using the weak instruments, but employing methods other than TSLS. Although this chapter has focused on TSLS some other methods for instrumental variable analysis are less sensitive to weak instruments than TSLS, and some of these methods are discussed in Appendix 12.5.

## Assumption #2: Instrument Exogeneity

If the instruments are not exogenous, then TSLS is inconsistent: The TSLS estimator converges in probability to something other than the population coefficient in the regression. After all, the idea of instrumental variables regression is that the instrument contains information about variation in $X_i$ that is unrelated to the error term $u_i$. If, in fact, the instrument is not exogenous, it cannot pinpoint this exogenous variation in $X_i$, and it stands to reason that IV regression fails to provide a consistent estimator. The math behind this argument is summarized in Appendix 12.4.

*Can you statistically test the assumption that the instruments are exogenous?* Yes and no. On the one hand, it is not possible to test the hypothesis that the instruments are exogenous when the coefficients are exactly identified. On the other hand, if the coefficients are overidentified, it is possible to test the overidentifying restrictions, that is, to test the hypothesis that the "extra" instruments are exogenous under the maintained assumption that there are enough valid instruments to identify the coefficients of interest.

First consider the case that the coefficients are exactly identified, so you have as many instruments as endogenous regressors. Then it is impossible to develop a statistical test of the hypothesis that the instruments are in fact exogenous. That is, empirical evidence cannot be brought to bear on the question of whether these

## A Scary Regression

One way to estimate the percentage increase in earnings from going to school for another year (the "return to education") is to regress the logarithm of earnings against years of school using data on individuals. But if more able individuals are both more successful in the labor market and attend school longer (perhaps because they find it easier), then years of schooling will be correlated with the omitted variable, innate ability, and the OLS estimator of the return to education will be biased. Because innate ability is extremely difficult to measure and thus cannot be used as a regressor, some labor economists have turned to IV regression to estimate the return to education. But what variable is correlated with years of education but not the error term in the earnings regression? That is, what is a valid instrumental variable?

Your birthday, suggested labor economists Joshua Angrist and Alan Krueger. Because of mandatory schooling laws, they reasoned, your birthday is correlated with your years of education: If the law requires you to attend school until your 16th birthday and you turn 16 in January while you are in tenth grade, you might drop out—but if you turn 16 in July you already will have completed tenth grade. If so, your birthday satisfies the instrument relevance condition. But being born in January or July should have no *direct* effect on your earnings (other than through years of education), so your birthday satisfies the instrument exogeneity condition. They implemented this idea by using the individual's quarter (three-month period) of birth as an instrumental variable. They used a very large sample of data from the U.S. Census (their regressions had at least 329,000 observations!), and they controlled for other variables such as the worker's age.

But John Bound, another labor economist, was skeptical. He knew that weak instruments cause TSLS to be unreliable and worried that, despite the extremely large sample size, the quarter of birth might be a weak instrument in some of their specifications. So when Bound and Krueger next met over lunch, the conversation inevitably turned to whether the Angrist–Krueger instruments were weak. Krueger thought not and suggested a creative way to find out: Why not rerun the regressions using a truly irrelevant instrument—replace each individual's real quarter of birth by a fake quarter of birth, randomly generated by the computer—and compare the results using the real and fake instruments? What they found was amazing: It didn't matter whether you used the real quarter of birth or the fake one as the instrument—TSLS gave basically the same answer!

This was a scary regression for labor econometricians. The TSLS standard error computed using the real data suggests that the return to education is precisely estimated—but so does the standard error computed using the fake data. Of course, the fake data *cannot* estimate the return to education precisely, because the fake instrument is totally irrelevant. The worry, then, is that the TSLS estimates based on the real data are just as unreliable as those based on the fake data.

The problem is that the instruments are in fact very weak in some of Angrist and Krueger's regressions. In some of their specifications, the first-stage $F$-statistic is less than 2, far less than the rule-of-thumb cutoff of 10. In other specifications, Angrist and Krueger have larger first-stage $F$-statistics, and in those cases the TSLS inferences are not subject to the problem of weak instruments. By the way, in those specifications the return to education is estimated to be approximately 8%, somewhat *greater* than estimated by OLS.[1]

---

[1]The original IV regressions are reported in Angrist and Krueger (1991), and the re-analysis using the fake instruments is published in Bound, Jaeger, and Baker (1995).

instruments satisfy the exogeneity restriction. In this case, the only way to assess whether the instruments are exogenous is to draw on expert opinion and your personal knowledge of the empirical problem at hand. For example, Philip Wright's knowledge of agricultural supply and demand led him to suggest that below-average rainfall would plausibly shift the supply curve for butter but would not directly shift the demand curve.

Assessing whether the instruments are exogenous *necessarily* requires making an expert judgment based on personal knowledge of the application. If, however, there are more instruments than endogenous regressors, then there is a statistical tool that can be helpful in this process: the so-called test of overidentifying restrictions.

*The overidentifying restrictions test.*   Suppose that you have a single endogenous regressor and two instruments. Then you could compute two different TSLS estimators: one using the first instrument, the other using the second. These two estimators will not be the same because of sampling variation, but if both instruments are exogenous, then they will tend to be close to each other. But what if these two instruments produce very different estimates? You might sensibly conclude that there is something wrong with one or the other of the instruments, or both. That is, it would be reasonable to conclude that one or the other, or both, of the instruments are not exogenous.

The **test of overidentifying restrictions** implicitly makes this comparison. We say implicitly, because the test is carried out without actually computing all of the different possible IV estimates. Here is the idea. Exogeneity of the instruments means that they are uncorrelated with $u_i$. This suggests that the instruments should be approximately uncorrelated with $\hat{u}_i^{TSLS}$, where $\hat{u}_i^{TSLS} = Y_i - (\hat{\beta}_0^{TSLS} + \hat{\beta}_1^{TSLS}X_{1i} + \cdots + \hat{\beta}_{k+r}^{TSLS}W_{ri})$ is the residual from the estimated TSLS regression using all the instruments (approximately rather than exactly because of sampling variation). (Note that these residuals are constructed using the true $X$'s rather than their first-stage predicted values.) Accordingly, if the instruments are in fact exogenous, then the coefficients on the instruments in a regression of $\hat{u}_i^{TSLS}$ on the instruments and the included exogenous variables should all be zero, and this hypothesis can be tested.

This method for computing the overidentifying restriction test is summarized in Key Concept 12.6. This statistic is computed using the homoskedasticity-only $F$-statistic. The test statistic is commonly called the $J$-statistic and is computed as $J = mF$.

In large samples, if the instruments are not weak and the errors are homoskedastic, then, under the null hypothesis that the instruments are exogenous, the $J$-statistic has a chi-squared distribution with $m - k$ degrees of freedom ($\chi^2_{m-k}$). It is important to remember that even though the number of restrictions being tested

**KEY CONCEPT**

**12.6**

## The Overidentifying Restrictions Test (The *J*-Statistic)

Let $\hat{u}_i^{TSLS}$ be the residuals from TSLS estimation of Equation (12.12). Use OLS to estimate the regression coefficients in

$$\hat{u}_i^{TSLS} = \delta_0 + \delta_1 Z_{1i} + \cdots + \delta_m Z_{mi} + \delta_{m+1} W_{1i} + \cdots + \delta_{m+r} W_{ri} + e_i,$$

where $e_i$ is the regression error term. Let $F$ denote the homoskedasticity-only $F$-statistic testing the hypothesis that $\delta_1 = \cdots = \delta_m = 0$. The overidentifying restrictions test statistic is $J = mF$. Under the null hypothesis that all the instruments are exogenous, if $e_i$ is homoskedastic, in large samples $J$ is distributed $\chi^2_{m-k}$, where $m - k$ is the "degree of overidentification," that is, the number of instruments minus the number of endogenous regressors.

is $m$, the degrees of freedom of the asymptotic distribution of the $J$-statistic is $m - k$. The reason is that it is only possible to test the *over*identifying restrictions, of which there are $m - k$. The modification of the $J$-statistic for heteroskedastic errors is given in Section 18.7.

The easiest way to see that you cannot test the exogeneity of the regressors when the coefficients are exactly identified ($m = k$) is to consider the case of a single included endogenous variable ($k = 1$). If there are two instruments, then you can compute two TSLS estimators, one for each instrument, and you can compare them to see if they are close. But if you have only one instrument, then you can compute only one TSLS estimator and you have nothing to compare it to. In fact, if the coefficients are exactly identified, so that $m = k$, then the overidentifying test statistic $J$ is exactly zero.

## 12.4 Application to the Demand for Cigarettes[1]

Our attempt to estimate the elasticity of demand for cigarettes left off with the TSLS estimates summarized in Equation (12.16), in which income was an included exogenous variable and there were two instruments, the general sales tax and the cigarette-specific tax. We can now undertake a more thorough evaluation of these instruments.

---

[1]This section assumes knowledge of the material in Sections 10.1 and 10.2 on panel data with $T = 2$ time periods.

As in Section 12.1, it makes sense that the two instruments are relevant because taxes are a big part of the after-tax price of cigarettes, and shortly we will look at this empirically. First, however, we focus on the difficult question of whether the two tax variables are plausibly exogenous.

The first step in assessing whether an instrument is exogenous is to think through the arguments for why it may or may not be. This requires thinking about which factors account for the error term in the cigarette demand equation and whether these factors are plausibly related to the instruments.

Why do some states have higher per capita cigarette consumption than others? One reason might be variation in incomes across states, but state income is included in Equation (12.16), so this is not part of the error term. Another reason is that there are historical factors influencing demand. For example, states that grow tobacco have higher rates of smoking than most other states. Could this factor be related to taxes? Quite possibly: If tobacco farming and cigarette production are important industries in a state, then these industries could exert influence to keep cigarette-specific taxes low. This suggests that an omitted factor in cigarette demand—whether the state grows tobacco and produces cigarettes—could be correlated with cigarette-specific taxes.

One solution to this possible correlation between the error term and the instrument would be to include information on the size of the tobacco and cigarette industry in the state; this is the approach we took when we included income as a regressor in the demand equation. But because we have panel data on cigarette consumption, a different approach is available that does not require this information. As discussed in Chapter 10, panel data make it possible to eliminate the influence of variables that vary across entities (states) but do not change over time, such as the climate and historical circumstances that lead to a large tobacco and cigarette industry in a state. Two methods for doing this were given in Chapter 10: constructing data on *changes* in the variables between two different time periods and using fixed effects regression. To keep the analysis here as simple as possible, we adopt the former approach and perform regressions of the type described in Section 10.2, based on the changes in the variables between two different years.

The time span between the two different years influences how the estimated elasticities are to be interpreted. Because cigarettes are addictive, changes in price will take some time to alter behavior. At first, an increase in the price of cigarettes might have little effect on demand. Over time, however, the price increase might contribute to some smokers' desire to quit, and, importantly, it could discourage nonsmokers from taking up the habit. Thus the response of demand to a price increase could be small in the short run but large in the long run. Said differently, for an addictive product like cigarettes, demand might be inelastic in the short

## The Externalities of Smoking

Smoking imposes costs that are not fully borne by the smoker; that is, it generates externalities. One economic justification for taxing cigarettes therefore is to "internalize" these externalities. In theory, the tax on a pack of cigarettes should equal the dollar value of the externalities created by smoking that pack. But what, precisely, are the externalities of smoking, measured in dollars per pack?

Several studies have used econometric methods to estimate the externalities of smoking. The negative externalities—costs—borne by others include medical costs paid by the government to care for ill smokers, health care costs of nonsmokers associated with secondhand smoke, and fires caused by cigarettes.

But, from a purely economic point of view, smoking also has *positive* externalities, or benefits. The biggest economic benefit of smoking is that smokers tend to pay much more in Social Security (public pension) taxes than they ever get back. There are also large savings in nursing home expenditures on the very old—smokers tend not to live that long. Because the negative externalities of smoking occur while the smoker is alive but the positive

ones accrue after death, the net present value of the per-pack externalities (the value of the net costs per pack, discounted to the present) depends on the discount rate.

The studies do not agree on a specific dollar value of the net externalities. Some suggest that the net externalities, properly discounted, are quite small, less than current taxes. In fact, the most extreme estimates suggest that the net externalities are *positive*, so smoking should be subsidized! Other studies, which incorporate costs that are probably important but difficult to quantify (such as caring for babies who are unhealthy because their mothers smoke), suggest that externalities might be $1 per pack, possibly even more. But all the studies agree that, by tending to die in late middle age, smokers pay far more in taxes than they ever get back in their brief retirement.[1]

_____

[1]An early calculation of the externalities of smoking was reported by Willard G. Manning et al. (1989). A calculation suggesting that health care costs would go *up* if everyone stopped smoking is presented in Barendregt et al. (1997). Other studies of the externalities of smoking are reviewed by Chaloupka and Warner (2000).

run—that is, it might have a short-run elasticity near zero—but it might be more elastic in the long run.

In this analysis, we focus on estimating the long-run price elasticity. We do this by considering quantity and price changes that occur over 10-year periods. Specifically, in the regressions considered here, the 10-year change in log quantity, $\ln(Q_{i,1995}^{cigarettes}) - \ln(Q_{i,1985}^{cigarettes})$, is regressed against the 10-year change in log price, $\ln(P_{i,1995}^{cigarettes}) - \ln(P_{i,1985}^{cigarettes})$, and the 10-year change in log income, $\ln(Inc_{i,1995}) - \ln(Inc_{i,1985})$. Two instruments are used: the change in the sales tax over 10 years, $SalesTax_{i,1995} - SalesTax_{i,1985}$, and the change in the cigarette-specific tax over 10 years, $CigTax_{i,1995} - CigTax_{i,1985}$.

**TABLE 12.1** Two Stage Least Squares Estimates of the Demand for Cigarettes Using Panel Data for 48 U.S. States

Dependent variable: $\ln(Q^{cigarettes}_{i,1995}) - \ln(Q^{cigarettes}_{i,1985})$

| Regressor | (1) | (2) | (3) |
|---|---|---|---|
| $\ln(P^{cigarettes}_{i,1995}) - \ln(P^{cigarettes}_{i,1985})$ | −0.94** (0.21) | −1.34** (0.23) | −1.20** (0.20) |
| $\ln(Inc_{i,1995}) - \ln(Inc_{i,1985})$ | 0.53 (0.34) | 0.43 (0.30) | 0.46 (0.31) |
| Intercept | −0.12 (0.07) | −0.02 (0.07) | −0.05 (0.06) |
| Instrumental variable(s) | Sales tax | Cigarette-specific tax | Both sales tax and cigarette-specific tax |
| First-stage $F$-statistic | 33.70 | 107.20 | 88.60 |
| Overidentifying restrictions $J$-test and $p$-value | — | — | 4.93 (0.026) |

These regressions were estimated using data for 48 U.S. states (48 observations on the 10-year differences). The data are described in Appendix 12.1. The $J$-test of overidentifying restrictions is described in Key Concept 12.6 (its $p$-value is given in parentheses), and the first-stage $F$-statistic is described in Key Concept 12.5. Individual coefficients are statistically significant at the *5% significance level or **1% significance level.

The results are presented in Table 12.1. As usual, each column in the table presents the results of a different regression. All regressions have the same regressors, and all coefficients are estimated using TSLS; the only difference between the three regressions is the set of instruments used. In column (1), the only instrument is the sales tax; in column (2), the only instrument is the cigarette-specific tax; and in column (3), both taxes are used as instruments.

In IV regression, the reliability of the coefficient estimates hinges on the validity of the instruments, so the first things to look at in Table 12.1 are the diagnostic statistics assessing the validity of the instruments.

First, are the instruments relevant? We need to look at the first-stage $F$-statistics. The first-stage regression in column (1) is

$$\ln(\widehat{P^{cigarettes}_{i,1995}}) - \ln(P^{cigarettes}_{i,1985}) = 0.53 - 0.22[\ln(Inc_{i,1995}) - \ln(Inc_{i,1985})]$$
$$(0.03) \quad (0.22)$$
$$+ 0.0255(SalesTax_{i,1995} - SalesTax_{i,1985}). \quad (12.18)$$
$$(0.0044)$$

Because there is only one instrument in this regression, the first-stage $F$-statistic is the square of the $t$-statistic testing that the coefficient on the instrumental variable, $SalesTax_{i,1995} - SalesTax_{i,1985}$, is zero; this is $F = t^2 = (0.0255/0.0044)^2 = 33.7$. For the regressions in columns (2) and (3), the first-stage $F$-statistics are 107.2 and 88.6, so in all three cases the first-stage $F$-statistics exceed 10. We conclude that the instruments are not weak, so we can rely on the standard methods for statistical inference (hypothesis tests, confidence intervals) using the TSLS coefficients and standard errors.

Second, are the instruments exogenous? Because the regressions in columns (1) and (2) each have a single instrument and a single included endogenous regressor, the coefficients in those regressions are exactly identified. Thus we cannot deploy the $J$-test in either of those regressions. The regression in column (3), however, is overidentified because there are two instruments and a single included endogenous regressor, so there is one ($m - k = 2 - 1 = 1$) overidentifying restriction. The $J$-statistic is 4.93; this has a $\chi_1^2$ distribution, so the 5% critical value is 3.84 (Appendix Table 3) and the null hypothesis that both the instruments are exogenous is rejected at the 5% significance level (this deduction also can be made directly from the $p$-value of 0.026, reported in the table).

The reason the $J$-statistic rejects the null hypothesis that both instruments are exogenous is that the two instruments produce rather different estimated coefficients. When the only instrument is the sales tax [column (1)], the estimated price elasticity is $-0.94$, but when the only instrument is the cigarette-specific tax, the estimated price elasticity is $-1.34$. Recall the basic idea of the $J$-statistic: If both instruments are exogenous, then the two TSLS estimators using the individual instruments are consistent and differ from each other only because of random sampling variation. If, however, one of the instruments is exogenous and one is not, then the estimator based on the endogenous instrument is inconsistent, which is detected by the $J$-statistic. In this application, the difference between the two estimated price elasticities is sufficiently large that it is unlikely to be the result of pure sampling variation, so the $J$-statistic rejects the null hypothesis that both the instruments are exogenous.

The $J$-statistic rejection means that the regression in column (3) is based on invalid instruments (the instrument exogeneity condition fails). What does this imply about the estimates in columns (1) and (2)? The $J$-statistic rejection says that at least one of the instruments is endogenous, so there are three logical possibilities: The sales tax is exogenous but the cigarette-specific tax is not, in which case the column (1) regression is reliable; the cigarette-specific tax is exogenous but the sales tax is not, so the column (2) regression is reliable; or neither tax is exogenous, so neither regression is reliable. The statistical evidence cannot tell us which possibility is correct, so we must use our judgment.

We think that the case for the exogeneity of the general sales tax is stronger than that for the cigarette-specific tax, because the political process can link changes in the cigarette-specific tax to changes in the cigarette market and smoking policy. For example, if smoking decreases in a state because it falls out of fashion, there will be fewer smokers and a weakened lobby against cigarette-specific tax increases, which in turn could lead to higher cigarette-specific taxes. Thus changes in tastes (which are part of $u$) could be correlated with changes in cigarette-specific taxes (the instrument). This suggests discounting the IV estimates that use the cigarette-only tax as an instrument and adopting the price elasticity estimated using the general sales tax as an instrument, −0.94.

The estimate of −0.94 indicates that cigarette consumption is somewhat elastic: An increase in price of 1% leads to a decrease in consumption of 0.94%. This may seem surprising for an addictive product like cigarettes. But remember that this elasticity is computed using changes over a 10-year period, so it is a long-run elasticity. This estimate suggests that increased taxes can make a substantial dent in cigarette consumption, at least in the long run.

When the elasticity is estimated using 5-year changes from 1985 to 1990 rather than the 10-year changes reported in Table 12.1, the elasticity (estimated with the general sales tax as the instrument) is −0.79; for changes from 1990 to 1995, the elasticity is −0.68. These estimates suggest that demand is less elastic over horizons of 5 years than over 10 years. This finding of greater price elasticity at longer horizons is consistent with the large body of research on cigarette demand. Demand elasticity estimates in that literature typically fall in the range −0.3 to −0.5, but these are mainly short-run elasticities; some studies suggest that the long-run elasticity could be perhaps twice the short-run elasticity.[2]

## 12.5  Where Do Valid Instruments Come From?

In practice the most difficult aspect of IV estimation is finding instruments that are both relevant and exogenous. There are two main approaches, which reflect two different perspectives on econometric and statistical modeling.

The first approach is to use economic theory to suggest instruments. For example, Philip Wright's understanding of the economics of agricultural markets led him to look for an instrument that shifted the supply curve but not the demand

---

[2]A sobering economic study by Adda and Cornaglia (2006) suggests that smokers compensate for higher taxes by smoking more intensively, thus extracting more nicotine per cigarette. If you are interested in learning more about the economics of smoking, see Chaloupka and Warner (2000), Gruber (2001), and Carpenter and Cook (2008).

curve; this in turn led him to consider weather conditions in agricultural regions. One area where this approach has been particularly successful is the field of financial economics. Some economic models of investor behavior involve statements about how investors forecast, which then imply sets of variables that are uncorrelated with the error term. Those models sometimes are nonlinear in the data and in the parameters, in which case the IV estimators discussed in this chapter cannot be used. An extension of IV methods to nonlinear models, called generalized method of moments estimation, is used instead. Economic theories are, however, abstractions that often do not take into account the nuances and details necessary for analyzing a particular data set. Thus this approach does not always work.

The second approach to constructing instruments is to look for some exogenous source of variation in $X$ arising from what is, in effect, a random phenomenon that induces shifts in the endogenous regressor. For example, in our hypothetical example in Section 12.1, earthquake damage increased average class size in some school districts, and this variation in class size was unrelated to potential omitted variables that affect student achievement. This approach typically requires knowledge of the problem being studied and careful attention to the details of the data, and it is best explained through examples.

## Three Examples

We now turn to three empirical applications of IV regression that provide examples of how different researchers used their expert knowledge of their empirical problem to find instrumental variables.

*Does putting criminals in jail reduce crime?* This is a question only an economist would ask. After all, a criminal cannot commit a crime outside jail while in prison, and that some criminals are caught and jailed serves to deter others. But the magnitude of the combined effect—the change in the crime rate associated with a 1% increase in the prison population—is an empirical question.

One strategy for estimating this effect is to regress crime rates (crimes per 100,000 members of the general population) against incarceration rates (prisoners per 100,000), using annual data at a suitable level of jurisdiction (for example, U.S. states). This regression could include some control variables measuring economic conditions (crime increases when general economic conditions worsen), demographics (youths commit more crimes than the elderly), and so forth. There is, however, a serious potential for simultaneous causality bias that undermines such an analysis: If the crime rate goes up and the police do their job, there will be more prisoners. On the one hand, increased incarceration reduces the crime rate; on the other hand, an increased crime rate increases incarceration. As in the butter example in Figure 12.1, because of this simultaneous causality an OLS regression of the crime rate on the incarceration rate will estimate some complicated combination of these two effects. This problem cannot be solved by finding better control variables.

This simultaneous causality bias, however, can be eliminated by finding a suitable instrumental variable and using TSLS. The instrument must be correlated with the incarceration rate (it must be relevant), but it must also be uncorrelated with the error term in the crime rate equation of interest (it must be exogenous). That is, it must affect the incarceration rate but be unrelated to any of the unobserved factors that determine the crime rate.

Where does one find something that affects incarceration but has no direct effect on the crime rate? One place is exogenous variation in the capacity of existing prisons. Because it takes time to build a prison, short-term capacity restrictions can force states to release prisoners prematurely or otherwise reduce incarceration rates. Using this reasoning, Levitt (1996) suggested that lawsuits aimed at reducing prison overcrowding could serve as an instrumental variable, and he implemented this idea using panel data for the U.S. states from 1972 to 1993.

Are variables measuring overcrowding litigation valid instruments? Although Levitt did not report first-stage $F$-statistics, the prison overcrowding litigation slowed the growth of prisoner incarcerations in his data, suggesting that this instrument is relevant. To the extent that overcrowding litigation is induced by prison conditions but not by the crime rate or its determinants, this instrument is exogenous. Because Levitt breaks down overcrowding legislation into several types and thus has several instruments, he is able to test the overidentifying restrictions and fails to reject them using the $J$-statistic, which bolsters the case that his instruments are valid.

Using these instruments and TSLS, Levitt estimated the effect on the crime rate of incarceration to be substantial. This estimated effect was three times larger than the effect estimated using OLS, suggesting that OLS suffered from large simultaneous causality bias.

*Does cutting class sizes increase test scores?* As we saw in the empirical analysis of Part II, schools with small classes tend to be wealthier, and their students have access to enhanced learning opportunities both in and out of the classroom. In Part II, we used multiple regression to tackle the threat of omitted variables bias by controlling for various measures of student affluence, ability to speak English, and so forth. Still, a skeptic could wonder whether we did enough: If we left out something important, our estimates of the class size effect would still be biased.

This potential omitted variables bias could be addressed by including the right control variables, but if these data are unavailable (some, like outside learning opportunities, are hard to measure), then an alternative approach is to use

IV regression. This regression requires an instrumental variable correlated with class size (relevance) but uncorrelated with the omitted determinants of test performance that make up the error term, such as parental interest in learning, learning opportunities outside the classroom, quality of the teachers and school facilities, and so forth (exogeneity).

Where does one look for an instrument that induces random, exogenous variation in class size, but is unrelated to the other determinants of test performance? Hoxby (2000) suggested biology. Because of random fluctuations in timings of births, the size of the incoming kindergarten class varies from one year to the next. Although the actual number of children entering kindergarten might be endogenous (recent news about the school might influence whether parents send a child to a private school), she argued that the *potential* number of children entering kindergarten—the number of 4-year-olds in the district—is mainly a matter of random fluctuations in the birth dates of children.

Is potential enrollment a valid instrument? Whether it is exogenous depends on whether it is correlated with unobserved determinants of test performance. Surely biological fluctuations in potential enrollment are exogenous, but potential enrollment also fluctuates because parents with young children choose to move into an improving school district and out of one in trouble. If so, an increase in potential enrollment could be correlated with unobserved factors such as the quality of school management, rendering this instrument invalid. Hoxby addressed this problem by reasoning that growth or decline in the potential student pool for this reason would occur smoothly over several years, whereas random fluctuations in birth dates would produce short-term "spikes" in potential enrollment. Thus, she used as her instrument not potential enrollment, but the deviation of potential enrollment from its long-term trend. These deviations satisfy the criterion for instrument relevance (the first-stage *F*-statistics all exceed 100). She makes a good case that this instrument is exogenous, but, as in all IV analysis, the credibility of this assumption is ultimately a matter of judgment.

Hoxby implemented this strategy using detailed panel data on elementary schools in Connecticut in the 1980s and 1990s. The panel data set permitted her to include school fixed effects, which, in addition to the instrumental variables strategy, attack the problem of omitted variables bias at the school level. Her TSLS estimates suggested that the effect on test scores of class size is small; most of her estimates were statistically insignificantly different from zero.

***Does aggressive treatment of heart attacks prolong lives?*** Aggressive treatments for victims of heart attacks (technically, acute myocardial infarctions, or AMI) hold the potential for saving lives. Before a new medical procedure—in this example, cardiac catheterization[3]—is approved for general use, it goes through clinical trials, a series of randomized controlled experiments designed to measure its effects and side effects. But strong performance in a clinical trial is one thing; actual performance in the real world is another.

A natural starting point for estimating the real-world effect of cardiac catheterization is to compare patients who received the treatment to those who did not. This leads to regressing the length of survival of the patient against the binary treatment variable (whether the patient received cardiac catheterization) and other control variables that affect mortality (age, weight, other measured health conditions, and so forth). The population coefficient on the indicator variable is the increment to the patient's life expectancy provided by the treatment. Unfortunately, the OLS estimator is subject to bias: Cardiac catheterization does not "just happen" to a patient randomly; rather, it is performed because the doctor and patient decide that it might be effective. If their decision is based in part on unobserved factors relevant to health outcomes not in the data set, the treatment decision will be correlated with the regression error term. If the healthiest patients are the ones who receive the treatment, the OLS estimator will be biased (treatment is correlated with an omitted variable), and the treatment will appear more effective than it really is.

This potential bias can be eliminated by IV regression using a valid instrumental variable. The instrument must be correlated with treatment (must be relevant) but must be uncorrelated with the omitted health factors that affect survival (must be exogenous).

Where does one look for something that affects treatment but not the health outcome, other than through its effect on treatment? McClellan, McNeil, and Newhouse (1994) suggested geography. Most hospitals in their data set did not specialize in cardiac catheterization, so many patients were closer to "regular" hospitals that did not offer this treatment than to cardiac catheterization hospitals. McClellan, McNeil, and Newhouse therefore used as an instrumental variable the difference between the distance from the AMI patient's home to the nearest cardiac catheterization hospital and the distance to the nearest hospital of any sort; this distance is zero if the nearest hospital is a cardiac catheterization hospital, and otherwise it is positive. If this relative distance affects the probability of receiving this treatment, then it is relevant. If it is distributed randomly across AMI victims, then it is exogenous.

Is relative distance to the nearest cardiac catheterization hospital a valid instrument? McClellan, McNeil, and Newhouse do not report first-stage $F$-statistics, but they do provide other empirical evidence that it is not weak. Is this distance

---

[3]Cardiac catheterization is a procedure in which a catheter, or tube, is inserted into a blood vessel and guided all the way to the heart to obtain information about the heart and coronary arteries.

measure exogenous? They make two arguments. First, they draw on their medical expertise and knowledge of the health care system to argue that distance to a hospital is plausibly uncorrelated with any of the unobservable variables that determine AMI outcomes. Second, they have data on some of the additional variables that affect AMI outcomes, such as the weight of the patient, and in their sample distance is uncorrelated with these *observable* determinants of survival; this, they argue, makes it more credible that distance is uncorrelated with the *unobservable* determinants in the error term as well.

Using 205,021 observations on Americans aged at least 64 who had an AMI in 1987, McClellan, McNeil, and Newhouse reached a striking conclusion: Their TSLS estimates suggest that cardiac catheterization has a small, possibly zero, effect on health outcomes; that is, cardiac catheterization does not substantially prolong life. In contrast, the OLS estimates suggest a large positive effect. They interpret this difference as evidence of bias in the OLS estimates.

McClellan, McNeil, and Newhouse's IV method has an interesting interpretation. The OLS analysis used actual treatment as the regressor, but because actual treatment is itself the outcome of a decision by patient and doctor, they argue that the actual treatment is correlated with the error term. Instead, TSLS uses *predicted* treatment, where the variation in predicted treatment arises because of variation in the instrumental variable: Patients closer to a cardiac catheterization hospital are more likely to receive this treatment.

This interpretation has two implications. First, the IV regression actually estimates the effect of the treatment not on a "typical" randomly selected patient, but rather on patients for whom distance is an important consideration in the treatment decision. The effect on those patients might differ from the effect on a typical patient, which provides one explanation of the greater estimated effectiveness of the treatment in clinical trials than in McClellan, McNeil, and Newhouse's IV study. Second, it suggests a general strategy for finding instruments in this type of setting: Find an instrument that affects the probability of treatment, but does so for reasons that are unrelated to the outcome except through their effect on the likelihood of treatment. Both these implications have applicability to experimental and "quasi-experimental" studies, the topic of Chapter 13.

## 12.6 Conclusion

From the humble start of estimating how much less butter people will buy if its price rises, IV methods have evolved into a general approach for estimating regressions when one or more variables are correlated with the error term. Instrumental variables regression uses the instruments to isolate variation in the endogenous regressors that is uncorrelated with the error in the regression of interest; this is the first stage of two stage least squares. This in turn permits estimation of the effect of interest in the second stage of two stage least squares.

Successful IV regression requires valid instruments, that is, instruments that are both relevant (not weak) and exogenous. If the instruments are weak, then the TSLS estimator can be biased, even in large samples, and statistical inferences based on TSLS $t$-statistics and confidence intervals can be misleading. Fortunately, when there is a single endogenous regressor, it is possible to check for weak instruments simply by checking the first-stage $F$-statistic.

If the instruments are not exogenous—that is, if one or more instruments is correlated with the error term—the TSLS estimator is inconsistent. If there are more instruments than endogenous regressors, instrument exogeneity can be examined by using the $J$-statistic to test the overidentifying restrictions. However, the core assumption—that there are at least as many exogenous instruments as there are endogenous regressors—cannot be tested. It is therefore incumbent on both the empirical analyst and the critical reader to use their own understanding of the empirical application to evaluate whether this assumption is reasonable.

The interpretation of IV regression as a way to exploit known exogenous variation in the endogenous regressor can be used to guide the search for potential instrumental variables in a particular application. This interpretation underlies much of the empirical analysis in the area that goes under the broad heading of program evaluation, in which experiments or quasi-experiments are used to estimate the effect of programs, policies, or other interventions on some outcome measure. A variety of additional issues arises in those applications—for example, the interpretation of IV results when, as in the cardiac catheterization example, different "patients" might have different responses to the same "treatment." These and other aspects of empirical program evaluation are taken up in Chapter 13.

## Summary

1. Instrumental variables regression is a way to estimate regression coefficients when one or more regressors are correlated with the error term.
2. Endogenous variables are correlated with the error term in the equation of interest; exogenous variables are uncorrelated with this error term.
3. For an instrument to be valid, it must be (1) correlated with the included endogenous variable and (2) exogenous.
4. IV regression requires at least as many instruments as included endogenous variables.

5. The TSLS estimator has two stages. First, the included endogenous variables are regressed against the included exogenous variables and the instruments. Second, the dependent variable is regressed against the included exogenous variables and the predicted values of the included endogenous variables from the first-stage regression(s).

6. Weak instruments (instruments that are nearly uncorrelated with the included endogenous variables) make the TSLS estimator biased and TSLS confidence intervals and hypothesis tests unreliable.

7. If an instrument is not exogenous, the TSLS estimator is inconsistent.

## Key Terms

instrumental variables (IV) regression (470)

instrumental variable (instrument) (470)

endogenous variable (471)

exogenous variable (471)

instrument relevance condition (472)

instrument exogeneity condition (472)

two stage least squares (472)

included exogenous variables (481)

exactly identified (481)

overidentified (481)

underidentified (481)

reduced form (483)

first-stage regression (484)

second-stage regression (484)

weak instruments (489)

first-stage $F$-statistic (490)

test of overidentifying restrictions (493)

---

**MyEconLab Can Help You Get a Better Grade**

**MyEconLab**   If your exam were tomorrow, would you be ready? For each chapter, **MyEconLab** Practice Tests and Study Plan help you prepare for your exams. You can also find similar Exercises and Review the Concepts Questions now in **MyEconLab**. To see how it works, turn to the **MyEconLab** spread on pages 2 and 3 of this book and then go to **www.myeconlab.com**.

For additional Empirical Exercises and Data Sets, log on to the Companion Website at **www.pearsonglobaleditions.com/Stock_Watson**.

---

## Review the Concepts

**12.1**  In the demand curve regression model of Equation (12.3), is $\ln(P_i^{butter})$ positively or negatively correlated with the error, $u_i$? If $\beta_1$ is estimated by OLS, would you expect the estimated value to be larger or smaller than the true value of $\beta_1$? Explain.

**12.2** Describe the key characteristics of a valid instrument. If you were a researcher, how would you determine if the variable you have selected as an instrument for an endogenous regressor is valid or not?

**12.3** In his study of the effect of incarceration on crime rates, suppose that Levitt had used the number of lawyers per capita as an instrument. Would this instrument be relevant? Would it be exogenous? Would it be a valid instrument?

**12.4** In their study of the effectiveness of cardiac catheterization, McClellan, McNeil, and Newhouse (1994) used as an instrument the difference in distance to cardiac catheterization and regular hospitals. How could you determine whether this instrument is relevant? How could you determine whether this instrument is exogenous?

## Exercises

**12.1** This question refers to the panel data regressions summarized in Table 12.1.

  **a.** Suppose that the Federal Government is considering a new tax on cigarettes that is estimated to increase the retail price by $0.25 per pack. If the current price per pack is $6.75, use the regression in column (1) to predict the change in demand. Construct a 95% confidence interval for the change in demand.

  **b.** Suppose that the United States enters a recession, and income falls by 5%. Use the regression in column (1) to predict the change in demand.

  **c.** Suppose you have additional data on the prices and quantities of cigarettes in 1993, 1994, 1996 and 1997. How do you think the estimated coefficients would change with an eight-year horizon? With a twelve-year horizon?

  **d.** Suppose that the $F$-statistic in column (1) were 63.7 instead of 33.7. Would the regression provide a reliable answer to the question posed in (a)? Why or why not?

**12.2** Consider the regression model with a single regressor: $Y_i = \beta_0 + \beta_1 X_i + u_i$. Suppose that the least squares assumptions in Key Concept 4.3 are satisfied.

  **a.** Show that $X_i$ is a valid instrument. That is, show that Key Concept 12.3 is satisfied with $Z_i = X_i$.

CHAPTER 12 Instrumental Variables Regression

**b.** Show that the IV regression assumptions in Key Concept 12.4 are satisfied with this choice of $Z_i$.

**c.** Show that the IV estimator constructed using $Z_i = X_i$ is identical to the OLS estimator.

**12.3** A classmate is interested in estimating the variance of the error term in Equation (12.1).

**a.** Suppose that she uses the estimator from the second-stage regression of TSLS: $\hat{\sigma}_a^2 = \frac{1}{n-2}\sum_{i=1}^{n}(Y_i - \hat{\beta}_0^{TSLS} - \hat{\beta}_1^{TSLS}\hat{X}_i)^2$, where $\hat{X}_i$ is the fitted value from the first-stage regression. Is this estimator consistent? (For the purposes of this question, suppose that the sample is very large and the TSLS estimators are essentially identical to $\beta_0$ and $\beta_1$.)

**b.** Is $\hat{\sigma}_b^2 = \frac{1}{n-2}\sum_{i=1}^{n}(Y_i - \hat{\beta}_0^{TSLS} - \hat{\beta}_1^{TSLS}X_i)^2$ consistent?

**12.4** Consider TSLS estimation with a single included endogenous variable and a single instrument. Then the predicted value from the first-stage regression is $\hat{X}_i = \hat{\pi}_0 + \hat{\pi}_1 Z_i$. Use the definition of the sample variance and covariance to show that $s_{\hat{X}Y} = \hat{\pi}_1 s_{ZY}$ and $s_{\hat{X}}^2 = \hat{\pi}_1^2 s_Z^2$. Use this result to fill in the steps of the derivation in Appendix 12.2 of Equation (12.4).

**12.5** Consider the instrumental variable regression model

$$Y_i = \beta_0 + \beta_1 X_i + \beta_2 W_i + u_i,$$

where $X_i$ is correlated with $u_i$ and $Z_i$ is an instrument. Suppose that the first three assumptions in Key Concept 12.4 are satisfied. Which IV assumption is not satisfied when:

**a.** $Z_i$ is independent of $(Y_i, X_i, W_i)$?

**b.** $Z_i = W_i$?

**c.** $W_i = 1$ for all $i$?

**d.** $Z_i = X_i$?

**12.6** In an instrumental variable regression model with one regressor, $X_i$, and one instrument, $Z_i$, the regression of $X_i$ onto $Z_i$ has $R^2 = 0.1$ and $n = 50$. Is $Z_i$ a strong instrument? [*Hint:* See Equation (7.14).] Would your answer change if $R^2 = 0.1$ and $n = 150$?

**12.7** In an instrumental variable regression model with one regressor, $X_i$, and two instruments, $Z_{1i}$ and $Z_{2i}$, the value of the $J$-statistic is $J = 2.2$.

**a.** Does this suggest that $E(u_i|Z_{1i}, Z_{2i}) \neq 0$? Explain.

**b.** What steps would you take if the $J$-statistic was 22.2?

**12.8** Consider a product market with a supply function $Q_i^s = \beta_0 + \beta_1 P_i + u_i^s$, a demand function $Q_i^d = \gamma_0 + u_i^d$, and a market equilibrium condition $Q_i^s = Q_i^d$, where $u_i^s$ and $u_i^d$ are mutually independent i.i.d. random variables, both with a mean of zero.

**a.** Show that $P_i$ and $u_i^s$ are correlated.

**b.** Show that the OLS estimator of $\beta_1$ is inconsistent.

**c.** How would you estimate $\beta_0$, $\beta_1$, and $\gamma_0$?

**12.9** A researcher is interested in the effect of military service on human capital. He collects data from a random sample of 4000 workers aged 40 and runs the OLS regression $Y_i = \beta_0 + \beta_1 X_i + u_i$, where $Y_i$ is a worker's annual earnings and $X_i$ is a binary variable that is equal to 1 if the person served in the military and is equal to 0 otherwise.

**a.** Explain why the OLS estimates are likely to be unreliable. (*Hint:* Which variables are omitted from the regression? Are they correlated with military service?)

**b.** During the Vietnam War there was a draft in which priority for the draft was determined by a national lottery. (The days of the year were randomly reordered 1 through 365. Those with birthdates ordered first were drafted before those with birthdates ordered second, and so forth.) Explain how the lottery might be used as an instrument to estimate the effect of military service on earnings. (For more about this issue, see Joshua D. Angrist, "Lifetime Earnings and the Vietnam Era Draft Lottery: Evidence from Social Security Administration Records," *American Economic Review*, June 1990: 313–336.)

**12.10** Consider the instrumental variable regression model $Y_i = \beta_0 + \beta_1 X_i + \beta_2 W_i + u_i$, where $Z_i$ is an instrument. Suppose that data on $W_i$ are not available and the model is estimated omitting $W_i$ from the regression.

**a.** Suppose that $Z_i$ and $W_i$ are uncorrelated. Is the IV estimator consistent?

**b.** Suppose that $Z_i$ and $W_i$ are correlated. Is the IV estimator consistent?

## Empirical Exercises

(Only three empirical exercises for this chapter are given in the text, but you can find more on the text website, **www.pearsonglobaleditions.com/Stock_Watson**.)

**E12.1** How does fertility affect labor supply? That is, how much does a woman's labor supply fall when she has an additional child? In this exercise you will estimate this effect using data for married women from the 1980 U.S. Census.[4] The data are available on the textbook website, **www.pearsonglobaleditions.com/Stock_Watson**, in the file **Fertility** and described in the file **Fertility_Description**. The data set contains information on married women aged 21–35 with two or more children.

    **a.** Regress *weeksworked* on the indicator variable *morekids*, using OLS. On average, do women with more than two children work less than women with two children? How much less?

    **b.** Explain why the OLS regression estimated in (a) is inappropriate for estimating the causal effect of fertility (*morekids*) on labor supply (*weeksworked*).

    **c.** The data set contains the variable *samesex*, which is equal to 1 if the first two children are of the same sex (boy–boy or girl–girl) and equal to 0 otherwise. Are couples whose first two children are of the same sex more likely to have a third child? Is the effect large? Is it statistically significant?

    **d.** Explain why *samesex* is a valid instrument for the instrumental variable regression of *weeksworked* on *morekids*.

    **e.** Is *samesex* a weak instrument?

    **f.** Estimate the regression of *weeksworked* on *morekids*, using *samesex* as an instrument. How large is the fertility effect on labor supply?

    **g.** Do the results change when you include the variables *agem1*, *black*, *hispan*, and *othrace* in the labor supply regression (treating these variable as exogenous)? Explain why or why not.

---

[4]These data were provided by Professor William Evans of the University of Maryland and were used in his paper with Joshua Angrist, "Children and Their Parents' Labor Supply: Evidence from Exogenous Variation in Family Size," *American Economic Review*, 1998, 88(3): 450–477.

**E12.2**  Does viewing a violent movie lead to violent behavior? If so, the incidence of violent crimes, such as assaults, should rise following the release of a violent movie that attracts many viewers. Alternatively, movie viewing may substitute for other activities (such as alcohol consumption) that lead to violent behavior, so that assaults should fall when more viewers are attracted to the cinema. On the textbook website, **www.pearsonglobaleditions.com/Stock_Watson**, you will find the data file **Movies**, which contains data on the number of assaults and movie attendance for 516 weekends from 1995 through 2004.[5] A detailed description is given in **Movies_Description**, available on the website. The dataset includes weekend U.S. attendance for strongly violent movies (such as *Hannibal*), mildly violent movies (such as *Spider-Man*), and nonviolent movies (such as *Finding Nemo*). The dataset also includes a count of the number of assaults for the same weekend in a subset of counties in the United States. Finally, the dataset includes indicators for year, month, whether the weekend is a holiday, and various measures of the weather.

**a.**  i.  Regress the logarithm of the number of assaults [$ln\_assaults = \ln(assaults)$] on the year and month indicators. Is there evidence of seasonality in assaults? That is, do there tend to be more assaults in some months than others? Explain.

   ii.  Regress total movie attendance ($attend = attend\_v + attend\_m + attend\_n$) on the year and month indicators. Is there evidence of seasonality in movie attendance? Explain.

**b.**  Regress $ln\_assaults$ on $attend\_v$, $attend\_m$, $attend\_n$, the year and month indicators, and the weather and holiday control variables available in the data set.

   i.  Based on the regression, does viewing a strongly violent movie increase or decrease assaults? By how much? Is the estimated effect statistically significant?

   ii.  Does attendance at strongly violent movies affect assaults differently than attendance at moderately violent movies? Differently than attendance at nonviolent movies?

   iii.  A strongly violent blockbuster movie is released, and the weekend's attendance at strongly violent movies increases by 6 million;

---

[5]These are aggregated versions of data provided by Gordon Dahl of University of California–San Diego and Stefano DellaVigna of University of California–Berkeley and were used in their paper "Does Movie Violence Increase Violent Crime?" *Quarterly Journal of Economics*, 2009, 124(2): 677–734.

meanwhile, attendance falls by 2 million for moderately violent movies and by 1 million for nonviolent movies. What is the predicted effect on assaults? Construct a 95% confidence interval for the change in assaults. [*Hint*: Review Section 7.3 and material surrounding Equations (8.7) and (8.8).)]

c. It is difficult to control for all the variables that affect assaults and that might be correlated with movie attendance. For example, the effect of the weather on assaults and movie attendance is only crudely approximated by the weather variables in the data set. However, the data set does include a set of instruments, *pr_attend_v*, *pr_attend_m*, and *pr_attend_n*, that are correlated with attendance but are (arguably) uncorrelated with weekend-specific factors (such as the weather) that affect both assaults and movie attendance. These instruments use historical attendance patterns, not information on a particular weekend, to predict a film's attendance in a given weekend. For example, if a film's attendance is high in the second week of its release, then this can be used to predict that its attendance was also high in the first week of its release. (The details of the construction of these instruments are available in the Dahl and DellaVigna paper referenced in footnote 5.) Run the regression from part (b) (including year, month, holiday, and weather controls) but now using *pr_attend_v*, *pr_attend_m*, and *pr_attend_n* as instruments for *attend_v*, *attend_m*, and *attend_n*. Use this regression to answer (b)(i)–(b)(iii).

d. The intuition underlying the instruments in (c) is that attendance in a given week is correlated with attendance in surrounding weeks. For each move category, the data set includes attendance in surrounding weeks. Run the regression using the instruments *attend_v_f*, *attend_m_f*, *attend_n_f*, *attend_v_b*, *attend_m_b*, and *attend_n_b* instead of the instruments used in part (c). Use this regression to answer (b)(i)–(b)(iii).

e. There are nine instruments listed in (c) and (d), but only three are needed for identification. Carry out the test for overidentification summarized in Key Concept 12.6. What do you conclude about the validity of the instruments?

f. Based on your analysis, what do you conclude about the effect of violent movies on (short-run) violent behavior?

**E12.3** (This requires Appendix 12.5) On the textbook website, **www.pearson-globaleditions.com/Stock_Watson**, you will find the data set **WeakInstrument**, which contains 200 observations on $(Y_i, X_i, Z_i)$ for the instrumental regression $Y_i = \beta_0 + \beta_1 X_i + u_i$.

**a.** Construct $\hat{\beta}_1^{TSLS}$, its standard error, and the usual 95% confidence interval for $\beta_1$.

**b.** Compute the $F$-statistic for the regression of $X_i$ on $Z_i$. Is there evidence of a "weak instrument" problem?

**c.** Compute a 95% confidence interval for $\beta_1$, using the Anderson–Rubin procedure. (To implement the procedure, assume that $-5 \le \beta_1 \le 5$.)

**d.** Comment on the differences in the confidence intervals in (a) and (c). Which is more reliable?

**APPENDIX**

# 12.1 The Cigarette Consumption Panel Data Set

The data set consists of annual data for the 48 contiguous U.S. states from 1985 to 1995. Quantity consumed is measured by annual per capita cigarette sales in packs per fiscal year, as derived from state tax collection data. The price is the real (that is, inflation-adjusted) average retail cigarette price per pack during the fiscal year, including taxes. Income is real per capita income. The general sales tax is the average tax, in cents per pack, due to the broad-based state sales tax applied to all consumption goods. The cigarette-specific tax is the tax applied to cigarettes only. All prices, income, and taxes used in the regressions in this chapter are deflated by the Consumer Price Index and thus are in constant (real) dollars. We are grateful to Professor Jonathan Gruber of MIT for providing us with these data.

**APPENDIX**

# 12.2 Derivation of the Formula for the TSLS Estimator in Equation (12.4)

The first stage of TSLS is to regress $X_i$ on the instrument $Z_i$ by OLS and then compute the OLS predicted value $\hat{X}_i$; the second stage is to regress $Y_i$ on $\hat{X}_i$ by OLS. Accordingly, the formula for the TSLS estimator, expressed in terms of the predicted value $\hat{X}_i$, is the formula for the OLS estimator in Key Concept 4.2, with $\hat{X}_i$ replacing $X_i$. That is,

$\hat{\beta}_1^{TSLS} = s_{\hat{X}Y}/s_{\hat{X}}^2$, where $s_{\hat{X}}^2$ is the sample variance of $\hat{X}_i$ and $s_{\hat{X}Y}$ is the sample covariance between $Y_i$ and $\hat{X}_i$.

Because $\hat{X}_i$ is the predicted value of $X_i$ from the first-stage regression, $\hat{X}_i = \hat{\pi}_0 + \hat{\pi}_1 Z_i$, the definitions of sample variances and covariances imply that $s_{\hat{X}Y} = \hat{\pi}_1 s_{ZY}$ and $s_{\hat{X}}^2 = \hat{\pi}_1^2 s_Z^2$ (Exercise 12.4). Thus, the TSLS estimator can be written as $\hat{\beta}_1^{TSLS} = s_{\hat{X}Y}/s_{\hat{X}}^2 = s_{ZY}/(\hat{\pi}_1 s_Z^2)$. Finally, $\hat{\pi}_1$ is the OLS slope coefficient from the first stage of TSLS, so $\hat{\pi}_1 = s_{ZX}/s_Z^2$. Substitution of this formula for $\hat{\pi}_1$ into the formula $\hat{\beta}_1^{TSLS} = s_{ZY}/(\hat{\pi}_1 s_Z^2)$ yields the formula for the TSLS estimator in Equation (12.4).

---

**APPENDIX**

## 12.3 Large-Sample Distribution of the TSLS Estimator

This appendix studies the large-sample distribution of the TSLS estimator in the case considered in Section 12.1—that is, with a single instrument, a single included endogenous variable, and no included exogenous variables.

To start, we derive a formula for the TSLS estimator in terms of the errors; this formula forms the basis for the remaining discussion, similar to the expression for the OLS estimator in Equation (4.30) in Appendix 4.3. From Equation (12.1), $Y_i - \overline{Y} = \beta_1(X_i - \overline{X}) + (u_i - \overline{u})$. Accordingly, the sample covariance between $Z$ and $Y$ can be expressed as

$$
\begin{aligned}
s_{ZY} &= \frac{1}{n-1} \sum_{i=1}^n (Z_i - \overline{Z})(Y_i - \overline{Y}) \\
&= \frac{1}{n-1} \sum_{i=1}^n (Z_i - \overline{Z})[\beta_1(X_i - \overline{X}) + (u_i - \overline{u})] \\
&= \beta_1 s_{ZX} + \frac{1}{n-1} \sum_{i=1}^n (Z_i - \overline{Z})(u_i - \overline{u}) \\
&= \beta_1 s_{ZX} + \frac{1}{n-1} \sum_{i=1}^n (Z_i - \overline{Z})u_i,
\end{aligned}
\tag{12.19}
$$

where $s_{ZX} = [1/(n-1)]\sum_{i=1}^n (Z_i - \overline{Z})(X_i - \overline{X})$ and where the final equality follows because $\sum_{i=1}^n (Z_i - \overline{Z}) = 0$. Substituting the definition of $s_{ZX}$ and the final expression in Equation (12.19) into the definition of $\hat{\beta}_1^{TSLS}$ and multiplying the numerator and denominator by $(n-1)/n$ yields

$$
\hat{\beta}_1^{TSLS} = \beta_1 + \frac{\dfrac{1}{n} \sum_{i=1}^n (Z_i - \overline{Z})u_i}{\dfrac{1}{n} \sum_{i=1}^n (Z_i - \overline{Z})(X_i - \overline{X})}.
\tag{12.20}
$$

## Large-Sample Distribution of $\hat{\beta}_1^{TSLS}$ When the IV Regression Assumptions in Key Concept 12.4 Hold

Equation (12.20) for the TSLS estimator is similar to Equation (4.30) in Appendix 4.3 for the OLS estimator, with the exceptions that $Z$ rather than $X$ appears in the numerator and the denominator is the covariance between $Z$ and $X$ rather than the variance of $X$. Because of these similarities, and because $Z$ is exogenous, the argument in Appendix 4.3 that the OLS estimator is normally distributed in large samples extends to $\hat{\beta}_1^{TSLS}$.

Specifically, when the sample is large, $\overline{Z} \cong \mu_Z$, so the numerator is approximately $\overline{q} = (\frac{1}{n})\sum_{i=1}^{n} q_i$, where $q_i = (Z_i - \mu_Z)u_i$. Because the instrument is exogenous, $E(q_i) = 0$. By the IV regression assumptions in Key Concept 12.4, $q_i$ is i.i.d. with variance $\sigma_q^2 = \text{var}[(Z_i - \mu_Z)u_i]$. It follows that var $(\overline{q}) = \sigma_{\overline{q}}^2 = \sigma_q^2/n$, and, by the central limit theorem, $\overline{q}/\sigma_{\overline{q}}$ is, in large samples, distributed $N(0, 1)$.

Because the sample covariance is consistent for the population covariance, $s_{ZX} \xrightarrow{p} \text{cov}(Z_i, X_i)$, which, because the instrument is relevant, is nonzero. Thus, by Equation (12.20) $\hat{\beta}_1^{TSLS} \cong \beta_1 + \overline{q}/\text{cov}(Z_i, X_i)$, so in large samples $\hat{\beta}_1^{TSLS}$ is approximately distributed $N(\beta_1, \sigma_{\hat{\beta}_1^{TSLS}}^2)$ where $\sigma_{\hat{\beta}_1^{TSLS}}^2 = \sigma_{\overline{q}}^2/[\text{cov}(Z_i, X_i)]^2 = (1/n)\text{var}[(Z_i - \mu_Z)u_i]/[\text{cov}(Z_i, X_i)]^2$, which is the expression given in Equation (12.8).

---

**APPENDIX**

## 12.4  Large-Sample Distribution of the TSLS Estimator When the Instrument Is Not Valid

This appendix considers the large-sample distribution of the TSLS estimator in the setup of Section 12.1 (one $X$, one $Z$) when one or the other of the conditions for instrument validity fails. If the instrument relevance condition fails, the large-sample distribution of the TSLS estimator is not normal; in fact, its distribution is that of a ratio of two normal random variables. If the instrument exogeneity condition fails, the TSLS estimator is inconsistent.

### Large-Sample Distribution of $\hat{\beta}_1^{TSLS}$ When the Instrument Is Weak

First consider the case that the instrument is irrelevant so that $\text{cov}(Z_i, X_i) = 0$. Then the argument in Appendix 12.3 entails division by zero. To avoid this problem, we need to take a closer look at the behavior of the term in the denominator of Equation (12.20) when the population covariance is zero.

We start by rewriting Equation (12.20). Because of the consistency of the sample average, in large samples, $\overline{Z}$ is close to $\mu_Z$, and $\overline{X}$ is close to $\mu_X$. Thus the term in the denominator of Equation (12.20) is approximately $\left(\frac{1}{n}\right)\sum_{i=1}^{n}(Z_i - \mu_Z)(X_i - \mu_X) = \left(\frac{1}{n}\right)\sum_{i=1}^{n}r_i = \overline{r}$, where $r_i = (Z_i - \mu_Z)(X_i - \mu_X)$. Let $\sigma_r^2 = \text{var}[(Z_i - \mu_Z)(X_i - \mu_X)]$, let $\sigma_{\overline{r}}^2 = \sigma_r^2/n$, and let $\overline{q}$, $\sigma_q^2$, and $\sigma_{\overline{q}}^2$ be as defined in Appendix 12.3. Then Equation (12.20) implies that, in large samples,

$$\hat{\beta}_1^{TSLS} \cong \beta_1 + \frac{\overline{q}}{\overline{r}} = \beta_1 + \left(\frac{\sigma_{\overline{q}}}{\sigma_{\overline{r}}}\right)\left(\frac{\overline{q}/\sigma_{\overline{q}}}{\overline{r}/\sigma_{\overline{r}}}\right) = \beta_1 + \left(\frac{\sigma_q}{\sigma_r}\right)\left(\frac{\overline{q}/\sigma_{\overline{q}}}{\overline{r}/\sigma_{\overline{r}}}\right). \tag{12.21}$$

If the instrument is irrelevant, then $E(r_i) = \text{cov}(Z_i, X_i) = 0$. Thus $\overline{r}$ is the sample average of the random variables $r_i$, $i = 1, \ldots, n$, which are i.i.d. (by the second least squares assumption), have variance $\sigma_r^2 = \text{var}[(Z_i - \mu_Z)(X_i - \mu_X)]$ (which is finite by the third IV regression assumption), and have a mean of zero (because the instruments are irrelevant). It follows that the central limit theorem applies to $\overline{r}$, specifically, $\overline{r}/\sigma_{\overline{r}}$ is approximately distributed $N(0, 1)$. Therefore, the final expression of Equation (12.21) implies that, in large samples, the distribution of $\hat{\beta}_1^{TSLS} - \beta_1$ is the distribution of $aS$, where $a = \sigma_q/\sigma_r$ and $S$ is the ratio of two random variables, each of which has a standard normal distribution (these two standard normal random variables are correlated).

In other words, when the instrument is irrelevant, the central limit theorem applies to the denominator as well as the numerator of the TSLS estimator, so in large samples the distribution of the TSLS estimator is the distribution of the ratio of two normal random variables. Because $X_i$ and $u_i$ are correlated, these normal random variables are correlated, and the large-sample distribution of the TSLS estimator when the instrument is irrelevant is complicated. In fact, the large-sample distribution of the TSLS estimator with irrelevant instruments is centered on the probability limit of the OLS estimator. Thus, when the instrument is irrelevant, TSLS does not eliminate the bias in OLS and, moreover, has a nonnormal distribution, even in large samples.

A weak instrument represents an intermediate case between an irrelevant instrument and the normal distribution derived in Appendix 12.3. When the instrument is weak but not irrelevant, the distribution of the TSLS estimator continues to be nonnormal, so the general lesson here about the extreme case of an irrelevant instrument carries over to weak instruments.

## Large-Sample Distribution of $\hat{\beta}_1^{TSLS}$ When the Instrument Is Endogenous

The numerator in the final expression in Equation (12.20) converges in probability to $\text{cov}(Z_i, u_i)$. If the instrument is exogenous, this is zero, and the TSLS estimator is consistent (assuming that the instrument is not weak). If, however, the instrument is not exogenous, then, if the instrument is not weak, $\hat{\beta}_1^{TSLS} \xrightarrow{p} \beta_1 + \text{cov}(Z_i, u_i)/\text{cov}(Z_i, X_i) \neq \beta_1$. That is, if the instrument is not exogenous, the TSLS estimator is inconsistent.

## 12.5　Instrumental Variables Analysis with Weak Instruments

This appendix discusses some methods for instrumental variables analysis in the presence of potentially weak instruments. The appendix focuses on the case of a single included endogenous regressor [Equations (12.13) and (12.14)].

### Testing for Weak Instruments

The rule of thumb in Key Concept 12.5 is that a first-stage $F$-statistic less than 10 indicates that the instruments are weak. One motivation for this rule of thumb arises from an approximate expression for the bias of the TSLS estimator. Let $\beta_1^{OLS}$ denote the probability limit of the OLS estimator $\beta_1$, and let $\beta_1^{OLS} - \beta_1$ denote the asymptotic bias of the OLS estimator (if the regressor is endogenous, then $\hat{\beta}_1 \xrightarrow{p} \beta_1^{OLS} \neq \beta_1$). It is possible to show that, when there are many instruments, the bias of the TSLS is approximately $E(\hat{\beta}_1^{TSLS}) - \beta_1 \approx (\beta_1^{OLS} - \beta_1)/[E(F) - 1]$, where $E(F)$ is the expectation of the first-stage $F$-statistic. If $E(F) = 10$, then the bias of TSLS, relative to the bias of OLS, is approximately 1/9, or just over 10%, which is small enough to be acceptable in many applications. Replacing $E(F) > 10$ with $F > 10$ yields the rule of thumb in Key Concept 12.5.

　　The motivation in the previous paragraph involved an approximate formula for the bias of the TSLS estimator when there are many instruments. In most applications, however, the number of instruments, $m$, is small. Stock and Yogo (2005) provide a formal test for weak instruments that avoids the approximation that $m$ is large. In the Stock–Yogo test, the null hypothesis is that the instruments are weak, and the alternative hypothesis is that the instruments are strong, where strong instruments are defined to be instruments for which the bias of the TSLS estimator is at most 10% of the bias of the OLS estimator. The test entails comparing the first-stage $F$-statistic (for technical reasons, the homoskedasticity-only version) to a critical value that depends on the number of instruments. As it happens, for a test with a 5% significance level, this critical value ranges between 9.08 and 11.52, so the rule of thumb of comparing $F$ to 10 is a good approximation to the Stock–Yogo test.

## Hypothesis Tests and Confidence Sets for $\beta$

If the instruments are weak, the TSLS estimator is biased and has a nonnormal distribution. Thus the TSLS $t$-test of $\beta_1 = \beta_{1,0}$ is unreliable, as is the TSLS confidence interval for $\beta_1$. There are, however, other tests of $\beta_1 = \beta_{1,0}$, along with confidence intervals based on those tests, that are valid whether instruments are strong, weak, or even irrelevant. When there is a single endogenous regressor, the preferred test is Moreira's (2003) conditional likelihood ratio (CLR) test. An older test, which works for any number of endogenous regressors, is based on the Anderson–Rubin (1949) statistic. Because the Anderson–Rubin (1949) statistic is conceptually less complicated, we describe it first.

The Anderson–Rubin test of $\beta_1 = \beta_{1,0}$ proceeds in two steps. In the first step, compute a new variable, $Y_i^* = Y_i - \beta_{1,0} X_i$. In the second step, regress $Y_i^*$ against the included exogenous regressors ($W$'s) and the instruments ($Z$'s). The Anderson–Rubin statistic is the $F$-statistic testing the hypothesis that the coefficient on the $Z$'s are all zero. Under the null hypothesis that $\beta_1 = \beta_{1,0}$, if the instruments satisfy the exogeneity condition (condition 2 in Key Concept 12.3), they will be uncorrelated with the error term in this regression, and the null hypothesis will be rejected in 5% of all samples.

As discussed in Sections (3.3) and (7.4), a confidence set can be constructed as the set of values of the parameters that are not rejected by a hypothesis test. Accordingly, the set of values of $\beta_1$ that are not rejected by a 5% Anderson–Rubin test constitutes a 95% confidence set for $\beta_1$. When the Anderson–Rubin $F$-statistic is computed using the homoskedasticity-only formula, the Anderson–Rubin confidence set can be constructed by solving a quadratic equation (see Empirical Exercise 12.3). The logic behind the Anderson–Rubin statistic never assumes instrument relevance, and the Anderson–Rubin confidence set will have a coverage probability of 95% in large samples, whether the instruments are strong, weak, or even irrelevant.

The CLR statistic also tests the hypothesis that $\beta_1 = \beta_{1,0}$. Likelihood ratio statistics compare the value of the likelihood (see Appendix 11.2) under the null hypothesis to its value under the alternative and reject it if the likelihood under the alternative is sufficiently greater than under the null. Familiar tests in this book, such as the homoskedasticity-only $F$-test in multiple regression, can be derived as likelihood ratio tests under the assumption of homoskedastic normally distributed errors. Unlike any of the other tests discussed in this book, however, the critical value of the CLR test depends on the data, specifically on a statistic that measures the strength of the instruments. By using the right critical value, the CLR test is valid whether instruments are strong, weak, or irrelevant. CLR confidence intervals can be computed as the set of $\beta_1$ that are not rejected by the CLR test.

The CLR test is equivalent to the TSLS $t$-test when instruments are strong and has very good power when instruments are weak. With suitable software, the CLR test is easy to use. The disadvantage of the CLR test is that it does not generalize readily to more than one endogenous regressor. In that case, the Anderson–Rubin test (and confidence set) is recommended; however, when instruments are strong (so TSLS is valid) and the coefficients are overidentified, the Anderson–Rubin test is inefficient in the sense that it is less powerful than the TSLS $t$-test.

### Estimation of $\beta$

If the instruments are irrelevant, it is not possible to obtain an unbiased estimator of $\beta_1$, even in large samples. Nevertheless, when instruments are weak, some IV estimators tend to be more centered on the true value of $\beta_1$ than is TSLS. One such estimator is the limited information maximum likelihood (LIML) estimator. As its name implies, the LIML estimator is the maximum likelihood estimator of $\beta_1$ in the system of Equations (12.13) and (12.14). (For a discussion of maximum likelihood estimation, see Appendix 11.2.) The LIML estimator also is the value of $\beta_{1,0}$ that minimizes the homoskedasticity-only Anderson–Rubin test statistic. Thus, if the Anderson–Rubin confidence set is not empty, it will contain the LIML estimator. In addition, the CLR confidence interval contains the LIML estimator.

If the instruments are weak, the LIML estimator is more nearly centered on the true value of $\beta_1$ than is TSLS. If instruments are strong, the LIML and TSLS estimators coincide in large samples. A drawback of the LIML estimator is that it can produce extreme outliers. Confidence intervals constructed around the LIML estimator using the LIML standard error are more reliable than intervals constructed around the TSLS estimator using the TSLS standard error, but are less reliable than Anderson–Rubin or CLR intervals when the instruments are weak.

The problems of estimation, testing, and confidence intervals in IV regression with weak instruments constitute an area of ongoing research. To learn more about this topic, visit the website for this book.

---

APPENDIX

## 12.6  TSLS with Control Variables

In Key Concept 12.4, the $W$ variables are assumed to be exogenous. This appendix considers the case in which $W$ is not exogenous, but instead is a control variable included to make $Z$ exogenous. The logic of control variables in TSLS parallels the logic in OLS: If a control variable effectively controls for an omitted factor, then the instrument is uncorrelated with the error term. Because the control variable is correlated with the error term, the coefficient on a control variable does not have a causal interpretation. The mathematics of control variables in TSLS also parallels the mathematics of control variables in OLS and entails relaxing the assumption that the error has conditional mean zero, given $Z$ and $W$, to be that the conditional mean of the error does not depend on $Z$. This appendix draws on Appendix 7.2 (Conditional Mean Independence), which should be reviewed first.

Consider the IV regression model in Equation (12.12) with a single $X$ and a single $W$:

$$Y_i = \beta_0 + \beta_1 X_i + \beta_2 W_i + u_i. \tag{12.22}$$

We replace IV Regression Assumption #1 in Key Concept 12.4 [which states that $E(u_i|W_i) = 0$] with the assumption that, conditional on $W_i$, the mean of $u_i$ does not depend on $Z_i$:

$$E(u_i|W_i, Z_i) = E(u_i|W_i). \tag{12.23}$$

Following Appendix 7.2, we further assume that $E(u_i|W_i)$ is linear in $W_i$, so $E(u_i|W_i) = \gamma_0 + \gamma_2 W_i$, where $\gamma_0$ and $\gamma_2$ are coefficients. Letting $\varepsilon_i = u_i - E(u_i|W_i, Z_i)$ and applying the algebra of Equation (7.25) to Equation (12.22), we obtain

$$Y_i = \delta_0 + \beta_1 X_i + \delta_2 W_i + \varepsilon_i, \tag{12.24}$$

where $\delta_0 = \beta_0 + \gamma_0$ and $\delta_2 = \beta_2 + \gamma_2$. Now $E(\varepsilon_i|W_i, Z_i) = E[u_i - E(u_i|W_i, Z_i)|W_i, Z_i] = E(u_i|W_i, Z_i) - E(u_i|W_i, Z_i) = 0$, which in turn implies corr$(Z_i, \varepsilon_i) = 0$. Thus IV Regression Assumption #1 and the instrument exogeneity requirement (condition #2 in Key Concept 12.3) both hold for Equation (12.24) with error term $\varepsilon_i$. Thus, if IV Regression Assumption #1 is replaced by conditional mean independence in Equation (12.23), the original IV regression assumptions in Key Concept 12.4 apply to the modified regression in Equation (12.24).

Because the IV regression assumptions of Key Concept 12.4 hold for Equation (12.24), all the methods of inference (both for weak and strong instruments) discussed in this chapter apply to Equation (12.24). In particular, if the instruments are strong, the coefficients in Equation (12.24) will be estimated consistently by TSLS and TSLS tests, and confidence intervals will be valid.

Just as in OLS with control variables, in general the TSLS coefficient on the control variable $W$ does not have a causal interpretation. TSLS consistently estimates $\delta_2$ in Equation (12.24), but $\delta_2$ is the sum of $\beta_2$, the direct causal effect of $W$, and $\gamma_2$, which reflects the correlation between $W$ and the omitted factors in $u_i$ for which $W$ controls.

In the cigarette consumption regressions in Table 12.1, it is tempting to interpret the coefficient on the 10-year change in log income as the income elasticity of demand. If, however, income growth is correlated with increases in education and if more education reduces smoking, income growth would have its own causal effect ($\beta_2$, the income elasticity) plus an effect arising from its correlation with education ($\gamma_2$). If the latter effect is negative ($\gamma_2 < 0$), the income coefficients in Table 12.1 (which estimate $\delta_2 = \beta_2 + \gamma_2$) would underestimate the income elasticity, but if the conditional mean independence assumption in Equation (12.23) holds, the TSLS estimator of the price elasticity is consistent.

# Experiments and Quasi-Experiments

In many fields, such as psychology and medicine, causal effects are commonly estimated using experiments. Before being approved for widespread medical use, for example, a new drug must be subjected to experimental trials in which some patients are randomly selected to receive the drug while others are given a harmless ineffective substitute (a "placebo"); the drug is approved only if this randomized controlled experiment provides convincing statistical evidence that the drug is safe and effective.

There are three reasons to study randomized controlled experiments in an econometrics course. First, an ideal randomized controlled experiment provides a conceptual benchmark to judge estimates of causal effects made with observational data. Second, the results of randomized controlled experiments, when conducted, can be very influential, so it is important to understand the limitations and threats to validity of actual experiments as well as their strengths. Third, external circumstances sometimes produce what appears to be randomization; that is, because of external events, the treatment of some individual occurs "as if" it is random, possibly conditional on some control variables. This "as if" randomness produces a "quasi-experiment" or "natural experiment," and many of the methods developed for analyzing randomized experiments can be applied (with some modifications) to quasi-experiments.

This chapter examines experiments and quasi-experiments in economics. The statistical tools used in this chapter are multiple regression analysis, regression analysis of panel data, and instrumental variables (IV) regression. What distinguishes the discussion in this chapter is not the tools used, but rather the type of data analyzed and the special opportunities and challenges posed when analyzing experiments and quasi-experiments.

The methods developed in this chapter are often used for evaluating social or economic programs. Program evaluation is the field of study that concerns estimating the effect of a program, policy, or some other intervention or "treatment." What is the effect on earnings of going through a job training program? What is the effect on employment of low-skilled workers of an increase in the minimum wage? What is the effect on college attendance of making low-cost student aid loans available to middle-class students? This chapter discusses how such programs or policies can be evaluated using experiments or quasi-experiments.

We begin in Section 13.1 by elaborating on the discussions in Chapters 1, 3, and 4 of the estimation of causal effects using randomized controlled experiments. In reality, actual experiments with human subjects encounter practical problems that constitute threats to their internal and external validity; these threats and some econometric tools for addressing them are discussed in Section 13.2. Section 13.3 analyzes an important randomized controlled experiment in which elementary students were randomly assigned to different-sized classes in the state of Tennessee in the late 1980s.

Section 13.4 turns to the estimation of causal effects using quasi-experiments. Threats to the validity of quasi-experiments are discussed in Section 13.5. One issue that arises in both experiments and quasi-experiments is that treatment effects can differ from one member of the population to the next, and the matter of interpreting the resulting estimates of causal effects when the population is heterogeneous is taken up in Section 13.6.

# 13.1 Potential Outcomes, Causal Effects, and Idealized Experiments

This section explains how the population mean of individual-level causal effects can be estimated using a randomized controlled experiment and how data from such an experiment can be analyzed using multiple regression analysis.

## Potential Outcomes and the Average Causal Effect

Suppose that you are considering taking a drug for a medical condition, enrolling in a job training program, or doing an optional econometrics problem set. It is reasonable to ask, what are the benefits of doing so—receiving the treatment—for *me*? You can imagine two hypothetical situations, one in which you receive the treatment and one in which you do not. Under each hypothetical situation, there would be a measurable outcome (the progress of the medical condition, getting a job, your econometrics grade). The difference in these two potential outcomes would be the causal effect, for you, of the treatment.

More generally, a **potential outcome** is the outcome for an individual under a potential treatment. The causal effect for that individual is the difference in the potential outcome if the treatment is received and the potential outcome if it is not. In general, the causal effect can differ from one individual to the next. For example, the effect of a drug could depend on your age, whether you smoke, or other health conditions. The problem is that there is no way to measure the causal effect for a single individual. Because the individual either receives the treatment or does not, one of the potential outcomes can be observed, but not both.

Although the causal effect cannot be measured for a single individual, in many applications it suffices to know the mean causal effect in a population. For example, a job training program evaluation might trade off the average expenditure per trainee against average trainee success in finding a job. The mean of the individual causal effects in the population under study is called the **average causal effect** or the **average treatment effect**.

The average causal effect for a given population can be estimated, at least in theory, using an ideal randomized controlled experiment. To see how, first suppose that the subjects are selected at random from the population of interest. Because the subjects are selected by simple random sampling, their potential outcomes, and thus their causal effects, are drawn from the same distribution, so the expected value of the causal effect in the sample is the average causal effect in the population. Next suppose that subjects are randomly assigned to the treatment or the control group. Because an individual's treatment status is randomly assigned, it is distributed independently of his or her potential outcomes. Thus the expected value of the outcome for those treated minus the expected value of the outcome for those not treated equals the expected value of the causal effect. Thus, when the concept of potential outcomes is combined with (1) random selection of individuals from a population and (2) random experimental assignment of treatment to those individuals, the expected value of the difference in outcomes between the treatment and control groups is the average causal effect in the population. That is, as was stated in Section 3.5, the average causal effect on $Y_i$ of treatment ($X_i = 1$) versus no treatment ($X_i = 0$) is the difference in the conditional expectations, $E(Y_i | X_i = 1) - E(Y_i | X_i = 0)$, where $E(Y_i | X_i = 1)$ and $E(Y_i | X_i = 0)$ are respectively the expected values of $Y$ for the treatment and control groups in an ideal randomized controlled experiment. Appendix 13.3 provides a mathematical treatment of the foregoing reasoning.

In general, an individual causal effect can be thought of as depending both on observable variables and on unobservable variables. We have already encountered the idea that a causal effect can depend on observable variables; for example, Chapter 8 examined the possibility that the effect of a class size reduction might depend on whether a student is an English learner. For most of this chapter, we focus on the case that variation in causal effects depends only on observable variables. Section 13.6 takes up unobserved heterogeneity in causal effects.

## Econometric Methods for Analyzing Experimental Data

Data from a randomized controlled experiment can be analyzed by comparing differences in means or by a regression that includes the treatment indicator and additional control variables. This latter specification, the differences estimator with additional regressors, can also be used in more complicated randomization schemes, in which the randomization probabilities depend on observable covariates.

*The differences estimator.* The **differences estimator** is the difference in the sample averages for the treatment and control groups (Section 3.5), which can be computed by regressing the outcome variable $Y$ on a binary treatment indicator $X$:

$$Y_i = \beta_0 + \beta_1 X_i + u_i, i = 1, \ldots, n. \tag{13.1}$$

As discussed in Section 4.4, if $X$ is randomly assigned, then $E(u_i | X_i) = 0$ and the OLS estimator of $\beta_1$ in Equation (13.1) is an unbiased and consistent estimator of the causal effect.

*The differences estimator with additional regressors.* The efficiency of the difference estimator often can be improved by including some control variables $W$ in the regression; doing so leads to the **differences estimator with additional regressors**:

$$Y_i = \beta_0 + \beta_1 X_i + \beta_2 W_{1i} + \cdots + \beta_{1+r} W_{ri} + u_i, i = 1, \ldots, n. \tag{13.2}$$

If $W$ helps to explain the variation in $Y$, then including $W$ reduces the standard error of the regression and, typically, the standard error of $\hat{\beta}_1$. As discussed in Section 7.5 and Appendix 7.2, for the estimator $\hat{\beta}_1$ of the causal effect $\beta_1$ in Equation (13.2) to be unbiased, the control variables $W$ must be such that $u_i$ satisfies conditional mean independence, that is, $E(u_i | X_i, W_i) = E(u_i | W_i)$. This condition is satisfied if $W_i$ are pretreatment individual characteristics, such as gender: If $W_i$ is a pretreatment characteristic and $X_i$ is randomly assigned, then $X_i$ is independent of $u_i$ and $W_i$ which implies that $E(u_i | X_i, W_i) = E(u_i | W_i)$. The $W$ regressors in Equation (13.2) should not include experimental outcomes ($X_i$ is not randomly assigned, given an experimental outcome). As always with control variables under conditional mean independence, the coefficient on the control variable does not have a causal interpretation.

*Estimating causal effects that depend on observables.* As discussed in Chapter 8, variation in causal effects that depends on observables can be estimated by including suitable nonlinear functions of, or interactions with, $X_i$. For example, if $W_{1i}$ is a binary indicator denoting gender, then distinct causal effects for men and women can be estimated by including the interaction variable $W_{1i} \times X_i$ in the regression in Equation (13.2).

*Randomization based on covariates.*   Randomization in which the probability of assignment to the treatment group depends on one or more observable variables $W$ is called **randomization based on covariates**. If randomization is based on covariates, then in general the differences estimator based on Equation (13.1) suffers from omitted variable bias. For example, Appendix 7.2 describes a hypothetical experiment to estimate the causal effect of mandatory versus optional homework in an econometrics course. In that experiment, economics majors ($W_i = 1$) were assigned to the treatment group (mandatory homework, $X_i = 1$ with higher probability than nonmajors ($W_i = 0$). But if majors tend to do better in the course than nonmajors anyway, then there is omitted variable bias because being in the treatment group is correlated with the omitted variable, being a major.

Because $X_i$ is randomly assigned given $W_i$, this omitted variable bias can be eliminated by using the differences estimator with the additional control variable $W_i$. The random assignment of $X_i$ given $W_i$ (combined with the assumption of a linear regression function) implies that, given $W_i$, $X_i$ is independent of $u_i$ in Equation (13.2). This conditional independence in turn implies conditional mean independence, that is, $E(u_i | X_i, W_i) = E(u_i | W_i)$ Thus the OLS estimator $\hat{\beta}_1$ in Equation (13.2) is an unbiased estimator of the causal effect when $X_i$ is assigned randomly based on $W_i$.

# 13.2   Threats to Validity of Experiments

Recall from Key Concept 9.1 that a statistical study is *internally valid* if the statistical inferences about causal effects are valid for the population being studied; it is *externally valid* if its inferences and conclusions can be generalized from the population and setting studied to other populations and settings. Various real-world problems pose threats to the internal and external validity of the statistical analysis of actual experiments with human subjects.

## Threats to Internal Validity

Threats to the internal validity of randomized controlled experiments include failure to randomize, failure to follow the treatment protocol, attrition, experimental effects, and small sample sizes.

*Failure to randomize.* If the treatment is not assigned randomly, but instead is based in part on the characteristics or preferences of the subject, then experimental outcomes will reflect both the effect of the treatment and the effect of the nonrandom assignment. For example, suppose that participants in a job training program experiment are assigned to the treatment group depending on whether their last name falls in the first or second half of the alphabet. Because of ethnic differences in last names, ethnicity could differ systematically between the treatment and control groups. To the extent that work experience, education, and other labor market characteristics differ by ethnicity, there could be systematic differences between the treatment and control groups in these omitted factors that affect outcomes. In general, nonrandom assignment can lead to correlation between $X_i$ and $u_i$ in Equations (13.1) and (13.2), which in turn leads to bias in the estimator of the treatment effect.

It is possible to test for randomization. If treatment is randomly received, then $X_i$ will be uncorrelated with observable pretreatment individual characteristics $W$. Thus, a **test for random receipt of treatment** entails testing the hypothesis that the coefficients on $W_{1i}, \ldots, W_{ri}$ are zero in a regression of $X_i$ on $W_{1i}, \ldots, W_{ri}$. In the job training program example, regressing receipt of job training ($X_i$) on gender, race, and prior education ($W$'s), and then computing the $F$-statistic testing whether the coefficients on the $W$'s are zero, provides a test of the null hypothesis that treatment was randomly received, against the alternative hypothesis that receipt of treatment depends on gender, race, or prior education. If the experimental design performs randomization conditional on covariates, then those covariates would be included in the regression and the $F$-test would test the coefficients on the remaining $W$'s.[1]

*Failure to follow the treatment protocol.* In an actual experiment, people do not always do what they are told. In a job training program experiment, for example, some of the subjects assigned to the treatment group might not show up for the training sessions and thus not receive the treatment. Similarly, subjects assigned to the control group might somehow receive the training anyway, perhaps by making a special request to an instructor or administrator.

The failure of individuals to follow completely the randomized treatment protocol is called **partial compliance** with the treatment protocol. In some cases, the

---

[1]In this example, $X_i$ is binary, so, as discussed in Chapter 11, the regression of $X_i$ on $W_{1i}, \ldots, W_{ri}$ is a linear probability model and heteroskedasticity-robust standard errors are essential. Another way to test the hypothesis that $E(X_i | W_{1i}, \ldots, W_{ri})$ does not depend on $W_{1i}, \ldots, W_{ri}$ when $X_i$ is binary is to use a probit or logit model (see Section 11.2).

experimenter knows whether the treatment was actually received (for example, whether the trainee attended class), and the treatment actually received is recorded as $X_i$. With partial compliance, there is an element of choice in whether the subject receives the treatment, so $X_i$ will be correlated with $u_i$ even if initially there is random assignment. Thus, failure to follow the treatment protocol leads to bias in the OLS estimator.

If there are data on both treatment actually received ($X_i$) and on the initial random assignment, then the treatment effect can be estimated by instrumental variables regression. **Instrumental variables estimation of the treatment effect** entails the estimation of Equation (13.1)—or Equation (13.2) if there are control variables—using the initial random assignment ($Z_i$) as an instrument for the treatment actually received ($X_i$). Recall that a variable must satisfy the two conditions of instrument relevance and instrument exogeneity (Key Concept 12.3) to be a valid instrumental variable. As long as the protocol is partially followed, then the actual treatment level is partially determined by the assigned treatment level, so the instrumental variable $Z_i$ is relevant. If initial assignment is random, then $Z_i$ is distributed independently of $u_i$ (conditional on $W_i$, if randomization is conditional on covariates), so the instrument is exogenous. Thus, in an experiment with randomly assigned treatment, partial compliance, and data on actual treatment, the original random assignment is a valid instrumental variable.

This instrumental variables strategy requires having data on both assigned and received treatment. In some cases, data might not be available on the treatment actually received. For example, if a subject in a medical experiment is provided with the drug but, unbeknownst to the researchers, simply does not take it, then the recorded treatment ("received drug") is incorrect. Incorrect measurement of the treatment actually received leads to bias in the differences estimator.

*Attrition.* **Attrition** refers to subjects dropping out of the study after being randomly assigned to the treatment or control group. Sometimes attrition occurs for reasons unrelated to the treatment program; for example, a participant in a job training study might need to leave town to care for a sick relative. But if the reason for attrition is related to the treatment itself, then the attrition results in bias in the OLS estimator of the causal effect. For example, suppose that the most able trainees drop out of the job training program experiment because they get out-of-town jobs acquired using the job training skills, so at the end of the experiment only the least able members of the treatment group remain. Then the distribution of unmeasured characteristics (ability) will differ between the control and treatment groups (the treatment enabled the ablest trainees to leave town). In other words, the treatment $X_i$ will be correlated with $u_i$ (which includes ability) for those

## The Hawthorne Effect

During the 1920s and 1930s, the General Electric Company conducted a series of studies of worker productivity at its Hawthorne plant. In one set of experiments, the researchers varied lightbulb wattage to see how lighting affected the productivity of women assembling electrical parts. In other experiments they increased or decreased rest periods, changed the workroom layout, and shortened workdays. Influential early reports on these studies concluded that productivity continued to rise whether the lights were dimmer or brighter, whether workdays were longer or shorter, or whether conditions improved or worsened. Researchers concluded that the productivity improvements were not the consequence of changes in the workplace, but instead came

about because their special role in the experiment made the workers feel noticed and valued, so they worked harder and harder. Over the years, the idea that being in an experiment influences subject behavior has come to be known as the Hawthorne effect.

But there is a glitch to this story: Careful examination of the actual Hawthorne data reveals no Hawthorne effect (Gillespie, 1991; Jones, 1992)! Still, in some experiments, especially ones in which the subjects have a stake in the outcome, merely being in an experiment could affect behavior. The Hawthorne effect and experimental effects more generally can pose threats to internal validity—even though the Hawthorne effect is not evident in the original Hawthorne data.

who remain in the sample at the end of the experiment and the differences estimator will be biased. Because attrition results in a nonrandomly selected sample, attrition that is related to the treatment leads to selection bias (Key Concept 9.4).

*Experimental effects.* In experiments with human subjects, merely because the subjects are in an experiment can change their behavior, a phenomenon sometimes called the **Hawthorne effect** (see the box on this page).

In some experiments, a "double-blind" protocol can mitigate the effect of being in an experiment: Although subjects and experimenters both know that they are in an experiment, neither knows whether a subject is in the treatment group or the control group. In a medical drug experiment, for example, sometimes the drug and the placebo can be made to look the same so that neither the medical professional dispensing the drug nor the patient knows whether the administered drug is the real thing or the placebo. If the experiment is double blind, then both the treatment and control groups should experience the same experimental effects, and so different outcomes between the two groups can be attributed to the drug.

Double-blind experiments are clearly infeasible in real-world experiments in economics: Both the experimental subject and the instructor know whether the subject is attending the job training program. In a poorly designed experiment, this experimental effect could be substantial. For example, teachers in an experimental program might try especially hard to make the program a success if they think their future employment depends on the outcome of the experiment. Deciding whether experimental results are biased because of the experimental effects requires making judgments based on details of how the experiment was conducted.

*Small samples.* Because experiments with human subjects can be expensive, sometimes the sample size is small. A small sample size does not bias estimators of the causal effect, but it does mean that the causal effect is estimated imprecisely. A small sample also raises threats to the validity of confidence intervals and hypothesis tests. Because inference based on normal critical values and heteroskedasticity-robust standard errors are justified using large-sample approximations, experimental data with small samples are sometimes analyzed under the assumption that the errors are normally distributed (Sections 3.6 and 5.6); however, the assumption of normality is typically as dubious for experimental data as it is for observational data.

## Threats to External Validity

Threats to external validity compromise the ability to generalize the results of the study to other populations and settings. Two such threats are when the experimental sample is not representative of the population of interest and when the treatment being studied is not representative of the treatment that would be implemented more broadly.

*Nonrepresentative sample.* The population studied and the population of interest must be sufficiently similar to justify generalizing the experimental results. If a job training program is evaluated in an experiment with former prison inmates, then it might be possible to generalize the study results to other former prison inmates. Because a criminal record weighs heavily on the minds of potential employers, however, the results might not generalize to workers who have never committed a crime.

Another example of a nonrepresentative sample can arise when the experimental participants are volunteers. Even if the volunteers are randomly assigned to treatment and control groups, these volunteers might be more motivated than the overall population and, for them, the treatment could have a greater effect. More generally, selecting the sample nonrandomly from the population of interest can compromise the ability to generalize the results from the population studied (such as volunteers) to the population of interest.

***Nonrepresentative program or policy.*** The policy or program of interest also must be sufficiently similar to the program studied to permit generalizing the results. One important feature is that the program in a small-scale, tightly monitored experiment could be quite different from the program actually implemented. If the program actually implemented is widely available, then the scaled-up program might not provide the same quality control as the experimental version or might be funded at a lower level; either possibility could result in the full-scale program being less effective than the smaller experimental program. Another difference between an experimental program and an actual program is its duration: The experimental program only lasts for the length of the experiment, whereas the actual program under consideration might be available for longer periods of time.

***General equilibrium effects.*** An issue related to scale and duration concerns what economists call "general equilibrium" effects. Turning a small, temporary experimental program into a widespread, permanent program might change the economic environment sufficiently that the results from the experiment cannot be generalized. A small, experimental job training program, for example, might supplement training by employers, but if the program were made widely available, it could displace employer-provided training, thereby reducing the net benefits of the program. Similarly, a widespread educational reform, such as offering school vouchers or sharply reducing class sizes, could increase the demand for teachers and change the type of person who is attracted to teaching, so the eventual net effect of the widespread reform would reflect these induced changes in school personnel. Phrased in econometric terms, an internally valid small experiment might correctly measure a causal effect, holding constant the market or policy environment, but general equilibrium effects mean that these other factors are not, in fact, held constant when the program is implemented broadly.

## 13.3 Experimental Estimates of the Effect of Class Size Reductions

In this section we return to a question addressed in Part II: What is the effect on test scores of reducing class size in the early grades? In the late 1980s, Tennessee conducted a large, multimillion-dollar randomized controlled experiment to ascertain whether class size reduction was an effective way to improve elementary education. The results of this experiment have strongly influenced our understanding of the effect of class size reductions.

## Experimental Design

The Tennessee class size reduction experiment, known as Project STAR (Student–Teacher Achievement Ratio), was a 4-year experiment designed to evaluate the effect on learning of small class sizes. Funded by the Tennessee state legislature, the experiment cost approximately $12 million. The study compared three different class arrangements for kindergarten through third grade: a regular class size, with 22 to 25 students per class, a single teacher, and no aides; a small class size, with 13 to 17 students per class and no aide; and a regular-sized class plus a teacher's aide.

Each school participating in the experiment had at least one class of each type, and students entering kindergarten in a participating school were randomly assigned to one of these three groups at the beginning of the 1985–1986 academic year. Teachers were also assigned randomly to one of the three types of classes.

According to the original experimental protocol, students would stay in their initially assigned class arrangement for the 4 years of the experiment (kindergarten through third grade). However, because of parent complaints, students initially assigned to a regular class (with or without an aide) were randomly reassigned at the beginning of first grade to regular classes with an aide or to regular classes without an aide; students initially assigned to a small class remained in a small class. Students entering school in first grade (kindergarten was optional), in the second year of the experiment, were randomly assigned to one of the three groups. Each year, students in the experiment were given standardized tests (the Stanford Achievement Test) in reading and math.

The project paid for the additional teachers and aides necessary to achieve the target class sizes. During the first year of the study, approximately 6400 students participated in 108 small classes, 101 regular classes, and 99 regular classes with aides. Over all 4 years of the study, a total of approximately 11,600 students at 80 schools participated in the study.

*Deviations from the experimental design.* The experimental protocol specified that the students should not switch between class groups, other than through the re-randomization at the beginning of first grade. However, approximately 10% of the students switched in subsequent years for reasons including incompatible children and behavioral problems. These switches represent a departure from the randomization scheme and, depending on the true nature of the switches, have the potential to introduce bias into the results. Switches made purely to avoid personality conflicts might be sufficiently unrelated to the experiment that they would not introduce bias. If, however, the switches arose because the parents most concerned with their children's education pressured the school into switching a child into a small class, then this failure to follow the experimental protocol could bias the results toward overstating the effectiveness of small classes. Another deviation from the experimental protocol was that the class sizes changed over time because students switched between classes and moved in and out of the school district.

## Analysis of the STAR Data

Because there are two treatment groups—small class and regular class with aide—the regression version of the differences estimator needs to be modified to handle the two treatment groups and the control group. This modification is done by introducing two binary variables, one indicating whether the student is in a small class and another indicating whether the student is in a regular-sized class with an aide, which leads to the population regression model

$$Y_i = \beta_0 + \beta_1 SmallClass_i + \beta_2 RegAide_i + u_i, \qquad (13.3)$$

where $Y_i$ is a test score, $SmallClass_i = 1$ if the $i^{th}$ student is in a small class and $= 0$ otherwise, and $RegAide_i = 1$ if the $i^{th}$ student is in a regular class with an aide and $= 0$ otherwise. The effect on the test score of a small class, relative to a regular class, is $\beta_1$, and the effect of a regular class with an aide, relative to a regular class, is $\beta_2$. The differences estimator for the experiment can be computed by estimating $\beta_1$ and $\beta_2$ in Equation (13.3) by OLS.

Table 13.1 presents the differences estimates of the effect on test scores of being in a small class or in a regular-sized class with an aide. The dependent

| **TABLE 13.1** | Project STAR: Differences Estimates of Effect on Standardized Test Scores of Class Size Treatment Group | | | |
|---|---|---|---|---|
| | **Grade** | | | |
| **Regressor** | **K** | **1** | **2** | **3** |
| Small class | 13.90** (2.45) | 29.78** (2.83) | 19.39** (2.71) | 15.59** (2.40) |
| Regular size with aide | 0.31 (2.27) | 11.96** (2.65) | 3.48 (2.54) | -0.29 (2.27) |
| Intercept | 918.04** (1.63) | 1039.39** (1.78) | 1157.81** (1.82) | 1228.51** (1.68) |
| Number of observations | 5786 | 6379 | 6049 | 5967 |

*Note:* The regressions were estimated using the Project STAR Public Access Data Set described in Appendix 13.1. The dependent variable is the student's combined score on the math and reading portions of the Stanford Achievement Test. Standard errors are given in parentheses under the coefficients. **The individual coefficient is statistically significant at the 1% significance level using a two-sided test.

variable $Y_i$ in the regressions in Table 13.1 is the student's total score on the combined math and reading portions of the Stanford Achievement Test. According to the estimates in Table 13.1, for students in kindergarten, the effect of being in a small class is an increase of 13.9 points on the test, relative to being in a regular class; the estimated effect of being in a regular class with an aide is 0.31 point on the test. For each grade, the null hypothesis that small classes provide no improvement is rejected at the 1% (two-sided) significance level. However, it is not possible to reject the null hypothesis that having an aide in a regular class provides no improvement, relative to not having an aide, except in first grade. The estimated magnitudes of the improvements in small classes are broadly similar in grades K, 2, and 3, although the estimate is larger for first grade.

The differences estimates in Table 13.1 suggest that reducing class size has an effect on test performance, but adding an aide to a regular-sized class has a much smaller effect, possibly zero. As discussed in Section 13.1, augmenting the regressions in Table 13.1 with additional regressors—the $W$ regressors in Equation (13.2)—can provide more efficient estimates of the causal effects. Moreover, if the treatment received is not random because of failures to follow the treatment protocol, then the estimates of the experimental effects based on regressions with additional regressors could differ from the difference estimates reported in Table 13.1. For these two reasons, estimates of the experimental effects in which additional regressors are included in Equation (13.3) are reported for kindergarten in Table 13.2; the first column of Table 13.2 repeats the results of the first column (for kindergarten) from Table 13.1, and the remaining three columns include additional regressors that measure teacher, school, and student characteristics.

The main conclusion from Table 13.2 is that the multiple regression estimates of the causal effects of the two treatments (small class and regular-sized class with aide) in the final three columns of Table 13.2 are similar to the differences estimate reported in the first column. That adding these observable regressors does not change the estimated causal effects of the different treatments makes it more plausible that the random assignment to the smaller classes also does not depend on unobserved variables. As expected, these additional regressors increase the $\overline{R}^2$ of the regression, and the standard error of the estimated class size effect decreases from 2.45 in column (1) to 2.16 in column (4).

Because teachers were randomly assigned to class types within a school, the experiment also provides an opportunity to estimate the effect on test scores of teacher experience. In the terminology of Section 13.1, randomization is conditional on the covariates $W$, where $W$ denotes a full set of binary variables indicating each school; that is, $W$ denotes a full set of school fixed effects. Thus, conditional on $W$, years of experience are randomly assigned, which in turn

| TABLE 13.2 | Project STAR: Differences Estimates with Additional Regressors for Kindergarten | | | |
|---|---|---|---|---|
| Regressor | (1) | (2) | (3) | (4) |
| Small class | 13.90** | 14.00** | 15.93** | 15.89** |
| | (2.45) | (2.45) | (2.24) | (2.16) |
| Regular size with aide | 0.31 | −0.60 | 1.22 | 1.79 |
| | (2.27) | (2.25) | (2.04) | (1.96) |
| Teacher's years of experience | | 1.47** | 0.74** | 0.66** |
| | | (0.17) | (0.17) | (0.17) |
| Boy | | | | −12.09** |
| | | | | (1.67) |
| Free lunch eligible | | | | −34.70** |
| | | | | (1.99) |
| Black | | | | −25.43** |
| | | | | (3.50) |
| Race other than black or white | | | | −8.50 |
| | | | | (12.52) |
| Intercept | 918.04** | 904.72** | | |
| | (1.63) | (2.22) | | |
| School indicator variables? | no | no | yes | yes |
| $\overline{R}^2$ | 0.01 | 0.02 | 0.22 | 0.28 |
| Number of observations | 5786 | 5766 | 5766 | 5748 |

*Note:* The regressions were estimated using the Project STAR Public Access Data Set described in Appendix 13.1. The dependent variable is the combined test score on the math and reading portions of the Stanford Achievement Test. The number of observations differ in the different regressions because of some missing data. Standard errors are given in parentheses under coefficients. The individual coefficient is statistically significant at the *5% level or **1% significance level using a two-sided test.

implies that $u_i$ in Equation (13.2) satisfies conditional mean independence, where the $X$ variables are the class size treatments and the teacher's years of experience and $W$ is the full set of school fixed effects. Because teachers were not reassigned randomly across schools, without school fixed effects in the regression [Table 13.2, column (2)] years of experience will in general be correlated with the error term, for example wealthier districts might have teachers with more years of experience. When school effects are included, the estimated coefficient on experience is cut in half, from 1.47 in column (2) of Table 13.2 to 0.74 in column (3). Because teachers were randomly assigned within a school, column (3) produces an unbiased estimator of the effect on test scores of an additional year of experience. The estimate, 0.74, is statistically significant and moderately large: Ten years of experience corresponds to a predicted increase in test scores of 7.4 points.

It is tempting to interpret some of the other coefficients in Table 13.2 but, like coefficients on control variables generally, those coefficients do not have a causal interpretation. For example, kindergarten boys perform worse than girls on these standardized tests. But these individual student characteristics are *not* randomly assigned (the gender of the student taking the test is not randomly assigned!), so these additional regressors could be correlated with omitted variables. Similarly, if race or eligibility for a free lunch is correlated with reduced learning opportunities outside school (which is omitted from the Table 13.2 regressions), then their estimated coefficients would reflect these omitted influences.

*Interpreting the estimated effects of class size.*   Are the estimated effects of class size reported in Table 13.1 and 13.2 large or small in a practical sense? There are two ways to answer this: first, by translating the estimated changes in raw test scores into units of standard deviations of test scores, so that the estimates in Table 13.1 are comparable across grades; and, second, by comparing the estimated class size effect to the other coefficients in Table 13.2.

Because the distribution of test scores is not the same for each grade, the estimated effects in Table 13.1 are not directly comparable across grades. We faced this problem in Section 9.4, when we wanted to compare the effect on test scores of a reduction in the student–teacher ratio estimated using data from California to the estimate based on data from Massachusetts. Because the two tests differed, the coefficients could not be compared directly. The solution in Section 9.4 was to translate the estimated effects into units of standard deviations of the test so that a unit decrease in the student–teacher ratio corresponds to a change of an estimated fraction of a standard deviation of test scores. We adopt this approach here so that the estimated effects in Table 13.1 can be compared across grades. For example, the standard deviation of test scores for children in kindergarten is 73.7, so the effect of being in a small class in kindergarten, based on the estimate in Table 13.1, is $13.9/73.7 = 0.19$, with a standard error of $2.45/73.7 = 0.03$. The estimated effects of class size from Table 13.1, converted into units of the standard deviation of test scores across students, are summarized in Table 13.3. Expressed in standard deviation units, the estimated effect of being in a small class is similar for grades K, 2, and 3 and is approximately one-fifth of a standard deviation of test scores. Similarly, the result of being in a regular-sized class with an aide is approximately zero for grades K, 2, and 3. The estimated treatment effects are larger for first grade; however, the estimated difference between the small class and the regular-sized class with an aide is 0.20 for first grade, the same as the other grades. Thus one interpretation of the first-grade results is that the students in the control group—the regular-sized class without an aide—happened

| | | | | | | |
|---|---|---|---|---|---|---|
| **TABLE 13.3** | Estimated Class Size Effects in Units of Standard Deviations of the Test Score Across Students | | | | | |

| | Grade | | | |
|---|---|---|---|---|
| **Treatment Group** | **K** | **1** | **2** | **3** |
| Small class | 0.19** (0.03) | 0.33** (0.03) | 0.23** (0.03) | 0.21** (0.03) |
| Regular size with aide | 0.00 (0.03) | 0.13** (0.03) | 0.04 (0.03) | 0.00 (0.03) |
| Sample standard deviation of test scores ($s_Y$) | 73.70 | 91.30 | 84.10 | 73.30 |

*Note:* The estimates and standard errors in the first two rows are the estimated effects in Table 13.1, divided by the sample standard deviation of the Stanford Achievement Test for that grade (the final row in this table), computed using data on the students in the experiment. Standard errors are given in parentheses under coefficients. **The individual coefficient is statistically significant at the 1% significance level using a two-sided test.

to do poorly on the test that year for some unusual reason, perhaps simply random sampling variation.

Another way to gauge the magnitude of the estimated effect of being in a small class is to compare the estimated treatment effects with the other coefficients in Table 13.2. In kindergarten, the estimated effect of being in a small class is 13.9 points on the test (first row of Table 13.2). Holding constant race, teacher's years of experience, eligibility for free lunch, and the treatment group, boys score lower on the standardized test than girls by approximately 12 points according to the estimates in column (4) of Table 13.2. Thus the estimated effect of being in a small class is somewhat larger than the performance gap between girls and boys. As another comparison, the estimated coefficient on the teacher's years of experience in column (4) is 0.66, so having a teacher with 20 years of experience is estimated to improve test performance by 13 points. Thus the estimated effect of being in a small class is approximately the same as the effect of having a 20-year veteran as a teacher, relative to having a new teacher. These comparisons suggest that the estimated effect of being in a small class is substantial.

*Additional results.* Econometricians, statisticians, and specialists in elementary education have studied this experiment extensively, and we briefly summarize some of those findings here. One is that the effect of a small class is concentrated in the earliest grades as can be seen in Table 13.3; except for the anomalous first-grade results, the test score gap between regular and small classes reported in Table 13.3 is essentially constant across grades (0.19 standard deviation unit in kindergarten, 0.23 in second grade, and 0.21 in third grade). Because the children initially assigned to a small class stayed in that small class, staying in a small class did not result in additional gains; rather, the gains made upon initial assignment were retained in the higher grades, but the gap between the treatment and control groups did not increase. Another finding is that, as indicated in the second row of Table 13.3, this experiment shows little benefit of having an aide in a regular-sized classroom. One potential concern about interpreting the results of the experiment is the failure to follow the treatment protocol for some students (some students switched from the small classes). If initial placement in a kindergarten classroom is random and has no direct effect on test scores, then initial placement can be used as an instrumental variable that partially, but not entirely, influences placement. This strategy was pursued by Krueger (1999), who used two stage least squares (TSLS) to estimate the effect on test scores of class size using initial classroom placement as the instrumental variable; he found that the TSLS and OLS estimates were similar, leading him to conclude that deviations from the experimental protocol did not introduce substantial bias into the OLS estimates.[2]

## Comparison of the Observational and Experimental Estimates of Class Size Effects

Part II presented multiple regression estimates of the class size effect based on observational data for California and Massachusetts school districts. In those data, class size was *not* randomly assigned, but instead was determined by local school officials trying to balance educational objectives against budgetary realities. How do those observational estimates compare with the experimental estimates from Project STAR?

To compare the California and Massachusetts estimates with those in Table 13.3, it is necessary to evaluate the same class size reduction and to express the predicted effect in units of standard deviations of test scores. Over the 4 years of the STAR experiment, the small classes had, on average, approximately 7.5 fewer students than the large classes, so we use the observational estimates to predict the effect on test scores of a reduction of 7.5 students per class. Based on the OLS estimates for the linear specifications summarized in the first column of Table 9.3, the California estimates predict an increase of 5.5 points on the test for a 7.5 student reduction in

---

[2]For further reading about Project STAR, see Mosteller (1995), Mosteller, Light, and Sachs (1996), and Krueger (1999). Ehrenberg, Brewer, Gamoran, and Willms (2001a, 2001b) discuss Project STAR and place it in the context of the policy debate on class size and related research on the topic. For some criticisms of Project STAR, see Hanushek (1999a), and for a critical view of the relationship between class size and performance more generally, see Hanushek (1999b). To learn about how the Project STAR subjects performed later in life, see Chetty, Friedman, Hilger, Saez, Schanzenbach, and Yagan (2011).

the student–teacher ratio ($0.73 \times 7.5 \cong 5.5$ points). The standard deviation of the test across students in California is approximately 38 points, so the estimated effect of the reduction of 7.5 students, expressed in units of standard deviations across students, is $5.5/38 \cong 0.14$ standard deviations.[3] The standard error of the estimated slope coefficient for California is 0.26 (Table 9.3), so the standard error of the estimated effect of a 7.5 student reduction in standard deviation units is $0.26 \times 7.5/38 \cong 0.05$. Thus, based on the California data, the estimated effect of reducing classes by 7.5 students, expressed in units of standard deviation of test scores across students, is 0.14 standard deviation, with a standard error of 0.05. These calculations and similar calculations for Massachusetts are summarized in Table 13.4, along with the STAR estimates for kindergarten taken from column (1) of Table 13.2.

The estimated effects from the California and Massachusetts observational studies are somewhat smaller than the STAR estimates. One reason that estimates from different studies differ, however, is random sampling variability, so it makes sense to compare confidence intervals for the estimated effects from the three studies. Based on the STAR data for kindergarten, the 95% confidence interval for the effect of being in a small class (reported in the final column of Table 13.4) is 0.13 to 0.25. The comparable 95% confidence interval based on the California observational data is 0.04 to 0.24, and for Massachusetts it is 0.02 to 0.22. Thus the 95% confidence intervals from the California and Massachusetts studies contain most of the 95% confidence interval from the STAR kindergarten data. Viewed in this way, the three studies give strikingly similar ranges of estimates.

There are many reasons the experimental and observational estimates might differ. One reason is that, as discussed in Section 9.4, there are remaining threats to the internal validity of the observational studies. For example, because children move into and out of districts, the district student–teacher ratio might not reflect the student–teacher ratio actually experienced by the students, so the coefficient on the student–teacher ratio in the Massachusetts and California studies could be biased toward zero because of errors-in-variables bias. Other reasons concern external validity. The district average student–teacher ratio used in the observational studies is not the same thing as the actual number of children in the class, the STAR experimental variable. Project STAR was in a southern state in the 1980s, potentially different from California and Massachusetts in 1998, and the grades

---

[3]In Table 9.3, the estimated effects are presented in terms of the standard deviation of test scores across *districts*; in Table 13.3, the estimated effects are in terms of the standard deviation of test scores across *students*. The standard deviation across students is greater than the standard deviation across districts. For California, the standard deviation across students is 38, but the standard deviation across districts is 19.1.

| TABLE 13.4 | Estimated Effects of Reducing the Student–Teacher Ratio by 7.5 Based on the STAR Data and the California and Massachusetts Observational Data | | | | |
|---|---|---|---|---|---|
| Study | $\hat{\beta}_1$ | Change in Student–Teacher Ratio | Standard Deviation of Test Scores Across Students | Estimated Effect | 95% Confidence Interval |
| STAR (grade K) | −13.90** (2.45) | Small class vs. regular class | 73.8 | 0.19** (0.03) | (0.13, 0.25) |
| California | −0.73** (0.26) | −7.5 | 38.0 | 0.14** (0.05) | (0.04, 0.24) |
| Massachusetts | −0.64* (0.27) | −7.5 | 39.0 | 0.12* (0.05) | (0.02, 0.22) |

*Note:* The estimated coefficient $\hat{\beta}_1$ for the STAR study is taken from column (1) of Table 13.2. The estimated coefficients for the California and Massachusetts studies are taken from the first column of Table 9.3. The estimated effect is the effect of being in a small class versus a regular class (for STAR) or the effect of reducing the student–teacher ratio by 7.5 (for the California and Massachusetts studies). The 95% confidence interval for the reduction in the student–teacher ratio is this estimated effect ± 1.96 standard errors. Standard errors are given in parentheses under estimated effects. The estimated effects are statistically significantly different from zero at the *5% significance level or **1% significance level using a two-sided test.

being compared differ (K through 3 in STAR, fourth grade in Massachusetts, fifth grade in California). In light of all these reasons to expect different estimates, the findings of the three studies are remarkably similar. That the observational studies are similar to the Project STAR estimates suggests that the remaining threats to the internal validity of the observational estimates are minor.

# 13.4 Quasi-Experiments

The statistical insights and methods of randomized controlled experiments can carry over to nonexperimental settings. In a **quasi-experiment**, also called a **natural experiment**, randomness is introduced by variations in individual circumstances that make it appear *as if* the treatment is randomly assigned. These variations in individual circumstances might arise because of vagaries in legal institutions, location, timing of policy or program implementation, natural randomness such as birth dates, rainfall, or other factors that are unrelated to the causal effect under study.

There are two types of quasi-experiments. In the first, whether an individual (more generally, an entity) receives treatment is viewed as if it is randomly determined. In this case, the causal effect can be estimated by OLS using the treatment, $X_i$, as a regressor. In the second type of quasi-experiment, the "as if" random variation only partially determines the treatment. In this case, the causal effect is estimated by instrumental variables regression, where the "as if" random source of variation provides the instrumental variable.

After providing some examples, this section presents some extensions of the econometric methods in Sections 13.1 and 13.2 that can be useful for analyzing data from quasi-experiments.

## Examples

We illustrate the two types of quasi-experiments by examples. The first example is a quasi-experiment in which the treatment is "as if" randomly determined. The second and third examples illustrate quasi-experiments in which the "as if" random variation influences, but does not entirely determine, the level of the treatment.

*Example #1: Labor market effects of immigration.* Does immigration reduce wages? Economic theory suggests that if the supply of labor increases because of an influx of immigrants, the "price" of labor—the wage—should fall. However, all else being equal, immigrants are attracted to cities with high labor demand, so the OLS estimator of the effect on wages of immigration will be biased. An ideal randomized controlled experiment for estimating the effect on wages of immigration would randomly assign different numbers of immigrants (different "treatments") to different labor markets ("subjects") and measure the effect on wages (the "outcome"). Such an experiment, however, faces severe practical, financial, and ethical problems.

The labor economist David Card (1990) therefore used a quasi-experiment in which a large number of Cuban immigrants entered the Miami, Florida, labor market in the "Mariel boatlift," which resulted from a temporary lifting of restrictions on emigration from Cuba in 1980. Half of the immigrants settled in Miami, in part because it had a large preexisting Cuban community. Card estimated the causal effect on wages of an increase in immigration by comparing the change in wages of low-skilled workers in Miami to the change in wages of similar workers in other comparable U.S. cities over the same period. He concluded that this influx of immigrants had a negligible effect on wages of less-skilled workers.

*Example #2: Effects on civilian earnings of military service.* Does serving in the military improve your prospects on the labor market? The military provides training that future employers might find attractive. However, an OLS regression of individual civilian earnings against prior military service could produce a biased estimator of the effect on civilian earnings of military service because military service is determined, at least in part, by individual choices and characteristics.

For example, the military accepts only applicants who meet minimum physical requirements, and a lack of success in the private sector labor market might make an individual more likely to sign up for the military.

To circumvent this selection bias, Joshua Angrist (1990) used a quasi-experimental design in which he examined labor market histories of those who served in the U.S. military during the Vietnam War. During this period, whether a young man was drafted into the military was determined in part by a national lottery system based on birthdays: Men randomly assigned low lottery numbers were eligible to be drafted, whereas those with high numbers were not. Actual entry into the military was determined by complicated rules, including physical screening and certain exemptions, and some young men volunteered for service, so serving in the military was only partially influenced by whether a man was draft-eligible. Thus being draft-eligible serves as an instrumental variable that partially determines military service but is randomly assigned. In this case, there was true random assignment of draft eligibility via the lottery, but because this randomization was not done as part of an experiment to evaluate the effect of military service, it is a quasi-experiment. Angrist concluded that the long-term effect of military service was to reduce earnings of white, but not nonwhite, veterans.

*Example #3: The effect of cardiac catheterization.*  Section 12.5 described the study by McClellan, McNeil, and Newhouse (1994) in which they used the distance from a heart attack patient's home to a cardiac catheterization hospital, relative to the distance to a hospital lacking catheterization facilities, as an instrumental variable for actual treatment by cardiac catheterization. This study is a quasi-experiment with a variable that partially determines the treatment. The treatment itself, cardiac catheterization, is determined by personal characteristics of the patient and by the decision of the patient and doctor; however, it is also influenced by whether a nearby hospital is capable of performing this procedure. If the location of the patient is "as if" randomly assigned and has no direct effect on health outcomes, other than through its effect on the probability of catheterization, then the relative distance to a catheterization hospital is a valid instrumental variable.

*Other examples.*  The quasi-experiment research strategy has been applied in other areas as well. Garvey and Hanka (1999) used variation in U.S. state laws to examine the effect on corporate financial structure (for example, the use of debt by corporations) of anti-takeover laws. Meyer, Viscusi, and Durbin (1995) used large discrete changes in the generosity of unemployment insurance benefits in Kentucky and Michigan, which differentially affected workers with high but not low earnings, to estimate the effect on time out of work of a change in unemployment benefits. The surveys of Meyer (1995), Rosenzweig and Wolpin (2000), and Angrist and Krueger (2001) give other examples of quasi-experiments in the fields of economics and social policy.

## The Differences-in-Differences Estimator

If the treatment in a quasi-experiment is "as if" randomly assigned, conditional on some observed variables $W$, then the treatment effect can be estimated using the differences regression (13.2). Because the researcher does not have control over the randomization, however, some differences might remain between the treatment and control groups even after controlling for $W$. One way to adjust for those remaining differences between the two groups is to compare not the outcomes $Y$, but the *change* in the outcomes pre- and post-treatment, thereby adjusting for differences in pre-treatment values of $Y$ in the two groups. Because this estimator is the difference across groups in the change, or difference over time, this estimator is called the differences-in-differences estimator. For example, in Card's (1990) study of the effect of immigration on low-skilled workers' wages, he used a differences-in-differences estimator to compare the *change* in wages in Miami with the *change* in wages in other U.S. cities. Another example of the use of the differences-in-differences estimator is given in the box "What Is the Effect on Employment of the Minimum Wage?"

***The differences-in-differences estimator.*** Let $\overline{Y}^{treatment, before}$ be the sample average of $Y$ for those in the treatment group before the experiment, and let $\overline{Y}^{treatment, after}$ be the sample average for the treatment group after the experiment. Let $\overline{Y}^{control, before}$ and $\overline{Y}^{control, after}$ be the corresponding pretreatment and post treatment sample averages for the control group. The average change in $Y$ over the course of the experiment for those in the treatment group is $\overline{Y}^{treatment, after} - \overline{Y}^{treatment, before}$, and the average change in $Y$ over this period for those in the control group is $\overline{Y}^{control, after} - \overline{Y}^{control, before}$. The **differences-in-differences estimator** is the average change in $Y$ for those in the treatment group, minus the average change in $Y$ for those in the control group:

$$\hat{\beta}_1^{diffs - in - diffs} = (\overline{Y}^{treatment, after} - \overline{Y}^{treatment, before}) - (\overline{Y}^{control, after} - \overline{Y}^{control, before})$$
$$= \Delta\overline{Y}^{treatment} - \Delta\overline{Y}^{control}, \tag{13.4}$$

where $\Delta\overline{Y}^{treatment}$ is the average change in $Y$ in the treatment group and $\Delta\overline{Y}^{control}$ is the average change in $Y$ in the control group. If the treatment is randomly assigned, then $\hat{\beta}_1^{diffs - in - diffs}$ is an unbiased and consistent estimator of the causal effect.

## What Is the Effect on Employment of the Minimum Wage?

How much does an increase in the minimum wage reduce demand for low-skilled workers? Economic theory says that demand falls when the price rises, but precisely how much is an empirical question. Because prices and quantities are determined by supply and demand, the OLS estimator in a regression of employment against wages has simultaneous causality bias (Key Concept 9.6). Hypothetically, a randomized controlled experiment might randomly assign different minimum wages to different employers and then compare changes in employment (outcomes) in the treatment and control groups, but how could this hypothetical experiment be done in practice?

The labor economists David Card and Alan Krueger (1994) decided to conduct such an experiment, but to let "nature"—or, more precisely, geography—perform the randomization for them. In 1992, the minimum wage in New Jersey rose from $4.25 to $5.05 per hour, but the minimum wage in neighboring Pennsylvania stayed constant. In this experiment, the "treatment" of the minimum wage increase—being located in New Jersey instead of Pennsylvania—is viewed "as if" randomly assigned in the sense that being subject to the wage hike is assumed to be uncorrelated with the other determinants of employment changes over this period. Card and Krueger collected data on employment at fast-food restaurants before and after the wage increase in the two states. When they computed the differences-in-differences estimator, they found a surprising result: There was no evidence that employment fell at New Jersey fast-food restaurants, relative to those in Pennsylvania. In fact, some of their estimates actually suggest that employment *increased* in New Jersey restaurants after its minimum wage went up, relative to Pennsylvania!

This finding conflicts with basic microeconomic theory and has been quite controversial. Subsequent analysis, using a different source of employment data, suggests that there might have been a small drop in employment in New Jersey after the wage hike, but even so the estimated labor demand curve is very inelastic (Neumark and Wascher, 2000). Although the exact wage elasticity in this quasi-experiment is a matter of debate, the effect on employment of a hike in the minimum wage appears to be smaller than many economists had previously thought.

The differences-in-differences estimator can be written in regression notation. Let $\Delta Y_i$ be the post experimental value of $Y$ for the $i^{th}$ individual minus the pre-experimental value. The differences-in-differences estimator is the OLS estimator of $\beta_1$ in the regression,

$$\Delta Y_i = \beta_0 + \beta_1 X_i + u_i. \tag{13.5}$$

The differences-in-differences estimator is illustrated in Figure 13.1. In that figure, the sample average of $Y$ for the treatment group is 40 before the experiment, whereas the pretreatment sample average of $Y$ for the control group is 20. Over the course of the experiment, the sample average of $Y$ increases in the control

---

**FIGURE 13.1** The Differences-in-Differences Estimator

The post-treatment difference between the treatment and control groups is $80 - 30 = 50$, but this overstates the treatment effect because before the treatment $\overline{Y}$ was higher for the treatment than the control group by $40 - 20 = 20$. The differences-in-differences estimator is the difference between the final and initial gaps, so $\hat{\beta}_1^{diffs-in-diffs} = (80 - 30) - (40 - 20) = 50 - 20 = 30$. Equivalently, the differences-in-differences estimator is the average change for the treatment group minus the average change for the control group, that is, $\hat{\beta}_1^{diffs-in-diffs} = \Delta \overline{Y}^{treatment} - \Delta \overline{Y}^{control} = (80 - 40) - (30 - 20) = 30$.

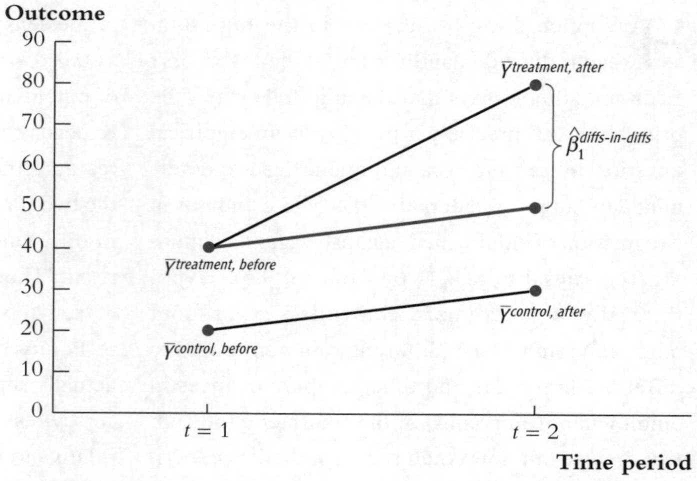

group to 30, whereas it increases to 80 for the treatment group. Thus the mean difference of the post-treatment sample averages is $80 - 30 = 50$. However, some of this difference arises because the treatment and control groups had different pretreatment means: The treatment group started out ahead of the control group. The differences-in-differences estimator measures the gains of the treatment group, relative to the control group, which in this example is $(80 - 40) - (30 - 20) = 30$. By focusing on the change in $Y$ over the course of the experiment, the differences-in-differences estimator removes the influence of initial values of $Y$ that vary between the treatment and control groups.

*The differences-in-differences estimator with additional regressors.* The differences-in-differences estimator can be extended to include additional regressors $W_{1i}, \ldots, W_{ri}$, which measure individual characteristics prior to the experiment. These additional regressors can be incorporated using the multiple regression model

$$\Delta Y_i = \beta_0 + \beta_1 X_i + \beta_2 W_{1i} + \cdots + \beta_{1+r} W_{ri} + u_i, i = 1, \ldots, n. \quad (13.6)$$

The OLS estimator of $\beta_1$ in Equation (13.6) is the **differences-in-differences estimator with additional regressors**. If $X_i$ is "as if" randomly assigned, conditional on $W_{1i}, \ldots, W_{ri}$, then $u_i$ satisfies conditional mean independence and the OLS estimator of $\hat{\beta}_1$ in Equation (13.6) is unbiased.

The differences-in-differences estimator described here considers two time periods, before and after the experiment. In some settings there are panel data with multiple time periods. The differences-in-differences estimator can be extended to multiple time periods using the panel data regression methods of Chapter 10.

*Differences-in-differences using repeated cross-sectional data.* A **repeated cross-sectional data** set is a collection of cross-sectional data sets, where each cross-sectional data set corresponds to a different time period. For example, the data set might contain observations on 400 individuals in the year 2004 and on 500 different individuals in 2005, for a total of 900 different individuals. One example of repeated cross-sectional data is political polling data, in which political preferences are measured by a series of surveys of randomly selected potential voters, where the surveys are taken at different dates and each survey has different respondents.

The premise of using repeated cross-sectional data is that if the individuals (more generally, entities) are randomly drawn from the same population, then the individuals in the earlier cross section can be used as surrogates for the individuals in the treatment and control groups in the later cross section.

When there are two time periods, the regression model for repeated cross-sectional data is

$$Y_{it} = \beta_0 + \beta_1 X_{it} + \beta_2 G_i + \beta_3 D_t + \beta_4 W_{1it} + \cdots + \beta_{3+r} W_{rit} + u_{it}, \quad (13.7)$$

where $X_{it}$ is the actual treatment of the $i^{th}$ individual (entity) in the cross section in period $t$ ($t = 1, 2$), $G_i$ is a binary variable indicating whether the individual is in the treatment group (or in the surrogate treatment group, if the observation is in the pretreatment period), and $D_t$ is the binary indicator that equals 0 in the first period and equals 1 in the second period. The $i^{th}$ individual receives treatment if he or she is in the treatment group in the second period, so in Equation (13.7), $X_{it} = G_i \times D_t$ that is, $X_{it}$ is the interaction between $G_i$ and $D_t$.

If the quasi-experiment makes $X_{it}$ "as if" randomly received, conditional on the $W$'s, then the causal effect can be estimated by the OLS estimator of $\beta_1$ in Equation (13.7). If there are more than two time periods, then Equation (13.7) is modified to contain $T - 1$ binary variables indicating the different time periods (see Section 10.4).

## Instrumental Variables Estimators

If the quasi-experiment yields a variable $Z_i$ that influences receipt of treatment, if data are available both on $Z_i$ and on the treatment actually received ($X_i$), and if $Z_i$ is "as if" randomly assigned (perhaps after controlling for some additional variables $W_i$), then $Z_i$ is a valid instrument for $X_i$ and the coefficients of Equation (13.2) can be estimated using two-stage least squares. Any control variables appearing in (13.2) also appear as control variables in the first stage of the two-stage least squares estimator of $\beta_1$.

## Regression Discontinuity Estimators

One situation that gives rise to a quasi-experiment is when receipt of the treatment depends in whole or in part on whether an observable variable $W$ crosses a threshold value. For example, suppose that students are required to attend summer school if their end-of-year grade point average (GPA) falls below a threshold.[4] Then one way to estimate the effect of mandatory summer school is to compare outcomes for students whose GPA was just below the threshold (and thus were required to attend) to outcomes for students whose GPA was just above the threshold (so they escaped summer school). The outcome $Y$ could be next year's GPA, whether the student drops out, or future earnings. As long as there is nothing special about the threshold value other than its use in mandating summer school, it is reasonable to attribute any jump in outcomes at that threshold to summer school. Figure 13.2 illustrates a hypothetical scatterplot of a data set in which the treatment (summer school, $X$) is required if GPA ($W$) is less than a threshold value ($w_0 = 2.0$). The scatterplot shows next year's GPA ($Y$) for a hypothetical sample of students as a function of this year's GPA, along with the population regression function. If the only role of the threshold $w_0$ is to mandate summer school, then the jump in next year's GPA at $w_0$ is an estimate of the effect of summer school on next year's GPA.

Because of the jump, or discontinuity, in treatment at the threshold, studies that exploit a discontinuity in the probability of receiving treatment at a threshold value are called **regression discontinuity** designs. There are two types of regression discontinuity designs, sharp and fuzzy.

*Sharp regression discontinuity designs.* In a sharp regression discontinuity design, receipt of treatment is entirely determined by whether $W$ exceeds the threshold: All students with $W < w_0$ attend summer school, and no students with $W \geq w_0$ attend; that is, $X_i = 1$ if $W < w_0$ and $X_i = 0$ if $W \geq w_0$. In this case, the jump in $Y$ at the threshold equals the average treatment effect for the subpopulation with $W = w_0$, which might be a useful approximation to the average treatment

---

[4]This example is a simplified version of the regression discontinuity study of the effect of summer school for elementary and middle school students by Jordan Matsudaira (2008), in which summer school attendance was based in part on end-of-year tests.

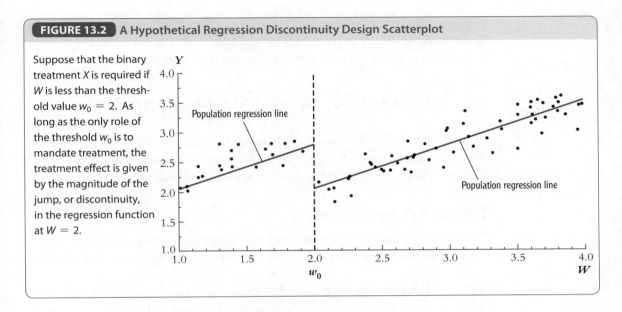

**FIGURE 13.2** A Hypothetical Regression Discontinuity Design Scatterplot

Suppose that the binary treatment $X$ is required if $W$ is less than the threshold value $w_0 = 2$. As long as the only role of the threshold $w_0$ is to mandate treatment, the treatment effect is given by the magnitude of the jump, or discontinuity, in the regression function at $W = 2$.

effect in the larger population of interest. If the regression function is linear in $W$, other than for the treatment-induced discontinuity, the treatment effect can be estimated by $\beta_1$ in the regression:

$$Y_i = \beta_0 + \beta_1 X_i + \beta_2 W_i + u_i. \tag{13.8}$$

If the regression function is nonlinear, then a suitable nonlinear function of $W$ can be used (Section 8.2).

*Fuzzy regression discontinuity design.* In a fuzzy regression discontinuity design, crossing the threshold influences receipt of the treatment but is not the sole determinant. For example, suppose that some students whose GPA falls below the threshold are exempted from summer school while some whose GPA exceeds the threshold nevertheless attend. This situation could arise if the threshold rule is part of a more complicated process for determining treatment. In a fuzzy design, $X_i$ will in general be correlated with $u_i$ in Equation (13.8). If, however, any special effect of crossing the threshold operates solely by increasing the probability of treatment—that is, the direct effect of crossing the threshold is captured by the linear term in $W$—then an instrumental variables approach is available. Specifically, the binary variable $Z_i$ which indicates crossing the threshold (so $Z_i = 1$ if $W_i < w_0$ and $Z_i = 0$ if $W_i \geq w_0$) influences receipt of treatment but is uncorrelated with $u_i$, so it is a valid instrument for $X_i$. Thus, in a fuzzy regression discontinuity design, $\beta_1$ can be estimated by instrumental variables estimation of Equation (13.8), using as an instrument the binary variable indicating that $W_i < w_0$.

## 13.5 Potential Problems with Quasi-Experiments

Like all empirical studies, quasi-experiments face threats to internal and external validity. A particularly important potential threat to internal validity is whether the "as if" randomization in fact can be treated reliably as true randomization.

### Threats to Internal Validity

The threats to the internal validity of true randomized controlled experiments listed in Section 13.2 also apply to quasi-experiments, but with some modifications.

*Failure of randomization.* Quasi-experiments rely on differences in individual circumstances—legal changes, sudden unrelated events, and so forth—to provide the "as if" randomization in the treatment level. If this "as if" randomization fails to produce a treatment level $X$ (or an instrumental variable $Z$) that is random, then in general the OLS estimator is biased (or the instrumental variable estimator is not consistent).

As in a true experiment, one way to test for failure of randomization is to check for systematic differences between the treatment and control groups, for example by regressing $X$ (or $Z$) on the individual characteristics (the $W$'s) and testing the hypothesis that the coefficients on the $W$'s are zero. If differences exist that are not readily explained by the nature of the quasi-experiment, then that is evidence that the quasi-experiment did not produce true randomization. Even if there is no relationship between $X$ (or $Z$) and the $W$'s, the possibility remains that $X$ (or $Z$) could be related to some of the unobserved factors in the error term $u$. Because these factors are unobserved, this possibility cannot be tested, and the validity of the assumption of "as if" randomization must be evaluated using expert knowledge and judgment applied to the application at hand.

*Failure to follow the treatment protocol.* In a true experiment, failure to follow the treatment protocol arises when members of the treatment group fail to receive treatment, members of the control group actually receive treatment, or both; in consequence, the OLS estimator of the causal effect has selection bias. The counterpart to failing to follow the treatment protocol in a quasi-experiment is when the "as if" randomization influences, but does not determine, the treatment level.

In this case, the instrumental variables estimator based on the quasi-experimental influence $Z$ can be consistent even though the OLS estimator is not.

*Attrition.*   Attrition in a quasi-experiment is similar to attrition in a true experiment in the sense that if it arises because of personal choices or characteristics, then attrition can induce correlation between the treatment level and the error term. The result is sample selection bias, so the OLS estimator of the causal effect is biased and inconsistent.

*Experimental effects.*   An advantage of quasi-experiments is that, because they are not true experiments, there typically is no reason for individuals to think that they are experimental subjects. Thus experimental effects such as the Hawthorne effect generally are not germane in quasi-experiments.

*Instrument validity in quasi-experiments.*   An important step in evaluating a study that uses instrumental variables regression is careful consideration of whether the instrument is in fact valid. This general statement remains true in quasi-experimental studies in which the instrument is "as if" randomly determined. As discussed in Chapter 12, instrument validity requires both instrument relevance and instrument exogeneity. Because instrument relevance can be checked using the statistical methods summarized in Key Concept 12.5, here we focus on the second, more judgmental requirement of instrument exogeneity.

Although it might seem that a randomly assigned instrumental variable is necessarily exogenous, that is not so. Consider the examples of Section 13.4. In Angrist's (1990) use of draft lottery numbers as an instrumental variable in studying the effect on civilian earnings of military service, the lottery number was in fact randomly assigned. But, as Angrist (1990) points out and discusses, if a low draft number results in behavior aimed at avoiding the draft and that avoidance behavior subsequently affects civilian earnings, then a low lottery number ($Z_i$) could be related to unobserved factors that determine civilian earnings ($u_i$); that is, $Z_i$ and $u_i$ are correlated even though $Z_i$ is randomly assigned. As a second example, McClellan, McNeil, and Newhouse's (1994) study of the effect on heart attack patients of cardiac catheterization treated the relative distance to a catheterization hospital as if it were randomly assigned. But, as the authors highlight and examine, if patients who live close to a catheterization hospital are healthier than those who live far away (perhaps because of better access to medical care generally), then the relative distance to a catheterization hospital would be correlated with omitted variables in the error term of the health outcome equation. In short, just because an instrument is randomly determined or "as if" randomly determined does not necessarily mean it is exogenous in the sense that $\text{corr}(Z_i, u_i) = 0$. Thus the case for exogeneity must be scrutinized closely even if the instrument arises from a quasi-experiment.

### Threats to External Validity

Quasi-experimental studies use observational data, and the threats to the external validity of a study based on a quasi-experiment are generally similar to the threats discussed in Section 9.1 for conventional regression studies using observational data.

One important consideration is that the special events that create the "as if" randomness at the core of a quasi-experimental study can result in other special features that threaten external validity. For example, Card's (1990) study of labor market effects of immigration discussed in Section 13.4 used the "as if" randomness induced by the influx of Cuban immigrants in the Mariel boatlift. There were, however, special features of the Cuban immigrants, Miami, and its Cuban community that might make it difficult to generalize these findings to immigrants from other countries or to other destinations. Similarly, Angrist's (1990) study of the labor market effects of serving in the U.S. military during the Vietnam War presumably would not generalize to peacetime military service. As usual, whether a study generalizes to a specific population and setting of interest depends on the details of the study and must be assessed on a case-by-case basis.

## 13.6 Experimental and Quasi-Experimental Estimates in Heterogeneous Populations

As discussed in Section 13.1, the causal effect can vary from one member of the population to the next. Section 13.1 discusses estimating causal effects that vary depending on observable variables, such as gender. In this section, we consider the consequences of *unobserved* variation in the causal effect. We refer to unobserved variation in the causal effect as having a heterogeneous population. To keep things simple and to focus on the role of unobserved heterogeneity, in this section we omit control variables $W$; the conclusions of this section carry over to regressions including control variables.

If the population is heterogeneous, then the $i^{th}$ individual now has his or her own causal effect, $\beta_{1i}$, which (in the terminology of Section 13.1) is the difference in the $i^{th}$ individual's potential outcomes if the treatment is or is not received. For example, $\beta_{1i}$ might be zero for a resume-writing training program if the $i^{th}$

individual already knows how to write a resume. With this notation, the population regression equation can be written

$$Y_i = \beta_{0i} + \beta_{1i}X_i + u_i. \tag{13.9}$$

Because $\beta_{1i}$ varies from one individual to the next in the population and the individuals are selected from the population at random, $\beta_{1i}$ is a random variable that, just like $u_i$, reflects unobserved variation across individuals (for example, variation in preexisting resume-writing skills). The average causal effect is the population mean value of the causal effect, $E(\beta_{1i})$; that is, it is the expected causal effect of a randomly selected member of the population under study.

What do the estimators of Sections 13.1, 13.2, and 13.4 estimate if there is population heterogeneity of the form in Equation (13.9)? We first consider the OLS estimator when $X_i$ is "as if" randomly determined; in this case, the OLS estimator is a consistent estimator of the average causal effect. That is generally not true for the IV estimator, however. Instead, if $X_i$ is partially influenced by $Z_i$, then the IV estimator using the instrument $Z$ estimates a weighted average of the causal effects, where those for whom the instrument is most influential receive the most weight.

## OLS with Heterogeneous Causal Effects

If there is heterogeneity in the causal effect and if $X_i$ is randomly assigned, then the differences estimator is a consistent estimator of the average causal effect. This result follows from the discussion in Section 13.1 and Appendix 13.3, which make use of the potential outcome framework; here it is shown without reference to potential outcomes by applying concepts from Chapters 3 and 4 directly to the random coefficients regression model in Equation (13.9).

The OLS estimator of $\beta_1$ in Equation (13.1) is $\hat{\beta}_1 = s_{XY}/s_X^2$ [Equation (4.7)]. If the observations are i.i.d., then the sample covariance and variance are consistent estimators of the population covariance and variance, so $\hat{\beta}_1 \xrightarrow{p} \sigma_{XY}/\sigma_X^2$. If $X_i$ is randomly assigned, then $X_i$ is distributed independently of other individual characteristics, both observed and unobserved, and in particular is distributed independently of $\beta_{0i}$ and $\beta_{1i}$. Accordingly, the OLS estimator $\hat{\beta}_1$ has the limit

$$\hat{\beta}_1 = \frac{s_{XY}}{s_X^2} \xrightarrow{p} \frac{\sigma_{XY}}{\sigma_X^2} = \frac{\mathrm{cov}(\beta_{0i} + \beta_{1i}X_i + u_i, X_i)}{\sigma_X^2}$$
$$= \frac{\mathrm{cov}(\beta_{0i} + \beta_{1i}X_i, X_i)}{\sigma_X^2} = E(\beta_{1i}), \tag{13.10}$$

where the third equality uses the facts about covariances in Key Concept 2.3 and $\text{cov}(u_i, X_i) = 0$, which is implied by $E(u_i|X_i) = 0$ [Equation (2.27)], and where the final equality follows from $\beta_{0i}$ and $\beta_{1i}$ being distributed independently of $X_i$, which they are if $X_i$ is randomly assigned (Exercise 13.9). Thus, if $X_i$ is randomly assigned, $\hat{\beta}_1$ is a consistent estimator of the average causal effect $E(\beta_{1i})$.

## IV Regression with Heterogeneous Causal Effects

Suppose that the causal effect is estimated by instrumental variables regression of $Y_i$ on $X_i$ (treatment actually received) using $Z_i$ (initial randomly or "as if" randomly assigned treatment) as an instrument. Suppose that $Z_i$ is a valid instrument (relevant and exogenous) and that there is heterogeneity in the effect on $X_i$ of $Z_i$. Specifically, suppose that $X_i$ is related to $Z_i$ by the linear model

$$X_i = \pi_{0i} + \pi_{1i}Z_i + v_i, \tag{13.11}$$

where the coefficients $\pi_{0i}$ and $\pi_{1i}$ vary from one individual to the next. Equation (13.11) is the first-stage equation of TSLS with the modification that the effect on $X_i$ of a change in $Z_i$ is allowed to vary from one individual to the next.

The TSLS estimator is $\hat{\beta}_1^{TSLS} = s_{ZY}/s_{ZX}$ [Equation (12.4)], the ratio of the sample covariance between $Z$ and $Y$ to the sample covariance between $Z$ and $X$. If the observations are i.i.d., then these sample covariances are consistent estimators of the population covariances, so $\hat{\beta}_1^{TSLS} \xrightarrow{p} \sigma_{ZY}/\sigma_{ZX}$. Suppose that $\pi_{0i}, \pi_{1i}, \beta_{0i}$, and $\beta_{1i}$ are distributed independently of $u_i$, $v_i$, and $Z_i$; that $E(u_i|Z_i) = E(v_i|Z_i) = 0$; and that $E(\pi_{1i}) \neq 0$ (instrument relevance). It is shown in Appendix 13.2 that, under these assumptions,

$$\hat{\beta}_1^{TSLS} = \frac{s_{ZY}}{s_{ZX}} \xrightarrow{p} \frac{\sigma_{ZY}}{\sigma_{ZX}} = \frac{E(\beta_{1i}\pi_{1i})}{E(\pi_{1i})}. \tag{13.12}$$

That is, the TSLS estimator converges in probability to the ratio of the expected value of the product of $\beta_{1i}$ and $\pi_{1i}$ to the expected value of $\pi_{1i}$.

The final ratio in Equation (13.12) is a weighted average of the individual causal effects $\beta_{1i}$. The weights are $\pi_{1i}/E\pi_{1i}$, which measure the relative degree to which the instrument influences whether the $i^{th}$ individual receives treatment. Thus the TSLS estimator is a consistent estimator of a weighted average of the individual causal effects, where the individuals who receive the most weight are those for whom the instrument is most influential. The weighted average causal effect that is estimated by TSLS is called the **local average treatment effect** (LATE). The term "local" emphasizes that it is the weighted average that places the most weight on those individuals (more generally, entities) whose treatment probability is most influenced by the instrumental variable.

There are three special cases in which the local average treatment effect equals the average treatment effect:

1. The treatment effect is the same for all individuals. This case corresponds to $\beta_{1i} = \beta_1$ for all $i$. Then the final expression in Equation (13.12) simplifies to $E(\beta_{1i}\pi_{1i})/E(\pi_{1i}) = \beta_1 E(\pi_{1i})/E(\pi_{1i}) = \beta_1$.

2. The instrument affects each individual equally. This case corresponds to $\pi_{1i} = \pi_1$ for all $i$. In this case, the final expression in Equation (13.12) simplifies to $E(\beta_{1i}\pi_{1i})/E(\pi_{1i}) = E(\beta_{1i})\pi_1/\pi_1 = E(\beta_{1i})$.

3. The heterogeneity in the treatment effect and heterogeneity in the effect of the instrument are uncorrelated. This case corresponds to $\beta_{1i}$ and $\pi_{1i}$ being random but $\text{cov}(\beta_{1i}, \pi_{1i}) = 0$. Because $E(\beta_{1i}\pi_{1i}) = \text{cov}(\beta_{1i}, \pi_{1i}) + E(\beta_{1i})E(\pi_{1i})$ [Equation (2.34)], if $\text{cov}(\beta_{1i}, \pi_{1i}) = 0$, then $E(\beta_{1i}\pi_{1i}) = E(\beta_{1i})E(\pi_{1i})$ and the final expression in Equation (13.12) simplifies to $E(\beta_{1i}\pi_{1i})/E(\pi_{1i}) = E(\beta_{1i})E(\pi_{1i})/E(\pi_{1i}) = E(\beta_{1i})$.

In each of these three cases, there is population heterogeneity in the effect of the instrument, in the effect of the treatment, or both, but the local average treatment effect equals the average treatment effect. That is, in all three cases, TSLS is a consistent estimator of the average treatment effect.

Aside from these three special cases, in general the local average treatment effect differs from the average treatment effect. For example, suppose that $Z_i$ has no influence on the treatment decision for half the population (for them, $\pi_{1i} = 0$) and that $Z_i$ has the same, nonzero influence on the treatment decision for the other half (for them, $\pi_{1i}$ is a nonzero constant). Then TSLS is a consistent estimator of the average treatment effect in the half of the population for which the instrument influences the treatment decision. To be concrete, suppose that workers are eligible for a job training program and are randomly assigned a priority number $Z$, which influences how likely they are to be admitted to the program. Half the workers know they will benefit from the program and thus may decide to enroll in the program; for them, $\beta_{1i} = \beta_1^+ > 0$ and $\pi_{1i} = \pi_1^+ > 0$. The other half know that, for them, the program is ineffective so they would not enroll even if admitted, that is, for them $\beta_{1i} = 0$ and $\pi_{1i} = 0$. The average treatment effect is $E(\beta_{1i}) = \frac{1}{2}(\beta_1^+ + 0) = \frac{1}{2}\beta_1^+$. The local average treatment effect is $E(\beta_{1i}\pi_{1i})/E(\pi_{1i})$. Now $E(\pi_{1i}) = \frac{1}{2}\pi_1^+$ and $E(\beta_{1i}\pi_{1i}) = E[\beta_{1i}E(\pi_{1i}|\beta_{1i})] = \frac{1}{2}(0 + \beta_1^+\pi_1^+) = \frac{1}{2}\beta_1^+\pi_1^+$, so $E(\beta_{1i}\pi_{1i})/E(\pi_{1i}) = \beta_1^+$. Thus, in this example, the local average treatment effect is the causal effect for those workers who are likely to enroll in the program, and it gives no weight to those who will not enroll under any circumstances. In contrast, the average treatment effect places equal weight on all individuals, regardless of whether they would enroll. Because individuals decide to enroll based in part on their knowledge of how effective the program will be for them, in this example the local average treatment effect exceeds the average treatment effect.

*Implications.*  If an individual's decision to receive treatment depends on the effectiveness of the treatment for that individual, then the TSLS estimator in general is not a consistent estimator of the average causal effect. Instead, TSLS estimates a local average treatment effect, where the causal effects of the individuals who are most influenced by the instrument receive the greatest weight. This conclusion leads to a disconcerting situation in which two researchers, armed with different instrumental variables that are both valid in the sense that both are relevant and exogenous, would obtain different estimates of "the" causal effect, even in large samples. The difference arises because each researcher is implicitly estimating a different weighted average of the individual causal effects in the population. In fact, a *J*-test of overidentifying restrictions can reject if the two instruments estimate different local average treatment effects, even if both instruments are valid. Although both estimators provide some insight into the distribution of the causal effects via their respective weighted averages of the form in Equation (13.12), in general neither estimator is a consistent estimator of the average causal effect.[5]

*Example: The cardiac catheterization study.*  Sections 12.5 and 13.4 discuss McClellan, McNeil, and Newhouse's (1991) study of the effect on mortality of cardiac catheterization of heart attack patients. The authors used instrumental variables regression, with the relative distance to a cardiac catheterization hospital as the instrumental variable. Based on their TSLS estimates, they found that cardiac catheterization had little or no effect on health outcomes. This result is surprising: Medical procedures such as cardiac catheterization are subjected to rigorous clinical trials prior to approval for widespread use. Moreover, cardiac catheterization allows surgeons to perform medical interventions that would have

---

[5]There are several good (but advanced) discussions of the effect of population heterogeneity on program evaluation estimators. They include the survey by Heckman, LaLonde, and Smith (1999, Section 7) and James Heckman's lecture delivered when he received the Nobel Prize in economics (Heckman, 2001, Section 7). The latter reference and Angrist, Graddy, and Imbens (2000) provide detailed discussion of the random effects model (which treats $\beta_{1i}$ as varying across individuals) and provide more general versions of the result in Equation (13.12). The concept of the local average treatment effect was introduced by Angrist and Imbens (1994), who showed that in general it does not equal the average treatment effect.

required major surgery a decade earlier, making these interventions safer and, presumably, better for long-term patient health. How could this econometric study fail to find beneficial effects of cardiac catheterization?

One possible answer is that there is heterogeneity in the treatment effect of cardiac catheterization. For some patients, this procedure is an effective intervention, but for others, perhaps those who are healthier, it is less effective or, given the risks involved with any surgery, perhaps on the whole ineffective. Thus the average causal effect in the population of heart attack patients could be, and presumably is, positive. The IV estimator, however, measures a marginal effect, not an average effect, where the marginal effect is the effect of the procedure on those patients for whom distance to the hospital is an important factor in whether they receive treatment. But those patients could be just the relatively healthy patients for whom, on the margin, cardiac catheterization is a relatively ineffective procedure. If so, McClellan, McNeil, and Newhouse's (1991) TSLS estimator measures the effect of the procedure for the marginal patient (for whom it is relatively ineffective), not for the average patient (for whom it might be effective).

## 13.7 Conclusion

In Chapter 1, we defined the causal effect in terms of the expected outcome of an ideal randomized controlled experiment. If a randomized controlled experiment is available or can be performed, it can provide compelling evidence on the causal effect under study, although even randomized controlled experiments are subject to potentially important threats to internal and external validity.

Despite their advantages, randomized controlled experiments in economics face considerable hurdles, including ethical concerns and cost. The insights of experimental methods can, however, be applied to quasi-experiments, in which special circumstances make it seem "as if" randomization has occurred. In quasi-experiments, the causal effect can be estimated using a differences-in-differences estimator, possibly augmented with additional regressors; if the "as if" randomization only partly influences the treatment, then instrumental variables regression can be used instead. An important advantage of quasi-experiments is that the source of the "as if" randomness in the data is usually transparent and thus can be evaluated in a concrete way. An important threat confronting quasi-experiments is that sometimes the "as if" randomization is not really random, so the treatment (or the instrumental variable) is correlated with omitted variables and the resulting estimator of the causal effect is biased.

Quasi-experiments provide a bridge between observational data sets and true randomized controlled experiments. The econometric methods used in this chapter for analyzing quasi-experiments are those developed in different contexts, in earlier chapters: OLS, panel data estimation methods, and instrumental variables regression. What differentiates quasi-experiments from the applications examined in Part II and the earlier chapters in Part III are the way in which these methods are interpreted and the data sets to which they are applied. Quasi-experiments provide econometricians with a way to think about how to acquire new data sets, how to think of instrumental variables, and how to evaluate the plausibility of the exogeneity assumptions that underlie OLS and instrumental variables estimation.[6]

## Summary

1.  The average causal effect in the population under study is the expected difference in the average outcomes for the treatment and control groups in an ideal randomized controlled experiment. Actual experiments with human subjects deviate from an ideal experiment for various practical reasons, including the failure of people to comply with the experimental protocol.

2.  If the *actual* treatment level $X_i$ is random, then the treatment effect can be estimated by regressing the outcome on the treatment. If the *assigned* treatment $Z_i$ is random but the actual treatment $X_i$ is partly determined by individual choice, then the causal effect can be estimated by instrumental variables regression, using $Z_i$ as an instrument. If the treatment (or assigned treatment) is random conditional on some variables $W$, those control variables need to be included in the regressions.

3.  In a quasi-experiment, variations in laws or circumstances or accidents of nature are treated "as if" they induce random assignment to treatment and control groups. If the actual treatment is "as if" random, then the causal effect can be estimated by regression (possibly with additional pretreatment characteristics as regressors); if the assigned treatment is "as if" random, then the causal effect can be estimated by instrumental variables regression.

---

[6]Shadish, Cook, and Campbell (2002) provide a comprehensive treatment of experiments and quasi-experiments in the social sciences and in psychology. An important line of research in development economics focuses on experimental evaluations of health and education programs in developing countries. For examples, see Kremer, Miguel, and Thornton (2009) and the website of MIT's Poverty Action Laboratory (http://www.povertyactionlab.org). Deaton (2010) provides a thoughtful critique of this research.

4. Regression discontinuity estimators are based on quasi-experiments in which treatment depends on whether an observable variable crosses a threshold value.

5. A key threat to the internal validity of a quasi-experimental study is whether the "as if" randomization actually results in exogeneity. Because of behavioral responses, the regression error may change in response to the treatment induced by the quasi-experiment, so the treatment is not exogenous.

6. When the treatment effect varies from one individual to the next, the OLS estimator is a consistent estimator of the average causal effect if the actual treatment is randomly assigned or "as if" randomly assigned. However, the instrumental variables estimator is a weighted average of the individual treatment effects, where the individuals for whom the instrument is most influential receive the greatest weight.

## Key Terms

program evaluation (521)
potential outcome (522)
average causal effect (523)
average treatment effect (523)
differences estimator (524)
differences estimator with additional regressors (524)
randomization based on covariates (525)
test for random receipt of treatment (526)
partial compliance (526)

instrumental variables estimation of the treatment effect (527)
attrition (527)
Hawthorne effect (528)
quasi-experiment (539)
natural experiment (539)
differences-in-differences estimator (542)
differences-in-differences estimator with additional regressors (544)
repeated cross-sectional data (545)
regression discontinuity (546)
local average treatment effect (552)

---

**MyEconLab Can Help You Get a Better Grade**

**MyEconLab**   If your exam were tomorrow, would you be ready? For each chapter, **MyEconLab** Practice Tests and Study Plan help you prepare for your exams. You can also find similar Exercises and Review the Concepts Questions now in **MyEconLab**.
To see how it works, turn to the **MyEconLab** spread on pages 2 and 3 of this book and then go to **www.myeconlab.com**.

For additional Empirical Exercises and Data Sets, log on to the Companion Website at **www.pearsonglobaleditions.com/Stock_Watson**.

## Review the Concepts

**13.1** A researcher studying the effects of a new fertilizer on crop yields plans to carry out an experiment in which different amounts of the fertilizer are applied to 100 different 1-acre parcels of land. There will be four treatment levels. Treatment level 1 is no fertilizer, treatment level 2 is 50% of the manufacturer's recommended amount of fertilizer, treatment level 3 is 100%, and treatment level 4 is 150%. The researcher plans to apply treatment level 1 to the first 25 parcels of land, treatment level 2 to the second 25 parcels, and so forth. Can you suggest a better way to assign treatment levels? Why is your proposal better than the researcher's method?

**13.2** A clinical trial is carried out for a new cholesterol-lowering drug. The drug is given to 500 patients, and a placebo is given to another 500 patients, using random assignment of the patients. How would you estimate the treatment effect of the drug? Suppose that you had data on the weight, age, and gender of each patient. Could you use these data to improve your estimate? Explain. Suppose that you had data on the cholesterol levels of each patient before he or she entered the experiment. Could you use these data to improve your estimate? Explain.

**13.3** Researchers studying the STAR data report anecdotal evidence that school principals were pressured by some parents to place their children in the small classes. Suppose that some principals succumbed to this pressure and transferred some children into the small classes. How would such transfers compromise the internal validity of the study? Suppose that you had data on the original random assignment of each student before the principal's intervention. How could you use this information to restore the internal validity of the study?

**13.4** What are experimental effects? How can they create biased treatment effects and what can a researcher do to reduce the bias?

**13.5** Consider the quasi-experiment described in Section 13.4 involving the draft lottery, military service, and civilian earnings. Explain why there might be heterogeneous effects of military service on civilian earnings; that is, explain why $\beta_{1i}$ in Equation (13.9) depends on $i$. Explain why there might be heterogeneous effects of the lottery outcome on the probability of military service; that is, explain why $\pi_{1i}$ in Equation (13.11) depends on $i$. If there are heterogeneous responses of the sort you described, what behavioral parameter is being estimated by the TSLS estimator?

## Exercises

**13.1**   How would you calculate the small class treatment effect from the results in Table 13.1. Can you distinguish this treatment effect from the aide treatment effect? How would you change the program to correctly estimate both effects?

**13.2**   For the following calculations, use the results in column (3) of Table 13.2. Consider two classrooms, A and B, with identical values of the regressors in column (3) of Table 13.2, except that:

**a.** Classroom A is a "small class," and classroom B is a "regular class." Construct a 90% confidence interval for the expected difference in average test scores.

**b.** Classroom A has a teacher with 6 years of experience, and classroom B has a teacher with 12 years of experience. Construct a 95% confidence interval for the expected difference in average test scores.

**c.** Classroom A is a small class with a teacher with 6 years of experience, and classroom B is a regular class with a teacher with 12 years of experience. Construct a 95% confidence interval for the expected difference in average test scores. (*Hint:* In STAR, the teachers were randomly assigned to the different types of classrooms.)

**d.** Why is the intercept missing from column (4)?

**13.3**   Suppose in a randomized controlled experiment of the effect of a SAT preparatory course on SAT scores, the following results are reported:

|  | Treatment Group | Control Group |
|---|---|---|
| Average SAT score ($\overline{X}$) | 1348 | 1395 |
| Standard deviation of SAT score ($S_X$) | 87.3 | 82.1 |
| Number of men | 60 | 40 |
| Number of women | 40 | 60 |

**a.** Estimate the average treatment effect on test scores.

**b.** Is there evidence of nonrandom assignment? Explain.

**13.4**   Read the box "What Is the Effect on Employment of the Minimum Wage?" in Section 13.4. Suppose, for concreteness, that Card and Krueger collected their data in 1991 (before the change in the New Jersey minimum wage) and in 1993 (after the change in the New Jersey minimum wage). Consider Equation (13.7) with the $W$ regressors excluded.

**a.** What are the values of $X_{it}$, $G_i$, and $D_t$ for:

   i. A New Jersey restaurant in 1991?

   ii. A New Jersey restaurant in 1993?

   iii. A Pennsylvania restaurant in 1991?

   iv. A Pennsylvania restaurant in 1993?

**b.** In terms of the coefficients $\beta_0$, $\beta_1$, $\beta_2$, and $\beta_3$, what is the expected number of employees in:

   i. A New Jersey restaurant in 1991?

   ii. A New Jersey restaurant in 1993?

   iii. A Pennsylvania restaurant in 1991?

   iv. A Pennsylvania restaurant in 1993?

**c.** In terms of the coefficients $\beta_0$, $\beta_1$, $\beta_2$, and $\beta_3$, what is the average causal effect of the minimum wage on employment?

**d.** Explain why Card and Krueger used a differences-in-differences estimator of the causal effect instead of the "New Jersey after—New Jersey before" differences estimator or the "1993 New Jersey—1993 Pennsylvania" differences estimator.

**13.5** Consider a study to evaluate the effect on college student grades of dorm room Internet connections. In a large dorm, half the rooms are randomly wired for high-speed Internet connections (the treatment group), and final course grades are collected for all residents. Which of the following pose threats to internal validity, and why?

**a.** Midway through the year, all the male athletes move into a fraternity and drop out of the study. (Their final grades are not observed.)

**b.** Engineering students assigned to the control group put together a local area network so that they can share a private wireless Internet connection that they pay for jointly.

**c.** The art majors in the treatment group never learn how to access their Internet accounts.

**d.** The economics majors in the treatment group provide access to their Internet connection to those in the control group, for a fee.

**13.6** Suppose that there are panel data for $T = 2$ time periods for a randomized controlled experiment, where the first observation ($t = 1$) is taken before the experiment and the second observation ($t = 2$) is for the post-treatment period. Suppose that the treatment is binary; that is, suppose that $X_{it} = 1$ if the $i^{th}$ individual is in the treatment group and $t = 2$, and $X_{it} = 0$ otherwise. Further suppose that the treatment effect can be modeled using the specification

$$Y_{it} = \alpha_i + \beta_1 X_{it} + u_{it},$$

where $\alpha_i$ are individual-specific effects [see Equation (13.11)] with a mean of zero and a variance of $\sigma_\alpha^2$ and $u_{it}$ is an error term, where $u_{it}$ is homoskedastic, $\text{cov}(u_{i1}, u_{i2}) = 0$, and $\text{cov}(u_{it}, \alpha_i) = 0$ for all $i$. Let $\hat{\beta}_1^{differences}$ denote the differences estimator — that is, the OLS estimator in a regression of $Y_{i2}$ on $X_{i2}$ with an intercept — and let $\hat{\beta}_1^{diffs-in-diffs}$ denote the differences-in-differences estimator — that is, the estimator of $\beta_1$ based on the OLS regression of $\Delta Y_i = Y_{i2} - Y_{i1}$ against $\Delta X_i = X_{i2} - X_{i1}$ and an intercept.

**a.** Show that $n\text{var}(\hat{\beta}_1^{differences}) \longrightarrow (\sigma_u^2 + \sigma_\alpha^2)/\text{var}(X_{i2})$. (*Hint:* Use the homoskedasticity-only formulas for the variance of the OLS estimator in Appendix 5.1.)

**b.** Show that $n\text{var}(\hat{\beta}_1^{diffs-in-diffs}) \longrightarrow 2\sigma_u^2/\text{var}(X_{i2})$. (*Hint:* Note that $X_{i2} - X_{i1} = X_{i2}$. Why?)

**c.** Based on your answers to (a) and (b), when would you prefer the differences-in-differences estimator over the differences estimator, based purely on efficiency considerations?

**13.7** Suppose that you have panel data from an experiment with $T = 2$ periods (so $t = 1, 2$). Consider the panel data regression model with fixed individual and time effects and individual characteristics $W_i$ that do not change over time, such as gender. Let the treatment be binary, so that $X_{it} = 1$ for $t = 2$ for the individuals in the treatment group and let $X_{it} = 0$ otherwise. Consider the population regression model

$$Y_{it} = \alpha_i + \beta_1 X_{it} + \beta_2(D_t \times W_i) + \beta_0 D_t + v_{it},$$

where $\alpha_i$ are individual fixed effects, $D_t$ is the binary variable that equals 1 if $t = 2$ and equals 0 if $t = 1$, $D_t \times W_i$ is the product of $D_t$ and $W_i$, and the $\alpha$'s and $\beta$'s are unknown coefficients. Let $\Delta Y_i = Y_{i2} - Y_{i1}$. Derive Equation (13.6) (in the case of a single $W$ regressor, so $r = 1$) from this population regression model.

**13.8**  Suppose that you have the same data as in Exercise 13.7 (panel data with two periods, $n$ observations), but ignore the $W$ regressor. Consider the alternative regression model

$$Y_{it} = \beta_0 + \beta_1 X_{it} + \beta_2 G_i + \beta_3 D_t + u_{it},$$

where $G_i = 1$ if the individual is in the treatment group and $G_i = 0$ if the individual is in the control group. Show that the OLS estimator of $\beta_1$ is the differences-in-differences estimator in Equation (13.4). (*Hint:* See Section 8.3.)

**13.9**  Derive the final equality in Equation (13.10). (*Hint:* Use the definition of the covariance and that, because the actual treatment $X_i$ is random, $\beta_{1i}$ and $X_i$ are independently distributed.)

**13.10**  Consider the regression model with heterogeneous regression coefficients

$$Y_i = \beta_{0i} + \beta_{1i} X_i + v_i,$$

where $(v_i, X_i, \beta_{0i}, \beta_{1i})$ are i.i.d. random variables with $\beta_0 = E(\beta_{0i})$ and $\beta_1 = E(\beta_{1i})$.

**a.**  Show that the model can be written as $Y_i = \beta_0 + \beta_1 X_i + u_i$, where $u_i = (\beta_{0i} - \beta_0) + (\beta_{1i} - \beta_1)X_i + v_i$.

**b.**  Suppose that $E[\beta_{0i} | X_i] = \beta_0$, $E[\beta_{1i} | X_i] = \beta_1$, and $E[v_i | X_i] = 0$. Show that $E[u_i | X_i] = 0$.

**c.**  Show that Assumption #1 and Assumption #2 of Key Concept 4.3 are satisfied.

**d.**  Suppose that outliers are rare so that $(u_i, X_i)$ have finite fourth moments. Is it appropriate to use OLS and the methods of Chapters 4 and 5 to estimate and carry out inference about the average values of $\beta_{0i}$ and $\beta_{1i}$?

**e.**  Suppose that $\beta_{1i}$ and $X_i$ are positively correlated so that observations with larger-than-average values of $X_i$ tend to have larger-than-average values of $\beta_{1i}$. Are the assumptions in Key Concept 4.3 satisfied? If not, which assumption(s) is (are) violated? Is it appropriate to use OLS and the methods of Chapters 4 and 5 to estimate and carry out inference about the average value of $\beta_{0i}$ and $\beta_{1i}$?

**13.11**  Results of a study by McClelan, McNeill, and Newhouse are reported in Chapter 12. They estimate the effect of cardiac catheterization on patient survival times. They instrument the use of cardiac catheterization by the distance between a patient's home and a hospital that offers the treatment. Do you think the local average treatment effect differs from the average treatment effect?

**13.12** Consider the potential outcomes framework from Appendix 13.3. Suppose that $X_i$ is a binary treatment that is independent of the potential outcomes $Y_i(1)$ and $Y_i(0)$. Let $TE_i = Y_i(1) - Y_i(0)$ denote the treatment effect for individual $i$.

    **a.** Can you consistently estimate $E[Y_i(1)]$ and $E[Y_i(0)]$? If yes, explain how; if not, explain why not.

    **b.** Can you consistently estimate $E(TE_i)$? If yes, explain how; if not, explain why not.

    **c.** Can you consistently estimate $\text{var}[Y_i(1)]$ and $\text{var}[Y_i(0)]$? If yes, explain how; if not, explain why not.

    **d.** Can you consistently estimate $\text{var}(TE_i)$? If yes, explain how; if not, explain why not.

    **e.** Do you think you can consistently estimate the median treatment effect in the population? Explain.

## Empirical Exercises

(Only one empirical exercise for this chapter is given in the text, but you can find more on the text Web site **www.pearsonglobaleditions.com/Stock_Watson**.)

**E13.1** A prospective employer receives two resumes: a resume from a white job applicant and a similar resume from an African American applicant. Is the employer more likely to call back the white applicant to arrange an interview? Marianne Bertrand and Sendhil Mullainathan carried out a randomized controlled experiment to answer this question. Because race is not typically included on a resume, they differentiated resumes on the basis of "white-sounding names" (such as Emily Walsh or Gregory Baker) and "African American–sounding names" (such as Lakisha Washington or Jamal Jones). A large collection of fictitious resumes was created, and the presupposed "race" (based on the "sound" of the name) was randomly assigned to each resume. These resumes were sent to prospective employers to see which resumes generated a phone call (a "call back") from the prospective employer. Data from the experiment and a detailed data description are on the textbook website, **www.pearsonglobaleditions.com/ Stock_Watson**, in the files **Names** and **Names_Description**.[7]

---

[7]These data were provided by Professor Marianne Bertrand of the University of Chicago and were used in her paper with Sendhil Mullainathan, "Are Emily and Greg More Employable Than Lakisha and Jamal? A Field Experiment on Labor Market Discrimination," *American Economic Review*, 2004, 94(4): 991–1013.

   **a.** Define the "call-back rate" as the fraction of resumes that generate a phone call from the prospective employer. What was the call-back rate for whites? For African Americans? Construct a 95% confidence interval for the difference in the call-back rates. Is the difference statistically significant? Is it large in a real-world sense?

   **b.** Is the African American/white call-back rate differential different for men than for women?

   **c.** What is the difference in call-back rates for high-quality versus low-quality resumes? What is the high-quality/low-quality difference for white applicants? For African American applicants? Is there a significant difference in this high-quality/low-quality difference for whites versus African Americans?

   **d.** The authors of the study claim that race was assigned randomly to the resumes. Is there any evidence of nonrandom assignment?

---

**APPENDIX**

## 13.1   The Project STAR Data Set

The Project STAR public access data set contains data on test scores, treatment groups, and student and teacher characteristics for the 4 years of the experiment, from academic year 1985–1986 to academic year 1988–1989. The test score data analyzed in this chapter are the sum of the scores on the math and reading portions of the Stanford Achievement Test. The binary variable "Boy" in Table 13.2 indicates whether the student is a boy ($= 1$) or girl ($= 0$); the binary variables "Black" and "Race other than black or white" indicate the student's race. The binary variable "Free lunch eligible" indicates whether the student is eligible for a free lunch during that school year. The teacher's years of experience are the total years of experience of the teacher whom the student had in the grade for which the test data apply. The data set also indicates which school the student attended in a given year, making it possible to construct binary school-specific indicator variables.

---

**APPENDIX**

## 13.2   IV Estimation When the Causal Effect Varies Across Individuals

This appendix derives the probability limit of the TSLS estimator in Equation (13.12) when there is population heterogeneity in the treatment effect and in the influence of the instrument on the receipt of treatment. Specifically, it is assumed that the IV regression assumptions in Key Concept 12.4 hold, except that Equations (13.9) and (13.11) hold with heterogeneous effects. Further assume that $\pi_{0i}$, $\pi_{1i}$, $\beta_{0i}$, and $\beta_{1i}$ are distributed independently of $u_i$, $v_i$, and $Z_i$; that $E(u_i|Z_i) = E(v_i|Z_i) = 0$; and that $E(\pi_{1i}) \neq 0$.

Because $(X_i, Y_i, Z_i)$, $i = 1, \ldots, n$ are i.i.d. with four moments, the law of large numbers in Key Concept 2.6 applies and

$$\hat{\beta}_1^{TSLS} = \frac{s_{ZY}}{s_{ZX}} \xrightarrow{p} \frac{\sigma_{ZY}}{\sigma_{ZX}}. \tag{13.13}$$

(See Appendix 3.3 and Exercise 17.2.) The task thus is to obtain expressions for $\sigma_{ZY}$ and $\sigma_{ZX}$ in terms of the moments of $\pi_{1i}$ and $\beta_{1i}$. Now $\sigma_{ZX} = E[(Z_i - \mu_Z)(X_i - \mu_X)] = E[(Z_i - \mu_Z)X_i]$. Substituting Equation (13.11) into this expression for $\sigma_{ZX}$ yields

$$\begin{aligned}
\sigma_{ZX} &= E[(Z_i - \mu_Z)(\pi_{0i} + \pi_{1i}Z_i + v_i)] \\
&= E(\pi_{0i}) \times 0 + E[\pi_{1i}Z_i(Z_i - \mu_Z)] + \text{cov}(Z_i, v_i) \\
&= \sigma_Z^2 E(\pi_{1i}),
\end{aligned} \tag{13.14}$$

where the second equality follows because $\text{cov}(Z_i, v_i) = 0$ [which follows from the assumption $E(v_i|Z_i) = 0$; see Equation (2.27)], because $E[(Z_i - \mu_Z)\pi_{0i}] = E\{E[(Z_i - \mu_Z)\pi_{0i}|Z_i]\} = E[(Z_i - \mu_Z)E(\pi_{0i}|Z_i)] = E(Z_i - \mu_Z) \times E(\pi_{0i})$ (which uses the law of iterated expectations and the assumption that $\pi_{0i}$ is independent of $Z_i$), and because $E[\pi_{1i}Z_i(Z_i - \mu_Z)] = E\{E[\pi_{1i}Z_i(Z_i - \mu_Z)|Z_i]\} = E(\pi_{1i})E[Z_i(Z_i - \mu_Z)] = \sigma_Z^2 E(\pi_{1i})$ (which uses the law of iterated expectations and the assumption that $\pi_{1i}$ is independent of $Z_i$).

Next consider $\sigma_{ZY}$. Substituting Equation (13.11) into Equation (13.9) yields $Y_i = \beta_{0i} + \beta_{1i}(\pi_{0i} + \pi_{1i}Z_i + v_i) + u_i$, so

$$\begin{aligned}
\sigma_{ZY} &= E[(Z_i - \mu_Z)Y_i] \\
&= E[(Z_i - \mu_Z)(\beta_{0i} + \beta_{1i}\pi_{0i} + \beta_{1i}\pi_{1i}Z_i + \beta_{1i}v_i + u_i)] \\
&= E(\beta_{0i}) \times 0 + \text{cov}(Z_i, \beta_{1i}\pi_{0i}) + E[\beta_{1i}\pi_{1i}Z_i(Z_i - \mu_Z)] \\
&\quad + E[\beta_{1i}v_i(Z_i - \mu_Z)] + \text{cov}(Z_i, u_i).
\end{aligned} \tag{13.15}$$

Because $(\beta_{1i}\pi_{0i})$ and $Z_i$ are independently distributed, $\text{cov}(Z_i, \beta_{1i}\pi_{0i}) = 0$; because $\beta_{1i}$ is distributed independently of $v_i$ and $Z_i$ and $E(v_i|Z_i) = 0$, $E[\beta_{1i}v_i(Z_i - \mu_Z)] = E(\beta_{1i}) \times E[v_i(Z_i - \mu_Z)] = 0$; because $E(u_i|Z_i) = 0$, $\text{cov}(Z_i, u_i) = 0$ ; and because $\beta_{1i}$ and $\pi_{1i}$ are distributed independently of $Z_i$, $E[\beta_{1i}\pi_{1i}Z_i(Z_i - \mu_Z)] = \sigma_Z^2 E(\beta_{1i}\pi_{1i})$. Thus the final expression in Equation (13.15) yields

$$\sigma_{ZY} = \sigma_Z^2 E(\beta_{1i}\pi_{1i}). \tag{13.16}$$

Substituting Equations (13.14) and (13.16) into Equation (13.13) yields $\hat{\beta}_1^{TSLS} \xrightarrow{p} \sigma_Z^2 E(\beta_{1i}\pi_{1i})/\sigma_Z^2 E(\pi_{1i}) = E(\beta_{1i}\pi_{1i})/E(\pi_{1i})$, which is the result stated in Equation (13.12).

## 13.3 The Potential Outcomes Framework for Analyzing Data from Experiments

This appendix provides a mathematical treatment of the potential outcomes framework discussed in Section 13.1. The potential outcomes framework, combined with a constant treatment effect, implies the regression model in Equation (13.1). If assignment is random, conditional on covariates, the potential outcomes framework leads to Equation (13.2) and conditional mean independence. We consider a binary treatment with $X_i = 1$ indicating receipt of treatment.

Let $Y_i(1)$ denote individual $i$'s potential outcome if treatment is received and let $Y_i(0)$ denote the potential outcome if treatment is not received, so individual $i$'s treatment effect is $Y_i(1) - Y_i(0)$. The average treatment effect in the population is $E[Y_i(1) - Y_i(0)]$. Because the individual is either treated or not, only one of the two potential outcomes is observed. The observed outcome, $Y_i$, is related to the potential outcomes by

$$Y_i = Y_i(1)X_i + Y_i(0)(1 - X_i). \tag{13.17}$$

If some individuals receive the treatment and some do not, the expected difference in observed outcomes between the two groups is $E(Y_i|X_i = 1) - E(Y_i|X_i = 0) = E[Y_i(1)|X_i = 1] - E[Y_i(0)|X_i = 0]$. This is true no matter how treatment is determined and simply says that the expected difference is the mean treatment outcome for the treated minus the mean no-treatment outcome for the untreated. If in addition the individuals are randomly assigned to the treatment and control groups, then $X_i$ is distributed independently of all personal attributes and in particular is independent of $[Y_i(1), Y_i(0)]$. With random assignment, the mean difference between the treatment and control groups is

$$E(Y_i|X_i = 1) - E(Y_i|X_i = 0) = E[Y_i(1)|X_i = 1] - E[Y_i(0)|X_i = 0] = E[Y_i(1) - Y_i(0)], \tag{13.18}$$

where the second equality uses the fact that $[Y_i(1), Y_i(0)]$ are independent of $X_i$ by random assignment and the linearity of expectations [Equation (2.28)]. Thus if $X_i$ is randomly assigned, the mean difference in the experimental outcomes between the two groups is the average treatment effect in the population from which the subjects were drawn.

The potential outcome framework translates directly into the regression notation used throughout this book. Let $u_i = Y_i(0) - E[Y_i(0)]$ and denote $E[Y_i(0)] = \beta_0$. Also denote

$Y_i(1) - Y_i(0) = \beta_{1i}$, so that $\beta_{1i}$ is the treatment effect for individual $i$. Starting with Equation (13.17), we have

$$
\begin{aligned}
Y_i &= Y_i(1)X_i + Y_i(0)(1 - X_i) \\
&= Y_i(0) + [Y_i(1) - Y_i(0)]X_i \\
&= E[Y_i(0)] + [Y_i(1) - Y_i(0)]X_i + \{Y_i(0) - E[Y_i(0)]\} \\
&= \beta_0 + \beta_{1i}X_i + u_i.
\end{aligned}
\tag{13.19}
$$

Thus, starting with the relationship between observed and potential outcomes and simply changing notation, we obtain the random coefficients regression model in Equation (13.9). [Equation (13.9) has $\beta_0$ varying across individuals, but that is equivalent to Equation (13.19) because $u_i$ also varies across individuals.] If $X_i$ is randomly assigned, then $X_i$ is independent of $[Y_i(1), Y_i(0)]$ and thus is independent of $\beta_{1i}$ and $u_i$. If the treatment effect is constant, then $\beta_{1i} = \beta_1$ and Equation (13.9) becomes Equation (13.1).

As discussed in Appendix 7.2 and Sections 13.1 and 13.3, in some designs $X_i$ is randomly assigned based on the value of a third variable, $W_i$. If $W_i$ and the potential outcomes are not independent, then in general the mean difference between groups does not equal the average treatment effect—that is, Equation (13.18) does not hold. However, random assignment of $X_i$ given $W_i$ implies that, conditional on $W_i$, $X_i$ and $[Y_i(1), Y_i(0)]$ are independent. This condition—that $X_i$ and $[Y_i(1), Y_i(0)]$ are independent, conditional on $W_i$—is often called *unconfoundedness*.

If the treatment effect does not vary across individuals and if $E(Y|X_i, W_i)$ is linear, then unconfoundedness implies conditional mean independence of the regression error in Equation (13.2). To see this, let $Y_i(0) = \beta_0 + \gamma W_i + u_i$, where $\gamma$ is the causal effect (if any) on $Y_i(0)$ of $W_i$, and let $Y_i(1) - Y_i(0) = \beta_1$ (constant treatment effect). Then the logic leading to Equation (13.19) yields $Y_i = \beta_0 + \beta_1 X_i + \gamma W_i + u_i$, which is Equation (13.2). Now $E(u_i|X_i, W_i) = E[Y_i(0) - \beta_0 - \gamma W_i|X_i, W_i] = E[Y_i(0) - \beta_0 - \gamma W_i|W_i] = E(u_i|W_i)$, where the second equality follows from unconfoundedness (if $[Y_i(1), Y_i(0)]$ is independent of $X_i$ given $W_i$, then $E[Y_i(0)|X_i, W_i] = E[Y_i(0)|W_i]$). Thus unconfoundedness implies that $E(u_i|X_i, W_i) = E(u_i|W_i)$ in Equation (13.2). The reasoning of Appendix 7.2 implies that, if $E(u_i|W_i)$ is linear in $W_i$, then the OLS estimator of $\beta_1$ in Equation (13.2) is unbiased, although in general the OLS estimator of $\gamma$ is biased because $E(u_i|W_i) \neq 0$.

# CHAPTER 14

# Introduction to Time Series Regression and Forecasting

Time series data—data collected for a single entity at multiple points in time—can be used to answer quantitative questions for which cross-sectional data are inadequate. One such question is, what is the causal effect on a variable of interest, $Y$, of a change in another variable, $X$, over time? In other words, what is the *dynamic* causal effect on $Y$ of a change in $X$? For example, what is the effect on traffic fatalities of a law requiring passengers to wear seatbelts, both initially and subsequently, as drivers adjust to the law? Another such question is, what is your best forecast of the value of some variable at a future date? For example, what is your best forecast of next month's unemployment rate, interest rates, or stock prices? Both of these questions—one about dynamic causal effects, the other about economic forecasting—can be answered using time series data. But time series data pose special challenges, and overcoming those challenges requires some new techniques.

This chapter and Chapters 15 and 16 introduce techniques for econometric analysis of time series data and apply these techniques to the problems of forecasting and estimating dynamic causal effects. This chapter introduces the basic concepts and tools of regression with time series data and applies them to economic forecasting. Chapter 15 applies the concepts and tools developed in this chapter to the problem of estimating dynamic causal effects using time series data. Chapter 16 takes up some more advanced topics in time series analysis, including forecasting multiple time series and modeling changes in volatility over time.

The empirical problem studied in this chapter is forecasting the growth rate of U.S. Gross Domestic Product (GDP)—that is, the percentage increase in the value of goods and services produced in the U.S. economy. While in a sense forecasting is just an application of regression analysis, forecasting is quite different from the estimation of causal effects, the focus of this book until now. As discussed in Section 14.1, models that are useful for forecasting need not have a causal interpretation: If you see pedestrians carrying umbrellas, you might forecast rain, even though carrying an umbrella does not *cause* rain. Section 14.2 introduces some basic concepts of time series analysis and presents some examples of economic time series data. Section 14.3 presents time series regression models in which the regressors are past values of the dependent variable; these "autoregressive" models use the history of GDP to forecast its future. Often, forecasts based on autoregressions can be improved by adding additional predictor variables and their past values, or "lags," as regressors, and these so-called autoregressive distributed lag models are introduced in Section 14.4. For example, we find that GDP forecasts made using lagged values of the term spread, the difference between the interest rate on long-term and short-term bonds, improve upon the autoregressive GDP forecasts. A practical issue is deciding how many past values to include in autoregressions and autoregressive distributed lag models, and Section 14.5 describes methods for making this decision.

The assumption that the future will be like the past is an important one in time series regression, sufficiently so that it is given its own name: "stationarity." Time series variables can fail to be stationary in various ways, but two are especially relevant for regression analysis of economic time series data: (1) The series can have persistent, long-run movements—that is, the series can have trends; and (2) the population regression can be unstable over time—that is, the population regression can have breaks. These departures from stationarity jeopardize forecasts and inferences based on time series regression. Fortunately, there are statistical procedures for detecting trends and breaks and, once detected, for adjusting the model specification. These procedures are presented in Sections 14.6 and 14.7.

## 14.1 Using Regression Models for Forecasting

The empirical application of Chapters 4 through 9 focused on estimating the causal effect on test scores of the student–teacher ratio. The simplest regression model relates in Chapter 4 related test scores to the student–teacher ratio ($STR$):

$$\widehat{TestScore} = 989.9 - 2.28 \times STR. \tag{14.1}$$

As was discussed in Chapter 6, a school superintendent, contemplating hiring more teachers to reduce class sizes, would not consider this equation to be very helpful. The estimated slope coefficient in Equation (14.1) fails to provide a useful estimate of the causal effect on test scores of the student–teacher ratio because of probable omitted variable bias arising from the omission of school and student characteristics that are determinants of test scores and that are correlated with the student–teacher ratio.

In contrast, as discussed in Chapter 9, a parent who is considering moving to a school district might find Equation (14.1) more helpful. Even though the coefficient does not have a causal interpretation, the regression could help the parent forecast test scores in a district for which they are not publicly available. More generally, a regression model can be useful for forecasting even if none of its coefficients has a causal interpretation. From the perspective of forecasting, what is important is that the model provides as accurate a forecast as possible. Although there is no such thing as a perfect forecast, regression models can nevertheless provide forecasts that are accurate and reliable.

The applications in this chapter differ from the test score/class size prediction problem because this chapter focuses on using time series data to forecast future events. For example, the parent actually would be interested in test scores next year, after his or her child had enrolled in a school. Of course, those tests have not yet been given, so the parent must forecast the scores using currently available information. If test scores are available for past years, then a good starting point is to use data on current and past test scores to forecast future test scores. This reasoning leads directly to the autoregressive models presented in Section 14.3, in which past values of a variable are used in a linear regression to forecast future values of the series. The next step, which is taken in Section 14.4, is to extend these models to include additional predictor variables such as data on class size. Like Equation (14.1), such a regression model can produce accurate and reliable forecasts even if its coefficients have no causal interpretation. In Chapter 15, we return to problems like that faced by the school superintendent and discuss the estimation of causal effects using time series variables.

## 14.2  Introduction to Time Series Data and Serial Correlation

This section introduces some basic concepts and terminology that arise in time series econometrics. A good place to start any analysis of time series data is by plotting the data, so that is where we begin.

### Real GDP in the United States

**Gross Domestic Product (GDP)** measures the value of goods and services produced in an economy over a given time period. Figure 14.1 a plots values of "real" GDP per year in the United States from 1960 through 2012, where "real" indicates that the values have been adjusted for inflation. The values of GDP are expressed in $1996, which means that the price level is held fixed at its 1996 value. Because U.S. GDP grows at approximately an exponential rate, Figure 14.1 a plots GDP on a logarithmic scale. GDP increased dramatically over a recent 52-year period, from approximately $3 trillion in 1960 to over $15 trillion in 2012. Measured on a logarithmic scale, this five-fold increase corresponds to an increase of 1.6 log points.

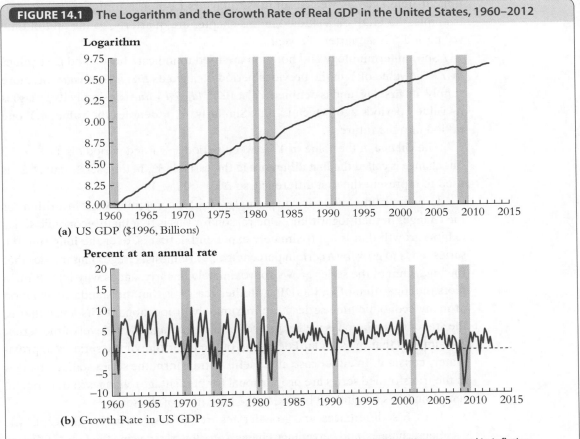

**FIGURE 14.1**   The Logarithm and the Growth Rate of Real GDP in the United States, 1960–2012

**(a)** US GDP ($1996, Billions)

**(b)** Growth Rate in US GDP

GDP increased from $3 trillion per year in 1960 to over $15 trillion per year in 2012, when measured in inflation-adjusted $1996. This five-fold increase corresponds to an increase of 1.6 log points. The growth rate of GDP was not constant, and it varied considerably from quarter to quarter.

The rate of growth was not constant, however, and the figure shows declines in GDP during the recessions of 1960–1961, 1970, 1974–1975, 1980, 1981–1982, 1990–1991, 2001, and 2007–2009, episodes denoted by shading in Figure 14.1.

## Lags, First Differences, Logarithms, and Growth Rates

The observation on the time series variable $Y$ made at date $t$ is denoted $Y_t$, and the total number of observations is denoted $T$. The interval between observations—that is, the period of time between observation $t$ and observation $t + 1$—is some unit of time such as weeks, months, quarters (3-month units), or years. For example, the GDP data studied in this chapter are quarterly, so the unit of time (a "period") is a quarter of a year.

Special terminology and notation are used to indicate future and past values of $Y$. The value of $Y$ in the previous period is called its *first lagged value* or, more simply, its **first lag**, and is denoted $Y_{t-1}$. Its $j^{th}$ *lagged value* (or simply its $j^{th}$ **lag**) is its value $j$ periods ago, which is $Y_{t-j}$. Similarly, $Y_{t+1}$ denotes the value of $Y$ one period into the future.

The change in the value of $Y$ between period $t-1$ and period $t$ is $Y_t - Y_{t-1}$; this change is called the **first difference** in the variable $Y_t$. In time series data, "$\Delta$" is used to represent the first difference, so $\Delta Y_t = Y_t - Y_{t-1}$.

Economic time series are often analyzed after computing their logarithms or the changes in their logarithms. One reason for this is that many economic series exhibit growth that is approximately exponential; that is, over the long run, the series tends to grow by a certain percentage per year on average. This implies that the logarithm of the series grows approximately linearly, and is why Figure 14.1a plots the logarithm of U.S. GDP. Another reason is that the standard deviation of many economic time series is approximately proportional to its level; that is, the standard deviation is well expressed as a percentage of the level of the series. This implies that the standard deviation of the logarithm of the series is approximately constant. In either case, it is useful to transform the series so that changes in the transformed series are proportional (or percentage) changes in the original series, and this is achieved by taking the logarithm of the series.[1]

Lags, first differences, and growth rates are summarized in Key Concept 14.1.

Lags, changes, and percentage changes are illustrated using the U.S. GDP data in Table 14.1. The first column shows the date, or period, where the first quarter of 2012 is denoted 2012:Q1, the second quarter of 2012 is denoted 2012:Q2, and so forth. The second column shows the value of the GDP in that quarter, the third column shows the logarithm of GDP, and the fourth column shows the growth rate of GDP (in percentage points at an annual rate). For example, from the first quarter to the second quarter of 2012, GDP increased from \$15,382 to \$15,428 billion,

---

[1] The change of the logarithm of a variable is approximately equal to the proportional change of that variable—that is, $\ln(X + a) - \ln(X) \cong a/X$, where the approximation works best when $a/X$ is small [see Equation (8.16) and the surrounding discussion]. Now, replace $X$ with $Y_{t-1}$ and $a$ with $\Delta Y_t$ and note that $Y_t = Y_{t-1} + \Delta Y_t$. This means that the proportional change in the series $Y_t$ between periods $t-1$ and $t$ is approximately $\ln(Y_t) - \ln(Y_{t-1}) = \ln(Y_{t-1} + \Delta Y_t) - \ln(Y_{t-1}) \cong \Delta Y_t / Y_{t-1}$. The expression $\ln(Y_t) - \ln(Y_{t-1})$ is the first difference of $\ln(Y_t)$, that is $\Delta \ln(Y_t)$. Thus $\Delta \ln(Y_t) \cong \Delta Y_t / Y_{t-1}$. The percentage change is 100 times the fractional change, so the percentage change in the series $Y_t$ is approximately $100\Delta \ln(Y_t)$.

## Lags, First Differences, Logarithms, and Growth Rates

**KEY CONCEPT**

**14.1**

- The first lag of a time series $Y_t$ is $Y_{t-1}$; its $j^{\text{th}}$ lag is $Y_{t-j}$.
- The first difference of a series, $\Delta Y_t$, is its change between periods $t-1$ and $t$, that is $\Delta Y_t = Y_t - Y_{t-1}$.
- The first difference of the logarithm of $Y_t$ is $\Delta \ln(Y_t) = \ln(Y_t) - \ln(Y_{t-1})$.
- The percentage change of a time series $Y_t$ between periods $t-1$ and $t$ is approximately $100\Delta\ln(Y_t)$, where the approximation is most accurate when the percentage change is small.

which is a percentage increase of $100 \times (15428 - 15382)/15382 = 0.30\%$. This is the percentage increase from one quarter to the next. It is conventional to report rates of growth in macroeconomic time series on an annual basis, which is the percentage increase in GDP that would occur over a year if the series were to continue to increase at the same rate. Because there are four quarters in a year, the annualized rate of GDP growth in 2012:Q2 is $0.30 \times 4 = 1.20$, or $1.20\%$.

This percentage change can also be computed using the differences-of-logarithms approximation in Key Concept 14.1. The difference in the logarithm of GDP from 2012:Q1 to 2012:Q2 is $\ln(15428) - \ln(15382) = 0.0030$, yielding the approximate quarterly percentage difference $100 \times 0.0030 = 0.30\%$. On an annualized basis, this is $0.30 \times 4 = 1.20$, or $1.20\%$, the same (to two decimal

| **TABLE 14.1** | GDP in the United States in 2012 and the First Quarter of 2013 | | | |
|---|---|---|---|---|
| Quarter | U.S. GDP (billions of $1996), $GDP_t$ | Logarithm of GDP, $\ln(GDP_t)$ | Growth Rate of GDP at an Annual Rate, $GDPGR_t = 400 \times \Delta\ln(GDP_t)$ | First Lag, $GDPGR_{t-1}$ |
| 2012:Q1 | 15382 | 9.641 | 3.64 | 4.75 |
| 2012:Q2 | 15428 | 9.644 | 1.20 | 3.64 |
| 2012:Q3 | 15534 | 9.651 | 2.75 | 1.20 |
| 2012:Q4 | 15540 | 9.651 | 0.15 | 2.75 |
| 2013:Q1 | 15584 | 9.654 | 1.14 | 0.15 |

*Note:* The quarterly rate of GDP growth is the first difference of the logarithm. This is converted into percentage points at an annual rate by multiplying by 400. The first lag is its value in the previous quarter. All entries are rounded to the nearest decimal.

places), as obtained by directly computing the percentage growth. These calculations can be summarized as

$$\text{Annualized rate of GDP Growth} = GDPGR_t \cong 400[\ln(GDP_t) - \ln(GDP_{t-1})]$$
$$= 400\Delta\ln(GDP_t), \qquad (14.2)$$

where $GDP_t$ is the value of GDP at date $t$. The factor of 400 arises from converting fractional change to percentages (multiplying by 100) and converting quarterly percentage change to an equivalent annual rate (multiplying by 4).

The final column of Table 14.1 illustrates lags. The first lag $GDPGR$ in 2012:Q2 is 3.64%, the value of $GDPGR$ in 2012:Q1.

Figure 14.1b plots $GDPGR_t$ from 1960:Q1 through 2012:Q4. It shows substantial variability in the growth rate of GDP. For example, GDP grew at an annual rate of over 15% in 1978:Q2 and fell at annual rate of over 8% in 2008:Q4. Over the entire period, the growth rate averaged 3.1% (which is responsible for the increase of GDP from $3.1 trillion in 1960 to $15.5 trillion in 2012), and the sample standard deviation was 3.4%.

## Autocorrelation

In time series data, the value of $Y$ in one period typically is correlated with its value in the next period. The correlation of a series with its own lagged values is called **autocorrelation** or **serial correlation**. The first autocorrelation (or

---

**KEY CONCEPT**

**14.2**

## Autocorrelation (Serial Correlation) and Autocovariance

The $j^{th}$ autocovariance of a series $Y_t$ is the covariance between $Y_t$ and its $j^{th}$ lag, $Y_{t-j}$, and the $j^{th}$ autocorrelation coefficient is the correlation between $Y_t$ and $Y_{t-j}$. That is,

$$j^{th} \text{ autocovariance} = \text{cov}(Y_t, Y_{t-j}) \qquad (14.3)$$

$$j^{th}\text{autocorrelation} = \rho_j = \text{corr}(Y_t, Y_{t-j}) = \frac{\text{cov}(Y_t, Y_{t-j})}{\sqrt{\text{var}(Y_t)\text{var}(Y_{t-j})}}. \qquad (14.4)$$

The $j^{th}$ autocorrelation coefficient is sometimes called the $j^{th}$ serial correlation coefficient.

**autocorrelation coefficient**) is the correlation between $Y_t$ and $Y_{t-1}$—that is, the correlation between values of $Y$ at two adjacent dates. The second autocorrelation is the correlation between $Y_t$ and $Y_{t-2}$, and the $j^{\text{th}}$ autocorrelation is the correlation between $Y_t$ and $Y_{t-j}$. Similarly, the $j^{\text{th}}$ **autocovariance** is the covariance between $Y_t$ and $Y_{t-j}$. Autocorrelation and autocovariance are summarized in Key Concept 14.2.

The $j^{\text{th}}$ population autocovariances and autocorrelations in Key Concept 14.2 can be estimated by the $j^{\text{th}}$ sample autocovariances and autocorrelations, $\widehat{\text{cov}(Y_t, Y_{t-j})}$ and $\hat{\rho}_j$:

$$\widehat{\text{cov}(Y_t, Y_{t-j})} = \frac{1}{T} \sum_{t=j+1}^{T} (Y_t - \overline{Y}_{j+1:\,T})(Y_{t-j} - \overline{Y}_{1:T-j}) \qquad (14.5)$$

$$\hat{\rho}_j = \frac{\widehat{\text{cov}(Y_t, Y_{t-j})}}{\widehat{\text{var}(Y_t)}}, \qquad (14.6)$$

where $\overline{Y}_{j+1:\,T}$ denotes the sample average of $Y_t$ computed using the observations $t = j + 1, \ldots, T$ and where $\widehat{\text{var}(Y_t)}$ is the sample variance of $Y$.[2]

The first four sample autocorrelations of $GDPGR$, the growth rate of GDP, are $\hat{\rho}_1 = 0.34$, $\hat{\rho}_2 = 0.27$, $\hat{\rho}_3 = 0.13$, and $\hat{\rho}_4 = 0.14$. These values suggest that GDP growth rates are mildly positively autocorrelated; if GDP grows faster than average in one period, it tends to also grow faster than average in the following period.

## Other Examples of Economic Time Series

Economic time series differ greatly. Four examples of economic time series are plotted in Figure 14.2: the U.S. unemployment rate; the rate of exchange between the dollar and the British pound; the logarithm of an index of industrial production in Japan; and the daily return on the Wilshire 5000 stock price index.

The U.S. unemployment rate (Figure 14.2a) is the fraction of the labor force out of work, as measured in the Current Population Survey (see Appendix 3.1). Figure 14.2a shows that the unemployment rate increases by large amounts during recessions (the shaded areas in Figure 14.1) and falls during recoveries and expansions.

---

[2]The summation in Equation (14.5) is divided by $T$, whereas in the usual formula for the sample covariance [see Equation (3.24)], the summation is divided by the number of observations in the summation, minus a degrees-of-freedom adjustment. The formula in Equation (14.5) is conventional for the purpose of computing the autocovariance. Equation (14.6) uses the assumption that $\text{var}(Y_t)$ and $\text{var}(Y_{t-j})$ are the same—an implication of the assumption that $Y$ is stationary, which is discussed in Section 14.4.

**FIGURE 14.2** Four Economic Time Series

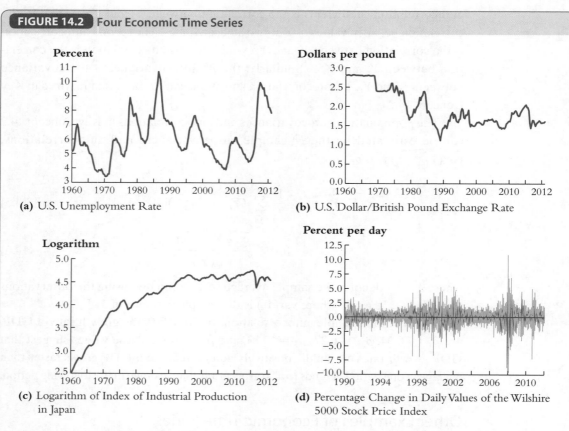

**(a)** U.S. Unemployment Rate

**(b)** U.S. Dollar/British Pound Exchange Rate

**(c)** Logarithm of Index of Industrial Production in Japan

**(d)** Percentage Change in Daily Values of the Wilshire 5000 Stock Price Index

The four time series have markedly different patterns. The unemployment rate (Figure 14.2a) increases during recessions and declines during recoveries and expansions. The exchange rate between the U.S. dollar and the British pound (Figure 14.2b) shows a discrete change after the 1972 collapse of the Bretton Woods system of fixed exchange rates. The logarithm of the index of industrial production in Japan (Figure 14.2c) shows a pattern of decreasing growth. The daily percentage changes in the Wilshire 5000 stock price index (Figure 14.2d) are essentially unpredictable, but the variance changes: This series shows "volatility clustering."

The dollar/pound exchange rate (Figure 14.2b) is the price of a British pound (£) in U.S. dollars. Before 1972, the developed economies ran a system of fixed exchange rates—called the "Bretton Woods" system—under which governments worked to keep exchange rates from fluctuating. In 1972, inflationary pressures led to the breakdown of this system; thereafter, the major currencies were allowed to "float"; that is, their values were determined by the supply and demand for currencies in the market for foreign exchange. Prior to 1972, the exchange rate was approximately constant, with the exception of a single devaluation in 1968, in which the official value of the pound, relative to the dollar, was decreased to $2.40. Since 1972 the exchange rate has fluctuated over a very wide range.

The index of industrial production for Japan (Figure 14.2c) measures Japan's output of industrial commodities. The logarithm of the series is plotted in Figure 14.2c, and changes in this series can be interpreted as (fractional) growth rates. During the 1960s and early 1970s, Japanese industrial production grew quickly, but this growth slowed in the late 1970s and 1980s, and industrial production has grown little since the early 1990s.

The Wilshire 5000 stock price index is an index of the share prices of all firms traded on exchanges in the United States. Figure 14.2d plots the daily percentage changes in this index for trading days from January 2, 1990, to December 31, 2013 (a total of 4003 observations). Unlike the other series in Figure 14.2, there is very little serial correlation in these daily percentage changes; if there were, then you could predict them using past daily changes and make money by buying when you expect the market to rise and selling when you expect it to fall. Although the changes are essentially unpredictable, inspection of Figure 14.2d reveals patterns in their volatility. For example, the standard deviation of daily percentage changes was relatively large in 1998–2003 and 2007–2008, and it was relatively small in 1994 and 2004. This "volatility clustering" is found in many financial time series, and econometric models for modeling this special type of heteroskedasticity are taken up in Section 16.5.

## 14.3 Autoregressions

How fast will GDP grow over the next year? Will growth be strong, so it will be a good year for the U.S. economy, or weak—perhaps even negative—signaling that the economy will be in a recession? Firms use growth forecasts when they forecast sales of their products, and local governments use growth forecasts when they develop their budgets for the upcoming year. Economists at central banks, like the U.S. Federal Reserve Bank, use growth forecasts when they set monetary policy. Wall Street investors rely on growth forecasts when deciding how much to pay for stocks and bonds. In this section, we consider forecasts made using an **autoregression**, a regression model that relates a time series variable to its past values.

### The First-Order Autoregressive Model

If you want to predict the future of a time series, a good place to start is in the immediate past. For example, if you want to forecast the rate of GDP growth in the next quarter, you might see how fast GDP grew in the last quarter.

A systematic way to forecast GDP growth, $GDPGR_t$, using the previous quarter's value, $GDPGR_{t-1}$, is to estimate an OLS regression of $GDPGR_t$ on $GDPGR_{t-1}$. Estimated using data from 1962 to 2012, this regression is

$$\widehat{GDPGR_t} = 1.991 + 0.344\, GDPGR_{t-1}, \tag{14.7}$$
$$\phantom{\widehat{GDPGR_t} = }(0.349)\ \ (0.075)$$

where, as usual, standard errors are given in parentheses under the estimated coefficients, and $\widehat{GDPGR}$ is the predicted value of $GDPGR$ based on the estimated regression line. The model in Equation (14.7) is called a *first-order autoregression*: an *autoregression* because it is a regression of the series onto its own lag, $GDPGR_{t-1}$, and *first-order* because only one lag is used as a regressor. The coefficient in Equation (14.7) is positive, so positive growth of GDP in one quarter is associated with positive growth in the next quarter.

A first-order autoregression is abbreviated AR(1), where the 1 indicates that it is first order. The population AR(1) model for the series $Y_t$ is

$$Y_t = \beta_0 + \beta_1 Y_{t-1} + u_t, \tag{14.8}$$

where $u_t$ is an error term.

*Forecasts and forecast errors.* Suppose that you have historical data on $Y$, and you want to forecast its future value. If $Y_t$ follows the AR(1) model in Equation (14.8) and if $\beta_0$ and $\beta_1$ are known, then the forecast of $Y_{T+1}$ based on $Y_T$ is $\beta_0 + \beta_1 Y_T$.

In practice, $\beta_0$ and $\beta_1$ are unknown, so forecasts must be based on estimates of $\beta_0$ and $\beta_1$. We will use the OLS estimators $\hat{\beta}_0$ and $\hat{\beta}_1$, which are constructed using historical data. In general, $\hat{Y}_{T+1|T}$ will denote the forecast of $Y_{T+1}$ based on information through period $T$, using a model estimated with data through period $T$. Accordingly, the forecast based on the AR(1) model in Equation (14.8) is

$$\hat{Y}_{T+1|T} = \hat{\beta}_0 + \hat{\beta}_1 Y_T, \tag{14.9}$$

where $\hat{\beta}_0$ and $\hat{\beta}_1$ are estimated using historical data through time $T$.

The **forecast error** is the mistake made by the forecast; this is the difference between the value of $Y_{T+1}$ that actually occurred and its forecasted value based on $Y_T$:

$$\text{Forecast error} = Y_{T+1} - \hat{Y}_{T+1|T}. \tag{14.10}$$

*Forecasts versus predicted values.* The forecast is *not* an OLS predicted value, and the forecast error is *not* an OLS residual. OLS predicted values are calculated for the observations in the sample used to estimate the regression. In contrast, the forecast is made for some date beyond the data set used to estimate the regression, so the data on the actual value of the forecasted dependent variable are not in the sample used to estimate the regression. Similarly, the OLS residual is the difference between the actual value of $Y$ and its predicted value for observations in the sample, whereas the forecast error is the difference between the future value of $Y$, which is not contained in the estimation sample, and the forecast of that future value. Said differently, forecasts and forecast errors pertain to "out-of-sample" observations, whereas predicted values and residuals pertain to "in-sample" observations.

*Root mean squared forecast error.* The **root mean squared forecast error (RMSFE)** is a measure of the size of the forecast error—that is, of the magnitude of a typical mistake made using a forecasting model. The RMSFE is the square root of the mean squared forecast error:

$$\text{RMSFE} = \sqrt{E[(Y_{T+1} - \hat{Y}_{T+1|T})^2]}. \tag{14.11}$$

The RMSFE has two sources of error: the error arising because future values of $u_t$ are unknown and the error in estimating the coefficients $\beta_0$ and $\beta_1$. If the first source of error is much larger than the second, as it can be if the sample size is large, then the RMSFE is approximately $\sqrt{\text{var}(u_t)}$, the standard deviation of the error $u_t$ in the population autoregression [Equation (14.8)]. The standard deviation of $u_t$ is in turn estimated by the standard error of the regression (*SER*; see Section 4.3). Thus, if uncertainty arising from estimating the regression coefficients is small enough to be ignored, the RMSFE can be estimated by the standard error of the regression. Estimation of the RMSFE including both sources of forecast error is taken up in Section 14.4.

*Application to GDP growth.* What is the forecast of the growth rate of GDP in the first quarter of 2013 (2013:Q1) that a forecaster would have made in 2012:Q4, based on the estimated AR(1) model in Equation (14.7) (which was estimated using data through 2012:Q4)? According to Table 14.1, the growth rate of GDP in 2012:Q4 was 0.15% (so $GDPGR_{2012:Q4} = 0.15$). Plugging this value into Equation (14.7), the forecast of the growth rate of GDP in 2013:Q1 is $\widehat{GDPGR}_{2013:Q1|2012:Q4} = 1.991 + 0.344 \times GDPGR_{2012:Q4} = 1.991 + 0.344 \times 0.15 = 2.0$ (rounded to the nearest tenth). Thus, the AR(1) model forecasts that the growth rate of GDP will be 2.0% in 2013:Q1.

How accurate is this AR(1) forecast? Table 14.1 shows that the actual growth rate of GDP in 2013:Q1 was 1.1%, so the AR(1) forecast is high by 0.9 percentage point; that is, the forecast error is −0.9. The $\overline{R}^2$ of the AR(1) model in Equation (14.7) is only 0.11, so the lagged value of GDP growth explains a small fraction of the variation in GDP growth in the sample used to fit the autoregression. This low $\overline{R}^2$ is consistent with the poor forecast of GDP growth in 2013:Q1 produced using Equation (14.7). More generally, the low $\overline{R}^2$ suggests that this AR(1) model will forecast only a small amount of the variation in the growth rate of GDP.

The standard error of the regression in Equation (14.7) is 3.16; ignoring uncertainty arising from estimation of the coefficients, our estimate of the RMSFE for forecasts based on Equation (14.7) is therefore 3.16 percentage points.

## The $p^{\text{th}}$-Order Autoregressive Model

The AR(1) model uses $Y_{t-1}$ to forecast $Y_t$, but doing so ignores potentially useful information in the more distant past. One way to incorporate this information is to include additional lags in the AR(1) model; this yields the $p^{\text{th}}$-order autoregressive, or AR($p$), model.

The **$p^{\text{th}}$-order autoregressive model** [the **AR($p$)** model] represents $Y_t$ as a linear function of $p$ of its lagged values; that is, in the AR($p$) model, the regressors are $Y_{t-1}, Y_{t-2}, \ldots, Y_{t-p}$, plus an intercept. The number of lags, $p$, included in an AR($p$) model is called the order, or lag length, of the autoregression.

For example, an AR(2) model of GDP growth uses two lags of GDP growth as regressors. Estimated by OLS over the period 1962–2012, the AR(2) model is

$$\widehat{GDPGR}_t = 1.63 + 0.28\,GDPGR_{t-1} + 0.17\,GDPGR_{t-2}. \qquad (14.12)$$
$$\phantom{\widehat{GDPGR}_t = }(0.40) \quad (0.08) \qquad\qquad (0.08)$$

The coefficient on the additional lag in Equation (14.1312) is significantly different from zero at the 5% significance level: The $t$-statistic is 2.27 ($p$-value = 0.02). This is reflected in an improvement in the $\overline{R}^2$ from 0.11 for the AR(1) model in Equation (14.7) to 0.14 for the AR(2) model. Similarly, the *SER* of the AR(2) model in Equation (14.12) is 3.11, an improvement over the *SER* of the AR(1) model, which is 3.16.

The AR($p$) model is summarized in Key Concept 14.3.

*Properties of the forecast and error term in the AR* (p) *model.* The assumption that the conditional expectation of $u_t$ is zero, given past values of $Y_t$ [that is, $E(u_t|Y_{t-1}, Y_{t-2}, \ldots) = 0$], has two important implications.

# Autoregressions

**KEY CONCEPT**

14.3

The $p^{\text{th}}$-order autoregressive model [the AR($p$) model] represents $Y_t$ as a linear function of $p$ of its lagged values:

$$Y_t = \beta_0 + \beta_1 Y_{t-1} + \beta_2 Y_{t-2} + \cdots + \beta_p Y_{t-p} + u_t, \qquad (14.13)$$

where $E(u_t | Y_{t-1}, Y_{t-2}, \dots) = 0$. The number of lags $p$ is called the order, or the lag length, of the autoregression.

The first implication is that the best forecast of $Y_{T+1}$ based on its entire history depends on only the most recent $p$ past values. Specifically, let $Y_{T+1|T} = E(Y_{T+1} | Y_T, Y_{T-1}, \dots)$ denote the conditional mean of $Y_{T+1}$, given its entire history. Then $Y_{T+1|T}$ has the smallest RMSFE of any forecast, based on the history of $Y$ (Exercise 14.5). If $Y_t$ follows an AR($p$), then the best forecast of $Y_{T+1}$ based on $Y_T, Y_{T-1}, \dots$ is

$$Y_{T+1|T} = \beta_0 + \beta_1 Y_T + \beta_2 Y_{T-1} + \cdots + \beta_p Y_{T-p+1}, \qquad (14.14)$$

which follows from the AR($p$) model in Equation (14.13) and the assumption that $E(u_t | Y_{t-1}, Y_{t-2}, \dots) = 0$. In practice, the coefficients $\beta_0, \beta_1, \dots, \beta_p$ are unknown, so actual forecasts from an AR($p$) use Equation (14.14) with estimated coefficients.

The second implication is that the errors $u_t$ are serially uncorrelated, a result that follows from Equation (2.27) (Exercise 14.5).

*Application to GDP growth.* What is the forecast of the growth rate of GDP in 2013:Q1, using data through 2012:Q4, based on the AR(2) model of GDP growth in Equation (14.12)? To compute this forecast, substitute the values of the GDP growth in 2012:Q3 and 2012:Q4 into Equation (14.12): $\widehat{GDPGR}_{2013:Q1|2012:Q4} = 1.63 + 0.28\,GDPGR_{2012:Q4} + 0.17\,GDPGR_{2012:Q3} = 1.63 + 0.28 \times 0.15 + 0.17 \times 2.75 \cong 2.1\%$, where the 2012 values for $GDPGR$ are taken from the fourth column of Table 14.1. The forecast error is the actual value, 1.1%, minus the forecast, or $1.1\% - 2.1\% = -1.0\%$, slightly greater in absolute value than the AR(1) forecast error of −0.9 percentage point.

## Can You Beat the Market? Part I

Have you ever dreamed of getting rich quickly by beating the stock market? If you think that the market will be going up, you should buy stocks today and sell them later, before the market turns down. If you are good at forecasting swings in stock prices, then this active trading strategy will produce better returns than a passive "buy and hold" strategy in which you purchase stocks and just hang onto them. The trick, of course, is having a reliable forecast of future stock returns.

Forecasts based on past values of stock returns are sometimes called "momentum" forecasts: If the value of a stock rose this month, perhaps it has momentum and will also rise next month. If so, then returns will be autocorrelated, and the autoregressive model will provide useful forecasts. You can implement a momentum-based strategy for a specific stock or for a stock index that measures the overall value of the market.

**TABLE 14.2    Autoregressive Models of Monthly Excess Stock Returns, 1960:M1–2002:M12**

| Dependent variable: Excess returns on the CRSP value-weighted index | | | |
|---|---|---|---|
| | (1) | (2) | (3) |
| Specification | AR(1) | AR(2) | AR(4) |
| Regressors | | | |
| excess return$_{t-1}$ | 0.050 (0.051) | 0.053 (0.051) | 0.054 (0.051) |
| excess return$_{t-2}$ | | −0.053 (0.048) | −0.054 (0.048) |
| excess return$_{t-3}$ | | | 0.009 (0.050) |
| excess return$_{t-4}$ | | | −0.016 (0.047) |
| Intercept | 0.312 (0.197) | 0.328 (0.199) | 0.331 (0.202) |
| F-statistic for coefficients on lags of excess return (p-value) | 0.968 (0.325) | 1.342 (0.261) | 0.707 (0.587) |
| $\overline{R}^2$ | 0.0006 | 0.0014 | −0.0022 |

Note: Excess returns are measured in percentage points per month. The data are described in Appendix 14.1. All regressions are estimated over 1960:M1–2002:M12 ($T = 516$ observations), with earlier observations used for initial values of lagged variables. Entries in the regressor rows are coefficients, with standard errors in parentheses. The final two rows report the F-statistic testing the hypothesis that the coefficients on lags of excess return in the regression are zero, with its p-value in parentheses, and the adjusted $R^2$.

Table 14.2 presents autoregressive models of the excess return on a broad-based index of stock prices, called the CRSP value-weighted index, using monthly data from 1960:M1 to 2002:M12, where "M1" denotes the first month of the year (January), "M2" denotes the second month, and so forth. The monthly excess return is what you earn, in percentage terms, by purchasing a stock at the end of the previous month and selling it at the end of this month, minus what you would have earned had you purchased a safe asset (a U.S. Treasury bill). The return on the stock includes the capital gain (or loss) from the change in price plus any dividends you receive during the month. The data are described further in Appendix 14.1.

Sadly, the results in Table 14.2 are negative. The coefficient on lagged returns in the AR(1) model is not statistically significant, and we cannot reject the null hypothesis that the coefficients on lagged returns are all zero in the AR(2) or AR(4) model. In fact, the adjusted $R^2$ of one of the models is negative and the other two are only slightly positive, suggesting that none of these models is useful for forecasting.

These negative results are consistent with the theory of efficient capital markets, which holds that excess returns should be unpredictable because stock prices already embody all currently available information. The reasoning is simple: If market participants think that a stock will have a positive excess return next month, then they will buy that stock now, but doing so will drive up the price of the stock to exactly the point at which there is no expected excess return. As a result, we should not be able to forecast future excess returns by using past publicly available information, and we cannot do it, at least using the regressions in Table 14.2.

## 14.4   Time Series Regression with Additional Predictors and the Autoregressive Distributed Lag Model

Economic theory often suggests other variables that could help forecast a variable of interest. These other variables, or predictors, can be added to an autoregression to produce a time series regression model with multiple predictors. When other variables and their lags are added to an autoregression, the result is an autoregressive distributed lag model.

### Forecasting GDP Growth Using the Term Spread

Interest rates on long-term and short-term bonds move together, but not one for one. Figure 14.3a plots interest rates on 10-year U.S. Treasury bonds and 3-Month Treasury bills from 1960 to 2012. Both interest rates show the same long-run tendencies: both were low in the 1960s, both rose through the 1970s and peaked

**FIGURE 14.3** Interest Rates and the Term Spread, 1960–2012

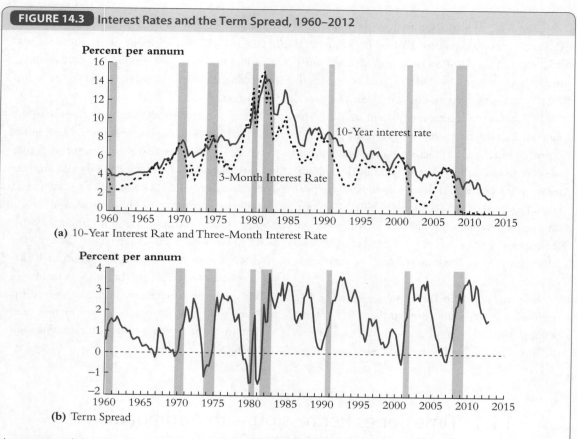

**(a)** 10–Year Interest Rate and Three–Month Interest Rate

**(b)** Term Spread

Long-term and short-term interest move together, but not one-for-one. The difference between long-term rates and short-term rates is called the term spread. The term spread has fallen sharply before U.S. recessions, which are shown as shaded regions in the figures.

in the early 1980s, and both fell subsequently. But the gap, or difference, between the two interest rates has not been constant: While short-term rates are generally below long-term rates, the gap between them narrows and even disappears shortly before the start of a recession; recessions are shown as the shaded bars in the figure. This difference between long-term and short-term interest rates is called the **term spread** and is plotted in Figure 14.3b. The term spread is generally positive, but it falls toward zero or below before recessions.

Figure 14.3 suggests that the term spread might contain information about the future growth of GDP that is not already contained in past values of GDP growth.

This conjecture is readily checked by augmenting the AR(2) model in Equation (14.12) to include the first lag of the term spread:

$$\widehat{GDPGR}_t = 0.95 + 0.27\,GDPGR_{t-1} + 0.19\,GDPGR_{t-2} + 0.44\,TSpread_{t-1}.$$
$$\quad\quad (0.49)\quad (0.08)\quad\quad\quad\quad (0.08)\quad\quad\quad\quad (0.18)\quad\quad\quad (14.15)$$

The $t$-statistic on $TSpread_{t-1}$ is $-2.43$, so this term is significant at the 1% level. The $\overline{R}^2$ of this regression is 0.16, an improvement over the AR(2) $\overline{R}^2$ of 0.14.

The forecast of the rate of change of GDP in 2013:Q1 is obtained by substituting the 2012:Q3 and 2012:Q4 values of the GDP growth into Equation (14.15), along with the value of the term spread in 2012:Q4 (which is 1.62); the resulting forecast is $\widehat{GDPGR}_{2013:Q1|2012:Q4} = 2.2\%$, and the forecast error is $-1.1\%$.

If one lag of the term spread is helpful for forecasting GDP growth, more lags might be even more helpful; adding an additional lag of the term spread yields

$$\widehat{GDPGR}_t = 0.97 + 0.24\,GDPGR_{t-1} + 0.18\,GDPGR_{t-2}$$
$$\quad (0.47)\quad (0.08)\quad\quad\quad\quad (0.08)$$
$$-\,0.14\,TSpread_{t-1} + 0.66\,TSpread_{t-2}. \quad\quad (14.16)$$
$$(0.43)\quad\quad\quad\quad\quad (0.43)$$

The $t$-statistic testing the significance of the second lag of the term spread is 1.53 ($p$-value $= 0.13$), so it falls just short of statistical significance at the 10% level. The $\overline{R}^2$ of the regression in Equation (14.16) is 0.17, a slight improvement over 0.16 for Equation (14.15). The $F$-statistic on all the term spread coefficients is 4.43 ($p$-value $= 0.01$), indicating that this model represents a statistically significant improvement over the AR(2) model of Section 14.3 [Equation (14.12)]. The standard error of the regression in Equation (14.16) is 3.06, a modest improvement over the $SER$ of 3.11 for the AR(2).

The forecasted rate of growth for GDP in 2013:Q1 using Equation (14.16) is computed by substituting the values of the variables into the equation. The term spread was 1.54 in 2012:Q3 and 1.62 in 2012:Q4. The forecast value of the rate of growth in GDP in 2013:Q1, based on Equation (14.16), is

$$\widehat{GDPGR}_{2013:Q1|2012:Q4} = 0.99 + 0.24 \times 0.15 + 0.18 \times 2.75$$
$$-\,0.14 \times 1.62 + 0.66 \times 1.54 = 2.3. \quad\quad (14.17)$$

The forecast error is $-1.2\%$.

***The autoregressive distributed lag model.*** Each model in Equations (14.15) and (14.16) is an **autoregressive distributed lag (ADL) model**: *autoregressive*

**KEY CONCEPT**

14.4

## The Autoregressive Distributed Lag Model

The autoregressive distributed lag model with $p$ lags of $Y_t$ and $q$ lags of $X_t$, denoted ADL($p, q$), is

$$Y_t = \beta_0 + \beta_1 Y_{t-1} + \beta_2 Y_{t-2} + \cdots + \beta_p Y_{t-p}$$
$$+ \delta_1 X_{t-1} + \delta_2 X_{t-2} + \cdots + \delta_q X_{t-q} + u_t, \qquad (14.18)$$

where $\beta_0, \beta_1, \ldots, \beta_p, \delta_1, \ldots, \delta_q$ are unknown coefficients and $u_t$ is the error term with $E(u_t | Y_{t-1}, Y_{t-2}, \ldots, X_{t-1}, X_{t-2}, \ldots) = 0$.

because lagged values of the dependent variable are included as regressors, as in an autoregression, and *distributed lag* because the regression also includes multiple lags (a "distributed lag") of an additional predictor. In general, an autoregressive distributed lag model with $p$ lags of the dependent variable $Y_t$ and $q$ lags of an additional predictor $X_t$ is called an **ADL(*p*, *q*)** model. In this notation, the model in Equation (14.15) is an ADL(2,1) model and the model in Equation (14.16) is an ADL(2,2) model.

The autoregressive distributed lag model is summarized in Key Concept 14.4. With all these regressors, the notation in Equation (14.18) is somewhat cumbersome, and alternative optional notation, based on the so-called lag operator, is presented in Appendix 14.3.

The assumption that the errors in the ADL model have a conditional mean of zero given all past values of $Y$ and $X$, that is, that $E(u_t | Y_{t-1}, Y_{t-2}, \ldots, X_{t-1}, X_{t-2}, \ldots) = 0$ implies that no additional lags of either $Y$ or $X$ belong in the ADL model. In other words, the lag lengths $p$ and $q$ are the true lag lengths, and the coefficients on additional lags are zero.

The ADL model contains lags of the dependent variable (the autoregressive component) and a distributed lag of a single additional predictor, $X$. In general, however, forecasts can be improved by using multiple predictors. But before turning to the general time series regression model with multiple predictors, we first introduce the concept of stationarity, which will be used in that discussion.

## Stationarity

Regression analysis of time series data necessarily uses data from the past to quantify historical relationships. If the future is like the past, then these historical relationships can be used to forecast the future. But if the future differs

## Stationarity

A time series $Y_t$ is *stationary* if its probability distribution does not change over time, that is, if the joint distribution of $(Y_{s+1}, Y_{s+2}, \ldots, Y_{s+T})$ does not depend on $s$ regardless of the value of $T$; otherwise, $Y_t$ is said to be *nonstationary*. A pair of time series, $X_t$ and $Y_t$, are said to be *jointly stationary* if the joint distribution of $(X_{s+1}, Y_{s+1}, X_{s+2}, Y_{s+2}, \ldots, X_{s+T}, Y_{s+T})$ does not depend on $s$, regardless of the value of $T$. Stationarity requires the future to be like the past, at least in a probabilistic sense.

fundamentally from the past, then those historical relationships might not be reliable guides to the future.

In the context of time series regression, the idea that historical relationships can be generalized to the future is formalized by the concept of **stationarity**. The precise definition of stationarity, given in Key Concept 14.5, is that the probability distribution of the time series variable does not change over time.

## Time Series Regression with Multiple Predictors

The general time series regression model with multiple predictors extends the ADL model to include multiple predictors and their lags. The model is summarized in Key Concept 14.6. The presence of multiple predictors and their lags leads to double subscripting of the regression coefficients and regressors.

*The time series regression model assumptions.* The assumptions in Key Concept 14.6 modify the four least squares assumptions of the multiple regression model for cross-sectional data (Key Concept 6.4) for time series data.

The first assumption is that $u_t$ has conditional mean zero, given all the regressors *and* the additional lags of the regressors beyond the lags included in the regression. This assumption extends the assumption used in the AR and ADL models and implies that the best forecast of $Y_t$ using all past values of $Y$ and the $X$'s is given by the regression in Equation (14.19).

The second least squares assumption for cross-sectional data (Key Concept 6.4) is that $(X_{1i}, \ldots, X_{ki}, Y_i)$, $i = 1, \ldots, n$, are independently and identically distributed (i.i.d.). The second assumption for time series regression replaces the i.i.d. assumption by a more appropriate one with two parts. Part (a) is that the data are drawn from a stationary distribution so that the distribution of the data

KEY CONCEPT

## 14.6

## Time Series Regression with Multiple Predictors

The general time series regression model allows for $k$ additional predictors, where $q_1$ lags of the first predictor are included, $q_2$ lags of the second predictor are included, and so forth:

$$
\begin{aligned}
Y_t = {} & \beta_0 + \beta_1 Y_{t-1} + \beta_2 Y_{t-2} + \cdots + \beta_p Y_{t-p} \\
& + \delta_{11} X_{1t-1} + \delta_{12} X_{1t-2} + \cdots + \delta_{1q_1} X_{1t-q_1} \\
& + \cdots + \delta_{k1} X_{kt-1} + \delta_{k2} X_{kt-2} + \cdots + \delta_{kq_k} X_{kt-q_k} + u_t,
\end{aligned}
\tag{14.19}
$$

where

1. $E(u_t \mid Y_{t-1}, Y_{t-2}, \ldots, X_{1t-1}, X_{1t-2}, \ldots, X_{kt-1}, X_{kt-2}, \ldots) = 0$;

2. (a) The random variables $(Y_t, X_{1t}, \ldots, X_{kt})$ have a stationary distribution, and (b) $(Y_t, X_{1t}, \ldots, X_{kt})$ and $(Y_{t-j}, X_{1t-j}, \ldots, X_{kt-j})$ become independent as $j$ gets large;

3. Large outliers are unlikely: $X_{1t}, \ldots, X_{kt}$ and $Y_t$ have nonzero, finite fourth moments; and

4. There is no perfect multicollinearity.

today is the same as its distribution in the past. This assumption is a time series version of the "identically distributed" part of the i.i.d. assumption: The cross-sectional requirement of each draw being identically distributed is replaced by the time series requirement that the joint distribution of the variables, *including lags*, does not change over time. In practice, many economic time series appear to be nonstationary, which means that this assumption can fail to hold in applications. If the time series variables are nonstationary, then one or more problems can arise in time series regression: The forecast can be biased, the forecast can be inefficient (there can be alternative forecasts based on the same data with lower MSFE), or conventional OLS-based statistical inferences (for example, performing a hypothesis test by comparing the OLS $t$-statistic to $\pm 1.96$) can be misleading. Precisely which of these problems occurs, and its remedy, depends on the source of the non-stationarity. In Sections 14.6 and 14.7, we study the problems posed by, tests for, and solutions to two empirically important types of nonstationarity in economic time series: trends and breaks. For now, however, we simply assume that the series are jointly stationary and accordingly focus on regression with stationary variables.

---

## Granger Causality Tests (Tests of Predictive Content)

The Granger causality statistic is the $F$-statistic that tests the hypothesis that the coefficients on all the values of one of the variables in Equation (14.19) (for example, the coefficients on $X_{1t-1}, X_{1t-2}, \ldots, X_{1t-q_1}$) are zero. This null hypothesis implies that these regressors have no predictive content for $Y_t$ beyond that contained in the other regressors, and the test of this null hypothesis is called the Granger causality test.

Part (b) of the second assumption requires that the random variables become independently distributed when the amount of time separating them becomes large. This replaces the cross-sectional requirement that the variables be independently distributed from one observation to the next with the time series requirement that they be independently distributed when they are separated by long periods of time. This assumption is sometimes referred to as **weak dependence**, and it ensures that in large samples there is sufficient randomness in the data for the law of large numbers and the central limit theorem to hold. We do not provide a precise mathematical statement of the weak dependence condition; rather, the reader is referred to Hayashi (2000, Chapter 2).

The third assumption, which is the same as the third least squares assumption for cross-sectional data, that large outliers are unlikely, is made mathematically precise by the assumption that all the variables have nonzero finite fourth moments.

Finally, the fourth assumption, which is also the same as for cross-sectional data, is that the regressors are not perfectly multicollinear.

*Statistical inference and the Granger causality test.* Under the assumptions of Key Concept 14.6, inference on the regression coefficients using OLS proceeds in the same way as it usually does using cross-sectional data.

One useful application of the $F$-statistic in time series forecasting is to test whether the lags of one of the included regressors has useful predictive content, above and beyond the other regressors in the model. The claim that a variable has no predictive content corresponds to the null hypothesis that the coefficients on all lags of that variable are zero. The $F$-statistic testing this null hypothesis is called the **Granger causality statistic**, and the associated test is called a **Granger causality test** (Granger, 1969). This test is summarized in Key Concept 14.7.

Granger causality has little to do with causality in the sense that it is used elsewhere in this book. In Chapter 1, causality was defined in terms of an ideal randomized controlled experiment, in which different values of $X$ are applied experimentally and we observe the subsequent effect on $Y$. In contrast, Granger causality means that if $X$ Granger-causes $Y$, then $X$ is a useful predictor of $Y$, given the other variables in the regression. While "Granger predictability" is a more accurate term than "Granger causality," the latter has become part of the jargon of econometrics.

As an example, consider the relationship between the growth rate of GDP and its past values and past values of the term spread. Based on the OLS estimates in Equation (14.16), the $F$-statistic testing the null hypothesis that the coefficients on both lags of the term spread are zero is 4.43 ($p$-value = 0.01): In the jargon of Key Concept 14.7, we can conclude (at the 1% significance level) that the term spread Granger-causes growth in GDP. This *does not* necessarily mean that a change in the term spread will cause—in the sense of Chapter 1—a subsequent change in GDP. It *does* mean that the past values of the term spread appear to contain information that is useful for forecasting changes in GDP, beyond that contained in past values of changes in GDP.

## Forecast Uncertainty and Forecast Intervals

In any estimation problem, it is good practice to report a measure of the uncertainty of that estimate, and forecasting is no exception. One measure of the uncertainty of a forecast is its root mean squared forecast error (RMSFE). Under the additional assumption that the errors $u_t$ are normally distributed, the RMSFE can be used to construct a forecast interval—that is, an interval that contains the future value of the variable with a certain probability.

*Forecast uncertainty.* The forecast error consists of two components: uncertainty arising from estimation of the regression coefficients and uncertainty associated with the future unknown value of $u_t$. For regression with few coefficients and many observations, the uncertainty arising from future $u_t$ can be much larger than the uncertainty associated with estimation of the parameters. In general, however, both sources of uncertainty are important, so we now develop an expression for the RMSFE that incorporates these two sources of uncertainty.

To keep the notation simple, consider forecasts of $Y_{T+1}$ based on an ADL(1,1) model with a single predictor—that is, $Y_t = \beta_0 + \beta_1 Y_{t-1} + \delta_1 X_{t-1} + u_t$—and suppose that $u_t$ is homoskedastic. The forecast is $\hat{Y}_{T+1|T} = \hat{\beta}_0 + \hat{\beta}_1 Y_T + \hat{\delta}_1 X_T$ and the forecast error is

$$Y_{T+1} - \hat{Y}_{T+1|T} = u_{T+1} - [(\hat{\beta}_0 - \beta_0) + (\hat{\beta}_1 - \beta_1)Y_T + (\hat{\delta}_1 - \delta_1)X_T]. \quad (14.20)$$

Because $u_{T+1}$ has conditional mean zero and is homoskedastic, $u_{T+1}$ has variance $\sigma_u^2$ and is uncorrelated with the final expression in brackets in Equation (14.20). Thus the mean squared forecast error (MSFE) is

$$\begin{aligned} \text{MSFE} &= E[(Y_{T+1} - \hat{Y}_{T+1|T})^2] \\ &= \sigma_u^2 + \text{var}[(\hat{\beta}_0 - \beta_0) + (\hat{\beta}_1 - \beta_1)Y_T + (\hat{\delta}_1 - \delta_1)X_T], \end{aligned} \quad (14.21)$$

and the RMSFE is the square root of the MSFE.

Estimation of the MSFE entails estimation of the two parts in Equation (14.21). The first term, $\sigma_u^2$, can be estimated by the square of the standard error of the regression, as discussed in Section 14.3. The second term requires estimating the variance of a weighted average of the regression coefficients, and methods for doing so were discussed in Section 8.1 [see the discussion following Equation (8.7)].

An alternative method for estimating the MSFE is to use the variance of pseudo out-of-sample forecasts, a procedure discussed in Section 14.7.

*Forecast intervals.* A forecast interval is like a confidence interval except that it pertains to a forecast. For example, a 95% **forecast interval** is an interval that contains the future value of the series in 95% of repeated applications.

One important difference between a forecast interval and a confidence interval is that the usual formula for a 95% confidence interval (the estimator $\pm 1.96$ standard errors) is justified by the central limit theorem and therefore holds for a wide range of distributions of the error term. In contrast, because the forecast error in Equation (14.20) includes the future value of the error $u_{T+1}$, computing a forecast interval requires either estimating the distribution of the error term or making some assumption about that distribution.

In practice, it is convenient to assume that $u_{T+1}$ is normally distributed. If so, Equation (14.20) and the central limit theorem applied to $\hat{\beta}_0$, $\hat{\beta}_1$, and $\hat{\delta}_1$ imply that the forecast error is the sum of two independent, normally distributed terms, so the forecast error is itself normally distributed, with variance equaling the MSFE. It follows that a 95% confidence interval is given by $\hat{Y}_{T+1|T} \pm 1.96\,SE(Y_{T+1} - \hat{Y}_{T+1|T})$, where $SE(Y_{T+1} - \hat{Y}_{T+1|T})$ is an estimator of the RMSFE.

## The River of Blood

As part of its efforts to inform the public about monetary policy decisions, the Bank of England regularly publishes forecasts of inflation. These forecasts combine output from econometric models maintained by professional econometricians at the bank with the expert judgment of the members of the bank's senior staff and Monetary Policy Committee. The forecasts are presented as a set of forecast intervals designed to reflect what these economists consider to be the range of probable paths that inflation might take. In its *Inflation Report*, the bank prints these ranges in red, with the darkest red reserved for the central band. Although the bank prosaically refers to this as the "fan chart," the press has called these spreading shades of red the "river of blood."

The river of blood for August 2013 is shown in Figure 14.4. (In this figure the blood is blue, not red, so you will need to use your imagination.) This chart shows that, as of August 2013, the bank's economists expected the rate of inflation to fall gradually from nearly 3% in early 2013 to 2%, the Bank's target rate of inflation, in 2015. The economists expressed considerable uncertainty about the forecast, however. They cited uncertainty about domestic spending, labor productivity, and economic growth in Europe and the emerging economies as important sources of inflation uncertainty. As it turns out, their near-term forecast was overly pessimistic: Inflation fell to their target of 2% by the end of 2013.

The Bank of England has been a pioneer in the movement toward greater openness by central banks, and other central banks now also publish inflation forecasts. The decisions made by monetary policy-makers are difficult ones and affect the lives—and wallets—of many of their fellow citizens. In a democracy in the information age, reasoned the economists at the Bank of England, it is particularly important for citizens to understand the bank's economic outlook and the reasoning behind its difficult decisions.

To see the river of blood in its original red hue, visit the Bank of England's website, at **http://www.bankofengland.co.uk**. To learn more about the performance of the Bank of England inflation forecasts, see Clements (2004).

### Figure 14.4  The River of Blood

The Bank of England's fan chart for August 2013 shows forecast ranges for inflation. The dashed line indicates the third quarter of 2015, 2 years after the release of the report.

Source: Reprinted with permission from the Bank of England.

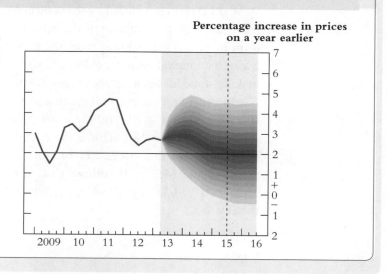

This discussion has focused on the case that the error term, $u_{T+1}$, is homoskedastic. If instead $u_{T+1}$ is heteroskedastic, then one needs to develop a model of the heteroskedasticity so that the term $\sigma_u^2$ in Equation (14.21) can be estimated, given the most recent values of $Y$ and $X$; methods for modeling this conditional heteroskedasticity are presented in Section 16.5.

Because of uncertainty about future events—that is, uncertainty about $u_{T+1}$ —95% forecast intervals can be so wide that they have limited use in decision making. Professional forecasters therefore often report forecast intervals that are tighter than 95%—for example, one standard error forecast intervals (which are 68% forecast intervals if the errors are normally distributed). Alternatively, some forecasters report multiple forecast intervals, as is done by the economists at the Bank of England when they publish their inflation forecasts (see "The River of Blood"on the previous page).

# 14.5  Lag Length Selection Using Information Criteria

The estimated GDP growth regressions in Sections 14.3 and 14.4 have either one or two lags of the predictors. One lag makes some sense, but why two and not three or four? More generally, how many lags should be included in a time series regression? This section discusses statistical methods for choosing the number of lags, first in an autoregression and then in a time series regression model with multiple predictors.

## Determining the Order of an Autoregression

In practice, choosing the order $p$ of an autoregression requires balancing the marginal benefit of including more lags against the marginal cost of additional estimation uncertainty. On the one hand, if the order of an estimated autoregression is too low, you will omit potentially valuable information contained in the more distant lagged values. On the other hand, if it is too high, you will be estimating more coefficients than necessary, which in turn introduces additional estimation error into your forecasts.

*The F-statistic approach.*  One approach to choosing $p$ is to start with a model with many lags and to perform hypothesis tests on the final lag. For example, you might start by estimating an AR(6) and test whether the coefficient on the sixth lag is significant at the 5% level; if not, drop it and estimate an AR(5), test the coefficient on the fifth lag, and so forth. The drawback to this method is that it will produce a model that is too large, at least some of the time: Even if the true AR order is five, so the sixth coefficient is zero, a 5% test using the $t$-statistic will incorrectly reject this null hypothesis 5% of the time just by chance. Thus, when the true value of $p$ is five, this method will estimate $p$ to be six 5% of the time.

*The BIC.* A way around this problem is to estimate $p$ by minimizing an "information criterion." One such information criterion is the **Bayes information criterion (BIC)**, also called the *Schwarz information criterion (SIC)*, which is

$$\text{BIC}(p) = \ln\left[\frac{SSR(p)}{T}\right] + (p+1)\frac{\ln(T)}{T}, \tag{14.22}$$

where $SSR(p)$ is the sum of squared residuals of the estimated AR($p$). The BIC estimator of $p$, $\hat{p}$, is the value that minimizes BIC($p$) among the possible choices $p = 0, 1, \ldots, p_{max,}$ where $p_{max}$ is the largest value of $p$ considered and $p = 0$ corresponds to the model that contains only an intercept.

The formula for the BIC might look a bit mysterious at first, but it has an intuitive appeal. Consider the first term in Equation (14.22). Because the regression coefficients are estimated by OLS, the sum of squared residuals necessarily decreases (or at least does not increase) when you add a lag. In contrast, the second term is the number of estimated regression coefficients (the number of lags, $p$, plus one for the intercept) times the factor $\ln(T)/T$. This second term increases when you add a lag. The BIC trades off these two forces so that the number of lags that minimizes the BIC is a consistent estimator of the true lag length. Appendix 14.5 provides the mathematics of this argument.

As an example, consider estimating the AR order for an autoregression of the growth rate of GDP. The various steps in the calculation of the BIC are carried out in Table 14.3 for autoregressions of maximum order six ($p_{max} = 6$). For example, for the AR(1) model in Equation (14.7), $SSR(1)/T = 9.866$, so $\ln[SSR(1)/T] = 2.289$. Because $T = 204$ (51 years, 4 quarters per year), $\ln(T)/T = 0.026$ and $(p+1)\ln(T)/T = 2 \times 0.026 = 0.052$ Thus BIC(1) $= 2.289 + 0.052 = 2.341$.

The BIC is smallest when $p = 2$ in Table 14.3. Thus the BIC estimate of the lag length is 2. As can be seen in Table 14.3, as the number of lags increases, the $R^2$ increases and the $SSR$ decreases. The increase in the $R^2$ is large from zero to one lag, smaller for one to two lags, and smaller yet for other lags. The BIC helps decide precisely how large the increase in the $R^2$ must be to justify including the additional lag.

| TABLE 14.3 | The Bayes Information Criterion (BIC) and the $R^2$ for Autoregressive Models of U.S. GDP Growth Rates, 1962–2012 | | | | |
|---|---|---|---|---|---|
| $p$ | $SSR(p)/T$ | $\ln[SSR(p)/T]$ | $(p+1)\ln(T)/T$ | $BIC(p)$ | $R^2$ |
| 0 | 11.198 | 2.416 | 0.026 | 2.442 | 0.000 |
| 1 | 9.866 | 2.289 | 0.052 | 2.341 | 0.119 |
| 2 | 9.546 | 2.256 | 0.078 | 2.334 | 0.148 |
| 3 | 9.546 | 2.256 | 0.104 | 2.360 | 0.148 |
| 4 | 9.508 | 2.252 | 0.130 | 2.382 | 0.151 |
| 5 | 9.366 | 2.237 | 0.156 | 2.394 | 0.164 |
| 6 | 9.359 | 2.236 | 0.183 | 2.419 | 0.164 |

*The AIC.* The BIC is not the only information criterion; another is the **Akaike information criterion (AIC)**:

$$\text{AIC}(p) = \ln\left[\frac{SSR(p)}{T}\right] + (p+1)\frac{2}{T}. \qquad (14.23)$$

The difference between the AIC and the BIC is that the term "$\ln(T)$" in the BIC is replaced by "2" in the AIC, so the second term in the AIC is smaller. For example, for the 204 observations used to estimate the GDP autoregressions, $\ln(T) = \ln(204) = 5.32$, so the second term for the BIC is more than twice as large as the term in AIC. Thus a smaller decrease in the $SSR$ is needed in the AIC to justify including another lag. As a matter of theory, the second term in the AIC is not large enough to ensure that the correct lag length is chosen, even in large samples, so the AIC estimator of $p$ is not consistent. As is discussed in Appendix 14.5, in large samples the AIC will overestimate $p$ with nonzero probability.

Despite this theoretical blemish, the AIC is widely used in practice. If you are concerned that the BIC might yield a model with too few lags, the AIC provides a reasonable alternative.

*A note on calculating information criteria.* How well two estimated regressions fit the data is best assessed when they are estimated using the same data sets. Because the BIC and AIC are formal methods for making this comparison, the autoregressions under consideration should be estimated using the same observations. For example, in Table 14.3 all the regressions were estimated using data from 1962:Q1 to 2012:Q4, for a total of 204 observations. Because the autoregressions involve lags of the growth rate of GDP, this means that earlier values of GDP growth (values before 1962:Q1) were used as regressors for the preliminary observations. Said differently, the regressions examined in Table 14.3 each include observations on $GDPGR_t$, $GDPGR_{t-1}, \ldots, GDPGR_{t-p}$ for $t = 1962{:}Q1, \ldots$, 2012:Q4 corresponding to 204 observations on the dependent variable and regressors, so $T = 204$ in Equations (14.22) and (14.24).

## Lag Length Selection in Time Series Regression with Multiple Predictors

The trade-off involved with lag length choice in the general time series regression model with multiple predictors [Equation (14.19)] is similar to that in an autoregression: Using too few lags can decrease forecast accuracy because valuable information is lost, but adding lags increases estimation uncertainty. The choice of lags must balance the benefit of using additional information against the cost of estimating the additional coefficients.

*The F-statistic approach.* As in the univariate autoregression, one way to determine the number of lags to include is to use $F$-statistics to test joint hypotheses that sets of coefficients are equal to zero. For example, in the discussion of Equation (14.16), we tested the hypothesis that the coefficient on the second lag of the term spread was equal to zero against the alternative that it was nonzero; this hypothesis was not rejected at the 10% significance level, suggesting that the second lag of the term spread could be dropped from the regression. If the number of models being compared is small, then this $F$-statistic method is easy to use. In general, however, the $F$-statistic method can produce models that are too large, in the sense that the true lag order is overestimated.

*Information criteria.* As in an autoregression, the BIC and AIC can be used to estimate the number of lags and variables in the time series regression model with multiple predictors. If the regression model has $K$ coefficients (including the intercept), the BIC is

$$BIC(K) = \ln\left[\frac{SSR(K)}{T}\right] + K\,\frac{\ln(T)}{T}. \tag{14.24}$$

The AIC is defined in the same way, but with 2 replacing $\ln(T)$ in Equation (14.24). For each candidate model, the BIC (or AIC) can be evaluated, and the model with the lowest value of the BIC (or AIC) is the preferred model, based on the information criterion.

There are two important practical considerations when using an information criterion to estimate the lag lengths. First, as is the case for the autoregression, all the candidate models must be estimated over the same sample; in the notation of Equation (14.24), the number of observations used to estimate the model, $T$, must be the same for all models. Second, when there are multiple predictors, this approach is computationally demanding because it requires computing many different models (many combinations of the lag parameters). In practice, a convenient shortcut is to require all the regressors to have the same number of lags, that is, to require that $p = q_1 = \cdots = q_k$, so that only $p_{max} + 1$ models need to be compared (corresponding to $p = 0, 1, \ldots, p_{max}$). Applying this lag-length selection method to the ADL for GDP growth and the term spread results in the ADL(2,2) model in Equation (14.16).

## 14.6   Nonstationarity I: Trends

In Key Concept 14.6, it was assumed that the dependent variable and the regressors are stationary. If this is not the case—that is, if the dependent variable and/or regressors are nonstationary—then conventional hypothesis tests, confidence intervals, and forecasts can be unreliable. The precise problem created by nonstationarity, and the solution to that problem, depends on the nature of that nonstationarity.

In this and the next section, we examine two of the most important types of nonstationarity in economic time series data: trends and breaks. In each section, we first describe the nature of the nonstationarity and then discuss the consequences for time series regression if this type of nonstationarity is present but ignored. We next present tests for nonstationarity and discuss remedies for, or solutions to, the problems caused by that particular type of nonstationarity. We begin by discussing trends.

### What Is a Trend?

A **trend** is a persistent long-term movement of a variable over time. A time series variable fluctuates around its trend.

Inspection of Figure 14.1a suggests that the logarithm of U.S. GDP has a clear upwardly increasing trend. The series in Figures 14.2a, b, and c also have trends, but their trends are quite different. The trend in the unemployment rate is increasing from the late 1960s through the early 1980s, then decreasing until the early 2000s, and then increasing again through 2012. The \$/£ exchange rate clearly had a prolonged downward trend after the collapse of the fixed exchange rate system in 1972. The logarithm of the industrial production index for Japan has a complicated trend: fast growth at first, then moderate growth, and finally no growth.

*Deterministic and stochastic trends.* There are two types of trends in time series data: deterministic and stochastic. A **deterministic trend** is a nonrandom function of time. For example, a deterministic trend might be linear in time; if the logarithm of U.S. GDP had a deterministic linear trend so that it increased by 0.75 percentage point per quarter, this trend could be written as $0.75t$, where $t$ is measured in quarters. In contrast, a **stochastic trend** is random and varies over time. For example, a stochastic trend might exhibit a prolonged period of increase followed by a prolonged period of decrease, like the unemployment rate trend in Figure 14.2a. But stochastic trends can be more subtle. For example, if you look carefully at Figure 14.1a, you will notice that the trend growth rate of GDP is not constant; for example, GDP grew faster in the 1960s than in the 1970s (the plot is steeper in the 1960s than in the 1970s), and it grew faster in the 1990s than in the 2000s.

Like many other econometricians, we think it is more appropriate to model economic time series as having stochastic rather than deterministic trends. Economics is complicated stuff. It is hard to reconcile the predictability implied by a deterministic trend with the complications and surprises faced year after year by workers, businesses, and governments. For example, although the U.S. unemployment rate rose through the 1970s, it was neither destined to rise forever nor destined to fall again. Rather, the slow rise of unemployment rates is now understood to have occurred because of a combination of demographic changes (such as an increase in female labor force participation), bad luck (such as oil price shocks and a productivity slowdown), and monetary policy mistakes. Similarly, the \$/£ exchange rate trended down from 1972 to 1985 and subsequently drifted up, but these movements too were the consequences of complex economic forces; because these forces change unpredictably, these trends are usefully thought of as having a large unpredictable, or random, component.

For these reasons, our treatment of trends in economic time series focuses on stochastic rather than deterministic trends, and when we refer to "trends" in time series data, we mean stochastic trends unless we explicitly say otherwise. This section presents the simplest model of a stochastic trend, the random walk model; other models of trends are discussed in Section 16.3.

*The random walk model of a trend.* The simplest model of a variable with a stochastic trend is the random walk. A time series $Y_t$ is said to follow a **random walk** if the change in $Y_t$ is i.i.d., that is, if

$$Y_t = Y_{t-1} + u_t, \tag{14.25}$$

where $u_t$ is i.i.d. We will, however, use the term *random walk* more generally to refer to a time series that follows Equation (14.25), where $u_t$ has conditional mean zero; that is, $E(u_t|Y_{t-1},Y_{t-2}, \dots) = 0$.

The basic idea of a random walk is that the value of the series tomorrow is its value today, plus an unpredictable change: Because the path followed by $Y_t$ consists of random "steps" $u_t$, that path is a "random walk." The conditional mean of $Y_t$ based on data through time $t - 1$ is $Y_{t-1}$; that is, because $E(u_t|Y_{t-1}, Y_{t-2}, \dots) = 0$, $E(Y_t|Y_{t-1}, Y_{t-2}, \dots) = Y_{t-1}$. In other words, if $Y_t$ follows a random walk, then the best forecast of tomorrow's value is its value today.

Some series, such as the logarithm of U.S. GDP in Figure 14.1a, have an obvious upward tendency, in which case the best forecast of the series must include an adjustment for the tendency of the series to increase. This adjustment leads to an extension of the random walk model to include a tendency to move, or "drift," in one direction or the other. This extension is referred to as a **random walk with drift**,

$$Y_t = \beta_0 + Y_{t-1} + u_t, \tag{14.26}$$

where $E(u_t|Y_{t-1},Y_{t-2}, \dots) = 0$, and $\beta_0$ is the "drift" in the random walk. If $\beta_0$ is positive, then $Y_t$ increases on average. In the random walk with drift model, the best forecast of the series tomorrow is the value of the series today, plus the drift $\beta_0$.

The random walk model (with drift, as appropriate) is simple yet versatile, and it is the primary model for trends used in this book.

*A random walk is nonstationary.* If $Y_t$ follows a random walk, then it is not stationary: The variance of a random walk increases over time, so the distribution of $Y_t$ changes over time. One way to see this is to recognize that, because $u_t$ is uncorrelated with $Y_{t-1}$ in Equation (14.25), $\text{var}(Y_t) = \text{var}(Y_{t-1}) + \text{var}(u_t)$; for $Y_t$ to be stationary, $\text{var}(Y_t)$ cannot depend on time, so in particular $\text{var}(Y_t) = \text{var}(Y_{t-1})$ must hold, but this can happen only if $\text{var}(u_t) = 0$. Another way to see this is to imagine that $Y_t$ starts out at zero—that is, $Y_0 = 0$. Then $Y_1 = u_1$, $Y_2 = u_1 + u_2$, and so forth so that $Y_t = u_1 + u_2 + \cdots + u_t$. Because $u_t$ is serially uncorrelated, $\text{var}(Y_t) = \text{var}(u_1 + u_2 + \cdots + u_t) = t\sigma_u^2$. Thus the variance of $Y_t$ depends on $t$; in fact, it increases as $t$ increases. Because the variance of $Y_t$ depends on $t$, its distribution depends on $t$; that is, it is nonstationary.

Because the variance of a random walk increases without bound, its *population* autocorrelations are not defined. (The first autocovariance and variance are infinite, and the ratio of the two is not well defined.) However, a feature of a random walk is that its *sample* autocorrelations tend to be very close to 1; in fact, the $j^{th}$ sample autocorrelation of a random walk converges to 1 in probability.

*Stochastic trends, autoregressive models, and a unit root.* The random walk model is a special case of the AR(1) model [Equation (14.8)] in which $\beta_1 = 1$. In other words, if $Y_t$ follows an AR(1) with $\beta_1 = 1$, then $Y_t$ contains a stochastic trend and is nonstationary. If, however, $|\beta_1| < 1$ and $u_t$ is stationary, then the joint distribution of $Y_t$ and its lags does not depend on $t$ (a result shown in Appendix 14.2), so $Y_t$ is stationary.

The analogous condition for an AR($p$) to be stationary is more complicated than the condition $|\beta_1| < 1$ for an AR(1). Its formal statement involves the roots of the polynomial, $1 - \beta_1 z - \beta_2 z^2 - \beta_3 z^3 - \cdots - \beta_p z^p$. (The roots of this polynomial are the values of $z$ that satisfy $1 - \beta_1 z - \beta_2 z^2 - \beta_3 z^3 - \cdots - \beta_p z^p = 0$.) For an AR($p$) to be stationary, the roots of this polynomial must all be greater than 1 in absolute value. In the special case of an AR(1), the root is the value of $z$ that solves $1 - \beta_1 z = 0$, so its root is $z = 1/\beta_1$. Thus the statement that the root be greater than 1 in absolute value is equivalent to $|\beta_1| < 1$.

If an AR($p$) has a root that equals 1, the series is said to have a *unit autoregressive root* or, more simply, a **unit root**. If $Y_t$ has a unit root, then it contains a stochastic trend. If $Y_t$ is stationary (and thus does not have a unit root), it does not contain a stochastic trend. For this reason, we will use the terms *stochastic trend* and *unit root* interchangeably.

## Problems Caused by Stochastic Trends

If a regressor has a stochastic trend (that is, has a unit root), then the OLS estimator of its coefficient and its OLS $t$-statistic can have nonstandard (that is, nonnormal) distributions, even in large samples. We discuss three specific aspects of this problem: (1) The estimator of the autoregressive coefficient in an AR(1) is biased toward 0 if its true value is 1; (2) the $t$-statistic on a regressor with a stochastic trend can have a nonnormal distribution, even in large samples; and (3) an extreme example of the risks posed by stochastic trends is that two series that are independent will, with high probability, misleadingly appear to be related if they both have stochastic trends, a situation known as spurious regression.

*Problem #1: Autoregressive coefficients that are biased toward zero.* Suppose that $Y_t$ follows the random walk in Equation (14.25), but this is unknown to the econometrician, who instead estimates the AR(1) model in Equation (14.8). Because $Y_t$ is nonstationary, the least squares assumptions for time series regression in Key Concept 14.6 do not hold, so as a general matter, we cannot rely on estimators and test statistics having their usual large-sample normal distributions. In fact, in this example, the OLS estimator of the autoregressive coefficient, $\hat{\beta}_1$, is consistent, but it has a nonnormal distribution, even in large samples: The asymptotic distribution of $\hat{\beta}_1$ is shifted toward zero. The expected value of $\hat{\beta}_1$ is approximately $E(\hat{\beta}_1) = 1 - 5.3/T$. This results in a large bias in sample sizes typically encountered in economic applications. For example, 20 years of quarterly data contain 80 observations, in which case the expected value of $\hat{\beta}_1$ is $E(\hat{\beta}_1) = 1 - 5.3/80 = 0.934$. Moreover, this distribution has a long left tail: The 5% percentile of $\hat{\beta}_1$ is approximately $1 - 14.1/T$, which, for $T = 80$, corresponds to 0.824, so 5% of the time $\hat{\beta}_1 < 0.824$.

One implication of this bias toward zero is that if $Y_t$ follows a random walk, then forecasts based on the AR(1) model can perform substantially worse than those based on the random walk model, which imposes the true value $\beta_1 = 1$. This conclusion also applies to higher-order autoregressions, in which there are forecasting gains from imposing a unit root (that is, from estimating the autoregression in first differences instead of in levels) when in fact the series contains a unit root.

*Problem #2: Nonnormal distributions of t-statistics.* If a regressor has a stochastic trend, then its usual OLS $t$-statistic can have a nonnormal distribution under the null hypothesis, even in large samples. This nonnormal distribution means that conventional confidence intervals are not valid, and hypothesis tests cannot be conducted as usual. In general, the distribution of this $t$-statistic is not readily tabulated because the distribution depends on the relationship between the regressor in question and the other regressors. An important example of this problem arises in regressions that attempt to forecast stock returns using regressors that could have stochastic trends (see the box in Section 14.7, "Can You Beat the Market? Part II").

One important case in which it *is* possible to tabulate the distribution of the $t$-statistic when the regressor has a stochastic trend is in the context of an autoregression with a unit root. We return to this special case when we take up the problem of testing whether a time series contains a stochastic trend.

*Problem #3: Spurious regression.* Stochastic trends can lead two time series to appear related when they are not, a problem called **spurious regression**.

For example, the U.S. unemployment rate was steadily rising from the mid-1960s through the early 1980s, and at the same time Japanese industrial production (plotted in logarithms in Figure 14.2c) was steadily rising. These two trends conspire to produce a regression that appears to be "significant" using conventional measures. Estimated by OLS using data from 1962 through 1985, this regression is

$$\overline{U.\,S.\;Unemployment\;Rate_t} = -2.37 + 2.22 \times \ln(Japanese\;IP_t),\;\overline{R}^2 = 0.34.$$
$$\qquad\qquad\qquad (1.19)\quad (0.32) \qquad\qquad\qquad\qquad (14.27)$$

The $t$-statistic on the slope coefficient is 7, which by usual standards indicates a strong positive relationship between the two series, and the $\overline{R}^2$ is moderately high. However, running this regression using data from 1986 through 2012 yields

$$\overline{U.\,S.\;Unemployment\;Rate_t} = 41.78 - 7.78 \times \ln(Japanese\;IP_t),\;\overline{R}^2 = 0.15.$$
$$\qquad\qquad\qquad (8.05)\quad (1.75) \qquad\qquad\qquad\qquad (14.28)$$

The regressions in Equations (14.27) and (14.28) could hardly be more different. Interpreted literally, Equation (14.27) indicates a strong positive relationship, while Equation (14.28) indicates an even stronger negative relationship.

The source of these conflicting results is that both series have stochastic trends. These trends happened to align from 1962 through 1985 but were reversed from 1986 through 2012. There is, in fact, no compelling economic or political reason to think that the trends in these two series are related. In short, these regressions are spurious.

The regressions in Equations (14.27) and (14.28) illustrate empirically the theoretical point that OLS can be misleading when the series contain stochastic trends. (See Exercise 14.6 for a computer simulation that demonstrates this result.) One special case in which certain regression-based methods *are* reliable is when the trend component of the two series is the same—that is, when the series contain a *common* stochastic trend; in such a case, the series are said to be cointegrated. Econometric methods for detecting and analyzing cointegrated economic time series are discussed in Section 16.4.

## Detecting Stochastic Trends: Testing for a Unit AR Root

Trends in time series data can be detected using informal and formal methods. The informal methods involve inspecting a time series plot of the data and computing the autocorrelation coefficients, as we did in Section 14.2. Because the first autocorrelation coefficient will be near 1 if the series has a stochastic trend, at least in large samples, a small first autocorrelation coefficient combined with a time series plot that has no apparent trend suggests that the series does not have a trend. If doubt remains, however, formal statistical procedures can be used to test the hypothesis that there is a stochastic trend in the series against the alternative that there is no trend.

In this section, we use the Dickey–Fuller test (named after its inventors David Dickey and Wayne Fuller, 1979) to test for a stochastic trend. Although the Dickey–Fuller test is not the only test for a stochastic trend (another test is discussed in Section 16.3), it is the most commonly used test in practice and is one of the most reliable.

*The Dickey–Fuller test in the AR(1) model.* The starting point for the **Dickey–Fuller test** is the autoregressive model. As discussed earlier, the random walk in Equation (14.26) is a special case of the AR(1) model with $\beta_1 = 1$. If $\beta_1 = 1$, $Y_t$ is nonstationary and contains a (stochastic) trend. Thus, within the AR(1) model, the hypothesis that $Y_t$ has a trend can be tested by testing

$$H_0: \beta_1 = 1 \text{ vs. } H_1: \beta_1 < 1 \text{ in } Y_t = \beta_0 + \beta_1 Y_{t-1} + u_t. \qquad (14.29)$$

If $\beta_1 = 1$, the AR(1) has an autoregressive root of 1, so the null hypothesis in Equation (14.29) is that the AR(1) has a unit root, and the alternative is that it is stationary.

This test is most easily implemented by estimating a modified version of Equation (14.29), obtained by subtracting $Y_{t-1}$ from both sides. Let $\delta = \beta_1 - 1$; then Equation (14.29) becomes

$$H_0: \delta = 0 \text{ vs. } H_1: \delta < 0 \text{ in } \Delta Y_t = \beta_0 + \delta Y_{t-1} + u_t. \qquad (14.30)$$

The OLS $t$-statistic testing $\delta = 0$ in Equation (14.30) is called the **Dickey–Fuller statistic**. The formulation in Equation (14.30) is convenient because regression software automatically prints out the $t$-statistic testing $\delta = 0$. Note that the Dickey–Fuller test is one-sided because the relevant alternative is that $Y_t$ is stationary, so $\beta_1 < 1$ or, equivalently, $\delta < 0$. The Dickey–Fuller statistic is computed using "nonrobust" standard errors—that is, the "homoskedasticity-only" standard errors presented in Appendix 5.1 [Equation (5.29) for the case of a single regressor and in Section 18.4 for the multiple regression model].[3]

---

[3]Under the null hypothesis of a unit root, the usual "nonrobust" standard errors produce a $t$-statistic that is in fact robust to heteroskedasticity, a surprising and special result.

*The Dickey–Fuller test in the AR(p) model.* The Dickey–Fuller statistic presented in the context of Equation (14.30) applies only to an AR(1). As discussed in Section 14.3, for some series the AR(1) model does not capture all the serial correlation in $Y_t$, in which case a higher-order autoregression is more appropriate.

The extension of the Dickey–Fuller test to the AR($p$) model is summarized in Key Concept 14.8. Under the null hypothesis, $\delta = 0$ and $\Delta Y_t$ is a stationary AR($p$). Under the alternative hypothesis, $\delta < 0$ so that $Y_t$ is stationary. Because the regression used to compute this version of the Dickey–Fuller statistic is augmented by lags of $\Delta Y_t$, the resulting $t$-statistic is referred to as the **augmented Dickey–Fuller (ADF) statistic**.

In general, the lag length $p$ is unknown, but it can be estimated using an information criterion applied to regressions of the form in Equation (14.31) for various values of $p$. Studies of the ADF statistic suggest that it is better to have too many lags than too few, so it is recommended to use the AIC instead of the BIC to estimate $p$ for the ADF statistic.[4]

*Testing against the alternative of stationarity around a linear deterministic time trend.* The discussion so far has considered the null hypothesis that a series has a unit root and the alternative hypothesis that it is stationary. This alternative hypothesis of stationarity is appropriate for series, such as the unemployment rate, that do not exhibit long-term growth. But other economic time series, such as U.S. GDP, exhibit long-run growth, and for such series the alternative of stationarity without a trend is inappropriate. Instead, a commonly used alternative is that the series are stationary around a deterministic time trend—that is, a trend that is a deterministic function of time.

One specific formulation of this alternative hypothesis is that the time trend is linear; that is, the trend is a linear function of $t$. Thus the null hypothesis is that the series has a unit root, and the alternative is that it does not have a unit root but does have a deterministic time trend. The Dickey–Fuller regression must be modified to test the null hypothesis of a unit root against the alternative that it is stationary around a linear time trend. As summarized in Equation (14.32) in Key Concept 14.8, this is accomplished by adding a time trend (the regressor $X_t = t$) to the regression.

A linear time trend is not the only way to specify a deterministic time trend; for example, the deterministic time trend could be quadratic, or it could be linear but have breaks (that is, be linear with slopes that differ in two parts of the

---

[4]See Stock (1994) and Haldrup and Jansson (2006) for reviews of simulation studies of the finite-sample properties of the Dickey–Fuller and other unit root test statistics.

## The Augmented Dickey–Fuller Test for a Unit Autoregressive Root

The augmented Dickey–Fuller (ADF) test for a unit autoregressive root tests the null hypothesis $H_0$: $\delta = 0$ against the one-sided alternative $H_1$: $\delta < 0$ in the regression

$$\Delta Y_t = \beta_0 + \delta Y_{t-1} + \gamma_1 \Delta Y_{t-1} + \gamma_2 \Delta Y_{t-2} + \cdots + \gamma_p \Delta Y_{t-p} + u_t. \quad (14.31)$$

Under the null hypothesis, $Y_t$ has a stochastic trend; under the alternative hypothesis, $Y_t$ is stationary. The ADF statistic is the OLS $t$-statistic testing $\delta = 0$ in Equation (14.31).

If instead the alternative hypothesis is that $Y_t$ is stationary around a deterministic linear time trend, then this trend, "$t$" (the observation number), must be added as an additional regressor, in which case the Dickey–Fuller regression becomes

$$\Delta Y_t = \beta_0 + \alpha t + \delta Y_{t-1} + \gamma_1 \Delta Y_{t-1} + \gamma_2 \Delta Y_{t-2} + \cdots + \gamma_p \Delta Y_{t-p} + u_t, \quad (14.32)$$

where $\alpha$ is an unknown coefficient and the ADF statistic is the OLS $t$-statistic testing $\delta = 0$ in Equation (14.32).

The lag length $p$ can be estimated using the BIC or AIC. When $p = 0$, lags of $\Delta Y_t$ are not included as regressors in Equations (14.31) and (14.32), and the ADF test simplifies to the Dickey–Fuller test in the AR(1) model. The ADF statistic does *not* have a normal distribution, even in large samples. Critical values for the one-sided ADF test depend on whether the test is based on Equation (14.31) or (14.32) and are given in Table 14.4.

---

sample). The use of alternatives like these with nonlinear deterministic trends should be motivated by economic theory. For a discussion of unit root tests against stationarity around nonlinear deterministic trends, see Maddala and Kim (1998, Chapter 13).

*Critical values for the ADF statistic.* Under the null hypothesis of a unit root, the ADF statistic does *not* have a normal distribution, even in large samples. Because its distribution is nonstandard, the usual critical values from the normal distribution cannot be used when using the ADF statistic to test for a unit root; a special set of critical values, based on the distribution of the ADF statistic under the null hypothesis, must be used instead.

The critical values for the ADF test are given in Table 14.4. Because the alternative hypothesis of stationarity implies that $\delta < 0$ in Equations (14.31) and (14.32), the ADF test is one-sided. For example, if the regression does not include a time trend, then the hypothesis of a unit root is rejected at the 5% significance level if the ADF statistic is less than $-2.86$. If a time trend is included in the regression, the critical value is instead $-3.41$.

The critical values in Table 14.4 are substantially larger (more negative) than the one-sided critical values of $-1.28$ (at the 10% level) and $-1.64$ (at the 5% level) from the standard normal distribution. The nonstandard distribution of the ADF statistic is an example of how OLS $t$-statistics for regressors with stochastic trends can have nonnormal distributions. Why the large-sample distribution of the ADF statistic is nonstandard is discussed further in Section 16.3.

*Does U.S. GDP have a stochastic trend?* The null hypothesis that the logarithm of U.S. GDP has a stochastic trend can be tested against the alternative that it is stationary by performing the ADF test for a unit autoregressive root. The ADF regression with two lags of $\Delta\ln(GDP_t)$ is

$$\widehat{\Delta\ln(GDP_t)} = 0.244 + 0.0002t - 0.030\ln(GDP_{t-1})$$
$$\phantom{\widehat{\Delta\ln(GDP_t)} = } (0.109) \quad (0.0001) \quad (0.014)$$

$$\phantom{\widehat{\Delta\ln(GDP_t)} = } + 0.269\Delta\ln(GDP_{t-1}) + 0.178\Delta\ln(GDP_{t-2}).$$
$$\phantom{\widehat{\Delta\ln(GDP_t)} = } (0.069) \phantom{+ 0.269\Delta\ln(GDP_{t-1}) } (0.070) \phantom{mmmmmmmmm} (14.33)$$

The ADF $t$-statistic is the $t$-statistic testing the hypothesis that the coefficient on $\ln(GDP_{t-1})$ is zero; this is $t = -2.18$. From Table 14.4, the 10% critical value is $-3.12$. Because the ADF statistic of $-2.18$ is less negative than $-3.12$, the test does not reject the null hypothesis at the 10% significance level. Based on the regression in Equation (14.33), we therefore cannot reject (at the 10% significance level) the null hypothesis that the logarithm of GDP has a unit autoregressive

| TABLE 14.4 Large-Sample Critical Values of the Augmented Dickey–Fuller Statistic | | | |
|---|---|---|---|
| **Deterministic Regressors** | **10%** | **5%** | **1%** |
| Intercept only | −2.57 | −2.86 | −3.43 |
| Intercept and time trend | −3.12 | −3.41 | −3.96 |

root—that is, that $\ln(GDP)$ has a stochastic trend—against the alternative that it is stationary around a linear trend.

The ADF regression in Equation (14.33) includes two lags of $\Delta\ln(GDP_t)$ to compute the ADF statistic. When the number of lags is estimated using the AIC, where $0 \leq p \leq 5$, the AIC estimator of the lag length is, however, one. When one lag is used (that is, when $\Delta\ln(GDP_{t-1})$ is included as a regressor), the ADF statistic is $-1.84$, which is less negative than $-3.12$. Thus, when the number of lags in the ADF regression is chosen by AIC, the hypothesis that the logarithm of U.S. GDP contains a stochastic trend is not rejected at the 10% significance level.

### Avoiding the Problems Caused by Stochastic Trends

The most reliable way to handle a trend in a series is to transform the series so that it does not have the trend. If the series has a stochastic trend—that is, if the series has a unit root—then the first difference of the series does not have a trend. For example, if $Y_t$ follows a random walk so that $Y_t = \beta_0 + Y_{t-1} + u_t$, then $\Delta Y_t = \beta_0 + u_t$ is stationary. Thus using first differences eliminates random walk trends in a series.

In practice, you can rarely be sure whether a series has a stochastic trend. Recall that, as a general point, failure to reject the null hypothesis does not necessarily mean that the null hypothesis is true; rather, it simply means that you have insufficient evidence to conclude that it is false. Thus failure to reject the null hypothesis of a unit root using the ADF test does not mean that the series actually *has* a unit root. For example, in an AR(1) model, the true coefficient $\beta_1$ might be very close to 1, say 0.98, in which case the ADF test would have low power—that is, a low probability of correctly rejecting the null hypothesis in samples the size of our GDP series. Even though failure to reject the null hypothesis of a unit root does not mean the series has a unit root, it still can be reasonable to approximate the true autoregressive root as equaling 1 and therefore to use differences of the series rather than its levels.[5]

## 14.7  Nonstationarity II: Breaks

A second type of nonstationarity arises when the population regression function changes over the course of the sample. In economics, this can occur for a variety of reasons, such as changes in economic policy, changes in the structure of the economy, or changes in a specific industry due to an invention. If such changes,

---

[5]For additional discussion of stochastic trends in economic time series variables and of the problems they pose for regression analysis, see Stock and Watson (1988).

or "**breaks**," occur, then a regression model that neglects those changes can provide a misleading basis for inference and forecasting.

This section presents two strategies for checking for breaks in a time series regression function over time. The first strategy looks for potential breaks from the perspective of hypothesis testing and entails testing for changes in the regression coefficients using $F$-statistics. The second strategy looks for potential breaks from the perspective of forecasting: You pretend that your sample ends sooner than it actually does and evaluate the forecasts you would have made had this been so. Breaks are detected when the forecasting performance is substantially poorer than expected.

## What Is a Break?

Breaks can arise either from a discrete change in the population regression coefficients at a distinct date or from a gradual evolution of the coefficients over a longer period of time.

One source of discrete breaks in macroeconomic data is a major change in macroeconomic policy. For example, the breakdown of the Bretton Woods system of fixed exchange rates in 1972 produced the break in the time series behavior of the $/£ exchange rate that is evident in Figure 14.2b. Prior to 1972, the exchange rate was essentially constant, with the exception of a single devaluation in 1968, in which the official value of the pound, relative to the dollar, was decreased. In contrast, since 1972 the exchange rate has fluctuated over a very wide range.

Breaks also can occur more slowly, as the population regression evolves over time. For example, such changes can arise because of slow evolution of economic policy and ongoing changes in the structure of the economy. The methods for detecting breaks described in this section can detect both types of breaks: distinct changes and slow evolution.

*Problems caused by breaks.* If a break occurs in the population regression function during the sample, then the OLS regression estimates over the full sample will estimate a relationship that holds "on average," in the sense that the estimate combines the two different periods. Depending on the location and the size of the break, the "average" regression function can be quite different from the true regression function at the end of the sample, and this leads to poor forecasts.

## Testing for Breaks

One way to detect breaks is to test for discrete changes, or breaks, in the regression coefficients. How this is done depends on whether the date of the suspected break (the **break date**) is known.

*Testing for a break at a known date.*   In some applications, you might suspect that there is a break at a known date. For example, if you are studying international trade relationships using data from the 1970s, you might hypothesize that there is a break in the population regression function of interest in 1972, when the Bretton Woods system of fixed exchange rates was abandoned in favor of floating exchange rates.

If the date of the hypothesized break in the coefficients is known, then the null hypothesis of no break can be tested using a binary variable interaction regression of the type discussed in Chapter 8 (Key Concept 8.4). To keep things simple, consider an ADL(1,1) model, so there is an intercept, a single lag of $Y_t$, and a single lag of $X_t$. Let $\tau$ denote the hypothesized break date and let $D_t(\tau)$ be a binary variable that equals 0 before the break date and 1 after, so $D_t(\tau) = 0$ if $t \leq \tau$ and $D_t(\tau) = 1$ if $t > \tau$. Then the regression including the binary break indicator and all interaction terms is

$$
\begin{aligned}
Y_t = \beta_0 &+ \beta_1 Y_{t-1} + \delta_1 X_{t-1} + \gamma_0 D_t(\tau) + \gamma_1 [D_t(\tau) \times Y_{t-1}] \\
&+ \gamma_2 [D_t(\tau) \times X_{t-1}] + u_t.
\end{aligned}
\tag{14.34}
$$

If there is not a break, then the population regression function is the same over both parts of the sample, so the terms involving the break binary variable $D_t(\tau)$ do not enter Equation (14.34). That is, under the null hypothesis of no break, $\gamma_0 = \gamma_1 = \gamma_2 = 0$. Under the alternative hypothesis that there is a break, the population regression function is different before and after the break date $\tau$, in which case at least one of the $\gamma$'s is nonzero. Thus the hypothesis of a break can be tested using the $F$-statistic that tests the hypothesis that $\gamma_0 = \gamma_1 = \gamma_2 = 0$ against the hypothesis that at least one of the $\gamma$'s is nonzero. This is often called a Chow test for a break at a known break date, named for its inventor, Gregory Chow (1960).

If there are multiple predictors or more lags, then this test can be extended by constructing binary variable interaction variables for all the regressors and testing the hypothesis that all the coefficients on terms involving $D_t(\tau)$ are zero.

This approach can be modified to check for a break in a subset of the coefficients by including only the binary variable interactions for that subset of regressors of interest.

*Testing for a break at an unknown break date.*   Often the date of a possible break is unknown or known only within a range. Suppose, for example, that you suspect that a break occurred sometime between two dates, $\tau_0$ and $\tau_1$. The Chow test can be modified to handle this by testing for breaks at all possible dates $\tau$ in between

$\tau_0$ and $\tau_1$ and then using the largest of the resulting $F$-statistics to test for a break at an unknown date. This modified Chow test is variously called the **Quandt likelihood ratio (QLR) statistic** (Quandt, 1960) (the term we shall use) or, more obscurely, the *sup-Wald statistic*.

Because the QLR statistic is the largest of many $F$-statistics, its distribution is not the same as an individual $F$-statistic. Instead, the critical values for the QLR statistic must be obtained from a special distribution. Like the $F$-statistic, this distribution depends on the number of restrictions being tested, $q$—that is, on the number of coefficients (including the intercept) that are being allowed to break, or change, under the alternative hypothesis. The distribution of the QLR statistic also depends on $\tau_0 / T$ and $\tau_1 / T$, that is, on the endpoints, $\tau_0$ and $\tau_1$, of the subsample over which the $F$-statistics are computed, expressed as a fraction of the total sample size.

For the large-sample approximation to the distribution of the QLR statistic to be a good one, the subsample endpoints, $\tau_0$ and $\tau_1$, cannot be too close to the beginning or the end of the sample. For this reason, in practice the QLR statistic is computed over a "trimmed" range, or subset, of the sample. A common choice is to use 15% trimming, that is, to set for $\tau_0 = 0.15T$ and $\tau_1 = 0.85T$ (rounded to the nearest integer). With 15% trimming, the $F$-statistic is computed for break dates in the central 70% of the sample.

The critical values for the QLR statistic, computed with 15% trimming, are given in Table 14.5. Comparing these critical values with those of the $F_{q,\infty}$ distribution (Appendix Table 4) shows that the critical values for the QLR statistics are larger. This reflects the fact that the QLR statistic looks at the largest of many individual $F$-statistics. By examining $F$-statistics at many possible break dates, the QLR statistic has many opportunities to reject the null hypothesis, leading to QLR critical values that are larger than the individual $F$-statistic critical values.

Like the Chow test, the QLR test can be used to focus on the possibility that there are breaks in only some of the regression coefficients. This is done by first computing the Chow tests at different break dates, using binary variable interactions only for the variables with the suspect coefficients, and then computing the maximum of those Chow tests over the range $\tau_0 \leq \tau \leq \tau_1$. The critical values for this version of the QLR test are also taken from Table 14.5, where the number of restrictions ($q$) is the number of restrictions tested by the constituent $F$-statistics.

If there is a discrete break at a date within the range tested, then the QLR statistic will reject with high probability in large samples. Moreover, the date at which the constituent $F$-statistic is at its maximum, $\hat{\tau}$, is an estimate of the break date $\tau$. This estimate is a good one in the sense that, under certain technical conditions, $\hat{\tau}/T \xrightarrow{p} \tau/T$; that is, the fraction of the way through the sample at which the break occurs is estimated consistently.

| TABLE 14.5 | Critical Values of the QLR Statistic with 15% Trimming | | |
|---|---|---|---|
| Number of Restrictions ($q$) | 10% | 5% | 1% |
| 1 | 7.12 | 8.68 | 12.16 |
| 2 | 5.00 | 5.86 | 7.78 |
| 3 | 4.09 | 4.71 | 6.02 |
| 4 | 3.59 | 4.09 | 5.12 |
| 5 | 3.26 | 3.66 | 4.53 |
| 6 | 3.02 | 3.37 | 4.12 |
| 7 | 2.84 | 3.15 | 3.82 |
| 8 | 2.69 | 2.98 | 3.57 |
| 9 | 2.58 | 2.84 | 3.38 |
| 10 | 2.48 | 2.71 | 3.23 |
| 11 | 2.40 | 2.62 | 3.09 |
| 12 | 2.33 | 2.54 | 2.97 |
| 13 | 2.27 | 2.46 | 2.87 |
| 14 | 2.21 | 2.40 | 2.78 |
| 15 | 2.16 | 2.34 | 2.71 |
| 16 | 2.12 | 2.29 | 2.64 |
| 17 | 2.08 | 2.25 | 2.58 |
| 18 | 2.05 | 2.20 | 2.53 |
| 19 | 2.01 | 2.17 | 2.48 |
| 20 | 1.99 | 2.13 | 2.43 |

*Note:* These critical values apply when $\tau_0 = 0.15T$ and $\tau_1 = 0.85T$ (rounded to the nearest integer), so the $F$-statistic is computed for all potential break dates in the central 70% of the sample. The number of restrictions $q$ is the number of restrictions tested by each individual $F$-statistic. Critical values for other trimming percentages are given in Andrews (2003).

The QLR statistic also rejects the null hypothesis with high probability in large samples when there are multiple discrete breaks or when the break comes in the form of a slow evolution of the regression function. This means that the QLR statistic detects forms of instability other than a single discrete break. As a result, if the QLR statistic rejects the null hypothesis, it can mean that there is a single discrete break, that there are multiple discrete breaks, or that there is slow evolution of the regression function.

The QLR statistic is summarized in Key Concept 14.9.

**KEY CONCEPT**

**14.9**

## The QLR Test for Coefficient Stability

Let $F(\tau)$ denote the $F$-statistic testing the hypothesis of a break in the regression coefficients at date $\tau$; in the regression in Equation (14.34), for example, this is the $F$-statistic testing the null hypothesis that $\gamma_0 = \gamma_1 = \gamma_2 = 0$. The QLR (or sup-Wald) test statistic is the largest of statistics in the range $\tau_0 \leq \tau \leq \tau_1$:

$$\text{QLR} = \max[F(\tau_0), F(\tau_0 + 1), \ldots, F(\tau_1)]. \qquad (14.35)$$

1. Like the $F$-statistic, the QLR statistic can be used to test for a break in all or just some of the regression coefficients.

2. In large samples, the distribution of the QLR statistic under the null hypothesis depends on the number of restrictions being tested, $q$, and on the endpoints $\tau_0$ and $\tau_1$ as a fraction of $T$. Critical values are given in Table 14.5 for 15% trimming ($\tau_0 = 0.15T$ and $\tau_1 = 0.85T$, rounded to the nearest integer).

3. The QLR test can detect a single discrete break, multiple discrete breaks, and/or slow evolution of the regression function.

4. If there is a distinct break in the regression function, the date at which the largest Chow statistic occurs is an estimator of the break date.

*Warning: You probably don't know the break date even if you think you do.* Sometimes an expert might believe that he or she knows the date of a possible break so that the Chow test can be used instead of the QLR test. But if this knowledge is based on the expert's knowledge of the series being analyzed, then in fact this date was estimated using the data, albeit in an informal way. Preliminary estimation of the break date means that the usual $F$ critical values cannot be used for the Chow test for a break at that date. Thus it remains appropriate to use the QLR statistic in this circumstance.

*Application: Has the predictive power of the term spread been stable?* The QLR test provides a way to check whether the GDP–term spread relation has been stable from 1962 to 2012. Specifically, we focus on whether there have been changes in the coefficients on the lagged values of the term spread and the intercept in the ADL(2,2) specification in Equation (14.16) containing two lags each, of $GDPGR_t$ and $TSpread_t$.

The Chow $F$-statistics testing the hypothesis that the intercept and the coefficients on $TSpread_{t-1}$, $TSpread_{t-2}$, and the intercept in Equation (14.16) are constant against the alternative that they break at a given date are plotted in Figure 14.5 for breaks in the central 70% of the sample. For example, the $F$-statistic testing for a break in 1975:Q1 is 1.93, the value plotted at that date in the figure. Each $F$-statistic tests three restrictions (no change in the intercept and in the two coefficients on lags of the term spread), so $q = 3$. The largest of these $F$-statistics is 6.39, which occurs in 1980:Q4; this is the QLR statistic. Comparing 6.39 to the critical values for $q = 3$ in Table 14.5 indicates that the hypothesis that these coefficients are stable is rejected at the 1% significance level. (The 1% critical value is 6.02.) Thus, there is statistically significant evidence that at least one of these coefficients changed over the sample.

## Pseudo Out-of-Sample Forecasting

The ultimate test of a forecasting model is its out-of-sample performance—that is, its forecasting performance in "real time," after the model has been estimated. **Pseudo out-of-sample forecasting** is a method for simulating the real-time performance of a forecasting model. The idea of pseudo out-of-sample forecasting is simple: Pick a date near the end of the sample, estimate your forecasting model using data up to that date, and then use that estimated model to make a forecast. Performing this exercise for multiple dates near the end of your sample yields a

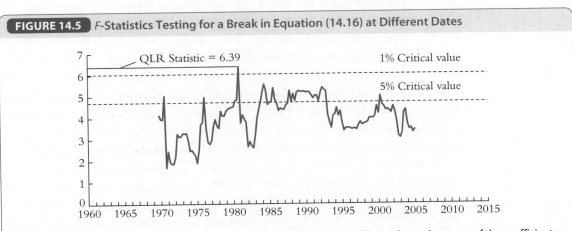

**FIGURE 14.5** *F*-Statistics Testing for a Break in Equation (14.16) at Different Dates

At a given break date, the $F$-statistic plotted here tests the null hypothesis of a break in at least one of the coefficients on $TSpread_{t-1}$, $TSpread_{t-2}$, or the intercept in Equation (14.16). For example, the $F$-statistic testing for a break in 1975:Q1 is 1.93. The QLR statistic is the largest of these $F$-statistics, which is 6.39. This exceeds the 1% critical value of 6.02.

**KEY CONCEPT**

**14.10**

## Pseudo Out-of-Sample Forecasts

Pseudo out-of-sample forecasts are computed using the following steps:

1. Choose a number of observations, $P$, for which you will generate pseudo out-of-sample forecasts; for example, $P$ might be 10% or 20% of the sample size. Let $s = T - P$.

2. Estimate the forecasting regression using the shortened data set for $t = 1, \ldots, s$.

3. Compute the forecast for the first period beyond this shortened sample, $s + 1$; call this $\widetilde{Y}_{s+1|s}$.

4. Compute the forecast error, $\widetilde{u}_{s+1} = Y_{s+1} - \widetilde{Y}_{s+1|s}$.

5. Repeat steps 2 through 4 for the remaining dates, $s = T - P + 1$ to $T - 1$ (re-estimate the regression at each date). The pseudo out-of-sample forecasts are $\{\widetilde{Y}_{s+1|s}, s = T - P, \ldots, T - 1\}$, and the pseudo out-of-sample forecast errors are $\{\widetilde{u}_{s+1}, s = T - P, \ldots, T - 1\}$.

series of pseudo forecasts and thus pseudo forecast errors. The pseudo forecast errors can then be examined to see whether they are representative of what you would expect if the forecasting relationship were stationary.

The reason this is called "pseudo" out-of-sample forecasting is that it is not true out-of-sample forecasting. True out-of-sample forecasting occurs in real time; that is, you make your forecast without the benefit of knowing the future values of the series. In pseudo out-of-sample forecasting, you simulate real-time forecasting using your model, but you have the "future" data against which to assess those simulated, or pseudo, forecasts. Pseudo out-of-sample forecasting mimics the forecasting process that would occur in real time, but without having to wait for new data to arrive.

Pseudo out-of-sample forecasting gives a forecaster a sense of how well the model has been forecasting at the end of the sample. This can provide valuable information, either bolstering confidence that the model has been forecasting well or suggesting that the model has gone off track in the recent past. The methodology of pseudo out-of-sample forecasting is summarized in Key Concept 14.10.

*Other uses of pseudo out-of-sample forecasting.* A second use of pseudo out-of-sample forecasting is to estimate the RMSFE. Because the pseudo out-of-sample forecasts are computed using only data prior to the forecast date, the pseudo out-of-sample forecast errors reflect both the uncertainty associated with future values of the error term and the uncertainty arising because the regression coefficients were estimated; that is, the pseudo out-of-sample forecast errors include both sources of error in Equation (14.20). Thus the sample standard deviation of the pseudo out-of-sample forecast errors is an estimator of the RMSFE. As discussed in Section 14.4, this estimator of the RMSFE can be used to quantify forecast uncertainty and to construct forecast intervals.

A third use of pseudo out-of-sample forecasting is to compare two or more candidate forecasting models. Two models that appear to fit the data equally well can perform quite differently in a pseudo out-of-sample forecasting exercise. When the models are different, such as when they include different predictors, pseudo out-of-sample forecasting provides a convenient way to compare the two models that focuses on their potential to provide reliable forecasts.

*Application: Did the predictive power of the term spread change during the 2000s?*  Using the QLR statistic, we rejected the null hypothesis that the predictive power of the term spread has been stable against the alternative of a break at the 1% significance level; that is, we rejected the joint hypothesis of no change in the intercept and the coefficients on the term spread in the ADL(2,2) model (see Figure 14.5). The maximal $F$-statistic occurred in 1980:Q4, indicating that a break occurred in the early 1980s. This suggests that a forecaster using lagged values of the term spread to forecast the growth rate of GDP should use an estimation sample starting after the break in 1980:Q4. Even so, a question remains: Does the ADL(2,2) model provide a stable forecasting model subsequent to the 1980:Q4 break?

If the coefficients of the ADL(2,2) model changed some time during the 1981:Q1–2012:Q4 period, then pseudo out-of-sample forecasts computed using data starting in 1981:Q1 should deteriorate. The pseudo out-of-sample forecasts of the growth rate of GDP for the period 2003:Q1–20012:Q4, computed using the ADL(2,2) model estimated with data starting in 1981:Q1, are plotted in Figure 14.6, along with the actual values of the growth rate of GDP. For example, the forecast of the growth rate of GDP for 2003:Q1 was computed by regressing $GDPGR_t$ on $GDPGR_{t-1}$, $GDPGR_{t-2}$, $TSpread_{t-1}$, and $TSpread_{t-2}$ with an intercept using the data through 2002:Q4, then computing the forecast $\overline{GDPGR}_{2003:Q1|2002:Q4}$ using these estimated coefficients and the data through 2002:Q4. This entire procedure was repeated using data through 2003:Q1 to compute the forecast $\overline{GDPGR}_{2003:Q2|2003:Q1}$. Doing this for all 40 quarters from 2003:Q1 to 2012:Q4

## Can You Beat the Market? Part II

Perhaps you have heard the advice that you should buy a stock when its earnings are high relative to its price. Buying a stock is, in effect, buying the stream of future dividends paid by that company out of its earnings. If the dividend stream is unusually large relative to the price of the company's stock, then the company could be considered undervalued. If current dividends are an indicator of future dividends, then the dividend yield—the ratio of current dividends to the stock price—might forecast future excess stock returns. If the dividend yield is high, the stock is undervalued, and returns would be forecasted to go up.

This reasoning suggests examining autoregressive distributed lag models of excess returns, where the predictor variable is the dividend yield. But a difficulty arises with this approach: The dividend yield is highly persistent and might even contain a stochastic trend. Using monthly data from 1960:M1 to 2002:M12 on the logarithm of the dividend–price ratio for the CRSP value-weighted index (the data are described in Appendix 14.1), a Dickey–Fuller unit root test including an intercept fails to reject the null hypothesis of a unit root at the 10% significance level. As always, this failure to reject the null hypothesis does not mean that the null hypothesis is true, but it does underscore that the dividend yield is a highly persistent regressor. Following the logic of Section 14.6, this result suggests that we should use the first difference of the log dividend yield as a regressor, not the level of the log dividend yield.

Table 14.6 presents ADL models of excess returns on the CRSP value-weighted index. In columns (1) and (2), the dividend yield appears in first differences, and the individual *t*-statistics and joint *F*-statistics fail to reject the null hypothesis of no predictability. But while these specifications accord with the modeling recommendations of Section 14.6, they do not correspond to the economic reasoning in the introductory paragraph, which relates returns to the *level* of the dividend yield. Column (3) of Table 14.6 therefore reports an ADL(1,1) model of excess returns using the log dividend yield, estimated through 1992:M12. The *t*-statistic is 2.25, which exceeds the usual 5% critical value of 1.96. However, because the regressor is highly persistent, the distribution of this *t*-statistic is suspect, and the 1.96 critical value may be inappropriate. (The *F*-statistic for this regression is not reported because it does not necessarily have a chi-squared distribution, even in large samples, because of the persistence of the regressor.)

One way to evaluate the apparent predictability found in column (3) of Table 14.6 is to conduct a pseudo out-of-sample forecasting analysis. Doing so over the out-of-sample period 1993:M1–2002:M12 provides a sample root mean squared forecast error of 4.08%. In contrast, the sample RMSFEs of always forecasting excess returns to be zero is 4.00%, and the sample RMSFE of a "constant forecast" (in which the recursively estimated forecasting model includes only an intercept) is 3.98%. The pseudo out-of-sample forecast based on the ADL(1,1) model with the log dividend yield does worse than forecasts in which there are no predictors!

This lack of predictability is consistent with the strong form of the efficient markets hypothesis, which holds that all publicly available information is incorporated into stock prices so that returns should not be predictable using publicly available information. (The weak form concerns forecasts based on past returns only.) The core message that excess returns are not easily predicted makes sense: If they were, the prices of stocks would be driven up to the point that no expected excess returns would exist.

The interpretation of results like those in Table 14.6 is a matter of heated debate among financial economists. Some consider the lack of predictability in predictive regressions to be a vindication of the efficient markets hypothesis (see, for example, Goyal and Welch, 2003). Others say that regressions over longer time periods and longer horizons, when analyzed using tools that are specifically designed to handle persistent regressors, show evidence of predictability (see Campbell and Yogo, 2006). This predictability might arise from rational economic behavior, in which investor attitudes toward risk change over the business cycle (Campbell, 2003), or it might reflect "irrational exuberance" (Shiller, 2005).

The results in Table 14.6 concern monthly returns, but some financial econometricians have focused on ever-shorter horizons. The theory of "market microstructure"—the minute-to-minute movements of the stock market—suggests that there can be fleeting periods of predictability and that money can be made by the clever and nimble. But doing so requires nerve, plus lots of computing power—and a staff of talented econometricians.

| TABLE 14.6 | Autoregressive Distributed Lag Models of Monthly Excess Stock Returns |

**Dependent variable: Excess returns on the CRSP value-weighted index**

| | (1) | (2) | (3) |
|---|---|---|---|
| Specification | ADL(1,1) | ADL(2,2) | ADL(1,1) |
| Estimation period | 1960:M1–2002:M12 | 1960:M1–2002:M12 | 1960:M1–1992:M12 |
| Regressors | | | |
| $excess\ return_{t-1}$ | 0.059 (0.158) | 0.042 (0.162) | 0.078 (0.057) |
| $excess\ return_{t-2}$ | | −0.213 (0.193) | |
| $\Delta\ln(dividend\ yield_{t-1})$ | 0.009 (0.157) | −0.012 (0.163) | |
| $\Delta\ln(dividend\ yield_{t-2})$ | | −0.161 (0.185) | |
| $\ln(dividend\ yield_{t-1})$ | | | 0.026[a] (0.012) |
| Intercept | 0.0031 (0.0020) | 0.0037 (0.0021) | 0.090[a] (0.039) |
| $F$-statistic on all coefficients ($p$- value) | 0.501 (0.606) | 0.843 (0.497) | |
| $\overline{R}^2$ | −0.0014 | −0.0008 | 0.0134 |

*Note:* The data are described in Appendix 14.1. Entries in the regressor rows are coefficients, with standard errors in parentheses. The final two rows report the $F$-statistic testing the hypothesis that all the coefficients in the regression are zero, with its $p$-value in parentheses, and the adjusted $R^2$.

[a] $|t| > 1.96$.

**FIGURE 14.6** U.S. GDP Growth Rates and Pseudo Out-of-Sample Forecasts

The pseudo out-of-sample forecasts made using the ADL(2,2) model of the form in Equation (14.16) generally track the actual growth rate of GDP from 2003 to 2012 but fail to forecast the sharp decline in GDP following the financial crisis of 2008.

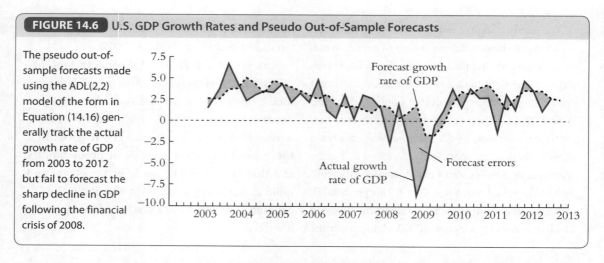

creates 40 pseudo out-of-sample forecasts, which are plotted in Figure 14.6. The pseudo out-of-sample forecast errors are the differences between the actual growth rate of GDP and its pseudo out-of-sample forecast—that is, the differences between the two lines in Figure 14.6. For example, in 2006:Q4, the growth rate of GDP was 3.1 percentage points (at an annual rate), but the pseudo out-of-sample forecast of $GDPGR_{2006:Q4}$ was 1.6 percentage points, so the pseudo out-of-sample forecast error was $GDPGR_{2006:Q4} - \widehat{GDPGR}_{2006:Q4|2006:Q3} = 1.5$ percentage points. In other words, a forecaster using the ADL(2,2), estimated through 2006:Q3, would have forecasted GDP growth of 1.6 percentage points in 2006:Q4, whereas in reality GDP grew by 3.1 percentage points.

How do the mean and standard deviation of the pseudo out-of-sample forecast errors compare with the in-sample fit of the model? The standard error of the regression of the ADL(2,2) model fit using data from 1981:Q1 through 2002:Q4 is 2.39, so based on the in-sample fit, we would expect the out-of-sample forecast errors to have mean zero and root mean squared forecast error of 2.39. In fact, over the 2003:Q1–2012:Q4 pseudo out-of-sample forecast period, the average forecast error is −0.73 and the *t*-statistic testing the hypothesis that the mean forecast error equals zero is −1.87; thus the hypothesis that the forecasts have mean zero is rejected at the 10% significance level but not at the 5% significance level. In addition, the RMSFE over the pseudo out-of-sample forecast period is 2.54, somewhat higher than the value of 2.39 for the standard error of the regression for the 1981:Q1–2002:Q4 period. Examination of Figure 14.6 shows that the pseudo out-of-sample forecasts track the actual values' GDP growth reasonably well except during late 2008 and early 2009, the period of steepest decline of GDP during the Great Recession. Excluding the single quarter 2008:Q4 lowers the pseudo out-of-sample RMSFE from 2.54 to 1.93.

According to the pseudo out-of-sample forecasting exercise, the performance of the ADL(2,2) forecasting model during the pseudo out-of-sample period 2003:Q1–2012:Q4 was, with the exception of the sharp decline in GDP in late 2008 following the financial crisis, comparable to its performance during the in-sample period of 1981:Q1–2002:Q4.[6] Although the QLR test points to instability in the ALD(2,2) model in the early 1980s, this pseudo out-of-sample analysis suggests that, after the early 1980s break, the forecasting model has been stable.

### Avoiding the Problems Caused by Breaks

The best way to adjust for a break in the population regression function depends on the source of that break. If a distinct break occurs at a specific date, that break will be detected with high probability by the QLR statistic, and the break date can be estimated. Thus the regression function can be estimated using a binary variable indicating the two subsamples associated with this break, interacted with the other regressors as needed. If all the coefficients break, then this regression takes the form of Equation (14.34), where $\tau$ is replaced by the estimated break date, $\hat{\tau}$, while if only some of the coefficients break, only the relevant interaction terms appear in the regression. If there is in fact a distinct break, then inference on the regression coefficients can proceed as usual—for example, using the usual normal critical values for hypothesis tests based on $t$-statistics. In addition, forecasts can be produced using the estimated regression function that applies to the end of the sample.

If the break is not distinct but rather arises from a slow, ongoing change in the parameters, the remedy is more difficult and goes beyond the scope of this book.[7]

## 14.8 Conclusion

In time series data, a variable generally is correlated from one observation, or date, to the next. A consequence of this correlation is that linear regression can be used to forecast future values of a time series, based on its current and past values. The starting point for time series regression is an autoregression, in which

---

[6]The ADL(2,2) was not alone in this failing to forecast GDP growth in 2008:Q4. Researchers at the Federal Reserve Bank of Philadelphia surveyed 47 professional forecasters in the third quarter of 2008 and asked for their forecasts of the growth rate of GDP in the fourth quarter. The median of the 47 forecasts was 0.7%, similar to the ADL(2,2) forecast of 1.0. The actual growth rate of GDP in 2008:Q4 was −8.7%.

[7]For additional discussion of estimation and testing in the presence of discrete breaks, see Hansen (2001). For an advanced discussion of estimation and forecasting when there are slowly evolving coefficients, see Hamilton (1994, Chapter 13).

the regressors are lagged values of the dependent variable. If additional predictors are available, then their lags can be added to the regression.

This chapter has considered several technical issues that arise when estimating and using regressions with time series data. One such issue is determining the number of lags to include in the regressions. As discussed in Section 14.5, if the number of lags is chosen to minimize the BIC, then the estimated lag length is consistent for the true lag length.

Another of these issues concerns whether the series being analyzed are stationary. If the series are stationary, then the usual methods of statistical inference (such as comparing $t$-statistics to normal critical values) can be used, and because the population regression function is stable over time, regressions estimated using historical data can be used reliably for forecasting. If, however, the series are nonstationary, then things become more complicated, and the specific complication depends on the nature of the nonstationarity. For example, if the series is nonstationary because it has a stochastic trend, then the OLS estimator and $t$-statistic can have nonstandard (nonnormal) distributions, even in large samples, and forecast performance can be improved by specifying the regression in first differences. A test for detecting this type of nonstationarity—the augmented Dickey–Fuller test for a unit root—was introduced in Section 14.6. Alternatively, if the population regression function has a break, then neglecting this break results in estimating an average version of the population regression function that in turn can lead to biased and/or imprecise forecasts. Procedures for detecting a break in the population regression function were introduced in Section 14.7.

In this chapter, the methods of time series regression were applied to economic forecasting, and the coefficients in these forecasting models were not given a causal interpretation. You do not need a causal relationship to forecast, and ignoring causal interpretations liberates the quest for good forecasts. In some applications, however, the task is not to develop a forecasting model but rather to estimate causal relationships among time series variables—that is, to estimate the *dynamic* causal effect on *Y over time* of a change in *X*. Under the right conditions, the methods of this chapter, or closely related methods, can be used to estimate dynamic causal effects, and that is the topic of the next chapter.

## Summary

1. Regression models used for forecasting need not have a causal interpretation.
2. A time series variable generally is correlated with one or more of its lagged values; that is, it is serially correlated.

3. An autoregression of order $p$ is a linear multiple regression model in which the regressors are the first $p$ lags of the dependent variable. The coefficients of an AR($p$) can be estimated by OLS, and the estimated regression function can be used for forecasting. The lag order $p$ can be estimated using an information criterion such as the BIC.

4. Adding other variables and their lags to an autoregression can improve forecasting performance. Under the least squares assumptions for time series regression (Key Concept 14.6), the OLS estimators have normal distributions in large samples, and statistical inference proceeds the same way as for cross-sectional data.

5. Using forecast intervals is one way to quantify forecast uncertainty. If the errors are normally distributed, an approximate 68% forecast interval can be constructed as the forecast plus or minus an estimate of the root mean squared forecast error.

6. A series that contains a stochastic trend is nonstationary, violating the second least squares assumption in Key Concept 14.6. The OLS estimator and $t$-statistic for the coefficient of a regressor with a stochastic trend can have a nonstandard distribution, potentially leading to biased estimators, inefficient forecasts, and misleading inferences. The ADF statistic can be used to test for a stochastic trend. A random walk stochastic trend can be eliminated by using first differences of the series.

7. If the population regression function changes over time, then OLS estimates neglecting this instability are unreliable for statistical inference or forecasting. The QLR statistic can be used to test for a break, and, if a discrete break is found, the regression function can be re-estimated in a way that allows for the break.

8. Pseudo out-of-sample forecasts can be used to assess model stability toward the end of the sample, to estimate the root mean squared forecast error, and to compare different forecasting models.

## Key Terms

gross domestic product (GDP) (570)
first lag (572)
$j^{th}$ lag (572)
first difference (572)
autocorrelation (574)
serial correlation (574)

autocorrelation coefficient (575)
$j^{th}$ autocovariance (575)
autoregression (577)
forecast error (578)
root mean squared forecast error
  (RMSFE) (579)

---

**MyEconLab Can Help You Get a Better Grade**

**MyEconLab** If your exam were tomorrow, would you be ready? For each chapter, **MyEconLab** Practice Tests and Study Plan help you prepare for your exams. You can also find similar Exercises and Review the Concepts Questions now in **MyEconLab**. To see how it works, turn to the **MyEconLab** spread on pages 2 and 3 of this book and then go to **www.myeconlab.com**.

For additional Empirical Exercises and Data Sets, log on to the Companion Website at **www.pearsonglobaleditions.com/Stock_Watson**.

---

## Review the Concepts

**14.1** Look at the four plots in Figure 14.2 — the US unemployment rate, the dollar-pound exchange rate, the logarithm of the index of industrial production, and the percentage change in stock prices. Which of these series appears to be non-stationary? Which of them appears to resemble a random walk?

**14.2** Many financial economists believe that the random walk model is a good description of the logarithm of stock prices. It implies that the percentage changes in stock prices are unforecastable. A financial analyst claims to have a new model that makes better predictions than the random walk model. Explain how you would examine the analyst's claim that his model is superior.

**14.3** A researcher estimates an AR(1) with an intercept and finds that the OLS estimate of $\beta_1$ is 0.88, with a standard error of 0.03. Does a 95% confidence interval include $\beta_1 = 1$? Explain.

**14.4** Suppose that you suspected that the intercept in Equation (14.16) changed in 1992:Q1. How would you modify the equation to incorporate this change? How would you test for a change in the intercept? How would you test for a change in the intercept if you did not know the date of the change?

## Exercises

**14.1** Consider the AR(1) model $Y_t = \beta_0 + \beta_1 Y_{t-1} + u_t$. Suppose that the process is stationary.

    **a.** Show that $E(Y_t) = E(Y_{t-1})$. (*Hint:* Read Key Concept 14.5.)

    **b.** Show that $E(Y_t) = \beta_0/(1 - \beta_1)$.

**14.2** The index of industrial production ($IP_t$) is a monthly time series that measures the quantity of industrial commodities produced in a given month. This problem uses data on this index for the United States. All regressions are estimated over the sample period 1986:M1 to 2013:M12 (that is, January 1986 through December 2013). Let $Y_t = 1200 \times \ln(IP_t/IP_{t-1})$.

    **a.** The forecaster states that $Y_t$ shows the monthly percentage change in *IP*, measured in percentage points per annum. Is this correct? Why?

    **b.** Suppose that a forecaster estimates the following AR(4) model for $Y_t$:

$$\hat{Y}_t = 0.787 + 0.052Y_{t-1} + 0.185Y_{t-2} + 0.234Y_{t-3} + 0.164Y_{t-4}.$$
$$\;\;(0.539)\;\;(0.093)\qquad(0.053)\qquad(0.078)\qquad(0.066)$$

Use this AR(4) to forecast the value of $Y_t$ in January 2014, using the following values of *IP* for July 2013 through December 2013:

| Date | 2013:M7 | 2013:M8 | 2013:M9 | 2013:M10 | 2013:M11 | 2013:M12 |
|------|---------|---------|---------|----------|----------|----------|
| IP   | 99.016  | 99.561  | 100.196 | 100.374  | 101.034  | 101.359  |

    **c.** Worried about potential seasonal fluctuations in production, the forecaster adds $Y_{t-12}$ to the autoregression. The estimated coefficient on $Y_{t-12}$ is −0.063 with a standard error of 0.045. Is this coefficient statistically significant?

**d.** Worried about a potential break, she computes a QLR test (with 15% trimming) on the constant and AR coefficients in the AR(4) model. The resulting QLR statistic was 3.94. Is there evidence of a break? Explain.

**e.** Worried that she might have included too few or too many lags in the model, the forecaster estimates AR($p$) models for $p = 0, 1, \ldots, 6$ over the same sample period. The sum of squared residuals from each of these estimated models is shown in the table. Use the BIC to estimate the number of lags that should be included in the autoregression. Do the results differ if you use the AIC?

| AR Order | 0 | 1 | 2 | 3 | 4 | 5 | 6 |
|---|---|---|---|---|---|---|---|
| SSR | 19,533 | 18,643 | 17,377 | 16,285 | 15,842 | 15,824 | 15,824 |

**14.3.** Using the same data as in Exercise 14.2, a researcher tests for a stochastic trend in $\ln(IP_t)$, using the following regression:

$$\widehat{\Delta \ln(IP_t)} = 0.030 + 0.000014t - 0.0085 \ln(IP_{t-1}) + 0.050\Delta\ln(IP_{t-1})$$
$$\phantom{xx}(0.015)\phantom{x}(0.000009)\phantom{xx}(0.0044)\phantom{xxxxxx}(0.054)$$

$$\phantom{xxxx} + 0.186\Delta\ln(IP_{t-2}) + 0.240\Delta\ln(IP_{t-3}) + 0.173\Delta\ln(IP_{t-4}),$$
$$\phantom{xxxx}(0.053)\phantom{xxxxxxxx}(0.053)\phantom{xxxxxxxx}(0.054)$$

where the standard errors shown in parentheses are computed using the homoskedasticity-only formula and the regressor $t$ is a linear time trend.

**a.** Use the ADF statistic to test for a stochastic trend (unit root) in $\ln(IP)$.

**b.** Do these results support the specification used in Exercise 14.2? Explain.

**14.4** The forecaster in Exercise 14.2 augments her AR(4) model for $IP$ growth to include four lagged values of $\Delta R_t$, where $R_t$ is the interest rate on 3-month U.S. Treasury bills (measured in percentage points at an annual rate).

**a.** The Granger-causality $F$-statistic on the four lags of $\Delta R_t$ is 4.16. Do interest rates help predict $IP$ growth? Explain.

**b.** The researcher also regresses $\Delta R_t$ on a constant, four lags of $\Delta R_t$ and four lags of $IP$ growth. The resulting Granger-causality $F$-statistic on the four lags of $IP$ growth is 1.52. Does $IP$ growth help to predict interest rates? Explain.

**14.5** Prove the following results about conditional means, forecasts, and forecast errors:

**a.** Let $W$ be a random variable with mean $\mu_W$ and variance $\sigma_W^2$ and let $c$ be a constant. Show that $E[(W - c)^2] = \sigma_W^2 + (\mu_W - c)^2$.

**b.** Consider the problem of forecasting $Y_t$, using data on $Y_{t-1}, Y_{t-2}, \ldots$. Let $f_{t-1}$ denote some forecast of $Y_t$, where the subscript $t - 1$ on $f_{t-1}$ indicates that the forecast is a function of data through date $t - 1$. Let $E[(Y_t - f_{t-1})^2 | Y_{t-1}, Y_{t-2}, \ldots]$ be the conditional mean squared error of the forecast $f_{t-1}$, conditional on values of $Y$ observed through date $t - 1$. Show that the conditional mean squared forecast error is minimized when $f_{t-1} = Y_{t|t-1}$, where $Y_{t|t-1} = E(Y_t | Y_{t-1}, Y_{t-2}, \ldots)$. (*Hint:* Review Exercise 2.27.)

**c.** Let $u_t$ denote the error in Equation (14.13). Show that $\text{cov}(u_t, u_{t-j}) = 0$ for $j \neq 0$. [*Hint:* Use Equation (2.27).]

**14.6** In this exercise you will conduct a Monte Carlo experiment to study the phenomenon of spurious regression discussed in Section 14.6. In a Monte Carlo study, artificial data are generated using a computer, and then those artificial data are used to calculate the statistics being studied. This makes it possible to compute the distribution of statistics for known models when mathematical expressions for those distributions are complicated (as they are here) or even unknown. In this exercise, you will generate data so that two series, $Y_t$ and $X_t$, are independently distributed random walks. The specific steps are as follows:

i. Use your computer to generate a sequence of $T = 100$ i.i.d. standard normal random variables. Call these variables $e_1, e_2, \ldots, e_{100}$. Set $Y_1 = e_1$ and $Y_t = Y_{t-1} + e_t$ for $t = 2, 3, \ldots, 100$.

ii. Use your computer to generate a new sequence, $a_1, a_2, \ldots, a_{100}$, of $T = 100$ i.i.d. standard normal random variables. Set $X_1 = a_1$ and $X_t = X_{t-1} + a_t$ for $t = 2, 3, \ldots, 100$.

iii. Regress $Y_t$ onto a constant and $X_t$. Compute the OLS estimator, the regression $R^2$, and the (homoskedastic-only) $t$-statistic testing the null hypothesis that $\beta_1$ (the coefficient on $X_t$) is zero.

Use this algorithm to answer the following questions:

**a.** Run the algorithm (i) through (iii) once. Use the $t$-statistic from (iii) to test the null hypothesis that $\beta_1 = 0$, using the usual 5% critical value of 1.96. What is the $R^2$ of your regression?

**b.** Repeat (a) 1000 times, saving each value of $R^2$ and the $t$-statistic. Construct a histogram of the $R^2$ and $t$-statistic. What are the 5%, 50%, and 95% percentiles of the distributions of the $R^2$ and the $t$-statistic? In what fraction of your 1000 simulated data sets does the $t$-statistic exceed 1.96 in absolute value?

**c.** Repeat (b) for different numbers of observations, such as $T = 50$ and $T = 200$. As the sample size increases, does the fraction of times that you reject the null hypothesis approach 5%, as it should because you have generated $Y$ and $X$ to be independently distributed? Does this fraction seem to approach some other limit as $T$ gets large? What is that limit?

**14.7** Suppose that $Y_t$ follows the stationary AR(1) model $Y_t = 2.5 + 0.7Y_{t-1} + u_t$, where $u_t$ is i.i.d. with $E(u_t) = 0$ and $\text{var}(u_t) = 9$.

**a.** Compute the mean and variance of $Y_t$. (*Hint:* See Exercise 14.1.)

**b.** Compute the first two autocovariances of $Y_t$. (*Hint:* Read Appendix 14.2.)

**c.** Compute the first two autocorrelations of $Y_t$.

**d.** Suppose that $Y_T = 102.3$. Compute $Y_{T+1|T} = E(Y_{T+1}|Y_T, Y_{t-1}, \ldots)$.

**14.8** Suppose that $Y_t$ is the monthly value of the number of new home construction projects started in the United States. Because of the weather, $Y_t$ has a pronounced seasonal pattern; for example, housing starts are low in January and high in June. Let $\mu_{Jan}$ denote the average value of housing starts in January and let $\mu_{Feb}, \mu_{Mar}, \ldots, \mu_{Dec}$ denote the average values in the other months. Show that the values of $\mu_{Jan}, \mu_{Feb}, \ldots, \mu_{Dec}$ can be estimated from the OLS regression $Y_t = \beta_0 + \beta_1 Feb_t + \beta_2 Mar_t + \cdots + \beta_{11}Dec_t + u_t$, where $Feb_t$ is a binary variable equal to 1 if $t$ is February, $Mar_t$ is a binary variable equal to 1 if $t$ is March, and so forth. (*Hint:* Show that $\beta_0 + \beta_2 = \mu_{Mar}$, and so forth.)

**14.9** The moving average model of order $q$ has the form

$$Y_t = \beta_0 + e_t + b_1e_{t-1} + b_2e_{t-2} + \cdots + b_qe_{t-q},$$

where $e_t$ is a serially uncorrelated random variable with mean 0 and variance $\sigma_e^2$.

**a.** Show that $E(Y_t) = \beta_0$.

**b.** Show that the variance of $Y_t$ is $\text{var}(Y_t) = \sigma_e^2(1 + b_1^2 + b_2^2 + \cdots + b_q^2)$.

**c.** Show that $\rho_j = 0$ for $j > q$.

**d.** Suppose that $q = 1$. Derive the autocovariances for $Y$.

**14.10** A researcher carries out a QLR test using 30% trimming, and there are $q = 5$ restrictions. Answer the following questions, using the values in Table 14.5 ("Critical Values of the QLR Statistic with 15% Trimming") and Appendix Table 4 ("Critical Values of the $F_{m,\infty}$ Distribution").

**a.** The QLR $F$-statistic is 3.9. Should the researcher reject the null hypothesis at the 5% level?

**b.** The QLR $F$-statistic is 1.1. Should the researcher reject the null hypothesis at the 5% level?

**c.** The QLR $F$-statistic is 3.6. Should the researcher reject the null hypothesis at the 5% level?

**14.11** Suppose that $\Delta Y_t$ follows the AR(1) model $\Delta Y_t = \beta_0 + \beta_1 \Delta Y_{t-1} + u_t$.

**a.** Show that $Y_t$ follows an AR(2) model.

**b.** Derive the AR(2) coefficients for $Y_t$ as a function of $\beta_0$ and $\beta_1$.

## Empirical Exercises

**E14.1** On the text website, **www.pearsonglobaleditions.com/Stock_Watson**, you will find the data file **USMacro_Quarterly**, which contains quarterly data on several macroeconomic series for the United States; the data are described in the file **USMacro_Description**. The variable *PCEP* is the price index for personal consumption expenditures from the U.S. National Income and Product Accounts. In this exercise you will construct forecasting models for the rate of inflation, based on *PCEP*. For this analysis, use the sample period 1963:Q1–2012:Q4 (where data before 1963 may be used, as necessary, as initial values for lags in regressions).

**a.** i. Compute the inflation rate, $Infl = 400 \times [\ln(PCEP_t) - \ln(PCEP_{t-1})]$. What are the units of *Infl*? (Is *Infl* measured in dollars, percentage points, percentage per quarter, percentage per year, or something else? Explain.)

ii. Plot the value of *Infl* from 1963:Q1 through 2012:Q4. Based on the plot, do you think that *Infl* has a stochastic trend? Explain.

**b.** i. Compute the first four autocorrelations of $\Delta Infl$.

ii. Plot the value of $\Delta Infl$ from 1963:Q1 through 2012:Q4. The plot should look "choppy" or "jagged." Explain why this behavior is consistent with the first autocorrelation that you computed in part (i).

**c** i. Run an OLS regression of $\Delta Infl_t$ on $\Delta Infl_{t-1}$. Does knowing the change in inflation this quarter help predict the change in inflation next quarter? Explain.

ii. Estimate an AR(2) model for $\Delta Infl$. Is the AR(2) model better than an AR(1) model? Explain.

iii. Estimate an AR($p$) model for $p = 0, \ldots, 8$. What lag length is chosen by BIC? What lag length is chosen by AIC?

iv. Use the AR(2) model to predict the change in inflation from 2012:Q4 to 2013:Q1—that is, predict the value of $\Delta Infl_{2013:Q1}$.

v. Use the AR(2) model to predict the level of the inflation rate in 2013:Q1—that is, $Infl_{2013:Q1}$.

**d.** i. Use the ADF test for the regression in Equation (14.31) with two lags of $\Delta Infl$ to test for a stochastic trend in $Infl$.

ii. Is the ADF test based on Equation (14.31) preferred to the test based on Equation (14.32) for testing for stochastic trend in $Infl$? Explain.

iii. In (i) you used two lags of $\Delta Infl$. Should you use more lags? Fewer lags? Explain.

iv. Based on the test you carried out in (i), does the AR model for $Infl$ contain a unit root? Explain carefully. (*Hint:* Does the failure to reject a null hypothesis mean that the null hypothesis is true?)

**e.** Use the QLR test with 15% trimming to test the stability of the coefficients in the AR(2) model for $\Delta Infl$. Is the AR(2) model stable? Explain.

**f.** i. Using the AR(2) model for $\Delta Infl$ with a sample period that begins in 1963:Q1, compute pseudo out-of-sample forecasts for the change in inflation beginning in 2003:Q1 and going through 2012:Q4. (That is, compute $\widehat{\Delta Infl}_{2003:Q1|2002:Q4}$, $\widehat{\Delta Infl}_{2003:Q2|2003:Q1}, \ldots, \widehat{\Delta Infl}_{2012:Q4|2012:Q3}$.)

ii. Are the pseudo out-of-sample forecasts biased? That is, do the forecast errors have a nonzero mean?

iii. How large is the RMSFE of the pseudo out-of-sample forecasts? Is this consistent with the AR(2) model for $\Delta Infl$ estimated over the 1963:Q1–2002:Q4 sample period?

iv. There is a large outlier in 2008:Q4. Why did inflation fall so much in 2008:Q4? (*Hint:* Collect some data on oil prices. What happened to oil prices during 2008?)

**E14.2** Read the boxes "Can You Beat the Market? Part I" and "Can You Beat the Market? Part II" in this chapter. Next, go to the course website, where you will find an extended version of the data set described in the boxes; the data are in the file **Stock_Returns_1931_2002** and are described in the file **Stock_Returns_1931_2002_Description**.

    **a.** Repeat the calculations reported in Table 14.2, using regressions estimated over the 1932:M1–2002:M12 sample period.

    **b.** Repeat the calculations reported in Table 14.6, using regressions estimated over the 1932:M1–2002:M12 sample period.

    **c.** Is the variable ln(*dividend yield*) highly persistent? Explain.

    **d.** Construct pseudo out-of-sample forecasts of excess returns over the 1983:M1–2002:M12 period, using regressions that begin in 1932:M1.

    **e.** Do the results in (a) through (d) suggest any important changes to the conclusions reached in the boxes? Explain.

---

**APPENDIX**

## 14.1 Time Series Data Used in Chapter 14

Macroeconomic time series data for the United States are collected and published by various government agencies. The Bureau of Economic Analysis in the Department of Commerce publishes the National Income and Product Accounts, which include the GDP data used in this chapter. The unemployment rate is computed from the Bureau of Labor Statistics's Current Population Survey (see Appendix 3.1). The quarterly data used here were computed by averaging the monthly values. The 10-year Treasury bond rate, 3-month Treasury bill rate, and the dollar/pound exchange rate data are quarterly averages of daily rates, as reported by the Federal Reserve. The index of industrial production for Japan is published by the Organisation for Economic Co-operation and Development (OECD). The daily percentage change in the Wilshire 5000 stock price index was computed as $100\Delta\ln(W5000_t)$, where $W5000_t$ is the daily value of the index; because the stock exchange is not open on weekends and holidays, the time period of analysis is a business day. We obtained all these data series from the Federal Reserve Economic Data (FRED) website at the Federal Reserve Bank of St. Louis. There you can find times series data on thousands of macroeconomic variables.

    The regressions in Table 14.2 and 14.6 use monthly financial data for the United States. Stock prices ($P_t$) are measured by the broad-based (NYSE and AMEX) value-weighted index of stock prices constructed by the Center for Research in Security Prices (CRSP). The monthly percentage excess return is $100 \times \{\ln[(P_t + Div_t)/P_{t-1}]\} - \ln(TBill_t)\}$, where $Div_t$ is the dividends paid on the stocks in the CRSP index and $TBill_t$ is the gross return (1 plus the interest rate) on a 30-day Treasury bill during month $t$. The dividend–price ratio is constructed as the dividends over the past 12 months, divided by the price in the current month. We thank Motohiro Yogo for his help and for providing these data.

**APPENDIX**

## 14.2 Stationarity in the AR(1) Model

This appendix shows that if $|\beta_1| < 1$ and $u_t$ is stationary, then $Y_t$ is stationary. Recall from Key Concept 14.5 that the time series variable $Y_t$ is stationary if the joint distribution of $(Y_{s+1}, \ldots, Y_{s+T})$ does not depend on $s$, regardless of the value of $T$. To streamline the argument, we show this formally for $T = 2$ under the simplifying assumptions that $\beta_0 = 0$ and $\{u_t\}$ are i.i.d. $N(0, \sigma_u^2)$.

The first step is deriving an expression for $Y_t$ in terms of the $u_t$'s. Because $\beta_0 = 0$, Equation (14.8) implies that $Y_t = \beta_1 Y_{t-1} + u_t$. Substituting $Y_{t-1} = \beta_1 Y_{t-2} + u_{t-1}$ into this expression yields $Y_t = \beta_1(\beta_1 Y_{t-2} + u_{t-1}) + u_t = \beta_1^2 Y_{t-2} + \beta_1 u_{t-1} + u_t$. Continuing this substitution another step yields $Y_t = \beta_1^3 Y_{t-3} + \beta_1^2 u_{t-2} + \beta_1 u_{t-1} + u_t$, and continuing indefinitely yields

$$Y_t = u_t + \beta_1 u_{t-1} + \beta_1^2 u_{t-2} + \beta_1^3 u_{t-3} + \cdots = \sum_{i=0}^{\infty} \beta_1^i u_{t-i}. \tag{14.36}$$

Thus $Y_t$ is a weighted average of current and past $u_t$'s. Because the $u_t$'s are normally distributed and because the weighted average of normal random variables is normal (Section 2.4), $Y_{s+1}$ and $Y_{s+2}$ have a bivariate normal distribution. Recall from Section 2.4 that the bivariate normal distribution is completely determined by the means of the two variables, their variances, and their covariance. Thus, to show that $Y_t$ is stationary, we need to show that the means, variances, and covariance of $(Y_{s+1}, Y_{s+2})$ do not depend on $s$. An extension of the argument used below can be used to show that the distribution of $(Y_{s+1}, Y_{s+2}, \ldots, Y_{s+T})$ does not depend on $s$.

The means and variances of $Y_{s+1}$ and $Y_{s+2}$ can be computed using Equation (14.36), with the subscript $s + 1$ or $s + 2$ replacing $t$. First, because $E(u_t) = 0$ for all $t$, $E(Y_t) = E(\sum_{i=0}^{\infty} \beta_1^i u_{t-i}) = \sum_{i=0}^{\infty} \beta_1^i E(u_{t-i}) = 0$, so the means of $Y_{s+1}$ and $Y_{s+2}$ are both zero and in particular do not depend on $s$. Second, $\text{var}(Y_t) = \text{var}(\sum_{i=0}^{\infty} \beta_1^i u_{t-i}) =$

$\sum_{i=0}^{\infty}(\beta_1^i)^2 \operatorname{var}(u_{t-i}) = \sigma_u^2 \sum_{i=0}^{\infty}(\beta_1^i)^2 = \sigma_u^2/(1 - \beta_1^2)$, where the final equality follows from the fact that if $|a| < 1$, $\sum_{i=0}^{\infty}a^i = 1/(1 - a)$; thus $\operatorname{var}(Y_{s+1}) = \operatorname{var}(Y_{s+2}) = \sigma_u^2/(1 - \beta_1^2)$, which does not depend on $s$ as long as $|\beta_1| < 1$. Finally, because $Y_{s+2} = \beta_1 Y_{s+1} + u_{s+2}$, $\operatorname{cov}(Y_{s+1}, Y_{s+2}) = E(Y_{s+1}Y_{s+2}) = E[Y_{s+1}(\beta_1 Y_{s+1} + u_{s+2})] = \beta_1 \operatorname{var}(Y_{s+1}) + \operatorname{cov}(Y_{s+1}, u_{s+2})$ $= \beta_1 \operatorname{var}(Y_{s+1}) = \beta_1 \sigma_u^2/(1 - \beta_1^2)$.

The covariance does not depend on $s$, so $Y_{s+1}$ and $Y_{s+2}$ have a joint probability distribution that does not depend on $s$; that is, their joint distribution is stationary. If $|\beta_1| \geq 1$, this calculation breaks down because the infinite sum in Equation (14.36) does not converge, and the variance of $Y_t$ is infinite. Thus $Y_t$ is stationary if $|\beta_1| < 1$ but not if $|\beta_1| \geq 1$.

The preceding argument was made under the assumptions that $\beta_0 = 0$ and $u_t$ is normally distributed. If $\beta_0 \neq 0$, the argument is similar except that the means of $Y_{s+1}$ and $Y_{s+2}$ are $\beta_0/(1 - \beta_1)$, and Equation (14.36) must be modified for this nonzero mean. The assumption that $u_t$ is i.i.d. normal can be replaced with the assumption that $u_t$ is stationary with a finite variance because, by Equation (14.36), $Y_t$ can still be expressed as a function of current and past $u_t$'s, so the distribution of $Y_t$ is stationary, as long as the distribution of $u_t$ is stationary and the infinite sum expression in Equation (14.36) is meaningful in the sense that it converges, which requires that $|\beta_1| < 1$.

**APPENDIX**

## 14.3  Lag Operator Notation

The notation in this and the next two chapters is streamlined considerably by adopting what is known as lag operator notation. Let L denote the **lag operator**, which has the property that it transforms a variable into its lag. That is, the lag operator L has the property $LY_t = Y_{t-1}$. By applying the lag operator twice, one obtains the second lag: $L^2 Y_t = L(LY_t) = LY_{t-1} = Y_{t-2}$. More generally, by applying the lag operator $j$ times, one obtains the $j^{\text{th}}$ lag. In summary, the lag operator has the property that

$$LY_t = Y_{t-1}, L^2 Y_t = Y_{t-2}, \text{ and } L^j Y_t = Y_{t-j}. \tag{14.37}$$

The lag operator notation permits us to define the **lag polynomial**, which is a polynomial in the lag operator:

$$a(L) = a_0 + a_1 L + a_2 L^2 + \cdots + a_p L^p = \sum_{j=0}^{p} a_j L^j, \tag{14.38}$$

where $a_0, \ldots, a_p$ are the coefficients of the lag polynomial and $L^0 = 1$. The degree of the lag polynomial $a(L)$ in Equation (14.38) is $p$. Multiplying $Y_t$ by $a(L)$ yields

$$a(L)Y_t = \left( \sum_{j=0}^{p} a_j L^j \right) Y_t = \sum_{j=0}^{p} a_j (L^j Y_t) = \sum_{j=0}^{p} a_j Y_{t-j} = a_0 Y_t + a_1 Y_{t-1} + \cdots + a_p Y_{t-p}. \quad (14.39)$$

The expression in Equation (14.39) implies that the AR($p$) model in Equation (14.13) can be written compactly as

$$a(L)Y_t = \beta_0 + u_t, \quad (14.40)$$

where $a_0 = 1$ and $a_j = -\beta_j$, for $j = 1, \ldots, p$. Similarly, an ADL($p, q$) model can be written

$$a(L)Y_t = \beta_0 + c(L)X_{t-1} + u_t, \quad (14.41)$$

where $a(L)$ is a lag polynomial of degree $p$ (with $a_0 = 1$) and $c(L)$ is a lag polynomial of degree $q - 1$.

APPENDIX

## 14.4 ARMA Models

The **autoregressive–moving average (ARMA) model** extends the autoregressive model by modeling $u_t$ as serially correlated, specifically as being a distributed lag (or "moving average") of another unobserved error term. In the lag operator notation of Appendix 14.3, let $u_t = b(L)e_t$, where $b(L)$ is a lag polynomial of degree $q$ with $b_0 = 1$ and $e_t$ is a serially uncorrelated, unobserved random variable. Then the ARMA($p,q$) model is

$$a(L)Y_t = \beta_0 + b(L)e_t, \quad (14.42)$$

where $a(L)$ is a lag polynomial of degree $p$ with $a_0 = 1$.

Both the AR and ARMA models can be thought of as ways to approximate the auto-covariances of $Y_t$. The reason for this is that any stationary time series $Y_t$ with a finite variance can be written either as an AR or as a MA with a serially uncorrelated error term, although the AR or MA models might need to have an infinite order. The second of these results, that a stationary process can be written in moving average form, is known as the Wold decomposition theorem and is one of the fundamental results underlying the theory of stationary time series analysis.

As a theoretical matter, the families of AR, MA, and ARMA models are equally rich, as long as the lag polynomials have a sufficiently high degree. Still, in some cases the autocovariances can be better approximated using an $ARMA(p,q)$ model with small $p$ and $q$ than by a pure AR model with only a few lags. As a practical matter, however, the estimation of ARMA models is more difficult than the estimation of AR models, and ARMA models are more difficult to extend to additional regressors than are AR models.

## 14.5 Consistency of the BIC Lag Length Estimator

This appendix summarizes the argument that the BIC estimator of the lag length, $\hat{p}$, in an autoregression is correct in large samples; that is, $\Pr(\hat{p} = p) \to 1$. This is not true for the AIC estimator, which can overestimate $p$ even in large samples.

### BIC

First consider the special case that the BIC is used to choose among autoregressions with zero, one, or two lags, when the true lag length is one. It is shown below that (i) $\Pr(\hat{p} = 0) \to 0$ and (ii) $\Pr(\hat{p} = 2) \to 0$, from which it follows that $\Pr(\hat{p} = 1) \to 1$. The extension of this argument to the general case of searching over $0 \leq p \leq p_{max}$ entails showing that $\Pr(\hat{p} < p) \to 0$ and $\Pr(\hat{p} > p) \to 0$; the strategy for showing these is the same as used in (i) and (ii) below.

### Proof of (i) and (ii)

*Proof of (i).* To choose $\hat{p} = 0$ it must be the case that $BIC(0) < BIC(1)$; that is, $BIC(0) - BIC(1) < 0$. Now $BIC(0) - BIC(1) = [\ln(SSR(0)/T) + (\ln T)/T] - [\ln(SSR(1)/T)] + 2(\ln T)/T = \ln(SSR(0)/T) - \ln(SSR(1)/T) - (\ln T)/T$. Now $SSR(0)/T = [(T-1)/T]s_Y^2 \xrightarrow{p} \sigma_Y^2$, $SSR(1)/T \xrightarrow{p} \sigma_u^2$, and $(\ln T)/T \longrightarrow 0$; putting these pieces together, $BIC(0) - BIC(1) \xrightarrow{p} \ln\sigma_Y^2 - \ln\sigma_u^2 > 0$ because $\sigma_Y^2 > \sigma_u^2$. It follows that $\Pr[BIC(0) < BIC(1)] \to 0$, so $\Pr(\hat{p} = 0) \longrightarrow 0$.

*Proof of (ii).* To choose $\hat{p} = 2$, it must be the case that $BIC(2) < BIC(1)$ or $BIC(2) - BIC(1) < 0$. Now $T[BIC(2) - BIC(1)] = T\{[\ln(SSR(2)/T) + 3(\ln T)/T] - [\ln(SSR(1)/T) + 2(\ln T)/T]\} = T\ln[SSR(2)/SSR(1)] + \ln T = -T\ln[1 + F/(T-2)] + \ln T$, where $F = [SSR(1) - SSR(2)]/[SSR(2)/(T-2)]$ is the homoskedasticity-only $F$-statistic [Equation (7.13)] testing the null hypothesis that $\beta_2 = 0$ in the AR(2). If $u_t$ is homoskedastic, then $F$ has a $\chi_1^2$ asymptotic distribution; if not, it has some other asymptotic distribution. Thus $\Pr[\mathrm{BIC}(2) - \mathrm{BIC}(1) < 0] = \Pr\{T[\mathrm{BIC}(2) - \mathrm{BIC}(1)] < 0\}$ $= \Pr\{-T\ln[1 + F/(T - 2)] + (\ln T) < 0\} = \Pr\{T\ln[1 + F/(T - 2)] > \ln T\}$. As $T$ increases, $T\ln[1 + F/(T - 2)] - F \xrightarrow{p} 0$ [a consequence of the logarithmic approximation $\ln(1 + a) \cong a$, which becomes exact as $a \longrightarrow 0$]. Thus $\Pr[\mathrm{BIC}(2) - \mathrm{BIC}(1) < 0] \longrightarrow \Pr(F > \ln T) \longrightarrow 0$, so $\Pr(\hat{p} = 2) \longrightarrow 0$.

## AIC

In the special case of an AR(1) when zero, one, or two lags are considered, (i) applies to the AIC where the term $\ln T$ is replaced by 2, so $\Pr(\hat{p} = 0) \longrightarrow 0$. All the steps in the proof of (ii) for the BIC also apply to the AIC, with the modification that $\ln T$ is replaced by 2; thus $\Pr[\mathrm{AIC}(2) - \mathrm{AIC}(1) < 0] \longrightarrow \Pr(F > 2) > 0$. If $u_t$ is homoskedastic, then $\Pr(F > 2) \longrightarrow \Pr(\chi_1^2 > 2) = 0.16$, so $\Pr(\hat{p} = 2) \longrightarrow 0.16$. In general, when $\hat{p}$ is chosen using the AIC, $\Pr(\hat{p} < p) \longrightarrow 0$, but $\Pr(\hat{p} > p)$ tends to a positive number, so $\Pr(\hat{p} = p)$ does not tend to 1.

# 15 Estimation of Dynamic Causal Effects

I n the 1983 movie *Trading Places*, the characters played by Dan Aykroyd and Eddie Murphy used inside information on how well Florida oranges had fared over the winter to make millions in the orange juice concentrate futures market, a market for contracts to buy or sell large quantities of orange juice concentrate at a specified price on a future date. In real life, traders in orange juice futures in fact do pay close attention to the weather in Florida: Freezes in Florida kill Florida oranges, the source of almost all frozen orange juice concentrate made in the United States, so its supply falls and the price rises. But precisely how much does the price rise when the weather in Florida turns sour? Does the price rise all at once, or are there delays; if so, for how long? These are questions that real-life traders in orange juice futures need to answer if they want to succeed.

This chapter takes up the problem of estimating the effect on $Y$ now and in the future of a change in $X$, that is, the **dynamic causal effect** on $Y$ of a change in $X$. What, for example, is the effect on the path of orange juice prices over time of a freezing spell in Florida? The starting point for modeling and estimating dynamic causal effects is the so-called distributed lag regression model, in which $Y_t$ is expressed as a function of current and past values of $X_t$. Section 15.1 introduces the distributed lag model in the context of estimating the effect of cold weather in Florida on the price of orange juice concentrate over time. Section 15.2 takes a closer look at what, precisely, is meant by a dynamic causal effect.

One way to estimate dynamic causal effects is to estimate the coefficients of the distributed lag regression model using OLS. As discussed in Section 15.3, this estimator is consistent if the regression error has a conditional mean of zero given current and past values of $X$, a condition that (as in Chapter 12) is referred to as exogeneity. Because the omitted determinants of $Y_t$ are correlated over time—that is, because they are serially correlated—the error term in the distributed lag model can be serially correlated. This possibility in turn requires "heteroskedasticity- and autocorrelation-consistent" (HAC) standard errors, the topic of Section 15.4.

A second way to estimate dynamic causal effects, discussed in Section 15.5, is to model the serial correlation in the error term as an autoregression and then to use this autoregressive model to derive an autoregressive distributed lag (ADL) model. Alternatively, the coefficients of the original distributed lag model can be estimated by generalized least squares (GLS). Both the ADL and GLS methods, however, require a stronger version of exogeneity than we have used so far: *strict* exogeneity, under which the regression errors have a conditional mean of zero given past, present, *and future* values of X.

Section 15.6 provides a more complete analysis of the relationship between orange juice prices and the weather. In this application, the weather is beyond human control and thus is exogenous (although, as discussed in Section 15.6, economic theory suggests that it is not necessarily strictly exogenous). Because exogeneity is necessary for estimating dynamic causal effects, Section 15.7 examines this assumption in several applications taken from macroeconomics and finance.

This chapter builds on the material in Sections 14.1 through 14.4 but, with the exception of a subsection (that can be skipped) of the empirical analysis in Section 15.6, does not require the material in Sections 14.5 through 14.7.

# 15.1 An Initial Taste of the Orange Juice Data

Orlando, the historical center of Florida's orange-growing region, is normally sunny and warm. But now and then there is a cold snap, and if temperatures drop below freezing for too long, the trees drop many of their oranges. If the cold snap is severe, the trees freeze. Following a freeze, the supply of orange juice concentrate falls and its price rises. The timing of the price increases is rather complicated, however. Orange juice concentrate is a "durable," or storable, commodity; that is, it can be stored in its frozen state, albeit at some cost (to run the freezer). Thus the price of orange juice concentrate depends not only on current supply but also on expectations of future supply. A freeze today means that future supplies of concentrate will be low, but because concentrate currently in storage can be used to meet either current or future demand, the price of existing concentrate rises today. But precisely how much does the price of concentrate rise when there is a freeze? The answer to this question is of interest not just to orange juice traders but more generally to economists interested in studying the operations of modern commodity markets. To learn how the price of orange juice changes in response to weather conditions, we must analyze data on orange juice prices and the weather.

Monthly data on the price of frozen orange juice concentrate, its monthly percentage change, and temperatures in the orange-growing region of Florida from January 1950 to December 2000 are plotted in Figure 15.1. The price, plotted in Figure 15.1a, is a measure of the average real price of frozen orange juice concentrate paid by wholesalers. This price was deflated by the overall producer price index for finished goods to eliminate the effects of overall price inflation.

**FIGURE 15.1**    Orange Juice Prices and Florida Weather, 1950–2000

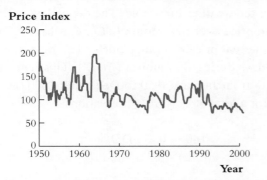

**(a)** Price Index for Frozen Concentrated Orange Juice

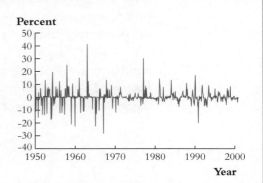

**(b)** Percent Change in the Price of Frozen Concentrated Orange Juice

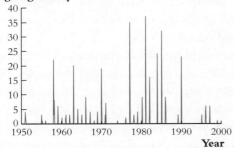

**(c)** Monthly Freezing Degree Days in Orlando, Florida

There have been large month-to-month changes in the price of frozen concentrated orange juice. Many of the large movements coincide with freezing weather in Orlando, home of many orange groves.

The percentage price change plotted in Figure 15.1b is the percent change in the price over the month. The temperature data plotted in Figure 15.1c are the number of "freezing degree days" at the Orlando, Florida, airport, calculated as the sum of the number of degrees Fahrenheit that the minimum temperature falls below freezing in a given day over all days in the month; for example, in November 1950 the airport temperature dropped below freezing twice, on the $25^{th}$ (31°) and on the $29^{th}$ (29°), for a total of 4 freezing degree days $[(32 − 31) + (32 − 29) = 4]$. (The data are described in more detail in Appendix 15.1.) As you can see by comparing the panels in Figure 15.1, the price of orange juice concentrate has large swings, some of which appear to be associated with cold weather in Florida.

We begin our quantitative analysis of the relationship between orange juice price and the weather by using a regression to estimate the amount by which orange juice prices rise when the weather turns cold. The dependent variable is the percentage change in the price over that month [$\%ChgP_t$, where $\%ChgP_t = 100 \times \Delta\ln(P_t^{OJ})$ and $P_t^{OJ}$ is the real price of orange juice]. The regressor is the number of freezing degree days during that month ($FDD_t$). This regression is estimated using monthly data from January 1950 to December 2000 (as are all regressions in this chapter), for a total of $T = 612$ observations:

$$\widehat{\%ChgP_t} = \ -0.40 + 0.47\,FDD_t. \tag{15.1}$$
$$(0.22)\ \ (0.13)$$

The standard errors reported in this section are not the usual OLS standard errors, but rather are heteroskedasticity- and autocorrelation-consistent (HAC) standard errors that are appropriate when the error term and regressors are auto-correlated. HAC standard errors are discussed in Section 15.4, and for now they are used without further explanation.

According to this regression, an additional freezing degree day during a month increases the price of orange juice concentrate over that month by 0.47%. In a month with 4 freezing degree days, such as November 1950, the price of orange juice concentrate is estimated to have increased by 1.88% ($4 \times 0.47\% = 1.88\%$), relative to a month with no days below freezing.

Because the regression in Equation (15.1) includes only a contemporaneous measure of the weather, it does not capture any lingering effects of the cold snap on the orange juice price over the coming months. To capture these we need to consider the effect on prices of both contemporaneous and lagged values of $FDD$, which in turn can be done by augmenting the regression in Equation (15.1) with, for example, lagged values of $FDD$ over the previous 6 months:

$$\widehat{\%ChgP_t} = -\,0.65 + 0.47\,FDD_t + 0.14\,FDD_{t-1} + 0.06\,FDD_{t-2}$$
$$(0.23)\ \ (0.14)\qquad\quad(0.08)\qquad\qquad(0.06)$$

$$+\ 0.07\,FDD_{t-3} + 0.03\,FDD_{t-4} + 0.05\,FDD_{t-5} + 0.05\,FDD_{t-6}. \tag{15.2}$$
$$(0.05)\qquad\qquad(0.03)\qquad\qquad(0.03)\qquad\qquad(0.04)$$

Equation (15.2) is a distributed lag regression. The coefficient on $FDD_t$ in Equation (15.2) estimates the percentage increase in prices over the course of the month in which the freeze occurs; an additional freezing degree day is estimated to increase prices that month by 0.47%. The coefficient on the first lag of $FDD_t$, $FDD_{t-1}$, estimates the percentage increase in prices arising from a freezing degree day in the preceding month, the coefficient on the second lag estimates the effect of a freezing degree day 2 months ago, and so forth. Equivalently, the coefficient on the first lag of *FDD* estimates the effect of a unit increase in *FDD* 1 month after the freeze occurs. Thus the estimated coefficients in Equation (15.2) are estimates of the effect of a unit increase in $FDD_t$ on current and future values of %$ChgP$; that is, they are estimates of the dynamic effect of $FDD_t$ on %$ChgP_t$. For example, the 4 freezing degree days in November 1950 are estimated to have increased orange juice prices by 1.88% during November 1950, by an additional $0.56\%(= 4 \times 0.14)$ in December 1950, by an additional $0.24\%(= 4 \times 0.06)$ in January 1951, and so forth.

## 15.2  Dynamic Causal Effects

Before learning more about the tools for estimating dynamic causal effects, we should spend a moment thinking about what, precisely, is meant by a dynamic causal effect. Having a clear idea about what a dynamic causal effect is leads to a clearer understanding of the conditions under which it can be estimated.

### Causal Effects and Time Series Data

Section 1.2 defined a causal effect as the outcome of an ideal randomized controlled experiment: When a horticulturalist randomly applies fertilizer to some tomato plots but not others and then measures the yield, the expected difference in yield between the fertilized and unfertilized plots is the causal effect on tomato yield of the fertilizer. This concept of an experiment, however, is one in which there are multiple subjects (multiple tomato plots or multiple people), so the data are either cross-sectional (the tomato yield at the end of the harvest) or panel data (individual incomes before and after an experimental job training program). By having multiple subjects, it is possible to have both treatment and control groups and thereby to estimate the causal effect of the treatment.

In time series applications, this definition of causal effects in terms of an ideal randomized controlled experiment needs to be modified. To be concrete, consider an important problem of macroeconomics: estimating the effect of an unanticipated change in the short-term interest rate on the current and future economic activity in a given country, as measured by GDP. Taken literally, the randomized controlled experiment of Section 1.2 would entail randomly assigning different economies to treatment and control groups. The central banks in the treatment group would apply the treatment of a random interest rate change, while those in the control group would apply no such random changes; for both groups, economic activity (for example, GDP) would be measured over the next few years. But what if we are interested in estimating this effect for a specific country, say the United States? Then this experiment would entail having different "clones" of the United States as subjects and assigning some clone economies to the treatment group and some to the control group. Obviously, this "parallel universes" experiment is infeasible.

Instead, in time series data it is useful to think of a randomized controlled experiment consisting of the same subject (e.g., the U.S. economy) being given different treatments (randomly chosen changes in interest rates) at different points in time (the 1970s, the 1980s, and so forth). In this framework, the single subject at different times plays the role of both treatment and control group: Sometimes the Fed changes the interest rate, while at other times it does not. Because data are collected over time, it is possible to estimate the dynamic causal effect, that is, the time path of the effect on the outcome of interest of the treatment. For example, a surprise increase in the short-term interest rate of two percentage points, sustained for one quarter, might initially have a negligible effect on output; after two quarters GDP growth might slow, with the greatest slowdown after $1\frac{1}{2}$ years; then over the next 2 years, GDP growth might return to normal. This time path of causal effects is the dynamic causal effect on GDP growth of a surprise change in the interest rate.

As a second example, consider the causal effect on orange juice price changes of a freezing degree day. It is possible to imagine a variety of hypothetical experiments, each yielding a different causal effect. One experiment would be to change the weather in the Florida orange groves, holding weather constant elsewhere—for example, holding weather constant in the Texas grapefruit groves and in other citrus fruit regions. This experiment would measure a partial effect, holding other weather constant. A second experiment might change the weather in all the regions, where the "treatment" is application of overall weather patterns. If weather is correlated across regions for competing crops, then these two dynamic causal effects differ. In this chapter, we consider the causal effect in the latter experiment, that is, the causal effect of applying general weather patterns. This corresponds to measuring the dynamic effect on prices of a change in Florida weather, *not* holding weather constant in other agricultural regions.

*Dynamic effects and the distributed lag model.*  Because dynamic effects necessarily occur over time, the econometric model used to estimate dynamic causal effects needs to incorporate lags. To do so, $Y_t$ can be expressed as a distributed lag of current and $r$ past values of $X_t$:

$$Y_t = \beta_0 + \beta_1 X_t + \beta_2 X_{t-1} + \beta_3 X_{t-2} + \cdots + \beta_{r+1} X_{t-r} + u_t, \qquad (15.3)$$

where $u_t$ is an error term that includes measurement error in $Y_t$ and the effect of omitted determinants of $Y_t$. The model in Equation (15.3) is called the **distributed lag model** relating $X_t$, and $r$ of its lags, to $Y_t$.

As an illustration of Equation (15.3), consider a modified version of the tomato/fertilizer experiment: Because fertilizer applied today might remain in the ground in future years, the horticulturalist wants to determine the effect on tomato yield *over time* of applying fertilizer. Accordingly, she designs a 3-year experiment and randomly divides her plots into four groups: The first is fertilized in only the first year; the second is fertilized in only the second year; the third is fertilized in only the third year; and the fourth, the control group, is never fertilized. Tomatoes are grown annually in each plot, and the third-year harvest is weighed. The three treatment groups are denoted by the binary variables $X_{t-2}$, $X_{t-1}$, and $X_t$, where $t$ represents the third year (the year in which the harvest is weighed), $X_{t-2} = 1$ if the plot is in the first group (fertilized two years earlier), $X_{t-1} = 1$ if the plot was fertilized 1 year earlier, and $X_t = 1$ if the plot was fertilized in the final year. In the context of Equation (15.3) (which applies to a single plot), the effect of being fertilized in the final year is $\beta_1$, the effect of being fertilized 1 year earlier is $\beta_2$, and the effect of being fertilized 2 years earlier is $\beta_3$. If the effect of fertilizer is greatest in the year it is applied, then $\beta_1$ would be larger than $\beta_2$ and $\beta_3$.

More generally, the coefficient on the contemporaneous value of $X_t$, $\beta_1$, is the contemporaneous or immediate effect of a unit change in $X_t$ on $Y_t$. The coefficient on $X_{t-1}$, $\beta_2$, is the effect on $Y_t$ of a unit change in $X_{t-1}$ or, equivalently, the effect on $Y_{t+1}$ of a unit change in $X_t$; that is, $\beta_2$ is the effect of a unit change in $X$ on $Y$ one period later. In general, the coefficient on $X_{t-h}$ is the effect of a unit change in $X$ on $Y$ after $h$ periods. The dynamic causal effect is the effect of a change in $X_t$ on $Y_t$, $Y_{t+1}$, $Y_{t+2}$, and so forth; that is, it is the sequence of causal effects on current and future values of $Y$. Thus, in the context of the distributed lag model in Equation (15.3), the dynamic causal effect is the sequence of coefficients $\beta_1$, $\beta_2, \ldots, \beta_{r+1}$.

*Implications for empirical time series analysis.* This formulation of dynamic causal effects in time series data as the expected outcome of an experiment in which different treatment levels are repeatedly applied to the same subject has two implications for empirical attempts to measure the dynamic causal effect with observational time series data. The first implication is that the dynamic causal effect should not change over the sample on which we have data. This in turn is implied by the data being jointly stationary (Key Concept 14.5). As discussed in Section 14.7, the hypothesis that a population regression function is stable over time can be tested using the QLR test for a break, and it is possible to estimate the dynamic causal effect in different subsamples. The second implication is that $X$ must be uncorrelated with the error term, and it is to this implication that we now turn.

## Two Types of Exogeneity

Section 12.1 defined an "exogenous" variable as a variable that is uncorrelated with the regression error term and an "endogenous" variable as a variable that is correlated with the error term. This terminology traces to models with multiple equations, in which an "endogenous" variable is determined within the model while an "exogenous" variable is determined outside the model. Loosely speaking, if we are to estimate dynamic causal effects using the distributed lag model in Equation (15.3), the regressors (the $X$'s) must be uncorrelated with the error term. Thus $X$ must be exogenous. Because we are working with time series data, however, we need to refine the definitions of exogeneity. In fact, there are two different concepts of exogeneity that we use here.

The first concept of exogeneity is that the error term has a conditional mean of zero given current and all past values of $X_t$, that is, that $E(u_t|X_t, X_{t-1}, X_{t-2}, \ldots) = 0$. This modifies the standard conditional mean assumption for multiple regression with cross-sectional data (Assumption #1 in Key Concept 6.4), which requires only that $u_t$ has a conditional mean of zero given the included regressors, that is, $E(u_t|X_t, X_{t-1}, \ldots, X_{t-r}) = 0$. Including all lagged values of $X_t$ in the conditional expectation implies that all the more distant causal effects—all the causal effects beyond lag $r$—are zero. Thus, under this assumption, the $r$ distributed lag coefficients in Equation (15.3) constitute all the nonzero dynamic causal effects. We can refer to this assumption—that $E(u_t|X_t, X_{t-1}, \ldots) = 0$—as *past and present exogeneity*, but because of the similarity of this definition and the definition of exogeneity in Chapter 12, we just use the term **exogeneity**.

The second concept of exogeneity is that the error term has mean zero, given all past, present, and *future* values of $X_t$, that is, that $E(u_t|\ldots, X_{t+2}, X_{t+1}, X_t, X_{t-1}, X_{t-2}, \ldots) = 0$. This is called **strict exogeneity**; for clarity, we also call it *past, present, and future exogeneity*. The reason for introducing the concept of strict exogeneity is that, when $X$ is strictly exogenous, there are more efficient estimators of dynamic causal effects than the OLS estimators of the coefficients of the distributed lag regression in Equation (15.3).

The difference between exogeneity (past and present) and strict exogeneity (past, present, and future) is that strict exogeneity includes future values of $X$ in the conditional expectation. Thus strict exogeneity implies exogeneity, but not the reverse. One way to understand the difference between the two concepts is to consider the implications of these definitions for correlations between $X$ and $u$. If $X$ is (past and present) exogenous, then $u_t$ is uncorrelated with current and past values of $X_t$. If $X$ is strictly exogenous, then in addition $u_t$ is uncorrelated with *future* values of $X_t$. For example, if a change in $Y_t$ causes *future* values of $X_t$ to change, then $X_t$ is not strictly exogenous even though it might be (past and present) exogenous.

As an illustration, consider the hypothetical multiyear tomato/fertilizer experiment described following Equation (15.3). Because the fertilizer is randomly applied in the hypothetical experiment, it is exogenous. Because tomato yield today does not depend on the amount of fertilizer applied in the future, the fertilizer time series is also strictly exogenous.

As a second illustration, consider the orange juice price example, in which $Y_t$ is the monthly percentage change in orange juice prices and $X_t$ is the number of freezing degree days in that month. From the perspective of orange juice markets, we can think of the weather—the number of freezing degree days—as if it were randomly assigned, in the sense that the weather is outside human control. If the effect of *FDD* is linear and if it has no effect on prices after $r$ months, then it follows that the weather is exogenous. But is the weather *strictly* exogenous? If the conditional mean of $u_t$ given future *FDD* is nonzero, then *FDD* is not strictly exogenous. Answering this question requires thinking carefully about what, precisely, is contained in $u_t$. In particular, if OJ market participants use forecasts of *FDD* when they decide how much they will buy or sell at a given price, then OJ prices, and thus the error term $u_t$, could incorporate information about future *FDD* that would make $u_t$ a useful predictor of *FDD*. This means that $u_t$ will be correlated with future values of $FDD_t$. According to this logic, because $u_t$ includes forecasts of future Florida weather, *FDD* would be (past and present) exogenous but not *strictly* exogenous. The difference between this and the tomato/fertilizer example is that, while tomato plants are unaffected by future fertilization, OJ market participants *are* influenced by forecasts of future Florida weather. We return to the question of whether *FDD* is strictly exogenous when we analyze the orange juice price data in more detail in Section 15.6.

The two definitions of exogeneity are summarized in Key Concept 15.1.

## 15.3 Estimation of Dynamic Causal Effects with Exogenous Regressors

If $X$ is exogenous, then its dynamic causal effect on $Y$ can be estimated by OLS estimation of the distributed lag regression in Equation (15.4). This section summarizes the conditions under which these OLS estimators lead to valid statistical inferences and introduces dynamic multipliers and cumulative dynamic multipliers.

**KEY CONCEPT**

**15.1**

## The Distributed Lag Model and Exogeneity

In the distributed lag model

$$Y_t = \beta_0 + \beta_1 X_t + \beta_2 X_{t-1} + \beta_3 X_{t-2} + \cdots + \beta_{r+1} X_{t-r} + u_t, \qquad (15.4)$$

there are two different types of exogeneity, that is, two different exogeneity conditions:
    Past and present exogeneity (exogeneity):

$$E(u_t | X_t, X_{t-1}, X_{t-2}, \ldots) = 0; \qquad (15.5)$$

Past, present, and future exogeneity (strict exogeneity):

$$E(u_t | \ldots, X_{t+2}, X_{t+1}, X_t, X_{t-1}, X_{t-2}, \ldots) = 0. \qquad (15.6)$$

If $X$ is strictly exogenous, it is exogenous, but exogeneity does not imply strict exogeneity.

## The Distributed Lag Model Assumptions

The four assumptions of the distributed lag regression model are similar to the four assumptions for the cross-sectional multiple regression model (Key Concept 6.4), modified for time series data.

The first assumption is that $X$ is exogenous, which extends the zero conditional mean assumption for cross-sectional data to include all lagged values of $X$. As discussed in Section 15.2, this assumption implies that the $r$ distributed lag coefficients in Equation (15.3) constitute all the nonzero dynamic causal effects. In this sense, the population regression function summarizes the entire dynamic effect on $Y$ of a change in $X$.

The second assumption has two parts: Part (a) requires that the variables have a stationary distribution, and part (b) requires that they become independently distributed when the amount of time separating them becomes large. This assumption is the same as the corresponding assumption for the ADL model (the second assumption in Key Concept 14.6), and the discussion of this assumption in Section 14.4 applies here as well.

The third assumption is that large outliers are unlikely, made mathematically precise by assuming that the variables have more than eight nonzero, finite moments.

## The Distributed Lag Model Assumptions

The distributed lag model is given in Key Concept 15.1 [Equation (15.4)], where

1. $X$ is exogenous, that is, $E(u_t | X_t, X_{t-1}, X_{t-2}, \dots) = 0$;
2. (a) The random variables $Y_t$ and $X_t$ have a stationary distribution, and
   (b) $(Y_t, X_t)$ and $(Y_{t-j}, X_{t-j})$ become independent as $j$ gets large;
3. Large outliers are unlikely: $Y_t$ and $X_t$ have more than eight nonzero, finite moments; and
4. There is no perfect multicollinearity.

This is stronger than the assumption of four finite moments that is used elsewhere in this book. As discussed in Section 15.4, this stronger assumption is used in the mathematics behind the HAC variance estimator.

The fourth assumption, which is the same as in the cross-sectional multiple regression model, is that there is no perfect multicollinearity.

The distributed lag regression model and assumptions are summarized in Key Concept 15.2.

**Extension to additional X's.** The distributed lag model extends directly to multiple $X$'s: The additional $X$'s and their lags are simply included as regressors in the distributed lag regression, and the assumptions in Key Concept 15.2 are modified to include these additional regressors. Although the extension to multiple $X$'s is conceptually straightforward, it complicates the notation, obscuring the main ideas of estimation and inference in the distributed lag model. For this reason, the case of multiple $X$'s is not treated explicitly in this chapter but is left as a straightforward extension of the distributed lag model with a single $X$.

## Autocorrelated $u_t$, Standard Errors, and Inference

In the distributed lag regression model, the error term $u_t$ can be autocorrelated; that is, $u_t$ can be correlated with its lagged values. This autocorrelation arises because, in time series data, the omitted factors included in $u_t$ can themselves be serially correlated. For example, suppose that the demand for orange juice also depends on income, so one factor that influences the price of orange juice is income, specifically, the aggregate income of potential orange juice consumers. Then aggregate income is an omitted variable in the distributed lag regression of orange juice price changes against freezing degree days. Aggregate income, however, is serially correlated: Income tends to fall in recessions and rise in expansions. Thus, income is serially correlated, and, because it is part of the error term, $u_t$ will be serially correlated. This example is typical: Because omitted determinants of $Y$ are themselves serially correlated, in general $u_t$ in the distributed lag model will be serially correlated.

The autocorrelation of $u_t$ does not affect the consistency of OLS, nor does it introduce bias. If, however, the errors are autocorrelated, then in general the usual OLS standard errors are inconsistent and a different formula must be used. Thus serial correlation of the errors is analogous to heteroskedasticity: The homoskedasticity-only standard errors are "wrong" when the errors are in fact heteroskedastic, in the sense that using homoskedasticity-only standard errors results in misleading statistical inferences when the errors are heteroskedastic. Similarly, when the errors are serially correlated, standard errors predicated upon i.i.d. errors are "wrong" in the sense that they result in misleading statistical inferences. The solution to this problem is to use heteroskedasticity- and autocorrelation-consistent (HAC) standard errors, the topic of Section 15.4.

## Dynamic Multipliers and Cumulative Dynamic Multipliers

Another name for the dynamic causal effect is the dynamic multiplier. The cumulative dynamic multipliers are the cumulative causal effects, up to a given lag; thus the cumulative dynamic multipliers measure the cumulative effect on $Y$ of a change in $X$.

*Dynamic multipliers.* The effect of a unit change in $X$ on $Y$ after $h$ periods, which is $\beta_{h+1}$ in Equation (15.4), is called the $h$-period **dynamic multiplier**. Thus the dynamic multipliers relating $X$ to $Y$ are the coefficients on $X_t$ and its lags in Equation (15.4). For example, $\beta_2$ is the one-period dynamic multiplier, $\beta_3$ is the two-period dynamic multiplier, and so forth. In this terminology, the zero-period (or contemporaneous) dynamic multiplier, or **impact effect**, is $\beta_1$, the effect on $Y$ of a change in $X$ in the same period.

Because the dynamic multipliers are estimated by the OLS regression coefficients, their standard errors are the HAC standard errors of the OLS regression coefficients.

*Cumulative dynamic multipliers.* The $h$-period **cumulative dynamic multiplier** is the cumulative effect of a unit change in $X$ on $Y$ over the next $h$ periods. Thus the cumulative dynamic multipliers are the cumulative sum of the dynamic multipliers. In terms of the coefficients of the distributed lag regression in Equation (15.4), the zero-period cumulative multiplier is $\beta_1$, the one-period cumulative multiplier is $\beta_1 + \beta_2$, and the $h$-period cumulative dynamic multiplier is $\beta_1 + \beta_2 + \cdots + \beta_{h+1}$. The sum of all the individual dynamic multipliers, $\beta_1 + \beta_2 + \cdots + \beta_{r+1}$, is the cumulative long-run effect on $Y$ of a change in $X$ and is called the **long-run cumulative dynamic multiplier**.

For example, consider the regression in Equation (15.2). The immediate effect of an additional freezing degree day is that the price of orange juice concentrate rises by 0.47%. The cumulative effect of a price change over the next month is the sum of the impact effect and the dynamic effect one month ahead; thus the cumulative effect on prices is the initial increase of 0.47% plus the subsequent smaller increase of 0.14% for a total of 0.61%. Similarly, the cumulative dynamic multiplier over 2 months is 0.47% + 0.14% + 0.06% = 0.67%.

The cumulative dynamic multipliers can be estimated directly using a modification of the distributed lag regression in Equation (15.4). This modified regression is

$$Y_t = \delta_0 + \delta_1 \Delta X_t + \delta_2 \Delta X_{t-1} + \delta_3 \Delta X_{t-2} + \cdots + \delta_r \Delta X_{t-r+1} + \delta_{r+1} X_{t-r} + u_t. \tag{15.7}$$

The coefficients in Equation (15.7), $\delta_1, \delta_2, \ldots, \delta_{r+1}$, are in fact the cumulative dynamic multipliers. This can be shown by a bit of algebra (Exercise 15.5), which demonstrates that the population regressions in Equations (15.7) and (15.4) are equivalent, where $\delta_0 = \beta_0$, $\delta_1 = \beta_1$, $\delta_2 = \beta_1 + \beta_2$, $\delta_3 = \beta_1 + \beta_2 + \beta_3$, and so forth. The coefficient on $X_{t-r}$, $\delta_{r+1}$, is the long-run cumulative dynamic multiplier; that is, $\delta_{r+1} = \beta_1 + \beta_2 + \beta_3 + \cdots + \beta_{r+1}$. Moreover, the OLS estimators of the coefficients in Equation (15.7) are the same as the corresponding cumulative sum of the OLS estimators in Equation (15.4). For example, $\hat{\delta}_2 = \hat{\beta}_1 + \hat{\beta}_2$. The main benefit of estimating the cumulative dynamic multipliers using the specification in Equation (15.7) is that, because the OLS estimators of the regression coefficients are estimators of the cumulative dynamic multipliers, the HAC standard errors of the coefficients in Equation (15.7) are the HAC standard errors of the cumulative dynamic multipliers.

## 15.4 Heteroskedasticity- and Autocorrelation-Consistent Standard Errors

If the error term $u_t$ is autocorrelated, then OLS coefficient estimators are consistent, but in general the usual OLS standard errors for cross-sectional data are not. This means that conventional statistical inferences—hypothesis tests and confidence intervals—based on the usual OLS standard errors will, in general, be misleading.

For example, confidence intervals constructed as the OLS estimator $\pm 1.96$ conventional standard errors need not contain the true value in 95% of repeated samples, even if the sample size is large. This section begins with a derivation of the correct formula for the variance of the OLS estimator with autocorrelated errors, then turns to heteroskedasticity- and autocorrelation-consistent (HAC) standard errors.

This section covers HAC standard errors for regression with time series data. Chapter 10 introduced a type of HAC standard errors, clustered standard errors, which are appropriate for panel data. Although clustered standard errors for panel data and HAC standard errors for time series data have the same goal, the different data structures lead to different formulas. This section is self-contained, and Chapter 10 is not a prerequisite.

## Distribution of the OLS Estimator with Autocorrelated Errors

To keep things simple, consider the OLS estimator $\hat{\beta}_1$ in the distributed lag regression model with no lags, that is, the linear regression model with a single regressor $X_t$:

$$Y_t = \beta_0 + \beta_1 X_t + u_t, \tag{15.8}$$

where the assumptions of Key Concept 15.2 are satisfied. This section shows that the variance of $\hat{\beta}_1$ can be written as the product of two terms: the expression for $\text{var}(\hat{\beta}_1)$, applicable if $u_t$ is not serially correlated, multiplied by a correction factor that arises from the autocorrelation in $u_t$ or, more precisely, the autocorrelation in $(X_t - \mu_X)u_t$.

As shown in Appendix 4.3, the formula for the OLS estimator $\hat{\beta}_1$ in Key Concept 4.2 can be rewritten as

$$\hat{\beta}_1 = \beta_1 + \frac{\frac{1}{T}\sum_{t=1}^{T}(X_t - \overline{X})u_t}{\frac{1}{T}\sum_{t=1}^{T}(X_t - \overline{X})^2}, \tag{15.9}$$

where Equation (15.9) is Equation (4.30) with a change of notation so that $i$ and $n$ are replaced by $t$ and $T$. Because $\overline{X} \xrightarrow{p} \mu_X$ and $\frac{1}{T}\sum_{t=1}^{T}(X_t - \overline{X})^2 \xrightarrow{p} \sigma_X^2$, in large samples $\hat{\beta}_1 - \beta_1$ is approximately given by

$$\hat{\beta}_1 - \beta_1 \cong \frac{\frac{1}{T}\sum_{t=1}^{T}(X_t - \mu_X)u_t}{\sigma_X^2} = \frac{\frac{1}{T}\sum_{t=1}^{T}v_t}{\sigma_X^2} = \frac{\overline{v}}{\sigma_X^2}, \tag{15.10}$$

where $v_t = (X_t - \mu_X)u_t$ and $\bar{v} = \frac{1}{T}\sum_{t=1}^{T} v_t$. Thus

$$\text{var}(\hat{\beta}_1) = \text{var}\left(\frac{\bar{v}}{\sigma_X^2}\right) = \frac{\text{var}(\bar{v})}{(\sigma_X^2)^2}. \tag{15.11}$$

If $v_t$ is i.i.d.—as assumed for cross-sectional data in Key Concept 4.3—then $\text{var}(\bar{v}) = \text{var}(v_t)/T$ and the formula for the variance of $\hat{\beta}_1$ from Key Concept 4.4 applies. If, however, $u_t$ and $X_t$ are not independently distributed over time, then in general $v_t$ will be serially correlated, so $\text{var}(\bar{v}) \neq \text{var}(v_t)/T$ and Key Concept 4.4 does not apply. Instead, if $v_t$ is serially correlated, the variance of $\bar{v}$ is given by

$$\begin{aligned}
\text{var}(\bar{v}) &= \text{var}[(v_1 + v_2 + \cdots + v_T)/T] \\
&= [\text{var}(v_1) + \text{cov}(v_1, v_2) + \cdots + \text{cov}(v_1, v_T) \\
&\quad + \text{cov}(v_2, v_1) + \text{var}(v_2) + \cdots + \text{var}(v_T)]/T^2 \\
&= [T\text{var}(v_t) + 2(T-1)\text{cov}(v_t, v_{t-1}) \\
&\quad + 2(T-2)\text{cov}(v_t, v_{t-2}) + \cdots + 2\text{cov}(v_t, v_{t-T+1})]/T^2 \\
&= \frac{\sigma_v^2}{T}f_T, \tag{15.12}
\end{aligned}$$

where

$$f_T = 1 + 2\sum_{j=1}^{T-1}\left(\frac{T-j}{T}\right)\rho_j, \tag{15.13}$$

where $\rho_j = \text{corr}(v_t, v_{t-j})$. In large samples, $f_T$ tends to the limit, $f_T \longrightarrow f_\infty = 1 + 2\sum_{j=1}^{\infty}\rho_j$.

Combining the expressions in Equation (15.10) for $\hat{\beta}_1$ and Equation (15.12) for $\text{var}(\bar{v})$ gives the formula for the variance of $\hat{\beta}_1$ when $v_t$ is autocorrelated:

$$\text{var}(\hat{\beta}_1) = \left[\frac{1}{T}\frac{\sigma_v^2}{(\sigma_X^2)^2}\right]f_T, \tag{15.14}$$

where $f_T$ is given in Equation (15.13).

Equation (15.14) expresses the variance of $\hat{\beta}_1$ as the product of two terms. The first, in square brackets, is the formula for the variance of $\hat{\beta}_1$ given in Key Concept 4.4, which applies in the absence of serial correlation. The second is the factor $f_T$, which adjusts this formula for serial correlation. Because of this additional factor

$f_T$ in Equation (15.14), the usual OLS standard error computed using Equation (5.4) is incorrect if the errors are serially correlated: If $v_t = (X_t - \mu_X)u_t$ is serially correlated, the estimator of the variance is off by the factor $f_T$.

## HAC Standard Errors

If the factor $f_T$, defined in Equation (15.13), was known, then the variance of $\hat{\beta}_1$ could be estimated by multiplying the usual cross-sectional estimator of the variance by $f_T$. This factor, however, depends on the unknown autocorrelations of $v_t$, so it must be estimated. The estimator of the variance of $\hat{\beta}_1$ that incorporates this adjustment is consistent whether or not there is heteroskedasticity and whether or not $v_t$ is autocorrelated. Accordingly, this estimator is called the **heteroskedasticity-and autocorrelation-consistent (HAC)** estimator of the variance of $\hat{\beta}_1$, and the square root of the HAC variance estimator is the **HAC standard error** of $\hat{\beta}_1$.

*The HAC variance formula.*   The heteroskedasticity- and autocorrelation-consistent estimator of the variance of $\hat{\beta}_1$ is

$$\tilde{\sigma}_{\hat{\beta}_1}^2 = \hat{\sigma}_{\hat{\beta}_1}^2 \hat{f}_T, \tag{15.15}$$

where $\hat{\sigma}_{\hat{\beta}_1}^2$ is the estimator of the variance of $\hat{\beta}_1$ in the absence of serial correlation, given in Equation (5.4), and where $\hat{f}_T$ is an estimator of the factor $f_T$ in Equation (15.13).

The task of constructing a consistent estimator $\hat{f}_T$ is challenging. To see why, consider two extremes. At one extreme, given the formula in Equation (15.13), it might seem natural to replace the population autocorrelations $\rho_j$ with the sample autocorrelations $\hat{\rho}_j$ [defined in Equation (14.6)], yielding the estimator $1 + 2\sum_{j=1}^{T-1}(\frac{T-j}{T})\hat{\rho}_j$. But this estimator contains so many estimated autocorrelations that it is inconsistent. Intuitively, because each of the estimated autocorrelations contains an estimation error, by estimating so many autocorrelations the estimation error in this estimator of $f_T$ remains large even in large samples. At the other extreme, one could imagine using only a few sample autocorrelations, for example, only the first sample autocorrelation, and ignoring all the higher autocorrelations. Although this estimator eliminates the problem of estimating too many autocorrelations, it has a different problem: It is inconsistent because it ignores the additional autocorrelations that appear in Equation (15.13). In short, using too many sample autocorrelations makes the estimator have a large variance, but using too few autocorrelations ignores the autocorrelations at higher lags, so in either of these extreme cases the estimator is inconsistent.

Estimators of $f_T$ used in practice strike a balance between these two extreme cases by choosing the number of autocorrelations to include in a way that depends on the sample size $T$. If the sample size is small, only a few autocorrelations are used, but if the sample size is large, more autocorrelations are included (but still far fewer than $T$). Specifically, let $\hat{f}_T$ be given by

$$\hat{f}_T = 1 + 2 \sum_{j=1}^{m-1} \left( \frac{m-j}{m} \right) \tilde{\rho}_j, \tag{15.16}$$

where $\tilde{\rho}_j = \sum_{t=j+1}^{T} \hat{v}_t \hat{v}_{t-j} / \sum_{t=1}^{T} \hat{v}_t^2$, where $\hat{v}_t = (X_t - \overline{X})\hat{u}_t$ (as in the definition of $\hat{\sigma}_{\hat{\beta}_1}^2$). The parameter $m$ in Equation (15.16) is called the **truncation parameter** of the HAC estimator because the sum of autocorrelations is shortened, or truncated, to include only $m - 1$ autocorrelations instead of the $T - 1$ autocorrelations appearing in the population formula in Equation (15.13).

For $\hat{f}_T$ to be consistent, $m$ must be chosen so that it is large in large samples, although still much less than $T$. One guideline for choosing $m$ in practice is to use the formula

$$m = 0.75T^{1/3}, \tag{15.17}$$

rounded to an integer. This formula, which is based on the assumption that there is a moderate amount of autocorrelation in $v_t$, gives a benchmark rule for determining $m$ as a function of the number of observations in the regression.[1]

The value of the truncation parameter $m$ resulting from Equation (15.17) can be modified using your knowledge of the series at hand. On the one hand, if there is a great deal of serial correlation in $v_t$, then you could increase $m$ beyond the value from Equation (15.17). On the other hand, if $v_t$ has little serial correlation, you could decrease $m$. Because of the ambiguity associated with the choice of $m$, it is good practice to try one or two alternative values of $m$ for at least one specification to make sure your results are not sensitive to $m$.

The HAC estimator in Equation (15.15), with $\hat{f}_T$ given in Equation (15.16), is called the **Newey–West variance estimator**, after the econometricians Whitney Newey and Kenneth West, who proposed it. They showed that, when used along with a rule like that in Equation (15.17), under general assumptions this estimator is a consistent estimator of the variance of $\hat{\beta}_1$ (Newey and West, 1987). Their

---

[1]Equation (15.17) gives the "best" choice of $m$ if $u_t$ and $X_t$ are first-order autoregressive processes with first autocorrelation coefficients 0.5, where "best" means the estimator that minimizes $E(\tilde{\sigma}_{\hat{\beta}_1}^2 - \sigma_{\hat{\beta}_1}^2)^2$. Equation (15.17) is based on a more general formula derived by Andrews [1991, Equation (5.3)].

proofs (and those in Andrews, 1991) assume that $v_t$ has more than four moments, which in turn is implied by $X_t$ and $u_t$ having more than eight moments, and this is the reason that the third assumption in Key Concept 15.2 is that $X_t$ and $u_t$ have more than eight moments.

*Other HAC estimators.*  The Newey–West variance estimator is not the only HAC estimator. For example, the weights $(m - j)/m$ in Equation (15.16) can be replaced by different weights. If different weights are used, then the rule for choosing the truncation parameter in Equation (15.17) no longer applies and a different rule, developed for those weights, should be used instead. Discussion of HAC estimators using other weights goes beyond the scope of this book. For more information on this topic, see Hayashi (2000, Section 6.6).

*Extension to multiple regression.*  All the issues discussed in this section generalize to the distributed lag regression model in Key Concept 15.1 with multiple lags and, more generally, to the multiple regression model with serially correlated errors. In particular, if the error term is serially correlated, then the usual OLS standard errors are an unreliable basis for inference and HAC standard errors should be used instead. If the HAC variance estimator used is the Newey–West estimator [the HAC variance estimator based on the weights $(m - j)/m$], then the truncation parameter $m$ can be chosen according to the rule in Equation (15.17) whether there is a single regressor or multiple regressors. The formula for HAC standard errors in multiple regression is incorporated into modern regression software designed for use with time series data. Because this formula involves matrix algebra, we omit it here and instead refer the reader to Hayashi (2000, Section 6.6) for the mathematical details.

HAC standard errors are summarized in Key Concept 15.3.

## 15.5  Estimation of Dynamic Causal Effects with Strictly Exogenous Regressors

When $X_t$ is strictly exogenous, two alternative estimators of dynamic causal effects are available. The first such estimator involves estimating an autoregressive distributed lag (ADL) model instead of a distributed lag model and calculating the dynamic multipliers from the estimated ADL coefficients. This method can entail estimating fewer coefficients than OLS estimation of the distributed lag model, thus potentially reducing estimation error. The second method is to estimate the coefficients of the distributed lag model, using **generalized least squares (GLS)**

## HAC Standard Errors

KEY CONCEPT

15.3

***The problem:*** The error term $u_t$ in the distributed lag regression model in Key Concept 15.1 can be serially correlated. If so, the OLS coefficient estimators are consistent but in general the usual OLS standard errors are not, resulting in misleading hypothesis tests and confidence intervals.

***The solution:*** Standard errors should be computed using a heteroskedasticity- and autocorrelation-consistent (HAC) estimator of the variance. The HAC estimator involves estimates of $m - 1$ autocovariances as well as the variance; in the case of a single regressor, the relevant formulas are given in Equations (15.15) and (15.16).

In practice, using HAC standard errors entails choosing the truncation parameter $m$. To do so, use the formula in Equation (15.17) as a benchmark, then increase or decrease $m$ depending on whether your regressors and errors have high or low serial correlation.

instead of OLS. Although the same number of coefficients in the distributed lag model are estimated by GLS as by OLS, the GLS estimator has a smaller variance. To keep the exposition simple, these two estimation methods are initially laid out and discussed in the context of a distributed lag model with a single lag and AR(1) errors. The potential advantages of these two estimators are greatest, however, when many lags appear in the distributed lag model, so these estimators are then extended to the general distributed lag model with higher-order autoregressive errors.

### The Distributed Lag Model with AR(1) Errors

Suppose that the causal effect on $Y$ of a change in $X$ lasts for only two periods; that is, it has an initial impact effect $\beta_1$ and an effect in the next period of $\beta_2$, but no effect thereafter. Then the appropriate distributed lag regression model is the distributed lag model with only current and past values of $X_{t-1}$:

$$Y_t = \beta_0 + \beta_1 X_t + \beta_2 X_{t-1} + u_t. \tag{15.18}$$

As discussed in Section 15.2, in general the error term $u_t$ in Equation (15.18) is serially correlated. One consequence of this serial correlation is that, if the distributed lag coefficients are estimated by OLS, then inference based on the usual OLS standard errors can be misleading. For this reason, Sections 15.3 and 15.4

emphasized the use of HAC standard errors when $\beta_1$ and $\beta_2$ in Equation (15.18) are estimated by OLS.

In this section, we take a different approach toward the serial correlation in $u_t$. This approach, which is possible if $X_t$ is strictly exogenous, involves adopting an autoregressive model for the serial correlation in $u_t$, then using this AR model to derive some estimators that can be more efficient than the OLS estimator in the distributed lag model.

Specifically, suppose that $u_t$ follows the AR(1) model

$$u_t = \phi_1 u_{t-1} + \tilde{u}_t, \tag{15.19}$$

where $\phi_1$ is the autoregressive parameter, $\tilde{u}_t$ is serially uncorrelated, and no intercept is needed because $E(u_t) = 0$. Equations (15.18) and (15.19) imply that the distributed lag model with a serially correlated error can be rewritten as an autoregressive distributed lag model with a serially uncorrelated error. To do so, lag each side of Equation (15.18) and subtract $\phi_1$ multiplied by this lag from each side:

$$Y_t - \phi_1 Y_{t-1} = (\beta_0 + \beta_1 X_t + \beta_2 X_{t-1} + u_t) - \phi_1(\beta_0 + \beta_1 X_{t-1} + \beta_2 X_{t-2} + u_{t-1})$$
$$= \beta_0 + \beta_1 X_t + \beta_2 X_{t-1} - \phi_1\beta_0 - \phi_1\beta_1 X_{t-1} - \phi_1\beta_2 X_{t-2} + \tilde{u}_t, \quad (15.20)$$

where the second equality uses $\tilde{u}_t = u_t - \phi_1 u_{t-1}$. Collecting terms in Equation (15.20), we have that

$$Y_t = \alpha_0 + \phi_1 Y_{t-1} + \delta_0 X_t + \delta_1 X_{t-1} + \delta_2 X_{t-2} + \tilde{u}_t, \tag{15.21}$$

where

$$\alpha_0 = \beta_0(1 - \phi_1), \delta_0 = \beta_1, \delta_1 = \beta_2 - \phi_1\beta_1, \text{ and } \delta_2 = -\phi_1\beta_2, \tag{15.22}$$

where $\beta_0$, $\beta_1$, and $\beta_2$ are the coefficients in Equation (15.18) and $\phi_1$ is the autocorrelation coefficient in Equation (15.19).

Equation (15.21) is an ADL model that includes a contemporaneous value of $X$ and two of its lags. We will refer to Equation (15.21) as the ADL representation of the distributed lag model with autoregressive errors given in Equations (15.18) and (15.19).

The terms in Equation (15.20) can be reorganized differently to obtain an expression that is equivalent to Equations (15.21) and (15.22). Let $\tilde{Y}_t = Y_t - \phi_1 Y_{t-1}$ be the **quasi-difference** of $Y_t$ ("quasi" because it is not the first difference, the difference between $Y_t$ and $Y_{t-1}$; rather, it is the difference between $Y_t$ and $\phi_1 Y_{t-1}$).

Similarly, let $\widetilde{X}_t = X_t - \phi_1 X_{t-1}$ be the quasi-difference of $X_t$. Then Equation (15.20) can be written

$$\widetilde{Y}_t = \alpha_0 + \beta_1 \widetilde{X}_t + \beta_2 \widetilde{X}_{t-1} + \widetilde{u}_t. \tag{15.23}$$

We will refer to Equation (15.23) as the quasi-difference representation of the distributed lag model with autoregressive errors given in Equations (15.18) and (15.19).

The ADL model Equation (15.21) [with the parameter restrictions in Equation (15.22)] and the quasi-difference model in Equation (15.23) are equivalent. In both models, the error term, $\widetilde{u}_t$, is serially uncorrelated. The two representations, however, suggest different estimation strategies. But before discussing those strategies, we turn to the assumptions under which they yield consistent estimators of the dynamic multipliers, $\beta_1$ and $\beta_2$.

***The conditional mean zero assumption in the ADL(1,2) and quasi-difference models.*** Because Equations (15.21) [with the restrictions in Equation (15.22)] and (15.23) are equivalent, the conditions for their estimation are the same, so for convenience we consider Equation (15.23).

The quasi-difference model in Equation (15.23) is a distributed lag model involving the quasi-differenced variables with a serially uncorrelated error. Accordingly, the conditions for OLS estimation of the coefficients in Equation (15.23) are the least squares assumptions for the distributed lag model in Key Concept 15.2, expressed in terms of $\widetilde{u}_t$ and $\widetilde{X}_t$. The critical assumption here is the first assumption, which, applied to Equation (15.23), is that $\widetilde{X}_t$ is exogenous; that is,

$$E(\widetilde{u}_t | \widetilde{X}_t, \widetilde{X}_{t-1}, \dots) = 0, \tag{15.24}$$

where letting the conditional expectation depend on distant lags of $\widetilde{X}_t$ ensures that no additional lags of $\widetilde{X}_t$, other than those appearing in Equation (15.23), enter the population regression function.

Because $\widetilde{X}_t = X_t - \phi_1 X_{t-1}$, so $X_t = \widetilde{X}_t + \phi_1 X_{t-1}$, conditioning on $\widetilde{X}_t$ and all of its lags is equivalent to conditioning on $X_t$ and all of its lags. Thus the conditional expectation condition in Equation (15.24) is equivalent to the condition that $E(\widetilde{u}_t | X_t, X_{t-1}, \dots) = 0$. Furthermore, because $\widetilde{u}_t = u_t - \phi_1 u_{t-1}$, this condition in turn implies that

$$
\begin{aligned}
0 &= E(\widetilde{u}_t | X_t, X_{t-1}, \dots) \\
&= E(u_t - \phi_1 u_{t-1} | X_t, X_{t-1}, \dots) \\
&= E(u_t | X_t, X_{t-1}, \dots) - \phi_1 E(u_{t-1} | X_t, X_{t-1}, \dots).
\end{aligned} \tag{15.25}
$$

For the equality in Equation (15.25) to hold for general values of $\phi_1$, it must be the case that both $E(u_t|X_t, X_{t-1}, \dots) = 0$ and $E(u_{t-1}|X_t, X_{t-1}, \dots) = 0$. By shifting the time subscripts forward one time period, the condition that $E(u_{t-1}|X_t, X_{t-1}, \dots) = 0$ can be rewritten as

$$E(u_t|X_{t+1}, X_t, X_{t-1}, \dots) = 0, \tag{15.26}$$

which (by the law of iterated expectations) implies that $E(u_t|X_t, X_{t-1}, \dots) = 0$. In summary, having the zero conditional mean assumption in Equation (15.24) hold for general values of $\phi_1$ is equivalent to having the condition in Equation (15.26) hold.

The condition in Equation (15.26) is implied by $X_t$ being strictly exogenous, but it is *not* implied by $X_t$ being (past and present) exogenous. Thus the least squares assumptions for estimation of the distributed lag model in Equation (15.23) hold if $X_t$ is strictly exogenous, but it is not enough that $X_t$ be (past and present) exogenous.

Because the ADL representation [Equations (15.21) and (15.22)] is equivalent to the quasi-differenced representation [Equation (15.23)], the conditional mean assumption needed to estimate the coefficients of the quasi-differenced representation [that $E(u_t|X_{t+1}, X_t, X_{t-1}, \dots) = 0$] is also the conditional mean assumption for consistent estimation of the coefficients of the ADL representation.

We now turn to the two estimation strategies suggested by these two representations: estimation of the ADL coefficients and estimation of the coefficients of the quasi-difference model.

## OLS Estimation of the ADL Model

The first strategy is to use OLS to estimate the coefficients in the ADL model in Equation (15.21). As the derivation leading to Equation (15.21) shows, including the lag of $Y$ and the extra lag of $X$ as regressors makes the error term serially uncorrelated (under the assumption that the error follows a first order autoregression). Thus the usual OLS standard errors can be used; that is, HAC standard errors are not needed when the ADL model coefficients in Equation (15.21) are estimated by OLS.

The estimated ADL coefficients are not themselves estimates of the dynamic multipliers, but the dynamic multipliers can be computed from the ADL coefficients. A general way to compute the dynamic multipliers is to express the estimated regression function as a function of current and past values of $X_t$, that is, to eliminate $Y_t$ from the estimated regression function. To do so, repeatedly substitute expressions for lagged values of $Y_t$ into the estimated regression function. Specifically, consider the estimated regression function

$$\hat{Y}_t = \hat{\phi}_1 Y_{t-1} + \hat{\delta}_0 X_t + \hat{\delta}_1 X_{t-1} + \hat{\delta}_2 X_{t-2}, \tag{15.27}$$

where the estimated intercept has been omitted because it does not enter any expression for the dynamic multipliers. Lagging both sides of Equation (15.27) yields $\hat{Y}_{t-1} = \hat{\phi}_1 Y_{t-2} + \hat{\delta}_0 X_{t-1} + \hat{\delta}_1 X_{t-2} + \hat{\delta}_2 X_{t-3}$, so replacing $\hat{Y}_{t-1}$ in Equation (15.27) by this expression for $\hat{Y}_{t-1}$ and collecting terms yields

$$\begin{aligned}\hat{Y}_t &= \hat{\phi}_1(\hat{\phi}_1 Y_{t-2} + \hat{\delta}_0 X_{t-1} + \hat{\delta}_1 X_{t-2} + \hat{\delta}_2 X_{t-3}) + \hat{\delta}_0 X_t + \hat{\delta}_1 X_{t-1} + \hat{\delta}_2 X_{t-2} \\ &= \hat{\delta}_0 X_t + (\hat{\delta}_1 + \hat{\phi}_1 \hat{\delta}_0) X_{t-1} + (\hat{\delta}_2 + \hat{\phi}_1 \hat{\delta}_1) X_{t-2} + \hat{\phi}_1 \hat{\delta}_2 X_{t-3} + \hat{\phi}_1^2 Y_{t-2}. \tag{15.28}\end{aligned}$$

Repeating this process by repeatedly substituting expressions for $Y_{t-2}$, $Y_{t-3}$, and so forth yields

$$\begin{aligned}\hat{Y}_t &= \hat{\delta}_0 X_t + (\hat{\delta}_1 + \hat{\phi}_1 \hat{\delta}_0) X_{t-1} + (\hat{\delta}_2 + \hat{\phi}_1 \hat{\delta}_1 + \hat{\phi}_1^2 \hat{\delta}_0) X_{t-2} \\ &\quad + \hat{\phi}_1(\hat{\delta}_2 + \hat{\phi}_1 \hat{\delta}_1 + \hat{\phi}_1^2 \hat{\delta}_0) X_{t-3} + \hat{\phi}_1^2(\hat{\delta}_2 + \hat{\phi}_1 \hat{\delta}_1 + \hat{\phi}_1^2 \hat{\delta}_0) X_{t-4} + \cdots. \tag{15.29}\end{aligned}$$

The coefficients in Equation (15.29) are the estimators of the dynamic multipliers, computed from the OLS estimators of the coefficients in the ADL model in Equation (15.21). If the restrictions on the coefficients in Equation (15.22) were to hold exactly for the *estimated* coefficients, then the dynamic multipliers beyond the second (that is, the coefficients on $X_{t-2}$, $X_{t-3}$, and so forth) would all be zero.[2] However, under this estimation strategy those restrictions will not hold exactly, so the estimated multipliers beyond the second in Equation (15.29) will generally be nonzero.

## GLS Estimation

The second strategy for estimating the dynamic multipliers when $X_t$ is strictly exogenous is to use generalized least squares (GLS), which entails estimating Equation (15.23). To describe the GLS estimator, we initially assume that $\phi_1$ is known. Because in practice it is unknown, this estimator is infeasible, so it is called the infeasible GLS estimator. The infeasible GLS estimator, however, can be modified using an estimator of $\phi_1$, which yields a feasible version of the GLS estimator.

---

[2]Substitute the equalities in Equation (15.22) to show that, if those equalities hold, then $\delta_2 + \phi_1 \delta_1 + \phi_1^2 \delta_0 = 0$.

*Infeasible GLS.* Suppose that $\phi_1$ were known; then the quasi-differenced variables $\widetilde{X}_t$ and $\widetilde{Y}_t$ could be computed directly. As discussed in the context of Equations (15.24) and (15.26), if $X_t$ is strictly exogenous, then $E(\widetilde{u}_t | \widetilde{X}_t, \widetilde{X}_{t-1}, \dots) = 0$. Thus, if $X_t$ is strictly exogenous and if $\phi_1$ is known, the coefficients $\alpha_0$, $\beta_1$, and $\beta_2$ in Equation (15.23) can be estimated by the OLS regression of $\widetilde{Y}_t$ on $\widetilde{X}_t$ and $\widetilde{X}_{t-1}$ (including an intercept). The resulting estimator of $\beta_1$ and $\beta_2$—that is, the OLS estimator of the slope coefficients in Equation (15.23) when $\phi_1$ is known—is the **infeasible GLS estimator**. This estimator is infeasible because $\phi_1$ is unknown, so $\widetilde{X}_t$ and $\widetilde{Y}_t$ cannot be computed and thus these OLS estimators cannot actually be computed.

*Feasible GLS.* The **feasible GLS estimator** modifies the infeasible GLS estimator by using a preliminary estimator of $\phi_1$, $\hat{\phi}_1$, to compute the estimated quasi-differences. Specifically, the feasible GLS estimators of $\beta_1$ and $\beta_2$ are the OLS estimators of $\beta_1$ and $\beta_2$ in Equation (15.23), computed by regressing $\hat{\widetilde{Y}}_t$ on $\hat{\widetilde{X}}_t$ and $\hat{\widetilde{X}}_{t-1}$ (with an intercept), where $\hat{\widetilde{X}}_t = X_t - \hat{\phi}_1 X_{t-1}$ and $\hat{\widetilde{Y}}_t = Y_t - \hat{\phi}_1 Y_{t-1}$.

The preliminary estimator, $\hat{\phi}_1$, can be computed by first estimating the distributed lag regression in Equation (15.18) by OLS, then using OLS to estimate $\phi_1$ in Equation (15.19) with the OLS residuals $\hat{u}_t$ replacing the unobserved regression errors $u_t$. This version of the GLS estimator is called the Cochrane–Orcutt (1949) estimator.

An extension of the Cochrane–Orcutt method is to continue this process iteratively: Use the GLS estimator of $\beta_1$ and $\beta_2$ to compute revised estimators of $u_t$; use these new residuals to re-estimate $\phi_1$; use this revised estimator of $\phi_1$ to compute revised estimated quasi-differences; use these revised estimated quasi-differences to re-estimate $\beta_1$ and $\beta_2$; and continue this process until the estimators of $\beta_1$ and $\beta_2$ converge. This is referred to as the iterated Cochrane–Orcutt estimator.

*A nonlinear least squares interpretation of the GLS estimator.* An equivalent interpretation of the GLS estimator is that it estimates the ADL model in Equation (15.21), imposing the parameter restrictions in Equation (15.22). These restrictions are nonlinear functions of the original parameters $\beta_0$, $\beta_1$, $\beta_2$, and $\phi_1$, so this estimation cannot be performed using OLS. Instead, the parameters can be estimated by nonlinear least squares (NLLS). As discussed in Appendix 8.1, NLLS minimizes the sum of squared mistakes made by the estimated regression function, recognizing that the regression function is a nonlinear function of the parameters being estimated. In general, NLLS estimation can require sophisticated algorithms for minimizing nonlinear functions of unknown parameters.

In the special case at hand, however, those sophisticated algorithms are not needed; rather, the NLLS estimator can be computed using the algorithm described previously for the iterated Cochrane–Orcutt estimator. Thus the iterated Cochrane–Orcutt GLS estimator is in fact the NLLS estimator of the ADL coefficients, subject to the nonlinear constraints in Equation (15.22).

*Efficiency of GLS.* The virtue of the GLS estimator is that when $X$ is strictly exogenous and the transformed errors $\tilde{u}_t$ are homoskedastic, it is efficient among linear estimators, at least in large samples. To see this, first consider the infeasible GLS estimator. If $\tilde{u}_t$ is homoskedastic, if $\phi_1$ is known (so that $\tilde{X}_t$ and $\tilde{Y}_t$ can be treated as if they are observed), and if $X_t$ is strictly exogenous, then the Gauss–Markov theorem implies that the OLS estimator of $\alpha_0$, $\beta_1$, and $\beta_2$ in Equation (15.23) is efficient among all linear conditionally unbiased estimators based on $\tilde{X}_t$ and $\tilde{Y}_t$, for $t = 2, \ldots, T$, where the first observation ($t = 1$) is lost because of quasi-differencing. That is, the OLS estimator of the coefficients in Equation (15.23) is the best linear unbiased estimator, or BLUE (Section 5.5). Because the OLS estimator of Equation (15.23) is the infeasible GLS estimator, this means that the infeasible GLS estimator is BLUE. The feasible GLS estimator is similar to the infeasible GLS estimator, except that $\phi_1$ is estimated. Because the estimator of $\phi_1$ is consistent and its variance is inversely proportional to $T$, the feasible and infeasible GLS estimators have the same variances in large samples, and the loss of information from the first observation ($t = 1$) is negligible when $T$ is large. In this sense, if $X$ is strictly exogenous, then the feasible GLS estimator is BLUE in large samples. In particular, if $X$ is strictly exogenous, then GLS is more efficient than the OLS estimator of the distributed lag coefficients discussed in Section 15.3.

The Cochrane–Orcutt and iterated Cochrane–Orcutt estimators presented here are special cases of GLS estimation. In general, GLS estimation involves transforming the regression model so that the errors are homoskedastic and serially uncorrelated, then estimating the coefficients of the transformed regression model by OLS. In general, the GLS estimator is consistent and BLUE in large samples if $X$ is strictly exogenous, but is not consistent if $X$ is only (past and present) exogenous. The mathematics of GLS involve matrix algebra, so they are postponed to Section 18.6.

## The Distributed Lag Model with Additional Lags and AR(*p*) Errors

The foregoing discussion of the distributed lag model in Equations (15.18) and (15.19), which has a single lag of $X_t$ and an AR(1) error term, carries over to the general distributed lag model with multiple lags and an AR($p$) error term.

*The general distributed lag model with autoregressive errors.* The general distributed lag model with $r$ lags and an $AR(p)$ error term is

$$Y_t = \beta_0 + \beta_1 X_t + \beta_2 X_{t-1} + \cdots + \beta_{r+1} X_{t-r} + u_t, \qquad (15.30)$$

$$u_t = \phi_1 u_{t-1} + \phi_2 u_{t-2} + \cdots + \phi_p u_{t-p} + \tilde{u}_t, \qquad (15.31)$$

where $\beta_1, \ldots, \beta_{r+1}$ are the dynamic multipliers and $\phi_1, \ldots, \phi_p$ are the autoregressive coefficients of the error term. Under the $AR(p)$ model for the errors, $\tilde{u}_t$ is serially uncorrelated.

Algebra of the sort that led to the ADL model in Equation (15.21) shows that Equations (15.30) and (15.31) imply that $Y_t$ can be written in ADL form:

$$Y_t = \alpha_0 + \phi_1 Y_{t-1} + \cdots + \phi_p Y_{t-p} + \delta_0 X_t + \delta_1 X_{t-1} + \cdots + \delta_q X_{t-q} + \tilde{u}_t, \quad (15.32)$$

where $q = r + p$ and $\delta_0, \ldots, \delta_q$ are functions of the $\beta$'s and $\phi$'s in Equations (15.30) and (15.31). Equivalently, the model of Equations (15.30) and (15.31) can be written in quasi-difference form as

$$\tilde{Y}_t = \alpha_0 + \beta_1 \tilde{X}_t + \beta_2 \tilde{X}_{t-1} + \cdots + \beta_{r+1} \tilde{X}_{t-r} + \tilde{u}_t, \qquad (15.33)$$

where $\tilde{Y}_t = Y_t - \phi_1 Y_{t-1} - \cdots - \phi_p Y_{t-p}$ and $\tilde{X}_t = X_t - \phi_1 X_{t-1} - \cdots - \phi_p X_{t-p}$.

*Conditions for estimation of the ADL coefficients.* The foregoing discussion of the conditions for consistent estimation of the ADL coefficients in the $AR(1)$ case extends to the general model with $AR(p)$ errors. The conditional mean zero assumption for Equation (15.33) is that

$$E(\tilde{u}_t | \tilde{X}_t, \tilde{X}_{t-1}, \ldots) = 0. \qquad (15.34)$$

Because $\tilde{u}_t = u_t - \phi_1 u_{t-1} - \phi_2 u_{t-2} - \cdots - \phi_p u_{t-p}$ and $\tilde{X}_t = X_t - \phi_1 X_{t-1} - \cdots - \phi_p X_{t-p}$, this condition is equivalent to

$$E(u_t | X_t, X_{t-1}, \ldots) - \phi_1 E(u_{t-1} | X_t, X_{t-1}, \ldots)$$
$$- \cdots - \phi_p E(u_{t-p} | X_t, X_{t-1}, \ldots) = 0. \qquad (15.35)$$

For Equation (15.35) to hold for general values of $\phi_1, \ldots, \phi_p$, it must be the case that each of the conditional expectations in Equation (15.35) is zero; equivalently, it must be the case that

$$E(u_t | X_{t+p}, X_{t+p-1}, X_{t+p-2}, \ldots) = 0. \qquad (15.36)$$

This condition is not implied by $X_t$ being (past and present) exogenous, but it is implied by $X_t$ being strictly exogenous. In fact, in the limit when $p$ is infinite (so that the error term in the distributed lag model follows an infinite-order autoregression), the condition in Equation (15.36) becomes the condition in Key Concept 15.1 for strict exogeneity.

*Estimation of the ADL model by OLS.* As in the distributed lag model with a single lag and an AR(1) error term, the dynamic multipliers can be estimated from the OLS estimators of the ADL coefficients in Equation (15.32). The general formulas are similar to, but more complicated than, those in Equation (15.29) and are best expressed using lag multiplier notation; these formulas are given in Appendix 15.2. In practice, modern regression software designed for time series regression analysis does these computations for you.

*Estimation by GLS.* Alternatively, the dynamic multipliers can be estimated by (feasible) GLS. This entails OLS estimation of the coefficients of the quasi-differenced specification in Equation (15.33), using estimated quasi-differences. The estimated quasi-differences can be computed using preliminary estimators of the autoregressive coefficients $\phi_1, \ldots, \phi_p$, as in the AR(1) case. The GLS estimator is asymptotically BLUE, in the sense discussed earlier for the AR(1) case.

Estimation of dynamic multipliers under strict exogeneity is summarized in Key Concept 15.4.

*Which to use: ADL or GLS?* The two estimation options, OLS estimation of the ADL coefficients and GLS estimation of the distributed lag coefficients, have both advantages and disadvantages.

The advantage of the ADL approach is that it can reduce the number of parameters needed for estimating the dynamic multipliers, compared to OLS estimation of the distributed lag model. For example, the estimated ADL model in Equation (15.27) led to the infinitely long estimated distributed lag representation in Equation (15.29). To the extent that a distributed lag model with only $r$ lags is really an approximation to a longer-lagged distributed lag model, the ADL model can provide a simple way to estimate those many longer lags using only a few unknown parameters. Thus in practice it might be possible to estimate the ADL model in Equation (15.39) with values of $p$ and $q$ much smaller than the value of $r$ needed for OLS estimation of the distributed lag coefficients in Equation (15.37). In other words, the ADL specification can provide a compact, or parsimonious, summary of a long and complex distributed lag (see Appendix 15.2 for additional discussion).

**KEY CONCEPT**

**15.4**

### Estimation of Dynamic Multipliers Under Strict Exogeneity

The general distributed lag model with $r$ lags and $AR(p)$ error term is

$$Y_t = \beta_0 + \beta_1 X_t + \beta_2 X_{t-1} + \cdots + \beta_{r+1} X_{t-r} + u_t \qquad (15.37)$$

$$u_t = \phi_1 u_{t-1} + \phi_2 u_{t-2} + \cdots + \phi_p u_{t-p} + \tilde{u}_t. \qquad (15.38)$$

If $X_t$ is strictly exogenous, then the dynamic multipliers $\beta_1, \ldots, \beta_{r+1}$ can be estimated by first using OLS to estimate the coefficients of the ADL model

$$Y_t = \alpha_0 + \phi_1 Y_{t-1} + \cdots + \phi_p Y_{t-p} + \delta_0 X_t + \delta_1 X_{t-1} + \cdots + \delta_q X_{t-q} + \tilde{u}_t, \qquad (15.39)$$

where $q = r + p$, and then computing the dynamic multipliers using regression software. Alternatively, the dynamic multipliers can be estimated by estimating the distributed lag coefficients in Equation (15.37) by GLS.

The advantage of the GLS estimator is that, for a given lag length $r$ in the distributed lag model, the GLS estimator of the distributed lag coefficients is more efficient than the ADL estimator, at least in large samples. In practice, then, the advantage of using the ADL approach arises because the ADL specification can permit estimating fewer parameters than are estimated by GLS.

## 15.6 Orange Juice Prices and Cold Weather

This section uses the tools of time series regression to squeeze additional insights from our data on Florida temperatures and orange juice prices. First, how long lasting is the effect of a freeze on the price? Second, has this dynamic effect been stable or has it changed over the 51 years spanned by the data and, if so, how?

We begin this analysis by estimating the dynamic causal effects using the method of Section 15.3, that is, by OLS estimation of the coefficients of a distributed lag regression of the percentage change in prices ($\%ChgP_t$) on the number of freezing degree days in that month ($FDD_t$) and its lagged values. For the distributed lag estimator to be consistent, $FDD$ must be (past and present) exogenous. As discussed in Section 15.2, this assumption is reasonable here. Humans cannot influence the weather, so treating the weather as if it were randomly assigned experimentally is appropriate. Because $FDD$ is exogenous, we can estimate the dynamic causal effects by OLS estimation of the coefficients in the distributed lag model of Equation (15.4) in Key Concept 15.1.

As discussed in Sections 15.3 and 15.4, the error term can be serially correlated in distributed lag regressions, so it is important to use HAC standard errors, which adjust for this serial correlation. For the initial results, the truncation parameter for the Newey–West standard errors ($m$ in the notation of Section 15.4) was chosen using the rule in Equation (15.17): Because there are 612 monthly observations, according to that rule $m = 0.75\,T^{1/3} = 0.75 \times 612^{1/3} = 6.37$, but because $m$ must be an integer, this was rounded up to $m = 7$; the sensitivity of the standard errors to this choice of truncation parameter is investigated below.

The results of OLS estimation of the distributed lag regression of $\%ChgP_t$ on $FDD_t$, $FDD_{t-1}$, ..., $FDD_{t-18}$ are summarized in column (1) of Table 15.1. The coefficients of this regression (only some of which are reported in the table) are estimates of the dynamic causal effect on orange juice price changes (in percent) for the first 18 months following a unit increase in the number of freezing degree days in a month. For example, a single freezing degree day is estimated to increase prices by 0.50% over the month in which the freezing degree day occurs. The subsequent effect on price in later months of a freezing degree day is less: After 1 month the estimated effect is to increase the price by a further 0.17%, and after 2 months the estimated effect is to increase the price by an additional 0.07%. The $R^2$ from this regression is 0.12, indicating that much of the monthly variation in orange juice prices is not explained by current and past values of $FDD$.

Plots of dynamic multipliers can convey information more effectively than tables such as Table 15.1. The dynamic multipliers from column (1) of Table 15.1 are plotted in Figure 15.2a along with their 95% confidence intervals, computed as the estimated coefficient $\pm 1.96$ HAC standard errors. After the initial sharp price rise, subsequent price rises are less, although prices are estimated to rise slightly in each of the first 6 months after the freeze. As can be seen from Figure 15.2a, for months other than the first the dynamic multipliers are not statistically significantly different from zero at the 5% significance level, although they are estimated to be positive through the seventh month.

Column (2) of Table 15.1 contains the cumulative dynamic multipliers for this specification, that is, the cumulative sum of the dynamic multipliers reported in

**TABLE 15.1** The Dynamic Effect of a Freezing Degree Day (*FDD*) on the Price of Orange Juice: Selected Estimated Dynamic Multipliers and Cumulative Dynamic Multipliers

| Lag Number | (1) Dynamic Multipliers | (2) Cumulative Multipliers | (3) Cumulative Multipliers | (4) Cumulative Multipliers |
|---|---|---|---|---|
| 0 | 0.50 (0.14) | 0.50 (0.14) | 0.50 (0.14) | 0.51 (0.15) |
| 1 | 0.17 (0.09) | 0.67 (0.14) | 0.67 (0.13) | 0.70 (0.15) |
| 2 | 0.07 (0.06) | 0.74 (0.17) | 0.74 (0.16) | 0.76 (0.18) |
| 3 | 0.07 (0.04) | 0.81 (0.18) | 0.81 (0.18) | 0.84 (0.19) |
| 4 | 0.02 (0.03) | 0.84 (0.19) | 0.84 (0.19) | 0.87 (0.20) |
| 5 | 0.03 (0.03) | 0.87 (0.19) | 0.87 (0.19) | 0.89 (0.20) |
| 6 . . . | 0.03 (0.05) | 0.90 (0.20) | 0.90 (0.21) | 0.91 (0.21) |
| 12 . . . | −0.14 (0.08) | 0.54 (0.27) | 0.54 (0.28) | 0.54 (0.28) |
| 18 | 0.00 (0.02) | 0.37 (0.30) | 0.37 (0.31) | 0.37 (0.30) |
| Monthly indicators? | No | No | No | Yes $F = 1.01$ ($p = 0.43$) |
| HAC standard error truncation parameter ($m$) | 7 | 7 | 14 | 7 |

All regressions were estimated by OLS using monthly data (described in Appendix 15.1) from January 1950 to December 2000, for a total of $T = 612$ monthly observations. The dependent variable is the monthly percentage change in the price of orange juice ($\%ChgP_t$). Regression (1) is the distributed lag regression with the monthly number of freezing degree days and 18 of its lagged values, that is, $FDD_t, FDD_{t-1}, \ldots, FDD_{t-18}$, and the reported coefficients are the OLS estimates of the dynamic multipliers. The cumulative multipliers are the cumulative sum of estimated dynamic multipliers. All regressions include an intercept, which is not reported. Newey–West HAC standard errors, computed using the truncation number given in the final row, are reported in parentheses.

**FIGURE 15.2**   The Dynamic Effect of a Freezing Degree Day (*FDD*) on the Price of Orange Juice

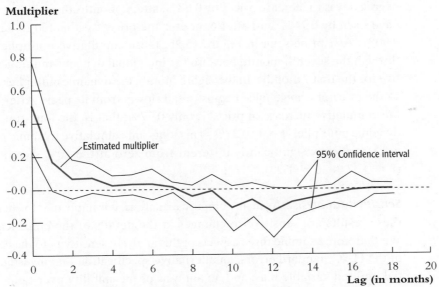

**(a)** Estimated Dynamic Multipliers and 95% Confidence Interval

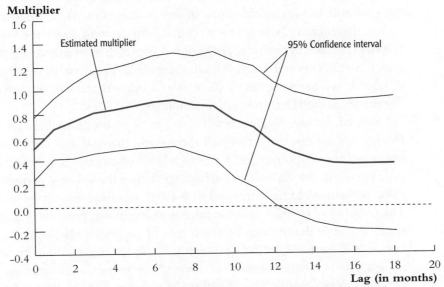

**(b)** Estimated Cumulative Dynamic Multipliers and 95% Confidence Interval

The estimated dynamic multipliers show that a freeze leads to an immediate increase in prices. Future price rises are much smaller than the initial impact. The cumulative multiplier shows that freezes have a persistent effect on the level of orange juice prices, with prices peaking seven months after the freeze.

column (1). These dynamic multipliers are plotted in Figure 15.2b along with their 95% confidence intervals. After 1 month, the cumulative effect of the freezing degree day is to increase prices by 0.67%, after 2 months the price is estimated to have risen by 0.74%, and after 6 months the price is estimated to have risen by 0.90%. As can be seen in Figure 15.2b, these cumulative multipliers increase through the seventh month, because the individual dynamic multipliers are positive for the first 7 months. In the eighth month, the dynamic multiplier is negative, so the price of orange juice begins to fall slowly from its peak. After 18 months, the cumulative increase in prices is only 0.37%; that is, the long-run cumulative dynamic multiplier is only 0.37%. This long-run cumulative dynamic multiplier is not statistically significantly different from zero at the 10% significance level ($t = 0.37/0.30 = 1.23$).

*Sensitivity analysis.* As in any empirical analysis, it is important to check whether these results are sensitive to changes in the details of the empirical analysis. We therefore examine three aspects of this analysis: sensitivity to the computation of the HAC standard errors; an alternative specification that investigates potential omitted variable bias; and an analysis of the stability over time of the estimated multipliers.

First, we investigate whether the standard errors reported in the second column of Table 15.1 are sensitive to different choices of the HAC truncation parameter $m$. In column (3), results are reported for $m = 14$, twice the value used in column (2). The regression specification is the same as in column (2), so the estimated coefficients and dynamic multipliers are identical; only the standard errors differ but, as it happens, not by much. We conclude that the results are insensitive to changes in the HAC truncation parameter.

Second, we investigate a possible source of omitted variable bias. Freezes in Florida are not randomly assigned throughout the year, but rather occur in the winter (of course). If demand for orange juice is seasonal (is demand for orange juice greater in the winter than the summer?), then the seasonal patterns in orange juice demand could be correlated with *FDD*, resulting in omitted variable bias. The quantity of oranges sold for juice is endogenous: Prices and quantities are simultaneously determined by the forces of supply and demand. Thus, as discussed in Section 9.2, including quantity would lead to simultaneity bias. Nevertheless, the seasonal component of demand can be captured by including seasonal variables as regressors. The specification in column (4) of Table 15.1 therefore includes 11 monthly binary variables, one indicating whether the month is January, one indicating February, and so forth (as usual one binary variable must be omitted to prevent perfect multicollinearity with the intercept). These monthly indicator variables are not jointly statistically significant at the 10% level ($p = 0.43$), and the estimated cumulative dynamic multipliers are essentially the same as for the specifications excluding the monthly indicators. In summary, seasonal fluctuations in demand are not an important source of omitted variable bias.

***Have the dynamic multipliers been stable over time?[3]*** To assess the stability of the dynamic multipliers, we need to check whether the distributed lag regression coefficients have been stable over time. Because we do not have a specific break date in mind, we test for instability in the regression coefficients using the Quandt likelihood ratio (QLR) statistic (Key Concept 14.9). The QLR statistic (with 15% trimming and HAC variance estimator), computed for the regression of column (1) with all coefficients interacted, has a value of 21.19, with $q = 20$ degrees of freedom (the coefficients on $FDD_t$, its 18 lags, and the intercept). The 1% critical value in Table 14.5 is 2.43, so the QLR statistic rejects at the 1% significance level. These QLR regressions have 40 regressors, a large number; recomputing them for six lags only (so that there are 16 regressors and $q = 8$) also results in rejection at the 1% level. Thus the hypothesis that the dynamic multipliers are stable is rejected at the 1% significance level.

One way to see how the dynamic multipliers have changed over time is to compute them for different parts of the sample. Figure 15.3 plots the estimated cumulative dynamic multipliers for the first third (1950–1966), middle third (1967–1983), and final third (1984–2000) of the sample, computed by running separate regressions on each subsample. These estimates show an interesting and noticeable pattern. In the 1950s and early 1960s, a freezing degree day had a large and persistent effect on the price. The magnitude of the effect on price of a freezing degree day diminished in the 1970s, although it remained highly persistent. In the late 1980s and 1990s, the short-run effect of a freezing degree day was the same as in the 1970s, but it became much less persistent and was essentially eliminated after a year. These estimates suggest that the dynamic causal effect on orange juice prices of a Florida freeze became smaller and less persistent over the second half of the twentieth century. The box "Orange Trees on the March" discusses one possible explanation for the instability of the dynamic causal effects.

***ADL and GLS estimates.*** As discussed in Section 15.5, if the error term in the distributed lag regression is serially correlated and $FDD$ is strictly exogenous, it is possible to estimate the dynamic multipliers more efficiently than by OLS

---

[3]The discussion of stability in this subsection draws on material from Section 14.7 and can be skipped if that material has not been covered.

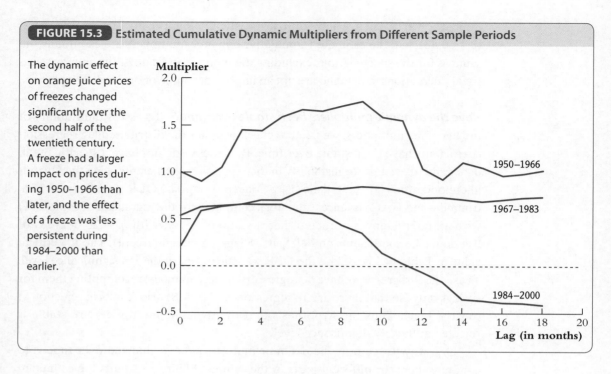

**FIGURE 15.3** Estimated Cumulative Dynamic Multipliers from Different Sample Periods

The dynamic effect on orange juice prices of freezes changed significantly over the second half of the twentieth century. A freeze had a larger impact on prices during 1950–1966 than later, and the effect of a freeze was less persistent during 1984–2000 than earlier.

estimation of the distributed lag coefficients. Before using either the GLS estimator or the estimator based on the ADL model, however, we need to consider whether *FDD* is in fact strictly exogenous. True, humans cannot affect the daily weather, but does that mean that the weather is *strictly* exogenous? Does the error term $u_t$ in the distributed lag regression have conditional mean zero, given past, present, and *future* values of *FDD*?

The error term in the population counterpart of the distributed lag regression in column (1) of Table 15.1 is the discrepancy between the price and its population prediction based on the past 18 months of weather. This discrepancy might arise for many reasons, one of which is that traders use forecasts of the weather in Orlando. For example, if an especially cold winter is forecasted, then traders would incorporate this into the price, so the price would be above its predicted value based on the population regression; that is, the error term would be positive. If this forecast is accurate, then in fact future weather would turn out to be cold. Thus future freezing degree days would be positive ($X_{t+1} > 0$) when the current price is unusually high ($u_t > 0$), so corr($X_{t+1}, u_t$) is positive. Stated more simply, although orange juice traders cannot influence the weather, they can—and do—predict it (see the box). Consequently, the error term in the price/weather regression

## Orange Trees on the March

Why do the dynamic multipliers in Figure 15.3 vary over time? One possible explanation is changes in markets, but another is that the trees moved south.

According to the Florida Department of Citrus, the severe freezes in the 1980s, which are visible in Figure 15.1(c), spurred citrus growers to seek a warmer climate. As shown in Figure 15.4, the number of acres of orange trees in the more frost-prone northern and western counties fell from 232,000 acres in 1981 to 53,000 acres in 1985, and orange acreage in southern and central counties subsequently increased from 413,000 in 1985 to 588,000 in 1993. With the groves farther south, northern frosts damage a smaller fraction of the crop, and—as indicated by the dynamic multipliers in Figure 15.3—price becomes less sensitive to temperatures in the more northern city of Orlando.

OK, the orange trees themselves might not have been on the march—that can be left to *MacBeth*—but southern migration of the orange groves does give new meaning to the term "nonstationarity."[4]

---

[4]We are grateful to Professor James Cobbe of Florida State University for telling us about the southern movement of the orange groves.

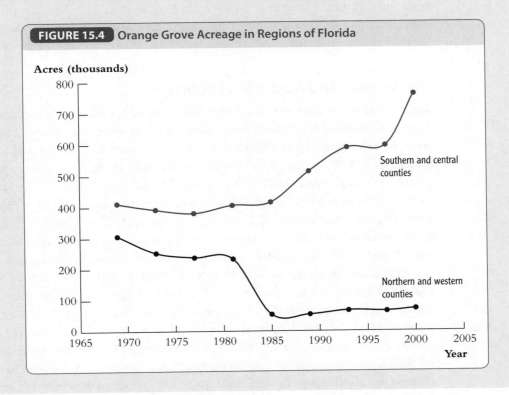

**FIGURE 15.4**  Orange Grove Acreage in Regions of Florida

is correlated with future weather. In other words, *FDD* is exogenous, but if this reasoning is true, it is not strictly exogenous, and the GLS and ADL estimators will not be consistent estimators of the dynamic multipliers. These estimators therefore are not used in this application.

## 15.7 Is Exogeneity Plausible? Some Examples

As in regression with cross-sectional data, the interpretation of the coefficients in a distributed lag regression as causal dynamic effects hinges on the assumption that $X$ is exogenous. If $X_t$ or its lagged values are correlated with $u_t$, then the conditional mean of $u_t$ will depend on $X_t$ or its lags, in which case $X$ is not (past and present) exogenous. Regressors can be correlated with the error term for several reasons, but with economic time series data a particularly important concern is that there could be simultaneous causality, which (as discussed in Sections 9.2 and 12.1) results in endogenous regressors. In Section 15.6, we discussed the assumptions of exogeneity and strict exogeneity of freezing degree days in detail. In this section, we examine the assumption of exogeneity in four other economic applications.

### U.S. Income and Australian Exports

The United States is an important source of demand for Australian exports. Precisely how sensitive Australian exports are to fluctuations in U.S. aggregate income could be investigated by regressing Australian exports to the United States against a measure of U.S. income. Strictly speaking, because the world economy is integrated, there is simultaneous causality in this relationship: A decline in Australian exports reduces Australian income, which reduces demand for imports from the United States, which reduces U.S. income. As a practical matter, however, this effect is very small because the Australian economy is much smaller than the U.S. economy. Thus U.S. income plausibly can be treated as exogenous in this regression.

In contrast, in a regression of European Union exports to the United States against U.S. income, the argument for treating U.S. income as exogenous is less convincing because demand by residents of the European Union for U.S. exports constitutes a substantial fraction of the total demand for U.S. exports. Thus a decline in U.S. demand for EU exports would decrease EU income, which in turn would decrease demand for U.S. exports and thus decrease U.S. income. Because of these linkages through international trade, EU exports to the United States and U.S. income are simultaneously determined, so in this regression U.S. income arguably is not exogenous. This example illustrates a more general point that

## NEWS FLASH: Commodity Traders Send Shivers Through Disney World

Although the weather at Disney World in Orlando, Florida, is usually pleasant, now and then a cold spell can settle in. If you are visiting Disney World on a winter evening, should you bring a warm coat? Some people might check the weather forecast on TV, but those in the know can do better: They can check that day's closing price on the New York orange juice futures market!

The financial economist Richard Roll undertook a detailed study of the relationship between orange juice prices and the weather. Roll (1984) examined the effect on prices of cold weather in Orlando, but he also studied the "effect" of changes in the price of an orange juice futures contract (a contract to buy frozen orange juice concentrate at a specified date in the future) on the weather. Roll used daily data from 1975 to 1981 on the prices of OJ futures contracts traded at the New York Cotton Exchange and on daily and overnight temperatures in Orlando. He found that a rise in the price of the futures contract during the trading day in New York predicted cold weather, in particular a freezing spell, in Orlando over the following night. In fact, the market was so effective in predicting cold weather in Florida that a price rise during the trading day actually predicted forecast errors in the official U.S. government weather forecasts for that night.

Roll's study is also interesting for what he did *not* find: Although his detailed weather data explained some of the variation in daily OJ futures prices, most of the daily movements in OJ prices remained unexplained. He therefore suggested that the OJ futures market exhibits "excess volatility," that is, more volatility than can be attributed to movements in fundamentals. Understanding why (and if) there is excess volatility in financial markets is now an important area of research in financial economics.

Roll's finding also illustrates the difference between forecasting and estimating dynamic causal effects. Price changes on the OJ futures market are a useful predictor of cold weather, but that does not mean that commodity traders are so powerful that they can *cause* the temperature to fall. Visitors to Disney World might shiver after an OJ futures contract price rise, but they are not shivering *because* of the price rise—unless, of course, they went short in the OJ futures market.

whether a variable is exogenous depends on the context: U.S. income is plausibly exogenous in a regression explaining Australian exports, but not in a regression explaining EU exports.

## Oil Prices and Inflation

Ever since the oil price increases of the 1970s, macroeconomists have been interested in estimating the dynamic effect of an increase in the international price of crude oil on the U.S. rate of inflation. Because oil prices are set in world markets in large part by foreign oil-producing countries, initially one might think that oil prices are exogenous. But oil prices are not like the weather: Members of OPEC set oil production levels strategically, taking many factors, including the state of the world economy, into account. To the extent that oil prices (or quantities) are set based on an assessment of current and future world economic conditions, including inflation in the United States, oil prices are endogenous.

## Monetary Policy and Inflation

The central bankers in charge of monetary policy need to know the effect on inflation of monetary policy. Because an important tool of monetary policy is the short-term interest rate (the "short rate"), they need to know the dynamic causal effect on inflation of a change in the short rate. Although the short rate is determined by the central bank, it is not set by the central bankers at random (as it would be in an ideal randomized experiment) but rather is set endogenously: The central bank determines the short rate based on an assessment of the current and future states of the economy, especially including the current and future rates of inflation. The rate of inflation in turn depends on the interest rate (higher interest rates reduce aggregate demand), but the interest rate depends on the rate of inflation, its past value, and its (expected) future value. Thus the short rate is endogenous, and the causal dynamic effect of a change in the short rate on future inflation cannot be consistently estimated by an OLS regression of the rate of inflation on current and past interest rates.

## The Growth Rate of GDP and the Term Spread

In Chapter 14 lagged values of the term spread were used to forecast future values of the growth rate of GDP. Because lags of the term spread happened in the past, one might initially think that there cannot be feedback from current growth rates of GDP to past values of the term spread, so past values of the term spread can be treated as exogenous. But past values of the term spread were not randomly assigned in an experiment; instead, the past term spread was simultaneously determined with past values of the growth rate of GDP. Because GDP and the interest rates making up the term spread are simultaneously determined, the other factors that determine the growth rate of GDP contained in $u_t$ are correlated with past values of the term spread; that is, the term spread is not exogenous. It follows that the term spread is not strictly exogenous, so the dynamic multipliers computed using an ADL model [for example, the ADL model in Equation (14.17)] are not consistent estimates of the dynamic causal effect on the growth rate of GDP of a change in the term spread.

# 15.8 Conclusion

Time series data provide the opportunity to estimate the time path of the effect on $Y$ of a change in $X$, that is, the dynamic causal effect on $Y$ of a change in $X$. To estimate dynamic causal effects using a distributed lag regression, however, $X$ must be exogenous, as it would be if it were set randomly in an ideal randomized experiment. If $X$ is not just exogenous but is *strictly* exogenous, then the dynamic causal effects can be estimated using an autoregressive distributed lag model or by GLS.

In some applications, such as estimating the dynamic causal effect on the price of orange juice of freezing weather in Florida, a convincing case can be made that the regressor (freezing degree days) is exogenous; thus the dynamic causal effect can be estimated by OLS estimation of the distributed lag coefficients. Even in this application, however, economic theory suggests that the weather is not strictly exogenous, so the ADL or GLS methods are inappropriate. Moreover, in many relations of interest to econometricians, there is simultaneous causality, so the regressor in these specifications are not exogenous, strictly or otherwise. Ascertaining whether the regressor is exogenous (or strictly exogenous) ultimately requires combining economic theory, institutional knowledge, and careful judgment.

## Summary

1.  Dynamic causal effects in time series are defined in the context of a randomized experiment, where the same subject (entity) receives different randomly assigned treatments at different times. The coefficients in a distributed lag regression of $Y$ on $X$ and its lags can be interpreted as the dynamic causal effects when the time path of $X$ is determined randomly and independently of other factors that influence $Y$.

2.  The variable $X$ is (past and present) exogenous if the conditional mean of the error $u_t$ in the distributed lag regression of $Y$ on current and past values of $X$ does not depend on current and past values of $X$. If in addition the conditional mean of $u_t$ does not depend on future values of $X$, then $X$ is strictly exogenous.

3.  If $X$ is exogenous, then the OLS estimators of the coefficients in a distributed lag regression of $Y$ on current and past values of $X$ are consistent estimators of the dynamic causal effects. In general, the error $u_t$ in this regression is serially correlated, so conventional standard errors are misleading, and HAC standard errors must be used instead.

4. If $X$ is strictly exogenous, then the dynamic multipliers can be estimated using OLS estimation of an ADL model or using GLS.

5. Exogeneity is a strong assumption that often fails to hold in economic time series data because of simultaneous causality, and the assumption of strict exogeneity is even stronger.

## Key Terms

dynamic causal effect (635)
distributed lag model (641)
exogeneity (642)
strict exogeneity (642)
dynamic multiplier (646)
impact effect (646)
cumulative dynamic multiplier (646)
long-run cumulative dynamic
    multiplier (647)

heteroskedasticity- and autocorrelation-
    consistent (HAC) standard error
    (650)
truncation parameter (651)
Newey–West variance estimator (651)
generalized least squares (GLS) (652)
quasi-difference (654)
infeasible GLS estimator (658)
feasible GLS estimator (658)

---

**MyEconLab Can Help You Get a Better Grade**

**MyEconLab**   If your exam were tomorrow, would you be ready? For each chapter, **MyEconLab** Practice Tests and Study Plan help you prepare for your exams. You can also find similar Exercises and Review the Concepts Questions now in **MyEconLab**. To see how it works, turn to the **MyEconLab** spread on pages 2 and 3 of this book and then go to **www.myeconlab.com**.

For additional Empirical Exercises and Data Sets, log on to the Companion Website at **www.pearsonglobaleditions.com/Stock_Watson**.

---

## Review the Concepts

**15.1** In the 1970s a common practice was to estimate a distributed lag model relating changes in nominal gross domestic product ($Y$) to current and past changes in the money supply ($X$). Under what assumptions will this regression estimate the causal effects of money on nominal GDP? Are these assumptions likely to be satisfied in a modern economy like that of the United States?

**15.2** Suppose that $X$ is strictly exogenous. A researcher estimates an ADL(1,1) model, calculates the regression residual, and finds the residual to be highly serially correlated. Should the researcher estimate a new ADL model with

additional lags or simply use HAC standard errors for the ADL(1,1) estimated coefficients?

**15.3** Suppose that a distributed lag regression is estimated, where the dependent
variable is $\Delta Y_t$ instead of $Y_t$. Explain how you would compute the dynamic
multipliers of $X_t$ on $Y_t$.

**15.4** Suppose that you added $FDD_{t+1}$ as an additional regressor in Equation
(15.2). If $FDD$ is strictly exogenous, would you expect the coefficient on
$FDD_{t+1}$ to be zero or nonzero? Would your answer change if $FDD$ is exogenous but not strictly exogenous?

## Exercises

**15.1** Increases in oil prices have been blamed for several recessions in developed
countries. To quantify the effect of oil prices on real economic activity,
researchers have run regressions like those discussed in this chapter. Let
$GDP_t$ denote the value of quarterly gross domestic product in the United
States and let $Y_t = 100\ln(GDP_t/GDP_{t-1})$ be the quarterly percentage
change in GDP. James Hamilton, an econometrician and macroeconomist,
has suggested that oil prices adversely affect that economy only when they
jump above their values in the recent past. Specifically, let $O_t$ equal the
greater of zero or the percentage point difference between oil prices at
date $t$ and their maximum value during the past 3 years. A distributed lag
regression relating $Y_t$ and $O_t$, estimated over 1960:Q1–2013:Q4, is

$$\hat{Y}_t = 1.0 - 0.007O_t - 0.015O_{t-1} - 0.019O_{t-2} - 0.024O_{t-3} - 0.037O_{t-4}$$
$$\quad (0.1) \quad (0.013) \quad (0.011) \quad\quad (0.011) \quad\quad (0.010) \quad\quad (0.012)$$

$$\quad -0.012O_{t-5} + 0.005O_{t-6} - 0.008O_{t-7} + 0.006O_{t-8}.$$
$$\quad\quad (0.008) \quad\quad (0.010) \quad\quad (0.008) \quad\quad (0.008)$$

**a.** Suppose that oil prices jump 25% above their previous peak value
and stay at this new higher level (so that $O_t = 25$ and $O_{t+1} = O_{t+2} =$
$\cdots = 0$). What is the predicted effect on output growth for each
quarter over the next 2 years?

**b.** Construct a 95% confidence interval for your answers in (a).

**c.** What is the predicted cumulative change in GDP growth over 8 quarters?

**d.** The HAC $F$-statistic testing whether the coefficients on $O_t$ and its lags
are zero is 5.79. Are the coefficients significantly different from zero?

**15.2** Macroeconomists have also noticed that interest rates change following oil price jumps. Let $R_t$ denote the interest rate on 3-month Treasury bills (in percentage points at an annual rate). The distributed lag regression relating the change in $R_t$ $(\Delta R_t)$ to $O_t$ estimated over 1960:Q1–2013:Q4 is

$$\widehat{\Delta R_t} = 0.03 + 0.013O_t + 0.013O_{t-1} - 0.004O_{t-2} - 0.024O_{t-3} - 0.000O_{t-4}$$
$$\quad (0.05) \ \ (0.010) \quad\ (0.010) \qquad (0.008) \qquad (0.015) \qquad\ (0.010)$$

$$\quad + 0.006O_{t-5} - 0.005O_{t-6} - 0.018O_{t-7} - 0.004O_{t-8}.$$
$$\qquad (0.015) \qquad\ (0.015) \qquad\ (0.010) \qquad\ (0.006)$$

**a.** Suppose that oil prices jump 25% above their previous peak value and stay at this new higher level (so that $O_t = 25$ and $O_{t+1} = O_{t+2} = \cdots = 0$). What is the predicted change in interest rates for each quarter over the next 2 years?

**b.** Construct 95% confidence intervals for your answers to (a).

**c.** What is the effect of this change in oil prices on the level of interest rates in period $t + 8$? How is your answer related to the cumulative multiplier?

**d.** The HAC $F$-statistic testing whether the coefficients on $O_t$ and its lags are zero is 1.93. Are the coefficients significantly different from zero?

**15.3** Consider two different randomized experiments. In experiment A, oil prices are set randomly, and the central bank reacts according to its usual policy rules in response to economic conditions, including changes in the oil price. In experiment B, oil prices are set randomly, and the central bank holds interest rates constant and in particular does not respond to the oil price changes. In both experiments, GDP growth is observed. Now suppose that oil prices are exogenous in the regression in Exercise 15.1. To which experiment, A or B, does the dynamic causal effect estimated in Exercise 15.1 correspond?

**15.4** Suppose that oil prices are strictly exogenous. Discuss how you could improve on the estimates of the dynamic multipliers in Exercise 15.1.

**15.5** Derive Equation (15.7) from Equation (15.4) and show that $\delta_0 = \beta_0$, $\delta_1 = \beta_1$, $\delta_2 = \beta_1 + \beta_2$, $\delta_3 = \beta_1 + \beta_2 + \beta_3$ (etc.). (*Hint:* Note that $X_t = \Delta X_t + \Delta X_{t-1} + \cdots + \Delta X_{t-p+1} + X_{t-p}$.)

**15.6** Consider the regression model $Y_t = \beta_0 + \beta_1 X_t + u_t$, where $u_t$ follows the stationary AR(1) model $u_t = \phi_1 u_{t-1} + \tilde{u}_t$ with $\tilde{u}_t$ i.i.d. with mean 0 and variance $\sigma_{\tilde{u}}^2$ and $|\phi_1| < 1$; the regressor $X_t$ follows the stationary AR(1) model $X_t = \gamma_1 X_{t-1} + e_t$ with $e_t$ i.i.d. with mean 0 and variance $\sigma_e^2$ and $|\gamma| < 1$; and $e_t$ is independent of $\tilde{u}_i$ for all $t$ and $i$.

**a.** Show that $\text{var}(u_t) = \dfrac{\sigma_{\tilde{u}}^2}{1 - \phi_1^2}$ and $\text{var}(X_t) = \dfrac{\sigma_e^2}{1 - \gamma_1^2}$.

**b.** Show that $\text{cov}(u_t, u_{t-j}) = \phi_1^j \text{var}(u_t)$ and $\text{cov}(X_t, X_{t-j}) = \gamma_1^j \text{var}(X_t)$.

**c.** Show that $\text{corr}(u_t, u_{t-j}) = \phi_1^j$ and $\text{corr}(X_t, X_{t-j}) = \gamma_1^j$.

**d.** Consider the terms $\sigma_v^2$ and $f_T$ in Equation (15.14).

    i. Show that $\sigma_v^2 = \sigma_X^2 \sigma_u^2$, where $\sigma_X^2$ is the variance of $X$ and $\sigma_u^2$ is the variance of $u$.

    ii. Derive an expression for $f_\infty$.

**15.7** Consider the regression model $Y_t = \beta_0 + \beta_1 X_t + u_t$, where $u_t$ follows the stationary AR(1) model $u_t = \phi_1 u_{t-1} + \tilde{u}_t$ with $\tilde{u}_t$ i.i.d. with mean 0 and variance $\sigma_{\tilde{u}}^2$ and $|\phi_1| < 1$.

**a.** Suppose that $X_t$ is independent of $\tilde{u}_j$ for all $t$ and $j$. Is $X_t$ exogenous (past and present)? Is $X_t$ strictly exogenous (past, present, and future)?

**b.** Suppose that $X_t = \tilde{u}_{t+1}$. Is $X_t$ exogenous? Is $X_t$ strictly exogenous?

**15.8** Consider the model in Exercise 15.7 with $X_t = \tilde{u}_{t+1}$.

**a.** Is the OLS estimator of $\beta_1$ consistent? Explain.

**b.** Explain why the GLS estimator of $\beta_1$ is not consistent.

**c.** Show that the infeasible GLS estimator $\hat{\beta}_1^{GLS} \xrightarrow{p} \beta_1 - \dfrac{\phi_1}{1 + \phi_1^2}$.

    [*Hint:* Use the omitted variable formula (6.1) applied to the quasi-differenced regression in Equation (15.23)].

**15.9** Consider the "constant-term-only" regression model $Y_t = \beta_0 + u_t$, where $u_t$ follows the stationary AR(1) model $u_t = \phi_1 u_{t-1} + \tilde{u}_t$ with $\tilde{u}_t$ i.i.d. with mean 0 and variance $\sigma_{\tilde{u}}^2$ and $|\phi_1| < 1$.

**a.** Show that the OLS estimator is $\hat{\beta}_0 = T^{-1} \sum_{t=1}^{T} Y_t$.

**b.** Show that the (infeasible) GLS estimator is $\hat{\beta}_0^{GLS} = (1 - \phi_1)^{-1}(T - 1)^{-1} \sum_{t=2}^{T}(Y_t - \phi_1 Y_{t-1})$. [*Hint:* The GLS estimator of $\beta_0$ is $(1 - \phi_1)^{-1}$ multiplied by the OLS estimator of $\alpha_0$ in Equation (15.23). Why?]

**c.** Show that $\hat{\beta}_0^{GLS}$ can be written as $\hat{\beta}_0^{GLS} = (T - 1)^{-1} \sum_{t=2}^{T-1} Y_t + (1 - \phi_1)^{-1}(T - 1)^{-1}(Y_T - \phi_1 Y_1)$. [*Hint:* Rearrange the formula in (b).]

**d.** Derive the difference $\hat{\beta}_0 - \hat{\beta}_0^{GLS}$ and discuss why it is likely to be small when $T$ is large.

**15.10** Consider the ADL model $Y_t = 5.3 + 0.2Y_{t-1} + 1.5X_t - 0.1X_{t-1} + \tilde{u}_t$, where $X_t$ is strictly exogenous.

    **a.** Derive the impact effect of $X$ on $Y$.

    **b.** Derive the first five dynamic multipliers.

    **c.** Derive the first five cumulative multipliers.

    **d.** Derive the long-run cumulative dynamic multiplier.

**15.11** Suppose that $a(L) = (1 - \phi L)$, with $|\phi_1| < 1$, and $b(L) = 1 + \phi L + \phi^2 L^2 + \phi^3 L^3 \ldots$.

    **a.** Show that the product $b(L)a(L) = 1$, so that $b(L) = a(L)^{-1}$.

    **b.** Why is the restriction $|\phi_1| < 1$ important?

## Empirical Exercises

(Only two empirical exercises for this chapter are given in the text, but you can find more on the text website, **www.pearsonglobaleditions.com/Stock_Watson**.)

**E15.1** In this exercise you will estimate the effect of oil prices on macroeconomic activity, using monthly data on the Index of Industrial Production (IP) and the monthly measure of $O_t$ described in Exercise 15.1. The data can be found on the textbook website, **www.pearsonglobaleditions.com/Stock_Watson**, in the file **USMacro_Monthly**.

    **a.** Compute the monthly growth rate in IP, expressed in percentage points, $ip\_growth_t = 100 \times \ln(IP_t / IP_{t-1})$. What are the mean and standard deviation of $ip\_growth$ over the 1960:M1–2012:M12 sample period? What are the units for $ip\_growth$ (percent, percent per annum, percent per month, or something else)?

    **b.** Plot the value of $O_t$. Why are so many values of $O_t$ equal to zero? Why aren't some values of $O_t$ negative?

    **c.** Estimate a distributed lag model by regressing $ip\_growth$ onto the current value and 18 lagged values of $O_t$, including an intercept. What value of the HAC standard truncation parameter $m$ did you choose? Why?

    **d.** Taken as a group, are the coefficients on $O_t$ statistically significantly different from zero?

    **e.** Construct graphs like those in Figure 15.2, showing the estimated dynamic multipliers, cumulative multipliers, and 95% confidence intervals. Comment on the real-world size of the multipliers.

   **f.** Suppose that high demand in the United States (evidenced by large values of *ip_growth*) leads to increases in oil prices. Is $O_t$ exogenous? Are the estimated multipliers shown in the graphs in (e) reliable? Explain.

**E15.2** In the data file **USMacro_Quarterly**, you will find data on two aggregate price series for the United States: the price index for personal consumption expenditures (PCEP) that you used in Empirical Exercise 14.1 and the Consumer Price Index (CPI). These series are alternative measures of consumer prices in the United States. The CPI prices a basket of goods whose composition is updated every 5–10 years. PCEP uses chain-weighting to price a basket of goods whose composition changes from month to month. Economists have argued that the CPI will overstate inflation because it does not take into account the substitution that occurs when relative prices change. If this substitution bias is important, then average CPI inflation should be systematically higher than PCEP inflation. Let $\pi_t^{CPI} = 400 \times [\ln(CPI_t) - \ln(CPI_{t-1})]$, and $\pi_t^{PCEP} = 400 \times [\ln(PCEP_t) - \ln(PCEP_{t-1})]$, and $Y_t = \pi_t^{CPI} - \pi_t^{PCEP}$, so $\pi_t^{CPI}$ is the quarterly rate of price inflation (measured in percentage points at an annual rate) based on the CPI, $\pi_t^{PCEP}$ is the quarterly rate of price inflation from the PCEP, and $Y_t$ is their difference. Using data from 1963:Q1 through 2012:Q4, carry out the following exercises.

   **a.** Compute the sample means of $\pi_t^{CPI}$ and $\pi_t^{PCED}$. Are these point estimates consistent with the presence of economically significant substitution bias in the CPI?

   **b.** Compute the sample mean of $Y_t$. Explain why it is numerically equal to the difference in the means computed in (a).

   **c.** Show that the population mean of $Y$ is equal to the difference of the population means of the two inflation rates.

   **d.** Consider the "constant-term-only" regression: $Y_t = \beta_0 + u_t$. Show that $\beta_0 = E(Y)$. Do you think that $u_t$ is serially correlated? Explain.

   **e.** Construct a 95% confidence interval for $\beta_0$. What value of the HAC standard truncation parameter $m$ did you choose? Why?

   **f.** Is there statistically significant evidence that the mean inflation rate for the CPI is greater than the rate for the PCEP?

   **g.** Is there evidence of instability in $\beta_0$? Carry out a QLR test. (*Hint:* Make sure you use HAC standard errors for the regressions in the QLR procedure.)

## 15.1   The Orange Juice Data Set

The orange juice price data are the frozen orange juice component of processed foods and feeds group of the Producer Price Index (PPI), collected by the U.S. Bureau of Labor Statistics (BLS series wpu02420301). The orange juice price series was divided by the overall PPI for finished goods to adjust for general price inflation. The freezing degree days series was constructed from daily minimum temperatures recorded at Orlando-area airports, obtained from the National Oceanic and Atmospheric Administration (NOAA) of the U.S. Department of Commerce. The *FDD* series was constructed so that its timing and the timing of the orange juice price data were approximately aligned. Specifically, the frozen orange juice price data are collected by surveying a sample of producers in the middle of every month, although the exact date varies from month to month. Accordingly, the *FDD* series was constructed to be the number of freezing degree days from the 11th of one month to the 10th of the next month; that is, *FDD* is the maximum of zero and 32 minus the minimum daily temperature, summed over all days from the 11th to the 10th. Thus %*ChgP*$_t$ for February is the percentage change in real orange juice prices from mid-January to mid-February, and *FDD*$_t$ for February is the number of freezing degree days from January 11 to February 10.

## 15.2   The ADL Model and Generalized Least Squares in Lag Operator Notation

This appendix presents the distributed lag model in lag operator notation, derives the ADL and quasi-differenced representations of the distributed lag model, and discusses the conditions under which the ADL model can have fewer parameters than the original distributed lag model.

### The Distributed Lag, ADL, and Quasi-Difference Models, in Lag Operator Notation

As defined in Appendix 14.3, the lag operator, L, has the property that $L^j X_t = X_{t-j}$, and the distributed lag $\beta_1 X_t + \beta_2 X_{t-1} + \cdots + \beta_{r+1} X_{t-r}$ can be expressed as $\beta(L)X_t$, where $\beta(L) = \sum_{j=0}^{r} \beta_{j+1} L^j$, where $L^0 = 1$. Thus the distributed lag model in Key Concept 15.1 [Equation (15.4)] can be written in lag operator notation as

$$Y_t = \beta_0 + \beta(\mathrm{L})X_t + u_t. \tag{15.40}$$

In addition, if the error term $u_t$ follows an $\mathrm{AR}(p)$, then it can be written as

$$\phi(\mathrm{L})u_t = \tilde{u}_t, \tag{15.41}$$

where $\phi(\mathrm{L}) = \sum_{j=0}^{p}\phi_j \mathrm{L}^j$, where $\phi_0 = 1$ and $\tilde{u}_t$ is serially uncorrelated [note that $\phi_1, \ldots,$ $\phi_p$ as defined here are the negatives of $\phi_1, \ldots, \phi_p$ in the notation of Equation (15.31)].

To derive the ADL model, premultiply each side of Equation (15.40) by $\phi(\mathrm{L})$ so that

$$\phi(\mathrm{L})Y_t = \phi(\mathrm{L})[\beta_0 + \beta(\mathrm{L})X_t + u_t] = \alpha_0 + \delta(\mathrm{L})X_t + \tilde{u}_t, \tag{15.42}$$

where

$$\alpha_0 = \phi(1)\beta_0 \text{ and } \delta(\mathrm{L}) = \phi(\mathrm{L})\beta(\mathrm{L}), \text{ where } \phi(1) = \sum_{j=0}^{p}\phi_j. \tag{15.43}$$

To derive the quasi-differenced model, note that $\phi(\mathrm{L})\beta(\mathrm{L})X_t = \beta(\mathrm{L})\phi(\mathrm{L})X_t = \beta(\mathrm{L})\tilde{X}_t,$ where $\tilde{X}_t = \phi(\mathrm{L})X_t$. Thus rearranging Equation (15.42) yields

$$\tilde{Y}_t = \alpha_0 + \beta(\mathrm{L})\tilde{X}_t + \tilde{u}_t, \tag{15.44}$$

where $\tilde{Y}_t$ is the quasi-difference of $Y_t$; that is, $\tilde{Y}_t = \phi(\mathrm{L})Y_t$.

## The Inverse of a Lag Polynomial

Let $a(x) = \sum_{j=0}^{p}a_j x^j$ denote a polynomial of order $p$. The inverse of $a(x)$, say $b(x)$, is a function that satisfies $b(x)a(x) = 1$. If the roots of the polynomial $a(x)$ are greater than 1 in absolute value, then $b(x)$ is a polynomial in nonnegative powers of $x$: $b(x) = \sum_{j=0}^{\infty}b_j x^j$. Because $b(x)$ is the inverse of $a(x)$, it is denoted as $a(x)^{-1}$ or as $1/a(x)$.

The inverse of a lag polynomial $a(\mathrm{L})$ is defined analogously: $a(\mathrm{L})^{-1} = 1/a(\mathrm{L}) = b(\mathrm{L}) = \sum_{j=0}^{\infty}b_j \mathrm{L}^j$, where $b(\mathrm{L})a(\mathrm{L}) = 1$. For example, if $a(\mathrm{L}) = (1 - \phi\mathrm{L})$, with $|\phi| < 1$, you can verify that $a(\mathrm{L})^{-1} = 1 + \phi\mathrm{L} + \phi^2\mathrm{L}^2 + \phi^3\mathrm{L}^3\ldots = \sum_{j=0}^{\infty}\phi^j\mathrm{L}^j$. (See Exercise 15.11.)

## The ADL and GLS Estimators

The OLS estimator of the ADL coefficients is obtained by OLS estimation of Equation (15.42). The original distributed lag coefficients are $\beta(\mathrm{L})$, which, in terms of the estimated coefficients, is $\beta(\mathrm{L}) = \phi(\mathrm{L})^{-1}\delta(\mathrm{L})$; that is, the coefficients in $\beta(\mathrm{L})$ satisfy the restrictions implied by $\phi(L)\beta(L) = \delta(L)$. Thus the estimator of the dynamic multipliers based on the OLS estimators of the coefficients of the ADL model, $\hat{\delta}(L)$ and $\hat{\phi}(L)$, is

$$\hat{\beta}^{ADL}(L) = \hat{\phi}(L)^{-1}\hat{\delta}(L). \tag{15.45}$$

The expressions for the coefficients in Equation (15.29) in the text are obtained as a special case of Equation (15.45) when $r = 1$ and $p = 1$.

The feasible GLS estimator is computed by obtaining a preliminary estimator of $\phi(L)$, computing estimated quasi-differences, estimating $\beta(L)$ in Equation (15.44) using these estimated quasi-differences, and (if desired) iterating until convergence. The iterated GLS estimator is the NLLS estimator computed by NLLS estimation of the ADL model in Equation (15.42), subject to the nonlinear restrictions on the parameters contained in Equation (15.43).

As stressed in the discussion surrounding Equation (15.36) in the text, it is not enough for $X_t$ to be (past and present) exogenous to use either of these estimation methods, for exogeneity alone does not ensure that Equation (15.36) holds. If, however, $X$ is strictly exogenous, then Equation (15.36) does hold, and assuming that Assumptions 2 through 4 of Key Concept 14.6 hold, these estimators are consistent and asymptotically normal. Moreover, the usual (cross-sectional heteroskedasticity-robust) OLS standard errors provide a valid basis for statistical inference.

*Parameter reduction using the ADL model.* Suppose that the distributed lag polynomial $\beta(L)$ can be written as a ratio of lag polynomials, $\theta_2(L)^{-1}\theta_1(L)$, where $\theta_1(L)$ and $\theta_2(L)$ are both lag polynomials of a low degree. Then $\phi(L)\beta(L)$ in Equation (15.43) is $\phi(L)\beta(L) = \phi(L)[\theta_2(L)^{-1}\theta_1(L)] = [\phi(L)\theta_2(L)^{-1}]\theta_1(L)$. If it so happens that $\phi(L) = \theta_2(L)$, then $\delta(L) = \phi(L)\beta(L) = \theta_1(L)$. If the degree of $\theta_1(L)$ is low, then $q$, the number of lags of $X_t$ in the ADL model, can be much less than $r$. Thus, under these assumptions, estimation of the ADL model entails estimating potentially many fewer parameters than the original distributed lag model. It is in this sense that the ADL model can achieve more parsimonious parameterizations (that is, use fewer unknown parameters) than the distributed lag model.

As developed here, the assumption that $\phi(L)$ and $\theta_2(L)$ happen to be the same seems like a coincidence that would not occur in an application. However, the ADL model is able to capture a large number of shapes of dynamic multipliers with only a few coefficients.

*ADL or GLS: Bias versus variance.* A good way to think about whether to estimate dynamic multipliers by first estimating an ADL model and then computing the dynamic multipliers from the ADL coefficients or, alternatively, by estimating the distributed lag model directly using GLS is to view the decision in terms of a trade-off between bias and variance. Estimating the dynamic multipliers using an approximate ADL model introduces bias; however, because there are few coefficients, the variance of the estimator of the dynamic multipliers can be small. In contrast, estimating a long distributed lag model using GLS produces less bias in the multipliers; however, because there are so many coefficients, their variance can be large. If the ADL approximation to the dynamic multipliers is a good one, then the bias of the implied dynamic multipliers will be small, so the ADL approach will have a smaller variance than the GLS approach with only a small increase in the bias. For this reason, unrestricted estimation of an ADL model with small number of lags of $Y$ and $X$ is an attractive way to approximate a long distributed lag when $X$ is strictly exogenous.

# CHAPTER 1

# Additional Topics in Time Series Regression

This chapter takes up some further topics in time series regression, starting with forecasting. Chapter 14 considered forecasting a single variable. In practice, however, you might want to forecast two or more variables, such as the growth rate of GDP and the rate of inflation. Section 16.1 introduces a model for forecasting multiple variables, vector autoregressions (VARs), in which lagged values of two or more variables are used to forecast future values of those variables. Chapter 14 also focused on making forecasts one period (e.g., one quarter) into the future, but making forecasts two, three, or more periods into the future is important as well. Methods for making multiperiod forecasts are discussed in Section 16.2.

Sections 16.3 and 16.4 return to the topic of Section 14.6, stochastic trends. Section 16.3 introduces additional models of stochastic trends and an alternative test for a unit autoregressive root. Section 16.4 introduces the concept of cointegration, which arises when two variables share a common stochastic trend—that is, when each variable contains a stochastic trend, but a weighted difference of the two variables does not.

In some time series data, especially financial data, the variance changes over time: Sometimes the series exhibits high volatility, while at other times the volatility is low, so the data exhibit clusters of volatility. Section 16.5 discusses volatility clustering and introduces models in which the variance of the forecast error changes over time, that is, models in which the forecast error is conditionally heteroskedastic. Models of conditional heteroskedasticity have several applications. One application is computing forecast intervals, where the width of the interval changes over time to reflect periods of high or low uncertainty. Another application is forecasting the uncertainty of returns on an asset, such as a stock, which in turn can be useful in assessing the risk of owning that asset.

## 16.1 Vector Autoregressions

Chapter 14 focused on forecasting the growth rate of GDP, but in reality economic forecasters are in the business of forecasting other key macroeconomic variables as well, such as the rate of inflation, the unemployment rate, and interest rates. One approach is to develop a separate forecasting model for each variable,

## Vector Autoregressions

A vector autoregression (VAR) is a set of $k$ time series regressions, in which the regressors are lagged values of all $k$ series. A VAR extends the univariate autoregression to a list, or "vector," of time series variables. When the number of lags in each of the equations is the same and is equal to $p$, the system of equations is called a VAR($p$).

In the case of two time series variables, $Y_t$ and $X_t$, the VAR($p$) consists of the two equations

$$Y_t = \beta_{10} + \beta_{11}Y_{t-1} + \cdots + \beta_{1p}Y_{t-p} + \gamma_{11}X_{t-1} + \cdots + \gamma_{1p}X_{t-p} + u_{1t} \quad (16.1)$$

$$X_t = \beta_{20} + \beta_{21}Y_{t-1} + \cdots + \beta_{2p}Y_{t-p} + \gamma_{21}X_{t-1} + \cdots + \gamma_{2p}X_{t-p} + u_{2t}, \quad (16.2)$$

where the $\beta$'s and the $\gamma$'s are unknown coefficients and $u_{1t}$ and $u_{2t}$ are error terms.

The VAR assumptions are the time series regression assumptions of Key Concept 14.6, applied to each equation. The coefficients of a VAR are estimated by estimating each equation by OLS.

using the methods of Section 14.4. Another approach is to develop a single model that can forecast all the variables, which can help to make the forecasts mutually consistent. One way to forecast several variables with a single model is to use a vector autoregression (VAR). A VAR extends the univariate autoregression to multiple time series variables, that is, it extends the univariate autoregression to a "vector" of time series variables.

### The VAR Model

A **vector autoregression (VAR)** with two time series variables, $Y_t$ and $X_t$, consists of two equations: In one, the dependent variable is $Y_t$; in the other, the dependent variable is $X_t$. The regressors in both equations are lagged values of both variables. More generally, a VAR with $k$ time series variables consists of $k$ equations, one for each of the variables, where the regressors in all equations are lagged values of all the variables. The coefficients of the VAR are estimated by estimating each of the equations by OLS.

VARs are summarized in Key Concept 16.1.

*Inference in VARs.* Under the VAR assumptions, the OLS estimators are consistent and have a joint normal distribution in large samples. Accordingly, statistical inference proceeds in the usual manner; for example, 95% confidence intervals on coefficients can be constructed as the estimated coefficient $\pm 1.96$ standard errors.

One new aspect of hypothesis testing arises in VARs because a VAR with $k$ variables is a collection, or system, of $k$ equations. Thus it is possible to test joint hypotheses that involve restrictions across multiple equations.

For example, in the two-variable VAR($p$) in Equations (16.1) and (16.2), you could ask whether the correct lag length is $p$ or $p - 1$; that is, you could ask whether the coefficients on $Y_{t-p}$ and $X_{t-p}$ are zero in these two equations. The null hypothesis that these coefficients are zero is

$$H_0: \beta_{1p} = 0, \beta_{2p} = 0, \gamma_{1p} = 0, \text{ and } \gamma_{2p} = 0. \tag{16.3}$$

The alternative hypothesis is that at least one of these four coefficients is nonzero. Thus the null hypothesis involves coefficients from *both* of the equations, two from each equation.

Because the estimated coefficients have a jointly normal distribution in large samples, it is possible to test restrictions on these coefficients by computing an $F$-statistic. The precise formula for this statistic is complicated because the notation must handle multiple equations, so we omit it. In practice, most modern software packages have automated procedures for testing hypotheses on coefficients in systems of multiple equations.

*How many variables should be included in a VAR?* The number of coefficients in each equation of a VAR is proportional to the number of variables in the VAR. For example, a VAR with 5 variables and 4 lags will have 21 coefficients (4 lags each of 5 variables, plus the intercept) in each of the 5 equations, for a total of 105 coefficients! Estimating all these coefficients increases the amount of estimation error entering a forecast, which can result in deterioration of the accuracy of the forecast.

The practical implication is that one needs to keep the number of variables in a VAR small and, especially, to make sure the variables are plausibly related to each other so that they will be useful for forecasting one another. For example, we know from a combination of empirical evidence (such as that discussed in Chapter 14) and economic theory that the growth rate of GDP, the term spread, and the rate of inflation are related to one another, suggesting that these variables could help forecast one another in a VAR. Including an unrelated variable in a

VAR, however, introduces estimation error without adding predictive content, thereby reducing forecast accuracy.

*Determining lag lengths in VARs.*  Lag lengths in a VAR can be determined using either *F*-tests or information criteria.

The information criterion for a system of equations extends the single-equation information criterion in Section 14.5. To define this information criterion, we need to adopt matrix notation. Let $\Sigma_u$ be the $k \times k$ covariance matrix of the VAR errors and let $\hat{\Sigma}_u$ be the estimate of the covariance matrix where the $i, j$ element of $\hat{\Sigma}_u$ is $\frac{1}{T}\sum_{t=1}^{T} \hat{u}_{it}\hat{u}_{jt}$, where $\hat{u}_{it}$ is the OLS residual from the $i^{\text{th}}$ equation and $\hat{u}_{jt}$ is the OLS residual from the $j^{\text{th}}$ equation. The BIC for the VAR is

$$ \text{BIC}(p) = \ln[\det(\hat{\Sigma}_u)] + k(kp + 1)\frac{\ln(T)}{T}, \tag{16.4} $$

where $\det(\hat{\Sigma}_u)$ is the determinant of the matrix $\hat{\Sigma}_u$. The AIC is computed using Equation (16.4), modified by replacing the term "$\ln(T)$" with "2."

The expression for the BIC for the $k$ equations in the VAR in Equation (16.4) extends the expression for a single equation given in Section 14.5. When there is a single equation, the first term simplifies to $\ln[SSR(p)/T]$. The second term in Equation (16.4) is the penalty for adding additional regressors; $k(kp + 1)$ is the total number of regression coefficients in the VAR. (There are $k$ equations, each of which has an intercept and $p$ lags of each of the $k$ time series variables.)

Lag length estimation in a VAR using the BIC proceeds analogously to the single equation case: Among a set of candidate values of $p$, the estimated lag length $\hat{p}$ is the value of $p$ that minimizes $\text{BIC}(p)$.

*Using VARs for causal analysis.*  The discussion so far has focused on using VARs for forecasting. Another use of VAR models is for analyzing causal relationships among economic time series variables; indeed, it was for this purpose that VARs were first introduced to economics by the econometrician and macroeconomist Christopher Sims (1980). (See the box "Nobel Laureates in Time Series Econometrics" at the end of this chapter.) The use of VARs for causal inference is known as *structural VAR modeling*, "structural" because in this application VARs are used to model the underlying structure of the economy. Structural VAR analysis uses the techniques introduced in this section in the context of forecasting, plus some additional tools. The biggest conceptual difference between using VARs for forecasting and using them for structural modeling, however, is that structural modeling requires very specific assumptions, derived from economic theory and institutional knowledge, of what is exogenous and what is not. The discussion of structural VARs is best undertaken in the context of estimation of systems of simultaneous equations, which goes beyond the scope of this book. For an introduction to using VARs for forecasting and policy analysis, see Stock and Watson (2001). For additional mathematical detail on structural VAR modeling, see Hamilton (1994) or Watson (1994).

## A VAR Model of the Growth Rate of GDP and the Term Spread

As an illustration, consider a two-variable VAR for the growth rate of GDP, $GDPGR_t$, and the term spread, $TSpread_t$. The VAR for $GDPGR_t$ and $TSpread_t$ consists of two equations: one in which $GDPGR_t$ is the dependent variable and one in which $TSpread_t$ is the dependent variable. The regressors in both equations are lagged values of $GDPGR_t$ and $TSpread_t$. Because of the apparent break in the relation in the early 1980s found in Section 14.7 using the QLR test, the VAR is estimated using data from 1981:Q1 to 2012:Q4.

The first equation of the VAR is the GDP growth rate equation:

$$\widehat{GDPGR_t} = 0.52 + 0.29\, GDPGR_{t-1} + 0.22\, GDPGR_{t-2}$$
$$\quad\;\; (0.52)\;\; (0.11) \qquad\qquad (0.09)$$

$$-0.90\, TSpread_{t-1} + 1.33\, TSpread_{t-2}. \qquad (16.5)$$
$$\;\;(0.36) \qquad\qquad (0.39)$$

The adjusted $R^2$ is $\overline{R}^2 = 0.29$.

The second equation of the VAR is the term spread equation, in which the regressors are the same as in the $GDPGR$ equation, but the dependent variable is the term spread:

$$\widehat{TSpread_t} = 0.46 + 0.01\, GDPGR_{t-1} - 0.06\, GDPGR_{t-2}$$
$$\quad\;\; (0.12)\;\; (0.02) \qquad\qquad (0.03)$$

$$+ 1.06\, TSpread_{t-1} - 0.22\, TSpread_{t-2}. \qquad (16.6)$$
$$\;\;(0.10) \qquad\qquad (0.11)$$

The adjusted $R^2$ is $\overline{R}^2 = 0.83$.

Equations (16.5) and (16.6), taken together, are a VAR(2) model of the growth rate of GDP, $GDPGR_t$, and the term spread, $TSpread_t$.

These VAR equations can be used to perform Granger causality tests. The $F$-statistic testing the null hypothesis that the coefficients on $TSpread_{t-1}$ and $TSpread_{t-2}$ are zero in the GDP growth rate equation [Equation (16.5)] is 5.91, which has a $p$-value less than 0.001. Thus the null hypothesis is rejected, so we can conclude that the term spread is a useful predictor of the growth rate of GDP, given lags in the growth rate of GDP (that is, the term spread rate Granger-causes the growth rate of GDP). The $F$-statistic testing the hypothesis that the coefficients on the two lags of $GDPGR_t$ are zero in the term spread equation [Equation (16.6)] is 3.48, which has a $p$-value of 0.03. Thus the growth rate of GDP Granger-causes the term spread at the 5% significance level.

Forecasts of the growth rate of GDP and the term spread one period ahead are obtained exactly as discussed in Section 14.4. The forecast of the growth rate of GDP for 2013:Q1, based on Equation (16.5), is $\widehat{GDP}_{2013:Q1|2012:Q4} = 1.7$ percentage point. A similar calculation using Equation (16.6) gives a forecast of the term spread 2013:Q1, based on data through 2012:Q4 of $\widehat{TSpread}_{2013:Q1|2012:Q4} = 1.7\%$. The actual values for 2013:Q1 are $GDPGR_{2013:Q1} = 1.1\%$ and $TSpread_{2013:Q1} = 1.9\%$.

## 16.2 Multiperiod Forecasts

The discussion of forecasting so far has focused on making forecasts one period in advance. Often, however, forecasters are called upon to make forecasts further into the future. This section describes two methods for making multiperiod forecasts. The usual method is to construct "iterated" forecasts, in which a one-period-ahead model is iterated forward one period at a time, in a way that is made precise in this section. The second method is to make "direct" forecasts by using a regression in which the dependent variable is the multiperiod variable that one wants to forecast. For reasons discussed at the end of this section, in most applications, the iterated method is recommended over the direct method.

### Iterated Multiperiod Forecasts

The essential idea of an iterated forecast is that a forecasting model is used to make a forecast one period ahead, for period $T + 1$, using data through period $T$. The model then is used to make a forecast for date $T + 2$, given the data through date $T$, where the forecasted value for date $T + 1$ is treated as data for the purpose of making the forecast for period $T + 2$. Thus the one-period-ahead forecast (which is also referred to as a one-step-ahead forecast) is used as an intermediate step to make the two-period-ahead forecast. This process repeats, or iterates, until the forecast is made for the desired forecast horizon $h$.

***The iterated AR forecast method: AR(1).*** An iterated AR(1) forecast uses an AR(1) for the one-period-ahead model. For example, consider the first-order autoregression for *GDPGR* [Equation (14.7)]:

$$\widehat{GDPGR}_t = 1.99 + 0.34\,GDPGR_{t-1}. \tag{16.7}$$
$$(0.35) \quad (0.08)$$

The first step in computing the two-quarter-ahead forecast of $GDPGR_{2013:Q2}$ based on Equation (16.7) using data through 2012:Q4 is to compute the one-quarter-ahead forecast of $GDPGR_{2013:Q1}$ based on data through 2012:Q4: $\widehat{GDPGR}_{2013:Q1|2012:Q4} = 1.99 + 0.34\,GDPGR_{2012:Q4} = 1.99 + 0.34 \times 0.15 = 2.0$. The second step is to substitute this forecast into Equation (16.7) so that $\widehat{GDPGR}_{2013:Q2|2012:Q4} = 1.99 + 0.34\,\widehat{GDPGR}_{2013:Q1|2012:Q4} = 1.99 + 0.34 \times 2.0 = 2.7$. Thus, based on information through the fourth quarter of 2012, this forecast states that the growth rate of GDP will be 2.7% in the second quarter of 2013.

***The iterated AR forecast method: AR(p).*** The iterated AR(1) strategy is extended to an AR($p$) by replacing $Y_{T+1}$ with its forecast, $\hat{Y}_{T+1|T}$, and then treating that forecast as data for the AR($p$) forecast of $Y_{T+2}$. For example, consider the iterated two-period-ahead forecast of the growth rate of GDP based on the AR(2) model from Section 14.3 [Equation (14.13)]:

$$\widehat{GDPGR}_t = 1.63 + 0.28\,GDPGR_{t-1} + 0.18\,GDPGR_{t-2}. \tag{16.8}$$
$$(0.40) \quad (0.08) \qquad\qquad (0.08)$$

The forecast of $GDPGR_{2013:Q1}$ based on data through 2012:Q4 using this AR(2), computed in Section 14.3, is $\widehat{GDPGR}_{2013:Q1|2012:Q4} = 2.1$. Thus the two-quarter-ahead iterated forecast based on the AR(2) is $\widehat{GDPGR}_{2013:Q2|2012:Q4} = 1.63 + 0.28\,\widehat{GDPGR}_{2013:Q1|2012:Q4} + 0.18\,GDPGR_{2012:Q4} = 1.63 + 0.28 \times 2.1 + 0.18 \times 0.15 = 2.2$. According to this iterated AR(2) forecast, based on data through the fourth quarter of 2012, the growth rate of GDP is predicted to be 2.2 percentage points in the second quarter of 2013.

***Iterated multivariate forecasts using an iterated VAR.*** Iterated multivariate forecasts can be computed using a VAR in much the same way as iterated univariate forecasts are computed using an autoregression. The main new feature of an iterated multivariate forecast is that the two-step-ahead (period $T + 2$) forecast of one variable depends on the forecasts of all variables in the VAR in period $T + 1$. For example, to compute the forecast of the growth rate of GDP in period $T + 2$ using a VAR with the variables $GDPGR_t$ and $TSpread_t$, one must forecast both $GDPGR_{T+1}$ and $TSpread_{T+1}$, using data through period $T$ as an intermediate step in forecasting $GDPGR_{T+2}$. More generally, to compute multiperiod iterated VAR forecasts $h$ periods ahead, it is necessary to compute forecasts of all variables for all intervening periods between $T$ and $T + h$.

As an example, we will compute the iterated VAR forecast of $GDPGR_{2013:Q2}$ based on data through 2012:Q4, using the VAR(2) for $GDPGR_t$ and $TSpread_t$ in Section 16.1 [Equations (16.5) and (16.6)]. The first step is to compute the one-quarter-ahead forecasts $\widehat{GDPGR}_{2013:Q1|2012:Q4}$ and $\widehat{TSpread}_{2013:Q1|2012:Q4}$ from that VAR. These one-period-ahead forecasts were computed in Section 16.1 based on Equations (16.5) and (16.6). The forecasts were $\widehat{GDPGR}_{2013:Q1|2012:Q4} = 1.7$ and $\widehat{TSpread}_{2013:Q1|2012:Q4} = 1.7$. In the second step, these forecasts are substituted into Equations (16.5) and (16.6) to produce the two-quarter-ahead forecast:

$$\widehat{GDPGR}_{2013:Q2|2012:Q4} = 0.52 + 0.29\,\widehat{GDPGR}_{2013:Q1|2012:Q4} + 0.22 GDPGR_{2012:Q4}$$
$$- 0.90\,\widehat{TSpread}_{2013:Q1|2012:Q4} + 1.33 TSpread_{2012:Q4}$$
$$= 0.52 + 0.30 \times 1.7 + 0.22 \times 0.15$$
$$- 0.90 \times 1.7 + 1.33 \times 1.6 = 1.7. \tag{16.9}$$

Thus the iterated VAR(2) forecast, based on data through the fourth quarter of 2012, is that the growth rate of GDP will be 1.7% in the second quarter of 2013.

Iterated multiperiod forecasts are summarized in Key Concept 16.2.

## Direct Multiperiod Forecasts

Direct multiperiod forecasts are computed without iterating by using a single regression in which the dependent variable is the multiperiod-ahead variable to be forecasted and the regressors are the predictor variables. Forecasts computed this way are called direct forecasts because the regression coefficients can be used directly to make the multiperiod forecast.

***The direct multiperiod forecasting method.***  Suppose that you want to make a forecast of $Y_{T+2}$ using data through time $T$. The direct multivariate method takes the ADL model as its starting point but lags the predictor variables by an additional time period. For example, if two lags of the predictors are used, then the

**KEY CONCEPT**

**16.2**

## Iterated Multiperiod Forecasts

The **iterated multiperiod AR forecast** is computed in steps: First compute the one-period-ahead forecast, then use that to compute the two-period-ahead forecast, and so forth. The two- and three-period-ahead iterated forecasts based on an AR($p$) are

$$\hat{Y}_{T+2|T} = \hat{\beta}_0 + \hat{\beta}_1\hat{Y}_{T+1|T} + \hat{\beta}_2 Y_T + \hat{\beta}_3 Y_{T-1} + \cdots + \hat{\beta}_p Y_{T-p+2} \quad (16.10)$$

$$\hat{Y}_{T+3|T} = \hat{\beta}_0 + \hat{\beta}_1\hat{Y}_{T+2|T} + \hat{\beta}_2\hat{Y}_{T+1|T} + \hat{\beta}_3 Y_T + \cdots + \hat{\beta}_p Y_{T-p+3}, \quad (16.11)$$

where the $\hat{\beta}$'s are the OLS estimates of the AR($p$) coefficients. Continuing this process ("iterating") produces forecasts further into the future.

The **iterated multiperiod VAR forecast** is also computed in steps: First compute the one-period-ahead forecast of all the variables in the VAR, then use those forecasts to compute the two-period-ahead forecasts, and continue this process iteratively to the desired forecast horizon. The two-period-ahead iterated forecast of $Y_{T+2}$, based on the two-variable VAR($p$) in Key Concept 16.1, is

$$\hat{Y}_{T+2|T} = \hat{\beta}_{10} + \hat{\beta}_{11}\hat{Y}_{T+1|T} + \hat{\beta}_{12}Y_T + \hat{\beta}_{13}Y_{T-1} + \cdots + \hat{\beta}_{1p}Y_{T-p+2}$$
$$+ \hat{\gamma}_{11}\hat{X}_{T+1|T} + \hat{\gamma}_{12}X_T + \hat{\gamma}_{13}X_{T-1} + \cdots + \hat{\gamma}_{1p}X_{T-p+2}, \quad (16.12)$$

where the coefficients in Equation (16.12) are the OLS estimates of the VAR coefficients. Iterating produces forecasts further into the future.

dependent variable is $Y_t$ and the regressors are $Y_{t-2}$, $Y_{t-3}$, $X_{t-2}$, and $X_{t-3}$. The coefficients from this regression can be used directly to compute the forecast of $Y_{T+2}$ using data on $Y_T$, $Y_{T-1}$, $X_T$, and $X_{T-1}$, without the need for any iteration. More generally, in a direct $h$-period-ahead forecasting regression, all predictors are lagged $h$ periods to produce the $h$-period-ahead forecast.

For example, the forecast of $GDPGR_t$ two quarters ahead using two lags each of $GDPGR_{t-2}$ and $TSpread_{t-2}$ is computed by first estimating the regression:

$$\widehat{GDPGR}_{t|t-2} = 0.57 + 0.34 GDPGR_{t-2} + 0.03 GDPGR_{t-3}$$
$$\quad (0.67) \quad (0.07) \quad\quad\quad (0.10)$$

$$+ 0.62 TSpread_{t-2} - 0.01 TSpread_{t-3}. \quad (16.13)$$
$$\quad (0.47) \quad\quad\quad (0.46)$$

The two-quarter-ahead forecast of the growth rate of GDP in 2013:Q2 based on data through 2012:Q4 is computed by substituting the values of $GDPGR_{2012:Q4}$, $GDPGR_{2012:Q3}$, $TSpread_{2012:Q4}$, and $TSpread_{2012:Q3}$ into Equation (16.13); this yields

$$\widehat{GDPGR}_{2013:Q2|2012:Q4} = 0.57 + 0.34 GDPGR_{2012:Q4} + 0.03 GDPGR_{2012:Q3}$$
$$+ 0.62 TSpread_{2012:Q4} - 0.01 TSpread_{2012:Q3} = 1.68.$$
$$(16.14)$$

The three-quarter-ahead direct forecast of $GDPGR_{T+3}$ is computed by lagging all the regressors in Equation (16.13) by one additional quarter, estimating that regression, and then computing the forecast. The $h$-quarter-ahead direct forecast of $GDPGR_{T+h}$ is computed by using $GPDGR_t$ as the dependent variable and the regressors $GPDGR_{t-h}$ and $TSpread_{t-h}$, plus additional lags of $GPDGR_{t-h}$ and $TSpread_{t-h}$, as desired.

*Standard errors in direct multiperiod regressions.* Because the dependent variable in a multiperiod regression occurs two or more periods into the future, the error term in a multiperiod regression is serially correlated. To see this, consider the two-period-ahead forecast of the growth rate of GDP and suppose that a surprise jump in oil prices occurs in the next quarter. Today's two-period-ahead forecast of the growth rate of GDP will be too low because it does not incorporate this unexpected event. Because the oil price rise was also unknown in the previous quarter, the two-period-ahead forecast made last quarter will also be too low. Thus the surprise oil price jump next quarter means that *both* last quarter's and this quarter's two-period-ahead forecasts are too low. Because of such intervening events, the error term in a multiperiod regression is serially correlated.

As discussed in Section 15.4, if the error term is serially correlated, the usual OLS standard errors are incorrect or, more precisely, they are not a reliable basis for inference. Therefore, heteroskedasticity- and autocorrelation-consistent (HAC) standard errors must be used with direct multiperiod regressions. The standard errors reported in Equation (16.13) for direct multiperiod regressions therefore are Newey–West HAC standard errors, where the truncation parameter $m$ is set according to Equation (15.17); for these data (for which $T = 128$), Equation (15.17) yields $m = 4$. For longer forecast horizons, the amount of overlap—and thus the degree of serial correlation in the error—increases: In general, the first $h - 1$ autocorrelation coefficients of the errors in an $h$-period-ahead regression are nonzero. Thus larger values of $m$ than indicated by Equation (15.17) are appropriate for multiperiod regressions with long forecast horizons.

Direct multiperiod forecasts are summarized in Key Concept 16.3.

**KEY CONCEPT**

**16.3**

## Direct Multiperiod Forecasts

The **direct multiperiod forecast** $h$ periods into the future based on $p$ lags each of $Y_t$ and an additional predictor $X_t$ is computed by first estimating the regression

$$Y_t = \delta_0 + \delta_1 Y_{t-h} + \cdots + \delta_p Y_{t-p-h+1} + \delta_{p+1} X_{t-h}$$
$$+ \cdots + \delta_{2p} X_{t-p-h+1} + u_t, \tag{16.15}$$

and then using the estimated coefficients directly to make the forecast of $Y_{T+h}$ using data through period $T$.

## Which Method Should You Use?

In most applications, the iterated method is the recommended procedure for multiperiod forecasting, for two reasons. First, from a theoretical perspective, if the underlying one-period-ahead model (the AR or VAR that is used to compute the iterated forecast) is specified correctly, then the coefficients are estimated more efficiently if they are estimated by a one-period-ahead regression (and then iterated) than by a multiperiod-ahead regression. Second, from a practical perspective, forecasters are usually interested in forecasts not just at a single horizon but at multiple horizons. Because they are produced using the same model, iterated forecasts tend to have time paths that are less erratic across horizons than do direct forecasts. Because a different model is used at every horizon for direct forecasts, sampling error in the estimated coefficients can add random fluctuations to the time paths of a sequence of direct multiperiod forecasts.

Under some circumstances, however, direct forecasts are preferable to iterated forecasts. One such circumstance is when you have reason to believe that the one-period-ahead model (the AR or VAR) is not specified correctly. For example, you might believe that the equation for the variable you are trying to forecast in a VAR is specified correctly, but that one or more of the other equations in the VAR is specified incorrectly, perhaps because of neglected nonlinear terms. If the one-step-ahead model is specified incorrectly, then in general the iterated multiperiod forecast will be biased, and the MSFE of the iterated forecast can exceed the MSFE of the direct forecast, even though the direct forecast has a larger variance. A second circumstance in which a direct forecast might be desirable arises in multivariate forecasting models with many predictors, in which case a VAR specified in terms of all the variables could be unreliable because it would have very many estimated coefficients.

# 16.3 Orders of Integration and the DF-GLS Unit Root Test

This section extends the treatment of stochastic trends in Section 14.6 by addressing two further topics. First, the trends of some time series are not well described by the random walk model, so we introduce an extension of that model and discuss its implications for regression modeling of such series. Second, we continue the discussion of testing for a unit root in time series data and, among other things, introduce a second test for a unit root, the DF-GLS test.

## Other Models of Trends and Orders of Integration

Recall that the random walk model for a trend, introduced in Section 14.6, specifies that the trend at date $t$ equals the trend at date $t - 1$, plus a random error term. If $Y_t$ follows a random walk with drift $\beta_0$, then

$$Y_t = \beta_0 + Y_{t-1} + u_t, \tag{16.16}$$

where $u_t$ is serially uncorrelated. Also recall from Section 14.6 that, if a series has a random walk trend, then it has an autoregressive root that equals 1.

Although the random walk model of a trend describes the long-run movements of many economic time series, some economic time series have trends that are smoother—that is, vary less from one period to the next—than is implied by Equation (16.16). A different model is needed to describe the trends of such series.

One model of a smooth trend makes the first difference of the trend follow a random walk—that is,

$$\Delta Y_t = \beta_0 + \Delta Y_{t-1} + u_t, \tag{16.17}$$

where $u_t$ is serially uncorrelated. Thus, if $Y_t$ follows Equation (16.17), $\Delta Y_t$ follows a random walk, so $\Delta Y_t - \Delta Y_{t-1}$ is stationary. The difference of the first differences, $\Delta Y_t - \Delta Y_{t-1}$, is called the **second difference** of $Y_t$ and is denoted $\Delta^2 Y_t = \Delta Y_t - \Delta Y_{t-1}$. In this terminology, if $Y_t$ follows Equation (16.17), then its second

KEY CONCEPT

16.4

## Orders of Integration, Differencing, and Stationarity

- If $Y_t$ is integrated of order one—that is, if $Y_t$ is $I(1)$—then $Y_t$ has a unit autoregressive root and its first difference, $\Delta Y_t$, is stationary.

- If $Y_t$ is integrated of order two—that is, if $Y_t$ is $I(2)$—then $\Delta Y_t$ has a unit autoregressive root and its second difference, $\Delta^2 Y_t$, is stationary.

- If $Y_t$ is **integrated of order** $d$—that is, if $Y_t$ is $I(d)$—then $Y_t$ must be differenced $d$ times to eliminate its stochastic trend; that is, $\Delta^d Y_t$ is stationary.

difference is stationary. If a series has a trend of the form in Equation (16.17), then the first difference of the series has an autoregressive root that equals 1.

*"Orders of integration" terminology.* Some additional terminology is useful for distinguishing between these two models of trends. A series that has a random walk trend is said to be **integrated of order one**, or $I(1)$. A series that has a trend of the form in Equation (16.17) is said to be **integrated of order two**, or $I(2)$. A series that does not have a stochastic trend and is stationary is said to be **integrated of order zero**, or $I(0)$.

The **order of integration** in the $I(1)$ and $I(2)$ terminology is the number of times that the series needs to be differenced for it to be stationary: If $Y_t$ is $I(1)$, then the first difference of $Y_t$, $\Delta Y_t$, is stationary, and if $Y_t$ is $I(2)$, then the second difference of $Y_t$, $\Delta^2 Y_t$, is stationary. If $Y_t$ is $I(0)$, then $Y_t$ is stationary.

Orders of integration are summarized in Key Concept 16.4.

*How to test whether a series is I(2) or I(1).* If $Y_t$ is $I(2)$, then $\Delta Y_t$ is $I(1)$, so $\Delta Y_t$ has an autoregressive root that equals 1. If, however, $Y_t$ is $I(1)$, then $\Delta Y_t$ is stationary. Thus the null hypothesis that $Y_t$ is $I(2)$ can be tested against the alternative hypothesis that $Y_t$ is $I(1)$ by testing whether $\Delta Y_t$ has a unit autoregressive root. If the hypothesis that $\Delta Y_t$ has a unit autoregressive root is rejected, then the hypothesis that $Y_t$ is $I(2)$ is rejected in favor of the alternative that $Y_t$ is $I(1)$.

*Examples of I(2) and I(1) series: The price level and the rate of inflation.* The rate of inflation is the growth rate of the price level. Recall from Section 14.2 that the growth rate of a time series $X_t$ can be computed as the first difference of the logarithm of $X_t$; that is $\Delta \ln(X_t)$ is the growth rate of $X_t$ (expressed as fraction). If $P_t$ is a time series for the price level measured quarterly, then $\Delta \ln(P_t)$ is its growth rate, and $Infl_t = 400 \times \Delta \ln(P_t)$ is the quarterly rate of inflation, measured in percentage points at an annual rate. As in the expression for the growth of GDP, $GDPGR$ in Equation (14.2), the factor 400 arises from converting fractional changes to percentage changes (multiplying by 100) and converting quarterly percentages to an annual rate (multiplying by 4).

In Empirical Exercise 14.1, you analyzed the rate of inflation, $Infl_t$, computed using the price index for personal consumption expenditures in the United States as $P_t$. In that exercise you concluded that the rate of inflation in the United States plausibly has a random walk stochastic trend—that is, that the rate of inflation is $I(1)$. If inflation is $I(1)$, then its stochastic trend is removed by first differencing, so $\Delta Inf_t$ is stationary. But treating inflation as $I(1)$ is equivalent to treating $\Delta \ln(P_t)$ as $I(1)$, but this in turn is equivalent to treating the logarithm of the price level, $\ln(P_t)$, as $I(2)$.

The logarithm of the price level and the rate of inflation are plotted in Figure 16.1. The long-run trend of the logarithm of the price level (Figure 16.1a) varies more smoothly than the long-run trend in the rate of inflation (Figure 16.1b). The smoothly varying trend in the logarithm of the price level is typical of $I(2)$ series.

## The DF-GLS Test for a Unit Root

This section continues the discussion of Section 14.6 regarding testing for a unit autoregressive root. We first describe another test for a unit autoregressive root, the so-called DF-GLS test. Next, in an optional mathematical section, we discuss why unit root test statistics do not have normal distributions, even in large samples.

*The DF-GLS test.* The ADF test was the first test developed for testing the null hypothesis of a unit root and is the most commonly used test in practice. Other tests subsequently have been proposed, however, many of which have higher power (Key Concept 3.5) than the ADF test. A test with higher power than the ADF test is more likely to reject the null hypothesis of a unit root against the stationary alternative when the alternative is true; thus a more powerful test is better able to distinguish between a unit AR root and a root that is large but less than 1.

This section discusses one such test, the **DF-GLS test** developed by Elliott, Rothenberg, and Stock (1996). The test is introduced for the case that, under the null hypothesis, $Y_t$ has a random walk trend, possibly with drift, and under the alternative $Y_t$ is stationary around a linear time trend.

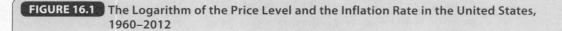

**FIGURE 16.1** The Logarithm of the Price Level and the Inflation Rate in the United States, 1960–2012

**Logarithm**

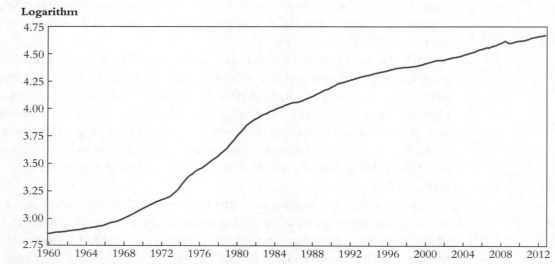

**(a)** Logarithm of the United States PCE Price Index

**Percent per annum**

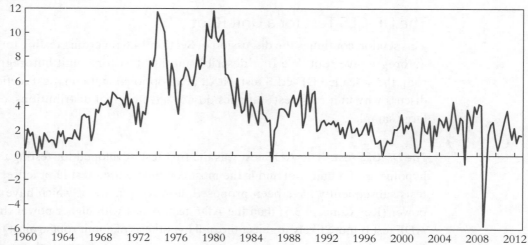

**(b)** United States PCE price inflation

The trend in the logarithm of prices (Figure 16.1a) is much smoother than the trend in inflation (Figure 16.1b).

The DF-GLS test is computed in two steps. In the first step, the intercept and trend are estimated by generalized least squares (GLS; see Section 15.5). The GLS estimation is performed by computing three new variables, $V_t$, $X_{1t}$, and $X_{2t}$, where $V_1 = Y_1$ and $V_t = Y_t - \alpha^* Y_{t-1}$, $t = 2, \ldots, T$, $X_{11} = 1$ and $X_{1t} = 1 - \alpha^*$, $t = 2, \ldots, T$, and $X_{21} = 1$ and $X_{2t} = t - \alpha^*(t - 1)$, where $\alpha^*$ is computed using the formula $\alpha^* = 1 - 13.5/T$. Then $V_t$ is regressed against $X_{1t}$ and $X_{2t}$; that is, OLS is used to estimate the coefficients of the population regression equation

$$V_t = \delta_0 X_{1t} + \delta_1 X_{2t} + e_t, \tag{16.18}$$

using the observations $t = 1, \ldots, T$, where $e_t$ is the error term. Note that there is no intercept in the regression in Equation (16.18). The OLS estimators $\hat{\delta}_0$ and $\hat{\delta}_1$ are then used to compute a "detrended" version of $Y_t$, $Y_t^d = Y_t - (\hat{\delta}_0 + \hat{\delta}_1 t)$.

In the second step, the Dickey–Fuller test is used to test for a unit autoregressive root in $Y_t^d$, where the Dickey–Fuller regression does not include an intercept or a time trend. That is, $\Delta Y_t^d$ is regressed against $Y_{t-1}^d$ and $\Delta Y_{t-1}^d, \ldots, \Delta Y_{t-p}^d$, where the number of lags $p$ is determined, as usual, either by expert knowledge or by using a data-based method such as the AIC or BIC, as discussed in Section 14.5.

If the alternative hypothesis is that $Y_t$ is stationary with a mean that might be nonzero but without a time trend, the preceding steps are modified. Specifically, $\alpha^*$ is computed using the formula $\alpha^* = 1 - 7/T$, $X_{2t}$ is omitted from the regression in Equation (16.18), and the series $Y_t^d$ is computed as $Y_t^d = Y_t - \hat{\delta}_0$.

The GLS regression in the first step of the DF-GLS test makes this test more complicated than the conventional ADF test, but it is also what improves its ability to discriminate between the null hypothesis of a unit autoregressive root and the alternative that $Y_t$ is stationary. This improvement can be substantial. For example, suppose that $Y_t$ is in fact a stationary AR(1) with autoregressive coefficient $\beta_1 = 0.95$, that there are $T = 200$ observations, and that the unit root tests are computed without a time trend [that is, $t$ is excluded from the Dickey–Fuller regression, and $X_{2t}$ is omitted from Equation (16.18)]. Then the probability that the ADF test correctly rejects the null hypothesis at the 5% significance level is approximately 31% compared to 75% for the DF-GLS test.

*Critical values for DF-GLS test.* Because the coefficients on the deterministic terms are estimated differently in the ADF and DF-GLS tests, the tests have different critical values. The critical values for the DF-GLS test are given in Table 16.1. If the DF-GLS test statistic (the $t$-statistic on $Y_{t-1}^d$ in the regression in the second

| **TABLE 16.1** Critical Values of the DF-GLS Test | | | |
|---|---|---|---|
| **Deterministic Regressors** **[Regressors in Equation (16.18)]** | **10%** | **5%** | **1%** |
| Intercept only ($X_{1t}$ only) | −1.62 | −1.95 | −2.58 |
| Intercept and time trend ($X_{1t}$ and $X_{2t}$) | −2.57 | −2.89 | −3.48 |

Source: Fuller (1976) and Elliott, Rothenberg, and Stock (1996, Table 1).

step) is less than the critical value (that is, it is more negative than the critical value), then the null hypothesis that $Y_t$ has a unit root is rejected. Like the critical values for the Dickey–Fuller test, the appropriate critical value depends on which version of the test is used—that is, on whether or not a time trend is included [whether or not $X_{2t}$ is included in Equation (16.18)].

*Application to the logarithm of GDP.* The DF-GLS statistic, computed for the logarithm of GDP, $\ln(GDP_t)$, over the period 1962:Q1 to 2012:Q4 with an intercept and time trend, is −2.85 when two lags of $\Delta Y_t^d$ are included in the Dickey–Fuller regression in the second stage, where the choice of two lags was based on the AIC (out of a maximum of six lags). This value is greater than the 5% critical value in Table 16.1, −2.89, so the DF-GLS test does not reject the null hypothesis of a unit root at the 5% significance level.

## Why Do Unit Root Tests Have Nonnormal Distributions?

In Section 14.6, it was stressed that the large-sample normal distribution on which regression analysis relies so heavily does not apply if the regressors are nonstationary. Under the null hypothesis that the regression contains a unit root, the regressor $Y_{t-1}$ in the Dickey–Fuller regression (and the regressor $Y_{t-1}^d$ in the modified Dickey–Fuller regression in the second step of the DF-GLS test) is nonstationary. The nonnormal distribution of the unit root test statistics is a consequence of this nonstationarity.

To gain some mathematical insight into this nonnormality, consider the simplest possible Dickey–Fuller regression, in which $\Delta Y_t$ is regressed against the single regressor $Y_{t-1}$ and the intercept is excluded. In the notation of Key Concept 14.8, the OLS estimator in this regression is $\hat{\delta} = \sum_{t=1}^{T} Y_{t-1}\Delta Y_t / \sum_{t=1}^{T} Y_{t-1}^2$, so

$$T\hat{\delta} = \frac{\frac{1}{T}\sum_{t=1}^{T} Y_{t-1}\Delta Y_t}{\frac{1}{T^2}\sum_{t=1}^{T} Y_{t-1}^2}. \tag{16.19}$$

Consider the numerator in Equation (16.19). Under the additional assumption that $Y_0 = 0$, a bit of algebra (Exercise 16.5) shows that

$$\frac{1}{T}\sum_{t=1}^{T} Y_{t-1}\Delta Y_t = \frac{1}{2}\left[\left(\frac{Y_T}{\sqrt{T}}\right)^2 - \frac{1}{T}\sum_{t=1}^{T}(\Delta Y_t)^2\right]. \tag{16.20}$$

Under the null hypothesis, $\Delta Y_t = u_t$, which is serially uncorrelated and has a finite variance, so the second term in Equation (16.20) has the probability limit $\frac{1}{T}\sum_{t=1}^{T}(\Delta Y_t)^2 \xrightarrow{p} \sigma_u^2$. Under the assumption that $Y_0 = 0$, the first term in Equation (16.20) can be written $Y_T/\sqrt{T} = \sqrt{\frac{1}{T}}\sum_{t=1}^{T}\Delta Y_t = \sqrt{\frac{1}{T}}\sum_{t=1}^{T}u_t$, which in turn obeys the central limit theorem; that is, $Y_T/\sqrt{T} \xrightarrow{d} N(0, \sigma_u^2)$. Thus $(Y_T/\sqrt{T})^2 - \frac{1}{T}\sum_{t=1}^{T}(\Delta Y_t)^2 \xrightarrow{d} \sigma_u^2(Z^2 - 1)$, where $Z$ is a standard normal random variable. Recall, however, that the square of a standard normal distribution has a chi-squared distribution with 1 degree of freedom. It therefore follows from Equation (16.20) that, under the null hypothesis, the numerator in Equation (16.19) has the limiting distribution

$$\frac{1}{T}\sum_{t=1}^{T} Y_{t-1}\Delta Y_t \xrightarrow{d} \frac{\sigma_u^2}{2}(\chi_1^2 - 1). \tag{16.21}$$

The large-sample distribution in Equation (16.21) is different than the usual large-sample normal distribution when the regressor is stationary. Instead, the numerator of the OLS estimator of the coefficient on $Y_t$ in this Dickey–Fuller regression has a distribution that is proportional to a chi-squared distribution with 1 degree of freedom minus 1.

This discussion has considered only the numerator of $T\hat{\delta}$. The denominator also behaves unusually under the null hypothesis: Because $Y_t$ follows a random walk under the null hypothesis, $\frac{1}{T}\sum_{t=1}^{T} Y_{t-1}^2$ does not converge in probability to a constant. Instead, the denominator in Equation (16.19) is a random variable, even in large samples: Under the null hypothesis, $\frac{1}{T^2}\sum_{t=1}^{T} Y_{t-1}^2$ converges in distribution jointly with the numerator. The unusual distributions of the numerator and denominator in Equation (16.19) are the source of the nonstandard distribution of the Dickey–Fuller test statistic and the reason that the ADF statistic has its own special table of critical values.

# 16.4 Cointegration

Sometimes two or more series have the same stochastic trend in common. In this special case, referred to as cointegration, regression analysis can reveal long-run relationships among time series variables, but some new methods are needed.

## Cointegration and Error Correction

Two or more time series with stochastic trends can move together so closely over the long run that they appear to have the same trend component; that is, they appear to have a **common trend**. For example, Figure 16.2 reproduces the plot of the 10-year and 3-month interest rates from Figure 14.3. The interest rates exhibit the same long-run tendencies or trends: Both were low in the 1960s, both rose through the 1970s to peaks in the early 1980s, then both fell through the 1990s. However, the difference between the long-term and short-term interest rates, the term spread, does not appear to have a trend. That is, subtracting the short-term rate from the long-term rate appears to eliminate the trends in both of the

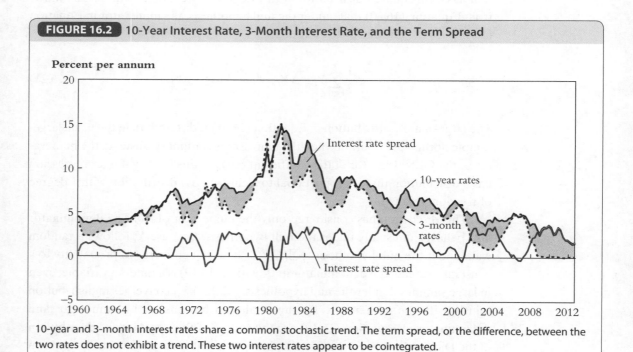

**FIGURE 16.2** 10-Year Interest Rate, 3-Month Interest Rate, and the Term Spread

10-year and 3-month interest rates share a common stochastic trend. The term spread, or the difference, between the two rates does not exhibit a trend. These two interest rates appear to be cointegrated.

## Cointegration

Suppose that $X_t$ and $Y_t$ are integrated of order one. If, for some coefficient $\theta$, $Y_t - \theta X_t$ is integrated of order zero, then $X_t$ and $Y_t$ are said to be *cointegrated*. The coefficient $\theta$ is called the **cointegrating coefficient**.

If $X_t$ and $Y_t$ are cointegrated, then they have the same, or common, stochastic trend. Computing the difference $Y_t - \theta X_t$ eliminates this common stochastic trend.

individual rates. Said differently, although the two interest rates differ, they appear to share a common stochastic trend: Because the trend in each individual series is eliminated by subtracting one series from the other, the two series must have the same trend; that is, they must have a common stochastic trend.

Two or more series that have a common stochastic trend are said to be cointegrated. The formal definition of **cointegration** (due to the econometrician Clive Granger, 1983; see the box "Nobel Laureates in Time Series Econometrics") is given in Key Concept 16.5. In this section, we introduce a test for whether cointegration is present, discuss estimation of the coefficients of regressions relating cointegrated variables, and illustrate the use of the cointegrating relationship for forecasting. The discussion initially focuses on the case that there are only two variables, $X_t$ and $Y_t$.

*Vector error correction model.* Until now, we have eliminated the stochastic trend in an $I(1)$ variable $Y_t$ by computing its first difference, $\Delta Y_t$; the problems created by stochastic trends were then avoided by using $\Delta Y_t$ instead of $Y_t$ in time series regressions. If $X_t$ and $Y_t$ are cointegrated, however, another way to eliminate the trend is to compute $Y_t - \theta X_t$, where $\theta$ is chosen to eliminate the common trend from the difference. Because the term $Y_t - \theta X_t$ is stationary, it too can be used in regression analysis.

In fact, if $X_t$ and $Y_t$ are cointegrated, the first differences of $X_t$ and $Y_t$ can be modeled using a VAR, augmented by including $Y_{t-1} - \theta X_{t-1}$ as an additional regressor:

$$\Delta Y_t = \beta_{10} + \beta_{11}\Delta Y_{t-1} + \cdots + \beta_{1p}\Delta Y_{t-p} + \gamma_{11}\Delta X_{t-1}$$
$$+ \cdots + \gamma_{1p}\Delta X_{t-p} + \alpha_1(Y_{t-1} - \theta X_{t-1}) + u_{1t} \qquad (16.22)$$

$$\Delta X_t = \beta_{20} + \beta_{21}\Delta Y_{t-1} + \cdots + \beta_{2p}\Delta Y_{t-p} + \gamma_{21}\Delta X_{t-1}$$
$$+ \cdots + \gamma_{2p}\Delta X_{t-p} + \alpha_2(Y_{t-1} - \theta X_{t-1}) + u_{2t}. \qquad (16.23)$$

The term $Y_t - \theta X_t$ is called the **error correction term**. The combined model in Equations (16.22) and (16.23) is called a **vector error correction model (VECM)**. In a VECM, past values of $Y_t - \theta X_t$ help to predict future values of $\Delta Y_t$ and/or $\Delta X_t$.

## How Can You Tell Whether Two Variables Are Cointegrated?

There are three ways to determine whether two variables can plausibly be modeled as cointegrated: Use expert knowledge and economic theory, graph the series and see whether they appear to have a common stochastic trend, and perform statistical tests for cointegration. All three methods should be used in practice.

First, you must use your expert knowledge of these variables to decide whether cointegration is in fact plausible. For example, the two interest rates in Figure 16.2 are linked together by the so-called expectations theory of the term structure of interest rates. According to this theory, the interest rate on January 1 on the 10-year Treasury bond is the average of the interest rate on a 3-month Treasury bill for the first quarter of the year and the expected interest rates on future 3-month Treasury bills issued in the subsequent 39 quarters, for total of 40 quarters, or 10 years. If this was not the case, then investors could expect to make money by holding either the 10-year Treasury note or a sequence of forty 3-month Treasury bills, and they would bid up prices until the expected returns were equalized. If the 3-month interest rate has a random walk stochastic trend, this theory implies that this stochastic trend is inherited by the 10-year interest rate and that the difference between the two rates—that is, the term spread—is stationary. Thus the expectations theory of the term structure implies that if the interest rates are $I(1)$, then they will be cointegrated with a cointegrating coefficient of $\theta = 1$ (Exercise 16.2).

Second, visual inspection of the series helps to identify cases in which cointegration is plausible. For example, the graph of the two interest rates in Figure 16.2 shows that each of the series appears to be $I(1)$ but that the term spread appears to be $I(0)$, so the two series appear to be cointegrated.

Third, the unit root testing procedures introduced so far can be extended to tests for cointegration. The insight on which these tests are based is that if $Y_t$ and $X_t$ are cointegrated with cointegrating coefficient $\theta$, then $Y_t - \theta X_t$ is stationary; otherwise, $Y_t - \theta X_t$ is nonstationary [is $I(1)$]. The hypothesis that $Y_t$ and $X_t$ are not cointegrated [that is, that $Y_t - \theta X_t$ is $I(1)$] therefore can be tested by testing the null hypothesis that $Y_t - \theta X_t$ has a unit root; if this hypothesis is rejected, then $Y_t$ and $X_t$ can be modeled as cointegrated. The details of this test depend on whether the cointegrating coefficient $\theta$ is known.

| TABLE 16.2 | Critical Values for the Engle–Granger ADF Statistic | | |
|---|---|---|---|
| **Number of X's in Equation (16.24)** | **10%** | **5%** | **1%** |
| 1 | −3.12 | −3.41 | −3.96 |
| 2 | −3.52 | −3.80 | −4.36 |
| 3 | −3.84 | −4.16 | −4.73 |
| 4 | −4.20 | −4.49 | −5.07 |

***Testing for cointegration when θ is known.*** In many cases expert knowledge or economic theory suggests a value for $\theta$. When $\theta$ is known, the Dickey–Fuller and DF-GLS unit root tests can be used to test for cointegration by first constructing the series $z_t = Y_t - \theta X_t$ and then testing the null hypothesis that $z_t$ has a unit autoregressive root.

***Testing for cointegration when θ is unknown.*** If the cointegrating coefficient $\theta$ is unknown, then it must be estimated prior to testing for a unit root in the error correction term. This preliminary step makes it necessary to use different critical values for the subsequent unit root test.

Specifically, in the first step the cointegrating coefficient $\theta$ is estimated by OLS estimation of the regression

$$Y_t = \alpha + \theta X_t + z_t. \tag{16.24}$$

In the second step, a Dickey–Fuller $t$-test (with an intercept but no time trend) is used to test for a unit root in the residual from this regression, $\hat{z}_t$. This two-step procedure is called the Engle–Granger Augmented Dickey–Fuller test for cointegration, or **EG-ADF test** (Engle and Granger, 1987).

Critical values of the EG-ADF statistic are given in Table 16.2.[1] The critical values in the first row apply when there is a single regressor in Equation (16.26), so there are two cointegrated variables ($X_t$ and $Y_t$). The subsequent rows apply to the case of multiple cointegrated variables, which is discussed at the end of this section.

## Estimation of Cointegrating Coefficients

If $X_t$ and $Y_t$ are cointegrated, then the OLS estimator of the coefficient in the cointegrating regression in Equation (16.24) is consistent. However, in general the OLS

[1]The critical values in Table 16.2 are taken from Fuller (1976) and Phillips and Ouliaris (1990). Following a suggestion by Hansen (1992), the critical values in Table 16.2 are chosen so that they apply whether or not $X_t$ and $Y_t$ have drift components.

estimator has a nonnormal distribution, and inferences based on its $t$-statistics can be misleading whether or not those $t$-statistics are computed using HAC standard errors. Because of these drawbacks of the OLS estimator of $\theta$, econometricians have developed a number of other estimators of the cointegrating coefficient.

One such estimator of $\theta$ that is simple to use in practice is the **dynamic OLS (DOLS) estimator** (Stock and Watson, 1993). The DOLS estimator is based on a modified version of Equation (16.24) that includes past, present, and future values of the change in $X_t$:

$$Y_t = \beta_0 + \theta X_t + \sum_{j=-p}^{p} \delta_j \Delta X_{t-j} + u_t. \tag{16.25}$$

Thus, in Equation (16.25), the regressors are $X_t, \Delta X_{t+p}, \dots, \Delta X_{t-p}$. The DOLS estimator of $\theta$ is the OLS estimator of $\theta$ in the regression of Equation (16.25).

If $X_t$ and $Y_t$ are cointegrated, then the DOLS estimator is efficient in large samples. Moreover, statistical inferences about $\theta$ and the $\delta$'s in Equation (16.25) based on HAC standard errors are valid. For example, the $t$-statistic constructed using the DOLS estimator with HAC standard errors has a standard normal distribution in large samples.

One way to interpret Equation (16.25) is to recall from Section 15.3 that cumulative dynamic multipliers can be computed by modifying the distributed lag regression of $Y_t$ on $X_t$ and its lags. Specifically, in Equation (15.7), the cumulative dynamic multipliers were computed by regressing $Y_t$ on $\Delta X_t$, lags of $\Delta X_t$, and $X_{t-r}$; the coefficient on $X_{t-r}$ in that specification is the long-run cumulative dynamic multiplier. Similarly, if $X_t$ were strictly exogenous, then in Equation (16.25) the coefficient on $X_t$, $\theta$ would be the long-run cumulative multiplier—that is, the long-run effect on $Y$ of a change in $X$. If $X_t$ is not strictly exogenous, then the coefficients do not have this interpretation. Nevertheless, because $X_t$ and $Y_t$ have a common stochastic trend if they are cointegrated, the DOLS estimator is consistent even if $X_t$ is endogenous.

The DOLS estimator is not the only efficient estimator of the cointegrating coefficient. The first such estimator was developed by Søren Johansen (Johansen, 1988). For a discussion of Johansen's method and of other ways to estimate the cointegrating coefficient, see Hamilton (1994, Chapter 20).

Even if economic theory does not suggest a specific value of the cointegrating coefficient, it is important to check whether the estimated cointegrating relationship makes sense in practice. Because cointegration tests can be misleading (they can improperly reject the null hypothesis of no cointegration more frequently than they should, and frequently they improperly fail to reject the null hypothesis), it is especially important to rely on economic theory, institutional knowledge, and common sense when estimating and using cointegrating relationships.

## Extension to Multiple Cointegrated Variables

The concepts, tests, and estimators discussed here extend to more than two variables. For example, if there are three variables, $Y_t$, $X_{1t}$, and $X_{2t}$, each of which is $I(1)$, then they are cointegrated with cointegrating coefficients $\theta_1$ and $\theta_2$ if $Y_t - \theta_1 X_{1t} - \theta_2 X_{2t}$ is stationary. When there are three or more variables, there can be multiple cointegrating relationships. For example, consider modeling the relationship among three interest rates: the 3-month rate ($R3m$), the 1-year ($R1y$) rate, and the 10-year rate ($R10y$). If they are $I(1)$, then the expectations theory of the term structure of interest rates suggests that they will all be cointegrated. One cointegrating relationship suggested by the theory is $R10y_t - R3m_t$, and a second relationship is $R1y_t - R3m_t$. (The relationship $R10y_t - R1y_t$ is also a cointegrating relationship, but it contains no additional information beyond that in the other relationships because it is perfectly multicollinear with the other two cointegrating relationships.)

The EG-ADF procedure for testing for a single cointegrating relationship among multiple variables is the same as for the case of two variables, except that the regression in Equation (16.24) is modified so that both $X_{1t}$ and $X_{2t}$ are regressors; the critical values for the EG-ADF test are given in Table 16.2, where the appropriate row depends on the number of regressors in the first-stage OLS cointegrating regression. The DOLS estimator of a single cointegrating relationship among multiple $X$'s involves including the level of each $X$ along with leads and lags of the first difference of each $X$. Tests for multiple cointegrating relationships can be performed using system methods, such as Johansen's (1988) method, and the DOLS estimator can be extended to multiple cointegrating relationships by estimating multiple equations, one for each cointegrating relationship. For additional discussion of cointegration methods for multiple variables, see Hamilton (1994).

*A cautionary note.* If two or more variables are cointegrated, then the error correction term can help to forecast these variables and, possibly, other related variables. However, cointegration requires the variables to have the same stochastic trends. Trends in economic variables typically arise from complex interactions of disparate forces, and closely related series can have different trends for subtle reasons. If variables that are not cointegrated are incorrectly modeled using a VECM, then the error correction term will be $I(1)$; this introduces a trend into the forecast that can result in poor out-of-sample forecast performance. Thus forecasting using a VECM must be based on a combination of compelling theoretical arguments in favor of cointegration and careful empirical analysis.

## Application to Interest Rates

As discussed earlier, the expectations theory of the term structure of interest rates implies that if two interest rates of different maturities are $I(1)$, then they will be cointegrated with a cointegrating coefficient of $\theta = 1$; that is, the spread between the two rates will be stationary. Inspection of Figure 16.2 provides qualitative support for the hypothesis that the 10-year and 3-month interest rates are cointegrated. We first use unit root and cointegration test statistics to provide more formal evidence on this hypothesis, then estimate a vector error correction model for these two interest rates.

*Unit root and cointegration tests.*  Various unit root and cointegration test statistics for these two series are reported in Table 16.3. The unit root test statistics in the first two rows examine the hypothesis that the two interest rates, the 3-month rate ($R3m$) and the 10-year rate ($R10y$), individually have a unit root. The ADF and DF-GLS test statistics are larger than the 10% critical values, so the null hypothesis of a unit root is not rejected for either series at the 10% significance level. Thus, these results suggest that the interest rates are plausibly modeled as $I(1)$.

The unit root statistics for the term spread, $R10y_t - R3m_t$, test the further hypothesis that these variables are not cointegrated against the alternative hypothesis that they are. The null hypothesis that the term spread contains a unit root is rejected at the 1% level, using both unit root tests. Thus we reject the hypothesis that the series are not cointegrated against the alternative that they are, with a cointegrating coefficient $\theta = 1$. Taken together, the evidence in the first three rows of Table 16.3 suggests that these variables plausibly can be modeled as cointegrated with $\theta = 1$.

| TABLE 16.3 | Unit Root and Cointegration Test Statistics for Two Interest Rates | |
|---|---|---|
| **Series** | **ADF Statistic** | **DF-GLS Statistic** |
| $R3m$ | −2.17 | −1.84 |
| $R10y$ | −1.03 | −0.96 |
| $R10y - R3m$ | −3.97** | −3.92** |
| $R10y - 0.814 \times R3m$ | −3.15 | — |

$R3m$ is the interest rate on 3-month U.S. Treasury bills, and $R10y$ is the interest rate on 10-year U.S. Treasury bonds. Regressions were estimated using quarterly data over the period 1962:Q1–2012:Q4. The number of lags in the unit root test statistic regressions were chosen by AIC (six lags maximum). Unit root test statistics are significant at the *5% or **1% significance level.

Because in this application economic theory suggests a value for $\theta$ (the expectations theory of the term structure suggests that $\theta = 1$) and because the error correction term is $I(0)$ when this value is imposed (the spread is stationary), in principle it is not necessary to use the EG-ADF test, in which $\theta$ is estimated. Nevertheless, we compute the test as an illustration. The first step in the EG-ADF test is to estimate $\theta$ by the OLS regression of one variable on the other; the result is

$$\widehat{R10y}_t = 2.46 + 0.81 R3m_t, \overline{R}^2 = 0.83. \tag{16.26}$$

The second step is to compute the ADF statistic for the residual from this regression, $\hat{z}_t$. The result, given in the final row of Table 16.3, is $-3.15$. This value is smaller than the 10% critical value (which is $-3.12$) but not smaller than the 5% critical value ($-3.41$), so the null hypothesis of no cointegration is rejected at the 10% significance level but not the 5% significance level. An interpretation of this result is that the EG-ADF test, which uses an estimated value of $\theta$, is less powerful than the test that uses what is arguably the correct value of $\theta = 1$.

*A vector error correction model of the two interest rates.* If $Y_t$ and $X_t$ are cointegrated, then forecasts of $\Delta Y_t$ and $\Delta X_t$ can be improved by augmenting a VAR of $\Delta Y_t$ and $\Delta X_t$ by the lagged value of the error correction term—that is, by computing forecasts using the VECM in Equations (16.22) and (16.23). If $\theta$ is known, then the unknown coefficients of the VECM can be estimated by OLS, including $z_{t-1} = Y_{t-1} - \theta X_{t-1}$ as an additional regressor. If $\theta$ is unknown, then the VECM can be estimated using $\hat{z}_{t-1}$ as a regressor, where $\hat{z}_t = Y_t - \hat{\theta} X_t$, and where $\hat{\theta}$ is an estimator of $\theta$.

In the application to the two interest rates, theory suggests that $\theta = 1$, and the unit root tests support modeling the two interest rates as cointegrated with a cointegrating coefficient of 1. We therefore specify the VECM using the theoretically suggested value of $\theta = 1$—that is, by adding the lagged value of the term spread, $R10y - R3m$, to a VAR in $\Delta R10y_t$ and $\Delta R3m_t$. Specified with two lags of first differences, the resulting VECM is

$$\widehat{\Delta R3m}_t = \underset{(0.12)}{-0.06} + \underset{(0.13)}{0.24\Delta R3m_{t-1}} - \underset{(0.18)}{0.16\Delta R3m_{t-2}} + \underset{(0.20)}{0.11\Delta R10y_{t-1}}$$

$$\underset{(0.15)}{-0.15\Delta R10y_{t-2}} + \underset{(0.05)}{0.03(R10y_{t-1} - R3m_{t-1})} \tag{16.27}$$

$$\widehat{\Delta R10y_t} = 0.12 - 0.00\Delta R3m_{t-1} - 0.07\Delta R3m_{t-2} + 0.22\Delta R10y_{t-1}$$
$$\phantom{\widehat{\Delta R10y_t} =} (0.06) \quad (0.09) \phantom{\Delta R3m_{t-1}} (0.07) \phantom{\Delta R3m_{t-2}} (0.11)$$

$$-0.07\Delta R10y_{t-2} - 0.09(R10y_{t-1} - R3m_{t-1}). \qquad (16.28)$$
$$(0.09) \phantom{\Delta R10y_{t-2}} (0.03)$$

In Equation (16.27), none of the coefficients is individually significant at the 5% level, and the coefficients on the lagged first differences of the interest rates are not jointly significant at the 5% level. In Equation (16.28), the coefficients on the lagged first differences are not jointly significant, but the coefficient on the lagged spread (the error correction term), which is estimated to be $-0.09$, has a $t$-statistic of $-2.74$, so it is statistically significant at the 1% level. Although lagged values of the first difference of the interest rates are not useful for predicting future interest rates, the lagged spread does help predict the change in the 10-year Treasury bond rate. When the 10-year rate exceeds the 3-month rate, the 10-year rate is forecasted to fall in the future.

## 16.5 Volatility Clustering and Autoregressive Conditional Heteroskedasticity

The phenomenon that some times are tranquil while others are not—that is, that volatility comes in clusters—shows up in many economic time series. This section presents a pair of models for quantifying volatility clustering or, as it is also known, conditional heteroskedasticity.

### Volatility Clustering

The volatility of many financial and macroeconomic variables changes over time. For example, daily percentage changes in the Wilshire 5000 stock price index, shown in Figure 16.3, exhibit periods of high volatility, such as in 2001 and 2008, and other periods of low volatility, such as in 2004. A series with some periods of low volatility and some periods of high volatility is said to exhibit **volatility clustering**. Because the volatility appears in clusters, the variance of the daily percentage price change in the Wilshire 5000 index can be forecasted, even though the daily price change itself is very difficult to forecast.

Forecasting the variance of a series is of interest for several reasons. First, the variance of an asset price is a measure of the risk of owning that asset: The larger

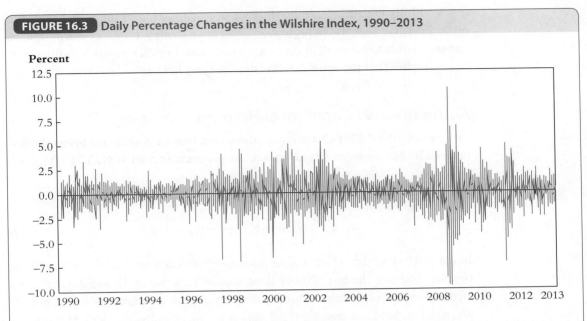

**FIGURE 16.3**   Daily Percentage Changes in the Wilshire Index, 1990–2013

Daily percentage price changes in the Wilshire 5000 index exhibit volatility clustering, in which there are some periods of high volatility, such as in 2008, and other periods of relative tranquility, such as in 2004.

the variance of daily stock price changes, the more a stock market participant stands to gain—or lose—on a typical day. An investor who is worried about risk would be less tolerant of participating in the stock market during a period of high—rather than low—volatility.

Second, the value of some financial derivatives, such as options, depends on the variance of the underlying asset. An options trader wants the best available forecasts of future volatility to help him or her know the price at which to buy or sell options.

Third, forecasting variances makes it possible to have accurate forecast intervals. Suppose that you are forecasting the rate of inflation. If the variance of the forecast error is constant, then an approximate forecast confidence interval can be constructed along the lines discussed in Section 14.4—that is, as the forecast plus or minus a multiple of the *SER*. If, however, the variance of the forecast error changes over time, then the width of the forecast interval should change over time: At periods when inflation is subject to particularly large disturbances or shocks, the interval should be wide; during periods of relative tranquility, the interval should be tighter.

Volatility clustering can be thought of as clustering of the variance of the error term over time: If the regression error has a small variance in one period, its variance tends to be small in the next period, too. In other words, volatility clustering implies that the error exhibits time-varying heteroskedasticity.

## Autoregressive Conditional Heteroskedasticity

Two models of volatility clustering are the **autoregressive conditional heteroskedasticity (ARCH)** model and its extension, the **generalized ARCH (GARCH)** model.

*ARCH.* Consider the ADL(1,1) regression

$$Y_t = \beta_0 + \beta_1 Y_{t-1} + \gamma_1 X_{t-1} + u_t. \tag{16.29}$$

In the ARCH model, which was developed by the econometrician Robert Engle (Engle, 1982; see the box "Nobel Laureates in Time Series Econometrics"), the error $u_t$ is modeled as being normally distributed with mean zero and variance $\sigma_t^2$, where $\sigma_t^2$ depends on past squared values $u_t$. Specifically, the ARCH model of order $p$, denoted ARCH($p$), is

$$\sigma_t^2 = \alpha_0 + \alpha_1 u_{t-1}^2 + \alpha_2 u_{t-2}^2 + \cdots + \alpha_p u_{t-p}^2, \tag{16.30}$$

where $\alpha_0, \alpha_1, \ldots, \alpha_p$ are unknown coefficients. If these coefficients are positive, then if recent squared errors are large, the ARCH model predicts that the current squared error will be large in magnitude, in the sense that its variance, $\sigma_t^2$, is large.

Although it is described here for the ADL(1,1) model in Equation (16.29), the ARCH model can be applied to the error variance of any time series regression model with an error that has a conditional mean of zero, including higher-order ADL models, autoregressions, and time series regressions with multiple predictors.

*GARCH.* The generalized ARCH (GARCH) model, developed by the econometrician Tim Bollerslev (Bollerslev, 1986), extends the ARCH model to let $\sigma_t^2$ depend on its own lags as well as lags of the squared error. The GARCH($p,q$) model is

$$\sigma_t^2 = \alpha_0 + \alpha_1 u_{t-1}^2 + \cdots + \alpha_p u_{t-p}^2 + \phi_1 \sigma_{t-1}^2 + \cdots + \phi_q \sigma_{t-q}^2, \tag{16.31}$$

where $\alpha_0, \alpha_1, \ldots, \alpha_p, \phi_1, \ldots, \phi_q$ are unknown coefficients.

The ARCH model is analogous to a distributed lag model, and the GARCH model is analogous to an ADL model. As discussed in Appendix 15.2, the ADL model (when appropriate) can provide a more parsimonious model of dynamic multipliers than can the distributed lag model. Similarly, by incorporating lags of $\sigma_t^2$, the GARCH model can capture slowly changing variances with fewer parameters than the ARCH model.

An important application of ARCH and GARCH models is to measuring and forecasting the time-varying volatility of returns on financial assets, particularly assets observed at high sampling frequencies such as the daily stock returns in Figure 16.3. In such applications, the return itself is often modeled as unpredictable, so the regression in Equation (16.29) only includes the intercept.

*Estimation and inference.*  ARCH and GARCH models are estimated by the method of maximum likelihood (Appendix 11.2). The estimators of the ARCH and GARCH coefficients are normally distributed in large samples, so in large samples, $t$-statistics have standard normal distributions, and confidence intervals can be constructed as the maximum likelihood estimate $\pm 1.96$ standard errors.

## Application to Stock Price Volatility

A GARCH(1,1) model of the Wilshire daily percentage stock price changes, $R_t$, estimated using data on all trading days from January 2, 1990, through December 31, 2013, is

$$\hat{R}_t = 0.057 \tag{16.32}$$
$$(0.010)$$

$$\hat{\sigma}_t^2 = 0.011 + 0.082\, u_{t-1}^2 + 0.908\sigma_{t-1}^2. \tag{16.33}$$
$$(0.002) \quad (0.007) \qquad (0.008)$$

No lagged predictors appear in Equation (16.32) because daily Wilshire 5000 percentage price changes are essentially unpredictable.

The two coefficients in the GARCH model (the coefficients on $u_{t-1}^2$ and $\sigma_{t-1}^2$) are both individually statistically significant at the 5% significance level. One measure of the persistence of movements in the variance is the sum of the coefficients on $u_{t-1}^2$ and $\sigma_{t-1}^2$ in the GARCH model (Exercise 16.9). This sum (0.99) is large, indicating that changes in the conditional variance are persistent. Said

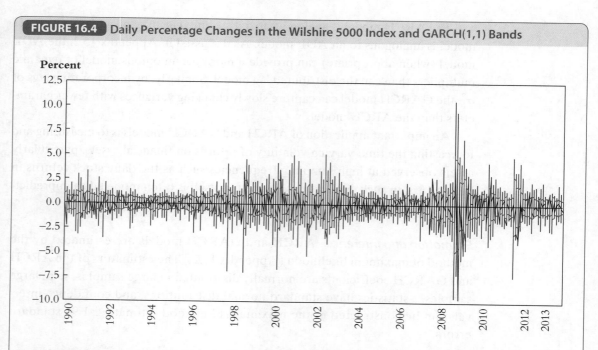

**FIGURE 16.4** Daily Percentage Changes in the Wilshire 5000 Index and GARCH(1,1) Bands

The GARCH(1,1) bands, which are $\pm \hat{\sigma}_t$, where $\hat{\sigma}_t$ is computed using Equation (16.33), are narrow when the conditional variance is small and wide when it is large. The conditional volatility of stock price changes varies considerably over the 1990–2013 period.

differently, the estimated GARCH model implies that periods of high volatility in stock prices will be long-lasting. This implication is consistent with the long periods of volatility clustering seen in Figure 16.3.

The estimated conditional variance at date $t$, $\hat{\sigma}_t^2$, can be computed using the residuals from Equation (16.32) and the coefficients in Equation (16.33). Figure 16.4 plots bands of plus or minus one conditional standard deviation (that is, $\pm \hat{\sigma}_t$), based on the GARCH(1,1) model, along with deviations of the percentage price change series from its mean. The conditional standard deviation bands quantify the time-varying volatility of the daily price changes. During the mid-1990s, the conditional standard deviation bands are tight, indicating lower levels of risk for investors holding a portfolio of stocks making up the Wilshire index. In contrast, during 2008, these conditional standard deviation bands are wide, indicating a period of greater daily stock price volatility.

## Nobel Laureates in Time Series Econometrics

In 2003 Robert Engle and Clive Granger won the Nobel Prize in economics for fundamental theoretical research in time series econometrics. Engle's work was motivated by the volatility clustering evident in plots like Figure 16.3. Engle wondered whether series like these could be stationary and whether econometric models could be developed to explain and predict their time-varying volatility. Engle's answer was to develop the autoregressive conditional heteroskedasticity (ARCH) model, described in Section 16.5. The ARCH model and

Clive W. J. Granger

Robert F. Engle

its extensions proved especially useful for modeling the volatility of asset returns, and the resulting volatility forecasts are used to price financial derivatives and to assess changes over time in the risk of holding financial assets. Today, measures and forecasts of volatility are a core component of financial econometrics, and the ARCH model and its descendants are the workhorse tools for modeling volatility.

Granger's work focused on how to handle stochastic trends in economic time series data. From his earlier work, he knew that two unrelated series with stochastic trends could, by the usual statistical measures of $t$-statistics and regression $R^2$'s, falsely appear to be meaningfully related; this is the "spurious regression" problem exemplified by the regressions in Equations (14.28) and (14.29). But are all regressions involving stochastic trending variables

spurious? Granger discovered that when variables shared common trends—in his terminology, were "co-integrated"—meaningful relationships could be uncovered by regression analysis using a vector error correction model. The methods of cointegration analysis are now a staple in modern macroeconometrics.

In 2011, Thomas Sargent and Christopher Sims won the Nobel Prize for their empirical research on cause and effect in the macroeconomy. Sargent was recognized for developing models that featured the important role that expectations about the future play in disentangling cause and effect. Sims was recognized for developing structural VAR (SVAR) models. Sims's key insight concerned the forecast errors in a VAR model—the $u_t$ errors in Equations (16.1) and (16.2). These errors, he realized, arose because of unforeseen "shocks" that buffeted the macroeconomy, and in many cases, these shocks had well defined sources like OPEC (oil price shocks), the

Christopher A. Sims

Lars Peter Hansen

Fed (interest rate shocks), or Congress (tax shocks). By disentangling the various sources of shocks that comprise the VAR errors, Sims was able to estimate the dynamic causal effect of these shocks on the variables appearing in the VAR. This disentangling of shocks is never without controversy, but SVARs are now a standard tool for estimating dynamic causal effects in macroeconomics.

*continued on next page*

In 2013, Eugene Fama, Lars Peter Hansen, and Robert Shiller won the Nobel Prize for their empirical analysis of asset prices. The work in the two "Can You Beat the Market" boxes in Chapter 14 and the box "Commodity Traders Send Shivers Through Disney World" in Chapter 15 was motivated in part by the "efficient markets" (unpredictability) work of Fama and the "irrational exuberance" (unexplained volatility) work of Shiller. Hansen was honored for developing "Generalized Method of Moments" (GMM) methods to investigate whether asset returns are consistent with expected utility theory. Microeconomics says that investors should equate the marginal cost of an investment (today's foregone utility from investing rather than consuming) with its marginal benefit (tomorrow's boost in utility from consumption financed by the investment's return). But a simple test of this proposition is complicated because marginal utility is difficult to measure, asset returns are uncertain, and the argument should hold across all asset returns. Hansen developed GMM methods to test asset-pricing models. As it turned out, Hansen's GMM methods had applications well beyond finance and are now widely used in econometrics. Section 18.7 introduces GMM.

For more information on these and other Nobel laureates in economics, visit the Nobel Foundation website, **http://www.nobel.se/economics**.

## 16.6 Conclusion

This part of the book has covered some of the most frequently used tools and concepts of time series regression. Many other tools for analyzing economic time series have been developed for specific applications. If you are interested in learning more about economic forecasting, see the introductory textbooks by Diebold (2007) and Enders (2009). For an advanced treatment of econometrics with time series data, see Hamilton (1994) and Hayashi (2000).

### Summary

1. Vector autoregressions model a "vector" of $k$ time series variables as each depends on its own lags and the lags of the $k - 1$ other series. The forecasts of each of the time series produced by a VAR are mutually consistent, in the sense that they are based on the same information.

2. Forecasts two or more periods ahead can be computed either by iterating forward a one-step-ahead model (an AR or a VAR) or by estimating a multiperiod-ahead regression.

3. Two series that share a common stochastic trend are cointegrated; that is, $Y_t$ and $X_t$ are cointegrated if $Y_t$ and $X_t$ are $I(1)$ but $Y_t - \theta X_t$ is $I(0)$. If $Y_t$ and

$X_t$ are cointegrated, the error correction term $Y_t - \theta X_t$ can help predict $\Delta Y_t$ and/or $\Delta X_t$. A vector error correction model is a VAR model of $\Delta Y_t$ and $\Delta X_t$, augmented to include the lagged error correction term.

4. Volatility clustering—in which the variance of a series is high in some periods and low in others—is common in economic time series, especially financial time series.

5. The ARCH model of volatility clustering expresses the conditional variance of the regression error as a function of recent squared regression errors. The GARCH model augments the ARCH model to include lagged conditional variances as well. Estimated ARCH and GARCH models produce forecast intervals with widths that depend on the volatility of the most recent regression residuals.

## Key Terms

vector autoregression (VAR) (685)
iterated multiperiod AR forecast (692)
iterated multiperiod VAR forecast (692)
direct multiperiod forecast (694)
second difference (695)
integrated of order $d[I(d)]$ (696)
integrated of order zero $[I(0)]$, one $[I(1)]$, or two $[I(2)]$ (696)
order of integration (696)
DF-GLS test (697)
common trend (702)

cointegration (703)
cointegrating coefficient (703)
error correction term (704)
vector error correction model (VECM) (704)
EG-ADF test (705)
dynamic OLS (DOLS) estimator (706)
volatility clustering (710)
autoregressive conditional heteroskedasticity (ARCH) (712)
generalized ARCH (GARCH) (712)

**MyEconLab Can Help You Get a Better Grade**

**MyEconLab**  If your exam were tomorrow, would you be ready? For each chapter, **MyEconLab** Practice Tests and Study Plan help you prepare for your exams. You can also find similar Exercises and Review the Concepts Questions now in **MyEconLab**. To see how it works, turn to the **MyEconLab** spread on pages 2 and 3 of this book and then go to **www.myeconlab.com**.

For additional Empirical Exercises and Data Sets, log on to the Companion Website at **www.pearsonglobaleditions.com/Stock_Watson**.

## Review the Concepts

**16.1**  A macroeconomist wants to construct forecasts for the following macroeconomic variables: GDP, consumption, investment, government purchases, exports, imports, short-term interest rates, long-term interest rates, and the rate of price inflation. He has quarterly time series for each of these variables from 1970 to 2014. Should he estimate a VAR for these variables and use this for forecasting? Why or why not? Can you suggest an alternative approach?

**16.2**  Suppose that $Y_t$ follows a stationary AR(1) model with $\beta_0 = 0$ and $\beta_1 = 0.5$. If $Y_t = 10$, what is your forecast of $Y_{t+2}$ (that is, what is $Y_{t+2|t}$)? What is $Y_{t+h|t}$ for $h = 20$? Does this forecast for $h = 20$ seem reasonable to you?

**16.3**  A version of the permanent income theory of consumption implies that the logarithm of real GDP ($Y$) and the logarithm of real consumption ($C$) are cointegrated with a cointegrating coefficient equal to 1. Explain how you would investigate this implication by (a) plotting the data and (b) using a statistical test.

**16.4**  What is meant by volatility clustering? Briefly describe two models that are used to describe data processes with volatility clustering.

**16.5**  What is a unit root? How does a researcher test for the presence of a unit root $n$ in the data?

## Exercises

**16.1**  Suppose that $Y_t$ follows a stationary AR(1) model, $Y_t = \beta_0 + \beta_1 Y_{t-1} + u_t$.

**a.**  Show that the $h$-period-ahead forecast of $Y_t$ is given by $Y_{t+h|t} = \mu_Y + \beta_1^h(Y_t - \mu_Y)$, where $\mu_Y = \beta_0/(1 - \beta_1)$.

**b.**  Suppose that $X_t$ is related to $Y_t$ by $X_t = \sum_{i=0}^{\infty} \delta^i Y_{t+i|t}$, where $|\delta| < 1$. Show that $X_t = [\mu_Y/(1 - \delta)] + [(Y_t - \mu_Y)/(1 - \beta_1\delta)]$.

**16.2**  One version of the expectations theory of the term structure of interest rates holds that a long-term rate equals the average of the expected values of short-term interest rates into the future, plus a term premium that is $I(0)$. Specifically, let $Rk_t$ denote a $k$-period interest rate, let $R1_t$ denote a one-period interest rate, and let $e_t$ denote an $I(0)$ term premium. Then $Rk_t = \frac{1}{k}\sum_{i=0}^{k-1} R1_{t+i|t} + e_t$, where $R1_{t+i|t}$ is the forecast made at date $t$ of the value of $R1$ at date $t + i$. Suppose that $R1_t$ follows a random walk so that $R1_t = R1_{t-1} + u_t$.

**a.** Show that $Rk_t = R1_t + e_t$.

**b.** Show that $Rk_t$ and $R1_t$ are cointegrated. What is the cointegrating coefficient?

**c.** Now suppose that $\Delta R1_t = 0.5\Delta R1_{t-1} + u_t$. How does your answer to (b) change?

**d.** Now suppose that $R1_t = 0.5R1_{t-1} + u_t$. How does your answer to (b) change?

**16.3** Suppose that $u_t$ follows the ARCH process, $\sigma_t^2 = 1.0 + 0.5u_{t-1}^2$.

**a.** Let $E(u_t^2) = \text{var}(u_t)$ be the unconditional variance of $u_t$. Show that $\text{var}(u_t) = 2$. (*Hint:* Use the law of iterated expectations, $E(u_t^2) = E[E(u_t^2|u_{t-1})]$.)

**b.** Suppose that the distribution of $u_t$ conditional on lagged values of $u_t$ is $N(0, \sigma_t^2)$. If $u_{t-1} = 0.2$, what is $\Pr(-3 \le u_t \le 3)$? If $u_{t-1} = 2.0$, what is $\Pr(-3 \le u_t \le 3)$?

**16.4** Suppose that $Y_t$ follows the AR($p$) model $Y_t = \beta_0 + \beta_1 Y_{t-1} + \cdots + \beta_p Y_{t-p} + u_t$, where $E(u_t|Y_{t-1}, Y_{t-2}, \dots) = 0$ Let $Y_{t+h|t} = E(Y_{t+h}|Y_t, Y_{t-1}, \dots)$. Show that $Y_{t+h|t} = \beta_0 + \beta_1 Y_{t-1+h|t} + \cdots + \beta_p Y_{t-p+h|t}$ for $h > p$.

**16.5** Verify Equation (16.20). [*Hint:* Use $\sum_{t=1}^{T} Y_t^2 = \sum_{t=1}^{T}(Y_{t-1} + \Delta Y_t)^2$ to show that $\sum_{t=1}^{T} Y_t^2 = \sum_{t=1}^{T} Y_{t-1}^2 + 2\sum_{t=1}^{T} Y_{t-1}\Delta Y_t + \sum_{t=1}^{T}\Delta Y_t^2$ and solve for $\sum_{t=1}^{T} Y_{t-1}\Delta Y_t$.]

**16.6** A regression of $Y_t$ onto current, past, and future values of $X_t$ yields

$$Y_t = 2.0 + 1.5X_{t+1} + 0.9X_t - 0.3X_{t-1} + u_t.$$

**a.** Rearrange the regression so that it has the form shown in Equation (16.25). What are the values of $\theta$, $\delta_{-1}$, $\delta_0$, and $\delta_1$?

**b.** i. Suppose that $X_t$ is $I(0)$ and $u_t$ is $I(0)$. Are $Y$ and $X$ cointegrated?

ii. Suppose that $X_t$ is $I(1)$ and $Y_t$ is $I(1)$. Are $Y$ and $X$ cointegrated?

iii. Suppose that $X_t$ is $I(1)$ and $u_t$ is $I(0)$. Are $Y$ and $X$ cointegrated?

**16.7** Suppose that $\Delta Y_t = u_t$, where $u_t$ is i.i.d. $N(0, 1)$, and consider the regression $Y_t = \beta X_t + error$, where $X_t = \Delta Y_{t+1}$ and *error* is the regression error.

Show that $\hat{\beta} \xrightarrow{d} \frac{1}{2}(\chi_1^2 - 1)$. [*Hint:* Analyze the numerator of $\hat{\beta}$ using analysis like that in Equation (16.21). Analyze the denominator using the law of large numbers.]

**16.8** Consider the following two-variable VAR model with one lag and no intercept:

$$Y_t = \beta_{11}Y_{t-1} + \gamma_{11}X_{t-1} + u_{1t}$$
$$X_t = \beta_{21}Y_{t-1} + \gamma_{21}X_{t-1} + u_{2t}.$$

**a.** Show that the iterated two-period-ahead forecast for $Y$ can be written as $Y_{t|t-2} = \delta_1 Y_{t-2} + \delta_2 X_{t-2}$ and derive values for $\delta_1$ and $\delta_2$ in terms of the coefficients in the VAR.

**b.** In light of your answer to (a), do iterated multiperiod forecasts differ from direct multiperiod forecasts? Explain.

**16.9 a.** Suppose that $E(u_t|u_{t-1}, u_{t-2}, \ldots) = 0$, that $\text{var}(u_t|u_{t-1}, u_{t-2}, \ldots)$ follows the ARCH(1) model $\sigma_t^2 = \alpha_0 + \alpha_1 u_{t-1}^2$, and that the process for $u_t$ is stationary. Show that $\text{var}(u_t) = \alpha_0/(1 - \alpha_1)$. (*Hint:* Use the law of iterated expectations $E(u_t^2) = E[E(u_t^2|u_{t-1})]$.)

**b.** Extend the result in (a) to the ARCH($p$) model.

**c.** Show that $\sum_{i=1}^{p}\alpha_i < 1$ for a stationary ARCH($p$) model.

**d.** Extend the result in (a) to the GARCH(1,1) model.

**e.** Show that $\alpha_1 + \phi_1 < 1$ for a stationary GARCH(1,1) model.

**16.10** Consider the cointegrated model $Y_t = \theta X_t + v_{1t}$ and $X_t = X_{t-1} + v_{2t}$, where $v_{1t}$ and $v_{2t}$ are mean zero serially uncorrelated random variables with $E(v_{1t}v_{2j}) = 0$ for all $t$ and $j$. Derive the vector error correction model [Equations (16.22) and (16.23)] for $X$ and $Y$.

## Empirical Exercises

(Only two empirical exercises for this chapter are given in the text, but you can find more on the text website, **www.pearsonglobaleditions.com/Stock_Watson**.)

**E16.1** This exercise is an extension of Empirical Exercise 14.1. On the text website, **www.pearsonglobaleditions.com/Stock_Watson**, you will find the data file **USMacro_Quarterly**, which contains quarterly data on several macroeconomic series for the United States; the data are described in the file **USMacro_Description**. Compute inflation, *Infl*, using the price index for personal consumption expenditures. For all regressions use the sample period 1963:Q1–2012:Q4 (where data before 1963 may be used as initial values for lags in regressions).

**a.** Using the data on inflation through 2012:Q4 and an estimated AR(2) model:

    i.  Forecast $\Delta Infl_{2013:Q1}$, the change in inflation from 2012:Q4 to 2013:Q1.

    ii.  Forecast $\Delta Infl_{2013:Q2}$, the change in inflation from 2013:Q1 to 2013:Q2. (Use an iterated forecast.)

    iii.  Forecast $Infl_{2013:Q2} - Infl_{2012:Q4}$, the change in inflation from 2012:Q4 to 2013:Q2.

    iv.  Forecast $Infl_{2013:Q2}$, the level of inflation in 2013:Q2.

**b.** Repeat (a) using the direct forecasting method.

**c.** In Exercise 14.1 you carried out an ADF test for a unit root in the autoregression for *Infl*. Now carry out the unit root test using the DF-GLS test. Are the conclusions based on the DF-GLS test the same as you reached using the ADF test? Explain.

**E16.2** On the text website, **www.pearsonglobaleditions.com/Stock_Watson**, you will find the data file **USMacro_Quarterly**, which contains quarterly data on real GDP, measured in $1996. Compute $GDPGR_t = 400 \times [\ln(GDP_t) - \ln(GDP_{t-1})]$, the growth rate of GDP.

**a.** Using data on $GDPGR_t$ from 1960:1 to 2012:4, estimate an AR(2) model with GARCH(1,1) errors.

**b.** Plot the residuals from the AR(2) model along with $\pm \hat{\sigma}_t$ bands as in Figure 16.4.

**c.** Some macroeconomists have claimed that there was a sharp drop in the variability of the growth rate of GDP around 1983, which they call the "Great Moderation." Is this Great Moderation evident in the plot that you formed in (b)?

# The Theory of Linear Regression with One Regressor

W hy should an applied econometrician bother learning any econometric theory? There are several reasons. Learning econometric theory turns your statistical software from a "black box" into a flexible tool kit from which you are able to select the right tool for the job at hand. Understanding econometric theory helps you appreciate why these tools work and what assumptions are required for each tool to work properly. Perhaps most importantly, knowing econometric theory helps you recognize when a tool will *not* work well in an application and when you should look for a different econometric approach.

This chapter provides an introduction to the econometric theory of linear regression with a single regressor. This introduction is intended to supplement—not replace—the material in Chapters 4 and 5, which should be read first.

This chapter extends Chapters 4 and 5 in two ways.

First, it provides a mathematical treatment of the sampling distribution of the OLS estimator and *t*-statistic, both in large samples under the three least squares assumptions of Key Concept 4.3 and in finite samples under the two additional assumptions of homoskedasticity and normal errors. These five extended least squares assumptions are laid out in Section 17.1. Sections 17.2 and 17.3, augmented by Appendix 17.2, mathematically develop the large-sample normal distributions of the OLS estimator and *t*-statistic under the first three assumptions (the least squares assumptions of Key Concept 4.3). Section 17.4 derives the exact distributions of the OLS estimator and *t*-statistic under the two additional assumptions of homoskedasticity and normally distributed errors.

Second, this chapter extends Chapters 4 and 5 by providing an alternative method for handling heteroskedasticity. The approach of Chapters 4 and 5 is to use heteroskedasticity-robust standard errors to ensure that statistical inference is valid even if the errors are heteroskedastic. This method comes with a cost, however: If the errors are heteroskedastic, then in theory a more efficient estimator than OLS is available. This estimator, called weighted least squares, is presented in Section 17.5. Weighted least squares requires a great deal of prior knowledge about the precise nature of the heteroskedasticity—that is, about the conditional variance of $u$ given $X$. When such knowledge is available, weighted least squares improves upon OLS. In most applications, however, such knowledge is unavailable; in those cases, using OLS with heteroskedasticity-robust standard errors is the preferred method.

# 17.1 The Extended Least Squares Assumptions and the OLS Estimator

This section introduces a set of assumptions that extend and strengthen the three least squares assumptions of Chapter 4. These stronger assumptions are used in subsequent sections to derive stronger theoretical results about the OLS estimator than are possible under the weaker (but more realistic) assumptions of Chapter 4.

## The Extended Least Squares Assumptions

*Extended least squares Assumptions #1, #2, and #3.* The first three extended least squares assumptions are the three assumptions given in Key Concept 4.3: that the conditional mean of $u_i$, given $X_i$, is zero; that $(X_i, Y_i), i = 1, \ldots, n$, are i.i.d. draws from their joint distribution; and that $X_i$ and $u_i$ have four moments.

Under these three assumptions, the OLS estimator is unbiased, is consistent, and has an asymptotically normal sampling distribution. If these three assumptions hold, then the methods for inference introduced in Chapter 4—hypothesis testing using the $t$-statistic and construction of 95% confidence intervals as $\pm 1.96$ standard errors—are justified when the sample size is large. To develop a theory of efficient estimation using OLS or to characterize the exact sampling distribution of the OLS estimator, however, requires stronger assumptions.

*Extended least squares Assumption #4.* The fourth extended least squares assumption is that $u_i$ is homoskedastic; that is, $\text{var}(u_i|X_i) = \sigma_u^2$, where $\sigma_u^2$ is a constant. As seen in Section 5.5, if this additional assumption holds, then the OLS estimator is efficient among all linear estimators that are unbiased, conditional on $X_1, \ldots, X_n$.

*Extended least squares Assumption #5.* The fifth extended least squares assumption is that the conditional distribution of $u_i$, given $X_i$, is normal.

Under least squares Assumptions #1 and #2 and the extended least squares Assumptions #4 and #5, $u_i$ is i.i.d. $N(0, \sigma_u^2)$, and $u_i$ and $X_i$ are independently distributed. To see this, note that the fifth extended least squares assumption states that the conditional distribution of $u_i|X_i$ is $N(0, \text{var}(u_i|X_i))$, where the distribution has mean zero by the first extended least squares assumption. By the fourth least

**KEY CONCEPT**

**17.1**

## The Extended Least Squares Assumptions for Regression with a Single Regressor

The linear regression model with a single regressor is

$$Y_i = \beta_0 + \beta_1 X_i + u_i, i = 1, \ldots, n. \qquad (17.1)$$

The extended least squares assumptions are

1. $E(u_i|X_i) = 0$ (conditional mean zero);
2. $(X_i, Y_i), i = 1, \ldots, n,$ are independent and identically distributed (i.i.d.) draws from their joint distribution;
3. $(X_i, u_i)$ have nonzero finite fourth moments;
4. $\text{var}(u_i|X_i) = \sigma_u^2$ (homoskedasticity); and
5. The conditional distribution of $u_i$ given $X_i$ is normal (normal errors).

squares assumption, however, $\text{var}(u_i|X_i) = \sigma_u^2$, so the conditional distribution of $u_i|X_i$ is $N(0, \sigma_u^2)$. Because this conditional distribution does not depend on $X_i$, $u_i$ and $X_i$ are independently distributed. By the second least squares assumption, $u_i$ is distributed independently of $u_j$ for all $j \neq i$. It follows that, under the extended least squares Assumptions #1, #2, #4, and #5, $u_i$ and $X_i$ are independently distributed and $u_i$ is i.i.d. $N(0, \sigma_u^2)$.

It is shown in Section 17.4 that, if all five extended least squares assumptions hold, the OLS estimator has an exact normal sampling distribution and the homoskedasticity-only $t$-statistic has an exact Student $t$ distribution.

The fourth and fifth extended least squares assumptions are much more restrictive than the first three. Although it might be reasonable to assume that the first three assumptions hold in an application, the final two assumptions are less realistic. Even though these final two assumptions might not hold in practice, they are of theoretical interest because if one or both of them hold, then the OLS estimator has additional properties beyond those discussed in Chapters 4 and 5. Thus we can enhance our understanding of the OLS estimator and the theory of estimation in the linear regression model by exploring estimation under these stronger assumptions.

The five extended least squares assumptions for the single-regressor model are summarized in Key Concept 17.1.

### The OLS Estimator

For easy reference, we restate the OLS estimators of $\beta_0$ and $\beta_1$ here:

$$\hat{\beta}_1 = \frac{\sum_{i=1}^{n}(X_i - \overline{X})(Y_i - \overline{Y})}{\sum_{i=1}^{n}(X_i - \overline{X})^2} \qquad (17.2)$$

$$\hat{\beta}_0 = \overline{Y} - \hat{\beta}_1\overline{X}. \qquad (17.3)$$

Equations (17.2) and (17.3) are derived in Appendix 4.2.

## 17.2 Fundamentals of Asymptotic Distribution Theory

Asymptotic distribution theory is the theory of the distribution of statistics—estimators, test statistics, and confidence intervals—when the sample size is large. Formally, this theory involves characterizing the behavior of the sampling distribution of a statistic along a sequence of ever-larger samples. The theory is asymptotic in the sense that it characterizes the behavior of the statistic in the limit as $n \to \infty$.

Even though sample sizes are, of course, never infinite, asymptotic distribution theory plays a central role in econometrics and statistics for two reasons. First, if the number of observations used in an empirical application is large, then the asymptotic limit can provide a high-quality approximation to the finite sample distribution. Second, asymptotic sampling distributions typically are much simpler, and thus easier to use in practice, than exact finite-sample distributions. Taken together, these two reasons mean that reliable and straightforward methods for statistical inference—tests using $t$-statistics and 95% confidence intervals calculated as $\pm 1.96$ standard errors—can be based on approximate sampling distributions derived from asymptotic theory.

The two cornerstones of asymptotic distribution theory are the law of large numbers and the central limit theorem, both introduced in Section 2.6. We begin this section by continuing the discussion of the law of large numbers and the central limit theorem, including a proof of the law of large numbers. We then introduce two more tools, Slutsky's theorem and the continuous mapping theorem, that extend the usefulness of the law of large numbers and the central limit theorem. As an illustration, these tools are then used to prove that the distribution of the $t$-statistic based on $\overline{Y}$ testing the hypothesis $E(Y) = \mu_0$ has a standard normal distribution under the null hypothesis.

## Convergence in Probability and the Law of Large Numbers

The concepts of convergence in probability and the law of large numbers were introduced in Section 2.6. Here we provide a precise mathematical definition of convergence in probability, followed by a statement and proof of the law of large numbers.

*Consistency and convergence in probability.* Let $S_1, S_2, \ldots, S_n, \ldots$ be a sequence of random variables. For example, $S_n$ could be the sample average $\overline{Y}$ of a sample of $n$ observations of the random variable $Y$. The sequence of random variables $\{S_n\}$ is said to **converge in probability** to a limit, $\mu$ (that is, $S_n \xrightarrow{p} \mu$), if the probability that $S_n$ is within $\pm\delta$ of $\mu$ tends to 1 as $n \to \infty$, as long as the constant $\delta$ is positive. That is,

$$S_n \xrightarrow{p} \mu \text{ if and only if } \Pr(|S_n - \mu| \geq \delta) \longrightarrow 0 \qquad (17.4)$$

as $n \to \infty$ for every $\delta > 0$. If $S_n \xrightarrow{p} \mu$ then $S_n$ is said to be a **consistent estimator** of $\mu$.

*The law of large numbers.* The law of large numbers says that, under certain conditions on $Y_1, \ldots, Y_n$, the sample average $\overline{Y}$ converges in probability to the population mean. Probability theorists have developed many versions of the law of large numbers, corresponding to various conditions on $Y_1, \ldots, Y_n$. The version of the law of large numbers used in this book is that $Y_1, \ldots, Y_n$ are i.i.d. draws from a distribution with finite variance. This law of large numbers (also stated in Key Concept 2.6) is

$$\text{if } Y_1, \ldots, Y_n \text{ are i.i.d., } E(Y_i) = \mu_Y, \text{ and var}(Y_i) < \infty, \text{ then } \overline{Y} \xrightarrow{p} \mu_Y. \quad (17.5)$$

The idea of the law of large numbers can be seen in Figure 2.8: As the sample size increases, the sampling distribution of $\overline{Y}$ concentrates around the population mean, $\mu_Y$. One feature of the sampling distribution is that the variance of $\overline{Y}$ decreases as the sample size increases; another feature is that the probability that $\overline{Y}$ falls outside $\pm\delta$ of $\mu_Y$ vanishes as $n$ increases. These two features of the sampling distribution are in fact linked, and the proof of the law of large numbers exploits this link.

*Proof of the law of large numbers.* The link between the variance of $\overline{Y}$ and the probability that $\overline{Y}$ is within $\pm\delta$ of $\mu_Y$ is provided by Chebychev's inequality, which is stated and proven in Appendix 17.2 [see Equation (17.42)]. Written in terms of $\overline{Y}$, Chebychev's inequality is

$$\Pr(|\overline{Y} - \mu_Y| \geq \delta) \leq \frac{\text{var}(\overline{Y})}{\delta^2}, \tag{17.6}$$

for any positive constant $\delta$. Because $Y_1, \ldots, Y_n$ are i.i.d. with variance $\sigma_Y^2$, $\text{var}(\overline{Y}) = \sigma_Y^2/n$; thus, for any $\delta > 0$, $\text{var}(\overline{Y})/\delta^2 = \sigma_Y^2/(\delta^2 n) \longrightarrow 0$. It follows from Equation (17.6) that $\Pr(|\overline{Y} - \mu_Y| \geq \delta) \longrightarrow 0$ for every $\delta > 0$, proving the law of large numbers.

*Some examples.* Consistency is a fundamental concept in asymptotic distribution theory, so we present some examples of consistent and inconsistent estimators of the population mean, $\mu_Y$. Suppose that $Y_i, i = 1, \ldots, n$ are i.i.d. with variance $\sigma_Y^2$ that is positive and finite. Consider the following three estimators of $\mu_Y$: (1) $m_a = Y_1$; (2) $m_b = (\frac{1 - a^n}{1 - a})^{-1} \sum_{i=1}^{n} a^{i-1} Y_i$, where $0 < a < 1$; and (3) $m_c = \overline{Y} + 1/n$. Are these estimators consistent?

The first estimator, $m_a$, is just the first observation, so $E(m_a) = E(Y_1) = \mu_Y$ and $m_a$ is unbiased. However, $m_a$ is not consistent: $\Pr(|m_a - \mu_Y| \geq \delta) = \Pr(|Y_1 - \mu_Y| \geq \delta)$, which must be positive for sufficiently small $\delta$ (because $\sigma_Y^2 > 0$), so $\Pr(|m_a - \mu_Y| \geq \delta)$ does not tend to zero as $n \to \infty$, so $m_a$ is not consistent. This inconsistency should not be surprising: Because $m_a$ uses the information in only one observation, its distribution cannot concentrate around $\mu_Y$ as the sample size increases.

The second estimator, $m_b$, is unbiased but is not consistent. It is unbiased because

$$E(m_b) = E\left[\left(\frac{1 - a^n}{1 - a}\right)^{-1} \sum_{i=1}^{n} a^{i-1} Y_i\right] = \left(\frac{1 - a^n}{1 - a}\right)^{-1} \sum_{i=1}^{n} a^{i-1} \mu_Y = \mu_Y,$$

$$\text{since } \sum_{i=1}^{n} a^{i-1} = \left(1 - a^n\right) \sum_{i=0}^{\infty} a^i = \frac{1 - a^n}{1 - a}.$$

The variance of $m_b$ is

$$\text{var}(m_b) = \left(\frac{1 - a^n}{1 - a}\right)^{-2} \sum_{i=1}^{n} a^{2(i-1)} \sigma_Y^2 = \sigma_Y^2 \frac{(1 - a^{2n})(1 - a)^2}{(1 - a^2)(1 - a^n)^2} = \sigma_Y^2 \frac{(1 + a^n)(1 - a)}{(1 - a^n)(1 + a)},$$

which has the limit $\text{var}(m_b) \to \sigma_Y^2 (1 - a)/(1 + a)$ as $n \to \infty$. Thus the variance of this estimator does not tend to zero, the distribution does not concentrate around $\mu_Y$, and the estimator, although unbiased, is not consistent. This is perhaps surprising, because all the observations enter this estimator. But most of the observations receive very small weight (the weight of the $i^{\text{th}}$ observation is proportional to $a^{i-1}$, a very small number when $i$ is large), and for this reason there is an insufficient amount of cancellation of sampling errors for the estimator to be consistent.

The third estimator, $m_c$, is biased but consistent. Its bias is $1/n$: $E(m_c) = E(\overline{Y} + 1/n) = \mu_Y + 1/n$, so the bias tends to zero as the sample size increases. To see why $m_c$ is consistent: $\Pr(|m_c - \mu_Y| \geq \delta) = \Pr(|\overline{Y} + 1/n - \mu_Y| \geq \delta)$. Now, from Equation (17.43) in Appendix 17.2, a generalization of Chebychev's inequality implies that for any random variable $W$, $\Pr(|W| \geq \delta) \leq E(W^2)/\delta^2$ for any positive constant $\delta$. Thus. $\Pr(|\overline{Y} + 1/n - \mu_Y| \geq \delta) \leq E[(\overline{Y} + 1/n - \mu_Y)^2]/\delta^2$. But $E[(\overline{Y} + 1/n - \mu_Y)^2] = \text{var}(\overline{Y}) + 1/n^2 = \sigma^2/n + 1/n^2 \longrightarrow 0$ as $n$ grows large. It follows that $\Pr(|\overline{Y} + 1/n - \mu_Y| \geq \delta) \longrightarrow 0$, and $m_c$ is consistent. This example illustrates the general point that an estimator can be biased in finite samples but, if that bias vanishes as the sample size gets large, the estimator can still be consistent (Exercise 17.10).

## The Central Limit Theorem and Convergence in Distribution

If the distributions of a sequence of random variables converge to a limit as $n \to \infty$, then the sequence of random variables is said to converge in distribution. The central limit theorem says that, under general conditions, the standardized sample average converges in distribution to a normal random variable.

*Convergence in distribution.* Let $F_1, F_2, \ldots, F_n, \ldots$ be a sequence of cumulative distribution functions corresponding to a sequence of random variables, $S_1, S_2, \ldots, S_n, \ldots$. For example, $S_n$ might be the standardized sample average, $(\overline{Y} - \mu_Y)/\sigma_{\overline{Y}}$. Then the sequence of random variables $S_n$ is said to **converge in distribution** to $S$ (denoted $S_n \xrightarrow{d} S$) if the distribution functions $\{F_n\}$ converge to $F$, the distribution of $S$. That is,

$$S_n \xrightarrow{d} S \text{ if and only if } \lim_{n \to \infty} F_n(t) = F(t), \tag{17.7}$$

where the limit holds at all points $t$ at which the limiting distribution $F$ is continuous. The distribution $F$ is called the **asymptotic distribution** of $S_n$.

It is useful to contrast the concepts of convergence in probability ($\xrightarrow{p}$) and convergence in distribution ($\xrightarrow{d}$). If $S_n \xrightarrow{p} \mu$, then $S_n$ becomes close to $\mu$ with high probability as $n$ increases. In contrast, if $S_n \xrightarrow{d} S$, then the *distribution* of $S_n$ becomes close to the *distribution* of $S$ as $n$ increases.

*The central limit theorem.* We now restate the central limit theorem using the concept of convergence in distribution. The central limit theorem in Key Concept 2.7 states that if $Y_1, \ldots, Y_n$ are i.i.d. and $0 < \sigma_Y^2 < \infty$, then the asymptotic distribution of $(\overline{Y} - \mu_Y)/\sigma_{\overline{Y}}$ is $N(0, 1)$. Because $\sigma_{\overline{Y}} = \sigma_Y/\sqrt{n}$, $(\overline{Y} - \mu_Y)/\sigma_{\overline{Y}} = \sqrt{n}(\overline{Y} - \mu_Y)/\sigma_Y$. Thus the central limit theorem can be restated as $\sqrt{n}(\overline{Y} - \mu_Y) \xrightarrow{d} \sigma_Y Z$, where $Z$ is a standard normal random variable. This means that the distribution of $\sqrt{n}(\overline{Y} - \mu_Y)$ converges to $N(0, \sigma_Y^2)$ as $n \longrightarrow \infty$. Conventional shorthand for this limit is

$$\sqrt{n}(\overline{Y} - \mu_Y) \xrightarrow{d} N(0, \sigma_Y^2). \tag{17.8}$$

That is, if $Y_1, \ldots, Y_n$ are i.i.d. and $0 < \sigma_Y^2 < \infty$, then the distribution of $\sqrt{n}(\overline{Y} - \mu_Y)$ converges to a normal distribution with mean zero and variance $\sigma_Y^2$.

*Extensions to time series data.* The law of large numbers and central limit theorem stated in Section 2.6 apply to i.i.d. observations. As discussed in Chapter 14, the i.i.d. assumption is inappropriate for time series data, and these theorems need to be extended before they can be applied to time series observations. Those extensions are technical in nature, in the sense that the conclusion is the same—versions of the law of large numbers and the central limit theorem apply to time series data—but the conditions under which they apply are different. This is discussed briefly in Section 16.4, but a mathematical treatment of asymptotic distribution theory for time series variables is beyond the scope of this book and interested readers are referred to Hayashi (2000, Chapter 2).

## Slutsky's Theorem and the Continuous Mapping Theorem

**Slutsky's theorem** combines consistency and convergence in distribution. Suppose that $a_n \xrightarrow{p} a$, where $a$ is a constant, and $S_n \xrightarrow{d} S$. Then

$$a_n + S_n \xrightarrow{d} a + S, a_n S_n \xrightarrow{d} aS, \text{ and, if } a \neq 0, S_n/a_n \xrightarrow{d} S/a. \tag{17.9}$$

These three results are together called Slutsky's theorem.

The **continuous mapping theorem** concerns the asymptotic properties of a continuous function, $g$, of a sequence of random variables, $S_n$. The theorem has two parts. The first is that if $S_n$ converges in probability to the constant $a$, then $g(S_n)$

converges in probability to $g(a)$; the second is that if $S_n$ converges in distribution to $S$, then $g(S_n)$ converges in distribution to $g(S)$. That is, if $g$ is a continuous function, then

$$\text{(i) if } S_n \xrightarrow{p} a, \text{ then } g(S_n) \xrightarrow{p} g(a), \text{ and}$$
$$\text{(ii) if } S_n \xrightarrow{d} S, \text{ then } g(S_n) \xrightarrow{d} g(S). \tag{17.10}$$

As an example of (i), if $s_Y^2 \xrightarrow{p} \sigma_Y^2$, then $\sqrt{s_Y^2} = s_Y \xrightarrow{p} \sigma_Y$. As an example of (ii), suppose that $S_n \xrightarrow{d} Z$, where $Z$ is a standard normal random variable, and let $g(S_n) = S_n^2$. Because $g$ is continuous, the continuous mapping theorem applies and $g(S_n) \xrightarrow{d} g(Z)$; that is, $S_n^2 \xrightarrow{d} Z^2$. In other words, the distribution of $S_n^2$ converges to the distribution of a squared standard normal random variable, which in turn has a $\chi_1^2$ distribution; that is, $S_n^2 \xrightarrow{d} \chi_1^2$.

## Application to the *t*-Statistic Based on the Sample Mean

We now use the central limit theorem, the law of large numbers, and Slutsky's theorem to prove that, under the null hypothesis, the *t*-statistic based on $\overline{Y}$ has a standard normal distribution when $Y_1, \ldots, Y_n$ are i.i.d. and $0 < E(Y_i^4) < \infty$.

The *t*-statistic for testing the null hypothesis that $E(Y_i) = \mu_0$ based on the sample average $\overline{Y}$ is given in Equations (3.8) and (3.11), and can be written

$$t = \frac{\overline{Y} - \mu_0}{s_Y/\sqrt{n}} = \frac{\sqrt{n}\,(\overline{Y} - \mu_0)}{\sigma_Y} \div \frac{s_Y}{\sigma_Y}, \tag{17.11}$$

where the second equality uses the trick of dividing both the numerator and the denominator by $\sigma_Y$.

Because $Y_1, \ldots, Y_n$ have two moments (which is implied by their having four moments; see Exercise 17.5), and because $Y_1, \ldots, Y_n$ are i.i.d., the first term after the final equality in Equation (17.11) obeys the central limit theorem: Under the null hypothesis, $\sqrt{n}(\overline{Y} - \mu_0)/\sigma_Y \xrightarrow{d} N(0, 1)$. In addition, $s_Y^2 \xrightarrow{p} \sigma_Y^2$ (as proven in Appendix 3.3), so $s_Y^2/\sigma_Y^2 \xrightarrow{p} 1$ and the ratio in the second term in Equation (17.11) tends to 1 (Exercise 17.4). Thus the expression after the final equality in Equation (17.11) has the form of the final expression in Equation (17.9), where [in the notation of Equation (17.9)] $S_n = \sqrt{n}(\overline{Y} - \mu_0)/\sigma_Y \xrightarrow{d} N(0, 1)$ and $a_n = s_Y/\sigma_Y \xrightarrow{p} 1$. It follows by applying Slutsky's theorem that $t \xrightarrow{d} N(0, 1)$.

## 17.3 Asymptotic Distribution of the OLS Estimator and *t*-Statistic

Recall from Chapter 4 that, under the assumptions of Key Concept 4.3 (the first three assumptions of Key Concept 17.1), the OLS estimator $\hat{\beta}_1$ is consistent and $\sqrt{n}(\hat{\beta}_1 - \beta_1)$ has an asymptotic normal distribution. Moreover, the *t*-statistic testing the null hypothesis $\beta_1 = \beta_{1,0}$ has an asymptotic standard normal distribution under the null hypothesis. This section summarizes these results and provides additional details of their proofs.

### Consistency and Asymptotic Normality of the OLS Estimators

The large-sample distribution of $\hat{\beta}_1$, originally stated in Key Concept 4.4, is

$$\sqrt{n}(\hat{\beta}_1 - \beta_1) \xrightarrow{d} N\left(0, \frac{\operatorname{var}(v_i)}{[\operatorname{var}(X_i)]^2}\right), \tag{17.12}$$

where $v_i = (X_i - \mu_X)u_i$. The proof of this result was sketched in Appendix 4.3, but that proof omitted some details and involved an approximation that was not formally shown. The missing steps in that proof are left as Exercise 17.3.

An implication of Equation (17.12) is that $\hat{\beta}_1$ is consistent (Exercise 17.4).

### Consistency of Heteroskedasticity-Robust Standard Errors

Under the first three least squares assumptions, the heteroskedasticity-robust standard error for $\hat{\beta}_1$ forms the basis for valid statistical inferences. Specifically,

$$\frac{\hat{\sigma}^2_{\hat{\beta}_1}}{\sigma^2_{\hat{\beta}_1}} \xrightarrow{p} 1, \tag{17.13}$$

where $\sigma^2_{\hat{\beta}_1} = \operatorname{var}(v_i)/\{n[\operatorname{var}(X_i)]^2\}$ and $\hat{\sigma}^2_{\hat{\beta}_1}$ is square of the heteroskedasticity-robust standard error defined in Equation (5.4); that is,

$$\hat{\sigma}^2_{\hat{\beta}_1} = \frac{1}{n} \frac{\dfrac{1}{n-2}\sum_{i=1}^{n}(X_i - \overline{X})^2 \hat{u}_i^2}{\left[\dfrac{1}{n}\sum_{i=1}^{n}(X_i - \overline{X})^2\right]^2}. \tag{17.14}$$

To show the result in Equation (17.13), first use the definitions of $\sigma^2_{\hat\beta_1}$ and $\hat\sigma^2_{\hat\beta_1}$ to rewrite the ratio in Equation (17.13) as

$$\frac{\hat\sigma^2_{\hat\beta_1}}{\sigma^2_{\hat\beta_1}} = \left[\frac{n}{n-2}\right]\left[\frac{\frac{1}{n}\sum_{i=1}^{n}(X_i-\overline{X})^2\hat{u}_i^2}{\text{var}(v_i)}\right] \div \left[\frac{\frac{1}{n}\sum_{i=1}^{n}(X_i-\overline{X})^2}{\text{var}(X_i)}\right]^2. \quad (17.15)$$

We need to show that each of the three terms in brackets on the right-hand side of Equation (17.15) converge in probability to 1. Clearly the first term converges to 1, and by the consistency of the sample variance (Appendix 3.3) the final term converges in probability to 1. Thus all that remains is to show that the second term converges in probability to 1, that is, that $\frac{1}{n}\sum_{i=1}^{n}(X_i-\overline{X})^2\hat{u}_i^2 \xrightarrow{p} \text{var}(v_i)$.

The proof that $\frac{1}{n}\sum_{i=1}^{n}(X_i-\overline{X})^2\hat{u}_i^2 \xrightarrow{p} \text{var}(v_i)$ proceeds in two steps. The first shows that $\frac{1}{n}\sum_{i=1}^{n}v_i^2 \xrightarrow{p} \text{var}(v_i)$; the second shows that $\frac{1}{n}\sum_{i=1}^{n}(X_i-\overline{X})^2\hat{u}_i^2 - \frac{1}{n}\sum_{i=1}^{n}v_i^2 \xrightarrow{p} 0$.

For the moment, suppose that $X_i$ and $u_i$ have eight moments [that is, $E(X_i^8) < \infty$ and $E(u_i^8) < \infty$], which is a stronger assumption than the four moments required by the third least squares assumption. To show the first step, we must show that $\frac{1}{n}\sum_{i=1}^{n}v_i^2$ obeys the law of large numbers in Equation (17.5). To do so, $v_i^2$ must be i.i.d. (which it is by the second least squares assumption) and $\text{var}(v_i^2)$ must be finite. To show that $\text{var}(v_i^2) < \infty$, apply the Cauchy–Schwarz inequality (Appendix 17.2): $\text{var}(v_i^2) \le E(v_i^4) = E[(X_i-\mu_X)^4u_i^4] \le \{E[(X_i-\mu_X)^8]E(u_i^8)\}^{1/2}$. Thus, if $X_i$ and $u_i$ have eight moments, then $v_i^2$ has a finite variance and thus satisfies the law of large numbers in Equation (17.5).

The second step is to prove that $\frac{1}{n}\sum_{i=1}^{n}(X_i-\overline{X})^2\hat{u}_i^2 - \frac{1}{n}\sum_{i=1}^{n}v_i^2 \xrightarrow{p} 0$. Because $v_i = (X_i - \mu_X)u_i$, this second step is the same as showing that

$$\frac{1}{n}\sum_{i=1}^{n}[(X_i-\overline{X})^2\hat{u}_i^2 - (X_i-\mu_X)^2u_i^2] \xrightarrow{p} 0. \quad (17.16)$$

Showing this result entails setting $\hat{u}_i = u_i - (\hat\beta_0 - \beta_0) - (\hat\beta_1 - \beta_1)X_i$, expanding the term in Equation (17.16) in brackets, repeatedly applying the Cauchy–Schwarz inequality, and using the consistency of $\hat\beta_0$ and $\hat\beta_1$. The details of the algebra are left as Exercise 17.9.

The preceding argument supposes that $X_i$ and $u_i$ have eight moments. This is not necessary, however, and the result $\frac{1}{n}\sum_{i=1}^{n}(X_i-\overline{X})^2\hat{u}_i^2 \xrightarrow{p} \text{var}(v_i)$ can be proven under the weaker assumption that $X_i$ and $u_i$ have four moments, as stated in the third least squares assumption. That proof, however, is beyond the scope of this textbook; see Hayashi (2000, Section 2.5) for details.

## Asymptotic Normality of the Heteroskedasticity-Robust $t$-Statistic

We now show that, under the null hypothesis, the heteroskedasticity-robust OLS $t$-statistic testing the hypothesis $\beta_1 = \beta_{1,0}$ has an asymptotic standard normal distribution if least squares Assumptions #1, #2, and #3 hold.

The $t$-statistic constructed using the heteroskedasticity-robust standard error $SE(\hat{\beta}_1) = \hat{\sigma}_{\hat{\beta}_1}$ [defined in Equation (17.14)] is

$$t = \frac{\hat{\beta}_1 - \beta_{1,0}}{\hat{\sigma}_{\hat{\beta}_1}} = \frac{\sqrt{n}(\hat{\beta}_1 - \beta_{1,0})}{\sqrt{n\sigma_{\hat{\beta}_1}^2}} \div \sqrt{\frac{\hat{\sigma}_{\hat{\beta}_1}^2}{\sigma_{\hat{\beta}_1}^2}}. \tag{17.17}$$

It follows from Equation (17.12) and the definition of $\sigma_{\hat{\beta}_1}^2$ that first term after the second equality in Equation (17.17) converges in distribution to a standard normal random variable. In addition, because the heteroskedasticity-robust standard error is consistent [Equation (17.13)], $\sqrt{\hat{\sigma}_{\hat{\beta}_1}^2/\sigma_{\hat{\beta}_1}^2} \xrightarrow{p} 1$ (Exercise 17.4). It follows from Slutsky's theorem that $t \xrightarrow{d} N(0, 1)$.

# 17.4 Exact Sampling Distributions When the Errors Are Normally Distributed

In small samples, the distribution of the OLS estimator and $t$-statistic depends on the distribution of the regression error and typically is complicated. As discussed in Section 5.6, however, if the regression errors are homoskedastic and normally distributed, then these distributions are simple. Specifically, if all five extended least squares assumptions in Key Concept 17.1 hold, then the OLS estimator has a normal sampling distribution, conditional on $X_1, \ldots, X_n$. Moreover, the $t$-statistic has a Student $t$ distribution. We present these results here for $\hat{\beta}_1$.

## Distribution of $\hat{\beta}_1$ with Normal Errors

If the errors are i.i.d. normally distributed and independent of the regressors, then the distribution of $\hat{\beta}_1$, conditional on $X_1, \ldots, X_n$, is $N(\beta_1, \sigma_{\hat{\beta}_1|X}^2)$, where

$$\sigma_{\hat{\beta}_1|X}^2 = \frac{\sigma_u^2}{\sum_{i=1}^{n}(X_i - \overline{X})^2}. \tag{17.18}$$

The derivation of the normal distribution $N(\beta_1, \sigma^2_{\hat{\beta}_{1|x}})$, conditional on $X_1, \ldots, X_n$, entails (i) establishing that the distribution is normal; (ii) showing that $E(\hat{\beta}_1 | X_1, \ldots, X_n) = \beta_1$; and (iii) verifying Equation (17.18).

To show (i), note that, conditional on $X_1, \ldots, X_n$, $\hat{\beta}_1 - \beta_1$ is a weighted average of $u_1, \ldots, u_n$:

$$\hat{\beta}_1 = \beta_1 + \frac{\frac{1}{n}\sum_{i=1}^{n}(X_i - \overline{X})u_i}{\frac{1}{n}\sum_{i=1}^{n}(X_i - \overline{X})^2}. \tag{17.19}$$

This equation was derived in Appendix 4.3 [Equation (4.30) and is restated here for convenience]. By extended least squares Assumptions #1, #2, #4, and #5, $u_i$ is i.i.d. $N(0, \sigma^2_u)$, and $u_i$ and $X_i$ are independently distributed. Because weighted averages of normally distributed variables are themselves normally distributed, it follows that $\hat{\beta}_1$ is normally distributed, conditional on $X_1, \ldots, X_n$.

To show (ii), take conditional expectations of both sides of Equation (17.19): $E[(\hat{\beta}_1 - \beta_1) | X_1, \ldots, X_n)] = E[\sum_{i=1}^{n}(X_i - \overline{X})u_i / \sum_{i=1}^{n}(X_i - \overline{X})^2 | X_1, \ldots, X_n] = [\sum_{i=1}^{n}(X_i - \overline{X}) \, E(u_i | X_1, \ldots, X_n)] / [\sum_{i=1}^{n}(X_i - \overline{X})^2] = 0$, where the final equality follows because $E(u_i | X_1, X_2, \ldots, X_n) = E(u_i | X_i) = 0$. Thus $\hat{\beta}_1$ is conditionally unbiased; that is,

$$E(\hat{\beta}_1 | X_1, \ldots, X_n) = \beta_1. \tag{17.20}$$

To show (iii), use that the errors are independently distributed, conditional on $X_1, \ldots, X_n$, to calculate the conditional variance of $\hat{\beta}_1$ using Equation (17.19):

$$\mathrm{var}(\hat{\beta}_1 | X_1, \ldots, X_n) = \mathrm{var}\left[\frac{\sum_{i=1}^{n}(X_i - \overline{X})u_i}{\sum_{i=1}^{n}(X_i - \overline{X})^2} \middle| X_1, \ldots, X_n\right]$$

$$= \frac{\sum_{i=1}^{n}(X_i - \overline{X})^2 \mathrm{var}(u_i | X_1, \ldots, X_n)}{\left[\sum_{i=1}^{n}(X_i - \overline{X})^2\right]^2}$$

$$= \frac{\sum_{i=1}^{n}(X_i - \overline{X})^2 \sigma^2_u}{\left[\sum_{i=1}^{n}(X_i - \overline{X})^2\right]^2}. \tag{17.21}$$

Canceling the term in the numerator in the final expression in Equation (17.21) yields the formula for the conditional variance in Equation (17.18).

## Distribution of the Homoskedasticity-Only *t*-Statistic

The homoskedasticity-only *t*-statistic testing the null hypothesis $\beta_1 = \beta_{1,0}$ is

$$t = \frac{\hat{\beta}_1 - \beta_{1,0}}{SE(\hat{\beta}_1)}, \tag{17.22}$$

where $SE(\hat{\beta}_1)$ is computed using the homoskedasticity-only standard error of $\hat{\beta}_1$. Substituting the formula for $SE(\hat{\beta}_1)$ [Equation (5.29) of Appendix 5.1] into Equation (17.22) and rearranging yields

$$t = \frac{\hat{\beta}_1 - \beta_{1,0}}{\sqrt{s_{\hat{u}}^2 / \sum_{i=1}^n (X_i - \overline{X})^2}} = \frac{\hat{\beta}_1 - \beta_{1,0}}{\sqrt{\sigma_u^2 / \sum_{i=1}^n (X_i - \overline{X})^2}} \div \sqrt{\frac{s_{\hat{u}}^2}{\sigma_u^2}}$$

$$= \frac{(\hat{\beta}_1 - \beta_{1,0})/\sigma_{\hat{\beta}_{1|X}}}{\sqrt{W/(n-2)}}, \tag{17.23}$$

where $s_{\hat{u}}^2 = \frac{1}{n-2}\sum_{i=1}^n \hat{u}_i^2$ and $W = \sum_{i=1}^n \hat{u}_i^2/\sigma_u^2$. Under the null hypothesis, $\hat{\beta}_1$ has an $N(\beta_{1,0}, \sigma_{\hat{\beta}_{1|X}}^2)$ distribution conditional on $X_1, \ldots, X_n$, so the distribution of the numerator in the final expression in Equation (17.23) is $N(0, 1)$. It is shown in Section 18.4 that $W$ has a chi-squared distribution with $n - 2$ degrees of freedom and moreover that $W$ is distributed independently of the standardized OLS estimator in the numerator of Equation (17.23). It follows from the definition of the Student *t* distribution (Appendix 17.1) that, under the five extended least squares assumptions, the homoskedasticity-only *t*-statistic has a Student *t* distribution with $n - 2$ degrees of freedom.

*Where does the degrees of freedom adjustment fit in?* The degrees of freedom adjustment in $s_{\hat{u}}^2$ ensures that $s_{\hat{u}}^2$ is an unbiased estimator of $\sigma_u^2$ and that the *t*-statistic has a Student *t* distribution when the errors are normally distributed.

Because $W = \sum_{i=1}^n \hat{u}_i^2/\sigma_u^2$ is a chi-squared random variable with $n - 2$ degrees of freedom, its mean is $E(W) = n - 2$. Thus $E[W/(n-2)] = (n-2)/(n-2) = 1$. Rearranging the definition of $W$, we have that $E(\frac{1}{n-2}\sum_{i=1}^n \hat{u}_i^2) = \sigma_u^2$. Thus the degrees of freedom correction makes $s_{\hat{u}}^2$ an unbiased estimator of $\sigma_u^2$. Also, by dividing by $n - 2$ rather than $n$, the term in the denominator of the final expression of

Equation (17.23) matches the definition of a random variable with a Student $t$ distribution given in Appendix 17.1. That is, by using the degrees of freedom adjustment to calculate the standard error, the $t$-statistic has the Student $t$ distribution when the errors are normally distributed.

# 17.5 Weighted Least Squares

Under the first four extended least squares assumptions, the OLS estimator is efficient among the class of linear (in $Y_1, \ldots, Y_n$), conditionally (on $X_1, \ldots, X_n$) unbiased estimators; that is, the OLS estimator is BLUE. This result is the Gauss–Markov theorem, which was discussed in Section 5.5 and proven in Appendix 5.2. The Gauss–Markov theorem provides a theoretical justification for using the OLS estimator. A major limitation of the Gauss–Markov theorem is that it requires homoskedastic errors. If, as is often encountered in practice, the errors are heteroskedastic, the Gauss–Markov theorem does not hold and the OLS estimator is not BLUE.

This section presents a modification of the OLS estimator, called **weighted least squares (WLS)**, which is more efficient than OLS when the errors are heteroskedastic.

WLS requires knowing quite a bit about the conditional variance function, $\mathrm{var}(u_i | X_i)$. We consider two cases. In the first case, $\mathrm{var}(u_i | X_i)$ is known up to a factor of proportionality, and WLS is BLUE. In the second case, the functional form of $\mathrm{var}(u_i | X_i)$ is known, but this functional form has some unknown parameters that can be estimated. Under some additional conditions, the asymptotic distribution of WLS in the second case is the same as if the parameters of the conditional variance function were in fact known, and in this sense the WLS estimator is asymptotically BLUE. The section concludes with a discussion of the practical advantages and disadvantages of handling heteroskedasticity using WLS or, alternatively, heteroskedasticity-robust standard errors.

## WLS with Known Heteroskedasticity

Suppose that the conditional variance $\mathrm{var}(u_i | X_i)$ is known up to a factor of proportionality; that is,

$$\mathrm{var}(u_i | X_i) = \lambda h(X_i), \tag{17.24}$$

where $\lambda$ is a constant and $h$ is a known function. In this case, the WLS estimator is the estimator obtained by first dividing the dependent variable and regressor by the square root of $h$ and then regressing this modified dependent variable on the modified regressor using OLS. Specifically, divide both sides of the single-variable regressor model by $\sqrt{h(X_i)}$ to obtain

$$\widetilde{Y}_i = \beta_0 \widetilde{X}_{0i} + \beta_1 \widetilde{X}_{1i} + \widetilde{u}_i, \tag{17.25}$$

where $\widetilde{Y}_i = Y_i/\sqrt{h(X_i)}$, $\widetilde{X}_{0i} = 1/\sqrt{h(X_i)}$, $\widetilde{X}_{1i} = X_i/\sqrt{h(X_i)}$, and $\widetilde{u}_i = u_i/\sqrt{h(X_i)}$.

The **WLS estimator** is the OLS estimator of $\beta_1$ in Equation (17.25); that is, it is the estimator obtained by the OLS regression of $\widetilde{Y}_i$ on $\widetilde{X}_{0i}$ and $\widetilde{X}_{1i}$, where the coefficient on $\widetilde{X}_{0i}$ takes the place of the intercept in the unweighted regression.

Under the first three least squares assumptions in Key Concept 17.1 plus the known heteroskedasticity assumption in Equation (17.24), WLS is BLUE. The reason that the WLS estimator is BLUE is that weighting the variables has made the error term $\widetilde{u}_i$ in the weighted regression homoskedastic. That is,

$$\text{var}(\widetilde{u}_i | X_i) = \text{var}\left[\frac{u_i}{\sqrt{h(X_i)}} \middle| X_i\right] = \frac{\text{var}(u_i | X_i)}{h(X_i)} = \frac{\lambda h(X_i)}{h(X_i)} = \lambda, \tag{17.26}$$

so the conditional variance of $\widetilde{u}_i$, $\text{var}(\widetilde{u}_i | X_i)$, is constant. Thus the first four least squares assumptions apply to Equation (17.25). Strictly speaking, the Gauss–Markov theorem was proven in Appendix 5.2 for Equation (17.1), which includes the intercept $\beta_0$, so it does not apply to Equation (17.25), in which the intercept is replaced by $\beta_0 \widetilde{X}_{0i}$. However, the extension of the Gauss–Markov theorem for multiple regression (Section 18.5) does apply to estimation of $\beta_1$ in the weighted population regression, Equation (17.25). Accordingly, the OLS estimator of $\beta_1$ in Equation (17.25)—that is, the WLS estimators of $\beta_1$—is BLUE.

In practice, the function $h$ typically is unknown, so neither the weighted variables in Equation (17.25) nor the WLS estimator can be computed. For this reason, the WLS estimator described here is sometimes called the **infeasible WLS** estimator. To implement WLS in practice, the function $h$ must be estimated, the topic to which we now turn.

## WLS with Heteroskedasticity of Known Functional Form

If the heteroskedasticity has a known functional form, then the heteroskedasticity function $h$ can be estimated and the WLS estimator can be calculated using this estimated function.

*Example #1: The variance of u is quadratic in X.* Suppose that the conditional variance is known to be the quadratic function

$$\text{var}(u_i|X_i) = \theta_0 + \theta_1 X_i^2, \tag{17.27}$$

where $\theta_0$ and $\theta_1$ are unknown parameters, $\theta_0 > 0$, and $\theta_1 \geq 0$.

Because $\theta_0$ and $\theta_1$ are unknown, it is not possible to construct the weighted variables $\tilde{Y}_i$, $\tilde{X}_{0i}$, and $\tilde{X}_{1i}$. It is, however, possible to estimate $\theta_0$ and $\theta_1$, and to use those estimates to compute estimates of $\text{var}(u_i|X_i)$. Let $\hat{\theta}_0$ and $\hat{\theta}_1$ be estimators of $\theta_0$ and $\theta_1$, and let $\widehat{\text{var}}(u_i|X_i) = \hat{\theta}_0 + \hat{\theta}_1 X_i^2$. Define the weighted regressors $\hat{\tilde{Y}}_i = Y_i/\sqrt{\widehat{\text{var}}(u_i|X_i)}$, $\hat{\tilde{X}}_{0i} = 1/\sqrt{\widehat{\text{var}}(u_i|X_i)}$, and $\hat{\tilde{X}}_{1i} = X_{1i}/\sqrt{\widehat{\text{var}}(u_i|X_i)}$. The WLS estimator is the OLS estimator of the coefficients in the regression of $\hat{\tilde{Y}}_i$ on $\hat{\tilde{X}}_{0i}$ and $\hat{\tilde{X}}_{1i}$ (where $\beta_0 \hat{\tilde{X}}_{0i}$ takes the place of the intercept $\beta_0$).

Implementation of this estimator requires estimating the conditional variance function, that is, estimating $\theta_0$ and $\theta_1$ in Equation (17.27). One way to estimate $\theta_0$ and $\theta_1$ consistently is to regress $\hat{u}_i^2$ on $X_i^2$ using OLS, where $\hat{u}_i^2$ is the square of the $i^{\text{th}}$ OLS residual.

Suppose that the conditional variance has the form in Equation (17.27) and that $\hat{\theta}_0$ and $\hat{\theta}_1$ are consistent estimators of $\theta_0$ and $\theta_1$. Under Assumptions #1 through #3 of Key Concept 17.1, plus additional moment conditions that arise because $\theta_0$ and $\theta_1$ are estimated, the asymptotic distribution of the WLS estimator is the same as if $\theta_0$ and $\theta_1$ were known. Thus the WLS estimator with $\theta_0$ and $\theta_1$ estimated has the same asymptotic distribution as the infeasible WLS estimator and is in this sense asymptotically BLUE.

Because this method of WLS can be implemented by estimating unknown parameters of the conditional variance function, this method is sometimes called **feasible WLS** or *estimated WLS*.

*Example #2: The variance depends on a third variable.* WLS also can be used when the conditional variance depends on a third variable, $W_i$, which does not appear in the regression function. Specifically, suppose that data are collected on three variables, $Y_i$, $X_i$, and $W_i$, $i = 1, \ldots, n$; the population regression function depends on $X_i$ but not $W_i$; and the conditional variance depends on $W_i$ but not $X_i$. That is, the population regression function is $E(Y_i|X_i, W_i) = \beta_0 + \beta_1 X_i$ and the conditional variance is $\text{var}(u_i|X_i, W_i) = \lambda h(W_i)$, where $\lambda$ is a constant and $h$ is a function that must be estimated.

For example, suppose that a researcher is interested in modeling the relationship between the unemployment rate in a state and a state economic policy variable ($X_i$). The measured unemployment rate ($Y_i$), however, is a survey-based estimate of the true unemployment rate $(Y_i^*)$. Thus $Y_i$ measures $Y_i^*$ with error, where the source of the error is random survey error, so $Y_i = Y_i^* + v_i$, where $v_i$ is the measurement error arising from the survey. In this example, it is plausible that the survey sample size, $W_i$, is not itself a determinant of the true state unemployment rate. Thus the population regression function does not depend on $W_i$; that is, $E(Y_i^* | X_i, W_i) = \beta_0 + \beta_1 X_i$. We therefore have the two equations

$$Y_i^* = \beta_0 + \beta_1 X_i + u_i^* \text{ and} \tag{17.28}$$

$$Y_i = Y_i^* + v_i, \tag{17.29}$$

where Equation (17.28) models the relationship between the state economic policy variable and the true state unemployment rate and Equation (17.29) represents the relationship between the measured unemployment rate $Y_i$ and the true unemployment rate $Y_i^*$.

The model in Equations (17.28) and (17.29) can lead to a population regression in which the conditional variance of the error depends on $W_i$ but not on $X_i$. The error term $u_i^*$ in Equation (17.28) represents other factors omitted from this regression, while the error term $v_i$ in Equation (17.29) represents measurement error arising from the unemployment rate survey. If $u_i^*$ is homoskedastic, then $\text{var}(u_i^* | X_i, W_i) = \sigma_{u*}^2$ is constant. The survey error variance, however, depends inversely on the survey sample size $W_i$; that is, $\text{var}(v_i | X_i, W_i) = a/W_i$ where $a$ is a constant. Because $v_i$ is random survey error, it is safely assumed to be uncorrelated with $u_i^*$, so $\text{var}(u_i^* + v_i | X_i, W_i) = \sigma_{u*}^2 + a/W_i$ Thus, substituting Equation (17.28) into Equation (17.29) leads to the regression model with heteroskedasticity

$$Y_i = \beta_0 + \beta_1 X_i + u_i, \tag{17.30}$$

$$\text{var}(u_i | X_i, W_i) = \theta_0 + \theta_1 \left( \frac{1}{W_i} \right), \tag{17.31}$$

where $u_i = u_i^* + v_i$, $\theta_0 = \sigma_{u*}^2$, $\theta_1 = a$, and $E(u_i | X_i, W_i) = 0$.

If $\theta_0$ and $\theta_1$ were known, then the conditional variance function in Equation (17.31) could be used to estimate $\beta_0$ and $\beta_1$ by WLS. In this example, $\theta_0$ and $\theta_1$ are unknown, but they can be estimated by regressing the squared OLS residual [from OLS estimation of Equation (17.30)] on $1/W_i$. Then the estimated conditional variance function can be used to construct the weights in feasible WLS.

It should be stressed that it is critical that $E(u_i | X_i, W_i) = 0$; if not, the weighted errors will have nonzero conditional mean and WLS will be inconsistent. Said differently, if $W_i$ is in fact a determinant of $Y_i$, then Equation (17.30) should be a multiple regression equation that includes both $X_i$ and $W_i$.

*General method of feasible WLS.*  In general, feasible WLS proceeds in five steps:

1.  Regress $Y_i$ on $X_i$ by OLS and obtain the OLS residuals $\hat{u}_i, i = 1, \ldots, n$.
2.  Estimate a model of the conditional variance function $\text{var}(u_i | X_i)$. For example, if the conditional variance function has the form in Equation (17.27), this entails regressing $\hat{u}_i^2$ on $X_i^2$. In general, this step entails estimating a function for the conditional variance, $\text{var}(u_i | X_i)$.
3.  Use the estimated function to compute predicted values of the conditional variance function, $\widehat{\text{var}}(u_i | X_i)$.
4.  Weight the dependent variable and regressor (including the intercept) by the inverse of the square root of the estimated conditional variance function.
5.  Estimate the coefficients of the weighted regression by OLS; the resulting estimators are the WLS estimators.

Regression software packages typically include optional weighted least squares commands that automate the fourth and fifth of these steps.

## Heteroskedasticity-Robust Standard Errors or WLS?

There are two ways to handle heteroskedasticity: estimating $\beta_0$ and $\beta_1$ by WLS or estimating $\beta_0$ and $\beta_1$ by OLS and using heteroskedasticity-robust standard errors. Deciding which approach to use in practice requires weighing the advantages and disadvantages of each.

The advantage of WLS is that it is more efficient than the OLS estimator of the coefficients in the original regressors, at least asymptotically. The disadvantage of WLS is that it requires knowing the conditional variance function and estimating its parameters. If the conditional variance function has the quadratic form in Equation (17.27), this is easily done. In practice, however, the functional form of the conditional variance function is rarely known. Moreover, if the functional form is incorrect, then the standard errors computed by WLS regression routines are invalid in the sense that they lead to incorrect statistical inferences (tests have the wrong size).

The advantage of using heteroskedasticity-robust standard errors is that they produce asymptotically valid inferences even if you do not know the form of the conditional variance function. An additional advantage is that heteroskedasticity-robust standard errors are readily computed as an option in modern regression packages, so no additional effort is needed to safeguard against this threat. The disadvantage of heteroskedasticity-robust standard errors is that the OLS estimator will have a larger variance than the WLS estimator (based on the true conditional variance function).

In practice, the functional form of $\text{var}(u_i|X_i)$ is rarely if ever known, which poses a problem for using WLS in real-world applications. This problem is difficult enough with a single regressor, but in applications with multiple regressors it is even more difficult to know the functional form of the conditional variance. For this reason, practical use of WLS confronts imposing challenges. In contrast, in modern statistical packages it is simple to use heteroskedasticity-robust standard errors, and the resulting inferences are reliable under very general conditions; in particular, heteroskedasticity-robust standard errors can be used without needing to specify a functional form for the conditional variance. For these reasons, it is our opinion that, despite the theoretical appeal of WLS, heteroskedasticity-robust standard errors provide a better way to handle potential heteroskedasticity in most applications.

## Summary

1. The asymptotic normality of the OLS estimator, combined with the consistency of heteroskedasticity-robust standard errors, implies that, if the first three least squares assumptions in Key Concept 17.1 hold, then the heteroskedasticity-robust $t$-statistic has an asymptotic standard normal distribution under the null hypothesis.

2. If the regression errors are i.i.d. and normally distributed, conditional on the regressors, then $\hat{\beta}_1$ has an exact normal sampling distribution, conditional on the regressors. In addition, the homoskedasticity-only $t$-statistic has an exact Student $t_{n-2}$ sampling distribution under the null hypothesis.

3. The weighted least squares (WLS) estimator is OLS applied to a weighted regression, where all variables are weighted by the square root of the inverse of the conditional variance, $\text{var}(u_i|X_i)$, or its estimate. Although the WLS estimator is asymptotically more efficient than OLS, to implement WLS you must know the functional form of the conditional variance function, which usually is a tall order.

## Key Terms

convergence in probability (726)

consistent estimator (726)

convergence in distribution (728)

asymptotic distribution (728)

Slutsky's theorem (729)

continuous mapping theorem (729)

weighted least squares (WLS) (736)

WLS estimator (736)

infeasible WLS (737)

feasible WLS (738)

normal p.d.f. (747)

bivariate normal p.d.f. (748)

**MyEconLab Can Help You Get a Better Grade**

**MyEconLab**  If your exam were tomorrow, would you be ready? For each chapter, **MyEconLab** Practice Tests and Study Plan help you prepare for your exams. You can also find similar Exercises and Review the Concepts Questions now in **MyEconLab**. To see how it works, turn to the **MyEconLab** spread on pages 2 and 3 of this book and then go to **www.myeconlab.com**.

For additional Empirical Exercises and Data Sets, log on to the Companion Website at **www.pearsonglobaleditions.com/Stock_Watson**.

## Review the Concepts

**17.1**  Suppose that Assumption #4 in Key Concept 17.1 is true, but you construct a 95% confidence interval for $\beta_1$ using the heteroskedastic-robust standard error in a large sample. Would this confidence interval be valid asymptotically in the sense that it contained the true value of $\beta_1$ in 95% of all repeated samples for large $n$? Suppose instead that Assumption #4 in Key Concept 17.1 is false, but you construct a 95% confidence interval for $\beta_1$ using the homoskedasticity-only standard error formula in a large sample. Would this confidence interval be valid asymptotically?

**17.2**  Suppose that $A_n$ is a sequence of random variables that converges in probability to 3. Suppose that $B_n$ is a sequence of random variables that converges in distribution to a standard normal. What is the asymptotic distribution of $A_n B_n$? Use this asymptotic distribution to compute an approximate value of $\Pr(A_n B_n < 2)$.

**17.3**  Suppose that $Y$ and $X$ are related by the regression $Y = 1.0 + 2.0X + u$. A researcher has observations on $Y$ and $X$, where $0 \leq X \leq 20$, where the conditional variance is $\text{var}(u_i | X_i = x) = 1$ for $0 \leq x \leq 10$ and $\text{var}(u_i | X_i = x) = 16$ for $10 < x \leq 20$. Draw a hypothetical scatterplot of the observations $(X_i, Y_i)$, $i = 1, \ldots, n$. Does WLS put more weight on observations with $x \leq 10$ or $x > 10$? Why?

**17.4**  Instead of using WLS, the researcher in the previous problem decides to compute the OLS estimator using only the observations for which $x \leq 10$, then using only the observations for which $x > 10$, and then using the average the two OLS of estimators. Is this estimator more efficient than WLS?

# Exercises

**17.1**  Consider the regression model without an intercept term, $Y_i = \beta_1 X_i + u_i$ (so the true value of the intercept, $\beta_0$, is zero).

**a.** Derive the least squares estimator of $\beta_1$ for the restricted regression model $Y_i = \beta_1 X_i + u_i$. This is called the restricted least squares estimator ($\hat{\beta}_1^{RLS}$) of $\beta_1$ because it is estimated under a restriction, which in this case is $\beta_0 = 0$.

**b.** Derive the asymptotic distribution of $\hat{\beta}_1^{RLS}$ under Assumptions #1 through #3 of Key Concept 17.1.

**c.** Show that $\hat{\beta}_1^{RLS}$ is linear [Equation (5.24)] and, under Assumptions #1 and #2 of Key Concept 17.1, conditionally unbiased [Equation (5.25)].

**d.** Derive the conditional variance of $\hat{\beta}_1^{RLS}$ under the Gauss–Markov conditions (Assumptions #1 through #4 of Key Concept 17.1).

**e.** Compare the conditional variance of $\hat{\beta}_1^{RLS}$ in (d) to the conditional variance of the OLS estimator $\hat{\beta}_1$ (from the regression including an intercept) under the Gauss–Markov conditions. Which estimator is more efficient? Use the formulas for the variances to explain why.

**f.** Derive the exact sampling distribution of $\hat{\beta}_1^{RLS}$ under Assumptions #1 through #5 of Key Concept 17.1.

**g.** Now consider the estimator $\tilde{\beta}_1 = \sum_{i=1}^{n} Y_i / \sum_{i=1}^{n} X_i$. Derive an expression for $\mathrm{var}(\tilde{\beta}_1 \mid X_1, \ldots, X_n) - \mathrm{var}(\hat{\beta}_1^{RLS} \mid X_1, \ldots, X_n)$ under the Gauss–Markov conditions and use this expression to show that $\mathrm{var}(\tilde{\beta}_1 \mid X_1, \ldots, X_n) \geq \mathrm{var}(\hat{\beta}_1^{RLS} \mid X_1, \ldots, X_n)$.

**17.2**  Suppose that $(X_i, Y_i)$ are i.i.d. with finite fourth moments. Prove that the sample covariance is a consistent estimator of the population covariance — that is, $s_{XY} \xrightarrow{p} \sigma_{XY}$, where $s_{XY}$ is defined in Equation (3.24). (*Hint:* Use the strategy outlined in Appendix 3.3 and the Cauchy–Schwarz inequality.)

**17.3.**  This exercise fills in the details of the derivation of the asymptotic distribution of $\hat{\beta}_1$ given in Appendix 4.3.

**a.** Use Equation (17.19) to derive the expression

$$\sqrt{n}(\hat{\beta}_1 - \beta_1) = \frac{\sqrt{\frac{1}{n}\sum_{i=1}^{n} v_i}}{\frac{1}{n}\sum_{i=1}^{n}(X_i - \overline{X})^2} - \frac{(\overline{X} - \mu_X)\sqrt{\frac{1}{n}\sum_{i=1}^{n} u_i}}{\frac{1}{n}\sum_{i=1}^{n}(X_i - \overline{X})^2},$$

where $v_i = (X_i - \mu_X)u_i$.

**b.** Use the central limit theorem, the law of large numbers, and Slutsky's theorem to show that the final term in the equation converges in probability to zero.

**c.** Use the Cauchy–Schwarz inequality and the third least squares assumption in Key Concept 17.1 to prove that $\text{var}(v_i) < \infty$. Does the term $\sqrt{\frac{1}{n}}\sum_{i=1}^{n} v_i / \sigma_v$ satisfy the central limit theorem?

**d.** Apply the central limit theorem and Slutsky's theorem to obtain the result in Equation (17.12).

**17.4** Show the following results:

**a.** Show that $\sqrt{n}(\hat{\beta}_1 - \beta_1) \xrightarrow{d} N(0, a^2)$, where $a^2$ is a constant, implies that $\hat{\beta}_1$ is consistent. (*Hint:* Use Slutsky's theorem.)

**b.** Show that $s_u^2 / \sigma_u^2 \xrightarrow{p} 1$ implies that $s_u / \sigma_u \xrightarrow{p} 1$.

**17.5** Suppose that $W$ is a random variable with $E(W^4) < \infty$. Show that $E(W^2) < \infty$.

**17.6** Show that if $\hat{\beta}_1$ is conditionally unbiased, then it is unbiased; that is, show that if $E(\hat{\beta}_1 | X_1, \ldots, X_n) = \beta_1$, then $E(\hat{\beta}_1) = \beta_1$.

**17.7** Suppose that $X$ and $u$ are continuous random variables and $(X_i, u_i)$, $i = 1, \ldots, n$, are i.i.d.

**a.** Show that the joint probability density function (p.d.f.) of $(u_i, u_j, X_i, X_j)$ can be written as $f(u_i, X_i) f(u_j, X_j)$ for $i \neq j$, where $f(u_i, X_i)$ is the joint p.d.f. of $u_i$ and $X_i$.

**b.** Show that $E(u_i u_j | X_i, X_j) = E(u_i | X_i) E(u_j | X_j)$ for $i \neq j$.

**c.** Show that $E(u_i | X_1, \ldots, X_n) = E(u_i | X_i)$.

**d.** Show that $E(u_i u_j | X_1, X_2, \ldots, X_n) = E(u_i | X_i) E(u_j | X_j)$ for $i \neq j$.

**17.8** Consider the regression model in Key Concept 17.1 and suppose that Assumptions #1, #2, #3, and #5 hold. Suppose that Assumption #4 is replaced by the assumption that $\text{var}(u_i | X_i) = \theta_0 + \theta_1 |X_i|$, where $|X_i|$ is the absolute value of $X_i$, $\theta_0 > 0$, and $\theta_1 \geq 0$.

**a.** Is the OLS estimator of $\beta_1$ BLUE?

**b.** Suppose that $\theta_0$ and $\theta_1$ are known. What is the BLUE estimator of $\beta_1$?

**c.** Derive the exact sampling distribution of the OLS estimator, $\hat{\beta}_1$, conditional on $X_1, \ldots, X_n$.

**d.** Derive the exact sampling distribution of the WLS estimator (treating $\theta_0$ and $\theta_1$ as known) of $\beta_1$, conditional on $X_1, \ldots, X_n$.

**17.9**  Prove Equation (17.16) under Assumptions #1 and #2 of Key Concept 17.1 plus the assumption that $X_i$ and $u_i$ have eight moments.

**17.10**  Let $\hat{\theta}$ be an estimator of the parameter $\theta$, where $\hat{\theta}$ might be biased. Show that if $E[(\hat{\theta} - \theta)^2] \longrightarrow 0$ as $n \longrightarrow \infty$ (that is, the mean squared error of $\hat{\theta}$ tends to zero), then $\hat{\theta} \xrightarrow{p} \theta$. [*Hint*: Use Equation (17.43) with $W = \hat{\theta} - \theta$.]

**17.11**  Suppose that $X$ and $Y$ are distributed bivariate normal with density given in Equation (17.38).

**a.**  Show that the density of $Y$ given $X = x$ can be written as

$$f_{Y|X=x}(y) = \frac{1}{\sigma_{Y|X}\sqrt{2\pi}} \exp\left[ -\frac{1}{2}\left(\frac{y - \mu_{Y|X}}{\sigma_{Y|X}}\right)^2 \right]$$

where $\sigma_{YX} = \sqrt{\sigma_Y^2(1 - \rho_{XY}^2)}$ and $\mu_{Y|X} = \mu_Y - (\sigma_{XY}/\sigma_X^2)(x - \mu_X)$. [*Hint*: Use the definition of the conditional probability density $f_{Y|X=x}(y) = [g_{X,Y}(x, y)]/[f_X(x)]$, where $g_{X,Y}$ is the joint density of $X$ and $Y$, and $f_X$ is the marginal density of $X$.]

**b.**  Use the result in (a) to show that $Y|X = x \sim N(\mu_{Y|X}, \sigma_{Y|X}^2)$.

**c.**  Use the result in (b) to show that $E(Y|X = x) = a + bx$ for suitably chosen constants $a$ and $b$.

**17.12**  **a.**  Suppose that $u \sim N(0, \sigma_u^2)$. Show that $E(e^u) = e^{\frac{1}{2}\sigma_u^2}$

**b.**  Suppose that the conditional distribution of $u$ given $X = x$ is $N(0, a + bx^2)$, where $a$ and $b$ are positive constants. Show that $E(e^u|X = x) = e^{\frac{1}{2}(a+bx^2)}$.

**17.13**  Consider the heterogeneous regression model $Y_i = \beta_{0i} + \beta_{1i}X_i + u_i$, where $\beta_{0i}$ and $\beta_{1i}$ are random variables that differ from one observation to the next. Suppose that $E(u_i|X_i) = 0$ and $(\beta_{0i}, \beta_{1i})$ are distributed independently of $X_i$.

**a.**  Let $\hat{\beta}_1^{OLS}$ denote the OLS estimator of $\beta_1$ given in Equation (17.2). Show that $\hat{\beta}_1^{OLS} \xrightarrow{p} E(\beta_1)$, where $E(\beta_1)$ is the average value of $\beta_{1i}$ in the population. [*Hint*: See Equation (13.10).]

**b.**  Suppose that $\text{var}(u_i|X_i) = \theta_0 + \theta_1 X_i^2$, where $\theta_0$ and $\theta_1$ are known positive constants. Let $\hat{\beta}_1^{WLS}$ denote the weighted least squares estimator. Does $\hat{\beta}_1^{WLS} \xrightarrow{p} E(\beta_1)$? Explain.

**17.14**  Suppose that $Y_i, i = 1, 2, \ldots, n$, are i.i.d. with $E(Y_i) = \mu$, $\text{var}(Y_i) = \sigma^2$, and finite fourth moment. Show the following:

    **a.** $E(Y_i^2) = \mu^2 + \sigma^2$

    **b.** $\overline{Y} \xrightarrow{p} \mu$

    **c.** $\dfrac{1}{n}\sum_{i=1}^{n} Y_i^2 \xrightarrow{p} \mu^2 + \sigma^2$

    **d.** $\dfrac{1}{n}\sum_{i=1}^{n}(Y_i - \overline{Y})^2 = \dfrac{1}{n}\sum_{i=1}^{n} Y_i^2 - \overline{Y}^2$

    **e.** $\dfrac{1}{n}\sum_{i=1}^{n}(Y_i - \overline{Y})^2 \xrightarrow{p} \sigma^2$

    **f.** $s^2 = \dfrac{1}{n-1}\sum_{i=1}^{n}(Y_i - \overline{Y})^2 \xrightarrow{p} \sigma^2$

**17.15** $Z$ is distributed $N(0,1)$, $W$ is distributed $\chi_n^2$, and $V$ is distributed $\chi_m^2$. Show, as $n \to \infty$ and $m$ is fixed, that:

    **a.** $W/n \xrightarrow{p} 1$.

    **b.** $\dfrac{Z}{\sqrt{W/n}} \xrightarrow{d} N(0,1)$. Use the result to explain why the $t_\infty$ distribution is the same as the standard normal distribution.

    **c.** $\dfrac{V/m}{W/n} \xrightarrow{d} \chi_m^2/m$. Use the result to explain why the $F_{m,\infty}$ distribution is the same as the $\chi_m^2/m$ distribution.

---

**APPENDIX**

# 17.1 The Normal and Related Distributions and Moments of Continuous Random Variables

This appendix defines and discusses the normal and related distributions. The definitions of the chi-squared, $F$, and Student $t$ distributions, given in Section 2.4, are restated here for convenient reference. We begin by presenting definitions of probabilities and moments involving continuous random variables.

## Probabilities and Moments of Continuous Random Variables

As discussed in Section 2.1, if $Y$ is a continuous random variable, then its probability is summarized by its probability density function (p.d.f.). The probability that $Y$ falls between two values is the area under its p.d.f. between those two values. Because $Y$ is continuous, however, the mathematical expressions for its probabilities involve integrals rather than the summations that are appropriate for discrete random variables.

Let $f_Y$ denote the probability density function of $Y$. Because probabilities cannot be negative, $f_Y(y) \geq 0$ for all $y$. The probability that $Y$ falls between $a$ and $b$ (where $a < b$) is

$$\Pr(a \leq Y \leq b) = \int_a^b f_Y(y)dy. \tag{17.32}$$

Because $Y$ must take on some value on the real line, $\Pr(-\infty \leq Y \leq \infty) = 1$, which implies that $\int_{-\infty}^{\infty} f_Y(y)dy = 1$.

Expected values and moments of continuous random variables, like those of discrete random variables, are probability-weighted averages of their values, except that summations [for example, the summation in Equation (2.3)] are replaced by integrals. Accordingly, the expected value of $Y$ is

$$E(Y) = \mu_Y = \int y f_Y(y)dy, \tag{17.33}$$

where the range of integration is the set of values for which $f_Y$ is nonzero. The variance is the expected value of $(Y - \mu_Y)^2$, the $r^{\text{th}}$ moment of a random variable is the expected value of $Y^r$, and the $r^{\text{th}}$ central moment is the expected value of $(Y - \mu_Y)^r$. Thus

$$\text{var}(Y) = E(Y - \mu_Y)^2 = \int (y - \mu_Y)^2 f_Y(y)dy, \tag{17.34}$$

$$E(Y^r) = \int y^r f_Y(y)dy, \tag{17.35}$$

and similarly for the $r^{\text{th}}$ central moment, $E(Y - \mu_Y)^r$.

## The Normal Distribution

*The normal distribution for a single variable.* The probability density function of a normally distributed random variable (the **normal p.d.f.**) is

$$f_Y(y) = \frac{1}{\sigma\sqrt{2\pi}} \exp\left[-\frac{1}{2}\left(\frac{y - \mu}{\sigma}\right)^2\right], \tag{17.36}$$

where $\exp(x)$ is the exponential function of $x$. The factor $1/(\sigma\sqrt{2\pi})$ in Equation (17.36) ensures that $\Pr(-\infty \leq Y \leq \infty) = \int_{-\infty}^{\infty} f_Y(y)dy = 1$.

The mean of the normal distribution is $\mu$, and its variance is $\sigma^2$. The normal distribution is symmetric, so all odd central moments of order three and greater are zero. The fourth central moment is $3\sigma^4$. In general, if $Y$ is distributed $N(\mu, \sigma^2)$, then its even central moments are given by

$$E(Y - \mu)^k = \frac{k!}{2^{k/2}(k/2)!} \sigma^k \text{ (}k\text{ even).} \tag{17.37}$$

When $\mu = 0$ and $\sigma^2 = 1$, the normal distribution is called the standard normal distribution. The standard normal p.d.f. is denoted $\phi$, and the standard normal c.d.f. is denoted $\Phi$. Thus the standard normal density is $\phi(y) = \frac{1}{\sqrt{2\pi}} \exp\left(-\frac{y^2}{2}\right)$ and $\Phi(y) = \int_{-\infty}^{y} \phi(s)ds$.

*The bivariate normal distribution.* The **bivariate normal p.d.f.** for the two random variables $X$ and $Y$ is

$$g_{X,Y}(x, y) = \frac{1}{2\pi\sigma_X\sigma_Y\sqrt{1 - \rho_{XY}^2}} \times \exp\left\{\frac{1}{-2(1 - \rho_{XY}^2)}\left[\left(\frac{x - \mu_X}{\sigma_X}\right)^2 - 2\rho_{XY}\left(\frac{x - \mu_X}{\sigma_X}\right)\left(\frac{y - \mu_Y}{\sigma_Y}\right) + \left(\frac{y - \mu_Y}{\sigma_Y}\right)^2\right]\right\}, \tag{17.38}$$

where $\rho_{XY}$ is the correlation between $X$ and $Y$.

When $X$ and $Y$ are uncorrelated ($\rho_{XY} = 0$), $g_{X,Y}(x, y) = f_X(x)f_Y(y)$, where $f$ is the normal density given in Equation (17.36). This proves that if $X$ and $Y$ are jointly normally distributed and are uncorrelated, then they are independently distributed. This is a special feature of the normal distribution that is typically not true for other distributions.

The multivariate normal distribution extends the bivariate normal distribution to handle more than two random variables. This distribution is most conveniently stated using matrices and is presented in Appendix 18.1.

*The conditional normal distribution.* Suppose that $X$ and $Y$ are jointly normally distributed. Then the conditional distribution of $Y$ given $X$ is $N(\mu_{Y|X}, \sigma_{Y|X}^2)$, with mean $\mu_{Y|X} = \mu_Y + (\sigma_{XY}/\sigma_X^2)(X - \mu_X)$ and variance $\sigma_{Y|X}^2 = (1 - \rho_{XY}^2)\sigma_Y^2$. The mean of this conditional distribution, conditional on $X = x$, is a linear function of $x$, and the variance does not depend on $x$ (Exercise 17.11).

## Related Distributions

*The chi-squared distribution.* Let $Z_1, Z_2, \ldots, Z_n$ be $n$ i.i.d. standard normal random variables. The random variable

$$W = \sum_{i=1}^{n} Z_i^2 \tag{17.39}$$

has a chi-squared distribution with $n$ degrees of freedom. This distribution is denoted $\chi_n^2$. Because $E(Z_i^2) = 1$ and $E(Z_i^4) = 3$, $E(W) = n$ and $\text{var}(W) = 2n$.

*The Student t distribution.* Let $Z$ have a standard normal distribution, let $W$ have a $\chi_m^2$ distribution, and let $Z$ and $W$ be independently distributed. Then the random variable

$$t = \frac{Z}{\sqrt{W/m}} \tag{17.40}$$

has a Student $t$ distribution with $m$ degrees of freedom, denoted $t_m$. The $t_\infty$ distribution is the standard normal distribution. (See Exercise 17.15.)

*The F distribution.* Let $W_1$ and $W_2$ be independent random variables with chi-squared distributions with respective degrees of freedom $n_1$ and $n_2$. Then the random variable

$$F = \frac{W_1/n_1}{W_2/n_2} \tag{17.41}$$

has an $F$ distribution with $(n_1, n_2)$ degrees of freedom. This distribution is denoted $F_{n_1, n_2}$.

The $F$ distribution depends on the numerator degrees of freedom $n_1$ and the denominator degrees of freedom $n_2$. As number of degrees of freedom in the denominator gets large, the $F_{n_1, n_2}$ distribution is well approximated by a $\chi_{n_1}^2$ distribution, divided by $n_1$. In the limit, the $F_{n_1, \infty}$ distribution is the same as the $\chi_{n_1}^2$ distribution, divided by $n_1$; that is, it is the same as the $\chi_{n_1}^2/n_1$ distribution. (See Exercise 17.15.)

---

**APPENDIX**

# 17.2 Two Inequalities

This appendix states and proves Chebychev's inequality and the Cauchy–Schwarz inequality.

## Chebychev's Inequality

Chebychev's inequality uses the variance of the random variable $V$ to bound the probability that $V$ is farther than $\pm\delta$ from its mean, where $\delta$ is a positive constant:

$$\Pr(|V - \mu_V| \geq \delta) \leq \frac{\text{var}(V)}{\delta^2} \quad \text{(Chebychev's inequality)}. \tag{17.42}$$

To prove Equation (17.42), let $W = V - \mu_V$, let $f$ be the p.d.f. of $W$, and let $\delta$ be any positive number. Now

$$E(W^2) = \int_{-\infty}^{\infty} w^2 f(w) dw$$

$$= \int_{-\infty}^{-\delta} w^2 f(w) dw + \int_{-\delta}^{\delta} w^2 f(w) dw + \int_{\delta}^{\infty} w^2 f(w) dw$$

$$\geq \int_{-\infty}^{-\delta} w^2 f(w) dw + \int_{\delta}^{\infty} w^2 f(w) dw$$

$$\geq \delta^2 \left[ \int_{-\infty}^{-\delta} f(w) dw + \int_{\delta}^{\infty} f(w) dw \right]$$

$$= \delta^2 \Pr(|W| \geq \delta), \tag{17.43}$$

where the first equality is the definition of $E(W^2)$, the second equality holds because the ranges of integration divides up the real line, the first inequality holds because the term that was dropped is nonnegative, the second inequality holds because $w^2 \geq \delta^2$ over the range of integration, and the final equality holds by the definition of $\Pr(|W| \geq \delta)$. Substituting $W = V - \mu_v$ into the final expression, noting that $E(W^2) = E[(V - \mu_V)^2] = \text{var}(V)$, and rearranging yields the inequality given in Equation (17.42). If $V$ is discrete, this proof applies with summations replacing integrals.

## The Cauchy–Schwarz Inequality

The Cauchy–Schwarz inequality is an extension of the correlation inequality, $|\rho_{XY}| \leq 1$, to incorporate nonzero means. The Cauchy–Schwarz inequality is

$$|E(XY)| \leq \sqrt{E(X^2)E(Y^2)} \quad \text{(Cauchy–Schwarz inequality)}. \tag{17.44}$$

The proof of Equation (17.44) is similar to the proof of the correlation inequality in Appendix 2.1. Let $W = Y + bX$, where $b$ is a constant. Then $E(W^2) = E(Y^2) + 2bE(XY) + b^2 E(X^2)$. Now let $b = -E(XY)/E(X^2)$ so that (after simplification) the expression becomes $E(W^2) = E(Y^2) - [E(XY)]^2/E(X^2)$. Because $E(W^2) \geq 0$ (since $W^2 \geq 0$), it must be the case that $[E(XY)]^2 \leq E(X^2)E(Y^2)$, and the Cauchy–Schwarz inequality follows by taking the square root.

# The Theory of Multiple Regression

This chapter provides an introduction to the theory of multiple regression analysis. The chapter has four objectives. The first is to present the multiple regression model in matrix form, which leads to compact formulas for the OLS estimator and test statistics. The second objective is to characterize the sampling distribution of the OLS estimator, both in large samples (using asymptotic theory) and in small samples (if the errors are homoskedastic and normally distributed). The third objective is to study the theory of efficient estimation of the coefficients of the multiple regression model and to describe generalized least squares (GLS), a method for estimating the regression coefficients efficiently when the errors are heteroskedastic and/or correlated across observations. The fourth objective is to provide a concise treatment of the asymptotic distribution theory of instrumental variables (IV) regression in the linear model, including an introduction to generalized method of moments (GMM) estimation in the linear IV regression model with heteroskedastic errors.

The chapter begins by laying out the multiple regression model and the OLS estimator in matrix form in Section 18.1. This section also presents the extended least squares assumptions for the multiple regression model. The first four of these assumptions are the same as the least squares assumptions of Key Concept 6.4 and underlie the asymptotic distributions used to justify the procedures described in Chapters 6 and 7. The remaining two extended least squares assumptions are stronger and permit us to explore in more detail the theoretical properties of the OLS estimator in the multiple regression model.

The next three sections examine the sampling distribution of the OLS estimator and test statistics. Section 18.2 presents the asymptotic distributions of the OLS estimator and $t$-statistic under the least squares assumptions of Key Concept 6.4. Section 18.3 unifies and generalizes the tests of hypotheses involving multiple coefficients presented in Sections 7.2 and 7.3, and provides the asymptotic distribution of the resulting $F$-statistic. In Section 18.4, we examine the exact sampling distributions of the OLS estimator and test statistics in the special case that the errors are homoskedastic and normally distributed. Although the assumption of homoskedastic normal errors is implausible in most econometric applications, the exact sampling distributions are of theoretical interest, and $p$-values computed using these distributions often appear in the output of regression software.

The next two sections turn to the theory of efficient estimation of the coefficients of the multiple regression model. Section 18.5 generalizes the Gauss–Markov theorem to multiple regression. Section 18.6 develops the method of generalized least squares (GLS).

The final section takes up IV estimation in the general IV regression model when the instruments are valid and strong. This section derives the asymptotic distribution of the TSLS estimator when the errors are heteroskedastic and provides expressions for the standard error of the TSLS estimator. The TSLS estimator is one of many possible GMM estimators, and this section provides an introduction to GMM estimation in the linear IV regression model. It is shown that the TSLS estimator is the efficient GMM estimator if the errors are homoskedastic.

*Mathematical prerequisite.* The treatment of the linear model in this chapter uses matrix notation and the basic tools of linear algebra and assumes that the reader has taken an introductory course in linear algebra. Appendix 18.1 reviews vectors, matrices, and the matrix operations used in this chapter. In addition, multivariate calculus is used in Section 18.1 to derive the OLS estimator.

## 18.1 The Linear Multiple Regression Model and OLS Estimator in Matrix Form

The linear multiple regression model and the OLS estimator can each be represented compactly using matrix notation.

### The Multiple Regression Model in Matrix Notation

The population multiple regression model (Key Concept 6.2) is

$$Y_i = \beta_0 + \beta_1 X_{1i} + \beta_2 X_{2i} + \cdots + \beta_k X_{ki} + u_i, i = 1, \ldots, n. \quad (18.1)$$

To write the multiple regression model in matrix form, define the following vectors and matrices:

$$Y = \begin{pmatrix} Y_1 \\ Y_2 \\ \vdots \\ Y_n \end{pmatrix}, U = \begin{pmatrix} u_1 \\ u_2 \\ \vdots \\ u_n \end{pmatrix}, X = \begin{pmatrix} 1 & X_{11} & \cdots & X_{k1} \\ 1 & X_{12} & \cdots & X_{k2} \\ \vdots & \vdots & \ddots & \vdots \\ 1 & X_{1n} & \cdots & X_{kn} \end{pmatrix} = \begin{pmatrix} X_1' \\ X_2' \\ \vdots \\ X_n' \end{pmatrix}, \text{ and } \beta = \begin{pmatrix} \beta_0 \\ \beta_1 \\ \vdots \\ \beta_k \end{pmatrix}, \quad (18.2)$$

so $Y$ is $n \times 1$, $X$ is $n \times (k + 1)$, $U$ is $n \times 1$, and $\boldsymbol{\beta}$ is $(k + 1) \times 1$. Throughout we denote matrices and vectors by bold type. In this notation,

- $Y$ is the $n \times 1$ dimensional vector of $n$ observations on the dependent variable.

- $X$ is the $n \times (k + 1)$ dimensional matrix of $n$ observations on the $k + 1$ regressors (including the "constant" regressor for the intercept).

- The $(k + 1) \times 1$ dimensional column vector $X_i$ is the $i^{\text{th}}$ observation on the $k + 1$ regressors; that is, $X_i' = (1 \ X_{1i} \dots X_{ki})$, where $X_i'$ denotes the transpose of $X_i$.

- $U$ is the $n \times 1$ dimensional vector of the $n$ error terms.

- $\boldsymbol{\beta}$ is the $(k + 1) \times 1$ dimensional vector of the $k + 1$ unknown regression coefficients.

The multiple regression model in Equation (18.1) for the $i^{\text{th}}$ observation, written using the vectors $\boldsymbol{\beta}$ and $X_i$, is

$$Y_i = X_i'\boldsymbol{\beta} + u_i, i = 1, \dots, n. \tag{18.3}$$

---

<table>
<tr><td>

## The Extended Least Squares Assumptions
## in the Multiple Regression Model

</td><td>

**KEY CONCEPT**

**18.1**

</td></tr>
</table>

The linear regression model with multiple regressors is

$$Y_i = X_i'\boldsymbol{\beta} + u_i, i = 1, \dots, n. \tag{18.4}$$

The extended least squares assumptions are

1. $E(u_i \mid X_i) = 0$ ($u_i$ has conditional mean zero);
2. $(X_i, Y_i)$, $i = 1, \dots, n$, are independently and identically distributed (i.i.d.) draws from their joint distribution;
3. $X_i$ and $u_i$ have nonzero finite fourth moments;
4. $X$ has full column rank (there is no perfect multicollinearity);
5. $\text{var}(u_i \mid X_i) = \sigma_u^2$ (homoskedasticity); and
6. The conditional distribution of $u_i$ given $X_i$ is normal (normal errors).

In Equation (18.3), the first regressor is the "constant" regressor that always equals 1, and its coefficient is the intercept. Thus the intercept does not appear separately in Equation (18.3); rather, it is the first element of the coefficient vector $\boldsymbol{\beta}$.

Stacking all $n$ observations in Equation (18.3) yields the multiple regression model in matrix form:

$$Y = X\boldsymbol{\beta} + U. \tag{18.5}$$

## The Extended Least Squares Assumptions

The extended least squares assumptions for the multiple regressor model are the four least squares assumptions for the multiple regression model in Key Concept 6.4, plus the two additional assumptions of homoskedasticity and normally distributed errors. The assumption of homoskedasticity is used when we study the efficiency of the OLS estimator, and the assumption of normality is used when we study the exact sampling distribution of the OLS estimator and test statistics.

The extended least squares assumptions are summarized in Key Concept 18.1.

Except for notational differences, the first three assumptions in Key Concept 18.1 are identical to the first three assumptions in Key Concept 6.4.

The fourth assumption in Key Concepts 6.4 and 18.1 might appear different, but in fact they are the same: They are simply different ways of saying that there cannot be perfect multicollinearity. Recall that perfect multicollinearity arises when one regressor can be written as a perfect linear combination of the others. In the matrix notation of Equation (18.2), perfect multicollinearity means that one column of $X$ is a perfect linear combination of the other columns of $X$, but if this is true, then $X$ does not have full column rank. Thus saying that $X$ has rank $k + 1$, that is, rank equal to the number of columns of $X$, is just another way to say that the regressors are not perfectly multicollinear.

The fifth least squares assumption in Key Concept 18.1 is that the error term is conditionally homoskedastic, and the sixth assumption is that the conditional distribution of $u_i$, given $X_i$, is normal. These two assumptions are the same as the final two assumptions in Key Concept 17.1, except that they are now stated for multiple regressors.

*Implications for the mean vector and covariance matrix of U.*  The least squares assumptions in Key Concept 18.1 imply simple expressions for the mean vector and covariance matrix of the conditional distribution of $U$ given the matrix of regressors $X$. (The mean vector and covariance matrix of a vector of random variables are defined in Appendix 18.2.) Specifically, the first and second assumptions in Key Concept 18.1 imply that $E(u_i|X) = E(u_i|X_i) = 0$ and that $\text{cov}(u_i, u_j|X) = E(u_iu_j|X) = E(u_iu_j|X_i, X_j) = E(u_i|X_i)E(u_j|X_j) = 0$ for $i \neq j$ (Exercise 17.7). The first, second, and fifth assumptions imply that $E(u_i^2|X) = E(u_i^2|X_i) = \sigma_u^2$. Combining these results, we have that

$$\text{under Assumptions \#1 and \#2, } E(U|X) = \mathbf{0}_n, \text{ and} \tag{18.6}$$

$$\text{under Assumptions \#1, \#2, and \#5, } E(UU'|X) = \sigma_u^2 I_n, \tag{18.7}$$

where $\mathbf{0}_n$ is the $n$-dimensional vector of zeros and $I_n$ is the $n \times n$ identity matrix.

Similarly, the first, second, fifth, and sixth assumptions in Key Concept 18.1 imply that the conditional distribution of the $n$-dimensional random vector $U$, conditional on $X$, is the multivariate normal distribution (defined in Appendix 18.2). That is,

$$\text{under Assumptions \#1, \#2, \#5, and \#6, the}$$
$$\text{conditional distribution of } U \text{ given } X \text{ is } N(\mathbf{0}_n, \sigma_u^2 I_n). \tag{18.8}$$

## The OLS Estimator

The OLS estimator minimizes the sum of squared prediction mistakes, $\sum_{i=1}^{n}(Y_i - b_0 - b_1X_{1i} - \cdots - b_kX_{ki})^2$ [Equation (6.8)]. The formula for the OLS estimator is obtained by taking the derivative of the sum of squared prediction mistakes with respect to each element of the coefficient vector, setting these derivatives to zero, and solving for the estimator $\hat{\boldsymbol{\beta}}$.

The derivative of the sum of squared prediction mistakes with respect to the $j^{\text{th}}$ regression coefficient, $b_j$, is

$$\frac{\partial}{\partial b_j} \sum_{i=1}^{n}(Y_i - b_0 - b_1X_{1i} - \cdots - b_kX_{ki})^2$$

$$= -2\sum_{i=1}^{n} X_{ji}(Y_i - b_0 - b_1X_{1i} - \cdots - b_kX_{ki}) \tag{18.9}$$

for $j = 0, \ldots, k$, where, for $j = 0$, $X_{0i} = 1$ for all $i$. The derivative on the right-hand side of Equation (18.9) is the $j^{\text{th}}$ element of the $k + 1$ dimensional vector, $-2X'(Y - Xb)$, where $b$ is the $k + 1$ dimensional vector consisting of $b_0, \ldots, b_k$. There are $k + 1$ such derivatives, each corresponding to an element of $b$. Combined, these yield the system of $k + 1$ equations that, when set to zero, constitute the first order conditions for the OLS estimator $\hat{\boldsymbol{\beta}}$. That is, $\hat{\boldsymbol{\beta}}$ solves the system of $k + 1$ equations

$$X'(Y - X\hat{\boldsymbol{\beta}}) = \mathbf{0}_{k+1}, \tag{18.10}$$

or, equivalently, $X'Y = X'X\hat{\boldsymbol{\beta}}$.

Solving the system of equations (18.10) yields the OLS estimator $\hat{\boldsymbol{\beta}}$ in matrix form:

$$\hat{\boldsymbol{\beta}} = (X'X)^{-1}X'Y, \tag{18.11}$$

where $(X'X)^{-1}$ is the inverse of the matrix $X'X$.

*The role of "no perfect multicollinearity."* The fourth least squares assumption in Key Concept 18.1 states that $X$ has full column rank. In turn, this implies that the matrix $X'X$ has full rank, that is, $X'X$ is nonsingular. Because $X'X$ is nonsingular, it is invertible. Thus the assumption that there is no perfect multicollinearity ensures that $(X'X)^{-1}$ exists, so Equation (18.10) has a unique solution and the formula in Equation (18.11) for the OLS estimator can actually be computed. Said differently, if $X$ does *not* have full column rank, there is not a unique solution to Equation (18.10) and $X'X$ is singular. Therefore, $(X'X)^{-1}$ cannot be computed and thus $\hat{\boldsymbol{\beta}}$ cannot be computed from Equation (18.11).

## 18.2 Asymptotic Distribution of the OLS Estimator and *t*-Statistic

If the sample size is large and the first four assumptions of Key Concept 18.1 are satisfied, then the OLS estimator has an asymptotic joint normal distribution, the heteroskedasticity-robust estimator of the covariance matrix is consistent, and the heteroskedasticity-robust OLS *t*-statistic has an asymptotic standard normal distribution. These results make use of the multivariate normal distribution (Appendix 18.2) and a multivariate extension of the central limit theorem.

### The Multivariate Central Limit Theorem

The central limit theorem of Key Concept 2.7 applies to a one-dimensional random variable. To derive the *joint* asymptotic distribution of the elements of $\hat{\boldsymbol{\beta}}$, we need a multivariate central limit theorem that applies to vector-valued random variables.

## The Multivariate Central Limit Theorem

Suppose that $W_1, \ldots, W_n$ are i.i.d. $m$-dimensional random variables with mean vector $E(W_i) = \mu_W$ and covariance matrix $E[(W_i - \mu_W)(W_i - \mu_W)'] = \Sigma_W$, where $\Sigma_W$ is positive definite and finite. Let $\overline{W} = \frac{1}{n}\sum_{i=1}^{n}W_i$. Then $\sqrt{n}(\overline{W} - \mu_W) \xrightarrow{d} N(0_m, \Sigma_W)$.

The multivariate central limit theorem extends the univariate central limit theorem to averages of observations on a vector-valued random variable, $W$, where $W$ is $m$-dimensional. The difference between the central limit theorems for a scalar as opposed to a vector-valued random variable is the conditions on the variances. In the scalar case in Key Concept 2.7, the requirement is that the variance is both nonzero and finite. In the vector case, the requirement is that the covariance matrix is both positive definite and finite. If the vector-valued random variable $W$ has a finite positive definite covariance matrix, then $0 < \text{var}(c'W) < \infty$ for all nonzero $m$-dimensional vectors $c$ (Exercise 18.3).

The multivariate central limit theorem that we will use is stated in Key Concept 18.2.

### Asymptotic Normality of $\hat{\beta}$

In large samples, the OLS estimator has the multivariate normal asymptotic distribution

$$\sqrt{n}(\hat{\beta} - \beta) \xrightarrow{d} N(0_{k+1}, \Sigma_{\sqrt{n}(\hat{\beta}-\beta)}), \text{ where } \Sigma_{\sqrt{n}(\hat{\beta}-\beta)} = Q_X^{-1}\Sigma_V Q_X^{-1}, \quad (18.12)$$

where $Q_X$ is the $(k+1) \times (k+1)$-dimensional matrix of second moments of the regressors, that is, $Q_X = E(X_iX_i')$, and $\Sigma_V$ is the $(k+1) \times (k+1)$-dimensional covariance matrix of $V_i = X_iu_i$, that is, $\Sigma_V = E(V_iV_i')$. Note that the second least squares assumption in Key Concept 18.1 implies that $V_i, i = 1, \ldots, n$, are i.i.d. Written in terms of $\hat{\beta}$ rather than $\sqrt{n}(\hat{\beta} - \beta)$, the normal approximation in Equation (18.12) is

$$\hat{\beta}, \text{ in large samples, is approximately distributed } N(\beta, \Sigma_{\hat{\beta}})$$
$$\text{where } \Sigma_{\hat{\beta}} = \Sigma_{\sqrt{n}(\hat{\beta}-\beta)}/n = Q_X^{-1}\Sigma_V Q_X^{-1}/n. \quad (18.13)$$

The covariance matrix $\Sigma_{\hat{\beta}}$ in Equation (18.13) is the covariance matrix of the approximate normal distribution of $\hat{\beta}$, whereas $\Sigma_{\sqrt{n}(\hat{\beta}-\beta)}$ in Equation (18.12) is the covariance matrix of the asymptotic normal distribution of $\sqrt{n}(\hat{\beta}-\beta)$. These two covariance matrices differ by a factor of $n$, depending on whether the OLS estimator is scaled by $\sqrt{n}$.

*Derivation of Equation (18.12).* To derive Equation (18.12), first use Equations (18.4) and (18.11) to write $\hat{\beta} = (X'X)^{-1}X'Y = (X'X)^{-1}X'(X\beta + U)$ so that

$$\hat{\beta} = \beta + (X'X)^{-1}X'U. \tag{18.14}$$

Thus $\hat{\beta} - \beta = (X'X)^{-1}X'U$, so

$$\sqrt{n}(\hat{\beta} - \beta) = \left(\frac{X'X}{n}\right)^{-1}\left(\frac{X'U}{\sqrt{n}}\right). \tag{18.15}$$

The derivation of Equation (18.12) involves arguing first that the "denominator" matrix in Equation (18.15), $X'X/n$, is consistent for $Q_X$ and second that the "numerator" matrix, $X'U/\sqrt{n}$, obeys the multivariate central limit theorem in Key Concept 18.2. The details are given in Appendix 18.3.

## Heteroskedasticity-Robust Standard Errors

The heteroskedasticity-robust estimator of $\Sigma_{\sqrt{n}(\hat{\beta}-\beta)}$ is obtained by replacing the population moments in its definition [Equation (18.12)] by sample moments. Accordingly, the heteroskedasticity-robust estimator of the covariance matrix of $\sqrt{n}(\hat{\beta}-\beta)$ is

$$\hat{\Sigma}_{\sqrt{n}(\hat{\beta}-\beta)} = \left(\frac{X'X}{n}\right)^{-1}\hat{\Sigma}_{\hat{V}}\left(\frac{X'X}{n}\right)^{-1}, \text{ where } \hat{\Sigma}_{\hat{V}} = \frac{1}{n-k-1}\sum_{i=1}^{n}X_iX_i'\hat{u}_i^2, \tag{18.16}$$

The estimator $\hat{\Sigma}_{\hat{V}}$ incorporates the same degrees-of-freedom adjustment that is in the *SER* for the multiple regression model (Section 6.4) to adjust for potential downward bias because of estimation of $k + 1$ regression coefficients.

The proof that $\hat{\Sigma}_{\sqrt{n}(\hat{\beta}-\beta)} \xrightarrow{p} \Sigma_{\sqrt{n}(\hat{\beta}-\beta)}$ is conceptually similar to the proof, presented in Section 17.3, of the consistency of heteroskedasticity-robust standard errors for the single-regressor model.

*Heteroskedasticity-robust standard errors.* The heteroskedasticity-robust estimator of the covariance matrix of $\hat{\beta}$, $\Sigma_{\hat{\beta}}$ is

$$\hat{\Sigma}_{\hat{\beta}} = n^{-1}\hat{\Sigma}_{\sqrt{n}(\hat{\beta}-\beta)}. \tag{18.17}$$

The heteroskedasticity-robust standard error for the $j^{th}$ regression coefficient is the square root of the $j^{th}$ diagonal element of $\hat{\Sigma}_{\hat{\beta}}$. That is, the heteroskedasticity-robust standard error of the $j^{th}$ coefficient is

$$SE(\hat{\beta}_j) = \sqrt{(\hat{\Sigma}_{\hat{\beta}})_{jj}}, \tag{18.18}$$

where $(\hat{\Sigma}_{\hat{\beta}})_{jj}$ is the $(j, j)$ element of $\hat{\Sigma}_{\hat{\beta}}$.

## Confidence Intervals for Predicted Effects

Section 8.1 describes two methods for computing the standard error of predicted effects that involve changes in two or more regressors. There are compact matrix expressions for these standard errors and thus for confidence intervals for predicted effects.

Consider a change in the value of the regressors for the $i^{th}$ observation from some initial value, say $X_{i,0}$, to some new value, $X_{i,0} + d$, so that the change in $X_i$ is $\Delta X_i = d$, where $d$ is a $k + 1$ dimensional vector. This change in $X$ can involve multiple regressors (that is, multiple elements of $X_i$). For example, if two of the regressors are the value of an independent variable and its square, then $d$ is the difference between the subsequent and initial values of these two variables.

The expected effect of this change in $X_i$ is $d'\beta$, and the estimator of this effect is $d'\hat{\beta}$. Because linear combinations of normally distributed random variables are themselves normally distributed, $\sqrt{n}(d'\hat{\beta} - d'\beta) = d'\sqrt{n}(\hat{\beta} - \beta) \xrightarrow{d} N(0, d'\Sigma_{\sqrt{n}(\hat{\beta} - \beta)}d)$. Thus the standard error of this predicted effect is $(d'\hat{\Sigma}_{\hat{\beta}}d)^{1/2}$. A 95% confidence interval for this predicted effect is

$$d'\hat{\beta} \pm 1.96\sqrt{d'\hat{\Sigma}_{\hat{\beta}}d}. \tag{18.19}$$

## Asymptotic Distribution of the *t*-Statistic

The $t$-statistic testing the null hypothesis that $\beta_j = \beta_{j,0}$, constructed using the heteroskedasticity-robust standard error in Equation (18.18), is given in Key Concept 7.1. The argument that this $t$-statistic has an asymptotic standard normal distribution parallels the argument given in Section 17.3 for the single-regressor model.

# 18.3    Tests of Joint Hypotheses

Section 7.2 considers tests of joint hypotheses that involve multiple restrictions, where each restriction involves a single coefficient, and Section 7.3 considers tests of a single restriction involving two or more coefficients. The matrix setup of

Section 18.1 permits a unified representation of these two types of hypotheses as linear restrictions on the coefficient vector, where each restriction can involve multiple coefficients. Under the first four least squares assumptions in Key Concept 18.1, the heteroskedasticity-robust OLS $F$-statistic testing these hypotheses has an $F_{q,\infty}$ asymptotic distribution under the null hypothesis.

## Joint Hypotheses in Matrix Notation

Consider a joint hypothesis that is linear in the coefficients and imposes $q$ restrictions, where $q \leq k + 1$. Each of these $q$ restrictions can involve one or more of the regression coefficients. This joint null hypothesis can be written in matrix notation as

$$R\beta = r, \tag{18.20}$$

where $R$ is a $q \times (k + 1)$ nonrandom matrix with full row rank and $r$ is a nonrandom $q \times 1$ vector. The number of rows of $R$ is $q$, which is the number of restrictions being imposed under the null hypothesis.

The null hypothesis in Equation (18.20) subsumes all the null hypotheses considered in Sections 7.2 and 7.3. For example, a joint hypothesis of the type considered in Section 7.2 is that $\beta_0 = 0, \beta_1 = 0, \ldots, \beta_{q-1} = 0$. To write this joint hypothesis in the form of Equation (18.20), set $R = [I_q \quad 0_{q \times (k+1-q)}]$ and $r = 0_q$.

The formulation in Equation (18.20) also captures the restrictions of Section 7.3 involving multiple regression coefficients. For example, if $k = 2$, then the hypothesis that $\beta_1 + \beta_2 = 1$ can be written in the form of Equation (18.20) by setting $R = [0 \quad 1 \quad 1]$, $r = 1$, and $q = 1$.

## Asymptotic Distribution of the $F$-Statistic

The heteroskedasticity-robust $F$-statistic testing the joint hypothesis in Equation (18.20) is

$$F = (R\hat{\beta} - r)'[R\hat{\Sigma}_{\hat{\beta}}R']^{-1}(R\hat{\beta} - r)/q. \tag{18.21}$$

If the first four assumptions in Key Concept 18.1 hold, then under the null hypothesis

$$F \xrightarrow{d} F_{q,\infty}. \tag{18.22}$$

This result follows by combining the asymptotic normality of $\hat{\boldsymbol{\beta}}$ with the consistency of the heteroskedasticity-robust estimator $\hat{\boldsymbol{\Sigma}}_{\sqrt{n}(\hat{\beta}-\beta)}$ of the covariance matrix. Specifically, first note that Equation (18.12) and Equation (18.74) in Appendix 18.2 imply that, under the null hypothesis, $\sqrt{n}(\boldsymbol{R}\hat{\boldsymbol{\beta}} - \boldsymbol{r}) = \sqrt{n}\boldsymbol{R}(\hat{\boldsymbol{\beta}} - \boldsymbol{\beta}) \xrightarrow{d} N(\boldsymbol{0}, \boldsymbol{R}\boldsymbol{\Sigma}_{\sqrt{n}(\hat{\beta}-\beta)}\boldsymbol{R}')$. It follows from Equation (18.77) that, under the null hypothesis, $(\boldsymbol{R}\hat{\boldsymbol{\beta}} - \boldsymbol{r})'[\boldsymbol{R}\boldsymbol{\Sigma}_{\hat{\beta}}\boldsymbol{R}']^{-1} (\boldsymbol{R}\hat{\boldsymbol{\beta}} - \boldsymbol{r}) = [\sqrt{n}\boldsymbol{R}(\hat{\boldsymbol{\beta}} - \boldsymbol{\beta})]'$ $[\boldsymbol{R}\boldsymbol{\Sigma}_{\sqrt{n}(\hat{\beta}-\beta)}\boldsymbol{R}']^{-1}[\sqrt{n}\boldsymbol{R}(\hat{\boldsymbol{\beta}} - \boldsymbol{\beta})] \xrightarrow{d} \chi_q^2$. However, because $\hat{\boldsymbol{\Sigma}}_{\sqrt{n}(\hat{\beta}-\beta)} \xrightarrow{p} \boldsymbol{\Sigma}_{\sqrt{n}(\hat{\beta}-\beta)}$, it follows from Slutsky's theorem that $[\sqrt{n}\boldsymbol{R}(\hat{\boldsymbol{\beta}} - \boldsymbol{\beta})]'$ $[\boldsymbol{R}\hat{\boldsymbol{\Sigma}}_{\sqrt{n}(\hat{\beta}-\beta)}\boldsymbol{R}']^{-1}[\sqrt{n}\boldsymbol{R}(\hat{\boldsymbol{\beta}} - \boldsymbol{\beta})] \xrightarrow{d} \chi_q^2$. or, equivalently (because $\hat{\boldsymbol{\Sigma}}_{\beta} = \hat{\boldsymbol{\Sigma}}_{\sqrt{n}(\hat{\beta}-\beta)}/n$), that $F \xrightarrow{d} \chi_q^2/q$, which is in turn distributed $F_{q,\infty}$.

## Confidence Sets for Multiple Coefficients

As discussed in Section 7.4, an asymptotically valid confidence set for two or more elements of $\boldsymbol{\beta}$ can be constructed as the set of values that, when taken as the null hypothesis, are not rejected by the $F$-statistic. In principle, this set could be computed by repeatedly evaluating the $F$-statistic for many values of $\boldsymbol{\beta}$, but, as is the case with a confidence interval for a single coefficient, it is simpler to manipulate the formula for the test statistic to obtain an explicit formula for the confidence set.

Here is the procedure for constructing a confidence set for two or more of the elements of $\boldsymbol{\beta}$. Let $\boldsymbol{\delta}$ denote the $q$-dimensional vector consisting of the coefficients for which we wish to construct a confidence set. For example, if we are constructing a confidence set for the regression coefficients $\beta_1$ and $\beta_2$, then $q = 2$ and $\boldsymbol{\delta} = (\beta_1\,\beta_2)'$. In general, we can write $\boldsymbol{\delta} = \boldsymbol{R}\boldsymbol{\beta}$, where the matrix $\boldsymbol{R}$ consists of zeros and ones [as discussed following Equation (18.20)]. The $F$-statistic testing the hypothesis that $\boldsymbol{\delta} = \boldsymbol{\delta}_0$ is $F = (\hat{\boldsymbol{\delta}} - \boldsymbol{\delta}_0)'[\boldsymbol{R}\hat{\boldsymbol{\Sigma}}_{\hat{\beta}}\boldsymbol{R}']^{-1}(\hat{\boldsymbol{\delta}} - \boldsymbol{\delta}_0)/q$, where $\hat{\boldsymbol{\delta}} = \boldsymbol{R}\hat{\boldsymbol{\beta}}$. A 95% confidence set for $\boldsymbol{\delta}$ is the set of values $\boldsymbol{\delta}_0$ that are not rejected by the $F$-statistic. That is, when $\boldsymbol{\delta} = \boldsymbol{R}\boldsymbol{\beta}$, a 95% confidence set for $\boldsymbol{\delta}$ is

$$\{\boldsymbol{\delta}: (\hat{\boldsymbol{\delta}} - \boldsymbol{\delta})'[\boldsymbol{R}\hat{\boldsymbol{\Sigma}}_{\hat{\beta}}\boldsymbol{R}']^{-1}(\hat{\boldsymbol{\delta}} - \boldsymbol{\delta})/q \leq c\}, \tag{18.23}$$

where $c$ is the 95th percentile (the 5% critical value) of the $F_{q,\infty}$ distribution.

The set in Equation (18.23) consists of all the points contained inside the ellipse determined when the inequality in Equation (18.23) is an equality (this is an ellipsoid when $q > 2$). Thus the confidence set for $\boldsymbol{\delta}$ can be computed by solving Equation (18.23) for the boundary ellipse.

## 18.4 Distribution of Regression Statistics with Normal Errors

The distributions presented in Sections 18.2 and 18.3, which were justified by appealing to the law of large numbers and the central limit theorem, apply when the sample size is large. If, however, the errors are homoskedastic and normally distributed, conditional on $X$, then the OLS estimator has a multivariate normal distribution in finite sample, conditional on $X$. In addition, the finite sample distribution of the square of the standard error of the regression is proportional to the chi-squared distribution with $n - k - 1$ degrees of freedom, the homoskedasticity-only OLS $t$-statistic has a Student $t$ distribution with $n - k - 1$ degrees of freedom, and the homoskedasticity-only $F$-statistic has an $F_{q,n-k-1}$ distribution. The arguments in this section employ some specialized matrix formulas for OLS regression statistics, which are presented first.

### Matrix Representations of OLS Regression Statistics

The OLS predicted values, residuals, and sum of squared residuals have compact matrix representations. These representations make use of two matrices, $\boldsymbol{P}_X$ and $\boldsymbol{M}_X$.

*The matrices $P_X$ and $M_X$.* The algebra of OLS in the multivariate model relies on the two symmetric $n \times n$ matrices, $\boldsymbol{P}_X$ and $\boldsymbol{M}_X$:

$$\boldsymbol{P}_X = \boldsymbol{X}(\boldsymbol{X}'\boldsymbol{X})^{-1}\boldsymbol{X}' \text{ and} \tag{18.24}$$

$$\boldsymbol{M}_X = \boldsymbol{I}_n - \boldsymbol{P}_X. \tag{18.25}$$

A matrix $\boldsymbol{C}$ is idempotent if $\boldsymbol{C}$ is square and $\boldsymbol{CC} = \boldsymbol{C}$ (see Appendix 18.1). Because $\boldsymbol{P}_X = \boldsymbol{P}_X\boldsymbol{P}_X$ and $\boldsymbol{M}_X = \boldsymbol{M}_X\boldsymbol{M}_X$ (Exercise 18.5), and because $\boldsymbol{P}_X$ and $\boldsymbol{M}_X$ are symmetric, $\boldsymbol{P}_X$ and $\boldsymbol{M}_X$ are symmetric idempotent matrices.

The matrices $\boldsymbol{P}_X$ and $\boldsymbol{M}_X$ have some additional useful properties (Exercise 18.5), which follow directly from the definitions in Equations (18.24) and (18.25):

$$\boldsymbol{P}_X\boldsymbol{X} = \boldsymbol{X} \text{ and } \boldsymbol{M}_X\boldsymbol{X} = \boldsymbol{0}_{n \times (k+1)};$$
$$\text{rank}(\boldsymbol{P}_X) = k + 1 \text{ and rank}(\boldsymbol{M}_X) = n - k - 1, \tag{18.26}$$

where $\text{rank}(\boldsymbol{P}_X)$ is the rank of $\boldsymbol{P}_X$.

The matrices $P_X$ and $M_X$ can be used to decompose an $n$-dimensional vector $Z$ into two parts: a part that is spanned by the columns of $X$ and a part orthogonal to the columns of $X$. In other words, $P_X Z$ is the projection of $Z$ onto the space spanned by the columns of $X$, $M_X Z$ is the part of $Z$ orthogonal to the columns of $X$, and $Z = P_X Z + M_X Z$.

*OLS predicted values and residuals.* The matrices $P_X$ and $M_X$ provide some simple expressions for OLS predicted values and residuals. The OLS predicted values, $\hat{Y} = X\hat{\beta}$, and the OLS residuals, $\hat{U} = Y - \hat{Y}$, can be expressed as follows (Exercise 18.5):

$$\hat{Y} = P_X Y \text{ and} \tag{18.27}$$

$$\hat{U} = M_X Y = M_X U. \tag{18.28}$$

The expressions in Equations (18.27) and (18.28) provide a simple proof that the OLS residuals and predicted values are orthogonal, that is, Equation (4.37) holds: $\hat{Y}'\hat{U} = Y'P_X' M_X Y = 0$, where the second equality follows from $P_X' M_X = 0_{n \times n}$, which in turn follows from $M_X X = 0_{n \times (k+1)}$ in Equation (18.26).

*The standard error of the regression.* The *SER*, defined in Section 4.3, is $s_{\hat{u}}$, where

$$s_{\hat{u}}^2 = \frac{1}{n-k-1} \sum_{i=1}^{n} \hat{u}_i^2 = \frac{1}{n-k-1} \hat{U}'\hat{U} = \frac{1}{n-k-1} U'M_X U, \tag{18.29}$$

where the final equality follows because $\hat{U}'\hat{U} = (M_X U)'(M_X U) = U'M_X M_X U = U'M_X U$ (because $M_X$ is symmetric and idempotent).

## Distribution of $\hat{\beta}$ with Normal Errors

Because $\hat{\beta} = \beta + (X'X)^{-1}X'U$ [Equation (18.14)] and because the distribution of $U$ conditional on $X$ is, by assumption, $N(0_n, \sigma_u^2 I_n)$ [Equation (18.8)], the conditional distribution of $\hat{\beta}$ given $X$ is multivariate normal with mean $\beta$. The covariance matrix of $\hat{\beta}$, conditional on $X$, is $\Sigma_{\hat{\beta}|X} = E[(\hat{\beta} - \beta)(\hat{\beta} - \beta)'|X] = E[(X'X)^{-1} X'UU'X(X'X)^{-1}|X] = (X'X)^{-1}X'(\sigma_u^2 I_n)X(X'X)^{-1} = \sigma_u^2(X'X)^{-1}$.

Accordingly, under all six assumptions in Key Concept 18.1, the finite-sample conditional distribution of $\hat{\boldsymbol{\beta}}$ given $\boldsymbol{X}$ is

$$\hat{\boldsymbol{\beta}} \sim N(\boldsymbol{\beta}, \boldsymbol{\Sigma}_{\hat{\beta}|X}), \text{ where } \boldsymbol{\Sigma}_{\hat{\beta}|X} = \sigma_u^2(\boldsymbol{X'X})^{-1}. \tag{18.30}$$

## Distribution of $s_{\hat{u}}^2$

If all six assumptions in Key Concept 18.1 hold, then $s_{\hat{u}}^2$ has an exact sampling distribution that is proportional to a chi-squared distribution with $n - k - 1$ degrees of freedom:

$$s_{\hat{u}}^2 \sim \frac{\sigma_u^2}{n - k - 1} \times \chi_{n-k-1}^2 \tag{18.31}$$

The proof of Equation (18.31) starts with Equation (18.29). Because $\boldsymbol{U}$ is normally distributed conditional on $\boldsymbol{X}$ and because $\boldsymbol{M_X}$ is a symmetric idempotent matrix, the quadratic form $\boldsymbol{U'M_XU}/\sigma_u^2$ has an exact chi-squared distribution with degrees of freedom equal to the rank of $\boldsymbol{M_X}$ [Equation (18.78) in Appendix 18.2]. From Equation (18.26), the rank of $\boldsymbol{M_X}$ is $n - k - 1$. Thus $\boldsymbol{U'M_XU}/\sigma_u^2$ has an exact $\chi_{n-k-1}^2$ distribution, from which Equation (18.31) follows.

The degrees-of-freedom adjustment ensures that $s_{\hat{u}}^2$ is unbiased. The expectation of a random variable with a $\chi_{n-k-1}^2$ distribution is $n - k - 1$; thus $E(\boldsymbol{U'M_XU}) = (n - k - 1)\sigma_u^2$, so $E(s_{\hat{u}}^2) = \sigma_u^2$.

## Homoskedasticity-Only Standard Errors

The homoskedasticity-only estimator $\widetilde{\boldsymbol{\Sigma}}_{\hat{\beta}}$ of the covariance matrix of $\hat{\boldsymbol{\beta}}$, conditional on $\boldsymbol{X}$, is obtained by substituting the sample variance $s_{\hat{u}}^2$ for the population variance $\sigma_u^2$ in the expression for $\boldsymbol{\Sigma}_{\hat{\beta}|X}$ in Equation (18.30). Accordingly,

$$\widetilde{\boldsymbol{\Sigma}}_{\hat{\beta}} = s_{\hat{u}}^2(\boldsymbol{X'X})^{-1} \quad \text{(homoskedasticity-only).} \tag{18.32}$$

The estimator of the variance of the normal conditional distribution of $\hat{\beta}_j$, given $\boldsymbol{X}$, is the $(j, j)$ element of $\widetilde{\boldsymbol{\Sigma}}_{\hat{\beta}}$. Thus the homoskedasticity-only standard error of $\hat{\beta}_j$ is the square root of the $j^{\text{th}}$ diagonal element of $\widetilde{\boldsymbol{\Sigma}}_{\hat{\beta}}$. That is, the homoskedasticity-only standard error of $\hat{\beta}_j$ is

$$\widetilde{SE}(\hat{\beta}_j) = \sqrt{(\widetilde{\boldsymbol{\Sigma}}_{\hat{\beta}})_{jj}} \quad \text{(homoskedasticity-only).} \tag{18.33}$$

## Distribution of the $t$-Statistic

Let $\tilde{t}$ be the $t$-statistic testing the hypothesis $\beta_j = \beta_{j,0}$, constructed using the homoskedasticity-only standard error; that is, let

$$\tilde{t} = \frac{\hat{\beta}_j - \beta_{j,0}}{\sqrt{(\tilde{\Sigma}_{\hat{\beta}})_{jj}}}. \tag{18.34}$$

Under all six of the extended least squares assumptions in Key Concept 18.1, the exact sampling distribution of $\tilde{t}$ is the Student $t$ distribution with $n - k - 1$ degrees of freedom; that is,

$$\tilde{t} \sim t_{n-k-1}. \tag{18.35}$$

The proof of Equation (18.35) is given in Appendix 18.4.

## Distribution of the $F$-Statistic

If all six least squares assumptions in Key Concept 18.1 hold, then the $F$-statistic testing the hypothesis in Equation (18.20), constructed using the homoskedasticity-only estimator of the covariance matrix, has an exact $F_{q,n-k-1}$ distribution under the null hypothesis.

*The homoskedasticity-only F-statistic.* The homoskedasticity-only $F$-statistic is similar to the heteroskedasticity-robust $F$-statistic in Equation (18.21), except that the homoskedasticity-only estimator $\tilde{\Sigma}_{\hat{\beta}}$ is used instead of the heteroskedasticity-robust estimator $\hat{\tilde{\Sigma}}_{\hat{\beta}}$. Substituting the expression $\tilde{\Sigma}_{\hat{\beta}} = s_{\hat{u}}^2(X'X)^{-1}$ into the expression for the $F$-statistic in Equation (18.21) yields the homoskedasticity-only $F$-statistic testing the null hypothesis in Equation (18.20):

$$\tilde{F} = \frac{(R\hat{\beta} - r)'[R(X'X)^{-1}R']^{-1}(R\hat{\beta} - r)/q}{s_{\hat{u}}^2}. \tag{18.36}$$

If all six assumptions in Key Concept 18.1 hold, then under the null hypothesis

$$\tilde{F} \sim F_{q,n-k-1}. \tag{18.37}$$

The proof of Equation (18.37) is given in Appendix 18.4.

The $F$-statistic in Equation (18.36) is called the Wald version of the $F$-statistic (named after the statistician Abraham Wald). Although the formula for the homoskedastic-only $F$-statistic given in Equation (7.13) appears quite different from the formula for the Wald statistic in Equation (18.36), the homoskedastic-only $F$-statistic and the Wald $F$-statistic are two versions of the same statistic. That is, the two expressions are equivalent, a result shown in Exercise 18.13.

## 18.5 Efficiency of the OLS Estimator with Homoskedastic Errors

Under the Gauss–Markov conditions for multiple regression, the OLS estimator of $\boldsymbol{\beta}$ is efficient among all linear conditionally unbiased estimators; that is, the OLS estimator is BLUE.

### The Gauss–Markov Conditions for Multiple Regression

The **Gauss–Markov conditions for multiple regression** are

$$(i) \ E(\boldsymbol{U}|\boldsymbol{X}) = \boldsymbol{0}_n,$$

$$(ii) \ E(\boldsymbol{U}\boldsymbol{U}'|\boldsymbol{X}) = \sigma_u^2 \boldsymbol{I}_n, \text{ and}$$

$$(iii) \ \boldsymbol{X} \text{ has full column rank.} \tag{18.38}$$

The Gauss–Markov conditions for multiple regression in turn are implied by the first five assumptions in Key Concept 18.1 [see Equations (18.6) and (18.7)]. The conditions in Equation (18.38) generalize the Gauss–Markov conditions for a single regressor model to multiple regression. [By using matrix notation, the second and third Gauss–Markov conditions in Equation (5.31) are collected into the single condition (ii) in Equation (18.38).]

### Linear Conditionally Unbiased Estimators

We start by describing the class of linear unbiased estimators and by showing that OLS is in that class.

*The class of linear conditionally unbiased estimators.* An estimator of $\boldsymbol{\beta}$ is said to be linear if it is a linear function of $Y_1, \ldots, Y_n$. Accordingly, the estimator $\tilde{\boldsymbol{\beta}}$ is linear in $\boldsymbol{Y}$ if it can be written in the form

$$\tilde{\boldsymbol{\beta}} = \boldsymbol{A}'\boldsymbol{Y}, \tag{18.39}$$

where $A$ is an $n \times (k + 1)$ dimensional matrix of weights that may depend on $X$ and on nonrandom constants, but not on $Y$.

An estimator is conditionally unbiased if the mean of its conditional sampling distribution, given $X$, is $\beta$. That is, $\tilde{\beta}$ is conditionally unbiased if $E(\tilde{\beta}|X) = \beta$.

***The OLS estimator is linear and conditionally unbiased.*** Comparison of Equations (18.11) and (18.39) shows that the OLS estimator is linear in $Y$; specifically, $\hat{\beta} = \hat{A}'Y$, where $\hat{A} = X(X'X)^{-1}$. To show that $\hat{\beta}$ is conditionally unbiased, recall from Equation (18.14) that $\hat{\beta} = \beta + (X'X)^{-1}X'U$. Taking the conditional expectation of both sides of this expression yields, $E(\hat{\beta}|X) = \beta + E[(X'X)^{-1}X'U|X] = \beta + (X'X)^{-1}X'E(U|X) = \beta$, where the final equality follows because $E(U|X) = 0$ by the first Gauss–Markov condition.

## The Gauss–Markov Theorem for Multiple Regression

The **Gauss–Markov theorem for multiple regression** provides conditions under which the OLS estimator is efficient among the class of linear conditionally unbiased estimators. A subtle point arises, however, because $\hat{\beta}$ is a vector and its "variance" is a covariance matrix. When the "variance" of an estimator is a matrix, just what does it mean to say that one estimator has a smaller variance than another?

The Gauss–Markov theorem handles this problem by comparing the variance of a candidate estimator of a *linear combination* of the elements of $\beta$ to the variance of the corresponding linear combination of $\hat{\beta}$. Specifically, let $c$ be a $k + 1$ dimensional vector and consider the problem of estimating the linear combination $c'\beta$ using the candidate estimator $c'\tilde{\beta}$ (where $\tilde{\beta}$ is a linear conditionally unbiased estimator) on the one hand and $c'\hat{\beta}$ on the other hand. Because $c'\tilde{\beta}$ and $c'\hat{\beta}$ are both scalars and are both linear conditionally unbiased estimators of $c'\beta$, it now makes sense to compare their variances.

The Gauss–Markov theorem for multiple regression says that the OLS estimator of $c'\beta$ is efficient; that is, the OLS estimator $c'\hat{\beta}$ has the smallest conditional variance of all linear conditionally unbiased estimators $c'\tilde{\beta}$. Remarkably, this is true no matter what the linear combination is. It is in this sense that the OLS estimator is BLUE in multiple regression.

The Gauss–Markov theorem is stated in Key Concept 18.3 and proven in Appendix 18.5.

**KEY CONCEPT**

**18.3**

## Gauss–Markov Theorem for Multiple Regression

Suppose that the Gauss–Markov conditions for multiple regression in Equation (18.38) hold. Then the OLS estimator $\hat{\boldsymbol{\beta}}$ is BLUE. That is, let $\tilde{\boldsymbol{\beta}}$ be a linear conditionally unbiased estimator of $\boldsymbol{\beta}$ and let $\boldsymbol{c}$ be a nonrandom $k + 1$ dimensional vector. Then $\text{var}(\boldsymbol{c}'\hat{\boldsymbol{\beta}}|\boldsymbol{X}) \leq \text{var}(\boldsymbol{c}'\tilde{\boldsymbol{\beta}}|\boldsymbol{X})$ for every nonzero vector $\boldsymbol{c}$, where the inequality holds with equality for all $\boldsymbol{c}$ only if $\tilde{\boldsymbol{\beta}} = \hat{\boldsymbol{\beta}}$.

## 18.6 Generalized Least Squares[1]

The assumption of i.i.d. sampling fits many applications. For example, suppose that $Y_i$ and $X_i$ correspond to information about individuals, such as their earnings, education, and personal characteristics, where the individuals are selected from a population by simple random sampling. In this case, because of the simple random sampling scheme, $(X_i, Y_i)$ are necessarily i.i.d. Because $(X_i, Y_i)$ and $(X_j, Y_j)$ are independently distributed for $i \neq j$, $u_i$ and $u_j$ are independently distributed for $i \neq j$. This in turn implies that $u_i$ and $u_j$ are uncorrelated for $i \neq j$. In the context of the Gauss–Markov assumptions, the assumption that $E(\boldsymbol{U}\boldsymbol{U}'|\boldsymbol{X})$ is diagonal therefore is appropriate if the data are collected in a way that makes the observations independently distributed.

Some sampling schemes encountered in econometrics do not, however, result in independent observations and instead can lead to error terms $u_i$ that are correlated from one observation to the next. The leading example is when the data are sampled over time for the same entity, that is, when the data are time series data. As discussed in Section 15.3, in regressions involving time series data, many omitted factors are correlated from one period to the next, and this can result in regression error terms (which represent those omitted factors) that are correlated from one period of observation to the next. In other words, the error term in one period will not, in general, be distributed independently of the error term in the

---

[1]The GLS estimator was introduced in Section 15.5 in the context of distributed lag time series regression. This presentation here is a self-contained mathematical treatment of GLS that can be read independently of Section 15.5, but reading that section first will help to make these ideas more concrete.

next period. Instead, the error term in one period could be correlated with the error term in the next period.

The presence of correlated error terms creates two problems for inference based on OLS. First, *neither* the heteroskedasticity-robust nor the homoskedasticity-only standard errors produced by OLS provide a valid basis for inference. The solution to this problem is to use standard errors that are robust to both heteroskedasticity and correlation of the error terms across observations. This topic—heteroskedasticity- and autocorrelation-consistent (HAC) covariance matrix estimation—is the subject of Section 15.4 and we do not pursue it further here.

Second, if the error term is correlated across observations, then $E(UU'|X)$ is not diagonal, the second Gauss–Markov condition in Equation (18.38) does not hold, and OLS is not BLUE. In this section we study an estimator, **generalized least squares (GLS)**, that is BLUE (at least asymptotically) when the conditional covariance matrix of the errors is no longer proportional to the identity matrix. A special case of GLS is weighted least squares, discussed in Section 17.5, in which the conditional covariance matrix is diagonal and the $i^{\text{th}}$ diagonal element is a function of $X_i$. Like WLS, GLS transforms the regression model so that the errors of the transformed model satisfy the Gauss–Markov conditions. The GLS estimator is the OLS estimator of the coefficients in the transformed model.

## The GLS Assumptions

There are four assumptions under which GLS is valid. The first GLS assumption is that $u_i$ has a mean of zero, conditional on $X_1, \ldots, X_n$; that is,

$$E(U|X) = \mathbf{0}_n. \tag{18.40}$$

This assumption is implied by the first two least squares assumptions in Key Concept 18.1; that is, if $E(u_i|X_i) = 0$ and $(X_i, Y_i)$, $i = 1, \ldots, n$, are i.i.d., then $E(U|X) = \mathbf{0}_n$. In GLS, however, we will not want to maintain the i.i.d. assumption; after all, one purpose of GLS is to handle errors that are correlated across observations. We discuss the significance of the assumption in Equation (18.40) after introducing the GLS estimator.

The second GLS assumption is that the conditional covariance matrix of $U$ given $X$ is some function of $X$:

$$E(UU'|X) = \Omega(X), \tag{18.41}$$

where $\Omega(X)$ is an $n \times n$ positive definite matrix-valued function of $X$.

KEY CONCEPT

18.4

# The GLS Assumptions

In the linear regression model $Y = X\beta + U$, the GLS assumptions are

1. $E(U|X) = 0_n$;
2. $E(UU'|X) = \Omega(X)$, where $\Omega(X)$ is an $n \times n$ positive definite matrix that can depend on $X$;
3. $X_i$ and $u_i$ satisfy suitable moment conditions; and
4. $X$ has full column rank (there is no perfect multicollinearity).

There are two main applications of GLS that are covered by this assumption. The first is independent sampling with heteroskedastic errors, in which case $\Omega(X)$ is a diagonal matrix with diagonal element $\lambda h(X_i)$, where $\lambda$ is a constant and $h$ is a function. In this case, discussed in Section 17.5, GLS is WLS.

The second application is to homoskedastic errors that are serially correlated. In practice, in this case a model is developed for the serial correlation. For example, one model is that the error term is correlated with only its neighbor, so $\text{corr}(u_i, u_{i-1}) = \rho \neq 0$ but $\text{corr}(u_i, u_j) = 0$ if $|i - j| \geq 2$. In this case, $\Omega(X)$ has $\sigma_u^2$ as its diagonal element, $\rho\sigma_u^2$ in the first off-diagonal, and zeros elsewhere. Thus $\Omega(X)$ does not depend on $X$, $\Omega_{ii} = \sigma_u^2$, $\Omega_{ij} = \rho\sigma_u^2$ for $|i - j| = 1$, and $\Omega_{ij} = 0$ for $|i - j| > 1$. Other models for serial correlation, including the first order autoregressive model, are discussed further in the context of GLS in Section 15.5 (also see Exercise 18.8).

One assumption that has appeared on all previous lists of least squares assumptions for cross-sectional data is that $X_i$ and $u_i$ have nonzero, finite fourth moments. In the case of GLS, the specific moment assumptions needed to prove asymptotic results depend on the nature of the function $\Omega(X)$, whether $\Omega(X)$ is known or estimated, and the statistic under consideration (the GLS estimator, $t$-statistic, etc.). Because the assumptions are case- and model-specific, we do not present specific moment assumptions here, and the discussion of the large-sample properties of GLS assumes that such moment conditions apply for the relevant case at hand. For completeness, as the third GLS assumption, $X_i$ and $u_i$ are simply assumed to satisfy suitable moment conditions.

The fourth GLS assumption is that $X$ has full column rank; that is, the regressors are not perfectly multicollinear.

The GLS assumptions are summarized in Key Concept 18.4.

We consider GLS estimation in two cases. In the first case, $\Omega(X)$ is known. In the second case, the functional form of $\Omega(X)$ is known up to some parameters that can be estimated. To simplify notation, we refer to the function $\Omega(X)$ as the matrix $\Omega$, so the dependence of $\Omega$ on $X$ is implicit.

## GLS When $\Omega$ Is Known

When $\Omega$ is known, the GLS estimator uses $\Omega$ to transform the regression model to one with errors that satisfy the Gauss–Markov conditions. Specifically, let $F$ be a matrix square root of $\Omega^{-1}$; that is, let $F$ be a matrix that satisfies $F'F = \Omega^{-1}$ (see Appendix 18.1). A property of $F$ is that $F\Omega F' = I_n$. Now premultiply both sides of Equation (18.4) by $F$ to obtain

$$\widetilde{Y} = \widetilde{X}\boldsymbol{\beta} + \widetilde{U}, \tag{18.42}$$

where $\widetilde{Y} = FY$, $\widetilde{X} = FX$, and $\widetilde{U} = FU$.

The key insight of GLS is that, under the four GLS assumptions, the Gauss–Markov assumptions hold for the transformed regression in Equation (18.42). That is, by transforming all the variables by the inverse of the matrix square root of $\Omega$, the regression errors in the transformed regression have a conditional mean of zero and a covariance matrix that equals the identity matrix. To show this mathematically, first note that $E(\widetilde{U}|\widetilde{X}) = E(FU|FX) = FE(U|FX) = \mathbf{0}_n$ by the first GLS assumption [Equation (18.40)]. In addition, $E(\widetilde{U}\widetilde{U}'|\widetilde{X}) = E[(FU)(FU)'|FX] = FE(UU'|FX)F' = F\Omega F' = I_n$, where the second equality follows because $(FU)' = U'F'$ and the final equality follows from the definition of $F$. It follows that the transformed regression model in Equation (18.42) satisfies the Gauss–Markov conditions in Key Concept 18.3.

The GLS estimator, $\widetilde{\boldsymbol{\beta}}^{GLS}$, is the OLS estimator of $\boldsymbol{\beta}$ in Equation (18.42); that is, $\widetilde{\boldsymbol{\beta}}^{GLS} = (\widetilde{X}'\widetilde{X})^{-1}(\widetilde{X}'\widetilde{Y})$. Because the transformed regression model satisfies the Gauss–Markov conditions, the GLS estimator is the best conditionally unbiased estimator that is linear in $\widetilde{Y}$. But because $\widetilde{Y} = FY$ and $F$ is (here) assumed to be known, and because $F$ is invertible (because $\Omega$ is positive definite), the class of estimators that are linear in $\widetilde{Y}$ is the same as the class of estimators that are linear in $Y$. Thus the OLS estimator of $\boldsymbol{\beta}$ in Equation (18.42) is also the best conditionally unbiased estimator among estimators that are linear in $Y$. In other words, under the GLS assumptions, the GLS estimator is BLUE.

The GLS estimator can be expressed directly in terms of $\Omega$, so in principle there is no need to compute the square root matrix $F$. Because $\tilde{X} = FX$ and $\tilde{Y} = FY$, $\tilde{\beta}^{GLS} = (X'F'FX)^{-1}(X'F'FY)$. But $F'F = \Omega^{-1}$, so

$$\tilde{\beta}^{GLS} = (X'\Omega^{-1}X)^{-1}(X'\Omega^{-1}Y). \qquad (18.43)$$

In practice, $\Omega$ is typically unknown, so the GLS estimator in Equation (18.43) typically cannot be computed and thus is sometimes called the **infeasible GLS** estimator. If, however, $\Omega$ has a known functional form but the parameters of that function are unknown, then $\Omega$ can be estimated and a feasible version of the GLS estimator can be computed.

## GLS When $\Omega$ Contains Unknown Parameters

If $\Omega$ is a known function of some parameters that in turn can be estimated, then these estimated parameters can be used to calculate an estimator of the covariance matrix $\Omega$. For example, consider the time series application discussed following Equation (18.41), in which $\Omega(X)$ does not depend on $X$, $\Omega_{ii} = \sigma_u^2$, $\Omega_{ij} = \rho\sigma_u^2$ for $|i - j| = 1$, and $\Omega_{ij} = 0$ for $|i - j| > 1$. Then $\Omega$ has two unknown parameters, $\sigma_u^2$ and $\rho$. These parameters can be estimated using the residuals from a preliminary OLS regression; specifically, $\sigma_u^2$ can be estimated by $s_{\hat{u}}^2$ and $\rho$ can be estimated by the sample correlation between all neighboring pairs of OLS residuals. These estimated parameters can in turn be used to compute an estimator of $\Omega$, $\hat{\Omega}$.

In general, suppose that you have an estimator $\hat{\Omega}$ of $\Omega$. Then the GLS estimator based on $\hat{\Omega}$ is

$$\hat{\beta}^{GLS} = (X'\hat{\Omega}^{-1}X)^{-1}(X'\hat{\Omega}^{-1}Y). \qquad (18.44)$$

The GLS estimator in Equation (18.44) is sometimes called the **feasible GLS** estimator because it can be computed if the covariance matrix contains some unknown parameters that can be estimated.

## The Zero Conditional Mean Assumption and GLS

For the OLS estimator to be consistent, the first least squares assumption must hold; that is, $E(u_i|X_i)$ must be zero. In contrast, the first GLS assumption is that $E(u_i|X_1, \ldots, X_n) = 0$. In other words, the first OLS assumption is that the error for the $i^{\text{th}}$ observation has a conditional mean of zero, given the values of the regressors for that observation, whereas the first GLS assumption is that $u_i$ has a conditional mean of zero, given the values of the regressors for *all* observations.

As discussed in Section 18.1, the assumptions that $E(u_i|X_i) = 0$ and that sampling is i.i.d. together imply that $E(u_i|X_1, \ldots, X_n) = 0$. Thus, when sampling is i.i.d. so that GLS is WLS, the first GLS assumption is implied by the first least squares assumption in Key Concept 18.1.

When sampling is not i.i.d., however, the first GLS assumption is not implied by the assumption that $E(u_i|X_i) = 0$; that is, the first GLS assumption is stronger. Although the distinction between these two conditions might seem slight, it can be very important in applications to time series data. This distinction is discussed in Section 15.5 in the context of whether the regressor is "past and present" exogenous or "strictly" exogenous; the assumption that $E(u_i|X_1, \ldots, X_n) = 0$ corresponds to strict exogeneity. Here, we discuss this distinction at a more general level using matrix notation. To do so, we focus on the case that $U$ is homoskedastic, $\Omega$ is known, and $\Omega$ has nonzero off-diagonal elements.

*The role of the first GLS assumption.* To see the source of the difference between these assumptions, it is useful to contrast the consistency arguments for GLS and OLS.

We first sketch the argument for the consistency of the GLS estimator in Equation (18.43). Substituting Equation (18.4) into Equation (18.43), we have $\widetilde{\boldsymbol{\beta}}^{GLS} = \boldsymbol{\beta} + (X'\Omega^{-1}X/n)^{-1}(X'\Omega^{-1}U/n)$. Under the first GLS assumption, $E(X'\Omega^{-1}U) = E[X'\Omega^{-1}E(U|X)] = \mathbf{0}_n$. If in addition the variance of $X'\Omega^{-1}U/n$ tends to zero and $X'\Omega^{-1}X/n \xrightarrow{p} \widetilde{Q}$, where $\widetilde{Q}$ is some invertible matrix, then $\widetilde{\boldsymbol{\beta}}^{GLS} \xrightarrow{p} \boldsymbol{\beta}$. Critically, when $\Omega$ has off-diagonal elements, the term $X'\Omega^{-1}U = \sum_{i=1}^{n}\sum_{j=1}^{n}X_i(\Omega^{-1})_{ij}u_j$ involves products of $X_i$ and $u_j$ for different $i, j$, where $(\Omega^{-1})_{ij}$ denotes the $(i, j)$ element of $\Omega^{-1}$. Thus, for $X'\Omega^{-1}U$ to have a mean of zero, it is not enough that $E(u_i|X_i) = 0$; rather $E(u_i|X_j)$ must equal zero for all $i, j$ pairs corresponding to nonzero values of $(\Omega^{-1})_{ij}$. Depending on the covariance structure of the errors, only some of or all the elements of $(\Omega^{-1})_{ij}$ might be nonzero. For example, if $u_i$ follows a first order autoregression (as discussed in Section 15.5), the only nonzero elements $(\Omega^{-1})_{ij}$ are those for which $|i - j| \leq 1$. In general, however, all the elements of $\Omega^{-1}$ can be nonzero, so in general for $X'\Omega^{-1}U/n \xrightarrow{p} \mathbf{0}_{(k+1)\times 1}$ (and thus for $\widetilde{\boldsymbol{\beta}}^{GLS}$ to be consistent) we need that $E(U|X) = \mathbf{0}_n$; that is, the first GLS assumption must hold.

In contrast, recall the argument that the OLS estimator is consistent. Rewrite Equation (18.14) as $\hat{\boldsymbol{\beta}} = \boldsymbol{\beta} + (X'X/n)^{-1}\frac{1}{n}\sum_{i=1}^{n}X_i u_i$. If $E(u_i|X_i) = 0$, then the term $\frac{1}{n}\sum_{i=1}^{n}X_i u_i$ has mean zero, and if this term has a variance that tends to zero, it converges in probability to zero. If in addition $X'X/n \xrightarrow{p} Q_X$, then $\hat{\boldsymbol{\beta}} \xrightarrow{p} \boldsymbol{\beta}$.

*Is the first GLS assumption restrictive?* The first GLS assumption requires that the errors for the $i^{th}$ observation be uncorrelated with the regressors for all other observations. This assumption is dubious in some time series applications. This issue is discussed in Section 15.6 in the context of an empirical example, the relationship between the change in the price of a contract for future delivery of frozen orange concentrate and the weather in Florida. As explained there, the error term in the regression of price changes on the weather is plausibly uncorrelated with current and past values of the weather, so the first OLS assumption holds. However, this error term is plausibly correlated with future values of the weather, so the first GLS assumption does *not* hold.

This example illustrates a general phenomenon in economic time series data that arises when the value of a variable today is set in part based on expectations of the future: Those future expectations typically imply that the error term today depends on a forecast of the regressor tomorrow, which in turn is correlated with the actual value of the regressor tomorrow. For this reason, the first GLS assumption is in fact much stronger than the first OLS assumption. Accordingly, in some applications with economic time series data the GLS estimator is not consistent even though the OLS estimator is.

## 18.7 Instrumental Variables and Generalized Method of Moments Estimation

This section provides an introduction to the theory of instrumental variables (IV) estimation and the asymptotic distribution of IV estimators. It is assumed throughout that the IV regression assumptions in Key Concepts 12.3 and 12.4 hold and, moreover, that the instruments are strong. These assumptions apply to cross-sectional data with i.i.d. observations. Under certain conditions the results derived in this section are applicable to time series data as well, and the extension to time series data is briefly discussed at the end of this section. All asymptotic results in this section are developed under the assumption of strong instruments.

This section begins by presenting the IV regression model, the two stage least squares (TSLS) estimator, and its asymptotic distribution in the general case of heteroskedasticity, all in matrix form. It is next shown that, in the special case of homoskedasticity, the TSLS estimator is asymptotically efficient among the class of IV estimators in which the instruments are linear combinations of the exogenous variables. Moreover, the *J*-statistic has an asymptotic chi-squared distribution in which the degrees of freedom equal the number of overidentifying restrictions. This section concludes with a discussion of efficient IV estimation and the test of overidentifying restrictions when the errors are heteroskedastic—a situation in which the efficient IV estimator is known as the efficient generalized method of moments (GMM) estimator.

## The IV Estimator in Matrix Form

In this section, we let $X$ denote the $n \times (k + r + 1)$ matrix of the regressors in the equation of interest, so $X$ contains the included endogenous regressors (the $X$'s in Key Concept 12.1) *and* the included exogenous regressors (the $W$'s in Key Concept 12.1). That is, in the notation of Key Concept 12.1, the $i^{th}$ row of $X$ is $X'_i = (1 \quad X_{1i} \quad X_{2i} \quad \ldots \quad X_{ki} \quad W_{1i} \quad W_{2i} \quad \ldots \quad W_{ri})$. Also, let $Z$ denote the $n \times (m + r + 1)$ matrix of all the exogenous regressors, both those included in the equation of interest (the $W$'s) *and* those excluded from the equation of interest (the instruments). That is, in the notation of Key Concept 12.1, the $i^{th}$ row of $Z$ is $Z'_i = (1 \quad Z_{1i} \quad Z_{2i} \quad \ldots \quad Z_{mi} \quad W_{1i} \quad W_{2i} \quad \ldots \quad W_{ri})$.

With this notation, the IV regression model of Key Concept 12.1, written in matrix form, is

$$Y = X\beta + U, \tag{18.45}$$

where $U$ is the $n \times 1$ vector of errors in the equation of interest, with $i^{th}$ element $u_i$.

The matrix $Z$ consists of all the exogenous regressors, so under the IV regression assumptions in Key Concept 12.4,

$$E(Z_i u_i) = 0 \quad \text{(instrument exogeneity).} \tag{18.46}$$

Because there are $k$ included endogenous regressors, the first stage regression consists of $k$ equations.

*The TSLS estimator.* The TSLS estimator is the instrumental variables estimator in which the instruments are the predicted values of $X$ based on OLS estimation of the first stage regression. Let $\hat{X}$ denote this matrix of predicted values so that the $i^{th}$ row of $\hat{X}$ is $(\hat{X}_{1i} \quad \hat{X}_{2i} \quad \ldots \quad \hat{X}_{ki} \quad W_{1i} \quad W_{2i} \quad \ldots \quad W_{ri})$, where $\hat{X}_{1i}$ is the predicted value from the regression of $X_{1i}$ on $Z$, and so forth. Because the $W$'s are contained in $Z$, the predicted value from a regression of $W_{1i}$ on $Z$ is just $W_{1i}$, and so forth, so $\hat{X} = P_Z X$, where $P_Z = Z(Z'Z)^{-1}Z'$ [see Equation (18.27)]. Accordingly, the TSLS estimator is

$$\hat{\beta}^{TSLS} = (\hat{X}'\hat{X})^{-1}\hat{X}'Y. \tag{18.47}$$

Because $\hat{X} = P_Z X$, $\hat{X}'\hat{X} = X'P_Z X$, and $\hat{X}'Y = X'P_Z Y$, the TSLS estimator can be rewritten as

$$\hat{\beta}^{TSLS} = (X'P_Z X)^{-1}X'P_Z Y. \tag{18.48}$$

## Asymptotic Distribution of the TSLS Estimator

Substituting Equation (18.45) into Equation (18.48), rearranging, and multiplying by $\sqrt{n}$ yields the expression for the centered and scaled TSLS estimator:

$$\sqrt{n}(\hat{\boldsymbol{\beta}}^{TSLS} - \boldsymbol{\beta}) = \left(\frac{\boldsymbol{X'P_ZX}}{n}\right)^{-1} \frac{\boldsymbol{X'P_ZU}}{\sqrt{n}}$$

$$= \left[\frac{\boldsymbol{X'Z}}{n}\left(\frac{\boldsymbol{Z'Z}}{n}\right)^{-1}\frac{\boldsymbol{Z'X}}{n}\right]^{-1}\left[\frac{\boldsymbol{X'Z}}{n}\left(\frac{\boldsymbol{Z'Z}}{n}\right)^{-1}\frac{\boldsymbol{Z'U}}{\sqrt{n}}\right], \quad (18.49)$$

where the second equality uses the definition of $\boldsymbol{P_Z}$. Under the IV regression assumptions, $\boldsymbol{X'Z}/n \xrightarrow{p} \boldsymbol{Q_{XZ}}$ and $\boldsymbol{Z'Z}/n \xrightarrow{p} \boldsymbol{Q_{ZZ}}$, where $\boldsymbol{Q_{XZ}} = E(X_iZ_i')$ and $\boldsymbol{Q_{ZZ}} = E(Z_iZ_i')$. In addition, under the IV regression assumptions, $Z_iu_i$ is i.i.d. with mean zero [Equation (18.46)] and a nonzero finite variance, so its sum, divided by $\sqrt{n}$, satisfies the conditions of the central limit theorem and

$$\boldsymbol{Z'U}/\sqrt{n} \xrightarrow{d} \boldsymbol{\Psi_{ZU}}, \text{ where } \boldsymbol{\Psi_{ZU}} \sim N(\boldsymbol{0}, \boldsymbol{H}), \boldsymbol{H} = E(Z_iZ_i'u_i^2) \quad (18.50)$$

and $\boldsymbol{\Psi_{ZU}}$ is $(m + r + 1) \times 1$.

Application of Equation (18.50) and of the limits $\boldsymbol{X'Z}/n \xrightarrow{p} \boldsymbol{Q_{XZ}}$ and $\boldsymbol{Z'Z}/n \xrightarrow{p} \boldsymbol{Q_{ZZ}}$ to Equation (18.49) yields the result that, under the IV regression assumptions, the TSLS estimator is asymptotically normally distributed:

$$\sqrt{n}\left(\hat{\boldsymbol{\beta}}^{TSLS} - \boldsymbol{\beta}\right) \xrightarrow{d} (\boldsymbol{Q_{XZ}}\boldsymbol{Q_{ZZ}^{-1}}\boldsymbol{Q_{ZX}})^{-1}\boldsymbol{Q_{XZ}}\boldsymbol{Q_{ZZ}^{-1}}\boldsymbol{\Psi_{ZU}} \sim N(\boldsymbol{0}, \boldsymbol{\Sigma}^{TSLS}), \quad (18.51)$$

where

$$\boldsymbol{\Sigma}^{TSLS} = (\boldsymbol{Q_{XZ}}\boldsymbol{Q_{ZZ}^{-1}}\boldsymbol{Q_{ZX}})^{-1}\boldsymbol{Q_{XZ}}\boldsymbol{Q_{ZZ}^{-1}}\boldsymbol{H}\boldsymbol{Q_{ZZ}^{-1}}\boldsymbol{Q_{ZX}}(\boldsymbol{Q_{XZ}}\boldsymbol{Q_{ZZ}^{-1}}\boldsymbol{Q_{ZX}})^{-1}, \quad (18.52)$$

where $\boldsymbol{H}$ is defined in Equation (18.50).

*Standard errors for TSLS.* The formula in Equation (18.52) is daunting. Nevertheless, it provides a way to estimate $\boldsymbol{\Sigma}^{TSLS}$ by substituting sample moments for the population moments. The resulting variance estimator is

$$\hat{\boldsymbol{\Sigma}}^{TSLS} = (\hat{\boldsymbol{Q}}_{XZ}\hat{\boldsymbol{Q}}_{ZZ}^{-1}\hat{\boldsymbol{Q}}_{ZX})^{-1}\hat{\boldsymbol{Q}}_{XZ}\hat{\boldsymbol{Q}}_{ZZ}^{-1}\hat{\boldsymbol{H}}\hat{\boldsymbol{Q}}_{ZZ}^{-1}\hat{\boldsymbol{Q}}_{ZX}(\hat{\boldsymbol{Q}}_{XZ}\hat{\boldsymbol{Q}}_{ZZ}^{-1}\hat{\boldsymbol{Q}}_{ZX})^{-1}, \quad (18.53)$$

where $\hat{\boldsymbol{Q}}_{XZ} = \boldsymbol{X'Z}/n$, $\hat{\boldsymbol{Q}}_{ZZ} = \boldsymbol{Z'Z}/n$, $\hat{\boldsymbol{Q}}_{ZX} = \boldsymbol{Z'X}/n$, and

$$\hat{\boldsymbol{H}} = \frac{1}{n}\sum_{i=1}^{n}Z_iZ_i'\hat{u}_i^2, \text{ where } \hat{\boldsymbol{U}} = \boldsymbol{Y} - \boldsymbol{X}\hat{\boldsymbol{\beta}}^{TSLS} \quad (18.54)$$

so that $\hat{U}$ is the vector of TSLS residuals and where $\hat{u}_i$ is the $i^{th}$ element of that vector (the TSLS residual for the $i^{th}$ observation).

The TSLS standard errors are the square roots of the diagonal elements of $\hat{\Sigma}^{TSLS}/n$.

## Properties of TSLS When the Errors Are Homoskedastic

If the errors are homoskedastic, then the TSLS estimator is asymptotically efficient among the class of IV estimators in which the instruments are linear combinations of the rows of $Z$. This result is the IV counterpart to the Gauss–Markov theorem and constitutes an important justification for using TSLS.

*The TSLS distribution under homoskedasticity.* If the errors are homoskedastic, that is, if $E(u_i^2|Z_i) = \sigma_u^2$, then $H = E(Z_iZ_i'u_i^2) = E[E(Z_iZ_i'u_i^2|Z_i)] = E[Z_iZ_i'E(u_i^2|Z_i)] = Q_{ZZ}\sigma_u^2$. In this case, the variance of the asymptotic distribution of the TSLS estimator in Equation (18.52) simplifies to

$$\Sigma^{TSLS} = (Q_{XZ}Q_{ZZ}^{-1}Q_{ZX})^{-1}\sigma_u^2 \quad \text{(homoskedasticity only).} \quad (18.55)$$

The homoskedasticity-only estimator of the TSLS variance matrix is

$$\tilde{\Sigma}^{TSLS} = (\hat{Q}_{XZ}\hat{Q}_{ZZ}^{-1}\hat{Q}_{ZX})^{-1}\hat{\sigma}_u^2, \text{ where } \hat{\sigma}_u^2 = \frac{\hat{U}'\hat{U}}{n-k-r-1}$$

$$\text{(homoskedasticity only),} \quad (18.56)$$

and the homoskedasticity-only TSLS standard errors are the square root of the diagonal elements of $\tilde{\Sigma}^{TSLS}/n$.

*The class of IV estimators that use linear combinations of Z.* The class of IV estimators that use linear combinations of $Z$ as instruments can be generated in two equivalent ways. Both start with the same moment equation: Under the assumption of instrument exogeneity, the errors $U = Y - X\beta$ are uncorrelated with the exogenous regressors; that is, at the true value of $\beta$, Equation (18.46) implies that

$$E[(Y - X\beta)'Z] = 0. \quad (18.57)$$

Equation (18.57) constitutes a system of $m + r + 1$ equations involving the $k + r + 1$ unknown elements of $\beta$. When $m > k$, these equations are redundant, in the sense that all are satisfied at the true value of $\boldsymbol{\beta}$. When these population moments are replaced by their sample moments, the system of equations $(\boldsymbol{Y} - \boldsymbol{Xb})'\boldsymbol{Z} = 0$ can be solved for $\boldsymbol{b}$ when there is exact identification ($m = k$). This value of $\boldsymbol{b}$ is the IV estimator of $\boldsymbol{\beta}$. However, when there is overidentification ($m > k$), the system of equations typically cannot all be satisfied by the same value of $\boldsymbol{b}$ because of sampling variation—there are more equations than unknowns—and in general this system does not have a solution.

The first approach to the problem of estimating $\boldsymbol{\beta}$ when there is overidentification is to trade off the desire to satisfy each equation by minimizing a quadratic form involving all the equations. Specifically, let $\boldsymbol{A}$ be an $(m + r + 1) \times (m + r + 1)$ symmetric positive semidefinite weight matrix and let $\hat{\boldsymbol{\beta}}_A^{IV}$ denote the estimator that minimizes

$$\min_b (\boldsymbol{Y} - \boldsymbol{Xb})'\boldsymbol{ZAZ}'(\boldsymbol{Y} - \boldsymbol{Xb}). \tag{18.58}$$

The solution to this minimization problem is found by taking the derivative of the objective function with respect to $\boldsymbol{b}$, setting the result equal to zero, and rearranging. Doing so yields $\hat{\boldsymbol{\beta}}_A^{IV}$, the IV estimator based on the weight matrix $\boldsymbol{A}$:

$$\hat{\boldsymbol{\beta}}_A^{IV} = (\boldsymbol{X'ZAZ'X})^{-1}\boldsymbol{X'ZAZ'Y}. \tag{18.59}$$

Comparison of Equations (18.59) and (18.48) shows that TSLS is the IV estimator with $\boldsymbol{A} = (\boldsymbol{Z'Z})^{-1}$. That is, TSLS is the solution of the minimization problem in Equation (18.58) with $\boldsymbol{A} = (\boldsymbol{Z'Z})^{-1}$.

The calculations leading to Equations (18.51) and (18.52), applied to $\hat{\boldsymbol{\beta}}_A^{IV}$, show that

$$\sqrt{n}(\hat{\boldsymbol{\beta}}_A^{IV} - \boldsymbol{\beta}) \xrightarrow{d} N(\boldsymbol{0}, \Sigma_A^{IV}), \text{ where}$$
$$\Sigma_A^{IV} = (\boldsymbol{Q_{XZ}AQ_{ZX}})^{-1}\boldsymbol{Q_{XZ}AHAQ_{ZX}}(\boldsymbol{Q_{XZ}AQ_{ZX}})^{-1}. \tag{18.60}$$

The second way to generate the class of IV estimators that use linear combinations of $\boldsymbol{Z}$ is to consider IV estimators in which the instruments are $\boldsymbol{ZB}$, where $\boldsymbol{B}$ is an $(m + r + 1) \times (k + r + 1)$ matrix with full row rank. Then the system of $(k + r + 1)$ equations, $(\boldsymbol{Y} - \boldsymbol{Xb})'\boldsymbol{ZB} = 0$, can be solved uniquely for the $(k + r + 1)$ unknown elements of $\boldsymbol{b}$. Solving these equations for $\boldsymbol{b}$ yields $\hat{\boldsymbol{\beta}}^{IV} = (\boldsymbol{B'Z'X})^{-1}(\boldsymbol{B'Z'Y})$, and substitution of $\boldsymbol{B} = \boldsymbol{AZ'X}$ into this expression yields Equation (18.59). Thus the two approaches to defining IV estimators that are linear combinations of the instruments yield the same family of IV estimators. It is conventional to work with the first approach, in which the IV estimator solves the quadratic minimization problem in Equation (18.58), and that is the approach taken here.

*Asymptotic efficiency of TSLS under homoskedasticity.* If the errors are homoskedastic, then $H = Q_{ZZ}\sigma_u^2$ and the expression for $\Sigma_A^{IV}$ in Equation (18.60) becomes

$$\Sigma_A^{IV} = (Q_{XZ}AQ_{ZX})^{-1}Q_{XZ}AQ_{ZZ}AQ_{ZX}(Q_{XZ}AQ_{ZX})^{-1}\sigma_u^2. \qquad (18.61)$$

To show that TSLS is asymptotically efficient among the class of estimators that are linear combinations of $Z$ when the errors are homoskedastic, we need to show that, under homoskedasticity,

$$c'\Sigma_A^{IV}c \geq c'\Sigma^{TSLS}c \qquad (18.62)$$

for all positive semidefinite matrices $A$ and all $(k + r + 1) \times 1$ vectors $c$, where $\Sigma^{TSLS} = (Q_{XZ}Q_{ZZ}^{-1}Q_{ZX})^{-1}\sigma_u^2$ [Equation (18.55)]. The inequality (18.62), which is proven in Appendix 18.6, is the same efficiency criterion as is used in the multivariate Gauss–Markov theorem in Key Concept 18.3. Consequently, TSLS is the efficient IV estimator under homoskedasticity, among the class of estimators in which the instruments are linear combinations of $Z$.

*The J-statistic under homoskedasticity.* The $J$-statistic (Key Concept 12.6) tests the null hypothesis that all the overidentifying restrictions hold against the alternative that some or all of them do not hold.

The idea of the $J$-statistic is that, if the overidentifying restrictions hold, $u_i$ will be uncorrelated with the instruments and thus a regression of $U$ on $Z$ will have population regression coefficients that all equal zero. In practice, $U$ is not observed, but it can be estimated by the TSLS residuals $\hat{U}$, so a regression of $\hat{U}$ on $Z$ should yield statistically insignificant coefficients. Accordingly, the TSLS $J$-statistic is the homoskedasticity-only $F$-statistic testing the hypothesis that the coefficients on $Z$ are all zero, in the regression of $\hat{U}$ on $Z$, multiplied by $(m + r + 1)$ so that the $F$-statistic is in its asymptotic chi-squared form.

An explicit formula for the $J$-statistic can be obtained using Equation (7.13) for the homoskedasticity-only $F$-statistic. The unrestricted regression is the regression of $\hat{U}$ on the $m + r + 1$ regressors $Z$, and the restricted regression has no regressors. Thus, in the notation of Equation (7.13), $SSR_{unrestricted} = \hat{U}'M_Z\hat{U}$ and $SSR_{restricted} = \hat{U}'\hat{U}$, so $SSR_{restricted} - SSR_{unrestricted} = \hat{U}'\hat{U} - \hat{U}'M_Z\hat{U} = \hat{U}'P_Z\hat{U}$ and the $J$-statistic is

$$J = \frac{\hat{U}'P_Z\hat{U}}{\hat{U}'M_Z\hat{U}/(n - m - r - 1)}. \qquad (18.63)$$

The method for computing the $J$-statistic described in Key Concept 12.6 entails testing only the hypothesis that the coefficients on the excluded instruments are zero. Although these two methods have different computational steps, they produce identical $J$-statistics (Exercise 18.14).

It is shown in Appendix 18.6 that, under the null hypothesis that $E(u_i \mathbf{Z}_i) = 0$,

$$J \xrightarrow{d} \chi^2_{m-k}. \tag{18.64}$$

## Generalized Method of Moments Estimation in Linear Models

If the errors are heteroskedastic, then the TSLS estimator is no longer efficient among the class of IV estimators that use linear combinations of $\mathbf{Z}$ as instruments. The efficient estimator in this case is known as the efficient generalized method of moments (GMM) estimator. In addition, if the errors are heteroskedastic, then the $J$-statistic as defined in Equation (18.63) no longer has a chi-squared distribution. However, an alternative formulation of the $J$-statistic, constructed using the efficient GMM estimator, does have a chi-squared distribution with $m - k$ degrees of freedom.

These results parallel the results for the estimation of the usual regression model with exogenous regressors and heteroskedastic errors: If the errors are heteroskedastic, then the OLS estimator is not efficient among estimators that are linear in $\mathbf{Y}$ (the Gauss–Markov conditions are not satisfied) and the homoskedasticity-only $F$-statistic no longer has an $F$ distribution, even in large samples. In the regression model with exogenous regressors and heteroskedasticity, the efficient estimator is weighted least squares; in the IV regression model with heteroskedasticity, the efficient estimator uses a different weighting matrix than TSLS, and the resulting estimator is the efficient GMM estimator.

*GMM estimation.*  **Generalized method of moments (GMM)** estimation is a general method for the estimation of the parameters of linear or nonlinear models, in which the parameters are chosen to provide the best fit to multiple equations, each of which sets a sample moment to zero. These equations, which in the context of GMM are called moment conditions, typically cannot all be satisfied simultaneously. The GMM estimator trades off the desire to satisfy each of the equations by minimizing a quadratic objective function.

In the linear IV regression model with exogenous variables $\mathbf{Z}$, the class of GMM estimators consists of all the estimators that are solutions to the quadratic minimization problem in Equation (18.58). Thus the class of GMM estimators based on the full set of instruments $\mathbf{Z}$ with different-weight matrices $\mathbf{A}$ is the same as the class of IV estimators in which the instruments are linear combinations of $\mathbf{Z}$.

In the linear IV regression model, GMM is just another name for the class of estimators we have been studying—that is, estimators that solve Equation (18.58).

*The asymptotically efficient GMM estimator.* Among the class of GMM estimators, the **efficient GMM** estimator is the GMM estimator with the smallest asymptotic variance matrix [where the smallest variance matrix is defined as in Equation (18.62)]. Thus the result in Equation (18.62) can be restated as saying that TSLS is the efficient GMM estimator in the linear model when the errors are homoskedastic.

To motivate the expression for the efficient GMM estimator when the errors are heteroskedastic, recall that when the errors are homoskedastic, $H$ [the variance matrix of $Z_i u_i$; see Equation (18.50)] equals $Q_{ZZ}\sigma_u^2$, and the asymptotically efficient weight matrix is obtained by setting $A = (Z'Z)^{-1}$, which yields the TSLS estimator. In large samples, using the weight matrix $A = (Z'Z)^{-1}$ is equivalent to using $A = (Q_{ZZ}\sigma_u^2)^{-1} = H^{-1}$. This interpretation of the TSLS estimator suggests that, by analogy, the efficient IV estimator under heteroskedasticity can be obtained by setting $A = H^{-1}$ and solving

$$\min_b (Y - Xb)'ZH^{-1}Z'(Y - Xb). \qquad (18.65)$$

This analogy is correct: The solution to the minimization problem in Equation (18.65) is the efficient GMM estimator. Let $\widetilde{\boldsymbol{\beta}}^{Eff.GMM}$ denote the solution to the minimization problem in Equation (18.65). By Equation (18.59), this estimator is

$$\widetilde{\boldsymbol{\beta}}^{Eff.GMM} = (X'ZH^{-1}Z'X)^{-1}X'ZH^{-1}Z'Y. \qquad (18.66)$$

The asymptotic distribution of $\widetilde{\boldsymbol{\beta}}^{Eff.GMM}$ is obtained by substituting $A = H^{-1}$ into Equation (18.60) and simplifying; thus

$$\sqrt{n}(\widetilde{\boldsymbol{\beta}}^{Eff.GMM} - \boldsymbol{\beta}) \xrightarrow{d} N(0, \Sigma^{Eff.GMM}),$$
$$\text{where } \Sigma^{Eff.GMM} = (Q_{XZ}H^{-1}Q_{ZX})^{-1}. \qquad (18.67)$$

The result that $\widetilde{\boldsymbol{\beta}}^{Eff.GMM}$ is the efficient GMM estimator is proven by showing that $c'\Sigma_A^{IV}c \geq c'\Sigma^{Eff.GMM}c$ for all vectors $c$, where $\Sigma_A^{IV}$ is given in Equation (18.60). The proof of this result is given in Appendix 18.6.

*Feasible efficient GMM estimation.* The GMM estimator defined in Equation (18.66) is not a feasible estimator because it depends on the unknown variance matrix $H$. However, a feasible efficient GMM estimator can be computed by substituting a consistent estimator of $H$ into the minimization problem of Equation (18.65) or, equivalently, by substituting a consistent estimator of $H$ into the formula for $\hat{\boldsymbol{\beta}}^{Eff.GMM}$ in Equation (18.66).

The efficient GMM estimator can be computed in two steps. In the first step, estimate $\boldsymbol{\beta}$ using any consistent estimator. Use this estimator of $\boldsymbol{\beta}$ to compute the residuals from the equation of interest, and then use these residuals to compute an estimator of $\boldsymbol{H}$. In the second step, use this estimator of $\boldsymbol{H}$ to estimate the optimal weight matrix $\boldsymbol{H}^{-1}$ and to compute the efficient GMM estimator. To be concrete, in the linear IV regression model, it is natural to use the TSLS estimator in the first step and to use the TSLS residuals to estimate $\boldsymbol{H}$. If TSLS is used in the first step, then the feasible efficient GMM estimator computed in the second step is

$$\hat{\boldsymbol{\beta}}^{Eff.GMM} = (\boldsymbol{X}'\boldsymbol{Z}\hat{\boldsymbol{H}}^{-1}\boldsymbol{Z}'\boldsymbol{X})^{-1}\boldsymbol{X}'\boldsymbol{Z}\hat{\boldsymbol{H}}^{-1}\boldsymbol{Z}'\boldsymbol{Y}, \tag{18.68}$$

where $\hat{\boldsymbol{H}}$ is given in Equation (18.54).

Because $\hat{\boldsymbol{H}} \xrightarrow{p} \boldsymbol{H}, \sqrt{n}(\hat{\boldsymbol{\beta}}^{Eff.GMM} - \tilde{\boldsymbol{\beta}}^{Eff.GMM}) \xrightarrow{p} 0$ (Exercise 18.12), and

$$\sqrt{n}\,(\hat{\boldsymbol{\beta}}^{Eff.GMM} - \boldsymbol{\beta}) \xrightarrow{d} N(0, \boldsymbol{\Sigma}^{Eff.GMM}), \tag{18.69}$$

where $\boldsymbol{\Sigma}^{Eff.GMM} = (\boldsymbol{Q}_{XZ}\boldsymbol{H}^{-1}\boldsymbol{Q}_{ZX})^{-1}$ [Equation (18.67)]. That is, the feasible two-step estimator $\hat{\boldsymbol{\beta}}^{Eff.GMM}$ in Equation (18.68) is, asymptotically, the efficient GMM estimator.

*The heteroskedasticity-robust J-statistic.* The **heteroskedasticity-robust J-statistic**, also known as the **GMM J-statistic**, is the counterpart of the TSLS-based J-statistic, computed using the efficient GMM estimator and weight function. That is, the GMM J-statistic is given by

$$J^{GMM} = (\boldsymbol{Z}'\hat{\boldsymbol{U}}^{GMM})'\hat{\boldsymbol{H}}^{-1}(\boldsymbol{Z}'\hat{\boldsymbol{U}}^{GMM})/n, \tag{18.70}$$

where $\hat{\boldsymbol{U}}^{GMM} = \boldsymbol{Y} - \boldsymbol{X}\hat{\boldsymbol{\beta}}^{Eff.GMM}$ are the residuals from the equation of interest, estimated by (feasible) efficient GMM, and $\hat{\boldsymbol{H}}^{-1}$ is the weight matrix used to compute $\hat{\boldsymbol{\beta}}^{Eff.GMM}$.

Under the null hypothesis $E(\boldsymbol{Z}_i u_i) = \boldsymbol{0}$, $J^{GMM} \xrightarrow{d} \chi^2_{m-k}$ (see Appendix 18.6).

*GMM with time series data.* The results in this section were derived under the IV regression assumptions for cross–sectional data. In many applications, however, these results extend to time series applications of IV regression and GMM. Although a formal mathematical treatment of GMM with time series data is beyond the scope of this book (for such a treatment, see Hayashi, 2000, Chapter 6), we nevertheless will summarize the key ideas of GMM estimation with time series data. This summary assumes familiarity with the material in Chapters 14 and 15. For this discussion, it is assumed that the variables are stationary.

It is useful to distinguish between two types of applications: applications in which the error term $u_t$ is serially correlated and applications in which $u_t$ is serially uncorrelated. If the error term $u_t$ is serially correlated, then the asymptotic distribution of the GMM estimator continues to be normally distributed, but the formula for $H$ in Equation (18.50) is no longer correct. Instead, the correct expression for $H$ depends on the autocovariances of $Z_t u_t$ and is analogous to the formula given in Equation (15.14) for the variance of the OLS estimator when the error term is serially correlated. The efficient GMM estimator is still constructed using a consistent estimator of $H$; however, that consistent estimator must be computed using the HAC methods discussed in Chapter 15.

If the error term $u_t$ is not serially correlated, then HAC estimation of $H$ is unnecessary and the formulas presented in this section all extend to time series GMM applications. In modern applications to finance and macroeconometrics, it is common to encounter models in which the error term represents an unexpected or unforecastable disturbance, in which case the model implies that $u_t$ is serially uncorrelated. For example, consider a model with a single included endogenous variable and no included exogenous variables so that the equation of interest is $Y_t = \beta_0 + \beta_1 X_t + u_t$. Suppose that an economic theory implies that $u_t$ is unpredictable given past information. Then the theory implies the moment condition

$$E(u_t | Y_{t-1}, X_{t-1}, Z_{t-1}, Y_{t-2}, X_{t-2}, Z_{t-2}, \ldots) = 0, \qquad (18.71)$$

where $Z_{t-1}$ is the lagged value of some other variable. The moment condition in Equation (18.71) implies that all the lagged variables $Y_{t-1}, X_{t-1}, Z_{t-1}, Y_{t-2}, X_{t-2}, Z_{t-2}, \ldots$ are candidates for being valid instruments (they satisfy the exogeneity condition). Moreover, because $u_{t-1} = Y_{t-1} - \beta_0 - \beta_1 X_{t-1}$, the moment condition in Equation (18.71) is equivalent to $E(u_t | u_{t-1}, X_{t-1}, Z_{t-1}, u_{t-2}, X_{t-2}, Z_{t-2}, \ldots) = 0$. Because $u_t$ is serially uncorrelated, HAC estimation of $H$ is unnecessary. The theory of GMM presented in this section, including efficient GMM estimation and the GMM $J$-statistic, therefore applies directly to time series applications with moment conditions of the form in Equation (18.71), under the hypothesis that the moment condition in Equation (18.71) is, in fact, correct.

## Summary

1.  The linear multiple regression model in matrix form is $Y = X\beta + U$, where $Y$ is the $n \times 1$ vector of observations on the dependent variable, $X$ is the $n \times (k + 1)$ matrix of $n$ observations on the $k + 1$ regressors (including a constant), $\beta$ is the $k + 1$ vector of unknown parameters, and $U$ is the $n \times 1$ vector of error terms.

2.  The OLS estimator is $\hat{\boldsymbol{\beta}} = (\boldsymbol{X'X})^{-1}\boldsymbol{X'Y}$. Under the first four least squares assumptions in Key Concept 18.1, $\hat{\boldsymbol{\beta}}$ is consistent and asymptotically normally distributed. If in addition the errors are homoskedastic, then the conditional variance of $\hat{\boldsymbol{\beta}}$ is $\text{var}(\hat{\boldsymbol{\beta}} \mid \boldsymbol{X}) = \sigma_u^2(\boldsymbol{X'X})^{-1}$.

3.  General linear restrictions on $\boldsymbol{\beta}$ can be written as the $q$ equations $\boldsymbol{R\beta} = \boldsymbol{r}$, and this formulation can be used to test joint hypotheses involving multiple coefficients or to construct confidence sets for elements of $\boldsymbol{\beta}$.

4.  When the regression errors are i.i.d. and normally distributed, conditional on $\boldsymbol{X}$, $\boldsymbol{\beta}$ has an exact normal distribution and the homoskedasticity-only $t$- and $F$-statistics have exact $t_{n-k-1}$ and $F_{q,n-k-1}$ distributions, respectively.

5.  The Gauss–Markov theorem says that, if the errors are homoskedastic and conditionally uncorrelated across observations and if $E(u_i|\boldsymbol{X}) = 0$, the OLS estimator is efficient among linear conditionally unbiased estimators (that is, OLS is BLUE).

6.  If the error covariance matrix $\boldsymbol{\Omega}$ is not proportional to the identity matrix, and if $\boldsymbol{\Omega}$ is known or can be estimated, then the GLS estimator is asymptotically more efficient than OLS. However, GLS requires that, in general, $u_i$ be uncorrelated with *all* observations on the regressors, not just with $\boldsymbol{X}_i$, as is required by OLS, an assumption that must be evaluated carefully in applications.

7.  The TSLS estimator is a member of the class of GMM estimators of the linear model. In GMM, the coefficients are estimated by making the sample covariance between the regression error and the exogenous variables as small as possible—specifically, by solving $\min_b[(\boldsymbol{Y} - \boldsymbol{Xb})'\boldsymbol{Z}]\boldsymbol{A}[\boldsymbol{Z}'(\boldsymbol{Y} - \boldsymbol{Xb})]$, where $\boldsymbol{A}$ is a weight matrix. The asymptotically efficient GMM estimator sets $\boldsymbol{A} = [E(\boldsymbol{Z}_i\boldsymbol{Z}_i'u_i^2)]^{-1}$. When the errors are homoskedastic, the asymptotically efficient GMM estimator in the linear IV regression model is TSLS.

## Key Terms

Gauss–Markov conditions for multiple regression (766)

Gauss–Markov theorem for multiple regression (767)

generalized least squares (GLS) (769)

infeasible GLS (772)

feasible GLS (772)

generalized method of moments (GMM) (780)

efficient GMM (781)

heteroskedasticity-robust
   $J$-statistic (782)
GMM $J$-statistic (782)

mean vector (796)
covariance matrix (796)

---

**MyEconLab Can Help You Get a Better Grade**

**MyEconLab**   If your exam were tomorrow, would you be ready? For each chapter, **MyEconLab** Practice Tests and Study Plan help you prepare for your exams. You can also find similar Exercises and Review the Concepts Questions now in **MyEconLab**. To see how it works, turn to the **MyEconLab** spread on pages 2 and 3 of this book and then go to **www.myeconlab.com**.

For additional Empirical Exercises and Data Sets, log on to the Companion Website at **www.pearsonglobaleditions.com/Stock_Watson**.

---

## Review the Concepts

**18.1** A researcher studying the relationship between earnings and gender for a group of workers specifies the regression model $Y_i = \beta_0 + X_{1i}\beta_1 + X_{2i}\beta_2 + u_i$, where $X_{1i}$ is a binary variable that equals 1 if the $i^{th}$ person is a female and $X_{2i}$ is a binary variable that equals 1 if the $i^{th}$ person is a male. Write the model in the matrix form of Equation (18.2) for a hypothetical set of $n = 5$ observations. Show that the columns of $X$ are linearly dependent so that $X$ does not have full rank. Explain how you would respecifiy the model to eliminate the perfect multicollinearity.

**18.2** You are analyzing a linear regression model with 500 observations and one regressor. Explain how you would construct a confidence interval for $\beta_1$ if:

  **a.** Assumptions #1 through #4 in Key Concept 18.1 are true, but you think Assumption #5 or #6 might not be true.

  **b.** Assumptions #1 through #5 are true, but you think Assumption #6 might not be true. (Give two ways to construct the confidence interval.)

  **c.** Assumptions #1 through #6 are true.

**18.3** Suppose that Assumptions #1 through #5 in Key Concept 18.1 are true but that Assumption #6 is not. Does the result in Equation (18.31) hold? Explain.

**18.4** When is the GLS estimator more efficient than the OLS estimator within the class of linear conditionally unbiased estimators?

**18.5** Construct an example of a regression model that satisfies the assumption $E(u_i \mid X_i) = 0$ but for which $E(U \mid X) \neq \mathbf{0}_n$.

## Exercises

**18.1** Consider the population regression of test scores against income and the square of income in Equation (8.1).

    **a.** Write the regression in Equation (8.1) in the matrix form of Equation (18.5). Define $Y$, $X$, $U$, and $\beta$.

    **b.** Explain how to test the null hypothesis that the relationship between test scores and income is linear against the alternative that it is quadratic. Write the null hypothesis in the form of Equation (18.20). What are $R$, $r$, and $q$?

**18.2** Suppose that a sample of $n = 20$ households has the sample means and sample covariances below for a dependent variable and two regressors:

|  | Sample Means | Sample Covariances | | |
|---|---|---|---|---|
|  |  | $Y$ | $X_1$ | $X_2$ |
| $Y$ | 6.39 | 0.26 | 0.22 | 0.32 |
| $X_1$ | 7.24 |  | 0.80 | 0.28 |
| $X_2$ | 4.00 |  |  | 2.40 |

    **a.** Calculate the OLS estimates of $\beta_0$, $\beta_1$, and $\beta_2$. Calculate $s_{\hat{u}}^2$. Calculate the $R^2$ of the regression.

    **b.** Suppose that all six assumptions in Key Concept 18.1 hold. Test the hypothesis that $\beta_1 = 0$ at the 5% significance level.

**18.3** Let $W$ be an $m \times 1$ vector with covariance matrix $\Sigma_W$, where $\Sigma_W$ is finite and positive definite. Let $c$ be a nonrandom $m \times 1$ vector and let $Q = c'W$.

    **a.** Show that $\text{var}(Q) = c'\Sigma_W c$.

    **b.** Suppose that $c \neq 0_m$. Show that $0 < \text{var}(Q) < \infty$.

**18.4** Consider the regression model $Y_i = \beta_0 + \beta_1 X_i + u_i$ from Chapter 4 and assume that the least squares assumptions in Key Concept 4.3 hold.

    **a.** Write the model in the matrix form given in Equations (18.2) and (18.4).

    **b.** Show that Assumptions #1 through #4 in Key Concept 18.1 are satisfied.

    **c.** Use the general formula for $\hat{\beta}$ in Equation (18.11) to derive the expressions for $\hat{\beta}_0$ and $\hat{\beta}_1$ given in Key Concept 4.2.

    **d.** Show that the $(1, 1)$ element of $\Sigma_{\hat{\beta}}$ in Equation (18.13) is equal to the expression for $\sigma_{\hat{\beta}_0}^2$ given in Key Concept 4.4.

**18.5**  Let $P_X$ and $M_X$ be as defined in Equations (18.24) and (18.25).

    **a.** Prove that $P_X M_X = 0_{n \times n}$ and that $P_X$ and $M_X$ are idempotent.

    **b.** Derive Equations (18.27) and (18.28).

    **c.** Show that rank$(P_X) = k + 1$ and rank$(M_X) = n - k - 1$. [*Hint:* First solve Exercise 18.10 and then use the fact that trace$(AB) =$ trace$(BA)$ for conformable matrices $A$ and $B$.]

**18.6**  Consider the regression model in matrix form, $Y = X\beta + W\gamma + U$, where $X$ is an $n \times k_1$ matrix of regressors and $W$ is an $n \times k_2$ matrix of regressors. Then, as shown in Exercise 18.17, the OLS estimator $\hat{\beta}$ can be expressed

$$\hat{\beta} = (X'M_W X)^{-1}(X'M_W Y).$$

Now let $\hat{\beta}_1^{BV}$ be the "binary variable" fixed effects estimator computed by estimating Equation (10.11) by OLS and let $\hat{\beta}_1^{DM}$ be the "de-meaning" fixed effects estimator computed by estimating Equation (10.14) by OLS, in which the entity-specific sample means have been subtracted from $X$ and $Y$. Use the expression for $\hat{\beta}$ given above to prove that $\hat{\beta}_1^{BV} = \hat{\beta}_1^{DM}$. [*Hint:* Write Equation (10.11) using a full set of fixed effects, $D1_i, D2_i, \ldots, Dn_i$ and no constant term. Include all of the fixed effects in $W$. Write out the matrix $M_W X$.]

**18.7**  Consider the regression model $Y_i = \beta_1 X_i + \beta_2 W_i + u_i$, where for simplicity the intercept is omitted and all variables are assumed to have a mean of zero. Suppose that $X_i$ is distributed independently of $(W_i, u_i)$ but $W_i$ and $u_i$ might be correlated and let $\hat{\beta}_1$ and $\hat{\beta}_2$ be the OLS estimators for this model. Show that

    **a.** Whether or not $W_i$ and $u_i$ are correlated, $\hat{\beta}_1 \xrightarrow{p} \beta_1$.

    **b.** If $W_i$ and $u_i$ are correlated, then $\hat{\beta}_2$ is inconsistent.

    **c.** Let $\hat{\beta}_1^r$ be the OLS estimator from the regression of $Y$ on $X$ (the restricted regression that excludes $W$). Will $\hat{\beta}_1$ have a smaller asymptotic variance than $\hat{\beta}_1^r$, allowing for the possibility that $W_i$ and $u_i$ are correlated? Explain.

**18.8**  Consider the regression model $Y_i = \beta_0 + \beta_1 X_i + u_i$, where $u_1 = \tilde{u}_1$ and $u_i = 0.5 u_{i-1} + \tilde{u}_i$ for $i = 2, 3, \ldots, n$. Suppose that $\tilde{u}_i$ are i.i.d. with mean 0 and variance 1 and are distributed independently of $X_j$ for all $i$ and $j$.

    **a.** Derive an expression for $E(UU') = \Omega$.

    **b.** Explain how to estimate the model by GLS without explicitly invert-
ing the matrix $\boldsymbol{\Omega}$. (*Hint:* Transform the model so that the regression
errors are $\tilde{u}_1, \tilde{u}_2, \ldots, \tilde{u}_n$.)

**18.9**  This exercise shows that the OLS estimator of a subset of the regression coefficients is consistent under the conditional mean independence
assumption stated in Appendix 7.2. Consider the multiple regression
model in matrix form $\boldsymbol{Y} = \boldsymbol{X\beta} + \boldsymbol{W\gamma} + \boldsymbol{U}$, where $\boldsymbol{X}$ and $\boldsymbol{W}$ are, respectively, $n \times k_1$ and $n \times k_2$ matrices of regressors. Let $\boldsymbol{X}_i'$ and $\boldsymbol{W}_i'$ denote the
$i^{\text{th}}$ rows of $\boldsymbol{X}$ and $\boldsymbol{W}$ [as in Equation (18.3)]. Assume that (i) $E(u_i|\boldsymbol{X}_i, \boldsymbol{W}_i) = \boldsymbol{W}_i'\boldsymbol{\delta}$, where $\boldsymbol{\delta}$ is a $k_2 \times 1$ vector of unknown parameters; (ii) $(\boldsymbol{X}_i, \boldsymbol{W}_i, Y_i)$
are i.i.d.; (iii) $(\boldsymbol{X}_i, \boldsymbol{W}_i, u_i)$ have four finite, nonzero moments;
and (iv) there is no perfect multicollinearity. These are Assumptions
#1 through #4 of Key Concept 18.1, with the conditional mean inde-
pendence assumption (i) replacing the usual conditional mean zero
assumption.

    **a.** Use the expression for $\hat{\boldsymbol{\beta}}$ given in Exercise 18.6 to write $\hat{\boldsymbol{\beta}} - \boldsymbol{\beta} = (n^{-1}\boldsymbol{X}'\boldsymbol{M}_W\boldsymbol{X})^{-1}(n^{-1}\boldsymbol{X}'\boldsymbol{M}_W\boldsymbol{U})$.

    **b.** Show that $n^{-1}\boldsymbol{X}'\boldsymbol{M}_W\boldsymbol{X} \xrightarrow{p} \boldsymbol{\Sigma}_{XX} - \boldsymbol{\Sigma}_{XW}\boldsymbol{\Sigma}_{WW}^{-1}\boldsymbol{\Sigma}_{WX}$, where $\boldsymbol{\Sigma}_{XX} = E(\boldsymbol{X}_i\boldsymbol{X}_i')$, $\boldsymbol{\Sigma}_{XW} = E(\boldsymbol{X}_i\boldsymbol{W}_i')$, and so forth. [The matrix $\boldsymbol{A}_n \xrightarrow{p} \boldsymbol{A}$ if $\boldsymbol{A}_{n,ij} \xrightarrow{p} \boldsymbol{A}_{ij}$ for all $i, j$, where $\boldsymbol{A}_{n,ij}$ and $\boldsymbol{A}_{ij}$ are the $(i, j)$ elements of $\boldsymbol{A}_n$ and $\boldsymbol{A}$.]

    **c.** Show that assumptions (i) and (ii) imply that $E(\boldsymbol{U}|\boldsymbol{X}, \boldsymbol{W}) = \boldsymbol{W\delta}$.

    **d.** Use (c) and the law of iterated expectations to show that
$n^{-1}\boldsymbol{X}'\boldsymbol{M}_W\boldsymbol{U} \xrightarrow{p} \boldsymbol{0}_{k_1 \times 1}$.

    **e.** Use (a) through (d) to conclude that, under conditions (i) through (iv),
$\hat{\boldsymbol{\beta}} \xrightarrow{p} \boldsymbol{\beta}$.

**18.10** Let $\boldsymbol{C}$ be a symmetric idempotent matrix.

    **a.** Show that the eigenvalues of $\boldsymbol{C}$ are either 0 or 1. (*Hint:* Note that $\boldsymbol{Cq} = \gamma\boldsymbol{q}$
implies $0 = \boldsymbol{Cq} - \gamma\boldsymbol{q} = \boldsymbol{CCq} - \gamma\boldsymbol{q} = \gamma\boldsymbol{Cq} - \gamma\boldsymbol{q} = \gamma^2\boldsymbol{q} - \gamma\boldsymbol{q}$ and
solve for $\gamma$.)

    **b.** Show that $\text{trace}(\boldsymbol{C}) = \text{rank}(\boldsymbol{C})$.

    **c.** Let $\boldsymbol{d}$ be an $n \times 1$ vector. Show that $\boldsymbol{d}'\boldsymbol{Cd} \geq 0$.

**18.11** Suppose that $\boldsymbol{C}$ is an $n \times n$ symmetric idempotent matrix with rank $r$ and
let $\boldsymbol{V} \sim N(\boldsymbol{0}_n, \boldsymbol{I}_n)$.

**a.** Show that $C = AA'$, where $A$ is $n \times r$ with $A'A = I_r$. (*Hint:* $C$ is positive semidefinite and can be written as $Q \Lambda Q'$, as explained in Appendix 18.1.)

**b.** Show that $A'V \sim N(0_r, I_r)$.

**c.** Show that $V'CV \sim \chi_r^2$.

**18.12 a.** Show that $\widetilde{\beta}^{\,Eff.GMM}$ is the efficient GMM estimator—that is, that $\widetilde{\beta}^{\,Eff.GMM}$ in Equation (18.66) is the solution to Equation (18.65).

**b.** Show that $\sqrt{n}(\hat{\beta}^{Eff.GMM} - \widetilde{\beta}^{\,Eff.GMM}) \xrightarrow{p} 0$.

**c.** Show that $J^{GMM} \xrightarrow{d} \chi_{m-k}^2$.

**18.13** Consider the problem of minimizing the sum of squared residuals, subject to the constraint that $Rb = r$, where $R$ is $q \times (k + 1)$ with rank $q$. Let $\widetilde{\beta}$ be the value of $b$ that solves the constrained minimization problem.

**a.** Show that the Lagrangian for the minimization problem is $L(b, \gamma) = (Y - Xb)'(Y - Xb) + \gamma'(Rb - r)$, where $\gamma$ is a $q \times 1$ vector of Lagrange multipliers.

**b.** Show that $\widetilde{\beta} = \hat{\beta} - (X'X)^{-1}R'[R(X'X)^{-1}R']^{-1}(R\hat{\beta} - r)$.

**c.** Show that $(Y - X\widetilde{\beta})'(Y - X\widetilde{\beta}) - (Y - X\hat{\beta})(Y - X\hat{\beta}) = (R\hat{\beta} - r)'[R(X'X)^{-1}R']^{-1}(R\hat{\beta} - r)$.

**d.** Show that $\widetilde{F}$ in Equation (18.36) is equivalent to the homoskedasticity-only $F$-statistic in Equation (7.13).

**18.14** Consider the regression model $Y = X\beta + U$. Partition $X$ as $[X_1 \quad X_2]$ and $\beta$ as $[\beta_1' \quad \beta_2']'$, where $X_1$ has $k_1$ columns and $X_2$ has $k_2$ columns. Suppose that $X_2'Y = 0_{k_2 \times 1}$. Let $R = [I_{k_1} \quad 0_{k_1 \times k_2}]$.

**a.** Show that $\hat{\beta}'(X'X)\hat{\beta} = (R\hat{\beta})'[R(X'X)^{-1}R]^{-1}(R\hat{\beta})$.

**b.** Consider the regression described in Equation (12.17). Let $W = [1 \quad W_1 \quad W_2 \quad \ldots \quad W_r]$, where $1$ is an $n \times 1$ vector of ones, $W_1$ is the $n \times 1$ vector with $i^{\text{th}}$ element $W_{1i}$, and so forth. Let $\hat{U}^{TSLS}$ denote the vector of two-stage least squares residuals.

   i. Show that $W'\hat{U}^{TSLS} = 0$.

   ii. Show that the method for computing the $J$-statistic described in Key Concept 12.6 (using a homoskedasticity-only $F$-statistic) and the formula in Equation (18.63) produce the same value for the $J$-statistic. [*Hint:* Use the results in (a), (b, i), and Exercise 18.13.]

**18.15**  (Consistency of clustered standard errors.) Consider the panel data model $Y_{it} = \beta X_{it} + \alpha_i + u_{it}$, where all variables are scalars. Assume that Assumptions #1, #2, and #4 in Key Concept 10.3 hold and strengthen Assumption #3 so that $X_{it}$ and $u_{it}$ have eight nonzero finite moments. Let $M = I_T - T^{-1}\iota\iota'$, where $\iota$ is a $T \times 1$ vector of ones. Also let $Y_i = (Y_{i1} \quad Y_{i2} \quad \cdots \quad Y_{iT})'$, $X_i = (X_{i1} \quad X_{i2} \quad \cdots \quad X_{iT})'$, $u_i = (u_{i1} \quad u_{i2} \quad \cdots \quad u_{iT})'$, $\tilde{Y}_i = MY_i$, $\tilde{X}_i = MX_i$, and $\tilde{u}_i = Mu_i$. For the asymptotic calculations in this problem, suppose that $T$ is fixed and $n \longrightarrow \infty$.

**a.** Show that the fixed effects estimator of $\beta$ from Section 10.3 can be written as $\hat{\beta} = (\sum_{i=1}^{n} \tilde{X}_i'\tilde{X}_i)^{-1} \sum_{i=1}^{n} \tilde{X}_i'\tilde{Y}_i$.

**b.** Show that $\hat{\beta} - \beta = (\sum_{i=1}^{n} \tilde{X}_i'\tilde{X}_i)^{-1} \sum_{i=1}^{n} \tilde{X}_i'u_i$. (*Hint: $M$ is idempotent.*)

**c.** Let $Q_{\tilde{X}} = T^{-1}E(\tilde{X}_i'\tilde{X}_i)$ and $\hat{Q}_{\tilde{X}} = \frac{1}{nT}\sum_{i=1}^{n}\sum_{t=1}^{T}\tilde{X}_{it}^2$. Show that $\hat{Q}_{\tilde{X}} \xrightarrow{p} Q_{\tilde{X}}$.

**d.** Let $\eta_i = \tilde{X}_i'u_i/\sqrt{T}$ and $\sigma_\eta^2 = \text{var}(\eta_i)$. Show that $\sqrt{\frac{1}{n}}\sum_{i=1}^{n}\eta_i \xrightarrow{d} N(0, \sigma_\eta^2)$.

**e.** Use your answers to (b) through (d) to prove Equation (10.25); that is, show that $\sqrt{nT}(\hat{\beta} - \beta) \xrightarrow{d} N(0, \sigma_\eta^2/Q_{\tilde{X}}^2)$.

**f.** Let $\tilde{\sigma}_{\eta,clustered}^2$ be the infeasible clustered variance estimator, computed using the true errors instead of the residuals so that $\tilde{\sigma}_{\eta,clustered}^2 = \frac{1}{nT}\sum_{i=1}^{n}(\tilde{X}_i'u_i)^2$. Show that $\tilde{\sigma}_{\eta,clustered}^2 \xrightarrow{p} \sigma_\eta^2$.

**g.** Let $\hat{\tilde{u}}_1 = \tilde{Y}_i - \hat{\beta}\tilde{X}_i$ and $\hat{\sigma}_{\eta,clustered}^2 = \frac{n}{n-1}\frac{1}{nT}\sum_{i=1}^{n}(\tilde{X}_i'\hat{\tilde{u}}_i)^2$ [this is Equation (10.27) in matrix form]. Show that $\hat{\sigma}_{\eta,clustered}^2 \xrightarrow{p} \sigma_\eta^2$. [*Hint:* Use an argument like that used in Equation (17.16) to show that $\hat{\sigma}_{\eta,clustered}^2 - \tilde{\sigma}_{\eta,clustered}^2 \xrightarrow{p} 0$ and then use your answer to (f).]

**18.16**  This exercise takes up the problem of missing data discussed in Section 9.2. Consider the regression model $Y_i = X_i\beta + u_i, i = 1, \ldots, n$, where all variables are scalars and the constant term/intercept is omitted for convenience.

**a.** Suppose that the least squares assumptions in Key Concept 4.3 are satisfied. Show that the least squares estimator of $\beta$ is unbiased and consistent.

**b.** Now suppose that some of the observations are missing. Let $I_i$ denote a binary random variable that indicates the nonmissing observations; that is, $I_i = 1$ if observation $i$ is not missing and $I_i = 0$ if observation $i$ is missing. Assume that $\{I_i, X_i, u_i\}$ are i.i.d.

i. Show that the OLS estimator can be written as

$$\hat{\beta} = \left( \sum_{i=1}^{n} I_i X_i X_i' \right)^{-1} \left( \sum_{i=1}^{n} I_i X_i Y_i \right) = \beta + \left( \sum_{i=1}^{n} I_i X_i X_i' \right)^{-1} \left( \sum_{i=1}^{n} I_i X_i u_i \right).$$

ii. Suppose that data are missing, "completely at random," in the sense that $\Pr(I_i = 1 | X_i, u_i) = p$, where $p$ is a constant. Show that $\hat{\beta}$ is unbiased and consistent.

iii. Suppose that the probability that the $i^{th}$ observation is missing depends of $X_i$, but not on $u_i$; that is, $\Pr(I_i = 1 | X_i, u_i) = p(X_i)$. Show that $\hat{\beta}$ is unbiased and consistent.

iv. Suppose that the probability that the $i^{th}$ observation is missing depends on both $X_i$ and $u_i$; that is, $\Pr(I_i = 1 | X_i, u_i) = p(X_i, u_i)$. Is $\hat{\beta}$ unbiased? Is $\hat{\beta}$ consistent? Explain.

c. Suppose that $\beta = 1$ and that $X_i$ and $u_i$ are mutually independent standard normal random variables [so that both $X_i$ and $u_i$ are distributed $N(0, 1)$]. Suppose that $I_i = 1$ when $Y_i \geq 0$, but $I_i = 0$ when $Y_i < 0$. Is $\hat{\beta}$ unbiased? Is $\hat{\beta}$ consistent? Explain.

**18.17** Consider the regression model in matrix form $Y = X\beta + W\gamma + U$, where $X$ and $W$ are matrices of regressors and $\beta$ and $\gamma$ are vectors of unknown regression coefficients. Let $\tilde{X} = M_W X$ and $\tilde{Y} = M_W Y$, where $M_W = I - W(W'W)^{-1}W$.

a. Show that the OLS estimators of $\beta$ and $\gamma$ can be written as

$$\begin{bmatrix} \hat{\beta} \\ \hat{\gamma} \end{bmatrix} = \begin{bmatrix} X'X & X'W \\ W'X & W'W \end{bmatrix}^{-1} \begin{bmatrix} X'Y \\ W'Y \end{bmatrix}$$

b. Show that

$$\begin{bmatrix} X'X & X'W \\ W'X & W'W \end{bmatrix}^{-1}$$
$$= \begin{bmatrix} (X'M_W X)^{-1} & -(X'M_W X)^{-1} X' W(W'W)^{-1} \\ -(W'W)^{-1} W' X(X'M_W X)^{-1} & (W'W)^{-1} + (W'W)^{-1} W' X(X'M_W X)^{-1} X' W(W'W)^{-1} \end{bmatrix}.$$

(*Hint:* Show that the product of the two matrices is equal to the identity matrix.)

   **c.** Show that $\hat{\boldsymbol{\beta}} = (\boldsymbol{X'M_WX})^{-1}\boldsymbol{X'M_WY}$.

   **d.** The Frisch–Waugh theorem (Appendix 6.2) says that $\hat{\boldsymbol{\beta}} = (\tilde{\boldsymbol{X}}'\tilde{\boldsymbol{X}})^{-1}\tilde{\boldsymbol{X}}'\tilde{\boldsymbol{Y}}$. Use the result in (c) to prove the Frisch–Waugh theorem.

---

**APPENDIX**

## 18.1 Summary of Matrix Algebra

This appendix summarizes vectors, matrices, and the elements of matrix algebra used in Chapter 1. The purpose of this appendix is to review some concepts and definitions from a course in linear algebra, not to replace such a course.

### Definitions of Vectors and Matrices

A **vector** is a collection of $n$ numbers or elements, collected either in a column (a **column vector**) or in a row (a **row vector**). The $n$-dimensional column vector $\boldsymbol{b}$ and the $n$-dimensional row vector $\boldsymbol{c}$ are

$$\boldsymbol{b} = \begin{bmatrix} b_1 \\ b_2 \\ \vdots \\ b_n \end{bmatrix} \text{ and } \boldsymbol{c} = \begin{bmatrix} c_1 & c_2 & \cdots & c_n \end{bmatrix},$$

where $b_1$ is the first element of $\boldsymbol{b}$ and in general $b_i$ is the $i^{\text{th}}$ element of $\boldsymbol{b}$.

   Throughout, a boldface symbol denotes a vector or matrix.

   A **matrix** is a collection, or an array, of numbers or elements in which the elements are laid out in columns and rows. The dimension of a matrix is $n \times m$, where $n$ is the number of rows and $m$ is the number of columns. The $n \times m$ matrix $\boldsymbol{A}$ is

$$\boldsymbol{A} = \begin{bmatrix} a_{11} & a_{12} & \cdots & a_{1m} \\ a_{21} & a_{22} & \cdots & a_{2m} \\ \vdots & \vdots & \ddots & \vdots \\ a_{n1} & a_{n2} & \cdots & a_{nm} \end{bmatrix},$$

where $a_{ij}$ is the $(i, j)$ element of $\boldsymbol{A}$, that is, $a_{ij}$ is the element that appears in the $i^{\text{th}}$ row and $j^{\text{th}}$ column. An $n \times m$ matrix consists of $n$ row vectors or, alternatively, of $m$ column vectors.

   To distinguish one-dimensional numbers from vectors and matrices, a one-dimensional number is called a **scalar**.

## Types of Matrices

*Square, symmetric, and diagonal matrices.*  A matrix is said to be **square** if the number of rows equals the number of columns. A square matrix is said to be **symmetric** if its $(i, j)$ element equals its $(j, i)$ element. A **diagonal** matrix is a square matrix in which all the off-diagonal elements equal zero; that is, if the square matrix $A$ is diagonal, then $a_{ij} = 0$ for $i \neq j$.

*Special matrices.*  An important matrix is the **identity matrix**, $I_n$, which is an $n \times n$ diagonal matrix with ones on the diagonal. The **null matrix**, $0_{n \times m}$, is the $n \times m$ matrix with all elements equal to zero.

*The transpose.*  The **transpose** of a matrix switches the rows and the columns. That is, the transpose of a matrix turns the $n \times m$ matrix $A$ into the $m \times n$ matrix, which is denoted by $A'$, where the $(i, j)$ element of $A$ becomes the $(j, i)$ element of $A'$; said differently, the transpose of the matrix $A$ turns the rows of $A$ into the columns of $A'$. If $a_{ij}$ is the $(i, j)$ element of $A$, then $A'$ (the transpose of $A$) is

$$A' = \begin{bmatrix} a_{11} & a_{21} & \cdots & a_{n1} \\ a_{12} & a_{22} & \cdots & a_{n2} \\ \vdots & \vdots & \ddots & \vdots \\ a_{1m} & a_{2m} & \cdots & a_{nm} \end{bmatrix}.$$

The transpose of a vector is a special case of the transpose of a matrix. Thus the transpose of a vector turns a column vector into a row vector; that is, if $b$ is an $n \times 1$ column vector, then its transpose is the $1 \times n$ row vector

$$b' = \begin{bmatrix} b_1 & b_2 & \cdots & b_n \end{bmatrix}.$$

The transpose of a row vector is a column vector.

## Elements of Matrix Algebra: Addition and Multiplication

*Matrix addition.*  Two matrices $A$ and $B$ that have the same dimensions (for example, that are both $n \times m$) can be added together. The sum of two matrices is the sum of their elements; that is, if $C = A + B$, then $c_{ij} = a_{ij} + b_{ij}$. A special case of matrix addition is vector addition: If $a$ and $b$ are both $n \times 1$ column vectors, then their sum $c = a + b$ is the element-wise sum; that is, $c_i = a_i + b_i$.

*Vector and matrix multiplication.*  Let $a$ and $b$ be two $n \times 1$ column vectors. Then the product of the transpose of $a$ (which is itself a row vector) with $b$ is $a'b = \sum_{i=1}^{n} a_i b_i$. Applying this definition with $b = a$ yields $a'a = \sum_{i=1}^{n} a_i^2$.

Similarly, the matrices $A$ and $B$ can be multiplied together if they are conformable— that is, if the number of columns of $A$ equals the number of rows of $B$. Specifically, suppose that $A$ has dimension $n \times m$ and $B$ has dimension $m \times r$. Then the product of $A$ and $B$ is an $n \times r$ matrix, $C$; that is, $C = AB$, where the $(i, j)$ element of $C$ is $c_{ij} = \sum_{k=1}^{m} a_{ik} b_{kj}$. Said differently, the $(i, j)$ element of $AB$ is the product of multiplying the row vector that is the $i^{\text{th}}$ row of $A$ with the column vector that is the $j^{\text{th}}$ column of $B$.

The product of a scalar $d$ with the matrix $A$ has the $(i, j)$ element $da_{ij}$; that is, each element of $A$ is multiplied by the scalar $d$.

*Some useful properties of matrix addition and multiplication.* Let $A$ and $B$ be matrices. Then:

   **a.** $A + B = B + A$;

   **b.** $(A + B) + C = A + (B + C)$;

   **c.** $(A + B)' = A' + B'$;

   **d.** If $A$ is $n \times m$, then $AI_m = A$ and $I_n A = A$;

   **e.** $A(BC) = (AB)C$;

   **f.** $(A + B)C = AC + BC$; and

   **g.** $(AB)' = B'A'$.

In general, matrix multiplication does not commute; that is, in general $AB \neq BA$, although there are some special cases in which matrix multiplication commutes; for example, if $A$ and $B$ are both $n \times n$ diagonal matrices, then $AB = BA$.

## Matrix Inverse, Matrix Square Roots, and Related Topics

*The matrix inverse.* Let $A$ be a square matrix. Assuming that it exists, the **inverse** of the matrix $A$ is defined as the matrix for which $A^{-1}A = I_n$. If in fact the inverse matrix $A^{-1}$ exists, then $A$ is said to be **invertible** or **nonsingular**. If both $A$ and $B$ are invertible, then $(AB)^{-1} = B^{-1}A^{-1}$.

*Positive definite and positive semidefinite matrices.* Let $V$ be an $n \times n$ square matrix. Then $V$ is **positive definite** if $c'Vc > 0$ for all nonzero $n \times 1$ vectors $c$. Similarly, $V$ is **positive semidefinite** if $c'Vc \geq 0$ for all nonzero $n \times 1$ vectors $c$. If $V$ is positive definite, then it is invertible.

*Linear independence.* The $n \times 1$ vectors $a_1$ and $a_2$ are **linearly independent** if there do not exist nonzero scalars $c_1$ and $c_2$ such that $c_1 a_1 + c_2 a_2 = 0_{n \times 1}$. More generally, the set of $k$ vectors $a_1, a_2, \ldots, a_k$ are linearly independent if there do not exist nonzero scalars $c_1, c_2, \ldots, c_k$ such that $c_1 a_1 + c_2 a_2 + \cdots + c_k a_k = 0_{n \times 1}$.

*The rank of a matrix.* The **rank** of the $n \times m$ matrix $A$ is the number of linearly independent columns of $A$. The rank of $A$ is denoted rank$(A)$. If the rank of $A$ equals the number of columns of $A$, then $A$ is said to have full column rank. If the $n \times m$ matrix $A$ has full column rank, then there does not exist a nonzero $m \times 1$ vector $c$ such that $Ac = \mathbf{0}_{n \times 1}$. If $A$ is $n \times n$ with rank$(A) = n$, then $A$ is nonsingular. If the $n \times m$ matrix $A$ has full column rank, then $A'A$ is nonsingular.

*The matrix square root.* Let $V$ be an $n \times n$ square symmetric positive definite matrix. The matrix square root of $V$ is defined to be an $n \times n$ matrix $F$ such that $F'F = V$. The matrix square root of a positive definite matrix will always exist, but it is not unique. The matrix square root has the property that $FV^{-1}F' = I_n$. In addition, the matrix square root of a positive definite matrix is invertible, so $F'^{-1}VF^{-1} = I_n$.

*Eigenvalues and eigenvectors.* Let $A$ be an $n \times n$ matrix. If the $n \times 1$ vector $q$ and the scalar $\lambda$ satisfy $Aq = \lambda q$, where $q'q = 1$, then $\lambda$ is an **eigenvalue** of $A$, and $q$ is the **eigenvector** of $A$ associated with that eigenvalue. An $n \times n$ matrix has $n$ eigenvalues, which need not take on distinct values, and $n$ eigenvectors.

If $V$ is an $n \times n$ symmetric positive definite matrix, then all the eigenvalues of $V$ are positive real numbers, and all the eigenvectors of $V$ are real. Also, $V$ can be written in terms of its eigenvalues and eigenvectors as $V = Q\Lambda Q'$, where $\Lambda$ is a diagonal $n \times n$ matrix with diagonal elements that equal the eigenvalues of $V$, and $Q$ is an $n \times n$ matrix consisting of the eigenvectors of $V$, arranged so that the $i^{\text{th}}$ column of $Q$ is the eigenvector corresponding to the eigenvalue that is the $i^{\text{th}}$ diagonal element of $\Lambda$. The eigenvectors are orthonormal, so $Q'Q = I_n$.

*Idempotent matrices.* A matrix $C$ is idempotent if $C$ is square and $CC = C$. If $C$ is an $n \times n$ idempotent matrix that is also symmetric, then $C$ is positive semidefinite and $C$ has $r$ eigenvalues that equal 1 and $n - r$ eigenvalues that equal 0, where $r = \text{rank}(C)$ (Exercise 18.10).

APPENDIX

# 18.2  Multivariate Distributions

This appendix collects various definitions and facts about distributions of vectors of random variables. We start by defining the mean and covariance matrix of the $n$-dimensional random variable $V$. Next we present the multivariate normal distribution. Finally, we summarize some facts about the distributions of linear and quadratic functions of jointly normally distributed random variables.

## The Mean Vector and Covariance Matrix

The first and second moments of an $m \times 1$ vector of random variables, $V = (V_1 \quad V_2 \quad \cdots \quad V_m)'$, are summarized by its mean vector and covariance matrix.

Because $V$ is a vector, the vector of its means—that is, its **mean vector**—is $E(V) = \mu_V$. The $i^{\text{th}}$ element of the mean vector is the mean of the $i^{\text{th}}$ element of $V$.

The **covariance matrix** of $V$ is the matrix consisting of the variance $\text{var}(V_i), i = 1, \ldots, m$, along the diagonal and the $(i, j)$ off-diagonal elements $\text{cov}(V_i, V_j)$. In matrix form, the covariance matrix $\Sigma_V$ is

$$\Sigma_V = E[(V - \mu_V)(V - \mu_V)'] = \begin{bmatrix} \text{var}(V_1) & \cdots & \text{cov}(V_1, V_m) \\ \vdots & \ddots & \vdots \\ \text{cov}(V_m, V_1) & \cdots & \text{var}(V_m) \end{bmatrix}. \quad (18.72)$$

## The Multivariate Normal Distribution

The $m \times 1$ vector random variable $V$ has a multivariate normal distribution with mean vector $\mu_V$ and covariance matrix $\Sigma_V$ if it has the joint probability density function

$$f(V) = \frac{1}{\sqrt{(2\pi)^m \det(\Sigma_V)}} \exp\left[-\frac{1}{2}(V - \mu_V)'\Sigma_V^{-1}(V - \mu_V)\right], \quad (18.73)$$

where $\det(\Sigma_V)$ is the determinant of the matrix $\Sigma_V$. The multivariate normal distribution is denoted $N(\mu_V, \Sigma_V)$.

An important fact about the multivariate normal distribution is that if two jointly normally distributed random variables are uncorrelated (equivalently, have a block-diagonal covariance matrix), then they are independently distributed. That is, let $V_1$ and $V_2$ be jointly normally distributed random variables with respective dimensions $m_1 \times 1$ and $m_2 \times 1$. Then if $\text{cov}(V_1, V_2) = E[(V_1 - \mu_{V_1})(V_2 - \mu_{V_2})'] = \mathbf{0}_{m_1 \times m_2}$, $V_1$ and $V_2$ are independent.

If $\{V_i\}$ are i.i.d. $N(0, \sigma_v^2)$, then $\Sigma_V = \sigma_v^2 I_m$, and the multivariate normal distribution simplifies to the product of $m$ univariate normal densities.

## Distributions of Linear Combinations and Quadratic Forms of Normal Random Variables

Linear combinations of multivariate normal random variables are themselves normally distributed, and certain quadratic forms of multivariate normal random variables have a chi-squared distribution. Let $V$ be an $m \times 1$ random variable distributed $N(\mu_V, \Sigma_V)$, let $A$

and $\boldsymbol{B}$ be nonrandom $a \times m$ and $b \times m$ matrices, and let $\boldsymbol{d}$ be a nonrandom $a \times 1$ vector. Then

$$\boldsymbol{d} + \boldsymbol{AV} \text{ is distributed } N(\boldsymbol{d} + \boldsymbol{A\mu_V}, \boldsymbol{A\Sigma_V A'}); \tag{18.74}$$

$$\text{cov}\,(\boldsymbol{AV}, \boldsymbol{BV}) = \boldsymbol{A\Sigma_V B'}; \tag{18.75}$$

$$\text{if } \boldsymbol{A\Sigma_V B'} = \boldsymbol{0}_{a \times b}, \text{ then } \boldsymbol{AV} \text{ and } \boldsymbol{BV} \text{ are independently distributed; and} \tag{18.76}$$

$$(\boldsymbol{V} - \boldsymbol{\mu_V})'\boldsymbol{\Sigma_V^{-1}}(\boldsymbol{V} - \boldsymbol{\mu_V}) \text{ is distributed } \chi_m^2. \tag{18.77}$$

Let $\boldsymbol{U}$ be an $m$-dimensional multivariate standard normal random variable with distribution $N(\boldsymbol{0}, \boldsymbol{I_m})$. If $\boldsymbol{C}$ is symmetric and idempotent, then

$$\boldsymbol{U'CU} \text{ has a } \chi_r^2 \text{ distribution, where } r = \text{rank}(\boldsymbol{C}). \tag{18.78}$$

Equation (18.78) is proven as Exercise 18.11.

---

APPENDIX

## 18.3  Derivation of the Asymptotic Distribution of $\hat{\beta}$

This appendix provides the derivation of the asymptotic normal distribution of $\sqrt{n}(\hat{\boldsymbol{\beta}} - \boldsymbol{\beta})$ given in Equation (18.12). An implication of this result is that $\hat{\boldsymbol{\beta}} \xrightarrow{p} \boldsymbol{\beta}$.

First consider the "denominator" matrix $\boldsymbol{X'X}/n = \frac{1}{n}\sum_{i=1}^{n}\boldsymbol{X_i X_i'}$ in Equation (18.15). The $(j, l)$ element of this matrix is $\frac{1}{n}\sum_{i=1}^{n} X_{ji}X_{li}$. By the second assumption in Key Concept 18.1, $\boldsymbol{X_i}$ is i.i.d., so $X_{ji}X_{li}$ is i.i.d. By the third assumption in Key Concept 18.1, each element of $\boldsymbol{X_i}$ has four moments, so, by the Cauchy–Schwarz inequality (Appendix 17.2), $X_{ji}X_{li}$ has two moments. Because $X_{ji}X_{li}$ is i.i.d. with two moments, $\frac{1}{n}\sum_{i=1}^{n} X_{ji}X_{li}$ obeys the law of large numbers, so $\frac{1}{n}\sum_{i=1}^{n} X_{ji}X_{li} \xrightarrow{p} E(X_{ji}X_{li})$. This is true for all the elements of $\boldsymbol{X'X}/n$, so $\boldsymbol{X'X}/n \xrightarrow{p} E(\boldsymbol{X_i X_i'}) = \boldsymbol{Q_X}$.

Next consider the "numerator" matrix in Equation (18.15), $\boldsymbol{X'U}/\sqrt{n} = \sqrt{\frac{1}{n}}\sum_{i=1}^{n}\boldsymbol{V_i}$, where $\boldsymbol{V_i} = \boldsymbol{X_i}u_i$. By the first assumption in Key Concept 18.1 and the law of iterated expectations, $E(\boldsymbol{V_i}) = E[\boldsymbol{X_i}E(u_i|\boldsymbol{X_i})] = \boldsymbol{0}_{k+1}$. By the second least squares assumption, $\boldsymbol{V_i}$ is i.i.d. Let $\boldsymbol{c}$ be a finite $k + 1$ dimensional vector. By the Cauchy–Schwarz inequality, $E[(\boldsymbol{c'V_i})^2] = E[(\boldsymbol{c'X_i}u_i)^2] = E[(\boldsymbol{c'X_i})^2(u_i)^2] \leq \sqrt{E[(\boldsymbol{c'X_i})^4]E(u_i^4)}$, which is finite by the third least squares assumption. This is true for every such vector $\boldsymbol{c}$, so $E(\boldsymbol{V_i V_i'}) = \boldsymbol{\Sigma_V}$ is finite and, we assume, positive definite. Thus the multivariate central limit theorem of Key Concept 18.2 applies to $\sqrt{\frac{1}{n}}\sum_{i=1}^{n}\boldsymbol{V_i} = \frac{1}{\sqrt{n}}\boldsymbol{X'U}$; that is,

$$\frac{1}{\sqrt{n}}\boldsymbol{X'U} \xrightarrow{d} N(\boldsymbol{0}_{k+1}, \boldsymbol{\Sigma_V}). \tag{18.79}$$

The result in Equation (18.12) follows from Equations (18.15) and (18.79), the consistency of $X'X/n$, the fourth least squares assumption (which ensures that $(X'X)^{-1}$ exists), and Slutsky's theorem.

## 18.4 Derivations of Exact Distributions of OLS Test Statistics with Normal Errors

This appendix presents the proofs of the distributions under the null hypothesis of the homoskedasticity-only $t$-statistic in Equation (18.35) and the homoskedasticity-only $F$-statistic in Equation (18.37), assuming that all six assumptions in Key Concept 18.1 hold.

### Proof of Equation (18.35)

If (i) $Z$ has a standard normal distribution, (ii) $W$ has a $\chi_m^2$ distribution, and (iii) $Z$ and $W$ are independently distributed, then the random variable $Z/\sqrt{W/m}$ has the $t$-distribution with $m$ degrees of freedom (Appendix 17.1). To put $\tilde{t}$ in this form, notice that $\hat{\boldsymbol{\Sigma}}_{\hat{\boldsymbol{\beta}}} = (s_{\hat{u}}^2/\sigma_u^2)\boldsymbol{\Sigma}_{\hat{\boldsymbol{\beta}}|X}$. Then rewrite Equation (18.34) as

$$\tilde{t} = \frac{(\hat{\beta}_j - \beta_{j,0})/\sqrt{(\boldsymbol{\Sigma}_{\hat{\boldsymbol{\beta}}|X})_{jj}}}{\sqrt{W/(n-k-1)}}, \tag{18.80}$$

where $W = (n-k-1)(s_{\hat{u}}^2/\sigma_u^2)$, and let $Z = (\hat{\beta}_j - \beta_{j,0})/\sqrt{(\boldsymbol{\Sigma}_{\hat{\boldsymbol{\beta}}|X})_{jj}}$ and $m = n-k-1$. With these definitions, $\tilde{t} = Z/\sqrt{W/m}$. Thus, to prove the result in Equation (18.35), we must show (i) through (iii) for these definitions of $Z$, $W$, and $m$.

    i. An implication of Equation (18.30) is that, under the null hypothesis, $Z = (\hat{\beta}_j - \beta_{j,0})/\sqrt{(\boldsymbol{\Sigma}_{\hat{\boldsymbol{\beta}}|X})_{jj}}$ has an exact standard normal distribution, which shows (i).

    ii. From Equation (18.31), $W$ is distributed as $\chi_{n-k-1}^2$, which shows (ii).

    iii. To show (iii), it must be shown that $\hat{\beta}_j$ and $s_{\hat{u}}^2$ are independently distributed.

From Equations (18.14) and (18.29), $\hat{\boldsymbol{\beta}} - \boldsymbol{\beta} = (X'X)^{-1}X'U$ and $s_{\hat{u}}^2 = (M_X U)'(M_X U)/(n-k-1)$. Thus $\hat{\boldsymbol{\beta}} - \boldsymbol{\beta}$ and $s_{\hat{u}}^2$ are independent if $(X'X)^{-1}X'U$ and $M_X U$ are independent. Both $(X'X)^{-1}X'U$ and $M_X U$ are linear combinations of $U$, which has an $N(\mathbf{0}_{n\times 1}, \sigma_u^2 I_n)$ distribution, conditional on $X$. But because $M_X X(X'X)^{-1} = \mathbf{0}_{n\times(k+1)}$ [Equation (18.26)], it follows that $(X'X)^{-1}X'U$ and $M_X U$ are independently distributed [Equation (18.76)]. Consequently, under all six assumptions in Key Concept 18.1,

$$\hat{\boldsymbol{\beta}} \text{ and } s_{\hat{u}}^2 \text{ are independently distributed,} \tag{18.81}$$

which shows (iii) and thus proves Equation (18.35).

## Proof of Equation (18.37)

The $F_{n_1, n_2}$ distribution is the distribution of $(W_1/n_1)/(W_2/n_2)$, where (i) $W_1$ is distributed $\chi^2_{n_1}$; (ii) $W_2$ is distributed $\chi^2_{n_2}$; and (iii) $W_1$ and $W_2$ are independently distributed (Appendix 17.1). To express $\widetilde{F}$ in this form, let $W_1 = (R\hat{\beta} - r)'[R(X'X)^{-1}R'\sigma_u^2]^{-1}(R\hat{\beta} - r)$ and $W_2 = (n - k - 1)s_{\hat{u}}^2/\sigma_u^2$ Substitution of these definitions into Equation (18.36) shows that $\widetilde{F} = (W_1/q)/[W_2/(n - k - 1)]$. Thus, by the definition of the $F$ distribution, $\widetilde{F}$ has an $F_{q, n-k-1}$ distribution if (i) through (iii) hold with $n_1 = q$ and $n_2 = n - k - 1$.

i. Under the null hypothesis, $R\hat{\beta} - r = R(\hat{\beta} - \beta)$. Because $\hat{\beta}$ has the conditional normal distribution in Equation (18.30) and because $R$ is a nonrandom matrix, $R(\hat{\beta} - \beta)$ is distributed $N(0_{q\times 1}, R(X'X)^{-1}R'\sigma_u^2)$, conditional on $X$. Thus, by Equation (18.77) in Appendix 18.2, $(R\hat{\beta} - r)'[R(X'X)R'\sigma_u^2]^{-1}(R\hat{\beta} - r)$ is distributed $\chi^2_q$, proving (i).

ii. Requirement (ii) is shown in Equation (18.31).

iii. It has already been shown that $\hat{\beta} - \beta$ and $s_{\hat{u}}^2$ are independently distributed [Equation (18.81)]. It follows that $R\hat{\beta} - r$ and $s_{\hat{u}}^2$ are independently distributed, which in turn implies that $W_1$ and $W_2$ are independently distributed, proving (iii) and completing the proof.

---

APPENDIX

## 18.5 Proof of the Gauss–Markov Theorem for Multiple Regression

This appendix proves the Gauss–Markov theorem (Key Concept 18.3) for the multiple regression model. Let $\widetilde{\beta}$ be a linear conditionally unbiased estimator of $\beta$ so that $\widetilde{\beta} = A'Y$ and $E(\widetilde{\beta}|X) = \beta$, where $A$ is an $n \times (k + 1)$ matrix that can depend on $X$ and nonrandom constants. We show that $\text{var}(c'\hat{\beta}) \leq \text{var}(c'\widetilde{\beta})$ for all $k + 1$ dimensional vectors $c$, where the inequality holds with equality only if $\widetilde{\beta} = \hat{\beta}$.

Because $\widetilde{\beta}$ is linear, it can be written as $\widetilde{\beta} = A'Y = A'(X\beta + U) = (A'X)\beta + A'U$. By the first Gauss–Markov condition, $E(U|X) = 0_{n\times 1}$, so $E(\widetilde{\beta}|X) = (A'X)\beta$, but because $\widetilde{\beta}$ is conditionally unbiased, $E(\widetilde{\beta}|X) = \beta = (A'X)\beta$, which implies that $A'X = I_{k+1}$. Thus $\widetilde{\beta} = \beta + A'U$, so $\text{var}(\widetilde{\beta}|X) = \text{var}(A'U|X) = E(A'UU'A|X) = A'E(UU'|X)A = \sigma_u^2 A'A$, where the third equality follows because $A$ can depend on $X$ but not $U$, and the final equality follows from the second Gauss–Markov condition. That is, if $\widetilde{\beta}$ is linear and unbiased, then under the Gauss–Markov conditions,

$$A'X = I_{k+1} \text{ and } \text{var}(\widetilde{\beta}|X) = \sigma_u^2 A'A. \tag{18.82}$$

The results in Equation (18.82) also apply to $\hat{\beta}$ with $A = \hat{A} = X(X'X)^{-1}$, where $(X'X)^{-1}$ exists by the third Gauss–Markov condition.

Now let $A = \hat{A} + D$ so that $D$ is the difference between the matrices $A$ and $\hat{A}$. Note that $\hat{A}'A = (X'X)^{-1}X'A = (X'X)^{-1}$ [by Equation (18.82)] and $\hat{A}'\hat{A} = (X'X)^{-1}X'X(X'X)^{-1} = (X'X)^{-1}$, so $\hat{A}'D = \hat{A}'(A - \hat{A}) = \hat{A}'A - \hat{A}'\hat{A} = \mathbf{0}_{(k+1) \times (k+1)}$. Substituting $A = \hat{A} + D$ into the formula for the conditional variance in Equation (18.82) yields

$$
\begin{aligned}
\operatorname{var}(\tilde{\boldsymbol{\beta}}|X) &= \sigma_u^2(\hat{A} + D)'(\hat{A} + D) \\
&= \sigma_u^2[\hat{A}'\hat{A} + \hat{A}'D + D'\hat{A} + D'D] \\
&= \sigma_u^2(X'X)^{-1} + \sigma_u^2 D'D,
\end{aligned}
\tag{18.83}
$$

where the final equality uses the facts $\hat{A}'\hat{A} = (X'X)^{-1}$ and $\hat{A}'D = \mathbf{0}_{(k+1) \times (k+1)}$.

Because $\operatorname{var}(\hat{\boldsymbol{\beta}}|X) = \sigma_u^2(X'X)^{-1}$, Equations (18.82) and (18.83) imply that $\operatorname{var}(\tilde{\boldsymbol{\beta}}|X) - \operatorname{var}(\hat{\boldsymbol{\beta}}|X) = \sigma_u^2 D'D$. The difference between the variances of the two estimators of the linear combination $c'\boldsymbol{\beta}$ thus is

$$
\operatorname{var}(c'\tilde{\boldsymbol{\beta}}|X) - \operatorname{var}(c'\hat{\boldsymbol{\beta}}|X) = \sigma_u^2 c'D'Dc \geq 0.
\tag{18.84}
$$

The inequality in Equation (18.84) holds for all linear combinations $c'\boldsymbol{\beta}$, and the inequality holds with equality for all nonzero $c$ only if $D = \mathbf{0}_{n \times (k+1)}$—that is, if $A = \hat{A}$ or, equivalently, $\tilde{\boldsymbol{\beta}} = \hat{\boldsymbol{\beta}}$. Thus $c'\hat{\boldsymbol{\beta}}$ has the smallest variance of all linear conditionally unbiased estimators of $c'\boldsymbol{\beta}$; that is, the OLS estimator is BLUE.

---

**APPENDIX**

# 18.6 Proof of Selected Results for IV and GMM Estimation

## The Efficiency of TSLS Under Homoskedasticity [Proof of Equation (18.62)]

When the errors $u_i$ are homoskedastic, the difference between $\boldsymbol{\Sigma}_A^{IV}$ [Equation (18.61)] and $\boldsymbol{\Sigma}^{TSLS}$ [Equation (18.55)] is given by

$$
\begin{aligned}
\boldsymbol{\Sigma}_A^{IV} - \boldsymbol{\Sigma}^{TSLS} &= (Q_{XZ}AQ_{ZX})^{-1}Q_{XZ}AQ_{ZZ}AQ_{ZX}(Q_{XZ}AQ_{ZX})^{-1}\sigma_u^2 - (Q_{XZ}Q_{ZZ}^{-1}Q_{ZX})^{-1}\sigma_u^2 \\
&= (Q_{XZ}AQ_{ZX})^{-1}Q_{XZ}A[Q_{ZZ} - Q_{ZX}(Q_{XZ}Q_{ZZ}^{-1}Q_{ZX})^{-1}Q_{XZ}]AQ_{ZX}(Q_{XZ}AQ_{ZX})^{-1}\sigma_u^2,
\end{aligned}
\tag{18.85}
$$

where the second term in brackets in the second equality follows from $(Q_{XZ}AQ_{ZX})^{-1}Q_{XZ}AQ_{ZX} = I_{(k+r+1)}$. Let $F$ be the matrix square root of $Q_{ZZ}$, so $Q_{ZZ} = F'F$ and $Q_{ZZ}^{-1} = F^{-1}F^{-1'}$. [The latter equality follows from noting that $(F'F)^{-1} = F^{-1}F'^{-1}$ and $F'^{-1} = F^{-1'}$.] Then the final expression in Equation (18.85) can be rewritten to yield

$$
\begin{aligned}
\boldsymbol{\Sigma}_A^{IV} - \boldsymbol{\Sigma}^{TSLS} &= (Q_{XZ}AQ_{ZX})^{-1}Q_{XZ}AF'[I - F^{-1'}Q_{ZX}(Q_{XZ}F^{-1}F^{-1'}Q_{ZX})^{-1}Q_{XZ}F^{-1}] \\
&\quad \times FAQ_{ZX}(Q_{XZ}AQ_{ZX})^{-1}\sigma_u^2,
\end{aligned}
\tag{18.86}
$$

where the second expression in brackets uses $F'F^{-1'} = I$. Thus

$$c'(\Sigma_A^{IV} - \Sigma^{TSLS})c = d'[I - D(D'D)^{-1}D']d\sigma_u^2, \tag{18.87}$$

where $d = FAQ_{ZX}(Q_{XZ}AQ_{ZX})^{-1}c$ and $D = F^{-1'}Q_{ZX}$. Now $I - D(D'D)^{-1}D'$ is a symmetric idempotent matrix (Exercise 18.5). As a result, $I - D(D'D)^{-1}D'$ has eigenvalues that are either 0 or 1 and $d'[I - D(D'D)^{-1}D']d \geq 0$ (Exercise 18.10). Thus $c'(\Sigma_A^{IV} - \Sigma^{TSLS})c \geq 0$, proving that TSLS is efficient under homoskedasticity.

## Asymptotic Distribution of the *J*-Statistic Under Homoskedasticity

The *J*-statistic is defined in Equation (18.63). First note that

$$
\begin{aligned}
\hat{U} &= Y - X\hat{\beta}^{TSLS} \\
&= Y - X(X'P_ZX)^{-1}X'P_ZY \\
&= (X\beta + U) - X(X'P_ZX)^{-1}X'P_Z(X\beta + U) \\
&= U - X(X'P_ZX)^{-1}X'P_ZU \\
&= [I - X(X'P_ZX)^{-1}X'P_Z]U. 
\end{aligned}
\tag{18.88}
$$

Thus

$$
\begin{aligned}
\hat{U}P_Z\hat{U} &= U'[I - P_ZX(X'P_ZX)^{-1}X']P_Z[I - X(X'P_ZX)^{-1}X'P_Z]U \\
&= U'[P_Z - P_ZX(X'P_ZX)^{-1}X'P_Z]U, 
\end{aligned}
\tag{18.89}
$$

where the second equality follows by simplifying the preceding expression. Because $Z'Z$ is symmetric and positive definite, it can be written in terms of its matrix square root, $Z'Z = (Z'Z)^{1/2'}(Z'Z)^{1/2}$, and this matrix square root is invertible, so $(Z'Z)^{-1} = (Z'Z)^{-1/2}(Z'Z)^{-1/2'}$, where $(Z'Z)^{-1/2} = [(Z'Z)^{1/2}]^{-1}$. Thus $P_Z$ can be written as $P_Z = Z(Z'Z)^{-1}Z' = BB'$, where $B = Z(Z'Z)^{-1/2}$. Substituting this expression for $P_Z$ into the final expression in Equation (18.89) yields

$$
\begin{aligned}
\hat{U}'P_Z\hat{U} &= U'[BB' - BB'X(X'BB'X)^{-1}X'BB']U \\
&= U'B[I - B'X(X'BB'X)^{-1}X'B]B'U \\
&= U'BM_{B'X}B'U, 
\end{aligned}
\tag{18.90}
$$

where $M_{B'X} = I - B'X(X'BB'X)^{-1}X'B$ is a symmetric idempotent matrix.

The asymptotic null distribution of $\hat{U}'P_Z\hat{U}$ is found by computing the limits in probability and in distribution of the various terms in the final expression in Equation (18.90) under the null hypothesis. Under the null hypothesis that $E(Z_iu_i) = 0$, $Z'U/\sqrt{n}$ has mean zero and the central limit theorem applies, so $Z'U/\sqrt{n} \xrightarrow{d} N(0, Q_{ZZ}\sigma_u^2)$. In addition,

$Z'Z/n \xrightarrow{p} Q_{ZZ}$ and $X'Z/n \xrightarrow{p} Q_{XZ}$. Thus $B'U = (Z'Z)^{-1/2'}Z'U = (Z'Z/n)^{-1/2'}$ $(Z'U/\sqrt{n}) \xrightarrow{d} \sigma_u z$ where $z$ is distributed $N(0_{m+r+1}, I_{m+r+1})$. In addition, $B'X/\sqrt{n} = (Z'Z/n)^{-1/2'}(Z'X/n) \xrightarrow{p} Q_{ZZ}^{-1/2}Q_{ZX}$, so $M_{B'X} \xrightarrow{p} I - Q_{ZZ}^{-1/2}Q_{ZX}(Q_{XZ}Q_{ZZ}^{-1/2'}Q_{ZZ}^{-1/2}Q_{ZX})^{-1}$ $Q_{XZ}Q_{ZZ}^{-1/2'} = M_{Q_{ZZ}^{-1/2}Q_{ZX}}$. Thus

$$\hat{U}'P_Z\hat{U} \xrightarrow{d} (z'M_{Q_{XZ}Q_{ZZ}^{-1/2}}z)\sigma_u^2. \tag{18.91}$$

Under the null hypothesis, the TSLS estimator is consistent and the coefficients in the regression of $\hat{U}$ on $Z$ converge in probability to zero [an implication of Equation (18.91)], so the denominator in the definition of the $J$-statistic is a consistent estimator of $\sigma_u^2$:

$$\hat{U}'M_Z\hat{U}/(n - m - r - 1) \xrightarrow{p} \sigma_u^2. \tag{18.92}$$

From the definition of the $J$-statistic and Equations (18.91) and (18.92), it follows that

$$J = \frac{\hat{U}'P_Z\hat{U}}{\hat{U}'M_Z\hat{U}/(n - m - r - 1)} \xrightarrow{d} z'M_{Q_{ZZ}^{-1/2}Q_{XZ}}z. \tag{18.93}$$

Because $z$ is a standard normal random vector and $M_{Q_{ZZ}^{-1/2}Q_{ZX}}$ is a symmetric idempotent matrix, $J$ is distributed as a chi-squared random variable with degrees of freedom that equal the rank of $M_{Q_{ZZ}^{-1/2}Q_{ZX}}$ [Equation (18.78)]. Because $Q_{ZZ}^{-1/2}Q_{ZX}$ is $(m + r + 1) \times (k + r + 1)$ and $m > k$, the rank of $M_{Q_{ZZ}^{-1/2}Q_{ZX}}$ is $m - k$ [Exercise 18.5]. Thus $J \xrightarrow{d} \chi_{m-k}^2$, which is the result stated in Equation (18.64).

## The Efficiency of the Efficient GMM Estimator

The infeasible efficient GMM estimator, $\tilde{\beta}^{Eff.GMM}$, is defined in Equation (18.66). The proof that $\tilde{\beta}^{Eff.GMM}$ is efficient entails showing that $c'(\Sigma_A^{IV} - \Sigma^{Eff.GMM})c \geq 0$ for all vectors $c$. The proof closely parallels the proof of the efficiency of the TSLS estimator in the first section of this appendix, with the sole modification that $H^{-1}$ replaces $Q_{ZZ}\sigma_u^2$ in Equation (18.85) and subsequently.

## Distribution of the GMM $J$-Statistic

The GMM $J$-statistic is given in Equation (18.70). The proof that, under the null hypothesis, $J^{GMM} \xrightarrow{d} \chi_{m-k}^2$ closely parallels the corresponding proof for the TSLS $J$-statistic under homoskedasticity.

# Appendix

**TABLE 1** The Cumulative Standard Normal Distribution Function, $\Phi(z) = \Pr(Z \le z)$

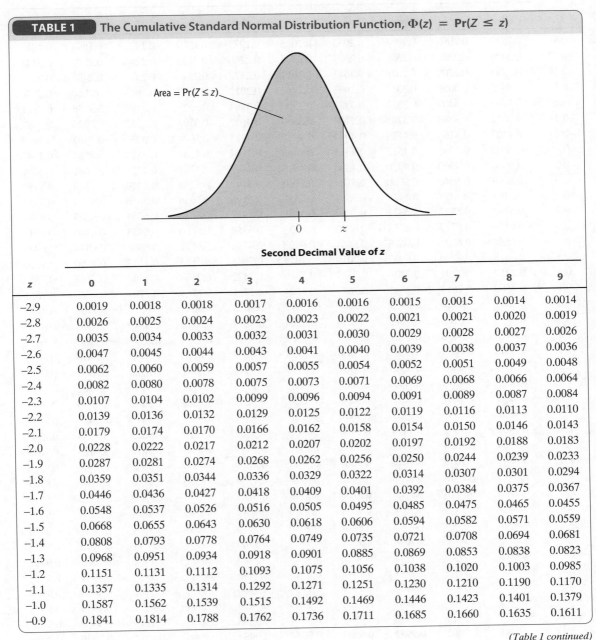

Area $= \Pr(Z \le z)$

| z | Second Decimal Value of z | | | | | | | | | |
|---|---|---|---|---|---|---|---|---|---|---|
| | 0 | 1 | 2 | 3 | 4 | 5 | 6 | 7 | 8 | 9 |
| −2.9 | 0.0019 | 0.0018 | 0.0018 | 0.0017 | 0.0016 | 0.0016 | 0.0015 | 0.0015 | 0.0014 | 0.0014 |
| −2.8 | 0.0026 | 0.0025 | 0.0024 | 0.0023 | 0.0023 | 0.0022 | 0.0021 | 0.0021 | 0.0020 | 0.0019 |
| −2.7 | 0.0035 | 0.0034 | 0.0033 | 0.0032 | 0.0031 | 0.0030 | 0.0029 | 0.0028 | 0.0027 | 0.0026 |
| −2.6 | 0.0047 | 0.0045 | 0.0044 | 0.0043 | 0.0041 | 0.0040 | 0.0039 | 0.0038 | 0.0037 | 0.0036 |
| −2.5 | 0.0062 | 0.0060 | 0.0059 | 0.0057 | 0.0055 | 0.0054 | 0.0052 | 0.0051 | 0.0049 | 0.0048 |
| −2.4 | 0.0082 | 0.0080 | 0.0078 | 0.0075 | 0.0073 | 0.0071 | 0.0069 | 0.0068 | 0.0066 | 0.0064 |
| −2.3 | 0.0107 | 0.0104 | 0.0102 | 0.0099 | 0.0096 | 0.0094 | 0.0091 | 0.0089 | 0.0087 | 0.0084 |
| −2.2 | 0.0139 | 0.0136 | 0.0132 | 0.0129 | 0.0125 | 0.0122 | 0.0119 | 0.0116 | 0.0113 | 0.0110 |
| −2.1 | 0.0179 | 0.0174 | 0.0170 | 0.0166 | 0.0162 | 0.0158 | 0.0154 | 0.0150 | 0.0146 | 0.0143 |
| −2.0 | 0.0228 | 0.0222 | 0.0217 | 0.0212 | 0.0207 | 0.0202 | 0.0197 | 0.0192 | 0.0188 | 0.0183 |
| −1.9 | 0.0287 | 0.0281 | 0.0274 | 0.0268 | 0.0262 | 0.0256 | 0.0250 | 0.0244 | 0.0239 | 0.0233 |
| −1.8 | 0.0359 | 0.0351 | 0.0344 | 0.0336 | 0.0329 | 0.0322 | 0.0314 | 0.0307 | 0.0301 | 0.0294 |
| −1.7 | 0.0446 | 0.0436 | 0.0427 | 0.0418 | 0.0409 | 0.0401 | 0.0392 | 0.0384 | 0.0375 | 0.0367 |
| −1.6 | 0.0548 | 0.0537 | 0.0526 | 0.0516 | 0.0505 | 0.0495 | 0.0485 | 0.0475 | 0.0465 | 0.0455 |
| −1.5 | 0.0668 | 0.0655 | 0.0643 | 0.0630 | 0.0618 | 0.0606 | 0.0594 | 0.0582 | 0.0571 | 0.0559 |
| −1.4 | 0.0808 | 0.0793 | 0.0778 | 0.0764 | 0.0749 | 0.0735 | 0.0721 | 0.0708 | 0.0694 | 0.0681 |
| −1.3 | 0.0968 | 0.0951 | 0.0934 | 0.0918 | 0.0901 | 0.0885 | 0.0869 | 0.0853 | 0.0838 | 0.0823 |
| −1.2 | 0.1151 | 0.1131 | 0.1112 | 0.1093 | 0.1075 | 0.1056 | 0.1038 | 0.1020 | 0.1003 | 0.0985 |
| −1.1 | 0.1357 | 0.1335 | 0.1314 | 0.1292 | 0.1271 | 0.1251 | 0.1230 | 0.1210 | 0.1190 | 0.1170 |
| −1.0 | 0.1587 | 0.1562 | 0.1539 | 0.1515 | 0.1492 | 0.1469 | 0.1446 | 0.1423 | 0.1401 | 0.1379 |
| −0.9 | 0.1841 | 0.1814 | 0.1788 | 0.1762 | 0.1736 | 0.1711 | 0.1685 | 0.1660 | 0.1635 | 0.1611 |

*(Table 1 continued)*

*(Table 1 continued)*

| | | | | Second Decimal Value of z | | | | | | |
|---|---|---|---|---|---|---|---|---|---|---|
| z | 0 | 1 | 2 | 3 | 4 | 5 | 6 | 7 | 8 | 9 |
| −0.8 | 0.2119 | 0.2090 | 0.2061 | 0.2033 | 0.2005 | 0.1977 | 0.1949 | 0.1922 | 0.1894 | 0.1867 |
| −0.7 | 0.2420 | 0.2389 | 0.2358 | 0.2327 | 0.2296 | 0.2266 | 0.2236 | 0.2206 | 0.2177 | 0.2148 |
| −0.6 | 0.2743 | 0.2709 | 0.2676 | 0.2643 | 0.2611 | 0.2578 | 0.2546 | 0.2514 | 0.2483 | 0.2451 |
| −0.5 | 0.3085 | 0.3050 | 0.3015 | 0.2981 | 0.2946 | 0.2912 | 0.2877 | 0.2843 | 0.2810 | 0.2776 |
| −0.4 | 0.3446 | 0.3409 | 0.3372 | 0.3336 | 0.3300 | 0.3264 | 0.3228 | 0.3192 | 0.3156 | 0.3121 |
| −0.3 | 0.3821 | 0.3783 | 0.3745 | 0.3707 | 0.3669 | 0.3632 | 0.3594 | 0.3557 | 0.3520 | 0.3483 |
| −0.2 | 0.4207 | 0.4168 | 0.4129 | 0.4090 | 0.4052 | 0.4013 | 0.3974 | 0.3936 | 0.3897 | 0.3859 |
| −0.1 | 0.4602 | 0.4562 | 0.4522 | 0.4483 | 0.4443 | 0.4404 | 0.4364 | 0.4325 | 0.4286 | 0.4247 |
| −0.0 | 0.5000 | 0.4960 | 0.4920 | 0.4880 | 0.4840 | 0.4801 | 0.4761 | 0.4721 | 0.4681 | 0.4641 |
| 0.0 | 0.5000 | 0.5040 | 0.5080 | 0.5120 | 0.5160 | 0.5199 | 0.5239 | 0.5279 | 0.5319 | 0.5359 |
| 0.1 | 0.5398 | 0.5438 | 0.5478 | 0.5517 | 0.5557 | 0.5596 | 0.5636 | 0.5675 | 0.5714 | 0.5753 |
| 0.2 | 0.5793 | 0.5832 | 0.5871 | 0.5910 | 0.5948 | 0.5987 | 0.6026 | 0.6064 | 0.6103 | 0.6141 |
| 0.3 | 0.6179 | 0.6217 | 0.6255 | 0.6293 | 0.6331 | 0.6368 | 0.6406 | 0.6443 | 0.6480 | 0.6517 |
| 0.4 | 0.6554 | 0.6591 | 0.6628 | 0.6664 | 0.6700 | 0.6736 | 0.6772 | 0.6808 | 0.6844 | 0.6879 |
| 0.5 | 0.6915 | 0.6950 | 0.6985 | 0.7019 | 0.7054 | 0.7088 | 0.7123 | 0.7157 | 0.7190 | 0.7224 |
| 0.6 | 0.7257 | 0.7291 | 0.7324 | 0.7357 | 0.7389 | 0.7422 | 0.7454 | 0.7486 | 0.7517 | 0.7549 |
| 0.7 | 0.7580 | 0.7611 | 0.7642 | 0.7673 | 0.7704 | 0.7734 | 0.7764 | 0.7794 | 0.7823 | 0.7852 |
| 0.8 | 0.7881 | 0.7910 | 0.7939 | 0.7967 | 0.7995 | 0.8023 | 0.8051 | 0.8078 | 0.8106 | 0.8133 |
| 0.9 | 0.8159 | 0.8186 | 0.8212 | 0.8238 | 0.8264 | 0.8289 | 0.8315 | 0.8340 | 0.8365 | 0.8389 |
| 1.0 | 0.8413 | 0.8438 | 0.8461 | 0.8485 | 0.8508 | 0.8531 | 0.8554 | 0.8577 | 0.8599 | 0.8621 |
| 1.1 | 0.8643 | 0.8665 | 0.8686 | 0.8708 | 0.8729 | 0.8749 | 0.8770 | 0.8790 | 0.8810 | 0.8830 |
| 1.2 | 0.8849 | 0.8869 | 0.8888 | 0.8907 | 0.8925 | 0.8944 | 0.8962 | 0.8980 | 0.8997 | 0.9015 |
| 1.3 | 0.9032 | 0.9049 | 0.9066 | 0.9082 | 0.9099 | 0.9115 | 0.9131 | 0.9147 | 0.9162 | 0.9177 |
| 1.4 | 0.9192 | 0.9207 | 0.9222 | 0.9236 | 0.9251 | 0.9265 | 0.9279 | 0.9292 | 0.9306 | 0.9319 |
| 1.5 | 0.9332 | 0.9345 | 0.9357 | 0.9370 | 0.9382 | 0.9394 | 0.9406 | 0.9418 | 0.9429 | 0.9441 |
| 1.6 | 0.9452 | 0.9463 | 0.9474 | 0.9484 | 0.9495 | 0.9505 | 0.9515 | 0.9525 | 0.9535 | 0.9545 |
| 1.7 | 0.9554 | 0.9564 | 0.9573 | 0.9582 | 0.9591 | 0.9599 | 0.9608 | 0.9616 | 0.9625 | 0.9633 |
| 1.8 | 0.9641 | 0.9649 | 0.9656 | 0.9664 | 0.9671 | 0.9678 | 0.9686 | 0.9693 | 0.9699 | 0.9706 |
| 1.9 | 0.9713 | 0.9719 | 0.9726 | 0.9732 | 0.9738 | 0.9744 | 0.9750 | 0.9756 | 0.9761 | 0.9767 |
| 2.0 | 0.9772 | 0.9778 | 0.9783 | 0.9788 | 0.9793 | 0.9798 | 0.9803 | 0.9808 | 0.9812 | 0.9817 |
| 2.1 | 0.9821 | 0.9826 | 0.9830 | 0.9834 | 0.9838 | 0.9842 | 0.9846 | 0.9850 | 0.9854 | 0.9857 |
| 2.2 | 0.9861 | 0.9864 | 0.9868 | 0.9871 | 0.9875 | 0.9878 | 0.9881 | 0.9884 | 0.9887 | 0.9890 |
| 2.3 | 0.9893 | 0.9896 | 0.9898 | 0.9901 | 0.9904 | 0.9906 | 0.9909 | 0.9911 | 0.9913 | 0.9916 |
| 2.4 | 0.9918 | 0.9920 | 0.9922 | 0.9925 | 0.9927 | 0.9929 | 0.9931 | 0.9932 | 0.9934 | 0.9936 |
| 2.5 | 0.9938 | 0.9940 | 0.9941 | 0.9943 | 0.9945 | 0.9946 | 0.9948 | 0.9949 | 0.9951 | 0.9952 |
| 2.6 | 0.9953 | 0.9955 | 0.9956 | 0.9957 | 0.9959 | 0.9960 | 0.9961 | 0.9962 | 0.9963 | 0.9964 |
| 2.7 | 0.9965 | 0.9966 | 0.9967 | 0.9968 | 0.9969 | 0.9970 | 0.9971 | 0.9972 | 0.9973 | 0.9974 |
| 2.8 | 0.9974 | 0.9975 | 0.9976 | 0.9977 | 0.9977 | 0.9978 | 0.9979 | 0.9979 | 0.9980 | 0.9981 |
| 2.9 | 0.9981 | 0.9982 | 0.9982 | 0.9983 | 0.9984 | 0.9984 | 0.9985 | 0.9985 | 0.9986 | 0.9986 |

This table can be used to calculate $\Pr(Z \leq z)$ where $Z$ is a standard normal variable. For example, when $z = 1.17$, this probability is 0.8790, which is the table entry for the row labeled 1.1 and the column labeled 7.

## TABLE 2  Critical Values for Two-Sided and One-Sided Tests Using the Student *t* Distribution

| Degrees of Freedom | Significance Level | | | | |
|---|---|---|---|---|---|
| | 20% (2-Sided) 10% (1-Sided) | 10% (2-Sided) 5% (1-Sided) | 5% (2-Sided) 2.5% (1-Sided) | 2% (2-Sided) 1% (1-Sided) | 1% (2-Sided) 0.5% (1-Sided) |
| 1 | 3.08 | 6.31 | 12.71 | 31.82 | 63.66 |
| 2 | 1.89 | 2.92 | 4.30 | 6.96 | 9.92 |
| 3 | 1.64 | 2.35 | 3.18 | 4.54 | 5.84 |
| 4 | 1.53 | 2.13 | 2.78 | 3.75 | 4.60 |
| 5 | 1.48 | 2.02 | 2.57 | 3.36 | 4.03 |
| 6 | 1.44 | 1.94 | 2.45 | 3.14 | 3.71 |
| 7 | 1.41 | 1.89 | 2.36 | 3.00 | 3.50 |
| 8 | 1.40 | 1.86 | 2.31 | 2.90 | 3.36 |
| 9 | 1.38 | 1.83 | 2.26 | 2.82 | 3.25 |
| 10 | 1.37 | 1.81 | 2.23 | 2.76 | 3.17 |
| 11 | 1.36 | 1.80 | 2.20 | 2.72 | 3.11 |
| 12 | 1.36 | 1.78 | 2.18 | 2.68 | 3.05 |
| 13 | 1.35 | 1.77 | 2.16 | 2.65 | 3.01 |
| 14 | 1.35 | 1.76 | 2.14 | 2.62 | 2.98 |
| 15 | 1.34 | 1.75 | 2.13 | 2.60 | 2.95 |
| 16 | 1.34 | 1.75 | 2.12 | 2.58 | 2.92 |
| 17 | 1.33 | 1.74 | 2.11 | 2.57 | 2.90 |
| 18 | 1.33 | 1.73 | 2.10 | 2.55 | 2.88 |
| 19 | 1.33 | 1.73 | 2.09 | 2.54 | 2.86 |
| 20 | 1.33 | 1.72 | 2.09 | 2.53 | 2.85 |
| 21 | 1.32 | 1.72 | 2.08 | 2.52 | 2.83 |
| 22 | 1.32 | 1.72 | 2.07 | 2.51 | 2.82 |
| 23 | 1.32 | 1.71 | 2.07 | 2.50 | 2.81 |
| 24 | 1.32 | 1.71 | 2.06 | 2.49 | 2.80 |
| 25 | 1.32 | 1.71 | 2.06 | 2.49 | 2.79 |
| 26 | 1.32 | 1.71 | 2.06 | 2.48 | 2.78 |
| 27 | 1.31 | 1.70 | 2.05 | 2.47 | 2.77 |
| 28 | 1.31 | 1.70 | 2.05 | 2.47 | 2.76 |
| 29 | 1.31 | 1.70 | 2.05 | 2.46 | 2.76 |
| 30 | 1.31 | 1.70 | 2.04 | 2.46 | 2.75 |
| 60 | 1.30 | 1.67 | 2.00 | 2.39 | 2.66 |
| 90 | 1.29 | 1.66 | 1.99 | 2.37 | 2.63 |
| 120 | 1.29 | 1.66 | 1.98 | 2.36 | 2.62 |
| ∞ | 1.28 | 1.64 | 1.96 | 2.33 | 2.58 |

Values are shown for the critical values for two-sided ($\neq$) and one-sided ($>$) alternative hypotheses. The critical value for the one-sided ($<$) test is the negative of the one-sided ($>$) critical value shown in the table. For example, 2.13 is the critical value for a two-sided test with a significance level of 5% using the Student *t* distribution with 15 degrees of freedom.

| TABLE 3 | Critical Values for the $\chi^2$ Distribution | | |

| Degrees of Freedom | Significance Level | | |
|---|---|---|---|
| | 10% | 5% | 1% |
| 1 | 2.71 | 3.84 | 6.63 |
| 2 | 4.61 | 5.99 | 9.21 |
| 3 | 6.25 | 7.81 | 11.34 |
| 4 | 7.78 | 9.49 | 13.28 |
| 5 | 9.24 | 11.07 | 15.09 |
| 6 | 10.64 | 12.59 | 16.81 |
| 7 | 12.02 | 14.07 | 18.48 |
| 8 | 13.36 | 15.51 | 20.09 |
| 9 | 14.68 | 16.92 | 21.67 |
| 10 | 15.99 | 18.31 | 23.21 |
| 11 | 17.28 | 19.68 | 24.72 |
| 12 | 18.55 | 21.03 | 26.22 |
| 13 | 19.81 | 22.36 | 27.69 |
| 14 | 21.06 | 23.68 | 29.14 |
| 15 | 22.31 | 25.00 | 30.58 |
| 16 | 23.54 | 26.30 | 32.00 |
| 17 | 24.77 | 27.59 | 33.41 |
| 18 | 25.99 | 28.87 | 34.81 |
| 19 | 27.20 | 30.14 | 36.19 |
| 20 | 28.41 | 31.41 | 37.57 |
| 21 | 29.62 | 32.67 | 38.93 |
| 22 | 30.81 | 33.92 | 40.29 |
| 23 | 32.01 | 35.17 | 41.64 |
| 24 | 33.20 | 36.41 | 42.98 |
| 25 | 34.38 | 37.65 | 44.31 |
| 26 | 35.56 | 38.89 | 45.64 |
| 27 | 36.74 | 40.11 | 46.96 |
| 28 | 37.92 | 41.34 | 48.28 |
| 29 | 39.09 | 42.56 | 49.59 |
| 30 | 40.26 | 43.77 | 50.89 |

This table contains the 90th, 95th, and 99th percentiles of the $\chi^2$ distribution. These serve as critical values for tests with significance levels of 10%, 5%, and 1%.

## TABLE 4    Critical Values for the $F_{m,\infty}$ Distribution

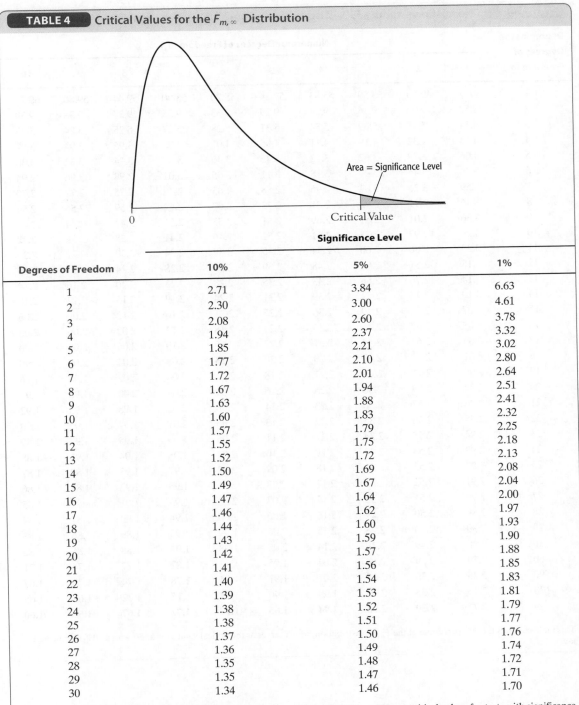

| Degrees of Freedom | Significance Level | | |
|---|---|---|---|
| | 10% | 5% | 1% |
| 1 | 2.71 | 3.84 | 6.63 |
| 2 | 2.30 | 3.00 | 4.61 |
| 3 | 2.08 | 2.60 | 3.78 |
| 4 | 1.94 | 2.37 | 3.32 |
| 5 | 1.85 | 2.21 | 3.02 |
| 6 | 1.77 | 2.10 | 2.80 |
| 7 | 1.72 | 2.01 | 2.64 |
| 8 | 1.67 | 1.94 | 2.51 |
| 9 | 1.63 | 1.88 | 2.41 |
| 10 | 1.60 | 1.83 | 2.32 |
| 11 | 1.57 | 1.79 | 2.25 |
| 12 | 1.55 | 1.75 | 2.18 |
| 13 | 1.52 | 1.72 | 2.13 |
| 14 | 1.50 | 1.69 | 2.08 |
| 15 | 1.49 | 1.67 | 2.04 |
| 16 | 1.47 | 1.64 | 2.00 |
| 17 | 1.46 | 1.62 | 1.97 |
| 18 | 1.44 | 1.60 | 1.93 |
| 19 | 1.43 | 1.59 | 1.90 |
| 20 | 1.42 | 1.57 | 1.88 |
| 21 | 1.41 | 1.56 | 1.85 |
| 22 | 1.40 | 1.54 | 1.83 |
| 23 | 1.39 | 1.53 | 1.81 |
| 24 | 1.38 | 1.52 | 1.79 |
| 25 | 1.38 | 1.51 | 1.77 |
| 26 | 1.37 | 1.50 | 1.76 |
| 27 | 1.36 | 1.49 | 1.74 |
| 28 | 1.35 | 1.48 | 1.72 |
| 29 | 1.35 | 1.47 | 1.71 |
| 30 | 1.34 | 1.46 | 1.70 |

This table contains the 90th, 95th, and 99th percentiles of the $F_{m,\infty}$ distribution. These serve as critical values for tests with significance levels of 10%, 5%, and 1%.

| TABLE 5A | Critical Values for the $F_{n_1,n_2}$ Distribution—10% Significance Level |

| Denominator Degrees of Freedom ($n_2$) | Numerator Degrees of Freedom ($n_1$) | | | | | | | | | |
|---|---|---|---|---|---|---|---|---|---|---|
|  | 1 | 2 | 3 | 4 | 5 | 6 | 7 | 8 | 9 | 10 |
| 1 | 39.86 | 49.50 | 53.59 | 55.83 | 57.24 | 58.20 | 58.90 | 59.44 | 59.86 | 60.20 |
| 2 | 8.53 | 9.00 | 9.16 | 9.24 | 9.29 | 9.33 | 9.35 | 9.37 | 9.38 | 9.39 |
| 3 | 5.54 | 5.46 | 5.39 | 5.34 | 5.31 | 5.28 | 5.27 | 5.25 | 5.24 | 5.23 |
| 4 | 4.54 | 4.32 | 4.19 | 4.11 | 4.05 | 4.01 | 3.98 | 3.95 | 3.94 | 3.92 |
| 5 | 4.06 | 3.78 | 3.62 | 3.52 | 3.45 | 3.40 | 3.37 | 3.34 | 3.32 | 3.30 |
| 6 | 3.78 | 3.46 | 3.29 | 3.18 | 3.11 | 3.05 | 3.01 | 2.98 | 2.96 | 2.94 |
| 7 | 3.59 | 3.26 | 3.07 | 2.96 | 2.88 | 2.83 | 2.78 | 2.75 | 2.72 | 2.70 |
| 8 | 3.46 | 3.11 | 2.92 | 2.81 | 2.73 | 2.67 | 2.62 | 2.59 | 2.56 | 2.54 |
| 9 | 3.36 | 3.01 | 2.81 | 2.69 | 2.61 | 2.55 | 2.51 | 2.47 | 2.44 | 2.42 |
| 10 | 3.29 | 2.92 | 2.73 | 2.61 | 2.52 | 2.46 | 2.41 | 2.38 | 2.35 | 2.32 |
| 11 | 3.23 | 2.86 | 2.66 | 2.54 | 2.45 | 2.39 | 2.34 | 2.30 | 2.27 | 2.25 |
| 12 | 3.18 | 2.81 | 2.61 | 2.48 | 2.39 | 2.33 | 2.28 | 2.24 | 2.21 | 2.19 |
| 13 | 3.14 | 2.76 | 2.56 | 2.43 | 2.35 | 2.28 | 2.23 | 2.20 | 2.16 | 2.14 |
| 14 | 3.10 | 2.73 | 2.52 | 2.39 | 2.31 | 2.24 | 2.19 | 2.15 | 2.12 | 2.10 |
| 15 | 3.07 | 2.70 | 2.49 | 2.36 | 2.27 | 2.21 | 2.16 | 2.12 | 2.09 | 2.06 |
| 16 | 3.05 | 2.67 | 2.46 | 2.33 | 2.24 | 2.18 | 2.13 | 2.09 | 2.06 | 2.03 |
| 17 | 3.03 | 2.64 | 2.44 | 2.31 | 2.22 | 2.15 | 2.10 | 2.06 | 2.03 | 2.00 |
| 18 | 3.01 | 2.62 | 2.42 | 2.29 | 2.20 | 2.13 | 2.08 | 2.04 | 2.00 | 1.98 |
| 19 | 2.99 | 2.61 | 2.40 | 2.27 | 2.18 | 2.11 | 2.06 | 2.02 | 1.98 | 1.96 |
| 20 | 2.97 | 2.59 | 2.38 | 2.25 | 2.16 | 2.09 | 2.04 | 2.00 | 1.96 | 1.94 |
| 21 | 2.96 | 2.57 | 2.36 | 2.23 | 2.14 | 2.08 | 2.02 | 1.98 | 1.95 | 1.92 |
| 22 | 2.95 | 2.56 | 2.35 | 2.22 | 2.13 | 2.06 | 2.01 | 1.97 | 1.93 | 1.90 |
| 23 | 2.94 | 2.55 | 2.34 | 2.21 | 2.11 | 2.05 | 1.99 | 1.95 | 1.92 | 1.89 |
| 24 | 2.93 | 2.54 | 2.33 | 2.19 | 2.10 | 2.04 | 1.98 | 1.94 | 1.91 | 1.88 |
| 25 | 2.92 | 2.53 | 2.32 | 2.18 | 2.09 | 2.02 | 1.97 | 1.93 | 1.89 | 1.87 |
| 26 | 2.91 | 2.52 | 2.31 | 2.17 | 2.08 | 2.01 | 1.96 | 1.92 | 1.88 | 1.86 |
| 27 | 2.90 | 2.51 | 2.30 | 2.17 | 2.07 | 2.00 | 1.95 | 1.91 | 1.87 | 1.85 |
| 28 | 2.89 | 2.50 | 2.29 | 2.16 | 2.06 | 2.00 | 1.94 | 1.90 | 1.87 | 1.84 |
| 29 | 2.89 | 2.50 | 2.28 | 2.15 | 2.06 | 1.99 | 1.93 | 1.89 | 1.86 | 1.83 |
| 30 | 2.88 | 2.49 | 2.28 | 2.14 | 2.05 | 1.98 | 1.93 | 1.88 | 1.85 | 1.82 |
| 60 | 2.79 | 2.39 | 2.18 | 2.04 | 1.95 | 1.87 | 1.82 | 1.77 | 1.74 | 1.71 |
| 90 | 2.76 | 2.36 | 2.15 | 2.01 | 1.91 | 1.84 | 1.78 | 1.74 | 1.70 | 1.67 |
| 120 | 2.75 | 2.35 | 2.13 | 1.99 | 1.90 | 1.82 | 1.77 | 1.72 | 1.68 | 1.65 |
| ∞ | **2.71** | **2.30** | **2.08** | **1.94** | **1.85** | **1.77** | **1.72** | **1.67** | **1.63** | **1.60** |

This table contains the 90th percentile of the $F_{n_1,n_2}$ distribution, which serves as the critical values for a test with a 10% significance level.

| TABLE 5B | Critical Values for the $F_{n_1, n_2}$ Distribution—5% Significance Level |

| Denominator Degrees of Freedom ($n_2$) | Numerator Degrees of Freedom ($n_1$) | | | | | | | | | |
|---|---|---|---|---|---|---|---|---|---|---|
| | 1 | 2 | 3 | 4 | 5 | 6 | 7 | 8 | 9 | 10 |
| 1 | 161.40 | 199.50 | 215.70 | 224.60 | 230.20 | 234.00 | 236.80 | 238.90 | 240.50 | 241.90 |
| 2 | 18.51 | 19.00 | 19.16 | 19.25 | 19.30 | 19.33 | 19.35 | 19.37 | 19.39 | 19.40 |
| 3 | 10.13 | 9.55 | 9.28 | 9.12 | 9.01 | 8.94 | 8.89 | 8.85 | 8.81 | 8.79 |
| 4 | 7.71 | 6.94 | 6.59 | 6.39 | 6.26 | 6.16 | 6.09 | 6.04 | 6.00 | 5.96 |
| 5 | 6.61 | 5.79 | 5.41 | 5.19 | 5.05 | 4.95 | 4.88 | 4.82 | 4.77 | 4.74 |
| 6 | 5.99 | 5.14 | 4.76 | 4.53 | 4.39 | 4.28 | 4.21 | 4.15 | 4.10 | 4.06 |
| 7 | 5.59 | 4.74 | 4.35 | 4.12 | 3.97 | 3.87 | 3.79 | 3.73 | 3.68 | 3.64 |
| 8 | 5.32 | 4.46 | 4.07 | 3.84 | 3.69 | 3.58 | 3.50 | 3.44 | 3.39 | 3.35 |
| 9 | 5.12 | 4.26 | 3.86 | 3.63 | 3.48 | 3.37 | 3.29 | 3.23 | 3.18 | 3.14 |
| 10 | 4.96 | 4.10 | 3.71 | 3.48 | 3.33 | 3.22 | 3.14 | 3.07 | 3.02 | 2.98 |
| 11 | 4.84 | 3.98 | 3.59 | 3.36 | 3.20 | 3.09 | 3.01 | 2.95 | 2.90 | 2.85 |
| 12 | 4.75 | 3.89 | 3.49 | 3.26 | 3.11 | 3.00 | 2.91 | 2.85 | 2.80 | 2.75 |
| 13 | 4.67 | 3.81 | 3.41 | 3.18 | 3.03 | 2.92 | 2.83 | 2.77 | 2.71 | 2.67 |
| 14 | 4.60 | 3.74 | 3.34 | 3.11 | 2.96 | 2.85 | 2.76 | 2.70 | 2.65 | 2.60 |
| 15 | 4.54 | 3.68 | 3.29 | 3.06 | 2.90 | 2.79 | 2.71 | 2.64 | 2.59 | 2.54 |
| 16 | 4.49 | 3.63 | 3.24 | 3.01 | 2.85 | 2.74 | 2.66 | 2.59 | 2.54 | 2.49 |
| 17 | 4.45 | 3.59 | 3.20 | 2.96 | 2.81 | 2.70 | 2.61 | 2.55 | 2.49 | 2.45 |
| 18 | 4.41 | 3.55 | 3.16 | 2.93 | 2.77 | 2.66 | 2.58 | 2.51 | 2.46 | 2.41 |
| 19 | 4.38 | 3.52 | 3.13 | 2.90 | 2.74 | 2.63 | 2.54 | 2.48 | 2.42 | 2.38 |
| 20 | 4.35 | 3.49 | 3.10 | 2.87 | 2.71 | 2.60 | 2.51 | 2.45 | 2.39 | 2.35 |
| 21 | 4.32 | 3.47 | 3.07 | 2.84 | 2.68 | 2.57 | 2.49 | 2.42 | 2.37 | 2.32 |
| 22 | 4.30 | 3.44 | 3.05 | 2.82 | 2.66 | 2.55 | 2.46 | 2.40 | 2.34 | 2.30 |
| 23 | 4.28 | 3.42 | 3.03 | 2.80 | 2.64 | 2.53 | 2.44 | 2.37 | 2.32 | 2.27 |
| 24 | 4.26 | 3.40 | 3.01 | 2.78 | 2.62 | 2.51 | 2.42 | 2.36 | 2.30 | 2.25 |
| 25 | 4.24 | 3.39 | 2.99 | 2.76 | 2.60 | 2.49 | 2.40 | 2.34 | 2.28 | 2.24 |
| 26 | 4.23 | 3.37 | 2.98 | 2.74 | 2.59 | 2.47 | 2.39 | 2.32 | 2.27 | 2.22 |
| 27 | 4.21 | 3.35 | 2.96 | 2.73 | 2.57 | 2.46 | 2.37 | 2.31 | 2.25 | 2.20 |
| 28 | 4.20 | 3.34 | 2.95 | 2.71 | 2.56 | 2.45 | 2.36 | 2.29 | 2.24 | 2.19 |
| 29 | 4.18 | 3.33 | 2.93 | 2.70 | 2.55 | 2.43 | 2.35 | 2.28 | 2.22 | 2.18 |
| 30 | 4.17 | 3.32 | 2.92 | 2.69 | 2.53 | 2.42 | 2.33 | 2.27 | 2.21 | 2.16 |
| 60 | 4.00 | 3.15 | 2.76 | 2.53 | 2.37 | 2.25 | 2.17 | 2.10 | 2.04 | 1.99 |
| 90 | 3.95 | 3.10 | 2.71 | 2.47 | 2.32 | 2.20 | 2.11 | 2.04 | 1.99 | 1.94 |
| 120 | 3.92 | 3.07 | 2.68 | 2.45 | 2.29 | 2.18 | 2.09 | 2.02 | 1.96 | 1.91 |
| ∞ | **3.84** | **3.00** | **2.60** | **2.37** | **2.21** | **2.10** | **2.01** | **1.94** | **1.88** | **1.83** |

This table contains the 95th percentile of the distribution $F_{n_1, n_2}$ which serves as the critical values for a test with a 5% significance level.

**TABLE 5C**   Critical Values for the $F_{n_1, n_2}$ Distribution—1% Significance Level

| Denominator Degrees of Freedom ($n_2$) | Numerator Degrees of Freedom ($n_1$) | | | | | | | | | |
|---|---|---|---|---|---|---|---|---|---|---|
| | 1 | 2 | 3 | 4 | 5 | 6 | 7 | 8 | 9 | 10 |
| 1 | 4052.00 | 4999.00 | 5403.00 | 5624.00 | 5763.00 | 5859.00 | 5928.00 | 5981.00 | 6022.00 | 6055.00 |
| 2 | 98.50 | 99.00 | 99.17 | 99.25 | 99.30 | 99.33 | 99.36 | 99.37 | 99.39 | 99.40 |
| 3 | 34.12 | 30.82 | 29.46 | 28.71 | 28.24 | 27.91 | 27.67 | 27.49 | 27.35 | 27.23 |
| 4 | 21.20 | 18.00 | 16.69 | 15.98 | 15.52 | 15.21 | 14.98 | 14.80 | 14.66 | 14.55 |
| 5 | 16.26 | 13.27 | 12.06 | 11.39 | 10.97 | 10.67 | 10.46 | 10.29 | 10.16 | 10.05 |
| 6 | 13.75 | 10.92 | 9.78 | 9.15 | 8.75 | 8.47 | 8.26 | 8.10 | 7.98 | 7.87 |
| 7 | 12.25 | 9.55 | 8.45 | 7.85 | 7.46 | 7.19 | 6.99 | 6.84 | 6.72 | 6.62 |
| 8 | 11.26 | 8.65 | 7.59 | 7.01 | 6.63 | 6.37 | 6.18 | 6.03 | 5.91 | 5.81 |
| 9 | 10.56 | 8.02 | 6.99 | 6.42 | 6.06 | 5.80 | 5.61 | 5.47 | 5.35 | 5.26 |
| 10 | 10.04 | 7.56 | 6.55 | 5.99 | 5.64 | 5.39 | 5.20 | 5.06 | 4.94 | 4.85 |
| 11 | 9.65 | 7.21 | 6.22 | 5.67 | 5.32 | 5.07 | 4.89 | 4.74 | 4.63 | 4.54 |
| 12 | 9.33 | 6.93 | 5.95 | 5.41 | 5.06 | 4.82 | 4.64 | 4.50 | 4.39 | 4.30 |
| 13 | 9.07 | 6.70 | 5.74 | 5.21 | 4.86 | 4.62 | 4.44 | 4.30 | 4.19 | 4.10 |
| 14 | 8.86 | 6.51 | 5.56 | 5.04 | 4.69 | 4.46 | 4.28 | 4.14 | 4.03 | 3.94 |
| 15 | 8.68 | 6.36 | 5.42 | 4.89 | 4.56 | 4.32 | 4.14 | 4.00 | 3.89 | 3.80 |
| 16 | 8.53 | 6.23 | 5.29 | 4.77 | 4.44 | 4.20 | 4.03 | 3.89 | 3.78 | 3.69 |
| 17 | 8.40 | 6.11 | 5.18 | 4.67 | 4.34 | 4.10 | 3.93 | 3.79 | 3.68 | 3.59 |
| 18 | 8.29 | 6.01 | 5.09 | 4.58 | 4.25 | 4.01 | 3.84 | 3.71 | 3.60 | 3.51 |
| 19 | 8.18 | 5.93 | 5.01 | 4.50 | 4.17 | 3.94 | 3.77 | 3.63 | 3.52 | 3.43 |
| 20 | 8.10 | 5.85 | 4.94 | 4.43 | 4.10 | 3.87 | 3.70 | 3.56 | 3.46 | 3.37 |
| 21 | 8.02 | 5.78 | 4.87 | 4.37 | 4.04 | 3.81 | 3.64 | 3.51 | 3.40 | 3.31 |
| 22 | 7.95 | 5.72 | 4.82 | 4.31 | 3.99 | 3.76 | 3.59 | 3.45 | 3.35 | 3.26 |
| 23 | 7.88 | 5.66 | 4.76 | 4.26 | 3.94 | 3.71 | 3.54 | 3.41 | 3.30 | 3.21 |
| 24 | 7.82 | 5.61 | 4.72 | 4.22 | 3.90 | 3.67 | 3.50 | 3.36 | 3.26 | 3.17 |
| 25 | 7.77 | 5.57 | 4.68 | 4.18 | 3.85 | 3.63 | 3.46 | 3.32 | 3.22 | 3.13 |
| 26 | 7.72 | 5.53 | 4.64 | 4.14 | 3.82 | 3.59 | 3.42 | 3.29 | 3.18 | 3.09 |
| 27 | 7.68 | 5.49 | 4.60 | 4.11 | 3.78 | 3.56 | 3.39 | 3.26 | 3.15 | 3.06 |
| 28 | 7.64 | 5.45 | 4.57 | 4.07 | 3.75 | 3.53 | 3.36 | 3.23 | 3.12 | 3.03 |
| 29 | 7.60 | 5.42 | 4.54 | 4.04 | 3.73 | 3.50 | 3.33 | 3.20 | 3.09 | 3.00 |
| 30 | 7.56 | 5.39 | 4.51 | 4.02 | 3.70 | 3.47 | 3.30 | 3.17 | 3.07 | 2.98 |
| 60 | 7.08 | 4.98 | 4.13 | 3.65 | 3.34 | 3.12 | 2.95 | 2.82 | 2.72 | 2.63 |
| 90 | 6.93 | 4.85 | 4.01 | 3.53 | 3.23 | 3.01 | 2.84 | 2.72 | 2.61 | 2.52 |
| 120 | 6.85 | 4.79 | 3.95 | 3.48 | 3.17 | 2.96 | 2.79 | 2.66 | 2.56 | 2.47 |
| ∞ | **6.63** | **4.61** | **3.78** | **3.32** | **3.02** | **2.80** | **2.64** | **2.51** | **2.41** | **2.32** |

This table contains the 99th percentile of the $F_{n_1, n_2}$ distribution, which serves as the critical values for a test with a 1% significance level.

# References

Acemoglu, Daron, Simon Johnson, James A. Robinson, and Pierre Yared. 2008. "Income and Democracy." *American Economic Review* 98(3): 808–842.

Adda, Jérôme, and Francesca Cornaglia. 2006. "Taxes, Cigarette Consumption, and Smoking Intensity." *American Economic Review* 96(4): 1013–1028.

Aggarwal, Rajesh K., and Philippe Jorion. 2010. "The Performance of Emerging Hedge Funds and Managers." *Journal of Financial Economics* 96: 238–256.

Almond, Douglas, Kenneth Y. Chay, and David S. Lee. 2005. "The Costs of Low Birth Weight." *Quarterly Journal of Economics* 120(3): 1031–1083.

Anderson, Theodore W., and Herman Rubin. 1950. "Estimators of the Parameters of a Single Equation in a Complete Set of Stochastic Equations." *Annals of Mathematical Statistics* 21: 570–582.

Andrews, Donald W. K. 1991. "Heteroskedasticity and Autocorrelation Consistent Covariance Matrix Estimation." *Econometrica* 59(3): 817–858.

Andrews, Donald W. K. 1993. "Tests for Parameter Instability and Structural Change with Unknown Change Point." *Econometrica* 61(4): 821–856.

Andrews, Donald W. K. 2003. "Tests For Parameter Instability and Structural Change with Unknown Change Point: A Corrigendum." *Econometrica* 71: 395–397.

Angrist, Joshua. 1990. "Lifetime Earnings and the Vietnam Era Draft Lottery: Evidence from Social Security Administrative Records." *American Economic Review* 80(3): 313–336.

Angrist, Joshua, and William Evans. 1998. "Children and Their Parents' Labor Supply: Evidence from Exogenous Variation in Family Size." *American Economic Review* 88(3): 450–477.

Angrist, Joshua, Kathryn Graddy, and Guido Imbens. 2000. "The Interpretation of Instrumental Variables Estimators in Simultaneous Equations Models with an Application to the Demand for Fish." *Review of Economic Studies* 67(232): 499–527.

Angrist, Joshua, and Alan B. Krueger. 1991. "Does Compulsory School Attendance Affect Schooling and Earnings?" *Quarterly Journal of Economics* 106(4): 979–1014.

Angrist, Joshua, and Alan B. Krueger. 2001. "Instrumental Variables and the Search for Identification: From Supply and Demand to Natural Experiments." *Journal of Economic Perspectives* 15(4), Fall: 69–85.

Arellano, Manuel. 2003. *Panel Data Econometrics.* Oxford: Oxford University Press.

Ayres, Ian, and John Donohue. 2003. "Shooting Down the 'More Guns Less Crime' Hypothesis." *Stanford Law Review* 55: 1193–1312.

Barendregt, Jan J. 1997. "The Health Care Costs of Smoking." *New England Journal of Medicine* 337(15): 1052–1057.

Beck, Thorsten, Ross Levine, and Norman Loayza. 2000. "Finance and the Sources of Growth." *Journal of Financial Economics* 58: 261–300.

Benartzi, Shlomo, and Richard H. Thaler. 2007. "Heuristics and Biases in Retirement Savings Behavior." *Journal of Economic Perspectives* 21(3): 81–104.

Bergstrom, Theodore A. 2001. "Free Labor for Costly Journals?" *Journal of Economic Perspectives* 15(4), Fall: 183–198.

Bertrand, Marianne, and Kevin Hallock. 2001. "The Gender Gap in Top Corporate Jobs." *Industrial and Labor Relations Review* 55(1): 3–21.

Bertrand, Marianne, and Sendhil Mullainathan. 2004. "Are Emily and Greg More Employable than Lakisha and Jamal? A Field Experiment on Labor Market Discrimination." *American Economic Review* 94(4): 991–1013.

Beshears, John, James J. Choi, David Laibson, and Brigitte C. Madrian. 2008. "The Importance of Default Options for Retirement Saving Outcomes: Evidence from the United States," in *Lessons from Pension Reform in the Americas*, edited by Stephen J. Kay and Tapen Sinha. Oxford: Oxford University Press, 59–87.

Bollersev, Tim. 1986. "Generalized Autoregressive Conditional Heteroskedasticity." *Journal of Econometrics* 31(3): 307–327.

Bound, John, David A. Jaeger, and Regina M. Baker. 1995. "Problems with Instrumental Variables Estimation When the Correlation Between the Instrument and the Endogenous Explanatory Variable Is Weak." *Journal of the American Statistical Association* 90(430): 443–450.

Campbell, John Y. 2003. "Consumption-Based Asset Pricing." Chap. 13 in *Handbook of the Economics of Finance,* edited by Milton Harris and Rene Stulz. Amsterdam: Elsevier.

Campbell, John Y., and Motohiro Yogo. 2005. "Efficient Tests of Stock Return Predictability." *Journal of Financial Economics* 81(1): 27–60.

Card, David. 1990. "The Impact of the Mariel Boatlift on the Miami Labor Market." *Industrial and Labor Relations Review* 43(2): 245–257.

Card, David. 1999. "The Causal Effect of Education on Earnings." Chap. 30 in *The Handbook of Labor Economics*, edited by Orley C. Ashenfelter and David Card. Amsterdam: Elsevier.

Card, David, and Alan B. Krueger. 1994. "Minimum Wages and Employment: A Case Study of the Fast Food Industry." *American Economic Review* 84(4): 772–793.

Carhart, Mark M. 1997. "On Persistence in Mutual Fund Performance." *Journal of Finance* 52(1): 57–82.

Carpenter, Christopher, and Philip J. Cook. 2008. "Cigarette Taxes and Youth Smoking: New Evidence from National, State, and Local Youth Risk Behavior Surveys," *Journal of Health* 27(2): 287–299

Case, Anne and Christina Paxson. 2008. "Stature and Status: Height, Ability, and Labor Market Outcomes." *Journal of Political Economy* 116(3): 499–532.

Chaloupka, Frank J., Michael Grossman, and Henry Saffer. 2002. "The Effect of Price on Alcohol Consumption and Alcohol-Related Problems." *Alcohol Research & Health* 26: 22–34.

Chaloupka, Frank J., and Kenneth E. Warner. 2000. "The Economics of Smoking." Chap. 29 in *The Handbook of Health Economics*, edited by Joseph P. Newhouse and Anthony J. Cuyler. New York: North Holland.

Chetty, Raj, John N. Friedman, Nathaniel Hilger, Emmanuel Saez, Diane Whitmore Schanzenbach, and Danny Yagan. 2011. "How Does Your Kindergarten Classroom Affect Your Earnings? Evidence from Project Star." *Quarterly Journal of Economics* CXXVI(4): 1593–1660.

Chow, Gregory. 1960. "Tests of Equality Between Sets of Coefficients in Two Linear Regressions." *Econometrica* 28(3): 591–605.

Clay, Karen, Werner Troesken, and Michael Haines. 2014. "Lead and Mortality." *The Review of Economics and Statistics* 96(3).

Clements, Michael P. 2004. "Evaluating the Bank of England Density Forecasts of Inflation." *Economic Journal* 114: 844–866.

Cochrane, D., and Guy Orcutt. 1949. "Application of Least Squares Regression to Relationships Containing Autocorrelated Error Terms." *Journal of the American Statistical Association* 44(245): 32–61.

Cook, Philip J., and Michael J. Moore. 2000. "Alcohol." Chap. 30 in *The Handbook of Health Economics*, edited by Joseph P. Newhouse and Anthony J. Cuyler. New York: North Holland.

Cooper, Harris, and Larry V. Hedges. 1994. *The Handbook of Research Synthesis*. New York: Russell Sage Foundation.

Dang, Jennifer N. 2008. "Statistical Analysis of Alcohol-Related Driving Trends, 1982–2005." Technical Report DOT HS 810 942. Washington, D.C.: U.S. National Highway Traffic Safety Administration.

Dahl, Gordon, and Stefano DellaVigna. 2009. "Does Movie Violence Increase Violent Crime," *Quarterly Journal of Economics* 124(2): 677–734.

Deaton, Angus. 2010. "Instruments, Randomization, and Learning about Development." *Journal of Economic Literature* 48(June): 424–455.

Dickey, David A., and Wayne A. Fuller. 1979. "Distribution of the Estimators for Autoregressive Time Series with a Unit Root." *Journal of the American Statistical Association* 74(366): 427–431.

Diebold, Francis X. 2007. *Elements of Forecasting* (fourth edition). Cincinnati: South-Western.

Ehrenberg, Ronald G., Dominic J. Brewer, Adam Gamoran, and J. Douglas Willms. 2001a. "Class Size and Student Achievement." *Psychological Science in the Public Interest* 2(1): 1–30.

Ehrenberg, Ronald G., Dominic J. Brewer, Adam Gamoran, and J. Douglas Willms. 2001b. "Does Class Size Matter?" *Scientific American* 285(5): 80–85.

Eicker, F. 1967. "Limit Theorems for Regressions with Unequal and Dependent Errors." *Proceedings of the Fifth Berkeley Symposium on Mathematical Statistics and Probability*, 1, 59–82. Berkeley: University of California Press.

Elliott, Graham, Thomas J. Rothenberg, and James H. Stock. 1996. "Efficient Tests for an Autoregressive Unit Root." *Econometrica* 64(4): 813–836.

Enders, Walter. 2009. *Applied Econometric Time Series*. 3rd Edition, New York: Wiley.

Engle, Robert F. 1982. "Autoregressive Conditional Heteroskedasticity with Estimates of the Variance of United Kingdom Inflation." *Econometrica* 50(4): 987–1007.

Engle, Robert F., and Clive W. J. Granger. 1987. "Cointegration and Error Correction: Representation, Estimation and Testing." *Econometrica* 55(2): 251–276.

Evans, William, Matthew Farrelly, and Edward Montgomery. 1999. "Do Workplace Smoking Bans Reduce Smoking?" *American Economic Review* 89(4): 728–747.

Foster, Donald. 1996. "Primary Culprit: An Analysis of a Novel of Politics." *New York Magazine* 29(8), February 26.

Fuller, Wayne A. 1976. *Introduction to Statistical Time Series*. New York: Wiley.

Garvey, Gerald T., and Gordon Hanka. 1999. "Capital Structure and Corporate Control: The Effect of Antitakeover Statutes on Firm Leverage." *Journal of Finance* 54(2): 519–546.

Gillespie, Richard. 1991. *Manufacturing Knowledge: A History of the Hawthorne Experiments.* New York: Cambridge University Press.

Goering, John, and Ron Wienk, eds. 1996. *Mortgage Lending, Racial Discrimination, and Federal Policy.* Washington, DC: Urban Institute Press.

Goyal, Amit, and Ivo Welch. 2003. "Predicting the Equity Premium with Dividend Ratios." *Management Science* 49(5): 639–654.

Granger, Clive W. J. 1969. "Investigating Causal Relations by Econometric Models and Cross-Spectral Methods." *Econometrica* 37(3): 424–438.

Granger, Clive W. J., and A. A. Weiss. 1983. "Time Series Analysis of Error-Correction Models." Pp. 255–278 in *Studies in Econometrics: Time Series and Multivariate Statistics,* edited by S. Karlin, T. Amemiya, and L. A. Goodman. New York: Academic Press.

Green, Richard K. and Susan M. Wachter. 2008, "The Housing Finance Revolution," Pp. 21–67 in *Housing, Housing Finance, and Monetary Policy: Symposium Proceedings*, Federal Reserve Bank of Kansas City.

Greene, William H. 2012. *Econometric Analysis* (seventh edition). Upper Saddle River, NJ: Prentice Hall.

Gruber, Jonathan. 2001. "Tobacco at the Crossroads: The Past and Future of Smoking Regulation in the United States." *Journal of Economic Perspectives* 15(2): 193–212.

Haldrup, Niels, and Michael Jansson, 2006. "Improving Size and Power in Unit Root Testing." Pp. 255–277 in *Palgrave Handbook of Econometrics, Volume 1: Econometric Theory,* edited by Terrence Mills and Kerry Patterson. Basingstoke U.K.: Palgrave MacMillan.

Hamilton, James D. 1994. *Time Series Analysis.* Princeton, NJ: Princeton University Press.

Hansen, Bruce. 1992. "Efficient Estimation and Testing of Cointegrating Vectors in the Presence of Deterministic Trends." *Journal of Econometrics* 53(1–3): 86–121.

Hansen, Bruce. 2001. "The New Econometrics of Structural Change: Dating Breaks in U.S. Labor Productivity." *Journal of Economic Perspectives* 15(4), Fall: 117–128.

Hansen, Lars Peter. 1982, "Large Sample Properties of Generalized Method of Moments Estimators." *Econometrica* 50(4): 1029–1054.

Hanushek, Eric. 1999a. "Some Findings from an Independent Investigation of the Tennessee STAR Experiment and from Other Investigations of Class Size Effects." *Educational Evaluation and Policy Analysis* 21: 143–164.

Hanushek, Eric. 1999b. "The Evidence on Class Size." Chap. 7 in *Earning and Learning: How Schools Matter*, edited by S. Mayer and P. Peterson. Washington, DC: Brookings Institution Press.

Hayashi, Fumio. 2000. *Econometrics.* Princeton, NJ: Princeton University Press.

Heckman, James J. 1974. "Shadow Prices, Market Wages, and Labor Supply," *Econometrica* 42: 679–694.

Heckman, James J. 2001. "Micro Data, Heterogeneity, and the Evaluation of Public Policy: Nobel Lecture." *Journal of Political Economy* 109(4): 673–748.

Heckman, James J., Robert J. LaLonde, and Jeffrey A. Smith. 1999. "The Economics and Econometrics of Active Labor Market Programs." Chap. 31 in *Handbook of Labor Economics*, edited by Orley Ashenfelter and David Card. Amsterdam: Elsevier.

Hedges, Larry V., and Ingram Olkin. 1985. *Statistical Methods for Meta-analysis.* San Diego: Academic Press.

Hetland, Lois. 2000. "Listening to Music Enhances Spatial-Temporal Reasoning: Evidence for the 'Mozart Effect.'" *Journal of Aesthetic Education* 34(3–4): 179–238.

Hoxby, Caroline M. 2000. "The Effects of Class Size on Student Achievement: New Evidence from Population Variation." *Quarterly Journal of Economics* 115(4): 1239–1285.

Huber, P. J. 1967. "The Behavior of Maximum Likelihood Estimates Under Nonstandard Conditions," *Proceedings of the Fifth Berkeley Symposium on Mathematical Statistics and Probability*, 1, 221–233. Berkeley: University of California Press.

Imbens, Guido W., and Joshua D. Angrist. 1994. "Identification and Estimation of Local Average Treatment Effects." *Econometrica* 62: 467–476.

Johansen, Søren. 1988. "Statistical Analysis of Cointegrating Vectors." *Journal of Economic Dynamics and Control* 12: 231–254.

Jones, Stephen R. G. 1992. "Was There a Hawthorne Effect?" *American Journal of Sociology* 98(3): 451–468.

Kremer, Michael, Edward Miguel, and Rebecca Thornton. 2009. "Incentives to Learn," *The Review of Economics and Statistics* 91: 437–456.

Krueger, Alan B. 1999. "Experimental Estimates of Education Production Functions." *Quarterly Journal of Economics* 14(2): 497–562.

Ladd, Helen. 1998. "Evidence on Discrimination in Mortgage Lending." *Journal of Economic Perspectives* 12(2), Spring: 41–62.

Levitt, Steven D. 1996. "The Effect of Prison Population Size on Crime Rates: Evidence from Prison Overcrowding Litigation." *Quarterly Journal of Economics* 111(2): 319–351.

Levitt, Steven D., and Jack Porter. 2001. "How Dangerous Are Drinking Drivers?" *Journal of Political Economy* 109(6): 1198–1237.

List, John. 2003. "Does Market Experience Eliminate Market Anomalies." *Quarterly Journal of Economics* 118(1): 41–71.

Maddala, G. S. 1983. *Limited-Dependent and Qualitative Variables in Econometrics.* Cambridge: Cambridge University Press.

Maddala, G. S., and In-Moo Kim. 1998. *Unit Roots, Cointegration, and Structural Change.* Cambridge: Cambridge University Press.

Madrian, Brigette C., and Dennis F. Shea. 2001. "The Power of Suggestion: Inertia in 401(k) Participation and Savings Behavior." *Quarterly Journal of Economics* 116(4): 1149–1187.

Malkiel, Burton G. 2007. *A Random Walk Down Wall Street.* New York: W. W. Norton.

Manning, Willard G., et al. 1989. "The Taxes of Sin: Do Smokers and Drinkers Pay Their Way?" *Journal of the American Medical Association* 261(11): 1604–1609.

Matsudaira, Jordan D. 2008. "Mandatory Summer School and Student Achievement." *Journal of Econometrics* 142: 829–850.

McClellan, Mark, Barbara J. McNeil, and Joseph P. Newhouse. 1994. "Does More Intensive Treatment of Acute Myocardial Infarction in the Elderly Reduce Mortality?" *Journal of the American Medical Association* 272(11): 859–866.

Meyer, Bruce D. 1995. "Natural and Quasi-Experiments in Economics." *Journal of Business and Economic Statistics* 13(2): 151–161.

Meyer, Bruce D., W. Kip Viscusi, and David L. Durbin. 1995. "Workers' Compensation and Injury Duration: Evidence from a Natural Experiment." *American Economic Review* 85(3): 322–340.

Moreira, M. J. 2003. "A Conditional Likelihood Ratio Test for Structural Models." *Econometrica* 71: 1027–1048.

Mosteller, Frederick. 1995. "The Tennessee Study of Class Size in the Early School Grades." *The Future of Children: Critical Issues for Children and Youths* 5(2), Summer/Fall: 113–127.

Mosteller, Frederick, Richard Light, and Jason Sachs. 1996. "Sustained Inquiry in Education: Lessons from Skill Grouping and Class Size." *Harvard Educational Review* 66(4), Winter: 631–676.

Mosteller, Frederick, and David L. Wallace. 1963. "Inference in an Authorship Problem." *Journal of the American Statistical Association* 58: 275–309.

Munnell, Alicia H., Geoffrey M. B. Tootell, Lynne E. Browne, and James McEneaney. 1996. "Mortgage Lending in Boston: Interpreting HMDA Data." *American Economic Review* 86(1): 25–53.

Neumark, David, and William Wascher. 2000. "Minimum Wages and Employment: A Case Study of the Fast-Food Industry in New Jersey and Pennsylvania: Comment." *American Economic Review* 90(5): 1362–1396.

Newey, Whitney, and Kenneth West. 1987. "A Simple Positive Semi-definite, Heteroskedastic and Autocorrelation Consistent Covariance Matrix." *Econometrica* 55(3): 703–708.

Newhouse, Joseph P., et. al. 1993. *Free for All? Lessons from the Rand Health Insurance Experiment.* Cambridge, MA: Harvard University Press.

Phillips, Peter C. B., and Sam Ouliaris. 1990. "Asymptotic Properties of Residual Based Tests for Cointegration." *Econometrica* 58(1): 165–194.

Porter, Robert. 1983. "A Study of Cartel Stability: The Joint Executive Committee, 1880–1886." *Bell Journal of Economics* 14(2): 301–314.

Quandt, Richard. 1960. "Tests of the Hypothesis That a Linear Regression System Obeys Two Separate Regimes." *Journal of the American Statistical Association* 55(290): 324–330.

Rauscher, Frances, Gordon L. Shaw, and Katherine N. Ky. 1993. "Music and Spatial Task Performance." *Nature* 365(6447): 611.

Roll, Richard. 1984. "Orange Juice and Weather." *American Economic Review* 74(5): 861–880.

Rosenzweig, Mark R., and Kenneth I. Wolpin. 2000. "Natural 'Natural Experiments' in Economics." *Journal of Economic Literature* 38(4): 827–874.

Ruhm, Christopher J. 1996. "Alcohol Policies and Highway Vehicle Fatalities." *Journal of Health Economics* 15(4): 435–454.

Ruud, Paul. 2000. *An Introduction to Classical Econometric Theory.* New York: Oxford University Press.

Shadish, William R., Thomas D. Cook, and Donald T. Campbell. 2002. *Experimental and Quasi-Experimental Designs for Generalized Causal Inference.* Boston: Houghton Mifflin.

Shiller, Robert J. 2005. *Irrational Exuberance* (second edition). Princeton, NJ: Princeton University Press.

Sims, Christopher A. 1980. "Macroeconomics and Reality." *Econometrica* 48(1): 1–48.

Stock, James H. 1994. "Unit Roots, Structural Breaks, and Trends." Chap. 46 in *Handbook of Econometrics*, volume IV, edited by Robert Engle and Daniel McFadden. Amsterdam: Elsevier.

Stock, James H., and Francesco Trebbi. 2003. "Who Invented Instrumental Variable Regression?" *Journal of Economic Perspectives* 17: 177–194.

Stock, James H., and Mark W. Watson. 1988. "Variable Trends in Economic Time Series." *Journal of Economic Perspectives* 2(3): 147–174.

Stock, James H., and Mark W. Watson. 1993. "A Simple Estimator of Cointegrating Vectors in Higher-Order Integrated Systems." *Econometrica* 61(4): 783–820.

Stock, James H., and Mark W. Watson. 2001. "Vector Autoregressions." *Journal of Economic Perspectives* 15(4), Fall: 101–115.

Stock, James H., and Motohiro Yogo. 2005. "Testing for Weak Instruments in Linear IV Regression." Chap. 5 in *Identification and Inference in Econometric Models: Essays in Honor of Thomas J. Rothenberg,* edited by Donald W. K. Andrews and James H. Stock. Cambridge: Cambridge University Press.

Tobin, James. 1958. "Estimation of Relationships for Limited Dependent Variables." *Econometrica* 26(1): 24–36.

Wagenaar, Alexander C., Matthew J. Salois, and Kelli A. Komro. 2009. "Effects of Beverage Alcohol Price and Tax Levels on Drinking: A Meta-Analysis of 1003 Estimates from 112 Studies." *Addiction* 104: 179–190.

Watson, Mark W. 1994. "Vector Autoregressions and Cointegration." Chap. 47 in *Handbook of Econometrics,* volume IV, edited by Robert Engle and Daniel McFadden. Amsterdam: Elsevier.

White, Halbert. 1980. "A Heteroskedasticity-Consistent Covariance Matrix Estimator and a Direct Test for Heteroskedasticity." *Econometrica* 48: 827–838.

Winner, Ellen, and Monica Cooper. 2000. "Mute Those Claims: No Evidence (Yet) for a Causal Link Between Arts Study and Academic Achievement." *Journal of Aesthetic Education* 34(3–4): 11–76.

Wooldridge, Jeffrey. 2010. *Economic Analysis of Cross Section and Panel Data.* (second edition) Cambridge, MA: MIT Press.

Wright, Philip G. 1915. "Moore's Economic Cycles." *Quarterly Journal of Economics* 29: 631–641.

Wright, Philip G. 1928. *The Tariff on Animal and Vegetable Oils.* New York: Macmillan.

Young, Douglas J., and Agnieszka Bielinska-Kwapisz. 2006. "Alcohol Prices, Consumption, and Traffic Fatalities." *Southern Economic Journal* 72: 690–703.

# Glossary

**Acceptance region:** The set of values of a test statistic for which the null hypothesis is accepted (is not rejected).

**Adjusted $R^2$ $(\overline{R}^2)$:** A modified version of $R^2$ that does not necessarily increase when a new regressor is added to the regression.

**ADL(*p*,*q*):** See *autoregressive distributed lag (ADL) model*.

**AIC:** See *information criterion*.

**Akaike information criterion (AIC):** See *information criterion*.

**Alternative hypothesis:** The hypothesis that is assumed to be true if the null hypothesis is false. The alternative hypothesis is often denoted $H_1$.

**ARCH:** See *autoregressive conditional heteroskedasticity*.

**AR(*p*):** See *autoregression*.

**Asymptotic distribution:** The approximate sampling distribution of a random variable computed using a large sample. For example, the asymptotic distribution of the sample average is normal.

**Asymptotic normal distribution:** A normal distribution that approximates the sampling distribution of a statistic computed using a large sample.

**Attrition:** The loss of subjects from a study after assignment to the treatment or control group.

**Augmented Dickey–Fuller (ADF) test:** A regression-based test for a unit root in an AR(*p*) model.

**Autocorrelation:** The correlation between a time series variable and its lagged value. The $j^{th}$ autocorrelation of $Y$ is the correlation between $Y_t$ and $Y_{t-j}$.

**Autocovariance:** The covariance between a time series variable and its lagged value. The $j^{th}$ autocovariance of $Y$ is the covariance between $Y_t$ and $Y_{t-j}$.

**Autoregression:** A linear regression model that relates a time series variable to its past (that is, lagged) values. An autoregression with *p* lagged values as regressors is denoted AR(*p*).

**Autoregressive conditional heteroskedasticity (ARCH):** A time series model of conditional heteroskedasticity.

**Autoregressive distributed lag (ADL) model:** A linear regression model in which the time series variable $Y_t$ is expressed as a function of lags of $Y_t$ and of another variable, $X_t$. The model is denoted ADL(*p*,*q*), where *p* denotes the number of lags of $Y_t$ and *q* denotes the number of lags of $X_t$.

**Average causal effect:** The population average of the individual causal effects in a heterogeneous population. Also called the average treatment effect.

**Balanced panel:** A panel data set with no missing observations, that is, in which the variables are observed for each entity and each time period.

**Base specification:** A baseline or benchmark regression specification that includes a set of regressors chosen using a combination of expert judgment, economic theory, and knowledge of how the data were collected.

**Bayes information criterion:** See *information criterion*.

**Bernoulli distribution:** The probability distribution of a Bernoulli random variable.

**Bernoulli random variable:** A random variable that takes on one of two values, 0 and 1. Also known as a binary random variable.

**Best linear unbiased estimator (BLUE):** An estimator that has the smallest variance of any estimator that is a linear function of the sample values $Y$ and is unbiased. Under the Gauss–Markov conditions, the ordinary least squares estimator is the best linear unbiased estimator of the regression coefficients conditional on the values of the regressors.

**Bias:** The expected value of the difference between an estimator and the parameter that it is estimating. If $\hat{\mu}_Y$ is an estimator of $\mu_Y$, then the bias of $\hat{\mu}_Y$ is $E(\hat{\mu}_Y) - \mu_Y$.

**BIC:** See *information criterion*.

**Binary variable:** A variable that is either 0 or 1. A binary variable is used to indicate a binary outcome. For example, $X$ is a binary (or indicator, or dummy) variable for a person's sex if $X = 1$ if the person is female and $X = 0$ if the person is male.

**Bivariate normal distribution:** A generalization of the normal distribution to describe the joint distribution of two random variables.

**BLUE:** See *best linear unbiased estimator (BLUE)*.

**Break date:** The date of a discrete change in population time series regression coefficient(s).

**Causal effect:** The expected effect of a given intervention or treatment as measured in an ideal randomized controlled experiment.

**Central limit theorem:** A result in mathematical statistics that says that, under general conditions, the sampling distribution of the standardized sample average is well approximated by a standard normal distribution when the sample size is large.

**Chi-squared distribution:** The distribution of the sum of $m$ squared independent standard normal random variables. The parameter $m$ is called the degrees of the freedom of the chi-squared distribution.

**Chow test:** A test for a break in a time series regression at a known break date.

**Clustered standard errors:** A method of computing standard errors that is appropriate for panel data.

**Coefficient of determination:** See $R^2$.

**Cointegration:** When two or more time series variables share a common stochastic trend.

**Common trend:** A trend shared by two or more time series.

**Conditional distribution:** The probability distribution of one random variable given that another random variable takes on a particular value.

**Conditional expectation:** The expected value of one random value given that another random variable takes on a particular value.

**Conditional heteroskedasticity:** The variance, usually of an error term, depends on other variables.

**Conditional mean:** The mean of a conditional distribution. See *conditional expectation*.

**Conditional mean independence:** The conditional expectation of the regression error $u_i$, given the regressors, depends on some but not all of the regressors.

**Conditional variance:** The variance of a conditional distribution.

**Confidence interval (confidence set):** An interval (or set) that contains the true value of a population parameter with a prespecified probability when computed over repeated samples.

**Confidence level:** The prespecified probability that a confidence interval (or set) contains the true value of the parameter.

**Consistency:** The property that an estimator is consistent. See *consistent estimator*.

**Consistent estimator:** An estimator that converges in probability to the parameter that it is estimating.

**Constant regressor:** The regressor associated with the regression intercept; this regressor is always equal to 1.

**Constant term:** The regression intercept.

**Continuous random variable:** A random variable that can take on a continuum of values.

**Control group:** The group that does not receive the treatment or intervention in an experiment.

**Control variable:** A regressor that controls for an omitted factor that determines the dependent variable.

**Convergence in distribution:** When a sequence of distributions converges to a limit; a precise definition is given in Section 17.2.

**Converge in probability:** When a sequence of random variables converges to a specific value; for example, when the sample average becomes close to the population mean as the sample size increases; see Key Concept 2.6 and Section 17.2.

**Correlation:** A unit-free measure of the extent to which two random variables move, or vary, together. The correlation (or correlation coefficient) between $X$ and $Y$ is $\sigma_{XY}/\sigma_X\sigma_Y$ and is denoted corr($X, Y$).

**Correlation coefficient:** See *correlation*.

**Covariance:** A measure of the extent to which two random variables move together. The covariance between $X$ and $Y$ is the expected value $E[(X - \mu_X)(Y - \mu_Y)]$ and is denoted cov($X, Y$) or by $\sigma_{XY}$.

**Covariance matrix:** A matrix composed of the variances and covariances of a vector of random variables.

**Critical value:** The value of a test statistic for which the test just rejects the null hypothesis at the given significance level.

**Cross-sectional data:** Data collected for different entities in a single time period.

**Cubic regression model:** A nonlinear regression function that includes $X$, $X^2$, and $X^3$ as regressors.

**Cumulative distribution function (c.d.f.):** See *cumulative probability distribution*.

**Cumulative dynamic multiplier:** The cumulative effect of a unit change in the time series variable $X$ on $Y$. The $h$-period cumulative dynamic multiplier is the effect of a unit change in $X_t$ on $Y_t + Y_{t+1} + \cdots + Y_{t+h}$.

**Cumulative probability distribution:** A function showing the probability that a random variable is less than or equal to a given number.

**Dependent variable:** The variable to be explained in a regression or other statistical model; the variable appearing on the left-hand side in a regression.

**Deterministic trend:** A persistent long-term movement of a variable over time that can be represented as a nonrandom function of time.

**Dickey–Fuller test:** A method for testing for a unit root in a first order autoregression [AR(1)].

**Differences estimator:** An estimator of the causal effect constructed as the difference in the sample average outcomes between the treatment and control groups.

**Differences-in-differences estimator:** The average change in $Y$ for those in the treatment group minus the average change in $Y$ for those in the control group.

**Discrete random variable:** A random variable that takes on discrete values.

**Distributed lag model:** A regression model in which the regressors are current and lagged values of $X$.

**Dummy variable:** See *binary variable*.

**Dummy variable trap:** A problem caused by including a full set of binary variables in a regression together with a constant regressor (intercept), leading to perfect multicollinearity.

**Dynamic causal effect:** The causal effect of one variable on current and future values of another variable.

**Dynamic multiplier:** The $h$-period dynamic multiplier is the effect of a unit change in the time series variable $X_t$ on $Y_{t+h}$.

**Endogenous variable:** A variable that is correlated with the error term.

**Errors-in-variables bias:** The bias in an estimator of a regression coefficient that arises from measurement errors in the regressors.

**Error term:** The difference between $Y$ and the population regression function, denoted $u$ in this textbook.

**Estimate:** The numerical value of an estimator computed from data in a specific sample.

**Estimators:** A function of a sample of data to be drawn randomly from a population. An estimator is a procedure for using sample data to compute an educated guess of the value of a population parameter, such as the population mean.

**Exact (finite-sample) distribution:** The exact probability distribution of a random variable.

**Exact identification:** When the number of instrumental variables equals the number of endogenous regressors.

**Exogenous variable:** A variable that is uncorrelated with the regression error term.

**Expectation:** See *expected value*.

**Expected value:** The long-run average value of a random variable over many repeated trials or occurrences. It is the probability-weighted average of all possible values that the random variable can take on. The expected value of $Y$ is denoted $E(Y)$ and is also called the expectation of $Y$.

**Experimental data:** Data obtained from an experiment designed to evaluate a treatment or policy or to investigate a causal effect.

**Explained sum of squares (ESS):** The sum of squared deviations of the predicted values of $Y_i$, $\hat{Y}_i$ from their average; see Equation (4.14).

**Explanatory variable:** See *regressor*.

**External validity:** Inferences and conclusions from a statistical study are externally valid if they can be generalized from the population and the setting studied to other populations and settings.

**Feasible GLS estimator:** A version of the generalized least squares (GLS) estimator that uses an estimator of the conditional variance of the regression errors and covariance between the regression errors at different observations.

**Feasible WLS:** A version of the weighted least squares (WLS) estimator that uses an estimator of the conditional variance of the regression errors.

**First difference:** The first difference of a time series variable $Y_t$ is $Y_t - Y_{t-1}$, denoted $\Delta Y_t$.

**First-stage regression:** The regression of an included endogenous variable on the included exogenous variables, if any, and the instrumental variable(s) in two stage least squares.

**Fitted value:** See *predicted values*.

**Fixed effects:** Binary variables indicating the entity or time period in a panel data regression.

**Fixed effects regression model:** A panel data regression that includes entity fixed effects.

**$F_{m,n}$ distribution:** The distribution of a ratio of independent random variables, where the numerator is a chi-squared random variable with $m$ degrees of freedom divided by $m$ and the denominator is a chi-squared random variable with $n$ degrees of freedom divided by $n$.

**$F_{m,\infty}$ distribution:** The distribution of a random variable with a chi-squared distribution with $m$ degrees of freedom divided by $m$.

**Forecast error:** The difference between the value of the variable that actually occurs and its forecasted value.

**Forecast interval:** An interval that contains the future value of a time series variable with a pre-specified probability.

**$F$-statistic:** A statistic used to a test joint hypothesis concerning more than one of the regression coefficients.

**Functional form misspecification:** When the form of the estimated regression function does not match the form of the population regression function; for example, when a linear specification is used but the true population regression function is quadratic.

**GARCH:** See *generalized autoregressive conditional heteroskedasticity*.

**Gauss–Markov theorem:** Mathematical result stating that, under certain conditions, the ordinary least squares estimator is the best linear unbiased estimator of the regression coefficients conditional on the values of the regressors.

**Generalized autoregressive conditional heteroskedasticity (GARCH):** A time series model for conditional heteroskedasticity.

**Generalized least squares (GLS):** A generalization of ordinary least squares that is appropriate when the regression errors have a known form of heteroskedasticity (in which case GLS is also referred to as weighted least squares, WLS) or a known form of serial correlation.

**Generalized method of moments (GMM):** A method for estimating parameters by fitting sample moments to population moments that are functions of the unknown parameters. Instrumental variables estimators are an important special case.

**GMM:** See *generalized method of moments*.

**Granger causality test:** A procedure for testing whether current and lagged values of one time series help predict future values of another time series.

**HAC standard errors:** See *heteroskedasticity- and autocorrelation-consistent (HAC) standard errors*.

**Hawthorne effect:** See *experimental effect*.

**Heteroskedasticity:** The situation in which the variance of the regression error term $u_i$, conditional on the regressors, is not constant.

**Heteroskedasticity- and autocorrelation-consistent (HAC) standard errors:** Standard errors for ordinary least squares estimators that are consistent whether or not the regression errors are heteroskedastic and autocorrelated.

**Heteroskedasticity-robust standard error:** A standard error for the ordinary least squares estimator that is appropriate whether or not the error term is homoskedastic or heteroskedastic.

**Heteroskedasticity-robust *t*-statistic:** A *t*-statistic constructed using a heteroskedasticity-robust standard error.

**Homoskedasticity:** The variance of the error term $u_i$, conditional on the regressors, is constant.

**Homoskedasticity-only *F*-statistic:** A form of the *F*-statistic that is valid only when the regression errors are homoskedastic.

**Homoskedasticity-only standard errors:** Standard errors for the ordinary least squares estimator that are appropriate only when the error term is homoskedastic.

**Hypothesis test:** A procedure for using sample evidence to help determine if a specific hypothesis about a population is true or false.

***I*(0), *I*(1), and *I*(2):** See *order of integration*.

**Identically distributed:** When two or more random variables have the same distribution.

**Impact effect:** The contemporaneous, or immediate, effect of a unit change in the time series variable $X_t$ on $Y_t$.

**Imperfect multicollinearity:** The condition in which two or more regressors are highly correlated.

**Included endogenous variables:** Regressors that are correlated with the error term (usually in the context of instrumental variable regression).

**Included exogenous variables:** Regressors that are uncorrelated with the error term (usually in the context of instrumental variable regression).

**Independence:** When knowing the value of one random variable provides no information about the value of another random variable. Two random variables are independent if their joint distribution is the product of their marginal distributions.

**Independently and identically distributed (i.i.d.):** When two or more independent random variables have the same distribution.

**Indicator variable:** See *binary variable*.

**Information criterion:** A statistic used to estimate the number of lagged variables to include in an autoregression or a distributed lag model. Leading examples are the Akaike information criterion (AIC) and the Bayes information criterion (BIC).

**Instrument:** See *instrumental variable*.

**Instrumental variable:** A variable that is correlated with an endogenous regressor (instrument relevance) and is uncorrelated with the regression error (instrument exogeneity).

**Instrumental variables (IV) regression:** A way to obtain a consistent estimator of the unknown coefficients of the population regression function when the regressor, $X$, is correlated with the error term, $u$.

**Interaction term:** A regressor that is formed as the product of two other regressors, such as $X_{1i} \times X_{2i}$.

**Intercept:** The value of $\beta_0$ in the linear regression model.

**Internal validity:** When inferences about causal effects in a statistical study are valid for the population being studied.

**Joint hypothesis:** A hypothesis consisting of two or more individual hypotheses, that is, involving more than one restriction on the parameters of a model.

**Joint probability distribution:** The probability distribution determining the probabilities of outcomes involving two or more random variables.

**J-statistic:** A statistic for testing overidentifying restrictions in instrumental variables regression.

**Kurtosis:** A measure of how much mass is contained in the tails of a probability distribution.

**Lags:** The value of a time series variable in a previous time period. The $j^{th}$ lag of $Y_t$ is $Y_{t-j}$.

**Law of iterated expectations:** A result in probability theory that says that the expected value of $Y$ is the expected value of its conditional expectation given $X$, that is, that $E(Y) = E[E(Y|X)]$

**Law of large numbers:** According to this result from probability theory, under general conditions the sample average will be close to the population mean with very high probability when the sample size is large.

**Least squares assumptions:** The assumptions for the linear regression model listed in Key Concept 4.3 (single variable regression) and Key Concept 6.4 (multiple regression model).

**Least squares estimator:** An estimator formed by minimizing the sum of squared residuals.

**Limited dependent variable:** A dependent variable that can take on only a limited set of values. For example, the variable might be a 0–1 binary variable or arise from one of the models described in Appendix 11.3.

**Linear-log model:** A nonlinear regression function in which the dependent variable is $Y$ and the independent variable is $\ln(X)$.

**Linear probability model:** A regression model in which $Y$ is a binary variable.

**Linear regression function:** A regression function with a constant slope.

**Local average treatment effect:** A weighted average treatment effect estimated, for example, by two stage least squares.

**Logarithm:** A mathematical function defined for a positive argument; its slope is always positive but tends to zero. The natural logarithm is the inverse of the exponential function; that is, $X = \ln(e^X)$.

**Logit regression:** A nonlinear regression model for a binary dependent variable in which the population regression function is modeled using the cumulative logistic distribution function.

**Log-linear model:** A nonlinear regression function in which the dependent variable is $\ln(Y)$ and the independent variable is $X$.

**Log-log model:** A nonlinear regression function in which the dependent variable is $\ln(Y)$ and the independent variable is $\ln(X)$.

**Longitudinal data:** See *panel data*.

**Long-run cumulative dynamic multiplier:** The cumulative long-run effect on the time series variable $Y$ of a change in $X$.

**Marginal probability distribution:** Another name for the probability distribution of a random variable $Y$, which distinguishes the distribution of $Y$ alone (the marginal distribution) from the joint distribution of $Y$ and another random variable.

**Maximum likelihood estimator (MLE):** An estimator of unknown parameters that is obtained by maximizing the likelihood function; see Appendix 11.2.

**Mean:** The expected value of a random variable. The mean of $Y$ is denoted $\mu_Y$.

**Moments of a distribution:** The expected value of a random variable raised to different powers. The $r^{th}$ moment of the random variable $Y$ is $E(Y^r)$.

**Multicollinearity:** See *perfect multicollinearity* and *imperfect multicollinearity*.

**Multiple regression model:** An extension of the single variable regression model that allows $Y$ to depend on $k$ regressors.

**Natural experiment:** See *quasi-experiment*.

**Natural logarithm:** See *logarithm*.

**95% confidence set:** A confidence set with a 95% confidence level. See *confidence interval*.

**Nonlinear least squares:** The analog of ordinary least squares that applies when the regression function is a nonlinear function of the unknown parameters.

**Nonlinear least squares estimator:** The estimator obtained by minimizing the sum of squared residuals when the regression function is nonlinear in the parameters.

**Nonlinear regression function:** A regression function with a slope that is not constant.

**Nonstationary:** When the joint distribution of a time series variable and its lags changes over time.

**Normal distribution:** A commonly used bell-shaped distribution of a continuous random variable.

**Null hypothesis:** The hypothesis being tested in a hypothesis test, often denoted $H_0$.

**Observational data:** Data based on observing, or measuring, actual behavior outside an experimental setting.

**Observation number:** The unique identifier assigned to each entity in a data set.

**OLS estimator:** See *ordinary least squares estimator*.

**OLS regression line:** The regression line with population coefficients replaced by the ordinary least squares estimators.

**OLS residual:** The difference between $Y_i$ and the ordinary least squares regression line, denoted $\hat{u}_i$ in this textbook.

**Omitted variables bias:** The bias in an estimator that arises because a variable that is a determinant of $Y$ and is correlated with a regressor has been omitted from the regression.

**One-sided alternative hypothesis:** The parameter of interest is on one side of the value given by the null hypothesis.

**Order of integration:** The number of times that a time series variable must be differenced to make it stationary. A time series variable that is integrated of order $d$ must be differenced $d$ times and is denoted $I(d)$.

**Ordinary least squares (OLS) estimators:** The estimators of the regression intercept and slope(s) that minimizes the sum of squared residuals.

**Outlier:** An exceptionally large or small value of a random variable.

**Overidentification:** When the number of instrumental variables exceeds the number of included endogenous regressors.

**Panel data:** Data for multiple entities where each entity is observed in two or more time periods.

**Parameters:** Constants that determine a characteristic of a probability distribution or population regression function.

**Partial compliance:** The failure of some participants to follow the treatment protocol in a randomized experiment.

**Partial effect:** The effect on $Y$ of changing one of the regressors, holding the other regressors constant.

**Perfect multicollinearity:** A situation in which one of the regressors is an exact linear function of the other regressors.

**Polynomial regression model:** A nonlinear regression function that includes $X, X^2, \ldots$ and $X^r$ as regressors, where $r$ is an integer.

**Population:** The group of entities—such as people, companies, or school districts—being studied.

**Population coefficients:** See *population intercept and slope*.

**Population intercept and slope:** The true, or population, values of $\beta_0$ (the intercept) and $\beta_1$ (the slope) in a single variable regression. In a multiple regression, there are multiple slope coefficients $(\beta_1, \beta_2, \ldots, \beta_k)$, one for each regressor.

**Population multiple regression model:** The multiple regression model in Key Concept 6.2.

**Population regression line:** In a single variable regression, the population regression line is $\beta_0 + \beta_1 X_i$, and in a multiple regression, it is $\beta_0 + \beta_1 X_{1i} + \beta_2 X_{2i} + \cdots + \beta_k X_{ki}$.

**Potential outcomes:** The set of outcomes that might occur to an individual (treatment unit) after receiving, or not receiving, an experimental treatment.

**Power:** The probability that a test correctly rejects the null hypothesis when the alternative is true.

**Predicted value:** The value of $Y_i$ that is predicted by the ordinary least squares regression line, denoted $\hat{Y}_i$ in this textbook.

**Price elasticity of demand:** The percentage change in the quantity demanded resulting from a 1% increase in price.

**Probability:** The proportion of the time that an outcome (or event) from a random experiment will occur in the long run.

**Probability density function (p.d.f.):** For a continuous random variable, the area under the probability density function between any two points is the probability that the random variable falls between those two points.

**Probability distribution:** For a discrete random variable, a list of all values that a random variable can take on and the probability associated with each of these values.

**Probit regression:** A nonlinear regression model for a binary dependent variable in which the population regression function is modeled using the cumulative standard normal distribution function.

**Program evaluation:** The field of study concerned with estimating the effect of a program, policy, or some other intervention or "treatment."

**Pseudo out-of-sample forecast:** A forecast computed over part of the sample using a procedure that is "as if" these sample data have not yet been realized.

*p*-value (significance pobability): The probability of drawing a statistic at least as adverse to the null hypothesis as the one actually computed, assuming the null hypothesis is correct. Also called the marginal significance probability, the $p$-value is the smallest significance level at which the null hypothesis can be rejected.

**Quadratic regression model:** A nonlinear regression function that includes $X$ and $X^2$ as regressors.

**Quasi-experiment:** A circumstance in which randomness is introduced by variations in individual circumstances that make it appear "as if" the treatment is randomly assigned.

**$R^2$:** In a regression, the fraction of the sample variance of the dependent variable that is explained by the regressors.

**$\overline{R}^2$:** See *adjusted $R^2$*.

**Randomized controlled experiment:** An experiment in which participants are randomly assigned to a control group, which receives no treatment, or to a treatment group, which receives a treatment.

**Random walk:** A time series process in which the value of the variable equals its value in the previous period plus an unpredictable error term.

**Random walk with drift:** A generalization of the random walk in which the change in the variable has a nonzero mean but is otherwise unpredictable.

**Regressand:** See *dependent variable*.

**Regression discontinuity:** A regression involving a quasi-experiment in which treatment depends on whether an observable variable crosses a threshold.

**Regression specification:** A description of a regression that includes the set of regressors and any nonlinear transformation that has been applied.

**Regressor:** A variable appearing on the right-hand side of a regression; an independent variable in a regression.

**Rejection region:** The set of values of a test statistic for which the test rejects the null hypothesis.

**Repeated cross-sectional data:** A collection of cross-sectional data sets, where each cross-sectional data set corresponds to a different time period.

**Restricted regression:** A regression in which the coefficients are restricted to satisfy some condition. For example, when computing the homoskedasticity-only $F$-statistic, it is the regression with coefficients restricted to satisfy the null hypothesis.

**Root mean squared forecast error (RMSFE):** The square root of the mean of the squared forecast error.

**Sample correlation coefficient (sample correlation):** An estimator of the correlation between two random variables.

**Sample covariance:** An estimator of the covariance between two random variables.

**Sample selection bias:** The bias in an estimator of a regression coefficient that arises when a selection process influences the availability of data and that process is related to the dependent variable. This bias induces correlation between one or more regressors and the regression error.

**Sample standard deviation:** An estimator of the standard deviation of a random variable.

**Sample variance:** An estimator of the variance of a random variable.

**Sampling distribution:** The distribution of a statistic over all possible samples; the distribution arising from repeatedly evaluating the statistic using a series of randomly drawn samples from the same population.

**Scatterplot:** A plot of $n$ observations on $X_i$ and $Y_i$, in which each observation is represented by the point $(X_i, Y_i)$.

**Serial correlation:** See *autocorrelation*.

**Serially uncorrelated:** A time series variable with all autocorrelations equal to zero.

**Significance level:** The prespecified rejection probability of a statistical hypothesis test when the null hypothesis is true.

**Simple random sampling:** When entities are chosen independently from a population using a method that ensures that each entity is equally likely to be chosen.

**Simultaneous causality:** When, in addition to the causal link of interest from $X$ to $Y$, there is a causal link from $Y$ to $X$. Simultaneous causality makes $X$ correlated with the error term in the population regression of interest.

**Simultaneous equations:** See *simultaneous causality*.

**Size of a test:** The probability that a test incorrectly rejects the null hypothesis when the null hypothesis is true.

**Skewness:** A measure of the aysmmetry of a probability distribution.

**Standard deviation:** The square root of the variance. The standard deviation of the random variable $Y$, denoted $\sigma_Y$, has the units of $Y$ and is a measure of the spread of the distribution of $Y$ around its mean.

**Standard error of an estimator:** An estimator of the standard deviation of the estimator.

**Standard error of the regression (SER):** An estimator of the standard deviation of the regression error $u$.

**Standardizing a random variable:** An operation accomplished by subtracting the mean and dividing by the standard deviation, which produces a random variable with a mean of 0 and a standard deviation of 1. The standardized value of $Y$ is $(Y - \mu_Y)/\sigma_Y$.

**Standard normal distribution:** The normal distribution with mean equal to 0 and variance equal to 1, denoted $N(0, 1)$.

**Stationarity:** When the joint distribution of a time series variable and its lagged values does not change over time.

**Statistically insignificant:** The null hypothesis (typically, that a regression coefficient is zero) cannot be rejected at a given significance level.

**Statistically significant:** The null hypothesis (typically, that a regression coefficient is zero) is rejected at a given significance level.

**Stochastic trend:** A persistent but random long-term movement of a variable over time.

**Strict exogeneity:** The requirement that the regression error has a mean of zero conditional on current, future, and past values of the regressor in a distributed lag model.

**Student $t$ distribution:** The Student $t$ distribution with $m$ degrees of freedom is the distribution of the ratio of a standard normal random variable, divided by the square root of an independently distributed chi-squared random variable with $m$ degrees of freedom divided by $m$. As $m$ gets large, the Student $t$ distribution converges to the standard normal distribution.

**Sum of squared residuals ($SSR$):** The sum of the squared ordinary least squares residuals.

**$t$-distribution:** See *Student t distribution*.

**Test for the difference between two means:** A procedure for testing whether two populations have the same mean.

**Time and entity fixed effects regression model:** A panel data regression that includes both entity fixed effects and time fixed effects.

**Time effects:** Binary variables indicating the time period in a panel data regression.

**Time fixed effects:** See *time effects*.

**Time series data:** Data for the same entity for multiple time periods.

**Total sum of squares ($TSS$):** The sum of squared deviations of $Y_i$ from its average.

**$t$-ratio:** See *t-statistic*.

**Treatment effect:** The causal effect in an experiment or a quasi-experiment. See *causal effect*.

**Treatment group:** The group that receives the treatment or intervention in an experiment.

**TSLS:** See *two stage least squares*.

**$t$-statistic:** A statistic used for hypothesis testing. See Key Concept 5.1.

**Two-sided alternative hypothesis:** When, under the alternative hypothesis, the parameter of interest is not equal to the value given by the null hypothesis.

**Two stage least squares:** An instrumental variable estimator, described in Key Concept 12.2.

**Type I error:** In hypothesis testing, the error made when the null hypothesis is true but is rejected.

**Type II error:** In hypothesis testing, the error made when the null hypothesis is false but is not rejected.

**Unbalanced panel:** A panel data set in which some data are missing.

**Unbiased estimator:** An estimator with a bias that is equal to zero.

**Uncorrelated:** Two random variables are uncorrelated if their correlation is zero.

**Underidentification:** When the number of instrumental variables is less than the number of endogenous regressors.

**Unit root:** An autoregression with a largest root equal to 1.

**Unrestricted regression:** When computing the homoskedasticity-only $F$-statistic, it is the regression that applies under the alternative hypothesis so that the coefficients are not restricted to satisfy the null hypothesis.

**VAR:** See *vector autoregression*.

**Variance:** The expected value of the squared difference between a random variable and its mean; the variance of $Y$ is denoted $\sigma_Y^2$.

**Vector autoregression:** A model of $k$ time series variables consisting of $k$ equations, one for each variable, in which the regressors in all equations are lagged values of all the variables.

**Volatility clustering:** When a time series variable exhibits some clustered periods of high variance and other clustered periods of low variance.

**Weak instruments:** Instrumental variables that have a low correlation with the endogenous regressor(s).

**Weighted least squares (WLS):** An alternative to ordinary least squares that can be used when the regression error is heteroskedastic and the form of the heteroskedasticity is known or can be estimated.

# Index

Page numbers followed by *f* indicate figures; those followed by *t* indicate tables.

## Large-Sample Critical Values for the t-statistic from the Standard Normal Distibution

| | Significance Level | | |
|---|---|---|---|
| | 10% | 5% | 1% |
| **2-Sided Test ( ≠ )** | | | |
| Reject if $|t|$ is greater than | 1.64 | 1.96 | 2.58 |
| **1-Sided Test (>)** | | | |
| Reject if $t$ is greater than | 1.28 | 1.64 | 2.33 |
| **1-Sided Test (<)** | | | |
| Reject if $t$ is less than | −1.28 | −1.64 | −2.33 |

# FOR STUDY AND DISCUSSION

1. In the midst of his perilous journey, Kino looks into the pearl for "his vision." But the pearl reflects only nightmares. What does each nightmare reveal about what has happened to Kino?

2. Is Kino in any way responsible for his little son's death? Why, or why not?

3. What is significant about the fact that the Song of the Family becomes "a battle cry" when Kino and Juana return with the pearl and the body of their son? What images now make the pair seem noble and powerful?

4. How does the melody of the pearl in Chapter 2 (page 721) compare with what Kino now sees in the pearl? What has caused Kino to associate the pearl with evil?

5. Kino at first saw the pearl as a means of gaining a kind of freedom. What would you say he finally gains from his tragic experience? How does Kino change? What does his final act reveal about his values?

6. Why do you think Kino and Juana throw the pearl away?

## THE NOVEL AS A WHOLE

### Plot

1. The plot of *The Pearl* consists of a series of connected incidents, all related in chronological order. Trace the major events of the plot. What are the *conflicts* in the story? What is the *climax* — that moment of greatest emotional intensity? How are the conflicts finally resolved? Would you describe the resolution as satisfying, or as something else?

2. To create suspense and tension, storytellers often use *foreshadowing* — that is, they drop hints about what is to happen later. Steinbeck often uses imagery from the natural world to foreshadow human conflicts. What human conflict is foreshadowed by the description of the ant lion on page 710? What human conflict is foreshadowed in the passage on page 728 that begins with the slaughter of the fish?

### Irony

1. To show us that life is unpredictable and not always comprehensible, writers often use *irony*. Ironic situations turn out to be just the reverse of what we expect or of what we think would be appropriate. What is ironic about the fact that it is Coyotito who is killed in this story? How did this irony affect you?

2. When Kino and Juana set out to sell the pearl at the opening of Chapter 4, they feel that it is "the morning of mornings of their lives, comparable only to the day when their baby was born. This was to be the day from which all other days would take their arrangement." Given what happens later, what is ironic about the parents' hopes? In what unexpected way does this turn out to be the "morning of mornings"?

3. Kino hoped to win freedom and knowledge through his son. He hoped that Coyotito would "break out of the pot that holds us in" (page 731). Ironically, how does Coyotito help his parents win a kind of "freedom"? What do Kino and Juana come to realize through the baby's death?

### Imagery

Kino and Juana are often compared to animals. After Kino finds the pearl, for example, he "howls," as a dog or a wolf would. What images in Chapter 6 compare Kino and Juana, as well as their trackers, to animals? In contrast, what images describe the pair when they return to La Paz on that golden afternoon, after their ordeal is over? How have they changed? What would you compare them to now?

## Symbol

A *symbol* is any object, action, person, or place that has a meaning in itself and that also stands for something broader than itself. The pearl in this story seems to stand for more than just an actual pearl. Steinbeck tells us on page 719 that the pearl is an accident, a "coated grain of sand." Find passages that reveal what the pearl symbolizes to various people at various times in the story. Does Steinbeck finally make us see the pearl again for what it really is — a beautiful "accident" of the sea? Explain.

## Theme

1. On page 709, Steinbeck says that everyone takes his or her own meaning from this story. *The Pearl* is a simple story, but what it means is anything but simple. One of the themes of the story might be illuminated by this statement made by Steinbeck on page 724:

> For it is said that humans are never satisfied, that you give them one thing and they want something more. And this is said in disparagement, whereas it is one of the greatest talents the species has and one that has made it superior to animals that are satisfied with what they have.

How does this statement apply to Kino and Juana and their quest? What desires eventually distinguish Kino and Juana from everyone else in La Paz? Are there other passages in the story supporting this as a theme?

2. The theme of *The Pearl* also might have something to do with tragic experience, and with the wisdom that can be gained from it. What tragic experience do Kino and Juana undergo? How do they change as a result of the experience? What wisdom do they gain?

3. Many people see the theme of the story as one concerning the dehumanizing nature of greed. In what passages is greed depicted as an evil? Tell specifically how it has dehumanized certain characters. Are there any major characters in the story who are not tainted at one time or another with greed? Is there a force in the story that finally triumphs over greed?

4. Throughout the story, Steinbeck develops the theme that the rich and powerful can dominate the poor and uneducated. What episodes dramatize this theme? Consider why Kino is unable to deal with the doctor and the pearl buyers. How does the priest's yearly sermon (page 734) relate to this theme? What do you think Steinbeck is saying about those who attempt to overcome this situation?

## Style

Because Steinbeck wanted this novel to serve as a parable, he wrote it in a style that is suggestive of a folk tale. Folk literature is usually told in simple, straightforward language; it makes use of repetition, which gives the prose a rhythmic effect; and its characters are often presented as either good or bad — they are not usually the complex individuals we know in actual life. Look back at the final scene of the novel, where Kino and Juana return to La Paz. How does the style here reflect some of the characteristics of a folk tale?

## Tone

*Tone* is the attitude that a writer takes toward the characters and events in a story. It is important to recognize a writer's tone, because if we misinterpret tone, we might misinterpret the entire story. How would you describe Steinbeck's tone in *The Pearl*? What does he think of the events that take place in La Paz? How does he feel about the various characters in the story?

## LANGUAGE AND VOCABULARY

### Using Precise Diction

Steinbeck's diction is simple, but he makes each word do exactly what he wants it to do. Look at his use of the word *lacy:*

> The hot sun beat on the earth so that Kino and Juana moved into the *lacy* shade of the brush . . . .

The word *lacy* means "like lace, having a delicate, open pattern." The word makes us visualize a shady area streaked with a delicate pattern of gentle sunlight. The word itself has a soft sound quality that adds to the impression of gentleness.

Using the dictionary when necessary, define the italicized words in the following sentences. Consider the precise meaning of each word, what the word makes you see, hear, or feel, and the word's sound quality. Notice that some of these words are used metaphorically. For such words, tell what comparisons they make and if you think the comparisons are effective.

> Kino had wondered often at the *iron* in his patient, fragile wife.
>
> His eyes rested in puffy little *hammocks* of flesh and his mouth drooped with discontent.
>
> It [the canoe] is the *bulwark* against starvation.
>
> Then in coordination Juana and Kino drove their double-bladed paddles into the sea, and the canoe *creased* the water and *hissed* with speed.
>
> The *liplike flesh* [of the oyster] *writhed* up and then *subsided.*
>
> "Kino will be a rich man," they *clamored.*
>
> He felt the evil *coagulating* about him, and he was helpless to protect himself.

> High slopes of the mountain are *swaddled* with pines.
>
> The third man *scrabbled* away like a crab, slipped into the pool, and then he began to climb frantically, to climb up the cliff where the water *penciled* down.

## FOR COMPOSITION

### Comparing Two Stories

In his book *The Sea of Cortez,* John Steinbeck narrates the experiences on which he based his novel *The Pearl.* As this part of his "sea log" opens, Steinbeck has reached the harbor town of La Paz in Mexico, a city he calls "beautiful out of all comparison."

> . . . It is a proud thing to have been born in La Paz, and a cloud of delight hangs over the distant city from the time when it was the great pearl center of the world. The robes of the Spanish kings and the stoles of bishops in Rome were stiff with the pearls from La Paz. There's a magic-carpet sound to the name, anyway. And it is an old city, as cities in the West are old, and very venerable in the eyes of Indians of the Gulf. Guaymas is busier, they say, and Mazatlán gayer, perhaps, but La Paz is *antigua.*
>
> The Gulf and Gulf ports have always been unfriendly to colonization. Again and again attempts were made before a settlement would stick. Humans are not much wanted on the peninsula. But at La Paz the pearl oysters drew men from all over the world. And, as in all concentrations of natural wealth, the terrors of greed were let loose on the city again and again. An event which happened at La Paz in recent years is typical of such places. An Indian boy by accident found a pearl of great size, an unbelievable pearl. He knew its value was so

great that he need never work again. In his one pearl he had the ability to be drunk as long as he wished, to marry any one of a number of girls, and to make many more a little happy too. In his great pearl lay salvation, for he could in advance purchase Masses sufficient to pop him out of Purgatory like a squeezed watermelon seed. In addition he could shift a number of dead relatives a little nearer to Paradise. He went to La Paz with his pearl in his hand and his future clear into eternity in his heart. He took his pearl to a broker and was offered so little that he grew angry, for he knew he was cheated. Then he carried his pearl to another broker and was offered the same amount. After a few more visits he came to know that the brokers were only the many hands of one head and that he could not sell his pearl for more. He took it to the beach and hid it under a stone, and that night he was clubbed into unconsciousness and his clothing was searched. The next night he slept at the house of a friend and his friend and he were injured and bound and the whole house searched. Then he went inland to lose his pursuers and he was waylaid and tortured. But he was very angry now and he knew what he must do. Hurt as he was he crept back to La Paz in the night and he skulked like a hunted fox to the beach and took out his pearl from under the stone. Then he cursed it and threw it as far as he could into the channel. He was a free man again with his soul in danger and his food and shelter insecure. And he laughed a great deal about it.

This seems to be a true story, but it is so much like a parable that it almost can't be. This Indian boy is too heroic, too wise. He knows too much and acts on his knowledge. In every way, he goes contrary to human direction. The story is probably true, but we don't believe it; it is far too reasonable to be true.

Write an essay in which you compare the story Steinbeck was told in La Paz with the details he uses in his own novel. Pay specific attention to the changes Steinbeck has made in the setting, the plot, the characterization, and the conflict of the original story. What central details has he maintained? What comment made about the Indian boy's final act might explain why Kino hurls the pearl into the sea? Use specific details from both stories as you write your comparison.

**Analyzing the Theme**
Using one of the discussion topics under the heading "Theme" (page 763), write an essay in which you analyze the theme of *The Pearl*. In your essay, state clearly and in detail what you believe is the major theme of the novel—what truth or insight about life and human behavior is Steinbeck revealing in his story? Cite specific passages from the novel to support your statement.

# Practice in Reading and Writing

## READING AND WRITING ABOUT LITERATURE

You are probably familiar with the work of some movie critics, music critics, and drama critics. Their reviews are found in popular magazines and in the daily and Sunday newspapers. Criticism of literature, like criticism of these other arts, is meant to stimulate us to form our own interpretations about the meaning of a novel, story, poem, or other work. Remember that good criticism is more than judgment. Judgment says merely that something is "good" or "bad." Good criticism is also a search for meaning.

Following is a portion of one critic's interpretation of Steinbeck's novel *The Pearl*. This writer opens by quoting Warren French, another critic of the same novel. Note that this writer disagrees with French. Note also how he uses specific details from the story to support his own interpretation of the meaning of Kino's experience.

Read the criticism carefully. Then write an essay in which you state your own ideas on the interpretation given here. Be sure to support your own conclusion with references to details in the novel itself.

It is difficult to understand how Warren French can interpret the "gesture [of flinging the pearl back into the sea] . . . as defeatism," how French can say that Kino "slips back not just half a step, but toboggans to the very bottom of the heap, for with his boat smashed, his baby dead, and the pearl cast into the sea, he has less when the story is over than he had when it started." Kino is not defeated. He has in a sense triumphed over his enemy, over the chief of the pearl buyers, who neither gets the pearl nor kills Kino to keep him from talking. Kino has rid himself of his pursuers; he has a clear road to the cities of the north, to the capital, where indeed he may be cheated again, but where he has infinitely more opportunity to escape his destiny as a hut-dwelling peasant on the edge of La Paz. He has proved that he cannot be cheated nor destroyed. But his real triumph, his real gain, the heights to which he has risen rather than the depths to which he has slipped back is the immense knowledge that he has gained about good and evil. This knowledge is the tool that he needs to help him on the final journey, the inescapable journey that everyman must take.

Harry Morris
"*The Pearl:* Realism and Allegory"

# For Further Reading

Agee, James, *A Death in the Family* (McDowell, Obolensky, 1956; paperback, Bantam, 1971)
Agee's Pulitzer Prize-winning novel tells a story of love and courage, as sudden, meaningless death changes the lives of a young boy and his family.

Brontë, Emily, *Wuthering Heights* (available in several paperback editions)
This is an unforgettable tale of two mismatched lovers, Cathy and the brooding Heathcliff. Their tragic love story is played out against the wild moors of England.

Cather, Willa, *Death Comes for the Archbishop* (Knopf, 1927; paperback, Vintage, 1971)
Perhaps Cather's best novel, this story chronicles the events of a single human life, that of the archbishop of Santa Fe, who "died of having lived" after forty years of service in the Southwest.

Clark, Arthur C., *Childhood's End* (Harcourt Brace Jovanovich, 1963; paperback, Ballantine, 1976)
Clark's fantasy is set in the future, when the Overlords of Earth are training a race of superhuman children, who will start a new life when their old planet is utterly destroyed.

Dickens, Charles, *A Tale of Two Cities* (available in several paperback editions)
The two cities are London and Paris. Dickens' story of love and sacrifice centers on people who are trying to escape the guillotine during the French Revolution.

Doyle, Sir Arthur Conan, *The Hound of the Baskervilles* (available in several paperback editions)
Doyle's famous horror story, set in a bleak place called Dartmoor, features Sherlock Holmes, an ancient curse, and a demonic killer hound.

Du Maurier, Daphne, *Rebecca* (Doubleday, 1948; paperback, Avon, 1976)
Rebecca is the dead wife of a man now married to the narrator—a young woman obsessed with finding out how Rebecca died. Du Maurier's Gothic romance was made into a movie under the direction of Alfred Hitchcock.

Eliot, George, *Silas Marner* (available in several paperback editions)
Eliot's great novel of greed and redemption is set in nineteenth-century England and centers on the character of Silas, a bitter, solitary miser whose life is changed when a little girl is left in his care.

Le Guin, Ursula, *The Left Hand of Darkness* (paperback, Ace Books, 1976)
This science-fiction fantasy by the author of *The Earthsea Trilogy* won both the Nebula and the Hugo Awards.

Orwell, George, *Animal Farm* (Harcourt Brace Jovanovich, 1946; paperback, Signet)
A witty satire, Orwell's short novel tells of a group of pigs who set up a utopia in which all animals are equal. We soon discover that the ruling pigs are just like their human enemies.

Paton, Alan, *Cry, the Beloved Country* (Scribner's, 1948; paperback, Scribner's)
This masterpiece by the great South African writer is about a Zulu pastor, his son Absalom, and the troubled and beautiful country they live in.

Wilder, Thornton, *The Bridge of San Luis Rey* (Harper & Row, 1967; paperback, Avon)
A bridge collapses in Peru and five people plunge to their deaths. Why these five? One character, who wonders if the accident is fated, proceeds to inquire into the secret lives of the five victims.

# Reading and Writing About Literature

## INTRODUCTION

In English class you will often be asked to write about the literature you read. The writing may be in response to a homework assignment, an examination question, or a research project. At times you may be assigned a topic to work on; at other times you may be instructed to choose your own subject.

In writing about literature your object is to demonstrate your understanding of a literary work or group of works by focusing on some specific aspect of the literature under study. For example, you may analyze the central character or characters in a short story. You may discuss the use of dramatic irony in a play. You may compare techniques or ideas in two poems. Such writing assignments are an important part of literary study, which aims at greater understanding and appreciation of the works you read.

The effort involved in writing about a literary work actually helps you get to know it better. Before you write, you must read the material carefully. You must think about what you have read, weigh the evidence, and come to conclusions. In putting your thoughts down on paper, you become more fully involved with the literature.

In your studies you will become familiar with a great many elents that are useful in analyzing literary works. You can safely assume that your readers will understand what you mean when you refer to a character as the *protagonist* or *antagonist,* or when you use such terms as *satire* and *tone.* These words are part of a common vocabulary used in writing about literature. (See the *Guide to Literary Terms and Techniques,* page 833.)

The material on the following pages offers help in planning and writing papers about literature. Here you will find suggestions for reading and analyzing literature, answering examination questions, choosing topics, gathering evidence, organizing essays, and writing and revising papers. Also included are model essays and several new selections for analysis along with suggested writing topics.

# READING LITERATURE

When you read a chapter in an economics or chemistry textbook, you read primarily to get the facts. Your purpose may be to learn the main principles of Keynesian economic theories or to understand how chlorophyll functions as a catalyst in photosynthesis. You read chiefly to gather information that is stated *directly* on the page.

Reading literature requires considerably more than understanding what all the words mean and getting the facts straight. Much of the meaning of a literary work may be stated *indirectly*. For example, a writer may not *tell* you directly that a character is mean and stingy. However, by referring to that individual as a *Scrooge,* an allusion to Ebenezer Scrooge in Dickens' "A Christmas Carol," the writer establishes the character's nature as hard and miserly. In other words, when you read literature, you depend a good deal on *inference,* drawing conclusions from different kinds of evidence. To read literature critically and grasp its meaning, you have to be an active reader, aware of *what* the author is doing, *how* the author is doing it, and *why.*

When you are asked to write about a literary work, be sure to read it carefully before you begin writing. Read actively, asking yourself questions as you work through the selection.

## Close Reading of a Short Story

A reader who enters imaginatively into a short story responds to several elements that are interdependent: plot (the sequence of related events); characters (persons, animals, or things presented as persons); point of view (the vantage point of the narrative); setting (the time and place of the action); and theme (the underlying idea about human life). The better you understand how these elements work together, the better you will understand and appreciate the author's intent and meaning.

Here is a brief story that has been read carefully by an experienced reader. The notes in the margin show how this reader thinks in working through a story. Read the story at least twice before proceeding to the commentary on page 774. You may wish to make notes of your own on a separate sheet of paper.

# The Trout    *Sean O'Faolain°*

One of the first places Julia always ran to when they arrived in G_____ was The Dark Walk. It is a laurel walk, very old; almost gone wild, a lofty midnight tunnel of smooth, sinewy branches. Underfoot the tough brown leaves are never dry enough to crackle: there is always a suggestion of damp and cool trickle.

She raced right into it. For the first few yards she always had the memory of the sun behind her, then she felt the dusk closing swiftly down on her so that she screamed with pleasure and raced on to reach the light at the far end; and it was always just a little too long in coming so that she emerged gasping, clasping her hands, laughing, drinking in the sun. When she was filled with the heat and glare she would turn and consider the ordeal again.

This year she had the extra joy of showing it to her small brother, and of terrifying him as well as herself. And for him the fear lasted longer because his legs were so short and she had gone out at the far end while he was still screaming and racing.

When they had done this many times they came back to the house to tell everybody that they had done it. He boasted. She mocked. They squabbled.

"Cry babby!"

"You were afraid yourself, so there!"

"I won't take you anymore."

"You're a big pig."

"I hate you."

Tears were threatening so somebody said, "Did you see the well?" She opened her eyes at that and held up her long, lovely neck suspiciously and decided to be incredulous. She was twelve and at that age little girls are beginning to suspect most stories: they have already found out too many, from Santa Claus to the Stork. How could there be a well! In The Dark Walk? That she had visited year after year? Haughtily she said, "Nonsense."

But she went back, pretending to be going somewhere else, and she found a hole scooped in the rock at the side of the walk, choked with damp leaves, so shrouded by ferns that she only uncovered it after much searching. At the back of this little cavern there was about a quart of water. In the water she suddenly perceived a panting trout. She rushed for Stephen and dragged him to see, and they were both so excited that they were no longer afraid of the darkness as

---

Description of walk—cool, dark, damp, uncultivated—gives a hint of mystery and secrecy.

This is a special place for Julia. She enjoys being frightened and has made a game of racing through the Dark Walk.

She gives impression of being high-spirited.

She initiates her young brother into the game.

Does she resent having shared the place with her brother?

Julia's rejection of children's stories shows emerging maturity.

She feels possessive about the walk.

Her curiosity outweighs her disbelief. She keeps searching until she discovers the well.

Children's interest in the fish is greater than their fear of the darkness.

---

° **Sean O'Faolain** (shôn ō-fə-lôn′, -lĭn).

they hunched down and peered in at the fish panting in his tiny prison, his silver stomach going up and down like an engine.

Nobody knew how the trout got there. Even old Martin in the kitchen garden laughed and refused to believe that it was there, or pretended not to believe, until she forced him to come down and see. Kneeling and pushing back his tattered old cap he peered in.

"You're right. How did that fella get there?"

She stared at him suspiciously.

"You knew?" she accused; but he said, "The divil a know"; and reached down to lift it out. Convinced she hauled him back. If she had found it then it was her trout.

Her mother suggested that a bird had carried the spawn. Her father thought that in the winter a small streamlet might have carried it down there as a baby, and it had been safe until the summer came and the water began to dry up. She said, "I see," and went back to look again and consider the matter in private. Her brother remained behind, wanting to hear the whole story of the trout, not really interested in the actual trout but much interested in the story which his mummy began to make up for him on the lines of, "So one day Daddy Trout and Mammy Trout . . ." When he retailed[1] it to her she said, "Pooh."

It troubled her that the trout was always in the same position; he had no room to turn; all the time the silver belly went up and down; otherwise he was motionless. She wondered what he ate and in between visits to Joey Pony, and the boat and a bathe to get cool, she thought of his hunger. She brought him down bits of dough; once she brought him a worm. He ignored the food. He just went on panting. Hunched over him she thought how, all the winter, while she was at school he had been in there. All the winter, in The Dark Walk, all day, all night, floating around alone. She drew the leaf of her hat down around her ears and chin and stared. She was thinking of it as she lay in bed.

It was late June, the longest days of the year. The sun had sat still for a week, burning up the world. Although it was after ten o'clock it was still bright and still hot. She lay on her back under a single sheet, with her long legs spread, trying to keep cool. She could see the D of the moon through the fir tree—they slept on the ground floor. Before they went to bed her mummy had told Stephen the story of the trout again, and she, in her bed, had resolutely presented her back to them and read her book. But she had kept one ear cocked.

---

1. **retailed** (rī-tāld′): told and retold.

Trout is trapped and gasping from exertion.

Julia doubts Martin.

She feels possessive about the trout.

She is not easily persuaded; likes to think for herself.

Her brother is interested in fantasy.

Julia has outgrown fairy tales.

Julia is taken up with thoughts of the trout's misery.
Her concern over the trout's hunger shows a grasp of real world and problems. Her own carefree happiness seems a cruel contrast to the fish's plight.

She has a lively imagination.

Summer—the time of maturation?

"And so, in the end, this naughty fish who would not stay at home got bigger and bigger and bigger, and the water got smaller and smaller. . . ."

Passionately she had whirled and cried, "Mummy, don't make it a horrible old moral story!" Her mummy had brought in a Fairy Godmother, then, who sent lots of rain, and filled the well, and a stream poured out and the trout floated away down to the river below. Staring at the moon she knew that there are no such things as Fairy Godmothers and that the trout, down in The Dark Walk, was panting like an engine. She heard somebody unwind a fishing reel. Would the *beasts* fish him out!

She sat up. Stephen was a hot lump of sleep, lazy thing. The Dark Walk would be full of little scraps of moon. She leaped up and looked out the window, and somehow it was not so lightsome now that she saw the dim mountains far away and the black firs against the breathing land and heard a dog say bark-bark. Quietly she lifted the ewer of water, and climbed out the window and scuttled along the cool but cruel gravel down to the maw[2] of the tunnel. Her pajamas were very short so that when she splashed water it wet her ankles. She peered into the tunnel. Something alive rustled inside there. She raced in, and up and down she raced, and flurried, and cried aloud, "Oh, gosh, I can't find it," and then at last she did. Kneeling down in the damp she put her hand into the slimy hole. When the body lashed they were both mad with fright. But she gripped him and shoved him into the ewer and raced, with her teeth ground, out to the other end of the tunnel and down the steep paths to the river's edge.

All the time she could feel him lashing his tail against the side of the ewer. She was afraid he would jump right out. The gravel cut into her soles until she came to the cool ooze of the river's bank where the moon-mice on the water crept into her feet. She poured out watching until he plopped. For a second he was visible in the water. She hoped he was not dizzy. Then all she saw was the glimmer of the moon in the silent-flowing river, the dark firs, the dim mountains, and the radiant pointed face laughing down at her out of the empty sky.

She scuttled up the hill, in the window, plonked down the ewer and flew through the air like a bird into bed. The dog said bark-bark. She heard the fishing reel whirring. She hugged herself and giggled. Like a river of joy her holiday spread before her.

Her outburst shows impatience with unbelievable, magical solutions.

The story has made her think.

She is troubled over trout's real danger.

Note emphasis on darkness.

Why does she take the water pitcher?

Why is she going to the walk?

What is the "Something" that is alive?

This requires greater courage than the "ordeal" described at the opening of the story.

Julia has decided to liberate the fish.

She empties the trout into the river.

She feels enormous relief; sees moon as having a radiant, laughing face.

She feels free now to enjoy her summer vacation.

---

2. **maw** (mô): here, a large opening.

In the morning Stephen rushed to her, shouting that "he" was gone, and asking "where" and "how." Lifting her nose in the air she said superciliously,[3] "Fairy Godmother, I suppose?" and strolled away patting the palms of her hands.

Julia decides to keep the reason for the trout's disappearance a secret. She enjoys playing the role of fairy godmother.

---

3. **superciliously** (sōō'pər-sĭl'ē-əs-lē): disdainfully.

## Commentary on "The Trout"

"The Trout" is a very special kind of story about growing up. The central figure is a delightful girl named Julia, who is on the brink of adolescence. Her untroubled, buoyant innocence is giving way to thoughtful and critical perceptions of the world around her. An experience involving a trout that is trapped in a natural well becomes an absorbing concern for her. It makes her aware of suffering and awakens in her a desire to relieve the creature's misery.

When we first meet Julia, she seems untouched by any knowledge of pain or solemnity. The long summer vacation stretches before her, offering days of unbounded joy. Most particularly she enjoys racing through an old laurel walk, overgrown with vegetation so dense that the trees block out the sunlight. The mingled feelings of terror and excitement that she feels in running through The Dark Walk are akin to the pleasure children experience in listening to a ghost story. It is fear stimulated by fantasy rather than by any real danger.

Although Julia is willing to share the pleasures of The Dark Walk with her young brother, Stephen, she feels possessive about the place. When he begins boasting about the game they've played, she becomes annoyed. When one of the adults mentions that there is a natural well in the walk, she is incredulous. She refuses to acknowledge any greater familiarity with the walk than her own. Curious, nevertheless, she hunts for the well and discovers a trout imprisoned in it. Because she has found the fish, she feels it is hers and refuses to let the gardener, Martin, remove it.

Julia becomes preoccupied with the trout's plight. She listens skeptically as her parents offer explanations for the trout's imprisonment, and rejects as babyish nonsense the story that her mother invents for Stephen's benefit. The pleasures of pony rides, boating, and swimming do not erase her concern over the trout. She worries about the creature's discomfort and its hunger. She attempts to feed it without success. She begins to imagine what its existence has been like all winter while she was at school, and she pictures it in its lonely misery, floating in the well.

Stephen serves as a foil to Julia, setting off her emerging maturity. Whereas Julia is beginning to teach herself the serious business of life, Stephen is still childishly naive and free of care. Julia has outgrown stories about Santa Claus and the Stork, but Stephen still relishes them. He has no interest in the actual trout but loves the story his mother makes up for him.

One night in late June, Julia becomes exasperated as her mother tells Stephen a bedtime story about the trout. She cries out at the "horrible old moral story." In the fairy tale, the trout is punished for its naughtiness, then rescued by a fairy godmother who sends rain to flush the trout out of the well and into the river. Julia knows there are no unbelievable, magical solutions, and she frets over the trout's real danger. She hears a fishing reel unwind and imagines that some cruel people are trying to catch the trout.

Her mother's story, with its happy ending, provides an incentive for Julia to act. She determines to go to The Dark Walk and rescue the fish. She is not deterred by the darkness, the lateness of the hour, or the night sounds of the "breathing land." Lifting a pitcher of water, she climbs out her bedroom window and heads down to the well. At the entrance to the walk, she hears something rustle, perhaps some creature moving through the leaves, but she is undaunted. She searches for the well and reaches into the slimy water for the trout, mastering her own panic and that of the fish. She transfers the trout into the ewer and races toward the river's edge, oblivious to her own discomfort. She pours the trout out of the ewer and watches until it disappears in the river.

Her great relief is mirrored imaginatively in the laughing face of the moon. When she reaches home, she is greatly pleased with herself and looks forward to a long, untroubled holiday. The next day when her brother notices that the fish is gone, she mocks his childish belief in magic deeds, preferring to keep her own role as "fairy godmother" a secret.

We feel at the conclusion of the story that, for Julia, this summer will mark a transition from the games and stories of childhood to the problems and challenges of life. The central action of the story is concerned with the reshaping and development of experience. The "ordeal" of racing through The Dark Walk in play, at the beginning of the story, seems almost a preparation for Julia's late-night race to save the trout. The make-believe story of the trout, with its happy ending, fuels Julia's imagination and suggests a solution to her problem. "The Trout" enables us to see how the worlds of fantasy and reality blend as a child grows up.

This analysis of "The Trout" tells more than the events of the story as they happen. It analyzes the various elements of the story, making apparent the interconnection of setting, characters, events, and theme. This reader has arrived at an interpretation of the story by actively pursuing the author's intent. The commentary accounts for the significant details of description and action; it comes to grips with the "point" of the story — its overall meaning or theme.

With practice you can develop skill in reading and analyzing a literary work. Here are some guidelines for close reading of fiction.

# Guidelines for Reading Fiction

1. *Look up unfamiliar words and references.* In "The Trout," O'Faolain uses *retail* as a verb meaning "to retell or repeat." If you feel uncertain about the meaning of a word and cannot get the meaning from context clues, be sure to check in a standard dictionary or other reference work.

2. *Learn to probe beneath the surface.* The author does not tell you directly that Julia is growing up. However, the reader draws this inference from several examples of her dawning maturity: her rejection of children's stories, her skeptical attitude, and her concern over the trout's misery.

3. *Actively question the author's purpose and method.* Ask yourself what significance there might be to details that the author gives you. For example, the action of this story takes place during summer, traditionally the season associated with maturation.

4. *Be alert to the author's emphasis.* The opening paragraph of "The Trout" gives a detailed description of The Dark Walk. This is a clue that this place will play an important role in the story.

5. *Account for all significant elements of the work.* Although Julia is the main character, it is important for the reader to understand the roles that other characters, and Stephen in particular, play in the story.

6. *Probe for the central idea or point — the underlying meaning of the work.* State this central idea, or theme, in a sentence. For example: *"The Trout" is concerned with the way the worlds of fantasy and reality blend as a child grows up.*

# Practice in Close Reading

The following passages are from short stories you are not likely to have read. Each passage is accompanied by a set of questions. Read carefully before answering the questions. If you need to, look up unfamiliar words or references.

## I

On a summer morning a hundred and fifty years ago a young Danish squire[1] and his wife went out for a walk on their land. They had been married a week. It had not been easy for them to get married, for the wife's family was higher in rank and wealthier than the husband's. But the two young people, now twenty-four and nineteen years old, had been set on their purpose for ten years; in the end her haughty parents had had to give in to them.

They were wonderfully happy. The stolen meetings and secret, tearful love letters were now things of the past. To God and man they were one; they could walk arm in arm in broad daylight and drive in the same carriage, and they would walk and drive so till the end of their days. Their distant paradise had descended to earth and had proved, surprisingly, to be filled with the things of everyday life: with jesting and railleries, with breakfasts and suppers, with dogs, haymaking and sheep. Sigismund, the young husband, had promised himself that from now there should be no stone in his bride's path, nor should any shadow fall across it. Lovisa, the wife, felt that now, every day and for the first time in her young life, she moved and breathed in perfect freedom because she could never have any secret from her husband.

To Lovisa—whom her husband called Lise—the rustic atmosphere of her new life was a matter of wonder and delight. Her husband's fear that the existence he could offer her might not be good enough for her filled her heart with laughter. It was not a long time since she had played with dolls; as now she dressed her own hair, looked over her linen press[2] and arranged her flowers she again lived through an enchanting and cherished experience: one was doing everything gravely and solicitously, and all the time one knew one was playing.

Isak Dinesen
*from* "The Ring"

---

1. **squire** (skwīr): a landowner.
2. **press:** a closet or case used for storage.

## FOR STUDY AND DISCUSSION

**1.** The young people in this story are from different social classes. How has their relationship been affected by the difference in their backgrounds?

**2.** What evidence is there in this passage that the wife, Lovisa, has led a sheltered life?

**3.** Where does the text suggest that she is innocent and inexperienced?

**4.** The young couple are perfectly happy. Is there any element in their characters or in their relationship that might threaten their happiness?

# II

It was quiet in the waiting room of the remote little station, except for the night sounds of insects. You could hear their embroidering movements in the weeds outside, which somehow gave the effect of some tenuous[1] voice in the night, telling a story. Or you could listen to the fat thudding of the light bugs and the hoarse rushing of their big wings against the wooden ceiling. Some of the bugs were clinging heavily to the yellow globe, like idiot bees to a senseless smell.

Under this prickly light two rows of people sat in silence, their faces stung, their bodies twisted and quietly uncomfortable, expectantly so, in ones and twos, not quite asleep. No one seemed impatient, although the train was late. A little girl lay flung back in her mother's lap as though sleep had struck her with a blow.

Ellie and Albert Morgan were sitting on a bench like the others waiting for the train and had nothing to say to each other. Their names were ever so neatly and rather largely printed on a big reddish-tan suitcase strapped crookedly shut, because of a missing buckle, so that it hung apart finally like a stupid pair of lips. "Albert Morgan, Ellie Morgan, Yellow Leaf, Mississippi." They must have been driven into town in a wagon, for they and the suitcase were all touched here and there with a fine yellow dust, like finger marks.

Ellie Morgan was a large woman with a face as pink and crowded as an old-fashioned rose. She must have been about forty years old. One of those black satchel purses hung over her straight, strong

---

1. **tenuous** (tĕn'yōo-əs): weak.

wrist. It must have been her savings which were making possible this trip. And to what place? you wondered, for she sat there as tense and solid as a cube, as if to endure some nameless apprehension[2] rising and overflowing within her at the thought of travel. Her face worked and broke into strained, hardening lines, as if there had been a death—that too-explicit evidence of agony in the desire to communicate.

Albert made a slower and softer impression. He sat motionless beside Ellie, holding his hat in his lap with both hands—a hat you were sure he had never worn. He looked homemade, as though his wife had self-consciously knitted or somehow contrived a husband when she sat alone at night. He had a shock of very fine sunburned yellow hair. He was too shy for this world, you could see. His hands were like cardboard, he held his hat so still; and yet how softly his eyes fell upon its crown, moving dreamily and yet with dread over its brown surface! He was smaller than his wife. His suit was brown, too, and he wore it neatly and carefully, as though he were murmuring, "Don't look—no need to look—I am effaced."[3] But you have seen that expression too in silent children, who will tell you what they dreamed the night before in sudden, almost hilarious, bursts of confidence.

Eudora Welty
*from* "The Key"

_____

2. **apprehension** (ăp′rĭ-hĕn′shən): dread; fearfulness.
3. **effaced** (ĭ-fāsd′): made inconspicuous, unnoticeable.

FOR STUDY AND DISCUSSION

**1.** Which details in the first two paragraphs emphasize the stillness in the railroad station?
**2.** What does this opening passage tell you about the background and economic circumstances of Albert and Ellie Morgan?
**3.** Show how details of physical appearance and gesture reveal the inner nature of these characters.
**4.** Where does the author suggest that the husband and wife are isolated from each other?

# Close Reading of a Poem

To experience a poem fully, you need to be aware of its special language and structure. Poets rely on the suggestive power of language and choose words for both their connotative and denotative meanings. Through images and figures of speech poets appeal to the reader's intellect and senses. Poets also make use of elements of sound, such as rhyme and rhythm, and special forms, such as the sonnet.

It is a good idea to read a poem several times, and aloud at least once. Often it is helpful to write a prose paraphrase of a poem (see page 317). A paraphrase is no substitute for the "meaning" of a poem, but it helps you clarify and simplify the author's ideas and language.

Read the following poem several times. Then turn to the explication on page 781. An *explication* is a line-by-line examination of the content and technique of a work.

# Autumn Chant  *Edna St. Vincent Millay*

Now the autumn shudders
   In the rose's root.
Far and wide the ladders
   Lean among the fruit.

Now the autumn clambers            5
   Up the trellised frame,°
And the rose remembers
   The dust from which it came.

Brighter than the blossom
   On the rose's bough            10
Sits the wizened,° orange,
   Bitter berry now;

Beauty never slumbers;
   All is in her name;
But the rose remembers            15
   The dust from which it came.

6. **trellised** (trĕl′ĭsd) **frame:** an open framework used for training vines.

11. **wizened** (wĭz′ənd): shriveled.

# Explication of "Autumn Chant"

Autumn is traditionally associated with ripeness and decline. It is a time of fruition, when crops are harvested from fields and orchards; it is also a time of decay, when the withering leaves and departing birds signal the onset of winter. In "Autumn Chant," Edna St. Vincent Millay makes the point that autumn is not only a time of endings, but also a time of new beginnings.

The opening stanza presents images of autumn's ripeness and decline. The ladders lean against trees in orchards where rich harvests of fruit are being picked. At the same time, the rose, one of nature's most beautiful creations, is approaching its end: "Now the autumn shudders/In the rose's root." The dread of impending death is conveyed by the verb *shudders*. There is, however, a promise of rebirth in the word *root*, which suggests the origin, the primary source, from which a new rose will grow.

As the season advances, vegetation changes color and gradually dies. This change becomes apparent on vines and creeping plants trained to ornament latticework. This image of encroaching death is set side by side with an image of rebirth in the refrain "And the rose remembers/The dust from which it came." The word *dust* refers to the remains of life after it disintegrates; dust also refers to the earth that nourishes new life. The lines suggest an interdependence of living and dying things.

In the third stanza the poet laments that the beauty of the rose is eclipsed by the brilliance of the rose hips, which are shriveled and bitter. Yet, although the rose is fading, the poet asserts in the last stanza that there is no loss of beauty: "Beauty never slumbers." The repetition of the refrain at the close of the poem affirms the theme that beauty in nature is inseparable from decay and death.

The basic meter of the poem is trochaic, which Millay varies in alternating lines by dropping the final unaccented syllables. The accents fall on the ear like the ticking of a clock, measuring out the season. The trochaic pattern gives way to iambic meter midway through the poem, in line 8, and again at the end, in line 16, to emphasize the refrain and to underscore the structure of the poem.

In addition to end rhyme which is exact, Millay uses approximate rhyme for subtle effects: *shudders/ladders; slumbers/remembers*. She also uses alliteration (*rose's root; rose remembers; bitter berry*) and assonance (*autumn, shudders; sits, wizened, bitter*) to link key words. This unobtrusive music is well suited to the theme of the poem.

# Guidelines for Reading a Poem

**1.** *Read the poem aloud at least once, following the punctuation for phrasing.* Commas, semicolons, periods, and other marks of punctuation tell you where to pause. Millay does not expect the reader to pause at the end of each line. In line 11, she signals more than one pause.

**2.** *Be alert to key words and references.* In poetry, a word often has special connotations, or associations. The word *shudders* in line 1, for example, has the denotative meaning "trembles or shivers." Its connotative meaning of "horror or extreme dread" gives the image added emotional meaning.

**3.** *Write a paraphrase of any lines that need clarification or simplification.* A paraphrase helps a reader understand imagery and figurative language. It also puts inverted word order into normal word order. For example, a paraphrase of lines 9–12 might read: The shriveled, orange bitter berries now occupying the branches are more vivid in color than the flowers on the rose boughs.

**4.** *Arrive at the central idea or meaning of the poem.* Try to state this idea in one or two sentences: *In "Autumn Chant," Millay suggests that although nature's beauty seems to wane in autumn, the promise of renewal is an integral part of the process that destroys that beauty.*

# Practice in Close Reading

## I

## Musician  *Louise Bogan*

Where have these hands been,
By what delayed,
That so long stayed
Apart from the thin

Strings which they now grace                    5
With their lonely skill?
Music and their cool will
At last interlace.

Now with great ease, and slow,
The thumb, the finger, the strong         10
Delicate hand plucks the long
String it was born to know.

And, under the palm, the string
Sings as it wished to sing.

## FOR STUDY AND DISCUSSION

**1.** Referring to clues in the poem, identify the instrument that the musician is playing.
**2.** In what way is the musician's artistry "lonely"?
**3.** The phrase "cool will" in line 7 refers to the control that the musician exercises over emotion. Why is such discipline necessary?
**4.** Where does the poet create the impression that both musician and instrument are incomplete without each other?
**5.** Although the title of the poem is "Musician," the poem concentrates on the musician's hands and on the strings of the instrument. What effect is gained by this focus?
**6.** Describe the poet's use of rhyme and assonance to increase the musicality of the poem and to reinforce its meaning.

# II

# Glass World  *Dorothy Donnelly*

The still scene scintillates;°
sparks swarm over the brier,
bare bushes blaze. Ice
is setting the world on fire.

A touch of sun on the sleet                     5
turns the teasel° to crystal,
and glances stars off the glass
stalks of the burdock and thistle.

On enamels of blue, a tree,
kindled by cold, air, and water,               10
lights up like a chandelier
in a flash of opals and amber.

1. **scintillates**  (sĭn′tə-lāts′):
sparkles brilliantly.

6. **teasel**  (tē′zəl): a plant
with thistlelike flowers.

## FOR STUDY AND DISCUSSION

**1.** A *paradox* is a statement that reveals a truth although it seems at first to present a contradiction. In your own words explain the paradox this poem is based on. Which sentence in the poem most clearly states the paradox?

**2.** What does the word *glass* in the title of the poem refer to? What other words does the poet use to suggest a glassy surface?

**3.** The phrase "fiery opal" is used to describe the brilliant, rainbow colors of that gemstone. In what similar way is the word *fire* used in this poem?

**4.** "To kindle" is to set on fire. Explain the metaphor in the last stanza.

# Close Reading of a Play

While many of the elements studied in connection with short stories and poetry are relevant to the study of drama, there are several additional elements that need to be taken into account. Drama has its own conventions, or practices. Classical Greek drama, for example, makes use of a chorus, a choragos, and odes (see page 485). Elizabethan drama makes use of asides and soliloquies (see page 533). Dramatists frequently make use of stage directions to create setting and to give players instructions for acting. A playwright may decide to use a chorus or a narrator to comment on the action. Sometimes a character will step out of the play to address the audience, as Gene does in *I Never Sang for My Father* (page 652). Generally, however, dialogue is the dramatist's most important device for presenting character and for moving the action along.

The following passage is from the Prologue of *Oedipus Rex* (*Oedipus the King*) by Sophocles. For the background of this play, see pages 487–490.

Read the passage several times, and aloud at least once. Then turn to the commentary on page 788.

# *from* Oedipus Rex    *Sophocles*    *Translated by Dudley Fitts and Robert Fitzgerald*

Scene: *Before the palace of* Oedipus, *King of Thebes. A central door and two lateral doors open onto a platform which runs the length of the façade. On the platform, right and left, are altars; and three steps lead down into the orchestra, or chorus-ground. At the beginning of the action these steps are crowded by suppliants who have brought branches and chaplets° of olive leaves and who sit in various attitudes of despair.* Oedipus *enters.*

## Prologue

**Oedipus.** My children, generations of the living
In the line of Cadmus,° nursed at his ancient hearth:
Why have you strewn yourselves before these altars
In supplication, with your boughs and garlands?

---

° **chaplets** (chăp′lĭts): wreaths or garlands.    2. **Cadmus** (kăd′məs): in Greek mythology, the founder of Thebes.

The breath of incense rises from the city                                    5
With a sound of prayer and lamentation.

                                  Children,
I would not have you speak through messengers,
And therefore I have come myself to hear you—
I, Oedipus, who bear the famous name.
(*To a* Priest) You, there, since you are eldest in the company,          10
Speak for them all, tell me what preys upon you,
Whether you come in dread, or crave some blessing:
Tell me, and never doubt that I will help you
In every way I can; I should be heartless
Were I not moved to find you suppliant here.                              15
**Priest.** Great Oedipus, O powerful King of Thebes!
You see how all the ages of our people
Cling to your altar steps: here are boys
Who can barely stand alone, and here are priests
By weight of age, as I am a priest of God,                                20
And young men chosen from those yet unmarried;
As for the others, all that multitude,
They wait with olive chaplets in the squares,
At the two shrines of Pallas,° and where Apollo°
Speaks in the glowing embers.                                             25
                                  Your own eyes
Must tell you: Thebes is in her extremity
And cannot lift her head from the surge of death.
A rust consumes the buds and fruits of the earth;
The herds are sick; children die unborn,
And labor is vain. The god of plague and pyre                            30
Raids like detestable lightning through the city,
And all the house of Cadmus is laid waste,
All emptied, and all darkened: Death alone
Battens upon the misery of Thebes.

You are not one of the immortal gods, we know;                           35
Yet we have come to you to make our prayer
As to the man of all men best in adversity
And wisest in the ways of God. You saved us
From the Sphinx, that flinty singer, and the tribute
We paid to her so long; yet you were never                              40
Better informed than we, nor could we teach you:
It was some god breathed in you to set us free.

---

24. **Pallas** (păl′əs): Pallas Athena, the Greek goddess of wisdom. **Apollo** (ə-pŏl′ō): the Greek god of the sun, music, poetry, healing, and prophecy.

Therefore, O mighty King, we turn to you:
Find us our safety, find us a remedy,
Whether by counsel of the gods or of men.                                    45
A king of wisdom tested in the past
Can act in a time of troubles, and act well.
Noblest of men, restore
Life to your city! Think how all men call you
Liberator for your triumph long ago;                                         50
Ah, when your years of kingship are remembered,
Let them not say *We rose, but later fell*—
Keep the State from going down in the storm!
Once, years ago, with happy augury,
You brought us fortune; be the same again!                                   55
No man questions your power to rule the land:
But rule over men, not over a dead city!
Ships are only hulls, citadels are nothing,
When no life moves in the empty passageways.

**Oedipus.** Poor children! You may be sure I know                           60
All that you longed for in your coming here.
I know that you are deathly sick; and yet,
Sick as you are, not one is as sick as I.
Each of you suffers in himself alone
His anguish, not another's; but my spirit                                    65
Groans for the city, for myself, for you.

I was not sleeping, you are not waking me.
No, I have been in tears for a long while
And in my restless thought walked many ways.
In all my search I found one helpful course,                                 70
And that I have taken: I have sent Creon,
Son of Menoikeus,° brother of the Queen,
To Delphi, Apollo's place of revelation,°
To learn there, if he can,
What act or pledge of mine may save the city.                               75

---

72. **Menoikeus** (mĕ-noi′kē-əs). 73. **To Delphi . . . revelation:** At Delphi, there was a shrine to Apollo, the god of prophecy. The oracle at Delphi was famous for issuing its prophecies as mysterious puzzles.

# Commentary on Scene from *Oedipus Rex*

The opening scene of the play provides background information showing how Oedipus' fate is linked to the fate of Thebes. It also gives us insight into the character of Oedipus, the tragic hero of the play.

The Prologue begins on a solemn note. The city of Thebes is polluted. In despair the people have come to the palace as suppliants, to beg the King's help. Oedipus appears and in his first words, "My children," reveals his compassionate and paternal attitude toward his subjects. He has chosen to speak directly to his people rather than use messengers, and he promises that he will help them in any way he can.

A Priest, acting as spokesperson, tells Oedipus of the widespread misery that is afflicting Thebes. Plague and famine are threatening the very existence of the city: "all the house of Cadmus is laid waste/All emptied, and all darkened." The people have turned to Oedipus as their savior. In the past his wisdom saved them. He freed the Thebans from the curse of the Sphinx by answering her riddle correctly. The Priest calls Oedipus the man "best in adversity/And wisest in the ways of God." Because his wisdom was tested in the past, they believe he can save them now.

The people's faith in the wisdom of their king appears justified. Oedipus identifies with the plight of his people; he tells them "not one is as sick as I." He acknowledges proudly that he once saved the land, referring to himself as "I, Oedipus, who bear the famous name." He believes he can unravel the mystery of the plague just as he solved the riddle of the Sphinx years before. In order to find a remedy he has sent his brother-in-law, Creon, to Delphi to consult the oracle. He is waiting to hear "What act or pledge of mine may save the city." Thus the main action of the play—Oedipus' quest for knowledge—is set into motion.

# Guidelines for Reading a Play

**1.** *Note any information that establishes the setting or explains the situation.* We are told immediately that the scene is the royal palace of Thebes. The opening speech tells us that the city of Thebes is being devastated by plague.

**2.** *Note clues that tell you what the players are doing or how the lines are spoken.* In lines 3–4 Oedipus reveals that the suppliants are spread over the steps before the altars, carrying boughs and garlands.

**3.** *Anticipate the action that will develop out of each scene.* In lines 70–75 Oedipus reveals that he has sent a messenger to the Delphic Oracle to learn how he might help the city. He arouses our interest in what will be the outcome of this action.

**4.** *Be alert to the mood of the play.* The tragic nature of the play is set at once by the despair and the lamentations of the Thebans.

# Practice in Close Reading

Creon brings back the message of the oracle. Thebes has been defiled by the murder of King Laios, who ruled the land before Oedipus. The gods demand that the murderer be found and expelled from the land. Oedipus seeks help from Teiresias, the blind seer.

**Choragos.** But there is one man who may detect the criminal.
    This is Teiresias, this is the holy prophet        285
    In whom, alone of all men, truth was born.
**Oedipus.** Teiresias: seer: student of mysteries,
    Of all that's taught and all that no man tells,
    Secrets of Heaven and secrets of the earth:
    Blind though you are, you know the city lies        290
    Sick with plague; and from this plague, my lord,
    We find that you alone can guard or save us.

    Possibly you did not hear the messengers?
    Apollo, when we sent to him,
    Sent us back word that this great pestilence        295
    Would lift, but only if we established clearly
    The identity of those who murdered Laios.
    They must be killed or exiled.
                    Can you use

Birdflight° or any art of divination
To purify yourself, and Thebes, and me                                      300
From this contagion? We are in your hands.
There is no fairer duty
Than that of helping others in distress.
**Teiresias.** How dreadful knowledge of the truth can be
When there's no help in truth! I knew this well,                            305
But did not act on it: else I should not have come.
**Oedipus.** What is troubling you? Why are your eyes so cold?
**Teiresias.** Let me go home. Bear your own fate, and I'll
Bear mine. It is better so: trust what I say.
**Oedipus.** What you say is ungracious and unhelpful                        310
To your native country. Do not refuse to speak.
**Teiresias.** When it comes to speech, your own is neither temperate
Nor opportune. I wish to be more prudent.
**Oedipus.** In God's name, we all beg you——
**Teiresias.**                                    You are all ignorant.
No; I will never tell you what I know.                                       315
Now it is my misery; then, it would be yours.
**Oedipus.** What! You do know something, and will not tell us?
You would betray us all and wreck the State?
**Teiresias.** I do not intend to torture myself, or you.
Why persist in asking? You will not persuade me.                            320
**Oedipus.** What a wicked old man you are! You'd try a stone's
Patience! Out with it! Have you no feeling at all?
**Teiresias.** You call me unfeeling. If you could only see
The nature of your own feelings . . .
**Oedipus.**                             Why,
Who would not feel as I do? Who could endure                                325
Your arrogance toward the city?
**Teiresias.**                             What does it matter?
Whether I speak or not, it is bound to come.
**Oedipus.** Then, if "it" is bound to come, you are bound to tell me.
**Teiresias.** No, I will not go on. Rage as you please.
**Oedipus.** Rage? Why not!
                              And I'll tell you what I think:                330
You planned it, you had it done, you all but
Killed him with your own hands: if you had eyes,
I'd say the crime was yours, and yours alone.
**Teiresias.** So? I charge you, then,
Abide by the proclamation you have made:                                    335

---

299. **Birdflight:** The flight of birds was observed by prophets and used in interpreting the future.

From this day forth
Never speak again to these men or to me;
You yourself are the pollution of this country.

**Oedipus.** You dare say that! Can you possibly think you have
Some way of going free, after such insolence?                     340

**Teiresias.** I have gone free. It is the truth sustains me.

**Oedipus.** Who taught you shamelessness? It was not your craft.

**Teiresias.** You did. You made me speak. I did not want to.

**Oedipus.** Speak what? Let me hear it again more clearly.

**Teiresias.** Was it not clear before? Are you tempting me?        345

**Oedipus.** I did not understand it. Say it again.

**Teiresias.** I say that you are the murderer whom you seek.

**Oedipus.** Now twice you have spat out infamy. You'll pay for it!

**Teiresias.** Would you care for more? Do you wish to be really angry?

**Oedipus.** Say what you will. Whatever you say is worthless.      350

**Teiresias.** I say you live in hideous love with her
Who is nearest you in blood. You are blind to the evil.

**Oedipus.** It seems you can go on mouthing like this forever.

**Teiresias.** I can, if there is power in truth.

**Oedipus.**                               There is:
But not for you, not for you,                                      355
You sightless, witless, senseless, mad old man!

**Teiresias.** You are the madman. There is no one here
Who will not curse you soon, as you curse me.

**Oedipus.** You child of endless night! You cannot hurt me
Or any other man who sees the sun.                                 360

**Teiresias.** True: it is not from me your fate will come.


## FOR STUDY AND DISCUSSION

**1.** In the opening scene of the play, Oedipus is revealed as a noble, compassionate ruler who seems to be in complete control of himself. What new facet of his nature is revealed in the scene with Teiresias?

**2.** What is Teiresias' motive for withholding the truth? Why does his refusal to speak anger Oedipus?

**3.** How does Oedipus provoke Teiresias into naming the murderer of Laios? How does he react to Teiresias' accusation?

**4.** What dramatic irony lies in the contrast between "blindness" and "seeing" in this scene?

**5.** Given Oedipus' powerful drive to pursue the truth, what do you anticipate will be his next move?

# WRITING ABOUT LITERATURE

## The Writing Process

We often refer to writing an essay as a *process*, which consists of three key stages or phases: **prewriting**, **writing**, and **revising**. In this process, much of the crucial work precedes the actual writing of the paper. In the prewriting stage, the writer makes decisions about what to say and how to say it. Prewriting activities include choosing and limiting a topic, gathering ideas, organizing ideas, and arriving at a *thesis*—the controlling idea for the paper. In the next stage, the writer uses the working plan to write a first draft of the essay. In the revising stage, the writer rewrites the draft, several times perhaps, adding or deleting ideas, rearranging order, rephrasing for clarity, and correcting errors in spelling, punctuation, and grammar. The steps in this process are interdependent. For example, new ideas may emerge as the paper is written, necessitating a restatement of the thesis or additional evidence.

The amount of time devoted to each stage will vary with individual assignments. During a classroom examination, you will have limited time to plan your essay and to proofread your paper. For a term paper, you may have weeks or months to prepare your essay.

On the following pages the steps in this process are illustrated through the development of several model papers.

## Answering Examination Questions

From time to time you will be asked to demonstrate your understanding of a literary work or topic by writing a short essay in class. Usually, your teacher will select the subject of the essay. How well you do will depend not only on how carefully you have prepared for the examination but on how carefully you read and interpret the essay question.

Before you begin to answer an examination question, be sure you understand what the question calls for. Suppose you are asked to discuss the different kinds of irony in a particular short story. Should you limit yourself to one type of irony, your essay will not fulfill the requirements of the question. If you are asked to state the theme of a novel and you give instead a summary of its plot, your answer will be unacceptable. No matter how good your essay is, it will be unsatisfactory if you do not respond to the question accurately. Always take some time to read the essay question carefully in order to determine how it should be answered.

Remember that you are expected to demonstrate specific knowledge of the literature. Any general statement should be supported by evidence. If you wish to demonstrate the tone of a poem, refer to individual words, sounds, images, and any other elements of style that make up the writer's voice. If you are allowed to use your textbook during the examination, you may occasionally quote short passages or refer to a specific page in order to provide supporting evidence.

At the start, it may be helpful to jot down some notes to guide you in writing the essay. If you have several points to make, decide what the most effective order of presentation will be. You might build up to your strongest point, or you might present your points to develop a striking contrast. Aim for a logical organization that helps your reader follow your thinking.

Also remember that length alone is not satisfactory. Your answer must be relevant, and it must be presented in acceptable, correct English. Always take time to proofread your paper.

The key word in examination questions is the *verb*. Let us look briefly at some common instructions used in examinations.

**ANALYSIS**   A question may ask you to *analyze* some aspect of a literary work or topic. When you analyze something, you take it apart to see how each part works. On an examination, you will generally be directed to focus on some limited but essential aspect of a work in order to demonstrate your knowledge and understanding. A common type of exercise is *character analysis,* in which you draw on the most significant details of characterization in order to reach conclusions about a specific figure. For example, you might be asked to analyze the characters of the fathers in "The Duke's Children" (page 128). You might be asked to analyze the ballad conventions in "Johnny Armstrong" (page 372). You might be asked to analyze the theme of *The Pearl* (page 709). Analysis may be applied to form, technique, or ideas.

**COMPARISON CONTRAST**    A question may ask that you *compare* (or *contrast*) two things, such as techniques, ideas, characters, or works. When you *compare*, you point out likenesses; when you *contrast*, you point out differences. If you are asked to *compare and contrast*, you will have to deal with similarities and differences. You might be asked to compare characters in two stories: Sylvia in "A White Heron" (page 118) and Jerry in "Through the Tunnel" (page 150). You might be asked to compare points of view in two essays: "The Hawk Is Flying" (page 174) and "Travels with Charley" (page 181). You might be asked to contrast the moods of two poems: "To the Thawing Wind" (page 300) and "The Lake Isle of Innisfree" (page 293). You might be asked to compare and contrast the images in two poems. Sometimes the instruction to *compare* implies both comparison and contrast. Always check with your teacher to make sure how inclusive the term *compare* is intended to be.

**DESCRIPTION**    If a question asks you to *describe* a setting or a character, you are expected to give a picture in words. In describing a setting, include details that establish the historical period as well as the locale. Be sure also to include details that establish mood or build emotional intensity. In describing a character, deal with both direct and indirect methods of characterization (see page 836). You might be asked to describe details in the story "María Tepache" (page 76) that render the flavor of its particular setting. You might be asked to describe the seven rooms of the prince's suite in "The Masque of the Red Death" (page 111) in order to point out the significance of color and the arrangement from east to west. You might be asked to describe the character of the Model T in White's essay "Farewell, My Lovely!" (page 192).

**DISCUSSION**    The word *discuss* in a question is much more general than the other words we've looked at. When you are asked to discuss a subject, you are expected to examine it in detail. If you were directed to discuss the characteristics of the medieval romance as illustrated in "The Tale of Sir Gareth" (page 449), you would be obligated to stress its chivalric exploits, since the code of chivalry is primary in the Arthurian legends. In discussing the moral issues in *Antigone* (page 491), you would have to take into account not only the position of the heroine but that of her adversary, Creon. If you were asked to discuss Shakespeare's use of superstition in *Julius Caesar* (page 536), you would need to include such important instances as the prophecy of the Soothsayer and the tempest in Act One, Calpurnia's dream in Act Two, and the appearance of Caesar's ghost in Act Four.

| EXPLANATION | A question may ask you to *explain* something. When you explain, you give reasons for something being the way it is. You make clear a character's actions, or you show how something has come about. You might, for example, be asked to explain how the author uses point of view in "A White Heron" (page 118) to control the reader's reaction to characters and events. You might be asked to explain how May Swenson uses language in "Ornamental Sketch with Verbs" (page 302) to transform an ordinary scene into something magical. You might be asked to explain the anachronistic references in "Arthur Becomes King" (page 427). You might be asked to explain a title, an allusion, or a convention. |
| --- | --- |
| ILLUSTRATION | The word *illustrate, demonstrate,* or *show* asks that you provide examples to support a point. You might be asked to provide examples of images in *The Pearl* (page 709) that depict characters in terms of animals. You might be asked to illustrate Antony's skill in manipulating the conspirators and the mob in *Julius Caesar* (page 536). You might be asked to demonstrate musical effects in "Summer Remembered" (page 354). Or you might be asked to show the kinds of artistic license that William Luce uses in *The Belle of Amherst* (page 253). |
| INTERPRETATION | The word *interpret* in a question asks that you give the meaning or significance of something. For example, you might be asked to provide an interpretation for a particular symbol, such as the sheet of yellow paper in "Contents of the Dead Man's Pockets" (page 20). You might be asked to interpret the meaning of a satire such as "The Phoenix" (page 164). Sometimes you will be asked to agree or disagree with a stated interpretation of a work, giving specific evidence to support your position. For example, see the essay topics on pages 699–700 and 766–767. |

You will find that there is frequent overlapping of approaches. In discussing a subject, you will draw upon illustration, explanation, analysis, or any other approach that is useful. In comparing or contrasting two works, you may rely on description or interpretation. However, an examination question generally will have a central purpose, and it is important that you focus on this purpose in preparing your answer.

On the following pages you will find some sample examination questions and answers for study and discussion. Note that the assignments (shown in italics) may be phrased as direct questions or as essay topics.

# I

**QUESTION**   *In a paragraph, explain the significance of the following lines that Cassius speaks in* Julius Caesar:

> *Men at some time are masters of their fates.*
> *The fault, dear Brutus, is not in our stars*
> *But in ourselves, that we are underlings.*
> *(I, 2, 139–141)*

**METHOD OF ATTACK**   This assignment asks you to explain the significance of some key lines in the play. What you need to demonstrate in your answer is that you understand not only the meaning of the lines, but their importance to the drama. Since you are instructed to write a single paragraph, the opening sentence should state the controlling idea of your essay.

Before you write the essay, jot down some notes to guide you. Be sure that you understand exactly what Cassius is saying. If necessary, paraphrase the lines in your notes.

### Paraphrase

Cassius tells Brutus that human beings control their own destiny. He does not believe that the stars influence human behavior. If human beings are inferior, it is their own fault.

### Cassius' Motives

Cassius wishes to have Brutus join the conspiracy. He knows that Brutus will not act out of base or selfish motives. Therefore, he appeals to Brutus' pride as a Roman. He suggests that the Romans are cowards who willingly subject themselves to the tyranny of Caesar. He implies that they can control what happens by taking matters into their own hands.

### Conclusion

This is one example of Cassius' skill in manipulating people.

Here is a model paragraph developed from the notes.

**ANSWER**
Topic Sentence

**This brief passage is one example of Cassius' persuasive tactics as master conspirator.** A shrewd judge of character, he knows that Brutus will not act out of base or selfish motives, so he appeals to Brutus' pride as a Roman. Denying a superstitious belief in the influence of the stars, Cassius urges Brutus to take control of his own destiny. He suggests that the Romans are cowards who will-

Supporting Statements

ingly accept their role as "underlings" to Caesar. Without naming the conspiracy, he implies that Romans can free themselves from Caesar's tyranny by becoming "masters of their fates."

Length: 96 words

The topic sentence of this paragraph states a *thesis*—a central idea that gives focus to the essay. Although the thesis appears at the opening of the essay, it represents the end product of thinking.

# II

**QUESTION**  *Analyze the character of the speaker in Browning's "The Laboratory" (page 384).*

**METHOD OF ATTACK**  This is an exercise in *character analysis*. This assignment is more demanding than the first assignment because you have to exercise your own judgment in setting limits to your answer. You may need one paragraph or several paragraphs. The assignment also requires that you supply a thesis statement. Your thesis statement should be formulated *after* you have examined the evidence and come to a conclusion about the subject.

Assuming that you have the text of the poem to work from, you might go through it line by line, noting explicit and implicit clues to the speaker's character. You might jot down line references alongside your notes to guide you in writing your paper. As you work, look for major characteristics that will provide a focus for your paper.

This is one way to approach the assignment.

**Character of Speaker**

Speaker is a "minion"—petite and delicate (29).
Men find her attractive since they are waiting for her at the court (12).
She is sure of her charms and offers the apothecary a kiss (46).
She possesses many jewels and gold (45).

**APPEARANCE: BEAUTY GRACE WEALTH**

She has been spurned by the King and is enraged (5).
She wants revenge against her rival, who has "ensnared" the King (27–30).
She furiously imagines the King and his new favorite laughing at her (7).
She takes pleasure in contemplating her rival's death; she wants her to die hideously and in agony (37–40).
She entertains fantasies of killing other women with poison carried in innocent-looking ornaments (17–24).
She feels no remorse about her crime or pity for her intended victim (43–44).
Her sole concern is whether the poison will be effective (29).

**PASSIONS: JEALOUSY ANGER HATRED CRUELTY**

She shows a will of iron in planning the murder.
She shows no dread of the apothecary shop, which is compared to hell—"devil's smithy" (3).
She does not shrink from the sight of the poisons—she ties on a glass mask (1).
She takes an interest in the different poisons and in the apothecary's art (9–16).
She even instructs him in changing the color of the poison (25–28).
She has the dust brushed from her clothing so that no one will suspect where she has been (47–48).

**NERVES OF STEEL**

What you might conclude from this set of notes is that the speaker is a diabolically evil woman whose monstrous nature is hidden beneath a façade of beauty and grace. Each of the overall characteristics shown in the notes can become the subject of a paragraph.

**ANSWER**     This is what the final essay might look like.

**INTRODUCTION**
Thesis Statement

*In "The Laboratory," Browning creates a portrait of a diabolically evil woman whose monstrous nature is hidden beneath a façade of beauty and grace.* Because she has been spurned by the King, she decides to be revenged by murdering the woman who has supplanted her in the King's affections.

**BODY**
Topic Sentence

**Her physical appearance belies the ugly, raging emotions that drive her to commit murder.** She is petite and delicate, by her own description a "minion" (line 29). Men find her desirable, for they are waiting to dance with her at the court. We get an image of her coquettish nature when she offers the apothecary one of her favors — a kiss on the mouth. She is sure of her charms. No doubt the jewels she offers as payment for the poison are gifts from her admirers.

**Underneath this veneer, she is consumed by jealousy, anger, and hatred.** Her overwhelming desire is to destroy the woman who has

"ensnared" the King (line 30). She furiously imagines the two of them laughing at her. She takes pleasure in contemplating her rival's death; she wants her to die hideously and in agony. She entertains fantasies of killing other women, perhaps potential rivals, with poison carried in innocent-looking ornaments. Although the apothecary looks "morose" (line 41), she is lighthearted. She feels no remorse about her crime or pity for her intended victim. Her sole concern is whether the poison will be effective.

**She shows great daring in planning and carrying out the murder.** She has no dread of the apothecary shop, which is compared to hell — the "devil's smithy" (line 3). She does not shrink from the sight of the poisons; she calmly ties on a glass mask for protection against the vapors. She takes an interest in the different poisons and in the

apothecary's art. Moreover, she instructs him in changing the color of the poison so that it will make the fatal drink more enticing. She takes care to have the dust brushed from her clothing so that no one will suspect where she has been.

Although the events of the poem are set in the *"Ancien Régime,"* the period before the French Revolution, the poem has immediacy and relevance. The corrupt passions of the speaker are not confined to any age but are found throughout history.

Length: 384 words

## III

*Some critics argue that the tragic figure in* Antigone *(page 491) is not the heroine for whom the play is named, but Creon. Other critics argue that there are two tragic figures in the play. Are there two tragic figures in the play or only one? If there is only one, who is it? Write an essay stating your opinion.*

This is an exercise in *interpretation*. There is no "right" answer. The effectiveness of your essay will depend on how well you build your case and how much supporting evidence you use. Note that the key term in the assignment is *tragic figure*. You must be clear about how you use this term in your essay.

Let us suppose that you wish to argue that Creon is the tragic hero of the play. This is what your notes might look like:

### Aristotle's Definition of Tragic Figure

Character must be a person of stature.

Character must be neither totally good nor evil.

An error in judgment or weakness in character causes tragic misfortune.

Character must be responsible for tragic events.

Action involves a change in fortune from happiness to misery.

Character undergoes a change.

### Creon as Tragic Figure

Creon is foremost figure in Thebes—King.

Creon wishes to preserve peace in Thebes.

Creon suffers from overweening pride and rashness.

Creon brings about the deaths of 3 people.

Creon loses both his son and his wife.

Creon gains knowledge of his own character.

### Creon at Center of Drama

Action focuses on Creon's dilemma, rather than on Antigone's.

She disappears after the fourth scene of the play.

Creon is seen in conflict with Antigone, with Haimon, and with Teiresias.

Whereas Antigone does not undergo a change, there is a significant change in Creon's character.

He understands that his own pride and rashness have been responsible for tragic events.

At end of play, he is a broken figure who longs for death.

**ANSWER**

*Thesis Statement* — Creon is the tragic figure in *Antigone. He exemplifies the tragic protagonist defined by Aristotle, and it is he rather than Antigone who is at the center of Sophocles' drama.*

*Topic Sentence* — **If we examine Aristotle's concept of the tragic hero, we see that Creon meets all the criteria of the role.** Creon is a person of stature; as King, he is the foremost figure in Thebes. He is neither totally good nor evil. He takes stern measures in order to preserve peace in Thebes. He brings about the tragic events in the play through his own pride and rashness. His own downfall involves a change from relative happiness to misery. Finally, through suffering, he gains insight into his own character.

*Supporting Evidence*

*Topic Sentence* — **The action of the play focuses on Creon's dilemma rather than on Antigone's.** She disappears after the fourth scene of the play. Creon, on the other hand, is dominant throughout the play. He is

Supporting Evidence seen in conflict with Antigone, with Haimon, and with Teiresias. Whereas Antigone undergoes no change, there is a significant change in Creon's character. He comes to understand that his own pride and rashness have been responsible for the tragic deaths of three people. At the end of the play, he is a broken figure who longs for death.

Length: 211 words

# Writing on a Topic of Your Own

## Choosing a Topic

At times you may be asked to write an essay on a topic of your own choosing. Often it will be necessary to read a work or group of works more than once before a suitable topic presents itself.

Although any literary subject that interests you is usually acceptable as a topic for study, it is a good idea to steer away from broad topics that invite generalizations and sweeping statements. You may be interested in the attitude toward women in the Arthurian legend, but in a 350–500 word essay, you would be forced to cover the subject too superficially to demonstrate any real mastery of the material. It might be better to restrict yourself to one tale, such as "The Tale of Sir Gareth."

Students sometimes worry that if they choose a narrow topic, they won't have enough to say. This will seldom present a problem if you have developed the habit of digging into a selection and examining it in depth.

A topic may focus on one element or technique in a work. If you are writing about fiction, you might concentrate on some aspect of plot, such as conflict. Or you might concentrate on character, setting, or theme. If you are writing about poetry, you might choose to analyze imagery or figurative language. In writing about drama, you might focus on dramatic irony or stage conventions. A topic may deal with more than one aspect of a work. You might, for example, discuss several elements of a short story in order to show how an idea or theme is developed. Keep the key verbs, such as *analyze, compare, illustrate,* in mind (see pages 793–795) as guides in limiting a topic.

Once you have a topic in mind, your object is to form it into a *thesis*, a controlling idea that represents the conclusion of your findings. This thesis, of course, will appear at the opening of your paper. It may be necessary to read a work several times before you can formulate a thesis. You would then need to present the evidence supporting your position. Here are some examples showing how a thesis differs from a topic:

**Topic**    The Central Conflict in "Chee's Daughter" (page 65)

**Thesis**    The central conflict is a clash between two sets of values—the traditional humanizing values embraced by Chee and the materialistic values adopted by his in-laws.

**Topic**    The Object of the Author's Satire in "The Phoenix" (page 164)

**Thesis**    The author's satire is directed against people who exploit nature for personal gain and an insensitive public that prefers violence and sensationalism to beauty and dignity.

**Topic**    Tone in "Blue Girls" (page 390)

**Thesis**    The poem opens on a lightly mocking tone in which the poet identifies with the carefree, irreverent attitudes of youth and then shifts to a harsh, bitter tone when he contemplates the ravages of age.

# Gathering Evidence

It is a good idea to take notes as you read, even if you do not yet have a topic in mind. Later on, when you have settled on a topic, you can discard any notes that are not relevant. Some people prefer a worksheet, others index cards. In the beginning, you should record all your reactions. A topic may emerge during this early stage.

When you take notes, make an effort to state ideas in your own words. If a specific phrase or line is so important that it deserves to be quoted directly, be sure to enclose the words in quotation marks. When you transfer your notes to your final paper, be sure to copy quotations exactly.

If you cite lines in a poem, you should enclose the line numbers in parentheses following the quotation. The following note, which is for "The Passing of Arthur" (page 469), shows you how to incorporate two lines of a poem into your own text:

Reluctant to cast Excalibur into the lake, Sir Bedivere finds an excuse to disobey Arthur: "Were it well to obey then, if a king demand/An act unprofitable, against himself?" (lines 57–58)

The slash (/) shows the reader where line 57 ends and line 58 begins. If you cite three or more lines, you should separate the quotation from your own text in this way:

> When Bedivere, the last of Arthur's knights, laments that the Round Table is dissolved and that he is now alone, Arthur replies, expressing a belief in the future:
>
> > "The old order changeth, yielding place to new,
> > And God fulfills himself in many ways,
> > Lest one good custom should corrupt the world."
> > (lines 202–204)

When a quotation is separated from your own text, you do not need quotation marks unless the lines cited are dialogue, as in this excerpt from Tennyson's poem.

Sometimes a direct quotation from a literary work can be the springboard to a topic. In his essay "Emily Dickinson," Van Wyck Brooks notes that Dickinson's "constant theme was deprivation" (page 250). You might decide to find illustrations of this theme in selected poems by Dickinson, or you might decide to elaborate Brooks's ideas. It is perfectly all right to use another person's idea as long as you give credit and acknowledge your source.

Let us suppose that you have just concluded the unit on Poetry in this textbook (pages 289–419). You are instructed to write an essay of approximately 500 words on a topic of your own choice. You realize that you must choose a relatively limited topic if you are to treat it thoroughly.

You haven't any ideas at the outset so you skim through the unit, refreshing your memory of poems studied in class and reading additional poems that interest you. You reread introductions and head-notes, sifting through this material for approaches and ideas. You become aware that two poems in the unit deal with a similar subject: May Swenson's "Ornamental Sketch with Verbs" (page 302) and Emily Dickinson's "She Sweeps with Many-Colored Brooms" (page 318). You wonder whether a comparison of subject matter and technique would help to illuminate both works. You decide to investigate.

You read each poem several times, paraphrasing lines for clarity wherever necessary. You might work out a chart of this kind for recording your notes, letting the letter A stand for "Ornamental Sketch with Verbs" and B stand for "She Sweeps with Many-Colored Brooms":

| | | |
|---|---|---|
| **SUBJECT** | Both poems describe the beauty of a sunset. | Setting of A is a city scene. |
| | | Focus is on mundane objects transformed into things rare and beautiful. |
| | Both unite the commonplace and the sublime. | Setting of B is a New England countryside. |
| | | Focus is on the grandeur of the western sky at sunset. |
| **TECHNIQUE** | Both poems are rich in visual images, particularly images of color. | A uses many vivid images; e.g., "gilded stagger," "salamander-red," "brindled light," "golden sled." |
| | | B uses an extended metaphor from domestic life to describe the colors of the sky: e.g., "many-colored brooms," "purple raveling," "amber thread," "duds of emerald." |
| | Both use diction with suggestive meanings and associations. | A uses words that have romantic or exotic associations: e.g., *salamander, flamingos, urns.* |
| | | B uses common words: e.g., *sweeps, purple.* |
| **TONE** | Both poems have a whimsical tone. | In A, there is humor in the incongruity, or contrast, between the object and what it becomes: e.g., pigeons to flamingos, ash cans to urns. |
| | | In B, the comparison of sunset to an absentminded, untidy housewife who forgets to dust and keeps dropping things is both playful and fantastic. |

# Organizing the Material

Before you begin writing, organize your main ideas into an outline. Your outline should provide for an introduction, a body, and a conclusion. The introduction should identify the authors, the works, or the problem that is under study. It should contain a statement of your thesis as well. The body of your paper should present the evidence supporting your thesis. The conclusion should restate or bring together your main ideas briefly.

This is one kind of outline you might use for a short paper. It indicates the main idea of each paragraph.

## INTRODUCTION

**Paragraph 1**   *Thesis*   Through the gift of observation and imagination, both poets invest ordinary scenes with magic.

## BODY

**Paragraph 2**   Both poems unite the commonplace and the sublime.

**Paragraph 3**   Both poems are rich in visual images, particularly images of color. Swenson sees the sunset creating decorative patterns along the street.

**Paragraph 4**   Like Swenson, Dickinson captures the dramatic splendor of the sunset, but she focuses on the brilliant colors of the sky.

**Paragraph 5**   Both poets use diction with suggestive meanings and associations.

**Paragraph 6**   Both poets adopt a whimsical tone toward their subject.

## CONCLUSION

**Paragraph 7**   Although there are differences in the settings chosen by the poets and in their styles, both poems convey a sense of wonder and delight to be found in the simple, everyday beauty of nature.

# Writing the Essay

Here is a model essay developing the thesis statement.

**TITLE**   A COMPARISON OF "ORNAMENTAL SKETCH WITH VERBS" AND "SHE SWEEPS WITH MANY-COLORED BROOMS"

**INTRODUCTION**
Identify works by title and author.

Thesis Statement

May Swenson, in "Ornamental Sketch with Verbs," and Emily Dickinson, in "She Sweeps with Many-Colored Brooms," have taken as their subject the beauty of a sunset. *Through the gift of observation and imagination, both poets invest ordinary scenes with magic.*

**BODY**

| | |
|---|---|
| Topic Sentence | **Both poems unite the commonplace and the sublime.** The setting of Swenson's poem is an ordinary city street. Sunset spilling over |
| Supporting Evidence | the street transforms such common sights as a girl on skates, an iceman, gutters, and sooty roofs into a golden and fabulous scene. The setting of Dickinson's poem is a New England countryside, where the glorious colors of the western sky are compared to precious gems—amber and emerald. |
| Topic Sentence | **Both poems are rich in visual images, particularly images of color.** Swenson sees the sunset creating decorative patterns along the street. The street becomes a "gilded stagger" as the light zigzags across it. The golden light covers the walls of buildings with spots |
| Supporting Evidence | of sunlight that look like shiny "salamander-red" scales. The spotted and streaked light falls across the gutter in fine, hairlike lines. It covers the tops of cars and boys' heads with "helmets." The coal truck is ringed with light that looks like a halo. Even the coal sliding down its chute is transformed into "nuggets" racing "from a golden sled." Lampposts are wreathed with light so that they look like "fantastic trees." Ordinary creatures like pigeons and dogs are transformed into exotic flamingos and chows; ash cans become urns; and homely fire escapes are changed to elegant balconies. |
| Transitional Sentence | **Like Swenson, Dickinson captures the dramatic splendor of the sunset, but she focuses on the brilliant colors of the sky.** She compares the sunset to a housewife who sweeps the sky with multicolored brooms. As she sweeps, she leaves streaks of color across the sky. She is inefficient and leaves "shreds" of her brooms behind |
| Supporting Evidence | her. She forgets to "dust the pond," and she drops purple and amber threads. She litters the eastern sky with her clothing, "duds of emeralds." The clouds become her aprons, which fly as she works. She continues to sweep until the sun settles behind the horizon and the stars come out. |
| Topic Sentence | **Both poets use diction with suggestive meanings and associations.** Swenson uses language with romantic or exotic associations. The word *salamander*, for example, calls to mind the mythological crea- |
| Supporting Evidence | ture that lives in fire; *urn* has connotations of elegance and dignity. Dickinson, on the other hand, uses common words with rich connotative meanings. The word *sweeps*, for example, carries with it not only the commonplace meaning of clearing a surface, but that of a flowing, majestic movement. *Purple* is the imperial color used to symbolize royalty. |
| Topic Sentence | **Both poets adopt a whimsical tone toward their subject.** The underlying humor in Swenson's poem arises from the incongruity between each object and what it becomes: pigeons to flamingos; |
| Supporting Evidence | ash cans to urns. There is something playful and fantastic also in |

**CONCLUSION** Dickinson's notion of sunset as an absentminded, untidy housewife who neglects to dust and who litters the sky.

Although there are differences in the settings chosen by the poets and in their styles, both poems convey a sense of wonder and delight to be found in the simple, everyday beauty of nature.

Length: 534 words

# Revising Papers

When you write an essay in class, you have a limited amount of time to plan and develop your essay. Nevertheless, you should save a few minutes to read over your work and make necessary corrections.

When an essay is assigned as homework, you have more time to prepare it carefully. Get into the habit of revising your work. A first draft of an essay should be treated as a rough copy of your manuscript. Chances are that reworking your first draft will result in a clearer and stronger paper. See the revision of the draft on pages 808–810.

When you revise your paper, examine it critically for awkward sentences, inexact language, errors in capitalization, punctuation, and spelling. Rewrite any passages that are unclear or incomplete.

Here are some guidelines to help you in revision.

# Guidelines for Revising a Paper

**1.** *Check to see that your major point, a thesis, is clearly stated.* In a short essay, the thesis should be stated in the first sentence. In a longer composition, the thesis should appear in the introductory paragraph.

**2.** *Follow a logical organization.* A long composition should have an introduction, a body, and a conclusion. Each part of the essay should be clearly related to the thesis.

**3.** *Make sure that ideas are adequately developed.* Support any generalizations with specific evidence.

**4.** *Check for errors in capitalization, punctuation, spelling, and sentence structure.*

Here is an early draft of the essay on pages 805–807, showing how it
was revised for greater clarity, accuracy, and conciseness.

~~The beauty of nature is a popular subject with poets. Two~~
¶
~~poems that deal with the beauty of a sunset are~~ May Swenson's _in_

"Ornamental Sketch with Verbs" and Emily Dickinson*in* "She Sweeps
_have taken as their subject the beauty of a sunset._
with Many-Colored Brooms." Through the gift of observation and

imagination, both poets invest ordinary scenes with magic.

_The setting of_
Both poems unite the commonplace and the sublime. Swenson's
_is_                                    _street. Sunset spilling over the street transforms such common_
poem ~~uses~~ an ordinary city ~~setting, where we see~~ a girl on skates,   _sights as_

an iceman, gutters, and sooty roofs, ~~The street is transformed~~ into
_golden and_                 _The setting of_  _'s poems_
a fabulous scene ~~by the sunset.~~ Dickinson ~~uses a~~ New England
_glorious_        _western_
countryside, where the colors of the sky are compared to precious

gems--amber and emerald.

Both poems are rich in visual images, particularly images of
_sees_                        _ing_
color. ~~In Swenson's poem~~ the sunset creates decorative patterns
_The street_
along the street. ~~It~~ becomes a "gilded stagger" as the light
_The golden light covers_   _with spots of sunlight that_
zigzags across it. The walls of buildings look like shiny "salamander-
_spotted and streaked_
red" scales. The light falls across the gutter in fine, hairlike lines.

It covers the tops of cars and boys' heads with "helmets."

Ordinary creatures like pigeons and dogs are transformed into
*exotic*
flamingos and chows; ash cans become urns; and fire escapes are
^ *homely*
changed to elegant balconies. The coal truck looks like ~~it has~~ *is ringed with light that*
*sliding down its chute*
a halo. Even the coal is transformed into "nuggets" racing "from
*are unearthed with light so that they*
a golden sled." ~~The~~ lampposts look like "fantastic trees."

Like Swenson, Dickinson captures the dramatic splendor of

the sunset, but she focuses on the brilliant colors of the sky.
*who sweeps the sky with multi-colored brooms.*
She compares the sunset to a housewife. As she sweeps, she leaves

streaks of color across the sky. She is inefficient and leaves
*She forgets to "dust the pond," and she drops purple and amber threads.*
"shreds" of her brooms behind her. She litters the eastern sky
*her clothing;*
with "duds of emeralds." The clouds become her aprons, which fly

as she works. She continues to sweep until the sun settles behind

the horizon and the stars come out.

Both poets use diction with suggestive meanings and associations.

Swenson uses language with romantic or exotic associations. The word salamander ~~is one~~ example, *for* ~~A salamander is a~~ *calls to mind the* mythological creature

that lives in fire. ~~The word~~ urn ~~is another example.~~ Dickinson uses *has connotations of elegance and dignity. on the other hand,*

~~words~~ ~~that are~~ common ~~but that have~~ *with* rich connotative meanings. ~~One~~

~~example is~~ the word sweeps, *for example, carries with it not only the* ~~It has a~~ commonplace meaning *of* clearing a

surface, ~~It also stands for~~ *but that of* a flowing, majestic movement. Purple

is the imperial color used to symbolize royalty.

Both poets adopt a whimsical tone toward their subject. ~~There~~ *The underlying humor in Swenson's poem arises from the* ~~is~~ incongruity between each object and what it becomes: ~~in Swenson's~~

~~poem:~~ pigeons to flamingos; ash cans to urns, ~~resulting in an~~

~~underlying humor.~~ ~~Dickinson's notion~~ *There* is *something* playful and fantastic in *also* ~~that~~

*of* sunset ~~is treated~~ as an absentminded, untidy housewife who neglects

to dust *who* and litters the sky.

Although there are differences in the settings chosen by the

poets and in their styles, both poems convey a sense of wonder and

delight to be found in the simple, everyday beauty of nature.

# ADDITIONAL SELECTIONS

# The Piece of Yarn     *Guy de Maupassant*

On all the roads around Goderville, farmers and their wives were streaming into town, for this was market day. The men strode calmly along, their bodies hunching forward with each movement of their long, crooked legs, misshapen from hard labors—from leaning on the plow, which simultaneously elevated the left shoulder and threw the back out of line; from swinging the scythe, in which the need for a solid stance bowed the legs at the knees; from all the slow and laborious tasks of work in the field. Their blue smocks, starched until they glistened like varnish, embroidered at neck and wrist with a small design in white thread, puffed out around their bony chests like balloons about to take flight with a head, two arms, and two feet attached.

The men tugged after them, at the end of a rope, a cow or a calf. And their wives, behind the animal, tried to hasten it on by flicking its rump with a small branch still bearing leaves. In the crook of their arms they carried large covered baskets from which heads of chickens and ducks protruded here and there. They walked with shorter and more lively steps than their husbands; their figures lean, erect, and wrapped in a tightfitting shawl pinned together over their chests; their hair swathed in a piece of white linen and topped off by a tight brimless cap.

Now and then a farm wagon would overtake them, drawn at a brisk trot by a small sturdy horse, grotesquely jouncing two men side by side, and a woman in the back clinging to the frame to cushion the rough jolts.

What a milling around, what a jostling mob of people and animals there was on Goderville square! Above the surface of the assemblage protruded the horns of cattle, the high-crowned, long-furred hats of wealthy farmers, and the headdresses of their ladies. The bawling, shrill, piercing voices raised a continuous din, above which echoed an occasional hearty laugh from the robust lungs of a merrymaking farmhand or the long lowing of a cow tied to a house wall.

Everything smelled of the stable, milk and manure, hay and sweat, and gave off the pungent, sour odor of man and beast so characteristic of those who work in the fields.

Maître Hauchecorne, of Bréauté,[1] had just reached Goderville and was making his way toward the square when he glimpsed a piece of yarn on the ground. Maître Hauchecorne, thrifty like the true Norman he was, thought it worthwhile to pick up anything that could be useful; and he stooped down painfully, for he suffered from rheumatism. He plucked up the thin piece of yarn and was just starting to wind it up carefully when he caught sight of Maître Malandain,[2] the harness maker, eyeing him from his doorstep. They had once disagreed over the price of a harness, and since

---

1. **Maître Hauchecorne, of Bréauté** (mā'trə ōsh'kôrn of brä'ō-tā').
2. **Malandain** (mál'ån-dāɴ').

both had a tendency to hold grudges, they had remained on bad terms with each other. Maître Hauchecorne felt a bit humiliated at having been seen by his enemy scrabbling in the dirt for a bit of yarn. He quickly thrust his find under his smock, then into his trousers pocket; afterwards he pretended to search the ground for something he had lost, and at last he went off toward the market-place with his head bent forward and his body doubled over by his aches and pains.

He lost himself at once in the shrill and slow-moving crowd, keyed up by long-drawn-out bargaining. The farmers would run their hands over the cows, go away, come back, undecided, always in fear of being taken in, never daring to commit themselves, slyly watching the seller's eye, endlessly hoping to discover the deception in the man and the defect in the beast.

The women, after placing their baskets at their feet, had drawn out their poultry, which sprawled on the ground, their feet tied together, with fear-glazed eyes and scarlet combs.

Standing rigidly, their faces giving away nothing, the women would listen to offers and hold to their prices; or else, on impulse deciding to accept an offer, would shout after a customer who was slowly moving off: "All right, Maît' Anthime.[3] It's yours."

Then, little by little, the square emptied, and as the bells rang the noonday angelus,[4] those who lived too far away scattered to the inns.

At Jourdain's, the large hall was filled with diners just as the great courtyard was filled with vehicles of all descriptions: two-wheeled carts, buggies, farm wagons, carriages, name-less carryalls, yellow with mud, battered, patched together, with shafts raised heaven-ward like two arms or with front down and rear pointing upward.

Next to the seated diners the immense fireplace, flaming brightly, cast a lively warmth on the backs of the right-hand row. Three spits were turning, loaded with chickens, pigeons, and legs of mutton, and a delectable aroma of roasting meat and of juices trickling over the heat-browned skin wafted from the hearth, making hearts gay and mouths drool.

All the carriage aristocracy was eating here at the table of Maît' Jourdain, innkeeper and horse dealer, a sly man who had a knack for making money.

The dishes were passed and emptied, along with jugs of yellow cider. Each man told of his dealings, what he had bought and sold. They asked one another about how they thought the crops would do. The weather was fine for hay, but a bit damp for grain.

All of a sudden the rolling beat of a drum echoed in the courtyard before the inn. At once all the diners, except a few indifferent ones, leaped to their feet, and with mouths still full and napkins in hand, rushed to the door and windows.

When the drum roll ended, the town crier announced in a jerky voice, breaking his sentences in the wrong places:

"It is made known to the inhabitants of Goderville, and in general to all—the persons attending the market fair, that there was lost this morning, on the Beuzeville[5] road, between—nine and ten o'clock, a black leather pocketbook containing five hundred francs[6] and some business documents. It is

---

3. **Maît' Anthime** (māt′áṇ-tēm′).
4. **angelus** (ăn′jə-ləs): a prayer said at morning, noon, and night.

5. **Beuzeville** (bœz′vēl′).
6. **five hundred francs:** about one hundred dollars, a considerable sum at that time.

requested that the finder return it—to the town hall, at once, or to Maître Fortuné Houlbrèque[7] of Manneville. There will be a reward of twenty francs."

The man then went off. Once more in the distance the beat of the drum rolled out hollowly, followed by the receding voice of the crier.

Now everyone began to discuss the announcement, weighing the chance Maître Houlbrèque had of getting his pocketbook back.

And the meal came to an end.

They were finishing coffee when the police sergeant appeared in the doorway.

He asked: "Is Maître Hauchecorne, of Bréauté, here?"

Maître Hauchecorne, sitting at the far end of the table, spoke up: "That's me!"

And the sergeant continued: "Maître Hauchecorne, please be good enough to come with me to the town hall. The mayor wants to talk with you."

The farmer, surprised and uneasy, gulped down his after-dinner glass of brandy, got up, and more stooped over than earlier in the morning, because his first steps after each meal were especially painful, started on his way, saying over and over:

"That's me! That's me!"

And he followed the sergeant out.

The mayor was waiting for him, presiding in an armchair. He was the local notary, a large man, grave in manner and given to pompous phrases.

"Maître Hauchecorne," he said, "you were seen this morning on the Beuzeville road picking up the pocketbook lost by Maître Houlbrèque, of Manneville."

The old farmer, struck speechless, in a panic over being suspected and not understanding why, stared at the mayor:

"Me? Me? Me pick up that pocketbook?"

"Yes, you are indeed the one."

"I swear! I don't know anything at all about it."

"You were seen."

"Seen? Me? Who says he saw me?"

"Monsieur[8] Malandain, the harness maker."

Then the old man remembered, understood, and flushing with anger, said: "Hah! He saw me, that old good-for-nothing! He saw me pick up this bit of yarn. Look, Mr. Mayor." And, fumbling in the depths of his pocket, he pulled out the little piece of yarn.

But the mayor, incredulous, shook his head: "You would have me believe, Maître Hauchecorne, that Monsieur Malandain, who is a trustworthy man, mistook that piece of yarn for a pocketbook?"

The farmer, enraged, raised his hand, spit to one side to reinforce his word, and said again: "But it's God's honest truth, the sacred truth, Mister Mayor. There! On my soul and salvation, I swear."

The major resumed his accusation: "After having picked up the article, you kept on searching in the mud for some time to see if some coin might have slipped out."

The old man was choking with indignation and fear.

"How can anyone say such things! . . . How can anyone say such lies to ruin a man's good name! How can anyone . . ."

No matter how much he protested, no one believed him.

He was confronted by Monsieur Malandain, who repeated his statement under oath. They hurled insults at each other for a full hour.

---

7. **Fortuné Houlbrèque** (fôr-tü-nāꞌo͞olꞌbrĕkꞌ).

8. **Monsieur** (mə-syœꞌ): French title equivalent to "Mr."

Maître Hauchecorne was searched at his own request. They found nothing on him.

Finally the mayor, completely baffled, sent him away with the warning that he was going to inform the public prosecutor and ask what should be done.

The news had spread. On leaving the town hall, the old man was surrounded and questioned with serious or good-humored curiosity, but without any hint of blame. He began to tell the story of the piece of yarn. They didn't believe him. They laughed.

He went here and there, stopped by everyone, buttonholing his acquaintances, beginning over and over again his story and his protestations, turning his pockets inside out to prove that he had nothing in them.

People said to him: "You sly old rascal, you!"

He got more and more annoyed, upset, feverish in his distress because no one believed him, not knowing what to do, and always telling his story.

Night came. It was time to go home. He set off with his three neighbors, showed them the place where he had picked up the piece of yarn, and all the way talked about his experience.

That evening he made the rounds of the village of Bréauté, telling his tale to everyone. He met no one who believed him.

He was sick about it all night.

The next day, about one in the afternoon, Marius Paumelle,[9] a farmhand working for Maître Breton, a landowner of Ymauville,[10] returned the pocketbook and its contents to Maître Houlbrèque, of Manneville.

This man claimed he had actually found the article on the highway, but being unable to read, he had taken it home and given it to his employer.

The news spread through the neighborhood. Maître Hauchecorne was informed. He began immediately to make the rounds, telling his story all over again, including the ending. He was exultant.

"What made me mad," he said, "wasn't so much the accusation, you know; it was all that lying. Nothing burns you up as much as being hauled into court on the word of a liar."

All day he kept talking about his experience, retelling it on the street to passersby, in the tavern to people having a drink, outside the church on the following Sunday. He would stop complete strangers to tell them. He felt calm about it now, but something still bothered him that he could not quite figure out. People listening to him seemed to be amused. They didn't appear to be convinced. He sensed that they were making remarks behind his back.

On Tuesday of the following week he returned to the marketplace in Goderville, driven by his need to state his case.

Malandain, standing in his doorway, began to laugh when he saw him going by. Why?

He accosted a farmer from Criquetot,[11] who didn't let him finish but punched him in the pit of the stomach and shouted in his face: "Knock it off, you old rascal!" Then he turned on his heel and walked away.

Maître Hauchecorne was struck speechless and grew more and more upset. Why would anyone call him an "old rascal"?

When he had taken his usual place at Jourdain's table, he launched into another explanation of the incident.

---

9. **Marius Paumelle** (mȧ-rē-üs′ pō-mĕl′).
10. **Breton . . . Ymauville** (brĕ-tôn′ē′mȯv-vēl′).

11. **Criquetot** (krĭk′tō′).

A horse dealer of Montivilliers[12] shouted at him: "Oh, come off it! I'm wise to that old trick. We know all about your yarn!"

Hauchecorne stammered: "But they found the pocketbook!"

"Sure old man! Somebody found it, and somebody took it back. Seeing is believing. A real pretty tangle to unsnarl!"

The farmer was stunned. At last he understood. People were accusing him of having gotten an accomplice to return the pocketbook.

He tried to deny it. The whole table burst into laughter.

Unable to finish his dinner, he left, the butt of jokes and mockery.

He went home, feeling humiliated and indignant, strangled with anger and mental confusion, especially crushed because, as a shrewd Norman, he knew himself capable of doing what he was accused of, and even boasting about it as a good trick. In his confusion, he could not see how he could prove his innocence, since he was well known for driving a sharp bargain. He was heartsick over the injustice of being suspected.

He set about telling his experience all over again, each day embroidering his recital, with each retelling adding new reasons, more vigorous protestations, more solemn vows that he dreamed up and repeated during his hours alone, his whole mind occupied with the yarn. He was believed less and less as his defense became more and more intricate and his explanations more and more involved.

"Ha! With such an explanation, he must be lying!" they said behind his back. He sensed this, ate his heart out, and exhausted his strength in useless efforts. He visibly began to weaken.

Jokers now encouraged him, for their amusement, to tell "The Yarn" as one encourages a soldier back from the wars to tell about his battles. His mind, hurt to the depths, began to weaken.

Toward the end of December he took to his bed.

He died during the early days of January, and, in his dying delirium, kept protesting his innocence, repeating:

"Just a bit of yarn . . . a little bit of yarn . . . see, Mr. Mayor, there it is!"

## FOR STUDY AND DISCUSSION

1. Besides giving us the setting of the story, the opening paragraphs also reveal important aspects of the villagers' characters. How does de Maupassant emphasize the peasants' frugality? How does he show their suspicion of one another? How do these details prepare us for their behavior later in the story?

2. Why does Hauchecorne attempt to conceal the yarn he has picked up? What does this incident reveal about his character?

3. Does Malandain believe that Hauchecorne found the pocketbook or is he deliberately lying? Is either answer reasonable, given the character of the peasants?

4. Why do the peasants refuse to believe that Hauchecorne is innocent?

## SUGGESTIONS FOR WRITING

1. Describe the major conflict in the story. Tell how it develops and how it is resolved.

2. A situation is said to be ironic when a character's actions bring about results that are unexpected or contrary to intent. Show that the plot of "The Piece of Yarn" hinges on irony of situation.

---

12. **Montivilliers** (môɴ′tə-vēl-yā′).

# A Pair of Silk Stockings  *Kate Chopin*

Little Mrs. Sommers one day found herself the unexpected possessor of fifteen dollars. It seemed to her a very large amount of money, and the way in which it stuffed and bulged her worn old *porte-monnaie*[1] gave her a feeling of importance such as she had not enjoyed for years.

The question of investment was one that occupied her greatly. For a day or two she walked about apparently in a dreamy state, but really absorbed in speculation and calculation. She did not wish to act hastily, to do anything she might afterward regret. But it was during the still hours of the night when she lay awake revolving plans in her mind that she seemed to see her way clearly toward a proper and judicious use of the money.

A dollar or two should be added to the price usually paid for Janie's shoes, which would insure their lasting an appreciable time longer than they usually did. She would buy so and so many yards of percale for new shirtwaists for the boys and Janie and Mag. She had intended to make the old ones do by skillful patching. Mag should have another gown. She had seen some beautiful patterns, veritable bargains in the shop windows. And still there would be left enough for new stockings—two pairs apiece—and what darning that would save for a while! She would get caps for the boys and sailor hats for the girls. The vision of her little brood looking fresh and dainty and new for once in their lives excited her and made her restless and wakeful with anticipation.

The neighbors sometimes talked of certain "better days" that little Mrs. Sommers had known before she had ever thought of being Mrs. Sommers. She herself indulged in no such morbid retrospection.[2] She had no time —no second of time to devote to the past. The needs of the present absorbed her every faculty. A vision of the future like some dim, gaunt monster sometimes appalled her, but luckily tomorrow never comes.

Mrs. Sommers was one who knew the value of bargains; who could stand for hours making her way inch by inch toward the desired object that was selling below cost. She could elbow her way if need be; she had learned to clutch a piece of goods and hold it and stick to it with persistence and determination till her turn came to be served, no matter when it came.

But that day she was a little faint and tired. She had swallowed a light luncheon—no! when she came to think of it, between getting the children fed and the place righted, and preparing herself for the shopping bout, she had actually forgotten to eat any luncheon at all!

She sat herself upon a revolving stool before a counter that was comparatively deserted, trying to gather strength and courage to charge through an eager multitude that was besieging breastworks[3] of shirting and figured lawn.[4] An all-gone limp feeling had come over her and she rested her hand aimlessly upon the counter. She wore no gloves. By degrees she grew aware that her hand had encoun-

---

1. *porte-monnaie* (pôrt' môn-nĕ'): a small pocketbook.

2. **morbid retrospection:** looking back on the past in a way that is unwholesome or psychologically unhealthy.
3. **breastworks:** low walls, here used metaphorically.
4. **figured lawn:** fine fabric decorated with a pattern.

tered something very soothing, very pleasant to touch. She looked down to see that her hand lay upon a pile of silk stockings. A placard nearby announced that they had been reduced in price from two dollars and fifty cents to one dollar and ninety-eight cents; and a young girl who stood behind the counter asked her if she wished to examine their line of silk hosiery. She smiled, just as if she had been asked to inspect a tiara of diamonds with the ultimate view of purchasing it. But she went on feeling the soft, sheeny luxurious things — with both hands now, holding them up to see them glisten, and to feel them glide serpentlike through her fingers.

Two hectic blotches came suddenly into her pale cheeks. She looked up at the girl.

"Do you think there are any eights-and-a-half among these?"

There were any number of eights-and-a-half. In fact, there were more of that size than any other. Here was a light-blue pair; there were some lavender, some all black and various shades of tan and gray. Mrs. Sommers selected a black pair and looked at them very long and closely. She pretended to be examining their texture, which the clerk assured her was excellent.

"A dollar and ninety-eight cents," she mused aloud. "Well, I'll take this pair." She handed the girl a five-dollar bill and waited for her change and for her parcel. What a very small parcel it was! It seemed lost in the depths of her shabby old shopping bag.

Mrs. Sommers after that did not move in the direction of the bargain counter. She took the elevator, which carried her to an upper floor into the region of the ladies' waiting rooms. Here, in a retired corner, she exchanged her cotton stockings for the new silk ones which she had just bought. She was not going through any acute mental process or reasoning with herself, nor was she striving to explain to her satisfaction the motive of her action. She was not thinking at all. She seemed for the time to be taking a rest from that laborious and fatiguing function and to have abandoned herself to some mechanical impulse that directed her actions and freed her of responsibility.

How good was the touch of the raw silk to her flesh! She felt like lying back in the cushioned chair and reveling for a while in the luxury of it. She did for a little while. Then she replaced her shoes, rolled the cotton stockings together and thrust them into her bag. After doing this she crossed straight over to the shoe department and took her seat to be fitted.

She was fastidious. The clerk could not make her out; he could not reconcile her shoes with her stockings, and she was not too easily pleased. She held back her skirts and turned her feet one way and her head another as she glanced down at the polished, pointed-tipped boots. Her foot and ankle looked very pretty. She could not realize that they belonged to her and were a part of herself. She wanted an excellent and stylish fit, she told the young fellow who served her, and she did not mind the difference of a dollar or two more in the price so long as she got what she desired.

It was a long time since Mrs. Sommers had been fitted with gloves. On rare occasions when she had bought a pair they were always "bargains," so cheap that it would have been preposterous and unreasonable to have expected them to be fitted to the hand.

Now she rested her elbow on the cushion of the glove counter, and a pretty, pleasant young creature, delicate and deft of touch, drew a long-wristed "kid" over Mrs. Sommers' hand. She smoothed it down over the wrist and buttoned it neatly, and both lost themselves for a second or two in admiring contemplation of the little symmetrical gloved hand. But there were other places where money might be spent.

There were books and magazines piled up in the window of a stall a few paces down the street. Mrs. Sommers bought two high-priced magazines such as she had been accustomed to read in the days when she had been accustomed to other pleasant things. She carried them without wrapping. As well as she could she lifted her skirts at the crossings. Her stockings and boots and well-fitting gloves had worked marvels in her bearing—had given her a feeling of assurance, a sense of belonging to the well-dressed multitude.

She was very hungry. Another time she would have stilled the cravings for food until reaching her own home, where she would have brewed herself a cup of tea and taken a snack of anything that was available. But the impulse that was guiding her would not suffer her to entertain any such thought.

There was a restaurant at the corner. She had never entered its doors; from the outside she had sometimes caught glimpses of spotless damask and shining crystal, and soft-stepping waiters serving people of fashion.

When she entered her appearance created no surprise, no consternation, as she had half feared it might. She seated herself at a small table alone, and an attentive waiter at once approached to take her order. She did not want a profusion; she craved a nice and tasty bite—a half dozen bluepoints,[5] a plump chop with cress, a something sweet—a crème-frappée,[6] for instance; a glass of Rhine wine, and after all a small cup of black coffee.

While waiting to be served she removed her gloves very leisurely and laid them beside her. Then she picked up a magazine and glanced through it, cutting the pages with a blunt edge of her knife. It was all very agreeable. The damask was even more spotless than it had seemed through the window, and the crystal more sparkling. There were quiet ladies and gentlemen, who did not notice her, lunching at the small tables like her own. A soft, pleasing strain of music could be heard, and a gentle breeze was blowing through the window. She tasted a bite, and she read a word or two, and she sipped the amber wine and wiggled her toes in the silk stockings. The price of it made no difference. She counted the money out to the waiter and left an extra coin on his tray, whereupon he bowed before her as before a princess of royal blood.

There was still money in her purse, and her next temptation presented itself in the shape of a matinée poster.

It was a little later when she entered the theater, the play had begun and the house seemed to her to be packed. But there were vacant seats here and there, and into one of them she was ushered, between brilliantly dressed women who had gone there to kill time and eat candy and display their gaudy attire. There were many others who were there solely for the play and acting. It is safe to say there was no one present who bore quite the attitude which Mrs. Sommers did to her surroundings. She gathered in the whole—stage and players and people in one wide impression, and absorbed it and enjoyed it. She laughed at the comedy and wept—she and the gaudy woman next to her wept over the tragedy. And they talked a little together over it. And the gaudy woman wiped her eyes and sniffled on a tiny square of filmy, perfumed lace and passed little Mrs. Sommers her box of candy.

The play was over, the music ceased, the

---

5. **bluepoints:** oysters from the south shore of Long Island.
6. **crème-frappée** (krĕm frä-pā′): a chilled dessert.

crowd filed out. It was like a dream ended. People scattered in all directions. Mrs. Sommers went to the corner and waited for the cable car.

A man with keen eyes, who sat opposite to her, seemed to like the study of her small, pale face. It puzzled him to decipher what he saw there. In truth, he saw nothing—unless he were wizard enough to detect a poignant wish, a powerful longing that the cable car would never stop anywhere, but go on and on with her forever.

## FOR STUDY AND DISCUSSION

**1.** What impression do you form of Mrs. Sommers' day-to-day life from the opening paragraphs of the story?
**2.** What need is awakened in her by the pair of silk stockings?
**3.** Mrs. Sommers spends all of the precious money on herself. Given the responsible nature of her character, what do you think accounts for this self-indulgence?
**4.** Early in the story we are told that Mrs. Sommers is not in the habit of dwelling on the "better days" she had once known. At the end of the story, is she ready to resume her practical attitude toward the deprivations of her life, or has she changed in some way?

## SUGGESTIONS FOR WRITING

**1.** Write a brief essay explaining your own attitude toward Mrs. Sommers. Do you find her sympathetic? pathetic? weak? or something else? Support your opinion with evidence from the story.
**2.** Compare Mrs. Sommers with Hester Tavener in "The Sentimentality of William Tavener" (page 52). What sense of loss do both women experience?

# Love   *William Maxwell*

*Miss Vera Brown,* she wrote on the blackboard, letter by letter in flawlessly oval Palmer method.[1] Our teacher for the fifth grade. The name might as well have been graven in stone.

As she called the roll, her voice was as gentle as the expression in her beautiful dark brown eyes. She reminded me of pansies.

When she called on Alvin Ahrens to recite and he said, "I know but I can't say," the class snickered but she said, "Try," encouragingly, and waited, to be sure that he didn't know the answer, and then said, to one of the hands waving in the air, "Tell Alvin what one-fifth of three-eighths is." If we arrived late to school, red-faced and out of breath and bursting with the excuse we had thought up on the way, before we could speak she said, "I'm sure you couldn't help it. Close the door, please, and take your seat." If she kept us after school

---

1. **Palmer method:** a method of teaching handwriting, popular earlier in this century.

it was not to scold us but to help us past the hard part.

Somebody left a big red apple on her desk for her to find when she came into the classroom, and she smiled and put it in her desk, out of sight. Somebody else left some purple asters, which she put in her drinking glass. After that the presents kept coming. She was the only pretty teacher in the school. She never had to ask us to be quiet or to stop throwing erasers. We would not have dreamed of doing anything that would displease her.

Somebody wormed it out of her when her birthday was. While she was out of the room the class voted to present her with flowers from the greenhouse. Then they took another vote and sweet peas won. When she saw the florist's box waiting on her desk, she said, "Oh?"

"Look inside," we all said.

Her delicate fingers seemed to take forever to remove the ribbon. In the end, she raised the lid of the box and exclaimed.

"Read the card!" we shouted.

*Many Happy Returns to Miss Vera Brown, from the Fifth Grade,* it said.

She put her nose in the flowers and said, "Thank you all very, very much," and then turned our minds to the spelling lesson for the day.

After school we escorted her downtown in a body to a special matinée of D. W. Griffith's[2] "Hearts of the World." She was not allowed to buy her ticket. We paid for everything.

We meant to have her for our teacher forever. We intended to pass right up through the sixth, seventh, and eighth grades and on into high school taking her with us. But that isn't what happened. One day there was a substitute teacher. We expected our real teacher to be back the next day but she wasn't. Week after week passed, and the substitute continued to sit at Miss Brown's desk, calling on us to recite and giving out tests and handing them back with grades on them, and we went on acting the way we had when Miss Brown was there because we didn't want her to come back and find we hadn't been nice to the substitute. One Monday morning she cleared her throat and said that Miss Brown was sick and not coming back for the rest of the term.

In the fall we had passed on into the sixth grade and she was still not back. Benny Irish's mother found out that she was living with an aunt and uncle on a farm a mile or so beyond the edge of town, and told my mother, who told somebody in my hearing. One afternoon after school Benny and I got on our bikes and rode out to see her. At the place where the road turned off to go to the cemetery and the Chautauqua[3] grounds, there was a red barn with a huge circus poster on it, showing the entire inside of the Sells-Floto Circus tent and everything that was going on in all three rings. In the summertime, riding in the back seat of my father's open Chalmers,[4] I used to crane my neck as we passed that turn, hoping to see every last tiger and flying-trapeze artist, but it was never possible. The poster was weather-beaten now, with loose strips of paper hanging down.

It was getting dark when we wheeled our bikes up the lane of the farmhouse where Miss Brown lived.

---

2. **D. W. Griffith:** a pioneer in the motion-picture industry (1875–1948).

3. **Chautauqua** (shə-tô'kwə): a program of educational assemblies which flourished during the late nineteenth and early twentieth centuries.
4. **Chalmers:** an automobile. The last year of production of Chalmers cars was 1923.

"You knock," Benny said as we started up on the porch.

"No, you do it," I said.

We hadn't thought ahead to what it would be like to see her. We wouldn't have been surprised if she had come to the door herself and thrown up her hands in astonishment when she saw who it was, but instead a much older woman opened the door and said, "What do you want?"

"We came to see Miss Brown," I said.

"We're in her class at school," Benny explained.

I could see that the woman was trying to decide whether she should tell us to go away, but she said, "I'll find out if she wants to see you," and left us standing on the porch for what seemed like a long time. Then she appeared again and said, "You can come in now."

As we followed her through the front parlor I could make out in the dim light that there was an old-fashioned organ like the kind you used to see in country churches, and linoleum on the floor, and stiff uncomfortable chairs, and family portraits behind curved glass in big oval frames.

The room beyond it was lighted by a coal-oil lamp but seemed ever so much darker than the unlighted room we had just passed through. Propped up on pillows in a big double bed was our teacher, but so changed. Her arms were like sticks, and all the life in her seemed concentrated in her eyes, which had dark circles around them and were enormous. She managed a flicker of recognition but I was struck dumb by the fact that she didn't seem glad to see us. She didn't belong to us anymore. She belonged to her illness.

Benny said, "I hope you get well soon."

The angel who watches over little boys who know but they can't say it saw to it that we didn't touch anything. And in a minute we were outside, on our bicycles, riding through the dusk toward the turn in the road and town.

A few weeks later I read in the Lincoln *Evening Courier* that Miss Vera Brown, who taught the fifth grade in Central School, had died of tuberculosis, aged twenty-three years and seven months.

Sometimes I went with my mother when she put flowers on the graves of my grandparents. The cinder roads wound through the cemetery in ways she understood and I didn't, and I would read the names on the monuments: Brower, Cadwallader, Andrews, Bates, Mitchell. In loving memory of. Infant daughter of. Beloved wife of. The cemetery was so large and so many people were buried there, it would have taken a long time to locate a particular grave if you didn't know where it was already. But I know, the way I sometimes know what is in wrapped packages, that the elderly woman who let us in and who took care of Miss Brown during her last illness went to the cemetery regularly and poured the rancid water out of the tin receptacle that was sunk below the level of the grass at the foot of her grave, and filled it with fresh water from a nearby faucet and arranged the flowers she had brought in such a way as to please the eye of the living and the closed eyes of the dead.

## FOR STUDY AND DISCUSSION

**1.** In this story the narrator recalls how a teacher made an unforgettable impression on her students. Why were the children so deeply touched by Miss Brown?

**2.** What characteristics of Miss Brown led the children to associate her with flowers?

**3.** In the opening paragraph of the story, the narrator says that the teacher's name "might as well have been graven in stone." In the light of later events, why is this statement tragically ironic?

**4.** At the conclusion of the story, the narrator has an image of someone placing fresh flowers on Miss Brown's grave. Why does he find comfort in this thought?

## SUGGESTIONS FOR WRITING

**1.** Tone, as you have learned, is the attitude a writer takes toward a subject or an audience. In a brief essay discuss the tone of "Love." Take into account matters of language, events, and feelings.

**2.** Explain the title of the story. In what way does it pinpoint the theme?

# One Art    *Elizabeth Bishop*

The art of losing isn't hard to master;
so many things seem filled with the intent
to be lost that their loss is no disaster.

Lose something every day. Accept the fluster
of lost door keys, the hour badly spent.                          5
The art of losing isn't hard to master.

Then practice losing farther, losing faster:
places, and names, and where it was you meant
to travel. None of these will bring disaster.

I lost my mother's watch. And look! my last, or          10
next-to-last, of three loved houses went.
The art of losing isn't hard to master.

I lost two cities, lovely ones. And, vaster,
some realms I owned, two rivers, a continent.
I miss them, but it wasn't a disaster.                            15

—Even losing you (the joking voice, a gesture
I love) I shan't have lied. It's evident
the art of losing's not too hard to master
though it may look like (*Write* it!) like disaster.

## FOR STUDY AND DISCUSSION

**1.** An art is a skill acquired by experience or training. According to the speaker, how does one master the "art of losing"?

**2.** What examples does the speaker give of her own experiences of loss? Which of these are metaphorical rather than literal?

**3.** Study the last stanza of the poem carefully. Does the speaker really believe that practicing the "art of losing" things prepares one for the disastrous loss of someone dear?

**4.** This poem is a modified *villanelle* (vĭl'ə-nĕl'), an intricate 19-line poem of French origin. Only two rhymes are allowed in the villanelle, and 8 lines are refrains. How does repetition gain emphasis for the poet's ideas?

**5.** What do you think the title refers to? Does the speaker believe there is "One Art," or is the title ironic?

## SUGGESTIONS FOR WRITING

**1.** How would you describe the speaker's attitude in this poem? Is it casual and indifferent? controlled and restrained? or something else?

**2.** *Hyperbole* is a figure of speech that uses exaggeration for special effect. Show how Bishop uses hyperbole in "One Art."

*When Synge went to the Aran Islands in 1898, he observed the custom that gives this play its title. Islanders who wished to ship cattle and horses to the mainland would ride the animals out to sea, where they would be towed through hazardous currents to steamers far offshore.*

# Riders to the Sea     *John Millington Synge°*

## Characters

Maurya, an old woman
Bartley, her son
Cathleen, her daughter
Nora, a younger daughter
Men and Women

Scene: *An island off the west of Ireland. Cottage kitchen, with nets, oilskins, spinning wheel, some new boards standing by the wall, etc. Cathleen, a girl of about twenty, finishes kneading cake, and puts it down in the pot oven[1] by the fire; then wipes her hands, and begins to spin at the wheel. Nora, a young girl, puts her head in at the door.*

**Nora** (*in a low voice*). Where is she?
**Cathleen.** She's lying down. God help her, and may be sleeping, if she's able.

---

° **Synge** (sĭng).

---

1. **pot oven:** An oven consisting of a heated iron plate covered by a pot.

[Nora *comes in softly, and takes a bundle from under her shawl.*]

**Cathleen** (*spinning the wheel rapidly*). What is it you have?

**Nora.** The young priest is after bringing them. It's a shirt and a plain stocking were got off a drowned man in Donegal.

[Cathleen *stops her wheel with a sudden movement, and leans out to listen.*]

**Nora.** We're to find out if it's Michael's they are, some time herself will be down looking by the sea.

**Cathleen.** How would they be Michael's, Nora? How would he go the length of that way to the far north?

**Nora.** The young priest says he's known the like of it. "If it's Michael's they are," says he, "you can tell herself he's got a clean burial by the grace of God, and if they're not his, let no one say a word about them, for she'll be getting her death," says he, "with crying and lamenting."

[*The door which* Nora *half closed is blown open by a gust of wind.*]

**Cathleen** (*looking out anxiously*). Did you ask him would he stop Bartley going this day with the horses to the Galway fair?

**Nora.** "I won't stop him," says he, "but let you not be afraid. Herself does be saying prayers half through the night, and the Almighty God won't leave her destitute," says he, "with no son living."

**Cathleen.** Is the sea bad by the white rocks, Nora?

**Nora.** Middling bad, God help us. There's a great roaring in the west, and it's worse it'll be getting when the tide's turned to the wind. (*She goes over to the table with the bundle.*) Shall I open it now?

**Cathleen.** Maybe she'd wake up on us, and come in before we'd done. (*Coming to the table*) It's a long time we'll be, and the two of us crying.

**Nora** (*goes to the inner door and listens*). She's moving about on the bed. She'll be coming in a minute.

**Cathleen.** Give me the ladder, and I'll put them up in the turf loft,[2] the way she won't know of them at all, and maybe when the tide turns she'll be going down to see would he be floating from the east.

[*They put the ladder against the gable of the chimney;* Cathleen *goes up a few steps and hides the bundle in the turf loft.* Maurya *comes from the inner room.*]

**Maurya** (*looking up at* Cathleen *and speaking querulously*[3]). Isn't it turf enough you have for this day and evening?

**Cathleen.** There's a cake baking at the fire for a short space (*throwing down the turf*) and Bartley will want it when the tide turns if he goes to Connemara.

[Nora *picks up the turf and puts it round the pot oven.*]

**Maurya** (*sitting down on a stool at the fire*). He won't go this day with the wind rising from the south and west. He won't go this day, for the young priest will stop him surely.

**Nora.** He'll not stop him, mother, and I heard Eamon Simon and Stephen Pheety and Colum Shawn saying he would go.

**Maurya.** Where is he itself?

**Nora.** He went down to see would there be another boat sailing in the week, and I'm thinking it won't be long till he's here now, for the tide's turning at the green head,[4] and the hooker's[5] tacking from the east.

---

2. **turf loft:** loft or attic where peat, used for fuel, was stored.

3. **querulously** (kwĕr′ə-ləs-lē): in a complaining or fretful manner.

4. **head:** headland.

5. **hooker:** a fishing boat with one mast.

**Cathleen.** I hear someone passing the big stones.

**Nora** (*looking out*). He's coming now, and he in a hurry.

**Bartley** (*comes in and looks round the room. Speaking sadly and quietly*). Where is the bit of new rope, Cathleen, was bought in Connemara?

**Cathleen** (*coming down*). Give it to him, Nora; it's on a nail by the white boards. I hung it up this morning, for the pig with the black feet was eating it.

**Nora** (*giving him a rope*). Is that it, Bartley?

**Maurya.** You'd do right to leave that rope, Bartley, hanging by the board. (Bartley *takes the rope.*) It will be wanting in this place, I'm telling you, if Michael is washed up tomorrow morning, or the next morning, or any morning in the week, for it's a deep grave we'll make him by the grace of God.

**Bartley** (*beginning to work with the rope*). I've no halter the way[6] I can ride down on the mare, and I must go now quickly. This is the one boat going for two weeks or beyond it, and the fair will be a good fair for horses I heard them saying below.

**Maurya.** It's a hard thing they'll be saying below if the body is washed up and there's no man in it[7] to make the coffin, and I after giving a big price for the finest white boards you'd find in Connemara. (*She looks round at the boards.*)

**Bartley.** How would it be washed up, and we after looking each day for nine days, and a strong wind blowing a while back from the west and south?

**Maurya.** If it wasn't found itself, that wind is raising the sea, and there was a star up against the moon, and it rising in the night. If it was a hundred horses, or a thousand horses you had itself, what is the price of a thousand horses against a son where there is one son only?

**Bartley** (*working at the halter, to* Cathleen). Let you go down each day, and see the sheep aren't jumping in on the rye, and if the jobber comes you can sell the pig with the black feet if there is a good price going.

**Maurya.** How would the like of her get a good price for a pig?

**Bartley** (*to* Cathleen). If the west wind holds with the last bit of the moon let you and Nora get up weed enough for another cock for the kelp.[8] It's hard set we'll be from this day with no one in it but one man to work.

**Maurya.** It's hard set we'll be surely the day you're drownd'd with the rest. What way will I live and the girls with me, and I an old woman looking for the grave?

[Bartley *lays down the halter, takes off his old coat, and puts on a newer one of the same flannel.*]

**Bartley** (*to* Nora). Is she coming to the pier?

**Nora** (*looking out*). She's passing the green head and letting fall her sails.

**Bartley** (*getting his purse and tobacco*). I'll have half an hour to go down, and you'll see me coming again in two days, or in three days, or maybe in four days if the wind is bad.

**Maurya** (*turning round to the fire, and putting her shawl over her head*). Isn't it a hard and cruel man won't hear a word from an old woman, and she holding him from the sea?

**Cathleen.** It's the life of a young man to be going on the sea, and who would listen to an old woman with one thing and she saying it over?

---

6. **the way:** so that.
7. **in it:** there.

---

8. **get up . . . kelp:** get enough seaweed to make another pile. Seaweed, used for chemical purposes, was a source of income.

**Bartley** (*taking the halter*). I must go now quickly. I'll ride down on the red mare, and the gray pony'll run behind me. . . . The blessing of God on you. (*He goes out.*)

**Maurya** (*crying out as he is in the door*). He's gone now, God spare us, and we'll not see him again. He's gone now, and when the black night is falling I'll have no son left me in the world.

**Cathleen.** Why wouldn't you give him your blessing and he looking round in the door? Isn't it sorrow enough is on everyone in this house without your sending him out with an unlucky word behind him, and a hard word in his ear?

[Maurya *takes up the tongs and begins raking the fire aimlessly without looking round.*]

**Nora** (*turning towards her*). You're taking away the turf from the cake.

**Cathleen** (*crying out*). The Son of God forgive us, Nora, we're after forgetting his bit of bread. (*She comes over to the fire.*)

**Nora.** And it's destroyed he'll be going till dark night, and he after eating nothing since the sun went up.

**Cathleen** (*turning the cake out of the oven*). It's destroyed he'll be, surely. There's no sense left on any person in a house where an old woman will be talking forever.

[Maurya *sways herself on her stool.*]

**Cathleen** (*cutting off some of the bread and rolling it in a cloth; to* Maurya). Let you go down to the spring well and give him this and he passing. You'll see him then and the dark word will be broken, and you can say "God speed you," the way he'll be easy in his mind.

**Maurya** (*taking the bread*). Will I be in it as soon as himself?

**Cathleen.** If you go now quickly.

**Maurya** (*standing up unsteadily*). It's hard set I am to walk.

**Cathleen** (*looking at her anxiously*). Give her the stick, Nora, or maybe she'll slip on the big stones.

**Nora.** What stick?

**Cathleen.** The stick Michael brought from Connemara.

**Maurya** (*taking a stick* Nora *gives her*). In the big world the old people do be leaving things after them for their sons and children, but in this place it is the young men do be leaving things behind for them that do be old.

[*She goes out slowly.* Nora *goes over to the ladder.*]

**Cathleen.** Wait, Nora, maybe she'd turn back quickly. She's that sorry,[9] God help her, you wouldn't know the thing she'd do.

**Nora.** Is she gone round by the bush?

**Cathleen** (*looking out*). She's gone now. Throw it down quickly, for the Lord knows when she'll be out of it again.

**Nora** (*getting the bundle from the loft*). The young priest said he'd be passing tomorrow, and we might go down and speak to him below if it's Michael's they are surely.

**Cathleen** (*taking the bundle*). Did he say what way they were found?

**Nora** (*coming down*). "There were two men," says he, "and they rowing round with poteen[10] before the cocks crowed, and the oar of one of them caught the body, and they passing the black cliffs of the north."

**Cathleen** (*trying to open the bundle*). Give me a knife, Nora, the string's perished[11] with the salt water, and there's a black knot on it you wouldn't loosen in a week.

**Nora** (*giving her a knife*). I've heard tell it was a long way to Donegal.

---

9. **sorry:** wretched.
10. **poteen** (pō-tēn´): Irish whiskey manufactured illegally.
11. **perished:** stiffened.

**Cathleen** (*cutting the string*). It is surely. There was a man in here a while ago—the man sold us that knife—and he said if you set off walking from the rocks beyond, it would be seven days you'd be in Donegal.

**Nora.** And what time would a man take, and he floating?

[Cathleen *opens the bundle and takes out a bit of a stocking. They look at them eagerly.*]

**Cathleen** (*in a low voice*). The Lord spare us, Nora! Isn't it a queer hard thing to say if it's his they are surely?

**Nora.** I'll get his shirt off the hook the way we can put the one flannel on the other. (*She looks through some clothes hanging in the corner.*) It's not with them, Cathleen, and where will it be?

**Cathleen.** I'm thinking Bartley put it on him in the morning, for his own shirt was heavy with the salt in it. (*Pointing to the corner*) There's a bit of sleeve was of the same stuff. Give me that and it will do.

[Nora *brings it to her and they compare the flannel.*]

**Cathleen.** It's the same stuff, Nora; but if it is itself aren't there great rolls of it in the shops of Galway, and isn't it many another man may have a shirt of it as well as Michael himself?

**Nora** (*who has taken up the stocking and counted the stitches, crying out*). It's Michael, Cathleen, it's Michael; God spare his soul, and what will herself say when she hears this story, and Bartley on the sea?

**Cathleen.** (*taking the stocking*). It's a plain stocking.

**Nora.** It's the second one of the third pair I knitted, and I put up three score stitches, and I dropped four of them.

**Cathleen** (*counts the stitches*). It's that number is in it. (*Crying out*) Ah, Nora, isn't it a bitter thing to think of him floating that way to the far north, and no one to keen[12] him but the black hags that do be flying on the sea?

**Nora** (*swinging herself round, and throwing out her arms on the clothes*). And isn't it a pitiful thing when there is nothing left of a man who was a great rower and fisher, but a bit of an old shirt and a plain stocking?

**Cathleen** (*after an instant*). Tell me is herself coming, Nora? I hear a little sound on the path.

**Nora** (*looking out*). She is, Cathleen. She's coming up to the door.

**Cathleen.** Put these things away before she'll come in. Maybe it's easier she'll be after giving her blessing to Bartley, and we won't let on we've heard anything the time he's on the sea.

**Nora** (*helping Cathleen to close the bundle*). We'll put them here in the corner.

[*They put them into a hole in the chimney corner. Cathleen goes back to the spinning wheel.*]

**Nora.** Will she see it was crying I was?

**Cathleen.** Keep your back to the door the way the light'll not be on you.

[Nora *sits down at the chimney corner, with her back to the door. Maurya comes in very slowly, without looking at the girls, and goes over to her stool at the other side of the fire. The cloth with the bread is still in her hand. The girls look at each other, and* Nora *points to the bundle of bread.*]

**Cathleen** (*after spinning for a moment*). You didn't give him his bit of bread?

[Maurya *begins to keen softly, without turning round.*]

**Cathleen.** Did you see him riding down?

---

12. **keen:** wail in mourning.

[Maurya *going on keening.*]

**Cathleen** (*a little impatiently*). God forgive you; isn't it a better thing to raise your voice and tell what you seen, than to be making lamentation for a thing that's done? Did you see Bartley, I'm saying to you.

**Maurya** (*with a weak voice*). My heart's broken from this day.

**Cathleen** (*as before*). Did you see Bartley?

**Maurya.** I seen the fearfulest thing.

**Cathleen** (*leaves her wheel and looks out*). God forgive you; he's riding the mare now over the green head, and the gray pony behind him.

**Maurya** (*starts, so that her shawl falls back from her head and shows her white tossed hair. With a frightened voice*). The gray pony behind him.

**Cathleen** (*coming to the fire*). What is it ails you, at all?

**Maurya** (*speaking very slowly*). I've seen the fearfulest thing any person has seen, since the day Bride Dara seen the dead man with the child in his arms.

**Cathleen** and **Nora.** Uah.

[*They crouch down in front of the old woman at the fire.*]

**Nora.** Tell us what it is you seen.

**Maurya.** I went down to the spring well, and I stood there saying a prayer to myself. Then Bartley came along, and he riding on the red mare with the gray pony behind him. (*She puts up her hands, as if to hide something from her eyes.*) The Son of God spare us, Nora!

**Cathleen.** What is it you seen?

**Maurya.** I seen Michael himself.

**Cathleen** (*speaking softly*). You did not, Mother; it wasn't Michael you seen, for his body is after being found in the far north, and he's got a clean burial by the grace of God.

**Maurya** (*a little defiantly*). I'm after seeing him this day, and he riding and galloping. Bartley came first on the red mare; and I tried to say "God speed you," but something choked the words in my throat. He went by quickly; and "the blessing of God on you," says he, and I could say nothing. I looked up then, and I crying, at the gray pony, and there was Michael upon it—with fine clothes on him, and new shoes on his feet.

**Cathleen** (*begins to keen*). It's destroyed we are from this day. It's destroyed, surely.

**Nora.** Didn't the young priest say the Almighty God wouldn't leave her destitute with no son living?

**Maurya** (*in a low voice, but clearly*). It's little the like of him knows of the sea. . . . Bartley will be lost now, and let you call in Eamon and make me a good coffin out of the white boards, for I won't live after them. I've had a husband, and a husband's father, and six sons in this house—six fine men, though it was a hard birth I had with every one of them and they coming to the world—and some of them were found and some of them were not found, but they're gone now the lot of them. . . . There were Stephen, and Shawn, were lost in the great wind, and found after in the Bay of Gregory of the Golden Mouth, and carried up the two of them on the one plank, and in by that door.

[*She pauses for a moment; the girls start as if they heard something through the door that is half open behind them.*]

**Nora** (*in a whisper*). Did you hear that, Cathleen? Did you hear a noise in the northeast?

**Cathleen** (*in a whisper*). There's someone after crying out by the seashore.

**Maurya** (*continues without hearing anything*). There was Sheamus and his father, and his own father again, were lost in a dark night, and not a stick or sign was seen of them when the sun went up. There was Patch after was drowned out of a curragh[13] that turned over. I was sitting here with Bartley, and he a baby, lying on my two knees, and I seen two women, and three women, and four women coming in, and they crossing themselves, and not saying a word. I looked out then, and there were men coming after them, and they holding a thing in the half of a red sail, and water dripping out of it—it was a dry day, Nora—and leaving a track to the door.

[*She pauses again with her hand stretched out towards the door. It opens softly and old women begin to come in, crossing themselves on the threshold, and kneeling down in front of the stage with red petticoats over their heads.*]

**Maurya** (*half in a dream, to* Cathleen). Is it Patch, or Michael, or what is it at all?
**Cathleen.** Michael is after being found in the far north, and when he is found there how could he be here in this place?
**Maurya.** There does be a power of young men floating round in the sea, and what way would they know if it was Michael they had, or another man like him, for when a man is nine days in the sea, and the wind blowing, it's hard set his own mother would be to say what man was it.
**Cathleen.** It's Michael, God spare him, for they're after sending us a bit of his clothes from the far north.

[*She reaches out and hands* Maurya *the clothes that belonged to Michael.* Maurya *stands up slowly and takes them in her hands.* Nora *looks out.*]

**Nora.** They're carrying a thing among them and there's water dripping out of it and leaving a track by the big stones.
**Cathleen** (*in a whisper to the women who have come in*). Is it Bartley it is?
**One of the Women.** It is surely, God rest his soul.

[*Two younger women come in and pull out the table. Then men carry in the body of* Bartley, *laid on a plank, with a bit of a sail over it, and lay it on the table.*]

**Cathleen** (*to the women, as they are doing so*). What way was he drowned?
**One of the Women.** The gray pony knocked him into the sea, and he was washed out where there is a great surf on the white rocks.

[Maurya *has gone over and knelt down at the head of the table. The women are keening softly and swaying themselves with a slow movement.* Nora *and* Cathleen *kneel at the other end of the table. The men kneel near the door.*]

**Maurya** (*raising her head and speaking as if she did not see the people around her*). They're all gone now, and there isn't anything more the sea can do to me. . . . I'll have no call now to be up crying and praying when the wind breaks from the south, and you can hear the surf is in the east, and the surf is in the west, making a great stir with the two noises, and they hitting one on the other. I'll have no call now to be going down and getting Holy Water in the dark nights after Samhain,[14] and I won't care what way the sea is when the other women will be keening. (*To* Nora) Give me the Holy Water, Nora, there's a small sup still on the dresser.

[Nora *gives it to her.*]

---

13. **curragh** (kûr′ə ᴋʜ, kûr′ə); a small boat.

14. **Samhain** (sä′wĭn): November 1, the beginning of the Celtic winter half year and also a feast of the dead.

**Maurya** (*drops Michael's clothes across* Bartley's *feet, and sprinkles the Holy Water over him*). It isn't that I haven't prayed for you, Bartley, to the Almighty God. It isn't that I haven't said prayers in the dark night till you wouldn't know what I'd be saying; but it's a great rest I'll have now, and it's time surely. It's a great rest I'll have now, and great sleeping in the long nights after Samhain, if it's only a bit of wet flour we do have to eat, and maybe a fish that would be stinking. (*She kneels down again, crossing herself, and saying prayers under her breath.*)

**Cathleen** (*to an old man*). Maybe yourself and Eamon would make a coffin when the sun rises. We have fine white boards herself bought, God help her, thinking Michael would be found, and I have a new cake you can eat while you'll be working.

**The Old Man** (*looking at the boards*). Are there nails with them?

**Cathleen.** There are not, Colum; we didn't think of the nails.

**Another Man.** It's a great wonder she wouldn't think of the nails, and all the coffins she's seen made already.

**Cathleen.** It's getting old she is, and broken.

[Maurya *stands up again very slowly and spreads out the pieces of Michael's clothes beside the body, sprinkling them with the last of the Holy Water.*]

**Nora** (*in a whisper to* Cathleen). She's quiet now and easy; but the day Michael was drowned you could hear her crying out from this to the spring well.[15] It's fonder she was of Michael, and would anyone have thought that?

**Cathleen** (*slowly and clearly*). An old woman will be soon tired with anything she will do, and isn't it nine days herself is after crying and keening, and making great sorrow in the house?

**Maurya** (*puts the empty cup mouth downwards on the table, and lays her hands together on* Bartley's *feet*). They're all together this time, and the end is come. May the Almighty God have mercy on Bartley's soul, and on Michael's soul, and on the souls of Sheamus and Patch, and Stephen and Shawn (*bending her head*); and may He have mercy on my soul, Nora, and on the soul of everyone is left living in the world.

[*She pauses, and the keen rises a little more loudly from the women, then sinks away.*]

**Maurya** (*continuing*). Michael has a clean burial in the far north, by the grace of the Almighty God. Bartley will have a fine coffin out of the white boards, and a deep grave surely. What more can we want than that? No man at all can be living forever, and we must be satisfied.

[*She kneels down again and the curtain falls slowly.*]

---

15. **spring well:** a place where a spring rises from the ground.

## FOR STUDY AND DISCUSSION

**1.** In a classical tragedy such as *Antigone,* the protagonist meets destruction through some error in judgment or weakness in character. What is responsible for the catastrophe in *Riders to the Sea*?

**2.** How is Bartley's death foreshadowed?

**3.** Despite her great sorrow and lamentation, does Maurya behave with dignity and courage? Explain your answer.

**4.** The play ends on a note of resignation. Do you think that Maurya has gained a measure of wisdom from her suffering?

**5.** How does the author convince you that this is not only a personal tragedy for Maurya's family, but a universal tragedy?

## SUGGESTIONS FOR WRITING

**1.** The Introduction on page 650 states that in the modern theater, realism "explores in detail the characters of ordinary people and the world they live in." Show how this statement applies to *Riders to the Sea*.

**2.** Discuss the role of superstition in *Riders to the Sea*. In your discussion, tell how superstitition affects the mood of the play.

## ABOUT THE AUTHORS

Guy de Maupassant (1850–1893) was born and grew up in Normandy, a French province. When he was twenty, he enlisted in the French army and served in the Franco-Prussian War. After the war he worked as a government clerk in Paris. His first published story, *Boule de suif* ("Ball of Fat"), was hailed as a masterpiece. Although he wrote novels, travel sketches, and poems, he is best known as a short-story writer. His most famous story is "The Necklace." Maupassant's fame rests on his close and accurate observation of human life. Many of his tales, like "The Piece of Yarn," have an ironic ending.

Kate Chopin (1850–1904) was born in St. Louis, Missouri. After graduating from school she became part of the fashionable social scene in St. Louis, although she did not relish the role of society belle. She married in 1870 and settled in Louisiana, which became the setting for many of her stories. After her husband's death she took over the management of the family plantation and the village store. In 1884 she returned to St. Louis with her children and began her literary career. Her first collection of stories, *Bayou Folk*, appeared in 1894. Chopin valued spontaneity in literature and tended to write quickly, with a minimum of revision. In addition to short stories she wrote poems and novels.

William Maxwell (1908– ) was born in Lincoln, Illinois. His mother died when he was ten. His family moved to Chicago when he was fourteen. He attended the University of Illinois and after graduation received a scholarship to Harvard. He taught at the University of Illinois until 1933, when he decided to become a novelist. *Bright Center of Heaven*, which came out in 1934, was well received. Maxwell writes of family life with warmth and sensitivity. His work shows a deep understanding of young people. His third novel, *The Folded Leaf* (1945), is about the friendship of two boys growing up in the Midwest in the 1920's. The story "Love" which appeared in *The New Yorker*, is based on an incident in Maxwell's childhood.

Elizabeth Bishop (1911–1979) was born in Worcester, Massachusetts. She was raised in Nova Scotia and in Boston. She attended Vassar College. In 1934 she met Marianne Moore, whose poetry was an important influence on her own work. Bishop traveled widely and lived for periods in Key West, Florida, in Mexico, and in Brazil. Her first volume of verse was published in 1946. She received a number of awards and grants for her poetry, including the Pulitzer Prize in 1955 and the National Book Award in 1970. Her poetry is characterized by detailed observation and a disciplined technique. Among her collections of poetry are *Poems: North and South—A Cold Spring, Questions of Travel, Selected Poems*, and *Complete Poems*. In addition to poetry she wrote short stories.

John Millington Synge (1871–1909) was born near Dublin, Ireland. After graduating from Trinity College in 1892, Synge went abroad to continue his studies. Acting on a suggestion from William Butler Yeats, the Irish poet, Synge went to the Aran Islands, off the west coast of Ireland. In *Riders to the Sea* he depicts the hard life of the people who live in these bleak, rocky islands. Synge became one of the contributors to the Abbey Theatre, a repertory theater in Dublin associated with the Irish literary revival. When he died at the height of his career, he had completed only six plays. His masterpiece is generally acknowledged to be a comedy, *The Playboy of the Western World*.

# Guide to Literary Terms and Techniques

**ALLITERATION** *The repetition of consonant sounds in a group of words close together.* Most often, alliteration comes at the beginning of words, although it can appear in the middle and at the end of words as well.

One important function of alliteration is to give special emphasis to the words alliterated. Our ear hears them as having special value. This is one reason why advertising jingles use alliteration frequently. Advertisers and politicians have discovered that alliteration helps people remember what they have said. Abraham Lincoln once alliterated the beginning, middle, and end of two words: "Among free men there can be no successful appeal from the b̲a̲l̲l̲o̲t̲ to the b̲u̲l̲l̲e̲t̲."

Alliteration is most commonly used in poetry. An example of a heavily alliterated passage is this, from Ted Hughes's "The Lake":

S̲n̲uffles̲ at my feet̲ for what̲ I might̲ drop or kick̲ up,
S̲ucks̲ and s̲lobbers̲ the s̲tones̲, s̲norts̲ through its̲ lips̲

See **Assonance, Onomatopoeia.**
See also pages 344, 356.

**ALLUSION** *A reference to a work of literature or to a well-known historical event, person, or place.* The purpose of an allusion is to give us a fuller understanding of one thing by helping us to see it in comparison with something else we may know better.

Allusions to the Bible and to the works of Shakespeare are common because so many people have had exposure to both. Allusions to famous people and historical events are common for the same reason.

In older literature, allusion to Greek and Roman deities is common because classical literature was once basic to everyone's education. Apollo, when alluded to, implies the values of moderation, reason, and the arts. Dionysos implies passion and abandon, since he was associated with the use of wine. Aphrodite implies beauty, while her son, Eros, suggests love. Any allusion to these figures would carry a special meaning.

An allusion to the Ark would suggest the story of Noah and the Flood in the Bible. An allusion to Cain would suggest murder, since, according to Genesis, Cain was the first person to take another's life. An allusion to Jonah would suggest God's trial of Jonah who was swallowed by a whale but restored to the world of the living. In his poem "A Black Man Talks of Reaping," Arna Bontemps

alludes to a statement in the Bible that people reap what they sow, or get back what they put into something—or, at least they ought to. The speaker of the poem wonders why this has not been so for his people.

Historical events yield many sources of allusions. "Crossing the Rubicon," for example, refers to Julius Caesar's decision to defy Pompey by crossing the river that was to have been the limit of his territory. When he declared defiantly, but triumphantly, *"Veni. Vidi. Vici.,"* Caesar gave us another source of allusion—his statement "I came. I saw. I conquered."

See page 327.

**ANACHRONISM** *An event or a detail that is chronologically out of its proper time in history.* Anachronism comes from a Greek word meaning "out of time." If a character in an ancient Greek tragedy were shown driving off in a car, that would be an anachronism. Obviously, there were no cars in ancient Greece. Sometimes an anachronism is unintentional, with no particular effect, as when the clock strikes in William Shakespeare's play *Julius Caesar.* (There were, of course, no striking clocks in ancient Rome.) At other times, an anachronism may be used deliberately for effect, as in Mark Twain's *A Connecticut Yankee in King Arthur's Court.* Here, the intrusion of a modern figure into a medieval world provides a source of humor and satire, as when the Yankee holds off a group of knights who are astounded at the "magic" of his death-dealing revolvers.

See pages 437, 530.

**ANALOGY** *A comparison of two things, stressing their similarities.* Often analogies are used in arguments to convince someone of a point, but analogies are used in other types of writing and speaking as well. Emily Dickinson uses an analogy in her famous poem called "I Never Saw a Moor." She says that just as she believes in moors and the sea, though she has never seen them, so does she also believe in God and Heaven.

See page 227.

**ANTAGONIST** *A person or force that opposes the protagonist in a story or drama; an enemy of the hero or heroine.* Antagonist comes from a Greek word meaning "to struggle against." Famous antagonists in literature include the evil Professor Moriarty, in Arthur Conan Doyle's stories about Sherlock Holmes; and the great white whale, Captain Ahab's antagonist in Herman Melville's novel *Moby-Dick*.

See page 626.

**ARGUMENT** *A kind of speaking or writing which uses reason to try to change the way people think.* The most famous arguments in literature are the carefully reasoned arguments of the philosopher Socrates. We usually think of good argument as being like Socrates' discourses: he advanced from point to point according to logical principles of reasoning, in order to convince someone of the truth of a certain point of view. Argument is one of the major forms of discourse. Others are **description, exposition, narration,** and **persuasion.**

**ARTISTIC LICENSE** *Freedom to depart from known facts to create a story.* By the use of artistic license, a writer treating a historical person or event can change details to suit the purposes of his or her own work of literature. In their play *The Diary of Anne Frank*, dramatists Frances Goodrich and Albert Hackett use artistic license when they have Anne write an entry in her diary describing how the Nazis stormed her hiding place. In actual fact, the diary ends on August 1, and the Nazis arrived on August 4. There is no entry in Anne's diary recording the tragic events of August 4.

See page 272.

**ASIDE** *A dramatic convention in which a character turns "aside" to speak a few words directly to the audience or to another character, but is not supposed to be heard by others on the stage.* An aside allows the character to reveal plans or feelings unknown to others on the stage, or to make secret comments about other characters. For instance, in William Shakespeare's play *Othello*, the villain, Iago, has been working on a plan to ruin Othello. When Iago delivers the following speech, his plans are close to being realized, as he reminds the audience in an aside:

> Emilia, run you to the citadel,
> And tell my lord and lady what hath happed!
> Will you go on? I pray. [*Aside*] This is the night
> That either makes me or fordoes me quite.

See **Monologue, Soliloquy.**
See also page 533.

**ASSONANCE** *The repetition of vowel sounds in a group of words close together.* Assonance is used most frequently in poetry, both within a single line or within a group of lines.

Assonance differs from full **rhyme** in that in assonance only the vowels repeat; in full rhyme, the vowels and consonants repeat. *Find* and *mind* are an example of full rhymes, but *find* and *hive*, because of their repeated "i" sound, are an example of assonance. Another example of assonance appears in this line from Edgar Allan Poe's poem "The Bells," where the "o" sound is repeated three times:

> From the molten golden notes

See **Alliteration, Onomatopoeia.**
See also pages 344, 356.

**ATMOSPHERE** *The general mood or feeling established in a work of literature.* Atmosphere is usually produced by careful **description.** Landscapes, especially places like dark, dank moors, are effective in producing atmosphere.

See page 64.

**AUTOBIOGRAPHY** *Someone's account of his or her own life.* Generally, an autobiography is a narrative account, often chronological, of the important events of a person's life. Such accounts often relate the person's life story to crucial historical events that are happening at the same time. They also offer personal evaluation of actions, as well as some speculation on the significance of certain actions and events. People in the public eye frequently offer autobiographies as a way of setting the record straight as they see it. Benjamin Franklin's *Autobiography* and Winston Churchill's *My Early Life* are two classic autobiographies.

See **Biography.**
See also page 207.

**BALLAD** *A narrative poem that depends on regular verse patterns and strong rhymes for its effect.* Folk ballads, such as "Johnny Armstrong," originate as anonymous songs and are passed on orally before being written down. The so-called *literary ballad* is composed by a known writer, and it may or may not be sung. John Keats's "La Belle Dame sans Merci" is an example of a literary ballad. Most ballads have lots of action and adventure, and most are tragic. Desperadoes, such as Jesse James or Billy the Kid, are favorite ballad subjects.

See pages 371, 374.

**BIOGRAPHY** *An account of someone's life, written by another person.* Most libraries have an entire section devoted to biography because it is among the most popular forms of nonfiction. The biographical portraits of Emily Dickinson, the interesting American poet who became a kind of hermit, by Van Wyck Brooks ("Emily Dickinson") and William Luce (*The Belle of Amherst*) show that the art of writing biography is anything but matter-of-fact. Different ages see important people in different ways; that is one reason why new biographies of significant people appear all the time.

See **Autobiography.**
See also pages 207, 280.

**BLANK VERSE**  *Verse written in unrhymed iambic pentameter — that is, with each line usually containing five iambs, which consist of an unstressed syllable followed by a stressed syllable* (⌣ ´). The word *blank* means that the verse is not rhymed. The blank-verse line has become the great line for epic and dramatic poetry in English, perhaps because the English language seems to be strongly iambic. William Shakespeare's plays and John Milton's epics are written in blank verse. Usually a line of blank verse has exactly ten syllables; it almost always has five strong stresses.

When the Queen in William Shakespeare's play *Hamlet* describes the drowning of Ophelia, she uses blank verse:

> Whĕn dówn hĕr wéedў tróphĭes ănd hĕrsélf
> Fĕll ĭn thĕ wéepĭng brook. Hĕr clóthĕs spréad wíde,
> Ănd mérmaĭd-líke ăwhíle thĕy bóre hĕr úp

Modern poets — notably Robert Frost — also use the blank-verse line. Because it has no rhyme, blank verse seems very natural, but with the underlying iambic meter ever present, it also has a tightness and dependability.

See **Iambic Pentameter, Meter.**
See also pages 367, 626.

**CATASTROPHE**  *The conclusion of a tragic drama or story, following the period of falling action.* At the point of catastrophe, the conflicts have been resolved, with disastrous consequences for the tragic hero or heroine, and possibly for others as well. Thus, the catastrophe of William Shakespeare's play *Julius Caesar* occurs when Brutus kills himself. At this point, all the conspirators are dead, the inevitable result of the machinations and decisions made throughout the body of the play.

See page 594.

**CATHARSIS**  *In tragedy, the release of strong emotions in the audience.* The word comes from a Greek word meaning "cleanse." The philosopher Aristotle felt that it was good for people to watch a noble figure fall from power for daring to test fate or the gods. Tragedies were supposed to make people feel pity for the fallen hero or heroine, and terror that such things could happen. Aristotle felt that such tragedies would "cleanse" members of the audience of their own urges to rebel against fate or the gods, as the tragic figure did. Such catharsis, then, would improve the stability of society.

See page 526.

**CHARACTERIZATION**  *The methods used to present the personality of a character in a work of literature.* A writer can develop a character in many ways: by showing the character's actions and speech, by giving a physical description of the character, by revealing the character's thoughts, by revealing what others think about the character, and by commenting directly on the character. Any or all of these methods may be used in a given characterization.

Characterization may be *direct* or *indirect.* In *direct characterization,* the writer tells us explicitly what kind of person the character is. If the character is a disgusting person with disagreeable habits and a past record of mischief making, we will be told. In *indirect characterization,* the writer makes us figure out the character for ourselves. We are allowed to see the character in action, to hear the character speak, and to hear others talk about him or her, but we have to use our own minds to generalize about the *kind* of person we are reading about — whether good, bad, trustworthy, sneaky, cruel, and so on. Most writers use both direct and indirect methods of characterization.

See **Characters.**
See also pages 42, 50, 63, 553, 704.

**CHARACTERS**  *Persons — or animals or natural forces represented as persons — in a work of literature.* Characters may be classified in several ways. For instance, they may be called *static* or *dynamic,* depending on whether they stay the same throughout a work (static) or undergo a change in personality or attitude (dynamic). Leiningen, the plantation owner in Carl Stephenson's story "Leiningen Versus the Ants," is a static character. Though he has great adventures, he does not undergo any change in attitude or in personality in the story. On the other hand, Cress Delahanty, in Jessamyn West's story "Road to the Isles," is a dynamic character. The entire point of the story is to trace her change from naive confidence in her dancing abilities to a realization that she is not a good dancer at all.

Characters may also be classified as *flat* or *round.* *Flat* characters are merely sketched out for us and are not fully developed; they are called "flat" because they have only one dimension, or "side." Like Old Man Fat in Platero and Miller's story "Chee's Daughter," a flat character may be a *stereotype,* with one recognizable personality trait. *Round* characters are more fully developed; we see many sides of their personality and we come to appreciate their complexity, as if they were actual persons. For example, because we see many sides of the father in Woiwode's story "The Beginning of Grief," we recognize him as a fully developed, complex individual.

See **Characterization.**
See also pages 42, 56.

**CLIMAX** *The moment of highest emotional intensity in a plot, when the outcome of the conflict is finally made clear to us.* While the term may refer to any of several moments of intensity, it usually refers to the climax of the main conflict. The climax of William Shakespeare's play *Julius Caesar* takes place in the last act, when we watch the noble Brutus die.

In Jack Finney's story "Contents of the Dead Man's Pockets," the climax occurs four paragraphs from the end, when the man has succeeded in inching his way along the ledge of the building to the point where he can shoot his arm forward and break the glass of his apartment window. It is at this very suspenseful and tense moment that we know for certain that man has won his conflict and that he will *not* plunge to his death in the street below.

See **Plot.**
See also pages 19, 704.

**COMEDY** *A literary work, generally amusing, which usually ends happily because the hero or heroine is able to overcome obstacles and get what he or she wants.* Though comedy and tragedy are often associated with drama, both terms can also apply to novels and short stories.

Comedy is distinct from **tragedy** in that the comic characters normally find a satisfactory resolution of their difficulties. The focus of most comedies is not on a single figure, as is the case with tragedies, but on a group of figures, placed in a recognizable society. Very frequently, a comedy will have sev-

eral plots, each with a group of central characters. Part of the humor comes from seeing how these plots interact.

Comedy often seeks to poke fun at the social customs and "rules" held by some of the characters—quite often the very same customs and "rules" held by the audience. Such comedies often include a young couple (or several) who defy the conventions and "rules," and whose marriage is delayed because of the shortsightedness of the adults. Usually the adults reform, see the error of their ways, and permit the youngsters to marry. One of the great masters of dramatic comedy, apart from William Shakespeare, is George Bernard Shaw, whose comedies have also been popular as movies and as Broadway musicals.

Modern comedy seems to have developed from the Greek comedies of the fifth and sixth centuries B.C.

See page 482.

**CONFLICT** *A struggle between two opposing forces in a piece of literature.* Conflict may take many forms, and it may be *external* or *internal.*

1. Conflict may take place between two or more characters, as in Platero and Miller's "Chee's Daughter," in which Chee opposes his father-in-law for custody of his daughter.

2. Conflict may occur between a character and society, as in Kurt Vonnegut's "Harrison Bergeron," in which Harrison challenges the rules of a society which forces everyone to be the same.

3. Conflict may occur between a character and nature, as in Carl Stephenson's "Leiningen Versus the Ants," where the main character struggles against an army of flesh-eating ants.

4. Conflict may take place within a character's own mind, as in Sarah Orne Jewett's "A White Heron," where Sylvia's desire to please the young hunter conflicts with her love for the wild white heron.

Longer narratives may contain several conflicts, which are usually interrelated in some way. William Shakespeare's play *Julius Caesar* includes the following conflicts: a conflict within Brutus, about whether to take action against Caesar or not; a conflict between the ruler, Caesar, and the conspirators; and a conflict between the conspirators and Antony for the rule of Rome. All these conflicts are resolved by the last scene of the play, when each form of disorder, within and between characters and groups, is resolved into order.

It is the staging of conflict, and its resolution or lack of resolution, that often provides the impetus behind a work of literature.

See **Plot.**
See also pages 2, 19, 594, 704.

**CONNOTATION**  *The suggested meanings of a word or phrase; the meanings and feelings that have become associated with the word, in addition to its explicit meaning.* The dictionary explicitly defines *rat,* for example, as a long-tailed rodent. But the connotations of the word *rat* go beyond this literal meaning; the word suggests dirt, disease, and danger. When applied to a person, the word *rat* suggests someone untrustworthy, dangerous, and unable to keep a secret. The word *autumn* is defined explicitly as the season that comes between summer and winter. But *autumn* suggests more than this: it suggests the beginning of decay, the end of youth, the death of the year. Advertisers are very sensitive to the connotations of words. In advertising an apartment, for example, the owner would probably not call the rooms "small," but would describe them as "cozy," a word with pleasant connotations.

See **Denotation.**
See also pages 117, 303, 313.

**CONVENTIONS**  *Certain practices or methods that are accepted by a reader or an audience even though they are not realistic.* For example, one of the conventions of the Elizabethan theater was the use of verse in speech, something that is no longer a convention in drama today.

See page 533.

**COUPLET**  *A pair of successive rhymed lines of poetry.* The following poem is written in couplets:

**A Recollection**
*Frances Cornford*

My father's friend came once to tea.
He laughed and talked. He spoke to me.
But in another week they said
That friendly pink-faced man was dead.

"How sad . . ." they said, "the best of men . . ."
So I said too, "How sad"; but then
Deep in my heart I thought, with pride,
"I know a person who has died."

Couplets usually emphasize a completed thought. The rhyme establishes a tight sense of closure. This is particularly true in the **Shakespearean sonnet,** as in this final couplet from Sonnet 73:

This thou perceivest, which makes thy love more strong,
To love that well which thou must leave ere long.

See pages 337, 348, 391.

**DENOTATION**  *The explicit meaning of a word, as listed in a dictionary.* We distinguish denotation as a special quality because many writers also use the **connotations** of words to intensify meaning. Connotation differs from denotation in that connotation depends on associated or related meanings in addition to, or in place of, the strict, explicit definition of a word. The word *informer,* for example, has a denotation of one who gives information. However, its connotation is that of a person who sells out friends and is a kind of traitor.

See **Connotation.**
See also pages 117, 303.

**DESCRIPTION**  *A kind of writing that uses sensory details to re-create a person, a place, a thing, or an event.* Sensory details are those that appeal to the senses of sight, sound, smell, touch, and taste. Description often works to establish a mood, or to stir up emotion.

Description is one of the major forms of discourse. Others are **argument, exposition, narration,** and **persuasion.**

See pages 64, 169.

**DIALECT**  *Speech that is flavored by the usages of particular regional, social, or cultural groups.* Formal writing usually uses a variant of English known as standard English. Most people, however, speak an English which is characteristic of their region or their associations. Mark Twain, for example, represented the diction and the pronunciation of the Mississippi Valley in *The Adventures of Huckleberry Finn* and other writings.

See pages 389, 466.

**DIALOGUE**  *Conversation or speech among two or more characters.* Plays are usually constructed entirely out of dialogue.

The use of dialogue is especially prominent in modern fiction, perhaps because it makes a story seem more natural and fast-moving. Modern writers use dialogue to reveal character, to establish the conflict, to build suspense, and to move the action forward.

See page 171.

**DICTION** *A writer's choice of words.* One of the prime ingredients of a writer's style is *words*. The French master of the novel, Gustave Flaubert, often struggled for half a day trying to get *"le mot juste"*: the precisely correct word for what he wanted to say.

An old song uses two forms of diction to show what a difference words make:

> Show me the way to go home,
> I'm tired and I want to go to bed . . .

> Indicate the way to my habitual abode,
> I'm fatigued and I want to retire . . .

Writers use an informal diction to produce a natural-sounding easiness, as contemporary poet Mari Evans does in these opening lines from "When in Rome":

> Mattie dear
> the box is full . . .
> take
> whatever you like
> to eat . . .

Phyllis Wheatley, on the other hand, writing in the eighteenth century, used formal diction to produce a more "literary" effect, as in these lines from her poem written to the Earl of Dartmouth:

> Should you, my lord, while you pursue my song
> Wonder from whence my love of Freedom sprung,
> Whence flow these wishes for the common good,
> By feeling hearts alone best understood,
> I, young in life, by seeming cruel fate
> Was snatch'd from Afric's fancied happy seat

See pages 333, 764.

**DRAMA** *A story written to be acted out on a stage.* The playwright usually emphasizes character, conflict, and action which are developed by the use of dialogue. Stage directions are provided to help the actors and the director bring the characters and the action to life. When the play is presented, additional elements — such as the set, props, and lighting effects — are used to enhance the emotional impact of the story. Thus, drama is truly a living form of literature; the same drama can take on new shape and nuance each time it is represented on the stage by different actors, under different direction.

See **Comedy, Tragedy.**
See also page 481.

**DRAMATIC IRONY** *A device which allows an audience or a reader to know something that a character in a drama or story is unaware of.* When we understand something that a character does not yet know, we are drawn into the play or story, and we usually feel a heightened sense of suspense, anxiety, or secret pleasure.

One of the most famous examples of extended dramatic irony occurs in Sophocles' play *Oedipus the King.* Throughout the play, Oedipus tries to discover the murderer of the previous king, threatening to destroy the murderer once he is found. But it is Oedipus himself who has killed the king, though he does not know it. Ironically, every time he speaks in condemnation of the murderer, Oedipus is condemning himself.

In William Luce's play *The Belle of Amherst,* we hear Emily Dickinson worry about being a failure as a poet: "Perhaps no one will ever read my poems. They seem to me like an undelivered letter lost in transit." We feel the dramatic irony here very sharply because *we* know, as Dickinson did not, that in fact she does become a major American poet. A further irony is that Mr. Higginson, who is famous at the time of the play and who judges Dickinson's poems so harshly, is heard of no more today.

See **Irony.**
See also pages 127, 136, 595.

**DRAMATIC POETRY** *Poetry in which one or more characters speak.* Dramatic poetry allows the writer to reveal character directly through dialogue, just as a playwright does. For example, Robert Frost's poem "Death of the Hired Man" is written mainly as a conversation between a husband and wife. The dialogue reveals their personalities, their differences of opinion, and the plight and life story of the hired man who has worked for them over the years and has come home to die. John Keats's poem "La Belle Dame sans Merci" is a dramatic poem, written as a conversation between a traveler and a sickly knight encountered on the roadside.

One type of dramatic poem is the *dramatic monologue,* in which only one character speaks; the listener's replies are suggested but not quoted. Robert Browning is the most famous writer of dramatic monologues. His poem "The Laboratory" is spoken by a jealous woman. The entire poem consists of her speech to a pharmacist as he mixes a deadly poison which she plans to use on her rival.

See page 383.

**ELEGY** *A lyric poem which expresses mourning, usually over the death of an individual.* An elegy may also be a lament over the passing of life and beauty, or a meditation on the nature of death. An elegy is usually formal in language and structure, and solemn or even melancholy in tone. Most elegies are long. Some famous elegies in the English language include Thomas Gray's 128-line "Elegy Written in a Country Churchyard" and Walt Whitman's "When Lilacs Last in the Dooryard Bloom'd," a 16-part elegy mourning the assassination of President Lincoln.

See page 395.

**EPIC** *A long narrative poem that usually centers on a single important character who embodies the values of a particular society.* The term is often misused to mean anything huge in scope. However, the literary meaning of *epic* implies a heroic character, an action of great importance, and a range of adventures that often span hell (or the underworld), earth, and heaven (or the upper world of the gods). Some of the oldest known stories are told in epic form.

See page 371.

**EPITHET** *An adjective phrase used to set apart, describe, and characterize a person, place, or thing.* Some of the most well-known epithets are from literature: "wine-dark sea," "ox-eyed Hera," "rosy-fingered Dawn." All of these are from Homer's *Odyssey.* But many popular expressions, such as "Catherine the Great" or "America the Beautiful," are also useful epithets.

**ESSAY** *A brief examination of a subject in prose, usually expressing a personal or limited view of the topic.* The essay is a modern literary form, probably dating back to Michel de Montaigne's *Essais,* written in the sixteenth century. Along with Francis Bacon in the seventeenth century and Ralph Waldo Emerson in the nineteenth century, Montaigne gave us an approach that has remained standard for years. It is an approach that takes a single subject, such as "Friendship," "Style," or "Duty," and examines it from a personal point of view.

We expect that modern essays will reveal almost as much about the writer as about the subject. This is one of the qualities that helps keep the essay distinct from journalism and from the kinds of reports that scholars and scientists prepare from their research.

See pages 173, 286.

**EXAGGERATION** *Saying more than what is literally true, usually for humor or for emphasis.* Other terms for exaggeration are overstatement and **hyperbole.** We use exaggeration all the time in everyday conversation: "I'm so hungry I could eat a bear." "She hit the ball a mile." "It's raining cats and dogs." Exaggeration is a stock device used by humorists. Mark Twain uses exaggeration often, as in this statement from "I Find Fool Gold":

> One of the pleasantest and most invigorating exercises one can contrive is to run and jump across the Humboldt River till he is overheated, and then drink it dry.

The point of this comic lie is that the Humboldt is a very small river.

See **Hyperbole.**

**EXPOSITION** *The kind of writing that explains a subject or provides information.* The most familiar form of exposition is probably the informative magazine article, or the news account in the daily papers. The parts of Harry Crews' essay called "The Hawk Is Flying" in which he explains the process of hooding a hawk is exposition. R. J. Heathorn's entire essay "Learn with BOOK" is expository: it explains how this imaginary new product, BOOK, works. Other examples of exposition include the introductions to parts of this book.

In drama and novels and some short stories, exposition is the part of the **plot** that provides information about setting and about what has happened to the characters before the story starts. A remarkable use of exposition is made in William Shakespeare's play *The Tempest.* Just after the play opens, we are on an island, and Prospero starts to explain to his daughter Miranda (and to the audience) how they came to be living on this empty island. Prospero's exposition is so long and clumsy that Miranda begins to doze. Shakespeare, in providing this traditional bit of exposition, is having some fun with his audience and himself.

Exposition is one of the major forms of discourse. Others are **argument, description, narration,** and **persuasion.**

See pages 179, 286, 594.

**FABLE** *A very brief story told to teach a moral or lesson.* Often the characters in fables are animals who speak and act like humans. The best-known fables are those of Aesop, who may have been a slave in Greece, living around 600 B.C. Aesop's shrewd, satirical fables are still told today. "Belling the Cat" is one of his most famous:

The mice gathered to solve the problem of the cat who was making their lives miserable. All the mice agreed that the best solution was to place a noisy bell around the cat's neck, so that they could hear its approach and run away. Then came the terrible problem: Who would volunteer to put the bell on the cat? The moral is: "It is easy to propose impossible remedies."

The seventeenth-century writer Jean de La Fontaine also wrote fables, including the favorite called "The Fox and the Grapes."

The American humorist James Thurber's fables continue in the Aesop tradition. His "Fables for Our Time" use barbed wit to puncture our modern pretensions. See "The Scotty Who Knew Too Much" for an example.

See page 184.

**FALLING ACTION** *All the action in a play that follows the turning point.* In William Shakespeare's *Julius Caesar*, the **turning point** takes place in Act Three, when Antony delivers his emotional speech persuading the populace to see Caesar as a martyr and the conspirators as their enemies. The people do believe Antony, and from this moment Brutus and the other conspirators are doomed. From here on, the action is called "falling action" because it is falling toward a **catastrophe**, the deaths of the conspirators that take place in Act Five. The terms "rising" and "falling" action make us see the plot of tragic plays as being something like a pyramid: the rising action leads toward a peak, or turning point; the falling action takes place after this, and leads down toward a catastrophe (usually death) for the tragic hero.

See **Rising Action**.
See also page 594.

**FARCE** *A type of comic play in which ridiculous situations and characters, coarse wit, and physical buffoonery are used to make us laugh.* The American movies starring Abbott and Costello, Laurel and Hardy, and the Three Stooges are farces. Farce is used all the time in popular television comedies—such as when characters walk into doors, slip on banana peels, or hide under beds or in closets.

Serious plays, even tragedies, often use farcical elements for comic relief. William Shakespeare, who had a genius for farce, often puts his commoners into hilarious farcical situations. These scenes contrast with the more serious problems that his noble characters find themselves faced with. See the conversation of the workmen that opens his play *Julius Caesar*.

**FICTION** *Any work of literature that includes material that is invented or imagined, that is not a record of things as they actually happened.* In literature, the term *fiction* usually refers to the **novel** or the **short story**. Much fiction is based on actual personal experience, but it almost always involves invented characters, or invented actions or settings, or other details which are made up for the sake of the story itself.

In *The House of the Seven Gables*, Nathaniel Hawthorne uses a real setting, that of a house in Salem, Massachusetts. He also mentions some historical incidents, such as the Salem witch trials. But the main characters and events of his novel are fictional, created for the sake of developing the novel's themes.

John Steinbeck's novel *The Pearl* is set in an actual place, and it is based on a true story. Steinbeck, however, simply uses this true account and the actual setting as the springboard for a novel that is obviously fictional.

**FIGURATIVE LANGUAGE** *Language that is used to describe one thing in terms of something else; language that is not intended to be taken literally.* Figurative language depends upon a comparison made between two or more things that are basically unlike.

Figurative language is used in everyday conversation. For example, we might refer to someone as a "turkey." This is not suggesting that the person gobbles and would make a good meal; it is simply a way of insulting someone because turkeys are not very bright, nor very industrious. To say that someone is a "shrimp" does not mean that the person is an edible sea animal; it simply means, figuratively, that the person is rather small (as a shrimp is, compared with a whale).

**Metaphor** is the main form of figurative language. Metaphor is an identification of two things that can be directly stated ("My love *is* a red rose"), or that can be implied or suggested ("My love has a rosy bloom"). Neither of these descriptions is meant to be taken literally (no one *is* a rose, nor does anyone bloom and open petals). Each description is figurative.

**Simile** is another common form of figurative language. A simile is straightforward. It always makes its comparison by using a specific word, such as *like, as, than,* or an equivalent ("My love is *like* a red rose").

**Personification**— speaking of an animal or an inanimate thing as if it were human — is a special form of metaphor. When Isabella Gardener in "Summer Remembered" speaks of the "quarreling of oarlocks," she is personifying the oarlocks as people. She is comparing the sounds made by the wooden oars to the noise of human argument.

A **symbol** is something (such as a dove, or a rose, or a journey) that is used to stand for itself and for something more than itself as well (such as peace, or love, or life).

See **Metaphor, Personification, Simile, Symbol.**
See also pages 96, 216, 308.

**FIGURE OF SPEECH** *Any expression that uses language figuratively, not literally.* **Metaphors, similes, personifications,** and **symbols** are all figures of speech.

See **Figurative Language.**

**FLASHBACK** *A scene in a story or play that interrupts the present action to tell about events that happened at an earlier time.* Most narratives are told in chronological order — that is, the order in which they occur in time. But often a flashback is needed to make the present action more understandable to the reader. Sarah Orne Jewett uses a flashback in her story "A White Heron." The second and third paragraphs flash back in time to tell us something about the little girl's background. The fourth paragraph picks up the chronological order begun in the first paragraph.

See page 143.

**FOIL** *A character (or a place or an event) that is used to contrast with another character (or place or event).* For example, in William Shakespeare's play *Julius Caesar,* the character of Cassius — a scheming and ambitious man — is used as a foil to the character of Brutus — an idealistic and unselfish man. *Foil* is also the word for a metallic material that gives off a reflection (as in *tinfoil*). A character who is a *foil* to someone else sets the other person off, and brings out his or her particular characteristics.

**FORESHADOWING** *The use of clues that hint at important plot developments that are to follow*
*in a story or drama.* While foreshadowing is primarily used as a plot device, it may also help in the creation of mood, causing us to feel suspense and anxiety. Charles Dickens is a master of this technique. In his novel *Oliver Twist* he hints many times at the true parentage of Oliver, who is an orphan. Soon after Oliver is born in a workhouse, his mother dies. She never tells anyone who she is or where she comes from. When Mr. Brownlow (who turns out later to be Oliver's grandfather) sees Oliver for the first time, he mutters to himself: "There is something in that boy's face . . . . Where have I seen something like that before?" When Oliver goes to Mr. Brownlow's house and sees the picture of a lady (who turns out later to be Oliver's dead mother), he feels "as if it was alive, and wanted to speak to me, but couldn't." These and other foreshadowings in the story help to create a mood of suspense and doubt. They intrigue us as readers, so that we anxiously read on to find out whether Oliver will discover his true identity and be rescued from his perilous situation.

See page 41.

**FRAMEWORK STORY** *A story that contains another story within it.* Saki's "The Storyteller" is an example of a framework story. The frame story is the story about the bachelor meeting the aunt and her rebellious charges in a railway car. The inner story is the tale the bachelor tells about the horribly good heroine, Bertha, who is devoured by a wolf.

**FREE VERSE** *Poetry that doesn't have a fixed line length, stanza form, rhyme scheme, or meter.* Free verse is an important modern verse technique and has caused some confusion. Older poetry was always written in regular form, with meter and rhyme, and many people still expect poets to follow this tradition. But modern poets, in order to strike out in new directions, often employ free verse to give expression to their own thoughts and to reorganize our expectations. Sometimes free verse relies on the kinds of pauses we hear in conversation, thus giving an easiness to the poetry. Although it does not use fixed rhymes or fixed rhythms, free verse may make use of rhyme and rhythm, as well as other poetic techniques, such as **alliteration, figurative language,** and **onomatopoeia.**

Marge Piercy uses free verse in this short poem, which is about love. Notice how rhythm in the poem is created by the use of repetition.

**Simple-Song**
*Marge Piercy*

When we are going toward someone we say
you are just like me
your thoughts are my brothers
word matches word
how easy to be together.

When we are leaving someone we say
how strange you are
we cannot communicate
we can never agree
how hard, hard and weary to be together.

We are not different nor alike
but each strange in his leather body
sealed in skin and reaching out clumsy hands
and loving is an act
that cannot outlive
the open hand
the open eye
the door in the chest standing open.

See pages 361, 369.

**HYPERBOLE**   *A figure of speech that uses exaggeration or overstatement for effect.* In these opening lines from her poem "Notes Written on a Damp Veranda," Phyllis McGinley uses hyperbole to emphasize how often it rains on her vacation.

Do they need any rain
In Portland, Maine?
   Does Texas pray for torrents,
The water supply
Run dry, run dry,
   From the ancient wells of Florence?
Is the vintage grape
In perilous shape
   On the slopes of Burgundy?
Let none despair
At the arid air—
   They've only to send for me.
Invite me to stay for a holiday
   And the rain will follow me.

See **Exaggeration**.
See also page 389.

**IAMBIC PENTAMETER**   *Five iambs ($\smile$ $'$) in a line of poetry.* An *iamb* is an unaccented syllable followed by an accented syllable ($\smile$ $'$). Iambic pentameter is one of the most basic and natural of English verse lines. *Penta-* is the Greek prefix for "five"; *meter* is the Greek for "measure." Most of Shakespeare's plays, all of Milton's *Paradise Lost*, and a great deal of modern poetry is written in iambic pentameter. Anne Bradstreet, the first American poet of note, uses iambic pentameter in her poem "To My Dear and Loving Husband":

My love is such that rivers cannot quench

See **Meter**.
See also pages 361, 367.

**IMAGERY**   *Words or phrases that use description to create pictures, or images, in the reader's mind.* Most images appeal directly to our sense of sight, but images can also appeal to our senses of sound, taste, smell, or touch.

The purpose of imagery is to help us re-create in our own minds the situation which the writer imagines, so that we can react as we would to the thing or the experience itself.

In these final lines from her poem "Venus Transiens," Amy Lowell describes a beautiful woman in several striking images that appeal to our senses of sight, sound, and touch:

For me,
You stand poised
In the blue and buoyant air,
Cinctured by bright winds,
Treading the sunlight.
And the waves which precede you
Ripple and stir
The sands at my feet.

See pages 291, 573, 762.

**INVERSION**   *The reversal of the usual order of words in a sentence.* Emily Dickinson, in the first stanza of her poem "For Each Ecstatic Instant," inverts the normal order of the verb *pay* and of its object *anguish*. This inversion emphasizes the word *anguish*—what the poet feels we must pay for the intense moments we experience:

For each ecstatic instant
We must an anguish pay
In keen and quivering ratio
To the ecstasy.

Sometimes the inversion is used for technical reasons. Edgar Allan Poe, for instance, in his poem "The Raven," almost certainly inverted words in the following sentence to get a rhyme for the word *nevermore* (which appears in a preceding line):

But the Raven, sitting lonely on the placid bust, spoke only
That one word, as if his soul in that one word he did outpour.

See page 333.

**IRONY** *A contrast or discrepancy between what is stated and what is really meant, or between what is expected to happen and what actually does happen.* Three kinds of irony are (1) *verbal irony,* in which a writer or speaker says one thing and means something entirely different; (2) *dramatic irony,* in which a reader or an audience perceives something that a character in the story or play does not know; and (3) *irony of situation,* in which the writer shows a discrepancy between the expected result of some action or situation and its actual result.

The character Antony in William Shakespeare's play *Julius Caesar* uses *verbal irony* when he keeps repeating in his funeral oration over Caesar's body: "For Brutus is an honorable man." Anthony is a political enemy of Brutus and does not think his participation in Caesar's murder was honorable.

Examples of *dramatic irony* are also found throughout *Julius Caesar.* For example, the audience knows from history that Caesar will be murdered by members of the Senate, but Caesar himself does not know this. The audience also hears the conspirators actually planning to murder Caesar, but Caesar himself is ignorant of the plot.

An example of *irony of situation* is found in Saki's story "The Storyteller." We would expect children to like stories that end with people living happily ever after. But in Saki's tale, we have a situation in which three children think the most beautiful story they have ever heard is one in which the heroine provides supper for a wolf with a black tongue. This situation reminds us, as irony often does, that life is unpredictable and that what we think is appropriate is not always what is true.

See pages 127, 136, 143, 338, 594, 762.

**LITERAL LANGUAGE** *Language that states facts or ideas directly.* Literal language means exactly what it says; it does not depend on hidden meanings. Literal language is the opposite of **figurative language.** We expect to find literal language used in factual writings, where precision and clarity are important.

**LOCAL COLOR** *The use of specific details describing the speech, dress, customs, and scenery associated with a particular region or section of a country.* The purpose of local color is to suggest the unique flavor of a specific locale. In the years following the Civil War, stories of local color flourished in the United States. Bret Harte uses the local color of the West in such stories as "The Outcasts of Poker Flat." Mark Twain re-creates the local color of a small town along the Mississippi in his novels *The Adventures of Tom Sawyer* and *The Adventures of Huckleberry Finn.* Sarah Orne Jewett uses the local color of rural Maine in her stories, such as "A White Heron."

See page 79.

**LYRIC POETRY** *Verse, usually brief, which focuses on the emotions or thoughts of the speaker.* Originally, the term *lyric* derived from the fact that in ancient Greece, certain poems were recited to the strumming of a lyre—a guitarlike instrument. The musical accompaniment helped intensify the emotional quality of the poem.

It is usual, as in John Crowe Ransom's lyric "Blue Girls," for the lyric poet to express a single or primary emotion, to which we relate as readers. It is also usual, as in Ransom's poem, for the emotion to be implied, rather than stated or named directly.

See **Poetry.**
See also page 387.

**METAPHOR** *A comparison made between two things which are basically dissimilar, with the intent of giving added meaning to one of them.* Metaphor is one of the most important forms of **figurative language.** Gwendolyn Brooks uses a metaphor in the opening lines of her poem "The Ballad of Rudolph Reed," when she says:

Rudolph Reed was oaken.
His wife was oaken too.

This metaphor compares two people to oak trees. On one level, this metaphor suggests that Rudolph Reed and his wife are dark-skinned. But it suggests much more than this. Rudolph Reed and his wife, the metaphor suggests, also have the solidity and the strength of the oak tree.

Many metaphors are not directly stated but implied, or suggested. An *implied metaphor* does not directly tell us that one thing *is* another different thing. When Walt Whitman exclaims, "Old age superbly rising!" he uses an implied metaphor. The word *rising* implies that he is comparing the onset of age with the rising of the sun. This is a particularly rich metaphor because it reverses our usual notion that age is a decline; according to this metaphor, old age is a new beginning.

Marianne Moore uses implied metaphors in the following poem about an American dancer, director of the Harlem Dance Theater. Three metaphors basic to this poem are the comparisons of the dancer to a dragon-fly, to a gem, and to a peacock:

**Arthur Mitchell**
*Marianne Moore*

Slim dragon-fly
  too rapid for the eye
    to cage.

contagious gem of virtuosity
make visible, mentality.
Your jewels of mobility

reveal
  and veil
    a peacock-tail.

An *extended metaphor* is a metaphor that is extended throughout a poem. In "She Sweeps with Many-Colored Brooms" by Emily Dickinson, the metaphor comparing the sunset to a housewife is extended throughout the entire poem.

A *dead metaphor* is a metaphor which has become so commonplace that it has lost its force, and we forget that it is not literally true. Some examples are the *foot* of a hill, the *head* of the class, and the *eye* of the needle.

A *mixed metaphor* is the use of two or more inconsistent metaphors in one expression. When they are examined, mixed metaphors make no sense. Mixed metaphors are often unintentionally humorous: "To hold the fort, he'd have to shake a leg" or "We're skating on a very gray area."

See **Figurative Language.**
See also pages 199, 308, 315, 317, 319, 610.

**METER**  *The regular pattern of rhythm—that is, of stressed and unstressed syllables in a line of verse.* Most poetry respects the normal stress that words ordinarily have. For example, we know that the accent should fall on the second syllable of *indeed.* This is the way most English-speaking people pronounce the word. In a line of poetry, the word would also be sounded to respect this pronunciation.

In metrical analysis the sign (⌣) means the syllable is unstressed. The sign (ˊ) means the syllable receives stress. The sign (|||) is used to separate metrical feet. A *metrical foot* usually consists of one stressed syllable and one or more unstressed syllables. Some of the principal metrical feet in English (with their adjectival forms in parentheses) are the following:

*Iamb* (iambic):⌣ˊ as in indeed.
*Trochee* (trochaic):ˊ⌣ as in hárkĕn.
*Anapest* (anapestic):⌣⌣ˊ as in comprehend.
*Dactyl* (dactylic):ˊ⌣⌣ as in fávŏrĭte.
*Spondee* (spondaic):ˊˊ as in upsét.

**Iambic pentameter** is one of the basic meters in English. Verse in iambic pentameter has five feet (*penta-* is the Greek prefix for "five"), most of which are iambs (⌣ˊ). The following line from "On Hearing a Symphony of Beethoven" by Edna St. Vincent Millay uses absolutely regular iambic pentameter:

This móment is the bést the wórld căn gíve

A metrical line is named for its pattern and number of feet: *iambic pentameter* has five iambs; *iambic tetrameter* has four iambs; *trochaic trimeter* has three trochees; and so on.

There are several "secrets" to keep in mind when you are *scanning* a line, or determining its metrical pattern. First, look for the most important words. They usually get an accent. Second, speak the line aloud, listening to where you give emphasis. Third, rely on a good dictionary to help with difficult words.

See **Iambic Pentameter, Rhythm.**
See also pages 361, 364.

**MONOLOGUE**  *A long speech in a play or story, delivered by a single person.* A monologue is delivered in the presence of one or more other characters; a **soliloquy** is delivered while the speaker is alone.

In William Shakespeare's play *Julius Caesar,* the characters frequently use monologues. An example is Cassius' speech in Act One, Scene 2, beginning "Why, man, he doth bestride the narrow world."

In poetry, a monologue may constitute the entire poem. This is called a *dramatic monologue,* a technique Robert Browning often uses. In his poem "The Laboratory," a woman talks to a silent chemist, revealing her twisted character as she watches poison being made for her rival.

See page 383.

**MORAL**  *A practical lesson about right and wrong conduct, often stated at the conclusion of an instructive story such as a fable.* Morals usually instruct us to "do" or "not do" certain things. The moral in the following verse is stated in the last two lines.

**Advice to Travelers**
*Walker Gibson*

A burro once, sent by express,
His shipping ticket on his bridle,
Ate up his name and his address,
And in some warehouse, standing idle,
He waited till he like to died.
The moral hardly needs the showing:
Don't keep things locked up deep inside—
Say who you are and where you're going.

See page 149.

**MOTIVATION** *The reasons, either stated or implied, for a character's behavior.* To make a story believable, a writer must provide characters with motivation that explains what they do. Characters may be motivated by outside events, or they may be motivated by inner needs or fears.

See page 63.

**NARRATION** *The kind of writing or speaking that relates a series of events (a narrative).* Narration explains what happened, when it happened, and to whom it happened. While narration is usually associated with fiction, it may also be used in nonfiction, such as in an essay or a biography. A narrative may be of almost any length, from short anecdotes, fables, and ballads; to longer narrative poems and short stories; to lengthy works such as epics and novels.

Narration is one of the major forms of discourse. Others are **argument, description, exposition,** and **persuasion.**

See page 169.

**NARRATIVE POETRY** *Poetry that tells a story.* A narrative poem can be as long as an **epic,** that is, several thousand lines, or it can be as short as a popular **ballad.** Homer's *Odyssey,* Keats's "La Belle Dame sans Merci," and Tennyson's "The Passing of Arthur" are all narrative poems.

See page 371.

**NARRATOR** *One who narrates, or tells, a story.* A writer may choose to have a story told by a *first-person* narrator, someone who is either a major or minor character in the story. Or a writer may choose to use a *third-person* narrator, someone who is not in the story at all. In this case, we think of the author of the story as being the narrator. Third-person narrators are often *omniscient,* or "all-knowing"—that is, they are able to enter into the minds of all the characters in the story.

Frank O'Connor's short story "The Duke's Children" is told by an "I" who is one of the characters in the story. This narrator is named Larry Delaney. He can reveal his own thoughts, of course, but he can report only what he *thinks* goes on in the minds of other characters.

Maurice Walsh's short story "The Quiet Man" is told by a third-person narrator. This narrator, who is not in the story at all, is omniscient and so can tell us what any one of the characters is thinking and feeling.

The word *narrator* can also refer to a character in a drama who guides the audience through the play, often commenting on the action and sometimes participating in it. Thornton Wilder uses such a narrator in his play *Our Town.*

An awareness of who the narrator is, of what the narrator's attitudes are, and of whether the narrator is trustworthy is of key importance in understanding a story. For instance, in Toni Cade Bambara's story "Blues Ain't No Mockin Bird," the reader must keep in mind that the events of the story are being narrated by a character who is a young girl. We can only guess at the way the adults in that story feel about the conflict with the cameraman, but we gain a vivid insight into the way the adults' behavior affects the children who are looking on.

See **Point of View.**
See also page 80.

**NONFICTION** *Prose that deals with real events and people, not with imagined events and imagined people.* In nonfiction, the characters, settings, and actions must conform to what is true; they cannot be manipulated by the imagination of the writer.

Two of the most popular forms of nonfiction are the **biography** and **autobiography,** which narrate the events of someone's life. **Essays** are another form, as are newspaper articles, journals, diaries, and magazine articles.

Nonfiction relies on all major forms of discourse: **description,** which gives sensory information; **narration,** which tells of a series of events; **exposition,** which explains a process or situation; and **persuasion** or **argument,** which tries to change the way a reader acts or thinks about something.

See page 173.

**NOVEL** *A long fictional narrative written in prose, usually having many characters and a* strong plot. Because it is longer than a short story, the novel usually allows for greater complexity of character and plot development. However, since the novel is a relatively new form of literature, first taking shape in the eighteenth century, it is constantly being redefined as writers continue to experiment with the form.

The broad term *novel* includes a variety of subclassifications or types. The *Gothic novel* is one of the earliest forms, and it remains popular today. Gothic novels create an atmosphere of mystery and danger in a picturesque setting, usually involving a threat combined with love intrigue for a romantic young heroine. Charlotte Brontë's *Jane Eyre* is an early example of a Gothic novel. The *historical novel* creates the atmosphere, customs, and events of an actual historical period, and may even include actual historical figures. William Thackeray's *Vanity Fair* is an early example of a historical novel; James Michener's *Chesapeake* is a more recent one. The *psychological novel* explores the complex emotional lives of the characters. *Crime and Punishment* by the Russian writer Fyodor Dostoyevsky is an example. Other popular forms of the novel include *detective stories*, *spy thrillers*, *science fiction*, and *fantasies*.

See page 703.

**OCTAVE** *A grouping of eight lines of verse, as in the first eight lines of a Petrarchan (or Italian) sonnet.* The eight lines are usually grouped together because they develop a single subject. The last six lines of a Petrarchan sonnet are also a group, called a **sestet**.

See **Petrarchan Sonnet.**

**ODE** *A complex and often lengthy lyric poem, written in a dignified, formal style on some serious subject.* Odes are used in Sophocles' Greek drama *Antigone* to conclude each scene, where they comment on such profound topics as the wonders of human creation, the workings of fate, and the power of love.

**ONOMATOPOEIA** *The use of a word whose sound imitates or reinforces its meaning.* In everyday speech, words such as *whoosh*, *tick-tock*, *zoom*, and *purr* are onomatopoetic. Another example is *popcorn*, which is named to echo its peculiar behavior.

See pages 344, 356.

**PARABLE** *A short, simple tale, usually about an ordinary, familiar event, from which a moral or religious lesson is drawn.* The Zen masters in Japan frequently use parables for religious or moral instructions. Some of the most famous parables are those used by Jesus in the New Testament. John Steinbeck considered his short novel *The Pearl* a kind of parable that reveals something about the nature of good and evil. Steinbeck tells his story in the simple style typical of traditional parables.

**PARADOX** *A statement that reveals a kind of truth, although it seems at first to be self-contradictory and untrue.* In the following poem, Countee Cullen presents a paradox. Though his grandmother is dead, he believes she will grow again.

### For My Grandmother
*Countee Cullen*

This lovely flower fell to seed;
Work gently sun and rain;
She held it as her dying creed
That she would grow again.

See page 340.

**PARALLELISM** *The repetition of words, phrases, or clauses that are similar in structure or in meaning.* Parallelism is used extensively in the Psalms in the Bible, where the meaning of one statement is often repeated, in a different way, in the next. This example is from Psalm 34:

I will bless the Lord at all times:
his praise shall continually be in my mouth.

Several famous uses of parallelism are found in Abraham Lincoln's Gettysburg Address. In this sentence from the speech, the repetition of the subject and part of the verb emphasizes Lincoln's point and gives his words a stately rhythm:

But, in a larger sense, we cannot dedicate — we cannot consecrate — we cannot hallow — this ground.

Christina Rossetti uses parallelism several times in this poem:

### Song
*Christina Rossetti*

When I am dead, my dearest,
  Sing no sad songs for me;
Plant thou no roses at my head,
  Nor shady cypress tree:
Be the green grass above me
  With showers and dewdrops wet;
And if thou wilt, remember,
  And if thou wilt, forget.

*Guide to Literary Terms and Techniques*  **847**

I shall not see the shadows,
   I shall not feel the rain;
I shall not hear the nightingale
   Sing on, as if in pain;
And dreaming through the twilight
   That doth not rise nor set,
Haply I may remember,
   And haply may forget.

**PARAPHRASE**   *A rewording of a text or of a passage from a text, often for the purpose of clarification or simplification.* A paraphrase differs from a summary in that it may be as long as, or even longer than, the original text. While the paraphrase may help us to understand more clearly what happens in the passage at hand, it does so at the expense of style, or atmosphere, or ambiguity — effects that may have been an important part of the original work. For example, here is a poem by Emily Dickinson, and a paraphrase:

### My Life Closed Twice Before Its Close
*Emily Dickinson*

My life closed twice before its close;
It yet remains to see
If Immortality unveil
A third event to me,

So huge, so hopeless to conceive
As these that twice befell.
Parting is all we know of heaven,
And all we need of hell.

I have felt as if I had died twice in my life, when I parted from a person I loved, and I am wondering whether my own death will reveal such deep emotions, impossible to put into words, as these previous "deaths" did. When we part from someone we love, our memory of why we loved them, of our happiness with them, can help us understand what heaven might be like; at the same time, our grief and pain at losing them makes us feel that we know what hell might be like.

The paraphrase might help someone who is reading the poem for the first time to understand what the poem "says," but it loses the impact and possibilities of meaning contained in the original.

See pages 317, 340, 418.

**PARODY**   *The imitation of a piece of literature or music or art, for amusement or instruction.* Literary parodies are ways of poking fun at the high seriousness of some writers and of some forms of literature. Parodies are also ways of poking fun at those who take the literature too seriously.

Dorothy Parker's poem "One Perfect Rose" opens with the kind of language used in some poems celebrating love. The parody begins when the poet shifts her tone and suggests that a limousine might be a better gift than a rose.

The more pronounced and distinct a style is, the easier it is to write a parody. "Sea Fever" by John Masefield is a case in point, as this parody of the opening lines suggests:

### C Fever: Bringing Home the Report Card

I must go down to the living room, to face
   the music go I,
And all I ask is a feeble excuse and some
   luck to get me by,
And my mom is miffed and I can't speak up
   and my knees are shaking,
And a gray mist's on my dad's face, and my
   voice starts quaking.

**PERSONIFICATION**   *A figure of speech in which something nonhuman is given human characteristics or feelings.* Elizabeth Bishop personifies factories in the opening lines of her poem "Varick Street." She describes the factories as if they were people who have to work at night.

At night the factories
struggle awake,
wretched uneasy buildings
veined with pipes
attempt their work.
Trying to breathe,
the elongated nostrils
haired with spikes
give off such stenches, too.

See **Figurative Language.**
See also page 308.

**PERSUASION**   *A kind of speaking or writing that is intended to influence people's actions.* Newspaper editorials and other essays that present a particular opinion on an issue, commercials and other advertisements, propaganda and other kinds of political speeches and handbills are all forms of persuasion. Persuasion is one of the principal forms of discourse; others are **argument, description, exposition,** and **narration.**

**PETRARCHAN SONNET**   *A lyric poem of fourteen lines, written in iambic pentameter, with an octave (first eight lines) that establishes a position or problem, and a sestet (last six lines) that resolves it.* Usually the **octave** is rhymed *abbaabba* and the **sestet** *cdecde; cdccdc;* or *cdedce.* The form was popularized by the Italian poet Francesco Petrarch in the thirteenth century. It is also called the *Italian sonnet.*

The American poet Edna St. Vincent Millay became an expert at the sonnet form. The following poem is written in the Petrarchan style, though Millay has departed from the traditional rhyme scheme in the sestet.

### I Shall Go Back
*Edna St. Vincent Millay*

a  I shall go back again to the bleak shore
b  And build a little shanty on the sand
b  In such a way that the extremist band
a  Of brittle seaweed will escape my door
a  But by a yard or two, and nevermore
b  Shall I return to take you by the hand;
b  I shall be gone to what I understand
a  And happier than I ever was before.

c  The love that stood a moment in your eyes,
d  The words that lay a moment on your tongue,
c  Are one with all that in a moment dies,
d  A little under-said and over-sung;
c  But I shall find the sullen rocks and skies
d  Unchanged from what they were when I was young.

See **Sonnet.**
See also page 391.

**PLOT** *The sequence of related events that make up a story or a drama.* It is important to remember that a plot shows us a *relationship* among events. Plots may be very simple, or, as in many novels, they may be complex and consist of a major plot plus one or more **subplots**. The major element in most plots is **conflict**.

In the past, plot has been of greater importance in the novel or short story than it often is today. A traditional plot structure might have the following elements: a section of **exposition**, which gives background information on such things as character and setting; a series of complications that develop the **conflict**; a **climax**, the point where the main conflict is finally solved; and a denouement, or a final unraveling of all the complications of the plot. A traditional plot of this sort is found in Maurice Walsh's short story "The Quiet Man," where our interest focuses on what happens in the conflict between the bully and the quiet man.

In more modern writings, however, plot is often minor, and might be almost nonexistent; in such a case, character and the inner states of the mind are dominant. This kind of minimal plot can be seen in Woiwode's story "The Beginning of Grief," where our major interest is not in what happens but in what the characters are experiencing emotionally.

See pages 2, 594, 704, 762.

**POETRY** *Traditionally, poetry is language arranged in lines with a regular rhythm and often with a definite rhyme scheme. Experimental poetry often does away with regular patterns of meter and rhyme, but it usually is set up in lines.* The density of meaning suggested by **imagery**, by **figurative language**, and by **rhythm** distinguishes poetry from other uses of language. As with many things, it is more difficult to define poetry than it is to recognize it. It surprises many people to discover that poetry is a very old form of human expression; prose, on the other hand, is fairly recent.

Poetry can tell a story (**narrative poetry**) or it can express an emotion or idea (**lyric poetry**). We often expect poetry to be set up in groups of lines called **stanzas**. Some of the common poetic forms are the **ballad**, the **epic**, and the **sonnet**.

See pages 298, 417.

**POINT OF VIEW** *The vantage point from which a narrative is told.* There are numerous possibilities for point of view, but three are most frequent: (1) *omniscient point of view*, (2) *limited third-person point of view*, and (3) *first-person point of view*.

In the *omniscient point of view* (often called the "all-knowing" point of view), the narrator can take us all over the world, allow us to see into the minds of all the characters, and help us to see events from several points of view. Ursula Le Guin, in her fantasy novel *A Wizard of Earthsea*, writes from an omniscient point of view:

> The island of Gont, a single mountain that lifts its peak a mile above the storm-racked Northeast Sea, is a land famous for wizards. From the towns in its high valleys and the ports on its dark narrow bays many a Gontishman has gone forth to serve the Lords of the Archipelago in their cities as wizard or mage, or, looking for adventure, to wander working magic from isle to isle of all Earthsea. Of these some say the greatest, and surely the greatest voyager, was the man called Sparrowhawk, who in his day became both dragonlord and Archmage. His life is told of in the *Deed of Ged* and in many songs, but this is a tale of the time before his fame, before the songs were made.

In the *limited third-person point of view*, the writer tells the story from the vantage point of one character in that story. In her novel *A Tree Grows in Brooklyn*, Betty Smith tells a story from the vantage point of her main character, a young girl named Francie. This helps us feel as if we are inside Francie's mind, participating in events in just the way she does:

The library was a little old shabby place. Francie thought it was beautiful. The feeling she had about it was as good as the feeling she had about church. She pushed open the door and went in. She liked the combined smell of worn leather bindings, library paste and freshly inked stamping pads better than she liked the smell of burning incense at High Mass.

In the *first-person point of view*, an "I" tells the story. This "I" is usually a character in the story. Our perception of all the other characters and events in the story is limited to the way this one character sees them and tells us about them. Richard Wright uses the first-person point of view to tell the story of his own life in *Black Boy*:

One winter morning in the long-ago, four-year-old days of my life I found myself standing before a fireplace, warming my hands over a mound of glowing coals, listening to the wind whistle past the house outside. All morning my mother had been scolding me, telling me to keep still, warning me that I must make no noise. And I was angry, fretful, and impatient. In the next room Granny lay ill and under the day and night care of a doctor and I knew that I would be punished if I did not obey. I crossed restlessly to the window and pushed back the long fluffy white curtains—which I had been forbidden to touch—and looked yearningly out into the empty street.

See **Narrator**.
See also pages 80, 95, 102, 108, 705.

**PROTAGONIST** *The central character in a story or drama, the one whom we, as readers or audience, are supposed to sympathize with.* The protagonist's enemy is the **antagonist.** The protagonist can be admirable and distinguished, such as Brutus in Shakespeare's play *Julius Caesar*, or foolish and very ordinary, such as Tom Benecke in Jack Finney's story "Contents of the Dead Man's Pockets."

See **Antagonist**.
See also page 626.

**PUN** *A humorous play on words, using either (1) two or more different meanings of the same word, or (2) two or more words that are spelled and pronounced somewhat the same but have different meanings.* William Shakespeare uses puns frequently. In his play *Romeo and Juliet*, a character named Mercutio, who is always joking, is fatally wounded and knows he does not have long to live. Punning on the word *grave*, Mercutio says, "Ask for me tomorrow and you shall find me a grave man."

In the following poem, Arthur Guiterman puns on the words *pause/paws* and on the different meanings of the word *bark*:

**Motto for a
Dog House**
*Arthur Guiterman*

I love this little house because
  It offers, after dark,
A pause for rest, a rest for paws,
  A place to moor my bark.

See page 554.

**QUATRAIN** *A group of four lines of verse which are unified in thought and sometimes in rhyme.* Quatrains are commonly rhymed *abab, abba,* or *abcb.* Sometimes quatrains are set apart as **stanzas.** Sometimes, as in the case of Shakespeare's sonnets, they are run together. A **Shakespearean sonnet** is made up of three quatrains and a concluding **couplet.**

See **Sonnet, Stanza**.
See also page 391.

**REFRAIN** *One or more words, phrases, or lines that are repeated regularly in a poem, usually at the end of each stanza.* Refrains are especially common in ballads and in songs meant to be sung by groups. Refrains can aid memory and emphasize an idea. An example of a refrain in modern poetry is found in the first stanza of Elizabeth Bishop's poem to a Brooklyn poet, "Invitation to Miss Marianne Moore":

From Brooklyn, over the Brooklyn Bridge, on this fine
  morning, please come flying.
In a cloud of fiery pale chemicals,
  please come flying.
to the rapid rolling of thousands of small blue drums
descending out of the mackerel sky
over the glittering grandstand of harbor-water,
  please come flying.

The invitation "please come flying" is repeated in each of the remaining eight stanzas. Doubtless, Miss Moore got the message.

See **Repetition**.
See also pages 344, 359.

**REPETITION** *The reappearance of a word, phrase, stanza, or structure in any literary work.* Repetition is one of the most reliable and widely used means of bringing intensity to a piece of literature. It takes an enormous number of forms. Three common forms used in poetry are **refrain, rhyme,** and **alliteration. Parallelism,** which is the repetition of structures or ideas, is useful in both poetry and prose.

One of the most famous examples of repetition occurs at the end of Robert Frost's poem "Stopping by

Woods on a Snowy Evening." Not only is an entire line repeated, but also the meter is repetitive and so is the rhyme:

The woods are lovely, dark, and deep,
But I have promises to keep,
And miles to go before I sleep,
And miles to go before I sleep.

The daring quality of these lines, with the total repetition of one line, has often caught readers' attention. The repetition has a calming effect, in one sense. But it also is a way of forcing us to reflect more deeply on the poet's words, and we sense that they may mean more than they seem to.

See **Alliteration, Parallelism, Refrain, Rhyme.**

**RHYME** *The repetition of accented vowel sounds and all succeeding sounds in words that appear close together in verse.*

*End rhyme,* the most common form of rhyme, places the rhyme sound at the end of the line of verse. The effect is one of closure, rest, and a sense of completion and fulfillment of expectation. An end rhyme is used in this short poem (a **couplet**):

O, God of dust and rainbows, help us see
That without dust the rainbow would not be.

*Langston Hughes*

*Internal rhyme* repeats sounds within the lines of verse. A famous use of internal rhyme occurs in the first line of Edgar Allan Poe's poem "The Raven":

Once upon a midnight dreary, while I pondered weak and weary

*Approximate rhyme* is very popular with modern poets. In approximate rhyme, the final rhyming sounds are close, but not the same. Emily Dickinson often uses approximate rhyme. Her approximate rhymes surprise us and add a slightly discordant note to a poem, as a flat or sharp note does to music. Here is an example:

**Lightly Stepped a Yellow Star**
*Emily Dickinson*

Lightly stepped a yellow star
To its lofty place,
Loosed the Moon her silver hat
From her lustral face.

All of evening softly lit
As an astral hall—
"Father," I observed to Heaven,
"You are punctual!"

The approximate rhyme here occurs in the words *hall* and *punctual*—they sound nearly alike, but they are slightly different.

One of the chief functions of rhyme is to insure the unity of a poem. The repetition of rhyming sounds emphasizes the relationship of certain lines. Another function of rhyme is to build our anticipation, which can be either satisfied or frustrated. Finally, a very happy function of rhyme is that it can produce humor, as in this verse from Gilbert and Sullivan's operetta *Iolanthe.* The lines describe someone who has had a bad night:

You're a regular wreck, with a crick in your neck; and no wonder you snore, for your head's on the floor, and you're needles and pins from your soles to your shins; and your flesh is a-creep, for your left leg's asleep; and you've cramps in your toes, and a fly on your nose, and some fluff in your lung, and a feverish tongue, and a thirst that's intense, and a general sense that you haven't been sleeping in clover . . . .

See **Rhyme Scheme.**
See also pages 344, 348, 351, 353.

**RHYME SCHEME** *The pattern of rhymes in a stanza or poem.* A rhyme scheme is usually indicated by using small letters to stand for each rhyme, starting with *a* for the first rhyme. Each *a* indicates the first rhyme, each *b* indicates the second rhyme, and so on. Letters indicating the rhyme scheme of Mary Coleridge's lovely "inside-out" poem appear on the left.

**Slowly**
*Mary Coleridge*

| | |
|---|---|
| a | Heavy is my heart, |
| b | Dark are thine eyes. |
| a | Thou and I must part |
| b | Ere the sun rise. |
| | |
| b | Ere the sun rise |
| a | Thou and I must part. |
| b | Dark are thine eyes, |
| a | Heavy is my heart. |

When analyzing a rhyme scheme, be sure to give the same rhyme sound the same letter, even if, as in the above poem, it appears in a different position in subsequent stanzas.

See **Rhyme.**
See also pages 351, 391.

**RHYTHM** *In language, the arrangement of stressed and unstressed syllables.* Rhythm is natural in all speech. Rhythm in poetry, as in music, can be fast, slow, soothing, disturbing, and so on.

When rhythm follows a generally regular pattern, we call it **meter**. Rhythm is used to lend musicality to a poem and to support the meaning of its lines. Occasionally, a tension between meter and rhythm will be felt, particularly in lines where meter makes us want to stop, but rhythm and meaning push us onward. An example of this appears in the beginning stanzas of Marya Zaturenska's poem "Song":

> Life with her weary eyes,
> Smiles, and lifts high her horn
> Of plenty and surprise,
> Not so where I was born
>
> In the dark streets of fear,
> In the damp houses where greed
> Grew sharper every year
> Through hunger and through need.

The reader expects the word *horn* to have a rhyme, and the tendency to want to stop at that word is strong. But the phrase is not meaningfully complete until the next line, so we move on. The break between stanzas is also surprising. We want to stop because the expectation of meter tells us to. But meaning tells us to go on. The effect here is to force us to pay close attention to what the poet is saying about life.

See **Meter**.
See also pages 361, 364.

**RISING ACTION** *The series of events in a drama that lead up to a turning point, where the central character's fate is sealed.* In William Shakespeare's play *Julius Caesar*, the rising action begins when the conspiracy is formed to murder Caesar, and it ends after Antony's speech in Act Three, when the populace has turned its back on Brutus. All the action that follows is **falling action.**

See **Falling Action.**
See also page 594.

**ROMANCE** *Originally, a term used to describe a medieval tale dealing with the loves and adventures of kings, queens, knights, and ladies, and including unlikely or supernatural happenings.* One of the most famous romances is the legend of King Arthur and his Knights of the Round Table.

In a more general sense, a romance is *any work of imaginative literature that is set in an idealized world and that deals with heroic adventures and battles in which brave heroes or heroines struggle against evil villains or monsters.* The conflict in a romance is almost always one of good versus evil. Often the heroes and heroines in a romance are aided by magic, such as a magical sword or a magical ring. The modern trilogy of novels called *The Lord of the Rings*, by J. R. R. Tolkien, is a romance. A movie that uses all the traditional elements of romance and sets its actions in a world of startling technological ("magical") achievements is *Star Wars*.

See pages 448, 466.

**SATIRE** *A literary work which mocks or ridicules the stupidity or vices of individuals, groups, institutions, or society in general.* Satire is generally of two sorts: that which is gentle, witty, and amusing; and that which is forceful, bitter, and even vicious.

In his novel *The House of the Seven Gables*, Nathaniel Hawthorne gently satirizes the aristocratic pride of one of his main characters, Hepzibah Pyncheon. He shows her affectations in dress, her cringing from the need to earn an honest living as a shopkeeper, and her disdain of what she would call "common folk." But Hawthorne is careful to show that Hepzibah is a sensitive human being as well, and his affection for his character prevents us from viewing her too harshly.

A classic example of bitter satire is found in Jonathan Swift's *Gulliver's Travels*, which mocks the corruption in every revered British institution of the early eighteenth century. Swift ridicules the British Empire, for example, by reducing it to a place called Lilliput, which is twelve miles in circumference, ruled over by an Emperor who is six inches high and who is addressed as Golbasto Momaren Evlame Gurdilo Shefin Mully Ully Gue.

See pages 163, 187.

**SESTET** *The final six lines of a Petrarchan (or Italian) sonnet.* The sestet (from the Italian for "six") has a rhyme scheme of *cdecde, cdccdc, cdedce,* or a variant. The first eight lines of the Petrarchan sonnet (the **octave**) usually state a thought, theme, or idea which is developed and resolved in the sestet. Sometimes the sestet is set apart as a **stanza**, and sometimes it is run together with the octave.

See **Petrarchan Sonnet.**

**SETTING** *The time and place in which the events of a literary work take place.* In short stories, novels, poetry, and nonfiction, the setting is generally created by **description**. In drama, setting is usually established by stage sets and dialogue.

Setting can be very important in establishing **atmosphere** or in making a comment about character. In his novel *Tess of the D'Urbervilles*, Thomas Hardy emphasizes the fall of his heroine, from a period of happiness to one of bleak despair, by changing her environment. At her happiest time, Tess lives on a prosperous dairy farm, in summer, at the height of the land's luxuriant fruitfulness; in her despair, she lives on a poor vegetable farm in the north of England, in the winter, when the land is most bare.

See **Atmosphere**.
See also pages 64, 79, 157.

**SHAKESPEAREAN SONNET** *A lyric poem of fourteen lines written in iambic pentameter, with three quatrains and a concluding couplet.* Shakespeare inherited the form from other English writers (it is also called the *English sonnet*), but he made the form so much his own that it has been named for him. The rhyme scheme of a Shakespearean sonnet is usually *abab cdcd efef gg*. If you read Shakespeare's sonnet "Shall I Compare Thee to a Summer's Day?", you can see how each **quatrain** deals with a single thought or problem, which is finally summed up or resolved in the **couplet**.

See **Sonnet**.
See also page 391.

**SHORT STORY** *A fictional narrative written in prose, which is shorter than a novel.* Because of its relative brevity, the short story often limits itself to one main event and the development of one character or a single aspect of character. A short story lacks the complexity and detail of the novel, but it may gain in impact through the compression of character and events.

See page 1.

**SIMILE** *A direct comparison made between two unlike things, using a word of comparison such as like, as, than, such as, or resembles.* Similes are one of the most frequently used **figures of speech;** not only are they common in prose and poetry, but they are also used in everyday speech. When we say, "His grip was like a vise" or "Her memory was like a computer," we are using a simile. In her poem "A Narrow Fellow in the Grass," Emily Dickinson describes a snake with this homely simile: "The grass divides as with a comb." The simile compares the grass to hair and the snake's path to a part made by a comb. In these lines from his poem "A Youth Mowing," D. H. Lawrence uses a simile to describe the pride of a young boy:

And he sees me bringing the dinner, he lifts
His head as proud as a deer that looks
Shoulder-deep out of the corn

See **Figurative Language, Metaphor**.
See also page 308.

**SOLILOQUY** *A dramatic convention in which a character makes an extended speech while alone on the stage.* This device allows the dramatist to convey a character's most private thoughts to the audience. In fact, soliloquies are actually "verbalized thoughts."

The convention of the soliloquy was primarily used in the Elizabethan theater, and it is not much used today. In *Hamlet*, for instance, William Shakespeare frequently uses the soliloquy to reveal his hero's uncertainties and innermost feelings. Without the soliloquies, we would not know very much about Hamlet's plans to murder his uncle, nor about his motives for doing so. One of the most famous soliloquies in literature is Hamlet's speech in Act Three, Scene 1, which begins, "To be, or not to be—that is the question."

See **Aside, Monologue**.
See also page 533.

**SONNET** *A lyric poem having fourteen rhymed lines, usually written in iambic pentameter.* The most important kinds of sonnets are the **Petrarchan** (or Italian) and the **Shakespearean** (or English). Both forms usually take a single topic and develop it fully. The Petrarchan sonnet has an eight-line beginning called the **octave**, and a six-line conclusion called the **sestet**. The feelings expressed in the octave often contrast with those expressed in the sestet. The Shakespearean sonnet often develops aspects of its topic in each of three **quatrains**, and uses the final **couplet** as a conclusion.

The sonnet form originated in Italy in the thirteenth century. It was very popular for love poems, but it was also popular for any meditation on a limited subject. During the Renaissance, entire books of poems were written using only the sonnet form. Writing a "Century of Sonnets" (100 sonnets) to a loved one was popular for a time in Elizabethan England.

Modern sonnets follow the older patterns, but often with variations. The American poet Edna St. Vincent Millay has used the Shakespearean sonnet form; one example is her wry "Oh, Oh, You Will Be Sorry for That Word." This sonnet clearly replies to some insult the speaker received. Each of the quatrains discloses a response to the insult. Finally, the couplet poses the last, surprising threat.

See **Petrarchan Sonnet,**
**Shakespearean Sonnet.**
See also page 391.

**SPEAKER** *The voice in a poem.* The voice of a poem can be the poet, or a character (person, animal, or thing) created by the poet. Except in the most personal of lyric poems, the poet will frequently speak in a voice invented for the poem. This is similar to a playwright who creates a speaker — a dramatic character — to speak lines on stage.

Even when a poem begins with "I," we cannot assume the speaker is the poet. Therefore, it is best to treat the voice in any poem as a speaker invented, like any other literary character, for the sake of the poem.

When Alexander Pope writes these lines, we know for certain that the speaker is not the poet:

I am his Highness' dog at Kew;
Pray tell me, sir, whose dog are you?

This little verse, engraved on a dog collar, contains a wry bit of humor. The dog himself is the speaker. Of course, we must wonder who the reader is.

See page 323.

**STANZA** *A group of related lines that forms a division of a poem or a song.* In some poems, each stanza has the same pattern; in others, each stanza is different.

"Report from a Far Place" by William Stafford is clearly broken into four stanzas. Yet there is no rhyme and no recognizable meter to unify each stanza. Each stanza consists of a sentence that takes three lines to "say."

More traditional is Sara Teasdale's "The Long Hill," which has three **quatrains** (groups of four lines) for its stanzas. Each stanza is rhymed in the same pattern, so the rhyme scheme of the entire poem is *abab cdcd efef.* As in many traditional poems, each stanza here states a complete thought that is related to the overall theme.

Isabella Gardner's "Summer Remembered" does not use regular stanza patterns at all. Instead, the poem is broken up into two large stanzas focusing on two aspects of the poem's theme.

Some of the best known of the regular stanza patterns are the **couplet,** the **quatrain,** the **sestet,** and

the **octave** — all named for the number of lines they possess.

See page 294.

**STYLE** *A writer's characteristic way of writing — his or her choice of words, sentence structure, and use of imagery and figurative language.* For example, a writer such as Dylan Thomas coins new words, writes in long, rhythmic sentences, and creates striking images and metaphors. Another writer such as Joan Didion uses sentences that are straightforward and very precise in diction. Dylan Thomas' style may remind us of poetry; Joan Didion's may remind us of good journalistic prose.

See pages 205, 216, 706, 763.

**SUBPLOT** *A plot in a story or play that is secondary to the main plot.* There may, in fact, be several subplots in longer literary forms like dramas or novels.

Usually the subplots are closely related to the main plot and support one general, unified theme. For instance, in Lorraine Hansberry's play *A Raisin in the Sun,* the main plot concerns Walter's struggle to become a responsible person. This plot is supported by two parallel subplots: his mother's desire to move the family to a better house and his sister Beneatha's drive to become a doctor. Each plot develops the general theme of our human need to become the best people we can become, despite considerable obstacles.

Subplots may also be *counterplots;* that is, they may provide a contrast to the main plot of the narrative. In her novel *Emma,* Jane Austen uses the rather comic subplot of Mrs. Elton's shallow marriage to the vicar as a mild contrast to the main plot of Emma's more meaningful relationship with Mr. Knightly.

See **Plot.**

**SUSPENSE** *A sense of uncertainty or anxiety about the outcome of events in a story or drama.* Generally, the purpose of suspense is to keep us in a state of high interest, so that we will read on eagerly to find out what happens next.

In the traditional novel, suspense is often most intense at the ends of chapters, where a character may be left at the point of death or in great peril. When novels were published in magazine installments, this made the reader want to buy the next issue to read the next chapter. In traditional drama, suspense has also been most intense at the ends of acts. This maintains the audience's curiosity about the next act, and makes them want to return after intermission. Some short stories concentrate solely on evoking a state of suspense. In "Contents of the Dead Man's Pockets," Jack Finney places his main character in a perilous situation, intensifying our suspense as we read along and increasing our fear and uncertainty until we reach the story's end.

See pages 41, 573.

**SYMBOL** *Something in a literary work which maintains its own meaning while at the same time standing for something broader than itself.* When a symbol is used in literature, its "double nature" can make it very complex and sometimes difficult to recognize.

There are many common, "reusable" symbols— symbols used over and over again. For example, the rose is often used as a symbol of beauty and love; the west is often used as a symbol of death; the seasons are often used as symbols of the human "seasons" of birth, youth, maturity, and old age; the dove is often used as a symbol of peace; a journey is often used as a symbol of life itself.

An interesting use of a symbol in literature is made in Robert Frost's poem "Birches." In that poem, the birches are themselves: trees that a boy can swing on and that can break under the weight of ice. But the birches also point toward heaven, and so they can be seen as symbolic ladders to the afterlife. Frost says it would be nice to experiment with the birches and "get away from earth awhile." But then he realizes he must die to have birches do their symbolic job, so he worries that his symbol may be taken too literally:

May not fate willfully misunderstand me
And half grant what I wish and snatch me away
Not to return. . . .

He can wait, he decides.

Writers usually let us know through the context when they wish us to interpret something as a symbol. Once we recognize a symbol, its further meanings seem to radiate outward in our imagination like the ripples from a stone dropped in a deep well.

See **Figurative Language.**
See also pages 110, 308, 325, 763.

**THEME** *The main idea expressed in a literary work; the central insight that the work gives us about human life.* If the work is relatively brief, such as a short story or a lyric poem, it will probably have only one theme. If it is a longer work, such as a novel or play, it will probably have several themes, which may work together. Theme is different from **plot** and from subject. For example, in the following poem, the subject is joy, but the theme has to do with two human needs: our need to give thanks for the joy that comes from ordinary things, and our need to share joy, lest we lose it:

**Welcome Morning**
*Anne Sexton*

There is joy
in all:
in the hair I brush each morning,
in the Cannon towel, newly washed,
that I rub my body with each morning,
in the chapel of eggs I cook
each morning,
in the outcry from the kettle
that heats my coffee
each morning,
in the spoon and the chair
that cry "hello there, Anne"
each morning,
in the godhead of the table
that I set my silver, plate, cup upon
each morning.

All this is God,
right here in my pea-green house
each morning
and I mean,
though often forget,
to give thanks,
to faint down by the kitchen table
in a prayer of rejoicing
as the holy birds at the kitchen window
peck into their marriage of seeds.

So while I think of it,
let me paint a thank-you on my palm
for this God, this laughter of the morning,
lest it go unspoken.

The Joy that isn't shared, I've heard,
dies young.

While a writer may state the theme directly, as is sometimes done in an essay, more often theme is only suggested and requires analysis and thought to be brought out. The theme of a work sometimes is a statement about life, but it often simply is the raising of an important question for which the writer gives no ready answers. Theme does not by any means have to be a **moral** or lesson, giving a prescription for behavior; rather, theme is an exploration of important ideas about human life.

Theme might be compared to a piece of colored thread being woven into a tapestry; it appears, disappears, reappears, perhaps in a different guise, until the final pattern emerges at the end of the work.

See pages 149, 157, 400, 704, 763.

**TONE** *The attitude a writer takes toward the subject or the reader of a work of literature.* In some cases, such as in Lincoln's Gettysburg Address, the tone is straightforward and serious. In other cases, as in Mark Twain's novel *The Adventures of Huckleberry Finn*, the tone shifts from seriousness to humor. At times Twain is amused by some of his characters, while at other times he takes them very seriously. It is always important to recognize tone, because a misunderstanding of tone can distort the entire meaning of a work. For example, many readers have failed to recognize Jonathan Swift's tone in his essay "A Modest Proposal," which suggests that the English solve the Irish problem by serving Irish infants as roasts and stews. Some horrified readers have thought Swift really was serious and have not caught the satire. Thus they have missed Swift's point, which is to show how the British had failed to treat the Irish as human beings.

See pages 109, 143, 330, 706, 763.

**TRAGEDY** *A literary work dealing with very serious and important themes, in which a dignified tragic figure meets destruction, usually through some personal flaw or weakness.* Although tragedy ends in destruction, its impact may not be depressing, but uplifting, for the hero or heroine often gains a measure of wisdom or self-awareness from failure. Although it is too late for the tragic hero or heroine to change the tragic outcome, he or she faces the catastrophe with dignity and courage.

In classic tragedy the hero is a person of high birth, whose personal destruction is in some way involved with the well-being of the state. The most famous tragedies of this type are those of ancient Greece, such as Sophocles' *Antigone*. Shakespeare's tragedies, such as *Julius Caesar*, also follow this pattern.

See pages 482, 626.

**TURNING POINT** *That crucial moment in a drama or story in which the fate of the hero or heroine is sealed, when the events of the plot must begin to move toward a happy ending or toward an unhappy one.* For example, in Shakespeare's play *Julius Caesar*, the turning point occurs in Act Three, when Antony manages, through his skillful oratory, to win the people over to his side and away from Brutus and the other conspirators. At this moment, Brutus' fate is sealed, and we know he cannot win over Antony. The rest of the play, Acts Four and Five, dramatize the events that lead finally to Brutus' tragic downfall.

See pages 594, 747.

**VERSE DRAMA** *A play written mostly or entirely in verse.* All of Shakespeare's plays are verse dramas. He uses **blank verse** (poetic lines written in unrhymed **iambic pentameter**) for most of his plays. *Antigone*, like all the Greek dramas, is a verse drama. Maxwell Anderson's *Winterset* is one of the better known examples of modern verse drama. Archibald MacLeish's verse drama *J. B.*, based on the Book of Job, is probably the most recent notable example in English.

# Glossary

Strictly speaking, the word *glossary* means a collection of technical, obscure, or foreign words found in a certain field of work. The words in this glossary are not "technical, obscure, or foreign," but are those that might present difficulty as you read the selections in this textbook.

Many words in the English language have several meanings. In this glossary, the meanings given are the ones that apply to the words as they are used in the selections in the textbook. Words closely related in form and meaning are generally listed together in one entry (**abstemious** and **abstemiousness**), and the definition is given for the first form. Related words that generally appear as separate entries in dictionaries are listed separately (**apathetic** and **apathy**). Regular adverbs (ending in *-ly*) are defined in their adjective form, with the adverb form shown at the end of the definition.

For complete definitions of these words, a good dictionary must be consulted.

The following abbreviations are used:

| | | |
|---|---|---|
| *adj.* adjective | *n.* noun | *v.* verb |
| *adv.* adverb | *prep.* preposition | |

## A

**abate** (ə-bāt′) *v.* To lessen.

**aberration** (ăb′ə-rā′shən) *n.* A deviation from the normal or usual.

**abhorrent** (ăb-hôr′ənt, -hŏr′ənt) *adj.* Hateful; disgusting. —**abhorrently** *adv.*

**abrasive** (ə-brā′sĭv, -zĭv) *adj.* Harsh; rough.

**absolve** (ăb-zŏlv′, -sŏlv′) *v.* To free from blame or guilt.

**abstemious** (ăb-stē′mē-əs) *adj.* Moderate in eating and drinking. —**abstemiousness** *n.*

**abstract** (ăb-străkt′, ăb′străkt′) *adj.* **1.** Difficult to understand; theoretical. **2.** Removed from reality; dreamy.

**abyss** (ə-bĭs′) *n.* A bottomless, empty space.

**accentuate** (ăk-sĕn′chōō-āt′) *v.* To emphasize.

**accredit** (ə-krĕd′ĭt) *v.* To authorize; appoint.

**acrid** (ăk′rĭd) *adj.* Harsh; bitter.

**administer** (ăd-mĭn′ĭs-tər) *v.* To give; dispense.

**admonish** (ăd-mŏn′ĭsh) *v.* To scold mildly.

**advent** (ăd′vĕnt) *n.* A coming or arrival, as of an important event or person.

**affable** (ăf′ə-bəl) *adj.* Friendly. —**affability** *n.*

**affiliate** (ə-fĭl′ē-āt′) *v.* To associate with.

**agitation** (ăj′ə-tā′shən) *n.* **1.** A violent movement or stirring. **2.** Emotional disturbance.

**alacrity** (ə-lăk′rə-tē) *n.* Quickness and liveliness in movement; eagerness.

**alight** (ə-līt′) *v.* To get off or down.

**alms** (ämz) *n. pl.* Money or goods given to the needy. —**almsgiver** *n.*

**amble** (ăm′bəl) *v.* To walk in a slow, relaxed way.

**amenity** (ə-mĕn′ə-tē, ə-mē′nə-) *n.* Something that makes a place more pleasant or comfortable.

**amiable** (ā′mē-ə-bəl) *adj.* Friendly. —**amiably** *adv.*

**ample** (ăm′pəl) *adj.* Plentiful.

**amulet** (ăm′yə-lĭt) *n.* A charm against evil or injury.

**animosity** (ăn′ə-mŏs′ə-tē) *n.* Hatred.

**antics** (ăn′tĭks) *n. pl.* Funny, playful behavior.

**apathetic** (ăp′ə-thĕt′ĭk) *adj.* Without emotion; indifferent. —**apathetically** *adv.*

**apathy** (ăp′ə-thē) *n.* The absence of emotion; indifference.

**aphorism** (ăf′ə-rĭz′əm) *n.* A short and wise or clever statement.

**apocalypse** (ə-pŏk′ə-lĭps′) *n.* A revelation or prophecy, particularly of destruction.

**appall** (ə-pôl′) *v.* To shock; horrify.

**apparition** (ăp′ə-rĭsh′ən) *n.* **1.** A ghost. **2.** A sudden appearance of an unusual sight or form.

**appease** (ə-pēz′) *v.* To soothe; satisfy.

**appertain** (ăp′ər-tān′) *v.* To have to do with.

**apprehensive** (ăp′rĭ-hĕn′sĭv) *adj.* Fearful. —**apprehensive** *adv.*

**apropos** (ăp′rə-pō′) *adj.* Relevant. —**apropos of** With regard to.

**arabesque** (ăr′ə-bĕsk′) *adj.* Fanciful; elaborate.

**arbiter** (är′bə-tər) *n.* A person who settles a dispute.

**arbitrary** (är′bə-trĕr′ē) *adj.* Determined by whim or personal preference. —**arbitrarily** *adv.*

**arbor** (är′bər) *n.* An area shaded by trees.

**ardent** (är′dənt) *adj.* Enthusiastic.

**array** (ə-rā′) *n.* **1.** A large display. **2.** An orderly grouping.

**arrogant** (ăr′ə-gənt) *adj.* Excessively self-important and proud. —**arrogantly** *adv.* —**arrogance** *n.*

**ascent** (ə-sĕnt′) *n.* The act of moving upward.

**aspiration** (ăs′pə-rā′shən) *n.* High ambition.

**assail** (ə-sāl′) *v.* To attack.

**assent** (ə-sĕnt′) *n.* Agreement.

**assimilate** (ə-sĭm′ə-lāt′) *v.* To absorb; make part of one's thinking.

© 1969, 1970, 1971, 1973, 1975, 1976, Houghton Mifflin Company.
The pronunciation system in this glossary is used by permission from *The American Heritage Dictionary of the English Language.*

ă pat/ā pay/âr care/ä father/b bib/ch church/d deed/ĕ pet/ē be/f fife/g gag/h hat/hw which/ĭ pit/ī pie/îr pier/j judge/k kick/l lid, needle/m mum/
n no, sudden/ng thing/ŏ pot/ō toe/ô paw, for/oi noise/ou out/ŏŏ took/ōō boot/p pop/r roar/s sauce/sh ship, dish/t tight/th thin, path/th this, bathe/
ŭ cut/ûr urge/v valve/w with/y yes/z zebra, size/zh vision/ə about, item, edible, gallop, circus/ à *Fr.* ami/œ *Fr.* feu, *Ger.* schön/ü *Fr.* tu, *Ger.* über/
кн *Ger.* ich, *Scot.* loch/ɴ *Fr.* bon.

**assumption** (ə-sŭmp'shən) *n.* An act of arrogance or forwardness.

**astound** (ə-stound') *v.* To amaze; bewilder.

**attain** (ə-tān') *v.* To arrive at; reach.

**audacious** (ô-dā'shəs) *adj.* Fearless; daring.

**audible** (ô'də-bəl) *adj.* Able to be heard.

**aught** (ôt) *n.* Anything at all.

**augment** (ôg-měnt') *v.* To increase; make greater.

**augur** (ô'gər) *v.* To predict the future from signs or omens. — **augurer** (ô'gyər-ər) *n.*

**august** (ô-gŭst') *adj.* Dignified; majestic.

**auspicious** (ô-spĭsh'əs) *adj.* Favorable; boding well.

**austere** (ô-stîr') *adj.* Solemn; dignified.

**authenticate** (ô-thĕn'tĭ-kāt') *v.* To confirm as true or genuine.

**avaricious** (ăv'ə-rĭsh'əs) *adj.* Greedy.

**avert** (ə-vûrt') *v.* To turn away.

**awry** (ə-rī') *adv.* Twisted toward one side.

**B**

**banter** (băn'tər) *n.* Quick, witty conversation.

**baroque** (bə-rōk') *adj.* Irregular or odd in shape.

**base** (bās) *adj.* Dishonorable; mean. — **basely** *adv.*

**bay** (bā) *v.* To force into being cornered so that escape is impossible.

**beleaguer** (bĭ-lē'gər) *v.* To attack by surrounding on all sides.

**belligerent** (bə-lĭj'ər-ənt) *adj.* Ready to fight or argue. — **belligerently** *adv.*

**bellow** (bĕl'ō) *v.* To roar.

**benediction** (bĕn'ə-dĭk'shən) *n.* A blessing.

**benefactor** (bĕn'ə-făk'tər) *n.* Someone who gives help, particularly financial help.

**benign** (bĭ-nīn') *adj.* Not harmful.

**bequeath** (bĭ-kwēth', -kwēth') *v.* To leave to someone by will; hand down.

**bereave** (bĭ-rēv') *v.* To leave sad or forlorn, as by death. — **bereavement** *n.*

**beseech** (bĭ-sēch') *v.* To ask seriously; beg.

**bestow** (bĭ-stō') *v.* To give; grant.

**betide** (bĭ-tīd') *v.* To happen to.

**betimes** (bĭ-tīmz') *adv. Archaic.* Early; quickly.

**blanch** (blănch, blänch) *v.* To become pale or white.

**bland** (blănd) *adj.* Mild; dull.

**blasphemy** (blăs'fə-mē) *n.* Any irreverent or contemptuous act or remark. — **blasphemous** *adj.*

**blithe** (blīth, blīth) *adj.* Carefree; cheerful. — **blitheness** *n.*

**bodice** (bŏd'ĭs) *n.* The fitted upper part of a dress.

**bouffant** (boo-fänt') *adj.* Full; puffed out.

**bower** (bou'ər) *n.* A leafy, shaded place. — **bowery** *adj.*

**brackish** (brăk'ĭsh) *adj.* Containing some salt (describing water).

**brand** (brănd) *n.* A burning stick.

**brandish** (brăn'dĭsh) *v.* To wave in a threatening way.

**brazen** (brā'zən) *adj.* **1.** Made of or like brass in color and hardness. **2.** Shameless.

**brazier** (brā'zhər) *n.* An open pan used to hold burning coals.

**broach** (brōch) *v.* To bring up a topic for discussion.

**brood** (brood) *v.* To cover in a protective way, as birds do with their young.

**brusque** (brŭsk) *adj.* Abrupt; rude.

**buffet** (bŭf'ĭt) *v.* To struggle against.

**bulwark** (bool'wərk, bŭl'-, -wôrk') *n.* Someone or something that acts as a defense or protection.

**C**

**caldron** (kôl'drən) *n.* A large kettle or vat.

**calibrate** (kăl'ə-brāt') *v.* To mark the measure or capacity of something.

**callous** (kăl'əs) *adj.* Unfeeling; pitiless. — **callousness** *n.*

**cameo** (kăm'ē-ō') *n.* A raised, carved design on a gemstone or shell.

**camphor** (kăm'fər) *n.* A chemical substance generally used to protect fabric against moths, but sometimes used in medicine as a stimulant.

**candelabrum** (kăn'də-lä'brəm) *n.* A large, branched candleholder.

**canter** (kăn'tər) *v.* To ride at a slow gallop.

**cape** (kāp) *n.* A piece of land projecting into a body of water.

**caper** (kā'pər) *v.* To jump about playfully.

**caprice** (kə-prēs') *n.* A sudden, impulsive change of mind or way of thinking.

**capricious** (kə-prĭsh'əs, -prē'shəs) *adj.* Fickle; subject to whim.

**cardiogram** (kär'dē-ə-grăm') *n.* A tracing of the contractions of the heart, used in diagnosing heart disease.

**carrion** (kăr'ē-ən) *adj.* **1.** Rotten or decaying. **2.** Feeding on decaying flesh.

**catapult** (kăt'ə-pŭlt') *v.* To leap or spring up suddenly.

**cataract** (kăt'ə-răkt') *n.* A large waterfall.

**cavalcade** (kăv'əl-kād', kăv'əl-kād') *n.* A formal parade of horsemen.

**cavalier** (kăv'ə-lîr') *adj.* Arrogant; haughty.

**celestial** (sə-lĕs'chəl) *adj.* Relating to heaven.

**cessation** (sĕ-sā'shən) *n.* A stopping, either permanent or temporary.

**chafe** (chāf) *v.* **1.** To rub in order to stimulate. **2.** To wear away by rubbing.

**chaff** (chăf) *n.* Straw or hay used to feed animals.

**chaise longue** (shāz' lông') A "long chair," having an extended seat to support the sitter's legs.

**chasm** (kăz'əm) *n.* A narrow, deep opening in the earth's surface.

**chasten** (chā'sən) *v.* **1.** To punish in order to make better. **2.** To purify; refine.

**chastise** (chăs-tīz') *v.* To punish; condemn. — **chastisement** *n.*

**chide** (chīd) *v.* To scold mildly.

**chortle** (chôrt'l) *v.* To chuckle with a snorting sound.

**cinch** (sĭnch) *v.* To fasten something tightly around another thing.

**circuit** (sûr'kĭt) *n.* A regular route taken by someone in the performance of his or her duties.

**citadel** (sĭt'ə-dəl, -dĕl') *n.* A fort that protects a city.

**citron** (sĭt'rən) *n.* The candied rind of a lemonlike fruit, used in baking.

**clamber** (klăm'ər, klăm'bər) *v.* To climb with difficulty, on all fours; scramble.

**cleave** (klēv) *v.* To split; pierce.

**cleft** (klĕft) *adj.* Split; divided.

**clique** (klēk, klĭk) *n.* A small, select group of people sharing a common interest.

**clod** (klŏd) *n.* A lump of soil or clay.

**cogitation** (kŏj′ə-tā′shən) *n.* Serious thought or meditation.

**commend** (kə-mĕnd′) *v.* 1. To make a favorable impression. 2. To be praiseworthy. 3. To express praise. 4. To transmit regards.

**complacence** (kəm-plā′səns) *n.* Satisfaction, especially self-satisfaction.

**compound** (kŏm′pound) *n.* An enclosed area or group of buildings where people live.

**comprehensive** (kŏm′prĭ-hĕn′sĭv) *adj.* Including all necessary details; extensive.

**concave** (kŏn-kāv′) *adj.* Curved inward.

**conceive** (kən-sēv′) *v.* To think of, as an idea.

**conceivable** (kən-sēv′ə-bəl) *adj.* Able to be thought of or imagined.

**conception** (kən-sĕp′shən) *n.* An idea; thought.

**condole** (kən-dōl′) *v.* To sympathize.

**confer** (kən-fûr′) *v.* To give; grant.

**congenial** (kən-jēn′yəl) *adj.* 1. Friendly. 2. Sharing similar tastes or habits.

**conjecture** (kən-jĕk′chər) *n.* A conclusion based on guesswork or insufficient evidence. — **conjectural** *adj.*

**conjoint** (kən-joint′) *adj.* United. — **conjointly** *adv.*

**conjunction** (kən-jŭngk′shən) *n.* An association; union.

**conjure** (kŏn′jər, kən-jōōr′) *v.* To bring a particular image to mind (used with **up**).

**consecrate** (kŏn′sə-krāt′) *v.* 1. To make holy. 2. To dedicate to a special service or goal.

**conservatory** (kən-sûr′və-tôr′ē, -tōr′ē) *n.* A glass-enclosed room used to grow plants.

**console** (kən-sōl′) *v.* To comfort.

**constancy** (kŏn′stən-sē) *n.* Steadfastness; firmness of purpose.

**consternation** (kŏn′stər-nā′shən) *n.* Sudden fear or confusion.

**construe** (kən-strōō′) *v.* To interpret.

**consul** (kŏn′səl) *n.* In ancient Rome, a high-ranking judge.

**contemplate** (kŏn′təm-plāt′) *v.* To look at thoughtfully and intently.

**contempt** (kən-tĕmpt′) *n.* Scorn; disdain.

**contort** (kən-tôrt′) *v.* To twist into an unusual shape.

**contour** (kŏn′tōōr) *n.* The outline or form of a figure or piece of land.

**contrition** (kən-trĭsh′ən) *n.* A feeling of regret for wrongdoing.

**contrive** (kən-trīv′) *v.* To plan cleverly; scheme.

**conventional** (kən-vĕn′shən-əl) *adj.* Conforming to accepted standards; customary.

**convoluted** (kŏn′və-lōō′tĭd) *adj.* Twisted; intricate.

**convulse** (kən-vŭls′) *v.* To agitate; cause to shake.

**coquette** (kō-kĕt′) *n.* A flirt. — **coquettish** *adj.*

**cordial** (kôr′jəl) *adj.* Friendly.

**cordon** (kôr′dən) *n.* A line or circle of individuals.

**corrugated** (kôr′ə-gāt′-ĭd) *adj.* Made of metal or paper that is furrowed or ridged for added strength.

**counsel** (koun′səl) *n.* 1. A private thought; secret. 2. An intention; purpose.

**countenance** (koun′tə-nəns) *n.* 1. The expression on a person's face. 2. The face. — *v.* To tolerate.

**counteract** (koun′tər-ăkt′) *v.* To act against; offset.

**covert** (kŭv′ərt, kō′vərt) *n.* A covered place. — *adj.* hidden; secret.

**covet** (kŭv′ĭt) *v.* To have a strong desire for something, especially something belonging to another.

**covey** (kŭv′ē) *n.* A small flock of birds.

**cow** (kou) *v.* To subdue by instilling fear.

**cower** (kou′ər) *v.* To shrink away or fall down in fear.

**cowl** (koul) *n.* Hood.

**cranny** (krăn′ē) *n.* A small, narrow opening in a rock or wall.

**credulity** (krĭ-dōō′lə-tē, -dyōō′lə-tē) *n.* A tendency to believe something too quickly and without sufficient evidence.

**crest** (krĕst) *n.* 1. The peak or highest point of something. 2. A bunch of feathers or growth on the head of some birds. — *v.* To reach the highest level.

**crevice** (krĕv′ĭs) *n.* 1. A narrow crack. 2. A deep opening in the earth's surface.

**cryptic** (krĭp′tĭk) *adj.* Mysterious; obscure.

**cumbersome** (kŭm′bər-səm) *adj.* Clumsy; burdensome; troublesome. — also **cumbrous.**

**cunning** (kŭn′ĭng) *adj.* Clever; skillful.

**curate** (kyōōr′ĭt) *n.* A clergyman who is in charge of a parish or who assists a clergyman of higher rank.

**curt** (kûrt) *adj.* Rude; blunt. — **curtly** *adv.*

## D

**dank** (dăngk) *adj.* Unpleasantly damp and chilly.

**daunt** (dônt, dänt) *v.* To make afraid.

**dauntless** (dônt′lĭs, dänt′-) *adj.* Fearless; bold.

**decorum** (dĭ-kôr′əm, -kōr′-) *n.* Conformity to standards of good taste in behavior, dress, etc.

**decree** (dĭ-krē′) *n.* An official order.

**deference** (dĕf′ər-əns) *n.* 1. Submission to the wishes of another. 2. Respect; courtesy.

**defile** (dĭ-fīl′) *v.* To make unclean or impure; soil.

**deflect** (dĭ-flĕkt′) *v.* To turn aside.

**deft** (dĕft) *adj.* Skillful in a quick and sure way. — **deftly** *adv.* — **deftness** *n.*

**deign** (dān) *v.* To think it proper to one's dignity to behave in a certain way.

**deluge** (dĕl′yōōj) *n.* A flood.

**dementia** (dĭ-mĕn′shə, -shē-ə) *n.* Insanity.

**demolition** (dĕm′ə-lĭsh′ən) *n.* The act of wrecking or destroying.

**demoralize** (dĭ-môr′əl-īz′, dĭ-mŏr′-) *v.* To corrupt.

**demure** (dĭ-myōōr′) *adj.* Modest; reserved.

**denizen** (dĕn′ə-zən) *n.* A resident; inhabitant.

---

ă pat/ā pay/âr care/ä father/b bib/ch church/d deed/ĕ pet/ē be/f fife/g gag/h hat/hw which/ĭ pit/ī pie/îr pier/j judge/k kick/l lid, needle/m mum/ n no, sudden/ng thing/ŏ pot/ō toe/ô paw, for/oi noise/ou out/ŏŏ took/ōō boot/p pop/r roar/s sauce/sh ship, dish/t tight/th thin, path/t*h* this, bathe/ ū cut/ûr urge/v valve/w with/y yes/z zebra, size/zh vision/ə about, item, edible, gallop, circus/ä *Fr.* ami/œ *Fr.* feu, *Ger.* schön/ü *Fr.* tu, *Ger.* über/ ᴋʜ *Ger.* ich, *Scot.* loch/ɴ *Fr.* bon.

**deplorable** (dĭ-plôr′ə-bəl, dĭ-plōr′-) *adj.* Worthy of condemnation. —**deplorably** *adv.*

**deploy** (dĭ-ploi′) *v.* To spread out troops.

**depravity** (dĭ-prăv′ə-tē) *n.* The state of being morally evil.

**deprivation** (dĕp′rə-vā′shən) *n.* The condition of being denied the means of comfort or enjoyment.

**derision** (dĭ-rĭzh′ən) *n.* Ridicule; contempt.

**derisive** (dĭ-rī′sĭv) *adj.* Contemptuous; mocking. —**derisively** *adv.*

**deter** (dĭ-tûr′) *v.* To prevent someone from acting through fear or doubt.

**device** (dĭ-vīs′) *n.* A decorative figure or design.

**dewlap** (dōō′lăp′, dyōō′-) *n.* Loose skin hanging from the neck. —**dewlapped** *adj.*

**diaphanous** (dī-ăf′ə-nəs) *adj.* So fine that light can shine through; airy.

**diffident** (dĭf′ə-dənt, -dĕnt′) *adj.* Without confidence; shy. —**diffidently** *adv.*

**dilatory** (dĭl′ə-tôr′ē, -tōr′ē) *adj.* Slow; delaying.

**diminutive** (dĭ-mĭn′yə-tĭv) *adj.* Very small; tiny.

**dirge** (dûrj) *n.* A funeral hymn.

**disapprobation** (dĭs-ăp′rə-bā′shən) *n.* Disapproval.

**disarm** (dĭs-ärm′) *v.* To make friendly; overcome hostility.

**disconsolate** (dĭs′kŏn′sə-lĭt) *adj.* Hopelessly unhappy.

**discourse** (dĭs′kôrs′, -kōrs′) *v.* To carry on a conversation about something.

**discredit** (dĭs-krĕd′ĭt) *v.* To disgrace; dishonor.

**discreet** (dĭs-krēt′) *adj.* Careful. —**discreetly** *adv.*

**discretion** (dĭs-krĕsh′ən) *n.* Caution.

**disjoin** (dĭs-join′) *v.* To separate.

**dismantle** (dĭs-mănt′l) *v.* To take apart.

**dismember** (dĭs-mĕm′bər) *v.* To remove the limbs from a body; to cut or tear to pieces.

**disparage** (dĭs-păr′ĭj) *v.* To belittle. —**disparagement** *n.*

**dispassionate** (dĭs-păsh′ən-ĭt) *adj.* Impartial; unemotional.

**dispatch** (dĭs-păch′) *v.* To send off or out quickly.

**disperse** (dĭs-pûrs′) *v.* **1.** To scatter in various directions. **2.** To cause to disappear.

**dissemble** (dĭ-sĕm′bəl) *v.* To disguise one's true feelings or motives.

**dissipate** (dĭs′ə-pāt′) *v.* To cause to disappear.

**dissolution** (dĭs′ə-lōō′shən) *n.* **1.** Disintegration. **2.** Death.

**dissuade** (dĭ-swād′) *v.* To stop someone from doing something through persuasion.

**distend** (dĭs-tĕnd′) *v.* To become swollen.

**distillate** (dĭs′tə-lāt′, dĭs-tĭl′ĭt) *n.* The concentrated, purified liquid left after the refining process; essence.

**diversion** (dĭ-vûr′zhən, -shən, dī-) *n.* Something that causes one's attention to be turned away.

**divert** (dĭ-vûrt′, dī-) *v.* **1.** To cause to turn aside. **2.** To entertain.

**divine** (dĭ-vīn′) *v.* To guess.

**docile** (dŏs′əl) *adj.* Tame; easily handled.

**doctrine** (dŏk′trĭn) *n.* A belief; principle.

**dodder** (dŏd′ər) *v.* To shake; tremble.

**dogged** (dô′gĭd, dŏg′ĭd) *adj.* Persistent; stubborn. —**doggedly** *adv.*

**domesticate** (də-mĕs′tĭ-kāt′) *v.* To make something strange or foreign familiar.

**dominion** (də-mĭn′yən) *n.* **1.** Power; supreme authority. **2.** Territory ruled; realm.

**dote** (dōt) *v.* To be extremely fond of something (used with **on**).

**doughty** (dou′tē) *adj.* Brave.

**dour** (dōōr, dour) *adj.* Ill-tempered.

**dowager** (dou′ə-jər) *n.* A well-to-do, elderly woman, especially a widow.

**down** (doun) *n.* Soft feathers used to stuff pillows.

**dowry** (dour′ē) *n.* Money or property brought by a woman to her husband at marriage.

**drawn** (drôn) *adj.* Haggard.

**droll** (drōl) *adj.* Humorous in a whimsical way.

**dubious** (dōō′bē-əs, dyōō′-) *adj.* Doubtful. —**dubiously** *adv.*

**dullard** (dŭl′ərd) *n.* A stupid person.

**ducal** (dōō′kəl) *adj.* Belonging to a duke or dukedom.

**duly** (dōō′lē) *adv.* In a fitting manner; rightfully.

**E**

**ebb** (ĕb) *n.* A gradual decrease in intensity or strength.

**eccentric** (ĕk-sĕn′trĭk, ĭk-) *n.* An odd or unusual person. —*adj.* strange; straying from the usual. —**eccentrically** *adv.*

**ecstacy** (ĕk′stə-sē) *n.* Great joy.

**eddy** (ĕd′ē) *v.* To move in a whirling motion against the current.

**edict** (ē′dĭkt′) *n.* An official order or decision.

**edifice** (ĕd′ə-fĭs) *n.* A large building or something resembling one.

**effete** (ĭ-fēt′) *adj.* Weak; unproductive.

**egress** (ē′grĕs) *n.* A way out; exit.

**ejaculate** (ĭ-jăk′yə-lāt′) *v.* To exclaim suddenly.

**elocution** (ĕl′ə-kyōō′shən) *n.* The art of reading or speaking in public.

**elusive** (ĭ-lōō′sĭv) *adj.* Able to avoid being seen or caught.

**emaciate** (ĭ-mā′shē-āt′) *v.* To become abnormally thin.

**emanate** (ĕm′ə-nāt′) *v.* To come forth; flow out.

**embellishment** (ĕm-bĕl′ĭsh-mənt) *n.* An ornament.

**eminent** (ĕm′ə-nənt) *adj.* Outstanding. —**eminently** *adv.*

**emissary** (ĕm′ə-sĕr′ē) *n.* Someone sent out as a messenger or representative.

**encompass** (ĕn-kŭm′pəs) *v.* To surround.

**engender** (ĕn-jĕn′dər) *v.* To produce.

**enigmatic** (ĕn′ĭg-măt′ĭk) *adj.* Puzzling.

**enkindle** (ĕn-kĭnd′l) *v.* To arouse; stir up.

**enmity** (ĕn′mə-tē) *n.* Hostility.

**enshroud** (ĕn-shroud′) *v.* To wrap so as to hide from view; conceal.

**ensue** (ĕn-sōō′) *v.* To follow immediately.

**enthrall** (ĕn-thrôl′) *v.* To spellbind; fascinate.

**entity** (ĕn′tə-tē) *n.* Something that has a definite and separate existence; something real.

**entrails** (ĕn′trālz′, -trəlz) *n. pl.* The internal organs of a human or an animal.

**entrance** (ĕn-trăns′) *v.* To fill with delight.

**entreat** (ĕn-trēt′, ĭn-) *v.* To ask for earnestly; beg.

**enunciate** (ĭ-nŭn′sē-āt′) *v.* To pronounce words clearly.

**escarpment** (ĕ-skärp′mənt) *n.* A steep slope.

**esoteric** (ĕs′ə-tĕr′ĭk) *adj.* Mysterious; open to or understood by only a select few.

**essence** (ĕs′əns) n. **1.** The most basic or important element of something. **2.** An extract containing a concentrated fragrance or flavor.

**ethereal** (ĭ-thîr′ē-əl) adj. **1.** Having to do with the upper regions of space. **2.** Light and airy.

**eulogy** (yōō′lə-jē) n. A speech delivered at a funeral in praise of the deceased person.

**evanescent** (ĕv′ə-nĕs′ənt) adj. Fleeting; short-lived.

**evocative** (ĭ-vŏk′ə-tĭv) adj. Tending to call forth memories, thoughts, and feelings.

**exalted** (ĕg-zôl′tĭd) adj. Noble; sublime.

**exasperation** (ĕg-zăs′pə-rā′shən) n. Extreme annoyance.

**excruciating** (ĕk-skrōō′shē-ā′tĭng) adj. Intensively painful.

**executor** (ĕg-zĕk′yə-tər) n. Someone appointed to carry out the instructions in a will.

**exhalation** (ĕks′hə-lā′shən) n. Something given off, as air or stream.

**exhilaration** (ĕg-zĭl′ə-rā′shən) n. Stimulation; liveliness; high spirits.

**exotic** (ĕg-zŏt′ĭk) adj. Foreign or unfamiliar.

**expansive** (ĕk-spăn′sĭv) adj. Behaving in a grand or self-important way. — **expansively** adv.

**expedient** (ĕk-spē′dē-ənt) n. A quick or convenient means of accomplishing a desired result.

**exploitation** (ĕks′ploi-tā′shən) n. The use of another person or a thing for selfish or improper reasons.

**extort** (ĕk-stôrt′) v. To get money from someone through threats, violence, or misuse of authority.

**exultation** (ĕg′zŭl-tā′shən) n. Rejoicing, especially in triumph.

**F**

**facilitate** (fə-sĭl′ə-tāt′) v. To make easy.

**faction** (făk′shən) n. A group within an organization working together against the main body or other groups.

**fatuous** (făch′ōō-əs) adj. Foolish. — **fatuously** adv.

**fawn** (fôn) v. To get attention or favor through flattery or excessive humility, as a dog will show friendliness by licking hands.

**feint** (fānt) v. To deliver pretended blows to confuse an opponent; to pretend to attack.

**fervent** (fûr′vənt) adj. Intense in feeling. — **fervently** adv.

**fervid** (fûr′vĭd) adj. Intensely enthusiastic. — **fervidly** adv.

**festoon** (fĕs-tōōn′) n. A wreath of flowers, leaves, and ribbons. — v. To hang such a wreath around.

**fetter** (fĕt′ər) n. Something attached to the body to prevent freedom of movement; a chain.

**fey** (fā) adj. Appearing as if under a spell.

**filigree** (fĭl′ə-grē′) adj. Delicate and lacelike.

**flagstone** (flăg′stōn′) n. A hard stone used for paving.

**flail** (flāl) v. To strike.

**flank** (flăngk) n. A side part of anything.

**flatulent** (flăch′ōō-lənt) adj. Full of or resembling gas.

**flaunt** (flônt) v. To show off.

**fleur-de-lys** (flûr′də-lē′, flōōr′-) n. A three-petaled flower design, used as an emblem of the kings of France.

**flint** (flĭnt) n. A small stone used to start a fire.

**flounce** (flouns) v. To move in quick, exaggerated movements.

**flounder** (floun′dər) v. To struggle or move with great difficulty.

**floweret** (flou′ər-ĭt) n. Poetic. A small flower.

**flute** (flōōt) n. A vertical groove with a rounded inner surface.

**fluctuate** (flŭk′chōō-āt′) v. To change continuously; rise and fall.

**forage** (fôr′ĭj, fŏr′-) n. Food for cattle, sheep, or horses.

**foray** (fôr′ā′) n. A raid.

**forbear** (fôr-bâr′) v. To be patient or tolerant.

**ford** (fôrd, fōrd) n. A place in a river that is shallow enough to cross on foot.

**foreboding** (fôr-bō′dĭng, fōr-) n. A feeling that something harmful is going to happen.

**forestall** (fôr-stôl′, fōr-) v. To prevent.

**formidable** (fôr′mə-də-bəl) adj. **1.** Causing fear. **2.** Very impressive because of strength or skill.

**freshet** (frĕsh′ĭt) n. A stream flowing into the sea.

**fretful** (frĕt′fəl) adj. Irritable. — **fretfully** adv.

**frivolous** (frĭv′ə-ləs) adj. Not serious; playful.

**frond** (frŏnd) n. A leaf or leaflike part of a plant.

**frowzy** (frou′zē) adj. Untidy; shabby.

**frugal** (frōō′gəl) adj. Thrifty. — **frugally** adv.

**furrow** (fûr′ō) n. A rut or groove made by a plow.

**furtive** (fûr′tĭv) adj. Sly; secret. — **furtively** adv.

**fusillade** (fyōō′sə-läd′, -läd′) n. A rapid and continuous barrage of gunfire; any rapid outburst or attack of something.

**G**

**gait** (gāt) n. A manner of walking.

**gall** (gôl) v. To irritate; annoy.

**gambol** (găm′bəl) v. To skip about playfully.

**gargoyle** (gär′goil′) n. A carved, jutting-out decoration on a building, featuring a fantastic and grotesque animal or human.

**garish** (gâr′ĭsh) adj. Overly showy; gaudy.

**garland** (gär′lənd) n. A wreath of flowers.

**garnish** (gär′nĭsh) v. To decorate; trim.

**gaunt** (gônt) adj. Extremely thin.

**gauntlet** (gônt′lĭt, gänt′-) n. **1.** A long protective glove. **2.** An ordeal once used as a means of punishment, in which the guilty person had to run between two rows of men who struck him with clubs or other weapons. **3.** A severe trial; an ordeal.

**gelatin** (jĕl′ə-tən) n. A thin, transparent, soluble material used in the preparation of food, medicine capsules, etc.

**germane** (jər-mān′) adj. Naturally related to the subject at hand.

**gibe** (jīb) v. To make sarcastic remarks.

**glean** (glēn) v. To gather grain from a field that has been reaped.

**glen** (glĕn) n. A valley.

---

ă pat/ā pay/âr care/ä father/b bib/ch church/d deed/ĕ pet/ē be/f fife/g gag/h hat/hw which/ĭ pit/ī pie/îr pier/j judge/k kick/l lid, needle/m mum/ n no, sudden/ng thing/ŏ pot/ō toe/ô paw, for/oi noise/ou out/ŏŏ took/ōō boot/p pop/r roar/s sauce/sh ship, dish/t tight/th thin, path/th this, bathe/ ŭ cut/ûr urge/v valve/w with/y yes/z zebra, size/zh vision/ə about, item, edible, gallop, circus/ à Fr. ami/œ Fr. feu, Ger. schön/ü Fr. tu, Ger. über/ KH Ger. ich, Scot. loch/N Fr. bon.

**glint** (glĭnt) *n.* To sparkle.

**gloaming** (glō'mĭng) *n.* Twilight.

**globular** (glŏb'yə-lər) *adj.* Globe-shaped; round.

**goad** (gōd) *n.* A pointed stick used to drive cattle. — *v.* To urge into action.

**gorge** (gôrj) *v.* To fill oneself, as when eating greedily.

**gourd** (gôrd, gōrd, gōōrd) *n.* The dried, hollow shell of a kind of plant (like a pumpkin), used as a container.

**gout** (gout) *n.* 1. A disease that affects the joints. 2. A spurt or splash.

**gramophone** (grăm'ə-fōn') *n.* A phonograph.

**granary** (grăn'ə-rē, grā'nə-) *n.* A storage place for grain that is ready to be used.

**grimace** (grĭ-mās', grĭm'ĭs) *n.* A facial expression of disgust or pain.

**grope** (grōp) *v.* To feel one's way.

**guttural** (gŭt'ər-əl) *adj.* Coming from the throat.

**H**

**habiliments** (hə-bĭl'ə-mənts) *n. pl.* Clothing and accessories suitable to a particular occasion.

**haggle** (hăg'əl) *v.* To argue about the price or terms of a deal.

**halcyon** (hăl'sē-ən) *adj.* Calm, peaceful.

**haply** (hăp'lē) *adv. Archaic.* Perhaps.

**harry** (hăr'ē) *v.* To torment, worry.

**hawk** (hôk) *n.* Any of a large group of birds of prey.

**hawk** (hôk) *n.* A small board used to hold plaster.

**hearken** (här'kən) *v.* To listen carefully.

**heraldry** (hĕr'əl-drē) *n.* Coats of arms or other family insignia. — **heraldric** (hə-răl'dĭk) *adj.*

**hermitage** (hûr'mə-tĭj) *n.* A place to live that is far away from other people.

**herbage** (ûr'bĭj, hûr'-) *n.* Green plant growth, especially grass.

**hew** (hyōō) *v.* To chop or cut.

**hilarity** (hĭ-lăr'ə-tē, hī-) *n.* Extreme merriment or laughter.

**holocaust** (hŏl'ə-kôst', hō'lə-) *n.* A large and destructive fire.

**homage** (hŏm'ĭj, ŏm'-) *n.* Honor and loyalty.

**hostelry** (hŏs'təl-rē) *n.* An inn.

**hove** (hōv) *v.* Headed into the wind, like a ship.

**hovel** (hŭv'əl, hŏv'-) *n.* A small, poor dwelling.

**hover** (hŭv'ər, hŏv'-) *v.* To move around while staying over a particular place.

**humane** (hyōō-mān') *adj.* Merciful; kind.

**hummock** (hŭm'ək) *n.* A small hill.

**I**

**ignominy** (ĭg'nə mĭn'ē) *n.* Dishonor; shame.

**illusory** (ĭ-lōō'sə-rē, -zə-rē) *adj.* Unreal.

**immerse** (ĭ-mûrs') *v.* To involve completely.

**imminent** (ĭm'ə-nənt) *adj.* About to happen. — **imminence** *n.*

**immolate** (ĭm'ə-lāt) *v.* To kill, as if for a sacrifice.

**impale** (ĭm-pāl') *v.* To pierce through and fix on something pointed.

**impalpable** (ĭm-păl'pə-bəl) *adj.* Unable to be felt.

**impart** (ĭm-pärt') *v.* To tell; reveal.

**impassive** (ĭm-păs'ĭv) *adj.* Showing no emotion.

**impede** (ĭm-pēd') *v.* To block; hinder.

**imperative** (ĭm-pĕr'ə-tĭv) *adj.* Commanding; urgent. — *n.* A compelling force.

**imperceptible** (ĭm'pər-sĕp'tə-bəl) *adj.* Not or barely noticeable. — **imperceptibly** *adv.*

**imperial** (ĭm-pîr'ē-əl) *adj.* Of great size and outstanding quality; majestic.

**impetuous** (ĭm-pĕch'ōō-əs) *adj.* Acting suddenly without thinking; reckless. — **impetuosity** (ĭm-pĕch'ōō-ŏs'ə-tē) *n.*

**implicit** (ĭm-plĭs'ĭt) *adj.* Characteristic of but not directly expressed; suggested.

**implore** (ĭm-plôr', -plōr') *v.* To beg.

**imposture** (ĭm-pŏs'chər) *n.* Deception; trickery.

**imprecation** (ĭm'prə-kā'shən) *n.* A curse.

**impregnable** (ĭm-prĕg'nə-bəl) *adj.* Incapable of being captured or entered; unyielding.

**impudent** (ĭm'pyə-dənt) *adj.* Boldly disrespectful.

**inanimate** (ĭn-ăn'ə-mĭt) *adj.* Not containing or showing life.

**inarticulate** (ĭn'är-tĭk'yə-lĭt) *adj.* 1. Uttered without the distinct sounds of speech. 2. Speechless.

**inaudible** (ĭn-ô'də-bəl) *adj.* Unable to be heard. — **inaudibly** *adv.*

**inauspicious** (ĭn'ô-spĭsh'əs) *adj.* Boding ill; unlucky.

**incandescent** (ĭn'kən-dĕs'ənt) *adj.* Very bright; brilliant. — **incandescence** *n.*

**incapacitate** (ĭn'kə-păs'ə-tāt') *v.* To take away strength or ability from.

**incendiary** (ĭn-sĕn'dē-ĕr'ē) *adj.* Capable of causing a fire.

**incessant** (ĭn-sĕs'ənt) *adj.* Unceasing; continuous. — **incessantly** *adv.*

**incite** (ĭn-sīt') *v.* To urge on to action.

**incomprehensible** (ĭn'kŏm-prĭ-hĕn'sə-bəl) *adj.* Not understandable.

**incongruous** (ĭn'kong'grōō-əs) *adj.* Lacking in suitability, harmony, or logic. — **incongruity** (ĭn'kŏng-grōō'ə-tē, ĭn'kən-) *n.*

**incorporate** (ĭn-kôr'pə-rāt') *v.* To combine; bring together into a single unit.

**incredulous** (ĭn-krĕj'ə-ləs) *adj.* Unable to believe.

**indigent** (ĭn'də-jənt) *adj.* Very poor.

**indigo** (ĭn'dĭ-gō') *n.* A deep purplish-blue.

**indiscreet** (ĭn'dĭs-krēt') *adj.* Showing poor judgment.

**indiscriminate** (ĭn'dĭs-krĭm'ə-nĭt) *adj.* Haphazard; random. — **indiscriminately** *adv.*

**indolent** (ĭn'də-lənt) *adj.* Lazy. — **indolence** *n.*

**indulge** (ĭn-dŭlj') *v.* To give in to an urge or whim.

**inert** (ĭn-ûrt') *adj.* Not moving or unable to move.

**infallible** (ĭn-făl'ə-bəl) *adj.* Incapable of error; certain. — **infallibly** *adv.*

**infuse** (ĭn-fyōōz') *v.* To fill, as if by pouring.

**ingenious** (ĭn-jēn'yəs) *adj.* Clever; inventive. — **ingeniously** *adv.*

**ingress** (ĭn'grĕs') *n.* A way in; entrance.

**insensible** (ĭn-sĕn'sə-bəl) *adj.* Unconscious. — **insensibility** *n.*

**insolent** (ĭn'sə-lənt) *adj.* Shamelessly disrespectful. — **insolence** *n.*

**instigate** (ĭn'stĭ-gāt') *v.* To urge on to action. — **instigation** (ĭn'stĭ-gā'shən) *n.*

**integrity** (ĭn-tĕg'rə-tē) *n.* The quality of being complete or sound, especially morally.

**intercession** (ĭn'tər-sĕsh'ən) *n.* Prayer or pleading on behalf of another.

**interim** (ĭn'tər-ĭm) *n.* The time between one event and another.

**interminable** (ĭn-tûr'mə-nə-bəl) *adj.* Seeming to be endless.

**interpose** (ĭn'tər-pōz') *v.* To introduce an interruption of speech or motion.

**interrogate** (ĭn-tĕr'ə-gāt') *v.* To question.

**intolerable** (ĭn-tŏl'ər-ə-bəl) *adj.* Unbearable.

**intricate** (ĭn'trĭ-kĭt) *adj.* Having many parts or details; complicated.

**intuitive** (ĭn-tōō'ə-tĭv, ĭn-tyōō'-) *adj.* Understood or known without conscious reasoning.

**inundate** (ĭn'ŭn-dāt') *v.* To flood. — **inundation** (ĭn'ŭn-dā'shən) *n.*

**invective** (ĭn-vĕk'tĭv) *n.* Strong verbal abuse characterized by curses and insults.

**invest** (ĭn-vĕst') *v.* To provide or endow with some particular quality.

**invigorate** (ĭn-vĭg'ə-rāt') *v.* To fill with strength and energy.

**irate** (ī'rāt, ī-rāt') *adj.* Very angry.

**irresolute** (ĭ-rĕz'ə-lōōt') *adj.* Unable to make a decision. — **irresolution** (ĭ-rĕz'ə-lōō'shən) *n.*

**irrevocable** (ĭ-rĕv'ə-kə-bəl) *adj.* Incapable of being undone or brought back. — **irrevocably** *adv.*

**J**

**jar** (jär) *v.* To shock; irritate.

**jest** (jĕst) *n.* Something said or done to amuse; a joke.

**jostle** (jŏs'əl) *v.* To bump and shove.

**jounce** (jouns) *v.* To bounce or shake; jolt.

**joust** (joust, jŭst, jōōst) *n.* A fight with lances between two people on horseback.

**judicious** (jōō-dĭsh'əs) *adj.* Showing good judgment; wise. — **judiciously** *adv.*

**juncture** (jŭng'chər) *n.* A point in time, especially a decisive moment.

**juxtapose** (jŭk'stə-pōz') *v.* To place side by side.

**K**

**kelp** (kĕlp) *n.* Brown seaweed.

**kindle** (kĭnd'l) *v.* To inflame; excite.

**kindred** (kĭn'drĭd) *adj.* Similar; related.

**knave** (nāv) *n.* **1.** *Archaic.* A male servant; a man of humble status. **2.** A dishonest, deceitful person.

**knead** (nēd) *v.* To rub or press with the hands.

**knoll** (nōl) *n.* A small hill.

**L**

**lacerate** (lăs'ə-rāt') *v.* To cut or tear jaggedly.

**laconic** (lə-kŏn'ĭk) *adj.* Using few words.

**lament** (lə-mĕnt') *v.* To grieve; mourn. — *n.* An expression of grief. — also **lamentation** (lăm'ən-tā'shən) *n.*

**languid** (lăng'gwĭd) *adj.* Without spirit; listless.

**languish** (lăng'gwĭsh) *v.* To become weak or slow.

**languor** (lăng'gər) *n.* An air of softness or gentleness. — **languorous** *adj.*

**lap** (lăp) *v.* To make a light, splashing sound.

**laurel** (lô'rəl) *n.* A plant with large leaves that are woven into a wreath to crown the victor in a contest. — *v.* To crown a victor with such a wreath.

**leer** (lîr) *v.* To look from the side with an expression of spite or ill will.

**leeward** (lē'wərd, lōō'ərd) *adj.* In the direction toward which the wind blows.

**legacy** (lĕg'ə-sē) *n.* Anything inherited through a will.

**legend** (lĕj'ənd) *n.* **1.** A story handed down from generation to generation, believed to have a historical basis. **2.** An inscription on a coin, etc. **3.** A caption or key for an illustration or a map.

**legion** (lē'jən) *n.* In ancient Rome, a major division of an army.

**lethargy** (lĕth'ər-jē) *n.* A condition of extreme sluggishness.

**lewd** (lōōd) *adj.* **1.** *Obsolete.* Ignorant; uncouth. **2.** Wicked; lustful.

**license** (lī'səns) *n.* Excessive and undisciplined freedom.

**liege** (lēj) *n.* A lord in medieval times.

**limber** (lĭm'bər) *adj.* Able to move easily.

**linguist** (lĭng'gwĭst) *n.* **1.** A person who speaks many languages. **2.** A language specialist.

**lintel** (lĭnt'l) *n.* The horizontal beam over a door or window.

**listless** (lĭst'lĭs) *adj.* Not showing interest or enthusiasm. — **listlessly** *adv.*

**lithe** (līth) *adj.* Easily graceful; limber.

**loath** (lōth, lōth) *adj.* Unwilling.

**lope** (lōp) *n.* A steady, easy stride.

**lore** (lôr, lōr) *n.* The accumulated information on a particular subject.

**lout** (lout) *n.* A stupid, awkward person.

**lubber** (lŭb'ər) *n.* A slow, clumsy person. — **lubberly** *adj.*

**lucent** (lōō'sənt) *adj.* Bright. — **lucence** *n.*

**lucid** (lōō'sĭd) *adj.* Clear.

**lumber** (lŭm'bər) *v.* To move clumsily.

**luminous** (lōō'mə-nəs) *adj.* **1.** Giving off light. **2.** Clear.

**lurch** (lûrch) *v.* To pitch forward suddenly.

**lurid** (lōōr'ĭd) *adj.* **1.** Glowing. **2.** Vivid, in a shocking way.

**lustrous** (lŭs'trəs) *adj.* Bright.

**lusty** (lŭs'tē) *adj.* Full of intense enthusiasm. — **lustily** *adv.*

**M**

**mace** (mās) *n.* An aromatic spice made from the outer covering of the nutmeg.

**mail** (māl) *n.* A flexible protective body covering, made of overlapping metal rings.

**maim** (mām) *v.* To cripple.

---

ă pat/ā pay/âr care/ä father/b bib/ch church/d deed/ĕ pet/ē be/f fife/g gag/h hat/hw which/ĭ pit/ī pie/îr pier/j judge/k kick/l lid, needle/m mum/ n no, sudden/ng thing/ŏ pot/ō toe/ô paw, for/oi noise/ou out/ŏŏ took/ōō boot/p pop/r roar/s sauce/sh ship, dish/t tight/th thin, path/*th* this, bathe/ ū cut/ûr urge/v valve/w with/y yes/z zebra, size/zh vision/ə about, item, edible, gallop, circus/à *Fr.* ami/œ *Fr.* feu, *Ger.* schön/ü *Fr.* tu, *Ger.* über/ кн *Ger.* ich, *Scot.* loch/ɴ *Fr.* bon.

**maize** (māz) n. Corn.

**malaise** (măl-āz′) n. A feeling of physical or mental discomfort.

**malevolent** (mə-lĕv′ə-lənt) adj. Showing ill will; wishing harm to others.

**malice** (măl′ĭs) n. Ill will; spite.

**malign** (mə-līn′) v. To speak evil of. – adj. harmful.

**malignant** (mə-lĭg′nənt) adj. Very harmful; likely to cause death.

**mandible** (măn′də-bəl) n. The jaw.

**manifest** (măn′ə-fĕst) adj. Obvious. – **manifestly** adv.

**mantle** (măn′təl) n. A sleeveless cloak or cape.

**marshal** (mär′shəl) v. To arrange in order.

**martial** (mär′shəl) adj. Pertaining to war or the military.

**matriarch** (mā′trē-ärk′) n. A woman who is the head of a family or tribe.

**mattock** (măt′ək) n. A digging tool similar to a pickax.

**memento** (mə-mĕn′tō) n. A souvenir.

**meticulous** (mə-tĭk′yə-ləs) adj. Extremely precise concerning details; fussy.

**mettle** (mĕt′l) n. An extremely fine character, especially in regard to courage.

**milch** (mĭlch) adj. Giving milk (describing a cow).

**milliner** (mĭl′ə-nər) n. A person who makes or sells women's hats.

**minute** (mī-nōot′) adj. Tiny.

**mollify** (mŏl′ə-fī′) v. To soothe.

**moniker** (mŏn′ĭ-kər) n. Slang. A person's name or nickname.

**monosyllable** (mŏn′ə-sĭl′ə-bəl) n. A word with one syllable.

**morbid** (môr′bĭd) adj. Concerned with gloomy or gruesome matters.

**mordant** (môr′dənt) adj. Biting; cutting.

**morose** (mə-rōs′ mô-) adj. Gloomy. – **morosely** adv.

**mortal** (môrt′l) adj. 1. Human; not able to live forever. 2. To the point of death; extreme. – **mortally** adv.

**mortality** (môr-tăl′ə-tē) n. The condition of being subject to death.

**mortify** (môr′tə-fī′) v. 1. Obsolete To deprive of life or strength. 2. To humiliate.

**motif** (mō-tēf′) n. The main idea or most distinctive quality of a work of art.

**myriad** (mĭr′ē-əd) n. A vast number. – adj. Countless.

**myrrh** (mûr) n. A fragrant plant fluid used in making incense or perfume.

**mystic** (mĭs′tĭk) adj. Mysterious; beyond human understanding. – also **mystical.**

**mysticism** (mĭs′tə-sĭz′əm) n. The belief that certain basic truths can be known or understood by intuition alone, without the use of reason.

**N**

**naive** (nä-ēv′) adj. Childlike; not worldy-wise.

**nape** (nāp) n. The back of the neck.

**nocturnal** (nŏk-tûr′nəl) adj. Occurring at night.

**nondescript** (nŏn′dĭ-skrĭpt′) adj. Not having any distinguishing qualities or characteristics.

**novelty** (nŏv′əl-tē) n. Something new or recently invented.

**nubbin** (nŭb′ĭn) n. Anything small and not yet developed.

**O**

**oblique** (ō-blēk′, ə-) adj. Not straightforward; unclear in meaning.

**oddments** (ŏd′mənts) n. pl. Various, miscellaneous items.

**odious** (ō′dē-əs) adj. Hateful; disgusting.

**omen** (ō′mən) n. Something that foretells the future.

**ominous** (ŏm′ə-nəs) adj. Threatening. – **ominously** adv.

**oppressive** (ə-prəs′ĭv) adj. Difficult to bear.

**optical** (ŏp′tĭ-kəl) adj. Having to do with the sense of sight. – **optically** adv.

**oracle** (ôr′ə-kəl, ŏr′-) n. A person believed in ancient times to be in contact with the gods.

**ordain** (ôr-dān′) v. To determine beforehand.

**ostentatious** (ŏs′tĕn-tā′shəs, ŏs′tən-) adj. Extremely showy.

**P**

**paling** (pāl′ĭng) n. A piece of wood that is part of a fence.

**pallid** (păl′ĭd) adj. Extremely pale.

**palmy** (pä′mē) adj. Prosperous; flourishing.

**palpable** (păl′pə-bəl) adj. Capable of being easily grasped mentally; obvious.

**panacea** (păn′ə-sē′ə) n. A supposed remedy; a cure-all.

**pandemonium** (păn′də-mō′nē-əm) n. Wild noise and disorder.

**parabolic** (păr′ə-bŏl′ĭk) adj. Bowl-shaped.

**paradox** (păr′ə-dŏks′) n. A situation or statement that seems self-contradictory but is nevertheless true.

**paramour** (păr′ə-mōor′) n. A lover.

**parley** (pär′lē) n. A discussion or conference.

**passive** (păs′ĭv) adj. Not active; making no effort.

**patent** (păt′ənt) adj. Obvious. – **patently** adv.

**patrimony** (păt′rə-mō′nē) n. Anything inherited from ancestors.

**patronize** (pā′trə-nīz′, păt′rə-) v. To treat others with an air of superiority. – **patronizing** adj. – **patronizingly** adv.

**peal** (pēl) n. The ringing of bells or chimes.

**peerless** (pîr′lĭs) adj. Without an equal; unmatched.

**pelt** (pĕlt) v. To pound steadily and heavily.

**pendulum** (pĕn′jōō-ləm, dyə-, də-) n. Something that swings freely back and forth.

**peon** (pē′ŏn′) n. In Latin America or the southwestern United States, a laborer or a farm worker.

**perceptible** (pər-sep′tə-bəl) adj. Noticeable; recognizable.

**perception** (pər-sĕp′shən) n. Understanding or insight; awareness.

**periphery** (pə-rĭf′ə-rē) n. The outside boundary of a particular area.

**perpetual** (pər-pĕch′ōō-əl) adj. Lasting forever; eternal.

**perplex** (pər-plĕks′) v. To confuse.

**perturbation** (pûr′tər-bā′shən) n. A confusion or disturbance.

**perverse** (pər-vûrs′) adj. Contrary to what is considered to be correct thinking or behavior.

**pestilence** (pĕs′tə-ləns) n. An epidemic of a contagious, deadly disease; plague.

**petulant** (pĕch′ōō-lənt) adj. Irritable; impatient.

**phantasm** (făn′tăz′əm) n. Something that seems to exist but actually has no physical reality; phantom. – also **phantasma.**

**phenomenon** (fĭ-nŏm′ə-nŏn′) *n.* Something that can be seen but is difficult to understand; an unusual occurrence.

**phosphorescence** (fŏs′fə-rĕs′əns) *n.* A continuous giving off of light.

**piazza** (pē-ăz′ə) *n.* A wide porch.

**piquant** (pē′kənt, -kǎnt′, pē-kǎnt′) *adj.* Stimulating; exciting. — **piquancy** *n.*

**pique** (pēk) *n.* Resentment due to injured pride. — *v.* To provoke such resentment by offending someone's pride.

**pirouette** (pĭr′ōō-ĕt′) *n.* A spinning movement on tiptoe.

**pith** (pĭth) *n.* The soft, spongy tissue in the center of the stems of most plants.

**placid** (plăs′ĭd) *adj.* Calm. — **placidly** *adv.*

**plaintive** (plān′tĭv) *adj.* Sad.

**plight** (plīt) *v.* To promise or bind by solemn oath, especially to promise to marry.

**plume** (plōōm) *n.* A cluster of feathers on a helmet worn as a decoration or symbol of rank.

**plunder** (plŭn′dər) *v.* To rob by force. — **plunderer** *n.*

**ply** (plī) *v.* **1.** To work diligently at an occupation requiring a particular skill. **2.** To travel back and forth between places.

**poignant** (poin′yənt) *adj.* Emotionally touching.

**poise** (poiz) *v.* To balance or remain steady in a certain position. — *n.* The state of being calm and self-assured.

**poll** (pōl) *n.* The head, especially the top of the head, where the hair is.

**pommel** (pŭm′əl, pŏm′-) *n.* The rounded front part of a saddle.

**porous** (pôr′əs, pōr′-) *adj.* Having tiny openings that allow liquids, gases, or odors to pass through.

**portal** (pôrt′l, pōrt′l) *n.* A point of entry, especially a large, imposing doorway or gate.

**portent** (pôr′tĕnt′, pōr′-) *n.* Something that predicts an event that is about to happen, usually an unfortunate one.

**portly** (pôrt′lē, pōrt′-) *adj.* Large; heavy.

**posterior** (pŏ-stîr′ē-ər, pō-) *n.* The rear end of the body or, figuratively, a part of something in a similar position.

**posterity** (pŏ-stĕr′ə-tē) *n.* All of a person's descendants.

**poultice** (pōl′tĭs) *n.* A hot pack applied to an inflamed part of the body.

**praetor** (prē′tər) *n.* In ancient Rome, an elected judge ranking just below a consul.

**precarious** (prĭ-kâr′ē-əs) *adj.* Uncertain; risky. — **precariously** *adv.*

**precede** (prĭ-sēd′) *v.* To come before.

**precincts** (prē-sĭngkts) *n. pl.* A neighborhood or particular area.

**precipitate** (prĭ-sĭp′ə-tāt′) *v.* **1.** To cause to happen sooner than expected; bring on. **2.** To cause a substance to separate and fall.

**premonition** (prē′mə-nĭsh′ən, prĕm′ə-) *n.* A feeling that a particular thing will happen.

**preoccupy** (prē-ŏk′yə-pī′) *v.* To completely fill one's thoughts.

**preside** (prĭ-zīd′) *v.* To be in charge or have control.

**presumptuous** (prĭ-zŭmp′chōō-əs) *adj.* Overconfident; arrogant.

**pretext** (prē′tĕkst′) *n.* A false reason; an excuse.

**prevail** (prĭ-vāl′) *v.* **1.** To be or remain in force. **2.** To have an effect. **3.** To have the greatest authority.

**prevalent** (prĕv′ə-lənt) *adj.* Generally accepted; widespread.

**prime** (prīm) *n.* The period of an individual's peak physical and mental condition.

**prink** (prĭngk) *v.* To primp; dress up in a fussy way.

**privation** (prī-vā′shən) *n.* A deprivation, especially of a basic need or comfort of life.

**procure** (prō-kyŏŏr′, prə-) *v.* To acquire; get.

**prodigious** (prə-dĭj′əs) *adj.* Enormous.

**prodigy** (prŏd′ə-jē) *n.* **1.** *Archaic.* An unusual happening, thought to foretell the future. **2.** An extraordinary person or thing.

**profane** (prō-fān′, prə-) *v.* To treat sacred things with contempt.

**proffer** (prŏf′ər) *v.* To offer.

**profuse** (prə-fyōōs′, prō-) *adj.* Abundant.

**promontory** (prŏm′ən-tôr′ē, -tōr′ē) *n.* A high ridge of land jutting out into a body of water.

**prone** (prōn) *adj.* Having a natural tendency (used with **to**).

**propriety** (prə-prī′ə-tē) *n.* The quality of being in accordance with what is accepted as proper in taste and behavior.

**prosaic** (prō-zā′ĭk) *adj.* Matter-of-fact; straightforward.

**proscription** (prō-skrĭp′shən) *n.* In ancient Rome, the publication of the name of someone condemned to death. Such a person was "fair game" and could be killed by anyone.

**prostrate** (prŏs′trāt′) *adj.* Lying face down, especially in humility.

**provender** (prŏv′ən-dər) *n.* Food, especially for livestock.

**providence** (prŏv′ə-dəns, -dĕns′) *n.* **1.** God's care or guidance. **2.** *cap.* God.

**prudent** (prōōd′ənt) *adj.* Careful; wise.

**pugnacious** (pŭg-nā′shəs) *adj.* Quarrelsome.

**pulsate** (pŭl′sāt′) *v.* To beat or throb.

**punctilious** (pŭngk-tĭl′ē-əs) *adj.* Very strict in carrying out details, especially details of proper behavior.

**purge** (pûrj) *v.* To make clean by removing impurities. — **purger** *n.*

**putrefactive** (pyōō′trə-făk′tĭv) *adj.* Causing decay or rotting.

**pyre** (pīr) *n.* A pile or structure, usually of wood, on which a dead body is burned as part of a funeral.

# Q

**quadrilateral** (kwŏd′rə-lăt′ər-əl) *n.* A four-sided figure.

---

ă pat/ā pay/âr care/ä father/b bib/ch church/d deed/ĕ pet/ē be/f fife/g gag/h hat/hw which/ĭ pit/ī pie/îr pier/j judge/k kick/l lid. needle/m mum/ n no. sudden/ng thing/ŏ pot/ō toe/ô paw, for/oi noise/ou out/ŏŏ took/ōō boot/p pop/r roar/s sauce/sh ship. dish/t tight/th thin. path/th this. bathe/ ū cut/ûr urge/v valve/w with/y yes/z zebra. size/zh vision/ə about. item. edible. gallop. circus/ä Fr. ami/œ Fr. feu. Ger. schön/ü Fr. tu, Ger. über/ KH Ger. ich, Scot. loch/N Fr. bon.

**quaint** (kwānt) *adj.* Pleasing in an unusual or old-fashioned way.

**qualm** (kwäm, kwôm) *n.* A sudden feeling of physical or mental discomfort or uneasiness.

**quarry** (kwôr'ē, kwŏr'ē) *n.* A place where building stone is taken from the ground.

**quicksilver** (kwĭk'sĭl'vər) *adj.* Fast-moving, like mercury.

**R**

**rail** (rāl) *v.* To complain bitterly; scold.

**rakish** (rā'kĭsh) *adj.* Dashing; carefree.

**rampant** (răm'pənt) *adj.* Wild in behavior; unrestrained.

**rampart** (răm'pärt) *n.* **1.** A protective wall encircling a fortress or city. **2.** Any structure that serves as a defense.

**rancor** (răng'kər) *n.* Hatred.

**range** (rānj) *v.* To wander about.

**rapport** (ră-pôr', -pōr') *n.* A harmonious relationship.

**rapt** (răpt) *adj.* Completely absorbed; engrossed.

**rationalism** (răsh'ən-əl-ĭz'əm) *n.* The belief that reason is the only authority in determining truth. — **rationalistic** (răsh'ən-əl-ĭs'tĭk) *adj.*

**rationalize** (răsh'ən-əl-īz') *v.* To think up self-satisfying but untrue reasons or excuses for one's behavior. — **rationalization** (răsh'ən-əl-ə-zā'shən) *n.*

**raze** (rāz) *v.* **1.** *Rare.* To erase. **2.** To tear down completely.

**rebuke** (rĭ-byōōk') *v.* To scold; reprimand.

**recede** (rĭ-sēd') *v.* To move or fade away.

**recluse** (rĕk'lōōs', rĭ-klōōs') *n.* A person who lives alone and shut off from other people.

**reconnoiter** (rē'kə-noi'tər, rĕk'ə-) *v.* To explore an area to get to know what it is like or what is happening there.

**recount** (rĭ-kount') *v.* To tell in detail; narrate.

**redress** (rĭ-drĕs') *v.* To set right; make amends. — (rĭ-drĕs', rē'drĕs') *n.* Correction of or compensation for something wrong.

**reel** (rēl) *v.* To spin or stagger; fall back.

**reflective** (rĭ-flĕk'tĭv) *adj.* Thoughtful.

**relentless** (rĭ-lĕnt'lĭs) *adj.* Not letting up; persistent. — **relentlessly** *adv.*

**relic** (rĕl'ĭk) *n.* Something from the past valued for its historic interest or personal association.

**remnant** (rĕm'nənt) *n.* Something left over, especially something indicating what has been; a trace.

**remorse** (rĭ-môrs') *n.* A feeling of guilt or regret for having done something wrong. — **remorseful** *adj.* — **remorsefully** *adv.*

**rend** (rĕnd) *v.* To pull at or rip forcefully.

**render** (rĕn'dər) *v.* **1.** To make a formal, public declaration. **2.** To deliver a personal expression or interpretation of something already written or said.

**rent** (rĕnt) *n.* A hole or opening made by ripping or tearing.

**repeal** (rĭ-pēl') *v.* *Obsolete.* To recall from exile. — *n.* *Obsolete.* The act of recalling from exile.

**repel** (rĭ-pĕl') *v.* To cause someone to turn away; disgust.

**repent** (rĭ-pĕnt') *v.* To feel sorry and eager to make amends for something one has done.

**repose** (rĭ-pōz') *v.* To lie quietly. — *n.* Sleep or rest; relaxation.

**reprieve** (rĭ-prēv') *n.* The postponement of punishment or trouble; temporary relief.

**reprove** (rĭ-prōōv') *v.* To scold.

**residue** (rĕz'ə-dōō', -dyōō') *n.* Something remaining after the major part has been removed.

**resolute** (rĕz'ə-lōōt') *adj.* Determined.

**resound** (rĭ-zound') *v.* To make a loud, echoing sound.

**restive** (rĕs'tĭv) *adj.* Nervous; restless.

**retain** (rĭ'tān') *v.* To hold or keep in a particular place or condition.

**retainer** (rĭ'tā'nər) *n.* Someone in the service of another, especially of one of the nobility in the Middle Ages.

**retentive** (rĭ'tĕn'tĭv) *adj.* Having the ability to keep or hold.

**reticent** (rĕt'ə-sənt) *adj.* Not inclined to speak; silent.

**retinue** (rĕt'n-ōō', -yōō') *n.* A group of people in the service of a person of high status.

**retort** (rĭ-tôrt') *v.* To answer in a sharp, quick way.

**retribution** (rĕt'-rə-byōō'shən) *n.* Punishment for having done something evil.

**revel** (rĕv'l) *v.* To engage in lively festivities. — *n.* A celebration; noisy merrymaking. — **reveler** *n.*

**reverberate** (rĭ-vûr'bə-rāt') *v.* To reecho.

**reverie** (rĕv'ər-ē) *n.* Fanciful thinking; a daydream.

**revile** (rĭ-vīl') *v.* To speak to with abusive language; insult.

**rhetorical** (rĭ-tôr'ĭ-kəl, rĭ-tōr'-) *adj.* Showy or complicated in one's style of writing or speaking.

**rheum** (rōōm) *n.* A watery discharge from the eyes or nose, as from a cold. — **rheumy** *adj.*

**rigor** (rĭg'ər) *n.* **1.** Strictness. **2.** Extreme difficulty. — **rigorous** *adj.*

**rile** (rīl) *v.* To anger.

**rite** (rīt) *n.* A ceremony for a special occasion, especially a religious ceremony.

**ritual** (rĭch'ōō-əl) *n.* A ceremony or practice performed according to set rules and at regular intervals. — **ritualistic** *adj.* — **ritualize** *v.*

**rivulet** (rĭv'yə-lĭt) *n.* A stream or brook.

**robust** (rō-bŭst', rō'bŭst) *adj.* Strong; healthy.

**root** (rōōt, rŏŏt) *v.* To dig in the earth as a pig does with its snout.

**rout** (rout) *n.* *Poetic.* A group of people; crowd.

**row** (rou) *n.* A noisy dispute.

**rueful** (rōō'fəl) *adj.* Sorrowful. — **ruefully** *adv.*

**S**

**sable** (sā'bəl) *adj.* Black or dark in color.

**sack** (săk) *v.* To loot a captured area.

**saffron** (săf'rən) *adj.* Orange-yellow.

**sagacious** (sə-gā'shəs) *adj.* Wise.

**salutation** (săl'yə-tā'shən) *n.* An expression or gesture of greeting.

**sanctimonious** (săngk'tə-mō'nē-əs) *adj.* Pretending to be righteous.

**sanitarium** (săn'ə-târ'ē-əm) *n.* An institution for the care of people with long-term illnesses.

**sate** (sāt) *v.* To satisfy to the fullest extent.

**saunter** (sôn'tər) *v.* To stroll.

**scabbard** (skăb'ərd) *n.* A container for a sword.

**scallop** (skŏl′əp, skăl′-) v. To make a decorative edging out of a series of curved projections.

**scavenge** (skăv′ĭnj) v. To search through rubbish heaps for something useful or edible.

**scoff** (skôf, skŏf) v. To mock; scorn.

**scrabble** (skrăb′əl) v. To scrape frantically with the hands.

**scrutinize** (skrōōt′n-īz) v. To examine carefully.

**scud** (skŭd) v. 1. To skim. 2. To be driven by the wind.

**scullery** (skŭl′ə-rē) n. A room where the dirty dishes are washed; kitchen.

**scuttle** (skŭt′l) n. To run quickly.

**seclusion** (sĭ-klōō′zhən) n. Being separated from others; isolation.

**sedan** (sĭ-dăn′) n. A closed automobile with wide front and back seats.

**sedate** (sĭ-dāt′) adj. Calm; unemotional.

**sedative** (sĕd′ə-tĭv) adj. Medication that calms and relaxes.

**seduce** (sĭ-dōōs′, -dyōōs′) v. 1. To persuade a person to do something wrong or to be disobedient. 2. To win someone over to one's side.

**seductive** (sĭ-dŭk′tĭv) adj. Tending to lead astray; enticing; charming.

**semblance** (sĕm′bləns) n. An outward appearance.

**senile** (sē′nīl′, sĕn′īl′) adj. Showing mental deterioration associated with old age. — **senility** (sĭ-nĭl′ə-tē) n.

**sensibilities** (sĕn′sə-bĭl′ə-tēz) n. pl. The ability to respond to stimuli with great feeling.

**sentinel** (sĕnt′n-əl) n. Someone who stands guard, usually a soldier.

**serpentine** (sûr′pən-tēn′, -tīn′) adj. Winding, like a serpent.

**servile** (sûr′vəl, -vīl′) adj. Slavish; submissive.

**shamble** (shăm-bəl) v. To walk in a shuffling way.

**shiftless** (shĭft′lĭs) adj. Lacking the will or ability to do anything; lazy. — **shiftlessness** n.

**shoal** (shōl) n. A sand bar or other elevation that creates a shallow place in a body of water.

**shroud** (shroud) v. To cover completely, as with a burial cloth.

**sickle** (sĭk′əl) n. A cutting tool with a rounded blade and a short handle.

**sidereal** (sī-dîr′ē-əl) adj. Having to do with the stars or constellations.

**sidle** (sīd′l) v. To move sideways, especially in a sly manner.

**sinew** (sĭn′yōō) n. 1. A tendon. 2. Muscular power.

**singular** (sĭng′gyə-lər) adj. Extraordinary; remarkable. — **singularly** adv.

**skitter** (skĭt′ər) v. To move quickly or skip along a surface.

**slake** (slāk) v. To make less intense; quench.

**slattern** (slăt′ərn) n. An untidy or dirty woman.

**slaver** (slăv′ər) v. To dribble saliva; drool.

**sloop** (slōōp) n. A small sailing vessel.

**sluggard** (slŭg′ərd) n. A lazy person.

**snood** (snōōd) n. A net worn over the back of the head to keep the hair in place.

**snuffle** (snŭf′əl) v. To breathe noisily; sniffle.

**sojourn** (sō′jûrn, sō-jûrn′) v. To stay somewhere temporarily.

**solicitous** (sə-lĭs′-ə-təs) adj. Showing concern; anxious.

**solicitude** (sə-lĭs′ə-tōōd, -tyōōd′) n. Concern.

**sordid** (sôr′dĭd) adj. 1. Depressingly drab; very shabby. 2. Morally low; vile. 3. Greedy; selfish.

**sovereign** (sŏv′ər-ən) adj. Supreme; chief.

**spar** (spär) n. A pole supporting a sail of a ship.

**spasmodic** (spăz-mŏd′ĭk) adj. Happening intermittently; on and off.

**spawn** (spôn) n. One of numerous young offspring, as from the eggs produced by some fish.

**spectral** (spĕk′trəl) adj. Ghostly.

**spectroscope** (spĕk′trə-skōp′) n. An instrument used to record bands of colored light coming from stars or other sources of radiant energy.

**speculation** (spĕk′yə-lā′shən) n. The pursuit of a risky financial venture.

**speculative** (spĕk′yə-lə-tĭv, -lā′tĭv) adj. In a reflective, wondering way. — **speculatively** adv.

**spew** (spyōō) v. To vomit; spit out.

**sphere** (sfîr) n. A globe-shaped object.

**spurn** (spûrn) v. To reject scornfully.

**stance** (stăns) n. A person's attitude or feelings concerning a particular situation.

**steadfast** (stĕd′făst′) adj. Not moving or changing; steady.

**stealthy** (stĕl′thē) adj. Moving or acting in secret.

**steed** (stēd) n. A spirited horse.

**strident** (strīd′ənt) adj. Shrill; harsh. — **stridently** adv.

**strategist** (străt′ə-jĭst) n. One skilled in making plans or schemes toward a certain end.

**suave** (swäv, swāv) adj. Gracious in manner; polished.

**subjugate** (sŭb′jə-gāt′) v. To keep under control; subdue. — **subjugation** (sŭb′jə-gā′shən) n.

**sublime** (sə-blīm′) adj. Inspiring awe; extremely impressive.

**subordinate** (sə-bôr′də-nāt′) v. To put in a less important position.

**sufferance** (sŭf′ər-əns, sŭf′rəns) n. The ability to endure pain or distress; tolerance.

**suffice** (sə-fīs′) v. To be enough; to satisfy the needs.

**suitor** (sōō′tər) n. Someone who requests or petitions.

**sultry** (sŭl′trē) adj. 1. Hot and humid; muggy. 2. Very hot; fiery.

**superfluity** (sōō′pər-flōō′ə-tē) n. Something not needed.

**suppliant** (sŭp′lĭ-ənt) adj. Beggarly; humble.

**supplication** (sŭp′lĭ-kā′shən) n. A humble prayer or request.

**supposition** (sŭp′ə-zĭsh′ən) n. Something supposed.

**surge** (sûrj) v. To rise up or increase suddenly.

**surmise** (sər-mīz′) v. To guess.

**susceptible** (sə-sĕp′tə-bəl) adj. Very sensitive; easily influenced or affected.

---

ă pat/ā pay/âr care/ä father/b bib/ch church/d deed/ĕ pet/ē be/f fife/g gag/h hat/hw which/ĭ pit/ī pie/îr pier/j judge/k kick/l lid, needle/m mum/ n no, sudden/ng thing/ŏ pot/ō toe/ô paw, for/oi noise/ou out/ŏŏ took/ōō boot/p pop/r roar/s sauce/sh ship, dish/t tight/th thin, path/th this, bathe/ ŭ cut/ûr urge/v valve/w with/y yes/z zebra, size/zh vision/ə about, item, edible, gallop, circus/ä Fr. ami/œ Fr. feu, Ger. schön/ü Fr. tu, Ger. über/ KH Ger. ich, Scot. loch/N Fr. bon.

**sustain** (sə-stān′) v. To support; strengthen.

**swathe** (swäth) v. To wrap.

**swivel** (swĭv′əl) v. To turn or rotate easily.

**synthetic** (sĭn-thĕt′ĭk) adj. Artificial.

**T**

**talisman** (tăl′ĭs-mən, tăl′ĭz-) n. Something supposed to have magical power, particularly to bring good luck.

**tallow** (tăl′ō) n. Animal fat used in preparing food or in making candles or soap.

**tangible** (tăn′jə-bəl) adj. Capable of being touched or felt; real.

**tarnish** (tär′nĭsh) v. To discolor; to spoil.

**tarry** (tăr′ē) v. To linger.

**taut** (tôt) adj. Tightly stretched; tense.

**teeter** (tē′tər) v. To move unsteadily; wobble.

**temperate** (tĕm′pər-ĭt, tĕm′prĭt) adj. Neither hot nor cold (describing weather).

**tenor** (tĕn′ər) n. General drift or meaning.

**terrain** (tə-rān′, tĕ-) n. A particular stretch of land or the physical features of it.

**testament** (tĕs′tə-mənt) n. A will.

**testy** (tĕs′tē) adj. Irritable.

**tether** (tĕth′ər) v. To confine an animal to a certain area by tying or chaining it.

**theology** (thē-ŏl′ə-jē) n. The study of religious doctrines or beliefs.

**throng** (thrŏng) n. A very large group of people or things. — v. To crowd together.

**thwart** (thwôrt) v. To block.

**tincture** (tĭngk′chər) n. A quality that colors or distinguishes something.

**tidings** (tī′dĭngz) n. pl. News.

**tine** (tīn) n. A slender, pointed projecting part.

**tolerable** (tŏl′ər-ə-bəl) adj. Bearable.

**tonic** (tŏn′ĭk) adj. Something that refreshes or restores.

**torrent** (tôr′ənt, tŏr′-) n. A violent flow, especially of water. — **torrential** (tô-rĕn′shəl, tə-) adj.

**transcend** (trăn-sĕnd′) v. To go beyond; surpass.

**transcendental** (trăn′sĕn-dĕnt′l) adj. Rising above or going beyond common thought or experiences; mystical.

**transfigure** (trăns-fĭg′yər) v. To change the form or appearance of something.

**transfix** (trăns-fĭks′) v. To make motionless with terror or awe.

**transgress** (trăns-grĕs′, trănz-) v. To go beyond the limits of something.

**transient** (trăn′shənt, -zhənt) adj. Not permanent; existing or lasting for only a short time.

**translucent** (trăns-lōō′sənt, trănz-) adj. Letting light pass through, but not enough to make objects on the other side clear.

**transverse** (trăns-vûrs′, trănz-) adj. Going crosswise.

**traverse** (trăv′ərs, trə-vûrs′) v. To go through or across.

**travesty** (trăv′ĭ-stē) v. To imitate in a ridiculing way.

**treatise** (trē′tĭs) n. A formal and lengthy written discussion of some subject.

**tremor** (trĕm′ər) n. A shivering or trembling movement.

**tremulous** (trĕm′yə-ləs) adj. **1.** Trembling; quivering. **2.** Fearful. — **tremulousness** n.

**trice** (trīs) n. An instant.

**truculent** (trŭk′yə-lənt) adj. Inclined to fight; fierce. — **truculently** adv. — **truculence** n.

**tumultuous** (tə-mŭl′chōō-əs) adj. Noisy in a wild and disorderly way.

**tureen** (tōō-rēn′, tyōō-) n. A deep, covered dish for serving soup or stew.

**tympany** (tĭm′pə-nē) n. The resounding sound coming from two objects striking against each other.

**U**

**unabashed** (ŭn′ə-băsht′) adj. Not ashamed or embarrassed.

**unassailable** (ŭn′ə-sā′lə-bəl) adj. Unable to be denied or attacked.

**unbraced** (ŭn′brāst′) adj. Unprotected; weakened.

**unbridle** (ŭn′brī′dəl) v. To release.

**uncanny** (ŭn′kăn′ē) adj. Weird; mysterious. — **uncannily** adv.

**undulate** (ŭn′jōō-lāt′, ŭn′dyə-, ŭn′də-) v. To move in a wavelike manner.

**unseemly** (ŭn′sēm′lē) adj. Not decent; improper.

**unsubstantial** (ŭn′səb-stăn′shəl) adj. Not real or solid; flimsy.

**untrammeled** (ŭn′trăm′əld) adj. Not hindered or confined; free.

**urchin** (ûr′chĭn) n. A mischievous youngster.

**usurer** (yōō′zhər-ər) n. Someone who lends money, usually at a high interest rate.

**V**

**vagrant** (vā′grənt) adj. Wandering.

**vair** (vâr) n. Squirrel fur used to decorate clothes during the Middle Ages.

**valor** (văl′ər) n. Bravery.

**vanguard** (văn′gärd′) n. The part of an army that advances before the rest.

**vanquish** (văng′kwĭsh, văn′-) v. To defeat in battle.

**veer** (vîr) v. To change direction.

**vehement** (vē′ə-mənt) adj. With great force; violent. — **vehemently** adv.

**versatile** (vûr′sə-təl) adj. Able to be used in many different ways.

**vestment** (vĕst′mənt) n. A robe worn by a clergyman. — **vestmented** adj.

**vesture** (vĕs′chər) n. **1.** Clothing. **2.** Something that covers or wraps.

**vex** (vĕks) v. To irritate.

**vibrant** (vī′brənt) adj. Very energetic; lively.

**victualize** (vĭt′l-īz) v. To supply with food. — also **victual.**

**vigilance** (vĭj′ə-ləns) n. Watchfulness.

**villa** (vĭl′ə) n. A large country house.

**vindicate** (vĭn′dĭ-kāt′) v. To clear of guilt or criticism.

**visage** (vĭz′ĭj) n. The face.

**vista** (vĭs′tə) n. An extended view.

**voracious** (vô-rā′shəs, vō-, və-) adj. Greedy; devouring.

**vouchsafe** (vouch′sāf′) v. To be gracious enough to give or grant.

**vulnerable** (vŭl′nər-ə-bəl) adj. Easily hurt or wounded.

**W**

**wallow** (wăl′ō) v. To roll about in something wet or dirty, especially mud. – n. A wet and muddy place.

**wane** (wān) v. To decrease gradually in size, intensity, or amount.

**wanton** (wŏn′tən) adj. Unrestrained; extravagant. – **wantonly** adv.

**wary** (wâr′ē) adj. Cautious.

**waver** (wāv′ər) v. To start giving way.

**weir** (wîr) n. An obstruction built in a river to change the direction of the flow of water.

**welter** (wĕl′tər) n. A jumbled mass.

**wend** (wĕnd) v. Archaic. Thought; imagined. – also **weened.**

**whelp** (hwĕlp, wĕlp) n. **1.** The young of various animals. **2.** A young child.

**whet** (hwĕt, wĕt) v. To sharpen.

**whimsy** (hwĭm′zē, wĭm′-) n. An imaginative or playful idea.

**whisk** (hwĭsk, wĭsk) v. To move rapidly.

**wistful** (wĭst′fəl) adj. Full of vague yearning; wishful.

**wizened** (wĭz′ənd) adj. Shriveled.

**wote** (wōt) v. Archaic. Knew. – also **wot.**

**wrack** (răk) n. To torture.

**wrath** (răth, räth) n. Extreme anger.

**writhe** (rīth) v. To twist and turn, as in agony.

**wrought** (rôt) v. Archaic. Created; performed. – adj. Formed; shaped by hammering.

**Y**

**yoke** (yōk) n. **1.** A wooden bar fitted around the necks of a pair of work animals to harness them together. **2.** Bondage; submission.

**Z**

**zealous** (zĕl′əs) adj. Enthusiastic; earnest. – **zealously** adv.

---

ă pat/ā pay/âr care/ä father/b bib/ch church/d deed/ĕ pet/ē be/f fife/g gag/h hat/hw which/ĭ pit/ī pie/îr pier/j judge/k kick/l lid, needle/m mum/ n no, sudden/ng thing/ŏ pot/ō toe/ô paw, for/oi noise/ou out/oo took/oo boot/p pop/r roar/s sauce/sh ship, dish/t tight/th thin, path/th this, bathe/ ū cut/ûr urge/v valve/w with/y yes/z zebra, size/zh vision/ə about, item, edible, gallop, circus/ à Fr. ami/œ Fr. feu, Ger. schön/ü Fr. tu, Ger. über/ KH Ger. ich, Scot. loch/N Fr. bon.

# Outline of Skills

Page numbers in italics refer to entries in the Guide to Literary Terms and Techniques

## LITERARY SKILLS

**Action** 573
**Alliteration** 217, 344, 356, *834*
**Allusion** 327, *834*
**Anachronism** 437, 530, *834*
**Analogy** 227, *834*
**Anecdote** 224
**Antagonist** 636, *834*
**Approximate Rhyme** 344, 348, 353, *851*
**Argument** *835*
**Artistic License** 272, *835*
**Aside** 533, *835*
**Assonance** 344, 356, *835*
**Atmosphere** 64, *835*
**Autobiography** 207, *835*
**Avenger** (in Tragedy) 626
**Ballad** 371, 374, *835*
**Biography** 207, 280, *835*
**Blank Verse** 367, 626, *836*
**Catastrophe** 594, *836*
**Catharsis** 536, *836*
**Characterization** 42, 50, 63, 553, 704, *836*
  Complex 63, *836*
  Direct and Indirect 42, 50, *836*
**Characters** 42, 56, *836*
  Flat and Round *836*
  Static and Dynamic 56, *836*
**Climax** 19, 704, *837*
**Comedy** 482, *837*
**Conflict** 2, 19, 594, 704, *837*
  External and Internal 2, 19, *837*
**Connotation** 117, 303, 313, *838*
**Conventions** 533, *838*
**Couplet** 337, 348, 391, *838*
**Denotation** 117, 303, *838*
**Description** 64, 169, *838*
  Reading Description (Practice in Reading and Writing) 169
**Dialogue** 171, *838*
  Reading Dialogue (Practice in Reading and Writing) 171
**Diction** 333, 764, *839*
**Drama** 481, 553, 573, 594, 626, 629, 649, 650, *839*
**Dramatic Irony** 127, 136, 595, *839*
**Dramatic Monologue** 383, *839*
**Dramatic Poetry** 383, *839*
**Elegy** 395, *839*
**End Rhyme** 344, 348, 351, *851*

**Epic** 371, *840*
**Epithet** *840*
**Essay** 173, 286, *840*
  Reading Essays of Opinion (Practice in Reading and Writing) 286
**Exaggeration** *840*
**Exposition** (as a Form of Discourse) 179, 286, *840*
**Exposition** (in Drama) 594, *840*
**Fable** 184, *840*
**Falling Action** 594, *841*
**Farce** *841*
**Fiction** *841*
**Figurative Language** 96, 216, 308, *841*
**Figure of Speech** 96, 126, 308, 216, *842*
**Flashback** 143, *842*
**Foil** *842*
**Folk Ballad** 371, 374, *835*
**Foreshadowing** 41, *842*
**Formal Essay** 173
**Framework Story** *842*
**Free Verse** 361, 369, *842*
**Hyperbole** *843*
**Iambic Pentameter** 361, 367, *843*
**Imagery** 291, 573, 762, *843*
**Implied Metaphor** 317, *844*
**Informal Essay** 173
**Internal Rhyme** 344, 348, 351, *851*
**Inversion** 333, *843*
**Irony** 127, 136, 143, 338, 594, 762, *839*, *844*
  Dramatic Irony 127, 136, 595, *839*, *844*
  Irony of Situation 127, 136, 143, 595, 762, *844*
  Verbal Irony 127, 136, 595, *844*
**Literal Language** *844*
**Literary Ballad** 371, *835*
**Local Color** 79, *844*
**Lyric Poetry** 387, *844*
**Metaphor** 199, 308, 315, 317, 319, 610, *844*
  Dead Metaphor 317, *845*
  Extended Metaphor 319, 610, *845*
  Implied Metaphor 317, *844*
  Mixed Metaphor *845*
**Meter** 361, 364, *845*
**Monologue** 383, *845*
**Moral** 149, *845*
**Motivation** 63, *846*
**Musical Devices** (in Poetry) 344
**Narration** 169, *846*
  Reading Narration (Practice in Reading and Writing) 169
**Narrative Poetry** 371, *846*
**Narrator** 80, *846*
**Nonfiction** 173, *846*
**Novel** 703, *846*

# Index of Titles by Themes

# Index of Fine Art

# Photo Credits

Page 20, Michael Wilson – De Wys; 24, Louis Goldman –Rapho/Photo Researchers; 65, F. Jensen – Monkmeyer; 67, Paul Conklin – Monkmeyer; 69, John Running; 82, Wm. Berssenbrugge – Shostal Associates; 86-94, Museum of Modern Art Film Still Archives; 120, The Learning Corporation of America; 125, Russ Kinne – Photo Researchers; 128, Everett C. Johnson – De Wys; 174, Gary Zahn – Bruce Coleman; 176, Willinger – Shostal Associates; 180, Courtesy, The Viking Press; 183, Fred Maroon – Photo Researchers; 185, Drawing by James Thurber; 188-189, David Burnett – De Wys; 193-198, Culver; 202, Tony Ray Jones – Magnum; 218-219, The Bettmann Archive; 220, California State Library; 221, Los Angeles County Museum; 222, The Bettmann Archive; 230, Art Resource; 231, Farrell Grehan – Photo Researchers; 237, from *The Shakespeare Plays*, BBC-TV and Time/Life Television co-production, courtesy Exxon Corp., Metropolitan Life Insurance and Morgan Guaranty Trust; 238, (top and bottom right and left) Alinari/ Art Resource, (center) The Bettmann Archive; 241, Culver; 243-248, Coco McCoy – Rainbow; 252-271, Sy Friedman; 273, Culver; 275, Brian Brake – Magnum; 284-285, The Bettmann Archive; 291, Grant Heilman; 292, Photo Researchers; 295, Hans Namuth; 297, Georg Gerster – Rapho/Photo Researchers; 300, Le Clair Bissell – Nancy Palmer; 309, Niklas Deak – Shostal Associates; 311, W. Bayer – Bruce Coleman; 312, Frederick Dodd – Peter Arnold; 314, Michael Collier – Stock, Boston; 318-319, Jen and Des Bartlett – Bruce Coleman; 320-321, David Hamilton – De Wys; 331, Eric Kroll – Taurus; 332, Jay Smith – Shostal Associates, 335, Scott Ransom – Taurus; 342, De Wys; 345, Raymond V. Schoder, S.J.; 346, Hans Reinhard – Bruce Coleman; 350, Gordon Johnson – Photo Researchers; 352-353, Elizabeth Resnick – Taurus; 357, Robert Carr – Bruce Coleman; 359, P. Choch – Stock, Boston; 365, Ed Cooper – Shostal Associates; 371, The Granger Collection; 383, Culver; 388, Ronny Jacques – Photo Researchers; 392, Howard Moss – Shostal Associates; 394, De Wys; 397, William Graham – Photo Researchers; 409, Larry Mulvihill – Photo Researchers; 410-411, National Maritime Museum, San Francisco; 412, Scala/Art Resource; 414, Jeremiah Bean, 422, (top) Erich Hartmann – Magnum; 424, Trevor Wood – Bruce Coleman; 425, Drawing by Howard Pyle; 426, Culver; 430-440, 445, 472, drawings by Howard Pyle; 468, N. Y. Public Library Print Room; 476, Robert Harding Associates; 481, Shostal Associates, 482, Dennis Stock – Magnum; 484, Culver; 485, The Bettmann Archive; 486, Dennis Stock – Magnum; 489-518, William Wurtzel; 527, The Bettmann Archive; 529, courtesy, The Stratford Festival, Canada; 530, The Folger Shakespeare Library; 531, The Bettmann Archive; 532, courtesy, The Stratford Festival, Canada; 533, Martha Swope – The American Shakespeare Theater; 535, Raymond V. Schoder, S.J.; 563-577, Museum of Modern Art Film Still Archives; 585, The Bettmann Archive; 587-623, Museum of Modern Art Film Still Archives; 628, Culver; 630, Edmunds Scientific Co.; 643-648, Wide World Photos; 650, © 1977, Paul Davis; 652-696, Martha Swope; 704, (top) The Bettmann Archive; 706, Giraudon/ Art Resource; 707, Hans Namuth.

# Art Credits

Beatrice Darwin   403, 404
Lois Ehlert   43
Jon Goodell   54, 57
Ron Himler   100, 103
Susan Jeschke   145, 148
Frances Jetter   164, 166, 168
Daniel Kirk   33, 35, 37, 39, 152–153
Judy Love   709, 712, 715, 718–719, 721, 723, 725, 727, 734–735, 738, 740–
741, 742, 744–745, 747, 750–751, 754, 756–757, 761
Lyle Miller   3, 6, 11, 76
Ed Parker   449, 451, 454, 458–459, 462–463, 465
Jos. A. Smith   104, 158, 162
Arvis Stewart   111, 114–115
Phero Thomas   137, 140–141

# Index of Authors and Titles

The page numbers in italics indicate where a brief biography of the author is located.

6
7
E 8
F 9
G 0
H 1
I 2
J 3